# Cosima Wagner's *Diaries*

# Cosima Wagner's
# DIARIES

## VOLUME I
## 1869-1877

Edited and annotated by
Martin Gregor-Dellin and Dietrich Mack

Translated and with an Introduction by
Geoffrey Skelton

A Helen and Kurt Wolff Book
Harcourt Brace Jovanovich
New York and London

Printed in the United States of America

LIBRARY OF CONGRESS CATALOGING IN PUBLICATION DATA
Wagner, Cosima Liszt, 1837–1930
Cosima Wagner's Diaries

Translation of Die Tagebücher 1
"A Helen and Kurt Wolff book."
Includes bibliographical references and indexes.
CONTENTS: v. 1. 1869–1877.
1. Wagner, Richard, 1813–1883. 2. Composers—
Germany—Biography. 3. Wagner, Cosima Liszt,
1837–1930. 4. Wives—Germany—Biography.
I. Gregor-Dellin, Martin, 1926–    II. Mack, Dietrich,
1940–    III. Skelton, Geoffrey.
ML410. W11C5253    1978    782.1'092'4 (B)
78-53919
ISBN 0-15-122635-0

First edition
BCDE

# Contents

# List of Illustrations

between pages 512 and 513

The "Nibelungen Kanzlei," 1872; the conductor Hans Richter in the center

The Wagner Theater, 1876
*Wood engraving; some details invented*

Sketches by Professor Josef Hoffman for Bayreuth *Ring* production
*Rheingold,* third scene
*Walküre,* second act
*Siegfried,* second act
*Götterdämmerung,* first act, second scene

The Rhinemaidens, 1876: Lilli Lehmann, Marie Lehmann, Minna Lammert

Swimming machine for the Rhinemaidens, who rode on bunks elevated on poles

The Nibelungs with their treasure, 1876

Amalie Materna as Brünnhilde, 1876
*Photo by J. Albert*

Franz Betz as Wotan, 1876

Judith Gautier-Mendès, 1875

Cosima Wagner

Siegfried Wagner as Young Siegfried, in the original costume of 1876
*Richard Wagner Gedenkstätte*

Cosima Wagner, 1877

Richard Wagner, 1877

*All photographs without source indication were supplied by Dr. Dietrich Mack, Bayreuth.*

*Photo reproduction by Jim Kalett*

# Introduction

## Richard and Cosima Wagner

Cosima, the younger daughter of the composer Franz Liszt, was still the wife of the conductor Hans von Bülow when, on November 16, 1868, she joined Richard Wagner at his home in Tribschen, near Lucerne in Switzerland. From then until Wagner's death on February 13, 1883, the two were never parted, except for a very few days at a time, and Cosima's Diaries, begun on January 1, 1869, provide a continuous and intimate picture of their fourteen years together—first at Lucerne, where, after Cosima's divorce from Hans von Bülow, they were married (on August 25, 1870), and then in Bayreuth in Germany. These were the years during which Wagner completed the huge *Ring* cycle, on which he had been working since 1849, and built the festival theater in Bayreuth in which to present it. He then went on to write his last work, *Parsifal*, which he produced at Bayreuth only a few months before his death at the age of sixty-nine.

All these events, and many more besides, are dealt with in detail in the Diaries, and there is consequently no need to say anything further about them here. But, in order that the reader can appreciate them to the full, it may be useful to describe the preceding events, which led Cosima, at the age of thirty-one, finally to abandon Hans von Bülow and devote the rest of her long life to Richard Wagner, a man twenty-four years older than she. It was a decision not lightly taken, as the very first pages of the Diaries show, and the agonies of conscience she suffered over her treatment of von Bülow continue unabated to the Diaries' end. She was less disturbed about the scandal caused by her conduct, but the reason she gives for starting to write her Diaries—so that her children might one day come to understand her and see her as she really was—suggests that this was not a matter of complete indifference to her.

When Cosima abandoned her husband and joined Richard Wagner at Tribschen, she was already the mother of four daughters, and another child was on the way. The two elder girls were Hans von Bülow's: Daniela, born in 1860, and Blandine, born in 1863. These two she left at her husband's home in Munich when she parted from him, though with the hope and intention that the arrangement would only be temporary. The two younger daughters, whom she took with her, were Richard Wagner's: Isolde, born in 1865, the year of the first production of *Tristan und Isolde*, and Eva, born in 1867, while he was composing *Die Meistersinger von Nürnberg*. The child as yet unborn when Cosima arrived at Tribschen was to be their last—and their crowning joy, for he was Wagner's first and only son. Like his sisters, he was named after the work on which Wagner was working at the time of his birth: *Siegfried*.

The acquisition of a family of his own so late in his life undoubtedly had a rejuvenating effect on Richard Wagner, and it gave him the stimulus he needed, at an age when most men would be thinking of a tranquil retirement, to realize his long-standing ambition of building a special theater of his own to stage his revolutionary *Ring*.

His 1836 marriage with his first wife, Minna, an actress four years older than he, had been childless, though she herself brought to the marriage an illegitimate daughter, Nathalie, whom she passed off in hublic as a younger sister. This marriage seems, after an initial crisis in which she left him for another man, to have functioned quite well for a number of years; by all accounts Minna was a good-looking woman and an efficient housewife, who coped resourcefully during the lean years when her husband was struggling to establish himself as a composer and a conductor. For her the pinnacle of happiness was reached when, in the early 1840s, he was appointed a conductor at the Dresden opera and brought out in quick succession his three operas *Rienzi* (1842), *Der Fliegende Holländer* (1843), and *Tannhäuser* (1845).

His subsequent involvement in the social revolution of 1849, which forced him to flee to Switzerland to avoid arrest and imprisonment in Dresden, was a shattering blow for Minna, from which she never really recovered. Though she eventually joined him in exile, she became embittered, having no sympathy for his desire to reform the theater which had provided him with a respectable living, and no belief in the huge work, *Der Ring des Nibelungen*, through which he planned to effect that reform. Wagner was obliged to turn for support to his friends, of whom the staunchest proved to be Franz Liszt, two years older than he. Courageously, in view of the composer's status as a wanted man in Germany, Liszt staged the first performance of *Lohengrin* in Weimar in 1850, and he also did all he could to help Wagner financially and encourage him to work on the *Ring*.

In his increasing estrangement from Minna, Wagner sought solace with other women—first with Jessie Laussot, an Englishwoman married to a Frenchman in Bordeaux, and then with Mathilde Wesendonck, whose husband, a well-to-do German businessman, had settled in Zurich. It was there, in the little house called Das Asyl on the grounds of the Wesendonck estate, that a jealous scene between Minna and Mathilde virtually brought the marriage to an end in 1858. Wagner, who had suspended work on *Siegfried* to write *Tristan und Isolde*, went off to Venice by himself.

When he had completed *Tristan und Isolde*, he made another attempt to resume his married life, and Minna accompanied him to Paris, where, in 1861, he produced his revised version of *Tannhäuser*. Neither this attempt to repair his marriage nor a subsequent one—in Biebrich, on the Rhine, when he was starting work on *Die Meistersinger*—proved successful; Minna returned to Dresden, and apart from an occasional meeting when he passed through that city, they saw nothing more of each other. Of the two women with whom he shared his life during this period, Friederike Meyer and Mathilde Maier, the second was the more significant; indeed, if his marriage with Minna had ended earlier, it is possible that she might have become his second wife. Both women figure in Cosima's Diaries, as, in fact, do Jessie Laussot and Mathilde Wesendonck. Whatever Wagner's relations with these various ladies may have been, it is interesting that both he and Cosima were able subsequently to remain on amicable terms with them.

During that summer of 1862 in Biebrich when he was working happily on *Die Meistersinger*, Wagner received visits from several friends, among them Hans von Bülow and his wife, Cosima. Hans von Bülow had been only sixteen, a promising pupil of Franz Liszt, when Wagner first met him in 1846 in Dresden. Cosima was even younger when Liszt and Wagner paid a visit to Paris in 1853, and Liszt took him to see his three children, Blandine, Cosima, and Daniel. Though he played no personal part in their lives in those early years, Wagner exerted through his music a very powerful influence on the two young people, and, as Cosima relates in the Diaries, it was a performance in Berlin, conducted by Hans, of the Overture to *Tannhäuser* that finally brought her and Hans together. The work was booed, and Cosima, who was staying with the von Bülows, remained up to console the young man on his return home. This was the beginning of the relationship that led to their marriage, on August 18, 1857. They visited Wagner in Zurich during their honeymoon and again a year later, when they were witnesses of the unhappy scenes involving Minna and Mathilde Wesendonck.

Cosima herself was no stranger to domestic trouble and unhappiness. She was the second child of Franz Liszt and the French Countess Marie d'Agoult, and was born on Christmas Day 1837, in Bellagio, Italy, on Lake Como. Her parents, who were never married, separated when she was not quite two years old, and she and her elder sister and younger brother were left in Paris in the care of Liszt's mother, actively discouraged from having anything to do with their own mother, who had by then devoted herself to a literary career under the pseudonym of Daniel Stern. Liszt himself continued to travel through Europe for a number of years, giving piano recitals, but in 1848 he abandoned his career as a virtuoso to settle down in Weimar as Court musical director. Here his companion was Princess Carolyne von Sayn-Wittgenstein, who, like Countess d'Agoult, had a daughter from her previous marriage. Thus Claire in Paris and Marie in Weimar received all the parental care of Countess d'Agoult and Liszt, respectively, and the three children of their own union were left to grow up virtually as orphans.

If Cosima had hoped to find in marriage a settled background to her life, she was disappointed. Hans's mother seems to have been unwilling to accept her, and it soon became apparent that Hans himself was not willing to allow her to share his life to the full. The death of her brother, Daniel, from consumption in 1859 was a further grief which much increased her sense of isolation.

Her meeting with Wagner in Biebrich, in an atmosphere very different from that of their previous encounters in Zurich, brought them closer together. His contentment with life at that time was such that he proved a gay and humorous companion, and in his autobiography, *Mein Leben* (*My Life*), he claimed to have noticed a melting of reserve in her, though her feelings toward him did not perhaps yet go so far as his toward her.

"Everything was still wrapped in silence and mystery," he wrote, "but the feeling inside me that she belonged to me assumed such certainty that it drove me in a moment of eccentricity to a display of rash high spirits. Once, when accompanying Cosima across an open square in Frankfurt to her hotel, I espied an empty wheelbarrow standing there, and on the spur of the moment I invited her to sit in it, so that I might wheel her to the hotel; she was instantly ready to comply, whereas I, astonished in turn by this, lost the courage to carry out my mad design. Bülow, who was following us, had seen the incident; Cosima explained very guilelessly to him what had been in our minds, and unfortunately I was unable to conclude that his high spirits matched ours, for he chided his wife for her temerity."

This little incident reveals quite a lot about all three characters. Humor and *joie de vivre*, much in evidence in the Diaries even at times of melancholy, had little or no place in the marriage between Cosima and Hans. Her feelings received yet another shattering blow when, later that same year, her sister, Blandine, who had married a French politician, Emile Ollivier, died after giving birth to a son.

It must have seemed to Cosima, in the period just before and after the birth of her second daughter, Blandine (so movingly described in the Diaries), that her only true friend in the world was Richard Wagner, though his visits to Berlin were rare and fleeting. It was on one of these, as they were driving to a concert to be conducted by Hans, that they at last admitted their love for each other and, as Wagner puts it in his autobiography, "sealed our vow to belong entirely to each other." This day, November 28, 1863, is frequently remembered in Cosima's Diaries.

However, their activities kept them apart for some time yet. While Cosima continued her life in Berlin as Hans von Bülow's wife and mother of his two children, Wagner moved to Vienna, attempting, with conducting engagements there and as far afield as Russia, to earn sufficient money to settle down and finish *Die Meistersinger*. His failure, due in some measure to his own extravagance, brought him to the verge of desperation. He was rescued from it, literally at the last moment, by what he himself described as a fairy story.

In May 1864, at the age of eighteen, a passionate admirer of his ascended the throne of Bavaria as King Ludwig II and immediately sent for him, to offer him generous financial support and complete freedom to write and produce his works in Munich. Wagner, who had been on the point of fleeing to some remote spot to escape his Viennese creditors, found himself all at once in possession of a villa beside Lake Starnberg in Bavaria. After first inviting Mathilde Maier to share it with him as his housekeeper (she refused), he hit upon the idea of asking Hans von Bülow to join him there for the summer, along with his wife and family.

Cosima came to Starnberg in June 1864 without her husband, who was detained a while longer in Berlin by ill health, and it was during this time that Wagner and Cosima's love was physically consummated, as the birth of their daughter Isolde in April 1865 proves.

During this summer visit, Wagner discussed with von Bülow the part the latter might play in the plans he was working out with the young King. These included, as well as new productions of his existing works at the Munich opera, the founding of a music school and (with the help of the architect Gottfried Semper, a friend from his Dresden years) the building of a special theater in the city in which to present the *Ring*. To begin with, von Bülow was appointed pianist to King Ludwig, with the promise of greater responsibilities to come, and thus, after settling his affairs in Berlin, he returned to Munich on a permanent basis, setting up house with his family there. Wagner was also living in Munich by that time, and together they brought *Tristan und Isolde* to the stage, Wagner directing and von Bülow conducting.

How much von Bülow knew at this point about the relationship between his wife and Wagner is unclear, but it is obvious that, even if he knew nothing definite (which seems unlikely), he must have had his suspicions; in August 1865, shortly after the production of *Tristan und Isolde*, he took Cosima off to Budapest for a long visit to her father, presumably in the hope of putting an end to the affair. Since she was forbidden to receive any letters from Wagner during her absence, she gave him a leather-bound book in which he could write his replies to the letters she sent him, to be read by her later. This, the so-called *Braunes Buch* (*Brown Book*), has only recently been published in full, and it, like the Diaries, reveals more about the relationship between Cosima, Hans von Bülow, and Wagner than has hitherto been known.

What that relationship was emerges—at least more clearly than before—in the Diaries, and thus need not be described in detail here. In any case, the period of living and working closely together did not long survive von Bülow and Cosima's return to Munich, for in December 1865, Wagner, having got himself at cross purposes with the government and people there, was forced to leave the city, and he went off to Switzerland.

The death of his wife in January 1866 removed at least one obstacle between him and Cosima, but there still remained von Bülow's reluctance to countenance a divorce. So the subterfuges continued, and were sustained partly for material reasons, since it was important for the fortunes of all concerned not to lose the good will of the young King, on whom Wagner still depended, both for his main income and for the opportunity to complete and stage his works under von Bülow's musical direction.

Cosima helped Wagner choose and furnish a permanent home for himself in Switzerland—Tribschen, a villa standing just outside Lucerne on a wooded tongue of land projecting into the Vierwaldstätter Lake—and she was able to pay him frequent visits there on the pretext of taking down from his dictation the autobiography the King had requested him to write, a project he had begun in Munich in July 1865.

Cosima was in Tribschen in February 1867, when she gave birth to Wagner's second daughter, Eva. At that time he had resumed work on *Die Meistersinger*. Officially, of course, Eva was the child of Hans von Bülow, but he was this time in no doubt as to who the true father was. In spite of this, he conducted the first performance of *Die Meistersinger* in Munich in June 1868, while Wagner sat in the royal box beside the King.

This was the culminating point of Wagner's personal relationship with Ludwig. Soon afterward the growing gossip about his venerated composer's scandalous love affair with the wife of his musical director came to the King's ears, bringing disillusionment and a measure of personal estrangement. Cosima's attempts to keep up the fiction of her marriage were now pointless. After a visit with Wagner to Italy, during which their third child was conceived, she returned to Munich only to settle her affairs with her husband; then, along with her two younger daughters, she joined Wagner at Tribschen, never to be parted from him again.

It is at this point that the Diaries begin.

In this short summary of preceding events, many of the persons who figure prominently in the Diaries have been mentioned. Further details about them, and about the many other people not mentioned here, will be found, as they make their initial appearance, in the notes at the back of this book. Cosima's family background has already been indicated; perhaps it might be helpful to the reader to have a similar account of Richard Wagner's, which is considerably more complicated.

He was born in Leipzig on May 22, 1813, as the ninth and youngest child of Carl Friedrich Wagner, a police actuary, and his wife, Johanna Paetz, whose father was a baker. Two of these nine children died in infant years. The eldest of the survivors, Albert, was 14 years older than Richard; he became a singer and theater manager and was instrumental in securing Richard his first job as chorus master in Würzburg. His eldest sister, Rosalie, an actress, married a university professor, Gotthard Oswald Marbach; she died in childbirth in 1837. His only other brother, Julius, remained unmarried and is not mentioned in the Diaries; he also died before they begin, and, besides, Richard had a low opinion of him. The remaining sisters were Luise, also an actress before her marriage to the publisher Friedrich Brockhaus; Klara, an opera singer who married Heinrich Wolfram and settled in Chemnitz; and Ottilie, who likewise married a Brockhaus, Hermann, a younger brother of her sister Luise's husband.

Carl Friedrich Wagner died in November 1813, when Richard was only six months old, and within a year of his death, in August 1814, his widow married Ludwig Geyer, an actor and playwright; they had one daughter, Cäcilie, who figures in the Diaries as the wife of Eduard Avenarius.

Geyer's close friendship with the Wagner family, which began before Carl Friedrich Wagner's death, has given rise to one of the famous unsolved mysteries of history—whether he was in fact the father of Richard as well as of Cäcilie. Nothing in the Diaries so far lends support to that speculation: the fact that Cosima refers to Geyer now and again as Richard's "father" is of little significance—the shortening of the word "stepfather" into "father" is quite normal German practice (Wagner employs it, too, in his autobiography), and in any case Geyer was the only father figure Richard consciously knew, and could therefore be considered entitled to the name. Short as their time together was, since he was only eight when Geyer died, Richard always had a great affection and respect for his stepfather, but it is noticeable in the Diaries that the member of his family in whom he took the greatest pride was his uncle Adolf Wagner, the younger brother of his legal father. Richard Wagner's pleasure in being descended from the same stock as this distinguished literary scholar who had once known Schiller would have been somewhat illogical if he had really believed himself to be the son of Geyer.

Of the nephews and nieces of Richard Wagner mentioned in the Diaries, Johanna Wagner-Jachmann was the adopted daughter of his brother, Albert. Franziska Ritter, wife of the musician Alexander Ritter, was Albert's true daughter. The Brockhaus brothers, Clemens and Fritz, were the sons of his sister Ottilie, and Doris Brockhaus was their sister. Klara Kessinger, the wife of Kurt von Kessinger, was the daughter of Wagner's sister Luise.

Before I leave the subject of family relationships, it might be helpful to catalogue the various nicknames under which Cosima's children usually appear in the Diaries. Daniela is Loulou, Lulu, Lusch, or Luschchen; Blandine is Boni or Bonichen; Isolde is Loldi or Loldchen; Eva is Evchen; and Siegfried is Fidi, Fidichen, Fidel, or Friedel.

The houses in which the Diaries were written—Tribschen and Wahnfried—are still in existence, the first being now a Wagner museum and the second the center of the combined Wagner archives and the Wagner museum of the city of Bayreuth (the Gedenkstätte). Neither house is exactly as it was in Richard Wagner's lifetime. Tribschen—or Triebschen, as Wagner himself called it, associating the name with the promontory formed by silt (*angetrieben*) on which it stands, an interpretation not backed up by any documentary evidence— had only been rented, and after Wagner's departure, other occupants made alterations (the last to occupy it was the American singer Minnie Hauk). The house was bought by the city of Lucerne in 1931 to be turned into a museum, its interior being restored as closely as possible to match its appearance in Wagner's time.

Wahnfried remained the Wagner family home until the death of Wieland Wagner, his eldest grandson, in 1966. The house had been severely damaged in a raid by American bombers on April 5, 1945, and during the rebuilding Wieland made several alterations to the interior, some of which were reversed when the house was bought, along with the festival theater, by the Richard Wagner Foundation in 1973 and converted for its present use as a research center.

The festival theater itself, though extended in various ways throughout the years and strengthened structurally, is still the one Wagner built and opened, in the summer of 1876, with the first performance of *Der Ring des Nibelungen*.

# *The Diaries*

Cosima's Diaries have a close connection, at least in preliminary intention, with Wagner's autobiography, *Mein Leben*, which he wrote at the request of King Ludwig II and dictated to Cosima. In notifying the King of his intention to bring the story of his life only up to the point at which he was summoned to Munich in 1864, Wagner said (in a letter to Ludwig dated July 21/22, 1865): "From then on, Cosima will continue the biography alone and will, I hope, one day complete it. She is best equipped to do this and will do it well."

The troubled events of the next three years, however, and the frequent separations between them hardly favored Cosima's role as biographer. Richard Wagner continued to jot down in telegraphic style (in the so-called *Annalen*) the events he wished eventually to be recorded for posterity, either by himself or by Cosima. He had always followed this practice, and his autobiography is based on similar jottings from an earlier period. These jottings cease in 1868, the year in which Cosima finally joined him, and from then on it was she who kept a daily record of their life together.

Whatever the original intention, it is clear from the very first page of her Diaries that Cosima considered them as much more than mere aids to memory for a future biography. Their avowed purpose was to provide a sort of apologia for her children, so that in later years they would be better able to understand her conduct in leaving Hans von Bülow for Richard Wagner, and would at the same time gain a proper appreciation of the man of genius to whom she had dedicated her life. If she frequently seems to lose sight of this maternal intention and to confide to her diary intimate reflections of a purely private kind, she never forgot that the focus of her attention was always Richard. On the only occasion when she left home alone with the children for a few days, she made no entries, since she had nothing to record about him. And the last entry (February 12, 1883) was made on the day before he died.

From Richard himself the Diaries were not kept concealed; indeed, in the first year, around the time she was giving birth to Siegfried, he wrote the entries himself, and occasional amendments and comments in his handwriting occur on subsequent pages. On October 11, 1879, he wrote to King Ludwig, "She is writing for our son a remarkably exact diary, in which there are entries for every day regarding my state of health, my work, and my occasional sayings, etc." It is clear, therefore, that he was familiar with the Diaries and regarded them as an accurate account of his life. He wrote again to King Ludwig on January 25, 1880, saying that he had promised Cosima to continue his autobiography, bringing it up to the time of their union, that is to say, 1868. "From that time on she herself has written about me, my daily life, and my doings, in the utmost detail, so that one day following my death my whole life down to my final hour will be available to my son."

It turned out otherwise. Not only did Richard Wagner leave his promise to continue his autobiography to 1868 unfulfilled, but Cosima's Diaries also did not pass, as they were intended to do, to their son, Siegfried.

Cosima's eyesight, which had already frequently caused her trouble while she was writing the Diaries, as several entries (and also their increasing illegibility) show, became even worse after Wagner's death, and in maintaining her correspondence she had to rely to a great extent on the help of her daughters. When Cosima's health finally broke down, in 1906, her daughter Eva took over the correspondence completely, and this led to a confidential relationship between mother and daughter which brought about, not surprisingly, family jealousies. These were still further exacerbated by Eva's marriage, in 1908, to the English-born historian Houston Stewart Chamberlain, whose influence on Cosima was considerable, and the tensions reached their woeful climax in a sensational court case in the years 1913–14, when Isolde took her mother to court in an attempt to gain recognition as a legal heir of Richard Wagner, rather than of Hans von Bülow (an attempt which, incidentally, failed). As Daniela, von Bülow's elder daughter, later bitterly wrote, "Our misery began in 1908, with Eva's marriage." It was in that year, too, that Cosima's Diaries came into the possession of Eva, who declared—and several times confirmed on oath—that her mother had presented them to her as part of her dowry.

Eva could not take immediate physical possession of the Diaries, since in the previous year Cosima had allowed Wagner's biographer, Carl Friedrich Glasenapp, to remove them from Wahnfried for consultation while completing the sixth and final volume of his biography of the composer. Glasenapp took all twenty-one volumes off to Riga, where he was then living, and did not return them until two years later. He made copious use of them in his own book, but since he did not reveal the source, this fact did not become known until much later, when Richard Graf du Moulin Eckart was commissioned to write the official biography of Cosima (first published in 1929), and was himself allowed to dip into the Diaries. He recognized many sentences which Glasenapp had lifted in entirety, a process he imitated, though, unlike his predecessor, he did reveal the source. After examining the Diaries he wrote to Eva, "When one day this book can be published without cuts, it will be seen as one of the most important pronouncements of our time, for it covers not only Tribschen, Bayreuth, and Wahnfried, but also to some extent the entire intellectual and political world of its time."

This is indeed true, and the relatively sparse use, in relation to its full scope, that both Glasenapp and Du Moulin Eckart made of the Diaries has in no way diminished their impact as a whole. It is surprising, moreover, to what extent both these biographers inaccurately reproduced much of what they chose to quote. There are actually instances in which their versions differ radically, even in sense, from the complete text as now published.

After Glasenapp returned the Diaries to Bayreuth in 1909, they remained in the archives at Wahnfried until 1911, during which time Siegfried and his other sisters apparently made no efforts to dispute Eva's claim to them. She finally removed them to her own home in Bayreuth, close to Wahnfried, and against the item "Cosima's Diaries" in the register of the archives she noted in her own handwriting, "All the Diaries were presented to her daughter Eva by her mother on October 22, 1911, and entrusted to her to look after." Eva claimed that Cosima had told her, "I know they will be safe with you."

The year 1930 brought a great change in the family fortunes. On April 1 of that year, Cosima died, at the age of 92; four months later, on August 4, her son, Siegfried, followed her to the grave. The sole heiress to the Wagner estate was Siegfried's English-born widow, Winifred. But Cosima's Diaries remained in the possession of Eva Chamberlain, whose legal right to them was not challenged at the time. Presumably in the following year, Eva copied from them a number of Richard Wagner's sayings, which she sent initially to the Italian conductor Arturo Toscanini, a friend of the family since he had first come to Bayreuth to conduct during the festival of 1930. After he returned them, these extracts, filling one hundred and thirty quarto pages, were published by Hans von Wolzogen in eight consecutive issues of the festival magazine, *Bayreuther Blätter*, between January 1936 and December 1937. Eva then presented the manuscript copy of her extracts to the Gedenkstätte. These extracts, along with those published by Glasenapp and Du Moulin Eckart, are all that was known of the Diaries before their present publication in full.

The reason why, after that time, Cosima's Diaries became even less accessible than they had been before again involves Eva Chamberlain.

In 1935 she presented the Diaries and a number of letters to the city of Bayreuth, "as a gift to the Richard Wagner Gedenkstätte." In the agreement, dated June 20/21, 1935, she laid down strict conditions for the gift, one of them being that the archivist at Wahnfried, Otto Strobel, should never be employed by the Gedenkstätte in any capacity. Eva's objections to Strobel, a renowned Wagner scholar, were for a long time believed to have been connected with the manner—hostile, in her view—in which he edited the correspondence between Richard Wagner and King Ludwig II of Bavaria, published under the aegis of Winifred Wagner in five volumes between the years 1936 and 1939. But there was a still more cogent reason for Eva's dislike of Strobel. In 1934 he discovered that the correspondence between Richard and Cosima was missing from the Wahnfried archives, and he reported the loss to the police. As a result, Eva made a written statement on oath, on November 9, 1934, declaring that she had burned these letters shortly after the death of her brother, Siegfried, on his specific instructions.

Eva gave further rein to her strong personal grudge against Strobel in the will which she made on April 28, 1939. In this, she not only repeated her condition that Strobel must not be allowed to have anything to do with the Gedenkstätte, but she also stipulated that he must never be permitted to see Cosima's Diaries, and she directed that these should be deposited in a bank, the Bayerischer Staatsbank in Munich, there to remain untouched until 30 years after her death. In a series of codicils added in 1941, Eva further laid down that the copyright in the Diaries should pass on her death to the city of Bayreuth, which, on the expiry of the thirty-year embargo, should be permitted to take possession of them. But even then she made certain conditions governing their publication and their availability for research purposes.

Thus in effect it was solely a personal quarrel between Eva Chamberlain and Otto Strobel which kept these Diaries from our sight for nearly a century after their completion. Eva died on May 26, 1942, and the embargo was designed to insure that Strobel would be dead by the time the Diaries were released to the city of Bayreuth. An effort by the Wagner family in 1954 to contest Eva's right in law to the Diaries was rejected by the German courts on the grounds that there was no evidence to upset her claim that she had received them as a gift from her mother; her rights in the Diaries thus upheld, her disposal of the copyright and the stipulations made by her in her will were held to be legally valid. In 1959, following Strobel's death, an application was made to have the embargo set aside on the grounds that the main reason for it had now been removed, but this was refused.

When at last, on May 26, 1972, the embargo expired and the time came for the city of Bayreuth to take actual possession of the Diaries, a further legal delay occurred, arising from a dispute between the executors of Eva's will and the city of Bayreuth about the terms on which the Diaries would be handed over. This effectively prolonged the embargo by two years. Not until March 12, 1974, were the Diaries able at last to make their return journey, under police protection, from the bank vault in Munich to Bayreuth, there to be subjected, under very strict control, to the processes of preservation, transcription, and publication.

Cosima wrote her Diaries in 21 identical volumes, 17.2 cm by 22 cm in size, and together they form a pile 35 cm high. Each volume is bound in black cardboard covers and secured on three sides by green ribbons. On the spine of each, the first and last dates of the entries are engraved in gilt letters. The number of pages in each book varies from 160 to 356, and all the sheets are covered in writing except in the final volume, which breaks off after 100 pages with Richard Wagner's death. The number of lines per page also varies from volume to volume, ranging from 14 to 36. The total number of words amounts to nearly one million.

Placed between the pages of the volumes are various telegrams, notes, and newspaper clippings, to which reference is made in the text, and in the present printed edition these are described and, where necessary, quoted, either in brackets in the text or in the notes at the back of the book. Most of the enclosures were no longer in their correct places when the Diaries were opened, having obviously fallen out and been replaced at random, but in almost all cases the German editors found it possible to restore them to their proper positions.

The text includes additions and amendments in Cosima's own hand, to which attention is drawn in the present volume, where necessary, by notes enclosed in brackets. There are also occasional additions and continuations in Richard Wagner's handwriting, and these, printed in italics, are also indicated by editorial notes. There is no discernible gap in the entries, and not a single page in all the 21 volumes has been removed or pasted over. In the final third of the full text, however, whole sentences have been crossed out and rendered illegible by an unknown hand, certainly at a later date. Since these do not affect the present volume in any way, it is unnecessary to examine them further here. In this first volume, which comprises one half of the full text, nothing was omitted in the German edition, apart from a very few words which had been rendered illegible by being written over, smudged, or obscured by ink blots. Attention is drawn to these by notes in brackets.

The German editors were considerably hampered in their task of reproducing the full text of the Diaries accurately by Cosima's handwriting, which, after the first few pages, becomes increasingly difficult to read. This was due in the main to the growing weakness of her eyesight, and in the later years of the Diaries many problems of deciphering were encountered. The task of transcription was carried out at the Gedenkstätte in Bayreuth, and in all questionable cases repeated checks were made by the editors and their assistants.

They faced still other problems in dealing with Cosima's often faulty German grammar and punctuation. Cosima was brought up speaking both French and German, and she had a good knowledge of other languages as well, but German was not her true native language, and its grammatical perils frequently defeated her. She also made occasional mistakes in the spelling of proper names, and here—as in their corrections of grammar and punctuation—the German editors have made the minimum number of alterations, being guided solely by the need to avoid confusion.


# *The Translation*

In this translation of the Diaries I have followed the example of the German editors as far as proper names are concerned, even though this means the constant misspelling by Cosima of her own daughter's name ("Daniella" for "Daniela") and the names of some of the family dogs ("Kos" for "Koss" and "Rus" for "Russ"). Cosima was, however, right in her spelling of "Tribschen" ("Triebschen," as already mentioned, was Wagner's own invention), and she was also correct to give the name "Wesendonck" its *c*—this was not dropped from the family name until some years later (by Mathilde's son, Karl Wesendonk).

On the other hand, I have not felt obliged, as the German editors contractually were, to follow Cosima in her manner of dating her entries, which is frequently confusing, for, after the first few entries, she did not always indicate the month or even the day of the week, and there are occasions when she became muddled and misdated entirely. Rather than become involved in putting matters right in footnotes, as in the German edition, I have followed a straightforward system of giving the full date for each entry.

Practicability has been my main aim throughout this translation, which is not (and cannot by its very nature be) a fully authentic document—that only the original German book, as edited by Martin Gregor-Dellin and Dietrich Mack, can be, since the Diaries were written in German. It is consequently to that edition that the reader in search of complete authenticity must go. Nevertheless, I have aimed, as far as is possible in translation, to match the authenticity of that edition, and in doing so I have been confronted with problems of my own.

For instance, should a translator attempt to reflect the frequent "foreignness" of Cosima's German by translating it into an equivalent "foreign" English? I felt that this would merely produce an artificial impression, and would prove distracting rather than illuminating, and so I resisted the temptation. On the other hand, stylistic clumsinesses, such as repetitions of individual words, mixture of tenses, and so on, can be regarded as a legitimate feature of any diary written for private purposes and not for publication, and presumably not revised by the author. Such shortcomings have nothing to do basically with the writer's command of a language as such, and consequently I have thought it right to reflect these clumsinesses in my translation.

Another problem arose for me in dealing with passages which are untranslatable because they involve a play on words which cannot be reproduced exactly in another language. In translating works of fiction one can frequently overcome this difficulty by substituting other words with which one *can* play around in a similar way, thus matching the original effect. But in a work as direct and personal as a diary, such a method introduces a note of unreality—indeed, almost of untruthfulness. The simplest way is of course to omit such passages, if they are not otherwise important, and this is the course I have followed when I have not been able to reflect the word play in similar and natural English words. This solution, however, unfortunately deprives us of several examples of Richard Wagner's humor, for he was an indefatigable and adroit punster. I have attempted to make up for this loss wherever possible by reproducing the pun in its original German form in the notes, with explanations where necessary.

My only other omissions are of occasional repeated entries, when Cosima seems to have forgotten that she had already recorded them. When such repetitions are very short, however, I have left them in. Apart from these omissions, of which there are in fact very few, amounting in all to not much more than a hundred words, the text of the Diaries is translated in full.

Cosima invariably gives the titles of books and plays in German, and most of her and Wagner's reading of foreign literature appears to have been in translation. My rule has been to give these titles in their original language, unless they are already so well known in English that the English titles can be safely used. For Richard Wagner's own literary works I have used the titles of the official English translation by W. Ashton Ellis. Other translations have been published of some of his literary works, but the Ashton Ellis titles are those most frequently used in English biographies of the composer (notably that of Ernest Newman) and are thus the easiest to identify.

The titles of Wagner's musical works are so well known in their original German form that they can safely be left that way. The same might be said of the passages from their texts which Cosima occasionally quotes: to any Wagnerian, "*Winterstürme wichen*," for instance, would be more easily identified than "Winter tempests have yielded," and thus I have usually preferred to leave them in this form. However, there can be no hard and fast rule on the matter: in cases where the *sense* of the quoted words is more important than their actual form, I have preferred to supply an English translation. But readers in any doubt will, I hope, find elucidation in the notes.

These notes, though based mainly on those in the German edition, differ from them in several aspects. An English or American reader naturally has a different cultural heritage and background from a German reader, and thus different points may call for elucidation; also, an opportunity has been provided by the passage of time and by second thoughts to supplement or amend annotations in the original German edition. In assembling the additional material for these notes I was greatly assisted by the late Mr. Wolfgang Sauerlander, who was also responsible for compiling the much-enlarged index. Fortunately for this book, his work on it was far advanced before his sudden death on October 27, 1977.

To the German editors, Martin Gregor-Dellin and Dietrich Mack, I am much indebted for help in solving specific factual problems.

Geoffrey Skelton

# The Diaries

This book belongs to my children.

Tribschen, near Lucerne.
1869.

Dedicated quite especially to Siegfried
by Mama.

# 1869

*Friday, January 1* On Christmas Day, my 31st birthday, this notebook was to have started; I could not get it in Lucerne. And so the
first day of the year will also contain the beginning of my reports to
you, my children. You shall know every hour of my life, so that one
day you will come to see me as I am; for, if I die young, others will be
able to tell you very little about me, and if I live long, I shall probably
only wish to remain silent. In this way you will help me do my duty—
yes, children, my duty. What I mean by that you will find out later.
Your mother intends to tell you everything about her present life,
and she believes she can do so.

The year 1868 marks the outward turning-point of my life: in this
year it was granted to me to put into action what for the past five years
had filled my thoughts. It is an occupation I have not sought after or
brought about myself: Fate laid it on me. In order that you may
understand, I must confess to you that up to the hour in which I
recognized my true inner calling, my life had been a dreary, unbeautiful dream, of which I have no desire to tell you anything, for I
do not understand it myself and reject it with the whole of my now
purified soul. The outward appearance was and remained calm, but
inside all was bleak and dreary, when there came into my life that being
who swiftly led me to realize that up to now I had never lived. My
love became for me a rebirth, a deliverance, a fading away of all that
was trivial and bad in me, and I swore to seal it through death, through
pious renunciation or complete devotion. What love has done for me
I shall never be able to repay. When the stars decreed that events,
about which you will find out elsewhere, should banish into isolation
my only friend, the guardian spirit and savior of my soul, the revealer
of all that is noble and true, that he should be left solitary, abandoned,
joyless, and unfriended, I cried out to him: I shall come to you and
seek my greatest and highest happiness in sharing the burdens of life
with you. It was then that I left you, my two precious eldest children.
I did it and would do it again at any moment, and yet I miss you both
and think of you day and night. For I love you all, each with an equal
love; in your hearts I seek the refuge for my earthly memory when my

time is past, and I would sacrifice everything to you—everything but the life of this one person. Our separation will be temporary, and you are still so small that you will not feel it as your mother does. This is my hope.

Early in the morning the Friend came to greet me and wish me a happy New Year. I am always so overcome by his kindness toward me, in my ever deeper awareness of his greatness, that in his presence I always feel I must dissolve into tears. Afterward I dressed Loldchen and Evchen prettily (white satin frocks and garlands of roses) and we went to give him our good wishes. Then we had breakfast, after which he went to work as usual (making a fair copy of the second act of *Siegfried* and completing his essay on the Jews). I took Evchen and Loldchen into the garden. Before lunch (at one o'clock) my beloved read me what he had written. At table he told me more of the range of his essay, and we discussed his position, that is to say, the position of art as laid down by the Jews, which made me see Mendelssohn for the first time as a tragic figure. After the meal he went for his usual walk, after receiving a telegram from the King and another from you. The latter affected him as it did me; my heart was heavy and full to bursting, because you were not here with me, but a glance at him consoled me and gave me courage—I was looking into a happy future. Then I arranged the Christmas tree, which was lit today for the second time. At about five o'clock Evchen and Loldchen, dressed again as angels, came down and found the Christmas gifts which had been kept back. Richard played for them, they danced, and I thought of you, my absent ones, so far away, and once again I watched the merry scene through a veil of tears, yet here, too, these tears were without bitterness. Then Richard started up a jumping jack, to Loldi's great joy. While the little ones were enjoying their supper, he played me the "Spring Song" from *Die Walküre*. When you one day hear these sounds, my children, you will understand me. I cannot hear them without being transported right away. — We had tea upstairs in my room; I asked my beloved to dictate something to me today (biography) for superstitious reasons (they say that whatever one does on the first day of the year one continues). Although it was an exertion for him, he wanted in his indescribable goodness toward me to do it, and so there emerged two pages about Schopenhauer which for me are beyond all price. At eleven we parted, after once more reviewing the day together and finding it harmonious and good. When he had gone, I sat down at my writing desk to talk to you. The Friend has given me the golden pen with which he wrote *Tristan* and *Siegfried*, and this I consecrate to these communications of mine to you. Thus I signify to you how sacredly I regard this work of a mother's confidences and anxieties; the pen which has traced the sublimest things ever created by a noble spirit shall now be dedicated solely to the depths of a woman's heart. So God bless you, my children, you who are far away, you who are close by, and you lying still unknown within my womb. May your mother's love be a friendly light to you in your path through life! Do not mistake your mother, though you yourselves will never be able to do what she has done, since what Fate has here decreed is something that will not recur. All whom I love are now at rest, and so I, too, will go to my bed. For you and for him my last and friendliest thoughts!

*Saturday, January 2* Cheered on opening my eyes by the sight of a rosy sky; the "foehn" had conjured up its most brilliant colors for the morning display of light. Soon afterward I was told that Evchen was ill, she had had a bad night. Concern, but no anxiety, for she was cheerful. Richard slightly indisposed but in good spirits. We visit the child, I stay upstairs while he goes to his work (essay on the Jews). At eleven I go to say goodbye before my walk with Loldi and can report that Evchen is well, if still a bit run down. Before lunch he reads me the continuation. Great delight in its terseness and pithiness. Our conversation at table arises from this. After the meal a feeling of intense happiness at having found each other. Later—in connection with the biography—I ask him whether I should read Schopenhauer. He advises me against it: a woman should approach philosophy through a man, a poet. I am in complete agreement. He goes for his walk, I to sleep with Musäus in my hand. In the evening to the children, Eva very lively, a great load off my mind. The children to bed (7 o'clock), then supper. Richard has no inclination to dictate; we decide to read a book. Plato? — Not yet bound. *Wallenstein?* — Read it again only a short time ago. Calderón? — Too emotional. So Shakespeare's histories or the *Odyssey*. We decide on the last. Most wonderful impression, a sublimely intimate evening, indelible images stamped on my mind. Untroubled sleep.

*Sunday, January 3* Bright Sunday sky. Eva healthy again. Richard well after a good night. Hoping for a letter from the children in Munich. First subject of conversation at breakfast—*Homer!* His influence on the artistic and earlier living ideals of my beloved. Daily visit to the children together. Richard to his work, I into the garden with Loldi. The frost pearls seen yesterday in the moss no longer to be found, but pleasure in the glistening, colorful scene. The soul at peace, Nature at peace, a lovely harmony. By one o'clock the Friend's essay finished; he reads me the ending (Schumann). The unexpectedly happy and mild mood of this ending. As usual at midday, the Friend takes a walk and I rest, reading Musäus's *"Rothmantel"* on my couch. In the evening to the children; Loldi has hit Evchen, but is good and repentant when I reproach her.

A cheerful "Good night." Supper in my room; conversation about the cavalrymen's songs of the Thirty Years' War and the Seven Years' War; Richard sings me two of them (*"Prinz Eugen"* and *"Die Prager Schlacht"*). Then he talks about Bernhard von Weimar and King Gustavus Adolphus; his indignation over present-day attempts to stamp the latter as a Jesuit. A typical feature, which Richard points out to me regarding the Battle of Lützen: Gustavus Adolphus's troops were not discouraged by his death, as happened with Pappenheim's death on the imperial side; proof that morality was on the side of the Protestants. Richard's delight in Bernhard von Weimar, pleasure in a German revealing himself thus. Magnificent demonstration of the whole Germanic character. He (Richard) seems to me to be the last true German. — The evening crowned with four cantos from the *Odyssey* (Calypso, Nausicaä, Leucothea). Only distraction during the reading in watching R.'s fine, radiant countenance and delighting in the sound of his voice. — Only shadows over the day: receiving no letter from Munich (the post office was closed in the afternoon), and the fact that the Friend entrusted some little service not to me, but to a servant. He does not yet realize how willingly I would do anything for him, the smallest things as well as the largest. — Tears came into my eyes once—when Loldi quite unexpectedly sang the songs she had learned from Loulou and Boni. Good night, my dear children, soon I shall have you all with me, as I keep you all together in my heart.

*Monday, January 4* Monday has always been my bad day. Evchen ill again (servants' carelessness!). My great concern about this coupled with some indecision, for it is not easy to make changes in the household. Patience and increased care on my part are called for. A letter from Hermine: the children there are well, they had a merry Christmas; melancholy pleasure in that. Spent the morning in the children's room, except for the hour in which R. read me his essay as a connected whole. This pleasure banished my worried mood at once. In the afternoon with the children; again much bother, for Evchen had inadvertently been given some milk, which again brought on tummy ache. However, she does not look too bad and has no temperature; she is also cheerful. I write to Hermine and Mathilde Maier so as not to give way to depression. A great longing for Loulou, who is perhaps missing me. Took up again the cantos of Homer which we read yesterday; a feeling that the book refuses to come to life when the Friend is not reading it out loud to me. To me the whole world is recognizable only in him and through him. — At R.'s wish the children are being given a second room; the move unsettles me, as does any outward change, however small. — After tea Richard plays for me the Prelude to *Tristan und Isolde* (which the *Signale* once described as "crudely sensual"!). Deeply moved by it, indeed hardly in control of myself. At such moments I can think of nothing else but Elsa's words, *"Für Dich möchte ich zum Tode gehen"* ["For you I would willingly lay down my life"], and even these I am unable to utter. Afterward two cantos from the *Odyssey* (Polyphemus and Circe); great delight in the former; Circe, however, whom we accompanied with punch, sent us to sleep. Genelli's Homer designs now no longer attract me, they are totally lacking in naïveté, even if the conception is frequently brilliant. Completely different pictures arise in our minds when we read this magnificent poem. At eleven Richard goes to his apartment; I go to bed, blessing the children.

*Tuesday, January 5 (Morning)* Evchen somewhat better, woke up only once during the night. From the moment of rising I was filled with great melancholy; harsh is the dream of life, my children, and in it I seem to myself a stranger. I fight against my depression. Evchen does not look well, but the sun is shining, and the day must certainly still hold some good and beautiful things in its lap.

*(Evening)* A walk in the bright sunshine was a great help to me; from the top of the hill I was enraptured by the ring of snow-capped mountains, which suggested to me a mysterious, unmoving dance. Absorbed long in watching the picture, my spirit heard the music which higher beings reproduce for us in sounds. — The transience of all individual existence, the eternity of the whole, was reflected to me in the blue mirror of the lake. My deep inner strength restored, I summoned the Friend from his work and together we wandered up the hill; the magnificent Mount Pilatus looked like a spectral shadow. Upstairs with the children I discovered there had been negligence again regarding their diet, and it worried me greatly; not for fear of the consequences, but because of the servants' indifference. The depression I had overcome returned and held sway over the whole day. From town Richard brought a toy for the children (a nutcracker), which gave them much joy. He also brought a letter informing him that no one was willing to publish the translation of his essay on Rossini. This letter gave me a new insight into conditions as they are in Paris. We could see very clearly how far removed we are from all these bustling activities, and how little we now really know of what is going on in the world, what is now the prevailing atmosphere there. — Put the children to bed; Evchen lively, if not yet entirely recovered. Three cantos from the *Odyssey* to finish the evening. The splendid happenings seem like a dream picture to me—so vital and distinct—when the Friend reads them out to me; when I read them for myself, it is as if they were real; but *thus* everything is experienced at a remove. His voice and his manner encompass the immortal work like music. "There is happiness, but we do not recognize it; if we do recognize it, we are unable to

appreciate it," says the Princess [in Goethe's *Tasso*]. I both recognize and appreciate it. Not all the sufferings and miseries of this earth can affect that happiness which lies concealed deep within the heart like a pearl in an oyster, and even in my heaviest hours I have known this blissful pearl in my soul. — Sleep well, my children, how your mother longs to see you all united!

*Wednesday, January 6*  Evchen still somewhat indisposed. Spent the morning with the children. Both good and in high spirits. Richard is copying out his essay. Apprehensive afternoon caused by a visit of the Bassenheims' servants to our servants. Since the former are in contact with Munich, and I can expect nothing but evil from there, I have the feeling that malicious curiosity has driven them here in the worst of weathers to find out whether I and the children are here. My imaginings upset Richard, since there is nothing he can do to help, but he is soon back in good spirits, and I console myself with the thought that in concealing my whereabouts I intended no harm to the world and acted only out of consideration for others. And if the trials I am expecting are to begin here and in this way, then in God's name I shall tell you, my children, how it all came about and how I am bearing it. Evening with the children; both full of fun. God give Eva a good night. — In the evening two cantos from the *Odyssey* (Odysseus and the Swineherd, Telemachus's Return); the former splendid in every detail, the second rather wearisome. Richard has finished copying his essay and is satisfied with it. Today I imagined myself in the children's room in Munich, unrecognized, but I did not wish to remain unrecognized; yet, recognized, I could not go. And so it is best as it is. May the gods but give us friendly guidance!

*Thursday, January 7*  The day began well; Evchen slept peacefully through the night, and Richard told me of the cheerful dream he had had, in which we were walking and talking intimately together. Even when Fate has hurled us beyond all revelations of this sort, such as premonitions, visions, dreams, so that we can scarcely continue to pay attention to them, all the same a pleasant image is of great value, it seems like a greeting from friendly gods to whom we no longer belong, and I am thankful for it as for a moment of happiness. — Unfortunately this ray of sunshine vanished all too soon. Richard brought up to me two issues of the *Süddeutsche Presse*, which some impudent person had sent him anonymously; they contained a lengthy article by Fröbel about *Opera and Drama*. I cannot describe the feelings of revulsion that filled me as I read it. May God preserve you, my children, from ever being obliged to see the things you love, honor, and believe in being dragged through the mud. Here there is no question of a contest, in which one courageously faces up to the opponent, not even of a martyrdom joyfully endured in order to bear witness to one's beliefs. This is nothing but a besmirching, which cannot be fought against, and the endurance of which does no good for one's cause. — Richard saw my deep dejection and read the article for himself. At first he took it calmly, for it gave him additional material for his *Judaism in Music* essay. At lunch, however, we sought in vain to dispel the grief which had taken hold of us, all our experiences rose up before us like the ghosts in Shakespeare's plays, and we wondered glumly why every word brought forth only dirt or met with apathetic non-recognition. The whole day remained under a cloud. From town someone brought my Friend the expected letter from Boni. Also two friendly greetings from afar (M. Muchanoff and Elisabeth Krockow), but I really do not know what to do with these friendships. No one will follow me when he knows whither I have come, and it is only by you that I still want to be loved and understood. — The children in good health; Loldi talks about Reynard the *Fish*. — In the evening the *Odyssey*; the finest thing in it the dog Argos, the profound mystery of Nature seemingly brought nearer and to some extent unveiled. The sick dog is the only living thing to recognize Odysseus through his change and disguise—then dies after awaiting him twenty years!

*Friday, January 8*   Dear Loulou and dear Boni, today is your father's birthday; I wish that he may spend it in a mood of peaceful reconciliation, though there is nothing I can contribute toward it. It was a great misunderstanding that bound us together in marriage; my feelings toward him are today still the same as 12 years ago: great sympathy with his destiny, pleasure in his qualities of mind and heart, genuine respect for his character, however completely different our temperaments. In the very first year of our marriage I was already in such despair over this confusion that I wished for death; many errors arose out of my distress, but I was always able to get a grip on myself again, and your father knew nothing of my sufferings—I do not think he will withhold his testimony that I always stood by him, in suffering as in joy, and that I helped him to the best of my powers. Never would he have lost me if Fate had not brought me together with the man for whom I had to recognize it as my task in life to live or die. I have not a single reproach to make to your father, even if our last years together were hard for me beyond all imagining. I wanted to try combining my former existence with my new life, I believed in the possibility of fusing together all the diverging feelings—abuse and insults proved to me that I was being a fool, and all that remained was for me to make the choice that was no choice. Thus I am now deprived of you, my children, and it worries me greatly, but there is a God who helps.

In the morning I wrote to Boni and Marie Muchanoff. I go around all day feeling rather wretched, for the weather is unfavorable. Richard and I recalled the previous year, in which we celebrated Hans's birthday all together and were still full of hopes and much good will. In the afternoon the Italian score of *Rienzi* arrived, as well as the *Cinque Canti* (which gave us less delight). Then with the children, until they were in bed. After a conversation on table turning, about which we are not of the same mind (Richard thinks it is the result of some mechanical law, I that it is fraud), we decided on three cantos from the *Odyssey*, only I am so tired that I can scarcely listen, and lose much of what is read. Today I felt in my womb the first stirrings of the unknown being within me.

*Saturday, January 9* A bad night; violent headaches combined with nightmares, worry about the children, dismal thoughts about my mother and father, painful memories of the past, and apprehensions about the children's future. My state of mind reaches the stage of blazing fear. "Oh, if only I had a sister!" I cry out in the silent darkness. Oh, my children, keep the ring of hearts intact! Only when joy and sorrow are sucked through the same root can trust and love emerge; the friendships which life brings in its course are all beset by humiliating doubts and misunderstandings. Unshakable, rewarding faith lies only in the love between sisters. — I rose, having slept little. The maid has gone for two days to visit her parents, and so I am now spending all my time in the children's room. The children are good and well behaved, I can write and read in their presence; and Eva is now well again. At midday Richard discussed with me the prospects for the immediate publication of the essay on the Jews; I told him I was incapable of saying anything at all about it, for, were one to tell me that it will cause him the greatest unpleasantness, or that it will be completely ignored or make a good impression, I should believe it all. — In connection with Fröbel's article, Richard tells me he feels as if he had knocked with friendly intentions on the door of a house in which everything was as still as death, and all he heard in reply was the grunt of a pig. I feel very unwell, violent headache, but a walk in the fresh air does me good. Finished the *Odyssey*.

*Sunday, January 10* Slight disappointment that the pen I had sent from New York for R. does not write well. I note this down because it bothered me during the night, and I had the feeling that my earlier luck has deserted me in the little as in the big things. Sleepless night with much worry about the children's future. Melancholy thoughts about my own upbringing, fears that I would not be able to bring up my children in accordance with my own ideas. Richard also none too well, but cheerful. Went for a walk with the two children, both well. Ate with them afterward. Later with Richard at table, arrival of the next installment of Fröbel's article on *Opera and Drama*. Though R. burned it without reading it, the mere thought of the unworthiness of people is upsetting. The King's silence is also curious and unkind. R.'s great depression in connection with his work, he really feels like abandoning the musical completion of his *Nibelungen* entirely. My objections only serve to increase his mood of dejection. I go sadly to lie down, R. goes off to town. Then with the children. In the evening, to my great joy, resumption of the dictation. Before going off to bed I say to R., "If only I could bring you real joy!" Deep melancholy grips me at the thought of his mood during the day, when he went through all his relationships and found not one of them serious and deep. Worst of all, his experiences with the King. We spoke of the possibility of spending our future life in a garret in Paris. A living room and two little bedrooms for ourselves and the children. God knows what Fate has in store for us.

*Monday, January 11* Eva unwell again; irritation over the way the whole house meddles; I am unjust enough to show R. my irritation. Prolonged sleeplessness is my only excuse for this injustice. He has sent off the essay on the Jews, which makes me apprehensive, yet I did not try to prevent it. Many thoughts about Boni and Loulou. A walk with the two children. Richard at work (*Die Meistersinger* is at last to be staged in Karlsruhe and Dresden). He tells me after lunch that he was in a state of alarm because he did not hear me come home, and he quotes Calderón: the most terrible thing of all is happy love, for then there is fear in everything. At lunch he said the curse of his life had been poverty and marriage. After the meal I again feel very unwell and go to lie down. Richard is finishing a page of his score; I am glad to see him restored in mood and appearance. It is only when he is out that I am beset by worry and anxiety that we shall not be left in peace; I see us abandoned to misery and malicious scorn. But once he is with me again, my evil thoughts vanish. It is for me downright agony to be separated from him, even for a single instant. No letter from the children. Hans keeps silent, my father must now be in Germany; how alien everything to do with the world has now become to me! And I know that nobody in it has ever loved me. — Eva somewhat better but still looking pale. Good evening, my Lusch, good evening, my Boni, I miss you even in moments of the greatest happiness. Never could I do without you entirely.

*Tuesday, January 12* A sleepless night was made bearable for me by the sight of the starlit sky. At dawn I fell asleep and then woke up. Richard is well—last night we had a moment of strain, because he did not want to dictate to me out of concern for my condition, and I urgently begged him to. But I gave in when I saw his great reluctance and his anxiety, and yesterday evening ended with the first canto of the *Iliad*. After such a moment of discord, however trivial, it is true happiness to exchange kind looks again. Eva still looking rather pale; I spend all morning with the children. Loldi often speaks of Loulou, which makes me glad and sad at the same time. She remembers the children's room in Munich in detail, and Eva cries out "Loulou, Loulou," as if trying to recall a dream. At lunch Richard tells me that he has been thinking a lot about his *Nibelungen*, and, he adds jokingly, it has made him feel very puffed up. It makes me happy to see him thinking of his divine work without repugnance. Apart from that, the *Odyssey* still forms the main topic of our conversation. Also Beethoven's symphonies—yesterday it was the A Major (with reference to the trio of the Presto, which German conductors always turn into a "Grandfather's Dance," whereas the tempo should quite unnoticeably become slower and the manner of playing should mark the great difference); today the F Major (in the first movement not a single repetition, yet everything seems the same). Richard has often pointed out to me with what sure instinct Beethoven in the symphonies (except for the Ninth, in which he uses words as a reconciling element) avoids touching on the regions in which he lets himself go in the more intimate forms of quartet and sonata. He knew that he was speaking to the people, and that here certain accents are out of place unless accompanied and softened by words. — After lunch a short sleep and a walk by myself in the garden. The cold has arrived, grass and trees are covered with frost. In this solitary hour I thought only of you, my children. I thought with apprehension of the future: if it should really be my lot to be separated from you, and if you should then find your mother's actions incomprehensible, may the heavens be merciful and grant me death! I have not selfishly pursued happiness, I have done only what could not have been done in any other way, and my only, yet heartfelt, pride is that I have helped and still help as far as I am able. Always remember, my children, that true peace will come to you only from complete dedication; the sufferings which flow from this source are unceasing, too, but gentle. From the garden to the children. There Richard found me; when he came in he was cheerful, indeed boisterous; my long meditation has tired me; also, I had been expecting him to bring me a letter from Munich, and since that was not the case, I felt sad. But I soon overcame it. In the evening, dictation; R. started off with great reluctance, but soon began to remember. We parted at about eleven, after having completed four pages. [*A sentence concerning a remark by Isolde omitted as untranslatable.*] — Talking of the world situation and a possible major upset this year, Richard said: "Even when one's expectations are blackly pessimistic, one is still being too optimistic, for things always come about by halves and loaded with so many compromises that only the baser elements gain anything. The only consolation is that the unworthy things are also incapable of starting anything." He added that twice in his life he had felt good and worthy: at the beginning of his exile, when, relieved of everything, he possessed and desired nothing; and in Vienna, after the *Tannhäuser* fiasco in Paris, when he had severed all ties and was not indebted to a single mortal soul.

*Wednesday, January 13*  Dreamed of Blandine, my sister. When I woke up, I looked for her: "Of course she is dead, alas." Richard well, the children lively, but the weather dull. Before going into the garden with the children I say adieu to Richard; he tells me his spirit is engulfed in heavy clouds; "the sort of thing one does not talk about." Oh, how well I understand him! Yet in the early morning—when he wakened me with "*Freude, schöner Götterfunken*" on the piano—I had hoped his mood would remain cheerful. When I return and go once more to greet him, he says, "Poor woman, all you have is me!" "Then I am not poor," I observe. However, he is working hard on his score. At table the conversation turns to Lola Montez. Describing her wretched ending, I say, "The poor creature!" Richard admonishes me severely, saying that such heartless, daemonic beings should not be grieved over, one should reserve one's pity for others. He is certainly right, yet badness seems to me always pitiable and nothing more worthy of our compassion than a wretched ending. We are delighted with the books he has bought (a new Lessing and the Simrock set of folk tales). The latter in particular delights me. While with the children in the evening he reads me two letters from Paris; the *Rienzi* venture there is being wretchedly handled. I continue to hope that it will not reach the stage. The Prelude to Act III of *Lohengrin* with the "Bridal Song" is reported to have been a tremendous success. — But no news of the children in Munich. I am not worried, just sorrowful. My worries concern the future, and it is for that reason that my nights are always bad and uneasy. — In the evening R. again spoke somberly; he believes that after his death they will drop his works entirely, and he will live on in human memory only as a phantom. However bad things look among the public, the theaters, and the press, I still cannot believe that he will disappear in this way. He maintains that not a soul studies his scores, and that seems to me, however widespread the stupidity and indifference, scarcely possible. In the evening he dictated to me again, and the day ended very merrily with his reminiscences of his second visit to London. I looked in once more on the sleeping children.

*Thursday, January 14*  Restless night, but good morning hours. Richard wakes me with the *Lohengrin* "Battle Song." But then he tells

me a bullfinch has dashed itself to death on the sides of the bird cage
in fright. He bought the little creatures only a few weeks ago; one of
them fretted itself to death and would not eat, wasted right away.
How sad it is! Kos is also always ill, and does not improve in spite of
all our attention. — After taking the children into the garden I go for
a little walk on my own, thinking of the little ones in Munich. Involuntarily the restless spirit, in its anxiety, implores its unmoving
surroundings for help and protection. They remain rigid and silent, but
deep inside the words resound: "Reconcile yourself with your heart
and your fate, control the former and bear the latter. In the end you
will not be given a burden greater than you can carry." I returned home
in peace. At lunch R. and I discuss once more the horrible episode
with Fröbel; that this man who is now foaming with rage is the same
man whom R. himself brought to Munich in order to help him pro-
pagate his ideas! R. tells me finally that Hebbel had once said to him
about Nestroy, "He is such a vile person that a rose he has sniffed must
itself begin to stink." His theories on love, as conveyed by Fröbel's
pen, seem to him, he says, rather like the rose beneath Nestroy's nose.
— A letter from his niece Ottilie in Dresden invites Richard to the
first performance there of *Die Meistersinger*. R. is undecided whether
to go; he would like to do something to prevent too poor a performance, but he dreads the thought of what he might experience there.
He goes into town and brings back a good letter from Milan (his
publisher), but nothing from my children. Much sorrow, but I manage
to control it. Richard is in a gloomy mood; the general silence in
Munich he finds very depressing. My father left Rome on the 7th;
R. thinks that an evil brew is being prepared for us on all sides. The
biography restores our spirits. Good night, my children. Your mother's
heart is concerned for you.

*Friday, January 15* Little sleep during the night; long hours of
quiet wakefulness in the dark. Thoughts of the children: are they
missing me? Few worries—perhaps all too few—about Hans; his
artistic activities are a source of pleasure to him, my sorrowful detachment from it after the failure of our great undertaking interrupted the
flow of this source. How different is R., how utterly he has only me to
understand him and to share his isolation from the world! I cannot
believe that I shall have to pay for my dedication to him through the
alienation of my elder children. Richard is not looking well: is it his
inner anxiety or the overcast weather which weighs so heavily on him?
The world around us remains silent. He asks me whether I am worrying
about the children, and he believes that my father has been a bad
influence in that matter. Unfortunately I believe so, too. However,
Loldi and Eva are well; the latter very wild. — Today R. woke me

up with *"Ein' feste Burg ist unser Gott."* Then he declared there would certainly be a war this year. How long will we be granted our Tribschen tranquillity? — Read some of Schiller's letters while the children are out walking. Fall asleep from weariness. R. is working on his score. Loldi very good, Eva so violent that she hits me. Solitary walk after lunch; the play of sun and mist gives the farther banks of the lake the appearance of a dream vision, the trees, covered with frost, greet me like gentle, friendly ghosts; Mount Pilatus, its peak surrounded by golden clouds, seems like the noble monarch of this dream world. *"Alles Vergängliche ist nur ein Gleichnis"* ["All transient things are but an image"], I find myself thinking as I reach the top of the hill and look around me. No happiness on earth, but in our hearts Eternity, that which echoes inside us with every noble sound, every profound poem, every picture in art or Nature, every great deed of the heart. — R. again brought me no letter; real pain; I know that I could pass on to my children teachings of imperishable, everlasting worth. Is this to be denied me? When will the change in my destiny come, so that I may live for my children and for him? — Loldchen and Evchen in good health and well behaved. In the evening, dictation—the return to Zurich and the busy year 1856. — R. told me during the evening that he loved me above all else in the world, and these words made me immeasurably happy—even if I know it already within my heart without his having to tell me.

*Saturday, January 16* Two months ago today I said goodbye to you, children—my heart is heavy when I think of it, and I am without any news of you! In order to get a little sleep I had a warm drink late last night; I went to sleep at once, but soon woke up again and thought of you. I desire nothing in this world but to be allowed to help my beloved, to give him some tranquil years of life, and to bring you up. Gladly will I sacrifice everything, everything, my contacts with the world, all music; will bear all disgrace, if only this is granted me! R. wished me good morning with the *Meistersinger* theme. He is well and has had a reassuring letter from Dresden (Mitterwurzer); he is glad that he does not need to go. The newspapers report that the King is giving many audiences; with a smile we observe that he is at last doing what we long in vain asked him to do! — I am apprehensive about Munich, all this silence; even the painter Lenbach, who was always good and loyal to me and promised to write, is silent. I stay with the children and write to Claire, asking her to find out news about Loulou and Boni. R. writes letters and turns down the invitation to Dresden. But he is not well; I am quite prepared to attribute it to the bad weather and the overcast sky, but all the same it worries me. We start talking about Schopenhauer, and he tells me Schopenhauer once said to Karl

Ritter, "I admire Wagner as a poet, but he is no musician." [*Added in the margin*: "Schopenhauer said: I admire how Wagner in his *Nibelungen* brings the dark, legendary figures humanly near to us. Then: He is a poet, but no musician."] R. is amused by Schopenhauer's use of the old-fashioned word "*admirieren*," but says it is at any rate better than if he had acknowledged him to be a musician and not a poet. After lunch the little Buddha (an earlier present of my mother's to Wagner) arrived, as well as the letters to his wife. Much good humor at their safe arrival. Richard says I have brought sense into his life and awakened in him a pleasure in good order. How glad he makes me with such statements! He plays the piano, the children come down and dance with me. Then he has more *Rienzi* trouble (the French). He goes for a walk and I stay with Schiller. Much delight and uplift from some of the poems ("The Words of Error" and "Fortune"). No letter from the children. Richard and I in low spirits because of it. A quiet evening, no dictation.

*Sunday, January 17 (Morning)* Slept only a little, but woke up quite fresh. Kept thinking about the possibility of a reunion with the children very soon. Great weakness and inner misery, but fought against both, for the little ones' and R.'s sake.

*(Evening)* My head feels heavy. How I should like to write to you cheerfully, so that you would read some of these pages with a smile; but cheerfulness I can only put into my actions; I do so with Loldchen and Evchen and shall do so with you when you are here. But writing down one's thoughts conjures up all the seriousness of life. And also I am still without letters, without news of you. I can look at your portrait, which is standing on the writing desk in front of me. My good Lulu, may Heaven bless you! This evening Richard hurt me—he, who is always such balm to my soul! When I begged him to continue with the biography, he observed that "this innocent life" could surely hold no attractions for me. Why did he say that? I do not know, for he certainly does not really think it. Alone, by myself, I have wept unceasingly today, though I have tried to keep myself in check through attending to the little ones and constant reading. On my own I am weak. At times I feel that death cannot be far away, but I chase the thought from my mind, for I want still to live, for him and for you. You look at me with your good and trusting eyes; surely you cannot be ill, my Luschchen? At table we talked a lot again about the drama. R. explained to me various verse meters, particularly in regard to Schiller, whose *Wallenstein* I am now rereading. He also feels that *Wallensteins Lager* and *Die Piccolomini* should be divided into three big acts, the *Lager*, with the arrival of the princess, of Max, and of Thekla accompanied by the dragoons (with marchlike music) at the end,

forming the first act. And the banquet at Terzky's, with the conversation between father and son at the conclusion of it, should end the whole play. — Richard is so worried about me that I do not know how to set about comforting him. It is after all my duty to keep him in good cheer. Good night, my children, it is now nearly midnight, the sacred hour. May all good angels accompany and protect you! Daniel and Blandine, bless my children!

*Monday, January 18* A better night, which I owe to the great extent of my worries; there comes a moment when the mind can no longer bear the load of all one's thoughts and takes refuge in sleep. Finished *Wallenstein* in the morning. How can we ever praise a poet enough who can take us right out of ourselves? I have always been especially affected by this particular work, in which a great spirit shows us the petty activities of the world in their largest dimensions, entertains us with the events, and uplifts us with his own feelings. Shakespeare's dramas are more powerful, more daemonic, more shattering; Goethe's style more tender perhaps, more intimate, more subtle; Calderón's fantasies more singular, more passionate and melancholy, but for me Schiller's creations remain the most affecting. For me it is as if he has found the right way of showing mankind its own image so as to give it courage. He is a benefactor of mankind, and the scope of his genius is not lessened by the fact that he avoids certain regions. — In Gordon's words [in *Wallenstein*]—misfortune has hope, fortune fear as its companion—lies for me the whole enigma of life: thus it is on earth, my children, that is how the poets see it and that is how we experience it. — Many newspapers came today, much news of musical activities. It all seems a grand muddle. Toward noon R. came up to see me, looking very gloomy; he feels set against completing his work. He began it, he says, at a time when life was to him a fantastic image, and now, when it has been given a basis through me and the children, he feels he could make better use of his powers than writing scores which will never be produced and will mean nothing to anybody. When I replied that times would change, he answered: "At best they will be terrible, at best they will become puritanical, and my work has no place there. But it would still be a thousand times better than the present situation." I find this a terrible statement; I feel that there can be no blessing on our bond if the *Nibelungen* remains unfinished. That R.'s state of health is just as much to blame for his lack of sympathy with his true calling as a passing glance at the world outside is no consolation for the pain I feel over his words; but I continue to hope that *his* God, the one that dwells in his own breast, will not forsake him. The children are playing beside me and keeping me from giving way to miserable thoughts. After lunch R. to town and I into the garden; I am still occupied with

*Wallenstein.* In this rereading, it has struck me above all that one is downright glad to see the hero suffering (Max's death, Buttler's treachery), and, however much one is affected by his fate, one has absolutely no desire to rescue him from it, for his downfall and the treachery alone constitute his greatness; completely different from Götz or Egmont, for whom one feels as do Georg and Klärchen. Very characteristically, Schiller has not given this ambitious, coolly calculating, yet rashly fanciful being a companion spirit true unto death, except for the sister, who, however, does not die with him, but *falls* with him. Wonderful is the absence of pathos in W.'s last appearance. It is as if—though not knowing he is to die—he is nevertheless aware of finality; calm and manly, he awaits his end. — From reflecting on this work just read, my thoughts soon transferred themselves to you, my children, and I sent you peaceful, loving greetings from afar. Five times I walked through the entire grounds of Tribschen, dusk fell, sky, mountains, lake stood gray and stiff before me like an impenetrable, threefold wall, and then there rose a sun in my soul, I felt inside me, deep and true, that you would remain by me, my children, whatever the world might do with me. Hardly had this light flared up in me in the enveloping darkness when I heard my name being called; R. had returned home, joyfully bringing me a letter from you. You are well and good and cheerful; your mother in her longing, melancholy happiness blesses you. In his unutterable kindness toward me R. was visibly full of cheer after handing me the letter. We went up to the children; Eva well and unruly, Loldi very peculiar. She had dropped a piece of wood. Eva picked it up and held it out to her, but she did not take it. "Take it and thank Eva," I said. At last, after long hesitation, she took it, but then went to the stove, picked up, without my seeing it, a large piece of wood, came back with it to me on the couch, and threw it at Eva, so close that it missed the little one by only a hair. To my astonished question why she had picked up the wood and thrown it, she replied, "Because I don't like the wood." I punished her, showed her what she might have done, she showed regret, but the whole thing remains a puzzle to me. — In the evening dictation, four large pages. How dearly I should like to stay up and write to you, children, but I promised R. to go to bed soon. So good night, my dear creatures, your mother is with you all.

(This evening R. pointed out to me that all the great poets—with the exception of Homer and Dante—were dramatists.)

*Tuesday, January 19* I intended last night to go to bed, but did not do so; as I closed the book I was overcome by such sad longing, the children's future seemed to me so dismal, I was so deeply aware that with the growing constriction of my soul I could be of no more help to Richard, that I resolved to go to him in this same midnight hour and tell him that I would go away, that henceforth I would and could live only for you, my children. But I did not do it; to sacrifice my own life and happiness, how happily I should do that; but then I visualized his life, his fate, and collapsed in a faint. When I came to myself I got into bed, and in the morning I could tell R. that I had slept well and —had dreamed of Bismarck. He smiled and told me that he had been thinking—since yesterday—of writing to Countess Bismarck and sending her a copy of *German Art and German Politics*. Perhaps she can influence her husband to take an interest in German art. — I advise him against it, because I anticipate only misunderstanding from such a step. Feeling unwell, I sat down at my writing desk and wrote with great effort to Lenbach concerning my portrait. Yesterday I had a letter from him, asking me to decide what to do about it. I went to lunch feeling very wretched, R. is also very unwell. But he has made a draft of the letter to Countess Bismarck. After lunch we played some of Loewe's ballades, which I found quite pleasing (particularly "*Elvershöh*"). He continues to insist that the emancipation of the Jews has stifled all German impulses. Then we discuss the difference between the former rough and robust German musicians and the present Jewish, elegant, educated ones. Into the garden then, R. to town. I go over and over again the way things stand, and was truly shocked when Richard told me at table, after I had asked him if he had ever really wished for death, that he had indeed longed for it, but had never really felt it as imminent: only at times when he had believed we would have to part had he felt that his life was at an end, that there was nothing more he could do. I trembled at this declaration's coming so close on the footsteps of my thoughts in the night. — After long musings my mind gave up, I walked unthinking out into the night and heard only the breaking of waves, stirred up by the wind, and the barking of dogs. Then to the children, where R. told me that I lived only for bringing up my children. In the evening a severe headache, R. reads me *Henry VI*.

*Wednesday, January 20* Off to sleep late, but slept well; sad thoughts, however, in the morning. R. once again mentions the letter to Countess Bismarck, I again try to dissuade him, and he gives in. But I do not know if I have done right. He is unutterably good to me. Yesterday evening we had to laugh heartily; he demanded something, I was at first against it, then I came round to it and explained to him how it was that I now wanted to follow his bidding, whereas I had not before; during this explanation he heard me use the words, "But, *my dear Wagner*." He mentioned it at first jokingly, and I did not properly understand him, so let it go, but he became increasingly vehement and said it had never happened before that I called him "my dear Wagner."

At last I understood him, and when I explained that it would never have occurred to me to call him that and he must have heard me wrong, we laughed heartily and long. — I have not gone to the children, because I want to write to Loulou and Hermine. That takes me the whole morning. In the meantime Richard comes up and shows me page 200, which he is now writing out. Feeling very unwell, weeping out of weakness, I have to pull myself together by force even just to bring myself to the table. We discuss Preller's illustrations to the *Odyssey*; Richard laughs and says that with my feelings for art I should have married a very rich man. After lunch a letter arrives from Esser, the musical director in Vienna, saying that the management there intends to stage *Die Meistersinger* in October of next year, that is to say, in two years' time!! Yet Dingelstedt had been in a great hurry with his contract, in which R. was to undertake not to let any fragments from his work be played in Vienna and also to give no other theater besides the Court theater the right to produce the opera. So the intention was to suppress *Die Msinger* entirely. Luckily R. was suspicious and did not accept the clause. — We are quite appalled at this new example of unworthiness. Here probably everything is working hand in hand—bureaucracy, Judaism, theater management (Dingelstedt), and perhaps even the Court. Through such experiences I realize very clearly how isolated he is and how he has utterly no one at his side but me. He goes into town, I take up the Schiller correspondence, read, and brood. Our recuperation and distraction are always the children, who are well and cheerful. Before tea I finish the correspondence. R. comes up, very despondent; he had now reached the stage where he could only keep silent. "Then let us be silent," I told him smiling. But with me, he said, it was always all right, he wanted to talk with me, but with nobody else; silence was the only thing that remained for him after all his experiences. He is not well. We started to talk again about the theater, and he observed that, if one wanted to present Goethe's *Faust*, it should be done without intermissions, played through without a break, as he had once seen done in London with a pantomime, which lasted three hours without an intermission and proved very gripping. — *Henry VI Part I* completed, having given us much enjoyment. I had read it years ago, but was quite incapable then of appreciating the remarkable nature of its fleeting portrayal or noting the wonderful characterization beneath the loose jumble. It had passed me by like a mirage, but now I saw every figure and felt every situation. — At parting Richard said that Schopenhauer was quite right: the sum total of wisdom would be to believe nothing and to say nothing. If he had not believed the King, for example, how much trouble would he have saved himself! We come back to the Viennese newspaper, and I advise Richard to use the announcement as a means of showing his acquaintances in Vienna and Berlin why his works are not being performed. Animatedly we discuss the situation; at times I, too, realize disconsolately how black things look. But he surely cannot have lived completely in vain; however hard they try, these people will not in the end be able to destroy him entirely. — I am so upset that I cannot get to sleep, and take up Schiller's poems ("The Fight with the Dragon"); it would really be enough for a lifetime to immerse oneself in such a poet, to understand and appreciate him thoroughly. How can people even begin to do so when they read all sorts of things at once, including mediocre stuff? — Good night, my children, I feel you close to me, you are both my sorrow and my hope.

*Thursday, January 21* Today is *Meistersinger* day; it is being produced in Dresden, and Richard wakes me with themes from the heavenly work. — At breakfast we speak again about what happened yesterday. — I am very tired, for I had a bad night, and dawn brought back to me my worries about the children. — Richard told me at breakfast that, if we had to live in a garret, he would publish a newspaper in which he would mercilessly expose everything. While the children are out walking I begin on the Lessing biography. Much enjoyment from it. After lunch R. reads to me from the book of folk tales, an act of the *Faust* comedy for puppets, which gives rise to great delight, indeed to a mood of unbelievable gaiety. But afterward I find myself reflecting sorrowfully that this splendid folk spirit must now, at a time when its manifestations are being carefully collected, have died out, much in the way that art galleries and museums coincide with a period of unproductivity in painting. — R. returns from his walk with the news that the article on the Jews is going to be printed. So be it! Then he goes to the children, telling me that he did not ask me to go with him since he had the feeling that this always cost me an effort. And so it is: where I was once used to finding four, I find it painful to see only two. However, the two here are flourishing. Kos on the other hand is ill, very ill; how sorry one feels for such a poor creature! In the evening we read the *Faust* puppet play to the end, amid hearty laughter, but with genuine interest. Kasperl is so entirely different in kind from the Spanish Grazioso or the Italian Harlequin, and what a striking testimony he is to the dramatic talents of the Germans! Glorious moonlight, enjoyed by us both.

*Friday, January 22* Sleepless night; if only I did not have these heavy thoughts! At times I feel that I shall go mad. How to get possession of the children without leaving R.? This I cannot, must not do. — In the morning R. sees in my face how I am suffering and suggests we go to the south. But I fear any disturbance in his situation and still hope that I shall recover. Our discussion about this is interrupted by a telegram from Mitterwurzer reporting that *Die Meistersinger* was a huge success in Dresden yesterday. Our nephew Clemens also telegraphed. It brought us great joy; perhaps Berlin will now have to do it. The sun is shining, for the first time in many days; if my children were with me I should be accounted happy, indeed overhappy, such as one has no right to expect here below, even when one renounces the world entirely. — After lunch, letters. Pasdeloup reports that the rehearsals for *Rienzi* have started after all; and arrival of the Italian *Holländer* score, which again brings much vexation. In the evening R.'s deep dissatisfaction with his artistic life. To conclude, *Henry VI Part II*—fearful impression, impossible to describe.

*Saturday, January 23* Very bad night; no sleep at all and anxiety over the children. I do not get up. R. comes, tells me about a letter from Weber (the publisher), who feels that the time is now right for the appearance of *Judaism in Music*. In good spirits about that. Then a letter from a Germano-Frenchman saying that there is talk in Paris of R.'s imminent arrival for *Rienzi*. I stay lying in bed the whole of the morning, very weak and with constant feelings of constriction in my heart. An Italian newspaper reports on the fight over the *Lohengrin* Prelude during Pasdeloup's concert. The Jews again. By lunch I am well once more; our conversation concerns yesterday's reading. Comparison with Aeschylus's *Agamemnon,* in which—as R. says—the choruses soften everything and give it a musical transfiguration, as it were, whereas in Shakespeare everything is spread before us and stays naked and terrifying. Beside it all other poetic works seem like divine lullabies, here it is as if Fate itself had removed its veil to appear before our mortal eyes. After lunch a communication from Hans; the *Signale* has printed a biography of him in which it is stated that when Hans was a young man Wagner had befriended him and cared for him like a father, while his own family left him penniless. This seems to have hurt Hans. How petty! I ask R. to write a correction at once in a proper tone of calm, which he then does, sending the draft to Hans. The weather is cold but fine; it does R. good, as one can see. I play games in the Froebel manner with the children, and Eva shows much intelligence. In the evening R. brings a letter from Mme Laussot to him: she will procure for him the manuscripts he needs for the edition of his works. — After tea, conclusion of *Henry VI Part II* and beginning of *Part III.* — Today R. gave me great joy when he told me that he was now so unwilling to write letters because he had resolved to complete his *Siegfried.*

*Sunday, January 24* A good night and in consequence a harmonious morning; at the same time thinking out a plan by which I might soon bring the other children to my side, and how I will arrange things generally in the uncertainties and difficulties of the situation. This gives me comfort. From Dresden R. has received a letter from Dr. Lang, who remains loyal in spite of our constant rebuffs, written at midnight after the *Meistersinger* performance. The success, it seems, was quite extraordinary. Happy mood embracing both report and reporter. Unfortunately R.'s passion for silk materials brought forth a remark from me which I should have done better to leave unsaid, for it produced a bit of ill feeling. Yesterday a carpenter, a plumber, a veterinary surgeon in the house—a singular stirring in my enchanted life; I had to laugh over my own impression and was unable at all to imagine that I would ever again want to visit a theater or even watch a large number of people moving about. I miss nothing in my seclusion—except the children. — In the morning arranged books. In the afternoon a letter from Mitterwurzer, who reports that the King of Saxony attended the performance and at the end was still applauding vigorously even after the singers' third curtain call, which is said never to have happened before. R. is replying to Mme Laussot and demanding through her the manuscript of *Jesus von Nazareth* from Princess Wittgenstein, who, although she was only lent it, does not want to give it back. Greed of possession or religious caution? Whichever it is, her cynical effrontery is the same. After lunch, in the children's presence, R. plays parts of the second act of *Tristan*. Whether I am becoming increasingly vulnerable or morbidly sensitive I do not know, but there are certain powerful impressions which I can hardly bear any longer. I literally shudder at the power of genius which suddenly lays bare before us the unfathomable secrets of existence, even when there is nothing I cherish and esteem more than this divinely daemonic power. I find myself thinking of R.'s words (on the death of Schnorr) [von Carolsfeld], "Art is perhaps a great crime"; and certainly those can be accounted happy who, like animals, know nothing of it, though this sort of happiness seems to me like eternal darkness. I watch till I am blind, hear till I am deaf, feel to the point of oblivion all its splendor; I am drawn to the shining, star-filled abyss, look irresistibly down, and sink senseless into it. We poor women who can only love, well may we be pitied when we divine the genius's secret! And yet what are we without this complicity in genius? Very exhausted, I lie down and pass from a sort of coma into sleep; afterward the children and the Lessing biography. In the evening Richard rather worn out, but we undertake the end of *Henry VI*. In the face of that, mortals can only be silent. But when one thinks that people stage *Richard III* separately—or, even worse, that some buffoon dares to turn the three parts of *Henry VI* into two and put these on the stage—then one asks oneself what is the point of genius, when after centuries it can command no respect, and its manifestations become the prey of charlatans. —

*Monday, January 25* A good night preceded by consideration of my plan. Letters from Richard's family giving their impressions of *Die Meistersinger*. Severe cold, the children affected by it. Move them into another room. R. miserable because he thinks I am sad. Comforting him and raising his spirits. He is pleased with his score. At table he tells me he was once warned against Fröbel by Al[exander] Müller, who told him Fröbel turned the evil conduct of his first wife to his own advantage. He had taken no notice. In the afternoon with the children, finished the Lessing biography. Germany treats its great men as Nature treats the individual, sacrificing them as if there were enough to spare. In the evening R. speaks with great indignation about the gambling lust. Some more dictation at last, giving me much pleasure. Punch and good night. — Vreneli told Richard about a poor dog she had seen *half* shot; its master had not wanted to buy the prescribed muzzle, and clumsily he tortured the poor creature. R. quite beside himself about it; we should bring our children up to be nuns or sisters of mercy; how can one even think of beauty in such a world?

*Tuesday, January 26* Glorious sunshine, the whole countryside dripping with light. Loldi four hours out in the garden today. I am well again. R. is working on his score and says he could not get through a morning without doing something on it. Cheerful spirits at lunchtime, the sunshine brings smiles to the whole house. Unfortunately, however, as R. is about to go out, a letter comes from Hans which is difficult to understand. He demands from R. the withdrawal of his correction for the *Signale* and reports the visit "of his wife to Versailles." R.'s whole appearance alters; he is in an utter frenzy. I understand at once that with the last sentence Hans intends just to let me know what he has told his family. In the afternoon with the children. Returning home very unwell, R. goes to lie down. At seven o'clock, when the children are sleeping, I go outside. The loveliest view of the countryside I have ever seen. Everything blue and silvery, the moon and the stars shining, the mountains glowing, the water glittering, all of it bright, yet veiled. Mood of elevation inside and around me; the unborn child moves in my womb, and I bless it. May its spirit be as clear and mild as this glowing night sky, as calm and noble as the mountain wrapped in its mantle of snow, may its disposition be as deep and gentle as this lightly ruffled water, may it regard the dark shadows around its feet as unmovingly as the dark wood at the foot of the mountain, while its head is bathed in light, may it illumine and raise up all wretched creatures as tenderly as the starlight transfigures the dry meadow and the withered trees! May it eternally think lovingly of the mother who bore it in love! — R. made even more weary by his afternoon sleep and in despondent mood. He bemoans the fact that I did not agree on that former occasion to stay in Genoa, to send for the children and then leave things to Fate. There is not much I can reply, for all the things which decided me then I explained to him at the time, and my inner voice tells me that I did right. Also, he is unwell, and it is only his sufferings speaking. — In the morning he received a very nice letter from his nephew Pastor Brockhaus about *Die Meistersinger*.

*Wednesday, January 27* R. is better, his night was good, it seems. Mine, too. Glorious weather. More news from Dresden. *Die Meistersinger* is being performed there four or five times in a row. The children are able to spend nearly the whole day in the garden. R. is unsettled in his work and even at lunch, because he thinks he tormented me yesterday evening. There is not much I can reply to him, for how could I tell him that his despondent mood had not upset me? And if I reassure him that I bear the distress willingly, I do not thus help him over his concern. All that remains for me is to be cheerful and unaffected. He does not look well, the letter from Hans yesterday has really shattered him. He says he feels as if he were living only by magic, and he can hardly bear anything more. A two-hour walk, sun setting, moon rising. Sudden fright in the "Robbers' Park," first a raven croaking near me, then a number of crows—their flight, together with their hoarse cries, filled me with alarm—were they prophesying some approaching evil? The golden brightness of the moon and its reflection on the water gradually calmed me. — R. has ordered Devrient's book about Mendelssohn—it looks somewhat comical, and the fact that Devrient is an uneducated play-actor and Mendelssohn a Jew emerges clearly. I read some of it to R. After that, dictation.

*Thursday, January 28* Tolerable night, not much sleep, but no worrying thoughts, either, read Devrient's book (while with the children). Much impatience with it, but much enlightenment, this account is like a confirmation of what R. wrote about Mendelssohn in his essay. Spoke about it to R. at table. He goes out, I am feeling weak again and have to lie down. Then with the children, who are lively and well behaved. Since R. reproaches me for not having been out of doors, I go out when it is already dark; the countryside is wrapped in gray dusk, I feel that the Greek underworld must have looked like this, and I could literally see the forms of its heroes as they wander across the calm gray water and vanish into the mists of the mountains and the clouds. Gradually the sky cleared, a pale star twinkled silently, the first I had seen this evening; "Greetings, gentle star, guide my fate kindly, shine benevolently on my children." As I spoke these words the star suddenly disappeared—was it because a tear dimmed my eye or because the emerging moon obscured its little light? — "Very well, you are as unyielding as all the rest, like them you teach me submissiveness." Then it came back into sight. "Are you now appeased? Give me a friendly sign that you will be merciful to my children"—and suddenly I saw Richard standing in front of me: he had been looking for me everywhere, calling out Siegfried's melody to me in all directions! Joyfully I acknowledged the sign; the whole countryside was gleaming, the clouds vanquished by the moon, the underworld atmosphere dispelled; I no longer looked for my little friend, having the large one at my side as pledge of the gentle direction of my fate. — R. said if only I knew all the things he called out to me when I was not there. Alas, I know that he loves me. — In the evening he dictates to me again, and we part affectionately. — The reason Nature exercises so beneficent an effect on us lies surely in the fact that it makes us so closely aware of how insignificant the individual is. Thousands of years have passed in which the mountains have stood unconcerned in the face of human suffering, the stars shone down indifferently on earthly woe. In the city, however, the individual thinks of himself as something special and important; the razing of houses, the erection of buildings, all the unrest he unceasingly causes, gives him a deceptive sense of his significance, and it is in this deception that his agitation lies; for is not Death telling him every hour that in fact he is nothing?

*Friday, January 29*   In the night, read Devrient's book to the end. In the morning, good, friendly letters from Mathilde [Maier]. Richard well, the children lively—I think of you, my absent ones, may you not miss your mother as much as she misses you! At lunch R. reminds me that yesterday during our conversation about the Battle of Marathon and the sudden noble assistance of the Plataeans tears came into our eyes, while during the reading of "The Fight with the Dragon" we actually wept. He thought we should not tell others what we were weeping about! — Then he told me he had the feeling that he really had always been surrounded by rogues. From this book he saw with utter disgust how Eduard Devrient, when he got to know of R.'s activities in Dresden and saw all that was being done, arranged for Mendelssohn to be offered a position there. Not a word of that had he heard at the time. Mendelssohn was of course wise enough not to respond to the proposals. — Amusing, too, to see the scene in which Sachs tries the shoe on Eva described in the press as "embarrassing"! R. says I should keep a list of all the nice things said about him; in the *A[ugsburger] A[llgemeine] Z[eitung]*, for instance, all that was said about the *Msinger* in Dresden was that servants stood in the cold outside the box office to secure tickets. A report on its success obviously omitted. And after the second performance it is "added" that Rietz, the conductor, was called to take a bow, and that in Dresden they had needed fewer rehearsals than in Munich. The work itself is passed by, simply the opportunity seized with delight to stir up vexation in Munich! — R. is very much occupied with his *Siegfried* and absorbed by it. The children are good—if I only knew how the little ones there are getting on! No report would be enough, but I have again had no letter for a long time. No dictation in the evening, but compiling an anthology of the "correct, counterjumping German" of E. Devrient. — Strong gale blowing.

*Saturday, January 30* Lovely sunshine. Mild weather; peaceful morning after a good night, in which as usual I dreamed about Blandine. Little to report on this day. In glorious spring weather spent a large part of the afternoon with the children in the garden. Richard well and I happy on that account. In the evening he tells me that between us there is only one danger: that we love each other too much; every morning when he goes to his score and writes the first line he would like to run upstairs again at once and see what I am doing. — Dictation. In the course of it I am overcome by a heavy, heavy feeling, I cannot describe it, hardly know in fact what it consists of. Suffering, eternal, inscrutable suffering, may you be borne in silence! This last lesson I leave to my children: that the drink contained in the fairest chalice of unearthly happiness is a tear! — Richard notices my mood and, to raise my spirits, tells me how his father Geyer, to give his mother a surprise on her birthday, staged a charade in which a councilor, Jeorgie, a gigantically huge man, laid himself in Mama's bed, dressed in her nightcap and bed jacket; he was given her big coffee cup, and the children summoned in their nightcaps and nightgowns to their mother's bedside, as usually happened in the morning; the mother was then called in, to their great delight. — I had to laugh a lot. Then, once again, weep. At last, in lovely moonlight, I fell asleep.

*Sunday, January 31* Richard very unwell, I despondent because of it; on top of that a stupid letter from Mme Laussot, who wishes to give him explanations (from 20 years ago!). That annoys him, because it is so utterly useless. The whole day passes gloomily. R. is weak and very limp, he cannot eat a thing. I in consequence feel deprived of my soul. At midday he says he cannot visualize what would have become of his life if I had not entered it. And if one were to say to him: But if your artistic plans had been carried through, if the King had proved steadfast, then you would not have been so utterly dependent on me? Nonsense! says R., he lives only through me, that had been his feeling from the very first hour. — He drags himself feebly through the whole day; in the evening I read to him (Goethe's correspondence with Knebel), but I suddenly begin to feel unwell and cause him anxiety. He fears that I am undermining my health through my seclusion here. Oh, indeed, my woe is great, but when I think of the possibility of *Siegfried* I am cured as if by magic!

*Monday, February 1* A good morning—it brought me news of the Munich children. Richard, however, is vexed by mail from Italy (*Rienzi* proofs). He says he would like to announce in all newspapers that he lives only through me, then hear nothing more. I let the children come downstairs, much joy from their liveliness and their good health. — But the day soon clouds over; when I went down to see how R. was faring, the poor man was quite beside himself. The botched scores which he receives constantly from Italy and Paris and the stupid waste of time caused by them upset him so—and he is unwell, too! When I later rejoined him at lunch, he had restored his spirits a little with Schopenhauer; he read me some of it during the meal, among other things a little excursus about the old Cologne School; since I found this insignificant, not to say trivial, I voice my feelings. To my profound regret R. misunderstood me and took my reply as evidence of ill humor toward him. He became angry, leaving me completely amazed and confused by his attitude. I went for a walk in the garden and considered in my heart what I had already so often considered, the meaning of life and our task within it; I know quite precisely that renunciation, self-sacrifice, is the only thing which gives our life value and meaning, and willingly I give up every happiness and every joy. If, through giving up everything and everybody, I would not become fully guilty of the murder of my beloved, how calmly would I go off and live for the children alone! — Never—even in the hours of severest trial—have I seriously thought of parting from R., because I know nobody who loves him as I love him. If an angel were to come and tell me, "You are superfluous," and to show me the prospect of a happy existence for him, how willingly would I embrace my cross, how calmly—my day's work done—look Death in the face! — I am utterly convinced that peace lies only in self-sacrifice—and it shocks me sometimes myself, the fact that it looks as if I had arrogantly pursued my own happiness. It seems like a contradiction between the way I think and the way I act—and yet I know that what urged me on was nothing selfish. All the same, I question myself often, question myself as to whether I did the right thing. — Then the daily task comes to my aid; to deal with that is to perform one's duty, according to Goethe. — R. reads to me from the correspondence.

*Tuesday, February 2* Candlemas, no sun and yet sun; the farmers want an overcast sky, and now it is indeed overcast, but a ray of sunshine breaks through. This brings our table conversation to the words of the oracle and the Greeks, in particular the Dorians. A letter from Hermine, the King has sent me three photographs—I am glad, for there seems to be no catastrophe in the offing. R. has received from Paris the very pleasant news that Pasdeloup has gone bankrupt, which means nothing will come of *Rienzi*. Walk in the garden in the dark. Hearing dogs bark in the distance, scattered lights shining in the lake; Tribschen itself is in darkness. After tea, dictation; it appears to me that the year 1858 was the true turning-point in R.'s destiny, and if Frau W[esendonck] had conducted herself well then, all the perplexities up to the appearance of the King could have been spared him. Then my participation in his life would also have been superfluous— even if we should always have loved each other deeply. This feeling makes me despondent. Above all, however, R.'s appearance, which is not good. Oh, if he could only be quite well again! The mild, unhealthy weather may also be to blame for his poor appearance. Bismarck's boastful behavior in the Chamber ("the reptiles and the miserable dynastic interests") gave R. a lot of joy. He returns to his letter to the Countess. Why do I stop him? It is surely very timid of me. Why have I lost all my courage, except the courage to suffer? If only I could see R. happy again and free of all care! But the gods are unmerciful—even if I were willing to purchase this happiness at the price of my total annihilation, they would still not grant it to me. Everything must be suffered to the end, my poor good children!

*Wednesday, February 3* Quiet day, its happy climax the arrival of the music box from Paris. Loldi and Eva blissful—so we, too, glad. Otherwise my heart is full of repressed tears. Richard is suffering so much—if only I could help! Oh, we poor mortal creatures! Evening, dictation.

*Thursday, February 4* R. well again, a bath helped him. His eyes gleam, and so my star is now shining again, too. In cheerful mood he writes letters and works on his score. After lunch I took a long walk with Loldi and watched a wonderfully exuberant sunset. Aglow with fire, one mountain was holding an exalted, silent conversation with the snow-covered, whitely gleaming mountain opposite. Light and heat, sun-drenched snow summit and sun-sparkling earth mass were telling each other things I did not understand, then both gave way to the majesty of night. In the morning I had been rereading the first letters R. wrote me (from Starnberg) and the accompanying poem about the sunset and the star. In the evening R. came up to my room, much affected by his *Nibelungen* work; I responded to his mood hardly at all, for I fear the effect of such excitement on his health. Dictation.

*Friday, February 5* Silver morning, mist, sun, and water. Greetings, my dear children! The day was quiet and active; R. seems entirely absorbed in the *Nibelungen,* and our conversation at table was earnest, indeed almost solemn. We thought of Schnorr, the singer, and the last time he sang—the "Forging Songs," "Now Begin," Siegmund's "Spring Song"—for the King and ourselves alone. The indelible impression of it resists both death and time. Glorious, cloudless sunset; the tender, rosy evening glow enfolds the snow-capped mountains and casts its reflection on the water, while a golden crown sinks down as if from the head of Mount Pilatus, between these two tones a pure, heavenly blue. The dark earth on which we wander resembles life, whereas the bright sky is art—or, better, love. One enters the house, after the heavenly vision has vanished, with one's inner feelings in peculiarly solemn mood; in pious concentration I think to myself that Paradise is only what we look at, observe; Paradise lost, on the other hand, is what we try to possess, grasp, and touch—in a word, the lost is the achieved. — From town R. brought me two lovely camellias— may they flourish; for I shall tend them carefully. And may *Siegfried* also flourish! We are willing, are we not, my children, to bear a little suffering together on that account? My dear, good children! — In the evening we had an interrupted dictation; I did not understand some of it and was foolish enough to say so, which caused a prolonged delay, though no real discord.

*Saturday, February 6* Last night I dreamed of a separation from R., my return to Munich, and a reunion with the children. Boni was very affected, Loulou indifferent, and I felt I could not go on living, floods of tears streamed from my eyes, and I asked all sorts of uncaring people how I could get to Paris, where Richard was staying. — Children, books, score, some letters, thus was the day filled, for R. as well as for me. A telegram brought news of *Die Meistersinger's* great success in Karlsruhe. A correspondent in Cologne brought to our notice the report in the *Kölnische Zeitung* concerning the Dresden success, which, says this friendly correspondent, would make Hiller and his comrades turn green and yellow with rage, for this large newspaper is literally bribed either to avoid all mention of Wagner's successes or to put a smear on them. — How strange and ugly seem even well-disposed notices from these spheres of the press, the theater and the musical world of the present, how jarring in our solitude their screeching tones! To me it seems it is not power which makes an enemy worthy of respect, but his inner worth. — Walk in the evening, the stars twinkling down on me one after another above the withered branches like friendly greetings.

*Sunday, February 7* Restless night and severe headache. — Today was Saint Richard's Day; in earlier times I should never have let this day pass without reminding my beloved jokingly of his supposed patron saint with a little gift. Now I cannot, for what little I have of my own I left at the household in Munich, and so the small pleasure must be done without. — Oh, I do not mind doing without things; it seems really always to have been my natural lot to abstain, to wish for nothing. I find it easy to believe that another age would have regarded me as a religious fanatic—now love has got me fully in its grasp, I know nothing else and am willing to suffer in and for it. Since the weather was fine, R. invited me to go for a walk with him; I did so. For the first time in two and a half months I walked outside the boundaries of Tribschen, with some concern lest I be seen. But I noticed nobody. — In the morning Levi, the conductor, sent a letter reporting the success of *Die Msinger* in Karlsruhe. As R. remarked at table, people are seeming to become a little nervous of being so much against him now, when, with his last work to be published, he has at the same time written his most popular. — A performance of *Tannhäuser* is announced for tomorrow in Basel. Our people are going to it. How hard it would have been for me previously not to go—I believe virtually impossible—and how calmly I now bear what is for me truly a great deprivation! I feel very low and would so much like to be cheerful. The children are well.

*Monday, February 8*  I start the morning with a little walk. R. and the children greet me from various windows. At breakfast R. tells me of an enthusiastic letter from Mme Viardot about *Die Msinger*. Also one from Dr. Nohl in Munich; he says all the signs point to the fact that the King has no sympathy for R. and his cause! I am alarmed when R. admits to me that he had written to this Herr Nohl, telling him that he was expecting a break with the King any moment. Besides these two letters there is an anonymous one containing nothing but abuse and the news that *Die Ms* was a failure in Karlsruhe. This pitiful scrap of paper arrives at the same time as the *A.A.Z.*, which reports an unprecedented success in Karlsruhe. — Today has belonged almost exclusively to the children, since the household is somewhat reduced. I share with them meals, games, walk, and R. calls me the good mother hen. He also said during the morning that we had already found happiness—it was just that nobody wanted us to enjoy it. — In the evening, dictation.

*Tuesday, February 9*  During the night I again took up *Proteus* by Dr. Marbach (Richard's brother-in-law), which we had read the evening before last. It is a remarkable production and testifies—like everything by Marbach—to a profound understanding of the subject, only the style—in spite of the very skillful construction—is much too flat. I told Richard that Marbach has the skeleton of a poet, but he lacks the flesh, whereas in people like Halm, Geibel, etc., etc., it is on the contrary precisely the bone structure which is lacking, for all their other talents. His (Marbach's) contemplation of the subject is profound, but the thoughts which arise from it are paltry. How strange! Richard agrees, and says that is the remarkable thing about the Germans, that they have so many qualities which are all aimed in the direction of real significance, but emerge incomplete and unconnected and therefore remain barren. In the course of the morning we discuss our situation, which cannot go on much longer as it now is. I tell R. I should like to write Hans that I could come to the children in Munich for two months and return from there to Tribschen at the beginning of May with all four of them, going on from there to Paris. What I am trying to do is avoid making a commotion, for the sake of the children and the King (that is to say, Richard). Richard, however, can see only one thing—the two-month separation—and will not hear of it. Deep worry in my soul; I really do believe that this way out, in this temporary stage, would be the best. — After lunch R. shows me Daumer's *Book of Ghosts*; I read some of the stories in it: the dumb child whom his sisters one day forget to feed, to whom the ghost of his mother appears and gives him food, an event of which he tells his suddenly concerned sisters himself (the miracle having freed his tongue), and then he dies. We are quite shattered by it—"It would all depend on whether one has contact with friendly ghosts," says Richard, who has a great tendency in this direction and has perhaps a deep, unconscious connection with these regions. — Since it is Shrove Tuesday, R. goes into town to get me some doughnuts, but there are none left. A little disappointment and a great joy, a deep absorption in love. I always in tears, not knowing whether of joy or sorrow. In the evening I put to R. the question whether our love never appears to him to be wrong; he does not quite understand me and thinks I mean by this what the world considers wrong, the betrayal of a friend; then he says that he knows only one thing—that since the world came into existence no man of his age had loved a woman as much as he loved me. The wrong I meant was not, however, concerned with what other people condemn, but with what it would perhaps be right for us to do according to our own conceptions of life and virtue of the highest kind. I would like to receive my directions from him. — We conclude the evening with Calderón's *Great Zenobia*. A wonderful first act, an incomparable scene in the second (Zenobia and Decius on the battlefield), and an utterly absurd, puppetlike third act give us a great deal to think about and consider. I wish Richard could decide to write something about Calderón, for nothing exhaustive has yet been said about this remarkable poet, so difficult to grasp. — In deep contemplation of my "plan" I fall asleep—("all crowns are dreams").

*Wednesday, February 10* In a dream I gave birth to a son. As I awoke and rose from my bed I found my camellia had blossomed; since I had involuntarily connected it in my mind with *Siegfried*, I am overjoyed. May the souls of my children blossom as handsomely and as tranquilly! In the morning read Winckelmann's biography (*Homo vagus et inconstans!*), much moved. How clearly the German genius speaks in this man; the poor cobbler's son, born in a land that at the time hardly possessed a language, bears within his spirit the Greek ideal. — His conversion to Catholicism an act of aesthetic infatuation which he resolved emotionally, carried out with terrible difficulty, and eternally regretted, but never regarded as frivolous. — At table R. told me he would be finished this month with the copying and wanted then to journey forth into the old land of romance. I say to him, "Once more you hover near me, forms and faces." In the morning he also began his article on Devrient, and he read it aloud to me. After lunch played passages from *Siegfried*. He leaves me, saying that, now that I am with him, he knows what he has lived for, only I should not weep so much. — I go with Loldi into the garden and reflect on what I have to do. — I am not arrogant and am always astonished that he needs me, but I believe with all my heart what he once again said to me today at lunch: that if I went away, his life and living, his thinking and his thoughts would be at an end, and for that reason I myself no longer hold to the idea of a two-month separation. Yet I do not know how to set about getting the children to me here; no plan seems right. Much grief on that account. Upstairs, read Calderón's *El secreto a voces* again, without being much absorbed by this masterpiece, because I am too worried. In the evening the delayed doughnuts with punch, and a reading of Albrecht Dürer's letter on receiving the news that Luther had been arrested. Profound and painful religious feelings; how different such a character is from the sunny, life-loving, divine Italian masters! And the powerful, helpless language! Wonderfully moving! Certainly no such son has ever been born to any Latin nation. — Yesterday R. told me he was stopped on the Reuss Bridge by a tympanist, who said he had been one of the musicians in R.'s concerts in Zurich in 1859. He declared that the whole Zurich orchestra was full of gratitude to R., since it had now been given what R. had previously demanded from the members of the Music Society, namely, a fixed salary and a permanent engagement. 32 people are now engaged summer and winter. R. sent his best wishes to the gentlemen of the Comité with the message that they could have introduced the measure somewhat earlier. —

*Thursday, February 11*    Hangover, rumors of war, and gray skies. The first oppresses R., the second clouds the newspaper, and the last troubles me. The children lively; Loldi, to whom I offer a doughnut, says she has already had one: on closer examination it turns out that she dreamed of a doughnut. — R. is unwell, but he is continuing to work, if with ever-increasing repugnance, on the Devrient article. I spend the whole morning with the children and am able in the course of it to finish Winckelmann's *Life*. Regarding my attitude toward the former, R. says I seem to have missed my vocation as a sister of mercy. He also thinks I am too good; but he should know that all the goodness he sees in me is only a reflection of his love. Our conversation about the Dürer picture brings us on to Luther; he would still like to find time to write that comedy with Luther as hero, and he says that in his thoughts he always literally lives with him, he feels related to him in many ways. In the afternoon a walk in the garden with R. and the children, the sun comes out ("more to listen than to shine") and we see a beautiful rainbow. Talked a lot about Calderón. R. stresses particularly how in the plays, after the characters have literally spent all their passion, the moment arrives when they experience a sudden reversal of will, and a mood of complete resignation diverts them from their violent misdeeds, making them appear magnanimous and noble. Thus Flerida in *El secreto a voces*, and the King almost throughout. — In the evening, dictation.

*Friday, February 12*    Settled springlike weather, a primrose has already appeared. That is indeed rather alarming—what will April and May be like? Richard is working on his Devrient article, I pass my time with Winckelmann and the children. The Italian newspapers report the success of the *Tannhäuser* Overture in Milan. At lunch our conversation scarcely moves from the Devrient book—where to publish R.'s article? In the garden with the children, then a letter from Claire, advising me to be as considerate of everyone as possible! — Read Calderón's comedy *Los enredos de la suerte*; in these comedies, R. says, chance takes the place of Fate in the tragedies. In the evening R. reads me the continuation of his article, much amusement from it. But I am unwell and have soon to take to my bed with a temperature.

*Saturday, February 13*    R. tells me in the morning how, having found the window of his dressing room open, he had angrily exclaimed: "I shall never reach old age at this rate! Maybe I shall always remain young!" Whereupon Jakob: "Yes, you'll always remain young." At two in the morning, he says, he came to see how I was, and since I was sleeping peacefully, he went to bed content. — Yesterday a score arrived which moved us very much. A 74-year-old musician (Claudius), who had earlier encouraged R. (in 1845), has revised his work *Der Gang nach dem Eisenhammer* and now sends it to R. for his opinion. The handwriting is very quavery; but what R. played from it is really rather good. It has been 24 years since R. last saw this nice man. I took the opportunity of asking R. whether he felt as I did: to me my whole former life seems in some way literally incredible. He says all the people he once knew now seem to him like shadows, like phantoms, at most he was ashamed of certain relationships. — My morning was given up again to Winckelmann and the children (also). R. works on his essay, which he is concluding in an unexpected and magnificently crushing way. One can see here as in other things how much he takes everything to heart, and how he can never desist from giving a matter its full, horrifying significance, even when this is not discernible to anybody else. I am downright shocked when he reads it to me. After lunch he tells me he received a letter from the King in the morning, but had not read it at once or wanted even to mention it, since he wished to keep his morning free for work. Now he read it out loud—the same old style of enthusiasm and love. A letter from the King's secretary Düfflipp was with it, and I started to read this aloud, suspecting nothing unpleasant. — R. had asked for an advance, to be deducted regularly from his allowance, to settle some outstanding debts. Now he is told by Councilor D[üfflipp] that Semper's claim (which has now been settled) and [Fröbel's] article on *Opera and Drama* had aroused the King's displeasure, and he would not listen to R.'s request. I told R. that Fr[öbel]'s article might perhaps have been commissioned expressly to arouse the King's displeasure, so that he would not grant R. a favor, and the people there would have the amusement of observing his embarrassment. This upsets R. so much that he becomes quite angry with me. I should indeed have realized that this subject is an unpleasant one for R., and should not have discussed it. I was now alarmed at the consequences of my clumsiness, for I had meant no harm. The children, whom we had sent for, were apprehensive, and this upset me very much, for I try above all to avoid making the children suffer from the worries of their parents. R. walked off abruptly, and I went in silence—as I had remained throughout—to my room. The children help to distract me from my sad thoughts. When they are in bed, R. comes up complaining of great tiredness. Together we read a chapter of Winckelmann, then he mentions today's incident and says I should regard all he said as having been spoken in a fever. I can only press his hand in silence; how could I ever take upon myself the right to forgive him? I stay up a long time and, restraining my tears with an effort, acknowledge that no suffering and no trial can absolve us from the fulfillment of our duty, and that my duty is to be good and kind toward R., whatever the hours may bring. I also reflect on the subject of *deserts*; without wishing it, I have nevertheless caused many people pain, I have wounded Hans, and my children are missing me. — How, therefore, can I ever complain of my own sorrows? — In bed a terrible thought strikes me—that Hans might finally go mad. In the morning I had read in the *Signale* that in Hanover he played nothing but Rubinstein compositions— that seems to me completely incomprehensible.

*Sunday, February 14* Fine, bright Sunday, I wake up melancholy, but at peace with myself. Unfortunately R. reports that he slept badly, and that always pains me more than anything. I have begun with great interest a charming book which R. received yesterday from Fräulein von Meysenbug. — Only it has been so long since I last received news of the children. That makes me sad. But spring is here; yesterday it was windy and dull, today everything glistens, the birds are flitting about, trees budding, mountains, sky, and lake are transformed, it is very beautiful and one enjoys it; but it is too early—how many poor seeds will be sacrificed and birds driven away! I find one of my main joys in tending my camellias, a real relationship is developing between these two living things and me, and I would not wish to have many flowers around me. These buds have received quite a few tears today. That is of course foolish, for what is causing me suffering is only the consequence of my situation—whoever steps beyond the boundaries must be prepared to be punished for it, however good his intentions, however difficult to achieve. Also, I ought to be glad when happiness deserts me—but mortals are weak and turn as avidly to pleasure as flowers to light. — After lunch we drove out toward Hergeschwyl, with Loldi. Time caught up with us, but the sunset was splendid, and the sickle of the rising moon slender and frail above Mount Pilatus. In the evening R. worked on his essay, I completed Fräulein von Meysenbug's book. At lunch R. asked me to develop the thought I had expressed in relation to Weber and Mendelssohn. He had observed that, when he had Weber's ashes moved to Dresden, only eighteen years had elapsed since the composer's death, whereas it was now 22 years since Mendelssohn died; yet at the time it had seemed to him an eternity since the tragic news was received, while now it seemed to him as if M.'s death had been reported only yesterday. — I said that, apart from the difference which his own age might make to his feelings, it seemed to me that a genius such as Weber would very soon be imbued with the nimbus and halo of the past, whereas a personality such as Mendelssohn's would be preserved in remembrance only because very many people who once knew him are still alive, and they keep the memory of him green. [*Added later:* "The sorrow that mankind feels at the loss of a genius also adds to the illusion.

Every time it is called to mind it produces pain, and that is doubled and tripled by Time. The passing 'What a shame' that a loss like that of Mendelssohn evokes from us does not engrave on our minds the sense of his being dead, and we must then always ask ourselves when he did in fact die."] Such a shadow does not grow, it can only disappear; the genius, however, is bound to become a legend immediately after his death; one can hardly believe that one knew him. The eternal worth of his work imprints itself also on the personality, so that it seems as if Life and Death have no real power over mortals such as Weber, Beethoven, and Mozart; it is as if they were of all time and had been with us only as the spirits they now are. With less gifted human beings life is everything, and they can only be forgotten, they cannot dominate the realm of shadows. As long as mortals who once knew them continue to live, their earthly presence remains fresh, whereas their spiritual essence fades, one remembers and talks of them without awe; in the case of true genius it is the other way around—the spirit becomes ever more alive, while the form in which it was clothed eventually takes on the appearance of a shadow.

*Monday, February 15* Kos is being taken to Zurich; he is ill. I have a letter from the children, things are not going well there, Hans's mother is making trouble. At breakfast I again discuss with R. what is to be done, but we could come to no conclusion. God give me strength, as He gave me the suffering! — When R. told me yesterday that I could not possibly know how much he loved me, and when he today observed that he was too much for me and my love for him was loading me down with too many sacrifices, I thought that my heart would burst. One thing I can feel—that I must remain brave and cheerful, whatever comes, so that I do truly help him. A day of peace will then arrive, for me, too, and the children will bless me after that.

Human intentions are pitiful, a puff of wind brings them to nought, and one finds oneself always in an open sea, rudderless, at the mercy of wind and waves, like Homer's hero; happy the person to whom in the somber whirlpools a helpful divinity mildly appears! — Love is this divine and beneficent Leucothea. Your mother is grieving today, my children, but she remains true to you and to her love. When she is no more, think of her and pray for her rest.

*Tuesday, February 16* After I had said good night to R. yesterday I fell into long meditation, from which I emerged as in a dream, then went downstairs once more to wish him pleasant rest. But when I reached his room I felt very shocked by my lack of discretion; it was as if I had been walking in my sleep and had suddenly woken up. I then said my good night in great embarrassment. — Vreneli, returning yesterday from Zurich, told us about Kos: he is very ill, God knows if he will get better. During the night I dreamed that he was very friendly toward the man in the institution and that the man rewarded him with kicks. I woke up with a start, sadly, to see a star twinkling down right through my window, and this gave me pleasure. — R. has finished his article, he read it to me yesterday evening. The day belongs to Winckelmann and the children; Loldi very talkative, thinking of Boni and the pond in Munich, having fun with me in the bathhouse and giving me much pleasure. R. settles the matter of *Rienzi* in Paris by declaring that the only interest he has in the performance is in keeping it from taking place, which he can and must do. At table he expresses his pleasure in the furniture, the books, the pictures, the butterflies, and says we are after all more dependent on the spirit than on Nature; the beauties of art are superior to the beauties of Nature, since they express what Nature desires; they are more limited, certainly, but for that reason their will is expressed all the more energetically. — I think with melancholy of our poor little Kos! — In the evening R. tells me with great joy that he has discovered a complete edition of *Die Horen,* Vasari, and the atlas to Winckelmann's works. We think a lot about the hours two years ago.

*Wednesday, February 17*  Dreamed of Blandine. On waking I hear the strains of the "Prize Song," the melody which brought Eva into the world and with which R. greeted my birthday (1866). Then R. brings our beautiful child to my bedside, she shines and sparkles, our little Eva! Spring is blooming outside; I hear and see everything as in a dream and like a departed spirit, I feel as if for me every kind of personal life has ceased and I am present now only in him and the children. — R. receives from his publishers the proofs of the Jewish article, which gladdens him, for he feared Weber had been intimidated. Presents for the children, meals with the children, much rejoicing. When we drink to Eva's health she is out of her mind with delight, in spite of having nothing to drink herself. Then I say she must go to bed; R. much dismayed, says this strictness is the Catholic side of my nature and that when my pleasure is greatest, I am always ready to renounce it. He is always asking himself how he would fare if I also took charge of him! This made us laugh. In the afternoon a walk with the children, at dusk fireworks in the *salon*. But Evchen is made ill by them; she has a dizzy spell, and I am very much alarmed, but she recovers. In the evening R. and I speak of former times, when we always passed each other like shadows, hardly spoke, and yet were so strangely close to each other. Then he read [Shakespeare's] *Coriolanus* to me in his unique way. — R. gave me flowers.

*Thursday, February 18*  Such nice dreams about Jesuits and Princess

Wittgenstein—a very bad night! Wrote letters—to Loulou and Mathilde. Great weariness. After lunch R. plays from *Die Walküre* (the ending) and I am literally overcome. Dear God! This work! — Its influence pervades my whole day, everything else I have to do is done as if in a dream, all that lives within me is these sounds and these words. — Whoever believes profoundly receives the reward for his faith in the form of delicious hope. As, today, I became so profoundly aware of how much I believe in R., in his mission in life, in his genius, in his kindness, in his love, there gradually arose in me out of my glowing emotions, unshakable though shadowed by unspeakable suffering, a gentle feeling, pale and tender as the new moon rising over a glowing sunset. It spoke, not of fortune or success, not of rest and joy, either— undefined and silent, it swelled up from my most intense feelings as that fairest of rewards, sweet hope.

*Friday, February 19* Good, eventless day; R. with his score, I with the children. After lunch went through some scenes of *A Midsummer Night's Dream* with R. Played with Loldi in the garden for two hours. She has christened her two dolls Pikasoki and Pulvia; the former is naughty—she will "shoot her up into the sky"—all this in the form of a story. In the evening finished *Coriolanus*.

*Saturday, February 20* As, at first dawn, the burden of thoughts and worries, of sufferings borne and expected, brought me a deep longing for death, I suddenly came to realize how happy I would be now if only I had a mother! A mother who understood everything, who comprehended my love, recognized my maternal cares, and would be able to advise me—who would say, "Give me your children, I will look after them and make them happy." And my longing died; if one day dire hours should come to you, my children, you will find me there at your side! — I slept all morning. At lunch R. showed me a letter from Mme Judith Mendès, who this summer wrote a very remarkable series of articles about him in the French *Presse*. The letter, too, is very nice and full of buoyant enthusiasm. That pleases us. In the morning R. greets me from below with the strains of the "Spring Song" from *Die Walküre*—I crept into the dining room to listen unseen.. Afternoon with the children—played the piano. Received a letter from Claire—she advises me to go to Munich— much melancholy. R. reads *Das Rheingold* to me. — During the day read some sonnets by Petrarch and found pleasure in a quotation from Goethe ("Whoever has good to do must be like a goading spirit"), which seems to me to be the right motto for R. He is the goading spirit for wretchedness and mediocrity. —

*Sunday, February 21* R. talks of a letter from Dr. Lang. Through his position in the ministry he has been able, by going through the bureaucratic hierarchy, to secure from Count Bismarck a command that Wagner's articles be published in the *N.A. Zeitung.* The article on the Devrient book will start things going. This is very pleasant news, for R. never before knew where he could place his things. In the morning I write a letter to Mme Mendès, in R.'s name, setting out his reasons for not going to see *Rienzi* in Paris. R. is satisfied with my letter. A gray day, everything wrapped in mist, R. does not go into town, we walk together in the garden. In the evening [Shakespeare's] *Julius Caesar.* R. reads it out loud to me wonderfully, it moves me so much that I go to bed quite ill.

*Monday, February 22* News of Kos, of whom the whole household has dreamed; the others happily, I sadly—so at any rate the honor of the oracle is saved. I am still suffering; a bud of one of the camellias has fallen off. — I am still unwell, and however much I make an effort to conceal it from myself, I have to give in. This morning I could pay only a little attention to the children. I am really feeling it now, that famous pale cast of thought! At times I feel as if I were literally turning pale beneath the swarm of cares which descends on me. In the afternoon, while R. was sleeping, I thought of the last letter from my father, in which he said to me, "Passion dies, but the pangs of conscience remain." What a superficial judgment! As if my coming to R. had been an act of passion, and as if I could ever feel pangs of conscience on that account! How little my father knows me, after all! — How willingly I would give up any sort of joy if I knew but one being to whom I could entrust R.'s isolated life! "To bear happiness is also a penance," Bettina wrote boldly to Goethe; how I feel this now, as I burden myself with so many heavy thoughts! Poets and sages teach us renunciation, life, too, teaches us renunciation, and renunciation is what my own heart bids me—but I could not apply it with a clear conscience; it would be like delivering the death blow just for the sake of my own peace of mind. The daily contemplation lies heavily on my heart; but R. does not notice it. He is working hard and happily. — My only sorrow is that he does not tell me about some things he writes and receives, for fear of upsetting me. On the contrary: I feel that all things become a game when they are shared. — In the evening we finish *J. Caesar.* Who could remain unmoved by this depiction of a melancholy which brings to nought the endeavors of great men? Brutus and Cassius feel that they are the last of the Romans, and this disconsolate feeling contains the seed of the death of their cause. It gives birth to madness; even before the battle has been lost, they believe themselves lost. — This is more or less the feeling I have had concerning all R.'s undertakings—I know the world belongs to other powers. — "O, that a man might know the end of this day's business ere it come! But it sufficeth that the day will end, and then the end is known." —

*Tuesday, February 23* R. has got me to copy out H. Franck's essay on *Tannhäuser* (written in '45, about 12 days after the first performance). It is excellent, indeed probably the most significant thing that has yet been written about *Tannhäuser*. R. talks much about a *Kasperl* which he had in mind to write and compose. The main characters are Kasperl and Wagner, Faust in the background. — During the night I thought it would perhaps be better and more salutary for both myself and others if I were a little cruel—I lack too much the power of causing trouble, and so I consume myself. — Around noon R. brings me the manuscript of the two acts of *Siegfried*. Indescribable joy! As I thank him, he says, "Everything belongs to you, even before I do it." — But at lunch he is despondent, indeed ill-humored; I had given him Claire's letter to read, and this had a bad effect on him. But he was soon cheerful again. After lunch with the children in the garden. In the evening R. writes letters and I arrange papers and fill in an address book. After tea *Twelfth Night*. Very gay mood.

*Wednesday, February 24* A good night, lovely deep sleep such as I have not known for a long time. — Yesterday R. and I talked about how one sometimes felt the urge to confide in another person. Then he said he believed that things would still turn out favorably for us, we must have our star somewhere. For the rest one must just ponder and wait to see which form of suffering one had chosen for oneself. R. writes to the King (16 pages) and I ink in two pages of the score; I see the notes as sacred runes which take on color beneath my hand. After lunch R. improvises. Then he tells me that a bad dream had impelled him during the night to send a telegram to Dr. Lang, telling him to make no use of the information he had given him. My alarm over this made R. regret having told me about it. After he has gone out I write him why I considered the information so important. — His improvisation—he went on from the *Lohengrin* Prelude to motives from the *Nibelungenring*—casts a spell once more over my whole soul. My soul is like a budding flower which opens only to the rays of his music. — In the evening the conclusion of *Twelfth Night*. — In the evening long reflection concerning our situation and how we should deal with it.

*Thursday, February 25* Richard dreamed that we were married, I wandered in a white satin robe (as in Terburg) through our roomy, well-furnished house and showed him Eva in a corner. I am dismayed, in view of this, to have had thoughts of death again during the night. But I am in good spirits; continuing to ink in the score gives me great pleasure—to follow in his footsteps like this! — In the afternoon,

however, I learn that he is suffering, and he does not look well. So
then I have to summon all my spiritual strength and comfort him.
He does not go into town, we walk with the children in the garden. —
Then he gets the children to dance. God grant him a good night, this
I now beseech on bended knees and feel that I could never bring myself
to part from him. He said today he believes we shall still be happy,
he feels that up till now he has really been pampered, for nothing he
had so far experienced in life has ever touched a vital nerve. A parting
from me, however, would spell his death. — Oh, may he sleep gently!
In the afternoon, while half asleep, I saw the children again and wept
copiously. — Today I told R. that I have never really heard his
*Lohengrin* Prelude, for with the very first notes I have always been
gripped by such an ecstasy that I do not hear this miracle like other
music, but experience it like a vision.

*Friday, February 26* Letters from the children and good, sympathetic
Frau Marenholtz. While with the children inked in the score; in the
afternoon a walk by myself. In the evening with the children, and wrote
to Boni. After tea searched for papers with R.

*Saturday, February 27* Letter from Eckert; they want to do *Die
Meistersinger* in Berlin, and Herr von Hülsen acts as if he had never
before negotiated with R. In the afternoon a letter from Hans about
the performance of *Tannhäuser* in Munich, enclosing a letter from the
King, who had not in fact attended the performance, but all the same
writes full of enthusiasm. I with the children almost all day. R. happy
about the letters, says he can still see us all reunited and assembled
here, my father, Hans, etc. Would Heaven but grant it—I cannot believe
it. Hans Richter announces a visit at Easter; perhaps I can arrange for
the children to visit me with him. R. has given me Gibbon (in English)
as a present. — Richard thinks I must be Loldi's daughter, owing to
the liveliness of my feelings. This reminds me of the terrible shock I
had yesterday when Loldi, after a mild scolding, had such violent
palpitations and got into such a state of agitation, her face glowing,
that I feared the worst and saw my child already dead! — Read one act
of *Antony and Cleopatra* with R.; strange feeling of discomfort.

*Sunday, February 28* All sorts of newspapers and reviews. I write
to Frau Marenholtz and spend my time with the children. It is Sunday,
which belongs to them, and they also eat with us. Unfortunately R.
decides after the meal to play something from *Siegfried*. Loldi became
restless during it, R. got impatient; to prevent an explosion I took her
up to my room and let Eva come, too; R. became very angry, and
unfortunately in the presence of the children, which distressed me
deeply. Whether I could have avoided any of it I do not know—
"activity, which never wearies," comes to my aid, I keep the children

amused and ink in two pages. R. seems to take the whole thing very lightly, and so no harm has been done. Good night, my children.

*Monday, March 1* Snow flurries, "winter tempests," yesterday Mount Pilatus dispatched a little avalanche, and today the whole country is covered with snow, the skies gray, the water a dirty green. Now winter is overtaking us. R., however, is busy on his work, may Heaven bless him! Richard says jokingly at lunch that, if he ever completes the *Nibelungen*, I shall deserve an order *pour le mérite*. After lunch the children again misbehave; it is difficult to combine bringing up children with an artistic life, but I am determined to succeed. — R. also explains why he was so angry the day before: he had been making music for me, through me, and with me, the disturbance caused by the child had caught him at a most sensitive moment, and the fact that, in order not to disturb him, I had intended to detach myself from him together with the child had upset him completely, since it showed I had not understood how he was producing these tones in conjunction with me. — At lunch he said he believed we would master our fate. I, on the other hand, am conscious of all sorts of trials ahead which I shall have to face, but I can await them calmly as long as my children's hearts are with me. Spent the evening conversing with R.

*Tuesday, March 2* At breakfast R. tells me that when anything came between us, it was because we loved each other too much and were too dependent on each other. His good fortune, he calls me! He goes off to work on the song with which Wotan wakes the Wala, I to the children, my life consists of bringing up and inking in [*in German a play on words: "Erziehen und Überziehen"*]. A violent foehn wind is raging outside. The market people cannot get across the lake to Lucerne, and wait with their wares in our boathouse; in the end they have to walk into town, carrying all their things, vegetables, poultry, eggs, on their backs. After lunch we play duets together on the piano, R. and I get much fun from it. R. says in his exhilaration, "What a lucky old donkey I am!," which makes us laugh a lot. In the evening with the children I read Shakespeare's *The Tempest*. A great and sublimely moral impression from it. The many horrible opera libretti had quite wiped the original poem from my mind—nymphs and specters were all that had remained in my memory. Now it seems to me so clear and so divine! I noticed particularly how uncommonly moderate Sh[ake]speare] remains in his use of expressions—as if the eccentricity of the situation and its framework had to be brought into balance by the simplicity of the speech (by which means the artlessness of natural life is also characterized). A less great writer would certainly have portrayed the love scene and Miranda with far more extravagance. Prospero's burial of his staff—incredibly sublime. — Later R. reads me the 3rd and 4th acts of *Antony and Cleopatra*. Well, who would dare to say a single word about that! I am utterly shattered. R. finds something of his *Tristan* reflected in it—inasmuch as it shows a being utterly consumed by love: in *Tristan* time renders it naïve and pure, whereas here it appears in a ghastly, voluptuous setting, yet no less destructively. Unfortunately R. then brings out Marbach's adaptation of the Sh.speare play. The tremendous agitation which the poet's work had brought about now gives way to real merriment. The good man appears to have wanted to *civilize* Sh.! — Inevitably we were led to discuss how Sh.'s life must have been: R. came back to his old precept that a poet cannot write about what he is currently experiencing, since he cannot see it clearly enough. — From the post office R. brings a tasteless letter from Mathilde.

*Wednesday, March 3*  In the morning R. plays the duet from the second act of *Die Meistersinger* and says he can never play it without being transported back to the time when he wrote it and I was carrying Evchen in my womb. Evchen was afraid of R. because he is wearing a different costume. I go up to the children, R. works in my room. But at lunch he reproaches me for not coming to him and censures vehemently but lovingly my fear of disturbing him. After lunch we play the *Faust* Overture as a piano duet. Then, in a lovely snow landscape, he goes out. The rooms are full of brightness in spite of gray skies in the morning, and in the afternoon the sun even emerges. From his walk he brings home the splendid edition of *Don Quixote* which Mme Viardot has given him. Great joy, for his passion for books grows daily, which leads him to say jokingly that he is well aware that I do not approve of it any more than of any other form of passion. In the evening, dictation resumed. "Bid that welcome which comes to punish us, and we punish it seeming to bear it lightly." "Let that be left which leaves itself." Three elements serve the species, R. says—love, in which the species desires to exist; the genius, in which it recognizes itself; and the saint, in whom it destroys the world.

*Thursday, March 4*  Still the snow landscape and sunshine with it, a calm and happy sight. R. working on his pencil sketches, I with the children; around noon I come downstairs and hear what he has just created! — He says he wanted to write down a page for me in which he would have contrasted his love with the love of Eduard, Tristan, and Antony; in me he had found the woman who could follow him in all respects, even as an artist, and now his genius must step in for the misfortunes of the other lovers and lead us on to happiness! — At lunch we again discussed the wonders and mysteries of Shakespearean tragedy: Cleopatra quite incomprehensible and yet so clear, so recognizable, so definite. It is that which distinguishes the true poet,

R. says, the ability to depict everything as it is, without explanation or solution. The latter is provided by the philosopher, and everyone who reads such poems must be his own philosopher. — While he is speaking to me, instructing and uplifting me, I am reminded of the verse at the conclusion of *Tasso*, though in an entirely different sense. I cling tight to the rock of his love, on which my "I," that is to say, my bad side, my self-will, my sinful limitations, was wrecked. To live for him is my salvation—in recognizing that I am always thinking of my absent children and hoping soon to have them here with me. — R. and I both had similar dreams: that we received visits and rejoiced in each other in a mood of harmonious well-being. Only in my dreams Blandine is always present. — Beethoven's grandnephew has come begging again. — As we continue to talk about Shakespeare's plays in increasing detail, he says he has often felt regret that in these works he could not enjoy each single ingredient for itself, for example, Henry IV by himself without interruption, and the young days of Prince Hal as a heroic comedy; this way would be artistically more consummate, though in a genius such as Shakesp. the very incompleteness serves to impart a true picture of the world. — He feels that with regard to artistic form we owe much to the French for having held so rigidly to the three unities, but one should be able to move about freely within these rules and project life into the prescribed magic circle. Sh. had exploded the whole machinery, and what one sees in him is not the world in a magic mirror, but something so real that one is startled. — Much else R. said to me about the nature of women—it makes me sad, deeply melancholy; we women cannot ponder these problems, we can only feel, love, yield ourselves. But how unworthy of R. I feel myself to be! — In the evening, dictation, after the children had provided me with much enjoyment. Good night, little ones here and yonder, and big one! — R. also reports that Rubinstein is to give a concert here. That is the last straw!

*Friday, March 5* Dreamed that my mother had published a pamphlet through Schuré, in which she made some scandalous assertions— that I had been besought by the Grand Duchess of Weimar and Princess Wittgenstein to keep my hands off R. and not to carry on the ill repute of my mother. — My own worries and thoughts are reflected back to me in this curious mirror! — Rich. at his work; I with the children; at lunch he talks a lot about Wotan and the Wala. — I tell him I believe that, if his friends knew how he was living and what satisfied him, instead of being pleased they would be angry and would despise me. He thinks that is not so, and that—as long as we demanded no active participation from them—we would find them sympathetic. I find that hard to believe, I do not even expect that in later years, when we are all peacefully at rest, my devotion and love will be remembered with good will—but my children at least shall know me. Snow is falling gently and copiously; it gives solitude a shining aspect; how quiet it is here! When have two beings ever before lived for and in each other, so cut off from the world? — From the post office R. brings back the first copies of his pamphlet on the Jews and a letter from Hermine. The children are fairly well, though Lusch has a cough. I am overcome with melancholy—when shall I see them again, when *have* them again? — While R. reads through the *Jews*, I look through the catalogue of Herr von zu Rhein's collection with a slightly heavy heart. When I still belonged to the world, I took great interest in such things. Later, dictation, and then discussed with R. my plan to request that the children visit me for a month. —

*Saturday, March 6* Great delight in the children, who are lively and healthy; yesterday they were sitting opposite each other on the floor of R.'s bedroom and playing. Loldi was putting on R.'s shoe, and Eva brushing her hair with his big brush. R. says he cannot ever forget the sight. — He has good news of Kos, we shall have him back probably at Easter. — Wrote to Hermine. R. at work, but after lunch to the law courts in connection with a dispute with his locksmith. In the evening a great shock, Eva falls down in a faint. One should never rejoice; we had been too happy about the children's good health. — As I sat silent and in tears beside her little bed, forcing myself not to move so that the child would go off to sleep, I heard in little Wilhelm's room opposite the sound of laughing, singing, and playing. In earlier days this contrast would have made me bitter, but now it gave me the consoling feeling that others at least were enjoying themselves while I was worrying myself to death. — R. came back from the courts very depressed: he never wants to get involved in a court case again, nothing but tricks, lies, evasions, his lawyer was frightened to death when he opened his mouth, for fear he would smash down the whole tissue of lies. The opposing lawyer a profiteer, a horribly prevaricating person, R.'s defending counsel a sheep, as was to be expected. Just think—says R.—throughout the world the judicial system is like that! In the evening, dictation.

*Sunday, March 7* R. still very much affected by the court session, but does some work; I with the children, who eat with us. After lunch a walk with Loldi and R. — Eva is well again. I feel very unwell and have to lie down. R. reads me a chapter from Schopenhauer ("Ethics") —shall I ever get the children? I am quite worn out.

*Monday, March 8* Richard did not find time today for his sketches, since he had to correct the proofs of his article on Devrient; this meant a dismal day. In the morning and afternoon I ink in pages of the score in the nursery. Eva alarms me with her temper. After lunch R. sends off *Die Meistersinger* to the "*Meistersängerin* Mme Viardot" and writes letters. I occupy myself with Winckelmann again. In the evening R. reads me the conclusion of the chapter by Schopenhauer. I can scarcely describe my present mood, everything is just expectation. Shall I see the children at Easter? — A good letter from Düfflipp, R.'s wishes are being fulfilled. [*In the margin:* "The advance granted, Schott given security, and Beethoven's nephew helped."]

*Tuesday, March 9*  Arrival of the author's copies of the pamphlet on the Jews; also of the *Gallery of Famous Germans*, which Breitkopf & Härtel have presented to R. R. at his work. The weather is fine. After lunch a walk with Loldi; since she will never leave my side, I make her a little speech; in the evening, when going to bed, she says, "Everything pleases me about you," meaning by that to assure me that she will do all I tell her. Since R. is still very much set against dictating, he reads me Shakespeare's *Love's Labour's Lost*. R. is very concerned for me, and I have to tell him how much worse other women in my condition frequently fare, in order to calm him down. In the night I wake up thinking of the children—shall I be able to make their lot a little bearable?

*Wednesday, March 10*  R. has received a letter from Hans, thanking him for the pamphlet on the Jews (sent to him directly by Weber) and announcing his journey to Vienna, where he is playing at Baron Sina's for 500 florins. The King has commanded *Tristan und Isolde* for May and *Rheingold* for August. Hans is delighted with the pamphlet. — R. is pleased by various things I say and declares that, if being able to converse daily with me were all he had, he would count himself lucky; he would ignore God knows whom—even Shakespeare himself if he came—just to converse with me. — (Winckelmann on the works of Bernini, "the common herd gone up in the world"; Poussin on Raphael: "An angel compared with the new, a donkey compared with the old.") At lunch R. is very exhausted, his work excites him so terribly that I am almost afraid to encourage him in it! Afterward a drive in the coach with Loldi—to Hergeschwyl. Rich. climbs on the rocks. In the coach he says that the peculiarities of my father's temperament could achieve harmonious expression only in a woman. Back home, played with the children. In the evening finished *Love's Labour's Lost*. At ten o'clock to bed—and woke up suddenly in the night in concern about R. A deep awareness that I have but one task— to make his life easier. Whatever may come, whether I die or whether I live, nothing shall lead me astray. The children's fate frightens me, since I shall one day leave them without provision, yet I hope for a friendly star for at least one of them, and this one will look after the others.

*Thursday, March 11*   Kos is cured and will soon return home—a great joy. R. works. Then he tells me that Berlioz has died; it brings back to my mind pictures of my childhood. R. and I discussed all the deaths in this year; the harvest has been terrible: Lamartine, Berryer, Genelli, Rossini, Berlioz, to name only the most renowned! — R. goes for a walk and brings "my Richard Wagner letter," printed in *La Liberté*. R. thinks it looks well and is glad that he decided as he did with regard to Paris. Pasdeloup writes that everything is going very well—he has completely new costumes after all and has engaged the top Paris ballerinas!! — Also two letters from Mathilde to R. and to me, giving an account of *Die Meistersinger* in Mannheim! — I am feeling rather despondent today in spite of the lovely spring air. Life is difficult, my children, oh so difficult! One must always remember that our highest good is suffering. — In the newspaper there was an article about the approaching Vatican Council, they wish to make the papal pagoda omnipotent and give the Jesuits the triple crown. Their tomfoolery may be all to the good. Did nothing in the evening, because Richard is tired.

*Friday, March 12*   In the night I woke with a start, no bad dream had troubled me, but I was so melancholy that it was a long time before I fell asleep again. I forced myself not to reflect, to think of nothing, however many troubles should come to roost in my heart; when it is too full, it will simply burst. And it is incredible how much the heart can hold—at times I can feel mine literally expanding to take in more. Early in the morning R. came up and played "*Ein Engel stieg aus Himmelsäther*" ["An angel descended from heavenly heights"]; he said he had seen me come into his room with the children, and this had come into his mind. — My life as a recluse is now almost ended, since recently, as we drove out, we met Colonel Am Rhyn, and when R. saw him again yesterday he had to tell him that I was here, I was expecting the children for Easter and had come early because I should not have been able to travel easily later. However, this will not make much difference to my seclusion, for I am shy of seeing other people. — R. worked long today and is terribly pent up on account of it, I avoid talking about it to him and divert the conversation to music in general; he says that up to Mozart music remained in a vegetable state, but with M. and particularly with Beethoven "anima" had entered into it. The Bachian fugue was like a great tree, so lofty and also imposing, yet in a completely different way from the human heart. — The weather is bad and one cannot go out, a fact of which I am indeed glad.

Winckelmann and the children fill in my time; R. is going through what he composed in the morning and is not satisfied with it, he thinks he has gone too far in the proliferation of his motives. At tea he said that, if he wanted to make things easy for himself, he would, from the moment Wotan says, *"Seit mein Wunsch es will,"* introduce recitative, which would certainly create a great effect, but would put an end to the work as art. Nobody has yet noticed with how much art he has employed all means to prevent the interruption of the flow of melody, while still achieving a romantic effect. — Music, he says, transfigures everything, it never permits the hideousness of the bare word, however terrible the subject. Afterward he read me various songs from the *Edda*: "Sinfiötli," "Harbard and Thor," "Wafrudiu," etc. I take delight above all in the sight of his face as he sits there opposite me, when his eyes grow dark and gleam and his resonant voice shatters my heart. — *Saturday, March 13* "The swan of Leipzig"—that is what the *Signale* today calls Rich. Much amused by it. A short notice in the *Karlsruher Zeitung* announces the publication of the pamphlet on the Jews and gives the opinion that by treating a whole race of people, including its eminent composer, ruthlessly, and also by treating all his opponents contemptuously, R. is harming both himself and his cause! . . . Unfortunately R. cannot go to his work, because the piano tuner is coming, he is agitated. We discuss our situation and my condition and resolve to engage a nurse from outside. Seldom indeed have two human beings lived in such isolation as we. R. goes for a walk, but brings no letter back from town for me. I still do not know whether I shall see the children again! In the evening R. reads me *"Ecken Ausfahrt,"* translated by Simrock. Dietrich von Bern the true German type: calm and deliberate, utterly lacking in aggression, but terrible strength when once roused. — The obituaries on Berlioz are all embarrassed in tone.

*Sunday, March 14* A poor soldier from the papal army came around begging yesterday, he had walked across the Gotthard and his right toe was frostbitten. He had good testimonials, and when on my instructions he was given five francs he wept with gratitude and joy. I was reminded then of the wish I had expressed as a child and still had as a girl to devote myself to the care of the poor. How far away from that I now am! And yet, when I see such misery, I have the feeling of having missed my vocation. — Snow has once more settled over the countryside—*le linceul*, as we call it! R. is extremely worried about my condition; we go for a walk in the garden. Then we get the children to dance. In the evening R. looks at me and says: if only he had not brought me such distress—if he had never entered my life, I should now be sitting quietly in Berlin, reading Winckelmann in peace! At that I can only laugh, but when he afterward reads me *Minna von Barnhelm* I have (foolish as it may sound) to weep; I cannot hear certain emotions, as spoken by his voice, without my whole inner being's trembling; and when I then contemplate him I have to acknowledge within my soul how unworthy of him I am, and swear to give him that loyalty which bears all suffering with rejoicing and without flinching. —

*Monday, March 15* Our reading kept us up until half past twelve; now R. has had a bad night and feels very unwell. On top of that comes the news that Pasdeloup will be here today to question R. about some things concerning *Rienzi*. Since R. declares he finds it less of a strain when I am there, I, too, shall see the good, muddled man. My letter to Judith Mendès was a distinct success, Truinet thinks it *"parfaite"* and Pasdeloup wants to bequeath it to his children as *"titre d'honneur."* Received a letter from Hermine, but she has not yet received mine, since Hans was in Vienna. At three Pasdeloup came and stayed till ten in the evening. All through this R. was so miserable that my heart bled. He recovered—or, rather, he exerted himself; God grant him a good night! To be prepared to die a thousand deaths for someone at every moment, yet to be unable to alleviate his suffering—what torture! — The mail brought an anonymous letter from Breslau "in the name of 7,000 Jews"—full of abuse and threats. It reminds me that Count Bismarck's assassin was a Jew. — They will drag us down into the mud, I will bear it all willingly just to remain at his side, they may revile me to the end of time, so long as I have helped him, have been permitted to give him my hand and say to him: I will follow you to the death! — Pasdeloup tells us that when, at his concert, some people hissed after the *Lohengrin* Prelude, a lady said to her neighbor, who was whistling ceaselessly into a key, *"Monsieur, si vous ne cessez pas, je vais vous casser la tête avec mon petit banc"* ["Sir, if you don't stop, I will hit you over the head with my footstool"]. My single prayer: one day to die with Richard in the selfsame hour. My greatest pride: to have rejected everything in order to live for him. My finest happiness: his joy. — Without him the world is to me no better than a sty, as Cleopatra says. — My blessings now on his night!

*Tuesday, March 16* R. slept well! At such times it is like a reunion after long separation. He brings upstairs with him a letter from Mme Viardot—about the Jewish pamphlet! This nonsense or this profound sense! She is a Jewess, that is now quite clear. When I tell R. I should like to write to her, he asks me to draft a few lines; these he finds good, and in fact, he copies them out. Then he goes to his work. I write to Loulou. A walk in the garden with Loldi; thought of the children! The evening is devoted to talk with R., since he is still too tired to undertake anything. Late in the evening wrote to Mathilde. I had ordered a gold pen for R. from New York, but the nib was too fine—that caused me a little worry. —

*Wednesday, March 17* R. brings a letter addressed to me from the King, which Hans has sent on to him. I cannot express the misery which fills me on reading these ecstatic phrases! R. has received another letter from Mme Viardot, she asks for a musical explanation—strange! R. suspects that she regrets her letter of yesterday. — While with the children I begin my embroidery. R. sketches. At lunch we talk about the children in Munich, particularly about Loulou, so good, so loyal. There is constantly this layer of black clouds around my heart. How easily I do without the world, or, rather, how utterly I do *not* miss it, and how hard to bear, how anxious my longing for my children! — Weber has sent newspapers (about the Jewish pamphlet). Everyone foaming, raging, jeering. In the evening, dictation.

*Thursday, March 18* R. unwell, unable to work. Vreneli to Zurich to fetch Kos. A friendly anonymous letter about the Jewish pamphlet. Letter from Richter, who is starting on a journey to find singers, for *Tristan und Isolde, Das Rheingold,* and *Die Walküre* have all been commanded for this year! — About the children, however, I learn nothing, and consequently ask R. to write a few lines to Hans, just so that he should not feel aggrieved at receiving no answer to various letters. Did a lot of embroidery and inking in, also much time in the garden; glorious spring day; "*Winterstürme wichen*"!

*Friday, March 19* Kos is now really back, but very much changed. R. works, I sit with the children, embroidering. The mail brings only an honorary diploma (Linzer Gesangsverein) and the *Signale* for R. The latter contains a report maintaining that in a letter R. wrote that the French were tailors, and he would only go to them to have his jackets made. R. is demanding a retraction. — Vreneli tells us that Semper had said in Zurich that it had been in Wagner's power to have the theater built, but W. had let the project drop!! — Still no news of the children. R. tells me the people who are behaving so badly toward us will live to regret it. I do not desire even that. But I do want to see my children again. — At this hour of the evening six years ago I was feeling very unwell; unwell and at the same time wretched. How wearily and gloomily I brought my baby into the world, without any assistance; how indifferently did the father greet it! Only Richard, far away, was concerned about me, and I did not know it. How dreary, how empty, how inwardly disturbed was my life at that time! How could I ever thank R. enough for what his love has done for me? At that time I was feeling so wretched that I told nobody that my labor pains had come, and that the baby was already there when they summoned the midwife. My mother-in-law was living in the house, Hans was at home, there were servants in plenty, and I was walking up and down in the *salon* all by myself, wriggling like a worm and whimpering; a cry I could not suppress woke the household and they carried me to my bed, where Boni then crept out. In every home a coming child is a time of joy, but I hardly dared tell Hans that I was pregnant, so unfriendly was his reaction, as if his comfort were being disturbed. I have never told anyone about this before; now I am writing it down—not to complain about Hans (he had many worries on his mind, and he did not know what pleases and what hurts a woman, for I had always kept silent), but because I cannot think without shuddering of that night in Berlin, which serves to make utterly clear to me the subsequent course of my destiny.

*Saturday, March 20*    The mail brings nothing but an abusive letter from Breslau (the third from there) and a large drawing (Sachs and Eva) from the King. Unfortunately this is very ugly. R. does a little work; I am doing my embroidery and busying myself with the children, when I notice a peculiar expression in Loldi's eyes which worries me, it seems like a touch of deceitfulness. Snow is falling again; spring and winter are locked in battle, likewise the evil and good spirits of my fate. I still do not know whether I shall see the children again! In the evening dictation, after we had inspected the plan of Odysseus's house.

*Sunday, March 21*    Still nothing from the children! — In the morning R. tells me he cannot imagine how we could once have thought we could contain our love within the rules of ordinary life. — He works a bit, I embroider and play with the children. Then Sunday lunch. Afterward a chapter of Otfried Müller on the Dorians, then a long, long sleep, for I am tired from worrying. In the garden when already getting late; at about 6:30, after dusk had fallen and everything was very gray and silent, a little bird twittered above my head, and at once I was seized with hope; then a rook cawed, and I heard my little friend no more. Richard is writing to the King. — Yesterday R. said, when he saw my hair undone, that it was true Geneviève hair, and he added: God, if I could lead you like that into the wilderness! Only there are no more wildernesses, everywhere *boardinghouses*—the wilder the country, the more luxurious the boardinghouse. — In the evening continued reading Otfried Müller.

*Monday, March 22*    There are days devoted to misfortune, and it has happened often in my life that such a day is the first of the week. Today, for instance, R. wanted to rise very early in order to finish his letter and also get down to his work. But the chimneysweep upsets it all. Then he reads me his letter, and I am overcome by deep melancholy. I wish he could find another form for his intercourse, it could be just as warm in tone and might look more genuine. He notices my reservations, though I do not voice them. — Hans has also written, and sends an article from a Catholic paper, in favor of the Jewish pamphlet. I divide the gloomy day between the children, embroidery, and inking in the score. During the night I found myself thinking melancholy thoughts about love: when the sexual emotions play no part, it is surely of a higher nature. Yet I cannot think that a love can be deeper, truer, purer than mine for Richard.

*Tuesday, March 23* Dismal indeed these first two days of spring have been, and I myself in despondent mood. At daybreak I wake and tell myself that suffering is good and salutary and that we must suffer with cheerful courage, still and silent, and only then will we feel strengthened, as if the whole world were waving palm fronds at our patience. Then, too, and only then, the choirs of angels descend, bringing us comfort and singing their "Hail to the Weepers," that fair cradle song of pain. The mortal being, however, takes up the cup reluctantly and prefers to lament, however much punishment he earns by it. — R. told me he had encountered the convicts who are working in the fields and they had exchanged friendly greetings, one of them even with the words *"Bonsoir, monsieur."* In spite of their chains, R. says, they are still members of society; whoever makes public redress for his crime is in a state of legality. — In the evening, dictation. (In the afternoon, inked in.)

*Wednesday, March 24* Many tears in the morning. God knows, they flow so fast that I cannot hold them back; but I do as much as possible to conceal them. The mail still brings nothing, it looks as if I shall not see the children at Easter. — At midday R. plays me some things (Wotan with Siegfried, powerfully gripping and moving!). At lunch Loldi gives me a shock by suddenly becoming unwell—fearing diphtheria, R. sends for the doctor, but it emerges with considerable certainty that she had drunk something out of the little brandy flask, and that has made her so ill. The doctor tells us in passing that he ha<sup></sup> read the Jewish pamphlet and he is glad to know the reason for the unceasing acts of enmity. A lady from Zurich had brought the pamphlet with her to read in the train. This amuses us. — When R. comes home from his walk we discuss my position; he says that, generally speaking, we have only the King to place us together and reckon us as one. The children I shall not now see. That will just have to be borne. Perhaps a fair reward will blossom in my heart! In the evening read Otfried Müller.

*Thursday, March 25* Maundy Thursday. — In the morning R. laments bitterly that I am so badly looked after in his house; I am sorry that he takes so to heart something which has always seemed to me so trivial. He works a little, I embroider and play with the children. After lunch he suggests that I walk into town with him, and is pleasantly surprised when I agree. So to town with the two children, in gay mood. Stopped for a rest in a hotel, drank coffee and ate cakes, also glanced through newspapers. Then at the post office found a letter from Hermine. It is still undecided whether the children will come—Hans's usual irresolution! Claire writes to me, too, and reports that my mother is again very unwell, a condition calling for profound pity. — Passed the evening conversing with R. He is happy, because I have had a letter.

*Good Friday, March 26*   Wrote to Hermine and to Claire. The former tells me, among other things, that Hans intends to give up the little apartment, so R. can send for his things. Around midday the sun comes out, which makes me very glad. My mood is quietly melancholy— how I should welcome the assurance that all are happy and well! — Just before noon the pamphlets arrive (*Herr Eduard Devrient and His Style*), and the complete songs of Schubert. Then I go to church, if only in order not to offend those people who cannot understand that such a day is better spent silently at home. It was three o'clock when I entered the Barfüsser church with Loldi; at this hour (I was told as a child) one may make a wish and it will be granted; so I wished for happiness and good health for the children and all who have come in close touch with me, and for the forgiveness of all to whom I have brought pain; in my spirit I then pardoned all who have either done me harm or wished me harm or are preparing to do so. R. comes to fetch me and we return home together. Lovely sunshine, clear air, birds twittering in the branches. How firmly I am resolved to suppress everything, to bear every worry by myself and to seek salvation in every act of suffering and self-sacrifice! Thus I participate in this sacred day and hope for my dear ones. — At home R. played and sang to me from the Schubert volumes. (The *Signale* has not accepted his denial of the false report—on the other hand Dr. Lang writes that the Jewish population is seething in Berlin.) Spent a wonderful evening with two of Plato's dialogues (*Ion, Hippias*).

*Saturday, March 27*   [*In the margin:* "Whoever desires the beautiful must endure much."] In the morning R. brings a new issue of the *Signale*, containing his correction. Then a pamphlet by a sentimental Jew, an admirer of Rich.'s, but indignant about *Judaism in Music*. At lunch spoke about this and then once more mainly about Plato. My eyes are much strained, perhaps from the embroidery. (Breslau sends us a 5th article!) In the afternoon I take the children downstairs and show them pictures (*Ring des Nibelungen*). R. returns home, finds us together, and is pleased by the sight. He tells me I can have no idea how happy he is. Read in the evening (*Hippias Minor*).

*Sunday, March 28*  R., coming to my room in the morning, says, "You have now been with me a whole winter, I can hardly believe it; you know nothing of me, have no idea how my heart rejoices when I think of it." — Yes, our love is a thing of truth in this world of lies and deception. — Yesterday we read together and were deeply moved by Shakespeare's sonnet "'Tis better to be vile than vile esteem'd," in which all the bitterness of a being who feels himself at odds with the world is so nobly expressed. — R. has a letter from Hans reporting on the impact of the pamphlet by Wilhelm Drach, and also further reactions to *Judaism*—the wealthy Jews in Munich are no longer so eager to see Wagner's operas; the theater management in Breslau has asked Nachbaur to choose a role other than Lohengrin for his guest appearance, since this work cannot very well be played in Breslau just now on account of the pamphlet. Then Hans relates that he visited Lachner with a deputation from the orchestra, requesting Lachner to conduct his latest suite (!) himself (in the Odeon concert); that is to take place this evening, and in all probability Lachner's supporters will stage the most ridiculous demonstrations. I do wish that these intrigues against Hans would stop at last. — Was in the garden looking for eggs with the children; the morning was nice, but the afternoon brought snow. — Richard was indisposed this morning and was unable to draw any "lines." — In the afternoon I read the French translation of *Tristan und Isolde*. Spent the evening going again through the Schubert songs— how much sifting one must do with Schubert before one attains a pure artistic enjoyment! In the night moonlight reflected in the snow; in the morning I heard the little finch singing, blackbirds came, too, to collect feathers from the hens, but now it will all stop, since more snow has been falling. R. writes to his friend Fräulein Meysenbug and mentions me kindly and lovingly. How that touches me! I can hardly say good night to him without tears starting in my eyes—he says we are as happy as lambs; if only there were not those wolves outside!

*Monday, March 29*  I am shocked at times by my appearance and ask myself if it is so bad on account of my condition, or because I am nearing my end, or just that I am getting older—I believe it is a sign of age. — Loldchen has a bad eye and Evchen a swollen cheek, yet one is glad to survive the winter with nothing worse. Rich. at work, I play throughout the morning with Loldi, who cannot go into the garden. At midday there arose between R. and myself the question of a change of faith; he said, "Your father would certainly not object to our relationship if, to make it possible, I were to become a Catholic." At that I asked him whether in order to marry me he would have become a Catholic, if that had been necessary. He replied that this was a "devilish" question, he could not even conceive of it. At first I

was disconcerted; my immediate feeling was that *I* am giving everything up, religion and all else besides, in order to ally myself with him,
but then I understood. A woman may and should sacrifice all for her
beloved, a man, on the other hand, can and should have a point from
which he neither shifts nor wavers. In addition, as R. observes, the
conversion from Catholicism to Protestantism is not the same as the
other way around; a Protestant is required to make a formal confession
of heresy. — This whole chapter did, however, bring me into a mood
of seriousness; it is difficult to achieve all at once an insight which
raises one above the painful realization of the difference between a
man's and a woman's love; and since with me everything moves
slowly, I spent just about the whole afternoon working on the matter.
— Colonel Am Rhyn visited me; that always produces a curious
situation. — In the evening began on *Alcibiades II.*

*Tuesday, March 30* Thick snow everywhere; it dazzles my eyes,
which are very weak. Munich is still wrapped in silence. Instead, R.
brings a letter from one of the editors of the monarchical *Wiener
Zeitung*, Dr. Leutner: he speaks enthusiastically of the Jewish pamphlet;
its "contemplative calm" and the "disregard for the comforts and trials
of life" propounded in it fill him with admiration. An article in a
newspaper (I do not know which one) calls R. the Hamann of the 19th
century. R. tells me he recently read somewhere that he had written
his *Judaism* because he envied Mendelssohn his genius and Meyerbeer
his success; this made him ask himself: What, not Hiller his wife?—for
he could envy Hiller neither for his genius nor for his success. — R. is
rather unwell, but he is working, and that puts him in good spirits.
The weather clears up and I walk with him into town; glorious sunset,
the whole of Tribschen transformed on our return. Was with R. at
the antiquarian's, then at the post office found a letter from Hermine.
In a week I shall see the children again! — In the evening R. unwell,
so I contain my joy inside myself. — I had a terrible shock during our
walk; not far from the railroad R. was reading out loud to me a letter
from Pohl ("This letter resembles not exactly a bad apple, but at any
rate a baked one," said R.); suddenly we see Kos in the middle of the
track fighting with another dog, the train almost on top of him!
R. seemed to shoot off like an arrow, and through his running and
shouting he rescues Kos, himself escaping only by a miracle—but the
sight! — In the evening finished reading *Alcibiades.* —

*Wednesday, March 31* [*In the margin:* "'Goethe, so intent on beauty.'
Richard."] A spring day. I can sit in the garden and embroider; the
children full of fun, dancing in the living room, outside much jumping
about and running. To me R. talks about the redecoration of the rooms;
strangely, it makes me feel sad; also I can think of nothing but the

children. — R. works and says he is now well into it: his Siegfried is rushing through the flames. — After lunch a letter from Loulou; its overformal French manner displeases R., and he tells me so, which makes me very melancholy. In the evening a letter from Mathilde— somewhat overwise. After tea read Plato's *Lysis* with indescribable delight. Otherwise, worry over a children's nurse.

*Thursday, April 1* Dreamed about the King, also of wild animals fighting with Rus; very little sleep. R. reports that he also did not sleep at all. But he goes off to his work and I to my letters (to J. Gerstenberg, who has asked me to sell a picture to the King; to Claire and to Hermine). Now I shall probably be going as far as Romanshorn to meet the children. Loldi is joyful, and even Eva, too. R. has now brought his Siegfried to the summit! I fear an interruption on account of the redecorating arrangements. — After lunch we drive into town to make some purchases (a hat for Evchen, a dress for Loldi). At home, start of all the moving muddle; I lie down, since I cannot help, and read Lewes. R. cheerful, he tells me that at times he has an unbounded confidence in his strength. The wicked are always with us, but in fact they never triumph, all that is needed is for the right one to come along (example: Odysseus). He says in dreams he often has the sense of flying, and that sometimes comes to him when he is awake, too; at times he feels he would need only an effort of will to find himself hovering high over everything. We will not go under, he declares. — This morning he had a letter from the Berlin Opera, which he did not immediately want to open, expecting something unpleasant as a consequence of his short note in the Jewish pamphlet. But, instead of that, Hülsen informs him very prettily of a production of *Die Msinger* in Berlin and Hanover. This is welcome, of course, but what miserable and pitiful creatures these people are! — In the evening R. speaks to me about the *Odyssey* and the *Iliad,* smoking and drinking beer. Since the joiners had been varnishing in the next room, all these various smells combine, and I gradually begin to feel dizzy and my head starts to ache; it robs me entirely of my vision and finally of my hearing, too. When I told R. of my condition he became very angry, seeing a reproach in what was only an explanation. He then said many things it would have been better for him not to have said. I up to my room where, feeling upset, I wept. Now I am wondering what would be the best thing to do—whether I should leave his temper to cool down or go to him, quietly explain again what had happened, and soothe him. Hardly had I written this when R. came in to wish me good night. I then went downstairs to him and calmed his fantasies.

*Friday, April 2* For me this was previously always Saint Francis's Day, now it just passes like all the others. The furniture moving continues, I help by beating and dusting the books. After lunch I take a rest and read Lewes's *Life of Goethe*. Then in the garden with the children and R. after his return from town. There he had found a delightful letter from a Comité Wagnerien, asking him for his permission to attend the first performance of *Rienzi*. Late in the evening Richter arrives from Munich with news, much of which is amusing, but there are some unpleasant things, too. Lachner's intrigues are still going on; and Hans has asked to be excused from conducting for several weeks. One miserable journalist completely dominates the Munich newspaper and denigrates everything that Hans does. The news tortures me; it was a great consolation for me to know that Hans was contented. But life is not interested in consolation.

*Saturday, April 3* Embroidered in the morning, while R. took Richter through his *Young Siegfried*. Family meal and then a walk in summery weather. Letters from Paris: Nuitter reports that the Jewish pamphlet has stirred up great indignation, and that this will probably harm *Rienzi*.

*Sunday, April 4* R. unwell, which makes it increasingly clear to me that the smallest alteration in our way of life and the slightest contact with the outside world is now unbearable to him, physically as well as morally. The projected production of *Das Rheingold* in Munich also distresses him deeply, the means are not at hand, and now things will be forced, his great work cut to pieces—it is a great shame, and I am in deadly fear that dealing with it, even if only from here, will completely rob him of his will to continue his work. — He looks bad and his whole nature is changed. — Again a day with the children; after lunch I am tired and lie down (with Lewes's *Life of Goethe*), late in the evening to town. Then took up *Das Rheingold*—but R. becomes impatient and ill-humored. — A Catholic paper praises the Jewish pamphlet and praises the young King who, like his ancestor who protected Orlando di Lasso, loves and honors R. Wagner, the composer of heroic song. Such is the world.

*Monday, April 5* Feelings of great nausea and worries about the redecorations. I spent the day on the sofa, listening to R. going through *Das Rheingold* with Richter, and embroidering. R. himself is very unwell —the trouble has so upset us both. I realize that we can indeed live only for and with each other, all contact with the outside world, however friendly the go-between, is harmful to us. In the evening read a little of *Charmides*, but did not get far. At 1 o'clock our good Richter made his departure.

*Tuesday, April 6* I am still unwell: the children's arrival is upsetting me. R. writes letters, I embroider and read Lewes's *Goethe*, a wretched book, but a noble subject. In the afternoon a long walk, in the evening

R. takes a bath—he is very, very run down. I read to him (the conclusion of *Charmides*). The children will not come tomorrow, but on Thursday. In the *Propyläen* I read letters by my grandfather about my father's first successes, and feel much moved. —

*Wednesday, April 7* Both R. and myself utterly run down; even being with the children I find difficult. I fight my weakness as much as I can and begin my letter to the King. Two telegrams arrive from Paris announcing the great success of *Rienzi* (yesterday was the first performance). R. was just then with me, to tell me that he is quite unable *now* to write about Berlioz. He would have liked to do it, and the impact of such an essay would perhaps have been good, but nobody should expect it of him. ("B[erlioz] the giant-sized pupil, too great to find himself a master.") At lunch a third telegram, from Pasdeloup with just the words: *Grand succès!* — Paid visits (Frau Am Rhyn, Countess Bassenheim). There and back with R. In the post office he finds a nice letter from Dr. Marbach, who tells him that all understanding people are pleased about the pamphlet and reports on the performance of *Hamlet* by Ambroise Thomas in Laube's theater!!! I found a letter from Claire, full of praise for Hans's chivalry in sending the children to me. — How willing I am to thank him for it! Played hide-and-seek with the little ones and discovered the first violets. In the evening read Plato's *Laches*, while reading got a fourth telegram, this time from Tausig in Berlin; it reads: "Huge success of *Lohengrin*, all Jews reconciled, your devoted Karl." In this way successes mean something. — At supper R. again spoke of his memories of Berlioz and said he would now only praise him, pointing out that his failures were due to the badness of the prevailing musical conditions; yet they were also due to something in himself, his temperament, he had been constrained, and the constraint of his spirit had led gradually to a deterioration in his character. Read much of Lewes, the subject remains constantly absorbing; but how frightful that affairs of the heart are discussed— how terrible is fame to a woman! It seems strange to me, too, that women who are loved by great men do not feel that they are what they are because of these men and this love, and imagine they are something else besides in themselves.

*Thursday, April 8* R. very unwell, has been told to expect the arrival of the stage director Hallwachs from Munich. I write to the King. At 12 o'clock lunch, and then departure with a heavy heart, since R. looks wretched. I feel more and more clearly how much a separation of even an hour upsets us both—it is really almost impossible. In Zurich met the children—an afternoon of joy. They are changed and look unwell, though not really ill. A cheerful journey home. R. still run down, though very satisfied with his conference (the machinist

Brandt is understanding and inventive). Everyone to bed. Great concern over the note Hermine gave me: Hans is ill, for the most part through annoyance over the eternal torments. He no longer visits the school or conducts the orchestra. — News from Paris, the success seems to have been great; also Mme Mendès has written another very good article ("*Richard Wagner—Liberté*").

*Friday, April 9*    Disturbed night, bad dreams of Father and Mother, the young people well, however; I feel that I must not leave the children. Finished my letter to the King. — R. continually unwell, he does not go to work. Family lunch; Boni very bright, but somewhat affected, Loulou seems nervous. A telegram brings news of the second performance of *Rienzi* in Paris; "*tous nos amis heureux*," cable Flaxland and Nuitter. In the garden with the children, violets and primroses! Loulou dictates to me a letter to her father and I enclose with it Claire's last letter praising Hans. Then received a few lines from Mathilde, with it an article from the *Wiener Revue*; reports that R. is to blame for the exhibition's not taking place; now that the King has had to give way, *Das Rheingold* will also not be staged!! R. sends this to Düfflipp and writes to the press. To town with the children, to the post office, the baker, then drove home. — I find the sight of the elder children painful; first, they do not look as well as the younger ones, then I see that their development has lacked my hand. A dark premonition tells me that I shall come to grief on this feeling.

*Saturday, April 10*    Woke up fresh after a good night; sunshine, birdsong, with this thoughts about the children. Overwhelming melancholy, but then the firm resolve to digest and overcome it all inwardly, so that R. does not suffer by it. — At breakfast R. reads me a letter which he had just received from Hans, who is living there isolated in the midst of the most despicable intrigues. It broke my heart and I spent the whole morning weeping and sobbing and reflecting. In the afternoon I wrote a complete account of things to the King. At ten in the morning Loldi was wished many happy returns and given her presents. Then family lunch and afterward read some of the report by Frederick the Great's doctor. Splendid impression. R. walks into town with Loulou, I stay behind with the three other children and play with them. There is a ton weight on my heart. From the town R. brings a letter from Mme Flaxland—in a very silly way she informs him that the Jewish pamphlet is detrimental to the success of *Rienzi*. There are no human beings left—just "pieces of paper"! In the evening read more of the little medical book, quite powerfully moved by several passages. I go to bed with most despondent thoughts, I feel as if I shall never be gay again—yet I do not wish for death, I see only too well how indispensable I am to the children, and perhaps life will show mercy on me after all, so that I can help! — Good night, my children, good night, my beloved, good night, poor Hans—if tears are of any value to the gods, you must all be granted peace, since I have wept for you all most sorely.

*Sunday, April 11* In the morning a package of newspapers, forwarded by Mme Flaxland. Much nonsense and much Jewish stuff. R. writes to Hans, but does not show me his letter. The children to church with Hermine. Afterward coffee with the children, a letter from Hans reporting nothing but bad things from Munich; on top of that a letter from Paul von Fels (formerly Prince Taxis), who wants an appointment of some kind and, in order to secure it, tells us a lot of gossip! At three o'clock a boat trip with the three little ones and R., and on our return found a tree in full blossom. In the evening occupied ourselves with Frederick the Great. Before that a short talk with Hermine, who seems loyal and attached. — Contemplated the four children as they slept and blessed them. A lovely starry night. Nature laughs— my heart weeps—"Fate is unmerciful, Man but little." — In Paris efforts are now being made to deny and thwart the success of R[*ienzi*]. —

*Monday, April 12* Woke up early from a nice dream, in which R. sang to me the theme he recently played for me, "*Sangst du mir,*" and asked me to sing with it the second theme from the love scene between Siegfried and Brünnhilde ("*Sie ist mir ein und eigen*"), which I did. — Worked with the children in the morning and afternoon, and about six o'clock with them into town, where R. caught up with us; he says that from afar we look like a walking cornfield, the children being poppies and cornflowers, I the field. I asked him what *he* was. "The happy husbandman, my one and only," he says. On the journey home we meet the convicts again, whose faces—in spite of their friendliness to us—frighten us; there is no hope in them, it is like a predestined leaning toward badness, and no compassionate excuses or well-meaning, reasonable considerations can prevail against the effect of such a physiognomy. — From the post office R. brings back two letters, one of them from Champfleury. In the evening began *Protagoras*; in spite of R.'s weariness, which comes from the games he played unceasingly with the children during our walk. — He also worked in the morning— for the first time since the interruption.

*Tuesday, April 13* Each day finer than the last, Nature is rejoicing and the children regaining their health. Worked with them in the morning, all four gathered around me; if I only knew Hans to be content, how happy I would be now! But we see the cloudless sky only in the world outside, not in our own souls, and we may not complain. When today I reflected with a sigh on my life, I told myself that I would erase none of it, except for my mistakes. — Teaching the children all day (telling them the life of Saint Elizabeth, among other things). R. working. In the evening *Protagoras*; I by myself, while resting, read Goethe's sonnets and his life. The absence of a reply to Beethoven's letter hurts me as if G[oethe] were a brother or a close friend of mine. — From Paris a newspaper clipping: Beckmann defends Wagner against the reproach of ingratitude (toward the King of Saxony) which *Charnacé* (!!) made. In talking about this bit of grotesqueness R. soon becomes very bitter. — Lovely, wonderful feeling between R. and me—I am reminded in connection with it of many a camellia flower I have seen unfold splendidly in spite of the evil worm, a black-and-yellow dot, lying in its heart. This black-and-yellow dot— my concern for Hans—it is simply there, as much a part of Nature's intention as the flowering of the plant itself! — The things have arrived from Munich. — In all my worries about the children I am upheld by the thought that, though their external life might perhaps be made more difficult on account of me, my union with R. allows me to help their inner development in a way I could not otherwise do; and since we can find happiness only within ourselves, this thought is a great consolation to me.

*Wednesday, April 14* Sun, buds, blossoms, for the first time the sound of cowbells. Rose at six, wrote letters for R. (Champfleury), then took a bath. Immediately after breakfast with the children in the garden, where I heard the cuckoo both yesterday and today. Spent the whole day with the good little ones, in the evening played with them at hoop bowling and skipping. Loulou and Boni are thoroughly good, willing, industrious, and gifted, too. In arithmetic today Lusch was more sure-footed than I! — The mail brings an abusive article from Petersburg and an abusive pamphlet from Leipzig. All Jews. In the evening I am very languid and worn out, my head full of troublesome thoughts. How shall I ever achieve what my heart bids me? How easy it is to die for what one loves, how hard to live for it! — A lovely moment of the day was that in which—after he had had the children dancing around—R. played them the *"Freude, schöner Götterfunken"* theme. What we poor mortals do not possess the genius gives us by lauding it in song—joy. "All wisdom, all art is forgotten," says R., "in the divine nature of this naïve theme, to which, through his noble bass voice, he imparts the whole force of human feeling. Here the naïve and the emotional are combined." — We finish *Protagoras*; but I am preoccupied with my maternal cares. I went once more to look at the four sleeping little ones. — (In Mannheim *Die Msinger* has been hissed on account of the pamphlet.)

*Thursday, April 15* In the morning a letter from Hans for Loulou. I again had to weep. R. came, and said it looked as if I would not after all be able to bear my lot. In the garden then, teaching the children in sultry weather. In the afternoon a long visit by Countess Bassenheim, whom I introduce to R. and who deports herself very well. Learned much from her about conditions in Bavaria (the pitiable character of King Max, who was afraid of the mayor, and appointments as gentlemen in waiting to be had for 300 florins). R. looked curiously dignified and respectable during the conversation. — In the evening with the children again, then together with R. read with much interest some letters of Frederick the Great to d'Argens. A great gale has arisen— it looks as if our spring has ended.

*Friday, April 16* My melancholy refuses to budge—in the night I wake up with a start, and in the evening I wonder how things are now with poor Hans. I meant little enough to him—but how hard I find it to withdraw even this little! — In the morning R. greeted me by telling me he had come upstairs because he had suddenly wondered whether I might not be a traditional legend, and he wished to assure himself I was really there! The weather is rough, we work and play, the children and I, in the children's *salon*. Then—because they were good—they eat with us. After lunch I finish reading Lewes—and, indication enough of the wretchedness of the book, afterward have to look up the dates he mentions in an encyclopedia. — In the evening Loulou dictates to me a nice letter to her father. — After tea read some more of Frederick the Great's letters—my mind not on it, thinking with concern and sorrow of Hans. My heart, I know, will never be freed of this burden, and I know no aid but to bear it without complaint, and not let either the children or my beloved have any idea how clouded my soul sometimes is. — (Newspapers. In the *Revue des Deux Mondes* a long article by Schuré about R. Wagner. The other papers, most of them favorable, confirm the success of *Rienzi*.)

*Saturday, April 17* "*Je ne [me] plains plus de la fortune par ennui.*" "*Pour connaître mes secrets il faut commencer par me corrompre, et cela n'est pas facile.*" — Fr. the Great. In the morning a large package of newspapers (Julius Lang, J. J. Weber). With the children as usual. After lunch they go to Countess Bassenheim's, I write to Mathilde and receive then from Claire the news that Mother has been put in a mental home! — A hard month, this. — The weather is overcast, the trees producing their green against a gray sky, it is like children's sorrow.

*Sunday, April 18* Very unwell, but constantly with the children; gave Lusch a lesson on the globe. Family lunch—cheerful and nice. Afterward puppet show and later magic lantern. Loldi plays Kasperl, and she and Eva rejoice over the slides. In the evening a little Schubert (without enjoyment) and a little Plato with R. Only he is tired and soon has to stop. — Curious news that Hiller is giving up his position as general factotum in Cologne; Judaism in music? R. had a very nice letter from Constantin Frantz; he says the pamphlet "is a true word spoken at the right time." Prof. Eckert in his lecture on R. Wagner in Berlin described the pamphlet as regrettable!

*Monday, April 19* Still mainly the children; R. does some work, although he is unwell. No letters, a Paris newspaper with a caricature and—a very enthusiastic article. R. goes out in very bad weather and returns very unwell. He goes to bed early and is much run down. I write to Claire. I read to the children about the way in which various birds build their nests, and I told R. about this. He observed: If a human being were to act with the certainty of truth and to look neither to the right nor to the left, no one could really do anything to him, and he would be as safe from other men as the bird's nest from the most violent gale. Christ's words—"Fear not, for the Father, who clothes the lilies, who protects the sparrows on the roof, for whom the very hairs of your head are numbered, will also care for you"—are difficult to understand (R. said), but of profound truth; the human being who truly lives for his own calling alone, has nothing to fear. This vision of an inwardly secure being has been perpetuated for mankind in the legend of Siegfried and the fairy tale of Tom Thumb. — Today, as I was searching for a book in the library, R. came into the next room and I heard him say to himself, "It is absolutely splendid." Later I asked him what was absolutely splendid. He said it was the sound of the children romping above, which he had just heard.

*Tuesday, April 20* I dream about *Das Rheingold* and a wonderful production of it in Munich, R. on the other hand sees me lying in my coffin surrounded by the children. This surprises me inasmuch as yesterday evening I did succumb to melancholy thoughts of death, affected by R.'s state of suffering. Children's day as usual. At lunch R. discusses the social problem with me and says he would gladly sacrifice all his art for a century to see the lower classes of society achieve a purification and reformation of the prevailing circumstances. The children in town, I at home with my embroidery. R. reads me Schopenhauer's chapter on "The Purposeful in the Fate of the Individual." — A letter from Nuitter speaks of the sixth performance of *Rienzi*, "which is now being given there three times a week and will probably make its way into the provinces." — (*Le bien et le mal que l'on prévoit n'arrive point.* — Frederick the Great. A disturbing or comforting saying, depending on how one looks at it.) — All my weeping has left me with a buzzing in my ears, which torments and also somewhat alarms me. R. had trouble with the furniture moving; I can never get over my surprise at how angry such admittedly irritating things make him, and yet he will persist with them.

*Wednesday, April 21* Said good night in the morning, since we did not take our leave of each other yesterday. Fine weather, but not warm enough to sit in the garden. I let the children off from their lessons so that they can run around a lot. I miss what has now become my habitual occupation; instead, wrote letters, preparations for R.'s birthday. Besides that a lot of furnishing bothers and a new maidservant. In the afternoon a telegram from Claire, "Some hope, Mother better," followed by a letter revealing that my mother had been on the brink of death. — My thoughts weigh heavily. — The children are good. In the evening finished Plato's *Critias*, with much enjoyment. R. also worked a little in the morning in spite of all the disturbances in the house.

*Thursday, April 22* Lovely day, outside the blossoms are opening, but Loldi ill; thus a worrying day for me. Claire writes that my mother is somewhat better, though not yet out of danger. R. manages some work. In the evening, letters of Frederick II, during the day with the invalid and Loulou. Wrote out a letter to her father. He has given a concert for the Pope in Regensburg; my father was present at it!

*Friday, April 23* Wretched days in splendid weather. Reports concerning my mother continue to be uncertain and alarming (I am writing to Claire), and Lulu joins Loldi in sickness. On top of that some hurt feelings, caused by people who do not matter, as well as by the only one who does matter. Hans's mother has taken all sorts of silly precautions with regard to the children, as if I were not looking after them properly—and as if she herself had ever taken good care of her own children, either morally or physically! When Hermine told me about it, I felt like approaching Hans and repudiating her insults, but on reflection I came to the conclusion that, even if I did not deserve the reproaches in this form, I should bear them willingly in return for pain I myself am perhaps causing, however ignoble it may seem. That R. today dealt very harshly with me, when he more or less accused me of not loving Eva because I could not take her with me on a late walk—that was indeed hard, and although many hours have since passed, I still have to weep bitterly as I write it down. But this, too, is surely deserved. — Since at the end of the day Loldi is somewhat better, I go out for a while with Boni and Lusch. Splendid view of the mountains. — From outside a letter from Dr. Lang, not much in it. May everyone in the house now rest peacefully, the dear good children and my poor friend—I must calm down my heart, which is beating violently. — My mother herself believes that she is about to die, and she will see nobody. —

*Saturday, April 24* Asked the doctor about my mother and received comfort from him, which a letter in the evening from Claire confirmed.

The children better. R. discusses with me the incident yesterday and feels that he was punished enough for his foolish anger by not going on the walk with me. Then he writes letters, among others to Semper, to let him know the truth concerning the Munich festival theater affair. — Arrival of a pamphlet, R. *W.—l'homme et le musicien*— much of it good, much wretched—always the same old stories of ingratitude, etc. Gave Loulou a geography lesson and then showed her on a hazel twig how blossoms and fruit evolve. Thundery evening. R. returns from town, having been bitten by a dog! Terrible shock. However, the doctor says it is nothing serious. Letters from Mathilde, Schuré (nice and manly), and Heim, who describes all the honors now being heaped on Semper. Appointed principal architect for the building of the cathedral in Berlin, then commissioned by the Emperor of Austria as a "famous master" to carry out work on the Hofburg and other buildings! R. feels the rebuff to the King of Bavaria very deeply. He says he can imagine in what a curious light he must appear to people, since he is the only person to whom the King has behaved well. It would have to happen to him that a case of royal enthusiasm should turn out to be a case of monomania.

*Sunday, April 25* Letter from Richter full of Munich news—as always unpleasant. The children are healthy, R.'s bite is healing, though he walks with difficulty. I feel worn out, having embroidered long into the night. With the children up to lunchtime, read and explained a Grimm legend to Lulu. Rested after lunch, then poured out my soul to R. In the afternoon a letter from Nuitter announcing the agreement of the string quartet, much to my delight. R. surprised to see me in correspondence with his friend. Some bantering, some serious talk. Then magic lantern, at last something from the Seven Years' War. —

*Monday, April 26* See from the newspapers that Hans did not conduct the last Odeon concert. So things look bad there! — R. worked a little. I with the children in the morning, in the afternoon at the Bassenheims'. In the evening read Apel's *Polyidos* with R. Till one-thirty in the morning writing a letter about Richard. — R.'s bite has got worse, and I am suffering from a buzzing in the ears and pains in the back.

*Tuesday, April 27* Splendid day, the children lively, R. works a little, we decide on an outing to Flüelen for tomorrow. In the afternoon a visit by Count Bassenheim. Before that R. reads me the description of Katte's death, written in an incredible style, and after that the arrangements made by Fried[rich] Wilh[elm] I for his burial. — Today was a muddled sort of day, from Nuitter I had a nasty letter—the gentlemen there are trying to swindle me and are demanding 2,000 francs!

This I cannot pay and am despondent about it, on top of being in great pain. Good night, children—

Mortals do not wish to die—that is their weakness, yet I must regard it as the rarest achievement of my soul that I no longer wish to die. (Sent the letter to Mathilde to copy.)

*Wednesday and Thursday, April 28 and 29* On Wednesday, despite dire prophecies concerning the weather, drove to Brunnen, there took a boat to the Grütli and then arrived at Flüelen. A night quaintly disturbed by the night watchman, then by Boni's falling out of bed and Loldi's calling for me, finally by Kos's barking at the night watchman. On Thursday morning drove to Bürklen, splendid weather, idyllic hours. In Flüelen R. had already told me during the evening how happy he was; on this morning beneath crowns of blossoms against a cloudless sky and the overwhelming birdsong we both feel how much we belong to each other. Via the Axenstrasse to Brunnen, then home by steamer. Here much trouble with the furniture—too crowded, as I feared. The disturbance in the house much greater than R. expected, he is vexed about it. — Letter from Claire: Mama is recovering, but her mind still frenzied. — Spoke much with R. about Munich, the political situation there is really too wretched. The School Law has been rejected (by the Upper Chamber), and Prince Otto, who was for the first time entitled to vote, came down *against* it! — I am concerned that Hans does not write to his children. Last night I dreamed I had gone to M[unich] in order to help him!

*Friday, April 30* A letter from Hans to Loulou, he has been unwell. Also from Countess Krockow, who wants to visit me. Lusch writes to her father. I sit beside her, embroidering. R. comes in and presses my hand fervently, he is in the midst of his work (*"Heil der Mutter, die mich gebar"*) ["Hail to the mother who bore me"]. — The doctor comes on account of Lulu, I am not happy with her appearance; she and Boni look lifeless beside Loldi and Eva. After lunch I sent them into town, then I work with Lusch, a little biblical history, then natural history, and I point out to her butterflies (swallowtail, orange-tip, peacock) which yesterday flew up in front of us. Then everyone to bed, and R. again read me some of Frederick the Great's letters.

*Saturday, May 1* R. tells me of a bat which he yesterday chased out of his room; involuntary alarm at this omen. — The day is fine, the witches on the Brocken have done their job properly, and R. observes that all Nature looks like a peasant bride with a wreath of myrtle. Studied geography with Loulou—she has to take medicine. Then unfortunately the paper hangers arrive, which exhausts me and makes me sad; to end it all, Loldi unwell again. R. works, however; after lunch he plays what he has written, and I am transported into melancholy bliss. He gets up and shows me my picture, saying that this is what he had seen! Alas, if only life could remain on such heights! But that only death can bring us. — In town, ordered flowers for R.'s birthday and learned that his father's play is unfortunately no longer to be found. Home very weary, Loldi very unwell, put her to bed, then pepper and camphor for the winter things, fell asleep after tea and slumbered a long time. Finally R. reads me a few more Fridericiana, glorious touches throughout.

*Sunday, May 2*   May delights out of doors! Got up early, sent Boni off to church with Hermine, I at home with the other three. The doctor finds Loldi indisposed and prescribes something for her. I tell Loulou about Saint Louis and read with her the scene in *Wilhelm Tell* in which the hero shoots the apple. She weeps, and I with her. At table R. asks her what a hero is; she does not know, whereupon he says: Someone who knows no fear. After lunch, with the two elder children and the little Am Rhyn girl to the fair in town, carrousel, menagerie, mines, panorama! R. had a letter from his friend Fräulein Meysenbug: she has received nothing, neither the Jewish pamphlet nor his letter of March 29. He replies to her, to my great astonishment he invites her to come here permanently. — R. is also not quite well, but he goes into town with me. — When I look at the children and feed on their joy I have to acknowledge how foolish it is to expect any personal joy in this world, to wish for something for oneself—such as a house or wealth or power or some such thing—when the only true happiness is the gleam of joy in the eyes of a cherished being. — While still in bed yesterday I read *Der arme Heinrich*; Goethe is said not to have liked it, which I can understand, even if there are many very moving features in it. — "Wounded love has a friend in Heaven," a fine old saying which contains all the consolation of renunciation. — In the menagerie R. and I had to laugh heartily when the man said about the hyena, "It murders not just for hunger, but also for lust."

*Monday, May 3*   My Monday began with a stream of vulgar abuse, which a bad maidservant, leaving our employment, flung at me while I was still in bed. Letting her talk, I reflected on the disparate nature of the world, in which the saint and the wise man put up with such curious surprises. At last she left, and I had paid my debt to the evil demon of the day. And indeed the day turned out to be a fine one. R. greeted me cheerfully; he said I was just a bundle of worry, and since in regard to him I had nothing more to worry about, knowing he was in good hands, I had no more thoughts for him. He also said he was too happy, he could no longer compose, he had everything he wanted —to which he added jokingly: when he now works, it is not for hunger, but lust! — He is working now, while I teach the children. Before lunch he played me what he had written—blissful hour of happiness, forgetting all miseries on earth and torments of life! I must always burst into tears and am at a loss for words when I hear his music. — Went out with the elder children, R. to town, then overtook me. Great weariness, but a mood of exaltation.

*Tuesday, May 4* In the early morning sent off letters to all corners of the earth, since I am in trouble about R.'s birthday. R. up late, he had a bad night. Telegram from the King: five years ago today R. arrived in Munich! R. works a little in spite of being unwell. I with the children, Loldi is somewhat better, but still looks run down. Could the dear creatures but know how anxious and worried I am about them! May they always find me in their hour of need, as I should so dearly like to find a mother now! At lunch R. says that in creative work the difficulty is not discovering ideas, but holding oneself in check—all too many things fly into his mind, his agitation and restlessness come from arranging and selecting them. He goes into town, the elde children, too, I at home with Eva and Loldi. Lovely mild air in the evening, true May delights earth and sky covered in blossom. — In the evening letters of Frederick the Great and anecdotes of his life. — During the night embroidered in bed.

*Wednesday, May 5* Loldi ill! She caught cold again yesterday. In consequence, the gray veil—as R. calls it—overshadows my day. I work in the morning with the healthy girls and in the afternoon tend the sick one. Toward evening things get a little better. Loulou today has her first piano lesson together with Marie Bassenheim. A letter from Mathilde, she has copied out mine to Herr Drumont. Yesterday a letter from Claire: my mother is improving.

*Thursday, May 6* Loldi still unwell and Lusch also indisposed, which means that I do not make them work, but let them spend Ascension Day in the garden. I with the little ones, embroidering more or less all day. Walked with R. in the garden morning and evening, splendid view of the fields and trees, he tells me he was listening to the birds in the early morning and had composed something based on them that he thought very beautiful, but now he sees it was nothing. A program arrived from Boston; in a grand musical festival to celebrate peace the *Tannhäuser* Overture is to be played (the "Pilgrims' Chorus" sung at the end!). R. dreams of it and that I come to it with Eva and he is beside himself at not having the appropriate dreams for my reception. — A letter from Flaxland, the publisher, with 3,000 francs from *Rienzi*. — In the evening Frederick the Great again; recommending movement to d'Argens, he says, "*La Nature paraît nous avoir plutôt destiné au métier de postillon qu'à celui de philosophe.*" — After lunch R. played me several passages from the B[eethoven] symphonies and promised to conduct one of them for me in the fall, either in Paris or in Milan.

*Friday, May 7*   Telegram from Pasdeloup that I shall at last receive the drawing of the heralds of peace; splendid weather, the "green-gold" of spring flourishing. The children outside, I with Loldi, embroidering; she is getting better, if not yet quite recovered. Vreneli comes to me to announce her second pregnancy, and she tells me she and her husband wish to open their business in the fall. It will cause a great upheaval in the house. After lunch R. fetches me my workbasket, sees Loldi, and becomes very despondent at the sight. His despondency becomes vehement, even harsh, because I asked him whether he was in a bad mood. I preserve silence, for what can I say? Was with the child, and at seven wandered around the garden a little by myself. Deep sorrow —should I not give it all up and live just for the children? Returning from town in the evening, R. says he had told himself he would still believe in his happiness if I came to meet him; now he realizes he had sinned, for I had not come. On top of that he told me that Loldi's look and her eccentric nature had caused him alarm. I listen to him calmly; afterward he reads me some more passages from Frederick II. During the night embroidered in bed. (Lusch dictated to me her letter to her father.)

*Saturday, Sunday, Monday, Tuesday, May 8–11*   Have written nothing for four days, have scarcely the strength for it, nor the time, for I wanted to get on with my embroidery. All sorts of evil omens appeared; on Sunday morning R. saw a large spider, Vreneli broke a window-pane during a night tour, Hermine dreamed of pearls—and trouble has indeed not been lacking. On Sunday Loldi had a relapse, she is still in bed and looks dreadful! — On Saturday I talk to Vreneli again about her affairs and we come to the conclusion that she should stay here a few more years. — On Sunday morning a visit from Count Bassenheim, discussed many things concerning Munich. In the evening a gloomy talk with R. about my confinement. I want it to be far away from here and in secret, for the sake of the elder children, he sees this as a humiliation for him and becomes very bitter. I can understand him and feel painfully for him—and yet it seems to me that here I have a duty in the face of which other feelings must be silenced. — On Monday morning into town to order the costumes for the heralds of peace. Spent the afternoon in deep distress at Loldi's bedside. In the evening a letter from Nuitter saying the people from Paris are coming. On Tuesday gave the elder children their lessons and embroidered, and also looked after Loldchen, who is still ill. After lunch R. goes out for a walk, I promise to go to meet him, which I do; since I wanted an address from a gardener concerning palm branches, I tell R. that I must go into town; this surprises him, since I otherwise find difficulty in walking, and he misunderstands the reason for this exception. Big, thundery rainstorm. In the evening he again brings up the dismal theme we recently discussed, I am incapable of answering and can only weep—oh, Star of Love, shine on me and illumine the heavy, dark paths for me! From outside a nice article by Mme Vallier in the *Réveil* and notification of honorary membership in the Berlin Academy. Tausig cables the news and begs R. "for the sake of the good cause" not to refuse it. What does Tausig call a good cause?

*Wednesday, May 12* Was up the whole night in order to get on with my embroidery, also because I am too agitated to sleep. At four o'clock heard the first bird and watched the sun rise, then wrote a greeting to R. and took it to his sitting room. To bed at 5, at 7 R. comes, writes something down for me, and wakes me up; fine morning, splendid day, Loldi looking better. From Hans a letter to Loulou that deeply depresses me. After lunch to Countess Bassenheim with Loulou for her piano lesson. In the evening R. reads me Apel's story *"Der Freischütz."* Much affected and stimulated by it. R. is fearful of putting out the lamps. I fall into a deep sleep.

*Thursday, May 13* Woke up early, refreshed; thundery atmosphere outside, gave the children their lessons and sat by Loldi, who is still not allowed out. Hans's mood lies heavily on my heart. My inner happiness, however, is when R. is working. Among the letters one from Richter, whom I have invited for R.'s birthday, also a very ridiculous one to me from Léon Leroy (a friend of the deceased Gaspérini). For the Wagner cause in Paris he offers a back-street journal—*La France Musicale*—which the King of Bavaria should purchase. How to make all these people understand that one wants nothing to do with any such things? For R. a letter from "A German" who, delighted with the Jewish pamphlet, informs him of a new bank project (Pronothon) to be put before the King. Then a recommendation from the Genelli estate, R. writes a couple of words to Düfflipp about it. Hans writes, to Loulou, that he feels a great urge to go away. Long visit from Countess Bassenheim, who gives me a letter from Marie Muchanoff—she wants to come here in August! We have no use for anybody. Children, art, and a smiling May morning.

*Friday, May 14* Since I had no time during the day, I embroidered at night till four in the morning. And I am also very tired on account of it. Loulou dictates to me a letter to her father. Then they go to try on their herald costumes. R. works, but says jokingly that he intends to write no more tragic things. He is concerned about me and feels I am attempting too much and destroying myself. When he plays the piano in the evening, I am so overcome that I have to sob and pray. A prayer for the man to whom I can be nothing and whose wretchedness arouses such deep pity in me, and for the children, who perhaps will never know how much I have suffered on their account. — R. is annoyed with my embroidery, he believes it is a strain on me—I may have to give it up! A letter from Heim in Zurich, Semper was pleased to have received R.'s letter. Letter from Pasdeloup, who now wants to do *Lohengrin.* "*Après cela j'aurai rendu service à mon pays, en lui prouvant la connaissance même des êtres privilégiés qui font la gloire de l'humanité.*" — Loldchen still indisposed.

*Saturday, May 15*  Took a bath, then gave Lusch a piano lesson, R. joins in and is kind and loving in everything. He has a nice letter from Frau Wille in Hamburg, where she saw *Tannhäuser.* To town with Boni to try on the herald costume, on my return home listen to R. A clumsy letter to me from Marie Muchanoff ("*On m'a inquiétée sur votre compte, Dieu veille sur vous.*" — !!). My only joy R.'s composition. Took Lusch to her piano lesson. Home at 5, met R., delight in the May pride. Arrival of the Paris bronze for his birthday. Lusch writes to her father. He is the only living being about whom I grieve.

*Sunday, May 16*  Whitsunday, Loldi somewhat better, we eat with the children. Afterward a visit from old Prince Wallerstein, who tells me many instructive things about Bavaria (under three kings). In the morning studied geography with Lusch. In the evening R. plays parts of *Euryanthe.* — Stayed up late in order to get on with my embroidery.

*Monday, May 17*  To bed at four, up at eight, fairly fresh, gave the children their lessons. R. has a letter from Düfflipp. He claims the evil things in Munich have been put right—God only knows! The King wishes to see R. on his birthday, but R. wants, to stay here. At lunch a philologist, Professor Nietzsche, whom R. first met at the Brockhaus home and who knows R.'s works thoroughly and even quotes from *Opera and Drama* in his lectures. A quiet and pleasant visit; at four we drive through light rain into town. R. is preoccupied, since he is not satisfied with his work this morning. In the evening I tell him that I should like my confinement to be away from here. Great weariness, asleep from eight o'clock onward. Loldi causes us concern with her excessive, exclusive attachment to me.

*Tuesday, May 18*  Rose early, wrote to Marie Muchanoff, declining her *sympathy.* R. still sad about our conversation yesterday, I tell him I will do what he thinks right. He writes to the King and says he will not come for his birthday. I embroider and work with the children. After lunch they go to Countess Bassenheim's, only Eva and Loldi remain with me. In the evening R. brings me a letter from the painter Lenbach; since it transpires from this that he is not sending my portrait R. is very dejected. In the evening several intermezzi by Cervantes.

*Wednesday, May 19*  Up late, very tired and worried, occupied as usual with the children and the embroidery. Before lunch R. plays for me what he has written and is delighted that several themes which date from the "Starnberg days" and which we had jokingly earmarked for quartets and symphonies have now found their niche (*"Ewig war ich, ewig bin ich"*). Great surge of joy at this coming together of life and art. The children out trying on their herald costumes. I, alone in the house, realize with concern that my work will not be ready in time for the birthday. R. returns home late from his walk. In the evening again considered the question of the birth of the new baby and the presence of the older children; I put consideration for Hans in the forefront; R., consideration for my comfort and well-being. We also talk about our servant Jakob—R. fears he is too much in the hands of the priests.

*Thursday, May 20*  Cramplike pains in the morning after a restful night. R. resumes our serious talk, during the night he has come closer to my view, we agree to send the elder children to Claire in Versailles. R. is not well, but works all the same. From outside the news that the King has attended the performance of *Tannhäuser*. Apart from this, Düfflipp complains of his withdrawal from public life. Wrote to M. Leroy, to make clear to him that W.'s cause has no need of back-street journals! Then invited Professor Nietzsche for R.'s birthday. Afterward to town, and a fine May day with R. Found a letter from Claire at the post office, she has seen my mother, sad description, but the insanity has disappeared. Much joy with the children on returning home; I have taught Lusch some folk songs, and she sings them prettily. In the evening R. and I begin *Don Quixote*.

*Friday, May 21*  Foehn wind, very sultry, with the children in the garden. Lusch writes to her father. R. works. The afternoon passes in the turmoil of preparations. Richter and the Paris quartet have arrived. I to the Hôtel du Lac to discuss everything. Trouble keeping R. at home. The children having their hair done, suddenly R. comes in, sees "holly" everywhere, rushes out, I tell him the King is here and will be coming to Tribschen tomorrow. R. does not know whether it is serious or a joke. — Yet the conversation with Richter has made me sad; returning by boat in stormy weather, I admit to myself that, were death to come to me now, I should not grieve. That I had to leave Hans appears cruel to me, but then I have to ask myself on whose account this cruelty arose. Also I feel plainly how within me some divinity rules, which determined my course—*I* did not wish or choose. But I do not hold it against anybody who cannot see this as I see it, who does not have the faith that I have, and who condemns me. Willingly and lightly will I bear the world's loathing—Hans's suffering, however, robs me of all joy. Good night, my good children!

*Saturday, May 22* In the night set up R.'s bust, surrounded by flowers. Early in the morning Richter blew Siegfried's call. Then the children were lined up as heralds of peace, and finally, at 10:30, the Paris quartet. R. very surprised and delighted. In the course of the day they play the B Minor, the A Minor, and the C-sharp Minor Quartets [of Beethoven]. I felt only like weeping. Telegrams from the King and from Hungary. The day goes by like a dream.

*Sunday, May 23* Schuré day; all day long the Schurés, that is to say, disruption of my customary life. R. very worn out, I always with my thoughts elsewhere. I can no longer talk except with the children. R. had letters of birthday greetings from Nohl, Lang (who reports that Marie Muchanoff completely denies that the Jewish pamphlet has had an effect in Berlin!), from the philologist Nietzsche (very nice letter) and from the postmaster Wickerle in Schwerin. All remaining friends and relations have kept silent. *How* mean! In the evening I feel very melancholy. Solitude is all we need.

*Monday, May 24* Great weariness, R. unwell, and on top of that much bother with the paper hangers. Nice letter from his sister Luise, who is, however, sad about the Jewish pamphlet. Played and worked with the children, supervised Lulu's piano practice. R. writes to Mathilde and to the Hungarians who sent him the telegram. In the evening a letter from Marie Muchanoff, she has retracted her unsealed letter and writes sensibly. She had heard that I had quarreled with my father and Hans. — When I tell R. in the evening that I had stayed awake several nights in order to finish my embroidery, he is very concerned and solemnly reproaches me for this lack of self-consideration.

*Tuesday, May 25* Very nice letter from the two Schurés. R. unwell and I feeling rather melancholy. The reason for it, as I also tell R., is my concern for the children and my fear that R., through his inability to economize, will be unable to provide for them. I still have to keep an eye on the paper hangers, but manage nonetheless to work with the children. In the afternoon to town with R. to look at an old bureau. In the evening read *Don Quixote*.

*Wednesday, May 26* Hermine off on a visit to her parents. I in earnest conclave with R. in the morning about what to do with the elder children in the coming days. Resolved to keep them with me and to put up with serious reproaches rather than to interrupt their upbringing now and expose them to instability. R. kneels down before me and says he has no other thought but to make himself worthy of me! In the morning and afternoon instructed the children, also went with them to their piano lesson, when I saw Count B[assenheim] and old Prince Wallerstein. Discussed the elections in Bavaria—they have turned out in favor of the Catholics, and the party is utterly jubilant. The King has thanked them in writing for the loyal attitude they have shown! Quite definitely Bavaria's downfall is impending, and it is the result of an alliance, manipulated by the priests, between Austria, France, and South Germany against Prussia. In all truth a very wretched state of affairs. The elections in Paris have gone decisively in the direction of the radicals. — Returning home with the children, I met R., who has written to the King. The news of the King's expression of gratitude grieves him deeply, it is too humiliating. In the evening *Don Quixote*. I, very tired, to bed at 9 o'clock, with the children.

*Thursday, May 27*   Corpus Christi day, proclaimed by cannon shots. The children merry and lively, eager to watch the procession, I pack them off, but spare myself the sight. R. comes to me, looking unwell, and harshly voices his objection to the children's outing. I say nothing and remind him only later that I had sought his opinion the day before, when I told him the little ones wanted to see the procession. R. now goes further and makes the reproach that I am literally killing myself with looking after the children, I am now all mother, and he is losing me entirely. He had been so pleased that I was to occupy the room next to his, but now I have gone to sleep with the children. He cannot reproach me for this, he says, but he feels it painfully. Deeply shattered by his words, I do not know what to say; if he does not feel happy with me, then I deserve his reproaches, and yet I feel I cannot do otherwise; but I shall have to try to arrange things so that nobody will fall short. R. does indeed tell me later that he is very unwell and that this had given rise to his mood. I write to Claire and to Mme Lucca. The children return home very cheerful. R. goes to bed, I read him Uncle Adolph's pamphlet *Theater and Public*. A very significant little essay. Lunch at 4 o'clock; visit from Count Bassenheim, something of a nuisance. Arrival of flowers sent by the King. In the evening some scenes from *The Merchant of Venice*. R. also told me in the morning that it looked as if I were expecting to die and had no wish but to sacrifice myself in all directions.

*Friday, May 28*   Focused my attention on arranging my twin duties in a way to satisfy all. I hope I have succeeded. The children to be set to work while R. is composing. I also wrote to Marie Muchanoff. After lunch make music with R., playing Haydn symphonies. Then with the children to meet him as he returns from town, after Lusch has dictated to me her letter to her father. In the evening he plays me his divine sketch; these immortal works will give you the answer, my children, when you ask yourselves: What was it Mama loved, for whom did she live? The weather very close, with thunderstorms—it almost does me good; when one's heart is filled with worry, outward disturbances are not unwelcome. Up to my room at midnight, then Jakob calls me: his little son is ill and is screaming. I go in and place my hand on him, and the child quiets down. Jakob tells R. about it, and R. says he is familiar with my hand and knows I could restore anyone from death to life with my touch. Sleepless night, since everyone restless, Loldi is afraid, Kos howls and snores, with it all storm winds and moonlight.

*Saturday, May 29* Very tired in the morning. Supervised Loulou's piano practice, then lay down for a while. In the afternoon the children went for their piano lesson; I had to punish Boni and keep her at home, which gave R. cause for some remarks. As in distress I listened to him, he said I should realize that everything about me was precious and sacred to him, and, if he sometimes spoke in this way, it was for him much like the Saturnalia, when one is permitted to take liberties with the gods. As far as he was concerned I was already hovering in the empyrean. — I had to weep terribly that *he* should say this to me, and I tried to think of other things, because I can neither grasp nor bear it that he should ascribe a value of any sort to me. After lunch played piano duets of Mozart symphonies. The weather very close. With R. did a little rearranging in the upper *salon*. In the morning came a letter from Hans to his daughter; he complains of his health and the lack of pleasant occupations. Late into town with R. and the children, they buy some oranges. In the evening an article by the "great" Riehl about Rheinberger's new opera. Blatant foolishness. A letter from Nuitter; the royalties from *Rienzi* will be small.

*Sunday, May 30* Anxious night—I almost thought my time had come. The thunderstorm must have unsettled me. Quiet, fine day, with Lulu geography and piano practice. Family lunch after R. did some work. Played piano duets of Mozart symphonies with R., then, while he was writing letters, read the children some of Grimm's fairy tales, played lotto and dominoes with them, and finally showed them the magic lantern. As I find pleasure in some sign of good disposition and remark to R. that I really ought to see other children in order to appreciate the agreeable inclinations of my own, he says what strikes one in this connection is not the good disposition, but the good upbringing; anyone who saw me with the children would have to feel respect for me. How happy these words made me!! — Regarding the King, R. feels it is in all respects providential that he comports himself as he does; if he had been even a hair's breadth bolder in acceding to everything, he would certainly no longer be king. — In the morning the children found two little birds, which they took for dead; but we soon saw that the little creatures were still alive and had probably been pitched out of their nest by some other bird. Now they are lying in cotton wool and being fed by us—whether we shall pull them through, God knows. They are robins.

*Monday, May 31* A day indoors, it is raining. Breakfasted with R. in the upper apartment. Then worked with the children. R. goes to his sketches. After lunch, the *Illustrirte Zeitung* has a biography of Hans with a portrait, the latter upsets me deeply. The rest of the day with R. and the children, we are all industrious and cheerful. But our little birds have been killed by the cat! In the evening *Don Quixote*, read by R. — R. and I much delighted with the development of Boni's character. It is as if my absence had made a very great impression on her. The spitefulness, indeed maliciousness, which previously distressed me in her, has now given way to great meekness and modesty. Yet she is very lively and healthy and is very contented.

*Tuesday, June 1* How shall I write down this terrible day? In the morning I worked with the children; it did in fact strike me that R. did not go to his *Siegfried* and seemed sad, but I did not ask him why. In the evening he told me he had the day before received a letter from Hans and was wrestling with himself over whether he should go to him. The King has commanded *Tristan* after all—with the two Vogls, a veritable disgrace! Now Hans has to conduct the rehearsals; this upsets his nerves, and he begs R. to help him secure his release. The letter is pitiable, and I wish he would go. R. feels nothing good can come of the meeting and is resisting. Very early evening—who, having lived through such hours, could still fear death? —

*Wednesday, June 2* Saint Blandina—previously a festival day for me! — Loldi very restless in the night; I weeping and trying to get a grip on myself. R. writes to Hans that he has decided to visit him if Hans wishes it, and in the meantime expects from him only that, before surrendering the work to the disgrace of such a performance, he should demand his dismissal. — The weather is nice, so I can let the children amuse themselves in the garden and keep my deathly feelings concealed from them. I lie down at last and go to sleep. R. comes to my room and guards my sleep; he reads his uncle's book and then at lunch tells me what he has read. Never before have I striven so hard to conceal my feelings. After lunch with the children to their piano lesson. With Countess B[assenheim] I can scarcely collect my thoughts. When I meet R., we no longer speak about what is alone in our minds. In the evening some reading (Ad[olph] Wagner on the three aspects of Dante's poetry: *Inferno*—sculpture, *Purgatorio*—painting, *Paradiso*—music). Sadly to bed.

*Thursday, June 3* Rose sadly, too, and feeling unwell. Wrote to the King and begged him to cancel *Tristan*. R. comes to my bed and asks me whether I will live or perish; he would follow me, that I must surely know. I get up and pull myself together—God helps when the need is greatest, as the proverb says. (Letters from Claire to me and Math[ilde] to R.) [*Continued from here in R. W.'s handwriting.*] *Oppressed feeling of weakness. R. tries in vain to occupy himself with his work. We sat in the garden while the children ate their meal there: R. had sent Loldi to fetch me. He complained about the constraints of his artistic calling— having, by obeying them, to leave his moral inclinations undeveloped: he could do nothing else, otherwise everything would turn out badly; to be a thoroughly moral person demanded complete self-sacrifice.* — I [R. W. started to write "*Cosima,*" then wrote "*I*" over it] *kept silent. Wretched lunch through Lulu's presence, but gradually a cheerful mood. Then garden again. R. reads out Wolfram's poem about the birth of Parzival. Great beauty; much affected.* — *Worked with Lulu.* — *R. into town; after putting the children to bed, I go to meet him on his return. At supper I felt sick; I withdrew to the upper floor, to go to the nursemaid. R., who saw in the exertion this put on me a reproach against himself for having, through the renewed and so much delayed rearrangement of the household, put considerable obstacles in my way, lost his head completely and gave way to excessive expressions of his concern. He complained that I continually and, as it seemed to him, with many excuses persisted in ignoring his daily appeals and representations to take possession of the apartment which had at last been put in order for me again, and to make it comfortable for myself. He said this gave him sad feelings of uneasiness, which constantly assailed him and tormented him like the fear of death. I at last won enough control over his ravings to make him listen to me when I explained to him that the reason for my hesitation in moving down to the apartment designed for me was that the proximity of his bedroom to mine (though indeed previously agreed on between us) was embarrassing to me now that the elder children were there. Since this bedroom of his was—as had also already been agreed—in the vicinity of the impending confinement and was to be prepared for the required nurse, I had to admit that I should prefer not to move down until the time for this arrangement arrived. This explanation seemed to surprise R. greatly and to arouse real bitterness in him. He said I should have told him this frankly a long time ago, since in this respect he had been misled concerning my views and my wishes. He became very quiet but, I believe, no less distressed. We parted very sadly.*

Friday, June 4 *Early. R. was up before 6 o'clock and gave orders that his bedroom should again be moved to the downstairs apartment.* [*At this point C. W.'s entries resume.*] When I come down R. hands me this book with the pages he has written in it. I should have preferred him not to have done so. I believe I was given the *coup de grâce* yesterday, and life confronts me as an insoluble enigma to which I intend to give no further thought. I keep the children occupied, rather than concern myself with them, for inside me all is sadness. R. seems unwell, I avoid all reference to yesterday evening—because I wish to say nothing about it. It appears to me like a judgment of God; and it must be borne. R. occupies himself with Beethoven and talks about his death (in his 57th year). He also says he has been overcome with a great longing to complete his *Siegfried*. May God give him the strength and spirits for it! I spend the whole day in a sort of daze, the only thing to arouse my repugnance being an enclosure from Dr. Lang—a Jewish pamphlet in which a letter from R. to Tausig is printed. I am not happy about this, but I suppose it does not really matter. To town with the children, returning by boat. Quiet, melancholy evening.

*Saturday, June 5* Splendid weather, summer heat. Prof. Nietzsche, the philologist, announces a visit, R. wishes to put him off, I feel it is better that he come. I have still not emerged from my dazed state, I hear everything like a very distant echo, and everything melts away as if in a fog. Long conversation with R.; he believes that I am capable of bearing grudges against him, whereas any harshness from him in fact simply annihilates me. [*Continued from here in R. W.'s handwriting.*] *A bearable evening spent with Nietzsche. Said good night about 11. The labor pains begin. At midnight leave the children's bedroom upstairs and, in order not to awake anybody, carry my bedclothes myself in two journeys down to the lower bedroom.*

*Sunday, June 6* *At 1 o'clock down to Richard to tell him and to insist that for the time being no fuss be made, that the arrangements for the day be adhered to, and that Nietzsche should stay for lunch with the children. R. throws his dressing gown over me and leads me upstairs to bed. The pains get more frequent; at 2 o'clock I have Vreneli woken and the midwife sent for. Necessary steps to make the adjoining room ready for the new arrival; but the time adjudged to be not yet so near; I fear the weakness which previously delayed Eva's birth. R. at my bedside in great concern. The midwife arrives after 3, to wait in the adjoining room, since I do not wish to speak to anybody. Things appear to quiet down somewhat. R. decides to use this period to get a few hours' sleep in order to strengthen himself for the coming day. He goes downstairs and gets into bed, but is so tortured by restlessness that he gets dressed again and comes upstairs; he rushes in and finds me in the most raging pain, being tended by the midwife. I was startled to see him suddenly standing before me and imagined I was seeing a ghost; I turned away in horror, thus driving him from the room into the open salon next door; when he again hears my cries, he rushes in once more, since the midwife has left me alone for a moment; I gripped his arm as I writhed, but signified to him that he should not speak. The midwife returned, R. withdrew again to the neighboring room; there he remained earwitness to the delivery and heard the cries of the laboring mother. As he hears Vreneli come in and then hears her exclaim in reply to some words from the midwife, "Oh, God in Heaven!," R. thinks something terrible has happened to me and hastens to the*

*landing to find out from Vreneli as she comes rushing out. But she greets him
with a joyful laugh: "A son has arrived!" Her previous exclamation had
simply been one of surprise that so little was prepared. Now R. went back into
the salon: from the unconscious mother he heard little more, yet on the other
hand he could clearly distinguish the lusty yells of the baby boy. With feelings
of sublime emotion he stared in front of him, was then surprised by an incredibly
beautiful, fiery glow which started to blaze with a richness of color never before
seen, first on the orange wallpaper beside the bedroom door; it was then reflected
in the blue jewel box containing my portrait, so that this, covered by glass and
set in a narrow gold frame, was transfigured in celestial splendor. The sun had
just risen above the Rigi and was putting forth its first rays, proclaiming a
glorious, sun-drenched day. R. dissolved into tears. Then to me, too, came from
across the lake the sound of the early-morning Sunday bells ringing in Lucerne.
He looked at the clock and noticed that his son had been born at 4 o'clock in the
morning. — Just before 6 o'clock R. was allowed in to see me; he told me of his
solemn emotions. I was in a mood of cheerfulness and gladness: the gift which
Fate had vouchsafed us through the birth of a son appeared to me to be one of
immeasurably consoling value. R.'s son is the heir and future representative of
the father for all his children; he will be the protector and guardian of his
sisters. We were very happy. The boy is big and strong: they say he weighs two
pounds more than other newborn boys. We discussed his name: Siegfried Richard.
R. felt an urge to give evidence of his joy throughout the house: he had handsome
gifts distributed to all the servants. — From 9 o'clock onward, my hand in R.'s,
I was granted my first strength-restoring sleep, even if short, lasting about 2
hours. At noon R. had to leave me in order to preside over the midday meal with
his guest (Nietzsche) and the children. During this time I was given the attention
necessary to my condition. At 4:30 R. was relieved of his onerous duties.
While the children went for a trip on the lake, we spent the time together,
quiet and full of hope. At 9 o'clock R. left me so that I could get some rest and
he himself recover from his exhaustion in sleep. —*

Monday, June 7   *Little sleep in the night, much pain: only in the morning
some rest. At our first meeting in the morning I could nevertheless give R.
reassuring news about my condition. Except for the times in which I had to
submit directly to the attentions required by a woman in childbed, R. sat
comfortingly at my bedside all day. But at noon he did drive into town to buy a
fine watch for Jakob (in the name of his own son Wilhelm); I was satisfied with
the purchase and gave the watch to Vreneli, who in her turn took it to her
husband to wear. The gift was accepted with touching emotion. — We discussed
the relationship we should like to see between Siegfried and the son of our loyal
house manager, who is about eight months older: R. said he wished he had at
the time insisted on the boy's being named "Kurwenal"; for he wished that
Wilhelm might one day behave toward Siegfried as Kurwenal to Tristan. —
There was much of good cheer, of melancholy pride in our talk. I also let the*

*children come to my bedside. The excitement of the younger ones soon exhausted me. On this day I suffered very much: the after-birth pains were significantly greater than at Eva's birth. But I faced the night consoled and with confidence, even though extremely weak, and on the whole it passed so well that I did not call on the nurse even once—and, since for the first time in her life she was able to sleep beside a mother in childbed undisturbed, she was very pleasantly surprised.*

Tuesday, June 8   *In the morning I was able to greet R. happily and cheerfully. He on the other hand seemed somewhat unwell, for which the thundery atmosphere was mainly responsible, and it made me also very restless and weak throughout the day. Our son is well: R. laughs about his strong fists; his well-shaped head delights us both. We spoke a lot about the significant change he has brought about in our fate. — Hermine had come back on the previous evening. The children were very content to have her with them again. Today R. went down to speak to her and found her, just as we desired, resolved to perform her duties loyally and perseveringly, in accordance with our trust in her. She, too, received a sizable present from R., who also assured her of his willingness to care for her throughout her life if she remained good and loyal. Much of what R. told me helped to put my mind at rest. But in general my condition remained very painful, and in particular my exhaustion and weakness were great. Toward evening R. was in town with the children for quite a while, making purchases. In regard to our son's christening, an attempt is being made to see whether the local Protestant priest thinks he can carry out the sacred task quietly here in the house without attracting the attention of the Catholic clergy. The day came to an end in a mood of mildness and harmony: Siegfried is flourishing, and his mother is glad to be alive. — R. leaves me about 10 o'clock, when I at last fall asleep. — (Letter from Villot.)*

Wednesday, June 9   *A good night: Siegf. somewhat restless. R. inquires after 5 o'clock and finds me sleeping. Then he comes to me at about 8 o'clock and recites the verse which he has just completed to his satisfaction:*

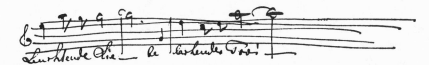

*Cheerful, harmonious day. From bed to the chaise-longue in the* salon. *R. has his meals upstairs. The children (except Eva) sent off to the Selisberg with Hermine: in the morning much together with them. They leave at 5. Many things discussed: news from Claire about Mama and Charnacé (Pasdeloup). In the evening pains: too long out of bed. R.'s concern. —*

Thursday, June 10   *Slept little: severe pains. Obliged to lie constantly in an outstretched position. R. unwell and despondent, concerned at my indisposition. Anxious dreams of the absent children unsettle me. Telegram not answered. Anxious, concerned mood the whole day. Discussions about the christening; about Hans. In between R.* reads Don Quixote, *with very refreshing results. (Letter from a Dresden Jew, "Ahasverus."* — *Declaration of the musician Altschul from Pest* [*a Jew*] *in the* Neue Freie Presse: R.*'s telegram: "Eljèn Altschul.") — Berlin advance (100 tr. d'or) on* Die Meistersinger. — *Laborious day. At last in the evening telegram from Selisberg: children arrived safely at the summit at 9 in the evening. Some comfort. After a warm bath in the evening R. also better; Hans discussed several times: earnestly, but without excitement. Much pain and tiredness.*

Friday, June 11   *Restored by good night's rest (first for a long time!), R. better, too. He declares he wants to see if he can take up composition again. Christening discussed; question: whether local priest? Schuré's father-in-law or R.'s nephew Clemens? Delay deemed expedient. (Letter from a lady harpist!) Improved condition: our son is to be taken for a walk in the garden for the first time. R. works on* Siegf. *again. I discuss in detail household affairs with Vreneli. Toward midday from bed to the* salon, *on the sofa. There ate with R. The boy taken out. Eva alone in the house.* — *In the evening letters: from Hermine, concerning the children: comforting; Chaillou; Flaxland to R.— little prospect of financial gain from the Paris success—for the time being.* — Don Quixote *splendid! Part of the afternoon and evening spent on it. Tender "good night."* —

Saturday, June 12   *Recovery continues. Dreamed of R. in Milan (but on the coast), secretly helping a refugee and at the same time performing the C Minor Symphony.* — *Rest, fine weather. Eva good, repeats everything well. Satisfaction with Siegfried's progress.* — *R. at work: he intends to finish the sketches in a few days. Today up to "O* kindischer Held." — *I am already writing letters, to Hermine, etc.* — *The swing in the garden is ready.* — *Nothing of significance happens.* — *In the evening* Don Quixote. *Parted at 10 o'clock.* — [*At this point C. W.'s entries resume.*]

Sunday, June 13   All hail the day which illumines us, hail to the sun which shines on us! — How shall I, poorest of creatures, describe the feelings with which I again take this book in my hands? . . . When the woman said to me, "Congratulations, it is a little boy," I had to weep and laugh and pray. — Preserve him, divinity which gave him to me, that he may be the support of his sisters, the heir of his adored father! Now that my happiness lies so sweetly in reach before my eyes, it seems to me ever more tremendous, more disembodied, I see it hovering, rising up high above all woes, and all I can do is to thank the universal spirit which proclaimed to us through this sign that it is kindly disposed toward us. The day is blazing gloriously, I did not sleep during the night, but all the same feel well. I reflected on a letter to be written to Hans, in which I shall describe my earlier, my present, and my future relationship with him [*added in the margin:* "if he will accept it!"]. May God reveal to me the right things to say in order to help him a little! R. is working, I hear it with bliss; when he comes up to me, he tells me how wonderfully it has turned out that his theme of joy (*"Sie ist mir alles"*) fits in excellently as accompaniment to the motive *"Heil der Mutter, die mich gebar,"* so that this expression of joy can be heard sounding in the orchestra up to the point where Siegfried himself sings it. Tomorrow he will probably finish his sketch! — As he comes up he wakes me, "the great Zenobia"—this name for me occurred to him while he was working. When I ask him why, he says I am great, truly great. — But what is great about me can only be the reflection of his own nature. At lunch he says to me that he knows I concern myself with others only when I see them in distress and in need of me, but when I see he is glad, only then am I really happy. And so it is in fact. Regarded our Siegfried; when R. saw him alone, the child appeared to him as he will once be, reflective and earnest; very moved, he tells me it was as if he had seen the eidolon of our precious boy. God preserve him for us! — R. tells me that my mother heard about the Paris quartet at Tribschen and assumed that the King of Bavaria had arranged for it, so it was no wonder he had no money left to engage Semper; he had enough on his hands with Wagner. We laugh heartily at this pitiful absurdity. "These poor people think of everything," says R., "except that it was the enthusiasm of a loving woman which provided me with this pleasure." — Against a most wonderful sunset I am writing these lines, lying at the window. Could I but sing a hymn to the Godhead! R. sings it for me, my hymn is my love for him. My Siegfried, crowning glory of my life, may you show how much I have loved your father! — Drank tea with R. To bed at 9. R. reads *Don Quixote* to me.

*Monday, June 14*   Fell asleep in the middle of Cardenio's adventure and did not wake up until six-thirty this morning. Saw our boy at once. I dreamed again of R. When he came to me, he said he now knew which little bird it was which, as I had told him, invariably started to twitter all by itself at three-thirty in the morning at the first sign of daybreak: it was Siegfried's bird, which had announced his arrival and now came to inquire after him. — R. brought a Chinese novel, sent to him by Mme Mendès (*"témoignage d'inexprimable admiration"*), which I have now almost finished. At one o'clock he comes with his sketches in his hand, inscribed "properly delivered," he says our son is now truly born. It is again divine, this act! — The only thing that distresses me is when R. says he will not live to see our boy's manhood and laments that we did not discover each other fifteen years ago. — The weather is nasty today, foehn atmosphere, and R. affected by it. Telegram from Hermine, the children in good health; in the evening *Don Quixote*.

*Tuesday, June 15*  R. had a bad night, which distresses me very much; I also fear that he will not start working out his sketches in the near future. Letter from Hermine, the children well and enjoying themselves. Eva blossoming here and Siegfried developing. I dressed, but am still very weak. Letter from Richter with the news that Hans has demanded his dismissal on the grounds of ill health! R. already knew. I write at length to Hans in great concern. Final attempt at an understanding. — With R. in quiet and earnest mood. Will I be granted the boon of seeing Hans at peace? . . . In the evening *Don Quixote*, I fall asleep and am very weary.

*Wednesday, June 16*  Feeling very worn out after a difficult night, I cannot yet bear much. Vreneli gives me a great shock by telling me of a letter from the maidservant in Munich, wanting urgently to know Hermine's present whereabouts. I imagined all sorts of terrible things and tried to get a grip on myself by assuming all these terrible things had already happened. R. came; before entering my room he put something to rights in the *salon*, causing me to remark jokingly that he must always fiddle about with things. The joke came near to upsetting him, and I made it only because the one single difference between R. and myself is that he takes pleasure in comfort and in pretty things, while I tend almost to prefer doing without to enjoying. I often think that one day I shall have to suffer complete deprivation in order to prove the value of this trait, which now sometimes causes trouble. Siegfried was brought in to us; how carefully I shall bring him up! Of course everything is ordained in the stars, and he is already what he will later become, yet his development can still be benefited by his upbringing; whether he will grow into a rugged oak or a lean poplar, that is already laid down, but whether the tree will remain beautiful, will not be damaged by parasite growths or plagued by maggots— that is what care, upbringing, is for. I shall be the loyal gardener who understands and protects you, my little boy, my good boy. R. declares he will be a genius, because he is my son, but all he himself wishes for is a *man*. — Since I feel very weak I stay in bed, R. plays through the whole of his third act. How lovely that we now have this! R. is sad to see me looking so worn out, and says that I suffer too much. He says the path of conciliatory discussion I have initiated with Hans will bring me much suffering, but I was right to do it—or, rather, I was Rightness itself. Then we discussed the completion of the library for Siegfried, he intends to learn Latin again with him. For the shaping of our happiness, he says, he would have no fears were it not for the existence of the things from which we are cutting ourselves off. Once more we went through all our sufferings in Munich—we, not even we, could have acted differently! Afterward read Eckermann-Goethe. R. went to the piano, a glance at the French songs of his youth (which he had copied out and presented to me at Christmas) filled him with great bitterness; he remembered how he was kept waiting outside the room in Mme Viardot's house and then had begged her to sing his "*Attente*," which "with radiant eyes" she had refused to do. He had had too much to put up with; not a single man had he discovered. I asked him whether he had done better with women. "Yes," he said, laughing, for he had me. Then he went to get ready for his walk. When he came up, he was weeping; inside him, he said, was nothing but praise and glory in connection with me, melancholy and bitterness in connection with everything else. Kos's condition is again causing us much worry, the poor dog's days are certainly numbered. — R. says he would like to return to Mme Viardot her Doré edition of *Don Quixote*; the illustrations displease us more and more. From Cervantes's story the Frenchman has extracted nothing but caricature; R. feels that even Cornelius, for instance, would for all his awkwardness have understood it better. The German Catholics are now firmly resisting the Council. Probably it will once more fall to the Germans to save the honor of mankind. Neither the French nor the English will bother about it, they will either simply bow to it or ignore the whole thing. — The weather is overcast, but in the evening becomes brighter. (On Wednesdays the witches are said to have power over one.) When it rained in the morning, I felt as if the good spirits were weeping with me. R. is giving up his intended cure in order to finish writing his third act; I feel he is right, for we have too many worries on our minds for him to be able to tend his health in peace and to good effect; and pleasure in one's work can also be beneficial.

*Thursday, June 17* R. had fears about me during the night and came up at two o'clock; but I was sound asleep. Siegfried continues well and Eva, too; of the children on the Selisberg I likewise have good news; the Godhead is treating me graciously and kindly, it is only the world which is inimical to me. Thus I cannot have Siegfried christened here, this would cause all sorts of difficulties, the Protestant clergyman told Vreneli when we sent her to ask. So we must consider in patience what to do. Today downstairs for the first time and in the garden, with R. to the pigeon house. Smiling reception everywhere! R. asked jokingly in the morning what more Siegfried had in store for him, now that he had already dislodged him from his bedroom. . . . There are lovely flowers in my sitting room, I see nothing but good all around me, yet worry lodges in my heart; I hope, dear children all, that things will be easier for you than for your mother. Surely there will never again be such a poor, bereft being as Hans. He feels so miserable in my absence, and yet I could never make him happy, never even please him. In the evening we discussed, R. and I, the oddly mysterious nature of our alliance. How timid and at the same time rapturous our first approaches, how unpremeditated our first union, how constantly were our unspoken thoughts centered only on renunciation, and how circumstances and people forced us to recognize that our love alone was genuine and that we were utterly indispensable to each other! — "The spirit of the universe desired me to have a son by you, and so it arranged things; we ourselves were forced to obey, without understanding why." — In the evening I feel very, very tired and worn out. Not even *D[on] Q[uixote]* restores us in its usual way, the sentimental episodes are too conventional.

*Friday, June 18* In the night R. again comes up to me in concern; I was just ringing for a light to be brought, so agitated were my spirits. He gave me the lamp, and now I continued to meditate in its brightness. I know that only complete sacrifice can assure us peace, I shall never be without worry, for I shall always grieve for the person whom I could not help, or, rather, who could do so little to help himself. Were I to sacrifice only myself—even though it be to utterly no avail—how willingly should I do it, yet—thus my thoughts spun on and on until in the morning I fell wearily asleep. Spent the morning in bed with the Eckermann *Conversations*, much edification from them. So great a being as G[oethe] remains an inexhaustible source of consolation. At lunch the ungrateful spite of a manservant produces a significant conversation. R. says one needs just as much Christian love to receive kindness as to show it; the subordinate asks himself: Why can I also not harbor these feelings, why can I not dispense alms? The unity of all Nature is expressed in the feelings of the poor person: I am a suffering mortal like you, we are equal. And this unconscious instinct for equality in turn creates the insuperable division. Only a saint, who does not dispense alms but turns himself into a poor person, a prisoner, can set this division aside. He says it was Alberich who made him profoundly aware of this mental condition. — Today R. has been rereading his essay *What Is German?*, and is very pleased with it. But what a severe judgment on the young King rises from it! — After lunch R. reads me some scenes from *Antigone*—that is the truly incomparable *par excellence*. But my head is very weak—it is as if I had not yet quite woken up out of a bad dream, and I fear it will remain like this my whole life through. When I yesterday, being very tired, gave in to my feelings, I reproached myself afterward severely: nothing, no suffering and no trial, must be allowed to make me forget my duty, which is to make R.'s days pleasant; I impressed this firmly on my mind during the night, and it must be my mainstay. In the evening letters from Lulu and Hermine. I write to both, also to Richter. In the evening I am very weak.

*Saturday, June 19* I had to stay in bed today, the doctor told me. R. is with me most of the time and reads to me (Eckermann). When he is there I always feel good, but once he is gone I am overcome by despondency and weakness; all my acts seem questionable, I ask myself whether I have not been striving for the impossible and through that, because of that, have done the wrong thing. Tears are my only solace, since I cannot be active. — The mail brings a nice letter from Champfleury with a book, *Les Chats*. I am very happy with the Goethe *Conversations*; in the weakest and most dismal hours communion with a great and wise man is an infinite solace.

*Sunday, June 20* Since I was worried that no reply had come from Hans, R. tells me that a letter arrived yesterday. He gives it to me, saying it is very fine. Deep, inexpressible agitation. Probably more because of that than because of getting up, I again feel unwell and have to take to my bed. In the evening the children back from the Selisberg, they are well and lively. They take great delight in Siegfried, who is shown to them. — In spirit now at this performance of *Tristan* in Munich, this dreadful one! At lunch R. and I smiled to think that poor *Tristan*, this night flower full of grace, has always been treated like a poisonous toadstool. R. is of the opinion that nobody wants tragedy, situations and feelings that cannot be changed or made better are anathema to all. Many tears shed today. — In connection with a saying by Goethe, R. declares that all poets seem to share the opinion that there is nothing at all for them in men, though they can make do with women in a pinch.

*Monday, June 21* Still in bed and weak, but worked with the children. In the night I was very worried that Hans might not have been able to get through the *Tristan* performance, and sent a telegram to Richter. The reply reads, "Bülow came to life during performance, afterward cheerful, calls of 'Bülow stay,' success tremendous." R. talks about the work and says that in it the cult of the earth goddess finds true expression; he feels as if he had thrown himself headlong into the paint pots and emerged dripping. He had had to make use of the richest resources of musical expression because the action of the drama is so simple. No one but a musician was in a position to explore such a subject to its very depths and remain at the same time attractive. The children have lunch at my bedside. In the evening read one of Grimm's fairy tales ("*M[eister] Pfriem*") to the little ones. Later Eckermann with R. Day and night I reflect on my reply to Hans; I intend to suggest that I come to Munich with the children and settle things with him there.

*Tuesday, June 22*   Still in bed and feeble, but feeling somewhat better. R. goes to work on his sketches. "All these primitive hotch-potches (Wotan storming in) I no longer care for at all," he says. All *five* children with me—the *"Cinque Canti,"* R. calls them in fun. With regard to the two eldest, who show none of my characteristics, he says one can see to what extent Woman is like the earth in relation to the sun: she is entirely passive, and all that comes out is what Man puts in; except when Earth itself is stirred by emotions, by enthusiasm, when Tellus falls in love with Sol, then it, too, takes an active part. Orientals rightly regard Woman as the plowed field in which they scatter the seed. The image of Tellus and Sol provides a parable that can explain much, and one has it constantly before one's eyes, since there is always day and night. In the afternoon a letter for R. from Hans arrives, a report on the *Tristan* performance. It induces R. to repeat what he said once before to me: "The King of B[avaria] is all daemon, I have been studying what he does, and he acts by instinct; when he stops to consider, he is lost. Without his even realizing it, his daemon tells him that, if he had gone along with me, had carried out my plans with real boldness, he and I would have gone completely to the dogs. In view of the wickedness and mediocrity of people he does whatever is possible to preserve my works for the world, but I cannot take much pleasure in his activities." — Some person was here again to request R.'s support in some unsavory Munich affair; Councilor Pfistermeister and Sauer, the adjutant, seem to think that only R. has any influence with the King!! Still Eckerm[ann], and with the children Grimm's fairy tales.

*Wednesday, June 23*   In bed! R. with his sketches; I get up, but soon have to lie down again. As I was playing with the feather on my bed, R. said, *"King Lear,"* and, since I could not remember the place, he fetched the play and read me the scene in which Lear comes in with his dead daughter in his arms. How terrible the effect of this one single scene! — "When one recalls the conventionality of speech in certain Italian and Spanish poets, how startled one is by the directness here; one sees that Sh[akespeare] must have been a Protestant." Concerning Gozzi, R. said it struck him as very significant that he had started out from the well-known acting talent of the Italians. To what levels things in Italy had now fallen could be seen in the fact that drama is banished from all the big theaters and only opera flourishes. — In the evening R. brings me a theater journal containing a nice article about Hans. I should like to write, but am too tired.

*Thursday, June 24*   Woke in the night and thought out a plan by which R. would give a reading of his *Nibelungen* in Munich and afterward tell everyone what we were trying to do, why we went away, and how we had now been forced to abandon all our plans. In the morning, *under the influence of Sol,* I found this idea absurd. I told R. about it and he said he had also once considered it, but afterward the mere thought of to whom he would want to speak had frightened him off; such a thing might be possible in Paris, where it would make an impression and have some effect, but in no town in Germany would he find an audience for anything like that. All one could do was to shed light from afar like a planet and not try to intervene directly. — Then he adds jokingly: when I am well again, he intends to enter his Goethe age, he has really made up his mind not to let things upset him any more. If only I would not let things affect me so! The greatest wisdom, and often the greatest humanity, is to let things take their course. Then he said, laughing, "It irritates you terribly that I cannot be happy without you; you want me to be cheerful and well, but you wish it could somehow be achieved without your help." I had to laugh and to say, "Yes, certainly that is so." — He goes to his sketches, and I begin my letter to Hans. When he comes in to lunch R. notices my emotional state and reproaches me for having written. He says I should have desisted, out of love for him. When I offer the letter to him to look at, he says he does not wish to read it. In the evening R. brings along an article by Cornelius about Genelli, which disgusts us both very much; R. says he throws in Dante, Homer, the Bible, as if they were nothing, and nothing comes out of it but false judgments; to stick strictly to the subject, nobody does that any more. — In the afternoon a visit from Countess Bassenheim.

*Friday, June 25* Still wretched nights, reflecting on my situation, my obligations; since personal sacrifice caused me no difficulty, it seems my life's test consists in having to offer up another life besides my own at the same time, a superior one! I got out of bed and was carried by R. into the garden. Great weakness. We spoke about *Lohengrin,* he told me that in the year '48 Röckel said to him, "What we now need is a sort of popular anthem." "Well," said R., "I have a theme," and sang him the motive from the March in the third act of *L.* Röckel found it too artificial, however. R. says he was right: one can tell that it comes from an artistic work. I told him then that I had first recognized the greatness of his art in this March and in the trumpet calls in the second act. When, utterly annihilated by the conclusion of the scene between Lohengrin and Elsa, I had come to believe that I could not possibly follow the further development, the trombone sounded—a somber, subterranean signal, so to speak, that he would give her an answer. Immediately following that, the bright trumpet calls, gripping my attention, and the art of music helped me over the shattering effect of the drama. In the same way, when in the second act Ortrud enters Elsa's dwelling and Telramund declares that calamity is now entrenched in the house, the morning calls of the trumpets, with their natural sounds, at once provide the soothing effect which Nature always brings to a troubled mind. After all this, R. says that the Berlin Academy should have nominated me (for he has now been officially informed that he is a member of this somewhat superfluous institute). A letter to me from Marie Muchanoff demands *Die Walküre* for Dresden, where Count Platen, the manager, is deporting himself very well. I have to inform her that the *Nibelungen* belongs to the King of Bavaria, which brings us back to the subject of the King, and R. once again asserts that without the King he and his works would no longer exist. — In the course of the day I have to return to bed, but all the same I spend a lot of time with the children. Another thing R. told me at lunch: "You are my idol, and it has certainly never happened before that a woman has so entirely fulfilled a man like me, has become virtually everything to him." — In the evening read Goethe's *Conversations with E[ckermann]* with ever-increasing pleasure. "All noble things seem to sleep until they are aroused by contradiction." What particularly pleases R. is that Goethe always places the significant personality in the forefront and wins sympathy for the works through this (as, for example, with Molière). In contrast, says R., one sees how little one nowadays cares about outstanding individuals in the fact that so many books go out of print (e.g., Riemer's *Lexicon*, Grimm's *German Grammar*). The practical results of these books are brought together in others, and nobody cares whether he is hearing the words of an intelligent man or not. "All just railway-carriage reading!" says R.

*Saturday, June 26* Night of brooding, going over things again and again—holding tight to one resolve: that R. should know nothing of my torturing thoughts; the only escape from tormenting, irrepressible worries is to have a firm purpose. With this I at last fell asleep. In the morning R. had breakfast with me and said that he had been thinking a lot yesterday about Joan of Arc, and what a pity it was that this subject, with all its sublime naïveté, was beyond the reach of art, since the world with which this heroine came into conflict is too despicable. — I find it easier to get up today, and the day's activities quell my restless thoughts. — Worked with the children in the garden and also ate there. Much pleasure in the flourishing of the little ones; in them I am given the likeness of the greatest happiness; if I did not have the torment of Hans, whose lot could even be compared with mine? How, in blissful innocence, the days pass! No noise from the world reaches us, here love alone rules supreme. I thank the God who gave me this: may He forgive me for having brought suffering to another being! R. now always works in the mornings. In the afternoon he wrote his letter to the Berlin

Academy: this, calm and serious, constitutes, in its outline of his position, the sharpest criticism of conditions in Germany. I remain in the
garden and write to M. Muchanoff. The doctor came, and R. found an
opportunity to remark to him what a great pity it is that Switzerland
has no better aim in life than to imitate Paris; instead of having some
capable person set up a technical college in Lucerne, they build one
hotel after another, and the women run around made up absurdly to
look like Parisians. On receiving the answer that such a little place
would never be able to compete with Paris, R. replied forcefully: "It
would be something different. What does it want with all this stupid
luxury? It should act according to its needs, have its own character, but
instead of that the rich gentlemen here prefer a nation of tricksters,
just lying in wait for the three months in the year when they can fleece
foreigners." — At seven o'clock I enter R.'s room, and he is quite
beside himself with joy at my appearance. We drink tea downstairs,
and upstairs continue reading Eck[ermann]-Goethe. —

*Sunday, June 27* The usual night thoughts, I was awakened abruptly
by the appearance of Hans in a dream. During the day I had read his
letter again, since I am determined never to conceal from myself the
evil I have done—however unwillingly—but on the contrary to impress
it ever more strongly on my mind, in order to repent and atone for
it as best I can. — In the morning R. came up to my room with a
letter from the King (addressed to *Herr R. W., the immortal poet and
composer, my great friend*). "When I am feeling gay as I am today, I sing
hymns to you, and yet I dreamed that you no longer loved me, and
went away." I, too, had dreamed that I had gone away! I then read
aloud the letter, which is very extravagant in tone. A conversation
about the Doré illustrations (which are at least an expression of their
times, something which can never be said of a similar German work)
leads us on to the splendid van Dycks we saw in Genoa, then to two
large copies made by Countess Nako, which R. had seen in her home
in Vienna. R. praised the Hungarian Countess's house, the Count's
fine character and enthusiasm for R. [*Unreadable sentence omitted.*] "If
I had been there in my G[oethe] age," he added with a smile, "I should
have been happy enough to stay there, but, restless as I was in Vienna,
always worrying about how to make do with the little I had and in
consequence exacting, I could not let anything make a friendly impact
on me. I should never wish to give up Austria," R. continued. "Through
its Slav inhabitants it possesses the poetry of reality we so much lack
in Germany." Then we considered what a different impression would
have been created if we had presented the model productions of
*T[annhäuser]*, *L[ohengrin]*, *Tr[istan] und I[solde]*, and *Die M[eister]s[inger]*
in Paris as in Munich, even in the German language; now everything

has been more or less scattered to the winds. "When I have finished the *Nibelungen*," R. also said, "I shall write some plays for the theater: Luther's marriage with C[atherine] v[on] Bora, Bernhard von Weimar (that would have to be set in a military camp), and also Barbarossa." "And Parzival?" I asked. "That will be done in my 80th year. I shall perhaps do *Die Sieger* as a play. [*In the margin, in R. W.'s handwriting: "And in addition publish a newspaper in which I should reveal all, all— speak my mind freely."*] But no more music. With my ten scores I should think I have done enough. I am presumptuous enough to believe that, in regard to musical richness and invention, there is little that can be compared, as far as diligence and wealth of detail is concerned, with *Tristan* and *Die Meistersinger*." — The King says he now wants to begin ruling! — Siegfried is three weeks old today, he looks fine. R. says that since his birth, which for me was the reason for living my life, he has had an unbounded confidence in Fate. — God bless you, my children, may you one day bless my peace, when my sufferings are at an end! R. had told the Academy of his willingness to supply them, if they should wish, with reports on the state of dramatic art in Germany. At my request R. struck out this sentence, saying, "You are right; anything that looks like a hope is stupid." The children to town with R., ate ices. I am tired and go to bed early.

*Monday, June 28* Wanted to get up early, but had another severe hemorrhage and had to remain in bed, to the great dismay of R. who, having risen in good spirits, soon found himself feeling miserable. Soon, however, he goes off to "Tellus and Sol" (Wotan and Erda). "If I had more of a philosophical bent," he says, "I should describe this prototype of all individualization; the separation of the planets from the sun is the beginning of all phenomena." I asked him whether he thought that much still remained to be discovered in the philosophical field after Schopenhauer. He replied, "To be described, much; to be discovered, I think not." Then he came to the conclusion that the symbols of Christianity offered less to the trained mind than those of the Indian religion, because the latter were the outcome of a very advanced culture, whereas the former originated in the poorest and most neglected classes. — Lusch does some copying for the King, I read some of Goethe's occasional verses ("*Lieben, leiden, lernen*"), and R. works, though reluctantly: "When I think that I shall never again hear a single note of my things, and that I am letting *Das Rheingold* be done without me, where should I find the urge to make music? I do it purely for you." In the afternoon I read Sophocles's *Ajax*—tremendous, morally uplifting impression. Gave Lusch her piano lesson, in the evening Eckermann.

*Tuesday, June 29* Long meditation during the night; the sin of

having deeply grieved another being cannot be redeemed, no explanation, no excuses suffice for it, and so I have burdened my soul with
a great sin; this I will expiate in whatever way I can, it shall work to
the advantage of the children and of my beloved; my self-will is broken,
broken, too, my self-respect, I recognize that we may not meddle in or
resist our fate, but must just bear and bear things as they come. Just
as the fairy tale tells us of little spirits standing by to aid the sorely
tried, so do my children stand by me; to love them as they will never
be loved again, this my woe teaches me, and the mother's soul is
filled with gratitude toward her little ones. For all grief affecting ourselves there is a consolation, but for the grief we inflict on others we
find no appeasement. Still weak; yet I get up. The doctor comes and
finds it necessary to consult an eye specialist. A great shock, which is
turned to worry by the eye specialist's visit. Siegfried has an inflammation of the cornea! The doctor has never before seen this in a newborn
child. I feel this trial as a punishment. Profound sorrow—would my
death bring atonement and salvation?

*Wednesday, June 30*  Hans does not write. At night I wake up and
question myself. My realization of the dreadfulness of life keeps me in a
state of anxiety about the children. I feel guilty ever since Hans told
me that he could not do without me. This—I did not believe! To keep
from R. and the children all knowledge of my worries—that is my
task. Wrote to Claire and told her everything; in this connection I came
to read an earlier letter of hers, in which she writes that people and
even Ollivier, my brother-in-law, are talking about my situation. In
the afternoon I was carried downstairs. R. has been working hard. In
the evening a conversation about Schiller brings us on to *Don Carlos*,
which we are reading.

*Thursday, July 1*  Another sleepless, thought-laden night! In the
morning so weak that I ask R. to come up to me, and I tell him my
worries; he talks splendidly and comfortingly to me; he is surely
right! I shall continue to hope. At breakfast R. spoke of the inestimable
boon which would come from a real fusion of the French and the
Germans—though certainly the French should not go to Heine,
Meyerbeer, and Kaulbach to find out about the German character. —
Siegfried has to be kept completely in the dark. A great worry. — The
joyful moment of the day was the arrival of Beethoven's portrait,
which R. has had copied (from the original, in Härtel's possession).
We receive the great man as a friend and benefactor, and R. says we
have pleasures which no others have, we lead a life like few others'.
— Previously all R.'s sublime impressions brought me closer to him—
now, when we are united, they bring me the consciousness of my
guilt. In the evening we spoke again about Goethe and Schiller, the

princess in *Tasso* and the queen in *Don Carlos*. The queen has always
been my ideal of womankind, the princess just a charming example of
femininity. Coming back once more to the portrait of Beethoven, R.
says to me: "This pleasure I also owe to you. Without you such an
idea would never have occurred to me. I should just have remained
excited and crazy." Seeing me still looking sad, he says: "I think only
of the beings whose whole existence depends on you, who are nothing
without you. There are six of us—and we are happy here." Yes, that
we are, for we live in love—it is only the thought of Hans and glimpses
into the children's future which fill me with sorrow. — R. writes to
the King, the eye specialist comes and finds Siegfried no worse. I
visit the children in the garden and give Lusch her piano lesson. Read
*Oedipus* by myself. In the evening Eckermann.

*Friday, July 2*  Similar night. I gladly abandon my nights to worry
and suffering, so long as I can devote my days to my beloved and to
the children. Rose very early; practiced on the piano with Lusch. Had
breakfast with R. The doctor with me, puts my mind at rest concerning
Siegfried; in the middle of his visit R. comes up and announces himself
as "Prince"; there is an article in *La Liberté* by Villiers de l'Isle-Adam
with the dedication: *à Richard Wagner, Prince de la musique profonde*.
While the children are working I read *Oedipus*; at lunch conversation
with R. about it. "Why could not Tiresias solve the riddle of the
Sphinx? It shows that a great human being is more than a prophet.
But why all these terrible things piled on Oedipus? In order to make
us aware of what life is and that *happiness is just an illusion*." — Down
to the children in the garden. Birds, roses, and cherries. There R.
says he must tell me in all soberness that for him I am a manifestation
of the divine. With what emotion I hear that—I, who am so miserably
conscious of my paltriness! — Trouble with Babli, Siegfried's nurse,
who constantly takes the baby into the light. In the evening Eckermann
again with R., much enjoyment. (Wrote to Prof. Nietzsche and returned
to him Lübke's wretched essay on *Die Msinger*.)

*Saturday, July 3*  Rainy day, and R. would have preferred sunshine
for his work, because he has to rewrite (Wotan's last words to Erda,
which have turned out too "idyllic"). The two doctors come and find
things looking better, Siegfried's eye is improving. Spent the day with
the children; R. stays indoors in good and cheerful spirits, in the evening he tells me: "How happy I was when today I really felt what I
enjoy under your protection! I took out a volume of Droysen and read
the death of Pyrrhus, then I opened Schopenhauer at the chapter on
music and discovered that, if I am ever to carry out my projected
writings, I must link them to this chapter." He added: "You never
read the right things: you should read this history of Hellenism, which

makes us aware of how at its dissolution this unique people was, as it were, returning to its heroic age; the things which occur in it could have come straight out of Homer. Everything so dramatic, so impassioned, so violent. And Sparta emerges again!" Against his reproach that I do not read what he recommends to me I have to say in my own defense that, since becoming a mother, I have really had no more time for reading, and today, while reading *Oedipus*, I literally reproached myself for not going yet again to see how the little ones were getting on. He reads me the death of Pyrrhus. We pass the evening in conversation; he is still delighted with the picture of Beethoven: "That is how he looked, this poor man who gave us back the language men spoke before they had ideas; it was to recover this language of the birds that Man created the divine art. But this is also the reason why a musician such as he is a being for whom there is absolutely no place in society." His other pleasure came from the children, for whom he played something and who played around him (Lulu already very earnestly fascinated by the music). I tell him how shattered I was by the passage in *Oedipus* in which Oe. says to his daughters that they will never marry, his shame would weigh on them, too. "It could be otherwise," R. replies. "Since you bore me a son I know that I must live to a ripe old age. The fact that I have won you shows me that Fate still has something extraordinary in store for me." I then tell him that I am resolved not to come out of my seclusion until it becomes necessary in order that the children may learn certain things. "Then we, too, shall enjoy the world," he said. You are happy now, my children, may God rain blessings on your more distant days! You, Lulu and Boni, will one day be to your father what I could never be; that is my comfort and my hope.

*Sunday, July 4* A good night, dreamed of distant travels with R., I showed him some Raphael drawings, met G[eorge] Sand, who reproached me for my deeds, I listen to her humbly and say merely that what I did was grave, but in my heart not evil. Mounted a puppet show for the children, then down to R. and am writing this as he composes; the true nature of music, as he has explained it to me, reveals itself to me thereby; it is as if something opens within my soul which is otherwise always held captive, and my mind relapses into a dream state; reality vanishes completely, and love alone holds sway. *"Diesen Kuss der ganzen Welt," "Seid umschlungen, Millionen"*—such things can really only be expressed in music, emotion has no place in the realm of words. As R. is playing me what he has written, Richter comes in, to our astonishment. Dismal news from Munich, the theater manager a coward, all the rest so crude that it defies description. Dear good Richter weeps as he recalls his happy days in Tribschen. I weep, too, and ask

R. to play something from *Tristan*. Deep emotion, tears—relief. R. then goes out with Richter, I write to the cook in Munich, who has written to me (Hans stays silent). And to Mathilde. Only Lulu caused me pain at lunch today, I felt she was taking advantage of my momentary embarrassment to be impertinent to me! At tea discussed with Richter the wretchedness of German conductors—the *great* Munich Lachner fails to notice mistakes in *Figaro* (among other things)! — Regarding Mannheim, Richter relates that at the 4th performance the Jews had hissed *Die Msinger*, but at the 5th the audience did not allow itself to be taken unawares and applauded vigorously throughout; when a few of the people of Israel began to hiss, a Dr. Werther stood up and cried "*hepp, hepp,*" whereupon the hissers went out. Late in the evening R. and I still lamenting our sorrows; I can feel in my indescribable suffering how sacred the bond of matrimony is, and how cautiously and reverently it should be tied. R. ever kind and lovingly concerned for me, showing me always that the world does not exist for him, that I am everything to him.

*Monday, July 5* Dream that I strayed with R. into a gathering of Jews and that I then went out begging with Hans, and stones were thrown at me. R. comes up. I show him the nice letter I received from Claire this morning; that brings us to the question of a divorce. I tell R. that I intend to write to Hans, asking if he wishes me to go to him, to give up everything here, to take just the four children with me, whether he really has the strength to be happy in view of all the stir our relationship has caused; if not, he should consent to a divorce, if only for his own sake. R. says that in this matter he must remain silent. He leaves me and writes to Düffl[ipp] about Hans's position. An atmosphere of stillness. After lunch, out in a boat with the children. Visited Countess Bassenheim, found her at home. In the evening with Richter. Wrote at a late hour to Claire.

*Tuesday, July 6* Thunder in the air; R. unwell, cannot work, I depressed. Grave discussion with R. about what I told him yesterday. I try to make him understand how—in my sense—the sacrifice of our happiness, indeed even of our life together, could never affect our love. He feels deeply hurt, but as always we have to admit, amid smiles and tears, that it is only the excess of our love which makes us so susceptible. Played with the children, little work because of the sultriness. In the evening R. and Richter play Mozart's C Major Symphony as a piano duet, in the course of which R. gets very indignant about the faulty arrangement: "That is just like the Germans—always carrying on about Mozart, and then they produce such editions!" Listening to the Andante, I found myself thinking of Beethoven, and I felt as if one might say to him, "Alas, alas, you have destroyed it, this beautiful world." But in his heart he built it up again. The gods have ceased their sweet and blessed playing, and instead of Paradise we have life, with all its terrible agony and the salvation which flows from it. There is no returning to Paradise, though there is to Heaven, and Mendelssohn, who perhaps flattered himself that he could restore the original state, is merely childish. With Beethoven musical creation becomes human, Mozart is the world of animal, vegetable, and mineral, the innocent, naïve world, unknowing both in gladness and sorrow; in the whole panoply Wagner appears as the revelation, as religion. In this history of creation the venerable Bach appears somewhat like the entire planetary system, before it separated itself from the sun. On such levels there is, however, no place for the gnat Mendelssohn to vaunt himself. — Good night, my children, good night, Hans, a very good night, my Richard! Today I really came to understand the idea of metempsychosis, I felt the need for atonement, it was a kind of consolation to tell myself that I should one day have to atone for the suffering I have caused by other means than sympathy and mourning, and yet no atonement can weigh more heavily on me than the knowledge of my guilt and my powerlessness to redeem it.

*Wednesday, July 7* Work everywhere, mine maternal, R.'s magnificent; at noon he calls out to me that he has found it—that is to say, the conclusion for Wotan and Erda. After lunch, as I give him my hand, he tells me that the slightest touch from me does him good, no more sympathetic creature exists, but that is also why nobody else can leave me alone! — To Frau Am Rhyn, who then accompanies me back here. The children play merrily with the Am Rhyn children. In the evening R. brings me a letter from Mathilde, she has heard about my 5th child from *Hornstein* and cannot understand why I told her nothing about it!!! R. very annoyed with her, reproaches me for being too weak toward everybody. I reply to her late in the evening, calmly and shortly. But all the same it has again raised a great worry in my mind, since Baron Hornstein lives—of all places—in Munich!

*Thursday, July 8* In the morning settled the Munich furniture-removal arrangements with Richter, he will supervise the packing. At breakfast discussed possible ways of regularizing Hans's position: he should take over the musical management, should no longer have such wretched men as Perfall over him. Then with the children, R. to his work. When I go to him, he says jokingly, "I love only my enemies, my friends I hate, that goes even beyond Christianity!" Wrote to Anna in Munich. At midday a letter from Dr. Lang; he again invites R. to write for the N[ord]*deutsche Zeitung*. After lunch R. wanted to play something from his sketches, but then did not feel in the mood. I suggested reading his *Parzival* draft and did so, amid occasional tears. I could feel deep within myself the purifying and ennobling effect which such sublime things have on us. To R[ichter] it was all completely new, and he listened in great emotion. We were interrupted by a visit from the eye specialist, great happiness over his pleasure at the improvement of the trouble; like a lightning flash Fate has once more revealed to me the abyss on whose edge we are always so blindly standing. R. goes out with Richter in a fine mood of exhilaration, Loldi and Eva come toward us, the elder children are on the swing. "Bless you," he calls out to me! I feel blessed, I am blessed. Oh, my children, if we still have much suffering to bear together, bear it bravely with me, and if Fate appears to deal more harshly with you because your mother broke with the world, be proudly glad that you can atone that one sin for her! — To the children once more, supervised Lulu's piano practice, then at 8 o'clock go to meet R. and Richter. In the evening said farewell to R[ichter], he will resign his position if Hans really goes. Late, worrying thoughts about Hans. R. told me he had felt so happy today. I think with hope of later times, when the children will be grown up and perhaps will be able to compensate for many things, if only heavy blows do not fall in the meantime. Good night, you sublime, good, great being whom I love, whom I serve, good night, my children, good night, Hans, on whom I have brought so much sorrow, I dream of worlds in which we shall all come together and love one another!

*Friday, July 9* Sultry. R. unwell. At breakfast he is given a card from Serov (the Russian R. Wagner!) and invites him to join us at table. [*Footnote in the diary:* "Serov has in consequence of his Russian national opera been appointed an active councilor of state and bears the title Excellency, about which R. good-humoredly teased him a lot."] S[erov] has just seen *Tristan* and *Die Msinger* in Munich and is quite intoxicated by them and also very satisfied with the performances. Before I join them, R. tells him a little about what has happened to us and why he will not go to see *Das Rheingold*; when in the course of it my name is mentioned, Serov cries, *"Quelle femme héroique!"* When R. tells me this, I am utterly astonished, so much have I got used to the thought of just being despised. — The children all well, Siegfried fine; R. was pleased today when Eva brought him his snuffbox as he was composing—"When a child appears like that one has such an indescribable sense of the grace and sweetness of life." Thought a lot and with much concern about Hans; then discussed with R. how best to save up my little income for the children. In the morning looked with R. through two newly ordered books (*Art Treasures of Venice* and *The Viennese Collections*). Beethoven has now been framed and is hanging on the wall. In the evening read Grimm's fairy tales to the

children. After dark wandered with R. in the garden under the silent
blessing of the stars. When I learn (through Grimm) that *"ach wach"*
means the same as *"o weh,"* I realize how related woe [*das Weh*] and
wide-awakeness [*das Wache*] are. My heart is filled with such anxiety,
I am afraid to live and do not wish to die. When I take precautionary
measures for the children, I immediately tell myself, "Fate will frustrate
it all." Today began *Oedipus at Colonus.*

*Saturday, July 10* R. had a very bad night, but he says in the morning,
"Lord, how happy I am, in spite of all indispositions." Worked with
the children, then received a letter from Mathilde and answered it
right away. She wants to know what to tell people when they ask
about me. I: "The truth!" R. is working hard and is in good and cheerful spirits, though worn out. After lunch to Countess B. with the
children. I tell her of the woman who bribed our stableboy to find out
things, in reply she tells me of her Munich experience. In the evening
told R. my concern for the children's future and my intentions; he
calms me down and ends with the words, "If I could only give you a
heaven on earth!" Thus do I experience here the complete *ideal* of
happiness. — Some words of Loldi's, of which I tell R., cause him to
suggest that I demand a divorce from Hans—but I cannot now make
demands on Hans; I have the strength to suffer, but no longer to wound.
— "Who never ate with tears his bread, who never through night's
heavy hours sat weeping on his lonely bed, *he* knows you not, ye
heavenly powers!" I should like to have reached the point at which
the children could gladden Hans's heart and I show how I intended
it all. Submissiveness—

*Sunday, July 11* R. yesterday brought home a newspaper (*Drama-
turgische Blätter?*) in which there was an article about *Judaism in Music.*
This morning R. tells me he has now read it and for the first time seen
mention of a Jewish Germanic culture in contrast to a Christian Germanic one. "Such impudence! One sees one is dealing .with people
who have no idea at all what things are about." Serov told us recently
that beside a waterfall in Finland he had discovered some verses cut
into the rock, signed "Richard Wagner." Yet R. has never been there.
R. goes to work despite the close atmosphere. I with the two younger
girls to pick strawberries and raspberries, the elder ones to church. —
During the morning R. comes up to my room to see whether I am
"still there." "I always believe you will run away." Then back to his
work. The children play, then family meal, a telegram from Tichatschek, to whom R. had sent some musical quotations on his birthday.
Chocolate for the children, I played a Beethoven quartet with R.,
afterward went for a walk with him. My grieving about Hans—never
expressed aloud—R. guesses, and it makes him sad. He recalls scenes,

at which he was present, when Hans struck me, and says he was
horrified at the calm indifference with which I had borne this. Very
painful feelings. — Back at home, so weary that I fell asleep on the
sofa. To bed at midnight.

*Monday, July 12*   R. comes up with a letter, Judith Mendès announces
a visit. For me a letter from Claire, good and affectionate. Work with
the children. R. dreamed that he was flying with me. Telegram from
Munich theater manager, asking whether it would be convenient to
send his scene painter to see R. In spite of being very unwell R. works
on his "*buffo* duet" (Wotan and Siegfried). Yesterday evening R. told
me how, after writing his *Columbus* Overture, he wanted to do a
Napoleon overture; he intended to depict his hero in all his glory up
to the Russian campaign, from then on in his decadence. For the apex
of the pyramid he needed a gong stroke, but began to doubt whether
this was permissible in music, and asked somebody. Since he could not
make up his mind to use the gong, he abandoned the whole thing. It
struck him as ironic when, listening in Paris to Berlioz's symphony
for the victims of the July Revolution, he had found the gong being
used frequently and very logically to a terrorizing point—whereas he
himself as a young man could not make up his mind to use a single
stroke! Music should be forceful, he said, we have the kettledrum and
the trumpet, but the gong is barbarous, what is needed is something
of that prudent quality the Greeks call "*sophrosyne*," the gong stroke
robs music of all ideality. — In the afternoon, when we wanted to rest,
the Serovs arrived with their son. Since the boy understands only
Russian, Loldi declares, "He doesn't know a thing." R. says of the
boy to his father: "Not a musician, but a councilor of state straight
away—*la mort sans phrase*." The visit was something of a burden to
us, inasmuch as it disturbed the routine of our accurtomed life. Mme
Ser. told me she would never have imagined that I lived so entirely
for my children. With the little ones until late in the evening beneath
the blossoming linden tree. Later looked at Raphael illustrations. R.
very worn out.

*Tuesday, July 13*   Supervised Lulu's piano exercises, then to R.,
who tells me at breakfast he would like to be able to bequeath Siegfried
a house and an income of 1,500 thalers, so that he would never have
to work for money and thereby lose his freedom. But he would have
to be modest in his wants. [*In the margin:* "In his will R. wants to stipu-
late that, if Siegf. works for money, he loses the income."] Then he
talks to me about Wolfram von Esch[enbach], Gottfried von Strass-
[burg], whom he calls great artists who attained great mastery. R.
works, I with the children, studying, playing, bathing. Wrote to
Claire, explained to her why I want the divorce. After lunch played

the piano with R. (Beethoven quartet). He receives a letter from an English lady, who sends him her English translation of *Judaism in Music* and asks for permission to publish it. Great surprise. Then R. takes up the Bach motet "*Als Christus zum Jordan kam*"—it moves us deeply. "The main thing is to put people at ease, to bring religious meditation companionably close to the heart, and the artist then decorates it further with his skill." This leads us to R.'s favorite idea of a school where things of this sort will be performed. "Perhaps I shall come to it yet, for after all my life is just beginning." In the evening Schopenhauer's chapter on music; so far as I can follow it, it seems to me to describe the nature of the divine art wonderfully well. — A word by Schop. about Giordano Bruno and his martyrdom fills us with horror, when we think of the fate of this devotee of truth after he was delivered over to the brutal power of the priests. "They would still like to burn people," R. says, "but it cannot be done."

*Wednesday, July 14* Rose with such a headache that I could not supervise Loulou's practice. Gradually got better. R. has had a nice letter from Chandon and with it a consignment of wine. After lunch the scene painter from Munich, *Rheingold* sketches! R. was jokingly indignant today about the summer—that it has already arrived: "I want to live terribly long." — Lulu dictated to me a letter to her father, it made my heart so heavy. In Paradise the serpent is concealed, it has settled in my heart, and all around is happiness, so beautiful and bright. Let us pray! . . . Thinking about my fate, I feel as if it is trying to make me recognize both deepest sorrow and highest happiness; my poor heart contains them both! Union with my beloved, unbounded happiness—grief over the suffering caused, inconsolable sorrow! — While R. is taking his walk and the children are in bed, I abandon myself to my thoughts; weeping, I sing to a tune of my own, "Who never ate with tears his bread"; the light starts to fade, nearby I hear Siegfried give a hiccup! The doctor was here today and unfortunately could see the spot more clearly than recently; R. comes home, I wipe away my tears, joy returns with him! We talk about the stories of Gottfried Keller, how much more significant they are than Auerbach's; of Tieck R. says that he lacked the painful concision which characterizes the great poet. After supper I read to R. Serov's essays on Berlioz—they are very good. As I write this down I have a feeling of anxiety which seems to me like a death agony. — How childish of my father to speak of "pangs of conscience"—how could I ever feel *those*? But fellow suffering—that is what oppresses my heart, I understand, too, how Parzival suffers and how he searches for Amfortas. Will I ever again be able to feel an unmixed pleasure?

*Thursday, July 15* In the morning with the children and at the same time draft a letter to the translator of the Jewish pamphlet. R. laughs, approves it, and says there is nothing more he can do, all he is now is a composing machine. Afternoon picnic with the children on the Sonnenberg, visit Serov. Returning home, I find R. sad, he was sorry that Eva was left behind, also he feels in a bad mood when I am not there. "Anything but change," he says. In the evening he says to me, "Good night, dream of paradises." I: "I know what would be heaven for me: to live our life here without having had another beforehand." R.: "I am freed of everything, not a soul has any claim on me—except you; when I imagine you gone, all is over."

*Friday, July 16* In France they are having revolutions again. In contrast, the King of Bavaria once again does *not* open the exhibition. One sees the aim is to get rid of the young King. R. thought yesterday evening with great concern about the forthcoming production of *Das Rheingold*—yet again a vast amount of money expended and a pitiful, not to say ridiculous result! All the same, R. does not intend to bother himself about it—how curious the ways of Fate, which fills precisely *this* incapable King with enthusiasm for R.'s works—how curiously terrible! The morning taken up with Siegfried, vexation over the stupid willfulness of his nurse and worry about his eye. At midday great weariness, yet played in the afternoon with the children. In the evening the Mendès couple (M. Villiers is also with them). She is very remarkable, so lacking in manners that I find it downright embarrassing, yet at the same time good-natured and terribly full of enthusiasm. She literally forces Rich. to play and sing pieces from *Die Walküre* and *Tristan*. When they have gone, R. says to me: "There are no women left in France—just think of that! My God, what a spirit you are!" he adds. He had noticed that I had been weeping while listening to his recital: "Yes, for us that is life, we are rooted in it, it is our heart's blood—the others amuse themselves with it, we live it." Late to bed.

*Saturday, July 17* "My God, Lusch, what a mother you have!" R. cries in the early morning when he finds me with my little girl, supervising her practice. Afterward he corrects my letter to the English translator. "How we really do work together!" he says. Boni's stubbornness causes me great concern; I have to punish her. In the afternoon the Mendès couple, I must entertain them. How curious their noisy enthusiasm seems to me! The woman says out loud all the things I believe in my inmost heart; the fact that she can say them aloud makes her seem strange to me. He is highly cultured and both of them thoroughly kind-hearted. They relate how R.'s publisher Schott advertised the translation of the Jewish pamphlet in Paris on the day of *Rienzi*'s first performance; Pasdeloup rushed out in alarm and, as he thought, bought up all the copies. Next day Schott offered him a thousand more copies which he had in stock, at the same price! Who could believe that of a publisher? And again, who was behind it? The last performance of *Rienzi* is reported to have aroused incredible enthusiasm and much presentation of bouquets! R. plays Wotan's farewell to Brünnhilde and several passages from *Lohengrin*. At eleven o'clock they tell us they have not eaten since lunch yesterday. We have nothing in the house, mood of gaiety. Of the movement of the waves in *Das Rheingold* R. says, "It is, so to speak, the world's lullaby."

*Sunday, July 18* R. rose late, is tired from yesterday. But he works. The children to church. I with the youngest ones. R. sends me the sketches which he has completed. Bathing with the little ones, then from two till ten the Mendès couple. She gives me a fan which a Chinese (an academician) has inscribed for her and which in the eyes of the Chinese is worth 100,000 francs; in exchange I have to give her a page of R.'s, which has indeed for me a different worth; I found it hard to part with it, though I do not begrudge it to this remarkable woman. R. regards her and her husband as a real enrichment of our lives, and they are certainly an extraordinary, noble couple. Unfortunately both of them seem in delicate health.

*Monday, July 19* In the morning a letter from Hans to his daughter, he is probably going to Italy with his mother. Melancholy mood, may the gods protect him! With the children. In the afternoon to the Hünendenkmal with our friends. Then home, R. again plays from his works. Judith M. tells me about her life, giving me a curious and terrible glimpse into conditions in Paris.

*Tuesday, July 20* With the children; only late in the evening the Mendès people, who had been to the riflemen's meeting in Zug. R. was just playing me the last thing he had written when they came in. In the morning I had read some pages of young Villiers's books—little that is edifying, much monstrosity.

*Wednesday, July 21* Still always the children; worry, because they are not well, Siegfried, Eva, and Boni. In the evening the Mendès people, music, and garden. They are excellent persons, but the French element is always something of a brake. R. already somewhat tired. He writes a friendly letter to Esser in Vienna, since I told him he was ill, then to Schott to tell him what he thinks about the Jewish-pamphlet affair.

*Thursday, July 22* Up at four o'clock, to Beckenried in the carriage, from there with our friends and Loulou by steamer to Brunnen, then up the Axenstein. Fine day, splendid, moonlit evening, spent the night in the Pension Aufdermauer. R. cheerful in spite of great fatigue. I deep in thought, the children's future hovers before my eyes,

Judith's unfortunate family life makes me really feel what I am to the children and what I can yet become to them. It is as if I have had to suffer such woe in order to gain knowledge in their behalf. Not for a moment, however, do I seek to relieve my heart of the pain which is racking it, I am downright frightened of feeling it less in the emotion of great happiness. As long as I live I wish to atone. —

*Friday, July 23* Up with Lusch at 4 o'clock, splendid sunrise, at 8 o'clock trip by boat to the Grütli, return journey at 11 o'clock. At home the children well. Letter to R. from Weissheimer, the bad impression left by this wretched letter causes a slight upset. A letter from Claire to me dealing with business matters. Early to bed after a bath with Lusch. Letter from Schuré, who is starting on the translation.

*Saturday, July 24* In the morning, while I am giving Lulu a piano lesson, R. comes up; he tells me that Prof. Braun has died; I am very upset by the news; of all people in Munich he and his wife were the friendliest toward me, and both were outstanding characters. R. is also affected by it and says that, if I were not there to hold him between Earth and Heaven, he would no longer be able to exist. He said yesterday that he could never for a moment forget how happy I had made him. His whole past life remains in his memory only as a state of weariness. Wrote to Rosalie Braun and showed the letter to R., asking him whether he can accuse me of an impertinence. R.: "All the better, then you will have learned something; it is like money which you have been swindled out of, that is a direct gain." In the afternoon the Serovs and the Mendès people, till late in the evening. R. plays and sings from *Die Msinger* and *Siegfried*. Braun's death causes in R. a violent outburst against the German princes who lend their support to nothing, to neither talent nor natural gifts, they let everything truly German die of neglect.

*Sunday, July 25* Delighted to observe Lulu's progress in piano playing; R. interrupts our practice; talk about the Mendès couple, she a child of Nature, he a highly cultured man, but unfortunately the French character is like a barrier, they put V. Hugo on the same level as Shakespeare. "The French lack poetic contemplation," says R. "Either they resort to tirades with exaggerated gestures, or they are terribly dry. Utterly untalented as they are as regards art, they could acquire their arrogant sense of superiority only on account of the wretched state of their neighbors. They see themselves being imitated everywhere, and must consequently come to regard themselves as the one true model. Only music might perhaps be able to widen their horizons." R. is very indignant that precisely at this point of time the newborn Saxon Prince has been given the Pope as his godfather, "whereas it is only the good nature of the people which allows its royal family to remain Catholics." — At noon the Mendès people, after lunch M. Villiers reads us his play; the same person in whom we could discern no talent has found in real life inspiration for a good play, which he read to us with marvelous skill. "There are at any rate established conditions there," says R. "Bad as they are, they nevertheless provide a picture—we Germans have no established conditions." — At lunch R. explained how differently one must work in the symphony and in music drama, where all is permissible except stupidities, since the action explains everything. Beethoven, he said, had only once forsaken serenity in the symphony, and there, with his infinite art, he had resorted to words. Take leave of our excellent friends; when they invite me to come with R. to Paris, to *Lohengrin*, and try to press me, I explain to them that I must make sacrifices in order to prove to another being how earnestly I regard a life which has imposed on me the sad necessity of wounding him. Moved silence. Painful thoughts of Hans and his fate, difficulty in going to sleep. — (At dessert, introduction of the children, who were judged very pretty and good.) In the morning a letter from Richter, who has requested his dismissal. He is being asked to stay on, R. answers that he should insist on his dismissal.

*Monday, July 26* Costumes for *Das Rheingold* arrived, very silly and unimaginative. Letter from the duped conductor Esser, very happy that R. wrote him a friendly letter. R. tells me it has occurred to him that he has now reached that state of happiness in which all he wants is to conserve it; he demands nothing more, no changes, just for it to endure. Lulu and Boni write to their father, dictating to me first. Rain. After lunch R. writes telling Munich the design of the costumes is as good as nonexistent. In the garden a little. Eva unwell. In the evening with the elder three to meet R. He has received a comical letter from Serov, whose wife seems to have taken umbrage at Judith; to state it briefly, he goes on at length about the French being unfitted to listen to R.'s works, whereas his wife, ah yes, his wife—! Much amusement over this.

*Tuesday, July 27* Awful dream that R. set his head on fire by carelessly turning a gas flame, after that a second, gentler, but all the same melancholy dream about R. In the morning constantly clutching my heart. R. comes up and tells me he had a very bad night with violent pains in the heart! At 5 o'clock he had written to Serov, telling him the French people who so disturbed him had now left, and his music could now proceed as earnestly and gloomily as his wife could wish. — We think with joy of our newly found friends, particularly of her. Then R. starts laughing at the fact that we always understand each other so well. "Oh, how happy we shall be—what is Goethe's happy old age compared with mine?" Then he says that he sometimes has the feeling that art is downright dangerous—it is as if in this great enjoyment of observing he is perhaps failing to recognize the presence of some hidden sorrow. Great pleasure in the children. Showed Lulu the *Orbis Pictus*, while Boni was copying out. Horrifying story of a nun in Cracow who went mad from being locked up. — Eva having trouble with her teeth. R. at his work, in the afternoon Grimm's fairy tales. Then with Lusch to meet R. On the way we meet Colonel Am Rhyn, who tells us it is reported in the *Luzerner Zeitung* that the King of Bavaria is at Tribschen, in Berne everybody had asked him about it, and the chief of police in Lucerne had said to him on the train that he had a good nose, he knew the King was at Tribschen!! — R. vexed by this. — Since I am surprised to have received no answer from M[athilde] M[aier], I ask R. whether he has withheld a letter from me; I then find out that a regular exchange of correspondence has been going on, and R. also thinks I was wrong not to have told her of the birth of Siegfried. This unfortunately hurt me deeply; with how much difficulty is self-will broken! When does a human being ever achieve complete renunciation? — Recently R. told me that things had changed between us after all, I was now only earnestly companionable toward him. And yet nothing has changed except that I now want no other joy but to see him happy and in good health and the children flourishing. Years ago, when I received the gift of his love, I was in an ecstasy; I hailed the light as if raised from the dead, I forgot everything I knew and believed in happiness on earth, believed in it and demanded it. Now I know everything again and in consequence am content to go around just like a shadow—and yet, so weak am I, I was hurt today, when all suffering should be welcome to me! — Wrote to Claire in the morning, sending her 1,000 francs to invest for Loulou. Eva somewhat better in the evening.

*Wednesday, July 28* Lessons with the children; showed them Raphael pictures. Eva still unwell. In the afternoon took Loulou to her piano lesson. Informed Countess Bassenheim of several things (warned her against our doctor as against a spy, since his relatives live in Munich). Colonel Am Rhyn reports that R. cannot deny the rumor of the King of Bavaria's presence, since this was printed in the Catholic newspaper! — Saw little of R. today. Letter from Judith in Munich. I reply at once.

*Thursday, July 29* Eva unwell. Boni to the dentist, R. at work; Lusch occupied with Raphael. Siegfried well (though still the little white spot!), Loldi picking red currants. In the afternoon a visit from the eye specialist, a stout-hearted man. In the evening showed the children the magic lantern and after tea played the piano with R. —

*Friday, July 30*    While I was asleep, R. came to me and gave me many kisses; I myself do not quite know yet whether this really happened or I just dreamed it. I have renounced all forms of personal joy, may God grant that my beloved and the children are made happy by my silent presence. At breakfast I read R. an account of the Humboldt celebrations, he says jokingly I will live to see his statue set up on his 100th birthday! I: "Siegfried might be there, not I." "Oh yes, you will. You will feel as if you have been swimming in a huge sea." To me any thought of a triumph, success, is almost unbearable. — Then I asked R. whether he thought every boy should lead a wild and dissolute life in his youth. He says: "Yes, if only for the sake of the salutary longing to return to one's senses. This is what always seemed to me questionable about Mendelssohn—that he never lost control of himself. Certainly this period does not need to be as petty as it was with me, it can be splendidly ennobled, as for example through wars in which one takes part (1813), or through travels accompanied by personal hardships, in Norway or somewhere like that." In the garden R. pays me a visit and says, "My happiness lacks but one happiness—that you may also be happy." Finished reading the life of Joan of Arc, afterward lost in thought over how I might preserve the children's simplicity and purity. Simplicity and purity, those inscrutable guardians of peace. — In the afternoon visit from Countess Bassenheim; telegram from Frau Laussot. — (Late in the evening.) If I could only make my children realize what I have now come to realize with so much pain—that a mortal can be great only in bearing what comes to him. He can do nothing except endure; and only through that can he also make others happy. Woe to him who attempts to meddle with Fate and to control and improve things through his own strength. With what mockery does Fate answer him, and how painful is this mockery! But whatever may come to you, children, bear it in stillness and silence and, whatever you do, do not think that you can do otherwise. There is nothing we can do, and whoever cannot learn to bear his lot until death surrenders the only thing he has. Your mother tells you this with bleeding heart and weeping eyes, listen to her, children, listen to her! — (A thunderstorm in the night.)

*Saturday, July 31*    Melancholy night, melancholy mood all morning. Lusch's practice dispels heavy thoughts. R. comes to us and reports that Hans has requested me, through Dr. Hallwachs, to sign a legal document enabling us to get a divorce. I find it good that it should happen in this way. But the thought that Hans has perhaps been brought to this point by acts of brutality disturbs me. The news appears to make R. happy, and so I, too, feel content, though very solemn. — Visit from Professor Nietzsche; a well-formed and pleasant human being. After lunch to Countess B.'s for the piano lesson; a moment of expansion, worried contemplation of life. At home found the Serovs. Heavy rain. Eva still in bed, the doctor not worried. Raging thunderstorm and dismal thoughts.

*Sunday, August 1* Every five minutes woke up abruptly, at first imagining Hans in sorrow, then had strange thoughts of a murderous attack on myself. Rose early, sat by Siegfried, and visited the other little ones. Before breakfast sorted through Weber's songs for Lusch, a simple little verse telling of the danger of wishes that come true arouses a melancholy mood in me. I have to weep. R. tells me he has written to Hallwachs, saying that the legal authorization I am required to give cannot be got so easily. R. would like to do it all by himself, in order to spare me the embarrassing details. I tell him the details and the so-called unpleasantness mean nothing to me; if he could free my heart of sad imaginings, I should accept with gratitude, but this he cannot do, and all the rest is a matter of indifference. Related to Lusch the life of Saint Anthony. At lunch Prof. Nietzsche, who is very pleasant and who feels happy at Tribschen. Afterward accompanied him to Hergeschwyl with the children and R.; he is climbing Mount Pilatus. We go for a walk; a fine Sunday evening, peasants playing skittles. Beer and cheese beneath an arbor. Playful journey home with the children, Boni a dwarf, Lusch and Loldi giants. [*In the margin:* "Telegram from Dresden: 'To the German Mastersinger R. W.: Reunion of German technical students, Elbschlösschen in Meissen. Performance of "Steersman's Song" from *Der Fliegende Holländer*. Enthusiastic cheers for the German composer Wagner.'"]

*Monday, August 2* Heavy rain, housework. Wrote to Claire to ask her to write belatedly to Hans. Suspicion that Hans might have received news of Siegfried's birth in a cruel manner and is offering me divorce as a sort of punishment. R. did not wish to show me Dr. Hallwachs's letter. I beg him never to try to spare me things, since the things I find hard to accept all lie elsewhere than in so-called vexations. I can bear abuse and ignominy and such things more easily in areas where the heart is not involved. Hans promises not to try to take advantage of his rights. In the morning with the children, inking in the *Siegfried* score. Afternoon with R., played the *Faust* Overture and two Haydn symphonies, during which we remarked that in matters of form Haydn is a greater master than Mozart. Arrival of the original score of the first act of *Tristan*. In the evening conversation about my father's works; R., very concerned about the turn his intellect has taken, speaks with preference of the *Faust* Symphony and even indeed of *Mazeppa* for its grand sweep, deplores the tiresome apotheosis fad and the use of the triangle, gong strokes, rattling chains in *Tasso*, etc.

His church music, he says, degenerates into a very childish juggling of certain intervals. Sorrow that he never lived in really close communion with him. Regret over the influence of Princess W[ittgenstein], who like a savage could only appreciate the most vulgar of effects, musical *chocs*. Concerning *Die heilige Elisabeth*, Nietzsche yesterday remarked to me that it smelled more of incense than of roses. — Today R. said that now, at the age of fifty, one knew what love was—everything prior to it had been mere amours. During the night I read *Tristan und Isolde*, and R., who knew I had taken the book upstairs with me, played some passages from it below as I read it in bed. — Catulle Mendès sends a Swedenborgian poem of his; unfortunately it makes impossible reading.

*Tuesday, August 3* R. reports that young Weissheimer is now quite simply demanding the return—with interest—of money which he spent in past days on himself. All on the assumption that R. has only to dip into the King of Bavaria's purse, and in revenge for R.'s not having secured a performance of Weissheimer's opera in Munich. Worked with the children. R. at his sketches. Walk with R. In the evening piano duets, Haydn symphonies. — Regarding a passage in my father's *Faust* Symphony, R. says he himself would have found it impossible to leave the accompaniment as it is, on the assumption that nobody would hear it and would notice only the melodic line. He had today spent a long time over one passage, he said. "Not a soul will hear it, but that does not worry me; and it is in things like that that the pleasure of working really lies." I: "But one does hear it—at least one is aware of the richness in the work." R.: "There are great harshnesses in Bach, too, but they arise from the fidelity with which he leads the individual voices, from the logic of the thought, not from a sort of sloppiness." — In great woe I ask myself today whether one can live long with such misery. My wish in regard to the children is (as I tell R.) that Lusch support her father, Boni marry a scholar, Loldi, Eva, and Siegfried live together. — May God only grant that Hans live long enough for me to be able still to give him some happiness through Lulu!

*Wednesday, August 4* A letter from Judith in Munich. In the evening also, unfortunately, an article by her husband: "*La Maison de R. Wagner à Lucerne.*" R. very upset by it. "The most important thing, my relationship with you and the children, they cannot mention, so they talk about the furniture." One hears no word about the King, even his excursions are no longer reported in the newspapers; very sinister. R. completes his sketch of the third act. After lunch with the children in the woods. Glorious weather; the finest summer I can ever remember has produced Siegfried.

*Thursday, August 5*  Arrival of the paper *La Poupée Modèle*, a great delight for the children. R. copies out his sketch for the King. Continued inking in the score. After lunch duets with R., a Haydn symphony. Visit from Count Bassenheim. The children cutting and pasting things from the book. — Letter from Lenbach, the painter. R. returns home from his walk, bringing a letter from Dr. Hallwachs. It is true that Hans learned in passing of Siegfried's birth. I regret not having informed him of it personally, R. reproves me for this thought and says it was proper that I did not do this. Heavy feelings, may Hans recover his spirits! — In the evening a Haydn symphony; great delight in its masterliness. "In him," says R., "one clearly sees how the popular genius finds its way. The form is more compact than in Mozart; *he* always went after the melody, had no time to spare for the work (with the exception of the four great symphonies). That is why these Haydn works are also much more interesting." — I hardly dare admit to myself how much I long for death. — A telegram from Richter reports that they could not get the right singer for Alberich, and he asks whether they might accept the wrong one. R. replies, "*Children* and *gentlemen*, do what you will and can, but leave me in peace."

*Friday, August 6*  "Undeserving man, how happy I am! When I wake up in the morning feeling rather tired, I have only to tell myself that you are still alive and I am full of cheer." I tell him that I had read "*Der Mann von 50 Jahren*" during the night and had been greatly moved by Hilarie's renunciation. "Yes, yes, I know, you would dearly like to introduce some of that renunciation stuff here, but—" He broke off his banter. My main aim is certainly to dispel all passionate feelings and in this way to atone until I can make things good again. I ink in the score, R. copies, Lusch dictates her letter to her father. — Letter from the Italian Boito, who writes that *Tristan* was a revelation to him, which reminds us that R. had intended his *Tristan* for Italian singers (though naturally not the present ignoramuses). Boito also says that the number of supporters for R. in Italy will continue to grow. (Kietz wrote yesterday that this music would make headway in France, like *homoeopathy* and many other German inventions!) In the evening again played two Haydn symphonies as piano duets. — Worried because Claire does not write to me.

*Saturday, August 7*  Lusch writes to her father, I ink in, R. copies; busy, rainy morning. At midday a letter from the cook in Munich, our things are being put up for sale there. Walk with R. He has had a letter from his sister Cäcilie, who wishes to visit him. We are both unwell, my heart is giving me pain. — After lunch we again play Haydn symphonies. — Read part of the foreword to Grimm's mythology. Also read Goethe's "*Der kluge Rechtsanwalt*"; very charmed by it, I discuss it with R., he says that he has rediscovered something of his Chandala maiden in it. In the evening wrote to Judith and sent off a telegram to Claire.

*Sunday, August 8* Richard very unwell! I in consequence in a mood of abstraction, glad it is Sunday and the children can just be left to play. Embark on Goethe's *Wanderjahre*. Serovs for lunch; he a good independent person, she as ugly as the night, interested in women's emancipation, while only yesterday R. and I were expressing our loathing for this so-called up-to-date rubbish. R. says: "The fact that Mill is for it shows that people today have no idea of even the simplest things, that they do not even know what being a mother means. They understand that in the East; there, where women are supposedly in a subordinate position, the mother is held sacred. The father is there to protect mother and child, that is to say, to take care of the external things; woman has nothing to do with the outside world. Of course she has immeasurable influence, but not by voting and trying to turn herself into a man, which she can never do." I find it impossible to understand how a woman with a child of her own can ever even consider doing anything beyond bringing up this child, in this field she is the indispensable ruler. Worried about Claire's failure to reply to my telegram. — Serov tells me how badly Berlioz spoke about my father in St. Petersburg. I feel almost like laughing over this baseless and superfluous malignancy.

*Monday, August 9* Letter from Claire; she has written to Hans! R. somewhat better. Children's morning. Afterward *Wanderjahre*. In the afternoon the botanist, a poor student who would like to be a naturalist, but now for lack of means is to become a theologian! His father was forced to join the Sonderbund, he was a ribbon maker, and the powers that be said they would not support him if he did not go over to them. Much joy in teaching the children. If I were rich, I should at once help this student to study natural history. Instead of founding [*adjective unreadable*] newspapers, these foolish Liberals should pay a little attention to individual needs; but they just go jogging along in their absurd way.

*Tuesday, August 10* I am unwell, but can see to the children, since Hermine is in bed. Wrote to Claire. Afterward read the *Wanderjahre*. In the evening R. fetches the medicine prescribed for me; on the bottle is written "For Mme Wagner." You see, says R., what state, church, and society are unable to do the apothecary puts right. R. at his copying for the King, about whom nothing is heard and who seems literally to have vanished.

*Wednesday, August 11* This morning, when I told R. that I was looking forward to the Italian translation of *Tristan* and asked whether

he was not, he said, "My pleasures now come from other things."
Unwell, I confine myself to my maternal duties. In the evening I read
in the newspaper that the King is getting Count Pocci to unveil the
Goethe monument he himself commissioned!! Discussion with R.
over whether the King was perhaps frightened off by what happened
between us. Certainly something is now being hatched out against the
King. R.'s last word: I care only about your recovery. R. works
assiduously on his copying.

*Thursday, August 12* Very unwell, the doctor is amazed that with
the weakness of my pulse I can still walk about. I spend the whole
morning lying down, distracting—or, rather, edifying—myself with
the *Wanderjahre*. The botany student here again. Hermine still ill;
in the afternoon I am again on my feet. [*A sentence containing an untranslatable word play omitted.*] Still nothing from Munich, it weighs like a
ton on my heart when I think of it. I was alarmed today when Loulou
told me of a pain in her side.

*Friday, August 13* Day for letters: wrote to Franz Lenbach; R.
receives news from Hermann Brockhaus and from Richter, who
describes the conditions in Munich as ever more horrible. Nothing
happened. R. at his copying. In the evening I read to him in astonishment the passage I found in the *Wanderjahre* concerning drama and
theater. "It does not disturb me," says R., who knows it well. We talk
about memoirs; R. said, "They can only be of value when they give
real facts—Napoleon told lies, it is said." I: "He was a play actor,
and that is why I cannot stand him, a hollow person." R: "When one
thinks that our courts are nothing but imitations of the court of Louis
XIV, which meant something in France in his day, and now all these
little Napoleons can think of is to surround themselves with the same
hocus-pocus! No nobler ambitions, in art only what is most vulgar;
and for that they spend all their money, yes, even spill blood." "One
cannot be angry with the poor German people, they have shed their
blood, have gone through thick and thin, but one can be angry with
its princes, who have so shamefully let it go to seed." An article in
the *A.A.Z.* "from Rome" interests us very much. All I say is: "Writing
articles makes people untruthful; the way the author speaks of Pius IX
is entirely different from the way he would speak of him in conversation, he ennobles him, even though he cannot avoid mentioning
the worthlessness of his plans and the cruelty of his methods. In the
same way you had to idealize Kings Max and Ludwig in your *Art and
Politics*." "You are right," says R., "they are false images, the present
time does not belong to us, one should not attempt to describe it."
In the late evening telegrams; Marie Muchanoff asking for Semper's
address. — "How will Siegfried feel when he one day sees the 3rd

act and learns that I wrote this scene just as he was being born?" [*Placed beside this page is a sheet of musical notation paper written in R.W.'s hand, containing on two lines the excerpt "Heil dem Tage . . ."*]

*Saturday, August 14* At breakfast we again mentioned the sufferings we went through before we came together. This longing for letters, this avidity for news and misery after the letter has been read, the telegrams—God, who can ever have any idea of it, unless he has loved so dreadfully? Arrival of the *Rheingold* pictures, the costumes have turned out somewhat better. In the afternoon Serov, entertaining conversation with him. In the evening overwhelming sense of the felicity of our love. R. maintains he would be nothing without me— O God! *Das Rheingold* to be performed on the 29th.

*Sunday, August 15* Feast of the Assumption. Showed the children Titian's *Assumpta*, then sat with them inking in, family lunch, in the afternoon R. plays me his third act, great emotion. "The kiss of love is the first intimation of death, the cessation of individuality, that is why a person is so terrified by it." In the evening visit from Count Bassenheim, who related to me an anecdote which happened to his father-in-law, Prince Wallerstein: Goethe wished to receive the Order of Saint Hubert, King Ludwig [I] was prepared to give it to him, but on condition that Goethe praised his poems. Goethe was unwilling, and so the King was also unwilling, and the Saint Hubert diamonds remained in the treasury! In the evening children's dance.

*Monday, August 16* In the morning R. still cheerful and well, he is happy and full of comfort and hope, he tells me. We speak about my father. R. says he first found out through him what Bach is. "One really cannot blame the world for being unwilling to accept that his gift of virtuosity was for him only of secondary importance. He was born to it—and what have time and duration to do with it?" "The main thing is that one should be out of the ordinary. In me the accent lies on the conjunction of poet and musician, as a pure musician I would not be of much significance." He adds, "All the world gets is the shell of the oyster, what can it possibly know of the joys of conceiving?" — In the afternoon a note from Judith, from which I see that a letter has got lost. Drove with R. to the Serovs, in the evening read Grimm's fairy tales to the children.

*Tuesday, August 17* Morning with children and *Wanderjahre*. R. exhausted by his work. In the afternoon work with the children. In the evening Richter. Still troubles in Munich. He has to stick by his resignation. Hans is in Kochel. In bed I remember how incapable he is of living in the country (those terrible holidays in Klampenborg!), and the bad weather on top of it. If only his health would improve!

*Wednesday, August 18* Up early; rehearsal with singers. I with the

Serovs in the next room. Overwhelming feelings of great melancholy. Deep awareness that I may no longer look on anything in *this world*. Heavy thoughts of Hans. — R. in the evening in a Falstaffian state, as he says, hoarse from choral singing. Read the *Wanderjahre*. — To the many bright ideas of the Munich theater director belongs the commissioning of a prologue for the reopening of the theater. A prologue for a new stage!! For that reason he has turned down the request of many friends for *Lohengrin*, and instead chooses *Jessonda*! R. telegraphs the King and asks for *Lohengrin* or *Die Meistersinger*.

[*End of the first notebook of the Diaries.*]

*Thursday, August 19* While I am working with the children, a package arrives from Professor Nietzsche: Semper's lecture on architectural styles. Read it with great interest, spoke about it to R. at lunch, both of us regretting we were no longer in touch with Semper. "When somebody has a bad conscience, there is no meanness one cannot expect from him." Mention of the two-faced game played by Semper's son in Munich. In the evening a telegram from the King, he will, "if possible," arrange a performance of *Lohengrin* for his birthday, and he sends greetings to *Will* and *Vorstel*. In the evening I read Semper's pamphlet to R. He is very tired from his copying. After lunch we discussed the present comprehensive letter from Hans. He feels my father must have advised Hans against a divorce. I am willing to bear anything and to await things in patience as long as Hans is not put in torment, but all the same I ask R., too, to keep silent.

*Friday, August 20* Letter from Judith, full of enthusiasm, I reply and ask her to use the occasion of *Das Rheingold* to make known the reasons why R. is staying away from Munich. In the afternoon R.'s sister Frau Avenarius arrives—he has not seen her for 21 years. When I express my pleasure for R.'s sake and ask him whether she has shown him love, he says with a smile, "We don't need love, we only need sincerity." In the evening I read Herwegh's foreword to the translation of *King Lear*, and R. deplores the facetious tone which is nowadays to be found everywhere, to which even Semper, with all his magnificent thoughts, is obliged to submit under the circumstances (a lecture to a mixed public in Zurich about matters which would require a whole book). R. also does not like talk about *"Menschtum"* ["mankind"], and altogether it is a great pity that Semper is now writing instead of building.

*Saturday, August 21* R. has completed his copying; I, concerned about Lusch's health, allow her to run around while I ink in my page of the score. At lunch the Serovs and Herr and Frau Avenarius, neither of the last two very pleasant, he in particular is terribly crude. Serov shows me an article by Mme Mendès which horrifies me. I do not think we shall be able to have much more to do with these people. R. is extremely hurt. In the evening a visit from Professor Nietzsche, very pleasant as always. The King is traveling to Landshut and has been to the exhibition.

*Sunday, August 22* In the morning breakfast with the professor, then with the children into the town, which is hung with flags and bunting for a singing festival. At two, family banquet with the poor student. Afterward music, the third act of *Siegfried*. Confusion concerning the professor's departure. He is staying until tomorrow morning. In the evening a very good letter from Countess Krockow, I reply to it during the night, which puts a great strain on me. She wished to know from me in my own words how things stand, and to describe that in detail cost me my night's rest. When I told Prof. Nietzsche of our experiences in Munich, he said they were truly horrifying. (In the morning R. wrote a beautiful poem for the King.)

*Monday, August 23* Very worn out by the writing in the night, rose mournfully, soon cheered up by R.'s presence. R. writes letters and teaches the children, who are now in my sole charge, since I have sent Hermine to Munich to settle some matters there. At lunch R. talked to me about Timoleon, telling how his brilliant career originated in the death of his brother, in which he was heavily involved; so there again I am presented with a symbol for happiness; amidst all the honors which accrued to him as the result of a long and glorious life of good deeds, the death of his brother must have been like a worm gnawing his heart. In the afternoon a drive with the children. Returned home very tired. To bed at 8 o'clock; downstairs R. had already fallen asleep, when he awoke he said to me, "I was far, far away, but always with you, in sleeping as in waking." — Nice letter from Lenbach.

*Tuesday, August 24* Letter from Marie Muchanoff, she is going to Munich, where she will meet my father, she asks whether I would not see him. This question leads to a conversation with R. from which I learn that he has been forced by a newspaper report to the conclusion that my father dissuaded Hans from his resolve to get a divorce from me! R. is now writing to Marie Muchanoff and giving her an outline of the whole situation, in the hope that she will show this to my father and perhaps cause him to reverse his unfortunate attitude. I also write her a few lines and send her Hans's last letter to me. In the afternoon a visit from Count Bassenheim; while on the Rigi he had seen Prince Georg of Prussia, who had spoken of me a lot—curious how surprised I am by every friendly word said about me! In the evening, after reading Grimm's fairy tales to the children, I receive a telegram from Hermine: "Old lady at home, humiliating reception, turned away from the house." Thus does the good lady avenge herself for the 10 years in which I treated her in such a way that R. was firmly convinced that she did and must love me, and was struck dumb when I once told him, "The woman is just waiting for an opportunity to do me harm." But that she should treat poor Hermine so badly! I write to Anna, so that she can show my remarks to Hans, who may perhaps be told God knows what by his mother. I comfort Hermine with a few words.

*Wednesday, August 25* During the night some distress, not because of the humiliation inflicted on me by Frau von B[ülow], but arising from thoughts about my father and my own situation, which he is making so much worse for me. In the morning a nice letter from Judith Mendès; she is beside herself, the theater director will not let her into rehearsals of *Das Rheingold.* Still the same old game! R. had telegraphed him (very curtly), he reads the text to me, I beg him to let Richter deal with the matter, which he does. I then write to Judith and tell her what my father has done to me, since she asks whether she should visit him. Also wrote to Franz Lenbach, who had replied with a simple expression of sympathy to my description of my situation. Meanwhile R. begins on the instrumentation of Act III. After lunch, with the children to Lulu's piano lesson, then did some botany with them, finally went to meet R. In the evening piano duets, a Mozart symphony and a Beethoven quartet. R. says to me we have time on our side, all we have to do is live long. Recently, when walking to the Lucerne cemetery, I said to him, "I have no wish to die." I have been supplied by Fate with a sorrow, a happiness, an activity—Hans, Richard, the children. The sorrow cannot pass, any more than the happiness can ever be clouded or the activity cease.

*Thursday, August 26* Very friendly letter from Professor Nietzsche, who sends us a lecture on Homer. Again children's day with inking in of score. R. orchestrating. Nothing from outside, thank God, except some articles by Judith Mendès about the exhibition and a letter from G. Herwegh, which astonishes R. particularly, since he had recently been thinking of giving a sign of life to this poor man who has fallen on hard times.

Herwegh is in Munich on account of *Das Rheingold* (R. says it is only the machinery they are all interested in), and R. had intended to invite him here, had not a word in H.'s letter made an unpleasant impression on him—the word *"drähtlich"* ["by wire"]. — At the last flush of sunset R. tells me how well and happy he feels, how his health has been restored and his whole being given new strength, and he says it is all my doing. I feel like going down on my knees to the gods in gratitude and, lest presumption corrupt my soul, I remember the being on whom I had to bring suffering, and in silence from afar I lament with him the grimness of our earthly lot. The happier I am, the more deeply am I aware of the existence of one who is not happy; against this feeling no sensible reasoning, no explanations, not even the consciousness that I could not have done otherwise, can help— or, rather, I do not seek such help, but suffer with him at all times. Read J. Mendès's article again, it is much better than I first thought in my excitement and annoyance at reading about R.'s personality in print. Nietzsche's lecture, on the other hand, excellent. — The midwife came today, and R. said he could never set eyes on her without feeling moved, she was for him a sacred being, since she had stood by me. — Wrote to Prof. Nietzsche.

*Friday, August 27* Dire dreams of persecutions. R. comes and says he will on no account let me go to my father, these people were capable of throwing me into a convent like Barbara Ubri (!!!). My father is now going to see *Rheingold* because he has been officially invited; previously, with *Tristan*, when we asked him to come and everything still gave grounds for hope, he did not wish to. Children's day as always, in the morning work, in the afternoon drive with them to Hergeschwyl; there fed the goats. R. suddenly meets his sister Frau Brockhaus, her family was on its way to Lucerne and wanted to visit him, he invites them for lunch tomorrow. — At lunch R. said to me, "The kiss of love and the procreation of a child is a *Kalpa*"; then, too: "In the newborn child, which does not remain what it was in the mother's womb, one can clearly perceive the *idea*; all states of becoming and being are nothing, the idea originating in the mother's womb is everything." As I come to the table, he reads me an Indian proverb: "You can attain the end of the world and the summits of mountains, but the thought of a king has never been attainable, not to a single soul." — I was reading some dates concerning Frederick the Great in the encyclopedia, and there I learned that, when bidden by his father to renounce the throne, he replied, "At once, if my father tells me I am not his true son." How great, how true to type! I am worried, Hermine is silent, Claire is silent, Hans does not write to his daughter, but I bury it all away, so that life here may remain pure and free, my children well, Richard active and content, I will bear my sorrow in silence to the end of my days.

*Saturday, August 28* After I had written this, Richard [*C. W. wrote "Hans" by mistake*] brought me a letter from the cook in Munich, saying that Hans had gone away, despondent and sad, without saying where. Terrible grief overcomes me, or, rather, bursts forth. I sob, completely possessed by the thought that my true duty would be to die. I remember being told by the botanist that a plant (spurge) would kill a person if he put its poison in an open wound. Continual brooding —oh, children, my children, remember your mother's words, no suffering is so hard to bear as the wrong we do, remember these words, wrought from pain in the most painful of hours! Sobbed the whole morning, uncontrollably. R. very concerned. At midday the Brockhaus family and Prof. Nietzsche, all very kind. I elsewhere. In the afternoon a letter from Judith, she tells me that my father wishes to settle my affairs for me, that he loves me, that Hans has gone away to expedite the matter. The letter did me infinite good, I began to breathe again. Then came telegram after telegram and letter after letter, all reporting that the dress rehearsal of *Das Rheingold* had been appalling, ridiculous to the highest degree, and that stupidity had joined hands with malice to ruin everything. R. telegraphs the King and asks for a postponement. — Late in the evening I write to Judith and Hermine (who has also written).

*Sunday, August 29* R. ill with grief about *Das Rheingold*. The telegrams continue: (1) The King—sends thanks for his birthday gift, otherwise nothing! (2) Richter announces his decision not to conduct. (3) Loën, the Weimar theater director, now in Munich, asks whether his conductor Lassen may take over, Perfall is demanding it. R. telegraphs a bravo to Richter, to Düfflipp a demand to put right all the deficiencies, to Loën saying no. In the evening news from Richter, he has really been suspended! In between all this Prof. Nietzsche; always pleasant. Gloomy day, what will come of this affair? The King's behavior puzzling. Very little with the children today and yesterday, which grieves me.

*Monday, August 30* R. writes to the King, explains the position to him, and suggests that he go to Munich, to make possible a good performance by Sunday. In the afternoon telegram from Düffl. (see the documents). Richard decides to make the journey. Great anxiety over this decision; R. says he knows he will return home fit; the reason why he was so ill following *Die Msinger* was not his vexation, but our separation.

*Tuesday, August 31* R. teases me because, even though this is the morning of his departure, I still give Loulou a piano lesson, "in youth love goes under!" In the morning visit from his sister Frau Avenarius; at midday letter from the stage director Hallwachs, giving a hopeless account of it all. We consider the possibility of a break with the King if he insists on the performance on Thursday. At 4 o'clock telegram from the King, he expects the performance on Sunday. Seeing R. off, great melancholy, but pleased that the King had listened to him. Journey home alone, R. has gone. I write to Claire, then *Wanderjahre*, finally wrote to R.

*Wednesday, September 1* Breakfast and all else with the children, in the afternoon telegram from R., he is well, the situation, however, uncertain. I write to him in the evening. — During the day just a serious word to Loulou; since she tells me she would like to go on the stage and sing, I describe to her in glaring colors how awful this profession is.

*Thursday, September 2* Industrious morning with the children, the botanist here. At midday visit from Professor Hermann Brockhaus, a nice little chat. Letters from Hermine and the head of the Marienanstalt. Hermine has seen my father, who is still well disposed toward me. At 4 o'clock surprise and joy: R. announces his return this evening. With the 4 children and the 2 dogs to fetch him; *Rheingold* impossible, the return of Richter to the conductor's desk would be the signal for the resumption of the old witch hunt against us and the King; and besides this the staging of the work is so abominable that the machinist is demanding three months to put it right. But the whole world is said to be in Munich. — Judith sends me a warning against Marie Muchanoff, I regret the confidences I made to the latter. R. well, he is only too glad to be here again!

*Friday, September 3* R. telegraphs the King, begs him to cancel the performance, so that the decision will at least come from him. News that the singer Betz has left Munich so as not to have to sing Wotan in such circumstances. R. writes to Düfflipp. What will come of all this? . . . Letter from Hermine, my father has told her Hans is in Berlin; I reply to her. Calmly as I accept all this news, my heart is nevertheless heavy! The warning against Marie Muchanoff also makes me anxious, she has Hans's letter to me, I sent it to her for my father's sake, but is she worthy of this confidence? — To town with the children and R., in the evening conversation about Bernhard von Weimar and Gustavus Adolphus, whom R. much reveres. — My heart is apprehensive, as in the face of a great disaster. "Woe on our mortal lot!" —

*Saturday, September 4* In the morning letter from Herr Schäfer (friend of Richter's with whom R. stayed), Betz, the singer of Wotan, has gone, does not wish to sing in these circumstances; that does not really worry the theater director, he gives the bass singer's role to the tenor Vogl, some musician or other will conduct, and so everything is all right. At the same time R. received a letter from his brother Albert Wagner, who at the end of his life can write nothing beyond a recommendation of a female singer! Letter from Hermine (a few more things about my father). To put my fears at rest, R. writes to Marie Muchanoff and asks for the return of Hans's letter. After lunch inspection of Siegfried's eye trouble makes me consider what a completely different fate is conferred in a moral sense on a person born blind, how much more purely he must be able to perceive truth through not seeing reality! All forms of temptation and deception must remain strangers to him. Great melancholy in the evening, life and the world horrify me ever more and more. Played duets with R., a Beethoven quartet.

*Sunday, September 5* Sent the two elder children to church, spent the morning with the two young ones. R. writes to Judith and to Schäfer and orchestrates. Family lunch, and afterward drive to the Alpine wildlife museum. In the evening read *Don Quixote*. Nothing from outside; only in the *A.A.Z.* reports that an intrigue against Perfall is the reason for the nonperformance of *Das Rheingold*, and that because of all the feeling against him in Munich, R. had to leave the city!!!

*Monday, September 6* Siegfried 3 months old today! Letter from Dr. Hallwachs on Hans's behalf, the petition has been filed, within two months I shall probably be divorced. Mood of solemnity. Botanist and children. Then a right worthy woman from Appenzell in her gay national costume sells me bits of embroidery (the nut-brown maid!). After lunch letter from Marie Muchanoff, she at last returns the letter from Hans and is coming here the day after next. Feeling of embarrassment, we have nothing to do with this world, however friendly it may be, and the confidence I placed in her weighs doubly on my heart. She also says my father was touched that I wanted to see him, "but does not wish to create a stir just now." As if I had either demanded or desired such a thing!! R. also annoyed by this. We drive to the Bassenheims' to report her coming. Terrible thunderstorm. R. returns home alone, I play and read with the children. When I come down, I look for R., he had fallen asleep after bitterly weeping—weeping about the King! We hear nothing about *Das Rheingold*. How can I console him? To weep with him is all I can do! Our mood is melancholy, we play piano duets, that restores our spirits. Only at the conclusion of the evening R.'s purchase of a baby carriage for Siegfried makes me concerned over our future existence, since R. is quite unable to save money. My concern annoys him, and he is right, I should have kept silent, for it is only with words of love that one helps, not with anxious talk.

*Tuesday, September 7* Letter from Judith, very nice and affectionate, reply to her at once. For R. a letter from Peter Cornelius, who also now intends to leave the music school; that pleases us, for we had assumed that P. C. was not at all interested in our sufferings. Richard takes the opportunity of writing to Düfflipp and describing the whole situation to him. — Beautiful autumn day which fills me with tranquillity, but unfortunately R. is not well, the letter and above all the remembrance of all our experiences are downright destroying him. He also finds Marie Muchanoff's visit very distasteful. He goes out for a walk, I remain at home with the children, Siegfried's new carriage arrives, great excitement among the children, go to meet R., he is unwell. Very quiet evening, he tells me about his uncle Adolph, whose memory is very precious to him. At supper he was overcome with great ill humor about the wretchedness of the world! If only he could get back to his work tomorrow!

*Wednesday, September 8* Lovely summer days still, the children lively out of doors. Visit from Countess Bassenheim in the morning; R. somewhat better, writes letters (to P[eter] C[ornelius], Schuré, Richter). Nothing at all happened today, Marie Muchanoff did not come. At times feelings of hope that Hans's life might take a turn for the better, but then once more melancholy thoughts. Delight in Siegfried.

*Thursday, September 9* Botanical walk, then inked in score beside the cradle, Siegfried in two versions before me. After lunch in the garden with R. and "Fidi" [Siegfried]; talked and talked about the child, what should we wish for him—earnestness, cheerfulness, a poetic spirit? R. tells me much about Bernhard von Weimar's heroism. — Letter to R. from Judith, *Rheingold* postponed, may later be performed for the King alone. Went for a drive with the children, encountered Countess Bassenheim at the railroad station, waiting in vain for Marie M. In the end a letter from Marie saying she is coming tomorrow to discuss important matters with me. Stupid, tiresome interference! — Fine evening, R. comes home cheerful, he says he always returns happy and gay, now that he knows I am in the house. — Emperor Louis Napoleon appears to be very ill, R. thinks he is on his deathbed.

*Friday, September 10* After parting from me yesterday evening in a very cheerful mood, R. comes up to my room in the morning looking most despondent; it is reported in the newspaper that *Das Rheingold* is now really to be performed within the next fortnight. When we had read in the newspapers that R. had been put off *"ad calendas Graecas"* we had breathed again, thinking the King had come to his senses at last—and now it is to be done after all! Grief over the King's behavior, rather than the sacrifice of his work, is making R. quite ill. I draft a letter to the King, but R. does not wish it to be sent, he feels he has already said enough. Mood of great sadness. Letter from Professor Nietzsche, who reports that all newspapers are full of infamous accounts, talking of a complete break between W. and the King, etc. He asks for news, which I then give him. Late in the afternoon Richter arrives. *Das Rheingold* is to be done in a fortnight, with all the roles changed; the singer R. rehearsed for *Loge* is to sing *Mime*, the orchestra has been reduced, etc., etc. The theater director is bribing newspapers on all sides, and now everyone is happily spreading lies. The members of the orchestra are much put out by all this and by the fact that they are to be directed by the most incapable of all conductors. But the wretches are within their rights. In the evening I am vexed by a day spent without any children's lessons. We discuss with R. the fact that he can only be silent, that his works belong to the King, and if the latter wishes to use them as mere toys, R. can do nothing to stop him, and there is absolutely nowhere one can look for support.

*Saturday, September 11* Contrary to his decision of yesterday, R. produces in the morning a letter to the conductor that horrifies me; I should have preferred him not to send it, but it does him good, for bearing things in silence gnaws at his heart. Worked with the children early in the morning, but then a gathering at Tribschen of Marie Muchanoff, Fräulein Holmès (poetess, composer, etc.), and others besides. The former pains me with various things she tells me about Hans. At midday a very affectionate letter from Countess Krockow, which also affects me, since it concerns my fate. In the afternoon the Brockhaus family, later the Holmèses, father and daughter, and thus till late in the night. Very un-Tribschen-like!

*Sunday, September 12* Letter from Claire, with it letter from Düfflipp, nothing really but the same old refrain, the King should not be dragged into it, etc., etc. Richard writes, making another proposal: Eberle as conductor and singers, etc., etc. Meanwhile, together with Richter, I draft a factual account of the situation. I am interrupted by Marie Muchanoff and Countess Bassenheim. Lively conversation, but no pleasure in it. R. is ill. Family lunch, rather quiet. With regard to the French, R. says jokingly, "We shall have to do it like Bernhard von Weimar—promote the German cause with French financial help." After lunch the *A.A.Z.*, with a shameful article about our affairs and ourselves personally. The poor wretches! But it is so sad that R. has been utterly deprived both of his beautiful peace and his spirits, and that his health is badly affected. Much discussion of our sad dilemma. Really, how wretched these people are! Saying good night to the children, a lot of fun; they play "dreams," and Boni is especially comical. When shall we return to our Tribschen peace?

*Monday, September 13* R. comes up and says he has it in mind to reply to the article in yesterday's *A.A.Z.*, and in fact he drafts out his reply in the morning, while I botanize with the children and work. Before lunch visit Frl. Holmès; on my return R. reads me his fine piece. Afterward visit from Frl. Holmès, later arrival of the Mendèses! Much pleasure again in Judith. Catulle tells me that in consequence of an article by Herr Schelle in the *Neue Freie Presse*, in which his wife is mentioned in an unbecoming way, he wrote this gentleman a letter in which he addressed him as a cowardly and ill-bred rascal and at the same time mentioned where he was to be found. I tell him that this choice gentleman will certainly not present himself. (A spider has just run across my book, "bringing delight at night"—may it delight poor Hans!) — R. is so tired that he can do no more than quickly greet all these good people. We then drink our tea together, just he and I, we are glad that he has written this article. — Hermine has returned.

*Tuesday, September 14* Richter has left for Paris. R. goes to visit Marie Muchanoff and the Mendèses. In the evening the Mendèses and the Holmèses. Judith still very dear to me. Babli [Siegfried's nurse] has left.

*Wednesday, September 15* Looked after Siegfried during the night with pleasure and solicitude. The fine weather is a help to the nursing. Long visit from Marie Muchanoff, thoroughly pleasant. She tells me that people blame the Jewish pamphlet on me, etc. Nice people! At lunch R. tells me with great concern that our Fritz has grazed his leg terribly. In the evening the Mendèses again. (Loldi to Hermine: "I was poor when you were away.")

*Thursday, September 16* Still looking after Siegfried. — Yesterday a letter came from Italy, *Lohengrin* is to be performed in Bologna, and an Italian newspaper wants to start doing publicity there. — At midday R. reads me a note in the *A.A.Z.*, which states that R.'s reply is so vehement that they hesitate to print it. We immediately guess that this is aimed at getting an order from the King to suppress the article. Great annoyance. What to do? Not a single weapon in our hands. R. very downcast. Visit from Schott (his publisher), then M. Muchanoff; I read her the *Parzival* draft. In the evening the Mendèses. Uneasy conversation, but afterward the third act of *Siegfried*.

*Friday, September 17* A good day! In the morning a telegram that announces that the article has been printed after all! It looks splendid. Farewell visit to Marie Muchanoff; she is kind and friendly. In the afternoon the Mendèses and Schotts, till late in the evening; they play charades. A friendly, cheerful gathering, my children like heralds of peace, R. in good spirits. With the article the last word has been spoken to the outside world.

*Saturday, September 18* Tired from looking after Siegfried through the night. Letter from a Herr Schäfer, who has drafted a very stupid statement for Richter. Unfortunately one's friends are rarely of much help. I write to Claire and Rothschild. R. still busy with Bernhard von Weimar. In the evening visit from Professor Nietzsche, who tells me of the most licentious things in the newspapers. Among much else it is asserted that the performance of *Das Rheingold* is connected with a plot whose strings can be sought in the Tuileries. W. is said to have made an alliance with the Catholic party; the proof: Frau von Muchanoff, whose daughter is a radical supporter of the Catholics, and so on—all this rubbish is screamed across the world in order to prevent people's recognizing the incompetence of the theater management with regard to *Das Rheingold.*

*Sunday, September 19*   Coffee with Prof. Nietzsche; unfortunately he vexes R. very much with an oath he has sworn not to eat meat, but only vegetables. R. considers this nonsense, arrogance as well, and when the Prof. says it is morally important not to eat animals, etc., R. replies that our whole existence is a compromise, which we can only expiate by producing some good. One cannot do that just by drinking milk—better, then, to become an ascetic. To do good in our climate we need good nourishment, and so on. Since the Prof. admits that Richard is right, yet nevertheless sticks to his abstinence, R. becomes angry. In the afternoon played with the children, lotto and dominoes. Very early to bed, being very tired. From outside all kinds of nonsense, conductors and theater directors offering their services. Nobody can really grasp what we are after.

*Monday, September 20*   Still Fidi-night and Fidi-morning. Dreamed that Hans had died, great melancholy. Yesterday R. told me a delightful dream he had had: he was walking with me across a bridge and advised me to go slowly, but I was careless and fell into the water, and yet I only got wet, which made R. say to himself, I shall always take shoes and stockings with me; then he suddenly heard the Siegfried theme, slightly varied, on a child's trumpet, and he was pleased that I had taught it to Siegfried. Then he woke up, and it was the soft cooing of the baby at the first crowing of Giölnir (that is what we call our tiny cock) which had brought it all about. — The botanist this morning, I gave him a copy of Goethe's *Wahrheit und Dichtung* along with his fee. — In the *A.A.Z.* two very ridiculous statements by Baron Perfall and Herr Julius Grosse (author of that recent choice article). In the afternoon visit from Herbeck, the conductor, concerning *Die Msinger,* which is shortly to be performed in Vienna. He asks R. whether something was cut in his reply to the *A.A.Z.,* for he could not otherwise understand the newspaper's preliminary remark about it. R. tells him that two acts of malice had here canceled each other out: when the editors saw the calmness of his reply, they had hoped for an order not to print the article; those in the Cabinet, on the other hand, had been glad that R. had allowed himself to be provoked, and had ordered it to be printed—in such ways is justice sometimes furthered. The extent to which people are interested in the *Rheingold* affair is demonstrated by the fact that the *Luzerner Tagblatt* publishes two articles about it—the first, to which the paper gives editorial support, is disgraceful, the second tolerable. — Wrote to Countess Krockow.

*Tuesday, September 21* In the morning argument with R. about the one point on which our opinions still differ; he feels the urge to spare me many things by concealing them; I am firmly in favor of being told all things good and bad. Report from the stage director Hallwachs that I am soon to be summoned to Berlin. Worry about Siegfried, who at first would not take his bottle, but calm soon restored. The whole day from early till late with the children—the weather is bad. Cheerful letter from Peter Cornelius; it seems that R.'s statement has after all been of great benefit to all the weaklings. Letter to me from Lenbach. Early to bed, to make up a little for the Siegfried-nights.

*Wednesday, September 22* In the night R. came to me, sat down beside me, and softly said, "You are everything to me"—I thought I was dreaming. Dull, cold day, work with the children. In the afternoon Loulou's piano lesson, in connection with which a visit to Countess Bassenheim, whom I like more and more each time. In the evening R. unfortunately unwell.

*Thursday, September 23* Semper's theater in Dresden completely burned down. This made me think of Semper's unlucky star. His great genius virtually unemployed, his works destroyed! — Following this news we receive two telegrams reporting the performance of *Das Rheingold* in Munich. So there it is—it is always the wicked who triumph. My only consolation is R.'s words: "I have the feeling that none of it really affects me, inside I remain unscathed; only when I am not in complete harmony with you does the ground tremble beneath me." — My melancholy impressions are increased by the unpacking of my Munich things. I shall remain sad to the end! In the evening a letter from Claire—Maman has again become insane! . . . Friendly letter from Judith. —

*Friday, September 24* The *A.A.Z.* reports a *succès d'estime* for *Das Rheingold*; the work is quite happily sacrificed, but the honor of the machinists, costume designer, director, etc., is saved—on paper, at any rate. I said to R. that Semper's theater had gone up in flames in indignation. — Striking sign of the way things are going in the world: Father Hyacinth, long persecuted by the Jesuits, has issued a protest against the whole Roman hierarchy. Very moving and significant. R. says the Pope is in the hands of the Jesuits, because they bring in the money. Antonelli cannot raise money and for that reason no longer has much say in things. — Fine letter from Heinrich Porges about *Das Rheingold*. Spent the whole day arranging furniture. Great tiredness. Fine autumn day, the mountains glisten with snow. Wrote to Claire and Judith. In the evening played a Beethoven quartet. When R. today visited his bookseller, the latter said to him, "You must certainly have already received your biography from Nohl, I sold out my copies (4) at once." We knew nothing about it. — In the evening great melancholy about life, we weep gently together, and, when he is gone, I have to continue weeping bitterly.

*Saturday, September 25* Finished my letter to Judith in the early morning in brilliant sunshine. R. comes and says, laughing, "Perfall has now been confirmed as theater director!" Such is the way of the world, fortunate is he who no longer has anything to do with it. After lunch with Lusch to her piano lesson and then made purchases for her birthday. In the evening a visit from Prince Georg of Prussia, to whom I present R.

*Sunday, September 26* Lovely day; with Richard to the star dance— that is what we call the play of the sun on the lake. Wrote to Marie M., from whom I yesterday received a report of the *Rheingold* performance in Munich! In the afternoon a letter from the producer Hall-wachs, who has been directed by Darmstadt to ask R. whether he would allow *Das Rheingold* to be performed elsewhere and under what conditions. R. intends to authorize this (to restore the honor of his work, which was mutilated in Munich) if the performance is a truly exemplary one. — Fine sunny afternoon in the garden. R. looked up with delight into the tree and told me that in his loneliness he had often looked up at it and always seen me as the blue of Heaven. In the morning, by summoning up all his energies, he managed to complete another page of his score. In the evening he brings me a copy of *Kladderadatsch*; it is the only paper which has depicted the events in Munich in a decently humorous manner ("Adonai's Revenge against Wotan"). In the evening a quartet (Beethoven).

*Monday, September 27* Lovely day, finest blessings of autumn, I can work with the children in the garden. R. writes to Darmstadt and Kassel (about *Rienzi*). In the morning a visit from Prince Georg; very well meaning, but scant! In the evening more about *Das Rheingold* in the newspaper—that it is a lavishly decorated, boring work! Letter from Peter Cornelius, birth of his daughter, and great depression over the situation in Munich. In the evening a long conversation with R. about whether, without saying a word, he should stop drawing his allowance. Or think only of the completion of the *Nibelungen* and give up the fight. I tell him to do what best accords with his inner feelings, with no thought for the possible consequences. Gnawing worry for R.—is he now to sacrifice all his works in this way? Deep melancholy; he says if I were not there it would be the end of him! — It was my name day today, he gave me flowers, also my father sent a telegram from Rome! — I can only keep silent.

*Tuesday, September 28* Nothing from outside. R. drafts a letter to Düffl., which he then discards. Always the question, to be or not to be. I ink in the score and work with the children. In the afternoon go for a drive with them. R. returns home upset, he has again seen an animal being tormented, which angers and distresses him. "The worst—and in some respects the ugliest—animal of all is the human being." We dip a little into Prince Georg's plays—very childish stuff. Beethoven quartets—indescribable delight! —

*Wednesday, September 29* Received Nohl's biography of R.! Nothing but trivialities. R. writes during the morning to P. Cornelius, I to Prof. Nietzsche about the portrait of Uncle Adolph. Occupied with the children as always. At lunch, in connection with a frightful murder case (a man has killed a whole family of 8 persons), R. speaks of the need for the death penalty. But it must be carried out in an entirely different way, he says—"not with that certain coy elegance." All the shops in the town should be closed, the public buildings draped in black, the judge in charge should accompany the criminal to the scaffold, the execution be in private; but the world must be reminded that a terrible fate has befallen it when one of its members has to be deprived of his life. People who are against the death penalty have no idea of the state of things, do not know what the world really consists of. Afternoon in the garden, R. goes for a walk, I practice the quartet. In the evening he brings me a letter from Prof. Nietzsche. The latter sends me a newspaper in which are printed quotations from R.'s correspondence with a "very dear" friend. Who this last is, is not stated, and I cannot guess. But this fresh piece of shamelessness horrifies me. In the evening I write to Prof. N., asking him to make known by means of an advertisement that R. knows nothing of this piece of impertinence. I say nothing to R. about it. Yesterday when he came home he called me his delight, and said I had no idea how happy he was.

*Thursday, September 30* In the night, before I dropped off to sleep, there came into my mind all my love for R. and what I owe to him. In the morning botany, then other work with the children. R. appears to be sketching out *Götterdämmerung.* In the afternoon R. startles me by informing me that *Kladderadatsch* has now referred to me, too, and dealt with me in a vulgarly malicious way. (*Cosima fan tutte.*) I had always maintained to him that *Kl.* would pass over things in silence, since Dohm was a decent man. R. says I can now see how impossible it is for a person to remain decent when he happens to be a journalist. In the evening a quartet. On going to bed, very dismal thoughts about Hans, deep melancholy. If people knew how I felt, would they have the heart to drag me through the mud?

*Friday, October 1* Letter from Prince Georg, sending another drama by himself. Attending to Siegfried. "But, Fidi," I say, "you would do better to stay here indoors." "Yes, there speaks the sage," R. observes, "but the know-it-all was there before the sage, and he wants to get to know everything the sage so regrets knowing." R. is still not very well. In the evening he brings a letter from Pasdeloup which sounds very gloomy. He is ill and business is not good! We discuss how impossible it is for R. to undertake anything outside. The world is closed to him; all his success still rests on the assumption that he is a composer of operas. But he is not that at all—hence the constant misunderstandings. We discuss the possibility of a journey to America, should the King withdraw his allowance. God knows what the future holds for us. — Beethoven quartet as a piano duet. —

*Saturday, October 2* It says in the newspaper that public demand for *Das Rheingold* has already begun to fall off!! R. in the morning in melancholy mood, but recovered himself in the course of it so much that at midday he could tell me, "I have something for you, something has arrived"—and then he showed me the beginning of the Norns' scene. At lunch he suddenly says to me: "No one in this world has proved his courage to me except you. People should at least show respect for that." I have to reply that I never possessed courage, but only love, which I still have. I know, alas, only too well how slight my strength is! — In the evening a letter from Claire; always only sad news of my mother. In the evening quartets with R.

*Sunday, October 3* A bad night, Siegfried awake every two hours; bore this slight torment with pleasure, how willing I am to suffer in order to earn my happiness and atone for the guilt of my existence! In the morning a visit from Countess Bassenheim, who much to my delight pleases R. greatly with her cordiality and her wit. Lunch with the children, then games with them. Siegfried well again. Wrote a letter to Claire. In the evening arrival of M. Schuré.

*Monday, October 4* Bad night with Siegfried, and R. still unwell. The expected letter does not arrive from Munich, so we assume the King is after all stopping the allowance. R. speaks to Schuré about our affairs and finds his outlook admirably sound. (Botanist.) After lunch I talk to Sch[uré] about the whole anomaly of R.'s coming into the world in our days. He should by rights have graced the world in Aeschylus's age; now, to clear up the insoluble misunderstanding between himself and the world, he relies on occasional explanations, and the more he talks, the wider the gap becomes. The theater of his thinking is a temple and the present theater a fairground stall, he speaks the language of the priest, and shopkeepers are supposed to understand him! I have to dedicate my whole life to him, for I have recognized his position. — In the morning he plays parts of the first act of *Siegfried.*

*Tuesday and Wednesday, October 5 and 6* Days devoted to our visitor; each morning some music from *Siegfried.* In the afternoon a walk; in the evening, reading. Have made the acquaintance of Lichtenberg, great delectation. From the outside world a letter from Judith and at last the expected letter from Mrazek. (Restless nights with Siegfried.)

*Thursday, October 7* Birth of the 2nd Stocker child. I assist Vreneli and am terribly moved by the sight of a creature coming into the world. Why are we so badly told in our youth what the world and life are like? — Letter from the maid in Munich, I receive some money from the sale and hear that Hans is on his way to Italy. I cannot hear his name mentioned without trembling in my heart. — I write to Judith and am afterward so tired that I have to spend the whole day in bed. This greatly affects R., and he reproves me for not sufficiently looking after myself. I should not tend Siegfried during the night, he says— but I feel I must and can do this. — Our mood, viewed from without, is a completely hopeless one. —

*Friday, October 8* Much time with Vreneli, and then with the children. R. orchestrates a page of his *Siegfried.* After lunch the arrival of the birds he is presenting to Loulou gives us much, much delight. Unfortunately R. returns home from his walk in a bad humor, and in connection with a letter from Claire he calls me to account in a manner which soon arouses angry impatience in me, for I know quite well that I have never failed him in anything and have guarded his honor more jealously than my own. This impatience, so foreign to my nature, upsets me terribly, and as I write this, my whole body is trembling and quaking, and I feel torn to pieces.

*Saturday, October 9* Of course R. realized that he had been unjust to me, and I that his irritability was only the result of the unpleasant impression Claire's letter had made on him (she urges me to be cautious about my marriage contract!). We have to fall into each other's arms without explanations—for anything which serves in the least to separate us is nonsense and madness. He does some orchestrating, I work with the children and nurse Fidi. After lunch, christening of the little Bernhard Stocker, the children to the church, I remain at home, for it would not be fitting for me to enter a church just now. In the evening R. reads me *Don Quixote.*

*Sunday, October 10* Quiet morning; we discuss peacefully and in detail the question which recently so upset us, and I write to Claire, asking her to attend to my little bit of business, namely to obtain for me the 40,000 francs my mother owes me, so that I can set it aside in an insurance company for the two elder children. Lunch with the children, with a christening cake. Then took a walk with R. to the little chapel; at the same time a farewell to Nature, everything is yellow, the sky overcast, the air, however, mild. We talk about Schopenhauer's rage against the veneration of women, and R. says laughingly that he can just imagine how he felt, with all his youthful passion and the problems occupying him, having to listen to all the intellectual chatter in his mother's home, knowing that his whole fortune was being dissipated on these junkets and he would have to write for money. There is a letter from Nau in the *Musikalische Zeitung* which displeases R. greatly; he thanks the pupils of the music school and at the same time praises all his fellow teachers, Perfall, etc., though he has repeatedly written here to say that everything is thoroughly wretched and bad. Now in Heaven's name—!

*Monday, October 11* Nothing to report on this day except preparations for Lulu's birthday. Telegrams from Herbeck that *Die Msinger* is in full swing in Vienna. Still great tiredness, I sleep almost the whole afternoon, in the evening *Don Quixote*.

*Tuesday, October 12* Lulu nine years old! Grand presentation of gifts—birds, a dress, all sorts of things; she is overjoyed. Children's party with puppet show (me!) and dancing. R. saddens me by claiming to have established through small, unimportant incidents that it would be better not to bring little girls together with boys. I almost reproach myself for having brought into his house as much disturbance as today, and intend to celebrate future birthdays in a different way. It also makes me melancholy that Hans did not send his child a greeting.

*Wednesday, October 13* Very cold, also despondent mood, because Fidi's rash continues to get worse. After lunch, with Lusch on foot to Countess Bassenheim's, also returned home on foot by moonlight. In the evening *Don Quixote*, which seems to us ever more splendid.

*Thursday, October 14* Raining heavily; a fire in the fireplace since early morning. R. has received an infinitely polite letter from Dingelstedt, telling him how pleased he is with *Die Msinger*! "It is incredible," R. says, "what such people will swallow—when one thinks of that note in the Jewish pamphlet!" In the afternoon a letter from Claire, saying I shall probably not get my little bit of capital! Arrival of a picture of Beethoven—a present from the King of Bavaria. R. put in a very bad mood by it; first, his behavior, and then this unusable gift. In the evening *Don Quixote*.

*Friday, October 15* Wretched night, since Siegfried woke up every two hours. Letter to Loulou from Aunt Isa, which filled me with melancholy, but also pleased me very much, since Loulou is so happy about it. I let her reply to it at once. With the children almost exclusively,

since I am sending the two maids to the theater. In the evening R.
brings back from his walk a Beethoven autograph, which young
Servais has presented to him, and a touching document from a former
musician in Saxony, who now for reasons of penury has become a
trimmings embroiderer; on this document, surrounded by ivy and
laurels, are inscribed all R.'s works up to *Judaism in Music*. R. is very
touched by this. Unfortunately a letter from Schuré has deeply upset
him. There are great difficulties regarding Siegfried's christening and
legalization, indeed it is virtually impossible for R. to give him his
name. — (Botanist.)

*Saturday, October 16* Very wretched night with Siegfried, who is
much plagued by his rash. I and R. in very melancholy mood. The
children to their lesson. I to meet them. Fine, warm moonlight, the
coloring almost southern. In the evening *Don Quixote*. We see how
unsatisfactorily one reads in one's youth and how superficially the
second part has been judged. R. says he would like a room expressly
devoted to honoring every single genius such as Cervantes. R. remarks
how C.'s genius creates exactly like Nature, and he and Shakespeare
belong among the poets in whom, as in Homer, one does not notice
the art, while (for example) the Greek tragedies, Schiller, Calderón,
seem like high priests, constructing their forms, as it were, out of a
thought. The figure of Don Q. is a counterpart of Hamlet, he says,
in regard to the mixture of the sublime with the ridiculous. And
everything always human. In this figure Cervantes has depicted himself,
he must often have felt like that in relation to the outside world, and
his glorious humanity (e.g., his judgment on the knights of the Court)
resembles the manner in which C. himself speaks about the poets of
the same period. What is striking about the second part is the development of the characters. Sancho has become a different person, yet
remains the same, he has gone on to personify the poet himself. He
sees everything, everything interests him, when D. Q. enters Don
Diego's house, the writer observes that it was above all the stillness of
it which pleased him. At supper we talk about Shakespeare's unknown
fate, R. believes that he wrote a good number of his plays after his
retirement to Stratford. Concerning Falconbridge and Edmund, those
two love children: I say that this cannot be discerned in Edmund, but
R. says it can—all regular relationships fall by the wayside, here we
see strife between father and daughter and there between father and
son, while in him Nature shows its power, having produced this one
resolute being. — Coming back to *D. Q.*, R. says that Goethe created
something similar in *Werther*, that is to say, a book in which one is not
conscious of the art behind it. When Cervantes tries to be an artist,
he turns into an academician, conventional—his genius is absolutely

unconscious, like an elemental force. Today he said much more in this manner, always divine, unique.

*Sunday, October 17* Lusch writes to her aunt; afterward family lunch. Wretched weather, all day keeping the children amused. I had a sad dream that my elder children caused me deep worry and that I saw Hans again, and he was so sad. Never again can I become like that! (In the evening *Don Quixote*.)

*Monday, October 18* Again wretched weather, the children in the garden; R. and I thinking only of our love. Letter from Prof. Nietzsche (very nice). After lunch the student, with whom we are starting on some geology. In town we miss R., each running in search of the other, in the end I hear the first theme of the 9th Symphony being whistled.

*Tuesday, October 19* Wretched nights, Siegfried's rash is worrying us very much. Lulu writes to her grandpapa on his birthday. I reply to Prof. Nietzsche. Visit from Frau Am Rhyn. After lunch very unwell, but with the children to meet R., who returns home from town in very despondent mood, having discovered in *Kladderadatsch* a terrible picture of the King, in which wicked things are suggested of him. I very unwell in the evening, so that we are not capable even of reading *Don Quixote*. (On Sunday R. sent Herr Servais a leaf for his album— concluding canon of Siegfried and Brünnhilde.)

*Wednesday, October 20* Wretched night, great concern over Siegfried, whose rash gets worse and worse. Worked with the children. R. working on his score. Our patience is being sorely tried by the fact that we hear nothing about the divorce, we decide to regard this present time as the acme of happiness and to await nothing from outside with impatience. R. asks me only not to tire myself out so much with teaching and tending the children—he says he knows I desire to purchase our happiness through self-sacrifice, but this upsets and pains him. In the afternoon with Lusch to her piano lesson at Countess Bassenheim's. — In the evening *D. Q.*, the wedding of Camacho. R. on Cervantes: "Certainly he is depicting himself in D. Q., thus playing around with himself and his fate." Letter from Judith.

*Thursday, October 21* Siegfried still unwell; wretched night. Morning with children; R. orchestrating but, he says, without pleasure. After lunch walk with the children, Loldi trouble, children's tea. In the evening Siegfried trouble.

*Friday, October 22* Father's birthday; sent him a telegram. First good night for a long time; Fidi slept from 11 to 6. R. unfortunately still rather unwell, but he keeps on working and seeks to help himself over it with a long walk. Much fun with the children in the evening, R. lifts them high into the air, carries them on his back like Henry IV, etc. In the evening *Don Quixote* (the cave of Montesinos, absolutely splendid). Great excitement in Switzerland over a book by the cantonal president about the instructional book used by the Jesuits in the seminary at Solothurn. It is certainly unbelievable!

*Saturday, October 23* R. not well and Fidi again restless. World history with Lulu and pleased how quickly she learns (a gift certainly inherited from her father). Very nice letter from Marie Muchanoff, she says that everything in Munich is in a state of complete confusion, that Wüllner cannot conduct *Le Postillon*, and so on. R. says jokingly he is glad, for if one had to assume that things are after all going well, that would be too bad. There is talk of closing down the school. In the afternoon with Lusch to Countess B.'s because of the lessons, home on foot late in the evening, when it was very dark. — R. in bed, a little dejected at my having been away so long. Three letters came, one from Esser, one from Munich (anonymous) which says that Hans has had an affair with an actress whom he wanted to marry, then about how things look in the Munich theater, the lack of discipline and order. Then in Berlin two performances of *Tannhäuser* have yielded 200 thalers—"a pure gift," says R.—In the evening R. gets up again, I bathe our little boy, then we read *Don Quixote*.

*Sunday, October 24* Letter from Prince Georg, who asks for an opinion on his plays, very embarrassing. Fine weather, I go for a walk with the children (to Frau Am Rhyn's). R. has a letter from his brother-in-law Avenarius, to whom he had gone for advice about the publication of his works. Avenarius advises him to publish them at his own expense! After laughing about this, R. says it is probably a good thing that difficulties are placed in his way, for he still does not know in what form he should bring out this edition, what he should leave out, and whether it should all be done simply as a supplement to the biography, for an author in the true sense of the word he has never been. Ate with the children. Afterward a long sleep, since truly overtired after a sleepless night. In the evening children's games and later *D. Quixote*.

*Monday, October 25* R. comes to breakfast with a letter from the King. All the old expressions of love and rapture, and with them a plea for pardon concerning his behavior over *Das Rheingold* ("my longing was too great"). Then we read in the *Signale* that *Die Walküre* is being prepared in the Munich Court theater; so much for the letter: it really is terrible! But we agree that R. is in fact living on his *Nibelungen*, he owes his existence to them, and so one really ought to thank God that a being such as the King has such curious fads in his head and truly wants to see and have the things, though indeed without being able to appreciate their sublimities. R. says: "He cannot kill the work, I am the only one who can kill it, by breaking with him and not completing it. The fact that he is ruining things now will not detract from the impression when they are one day presented in the way I want, for people still have me to thank for *Tannhäuser* and *Lohengrin*. This great presentation does, however, depend in a general sense on cultural conditions, and if these are not achieved, not even the most consummate performances in Munich would be of any avail. All this is in the hands of Fate. But to reply to all the King's enthusiastic assurances is difficult." — When I ask him whether he intends to go to Vienna for the production of *Die Msinger* he says no: "It is better thus; when I intervene in anything, some demonic urge always arises and puts things in jeopardy —in this way it will simply be a bad theatrical performance, which will pass, as all bad things pass." — Put away the summer things and brought out the winter things, the cold is already with us—and children's coughs, too, unfortunately.

In the afternoon the student for geology. R. comes home with letters. (1) Hallwachs writes that our case might well take six months. (2) Richter, who announces that he has been invited to Brussels to conduct *Lohengrin*. (3) Schuré, who simply addresses us as a good and loyal friend. I said to R. that it would be a good thing if our Mendès friends could learn something from Schuré in this regard. "Unfortunately," says R., "no development is possible in French people, there is at best only an inspired intuition; for the whole nation has virtually collapsed under the rule of the Jesuits, and their upbringing deprives them of all independent spirit." He then considers how Protestantism could by itself have saved France, and how the terrible disciplined schooling at all levels can only breed cynicism. In the evening he discusses with me the question of human progress, which has not changed in character, its essence remains the same; what we have lost in productivity, thereby giving our age the appearance of falling into decadence, is made up for by a wider distribution of culture; it is true that in this distribution art is losing a very great deal, but who can measure how gradually the level is rising? Music has now taken the place of the Renaissance arts. — In the evening *D. Quixote*: unfortunately the devil's masquerade, which has little appeal for us, since we find its purport and the pedantic manner of conveying it downright embarrassing.

*Tuesday, October 26* R.'s great distress in regard to the King's letter; how to reply—earnestly or circuitously, or keep completely silent? The day overshadowed by children's coughs. In the evening great sorrow concerning *D. Quixote*. The masquerade is intolerable, and this makes us very sad. Much pleasure, on the other hand, caused by a letter from Doris Brockhaus, who tells me I shall probably be able to obtain the picture of Uncle Adolph Wagner.

*Wednesday, October 27*  With the children, gave Boni and Loulou lessons, at the same time drafted for Prince Georg the wished-for review. Richard orchestrating. He is unfortunately still not well. In the afternoon a letter from P. Cornelius, he is intent on leaving Munich, because open hostilities are being waged there against R. In the evening to the theater with Countess Bassenheim: *Die bösen Zungen* by Laube, a famous play of the *"present age"*! We are quite horrified and do not stay to the end. As R. says, people understand nothing but newspaper gossip, that is their whole world!

*Thursday, October 28*  A good night, Fidi slept for eight hours straight. Yesterday another letter from Claire, who tells me I shall not receive my bit of capital. Loulou in bed, I write to Marie Muchanoff, sitting beside her. At lunch R. speaks of his pleasure in the house and our seclusion. "This is what I always wished for—and yet in wishing for it I always asked myself what I would get from it, I would be as alone here as anywhere else." The *moaning* of the open fire delights him. "Everything is contained in this *moaning*—the sound of ships at sea, a popular uprising, the rolling of carriage wheels, everything." In the evening R. plays with Fidi for half an hour quite alone. Great gladness that he is getting better. In the evening more enjoyment with *Don Quixote*. Q.'s instructions to Sancho Panza wonderful.

*Friday, October 29*  Letter from Dr. Hallwachs; the first legal deed concerning our divorce is on its way. With the children, wrote to Judith Mendès. Thick snow outside, much brightness indoors. R. is very delighted with his uncle's book on Erasmus. What a pleasant, warm tone literature possessed in those times (he says), so much youthful enthusiasm! I read by myself about Cervantes's life and am so terribly affected by his fate that in the evening I can scarcely take delight in his work, which is again splendid (governorship and episode with Dulcinea). — Yesterday when I glanced at a religiously inclined letter from Hermine, it made me truly melancholy to see to what extent the eternal and so deeply moving teachings of Christ have fallen into the hands of the exploiters. They haggle with the crucifix and eternally put the unsewn garment of the simple teaching up for auction. My thoroughly religious nature cannot do without the teaching, but cannot bear the manner in which it is conveyed! — R. reads me from the *A.A.Z.* some very excellent sentences written by the painter Pecht about the unworthy treatment of Semper in Saxony; this cry of indignation amidst the general indifference pleases me so much that I write Pecht a word of acknowledgment, but expect from him either no reply or an irrelevant one. — Great fright over R.'s fall from the ladder while arranging his library. At supper we discuss various matters from earlier days. "What would have happened if I had gone to live in Berlin at that time, as I wanted to?" "Who can say?" "Oh, it is inevitable that we, after being together for only a few hours, should have felt we could not do without each other," says R. — I stay up late and consider until midnight how I might give R. on his birthday a sign of what he means to me, to the world. — R. asks what I am thinking of all by myself. — "You will know in eight months' time!" —

*Saturday, October 30* Wrote to Claire while with the children; still thinking of Cervantes's life, always in connection with R.'s fate. Perhaps Hans is the only person who shares the feelings which move me when I consider what such beings mean to the world and the world to them. I am certain he is willing to suffer for R.'s sake, but he cannot admit it to himself, and it all has to remain unspoken. How often my thoughts linger with the poor man! In the afternoon to town with two of the children. In the evening *Don Quixote*. (R. tells me today, "I am nothing but concern for you and our little world.")

*Sunday, October 31* In bed, much pain, read Gibbon. R. writing down his views on conducting. Family lunch; on leaving, R. looks Eva long in the eye: "What is individuality? Nothing—one sees that when one looks at such a child's face, and a whole species answers." Visit from Countess Bassenheim. — Fidi in better health, which makes me very glad. — I forbid R. to read the life of Cervantes, because I do not wish him to read about the portrait of Cervantes, an engraving of which I am trying to get. — Wonderful out of doors, trees still green (the plane on the terrace), with snow, sunshine, and the radiant, rosy tints of the mountains. In the evening R. unwell and Fidi again afflicted with his rash,

*Monday, November 1* Wretched night with Fidi. All Saints' Day, or *the poor men*, as Loldi says after I have told her what All Saints' Day means. — R. comes to my bed in gloomy spirits and says that throughout the night he has been hearing songs for investiture and convent vows. I was also sad, treading once more the heavy path I trod last year at this time. Watched the sunrise with a crescent moon— such a sight always lifts my heart again. — At breakfast R. says: "How curious it is with nations—one sees how long it takes to produce fine blossoms; the Italians were marked out for something of which nobody in the Italy of ancient times had any idea. One can of course say that there was much mixing of blood, but I hold this to be far less important than the local factors. Out of this nation, which earlier seemed somewhat unproductive, suddenly there emerge from all directions beings who appear, every one of them, to be great, characteristic, and endowed with genius." Further: "The two things which have enriched the world since the disappearance of the ancient world are Christianity and music." — Then R. says he has decided to write to the King, saying he cannot write to him. He reads me his letter, which I should have liked to be severer still. During the day, great concern about Loulou and Boni, who have complained of my strictness. I feel shaken to my very soul—are my children really so estranged from me that they repay my love with resentment? — Gloomy night; "who never through night's heavy hours." But then the heavenly powers came to my aid, I know that I must bear everything, for my life is a sin.

*Tuesday, November 2* All Souls' Day, I make the children pray for the dead, then speak to them earnestly and solemnly. — R. in sad mood, has no desire to write another note of his *Nibelungen*, the newspaper says *Die Walküre* is being prepared for production in Munich. Much melancholy, in addition Siegfried unwell. To town with R., Christmas preparations already. Fine evening, the mountains wonderful, but the walk does us no good. Siegfried ill, fears of diphtheria; the doctor summoned in the night, feelings of despair. Oh, children, do not lay bold hands on Fate, not even to help others! Once it is done, gods, spirits, and mortals will turn their backs on the poor individual, worry will eat his heart as the eagle ate Prometheus's, and no Hercules can free him, but only Death. Accept, children, accept—do not seek to relieve anything, seek no happiness for yourselves, but also do not seek it for others, and bear what you are given to bear without boldly imploring still further burdens! Content yourselves with carrying out what the gods have imposed on you, do not demand to recognize and interpret Fate itself; otherwise, children, peace will flee forever! — Siegfried somewhat better, no danger, the cries of desperation were premature. — Thought of Hans, of our sad last days together, how content I am never to forget his suffering!

*Wednesday, November 3* Life is a dream in which we are expected to do evil to one another! Siegfried somewhat better, worked with the children and tended him. In the afternoon to Countess Bassenheim's with Lusch. Very tired in the evening. R. has finished his essay on conducting and sent it off.

*Thursday, November 4* Dreamed of taking leave of Hans; great melancholy. In the morning R. comes up to me, he is concerned about my health, then he says, "What should we give the first people who congratulate us on our marriage?" I ask who they are. "The Chaillous" —my tailors in Milan! We laugh. After that a letter from Claire informs me that my mother read the announcement of our marriage in *La Liberté*. I have to write to her, which I find very uncongenial. "Oh, your parents," says R. jokingly, "your dear papa—it soon turns out that sitting down to a piano is rather different from sitting down to life." — After lunch R. says he wants to write me a letter, he is too worried about my life, then he lights two candles and shows me a colossal shotgun in the corner of his room. He will shoot himself with this, he says, if I do not take care of myself. Much amusement over it, questions as to where the shotgun came from. "Well, that is a secret." In the evening *D. Quixote*, leaving the ducal court—"What a clever person he is!" Richard working.

*Friday, November 5* Arranged the study, or "thinking den." After lunch, with Lulu to her piano lesson. In the evening *D. Quixote*. In the morning a letter from Doris, saying the woman in Leipzig is trying to cheat me. In the evening letters from Judith and Catulle Mendès, they beg R. to come to Paris to conduct concerts. Litolff offers him hospitality. — A Paris newspaper announces our marriage in very dignified phrases, a Herr Beckmann protests against ugly rumors. R. laughs, embraces me, and says, "Oh, yes, you are being gossiped about with me." Then he takes Siegfried in his arms and plays with him for a long time; to me he says: "We shall have to send Siegfried away; when he is approaching manhood he will have to meet other people, to get to know adversity, have fun, and misbehave himself; otherwise he will become a dreamer, maybe an idiot, the sort of thing we see in the King of Bavaria." "But where?" "With Nietzsche—wherever Nietzsche is teaching—and we shall watch from afar, as Wotan watches the education of Siegfried. He will have free meals twice a week with Nietzsche, and every Saturday we shall expect a report."

*Saturday, November 6* Wrote to Mama and to Claire. R. to Catulle, telling him he is not in favor of taking on anything at all. With the children. After lunch with Colonel Am Rhyn, on R.'s advice I buy 20 shares in the new steamship company. Very perturbed by it, since frightened of losing the children's money. After lunch arranged the rooms. Great weariness. R. unwell, on top of that a very wretched night with Siegfried.

*Sunday, November 7* Feeling very weak, and R. unfortunately very unwell. He talks of assuring Siegfried's future in the event of sudden death! Noticing my dismay, he says, "I do not believe it, things only happen to me when I believe in them and most deeply, as for example with the King of Bavaria, when I really expected everything." Family lunch, all well and lively. After lunch, walked as far as the painter Zünd's house. It does much good. (In the evening I write to Doris Brockhaus and ask her to send me the picture of Uncle Adolph.)

*Monday, November 8* A good night, cheerful spirits, discussed with R. the children's future, the need to put all my interests aside for the elder children. Hopes of building a house for Siegfried, stipulating, however, that the girls should always find a refuge in it. — Afterward arranged the study. After lunch went out with R., then lessons with the children. (Prof. Nietzsche announces a visit.) —

*Tuesday, November 9* R. working; lovely weather, the children in the garden, I unwell in spite of a good night. R. is asked for a tribute to the firemen, which he immediately drafts. "He who forswears happiness is blessed"—this motto, says R., is worthy of the young Goethe (the grandson!), and it came to him as a word of Brahman wisdom.

*Wednesday, November 10* Worked with the children, in the afternoon to Countess B. with Lusch, who makes an impression with her good memory. In the evening R. bundled up in blankets, I read him the conclusion of *Don Quixote*. Then I feel so unwell that I have to go to bed.

*Thursday, November 11* R. very pleased, because I had a good night; he had taken Siegfried away and told the maid to watch over him in his own rooms. At breakfast I told him it was not right that we had ignored Schiller's birthday, which was yesterday. "Well," he said, "yesterday was the very day on which, while I was working, I felt inwardly pleased by Schiller's picture opposite me, and I pictured to myself his whole essence." I remembered then that I had also told Lulu about Sch. We had the same dream, R. and I—that we embraced each other. — In the morning arranged books in the study. At lunch R. declares: "I have been thinking again about *Don Quixote* and, considering it from the angle of its ironic outlook on the world, I was reminded of a dialogue by Plato; it is in him, too, this irony, but there it appears free, confident, nothing is pressing on it. Whereas one senses the horrible pressure of Catholicism on Cervantes's noble spirit; the way he finds it necessary to make the poor Moresco praise the Inquisition! In the Greek one sees the Olympic wreath, in the Spaniard the starving poet, treated by the nobility, just as D. Q. was treated, like a plaything, in a world hostile to things of the spirit. Oh, the misery of having been born in this millennium!" Then, concerning Luther: "How right my uncle was always to call him the godly man." In the evening R. reads "The Fight with the Dragon" to the two eldest children in his wonderful way, then says to me: "In my youth I did not at all understand the beauty of this poem, its masculine perfection. One must read such things from time to time in order to understand what such human beings mean." — Letter from Catulle Mendès: the Brussels director has gone back on his word—just as we expected.

*Friday, November 12* More conversation about the influence of Christianity. "This teaching is too lofty not to have had the most pernicious of influences; it could not be forced on the world, it could only become truth in the minds of those who took refuge in the Thebais. When one sees how such giant intellects as Dante and Calderón served this teaching, one must admit that their works, if not they themselves, have suffered. How free, in contrast, do such beings as Goethe and Schiller seem, though certainly as intellects they are no greater than the two former." — Eva ill, let us hope nothing serious. Letter from Lenbach, the painter. — Yesterday, in front of the children, R. made a remark about the aristocracy and *von*'s which upset me, for there are certain matters I prefer not to be touched on in front of the children; I was sitting there in silent reflection when suddenly R. rose from the piano, embraced me, and said I was the best and noblest woman in the world! I was startled to the point of tears. (Afterward he played a piece by Bach and said, "Certain features in Bach can only be explained by the fact that he was a great improviser and wanted to pin down what he was so lightly extemporizing; hence the many pedantic markings, the curious runs, etc.") — Wrote to Franz Lenbach. The eye specialist came on my account, my eyes are so weak.

*Saturday, November 13*  Added the finishing touches to the study. R. did some work on the second essay on conducting. He wants to write to the King again, to describe to him all we have been through, then describe all he is to him, what he owes to him, how without him he would never have been able to get down to his work, and finally to ask him to have nothing performed for the time being, to ignore the theater completely for a while. I ask R. not to send it yet. In the afternoon visit from Professor Nietzsche, who tells me it is quite incredible what lies are circulating in the world, both written and spoken, about R. (how, for instance, he stands before a mirror in an effort to equate himself with Goethe and Schiller—then about his luxury, his *harem*, his intimacy with the King of Bavaria, whom he incites to all his follies, etc.). We wonder what picture of him will go down in posterity. In the evening R. reads me his essay. In the morning Lulu had a letter from her father, who is now living in the Villa d'Este.

*Sunday, November 14*  In the morning a letter from Chaillou, the tailor in Milan, offering us a villa on Lake Como on very favorable terms. We are very much tempted. "Superstition is now my whole philosophy; for me the Chaillous are eudaemonic beings, their intervention in our lives has always been friendly. True, Wallenstein was deceived in this way about Piccolomini, but Wallenstein was a bad fellow, and I am not." Family lunch. Then a walk, lovely glow on the Rigi at sunset. In the evening R. and Prof. Nietzsche discuss the first conceptions of language, which R. describes jokingly as talking primitive philology. Talked a lot about the Villa Capuana. — Fidi is no longer sleeping beside me, R. wished me to get my rest. — R. says, half in fun and half in earnest: "Just wait—when I write my treatise on the philosophy of music, church and state will be abolished. Religion has assumed flesh and blood in a way quite different from these dogmatic forms—music, that is the direct product of Christianity, as is the saint, like Saint Francis of Assisi, who compensates for the whole church as well as for the whole world." (Yesterday evening R. played us the beginning of the Norns' scene.)

*Monday, November 15* The main topic of conversation is still the Villa Capuana; R. writes to Frau Lucca and I to Chaillou. In the morning work with the children. Much joy about a box arriving from Milan, R. loves it best of all when I am wearing new clothes. When I come down to him toward evening: "The joy," he says, "when you come in like that; you look like a child." With him to town; back home, I find the student and a letter from Pecht; then I have cause to regret ever having written to him, he has misunderstood me entirely and thinks I am assuming he would intervene on our behalf! R. tells me not to reply to him and also not even to regret having written to him, but just to—"forget it." Read Plato in the evening. —

*Tuesday, November 16* News that I am to receive only 10 shares in the steamship company. With the children in the study. R. works, but complains about his health and about his task ("when every note is supposed to convey the end of the world"). After lunch read parts of Lessing's *Emilia Galotti* and Schiller's *Fiesco* in consequence of a conversation with R. about them. In the evening R. reads me Plato's *Meno*; it arouses wonderful feelings in us. — In my solitary hours I think back on this time last year; with a heavy heart I tread this *Via Crucis*, may Hans forget those days! I cherish a fair hope in the thought that Loulou will one day bring him joy and share his life happily. (R. tells me today that I have recognized the entire state of the world in myself, it is a state of convulsion; every thought, every joy, every sorrow, is a convulsion, and if it is not that, it is not worth much.)

*Wednesday, November 17* Sleepless night of musing. Worked with the children. R. unfortunately still not well. In the afternoon to Countess Bassenheim. In the evening completed *Meno*. Letter from Mama, very melancholy, and from Claire; the latter tells me she is reading Aristophanes, which causes R. to talk about him. (The conflict between will and idea produces the tremendous comedy.)

*Thursday, November 18* Still concerned about R., who is looking wretched. In the morning he writes to the King; I beg him to alter some passages which might perhaps give offense, and he intends to do so. In the afternoon I am summoned to appear at the parsonage. First step toward divorce! In the evening Plato's *Euthyphro*.

*Friday, November 19* Wretched night; worries about Lulu's health, R. also still not well. I suffer gladly. Yesterday evening R. played to me from *Tristan*, melting my whole soul. He became sad as we considered how musicians fail to take heed of such a work. He does not want to send off his letter to the King, since it is Friday. I, on the other hand, make my mail orders for Christmas. In the evening a letter to the parsonage refusing to obey their summons. In the evening the *Apology* of Socrates (quite wonderful). This morning R. did some further work on his essay on conducting and read it to me after lunch.

*Saturday, November 20* At seven in the morning R. wishes me a good morning and says he has already been thinking a lot about Socrates. It is very remarkable (he says) that his whole approach is negative; this means he is wise, but no philosopher, he is always trying to fathom where wisdom can be found, in Heaven and beneath the ground in Hades, everywhere. In this sense he can be compared with Kant, who in his *Critique of Pure Reason* declares that this problem cannot be solved, and he stands in relation to Plato more or less as Schopenhauer's first book stands to his second. To this extent he is also the clearest example of a step forward in the development of the human spirit. He could only be mild and benevolent, since all around him he saw error. But he must have been terribly irritating, since he could not be put into any category, not even among the philosophers, and yet he attracted everyone to him; if he had only accepted money, all would have been well. Plato was the first philosopher—Socrates was simply his forerunner, of the greatest importance to him, since he threw doubt on all recognized values. Such earlier men as Anaxagoras, Pythagoras, etc., were practicians, they sought to explain the objective world. Plato was the first to recognize the world's ideality, that the species was everything, the individual nothing. — Much concern about Lulu; after I have scolded her about something, she waits until I have gone away and then gives vent to the ugliest of resentment. Today she is not being allowed to work with me. (Yesterday in the *A.A.Z.* I read a short biography of Papin, the scholar, whose experiences and death affected me terribly. Whether absolute wisdom—like that of Socrates— or remarkable significance like Papin's—all greatness must be rejected by this world. And all—here, because of lunch, I no longer know what I wanted to say.) In the evening Greek history with Lusch. Since I am coming down with a sore throat, R. tells me he does not know which is greater, his love or his concern for me. I go to bed, and R. reads *Crito* to me. R. reads me his letter to the King and sends it off.

*Sunday, November 21* In the morning we again talk about Socrates. "Beyond this moral code Christianity could not go—Christianity generated ecstasy, the complete destruction of the world, but as regards what the world itself can bring about, no one can ever go higher than Socrates. In the greatness of his heart the saint sees, but he can only speak in symbols, the symbols of religion, and those who do not see

the picture in the same way as he cannot understand the symbols."
— Visit from Countess Bassenheim; her little girl stays to lunch with us.
R. works on his essay and sends it off. In the evening read *Gorgias*.

*Monday, November 22* That "better to suffer injustice than to commit
it" makes me think a lot of Hans, with great melancholy; I dream that
I received a letter from him with the following inscription: "To the
delectable, adored one, from the poor exile or invalid." — I am still
worried about Lulu. — With regard to his essay, R. tells me he will
write down everything he can remember. "I want, like Socrates, to
be the gadfly which always spurs on. The manner in which all our art
is treated is too contemptible." Worked with the children in the study.
Loulou unwell, however, which makes me very anxious. In the afternoon a letter from the clergyman asking me to visit his office with regard
to my divorce. I decide to go, in order not to cause any delay in this
matter; in the evening setting up the theater for the children.

*Tuesday, November 23* In the morning with R. to the lawyer with
the clergyman's letter, I am dissuaded from going to see him and
give up the intention with pleasure. Afterward looked at children's
toys with R. Otherwise children's day. R. and Lulu both somewhat
better; fine, cold weather, sun and snow. In the evening *Gorgias*.

*Wednesday, November 24* R. works in my room, I with the children.
Friendly letter from Professor Nietzsche, replied to him. Letter from
the lawyer, saying I shall have to appear before the clergyman after all.
In the afternoon some concern that R. cannot be persuaded to curb
his inclinations. (Recently he said *à propos* of births or procreations,
"The time must be right, the position of the stars right, that's how it
was with me; that it didn't all turn out brilliantly you can see in my
restlessness and the fact that nothing much came of my brother
Albert.") In the evening a melancholy letter from Hans Richter, he
is conducting *Lohengrin* in Brussels, but is thoroughly despondent
about French musical conditions, would like to be back in Germany,
poor man. — Some pleasure in seeing the King of Bavaria behaving
well; for instance, Döllinger, the cathedral provost, was not invited
to the Vatican Council, now he is going after all as an embassy attaché.

*Thursday, November 25* R. does not work in my room, great concern
that he cannot bring himself into the right mood. Family lunch,
some disturbance in the house. R. Pohl does not come as expected,
read Mone's *Heroic Saga* with R. Letter from Claire, answered her the
following morning.

*Friday, November 26* Cheerful atmosphere, R. again in working
vein: "At least the Norns' rope has now got into a tangle." — Letter
from Judith, another from Königsberg—*Die Meistersinger* is to be
presented there; a new picture from Berlin very unpleasing—makes

him look like Mendelssohn and Meyerbeer! Arrival of R. Pohl. Visited Countess Bassenheim. — Incomparable impression from a new collection of Dürer pictures.

*Saturday, November 27*  The Catholic party has won in Bavaria, they are talking of arraigning the ministry and appointing a guardian for the King. R. works on his "Norns' Song," I with the children. Boni unfortunately very unwell. Around noon Jakob brings me an anonymous letter; amid abuse of the vulgarest sort someone sends me a photograph of Schopenhauer, saying he resembles Richard! When I have got over the first shock, I almost welcome this penance; the whole day long I am in very good spirits, conversing a lot with Pohl and then speaking of this curious letter, in the end it makes us— laugh. R. reads us his essay on conducting.

*Sunday, November 28*  Six years ago today R. came through Berlin, and then it happened that we fell in love; at that time I thought I should never see him again, we wanted to die together. — R. remembers it, and we drink to this day. Countess Bassenheim visits me and takes Lulu off to lunch. In the afternoon R. continues writing his essay, I read some stories by Turgenev with Pohl, very mediocre. In the evening R. reads from his biography; we had a great shock at first, thinking it was lost, R. could not find it anywhere, until he remembered that he had put the folder behind his books to hide a piece of the wallpaper. I laughed and observed that this was just like him, to forget his whole biography and use the folder as if he were a paper hanger. In the evening I reflected on how love works on us like a Plutonian eruption, it bursts through everything, throws all strata into confusion, raises mountains, and there it is—utmost transformation and utmost law. In the morning R. told me he had always wanted to come to me; now, when he is working on his Brünnhilde, I am constantly before his eyes.

*Monday, November 29*  Boni ill, not dangerously, but weak. The foehn has returned and is making us feel wretched. R. indisposed, but works all the same. After lunch talked much with Pohl, brought the conversation around to Hans, of whom he knew nothing definite; I saw he was vexed with him, so I did a lot of talking and made myself very melancholy thereby! God grant him the noble ability to recognize the felicity of suffering, and grant me the consolation of seeing his child, my Lulu, one day become a joy and consolation to him! If things go right with you, my child, a fine, heavenly task will perhaps be assigned to you one day—fulfill it! — R. then played Pohl and me the first scene of his third act. This always affects me terribly. — The student does geography with Lulu. I heard something which made me truly glad. Pohl told me that Dohm had fled to Weimar nine months ago because of his debts, so he is no longer editing *Kladderadatsch*. This proves that it was not *he* who permitted those nasty things to be printed about me; that was a relief. Abuse matters little, but what meant much to me was that someone whom I had always known and acknowledged to be a decent person had suddenly become vile. In the evening slight vexation because of too much talk—and R. always prefers doing something.

*Tuesday, November 30* Telegram from Weimar. *Die Meistersinger* has been received in Weimar with great enthusiasm. Richard not well, does no work, but writes letters instead. In the afternoon announcement of an engagement between Doris Brockhaus and Richard Wagner, which made us laugh a lot; then an anonymous letter: Master, compose a *Faust*. I read Pohl the *Parzival* sketch, in the evening read the biography.

*Wednesday, December 1* R. tries to force himself into working, but it cannot be done, he is unwell, and on top of that we have to suffer the piano tuner. I with the children as usual. In the afternoon R. goes through the third act of *Siegfried* with Pohl. In the evening the biography. — Saying good night, I confess to R. that the presence of any other person makes me sad; everyone who is in touch with the world and brings news of it disturbs the quiet rhythm of our life here, or, rather, evokes a mood of melancholy in me. —

*Thursday, December 2* Departure of Dr. Pohl. R. not very well, writes letters. A Herr Köhler has written to him in connection with *Die Meistersinger* in Königsberg and concludes his letter with the wish that R. be granted the greatest happiness in life. Because of this conclusion, R. replies and tells him his wish has been literally fulfilled. Family lunch; in the evening a letter from Claire, saying I should write to Count Flavigny concerning my money; I begin the letter at once. Wrote to Judith. In the evening read *Cratylus* with R.

*Friday, December 3* R. at his work, I in the study: get the children to write something for their father. At lunch we talk about the peculiarities of the Germans, like R. Pohl, for example, who, with his miserable job (subeditor with the *Baden-Badener Journal*), and in spite of keeping such terrible company, nevertheless remains so much of a German that, for the sake of his artistic convictions, he has turned down a position as correspondent with the English *Athenaeum*. Only a German has convictions in matters of art, all the rest consider such things puerile. — At the mention of bad company I said, "I shall save Fidi from that." "Then he really will be vulnerable to it. Things cannot be done *negatively*, only *positively*. The only way is to arouse in him a feeling for ideals, so that he can offer a manly resistance. If he can look on things in a thoughtful way, sensuousness and vulgarity will have no power over him. I know that my father and my mother encouraged this sense of the ideal in me, however unsettled and frugal our circumstances. Once that is done, disgust with all the baseness will appear at the proper time. I have experienced all the bad things it is possible to know." — After lunch R. goes to town and brings back a letter from the students at Jena; after the performance of *Die Meistersinger* in Weimar they drank a *Salamander* to R.'s health. — (Last night I dreamed about Hans—that he walked through the living room, pale and agitated.) In the evening *Cratylus* without much pleasure, since R. finds the philological treatment somewhat childish.

*Saturday, December 4*  R. at work; afterward very excited. I with the children. After lunch to town to do some Christmas shopping. R. catches cold in the process and returns home very indisposed. He fears he will be unable to work tomorrow. In the evening I consider my life and end with the prayer, "Forgive me the evil I have done in my life and on this day, and grant me the grace of still doing good."

*Sunday, December 5*  R. dreamed that I had to go to Munich and I looked so worn out. His concern about this dream, he says, took his mind entirely off his own condition. Yesterday his old friend Pusinelli wrote to him from Dresden, congratulating him on his engagement to Doris Brockhaus. — R. works, I play puppets with the children. Large and merry family lunch. Arrival of Kant's works for R. at Christmas. Toward evening magic lantern, dominoes, lotto with the children. In the evening a further attempt to finish *Cratylus*. (Wrote to my mother.)

*Monday, December 6*  Letter from Marie Muchanoff, which I answer at once; a wretched night; at nights my melancholy thoughts flood over me, I never go to sleep without tears, which then turn into dreams. Curious—Hans was in fact ill-disposed toward Christmas, and now when I think of him having to spend these days alone, I am overcome, as I prepare for them, by indescribable melancholy. R. still unwell, the children on the other hand lively.

*Tuesday, December 7*  Work with the children, R. at his sketches, he complains of feeling constantly unwell. Letter from Prof. Nietzsche, he is coming to us at Christmas. In the evening R. reads me *Tristram Shandy*, in which the diatribes against solemnity give me much enjoyment, reminding me of those bigots the Schumannians. Spoke with R. about Mendelssohn. Comparison to a crystal: the *Hebrides* Overture so clear, so smooth, so melodious, as definite in form as a crystal, but also just as cold; such an enormous talent as Mendelssohn's is frightening, it has no place in the development of our music. A landscape painter, incapable of depicting a *human being*. (I am occupying myself with Semper's textile art, which makes R. laugh and call me "you aesthetic soul.") In the morning R. reproached me for not going to him when he was at work, it had ruined his mood. Concern about this.

*Wednesday, December 8*  Opening of the Vatican Council, Immaculate Conception. At Tribschen nothing but confusion, all the men gone to church, hence no servants and R. annoyed. His morning's work spoiled; I take Lusch to Countess B.'s, where she has been invited. At midday arrival of a medallion of R. prepared in Berlin, very inadequate and unpleasing. The *Parnasso italiano* also arrived; Cornelius sends it to me. In the evening finished my chair. Read *Tristram Shandy*. On parting, R. looked long at me, and tears began to flow down my cheeks. Do not weep—he said—for Siegfried's words to Brünnhilde have just come into my mind—and he fetched his pencil and wrote the theme down. (Talked about Parcival, the first kiss of love, premonition of death.)

*Thursday, December 9*  Glorious day, blue sky and sunshine; R. works, I drive into town to do some Christmas shopping. Family lunch. Afterward a letter from Count Flavigny, he calls himself my uncle, but does not send me my money. In the evening *Tristram Shandy*. Talking of the bust of [Wilhelmine] Schröder-Devrient, which always moves R., he tells me: She was no longer very respectable when I came into contact with her, but for such a person, with that formidable talent, there was only one possible compensation, and that was sensuousness; without this she would have been unable to bear it. (Wrote to Prof. Nietzsche.)

*Friday, December 10*  Fog again, R. cannot work, I drive once more to Father Christmas. In the evening business letters (Count Flav., Rothschild, etc.). Later *Tristram Shandy*. R. very agitated. "A musician is a veritable ox," he says.

*Saturday, December 11*  Very nice letter to R. from Prof. N. — R. comes to my bed early in the morning to receive the orders of the day —if I am well, he says, he will dress luxuriantly. We decide on *Knecht Ruprecht* and the *Christkind* for Christmas. He works and is satisfied; in Brünnhilde's scene with Siegfried in *Götterdämmerung* none of the themes from the love scene reappear, because everything evolves out of the *mood*, not the underlying thought, and the mood here is different from that of the *heroic idyll* of *Siegfried*. — At lunch, amusement over the Vatican Council, where they are said to have been unable to understand one another because of the differing Latin. Joy in the children, their jubilant hubbub on the stairs interrupts our table talk. I constantly thanking the gods that they are well; R. tells me he cannot pray, but his feelings of gratitude take shape in him as an ardent desire for the destruction of the individual self. — How constantly I suffer about Hans! I should like to die before him, so that he might realize how every hour I suffered with him, through all happiness and all blessings. —

*Sunday, December 12* Through all these days I was preoccupied with Daniel, who died on December 4, 1859. I am worried about his grave. Children, my children, hold firm to one another—brotherly love, sisterly love, nothing else can make up for it! — R. completes the pencil sketch of the Prelude to *Götterdämmerung*. The picture of Uncle A[dolph] W[agner] arrives. I for a walk with the children to meet Mariechen B[assenheim], who is eating with us. In the evening magic lantern, then took the little girl back to her mother. After tea continued with *Tristram Shandy*. — R. does more work on his essay, with increasing vexation as he thinks of musical conditions in Germany.

*Monday, December 13* Christmas bits and pieces and work, R. laughs at my being so exclusively occupied with all this. He constantly working, on Siegfried and Brünnhilde as well as his essay. In the afternoon geography with the student. In the evening R. reads to me out of a volume of Heine (posthumous things). As always things of incomparable genius, but also very repulsive pieces. "He is the bad conscience of our whole era," R. says, "the most unedifying and demoralizing matters one can possibly imagine, and yet one feels closer to him than to the whole clique he is so naïvely exposing."

*Tuesday, December 14* Constant wretched nights, thoughts of my death. Then considered Schiller, how after his works there could only be musical drama, to which he, as it were, forms the bridge. Worked with the children. After lunch made Christmas purchases. In the evening gilded nuts while R. read out *Tristram Shandy*. Loulou causes me concern with her very stubborn behavior. — Curious, when I think of this world and its people, I feel there could not be too much censure and ill usage for me, but when I think of higher worlds and higher beings, there I know I am loved. The malice here below I gladly bear.

*Wednesday, December 15* Vreneli gave me great pleasure today when she said, "Now the master knows what he is working for," meaning me and Fidi. The *Christkind* came, a very poor girl from Bamberg; we intend to dress her nicely, so that she can summon the children after *Knecht Ruprecht*, and then give her presents too. R. works, I still very weak; it looks as if my strength will never return, I must just take care that R. never notices how weak I feel. In the afternoon to Countess B. with Lusch. In the evening, Christmas bits and pieces. (Letter from Claire, saying my new marriage raises doubts about paying me my capital—whereas my proposal is that it should be invested for me there! Very pretty!)

*Thursday, December 16* R. works on the sketch of the intermezzo;

when feeling so blissful about the flourishing state of his mind and heart, I fear always that I might forget Hans's suffering, I then invariably remind myself of it. — With the children at lunch. R. and I start talking about *Tristram Shandy*; R. remarks on the curiousness of this disquieting book, in which everything is attributed to procreation and birth, and in turn birth becomes the reason why Tristram Shandy cannot express himself except in this confused manner. The fact that Shandy's father refers constantly to *mother wit*, or the wit one derives from *oneself*, suggests that by this he means genius. — After lunch R. goes into town, I stay in the downstairs *salon* and gild nuts. Colorful sunset, the last glimmers of the open fire, the dark gleam on the Goethe frame, the nuts glittering in the dusk; my "better soul" awakens, and in my thoughts I look back on my life. Could I have done otherwise? Am I to reject my love for R.? . . . Never, and since not, that means I had no right to act differently. But since on account of it someone had to suffer, I acknowledge deep inside myself the sinfulness of this obedience, and I shall atone and do penance for it in all the ways I can.

*Friday, December 17* Foehn weather, R. still not well, does no work on his sketch and is despondent. Visit from Colonel Am Rhyn, discussion about the investment of savings for the children. Horrible weather, Loldi unwell, R. indisposed. In the evening painted Christmas names.

*Saturday, December 18* To town in the morning to make purchases for Christmas. Both R. and I had a very wretched night, R. ill, I immersed in gloomy thoughts. — In the morning a letter from Prince Hohenlohe, arrival of the Order of Iftekhar from the Bey of Tunis, a large silver brooch, which R. immediately puts to use on the roof of the puppet theater; he does not intend to acknowledge its receipt, since it is too ridiculous to be refused. R. still unwell. In the evening, when I intervene in a conversation with the children, he thinks I am worried that a quarrel might ensue, and in his misunderstanding he becomes heated about this supposed worry. A despondent evening in consequence! Reading newspapers, I told R. today, was for me the same as meddling in things with which one has nothing to do, relying on the reports of people who do not know.

*Sunday, December 19* Letter from Richter to R.; *Lohengrin* is to be performed in Brussels in the middle of January. Lunch and games with the children, in the evening read to Lusch some scenes from Goethe's *Iphigenie* (prose), because she is just learning this group of legends. Joy in Eva, who is incredibly lively and intelligent. In the evening took up *Tristram Shandy* again.

*Monday, December 20* Wretched nights still, because of either the foehn or melancholy feelings. I should never have regained my sleep if I had left R. to his dreary and disconsolate fate, that is certain, and now it is the thought of Hans's lonely existence which robs me of my rest. But I do not complain, for I feel this is as it should be. — If only, my children, I could instill my knowledge into your souls, enabling you to renounce all happiness here below without personal experience, consequently cheerfully and sinlessly! "Let him who calls no soul his own steal away from our bond" came into my mind while I was thinking of R. Loulou, my child, assume the task of living for your father, to compensate him for all he has lost! — I felt peculiarly sad when I heard Loulou reflecting in the evening that she would like to marry and have children. — The *Illustrirte Zeitung* publishes a portrait of Beethoven in the year 1805; it is very unattractive, bloated, almost devoid of intellectual expression. "Well, musicians must be ugly in appearance, in them the heart is everything; as a woman becomes clairvoyant through her nervous system, so a musician does through his heart, which does indeed have a mind of its own. The musician does not see people, their movements, and their actions, for him everything is tempo, structure, etc." He continues writing his essay and reads me what he has written. Afterward we discuss how *Knecht Ruprecht* should look. Then with him into town. Sent the student home; news that Eduard Devrient has been suddenly dismissed. For what reason? Have R.'s words perhaps had an indirect influence on the Grand Duke? — In the evening, looking at Fidi, R. says he has the glittering eyes of the Wälsungen; that brings us on to the *Edda*, then to *Götterdämmerung*; he shows me some lines in his composition notebook which Brünnhilde should sing in place of "*Selig in Leid und Lust,*" and in which the chorus should join; the burning of Siegfried's body to be done as a sort of ritual. But he has abandoned it—rightly—as not being stylistically in keeping with the whole. "Such things as final choruses have no place in this work." — In the evening much enjoyment with *Tristram Shandy*.

*Tuesday, December 21* Gift troubles; can giving pleasure to others make up for the distress of having been the cause of suffering? Certainly it does not, yet the pleasure remains great and pure. In the night I thought of an idea for a comedy, of which I worked out the whole first act. Afternoon outing with R. In the evening a letter from Judith, reporting that after a bad first performance of *Die Meistersinger* there was a great demonstration of hostility, whereupon a young man in great excitement pressed into her hand some pretty verses about R. Pasdeloup proudly and boldly repeated the Overture on the following Sunday, and a veritable storm of enthusiasm (*vive Wagner*) is said to have broken out. — R. works on his essay. In the evening *Tristram Shandy*.

*Wednesday, December 22*   Did not sleep; the cook in Munich writes to Hermine that Hans has been enjoying himself in Florence, but has been ill. During the night, when thinking of the children's delight, I consider ideas for a prayer for Christmas Eve.* Then in my head I work out my comedy. In the morning to town again, furnish the dollhouse. Christmas activities all day long. In the morning a letter to R. from Pohl. R. indisposed. —

*Thursday, December 23*   While gilding my apples I am given a letter from Counselor Bucher. It gave me much joy; I thought he belonged among that group of former friends who paid attention to the malicious things said about me. Now he has written in a friendly tone and with no other motive than to greet me on my birthday; since I think highly of him, I found this sign of life from him extremely welcome. In the evening I decorated the tree just as finely as I could. R. in cheerful mood as I did so. During the day I had a moment of distress. R.'s sister Cäcilie sent him the papers for which I had asked; she sends no greeting to me and writes in an obtuse and ugly manner. That hurt me—it would have been so much better if R.'s sister had felt for me.

*Friday, December 24*   Busy with arrangements. I have painted all the names (of the complete household) and distributed them around the living room. The aim is to give out the presents without the use of tables. Professor Nietzsche comes in the morning and helps me set up the puppet theater with Iftekhar on it. In the afternoon I still have a few things to take care of, and in the meantime R. rehearses *Knecht Ruprecht* and the *Christkindchen*. I return home, and we begin. I, with the professor in the nursery, invite Loulou to recite "The Fight with the Dragon," in order to exercise her mental powers; she says it up to "Thou, lord, must know the chapel well," then Hermine comes in and says she can hear such roaring! Suddenly our *Knecht Ruprecht* appears and roars; terrible alarm among the children, R. gradually pacifies him, he scatters his nuts, cries of delight from the children. While they are picking them

*There follow a page and a half of sketches for the prayer, and Christmas verses. The final version of the prayer is written out on the last page of this notebook of the Diaries, after the entry for August 12, 1870. It runs: "Dear *Christkindchen*, you have come to us and made us happy, we thank you, while remembering all those who are unhappy and begging you from our hearts to seek them out and to bless them. To those who are poor and hungry, in cold and darkness, give your nourishment and your heavenly kingdom; to those poor people who, without a friend, are lonely and weeping, bring your comfort and tell them they are blessed; greet the little children who have no mother to light their Christmas tree, and tell them that you are their best friend. As you have given us the many little lights, give to all others your great light, so that they may feel as happy as we now are."

up, the *Christkindchen* appears, brilliantly illumined. In silence the whole household follows, I with the children in front; the *Christkindchen* beckons with the tree and wanders slowly down the stairs, disappearing through the gallery. The children, dazzled by the gleaming of the tree and the presents, do not notice the disappearance. After the present-giving I pray with the children in front of the extinguished tree. Professor Nietzsche's gift to me is the dedication of his lecture on Homer. (In the evening *Der bethlehem|ische Kindermord.*)

*Saturday, December 25*   In the morning I sketched out the little poems. Then Loldi came to me, R. had sent her in with a little volume of manuscripts and 32 pages of the printed biography. Very moved, particularly by the former, for R. certainly must have gone to much trouble in acquiring them. Tears. A very nice parcel for the children from Frau Schuré (all sorts of toys). I tell the children that the dolls which gave them the most pleasure came from their father. Family lunch; afterward read *Parzival* with Prof. Nietzsche, renewed feelings of awe. Then some sublime words from R. on the philosophy of music, which, it is to be hoped, he will write down. — Letter from Lenbach. In the evening, passages from the biography. — R. still occupied with his essay on conducting. — Great tiredness.

*Sunday, December 26*   Children to church, then lunch together; later played my comedy for them. Letter to Lusch from her aunt, who virtually demands that I send her. Shall I? Great inner struggle. Boni unwell in the evening, I am writing this in the *salon* next to the nursery, and committing the *Christkindchen* poem to paper.

# 1870

*Monday, January 3*  Have not written in this book for a whole week. Spent most of the time with Prof. Nietzsche, who left us yesterday. Today a letter from my mother, whose health is improving. Otherwise, several signs of friendliness from the outside world, among them a parcel today from Judith M., with pictures of R.'s works painted by her. On New Year's Eve our tree was lit again, and I received from R. such presents that I was quite amazed. He sent Marie Muchanoff a telegram in verse, I write letters in all directions. On January 1 I received some money, which I took as a good omen. R. still very much occupied with his essay. We are now both tired. From Paris I received anonymously a nice *bonbonnière*, which I took to Countess B. Exchange of visits with the Am Rhyns and the whole B. family during this time. Many curious reports of the Vatican Council and from Paris (Ollivier's government).

*Tuesday, January 4*  Very unwell again, but wrote letters while the children were writing to their aunt (I to Mama, Judith, Lenbach, etc.). The children also unwell, which causes me worry.

*Wednesday, January 5*  Worked with the children. At lunch R. speaks about life, which is like the flickering flames eternally raging around Brünnhilde's rock. Now and again someone breaks through these flames and tames them, but most come to grief in them. In the evening *Tristram Shandy*. (Letter from both the Schurés, very nice.) With regard to my divorce, which is making no progress, R. says, "Laws are transmitted," etc. "Nature and love are prompt, but laws—they creep on all fours!"

*Thursday, January 6*  Loulou ill (a chill); I stay beside her and play with her all day. Lunch with the other children. Loldi now says, "I greet you a greeting for Uncle Richard." R. plays passages from the 3rd act of *Siegfried*—the sounds he creates are the sun of my life! (Letter from Rothschild.)

*Friday, January 7*  Because of R.'s playing yesterday I have been walking on clouds, though always with an anxious heart, since Lusch is still in bed and Boni unwell. To town for my money, then to Countess B., who tells me she knows the year will turn out well, since Richard visited her on the first day. An inquiry from Mathilde Maier about R.'s illness! Replied to her at once. — In the evening *Tristram Shandy*, pleasure alternating with dissatisfaction. Talent, but no genius.

*Saturday, January 8* Woke up in the night, remembered Hans's birthday; if I had thought solely of him, lived only for him, would this have been better in a moral sense? I believe it would, but I also firmly believe that it was not my mission in life. My hopes are founded on Loulou's cherishing her father above all others for my sake and devoting her life to him. R. worried over the lack of progress in our affairs, also worried on Fidi's account. Lusch still in bed, but the doctor unconcerned. Foehn, very oppressive weather. In Munich they have engaged Lucile Grahn, and work is continuing on *Die Walküre*, according to the *Musikalische Zeitung*. — Played a comedy for the children at Lusch's bedside. Nice letter from Claire; the French are satisfied with the Ollivier government. — In the evening, looking at the stars, I thought out the following poem:

*Zum 8ten Januar*

| | |
|---|---|
| *Ihr ruhigen Sterne* | *Enthüllt ew'gen Tanz,* |
| *grüsst aus der Ferne* | *dass er genese ganz* |
| *des Armen Nacht!* | *von jeder Erdentaumelqual,* |
| *Entsendet euer Licht,* | *und sich ergebe fromm* |
| *dass nicht mehr er ficht* | *dem Leiden wie es komm'* |
| *gen Schicksals Macht!* | *erblickend das Sternental.* |

["You peaceful stars, greet from afar the poor one's night! Send your light, that he may no longer fight against the power of Fate! Display eternal dance, that he recover quite from the frenzies of this mortal life and piously accept suffering as it comes, gazing on the starry vale."]

*Sunday, January 9* In the morning R. gets down again to his composing and sketches the opening to the prologue of *Götterdämmerung*. I read Grimm's fairy tales to Loulou and feel pleased that she much prefers these to the Andersen ones. Lunch with the children, without Lusch, who is still in bed; the others have colds, too. After lunch Bayer, the lawyer, who gladdens R. greatly by telling him that once we are married the christening of Fidi will cause no difficulties at all. R. very happy, as if a burden had been lifted from him! — At supper he spoke about his godfather, Träger, in Leipzig, whose bluestocking of a wife was his first encounter with an intellectual woman (Aspasia type!); from her he first heard the words "architectonic relationships": she used them to Rosalie in connection with the stage decorations at the Leipzig theater, which Rosalie thought bad. At the age of twelve R. had read *Die Jungfrau von Orleans* to her, she had asked him to do so. His godfather gave him a blue-gray dress coat and a red Turkish waistcoat from his own wardrobe; this caused his mother great amusement, but R. was impervious to her gibes, for his rich godfather's dress coat, altered to fit him, had a silk lining. — Letter to me from Krausse, the painter, about R.'s supposed illness, and from an unknown young man in Vienna came a very touching and anxious inquiry as to whether he really was ill. — In the evening finally laid *Tristram Shandy* aside with a feeling of aversion, and began on the *Vita nuova* (pedantically mystical, says R.). Profoundly moved by the canzona in which D[ante] sees Beatrice lying dead! "This is the genesis of all poetry," R. says. It leads me to the second act of *Tristan*, which I read again with delight.

*Monday, January 10* "I am going to write a new work," R. exclaims to me. "It begins with the second act of *Tristan* and ends with Hans Sachs's wedding." Letter from the King, still in the same old style. R. thinks he can use it as a pretext to beg him on no account to produce *Die Walküre* without R.'s aid, and he will suggest producing this as well as *Das Rheingold* for him. When I tell him I would not be able to attend the performances, he says: Then on no account. I then go to the children, all four of whom are unwell! I read to them and play with them. R. works and is in cheerful mood, then ruins both his mood and his state of health with a walk. He says it feels quite stuffy out of doors, like a peasant's living room, the air is so thick. — In the evening finished the *Vita nuova* (sketched poem for the 7th).

*Tuesday, January 11* All five unwell today, coughs, colds, etc., great concern. R. also unwell, forces himself to work. When he again says that he finds it unthinkable to produce a work without my being there, I kiss his hand in deep emotion, upon which he laughs and says, "Now one gets praised for a law of Nature." — Bishop Strossmayer's opposition to the Jesuits at the 5th meeting of the Council causes us much amusement. After lunch discussed the violin as a solo instrument (unmanly, ridiculous). I write to Claire and to Krausse, the painter. [*Some words concerning a Calderón quotation omitted.*] In the evening read with R. the letters of his stepfather, Geyer, very moved by them. R. says, "He sacrificed himself for us." (Early today, when Loldi went to R., he asked her why she was crying. "I'm not crying, tears are just coming!") R. tells me that as a child he was nicknamed *Amtmann Rührei*, because he was so sensitive. (R. has written to the King and made suggestions to him.)

*Wednesday, January 12* Again very restless in the night; the children also still unwell, concern, too, about Fidi, who is teething. Read in the newspaper that the King has commanded *Die Walküre*. A great shock, the urge to resume work utterly killed. On top of that the air very unpleasant. Read nothing in the evening.

*Thursday, January 13* Very unwell, chest pains; delight in Fidi, who visits me in the morning. R. is having breakfast beside my bed and says he would like to be a painter, to paint me with the child. — Amusement over the doctor's reply when R. shows him a tumor growing on a finger. "Good Heavens," he says, "how productive you are!" — R. works a little; in the afternoon he writes to his friend Pusinelli, announcing the birth of his son. Letter from Frau Schuré; Paris is literally in an uproar over the murder of Victor Noir by Prince Pierre Napoleon. In the evening began on Plato's *Theaetetus*, great and heavenly delight in it.

*Friday, January 14* Better again, R., too, he works, I go into town, make purchases, and visit Countess Bassenheim. Lusch tells me that she dreamed of her father and felt such joy at his arrival that she almost fell out of the window. I feel glad that I am succeeding in keeping her feelings for her father alive. R. works and, when I return home, gives me the first penciled pages of *Götterdämmerung*, with which I consecrate the little bureau in the corner. In the afternoon played with the children, read them fairy tales. In the evening R. writes to his sister Cäcilie, to my relief making no mention of the business between her and myself; but he forbids me to write a single word to her, he says she is not worth it. In the evening *Theaetetus*. — (Sunshine.)

*Saturday, January 15* I tell R. that Lessing's essay on the way in which the ancient Greeks depicted Death had been very vivid in my mind during the morning; it had reminded me of his Isolde, who, as she puts out the torch, appears to us in the smiling guise of loving heroine and goddess of Death simultaneously. Talked of the medieval skeleton; R. observes that the Germans had managed to give even this gruesome image a cheerful and homely aspect, which is what makes "the Germans so original and closest in kind to the Greeks." — The children in better health, I can take them for a drive (Boni and Loldi). After lunch went out with R.; he is not well and was not able to do much work. Springlike weather. In the evening the conclusion of *Theaetetus*. (Letter from M. Maier.)

*Sunday, January 16* In better spirits because of the children's improved health; games with them; in the afternoon sorted the files with R. (Yesterday R. played me the last movement of the Ninth Symphony—and we were once more quite overwhelmed by the naïveté of the faith which blows through Schiller's poem as well as Beethoven's music. Who could teach himself that? Certainly my father, for instance, is a believer, but I do not call this faith.) — In the evening R. read me *King Lear*.

*Monday, January 17* Letter from my mother, good and friendly; worked with the children while R. was revising his "Norns' Song" for the second sketch. Wrote to Prof. Nietzsche. He has sent me Gervinus on Handel; when in this connection I tell R. that Gervinus's book on Shakespeare is still selling well after 30 years, R. says: "That's because of the subject. If Shakespeare were to write a book about Gervinus, it would probably not sell at all." — "Arithmetic is to music what words are to an idea." "The musician who does nothing but write music from morning till night, entirely ignoring the world of ideas, must be an ox—he is missing far more than those who, knowing nothing of music, observe the rest of the world." — "Everything in Goethe and Schiller tends toward music. What alienates us here and there in Calderón is the Italian element, which brought forth opera; in our poets we sense the basic element of music drama." R. goes for a walk, then writes to Baron Werthern, asking him to send him the Berlin diploma. I with the children, Grimm's fairy tales. In the evening finished *King Lear*.

*Tuesday, January 18* Sleepless night; reason: my inner agitation about my mother's asking how Hans is. I pull myself together, however, as much as I can, and give the children their lesson. R. works. Everyone fairly well, snow outside. I start on my embroidery for R. Nothing from outside, the newspapers are full of Rochefort, Prince Bonaparte, Ollivier, etc. In the evening began *Timon of Athens*.

*Wednesday, January 19* R. tells me that last night he dreamed he had been a minister at the court of Queen Anne of England and had quarreled with a Lord Evans (Aha, R. had thought to himself, he doesn't yet know who I am, he still thinks I am a musician!). Much amusement from his description; R. then tells me how happy he is with me, because of me. "Yes, if only I knew of just a single person who could be in the least compared with you—of whom I could say; 'Ah, that was the first draft, that has been brought to fruition in C.' The only things I fear are change and illness. I do not appreciate anywhere near enough how happy I am. I do not enjoy it nearly enough. I never want to leave this house again." How I thank God for this happiness! Who could estimate what such words do to my heart? Letters arrive (from a man in Bremen, who thanks him for having so thoroughly drubbed the so-called conductors, from his friend Pusinelli, I one from Claire, very nice). Lusch is driven to Countess Bassenheim's. R., accompanying her to the carriage, falls on the steps in front of the house, a great shock. Thank goodness he soon recovers and feels nothing but negligible pain. In the evening, conclusion of *Timon*. In the afternoon the three children downstairs, Loldi says, "The wind talks so much." —

*Thursday, January 20* A letter to Lusch from her father, he was touched by our Christmas festivities. R. suffering from his fall, but working. I with the children, then lunch with them, glad that all are in good health. In the evening R. writes to C. Frantz (regarding the care of Daniel's grave). An evening of conversation. When I tell R. I intend to write once more to my father with a message for Hans and after that to keep silent, he says, "That's right, for people are divided not by what they are, but by how they see things, how they express themselves." My mother has written to R.: the publisher in Paris wants to purchase the old French songs for 500 francs.

*Friday, January 21*  Letter to R. from Baron Werthern: he did not send the diploma at once, but first sent an inquiry, so as to obtain an autograph from R.; at my request R. writes him a little verse [*see notes*]. R. at his spinning loom, I with my children; R. pleased with his work: "It sounds like the fluttering of night birds; everything depends on impressions of Nature, and here in the Norns' scene I can see the tall fir tree near the rock and hear the nocturnal rustling." At lunch, in connection with the wine, he tells me about a hunchbacked wine merchant in Königsberg named Tiplowski, in whose cellar he had first encountered the good Château d'[*unreadable*]. This man had said to him, after a curious excursus on something or other, "Remember that I told you this today, on December 2, on the day Napoleon proclaimed himself emperor, in the Blutgericht"—that was the name of the wine cellar, because it stood on the spot where the scaffold had previously stood, in an old castle. Later, when Louis Napoleon introduced *his* December 2, Richard was always reminded of the hunchback Tiplowski. — Much joy in Fidi, and, gazing on him, R. talks about Nature, which cares only for the species, never the individual, which is why it sometimes makes children so unlike their parents and develops some particular family predisposition; since it is so stupid, it attempts to produce creatures of intelligence—"here a small instead of a large nose might perhaps help; for it seeks everything in form, which in turn shows us how aesthetic its methods are." At lunch he says, "Since my union with you I have gained an incredible confidence in myself and my fate; I know I shall live to be old—my life is just beginning." After lunch he plays the Norns' scene to me, an inexpressible delight. In the evening I show Loulou Genelli's illustrations to Homer; no particular pleasure in them. R. says, "Homer is Homer and Genelli is Genelli"—beauty is lacking. In the evening I feel very unwell; thoughts of my death. Concern for the children. Listen to me, Lusch and Boni, Loldi, Eva, and Siegfried, should you after my death be divided against and alienated from one another, keep your love intact in your hearts, do not forsake one another, seek one another out again and unite in the memory of your mother; this bond will hold firm, do not forget my warning. — In the evening R. reads me passages from König's *Hohe Braut*; a very nice novel.

*Saturday, January 22* Still unwell, R. gives me *Sigufrid* to read, a drama by Ettmüller, a friend from Zurich. It is very archaic in style and irritates me. Since R. welded the *Edda* myths into his *Ring*, everyone has been making plays out of them, their work is discussed and praised, while R.'s unique and eternal work—but what does it matter? (Wrote yesterday to Frau Schuré.) At lunch R. informs me that he has received a letter from the lawyer, from which it seems the divorce is being held up; Hans has given no sign of life, and his presence in Berlin is required to complete the matter. I write to Hans's lawyer. Concern that Hans might be upset. I am willing to bear the wretched situation into which I have brought myself, and even the difficulties which arise for Fidi out of the uncertainties, as payment for my priceless happiness! Then I wrote to E. Ollivier, who has been attacked in the most despicable manner in the Lower Chamber; thus he will not think it is his advancement which has tempted me to approach him again. In the evening R. reads me passages from the first part of *Faust*; on reaching the verse "I am too old to be content with play," R. says, "Goethe discerned this highest wisdom in his early youth; so one sees how stupid it is to assume that poets must first live through what they write." — A lot of news in the papers; first, the very remarkable protest by the cathedral provost Döllinger, signed with his own name, against the infallibility speech; then—so R. tells us—the execution of *Uncle* Traupmann (who murdered a family of 8 people!); then the Ollivier government and its struggles.

*Sunday, January 23* Children's games day! R. calls me the good old mother hen; and truly my whole day is spent in entertaining the children. Only during the afternoon do I take up the *Eroica* with R.; at one point in the first movement he gets to his feet, much moved: "The only mortal who can be compared with Shakespeare!" In the evening he reads me passages from Schopenhauer on love ("Kant spoke of it without practical knowledge"). R. thought it might perhaps repel me, but, on the contrary, I am very moved and uplifted. — R. says, "Love without children is a sham." The final essay on conducting arrived today in print.

*Monday, January. 24* I am still ill, the children well, however; R. works. — Yesterday we felt some sort of comfort in reading that Hans had played several times to small gatherings in Florence. "[*Il*] *tempo è gentil uomo*"—perhaps it will bring him some balm. On his walk R. meets our lawyer, who tells him the priest is claiming Fidi for the Catholic church. We hope it will all turn out right eventually. In the evening *The Arabian Nights* with Lusch. (In the morning a retaliatory poem from Baron Werthern.) R. reads something to me, for we had a great fright. Fidi fell from the sofa with a loud bump. R. in great agitation; Boni, who was there, laughs; afterward I ask her why, she says the way he snatched his cap from his head (she shows how). We all laughed a lot, and R. pointed out to me that one must always be gentle with children, for they very seldom poke fun vindictively, but simply yield to immediate impressions.

*Tuesday, January 25* Letter from Düfflipp; R.'s suggestions have not been accepted, *Die Walküre* will be performed. Great anguish. At lunch, after having tried in vain to force himself to work, R. says: "If I did not have you, I should not know why I am on the earth at all. I think I should go mad—on the one hand unable to be other than one is, on the other, being not at all to the world's liking." For me a letter from Professor Nietzsche and arrival of a Semper drawing. I work unceasingly on my purse for Saint Richard's Day, which I manage to finish. Great cold, we have to give up the upstairs *salon*. In the evening I read Gervinus to R. (Shakespeare, Handel), great dismay over the style (not to speak of the contents), he writes like Eduard Devrient! Prof. N. also sent me a philosophical book (Hartmann), which arouses feelings of great repugnance. Time and time again R. harks back to the greatness of Schopenhauer.

*Wednesday, January 26* Amicable morning mood, we have breakfast in my bedroom. Afterward R. works, I as usual with the children. In the afternoon with Lusch to Countess Bassenheim's. A letter to R. from Prof. Marbach, who, delighted with *Die Meistersinger*, says that to hear the *Nibelungen* will be for him like the first sight of an alpenglow. — The *Walküre* performance casts its long and gloomy shadow over our lives. R. is also concerned that my divorce is dragging on so. — In the evening passages from Schopenhauer on books and reading (in connection with Gervinus!) —

*Thursday, January 27* The police making inquiries about me, the matter is referred to the lawyer. No reply to me from Berlin. So the constellations from outside are evilly disposed—*Die Walküre* clouds all our thoughts of the world. "If the fires of art and the warmth of love did not sustain me, I should no longer be alive," says R. Piano practice with Lusch. In the evening *The Arabian Nights* with her. After tea played piano duets with R., much appalled by the poor quality of these arrangements.

*Friday, January 28* Not a good night, but I got out of bed swiftly to bathe Fidi and then to have breakfast in comfort with R. Then to the children; Lusch unwell, no lessons, I write down my poem for Prince Wallerstein, which Lusch is to recite to him on Sunday. In the afternoon went for a walk with R. Unwell; in the evening read Schopenhauer.

*Saturday, January 29* Awake the whole night, plagued by anxious imaginings; but rise in the morning in cheerful spirits. R. is still working. "You are keeping me busy," he tells the statuette of Siegfried. Our lawyer comes to see us, he thinks that Simson, the lawyer in Berlin, is delaying the divorce out of malice. In the evening finished reading "Ali Baba" with Lusch. Early to bed, feeling very worn out.

*Sunday, January 30* Dressed the children so that they could accompany Loulou; during their absence I write down the first scene of my comedy. Lunch with the children, without Loulou; afterward puppet show, very well played by Boni. Loulou returns home and tells me that the old Prince had wept a lot as she recited her poem to him. — Nice letter from Schuré; R. praises his simple disposition, in contrast to Mendès: "In the French, education is not a liberating factor, but a shackle," R. remarks. — He works, but is in a very gloomy mood because of the *Walküre* affair. It makes me melancholy to think that he has to buy the possibility of completing his work by sacrificing the earlier parts of it. The nature of the world seems to me to stand revealed thereby. Letter to the children from Aunt Isa. At such a time a veil descends on my soul; or rises from it and clouds all my thoughts. —

*Monday, January 31* The Geyer-Wagner cup, which I gave to R., broken this morning by the maid; sorry as I am, I thank God that misfortune strikes in this way, leaving the children unharmed. R. works, I working with the children. In the afternoon a visit from the old Prince, who tells me he wept with emotion and pleasure when Lusch yesterday recited my poem to him. He speaks of his childhood— he has served under three Bavarian kings—his father a reigning prince, and now he ends up in Lucerne. R. in agitated mood, much in his sketch is not yet as he wants it. "I am no composer," he says, "I wanted only to learn enough to compose *Leubald und Adelaïde*; and that is how things have remained—it is only the subjects which are different."

*Tuesday, February 1* Sent Prof. N. his books back (Gervinus and Hartmann). Lessons with the children, Boni is making progress in French. After lunch to town with R. and the children. R.'s depressed mood. *Die Walküre* hangs over our heads like a curse. Besides that, things in Bavaria are looking bad: the Catholics, who have the majority in the Lower Chamber, are trying to unseat Prince Hohenlohe; the King is retaining his minister, refusing to accept the Address, and forbidding his family the court. Who can have advised him? Is it perhaps a trap?? I read Janus's book about the popes and the Vatican Council.

*Wednesday, February 2* Candlemas; wonderful weather, brightest sunshine, approach of spring; the children out of doors a lot; R., too, in the morning. He is very despondent. "If it were not for you, I should simply be thinking of ways to take leave of the world, so as no longer to have to look at it." In the afternoon drove to Countess B.'s with Lusch; they have hopes of seeing an improvement in their situation at last. Sincerely glad to hear it. In the evening, when I speak to R. about a dance for the children, he becomes annoyed; the evening passes gloomily. In the morning he comes to me and asks me to forgive (!!) him, he is so heavy-hearted, so sad, and when, to cap all that, he vents his sadness on me, he is inconsolable. He embraces me and says with a smile, *"il revient toujours à son seul amour."* — He told me during the day that he had written to the secretary of the Academy (Gruppe). When I ask him why, he says, "A drowning man clutches at every straw; perhaps God will send me an understanding voice."

*Thursday, February 3* Letters from Prof. N. enclosing his lecture on Socrates. With the children to the photographer's. Brought home letters (R. Pohl, Kietz, Klindworth, etc.). R. has been working. Returning from his walk in a somewhat more cheerful mood, he calls me and shows me the moon in the first quarter with the evening star, shining companionably in the clear twilight. "It always looks like hope." In the evening R. reads me the lecture, which we find very stimulating. "Beloved music," Socrates's dream, brings R. back to the subject of the musical theme. "How much more significant does such a theme appear than any spoken thought! Schopenhauer is right: music is a world in itself, the other arts only express a world."

*Friday, February 4* R. is again taking pleasure in his work; he is working out the orchestral Prelude to *Götterdämmerung* (violin accompaniment to the Siegfried theme). We play it and are delighted with it. — Pleasure in the King of Bavaria because he is supporting Prince Hohenlohe and refusing the Upper Chamber's Address. In the evening R. reads me *The Frogs* by Aristophanes, in connection with our discussions on the lecture ("Socrates and Greek Tragedy").

*Saturday, February 5* For R. a lively awakening to work, I with the children. Siegfried's passage down the Rhine, signaled by the extensive theme of the Rhinemaidens, who are glad of his arrival, puts us in fine spirits. R. talks about the song of Siegfried and Brünnhilde, *"O heil'ge Götter,"* and says to me: "If you only knew what it brought back to my mind! In Magdeburg, at the end of a gay Auber overture, my poodle, which had been waiting outside for me, came into the orchestra, ran to the bassoon, and sat there quite still, but then he suddenly let out a loud note of lament. Everybody laughed; it affected me terribly, and I can always hear that melancholy song above the merry orchestra." In the evening lesson in Greek history, I pay the student (16 francs) and make a note of it, because he appears to be dishonest. In the evening finished *The Frogs*.

*Sunday, February 6*  Wrote to Prof. N. while the children were playing. R. works. Lunch with the children, afterward theater, which I perform for the children. In the evening occupied with Mozart's G Minor Symphony, whose "teeming transcendencies" R. points out to me. He tells me about M[ozart] in Leipzig, when he first heard something by Bach: after that we play the first two movements. In the evening Aristophanes's *The Acharnians.*

*Monday, February 7*  Will the King of Bavaria lose his throne? This is being threatened in Rome, and the Clericals are saying in the Lower Chamber: We have the peasants. In any case we are glad that he is behaving well and supporting Prince H[ohenlohe]. — Today is Saint Richard's Day according to the Protestant calendar; I keep my celebrations to myself, however, since the framing has not been completed. — With the children; when I go to R., he plays me the Gibichungs' theme, which came to him in such a clear-cut form that he wrote it down in ink immediately. Great delight in it; conversation about these characters Gunther and Hagen, the latter repulsively mysterious, impassive, curt. On long-lost naïveté: "All these heroes appeared to me like a gathering of animals, lions, tigers, etc.; they also devour one another, but there is no disgusting convention, court etiquette, etc., mixed up in it—everything is naïve." — We drive into town, there I ask R. to call for me at the photographer's—when he arrives he looks utterly distraught. In the evening, when I ask the reason, he tells me that he had come across a pitiable, badly injured dog; the sight of it, and above all his inability to do anything to help it, had distressed him; and suddenly he realized the sublime greatness of Goethe's decision to make his W[ilhelm] Meister a surgeon. "Everyone must have a calling as well as a philosophical outlook, and there can be no finer or more humanitarian calling than that of a surgeon." He speaks with such excitement that the children think he is cross. — In the town met Count B., who paid me a long visit; during it the student's lesson, and it vexed me a little not to be able to attend it, because my mistrust of him is unfortunately growing. Possible that I am now very unfavorably disposed toward Catholic religious education. The newspaper reports that the Patriarch of Jerusalem spoke in favor of the neutralization of the church, whereupon he was summoned before the Pope *unaccompanied*; there Bishop Valerga gave him two documents to sign, either a withdrawal, or a renunciation of all the privileges of his church. The old man requested permission to go home to reflect, but there was no question of it, he was under arrest after a delay of two hours this 70-year-old Patriarch at last signed the renunciation! Is this true? — In the evening R. brings Fidi into the children's *salon*, then takes him into the study. "I am so happy," he says

when I join him there, "Fidi is the seal on our love." He writes to
Prof. N., who wrote us two very nice letters about his lecture. After
tea finished *The Acharnians*; and at the conclusion of the evening,
talking about a funeral cantata by Bach, R. says: "Bach and Dürer,
they are two of a kind, both possess in the same degree a quality of
inner sadness and also the same taste for mysteriously imaginative
ornamentation. Only in Bach there is unfortunately still too much
of what was then fashionable, the marks of a bad period." — When
R. was already in his bedroom I heard him cry out, "Now I absolutely
forbid a visit to the Wesendoncks—" (the previous night he had dreamed
he had been there and had had to listen to "bottled-up" and long-
stored-up notices of a pamphlet of his, while he was constantly seeking
his hat and unable to find it!). —

*Tuesday, February 8*   While I am greeting Fidi in my bed, R. notices
a spider on it and removes it quickly. "A spider in the morning
brings dire warning," I had to say aloud; R. denounces my superstition,
saying that the powers which weave our troubles lie within us. But
the troubles have turned up—my elder children gave me cause for
concern; but I will willingly bear it and keep silent about it. — R.
works, wants to play for me what he has written, but cannot do it,
which grieves him; at lunch he tells me that while he was composing,
it had occurred to him that his journey to Paris, when he saw me
for the first time (rue Casimir Perier, October 9–10, 1853), had been
his voyage in quest of a wife; but on that occasion I had been the Tristan, who noticed nothing. — He comes back to Mozart and says he
wants to build the whole philosophy of music out of one movement
of a Mozart symphony; precisely because it is so simple and melodically
so infinitely free. Beethoven would be a more difficult model—the
first movement of the *Eroica* is impossible to define. — Letters about
the Council, the story of the Patriarch of Chaldea is confirmed! —

*Wednesday, February 9*   The spider is still spinning troubles! Letter
from Councilor Düfflipp, to whom R. had not replied: the King is
demanding an answer. Now I shall have to reply for R. R. unwell.
I write to Munich that there is nothing more he can say. Wrote to
Claire. A lot of snow outside.

*Thursday, February 10*   R. writes to the conductor Eckert in Berlin;
I have advised him to give his support to the production of *Die
Msinger* there; perhaps he will even attend it. At lunch he announces
that on Eva's birthday (February 17) *Die Msinger* is to be given its
first performance in Vienna, which delights us. — In the afternoon I
discuss with him Janus's book, which I regret having read, since it
casts an all-too-dismal light on human history. R. replies: "Burning and
torture are no longer possible, but when one hears of people starving to

death in London, can one talk of progress? And isn't any common-or-garden Jesuit right when he asks, 'What use are all your parliaments and bills and all the rest of your fine institutions, when people are dying of hunger in the streets?'" He continues: "People are stupid, rather than evil; the fact that they are malicious, that of course comes from the illusion which deceives every individual into thinking that he is everything and the rest of the world nothing. But the fact that, when so good a person as Peabody appears, he achieves nothing with his charity, and knows no better than to give his donations to the aldermen of London to distribute, with the result that people go on dying of starvation—it is that which makes one despair." Letter from Prof. Gruppe in Berlin, reporting that the Academy will be very pleased if R. gives a lecture there. — Lunch with the children and afterward games. (Letter from Richter: *Lohengrin* held up on account of the scenery.)

*Friday, February 11* R.'s urge to work gone, concern about this; the light of my life goes out at such times. Discussions about the Council and the situation in Bavaria make up most of our conversation, during which R. says jokingly, "God is the spirit who always desires good and always creates evil," in contrast to Mephisto. Then: "Life is made for philosophy, not philosophy for life." Sleigh ride with Lusch. In the evening *Ion* by Euripides; great antipathy toward it, both in form and content.

*Saturday, February 12* Lusch ill again, which alarms me very much. Abandoned lessons. In the afternoon, as we are playing Beethoven symphonies in the old piano-duet arrangements, Prof. Nietzsche arrives. Lengthy conversation about his lecture. Then R. plays us passages from Mozart's *Entführung* and *Figaro*—he likes the old Simrock editions. When Prof. N. remarks that Mozart is said to have invented the music of intrigue, R. replies that, on the contrary, he resolved intrigue in melody. One has only to compare Beaumarchais's (incidentally excellent) play with Mozart's opera to see that the former contains cunning, clever, and calculating people who deal and talk wittily with one another, while in Mozart they are transfigured, suffering, sorrowing human beings.

*Sunday, February 13* Spent the morning with Prof. Nietzsche, talked of many things. He tells me that Dorn, the conductor, has published a book whose whole purpose is simply to denigrate R. Dorn attempts to conceal the base tricks he played in Riga by telling all sorts of lies. Unfortunately he has a number of R.'s youthful letters, which he has published. In them R. addresses him in a downright childlike way—what mean advantage is taken of this! I beg Prof. N. to say nothing to R. about it. Lunch with the children. Prof. N.'s departure.

— How solitary R. is in this world! — News that the King of Bavaria is renouncing his throne. — During the night I dreamed that I locked myself in the children's *salon* with Blandine and declared that Death would nevertheless find a way in; I then said to her: I shall call on you in the hour of my death. Conversation with R. about the King's abdication, which would remove the material foundations of our life.

*Monday, February 14*  R. again at work; fine weather, sleigh ride, a landscape of sugar candy and marzipan. When we return home, a letter from Claire, saying Mama has told her Hans does not want a divorce—this she heard through Mme Ollivier. Besides this, many unpropitious things about my mother. I write to them both and struggle against bitter feelings.

*Tuesday, February 15*  R. dreamed that he went walking with Goethe, conversed with him, and resolved to stay with him, "having found my mission in life in the company of such a man." He goes to work in good spirits, I with the children. At lunch he tells me he has been looking at *Käthchen von Heilbronn* and tears had come into his eyes as he recalled my dreams that Loldi would probably turn into a sort of Käthchen. Yesterday he told me that when he was a child the most terrible things he could imagine were a permanent separation through travel and the incurable illness of a beloved being. He was often indulgent toward bad books or pictures when these themes were touched on. — In the afternoon a letter from Mme Ollivier, very friendly, I reply at once. (Yesterday in the middle of our walk R. suddenly sighed; he told me later he had been thinking of my pains during my confinement.) A telegram from Herbeck that *Die Msinger* is really to be done on Thursday and that the whole company is full of enthusiasm; they are expecting R. to be there. — R. laughs and asks what he would be without me and the children. Ever-increasing joy in Fidi, who is blooming. "I suppose you would like him to become a sort of Parzival!" I: "Yes." In the evening I, too, looked through *Käthchen von Heilbronn*. When I remark to R. how strange it is that one is still so moved at the end, though one knows what is coming, R. replies that, since everything in it is musical, it is not surprise which counts, but fulfillment.

*Wednesday, February 16*  In the morning went by sleigh into town with Loldi. Made purchases for Loldi's birthday. After lunch the lawyer—he is to write to Florence. The advocate is of the opinion that matters have now gone so far that the whole thing could in fact be settled today or tomorrow. R.'s great annoyance. I hold my peace; as long as R. remains in good health and preserves the will to work, and the children flourish, I will gladly atone and offer my person to the world as a sacrifice! — Our mood of despondency is not lightened by outside events. "In the annals of the world one can only rejoice over those who are vanquished." — The French newspapers are rejoicing over the downfall of Prince Hohenlohe, which can lead to great conflict.

*Thursday, February 17* Eva's birthday; the "tune" is played. Great joy among the little ones. After lunch children, fancy-dress party. In the evening a letter from Prof. Nietzsche, which pleases us, for his mood had given us cause for concern. Regarding this, R. says he fears that Schopenhauer's philosophy might in the long run be a bad influence on young people of this sort, because they apply his pessimism, which is a form of thinking, contemplation, to life itself, and derive from it an active form of hopelessness. — I write to M. M. — A fright in the evening—Fidi fell off the sofa!

*Friday, February 18* Today, children, I committed a grave wrong; I offended our friend, and since this is something I wish never to do again, regarding it as the blackest of sins, I use this instance to identify the pitifulness of our human nature. We were speaking of Beethoven's C Minor Symphony, and I willfully insisted on a tempo which I felt to be right. That astonished and offended R., and now we are both suffering—I for having done it, he for having experienced willfulness at my hands. After lunch with the children to Countess Bassenheim, whose hard lot and excellent disposition always touch me.

*Saturday, February 19* R. cheerful again; he tells me, "All I now have in this world is my love for you, that is why, when the least discord arises between us, everything ends for me." With the children morning and afternoon. In the evening *Parmenides*. Letter from Claire. Read *The Arabian Nights* with Lusch. Wrote to L. Bucher and requested him to visit Hans's lawyer, to find out from him what is holding up the divorce.

*Sunday, February 20* R. well, working. Children's day, I play, read, sing with them. In the evening, when I give a mock dinner for them, R. plays, amid great delight, the *Gazza Ladra* Overture. Then, for ourselves, we take up Luther's hymn in a cantata by Bach, *"Das Wort sie sollen lassen stahn."* R. as always greatly moved by it. "A people which can produce such a thing is a people worthy of respect, and a Jew makes a French opera out of it—that says everything." And yet—say I—it is these very sounds, desecrated and ignorantly distorted, which have made that opera into a success. "And Bach is Luther," R. went on. "Just look at the calm way in which he writes the boldest, most daring of things." — In the evening read Nohl's *Gluck und Wagner*, some of it very good (e.g., on *Tristan*), but much of it unpleasantly bombastic.

*Monday, February 21* An article in the *A.A.Z.* about conditions in London produces from R. the following words at breakfast: "The world is so terrible, and self-deception through the individuation of the will so great, that everyone takes himself to be the whole. None can escape the guilt of existence, yet none can radically get the better of the world. So everyone has to try to maintain his battered position and atone for the guilt he has earned in bringing sorrow to others with great goodness of heart and deeds of the spirit, which bring benefit to so many." And then, also about London: "Such a city is the cancer of a nation, it sucks it dry; if Bismarck really wants to abolish great cities, he has had a truly German thought." "Misery of the kind we see before our eyes is something the Greeks never knew." Yesterday we felt pleased that in his portrait Tischbein had draped Schiller in purple. "Of all poets," I said, "he is the only one I like to imagine in purple." R.: "Because he no longer led a personal life, he knew he would die young, he wanted to complete his task, and for that reason there is something noble, heroic about him." "The Spaniards were right," he said jokingly. "I see Cervantes as a cripple, an old soldier in a brown coat, contemplating the world from his guardroom." — In the evening astronomy lesson with the children, and afterward back to Nohl's *Gluck und Wagner*. R. was rather tired out by his work today and remarked that the life we were leading was perhaps exhausting for the very reason that it always called for the highest, both in feelings and in creativeness.

*Tuesday, February 22* We are surprised to have received no reviews from Vienna of *Die Msinger* (due to illness or malice?). In the morning R. says to me: "You poor creature, having to look after so many things! First come I, the composing machine—there you have to take care that it is properly oiled and doesn't squeak—and then the dozen children, who all have to be trained." — Lulu reads me *Robinson Crusoe*, and this excellent book reminds me once more of the fate of great men: Daniel Defoe in the pillory—how dreadful! — In the evening *The Wasps* by Aristophanes.

*Wednesday, February 23* As a result of an agitated night in which all the deceased came back to me, I find myself speaking of Blandine's death. "One becomes a quite different person," says R., "when one has experienced things like that. To have to tell oneself that a person such as Blandine has vanished from the earth! Yes, and Schnorr's death, how terrible it was—one survives it, but one is never quite the same again. If Schnorr had not died, our fate would probably have been a different one, we should have sacrificed ourselves, as we did at the beginning. Without him there was no longer any hope for our kind of art." He ended his afternoon meditation with a smile: "In place of Schnorr we now have Fidi." Then he goes diligently to work. He has crossed out a passage—"I wanted to make things easy for myself, now it gives me no rest." — After lunch to Countess B., whose daughter is ill. Her son, just returned, tells me much about Vienna; an aristocratic cousin had told him that the reason why the present princes are so weak is that they are intimidated by the Freemasons! — In the evening finished *The Wasps*.

*Thursday, February 24*  Great excitement in the juvenile world— today is the Fritschi procession! We drive to the Hôtel du Lac, have a meal, and from there watch the very pretty procession. I find myself standing beside Archduke Heinrich, who married an actress and now lives in Lucerne in a kind of exile. In the afternoon R. brings me from the post office a letter from my friend L. Bucher, who assures me that Simson, the lawyer, is an honest man, then a letter from Hans to our lawyer—he intends to go to Berlin at the end of March. It moves me terribly, I can scarcely look at the handwriting. God preserve you, my children, from such emotions! — Last night, when I could not sleep, I watched the moon, which was just rising (3:30). "Star of the silent night!" I cried out to its friendly face, and sank into deep contemplation! The hardest thing, children, is to have brought sorrow on a human being—God save you from that fate! — What the children particularly enjoyed looking at were the stuffed birds. A duck drew R.'s attention, too. "What an expression—Tristan and Isolde, the whole melancholy of life!" In the evening *Hermes Odysseus*, as a sort of spring god. (The chief dancer at yesterday's carnival ball is reported to have been the rabbi!)

*Friday, February 25*  R. works hard. "A musician, when he is composing, falls into a sort of insane, somnambulistic state. How different from literary work—words are the gods living within a convention, but tones are the daemons." In the afternoon the children to their piano lesson, I write to L. Bucher. In the morning a letter from the Munich "Schäfer" who, having gone to Vienna to see *Die Msinger*, now reports that the performance was postponed on account of the singers' hoarseness.

*Saturday, February 26*  Nothing from outside—or inside, either, for R. is unwell and cannot work; I am also indisposed, but I give the children their lessons. In the afternoon a letter from my mother; I go out to order some things for R.'s birthday. Spring is coming. When I express to R. my joy over our budding hyacinths and tell him that watching a flower grow means almost more to me than contemplating a work of art, he laughs and says: "Yes, beside the hyacinths what does that head of Schiller look like? Like a flowerpot." — Much delight in *Robinson Crusoe* with Loulou.

*Sunday, February 27*  Letters to Claire and Judith. Sudden arrival of Heinrich Porges, who tells us many ridiculous things about musical conditions in Munich. *Tannhäuser* under the "bungler" Wüllner is said to have been utterly unrecognizable. — Since R. was a trifle vexed, he says, "Music making makes everyone either stupid or malicious." Very nice letter from Eberle, the rehearsal manager in Berlin, who voices his annoyance over the "lack of energy" of the singers in Berlin. R. says he is the type of German musician, fanatical and pedantic, rude, often drunk, who earns everybody's hatred with his importunate manner—importunate, however, only for the sake of the cause. The three of us go for a walk. In the evening H. Porges reads us his essay about *Lohengrin*, which contains many very good things. (Wonderful spring weather.)

*Monday, February 28* Unfortunately R. had a bad night, in consequence of which he cannot work. I with the children. R. gives me a lovely necklace, intended as a present on Eva's birthday. After lunch telegrams from Vienna: a great success, "despite Israel." I to town with Porges; returning home, find great indignation in the juvenile world; believing that some farmer's boys had killed a lamb, Loldi ran after them, hit them, and stuck out her tongue; now stamping her feet, she demanded that R. "slaughter" the boys! — Letter from Countess Krockow, very friendly, the only thing in it which grieves me is that my old friend Frau Marenholtz-Bülow feels, despite her "eternal great friendship," that she no longer ought to write to me. In the evening more of Porges's *Lohengrin* essay (his Jewishness becomes apparent only in his inability to listen in silence).

*Tuesday, March 1* Letter from Prof. Nietzsche enclosing another from the bookseller Lesimple, who reports that on his instigation (via Prof. N.) the question of R.'s being given the direction of the music festival in Bonn is being eagerly discussed. R. tells me he will accept if I go with him. Splendid weather, the children in the garden, R. goes for a long walk with Porges, which does him good. In the evening we go through the arrangements of the Beethoven symphonies made for solo piano by my father, then R. asks Porges in the manner of Socrates the meaning of the philosophical expressions with which his essay is unfortunately heavily larded. Nothing much emerges from P.'s answers, so then R. explains to him how it is that the Holy Grail can be regarded as freedom. Renunciation, repudiation of the will, the oath of chastity separate the Knights of the Grail from the world of appearances. The knight is permitted to break his oath through the condition which he imposes on the woman—for, if a woman could so overcome a natural propensity as not to ask, she would be worthy of admission to the Grail. It is the possibility of this salvation which permits the knight to marry. The Knight of the Grail is sublime and free because he acts, not in his own behalf, but for others. He desires nothing more for himself. — In the evening R. says to me, "Justice reigns in this world, only it is difficult to recognize."

*Wednesday, March 2*   Weather still splendid, I play at hoop bowling with the children. Then I write to Countess Krockow, R. works. He thinks I am sad and melancholy, whereas it is only that the things he told me yesterday about *Lohengrin* affected me deeply and are still echoing in my mind. After lunch he plays Porges the scene of the Wala's awakening by Wotan. A letter from Porges's brother Fritz, saying that the performance in Vienna was a quite execrable one. Yesterday P. told me several things about Semper in Vienna, which showed me that he has been conducting himself there in just such a childishly unreliable way as toward us in Munich.

*Thursday, March 3*   Splendid weather, games with the children in the garden. R. is working. In the hermitage I discuss some matters from the past with Heinrich Porges. He makes me very happy by telling me that he has never seen R. so tranquil and so lively as he is now; he is convinced that R. would never have taken up his *Nibelungen* again if this great change in his life had not occurred. This affects me so much that I have to weep. When I tell this to R.: "Nothing, not a single new note would I ever have produced if I had not found you. Now I have a life to live." — At lunch we discuss the curious distinction between Austrian pronunciation and that of the rest of the Germans, also how they pronounce Greek words, such as Zeus, Ze-us. R. attributes this to the fact that the schools were handed over to the Jesuits, who came from Italy and superimposed their Italian pronunciation on German. The Viennese pronunciation is not a *dialect*, but a foreign accent. In the afternoon a big outing to Stanzstad, all in fine spirits. In the evening R. plays Beethoven's A Major Symphony (as a piano duet with P.). He sends a telegram to Herbeck, calling on him to improve the production.

*Friday, March 4*   R. works and is in fine fettle; letter from his friend Champfleury, who is founding a journal on the arts and intends to begin it with a biography of Méhul, because he has constantly heard R. speaking of Méhul. I am to write R.'s reply. In the morning a little poem for Frau Schuré, to save Loulou a letter. In the afternoon to town with Loldi, purchases. In the evening I read Bismarck's speech on the death penalty, whereupon R.: "They can never think of anything but the protection of the citizen, just as, when they speak against cruelty to animals, they say: Animals are so useful. I say that a human being who has killed another and still wishes to go on living is a very doubtful character; the nobler his motives for the murder, the more keenly should he desire his own death. This is where religion should come in, a priest should go to the murderer, suffer with him the hardships of prison, until he has come to long for death. On the day of the execution, which would be held in secret, the town should be draped in black, the shops closed, bells should toll, and only the judges should watch the sentence being carried out. The death penalty would also provide an ethical factor, reminding the world of the seriousness of life. But people do not want to be serious. No paid priests, but monasteries, places of refuge, whose only task would be to suffer with the criminals." Then from that to his favorites: "I think I shall concern myself from now on only with Alexander, Bernhard von W[eimar], Luther, Frederick the Great"—and Cromwell, I add. "Yes. To think that stupid people have labeled him a hypocrite, when his whole impetus was his faith; he was someone who felt: I am a man beloved of God, and you, Charles, are a Godforsaken one. Such a man must hold communion with his God." — Telegram of 180 words from Herbeck, claiming that the performance was not as bad as people say. —

*Saturday, March 5* Telegram about the second performance of *Die Ms.* in Vienna; "Tremendous reception, countless curtain calls," etc. R. works, I with the children. After lunch I speak of the dog which Tristan gave to Isolde, and *Petitcriu*—read aloud by R.—makes a most powerful impression. In the evening *Die Walküre*. When we subsequently talk of the production of these works, I tell R. he should look up the article on *Baireuth* in the encyclopedia; R. had mentioned this place as the one he would choose. To our delight we read in the list of buildings of a splendid old opera house! He amused us with a story about his sister Rosalie: when she was playing Gretchen, the maidservant who came to fetch her and always watched the final scene from the pit, began to sob bitterly. A neighbor asked her: "What are you crying for? It's none of it true." "Excuse me, but I ought to know— I work with the Mamsell."

*Sunday, March 6* An army doctor in Brunswick has sent some fine sausages! We laugh a lot, for some days ago—thinking of the sausage which Richter brought us when he was looking for a singer for Walther von Stolzing—we had said, "We shall never find such a sausage again." This time it is for *Lohengrin*. In return R. sends his portrait with a little verse at the bottom. At lunch R. speaks of his renewed pleasure in Droysen's book about Alexander. "If I were locked up in prison, I should ask only for Greek literature and things about Greece. From these people we derive joy; I am well aware that they did not dot all the *i*'s, but from them we have learned happiness, they are without sin." (Seeing an emotional expression on Hermine's face, he asked: "Which nation pleases God most? Resignation.") After lunch *Die Walküre*, in the evening as well (Wotan's scene with Fricka and Brünnhilde). During this he gives a loud laugh: "And this is what Kindermann and Wüllner are now to bring off in Munich! — I begin to find it funny." In the evening he says: "You can understand that I felt the need, after writing these parts of the *Nibelungen*, to leave this element of dreadfulness and to write *Tristan und Isolde*, which was, so to speak, just a love scene; indeed, I thought of it as an Italian opera, that is to say, to be sung by Italian singers—and in Rio de Janeiro."

*Monday, March 7* The folder with the portrait of Geyer has arrived; I present it to R. with a little poem (it should have come just a month ago). It gives R. much pleasure. "Everything you do has resonance and meaning," he says, "like your dear voice and your pure soul." — Many curious embarrassments on account of Porges's Jewish origin, every moment brings the Lord Jesus to our lips! To town in the afternoon. In the evening *Die Walküre*. R. is delighted with the folder. (A letter from Karlsruhe: the new director, Kaiser, wants *Rienzi*. Previously R.'s *friend* E. Devrient refused to produce it, ostensibly *on principle*, and instead did—Lachner's *Catarina Cornaro*!)

*Tuesday, March 8* R. continues work on his "*Höllendämmerung*" (as the newspapers call it); I with the children. Toward noon a letter arrives from Herr Wesendonck, which makes an unpleasant impression on R. as well as on me. Around Christmas R. had asked him for copies of papers in the family's possession, and instead they sent back the originals. Embarrassed by this, R. wanted to give something in return, and sent the printed proofs of the biography with a long letter explaining its significance. To this Herr W. now replies so clumsily, advising him not to proceed with it in such minute detail, etc., that R. is greatly vexed.

In the afternoon I am overcome by melancholy, the old canon keeps over and over returning to my mind: happiness lies in renunciation alone. Children, it does not look as if I have renounced anything; God knows how my life will be judged, but I beg you to take to heart the knowledge I have gained through sorrow and joy: there is no happiness on earth except sacrifice. To wish nothing for oneself, to seek nothing, to give oneself up to serving the smallest, the most unimportant, to doing good—that, my children, is the way to freedom, believe me! — In the evening we tell Porges some of the things which led me to the break—and R. says, "People are so deceitful, so sham, that not one of them was prepared to believe in your sincerity and your truthfulness." — In the evening read from the second part of *Faust* with intense delight. Then from Osterwald's *Hermes Odysseus*. — Late in the evening R. speaks in more detail about the unpleasant experience with O[tto] W[esendonck], in whom he had confided only out of goodness of heart and who replied to him so insolently.

*Wednesday, March 9* "I not only love you, but *live* you," R. tells me this morning. "When you are in the least upset or worried, I am as lame as a bird with a broken wing." Great joy in Fidi, who is only too innocent and too good! At midday R. is very unwell, yesterday's letter is still annoying him. He stays at home, I go to Countess Bassenheim's with Loulou (lesson), there I learn that her relatives in Vienna have written to her enthusiastically about *Die Msinger*. Letter from Eckert—the minister's wife, Frau von Schleinitz, is keeping a dedicated eye on the rehearsals of *Die Msinger*.

*Thursday, March 10* Great alarm at the news, given to R. by Porges, that Düfflipp has written to Hans and asked him to accelerate the divorce! Obviously they cannot cope in Munich with *Die Walküre*, amd the King is wishing that R. might return to Munich. Hence this letter, which may perhaps—in view of Hans's character—ruin things for us entirely! I write at once to Düfflipp, expressing my indignation, and send a copy of this letter to *Hans* through my lawyer. — Porges departs; obviously he came with the idea of being chosen by R. to conduct *Die Walküre*. — Today's news has a very depressing effect on me; a vision of Hans's sad life keeps returning to my mind; the only way to atone for this is to let nobody, and above all my beloved, see how hurt I feel. — In the evening I sorted out papers; R. is somewhat better; when I tell him how sorry I am that the W[esendonck] letter [*one or two words obscured by a blot*], he replies: "Only because I saw that it vexed you. That is the only thing that matters to me, otherwise I am quite indifferent." — Snow.

*Friday, March 11* Yesterday evening, while I was sorting out the papers, R. was reading *Faust*; this morning he said, "There is absolutely nothing which can be compared with this prison scene in the first part; I maintain that this is German, this great clemency, though certainly it has nothing to do with the present fine state of the German nation." He then turned up, in Simrock's *Heldenbuch*, a poem in which an adulteress is exonerated by a judge and jury. Powerful moving impression. — R. today wears the turquoise I gave him. "May it bring you good fortune," I say to him. "Good fortune has brought it to me," he replies. He goes out, I play and work with the children. In the evening I am overcome by such melancholy that, when R. speaks to me about the children, tears stream from my eyes and I have to leave the room so that R. shall not see my state of mind. Hans will never know how much I suffer for him! R. reads to me from Droysen's *Alexander*.

*Saturday, March 12* Very melancholy feelings. Thoughts of death. Can it erase the consciousness of guilt? The four verses of Gottfried von Strassburg engrave themselves on my mind: "If ever anyone bore a constant sorrow in enduring felicity, then Tristan bore this constant sorrow." — For I am happy, yet I cannot forget that someone has suffered and is perhaps still suffering. All the time with the children; read *Robinson*, sang, etc. In the evening R. reads Gottfried's *Tristan und Isolde* to me.

*Sunday, March 13* Restless night with palpitations, I called out five or six times, "*Obag, Obag*, help me," meaning Richard. We joke a lot about this "*Obag*." Lovely March day, after lunch we go with the children to the dairy. All in fine, cheerful spirits. Returning home, we see two trees full of starlings, a whole flock of them has now arrived. They commune with one another, distribute themselves among the trees, a huge twittering surrounds the whole house, on the roadside saw the first daisies. — Much with R. again about Goethe's *Faust*, the second part of which he describes as a complete palingenesis. In the evening the quartet "*Es muss sein*" with R. Much, much pleasure from it.

*Monday, March 14* More snow! Our poor little birds! We want to give them some bread, but they have all flown away. "One more striking proof of the ideality of time and space, that the birds live now here and now there." — In the *Musikalische Zeitung* there is a report on the performance of *Die Msinger* in Vienna. Among other things the J[ews] are spreading a story around that "Beckmesser's Song" is an old Jewish song which R. was trying to ridicule. In consequence, some hissing in the second act and calls of "We don't want to hear any more," but complete victory for the *Germans*. R. says, "That is something none of our fine historians of culture notice: that things have reached the stage of Jews' daring to say in the imperial theater, 'We do not want this.'" — The newspapers are saying that the Bey of Tunis sent R. a decoration in diamonds—thus is history written! — Fidi unwell, he is having trouble with his teething. — In the evening arrival of the *Trois Mélodies*, which contain to our amazement and displeasure a dedication to the *Baronne de Caters*, whom R. does not even know. He writes at once demanding the withdrawal of the dedication. — In the evening read *Tr[istan] und I[sold]e*, which makes me realize ever more clearly how great and unique R.'s conception of it is. — My great melancholy persists; what would I not give to learn that Hans is contented and active! All the evils of the past have now vanished from my mind, and I see and feel only that I had to leave him. Could I but spare my children such suffering!

*Tuesday, March 15* Very cold. Letter from Prof. Nietzsche: in Bonn they have *unanimously* chosen F. Hiller as conductor of the music festival! So that is that. R. in cheerful mood, gets down to Siegfried's arrival, which has caused him a lot of work. He did not wish to make something very spectacular out of it, and he has assumed that the introduction will have set the basic mood, that we will know that Siegfried is on the Rhine and that the talk of the Gibichungs is just a parenthesis. In the afternoon letters from Schuré and his wife, very nice and friendly. In the evening we write letters, R. and I (to Champfleury, Villot, Schuré, Eckert, etc.).

*Wednesday, March 16*   Fine weather, though still cold. The children in the garden. I write to Prof. Nietzsche. R. at work, but not satisfied, he says Porges's visit was of no benefit to him. — I take Loulou to her lesson. In the evening R. reads me some of *Hamlet*; terrible impact; for the first time I realize that Hamlet, in recognizing the nature of the world, passes far beyond thoughts of revenge, and also indeed of suicide; the horrible deed which should spur him to revenge makes him at the same time aware of the nature of the world and also, in consequence, aware that no death can put things right. On top of that he is the seer of spirits, to whom reality can only appear as a terrible dream. — (Letters from Mathilde Maier and Claire.)

*Thursday, March 17*   R. is still working and is tolerably well. From the outside world only the very distasteful matter of the dedication of the three songs; I write on R.'s behalf to the lady and beg her to tell the publisher she does not wish for this imposed dedication. The publisher did it "in the interests of the works," as he expresses it. In the evening read *Hamlet* again from the beginning. — Much impressed by a missionary's account of his efforts to convert a Buddhist minister in Siam. The Buddhist emerges as a most noble figure. R. deplores the fact that the Jewish religion has been grafted on to Christianity and has completely spoiled it. —

*Friday, March 18*   I begin the folder with great difficulty. R. works. Letter from Councilor Düfflipp, saying it is not true that he wrote to Hans about the divorce; God knows who is telling lies. Teaching the children as usual. R. is reading about the death of Alexander and would like to write a play about it, "if only I were not a musician! This wretched note-writing—into what category of uneducated people has it pitched me?"

*Saturday, March 19*   Wrote letters (to Düfflipp, to pacify him; to my mother). In the morning R. again speaks about religion. "This need for religion shows that human beings are in fact disposed toward good. What a comforting example, after all, is offered by such a religion as that of Buddha, in which the reward is the gentle heart itself and the punishment the angry heart!" R. reads Lusch the account of the Battle of Thermopylae. I hope the child will retain the impression. After lunch R. is very despondent; *Die Msinger* so badly presented in Vienna, *Lohengrin* held up in Brussels, on top of that the unsuccessful

*Rienzi* in Paris and in Munich the bygone *Rheingold* and the impending *Walküre*—it is all vexatious, and then our personal affairs still remain unsolved. He says he really ought to insure personally that his things are better performed, and he talks of the possibility of traveling to Berlin. Meanwhile he has sent Betz a telegram, asking him whether he can guarantee that the performance will be a good one. —

*Sunday, March 20* Boni's birthday, celebrated by us all, children are invited, fine spring weather. Children's party, very merry. — R. is very agitated. In the evening he says, "I am just on 57, and it is high time that I should be sensible—or at least pass as such." — Letter from Betz, the singer, prophesying a very good performance in Berlin, then one from Esser, the former conductor, reporting the most deplorable things about the Viennese production. Not a single word of the text understandable, the Night Watchman's horn replaced by a trombone, the lute by a guitar! This does not exactly raise R.'s spirits.

*Monday, March 21* Letter from Heinrich Porges, according to which they do not really know in Munich what to do about *Die Walküre*. How strange is my fate, which keeps me eternally under a threatening cloud! There is always something bad ahead which cannot be averted. "How do you think it will end between the King and me?" Thinking of Kant's celebrated anecdote, I say, "That is something to be forgotten!" "Yes, if I had your fine equanimity," then, jokingly, "You will certainly bring up the children to be saints—to the eldest you will give a pension, and the others must run around with piously pale expressions on their faces!" — After his work he says he is in a state of nerves, but after taking a walk he reports that he is in a good, comfortable, bourgeois mood, which relieves me very much. — Arrival of presents and a letter from Aunt Isa; a photograph of Hans, which is enclosed, affects me very much. The tone of their aunt's letter is not right, it sets out to flatter the children, and that can prove very harmful in the long run. In the evening *As You Like It*, in which we are above all struck by the immediacy of Shakespeare's stage.

*Tuesday, March 22* Letter to me from Secretary Düfflipp; more *Walküre* machinations, deplorable. R. replies to it, again summarizing his whole life in Munich and simply asking the King at least to have *Die Walküre* performed *privatim*. I write to him as well and finish by considering and summarizing the whole Munich past. I also tell the secretary what a great artistic flowering could mean for Bavaria *now*, when everything is crumbling and chaotic.

*Wednesday, March 23* Telegrams from Brussels, *Lohengrin* a great success and much excitement among our friends. — Horrible weather here, snow drifts, etc. I drive to the dancing lesson with the children. — In the morning a letter from the lawyer; Hans is now on his way to

Berlin; but he is required to spend a month or two there, and he says he has to be back in Florence on May 1. Well, as God wills.

*Thursday, March 24* Still snow. Lunch with the children after work. Letter from R. Pohl, which gives me some hope for the goblet. I write to Brussels, to Dr. Pohl, and to Porges. In the evening read Gottfried's *Tristan*, with indignation (because of Brangäne!). — The conductor Hagen sends a telegram, offering his services as conductor for *Die Walküre!*

*Friday, March 25* Letter from C. Mendès; success of *Lohengrin* quite enormous; Richter summoned to the royal box, presented with a golden laurel wreath, etc. Biggest success the 2nd act. Also a letter from a lecturer at the University of Vienna, which says that all the scholars and the whole of Vienna's student body are on the side of *Die Msinger*, whereas the Jews are showing violent opposition. R. occupied with his answers to Brussels, etc. (unfortunately!). Arrival of the pamphlet on conducting. Telegram from Vienna that the fifth performance of *Die Msinger* is taking place that same evening. R. sends off a letter in French for publication. In the evening R. asks me how I think his relations with the King of B. will end. One is looking down into an abyss and cannot foretell what will happen. (In the afternoon took the children to their physical training and dancing lessons.) Through Dr. Pohl's agency I am able to present R. with a drawing of his Uncle Adolph in advanced age (as he knew him). R. very pleased. ("The Pope proclaims his infallibility, I proclaim your indefatigability.") Eva not very well.

*Saturday, March 26* R. dispatches his pamphlet in all directions. Letter from Prof. Nietzsche. Much joy in Fidi, R. wishes him to wear the cap which his father Geyer had made him wear himself from his earliest youth. R. says he can see whether people love him from whether or not they begrudge him the happiness of having a son. The children write under my supervision (to their father on his name day—Boni to Aunt Isa, Lulu a timetable for her father). R. cheerful, although he has not been working. We walk to town, splendid weather, on the trees we see the first buds. The children again in the garden. Joy in them; the tower bell rings, R.: "A tower like that always seems to me like a living being who—when it rings—is lazily and phlegmatically telling me something." Loldi says, "Lulu, for Christmas you must make a tree for your birds." — R. had the idea of writing an essay in French, in order, perhaps, to set something up there which would not be possible in Germany. Today he suddenly said to me: "I am giving it up; I could not tell the French the whole truth and achieve my aim; I should have to hush certain things up. So I prefer to say all I think to thin air and for my own satisfaction in German."

Letter from Kassel, saying *Rienzi* has been a big success there. (In the newspaper there was talk of a musical undertaking in which Hans took part—God grant him success and satisfaction!) In the evening until midnight *The Merchant of Venice*.

*Sunday, March 27* R. again at his work. I at my embroidery. Lunch with the children. Afterward R. talks about *The Merchant*. Shylock a completely axiomatic figure; the others under the influence of a single law and a harmony which is given expression in the 5th act, nocturnal atmosphere, the love of music. But what does Shylock care about music? No one in fact expresses this awareness, they are just immersed in it, and they forget Shylock as soon as he is overcome; but we see and feel it thus. — Lusch play-acts in front of us and in doing so mentions, to my consternation, "Prince Bonaparte, who murders people—that is French." — In the evening great weariness.

*Monday, March 28* I very tired, on the edge of tears, have to struggle hard to teach and embroider. Sorting out summer clothes. Bathed children. Wrote to Prof. Nietzsche. Yesterday evening, as we were reading the *Iliad*, R. said, "The fact that Alexander has found no poet to celebrate him shows the attitude of a poet toward experience— how for him everything is just intuition." (Doris Brockhaus's fiancé has died suddenly.) — In the evening R. gets very agitated, believing that I am being worn out by looking after the children so unremittingly. His habit of looking on the black side convinces him that I am trying to punish myself. "On the one hand the *Nibelungen* must be completed, on the other the children must be looked after by you alone. If you ruin yourself with it, you will say it was Fate." — This remark causes me much sorrow.

*Tuesday, March 29* Letter from C. Mendès: the success of *Lohengrin* is growing in Brussels. One thing in the letter annoys R.—that Catulle speaks of the director of the Grand Opéra and says, "He has expressed the intention of doing *L.*, but the road to hell is paved with such good intentions." "There one sees the sort of people one always has to deal with," R. says. "I refused to let Perrin have *Lohengrin*, although he offered me an advance of 10,000 francs and undertook to produce it within a year. But people always regard it as the greatest of favors to be taken up by the Paris Opera." In the evening R. reads me the beginning of his work on international theater. We discuss the matter and decide to come out against it, though at most in the form of a memorandum to Ollivier. In the evening read *The Arabian Nights* with the children. (Letter from Richter, who is arriving the day after tomorrow.)

*Wednesday, March 30* In the morning talked again about the memorandum, I am to write to Mendès, explaining why R. is not going to write it. R. works and plays for me the wonderfully moving passage in which Siegfried loses his memory of Brünnhilde. After lunch took the children to their dancing lesson; R. visits us there and conjures up some chocolate! — Evening of talk. Long letter from Herbeck, saying that everything had to be done in Vienna as it was because the audience was "thus and thus"—in fact, foolish nonsense.

*Thursday, March 31* Work with the children (recently much delight in Loldi, to whom I said, "All children have their ears pierced, in order to wear earrings," and she replied: "Even the poor people? When we are grown up, we shall give everything to the poor!"). When I tell R. about this, he says I should not be surprised, since I am always drawing the children's attention to the needy. He added shortly, with a smile, "I already see myself in Marburg under the scepter of Saint Elizabeth." Together we read the story of Saint Alexis, which so fascinated Goethe and which he so beautifully reconstructed from the woman's words. R. works. After lunch with the children, arrival of Richter, who tells us all about the difficulties of his time in Brussels. Many amusing things are interspersed with it, such as the celebrations for Fétis's 86th birthday, which occurred shortly after *Lohengrin*. Fétis's speech, according to him, went like this: "Gentlemen, it would be better if I were already in my grave, realism is winning ground everywhere, and I am an advocate of idealism; I respect the single-mindedness with which Wagner fights for the cause of realism, but I am an idealist," etc. At the end of this speech, it is said, not a hand was lifted, and there was no hint of applause, only on the words "better if I were in my grave" a protesting "no." — About Mathilde Mallinger, we learn from Richter that she is supposed to be the daughter of Bishop Strossmayer, at one time so much talked about in Rome. — Music in the evening; R. plays what he has already composed of *Götterdämmerung*. How happy I feel to be no longer personally of any consequence, deriving my pleasure solely from R.'s good progress and the children's well-being! Richter thinks the children are looking very well. — He tells us some very comical things about the aged Moscheles, which he had heard from pupils of his in Brussels. Since he received a small percentage from his music publisher for increased sales of printed music, he always feigned great indignation about loose pages and kept needle and thread handy, so that he could sew them together again—thus preventing the poor student from returning the book and forcing him to buy things instead of borrowing them.

*Friday, April 1* The music so affected me that I could not close my eyes for an instant. I feel extremely weak and "my mind" is only good for pulling the educational cart (R. told me about a Saxon peasant who once said to him: This dog has *no mind*, he will never pull a cart). In the morning a very nice letter from Frau Dr. Wille, to whom R.

sent his pamphlet. She speaks about me in a kind and friendly manner. R. says: "Why are we so pleased? Is it because we have received some of this kindness, or because it is a revenge for us, or something of that sort? No, certainly not—it is just unalloyed pleasure in a friend who is good and worthy of respect." — Letter from the theater manager in Magdeburg: he was present at the dress rehearsal of *Die Meistersinger* in Berlin, the King, the entire Court, and royal guests had been there, the impact profound. — But we learn nothing about the performance. — To town: Richter negotiates on my behalf concerning the serenade. In the evening 3rd act of *Siegfried*; yesterday *Götterdämmerung* (R. said he thought he had succeeded with Gutrune, she is a heathen child).

*Saturday, April 2* First real signs of spring, and in addition R. for the first time in his life called Papa! Fidi says and repeats it clearly. Telegram from Frau Schleinitz and the stage director Hallwachs in Berlin; she speaks of tendentious opposition which is being totally annihilated, he of a great triumph in spite of colossal deficiencies in the performance. Our good Richter leaves. We are sorry; he has prospects of going to Pest. After lunch letter from Louis Köhler in Königsberg, where *Die Msinger* has also been done and has made a great impression (nice letter from a Belgian journalist—the newspapers there seem to be entirely on our side). I sent our good Richter off with hopes for the future of our Bayreuth venture. As we went out, in the most splendid weather, I said to Richard, "We shall give up the Alps only for our Bayreuth venture." "We shall be *bereuter* [*approximate translation:* "sadder"]," he replied with a laugh. That reminds us that Richter told us the King has already appointed his stableboys for the Valkyries, whereas R. wants them to be depicted just as hazy images! In the evening R. reads to me from the *Iliad* and talks to me about the deep religious feeling of the Greeks (despite their having no real religion), something which is much too often ignored—for example, how Alexander could only be pacified after the death of Clitus by hearing it described as a punishment from Dionysus. — In the morning I read of the mutilations to which the papacy is subjecting monuments of art. R. says, "Instead of the French maintaining a garrison in Rome to defend the Pope, the various nations should put a garrison there to protect works of art."

*Sunday, April 3* Letter from the lawyer in Berlin, saying I should do nothing, but must simply wait. R. works, I embroider. At breakfast we talk about Hamlet, and R. says he is convinced that after the appearance of the ghost Hamlet is completely mad, not that he feigns madness, but has really become so. — Will Fidi succumb to the magic of music? "If he does not, he will be an ox!" "In relation to our world Beethoven is a human being rather like Eberle, but on account of his genius he is at home in a world of which he knows every nook and cranny, but of which we have no idea." "That is why they so hate and fear music, because they know nothing can hold up against it. It is not the representation of an idea, but the idea itself." "Mankind's whole feeling for beauty has found refuge in music," I say to R., and he agrees with me. — Richard's letter to Richter is in the newspaper, as also a report from Florence, according to which Hans played and conducted with great success in Florence and the King of Italy presented him with the order of the Corona d'Italia. Played in the garden with the children; splendid weather.

*Monday, April 4*  Bad start to the day with a letter from H. Porges, who actually wants to arrange discussions between R. and Herr von Perfall about *Die Walküre*. Sorrowful conversation with R. about this. How will it all end? — Children in the garden, I embroider. After lunch R. takes my head in his hands and says, "You are my last support, my only support." — Letter from Herr von Gersdorff in Berlin about *Die Msinger*; as in Vienna, Beckmesser's serenade was the cue for the hissers, who were completely crushed, however. Letter from Prof. Nietzsche. We send Richter a telegram for his birthday; I write to Porges, rebuking him. In the evening *Symposium*. (Copy of a French periodical, *Le Diable*, with a nice essay by Cat. Mendès on *Lohengrin*. But the whole disgusts us irremediably.)

*Tuesday, April 5*  Still worrying about *Die Walküre*; what to do, what to say, and how to find the will to work in such an atmosphere? R. forces himself, but with no enjoyment. R. reads in the paper that Hans has given a concert in Milan. Long letter from Councilor Düfflipp: R. should come, but in a *conciliatory* spirit! We go out in splendid weather, encounter close to the house an unknown priest, it is the papal nuncio; concern about Fidi's unchristened state. The Swiss are protesting against the Vatican Council and end their protest with Schiller's lines, "We want to be a single nation of brothers." R. replies to D. in the evening, very calmly and clearly: they must do what they can. (Letter from Schuré and his wife: prospects of a Wagner concert in Paris.) Prolonged contemplation (yesterday) of a sunset over the mountains, a lively breeze whipping up the blue lake, the peaks glowing serenely; thus our love amid the world's turmoil, it will glow until death. R. tells me of his stay in Blasewitz (as a child)—how for the first time he saw members of the Burschenschaft [fraternity] in their old German costumes.

*Wednesday, April 6*  Fidi 10 months old today. Letter from Herr Horawitz in Vienna, saying the 6th performance of *Die Ms.* had taken place and went very well. Nothing from Berlin except an abusive article, sent on to us in malice. The children in the garden, then to their dancing lesson. — Countess Bassenheim seems to have gathered from the newspapers that the performance in Berlin went badly. In the evening a quotation brings our conversation around to the prison scene in *Faust*. "This staying in one spot, this refusal to move, a sign of madness, appears in Gretchen in order to separate her from Faust and to enable her to become his redemptress. What in the saints is produced by higher knowledge is shown here as a pathological factor." Afterward read the *Symposium* until midnight; one of the deepest impressions of my whole life, as if I had seen the original beauty of which Diotima speaks. Tears of ravishment fill our eyes at the end of this wonderful poem.

*Thursday, April 7* To Richard in the morning with Fidi in my arms. "To create beauty from beauty," R. cries out to me. The *Symposium* forms the main topic of our conversation. R. works and is pleased in the evening; he has completed the Oath and is satisfied. "The difficulty," he says, "was to avoid bringing a new tempo into the scene, everything had to be continuous, but all the same it had to seem significant, like a heavy thundercloud." He has succeeded wonderfully. "Dear indispensability," he called me today—how sweet it is for me to hear what I already know: that he loves me! — Family lunch, Lulu touchy, has to be punished. In the evening great rudeness from the Am Rhyn boy toward the children, I instruct the children to show humility toward good, fearsome pride toward evil. In the evening Xenophon's *Memorabilia*. (Letter from Claire.) The first violets.

*Friday, April 8* Cheerful morning, the children constantly in the garden, on account of the weather. R. works, I embroider and prepare summer clothes. Letter from Heinrich Porges apologizing for the *Walküre* intervention. With Countess Bassenheim at the dancing lesson. On the wooden bridge encountered the former Lieutenant Müller, whom I had not seen since Zurich with R. (1857); this made me feel embarrassed. — "You must not cry because we are so happy," said R. to me yesterday, when he embraced me and I as usual could only weep. "I wrote *Art and Revolution* under just such an impression as that of the *Symposium* now," R. says, and, when I tell him how hard it is for me to talk to people when all they understand is just success and non-success, he says: "You are right; everything is a compromise, even the fact that I allow *Lohengrin* and *Tannhäuser* to be regarded as operas; it is terrible: if I were independent, a man of means, I would not give my things to any theater." "There ought really to be a prytaneum set up in Germany, which would say to me, for instance: Your things will be produced everywhere, for that you will receive such and such an allowance, but the works will belong to the nation, for it is shameful to receive money for such things, to see them regarded as mere goods," R. says to me on receiving a fee from Hamburg for *Der Fliegende Holländer*.

*Saturday, April 9*    As usual garden, embroidery, and composition. At lunch brought the conversation back to the *Symposium*. R. places this work above everything else: "In Shakespeare we see Nature as it is, here we have the artistic awareness of the benefactor added; what would the world know of redeeming beauty without Plato? And what human instinct can be seen in the fact that it is precisely Plato who has been preserved for us!" — As I go to lie down after lunch, I hear R. cry, "How happy I am!" R. shows me a wonderful poem he has received from an unknown man in Berlin, who tried thus to console himself for not having been able to get a ticket for the 2nd performance of *Die Msinger*.

[*Written after the April 10 entry but marked* "belongs to April 9."] A year ago the elder children came to me here; I think they are happy, and that is the best thing; may they one day be able to use this happiness to their father's advantage! — In the evening R. played a small passage from *Tristan* (A-flat major, second act) which so pierced my heart that I was quite unable to write a short note (to Porges). "My heart bites me like the asp," I said to R. "Yes," he said, "the *Symposium*. I, too, thought today of *Tristan* and the *Symposium*. In *Tristan* it is also Eros who holds sway, and what in the one is philosophy is music in the other." I had to admit to him that, when I heard his music, everything in life which occupied me, indeed, deeply worried and upset me, was suddenly swept away "like daytime ghosts," like bad and empty dreams, and I had but one feeling: to him, to him!

*Sunday, April 10*    Palm Sunday and Loldi's birthday, along with the first spring rain, bringing life but depriving us of a picnic in the country. Letter from Richter, who has seen my father in Munich and will travel with him to Hungary. Besides that, horrifying accounts of the artistic state of Munich; but *Die Walküre* is being worked on—by painters and machinists. R. is not well and cannot work, he confines himself to correcting the proofs of his biography. I exclusively occupied with the children and my embroidery. Letter from Prof. Nietzsche, who announces his promotion to professor *ordinarius* and speaks of newspaper reports making R. the musical director in Berlin.

*Monday, April 11*    Sudden arrival of Heinrich Porges, who, alarmed by the King's assumption that he will conduct *Die Walküre*, asks R. to forgive him his lack of caution. He has seen my father in Munich. In the evening a letter from Frl. Meysenbug. Dancing lesson, R. recognizes in the teacher the son of a very old female acquaintance from his Königsberg days, a member of the chorus and friend of his wife's.

*Tuesday, April 12*    R. works, I embroider, the children play. In the afternoon a walk to the dairy, there drank milk, lovely weather; I believe we shall never be able to live without the Alps. Letter from Herr Horawitz, who says that mendacious autograph copies of a correspondence have been sent from Berlin to all Viennese newspapers and received there with crows of delight (regarding the performance of *Die Ms.*). R. was pleased with Bismarck, who simply ordered his envoy to leave Rome and declared that he would not allow the Prussian bishops to return to their sees if the clause concerning Protestantism were permitted to stand. — Departure of H. Porges.

*Wednesday, April 13*   In the *A.A.Z.* there is a report on the musical situation in Florence; in it Hans is much praised, and it is said that he has been invited to conduct the Beethoven centennial concerts in Milan. R. writes a poem for the King (*dernier effort!*), he feels it will do good to address him in this way. — Yesterday R. said to me, "Let's just not have too much Makarie—with you I am always fearing some holy calamity." "You are so innocent," he tells me. If I can only give him the tranquillity he needs! Drive with the children to Countess Bassenheim's, glorious sunset. R. tells me with a laugh that the only man I care for is Fidi! Start on *Oedipus at Colonus*.

*Thursday, April 14*   Working and lunch with the children. Discussion of the letter received yesterday from Const[antin] Frantz concerning *Die Msinger* in Berlin, for which R. had given him a ticket. This letter is anything but pleasing, he thinks it a pity there is so little for the barrel organ in it! Yet I am glad that it came, since he informs me that Daniel's grave is being cared for. To town with R. to fetch Easter eggs. Letter from Prof. N., who reports that Doris B[rockhaus]'s fiancé killed himself. When I arrive home, R. says to me, "If you only knew what I thought, when you came bowling home: 'Here comes the only person in the world who means anything to you.'" I read something on his desk and he says, "As long as I can see your dear face, I shall not die." In the evening finished *Oedipus*; tremendous impression, and R. remarks: "A special feature of the Greeks, which I believe is not to be found among us, is the sanctity and divinity of the curse-laden individual who is being punished in behalf of a whole generation. Oedipus is quite godlike in his harshness against Polynices, it could be Zeus himself speaking, which is why, when he lays aside his last mortal frailty, he is at once summoned to the gods. That appears to us harsh, for we do not share the religious feelings of the Greeks." — In the morning I say I should be glad to hear old Italian church music as before: "That will be done in our school in Bayreuth." "But in this school," I say, "the piano must not be taught, the students must be able to play the piano only well enough to become good musicians, but they will get no training in it in our school, otherwise virtuosity will stifle everything." "You are right," says R., "but how bold you are!"

*Friday, April 15* Loulou all day with Countess Bassenheim, who took her to the graves. From the outside world a Berlin newspaper, according to which the reviews of *Die Msinger* overstepped all the bounds of decency. A weak article, but favorable, suggesting that the political party the paper represents is taking the side of the work; it is also stated that at the first performance the orchestra seats were full of "distinctive physiognomies," ready "to take their revenge on the author of 'Judaism in Music.'" — I discuss with R. my hope that Hans might feel contented in Florence, since he found Germany so uncongenial and Munich in particular insufferable. — In the afternoon a letter from a Herr *Brayer* in Chartres, offering his services as a conductor for Munich and *Die Walküre*!! Not much joy from outside, our young children are our only consolation and support; but for them, I think, we should be willing to die. "People imagined all sorts of things about our union, but that it was the result of a tremendous love and that our finding each other was no mere accident—that scarcely seems to occur to anybody." — R. today in gloomy mood, because he was disturbed during his work and is making no progress. (It is Siegfried's departure with Gunther.) "At such times," he says, "one feels one will never be able to do it." In the morning, when I called out to him, "Are you amicably disposed toward me?" he answered, "Quite amicably, and every day I love you more." — In the evening read the *Revue des Deux Mondes*, which Schuré sent me. R. to bed early.

*Saturday, April 16* We talk about women. R. says, "When they lose a certain timid modesty, try to be something other than wives and mothers, how unpleasantly stiff they become!" Talk about Easter eggs. R. relates how, when he was in Eisleben, some friends of his uncle sent him a basket of large crows' eggs with the inscription "Green eggs for Richard Geyer"; their green color gave him a great delight. A letter from Judith, they want to visit us. A "charitable hand," as R. calls it, has sent us a very ugly article by Heinrich Dorn about *Die Msinger*; wretched, pitiful creatures! A ridiculous, adulatory poem to R., with the request that he write some words under the cipher A. v. T., we see as one of those vulgar traps to which R. is always being exposed because he is regarded, alas, as an operatic composer! On the other hand, the turbulent enthusiasm of the French gives us little pleasure, either. So Schopenhauer is completely right! We read yesterday an article about Sch[openhauer] entitled "*Un bouddhiste contemporain*," in which the only thing which pleased us was some of Schopenhauer's own words on the subject of progress. The Jesuits are making approaches to the Jews, amusing account of a conversation between the Pope and the

*Lehmann* brothers! — R. still not quite well. — We burn winter in the form of a bogeyman bearing our Christmas tree on his head—great joy among the children. Marie Bassenheim with us overnight.

*Sunday, April 17* Easter joys, Easter sorrows, and dressed Easter lamb. I conceal the eggs and then have to retire, because I feel worn out by even this little exertion. R. comes to me and says, "'Hagen's Watch' will be colossal." Toward noon he plays me the glorious piece he has just composed. Very good report in a new musical periodical about the *Msinger* production in Berlin, the many rumors which were circulated, nonsense which made it impossible for people really to *hear* the work. Letter to R. from the conductor Schmidt in Leipzig, who says that for him, after hearing *Die Ms.* in Berlin, it is no longer just a question, but a duty to art and the public to stage the work in Leipzig. Letter to me from E. Schuré, he talks of a morning reception at my mother's. — I had just written to M. Maier when R. tells me she has written to him with news of Hans's distressed condition in Florence, conveyed to her by his mother and sister. I can hardly believe that this is true, for all reports maintain the contrary, but my peace of mind is again shattered. "Oh, this mortal life!" R. has received the proofs of his *Walküre* text. How depressing! — R. said with regard to his biography, "I believe it will turn out terribly monotonous for the reader; eternal new beginnings, and nothing ever comes of them."

*Monday, April 18* Very bad night, I have to call R. and spend the day in bed on account of a kind of sore throat. In the *A.A.Z.* a correspondent's report from Berlin (Julius *Cohen* Rodenberg) about *Die Msinger*; it pokes fun at the applauding "blond Germans," depicts the composer as a monster, but praises the work itself. — (Yesterday R. drew for me with a pencil the scenery for his *Götterdämmerung*.) — R. brings a letter from the poet Hans Herrig, who seems to be full of R.'s ideas to the point of obsession. R. had asked for his address in an advertisement in the *Norddeutsche Allgemeine*. He relates with indignation that at the 3rd performance cuts had already been introduced; R. writes to Eckert about them. R. has his meals with me; he talks of many model performances he brought about in small towns and says [Wilhelmine] Schröder-Devrient once humorously remarked that Reissiger would have to put in for an extra allowance for gymnastics lessons; since R. was constantly jumping on to the stage from the orchestra to lend a hand, Reissiger wanted to do the same, but could not manage it, hence the need for gymnastics lessons. — While R. is eating with me, he recalls my confinement and weeps, describing his condition and then his happiness. — Reverting to *Die Msinger* in Berlin, he says, "It is still just as I said to Hans in Munich on his birthday: we shall attain success only if we renounce all pleasure in it."

I tell him I have written to Judith and told her how offended I was to see *Lohengrin* praised in a paper so full of shameful stories. R.: "I wonder if she will understand? She has such good and deep qualities, but they are all such fragmented entities. You are the only complete person I have ever met, you are even more complete than I am"— which of course made me laugh. In the evening read *Henry IV*.

*Tuesday, April 19*   Still unwell: wrote to Prof. Nietzsche. Otherwise spent the whole day embroidering. R. works. The weather is fine, the children are in the garden.

*Wednesday, April 20*   The children with me again for lessons. We still hear nothing from Berlin. All is silent in Munich, too. But the weather is glorious, we delight in Tribschen. Coffee in the garden. —

*Thursday, April 21*   With the children; R. has received a letter from Councilor Düfflipp saying that the King was unpleasantly surprised by his last letter and asks him to choose Heinrich Porges after all. Our *Non possumus* to this. Then R. completes "Hagen's Watch." Afternoon in the garden. R. goes for a long walk. Go for a drive in the green outfit, to the children's joy.

*Friday, April 22*   Letter from an unknown enthusiast in Berlin (Lieutenant Schöning); he says the management in Berlin has put *Die Msinger* aside until the fall, so that passions will have time to cool. Great consternation about this—it means a few Jewboys have achieved their aim. R. is at first depressed, but he soon recovers his spirits, and we enjoy a splendid afternoon in the garden, Fidi beside us! In the evening I take the elder ones to their dancing lesson. (Read Berlioz's memoirs.)

*Saturday, April 23*   R. in gloomy mood. I embroider and teach. At lunch R. reads me a passage about old Italian music by Tieck, which he finds very significant. "We have discovered the magic formula with which to solve this dilemma—the large orchestra, which, like Nature, is all-embracing, and within whose confines the human being can roam." — Delight in a hedgehog which has made its nest beneath a bench in our garden. Fidi's first toy, brought home for him by R. (Letter from Claire.)

*Sunday, April 24*   Overcast weather, spring rain; R. in dull spirits because of it. He writes to Düfflipp to tell him that he feels no bitterness, and his only wish is that the King might get some enjoyment from *Die Walküre*. I am very much alarmed by some of the expressions in this letter, and that in turn worries R. I quickly get a grip on myself —I must remember that for me every sorrow is a blessing and my task is above all not to upset R. Then a happy lunch with the children. But concern hangs heavily over us. Showed the children Raphael and Doré's

Bible. Gave Lusch Tieck's "Red Riding Hood" to read. In the evening, *Henry IV Part II.*

*Monday, April 25*  R. had a sad dream about our separation. Our mood is melancholy; I have regained my self-control and am glad. Boni in bed on account of slight hoarseness. The cuckoo calls, the hedgehog has gone, the cat laboriously carries its kittens to the bed in the guest room. Go out after lunch with R., he tells me that in his youth he always dreaded spring, for it meant the theaters would be empty, the audience absent, the poor musical director shown the door. As he is telling me this, a man appears and hands me a court summons. If I do not return to Berlin within 4 weeks, proceedings for divorce will be inaugurated. Only inaugurated! — In the morning R. sent off a different letter to Councilor Düffl., though I begged him to send the first. But the later one seems to me more suited to both the situation and the man. Letter from Schmidt, the musical director in Leipzig; fee for *Die Msinger.* Dancing lesson; Lusch experienced her first rebuff; she took it well. — Before beginning our reading R. says: "I wish for nothing, I want only to preserve, and that is the most awful form of worry, as Calderón says so well in his sonnet. Whoever demands something has desire and hope; whoever possesses happiness has only the fear of losing it. A happy person is almost bound to have only apprehensive dreams—that he will lose what he has."

*Tuesday, April 26*  R. began the day with a conversation about the Greek attitude toward love, which we cannot ourselves envisage and which, when it did not degenerate into depravity, produced the highest qualities of aestheticism. "The adoration of women, on the other hand, is a completely new factor, and one which divides us entirely from the antique world. The ancient Germans respected women as something mysterious, closer to Nature—rather in the way the Egyptians worshiped animals—and, in order to preserve their divinity intact, did not wish to touch them. What this cult has led to today, whereby women since chignons and *bibi* hats have demanded to be adored and from which they derive all this emancipation nonsense—that we already know." — He goes to work again, for the first time in many days—I with the children. In the afternoon a walk with Loulou and Loldi, who fell in the lake, as she proudly relates. Stop for a rest in the dairy; the children talk of the first cockchafer. In the evening *Phaedrus.* (Letter from my mother.)

*Wednesday, April 27*  Truly awful night, I start up abruptly from sleep three or four times and cry out; in the end I have to get up, R. consoles me. I remember fearfully how I was so violently awoken at the time of Blandine's death. Who is suffering, who is dying?—my father, poor Hans? God protect us! Of R. I can and will not think in this connection; I no longer enjoy hearing the cuckoo, for three years ago he asked it how many years he had to live and received 3 calls in answer. Oh, eternal worry, when will you disappear? Only with life itself. — Nasty, stormy day. Lusch has to stay in bed on account of a cough, and R. has to write letters! — Yesterday R. said that he would like to have three little volumes of his essays, in which *Art and Revolution* would appear. He also said he felt like writing to Ollivier, telling him that "everything they do against the Jesuits, however tyrannical, however despotic, is salutary, but whatever they do *with* them is ruinous." He feels that something great might emerge from this plebiscite if one were to put a stop to the eternal talk in the Chamber, were to close it, also withdraw the freedom of the press, for on all this the "priests" were thriving. They should be utterly wiped out, the schools made free, all the people stirred up by the clerics should be shot down, and so on. Read Sicilian fairy tales with the children and in the evening *Phaedrus* with R. In the course of this R. observes "how lightly people talk of the Greeks and of Platonic love, whereas their world is simply inconceivable and incomprehensible to us unless we completely change our mental outlook, as in the study of philosophy."

*Thursday, April 28* Letter from the conductor Levi. ("I respect him," says R., "because he really calls himself *Levi* as in the Bible, and not Löwe, Lewy, etc.") He says he has been invited to conduct *Die Walküre*, and he asks for R.'s opinion. R. replies calmly and honestly. — Lusch still in bed. I concerned about I know not what, but happy. I asked R. whether he no longer wrote things down, no diary? "No, that has stopped, now I enjoy my happiness. I swear to you I am amazed at myself when I see that none of my old confidence has left me, my imagination is perhaps even improved, with the constant urge to create. Whom have I to thank for this?" "The King of Bavaria," I interpose jokingly. "Aha, that is your answer to my recent letter. Believe me, I should have wearily dropped his favor if I had not found you." — Yesterday, when he was surprised not to have received a letter from Hanover, I said our friend von Bronsart was probably shocked by our relationship. After some reflection he said, "That people cannot see that we knew exactly what we were doing, since after all I am no trickster and you also had sufficient knowledge of the world; that we braved everything and took it on ourselves in order to belong to each other, that should surely fill them with respect." "When I have brought the children up nicely and you have finished the *Nibelungen*, then perhaps we shall be respected." — At lunch (yesterday) he answered my question concerning the relationship of Plato's *soul* to Schopenhauer's *will*; I understood what he said, only I cannot write it down. —

Very nice and original letter from our new friend *Hans Herrig*. A devotee of Schopenhauer (obviously) and of Wagner, as is only proper. In the evening read *Ivanhoe* with great admiration.

*Friday, April 29* The mail brings nothing, and R. is able to do some work. The children still not quite well—and outside snow. Yet the whole world looks unsettled, so much so that R. told me that in his thoughts he had got to the stage of even making do with the Jesuits, who at least would bring peace to the world. "Their power is based, not on their atrocious methods, but on the idea underlying them, their recognition of the wickedness and foolishness of mankind." — "The animal divineness of the Greeks is so strange to us," he also says, when we again come to that topic. — Letters (in the evening) from Darmstadt, the conductor Marpurg, who reports his enthusiasm for *Die Walküre*, then (from Cologne) newspapers in which Herr Hiller is castigated for his management (that people send us such things!), then 5 thalers for the performance of the *Msinger* overture in Cologne.

*Saturday, April 30* Colds, wretched weather, but R. works and finishes the intermezzo ("Hagen's Watch"—Brünnhilde contemplating the ring), which, as he says, is more a sort of cadenza, like a parenthesis, not an intermezzo. — Our manservant is leaving us; apart from his *Knecht Ruprecht* nothing was good about him, but that was excellent. In the evening R. reads me *Ivanhoe*. Letter from Herr *Simson* in Berlin: in 4 weeks I must present myself to the priest, and then the proceedings will begin. Hans has returned to Florence.

*Sunday, May 1* Deceptiveness of the foehn, one moment fine weather, the next rain. Loldi sees a robin and says, "It's like Mama's shawl." Countess Bassenheim visits me, survey of the world, in which there are enough curious things going on (France-Rome plebiscite—infallibility—England-Greece Marathon — murder of the embassy people—international conspiracy—in Germany the three *J*'s). We read to the Countess yesterday's letter from Richter, in which he first says that since his dismissal the number of Jews has increased by *45,000* (!), then that at a performance of *Die Msinger* a Jew shouted after the Overture, "Oh, the poor orchestra!," hissed, and then, rebuked by his neighbor, joined in the applause himself, saying, "You see, the beautiful bits I applaud, too, but there are only one or two beautiful bits— *or let's say three.*" Lunch with the children. Later I read them Sicilian fairy tales. Then I go for a walk in wind and rain with R. In the evening R. says: "When one day in my old age I write *Die Sieger*, I shall give it a prelude in which the first part of the story (in which the Chandala maiden spurns Ananda) will be told. Only music can convey the mysteries of reincarnation."

*Monday, May 2* Children's work. R.'s work. Then he replies to

C. Frantz and compares the mania for detached pieces from opera with the mania for quotations from the tragedies. Nothing from outside, only newspapers and money from Berlin. Children's dances and fairy tales.

*Tuesday, May 3* Dire weather arrives with the new manservant. R. complains of not being able to work; with the children much time on geography, fairy tales, etc. —

*Wednesday, May 4* When our breakfast conversation brings us to Richter and his stay in Paris (he did *not* see Notre Dame and in the Louvre *only* Napoleon's boots), R. says: "People who learned nothing of the 'ancient Greeks' in their childhood have no eye for beauty. All my later feelings about the ugliness of our present world stem from looking at the illustrations in Moritz's mythology. Perseus with his fine helmet, but otherwise naked, delighted me and made me disgusted with our whole military system, with its buttoned-up uniforms plastered with decorations. When I read that crowned poets received only an olive wreath as prize, I was thrilled, and I despised the people who strutted about in all their ribbons. It was respect for the olive wreath which gave me my contempt for decorations, not democratic affectation or plebeian crudeness, as your father, for instance, certainly imagines." He works, I with the children. At lunch it cuts me to the quick when he says that in the excitement of work he has often wanted to come up to me, but, knowing that I was busy teaching the children, he stayed away. He said I should really engage a governess for the children. I have to weep, for I feel I have to make this sacrifice, yet how much I want him always to be contented! Letters—one to R. from the King in the usual strain—that he could never be unfaithful to him, etc.—one to me from a lieutenant: I am invited to write for a newspaper!!! Very unpleasant impression from the printing, with omissions, of a letter from R. to the music director Eberle; the omissions distort the letter so much that Eckert and Betz must feel offended, hence, no doubt, their silence. R. is very upset about this, he writes at once to Eckert and gets up at 4 o'clock in the morning (Thursday) to make his letter even more emphatic. Then he again sees the sunrise from the Orange Room, as at the time of Fidi's birth. — Last dancing lesson.

*Thursday, May 5* Letter to me from Prof. Nietzsche. R. not well and not satisfied with his work. Walk in the afternoon. A letter from the lawyer, trouble over the children's certificates of residence. Evening of conversation, preparations for the projected outing tomorrow.

*Friday, May 6* No outing, wretched cold weather; R. writes letters (to the King and to Hans Herrig), I look for poems for R.'s birthday.

Letter from Frau Schuré. R. not well, I am worried about him. Wrote to Claire. —

*Saturday, May 7* More children's coughs! — In the morning R. exclaims to me, "You really are a miraculous woman, I have just been considering your letter to Franziska Ritter, it is perhaps the finest thing you have ever done." (Some ill feeling had arisen, which I was attempting to dispel.) Then he comes to me and we get on the topic of Berlioz's memoirs, which he is now reading. "In him one can so clearly see the reciprocity between natural inclinations and external conditions and relationships. Everything in Paris is horrible to him, and yet he cannot give it up—this horribleness is for him the whole world. His main grief was opera, which he could never master." Newspapers from Vienna; a passage in which it is maintained that the *Eroica* foretells Wagner particularly displeases R.: "I find it horrible when people compare me with Beethoven; I always feel like saying, 'What do you know of B.?'" I explain to him how I think it is meant (a glorification of the Germanic character, not of Napoleon, hence a pointer toward Wagner). He laughs and says his consciousness has outgrown him. (In his letter to the King he had called me his consciousness.) — We really had to laugh yesterday when Jakob told us that the old lamplighter at the Schweizerhof (who always greets R. with a "Good morning, Herr *Richard Wagner*") has just recovered from a mortal illness; now he goes around picking camomile flowers and eating them; he also puts a few on his nose during the night, in order to prolong his life, yet all the while he is declaring, "Oh, dying is splendid!" — R. says that Berlioz's memoirs have strengthened his resolve never again to have anything to do with Paris. Fun over Fidi's profession (surgeon), but we stick to our opinion, for a person must have a definite calling. — R. is not well and in an agitated state, but all the same he works a little. I am very worried when he is indisposed, worried and grieved. In the evening began on *Phaedo*.

*Sunday, May 8* Nice but pale weather. R. works, I to a rehearsal of the *"Huldigungsmarsch"* at the barracks. God knows how this will turn out, perhaps my star will help me, but I am somewhat nervous. Meal with the children at 4 o'clock on account of the rehearsal. In the evening continued with *Phaedo*.

*Monday, May 9* To my surprise R. decides on the outing. We go in spite of the pale clouds. Great joy among the children, arrival in Brunnen; drive to the Grütli, I remember Grandmama's and Daniel's birthdays, both today. The weather turns bad, but we remain cheerful. In the evening, as I go to bed, I hear R. out on the Axenstrasse calling to me the theme from the love scene between Siegfried and Brünnhilde.

*Tuesday, May 10*   Terrible boardinghouse night in Brunnen. Kos barking, people shouting, Boni coughing, beds and doors creaking, etc. — I have to get up often to attend to Boni, and then I think of what Socrates said about pleasant and unpleasant things; my bed, otherwise unbearable, seemed very pleasant to me each time I leaped back into it after attending to the little ones, and so I laughed, recalling the *two ends*. R. got no sleep, either. We decide to return home at 10 o'clock. At home, plebiscite—yes; letters, Clemens Brockhaus reports on the terrible state of his family following the calamity, then an obituary notice, Constantin Frantz has lost his son, R.'s last letter once again gave him a commission for the cemetery!! Arrival of Prof. Nietzsche's speech in Latin, then of a lovely spring outfit which R. had ordered for me as a surprise! Letter from Frl. von Meysenbug (giving R. little pleasure). R. astonished to have received no reply from Eckert; so another enemy made! The latter will have taken advantage of the most convenient piece of gossip to divest himself of his gratitude. — When I come down to R. in the afternoon, he plays me a piece he has just thought out, "Blackbird Theme, Scherzo in the Beethoven Manner"—he copied it from our blackbird. "When I hear something like that, I call it quite simply a Beethoven allegro, meaning that he is the creator of this form, he is the master, without him it would not exist." "How I should like now to write poetry!" he says. "What easy, swift work—what is it compared with writing scores? It is the skeleton, like bare branches, the tree in winter; music is the blossom, the leaves." Music in the evening. He plays me passages from the first act of *Götterdämmerung*. — He then complains of the difficulty of the scene between Waltraute and Brünnhilde, the one in agitated haste, the other expansively moved that a friend has come to visit her.

*Wednesday, May 11*   The children busy with the poems; R. calls me down while he is working; he wants to embrace me. I leave him in haste, in order to embroider, on account of his birthday. In the afternoon to Countess B.'s, saw the old Prince perhaps for the last time. — Great alarm during the day; R. had a cuckoo in front of his window, he saw it and describes its powerful form to us. Everything makes me worry, I don't know why.

*Thursday, May 12*   Got up very early because of the folder. Nice letters from the former conductor *Esser* and R.'s old friend Pusinelli, who mentions me in the most friendly way. Worry about Fidi, whose hoarseness persists. Boni surprises me with a nice fairy tale, quite well told in French. Loldi says, "The moon has a cheek missing." R. not very well. (Much talk about the plebiscite.)

*Friday, May 13*   The Beethoven Committee in Vienna invites R. to conduct the 9th Symphony (Lachner *Fidelio*, my father the *Missa*

*Solemnis*); R. does not want to: "When I at last have a home of my own, I shall conduct the Symphony for you, but I want nothing to do with all that rabble." He is unfortunately not well. Marie Bassenheim with us for lunch. In the evening R. wrapped himself in blankets to ward off a cold; I read him scenes from *Wallenstein* and we come to the conclusion that the play—particularly the relationship between Thekla and Max—is far too little appreciated. R. tells me how impressed he was, when he came to Würzburg, to be told by a man named Seiffert that as a poet Heine was much better than Schiller. We talk about having the plays performed in Bayreuth, for the disgraceful way in which they are done spoils them for one—for example, Thekla is always shown as weak and tearful, whereas she possesses all the ruthlessness of true love. "There he is!" reminds us of Eva's blissful cry in *Die Msinger*. "It is magnetism which contrives, for example, that the sheep finds in the wide world the grass which is good for it, all the rest is shadowy show. Thus a woman in love—the whole world consists of phantoms, but she knows where *he* is."

*Saturday, May 14* R. at work, I visit him in a white gown, he laughs and says, "The White Lady, or, rather, Thekla, since for all fine things I have you as model; that's why I am happy; you knew I could be helped." Fidi is unfortunately still hoarse. R. romps around a lot with the children, who are really very sweet. In the newspaper I read that Hans has conducted a concert in Florence. To town with R.; a terrible rainstorm, over which we just laugh, however.

*Sunday, May 15* Very seemly letter from the conductor Levi, who has refused to conduct *Die Walküre*. Gloriously fine day; burning sunshine; to the sounds of Fidi's "Dadadada" R. sketches part of Waltraute's narration (he "sends off the ravens"). Family lunch in the best of spirits. Afterward R. reads Hoffmann's *"Das fremde Kind"* to me and the elder children; great enjoyment in this fine tale, which R. says expresses very well the pressures of civilization, the breach between Nature and culture. — Visit from our lawyer, who does not understand the procedure in Berlin and cannot at all foresee when it will end. Letter to Prof. Nietzsche. Fine evening, cicadas, cockchafers, great exuberance of growth, sap and strength everywhere.

*Monday, May 16* If only we could curb passion—if only it could be banished from our lives! Its approach now grieves me, as if it were the death of love. — Letter from Claire; worked with the children in the garden, R. meanwhile at his sketching. Drove to town with Lusch; R. writes Esser a statement, designed for publication, on his attitude toward the production of *Die Walküre*. Letter from Herr Hans Herrig; very curious—he seems really to be more obsessed than filled with R.'s ideas. — Fidi still hoarse, I very sad about it. — Yesterday evening we read *Phaedo*; I thought of what R. said to me about Socrates: that his wise circumspection, his absolute contemplation, which nothing could destroy, had been encountered only once in the world, whereas even the saints had been present in numbers. (Wrote off concerning the certificates of baptism.)

*Tuesday, May 17*   R. had a very bad night, got up, ran out into the garden, listened to the dawn, made "raven studies" (but it croaked horribly), and in the end felt very wretched. Yesterday evening a bat flew around him, which alarmed me considerably. Fidi still hoarse; I take the children to Countess Bassenheim's, her little daughter's birthday, Eva invited for the first time. In the evening read *Wallenstein* with R.

*Wednesday, May 18*   R. still unwell, I myself worn out, but Fidi somewhat better. Fine weather. First botany lesson with the children; fine afternoon out of doors with R. Nice letter to him from Prof. Nietzsche. In the evening started *Wallensteins Tod.*

*Thursday, May 19*   R. said at breakfast that *Wallenstein* had brought back to his mind what he wrote in *Opera and Drama* about the nature of drama; to make something clear to the audience, one needs to put in so much which in fact leaves it unaffected. R. is indisposed, I bothered by things going wrong for his birthday; I have been working on it for about six months, and almost everything is letting me down; at such times our only help is the acknowledgment that we cannot control external influences! Fidi getting better.

*Friday, May 20*   Continuation of the birthday contrarinesses, but glorious hot weather, the work in the garden more planned than carried out. The boats on the lake remind one of that image which R. gave for' melody in *Opera and Drama*: it floats above the element, is distinct from it, but cannot exist without it. Fidi, our prince, looks splendid: "Through him the Universal Spirit has shown what it wanted, why it put our love and our loyalty to the test." — I prepare Lusch to release the birds given to her on her birthday; it costs her a great struggle, but she decides to keep birds only in winter and to free them in summer. How much I praise the star which has allowed the children to pass their youth in this solitary place and in R.'s proximity! None of life's battles, no anguish will ever be able to affect this felicity. — After lunch, when we are reading *Wallenstein*, Jakob comes in struggling for breath: the King's head coachman is here, has brought a horse. The arrival of Grane, the children's joy, Thespis wagon (the little ones jump on to the wagon and dance). Poor Fritz! The coachman brings good news of the King. Happy walk with R. in the evening in the finest May weather. Fidi on the horse, earnest, wondering, but secure.

*Saturday, May 21*  Awake at 4 o'clock, rise at 4:30 and write a poem for Loulou to speak while freeing her birds tomorrow.

*Liebe Vöglein flieget fort,*
*gedenket mein am freien Ort,*
*ein Nest euch bauet*
*drin Kleine erschauet,*
*Männchen sing freier*
*Weibchen brüt Eier*

*Zu mir kommt wieder*
*fällt Schnee hernieder,*
*friert es auch draussen,*
*bei mir kommt hausen,*
*die Kleinen bringt her.*
*Willkommne Wiederkehr!*

*Und bleibt ihr fort so lebet wohl*
*nicht ist der Liebe Wesen hohl,*
*wie dürfte Liebe sie sich taufen*
*wollt sie Besitz mit Kummer erkaufen.*
*Und fallen, süsser Tau, wohl Tränen,*
*sie weihen zur Blume unser Trennen.*

*Schöner Fink*
*ink folg dem Wink,*
*liebster Zeisig*
*eifrig eilig zeige dich*
*die Tür ist auf*
*nehmt euren Lauf.*

*Der schönste Tag ist heut'*
*dass sein Vogel auch sich freut*
*will von Herzen das Kind,*
*drum liebe Vöglein, geschwind,*
*ziehet frei dahin*
*Es folget euch froh mein Sinn.*

["Dear birdies, fly away, think of me when you are free; build a nest for your young; cock, sing more freely, hen, hatch eggs. Come back to me if snow falls; and if outside it freezes, seek shelter here with me; bring your little ones: A welcome return! And if you come not again, then fare you well: nothing in love is vain; how could it be called love, if it paid for ownership in sorrow? And if tears, sweet dewdrops, should fall, they but dedicate our parting to the flowers. Lovely finch, swiftly follow the call; dearest siskin, show how you can hasten—the door is open: go your way. Today is the loveliest of days; that her bird should also be happy is the girl's dearest wish. So, dear birdies, quick: fly away to freedom! My thoughts follow you in joy."]

Did the children's hair and made further preparations. Letters from R.'s old acquaintance and companion in misery, E. Kietz, who wants to visit him. Arrival of the certificates of baptism. I drive to the rehearsal—as far as I can judge, the piece is going well. We finish *Wallenstein*, with the greatest of admiration for this masterpiece, which only the necessity of being divided into three separate plays has damaged in a few particulars.

*Sunday, May 22*  During the night decorated the stairs and the vestibule, but I note by my mood that I am no longer up to festive occasions, and now, even before the day begins, here I sit, writing this and weeping. God grant my children joy today; whoever has suffered much loses the capacity to laugh. On festive days in particular one realizes how sad life is! The unremarked passing of days without unspoken fears is surely the best thing for sore hearts. God bless all whom I love, and give me rest soon! — The pleasure R. felt soon swept my melancholy mood away. At 8 o'clock I positioned the children with wreaths of roses: Loldi and Eva at the front door; farther down in the bower, beneath a laurel, Boni; at the bottom of the steps, beside the bust loaded down with flowers, myself and Fidi; at the end of the tableau Loulou. The music *("Huldigungsmarsch")* began at 8:30, the 45 soldiers grouped under the fir tree, at the conclusion R. emerged sobbing from the house and thanked the conductor; he was deeply moved, making me almost regret having arranged this little ceremony. Afterward the children recited poems to him, we breakfasted in gay spirits and then went off to rest. In the afternoon the birds were to be released and some fireworks lit, but a huge storm came up and we ended the day quietly. Many letters and telegrams (King, Richter, Standhartner, etc.), a fine poem from Hans Herrig ("The Three Norns"), a nice letter from Prof. Nietzsche. A telegram from my father ("Forever with you, on bright as on gloomy days") pleased and moved me greatly.

*Monday, May 23*  Long sleep; then the delayed festivities. Arrival of the playpen designed by Hans, I put Fidi in it, the children gather around it, Loulou recites her poem in front of the cage, then we carry the cage into the garden; four of the birds fly away immediately; only a single chaffinch remained behind, unwilling to follow the calls of its brethren; for fear that the cat might get it, I tell Jakob to take it out and give it to Loulou to place on a bush; this is done, but probably the shock numbed it, for it flew, not upward, but downward, and Jakob's dog, which we had not even noticed, pounced on it—it was dead. Thus this little festival of joy ended in tragedy, the poor bird had sensed its coming death. What a grim lesson—how wretched the human being's pitiful good intentions in relation to Fate! The finch had to pay with its life for the freedom of its brethren. — I write to Prof. Nietzsche; after lunch, first drive with Grane to Stanz. In the evening our fireworks. Alluding to the morning serenade, R. calls me the conductor of his life.

*Tuesday, May 24*  R. writes letters (business and otherwise); Herr Weissheimer continues his shameless conduct toward R. Frl. von Meysenbug also sends birthday congratulations. R. sinks into meditation about the *second generation*, which was attracted to him but which was worthless, whereas the third, now 25 years old, appears through its earnestness and concentration to grasp R.'s *ideas*. I work with the children; in the afternoon visit of Agatha Aufdermauer from Brunnen, our Tribschen enchants her. Then to the jeweler, who has been to see Semper; the latter received him at first hostilely, but then gradually gave some explanations. In the evening *Philoctetes*. I write to Frau Schuré and quote to her R.'s saying about Wallenstein: "Born under Saturn and flirting with Jupiter, who does not repay his trust."

*Wednesday, May 25* Arrival of two pineapples from Paris, we suspect Judith. Letter from Esser (Richter reports that Wüllner is to conduct *Die Walküre* in Munich!!). Arrival of flowers, the King has sent them. Letter from Eckert; a misunderstanding, his wife was dangerously ill; pleasure at one ill-wisher the less. I write to Dr. Pusinelli about the hanging lamp. Bad news of Prince Wallerstein. — (R. calls me "my good consciousness.") Worked with the children, R. resumes *Götterdämmerung*. Drive to inquire about the Prince's condition. R. writes to Richter, asking him to go to the secretary of the Beethoven Committee and tell him that R. finds it impossible to reply to a letter signed by Messrs. *Hanslick* and *Schelle*. In the evening R. remarks that Fidi has literally blossomed in the open air; in the morning he had been so small, in the afternoon in the garden he was strong—"that is how we see it, anyway." I: "If we see it, then it must be so, for what brings about change in us will also affect the child." "That is just the problem," R. replies and, going on from there, explains to me the nature of Schopenhauer's Will (from Brahma to Buddha), "the urge toward life, then toward knowledge, and finally toward destruction. Remorse— that is to say, the knowledge that inside us something lives which is much more powerful than our idea of evil." R. spoke for a long time, beautifully and movingly, and I felt as if through him I were penetrating into the secrets of the world, but only through him. Afterward finished *Philoctetes*, with unbounded admiration. — The letters from the Council amuse us, the discussion on infallibility opened with the following argument: Saint Peter, crucified head downward, provides the symbol of the head bearing the limbs, for "the Sicilians, to whom Saint Peter had preached the doctrine of infallibility, had in their doubt called on the Virgin Mary, who replied that she did in fact remember her son's declaring Peter to be infallible!" — "The sun shines down on baseness," says R., reading in the newspapers about the *temps de l'empereur*.

*Thursday, May 26* Ascension Day. The newspapers write of an "ovation" given to R. by the military band; this amuses R. "Thus is history made," he says. "It would never occur to anybody that you engaged these people. There was not the slightest intention of giving me an ovation, but I am afraid that most of the ovations of which one hears are like that." — In the afternoon in the woods with the children, Loulou pleases me; in fun we had given her 50 centimes, an old lady approached and of her own accord she asked me to allow her to give the money to the woman. — In the evening Shakespeare's *Merry Wives.* (Visit of the young Count B.; we write to Judith.)

*Friday, May 27* Conference with the priest; little of benefit; among other things he reproaches me for the morning serenade. R. meanwhile writes to the King. He is greatly delighted with the doctor, who tells him he has never seen such a fine boy as Fidi. Fine afternoon. Fidi taking a sun bath; read in the hermitage. "Music is nothing but will," says R.

*Saturday, May 28* Sent the priest's attestation to the law courts in Berlin, then wrote to Claire. R. works. A drive in the afternoon; when we remark on Kos's intelligence, I ask, "Where does the soul of such an animal go?" "We must think of that as a really friendly place," R. replies. "It is only Death itself of which we must think solemnly, as a test of life; what comes after, however, in as friendly a light as possible." In the evening conclusion of *The Merry Wives* with great enjoyment and admiration; R. says that particularly on the stage this work comes splendidly to life, entertaining, many-sided. During the fifth act he says, "Shakespeare's head was full of these fairies, this elfin world—*Old England* lived inside him." "And so we have read three great poets one after another (Schiller, Sophocles, Shakespeare), and each of their works has both moved and surprised us, since the work of such geniuses always has something inconceivable about it." An article by Berthold Auerbach (no such genius he!) about woods is printed in the newspaper; R. says he found it unreadable on account of its affected closeness to Nature: "These fellows are a real nuisance" (the Jews).

*Sunday, May 29* All kinds of fun and games with the children while R. works. We hear that Laube has had to leave the theater in Leipzig, since the town, deeming it necessary to close it down, would not give him any compensation: "How degrading for such an old hand, to be caught up so in the common grind." Walk through the woods with the older children; R. could not bring himself to leave the little ones at home, so we turned back, fetched them in the carriage, and then had them driven home, while we walked home through the woods. At lunch we spoke of the need to possess Shakespeare in English, Walter Scott, too; regarding the latter, it suddenly occurs to R. that he covered the whole of English history in his novels, except for the period Shakespeare dealt with. — A murder case which is filling the newspapers (the entire family of an inoffensive smith murdered by a thief) reminds us of the terrible fate which governs us all. It is not the murder itself which fills us with horror, but the fearful lot which can be meted out to any one of us. On our return home, Vreneli tells us she heard in the town that a boat had been sucked into the paddle of the steamer, and the man and child in it killed; our people in Tribschen heard the screams of the passengers on the steamer. With such warnings, such signs, who can call himself fortunate here below? — Conversation at supper brings us to Mozart. Dealing with *Die Zauberflöte*, R. says, "Mozart is the founder of German declamation—what fine humanity resounds in the Priest's replies to Tamino! Think how stiff such high priests are in Gluck. When you consider this text, which was meant to be a farce, and the theater for which it was written, and compare what was written before Mozart's time (even Cimarosa's still-famous *Matrimonio Segreto*)—on the one side the wretched German *Singspiel*, on the other the ornate Italian opera—one is amazed by the soul he managed to breathe into such a text. And what a life he led! A bit of tinsel at the time of his popularity, but for that he had then to pay all the more dearly. He did not complete his work, which is why one cannot really compare him with Raphael, for there is still too much convention in him." — We begin *Die Jungfrau von Orleans*; at the conclusion of the prologue R. says, "Yes, it all begs for music, though that is not to say it fails as a work of art." When I tell him that just one thing offends me, the father, Arc, whom I should prefer to see handled in the Shakespearean manner, R. says, "Don't even think of it: Sh[akespeare] is a natural genius, Schiller an artistic one; he and Goethe wanted to wring true pathos from the German language and rescue the German stage from vulgar realism." As, in tears, we come to the end of the first act, R. says, "As Goethe touches us through his objectivity, Schiller touches us through his subjectivity."

*Monday, May 30* Buying clothes; R. tells me he has ordered fine bright trousers, having told himself, "In your wedding year you are entitled to look elegant." I am worried about Loulou, who is complaining of a headache. In the newspaper it is reported that the first rehearsal of *Die Walküre* took place on May 16 and that Herr Marpurg from Darmstadt is to conduct the performances. R. very upset, writes to Herr Marpurg to tell him it is not a question of his (R.'s) being short of conductors—just that all of them with any sense of decency are refusing to conduct the work in the composer's absence. Reflections about the King; gnawing grief. — There is talk in the paper of great disturbances in Florence, which worries me on Hans's account; how even the most favored of people are affected by the burdens of life! — Richter writes from Vienna, giving news of Herr Horawitz; in character the ambiguous counterpart of Herr Julius Lang; a true Falstaff's army! — In the evening *Die Jungfrau von Orleans*. (Letter

from Klindworth in Moscow, who is arranging *Siegfried* for the piano
and says how grateful we must all be to the King for providing R.
with the leisure to write such works. "It was something else which
made this leisure productive," says R.)

*Tuesday, May 31*   When we were talking yesterday evening about
the transmigration of souls, R. cried: "Thank God this is all a deep
mystery, otherwise mankind would by now have put it all on an official
basis. 'You will become a bird, you a dog,' a policeman would tell
us." — In the morning R. receives me wearing a tail coat and a stand-up
collar—"since you like formality so much." The children say he
looks like "a gentleman." At eleven o'clock arrival of the painter
Kietz; much confusion; from the lunchtime conversation I remember
R.'s words to Kietz: "You say painters stand closer to Nature than
musicians. Nonsense, a baby cries before it sees, and we hear this cry."
— Herr Kietz says of Fidi, "He has a sword in his eyes." — In the
evening we are rather tired from so much talking and listening; the
May wine helps a little, but we are off our usual track. It has an odd
effect on me, I relapse more and more into silence and feel that I
am incapable of sustaining any sort of contact with other people;
my mood becomes despondent, indefinable fears oppress me, my heart
is like a creature in flight. By chance I read that the drought in Florence
is so severe that it has led almost to starvation; this brought me into a
state of grief and alarm, speaking is no help, all that helps is the communion with great minds in the company of R. When I retired to my
room yesterday evening, I had to take up the correspondence of Goethe
and Schiller in order to calm my spirits. A feeling of quiet resignation
took possession of me—let come what must!   — Talking about R.'s
friend, the philologist Lehrs, Kietz told us that Lehrs had once asked
him to light a fire and had scolded him for having no sense of architecture; Kietz had then laid the fire according to his instructions
(L. could no longer rise from his chair); before the fire had burned
halfway down, Lehrs himself had expired! (Concern over Loulou's
headache.)

*Wednesday, June 1*   I often talk with R. about the French and their
curious influence on national costumes, which they have all spoiled,
the inability of their present-day actors to wear medieval or ancient
costumes; what best suits them is the dress of the Louis XIV period,
with its wigs, caparisons, etc. "It is remarkable how even in Shakespeare's time the French were called *M. Pardonnez-moi* and regarded as
ridiculously foppish. From the very start this Gallic race seems to have
powdered and prettified everything; all the barbaric juices and forces
seem to dry up in them." — When I come down to breakfast, R.
greets me in song with the melody from the Ninth Symphony: "Who

has pulled off the great triumph, husband of this wife to be," etc. "That is my 'Ode to Joy,' " he says. — While I was contemplating my happiness yesterday before going to sleep, I found myself thinking of the sufferings of others; I was appalled, and, just as I long ago renounced the sensual expression of love, so I now resolved to sacrifice any kind of little joy, even indeed of comfort, in order to pay down to the very last penny for this one single nameless happiness: to behold and to share in R.'s progress! — Yesterday a letter came from Russia, without address or even name; in it two enthusiastic secret lovers thank R. for the raptures his music has brought them. — No reply from Dr. P[usinelli], or from the lawyer; both cause me concern. — In the afternoon alarm over Rus's disappearance, but he was found again at the Adler inn. Wet day, Herr Kietz makes his outing with the steamer; in the evening reminiscences about R.'s dogs. (Arrival of the money order, which I at once send to the steamship company, and thus have put aside 5,500 francs for the children in the past year.)

*Thursday, June 2* During the night I hear R. calling from the next room: "No one will believe how happy I am to have you for my wife." — Yesterday morning I entered his room and he played and sang the sketch he had just made of Siegfried's arrival in disguise at Brünnhilde's rock. Dreadful the effect of the hero's inhuman address to his woman, and through the large web of themes which dominates all four works a language has been created of which the world as yet knows nothing. — Lunch with the children and Herr Kietz, who leaves at 4 o'clock; his visit has not given R. much pleasure, he finds he has sunk very low in the world. In the evening conclusion of *Die Jungfrau von O.* Previously we had tended to regard the episode with Lionel as a flaw in the work; this time we were quite amazed and full of admiration for it. "It is not sensual love which overcomes Joan; rather, her awesomely sacred calling has been destroyed, this is all very well motivated in the preceding scenes, by the heroes who woo her, and the whole Court life. But it is all so delicate and profound that most people are quite unable to grasp it. For them it does not exist." — Wonderful evening in the garden at sunset—Lusch as a dairymaid; our good Herr Kietz brought the bad weather with him and has taken it away again. The scent of acacia blossoms, children at play, people moving to and fro—the sun, a dying hero, greets us all as he takes his leave.

*Friday, June 3* "The words convey only the ghostliness of the apparition, the music sounds just innocently grieving," R. said yesterday. Before that he exclaimed: "When I have finished this first act, I shall have unloaded a formidable piece of work. To me the most singular thing of all is that I have managed to do the Norns' scene to my own satisfaction." I: "And yet it is a lovely piece!" "That is the music," he says, etc. Letter from our new friend Hans Herrig, who is having great difficulty with "the music drama," yet who seems a very remarkable person. R. replies to him. Letter from the conductor Marpurg, who is very indignant that anyone should have thought he would conduct *Die Walküre* in Munich in R.'s absence. — R. works; we are glad to be alone again. In the afternoon visit of Countess B. with her daughter; the child behaves very nastily to Loulou, her first experience of feeling offended; for her benefit I draw from it the moral that she must seek everything in the love of her brother and sisters, expect nothing from the outside world. — In the evening, *The Taming of the Shrew*: "How low we have sunk can be seen in what the German theaters have done with this play." — A Jew, Herr Strousberg, has bought the *A.A. Zeitung*, the only paper which was not hitherto in the hands of the Jews, having belonged to an old German firm!!

*Saturday, June 4* Letter from Herr Kietz. "The best thing about him is the silly boy," says R., "the adult man is horrible." — R. at his sketches, I with the children, alternately bathing, teaching, playing. R. shows me in the sketch the theme from the love scene between Br[ünnhilde] and Siegfried, which appears like a mirage as S. overpowers Br. and she subconsciously recognizes him. R. says, "When the ring was snatched from her I thought of Alberich; the noblest character suffers the same as the ignoble, in every creature the will is identical." — At lunch he again complains about music as a profession: "Every kind of work which is unconnected with reason is a joke compared with it; here nothing can be forced, just as one cannot resume a dream by an effort of will, one has just to wait until it literally flies into one's mind." — In the afternoon letters by R. to Nietzsche, Eckert, etc. Rubbish received: a theologian wants a recommendation to Austria, a man in Riga wants a position as concert-master, an embassy secretary wants a recommendation for his compositions, etc. — In the evening I suddenly abandon the children and wander to the piano, something I normally never do now; R., returning home from his walk, is quite put out, because he wanted to use the piano himself, or, rather, had to, since the musical treatment of Siegfried's sword-drawing was running through his head; laughing over our identity of thought, I left the room, he started writing, I put the children to bed. In the evening continued with *The Taming of the Shrew*.

*Sunday, June 5* Difficult, tortured night, in my heart I am always reflecting on the offense I have given, and immersing myself in it, knowing no other way to atone for it. — Letter from the music dealer *Kahnt* about the publication, but so petty and underhanded that R. does not intend to reply to him. R. today finishes the pencil sketch of the first act of *Götterdämmerung*. But he says the thought of completing it "in ink" makes him shudder. Lunch with the children. Afterward the children play at cooking dinner, mashing and splashing. R. plays through his *Götterdämmerung* sketches and complains at having to live so completely without music, but then on reflection decides that he could not listen to music in the way it is done today, he would have to perform it himself, and that in turn would put a stop to his creating. — In the evening finished *The Taming*. — Memories of last year!

*Monday, June 6* My child, my son, your birth—my highest happiness —is connected with the greatest affliction of another, this was my life's sin, never forget this, recognize in it a portrait of life, and atone for it as best you can. But my blessings on you as the realization of my most blissful dream! — At 4:30 I am awakened by sweet sounds, R. at the piano proclaiming to me the hour of birth. Flowers and stars (in a little golden frame) are then brought to me by Loldi and Eva; later Fidi, in white on the red blanket, receives the congratulations of his sisters and gives them gifts; at the foot of the "sacrificial altar," as in a pagoda, he looks like a little Buddha, bestowing favors as he is worshiped. R. exclaims: "What a beautiful morning! How happy I am!" — (To add to everything, a third letter from his friend Kietz!!) — Lulu pleases us with her affection for Fidi, the dear girl has a warm heart, may life's course not break it. —

*6ten Juni*
*Wenn von der Sonne Abschiedskosen*
*Die Erde die süsse Traube gewinnt,*
*Da haben in Lust und Leid wir geminnt,*
*Und erblüht bist Du mit den Rosen.*

*Die um das Grab von Tristan und Isolden,*
*Sich üppig umschlingend erheben,*
*Die Rosen so hold, die Reben so golden,*
*umschlingen sie sich um Dein Leben!*

*Dein Bild, urewig, segnete Tristan's Nacht,*
*Als in Todeswahn wir uns fanden,*
*Siegfried's Sonne hat der Geburt gelacht,*
*Wie Vater und Mutter neu erstanden.*

*Bei den Rosen und Reben, Tristan' und Isolden's Ruh*
*Bei Sonnen und Erden Abschieds-Kuss,*
*Stürme, mein Siegfried, was da stürmen muss,*
*Hell wie der Tag, tief wie die Nacht seist Du.*

["When from the sun's parting caresses Earth was bringing forth
sweet grapes, then did we make love in joy and sorrow, and thou didst
blossom with the roses. The leaves that so luxuriantly entwine the
tomb of Tristan and Isolde, the lovely rose, the golden vine—may they
entwine themselves about thy life! Thy eternal image blessed Tristan's
night when we came together in the illusion of death; on thy birth
did Siegfried's sun smile down—like father and mother, newly arisen.
Over the roses and vines of Tristan and Isolde's rest, over the parting
caress of sun and earth, let storms rage, my Siegfried, as they must—
be thou light as the day, deep as the night!"]

Very bad weather for Fidi's birthday; it does not worry the children,
but R. is unwell. Yesterday evening he spoke a long time about philosophy and said that from Plato to Kant there had been no real progress;
that Spinoza, for instance, who had acknowledged the wickedness of
the world, had still taken this world as it appears to us for the reality.
— He reads passages from Ranke's *Wallenstein* and praises Ranke,
because he is unemotional. — I act out comedies with the children. —
In the evening I read parts of the Schiller-Goethe correspondence to R.

*Tuesday, June 7*   "How much has faded from my life!" R. says.
"When I think of Zurich, where I spent 9 years, and nothing of it
remains; I performed the Beethoven symphonies there, it is all forgotten
—so we are quits." — Lindner, the engraver, arrives, and we begin our
work; almost everything in his copperplate has to be altered, but I
hope it will turn out well; the man himself, a peasant's son, appeals
to us for the simple integrity of his nature. — Yesterday, to the children's great delight, an Italian boy came, bringing a marmot. R. spoke
with him a little in Italian: "What it does to one to hear a boy like that
saying *Sì, signor*—the nobility, the sadness of it! One thinks of 'Mignon,'
'*Kennst du das Land*,' and it brings tears to one's eyes." In the evening
we start on *Wilhelm Meister*, unfortunately without much satisfaction
from the first book. — Letter to R. from the King; for myself a letter
from Councilor Pusinelli, which pleases me.

*Wednesday, June 8*   "You are all soul, love, kindness," R. said to me
yesterday, whereas I feel like Gretchen: "know not what he finds in
me." — Gave lessons to the children; R. unfortunately unwell and in
gloomy mood. Very inopportune the visit of *Friedrich* Porges and his
wife from Vienna, since R. has little inclination to talk, and they stay
a long time. Wretched cold weather, the sort of day one just has to put
up with. — Late supper, since R. has to correct the proofs of his biography. And we read nothing in the evening,

*Thursday, June 9*   Very bad weather, to which the month of June is
subject here. R. unwell, does not get around to working. Family
lunch: Loldi very beautiful, as if from another world, R. says, Sakuntala

or Cenerentola. A drive after lunch. In the evening read *Wilhelm Meister*. (R. writes to Herr Kietz, who is still "stuck" in Zurich.)

*Friday, June 10* Much joy in Fidi, who is becoming very lively and sturdy. — Yesterday I read in the newspaper that Hans is to play in Nuremberg and Würzburg on behalf of the Hans Sachs monument— for the last time in Germany. — Sent off Lulu's letter to her aunt and enclosed with it a photograph of the children; her tone toward the children does in fact displease me greatly, and I have considered whether I should not put a stop to the correspondence; but later it may be to the children's benefit to have this contact, and I willingly swallow my personal pride. — Yesterday morning we gave an innkeeper several pheasants' eggs to hatch; when I asked why our hen pheasant did not hatch them herself, I was told she would not hatch them in the aviary! This made me sad, and I thought of the poor finch. — I am very unwell and can only teach the children with an effort. R. does some work, but he is in a despondent mood, thinking of the production of *Die Walküre*. — After lunch we go for a drive in spite of the uncertain weather; on the journey we talk about the ugliness of present fashions. "What impression of femininity can a young man now have when he sees all these chignons?" R. says. "How can male propensities ever flourish?" — A book by A. Stahr about the female characters in Goethe reveals to us the wretched triviality of the modern book world. In the evening continuation of *W. Meister*; much enjoyment. We then start talking about Beethoven, and R. says: "The only time Beethoven was not concise is in the finale of the great B-flat Major Sonata, which your father alone can play, and in which I got more enjoyment out of his virtuosity than out of what was being played. Conciseness seems to be the secret of music; when melody ceases and is replaced by some kind of working out, the effect is lost. Beethoven is the first composer in whom everything is melody; it was he who showed how from one and the same theme a succession of new themes arise which are complete in themselves." —

*Saturday, June 11* Letter from the conductor Esser in Salzburg, reporting that *Die Walküre* is to be produced in Munich on June 26. R. laughs and says, "My contacts with Esser, now that he is retired from the theater, remind me of how it used to be with Pohlenz long ago, when he and I deplored the 'new era' led by Mendelssohn and together represented the worthy old artistic tastes of Leipzig." I suddenly feel very unwell and go for a drive with the children to recover a little. Returning home I find Prof. Nietzsche and his friend Herr Rohde, also a philologist, who had announced their coming yesterday. Lively and serious conversation. In the evening Prof. N. reads us a lecture on the Greek music drama, a title for which R. pulls him up, explaining the reason for his disapproval. The lecture is a good one and shows that he has a true feeling for Greek art. (Prof. N. has brought me Dürer's *Melancholie*.)

*Sunday, June 12*    Breakfast all together, then with our guests to the Lion of Lucerne, while R. works. At lunch R. is very lively and good-humored, he starts talking about musicians, "who are wild beasts, not educated creatures, very close in fact to actors. To demand of our present-day musicians, with their quintets, trios, cantatas, etc., that they conduct, is like suddenly demanding from a writer of novels that he play comic roles." At five o'clock we accompany our guests to the railroad station; then home; glorious weather, lovely moonlight; after supper *W. Meister*, R. reads the scene between Mignon and Wilhelm wonderfully (the egg dance).

*Monday, June 13*    Nothing from outside except beautiful weather, which refreshes us very much. Work with the children; R. at his sketches. In the afternoon a clumsy remark by me leads to slight discord; I almost feel grateful for the episode, since on such occasions we realize all the more strongly that we cannot bear the slightest lack of unity between us. — The student informs me that after long struggles he has given up theology and with it his scholarship, in order to devote himself to natural science—an almost heroic decision in his circumstances. — In the evening to Countess B.'s, the Prince is nearing his end. — Back home, *W. Meister*.

*Tuesday, June 14*    In the morning long discussion about *W. Meister*, which continues to enchant us. The children with the landlord, so I write to Judith and deal with some business letters; very close atmosphere. In the afternoon read *W. Meister* with R. In the evening, contemplation of the print *Die Melancholie*, which Prof. Nietzsche gave me, brings us to a comparison between A. Dürer and [J.] S. Bach. "Both," says R., "should be regarded as the conclusion of the Middle Ages, for it is nonsense to regard Bach as of our own time. Both endowed with this rich and mysterious imagination, dispensing with beauty but achieving sublimity, which is greater than all beauty. The poet one might put beside them is Dante, though he is less congenial because not so human, meaning not a Protestant." The *A.A.Z.* arrives and contains a nasty piece about *Die Walküre*: "Previously the interest in W[agner]'s work was great, now nobody talks about it." R. very upset by this malicious distortion of all known facts. "It is not the malice itself which constantly amazes one, but the new forms it continually and with downright genius manages to find." When I tell Vreneli always to hand the newspapers to me first, she informs me that in the spring some vile caricatures, the contents of which she is quite unable to confide to me, had been sent from Munich; she had burned them! (Letter from Claire.)

*Wednesday, June 15*  Arrival of my wedding dress, plans for Fidi's future, R. plays to him, he listens earnestly; R. works. In a long conversation in the morning he examines the nature of the world: "Nature did not intend human beings to aspire higher than building themselves something like an anthill; great minds are anomalies, and one must not judge the masses according to them; when the people themselves are gifted with imagination, they do not bring forth anthills as do the English and the Swiss, who are the unimaginative ones; but out of a state of disorder they produce interesting personalities." — Passing then to our plans for the production of the *Nibelungen*: "What is gratitude, what is time? Once it is there, it will exist for humanity forever. Even if I know I shall never change the masses, never transform anything permanent, all I ask is that the good things also have their place, their refuge. The common and the bad must occupy and retain the main expanse, but the good can perhaps still find asylum." "You'll see," he exclaimed yesterday, "you'll see, *Die Walküre* will still turn out to my advantage; it is true I can have nothing to do with it, but something will emerge which will be of more advantage to me, to my plans, than if the present silence persisted unbroken." — At the conclusion of the third book of *W. M.*, he said, as he laid the volume down: "How was it with us? Did we know how united we were? That is something only God decides." — Frau Ras, the charming embroiderer from Appenzell, visits us, then to town with R. In the evening more of *W. Meister*. Glorious moonlit night. "You have made three wishes, Dauphin," R. suddenly says. "Do you know," he adds, "what wish I have just made to the moon? That I may be spared ever having to leave your side in order to gain a living for us; it would be terrible to have to part from you under such conditions."

*Thursday, June 16*  Corpus Christi, people busy shooting, tinkling bells, etc.; but splendid weather. "Good morning, my little pride," says R. to me. The children with us, the two elder ones go to the procession. Letter from Dr. Herrig, very remarkable. We have received news from the Maderaner valley; since the reply was delayed I had already made up my mind that the guesthouse did not wish to accept us on account of our situation, and had resigned myself to it. Now things are different, and we shall probably be there within a fortnight. Very bad news of the old Prince, who is sinking. Family lunch. The newspapers report that the dogma of infallibility is to be promulgated, coupled with an anathema, and that the behavior of the bishops on the opposite side has throughout been full of character. — After lunch R. starts on the subject of Heine's remark about Schiller's poetry—"they are drunken ideas." "If one were chemically to analyze this witticism, which seems like a stroke of genius, one would discover at its base the Jewish outsider, who speaks about the conditions of our life as an Iroquois would speak of our railroads. Behind this 'drunken idea' lie experiences in student life, when someone is abused as a *scholar*, and out of this insult comes a drunken duel; here, too, the Jew is an outsider, he notices what is raw and flat, but he has no feeling for the ideals of our nature. The fact that in Schiller the very exact perception of our ideality sometimes shows itself too strongly—this is what he calls 'drunken ideas,' to which one can really only reply, 'You don't understand.'" — Little pleasure in the analysis of *Hamlet* in *W. Meister*—our interpretation, or, rather, our feeling about it, is deep in a different way. — Recently R. said to me, "In the style of declaiming the 'Ode to Joy,' which is only correct and worthy of the poem if it is *maestoso*, one can recognize the whole problem of words in relation to music." Regarding the analysis of *Hamlet* he said, "Goethe showed great genius in the observation of life, but his judgment concerning poets was unsound." — R. suddenly writes to the King, asking him to stage *Die Walküre* for himself alone. Continued reading of *W. Meister* restores his high spirits, then, as he seals his letter, he says, "One stands between the good spirit and the demon; you belong to the good spirits, the King to the demons." Gradually we become quite gay, a violent thunderstorm develops, R. is glad, for he cannot go out, "only love and create, and create because I love, you are the central sun around which everything revolves." "Are you cheerful again?" I asked. "In everything you set in motion I am cheerful and happy, but you cannot work wonders, the outside world remains the same, and yet—you have worked wonders." He corrects the proof sheets of the biography: "Will Fidi have to go through all this, too—could he not be spared it?"

*Friday, June 17*   As we learn from Dr. Herrig's letter, a Herr Ambros says in a Viennese newspaper that R. wrote his pamphlet on conducting solely in order to get himself appointed conductor of the Beethoven celebrations; wretched people, and nobody will ever learn that R. did not in fact reply at all to the invitation. — "My work, what a luxury!" said R. "Truthfully, I only do it so that you won't be cross." We read *W. Meister*: "Aurelie's remarks about the German nation— remarkable how she sees what every great man has felt; I am glad to see that my feelings have such roots." Great joy in Fidi: "One can see he is a child of the deepest love, and that this love had something to say." Letter from the publishers, they want to do *Rienzi* in Munich and Vienna. — Our talk in the evening brings us to Spanish dances, which made an indelible impression on R. in his youth. — In the garden the two little ones play with the convicts, who are cutting the grass under supervision and give them strawberries. Loldi takes one of them some money, which we gave her for this purpose; a touching picture, but the faces terrible. "What a study!" R. says. "The whole obstinacy of Nature's immutability is reflected in such faces." The older girls with M[arie] Bassenheim, I go to fetch them and am shocked by the sight of the old Prince in decline. When I return home, R. tells me I should really never leave him, not even for a short while. The conversation about Spanish dancing leads us to talk of nations in general, and I request from him an attestation that I am German.

*Saturday, June 18* R. remarks in the morning: "It is really very curious that King *Jérôme* offered Beethoven a pension, and only then did the Austrian nobles fix his allowance. I should like to point that out one day in order to show that the most favorable opportunity for German talent would still be afforded by Frenchmen or Russians coming to rule over us; they would at least think it worthwhile to inquire about a man of note." R. works; letter from Catulle Mendès, who tells R. they will not be able to resist the temptation of seeing *Die Walküre* in Munich; R. replies that in that case he (R.) must resist the temptation of seeing them at Tribschen. Toward evening, visit with R. the Pension Stutz, a property close by; sad and melancholy impression, much more cut off from the world than Tribschen.

*Sunday, June 19* R. worn out by work, but very much more so by the impending production of *Die Walküre*. I force myself to keep silent about it. R. reads in the *Illustrirte Zeitung* that he had refused with grateful appreciation the flattering invitation to conduct the 9th Symphony; this annoys him a great deal, and he sends a correction to the *Signale*. Sunday—that is to say, much observed—walk with the children. — Visit from our bookseller Prell, who tells us some very curious stories—how, for example, he sold a set of the Brockhaus encyclopedia to a rich peasant, but the latter had to bring it back, on the command of his priest, as being anticlerical. "Yes," says R., "our Liberal gentlemen do not go to the peasant and inquire what he is reading, they content themselves with boasting in the taverns." — The great news of the household is that for the first time our hen pheasant is broody. R. yesterday intentionally crushed an insect pest with his foot and said that while doing so he had felt a physical shock through his whole body.

*Monday, June 20* Melancholy night with strange dreams, thought much of Hans, with inner consciousness of his distress. Could I have spared it him? As I ask myself this question, R. comes in, looking quite worn out, and then I once more feel that I could not have done other than I did—may my deep fellow suffering atone for my sin! — Letter from Richter, he is also going to Munich, in order to meet the manager of the Brussels theater, who wants to perform *Lohengrin* in Paris—all this without even asking R. I write to the guesthouse proprietor in the Maderaner valley; we are giving up the idea of a six-week stay there, since it would cost too much. Telegram from Catulle Mendès begging pardon, they will not go to Munich. Telegram from Richter, who is coming here next week to copy out the sketch of the first act for the King. Boat ride to St. Nikolaus with the children, Loldi is the first to espy R., who came overland to meet us; Eva returns home in the boat with Hermine, from the heights Loldi catches sight of the ship again and we call out to one another. — In the evening *W. Meister*, with ever-increasing admiration for the unending richness of its inspiration.

*Tuesday, June 21*   I am sorrowful, my children, and must struggle to insure that nobody notices; during the night I thought of my parting from Hans a year ago last November; where did I find the strength— I who cannot look on any distress unmoved, even among strangers? Surely it was Fate which drove me, I was obeying a higher dispensation, but I shall never get over the distress I caused Hans—never, never. — Letter from the lawyer in Berlin, who tells me of an order according to which I have once again to declare that I do not intend to return home; following this statement comes the final hearing, in which "presumably the divorce will be promulgated." After lunch a drive with the two horses to the Rossloch, wonderful weather, the children in merry mood. In the evening read some more of *W. Meister*. Prof. Nietzsche writes very nicely of the impression Tribschen made on him and his friend, and he dedicates to me his lectures on Socrates and Greek art. Dr. Herrig sends some manuscripts, and the King a copy of the water color of Tribschen.

*Wednesday, June 22*   In the newspaper appear reports of Hans's concerts for the Hans Sachs monument. I give Loulou all these copies to preserve. — R. unfortunately very worn out by his work, but still more by worry about *Die Walküre*. A friendly letter from Marie Muchanoff, the Wagner performances in Weimar have begun with *Der [Fliegende] Holländer*. In the afternoon to Countess Bassenheim's, the Prince died in the morning; saw the corpse, the serenity of death, the agony of life, a profound impression. — In the evening R. very unwell; I read *W. Meister* to him; over Wilhelm's inquiry about his child, in the tower at the end of the 7th book, we have to weep. "In one's youth one cannot begin to understand that," R. says. —

*Thursday, June 23*   Sleepless night worrying about R. and thinking of the Prince. In the morning R. talks about Protestantism, "which can only be understood as a *protest* against every confession in favor of the true core of religion, which lies in its nature. This is what one must make clear to a child, while teaching him only the life of Christ, in all its simplicity and nobility. Besides that, tolerance toward other religions, familiarity with Greek myths, which as a diagnosis of life are very profound, even if they bring no salvation." — Then R. says he has long felt like writing a novel; a young man—somewhat like Lessing, but with a different name—is cursed by his parents for consorting with play actors, he flees, is captured by Prussian recruiting officers, has to take part in a big battle in the Seven Years' War, comes to know and admire Frederick, whom he previously hated, becomes his secretary. Their conversations, etc. — Letter—from Barcelona! — To Countess B.'s, R. shocked by my mourning clothes. He works eagerly and hard and is in somewhat better health. Family lunch; late in the evening a walk, afterward *W. Meister*, in which the way Mignon's death is passed over annoys us very much. I feel that after recognizing Mariane's innocence Wilhelm, a broken man, should devote himself entirely to the children; Mignon's death, which could not be averted, brings him heartbroken to Lothario and his family, with the sole ambition of bringing up Felix well; only then the meeting with Natalie. But the mixing up of the Mignon catastrophe with the educational plan is offensive.

*Friday, June 24* Very thundery day, but we can work in the garden in the morning; I write to Prof. Nietzsche (yesterday I wrote to Marie Muchanoff in Weimar). Just as I am about to bathe Fidi there comes thunder, hail, rain, hurricane. From town comes a letter from Franz Müller in Munich; he emphatically reports the enthusiasm of *all* for *Die Walküre*! *Die W.* is to be given there on Sunday, then three times in succession *Das Rheingold* and *Die Walküre*. "It really is wonderful," R. says bitterly. "Perfall as manager, Wüllner as conductor, Grandaur as producer, Müller as historian, and only then the King of Bavaria and my work." It pierces my heart like a dagger, and I ask myself whether this disgraceful act will really go unavenged? Shortly beforehand R. had said to me, "You are the King of Bavaria's sister, you have joined hands to save my life—he, it is true, as a foolish character, you as a good woman." I cannot make out the King's feelings—though, as an Indian proverb says, this one can never do with kings anywhere. As I write this, Fidi is sitting at my side, a bird is sitting on the catalpa tree, and they are babbling together. Our ray of sunshine, we call Fidi. — The evening shows the melancholy effects of that stupid letter: R. so beside himself and also so physically worn out that I stand there disconsolate, not knowing what to do. He gradually calms down outwardly. We read *W. Meister*, but in dissatisfaction give up reading at the point of Mignon's death. Incomprehensible that Natalie, in telling him the fate of the child, does not at the same time tell him to live now only for the children, to take Mignon to Italy and grant her at least a gentle death, and only later to seek out his friends and start on the course of study, in which he in any case behaves stupidly enough.

*Saturday, June 25*   Since the effects of yesterday's letter were so very bad, I gave instructions that all letters from Munich must first be handed to me. I am very glad to have made this rule; a letter from Councilor Düfflipp announces that not only will the King *not* command the production for himself alone, but also he himself will not attend the first performance—only the one to be given in conjunction with *Das Rheingold*! I reply as best I can and say I am keeping all reports from the master's eyes. R. did a lot of work yesterday, and today he resumes it. Arrival of the legal document, reply to it. Letter from Frau Dr. Wille inviting R. and me to stay with her. The great friendliness with which this is done touches us very much, R. thanks her and promises her the first visit after our marriage. "You knew about it," he suddenly says to me at lunch. "What?" "Something." Of the King he says, "He is a creature worthy of respect, he is Fate." Visit from Count Bassenheim, he asks me to write to Düfflipp: the Countess would like to have the Prince's estate changed to a female inheritance. I write. — Letter from von Bronsart, the theater manager in Hanover; *Die Msinger* has not been a success there. Visit to Frau Am Rhyn's; apart from that nothing but lack of peace and joy, because our poor Kos is going blind; one eye is already lost and the other will probably also be affected by his mange. How cruel everything is, everything! R. takes Kos to the eye specialist and returns home with the good news that the trouble is not too dangerous—it just looks very bad. — In the evening R. takes up *W. Meister* again and says what we must do now is to get to know Goethe, we are like children to be so swept away by this novel, so long familiar to us, what we are concerned with is understanding the poet.

*Sunday, June 26*   Kos very bad. "The way inanimate forces, chemical forces, fight over such a poor creature and destroy it truly demonstrates that life is just a condition, an agony," R. says. — Toward noon Richter arrives, to our great delight; he did not attend the rehearsal of *Die Walküre* in Munich, which was very nice of him. R. is in good spirits, we talk of Bayreuth and forget about Munich! Fidi, our Monsieur Sunbeam. Letter from the publisher Lucca: Breitkopf und Härtel have the effrontery to claim the publishing rights for Italy. Punch in the evening with Richter, for whom things seem to be going very badly in Vienna. After he has gone to bed we read another chapter of *W. Meister*—"Mignon's Exequies."

*Monday, June 27*   Yesterday we spoke not a single word about the performance, and that was what R. needed, for he can stand no more about it; Richter found that out when he told him he had regretted the "*correction.*" "Have you no sense of honor left?" R. exclaimed violently. "They can clap, applaud, but nothing else; it was possible, in short, for such names as Hanslick and Schelle to appear on that invitation." — The revival of *Tannhäuser* in Vienna seems to have achieved an unparalleled success. I write to the publisher Lucca in R.'s name. The day goes by, with no news from Munich, thank goodness—just in the evening there arrives a telegram whose signature put us in a good humor from the very start; a Herr Napoleon Homolatsch—probably a Bohemian—telegraphs of boundless rejoicing at the end of the first act. Yesterday there was the usual malevolent notice in the *A.A.Z.* about the dress rehearsal; I cut it out and hid it from R. In the evening continued *W. Meister.* R. derives from this characteristic work new proofs of the limited nature of poetry and the unlimited scope of music, which is not tied to any form of beauty, but quite naïvely produces the sublime. — At lunch he tells us about Hanslick (his mother a Jewess) and Herr Ambros, who allowed himself to be bought by the *Neue Freie Presse* (against R.), how both of them had approached him, made admissions to him, and then, reckoning on his good manners like the miserable creatures they are, had no fear that he would one day tell what he knew. —

*Tuesday, June 28* A Herr Marr (son of the actor) sends us a little pamphlet which appears to be not at all badly written. Letter from Herr Lindner, the engraver, touching in its clumsy simplicity. In the afternoon to Count B.'s to hear news of the Countess. Sad disclosures about his son. — In Rome they are now calling one another donkey, rogue, and rascal; *asino* is what the Pope called Prince Rauscher, and rogue and rascal the majority bishops called Cardinal Guidi in the assembly hall. — R. plays the Norns' scene with Richter; and we finish *W. Meister.* (I write to Herr Pohl, asking him, in the event that he writes about *Die Walküre*, to be sure to mention the one important point: that no musician should be prepared to conduct the work without the composer's participation.)

*Wednesday, June 29* "My eudaemon," R. calls Fidi. "You are my good spirit." — Yesterday a money order arrived from Pest, *Tannhäuser* has brought in an unexpected 500 florins, which pleases R. greatly. — Today the outside world brings us only a letter from Herr Schäfer in Munich; according to him the success of *Die Walküre* is very great, and the manager of the Berlin Court theater is said to have applauded unceasingly and to have made notes on the casting in Berlin (!!). R. has a cold, does not go out, plays duets with Richter: Haydn symphonies—that reminds me of the time when I used to play these works with Blandine. "*Le beau temps où j'étais si malheureuse,*" as Madame de Staël says, my sad, fatherless and motherless, and yet blissful youth! The children constantly around us.

*Thursday, June 30*   Yesterday I fully intended to write to Herr Wüllner to leave him in no doubt about the nature of his misdeed. Today I find it more sensible and dignified to remain silent. — Letter to R. from Frl. v. Meysenbug: she wants to come here. The Music Society in Vienna inquires whether R. has received the invitation, thereby ignoring all that has happened. — While Fidi is crawling on the carpet in front of me, R. thinks of the November day on which I arrived here; at once my final parting from Hans comes into my mind, and I shudder in agony. Who would require distractions, once he has looked down into the pit of sorrow and wandered on the highest heights of bliss? — Yesterday Richter took the children for a ride in a boat along the Tribschen banks; I did not wish to deprive the children of their enjoyment on account of my nervousness, and, so as not to make things difficult for Richter, I did not go into the boat. Thus I was running around on the bank in the most absurd, indescribable fear, unceasingly working out how best I could leap to the rescue in case of an accident. The ride was calm and pleasant, Rus swam behind the children's boat, 7 little ones enjoyed their pleasure (Willie and the Am Rhyn children as well), I suffered on my own behalf and rejoiced on theirs. — Two professors' wives from Berlin write to R. to express their pleasure in *Die Msinger* and to beg him to write another such lighthearted opera. — Family lunch, Boni rather unwell; her character has very noticeably taken a turn for the better. Italian newspaper, which reports on the great impression made by *Der Fliegende Holländer* in Weimar. My father's "Beethoven Cantata," unfortunately rendered unenjoyable by its text, and anyway its whole form (the *Eroica* theme is sung!), is disagreeable. — Nice letter from Frau Dr. Wille, she wants to visit us, since we do not wish to visit her before the wedding. In the evening R. plays with Richter Beethoven's C-sharp Minor Quartet; ever-recurring astonishment over this purest piece of Beethoveniana.

*Friday, July 1*   Stormy weather; R. works. In the afternoon the lawyer; he thinks that everything can be settled this month. This always gives me a feeling of earnestness, almost even of melancholy, and makes me feel unwell. From his walk R. brings back a telegram from Weimar with 46 signatures, the four performances are over and they are sending R. a silver laurel wreath. — Much joy in Fidi. "One has to have grown old like me to know what happiness this is," R. says to Richter. And: "If this boy does not turn out better and bigger than I, then physiognomy is a liar." — In the evening I play passages from Beethoven's quartets with Richter, then R. reads the first two acts of *Macbeth*, in which we are struck by the very bad translation (Tieck, not Schlegel).

*Saturday, July 2* Rain, a planned outing to Mount Pilatus thereby thwarted. R. works, and completes the sketch of the first act. Simultaneously with my great joy over this outcome I have to read in the *A.A.Z.* a contemptible review of his *Die Walküre*; I tear the wretched thing up. Pohl has written, too, in *Die Signale*; very weak and insipid. Another letter from the publisher Lucca which vexes R. very much; in the evening again quartets. — R. talks about his essay *Beethoven and the German Nation*, then about his three heroic comedies, Luther's Wedding, Bernhard von Weimar, and Frederick the Great. Letter from Claire.

*Sunday, July 3* I am unwell; write to Lucca on R.'s behalf, R. himself writes Härtel's a letter which I translate for Lucca. To town after family lunch. In the evening *Macbeth*, the impact of which is again a crushing one. "As with Antony, Hamlet, Othello, Shakespeare shows us in Macbeth a character entirely destroyed by Fate. Of the Macbeth as he is described to us and honored in the beginning there is no trace left, the demonic element takes control, and the individual ceases entirely to exist. That is the play's greatness and tragedy." At lunch during dessert Jakob brings us the silver laurel wreath from Weimar. It is truly handsome. — Letter from poor C. Frantz enclosing his *Naturlehre des Staats*; he had wanted to dedicate it to R. and asked if he might, but since R. did not reply he had not dared! The death of his son has robbed him forever of his joy in life.

*Monday, July 4* R. writes letters; I find myself very unwell, constant feelings of nausea, which render me helpless. I struggle against it as best I can and give the children their lessons. Go for a drive in the afternoon. A summons for July 18 arrives from the town law courts. Newspapers of all sorts with stupidities about *Die Walküre*; the King truly did not attend either the dress rehearsal or the first two performances, and for that he spent 40,000 florins and offended R.'s feelings! R. thinks he did not go because in his letter to Esser R. had said the King had wanted the performance, and now it was his whim to present him with a denial. In the evening we begin Tieck's *Dichterleben*.

*Tuesday, July 5* Glorious day, but I am feeling very unwell, can teach the children only with an effort. R. writes various letters, I to Herr Simson in Berlin. After lunch drive to Hergeschwyl, we decide on tomorrow for the outing to Mount Pilatus, since I believe that only a change of air can help me. In the carriage R. talks of the bringing together of several themes in music; the ear perceives only one, but the addition of the others as accompaniment to it tremendously sharpens and heightens the impact of this single melody which one hears. In poetry no comparable effect is possible, except perhaps through equivocation, humor, irony, such as we have seen and admired many times in *Don Carlos*, for instance (scene between Don C. and Alba); the whole of *Tasso* is based on a similar effect. But in literature this purpose is achieved by keeping silent about certain things, in music by positive means; however, one must be capable of arranging the themes in such a way that the main melody can really be heard; Berlioz, for example, was not successful in the *"Scène au Bal,"* where the love motive sounds like the bass line. — In the morning R. reads me the passage in which Schopenhauer compares Plato's ideas with Kant's "thing in itself" and at the same time criticizes the misunderstanding caused in this connection by Kant's successors. — In the evening I feel so ill that I have to take to my bed very soon.

*Wednesday, July 6*  R. has read and misunderstood some things in my diary, which pains me deeply. — The doctor comes and forbids me to go on the Pilatus outing. Terribly close, the children running around in their nightgowns. Visit from Count B. The King appears not to wish to receive the Countess— he never likes seeing women. In the afternoon I go for a drive, in the evening continue with *Dichterleben*. A great deal in it of significance, only Tieck, whatever he is, is no poet.

*Thursday, July 7*  I am still unwell and have not been able to eat a thing for the last four days; but my pains are gradually growing less. Family lunch; the *Illustrirte Zeitung* with its fashion pictures provokes from R. the remark that the Parisian world does at any rate show itself in its costumes as it really is—the gross indolence of the men, the provocative impudence of the women. It is a true portrait of a world with which we certainly have nothing to do. But the Germans who copy these fashions! The Parisian woman knows to a hair what she is, how she looks, and dresses herself accordingly; the German woman, however, looks at her neighbor, envies her, and tries to copy her, never mind how ill it suits her. Beauty has surely vanished forever from this world of ours; we may still have our thoughts and the religious world of music, but the type of beauty which manifests itself in costumes and in buildings—that can come only from a generously inclined aristocracy which feels at one with the people, and that has gone. The right moment to give the whole nation its impetus would have been after the wars of liberation, but that was when they all feared the word *German* like the red republic. Letter from an enthusiastic sculptor (Natter) who has only just read the *Ring des Nibelungen* and is utterly absorbed by it, he is sending a statuette of *Brünnhilde*. Visit from the conductor Herbeck; R. is vexed at having to tell him things which he described in detail in his pamphlet on the reform of the German operatic stage. R. goes through the Norns' scene with Richter. In the evening a walk in the garden by moonlight until eleven o'clock.

*Friday, July 8* Rumors of war, because of a Prussian pr .ce's ascending the Spanish throne; the French as always ridiculously excited by something happening without their consent. Loulou unwell, our Pilatus outing again in jeopardy; big thunderstorm, R. plays the A Major Symphony with Richter and says, "From time to time one must perform these wonderful things in order to recognize ever more clearly the power of a will which so confidently expresses what everyone understands but none can define." — In the evening Richter brings the student along to join in the discussion of the outing, and, since the latter stupidly gives himself airs about the celebration of the Battle of Sempach, R. gets very angry and tells him how pitiful such affectations look in a thoroughly demoralized nation which can do nothing but fleece foreigners and give a free hand to the Jesuits. Afterward R. much regrets his vehemence.

*Saturday, July 9* I am well again, but Lusch lies in bed—thus worry replaces suffering—such is life! The statuette has arrived; it is quite nicely worked, only I am sorry that the sculptor did not choose to depict the compassionate and loving Valkyrie Brünnhilde—R.'s own true creation—but, rather, the sinister figure brooding on revenge, which could just as well be Geibel's or Hebbel's; for in this mood she is—in R.'s poem—no longer herself. Loulou is recovering in bed, I read *The Arabian Nights* to her. — Yesterday R. once more made me happy when he said: "How happy I am! Only I should like to be 15 years younger—how much erring I could have been spared if I had had you then! And one thing is certain: without you I should never again have written a note." He writes to the publisher Kahnt, categorically laying down his terms. Apart from that he makes a draft for his essay on Beethoven. — In the evening continuation of *Dichterleben*, we enjoy the scenes with the Puritans.

*Sunday, July 10* Since Loulou has now recovered, we decide on the outing. Nice Italian article about *Die Msinger* in Weimar. Family lunch. At 4 o'clock drive to Hergeschwyl in very fine weather, from there the ascent of Mount Pilatus, a veritable caravan with guides, porters, sedan-chair attendants, the student, Richter, Jakob, and the two *big* girls. A gay ride; with the ascent a gradual alleviation of cares, love alone holds sway and manifests itself in the high, pure ether. Sublime impressions of stillness and solitude; on such impressions he based the life of the gods in the *Ring des Nibelungen*. Lovely moonlight on the Pilatus peak. The children merry.

*Monday, July 11* Watched the sunrise by myself, great and peaceful impression. — Otherwise we are very tired, the ride had wearied us, and rest was not possible during the night on account of the many guests. We take a walk across loose stones to a meadow covered with Alpine roses, settle ourselves down there, and the day passes in an attempt to make up our lost sleep. Finished reading the 1st part of *Dichterleben*; though in form it is awkward and ungainly throughout, we find the whole composition nevertheless very interesting. — Early to bed.

*Tuesday, July 12* The weather is uncertain and I am unwell, all the same we decide to climb the Esel, after having read in the temple something from Schopenhauer ("A Man's Place in the Estimation of Others"). I write my notes while still in the public room of the inn. — Having arrived in storm and rain, I go to my bed feeling ill.

*Wednesday, July 13* I spend the whole day in bed, most unwell. R. in his love and kindness reads to me; the second part of *Dichterleben* we find very gripping, the story of the marriage recalls R.'s marriage and seems entirely convincing, and in the figure of Southampton we rediscover the King of Bavaria. — A guide brings news that an ultimatum has been sent from Paris to the King of Prussia, saying he should forbid his relative to accept the crown, otherwise war!! I am quite beside myself over this example of French insolence; this nation deserves a merciless chastisement. —

*Thursday, July 14* Rain. I feel somewhat better and get up. R. says to me that it is wrong of us to seek diversions such as other people have need of, we could never make a success of an outing of this sort, in place of it we have our own happiness. He says he would like to live like this for twenty years without moving a step, just with me and the children. — When I yesterday childishly asked him whether he loved me, he replied, "I should like to know what else I do but love you." — We read more of *Dichterleben*, and I write my entry for yesterday in my book. In the evening the weather clears up and we are able to climb the Esel. Telegram from Richter reporting the presence in Lucerne of Karl Klindworth. (Richter had walked ahead in the morning with the student.)

*Friday, July 15* In the morning I hear the *"Morgentraumdeutweise"*; shortly afterward R. comes to me saying that Karl Klindworth is here, in fact with Richter, who, scarcely arrived below, has come up again. We prepare to take leave of the heights. Klindworth has seen Hans in Berlin. He says Hans is well and very contented with his stay in Florence; he is now planning a journey to America. If I am truly to be given, on top of all else, the consolation of knowing that things are well with Hans, then, dear God, there will never have been a happier woman than I! — K. Kl[indworth] saw *Die Walküre* in Munich and says it made an overwhelming impression on him; he also tells me that my father is traveling with a bevy of acquaintances to see *Die Walküre*, and is going on to the Passion play in Oberammergau. How different this life from our own, how turned outward, avid for distraction, how wide the gap between us! — Return home via Alpnach in very fine weather; merry greetings, good children! Fidi looks pale; Loldi had seen the convicts' *stable* (the prison); Eva sleepy. In the newspapers, however, the proclamation of the infallibility dogma and *war*! The arrogant and wicked French are not content with the withdrawal of the Prince of Hohenzollern, they are demanding through their envoy Benedetti a promise from the King of Prussia that he will never give his approval to the acceptance of the Spanish crown by any Prussian prince. The King quite rightly refuses to receive the envoy. So now they are arming! This news upsets us greatly.

*Saturday, July 16* Not a wink of sleep, the excitement is too great! According to a letter from Catulle Mendès, our friends will probably not visit us, and of that we are glad, for to see a Frenchman now would be very unpleasant. On top of this the newspaper provides the illuminating news that the Emperor was indeed well aware of the Prince of H.'s candidature for the throne and only annoyed because the latter refused to marry a niece of the Empress, Frl. d'Albe. *That* the ministers did not know, they were hoodwinked by their own Emperor!! So on account of a band of crooks a firebrand is to be thrown into Europe. And for this the people in Paris are singing the *"Marseillaise"* and *à bas la Prusse!* — I write to Councilor Düfflipp, because among other things K. Kl[indworth] brought us the curious news that they were not quite certain whether to refuse *Die Walküre* to the theater managers who offered to buy it. Things in Munich are said to be in such a muddle that they would like to have von Bülow back and to change every-thing. R. declares that he will never again set foot in Munich. — Yesterday a visit from Countess B., who tells me that all the hopes she has in her affairs she owes to me. Letter from Prof. Nietzsche, who out of consideration for us did not go to see *Die Walküre* in Munich; I reply to him and try as hard as I can to arouse his enthusiasm for Prussia's right to represent Germany. — (Many newspapers—foreign ones—on the performances in Weimar, all full of the most distasteful praise.) — What lies ahead of us, how will, how can this frightful war end? — The King of Bavaria ill, did not attend any performance of *Die Walküre*. — The newspapers allow a ray of hope for peace to shine through. Played through third act of *Siegfried*; in the evening, biography.

*Sunday, July 17* Frightful thunderstorm; I declare that the gods are angry with the French. War has been declared; in Paris nothing but phrases. The Prussians quietly firm and resolved. R. says, "Typical of a Frenchman: he does not keep his word, but when one reminds him of it, one is obliged to fight a duel with him." And: "The French are the putrefaction of the Renaissance." — I am so beside myself that I fear becoming a burden to R., but he calls me his life-giver, kind and loving as he always is. — Confidential talk with Herr Klindworth, who is departing for Germany and will see Hans there. I beg him to tell Hans everything I had intended to write to him. I am very moved by our conversation. — Klindworth finds R. rejuvenated and in his state of mind unrecognizable; Hans had told him that, if R. were ever again to write a single note, it would be thanks to me. — Letter from Herr Villiers, who sends his play and with typical French insolence makes fun of the *excellents Prussiens*. R. is against his visit and says all our sympathies are with the Prussians. We accompany Klindworth to the railroad station, a sad farewell. — In the morning I wrote to Claire and to L. Bucher. To the latter in order to express my complete sympathy with Prussia. Lucerne in a state of alarm; everybody worried—how hateful the French nation appears!

*Monday, July 18*   The more one hears of the French behavior, the more angry one becomes; a tissue of lies, ignorance, insolence, and conceit. As reason for the war Gramont and Ollivier cite the memorandum which Bismarck is said to have circulated to all foreign Courts. There never was such a note—just the telegram which was published in the newspapers, and so it is all pure lies. I tell R. that the war is Beethoven's jubilee, the declaration of war was made on July 17, 1870, on December 17, 1770, B. was born. I only hope to God that there is a lucky seven in all this! R. says he is beginning to feel hopeful; war is something noble, it shows the unimportance of the individual; at St. Jakob 2,000 *corpses* defeated the 40,000 feared Armagnacs—a case of an idea proving all-conquering; war is, so to speak, a dance performed with the most dreadful of powers, like a Beethoven finale in which he unleashes all the demons in a magnificent dance. In the afternoon we go to town to find out what is going on, but there is no news. In the newspapers all the enthusiasm which follows the King of Prussia everywhere. — R. writes to Herr Villiers that we shall hardly be in a position to see our French friends. — Except for my occupation with the children I am unable to put my mind to anything. Letter from Prof. Nietzsche, who, it seems, in order to escape both the French and the Germans, is going to the Axenstein.

*Tuesday, July 19*   The Bavarians, thank God, are going along with Prussia; the Austrians, disgraceful as always, with France. My heart is heavy; R., however, tends, rather, to be cheerful; conditions in Germany were too unsavory, this war could once again show what the Germans are. I think of the message I gave Herr Klindworth for Hans; what a hard school must a poor mortal go through in order to solve the riddles of life! — R., who had almost completed his essay *Beethoven and the German Nation* in his own mind, cannot now capture the mood to begin it. Outward events do not affect the core of the matter, but they are unsettling, and the inner lantern stops glowing, the winds of Fate blow the flame hither and thither. — In the afternoon a visit from Baron zu Weichs, who tells me many heartening things about the state of the German army, and, among other things, that Colonel Rüstow has been in Paris, acting on behalf of Count Bismarck, for the past 4 weeks. Telegram to Richter; Mendès, Villiers, etc., are arriving; and indeed in the evening they are with us. Feelings of great embarrassment, though the dear people are friendly. We make music.

*Wednesday, July 20* In the morning R. exclaims to me: "Do you know what I was thinking of in that great arpeggio at Brünnhilde's awakening? Of the movement of your fingers in a dream, when your hand glides through the air. That's why I am still not satisfied with it." — Lessons with the children, while R. begins on his *Beethoven*. To one of the Frenchmen I explain concisely my attitude toward the war. — Full table at dinner; before it the Norns' scene, later in the evening Wotan and Fricka; in between, presentation of Siegfried. — Very fine letter from Dr. Herrig, who in true German manner welcomes the war wholeheartedly, yet looks with apprehension on the outcome. R. replies to him at once.

*Thursday, July 21* R. and I are both very tired and decide to keep to ourselves as much as possible. Since Lulu has a headache I let her read *The Arabian Nights* (Sindbad) instead of working. Family lunch, then a drive with Judith Mendès, in the evening tea with her and her husband; the others we had put off. — Germany is united, may God bless its arms! — In the afternoon R. said to me, "Since your arrival I have had boundless confidence, a shameless belief in myself; even this most terrible of events, this war, will turn out, according to my belief, to be a blessing for me." He has been working on his *Beethoven* and declares that every day he enjoys the happiness of our life more deeply. When he was playing passages from *Die Walküre* yesterday, he thought of the last time he played it to me, in Biebrich (1862). "Those were sad days," he cries. Returning home with Judith, I find R. looking very upset and cannot understand why. After the visitors' departure I learn that the housekeeper had behaved improperly toward R. Against such rudeness he is defenseless, and he finds it hard to shrug off, for toward the servants he is always inexpressibly kind.

*Friday, July 22* Start of our spa cure; we walk in the morning in the garden, R. and I, and discuss the war. All at once one can feel where one belongs, there is a connection which in times of peace cannot make itself felt, since only the bad things float to the surface. Inside one feels something which cannot be talked about, yet it is present in everything, and in this emotion one puts all one's hopes and wishes. Thus says R. — The University of Kiel wants to join in, lock, stock, and barrel; the merchants are making great sacrifices, and the clerics are obliged to keep silent. In contrast, there is a great deal of lying and boasting going on in France. Bismarck says in the Lower Chamber that he has not even informed the King about Gramont's talk with Werther, since he found the demand for a letter of apology *ridiculous*. The Viennese students want to join Germany; the Catholic-dominated Chambers in Bavaria quite shameless. — Eva suddenly becomes ill, with convulsions. As I am standing beside her bed, Vreneli brings me the news that our dairy farmer, who supplied us with fish, has been drowned, and right in front of our house; what life can bring us, Vreneli says drily and rightly. — In the evening the Mendès couple; R. and Richter play the F Major Symphony and the last movement of the *Eroica*.

*Saturday, July 23*   Eva still unwell; a letter from Claire, her son has had to join the navy. The report in the *Bund* that the French have all the advantages through their position, their rail network, and their fleet depresses me; R. chides me for having so little faith in ideals. I reply to Claire. Judith with us at lunch, afterward I translate with her *Damayanti and Nala*. In the evening music from *Die Msinger*. (Letter from my mother.)

*Sunday, July 24*   I am sad, sad, and the doctor, reporting that two villages near Offenburg have been burned down by the Turcos, does not exactly raise my spirits. I continue translating at Eva's bedside; family lunch; we drink a toast to General Moltke. In the afternoon Judith, in the evening a boat ride "at the silencing of the light," as R. says. Fireworks on Mount Pilatus, later quartets by Beethoven. Eva still unwell. A report about 6,000 Austrians who have joined the French—a report coming from the French—annoys us profoundly, and R. demands of our friends that they understand how much we hate the French character.

*Monday, July 25*   Sad unto death! — Jakob returns from the dairy farmer's funeral and reports that a telegram has announced the imminent engagement of the troops, I pray with my children for the Germans. After lunch to Countess Bassenheim's. In the evening our friends. R. said at lunch that he is basing his whole essay on a sentence which I let slip: that music goes far beyond beauty. — In the afternoon Fidi in the "blue closet," then R.

*Tuesday, July 26*   No fighting has taken place. Great delight among us over the behavior of the Duke of Nassau; Napoleon had promised to return his dukedom to him, he sends his compliments and elects to serve with Prussia in the war. Worked with the children, Eva well again, made progress with the translation. When our French visitors arrive, there comes from R. a long speech on the German character and how difficult it is for us at this moment to consort with French people. I am much alarmed by the news that 50,000 Frenchmen are stationed in St. Louis, and altogether by the fact that the French are said to be ready and the Germans not. R. works on his *Beethoven*. (I write to my mother.)

*Wednesday, July 27* R. still at his *Beethoven*; I with the children. No war news. Drive in the afternoon with R. to our friends'; on our return Richter hands over a letter, it is from Hallwachs and reports that on July 18 the divorce was made final. There is no happiness on this earth, my children, for at this news I only had tears.

*Thursday, July 28* Worked with the children. The newspapers report some splendid revelations by Bismarck; he has had the *Times* informed of the proposals which Benedetti unceasingly made to him (French invasion of Austria, so that they might then conquer Belgium, then supplies for the Southern states, enabling them to take over French Switzerland, and other savory things of that sort). The French do not know what to say, except that the Emperor *knew nothing about it*, or that Bismarck had provoked it all. — Visit from Prof. Nietzsche, in the evening the French visitors, music, the Norns' scene, and *Tristan*.

*Friday, July 29* Spent the morning with Prof. N., R. reads passages from his essay on Beethoven, I am surprised that I can follow it so well, since I have never studied philosophy. After lunch Herr N. introduces his sister to me, a nice, modest girl. Later, sudden arrival of our friend R. Pohl, engaged in fleeing from Baden territory. Richard compares our motley company with the *Decameron*—as they fled from the plague, so we from the war. The French visitors arrive as usual and the conversation is lively. (Austria, as well as England, Italy, and Switzerland, is behaving abominably—that so-called sage objectivity which accords the same treatment to an honest man—Bismarck—as to a rogue—Napoleon.) —

*Saturday, July 30* Our little company is breaking up; the French people, having learned from R.'s visit to our lawyer that the wedding cannot take place for at least another four or five weeks, are visiting a friend in Avignon and will then return. R. Pohl is looking for a guesthouse, Prof. Nietzsche is going to the Maderaner valley with his sister. Our last dinner with the French; at the end of the evening a long conversation between Catulle M[endès] and R. in consequence of a reading by M. Villiers, whose hypocritical trend, bombastic style, and theatrical presentation had made us thoroughly indignant. R. draws their attention to the objectionable nature of their rhetorical poetry. Catulle listens, full of understanding and much affected; we have come really to like him because of his sensitive nature and fine intellect, but his friend is becoming increasingly intolerable. Parting from Catulle and Judith, that good, deeply distressed couple who both possess real beauty of soul. — In the morning I strolled with R. under the linden tree on the lakeside, and once again we felt clearly how much we mean to each other. —

*Sunday, July 31*  Peace again in the house; the previous turmoil still pursues me in bad dreams. — I have forgotten to note down that last Thursday we gave our children great joy with a visit to Tribschen of 15 trained dogs, mostly poodles. The day before I had promised them a party of children in fine jackets and pink hats, and when the very handsome, dressed-up dogs arrived in a cart, together with their trainer and a barrel organ, the jubilation was huge. The grownups in the household enjoyed themselves no less, and the dogs, who were given lumps of sugar, and the Italians, who put them through their tricks, did not go unrewarded. — France needs a *Moltke cure*, says R. when we discuss the incredible insolence and mendaciousness of the French behavior. A day and evening of lovely peace, R. drinks his beer in the garden outside the house, and the passing mention of a line in *Hamlet* brings him to a comparison between Sh[akespeare] and Beethoven; as in Shakespeare the characters, so in Beethoven the melodies—unmistakable, incomparable, an entire, inexplicable world.

*Monday, August 1*  Very bad night; dreams of being pursued; I force myself to continue my cure with R., but it has a bad effect on me. Letter from Frl. v. Meysenbug, she is on the Sonnenberg. At eleven, as a storm approaches, R. goes off to see the Protestant parson Tschudi, from whom he returns very content. When the document announcing my divorce is received here, we shall probably have no difficulties at all. R., when I ask him whether all of this is agreeable to him, says he knows of no creature anywhere in the world with whom he would wish to be united except me! If he had not had me, he says, he would have entered a monastery. — In the afternoon I order our wedding rings, in the traditional Lucerne form. In the evening a letter from Herr Praeger in London, reporting on the performance there of *Der Fl. Holländer* (in Italian) and its success. —

*Tuesday, August 2*  A wild night for R. and me, he dreams of his wife, who was insolent and malicious toward us and against whom he could defend himself only by crying out, "But you are dead." With this cry he woke up; I heard him, too, but, being still in the grip of a dream which robbed me of the German language, called out to him in French, "*J'ai bien dormi,*" although I only wanted to ask, "What is the matter?" He, already awake: "Why are you talking French?" I, half-awake: "You cried out in French." But his dream keeps on recurring throughout the night. In the morning it made us laugh a lot. And as usual R.'s dream was associated with my thoughts during the day. — R. reads me his continuation of the Beethoven essay: "To please you I have mentioned Palestrina." — The French have been repulsed by the Germans near Saarbrücken. Great enjoyment in the afternoon, R. reads aloud Xenophon's *Symposium*. Then he walks up the Sonnenberg to visit Frl. v. M[eysenbug]. I stay at home with the children.

*Wednesday, August 3* Very distasteful letter from R.'s nephew, R. Avenarius, demanding 100 thalers for his cousin Rosalie; the letter is foolish and importunate. — I read in the *Illustrirte Zeitung* a report about the promulgation of the Pope's infallibility; when the result of the vote was put in his hands and he was about to proclaim his infallibility, a thunderstorm plunged the assembly room into such darkness that two candles had to be brought in order that the Pope could read out his own deification. Worked with the children, at one o'clock Frl. v. M[eysenbug] with Frl. Herzen; a pleasant, sympathetic visit. At lunch I receive the document confirming my divorce. — News that Saarbrücken, often attacked in vain by the French, has now at last been taken by them. An unimportant outpost. — Grand presentation of children; our friend finds the little ones charming and well behaved.

*Thursday, August 4* Ever-mounting pleasure in Bismarck, whose revelations show ever more clearly how wisely and at the same time how righteously he has been acting; he says he did in fact have to temporize with the French in order to enjoy at least a few years of peace. The French diplomacy, which could make such proposals to a German minister, he described as *the most obtuse of diplomacies*. A German minister! One hears the words for the first time, and how noble and proud does this minister appear! He has also forced England, by casting ceaseless aspersions on its actions, to stop supplying France with coal and ammunition. — How uplifting it must be for Bavaria, Saxony, and Württemberg to be fighting now as a German army! — Visit from Countess Bassenheim, who is nevertheless concerned about our army. The French had indeed captured Saarbrücken. How despicable do the French reports sound, praising the great effectiveness of their mitrailleuses! — In the evening we read poems by Byron.

*Friday, August 5* Fidi in his corral; R. says it is all a dream—one cannot believe in such happiness! Then he adds, "I wonder how Frl. v. Meysenbug must have felt recently, seeing you come in, when she saw me ten years ago in Paris with my wife!" — Lunch brings us heaviness of heart; a report in the *Bund* says that the mitrailleuse strikes and wreaks havoc at 1,600 meters; and the horrible French report about the Saarbrücken affair praises these terrible things! Mitrailleuses for our men and finery for our women—that is what the French bring us, says R. — However, after lunch Jost, the Am Rhyns' manservant, brings news that the Austrians have beaten the French; in great excitement we drive into town and it is true—they have been beaten, but Prussia and Bavaria beat them, took the fort at Weissenburg, and put the enemy to flight. General Douay is dead. The report states simply, "Brilliant but bloody victory"; whereas the French bulletin speaks boastfully of Saarbrücken, at the same time of the "miracle of the mitrailleuses," "the verve of the troops." Napoleon III (and last) writes to Eugénie about Louis, who had his baptism of fire, and his fearlessness made the soldiers weep!! And the government bonds rose, too. Oh, the miserable, evil creatures! — We feel the need for stillness, so that in stillness and contemplation the good spirits may stand by our cause! Weeping, R. and I regard each other and felt no wish to speak. The situation is too big, too frightful, God bless Germany, the German army, as it is now called! — Empress Eugénie goes every day to pray before the picture of Notre Dame des Victoires (Notre Dame des Mitrailleuses, says R.), and the Pope appeals to this lady to insure that the French do not abandon him. We hardly dare think of the significance of our cause.

*Saturday, August 6* Letter from Judith. — We read in the newspaper that the citizens of Weissenburg themselves took up arms against the Germans, against their own brothers—shame on them! I should like to spend the whole day praying; each fresh piece of news summons my heart to meditation—how splendid the alliance between North and South Germany! — R. told us yesterday evening that, as he was returning from town, he met the policeman who guards the convicts; the man stopped him and asked him how things stood; Richter told him of the Prussian victory, whereupon the policeman: "Yes, the King of Prussia is a good man, he is the only one who will come to the Pope's aid, the Pope himself has said the time will come when he will have to ask a Protestant for help!" When Richter today tells people in the town about this, they reply that all the convicts in Lucerne revere Louis Napoleon; the priest who visits them and is supposed to make them pious speeches talks only politics to them. — The *Bund* contains an extract from an article by Charles Hugo (son of the poet), in which he describes the Prussian army and compares it with the French army in a way one would not expect even from a Frenchman: that the Prussian commandants are being followed by brigands in turbans, and other things of that kind!!! What does such a nation deserve? But now, at this very moment, our soldiers are fighting and bleeding; may they be blessed and fortified, oh, God of Righteousness, help them! I write out a prayer for my children. — (Letter from Graz with 100 florins; *Der Fl. Holländer* has been a great success there; the money is welcome, for we are very short of it.) Twice already R. has found an opportunity to protest vehemently against so-called Swiss neutrality; once to our lawyer, who, when R. informed him of the victory at Weissenburg, replied that it was all the same to him; and yesterday to General (in the Neapolitan army) Schuhmacher; R. met him in the cigar shop, where everybody was awaiting the dispatches, and when they at last arrived and R. was reading them, the general said, "One cannot make head or tail of them," and as a strategist he argued that the Prussians could not possibly have taken the fort if the French had intended to defend it, and other things of that kind, whereupon R. simply replied, "That is all very well, but one thing I can see—who is lying and who is telling the truth; the first the French are doing, the second the Germans." — With that he left and went to his bookseller's shop, where an English family was being shown the *Totentanz* [Dance of Death], painted here on the bridge. "*Totentanz, Franzosentanz*," said R. to Richter. As he walked through the post office on his way home, the bookseller met him again and said, rubbing his hands: "You have just helped me to make 40 francs. The English boy, who understands German, had to explain your joke to his parents; they asked me who you were, I told them, and, laughing, they at once bought the picture book." — We discuss in lively tones all the many things Germany owes to Count Bismarck; when one thinks of the previous Prussian ministers, and now of Beust and his consorts! He is a true German; that is why the French so hate him. — The French newspapers say the King of Prussia had telegraphed, "Bloody, *regrettable* victory"!!! (Instead of "Brilliant but bloody victory.")

*Sunday, August 7* I am writing these lines on Monday, yesterday went past in tears of the deepest emotion; at midday good Count Bassenheim rushed in and announced a German victory at Wörth; the Crown Prince had beaten MacMahon, the French troops had fled, there is talk of an uprising in Paris. In the evening the Countess sends her maid, to tell us that Marshal Bazaine has also been beaten, though this is not yet confirmed. Our spirits lifted tremendously! Siegfried, our Siegfried, will find himself in a different world.

*Monday, August 8* Restless night; yesterday evening Richter drove once again into town, but the dispatches he brought back were incomprehensible, all we could make of them was that the Northern army appears to have advanced, too; I scarcely dare believe it all. The terrible losses lie heavy on our hearts; of 3,000 men only 180 have survived, on account of the mitrailleuse fire! — Regarding Bismarck we hear the following story: after the declaration of war he was summoned to the Queen, who said to him, "So once again we face terrible times—what will this war cost us?" "Your Majesty, a few Napoleons," was Bismarck's reply! — In the afternoon to Countess B.'s with my lint, bandages, linen, etc. The newspapers (the Swiss ones, all in favor of the French) report that the French troops are regrouping and are in excellent shape. It was not Bazaine but Frossard who was beaten when he tried to go to MacMahon's aid; Napoleon, telegraphing the news, reported that the situation could be repaired. All the same, Paris is being placed in a state of siege. Countess B. tells me that the Viennese banker *Todesco* was with her when the news came of the victory at Wörth; he turned pale, spoke of the 30 millions which had been lost, and said the Austrians were now certain to commit the "folly" of joining in the war, etc. This makes the Countess suspect that Beust has accepted money under the table and that Austria will now join with France, for Herr Todesco is an intimate of Beust's. Among other things he also said: "And this man *Bray*, what on earth is he doing? We all thought he was well disposed"!!! Well disposed— that means, French! — We drive to the shop where the news is posted, there are rumors of a German defeat at Metz. Though without foundation, the mention of it is nevertheless enough to make one apprehensive. Fortune is fickle—will it remain true to our army? In melancholy concern I go on with my work and collect my faculties to pray for a deep wish.

*Tuesday, August 9* Mild the day, the Heavens gray, the heart is cowed, the spirit bowed, the breast beset, the eyes are wet, who'll come to tell that all is well? — Today R. rescued Fidi from great disaster; pieces of broken glass had been left on the floor, he was crawling over it and had a large piece in his hand. He was just about to put it in his mouth when R. happened to see it. Constant danger is our sky and suffering our earth, the air between, which brings us a little refreshment, is hope! — This mood prevails all day, rain falls, we wait in vain for news; Loulou becomes unwell and Fidi's inoculation takes effect. — Letter from Prof. Nietzsche, who has resolved to join the army. I reply to him, saying the time is not yet ripe. We are having trouble with Richter, for he, too, would like to join up. Our one consolation yesterday we found in scenes from Shakespeare's *Henry V*. — Letter from Claire, her son has departed without being able to say goodbye! — In the morning R. read me some splendid passages from his essay on Beethoven.

*Wednesday, August 10* Loulou in bed, no news; dismal weather, Fidi unwell, I spend the day preparing lint. In the evening I go to meet R.; the news from Paris is confused, there is talk of the Emperor's abdication, the Empress's flight, and about the state of the navy, which would require 120 ships but has only 23; but then again news that the French army is regrouping, the Empress forming a government (Palikao), that Gen. Changarnier is being given the supreme command. Nobody can make sense of it all. — After supper we read C. Frantz's excellent chapter on Napoleon's propaganda. R. full of confidence in the German victory. — The battle at Wörth takes on an ever-increasing significance.

*Thursday, August 11* Constant discussion of the situation, R. convinced that the Germans will win; I have the *faith*, but with it the apprehension. R. says: As the Indians believe that an unfulfilled wish is the reason for the life of another soul, so does the wish of all good people to see the German character flower at last lay the ground for our victory over this much-feared France and its unconvincing-looking organization. — Dissuading Richter the day before yesterday from joining in the war (on the grounds that it was useless), R. said to him: "It will turn you into an adventurer; for love of me you have given up your position, now hold out. When you were in Brussels, I received a letter, signed '*les mânes de Meyerbeer et de Mendelssohn*,' in which I was told that now I once again had a loyal friend, I should make haste to get him married, so that I could seduce his wife after destroying his life." I reflect on this slander: no blame falls on R.; if there is blame, it falls entirely on me; how I must atone for it is a matter between me and my God. But Richard is as innocent as a baby. — I write to Claire, then family lunch, later a drive in spite of very bad weather, R. to the parson, I to inspect the hanging lamp. — No news, except that the Alsatians, turned by the Church into fanatics, are shooting at wounded Germans, while the women pour hot water on the heads of our soldiers; some doctors have also been killed by the French. In consequence of this the Germans have shot 26 peasants. (Count Bassenheim suddenly polite to Richard!)

*Friday, August 12* My dear long life, R. exclaims to Fidi, who is now beginning to walk! As he embraces me, he says, "Yes, a fair wife, that is something poor Beethoven did not have, it was reserved for poor old me, which is why I have such ridiculous faith in myself." — Letter from Hans Herrig, as remarkable and original as ever. No news of the war, just constant horrible weather, which must make marching very difficult for our fine soldiers, God be with them. — The newspapers are printing poems by Messrs. Freiligrath, Bodenstedt, etc., etc., and R. remarks that in such times as these poets should meet the same fate as Cinna in *Julius Caesar*. — The hanging lamp is put up, but will not be used before Fidi's christening. It pleases R. and is really handsome. R. on the Sonnenberg, I go to meet him on a typical Swiss evening: yodeling, cowbells, and church bells, yet in spite of it all great stillness and peace. The weather has cleared up a little, and late in the evening the moon shines down brightly on us. — R. works on his *Beethoven*; we are without news.

[*End of the second notebook of the Diaries.*]

*Saturday, August 13* A new volume, almost a year gone by again. May I be given the grace to record only improvements in myself! An ever-deeper recognition of my own unworthiness, an ever more cheerful and voluntary atonement for this unworthiness, a more radical negation of self-will, repudiation of all life's vanities, concentration on the one single aim. May it be granted me to raise my children in love, so that their love will one day be my fair intercessor, and may my one happiness be to see them grow up in peace and joy! — For news, only the rumor that the Prince Imperial has been dispatched to London; should this be confirmed, then things would look bad for the Napoleons. Our troops are advancing ever farther, God be with them. We read the most frightful accounts of the inhumanity of the French, wounded men and doctors are being murdered, one of the former had his eyes gouged out by a 14-year-old boy! It is terrible. Talking to me yesterday about Eva, Richter said she would surely have a fine voice and should go on our ideal stage. I cannot resist giving vent to utter repugnance, and declare that in such an event my daughter would be lost to me. I do not consider it possible for a woman to live a public life and at the same time to fulfill her feminine duties; and above all not in a field of art which burdens her with playing the most terrible things. If this is to be Eva's fate, then I shall regard her as having been sacrificed, and myself as well. — Pleasure in Loulou and Boni, because they prefer working for the soldiers to playing. R. remarks on the prettiness of Loldi's cheeks, and says: "Even as a child I always sought for beauty in the cheeks; I did not realize that what I meant by that was a kind smile, spreading across the whole face. I once looked at myself in a mirror to find out whether my appearance was not too repellent. Handsome you are not, I thought to myself, but also not too ugly, for your cheeks are certainly not ugly." — In the evening now always the newspaper; the heroic, melancholy details of our victories.

*Sunday, August 14* These pansies R. picked for me on our walk to the fountain, after saying to me, "I have been thinking about our love; how one should describe it I don't know, but I know that it is a complete inner inability to do without the other." Toward midday, Countess Bassenheim, Frl. Meysenbug, and Frl. Herzen to lunch. Naturally the conversation revolved around the military situation; details of the atrocious acts of the French soldiers (Algerian Turcos and Zouaves) are becoming increasingly terrible. In the evening a telegram that Nancy has been occupied by our troops.

*Monday, August 15* As I prepare lint in the morning with Frl. von Meysenbug, who, along with Olga Herzen, spent the night with us, we talk about Hans; everything she tells me about his position in Florence is highly pleasing. He himself is supposed to have said, "If I ever become a likeable person, I shall have Florence to thank for it." Fidi slept last night in my room (Frl. Olga had his room); when, in the darkness, I touched the little cradle and heard the breathing of the sleeping child I felt as if I were in a blissful dream! — Today is Napoleon Day; as we are thinking of it and wondering how he will be celebrating it, Count B. arrives with a telegram from his son in Munich; Marshal Bazaine beaten by the Prussians, King Wilhelm himself was in command of the cavalry. A terrifying Last Judgment—what will now become of the French? And Napoleon? Ham, Boulogne, Strassburg, Mexico— must all these not appear to him now to be the core of his fate, and the Emperor's pomp the worthless, now ridiculous outer shell? . . . Marie Muchanoff wrote yesterday that my father sobbed throughout the whole of *Die Walküre*, and she had been unable to watch the scene between Brünnhilde and Siegmund for a 3rd time, so much was she affected by it. — Recently, when I spoke hopefully of an *emperor* of Germany in the near future, R. said he should not call himself emperor, but duke of Germany. Now I see in yesterday's newspaper that the rector of the University of Berlin, Herr Du Bois-Reymond, has had the same thought, which seemed to us very daring. — In the evening the conversation brings us to Minna, R.'s first wife; some things told me by Frl. Meysenbug brought me face to face with a veritable abyss of meanness. With tears in his eyes R. tells me more about it: "That was the main ingredient of my earlier life and all else linked with it, culminating in a complete fiasco." I must, he said, have patience with and understanding for him, for I could never imagine the atmosphere in which he had lived. "The first person ever to give me the impression of nobility was your father." How must such words affect me, whose only feelings for him are of admiration and respect!

*Tuesday, August 16* Napoleon claims to have repulsed the Prussians at Dongeville, but he is on the retreat to Verdun, and King Wilhelm reports to his consort: victory at Metz. It appears to have been an outpost skirmish. I receive two letters from Prof. Nietzsche, the first, delayed, from Basel, the other from Erlangen, where he is already tending the wounded. In a few days he will be going to Metz. I feel that Richter should also go, but he lacks the means, and we are in no position to support him adequately, either, which is sad, but must be borne. — From Paris 40,000 Germans have been banished in a scandalous manner, and there is no end to the barbarous behavior of the French troops.

*Wednesday, August 17* A report from my brother-in-law once more gives cause for concern: it seems the French are out steadily to weaken the Germans by withdrawing, which means the Germans have to maintain troops in the provinces (Alsace, Lorraine, etc.). There is also talk of an imminent battle at sea! The prefect of Verdun has reported that 10,000 Prussians fell in a single engagement, and the people of Lyon believe this and rejoice over it! At the moment we cannot understand the movements of our forces; it seems they wanted to cut off Bazaine's retreat, but the retreat was nevertheless effected. A correspondent for the *Times*, who viewed the Battle of Wörth from the top of a tower, told a certain Herr von Loë that the Germans, when repulsed, always retreated in exemplary fashion, as if under orders, whereas the French fled headlong, each man being likely to stab any fellow countryman in front of him in order to escape more quickly. R. says every body of soldiers has some distinguishing mark—the Macedonians their phalanx, the French of Napoleon's time their bold attack; the hallmark of our army is this calm confidence, but what do the French of today have? It is being said that the Austrians distinguished themselves much more (in '66). Yet I am still worried, for the entire French nation is ready to take up arms. God be with our Germans! — R. was unwell yesterday, he had worked too hard in the morning on his *Beethoven*, made much music in the afternoon with Richter, then in the evening the disturbing newspaper reports. We are afraid the Germans are giving the French too much time. (Letter to me from Peter Cornelius.)

*Thursday, August 18*  Richter, whom I sent to the Sonnenberg, brings me 50 francs for the wounded, I do some collecting myself and am able to give Countess B. 137 francs. In town there are once again two conflicting news reports: the French claim to have won at Gravelotte; on the other hand, a report comes from Pont-à-Mousson that after a battle lasting 12 hours, with many casualties, the French were thrown back, and also the projected splitting of the French army was accomplished. The news has been so conflicting ever since Sunday, but I prefer to believe the Germans. — Family lunch (Loulou begins swimming today). R. says he hopes Paris ("this kept woman of the world") will be burned down; in his youth he had not understood Blücher, who had desired this, and he had disapproved, but now he understood him—the burning of Paris would be a symbol of the world's liberation at last from the pressure of all that is bad. In 1815 the allies went out of their way not to harm this city, for they were soon to have need of it again to amuse themselves. R. would like to write to Bismarck, requesting him to shoot all of Paris down. — When I return home from town, Dr. Pohl is there, and R. is singing the last scene of the first act of *Götterdämmerung* for him. Discussion of the situation, R. believes the German reports implicitly. It is also said that Prussia has returned the millions demanded in '66 to Bavaria. — When R. saw me, he said: "There you are. I am always so happy when you come back, I enjoy again the crowning act of my life whenever I see you"—while for me, as I was returning, the ground burned beneath my feet in my longing to see him again, to know how he was. R. is very impatient at receiving no news from Cl[emens] Brockhaus, he much desires our marriage to take place on the 25th. I remembered everything in patience, for thoughts of the general situation are too grave. — As I came home, I met the widow of the dairy farmer who was recently drowned; I spoke to her and was very touched by the way she spoke of the disaster and her attitude toward it. Her face, ravaged by farm work, has fine, regular features, and her child looks fresh and alert.

*Friday, August 19* Thirteen years ago, in the same wet weather, my wedding day; I did not know what I was then promising, for I never kept to it; if I now know what has assumed control of me, I wish never to forget the sin, but to stare it constantly in the face, in order to learn humility and submissiveness. In the morning R. reads to me from his *Beethoven*; magnificent the description of the C-sharp Minor Quartet and the comparison with Shakespeare. The remainder of the day passes in a discussion of the situation; our troops have been fighting for 4 days now; the French are constantly reporting victories, but they do not mention any good results arising from their victories. In Paris one may no longer speak the name of the Emperor, and the shameful way in which these once-fêted people are now being treated is utterly disgusting; it is curious how what is happening in Paris, which previously interested everybody, has now become a matter of such complete indifference. They can do what they please as long as they are humbled. When R. goes to town, he is addressed by a man he does not recognize; he turns out eventually to be one of the Dresden revolutionaries, *Metzdorf*, who spent the last 20 years in Paris, earning his living by giving lessons, and has now been banished! All in the name of civilization! — We cannot understand the reports of the fighting, but R. thinks it is all designed to give the Crown Prince's army time to reach the scene. I downright forbid anyone to go in search of news; it is a sin to treat such events as an object of curiosity. R. agrees with me and says, "In such great times individuals deteriorate; they use the excitement and the news as an excuse for spending their time in cafés and strolling the streets." — Great amusement yesterday over Richter, who sang to us the duet of the two Pharaohs from Rossini's *Moses*, the young and the old, and thus exposed the ludicrous nature of this type of art. He had played in it (the horn) in Vienna, in connection with which R. remarks that it is a disgrace to expect Germans to participate in such things. — R. very incensed that his nephew does not reply to him, and sends off a telegram (to Ottilie); I beg him to wait, but he will not.

*Saturday, August 20*   A correspondent's report in the *Bund* yesterday upset me very much; it said that the Germans were facing guerrilla warfare, and today the *A.A.Z.* declares that if the Germans do not soon destroy Bazaine and march on Paris as hastily as possible, all their victories will be wasted.

I am still utterly consumed by my anxiety when Countess B. is announced, and she tells me of a victory at Metz, the French cut off from Paris. This is official. May the grace of God now descend on our magnificent German steadfastness, that the prize may be worthy of these dreadful and splendid struggles! — (Letter from Clemens Brockhaus arrives today after all—so you see one must always remain patient, says R.) I write to Mathilde M[aier] and to Judith Mendès; the latter we shall probably not see again. — Jakob brings news that all our papers have arrived at the parsonage, but the parson Tschudi is on a short tour, and that is why we have heard nothing from him! — The news of the victory is confirmed; R. drafts a fine poem for the King and copies it out on the title page of the first act of *Götterdämmerung*, which he is sending the King for his birthday. Today is a good day, but one goes about as if in a dream, all I can see is the battlefield. David Strauss has written an open letter to Renan, in which he explains to him Germany's entire position in relation to France; apart from a few errors of taste the description is excellent. A dispatch reports that Napoleon has been abused, not to say maltreated by the Mobile Guard and is being given no support by the army. MacMahon has sent him as a prisoner to Reims!! And this is the nation which wanted to hurl itself on Germany! The way German women prefer to look after the French wounded, in order to make use of their little bit of French, looks very indecorous. — Late in the evening a letter from Judith M., they want to come here after all, which is certainly rather curious. — Another poem by Freiligrath; it really is wretched, this verse-making in these terrible days when the heart jumps nervously at every piece of news. — Mazzini has been captured; thus the three figures whom my father most revered are now in unenviable positions: Mazzini in prison, the Pope beset by a thousand fears, and L[ouis] Napoleon—*in the gutter*, as Dr. Wille prophesied years ago, to my father's great indignation. — "My good spirit," R. calls me repeatedly during the evening as he thinks tenderly of our approaching marriage.

*Sunday, August 21*   Today our banns are called in the church; and on Thursday, the King's birthday, we are to be married. Loldi is lying ill in bed. Nice letter from Marie Muchanoff, to which I reply at once. Dr. Suiter reports that the King of Prussia has made peace proposals; God knows whether they will be accepted. (Letters to R.'s sisters, to E. Ollivier, to Claire, to Mme Schuré, etc.) In the afternoon visit from Pecht, the painter, which pleases us very much. (Letter from Prof. Nietzsche; he is composing music in the military hospital.)

*Monday, August 22* The elder children's certificates of residence arrive, which is very important for an undisturbed life here. The news of peace is not confirmed; the French people continue to live in complete ignorance of events, the war minister's face never revealing anything but mystery and joy. Each side has lost 50,000 men. R. writes a splendid letter to my mother; I write to Frau Wesendonck and ask R. if he is satisfied with the letter; he feels it goes too far, and says he had always thrown a poetic veil over this relationship, in order not to admit its triviality, but now he himself has lost his poetic feelings for it, and he does not care to be reminded. He thinks I might receive an unpleasant answer, but I do not believe that, for I believe my attitude is not lacking in delicacy. — Herr Pecht lunches with us, and we take great pleasure in showing him Tribschen. The wedding rings arrive. R. says he wants to laugh out loud like a child when he sees my signature: Cosima Wagner; it seems to him like a dream. I beg God, in his grace toward me in my joy, not to forget those who are mourning and suffering. (In the evening, yesterday and today, read *King John*, but it is almost impossible to keep one's mind even on Shakespeare in these disturbed times.) Letter from Claire.

*Tuesday, August 23* At Metz the French have fired on a soldier bearing a flag of truce and on his trumpeter; thus do they persist in their inhumanity. I write to Claire and explain to her the differences between the Germans and the French. Loldi still unwell, indeed worse than yesterday, which worries us; we shall not be married on Thursday, for I want none of the children to miss it. I write to Elisabeth Krockow. In the afternoon R. reads aloud some of Beethoven's letters; I feel as if I now understand everything. We talk about yesterday's visit and then go on to talk of the surprise most people show in seeing our life here in Tribschen. "What odd ideas they have about it!" "Yes," R. says, "about 5 months ago I received a letter from an anonymous woman, who told me she had wagered that I would not marry you. She asked me to tell her yes or no in the *N. Nachrichten*, saying my friends were worrying that you were a schemer, and the King was very angry about the rumor." One is always shocked by people's maliciousness; what does such a woman, whom I have certainly never harmed, what does she get from reviling me in this way? Has not every woman a sphere in which she moves and works? By what right does such a one throw mud at another unknown to her? It cannot be envy, for nobody in the world can envy me now that I have withdrawn from the world.

*Wednesday, August 24* To remind me that we should never lose sight of the seriousness of life, my Loldi is so unwell that she will not be able to attend the wedding tomorrow; we shall leave Eva with her for company. And so a veil is cast over the happy ceremony. R. drives to town to make the last preparations, and I explain to the children what is happening tomorrow. They weep with me and then smile with me, too, and finally Boni laughs, almost out loud: "You are marrying Uncle Richard." — We are very moved by the description of the battle at Wörth and its conclusion with the hymn *"Nun danket alle Gott."* — The French newspapers continue to spread lies, they say that the Germans maltreat the wounded and that they seize all the young French people and force them to fight in the front line; these lies are responsible for all the terrible reprisals practiced by the French. Napoleon has demanded to return to Paris, so that he can die beneath its walls, Palikao has replied they have no use for him, and if he really means what he says about dying, he can do that just as well in Reims. R. explains to us the whole operation against Bazaine, and we have to admire the cleverness of this plan. A soldier can feel it, too, says R., when he is being led well; like a member of an orchestra under a good conductor, each discovers the right way for himself, but the correct tempo must be given. Visit of Frl. Meysenbug with a professor from Palermo (Balerna?), who is extremely well disposed toward the Germans. — R. tells me jokingly that I will be annoyed at the lack of ancient symbolism in the Protestant marriage ceremony; we go on to talk about the ugly habit of gaping at weddings; all society is interested in is mine and thine, and the church is also concerned exclusively with this theme, thou hast and thou hast not, and thy reward is in Heaven! — The newspapers are constantly filled with shocking reports about the kindness of the German women toward French officers, so that they can make use of their little bit of French. "It is a great shame," says R., "that the Germans no longer beat their women; if that custom were to return, we should experience a revolution in the literature of today." I suggest an auto-da-fé of chignons, crinolines, etc., on the Odeonsplatz in Munich. — R. told us at lunch that during the consecration of the July Revolution memorial column (for which ceremony Berlioz wrote the music) he heard behind him a curious dialect which he at once recognized as German but could not properly understand; it came from a Lorrainean peasant. "So they are still Germans, I thought to myself, but it made me feel as sad as hearing birdsong in autumn." I am writing this at Loldi's bedside; I am concerned about her; our good Richter is to blame for her illness, because he allowed her to swim and kept her too long in the cold water. I have difficulty in restraining R. from showing Richter his annoyance over his lack of caution. Every worry is for me a warning sign, and I know that it must be thus; God give me the grace never again to cause suffering to anyone, knowingly or unknowingly!

*Thursday, August 25*   At 8 o'clock we were married; may I be worthy of bearing R.'s name! My prayers were concentrated on two points: R.'s well-being—that I might always promote it; Hans's happiness— that it might be granted him, separated from me, to lead a cheerful life. The Mendès couple did not come, also sent no word. We are worried about them. In the afternoon a letter from Judith: Catulle would be considered a deserter if he were now to leave Paris. Then a telegram from Marie Muchanoff, signed also by Tausig and Lenbach, congratulating us. In the afternoon we become very worried about Loldi, who still has a high temperature. We put off the christening, which was to have been next Sunday. Great worry! Besides this I am alarmed by a report in the *Bund*, describing the great danger for Germany of the advance on Paris. We part in the evening, worried and melancholy, but aware of our happiness.

*Friday, August 26*   The doctor, whom I ask for an honest opinion of Loldi's condition, gives me complete reassurance. Our spirits raised by this. Letter from Herr Lenbach, who is presenting me with a portrait, which delights me very much on R.'s account. Congratulatory telegram from the King. We pay our calls (to Frau Am Rhyn, the Bassenheims, the parson, and Frl. Meysenbug). Returning home, we send off the 120 *"faire part"*; a bouquet of edelweiss, sent to me by Frau Wesendonck. In contrast, a distasteful correspondence with Dr. Wille, whose wife is a dear and good friend, but there is a certain rudeness in the way he interposes himself between us. In the evening Frl. Meysenbug, Prof. Blazerna, and Frl. Herzen to tea (Loldi somewhat better).

*Saturday, August 27*   Night with no sleep at all, I can no longer bear any social activity. Loldi sleeps in my room, I watch over her sleep, which is fairly quiet. Letter from the Schurés, who see Strassburg in flames, and as good Alsatians do not really know what to think. Letter of congratulation from Councilor Düfflipp. Nice letter to R. from my mother, I thank her for it. The three healthy children with Frl. v. M[eysenbug] (yesterday Loulou distinguished herself by dancing the minuet very nicely); I go to fetch them. In the evening a letter from M[athilde] Maier, to whom I also write at once. R. writes to Schuré and urges him to be a German. Louis Blanc is the only Frenchman to speak a sensible word in these times, he advises a republic and then an alliance with Germany. — Yesterday evening Richter played passages from *Lohengrin*, and I felt how it was this work which really decided my fate; how much I desired to belong to a country which alone could produce such things. — (Loldi still ill.)

*Sunday, August 28*   In the morning R. calls out to me, "Cosima *Helferica* Wagner, that is what you should be named, for you have truly helped." At 10 o'clock we start out, and arrive in Mariafeld toward two o'clock. Very friendly reception from the whole family; Frau Dr. [Wille] says to me, "I have been watching you with great sympathy; you have taken and borne enormous things on your shoulders, though you are so young." She tells me my father said, "Now my daughter has a husband who is worthy of her." We spend a nice day there. Dr. W[ille] has a great many tales to tell, among them, about Napoleon III: how, when one of his protégés needs money, he takes to his bed, which then causes a slump in which his favorite can make a profit. — He compares the poet Georg Herwegh with a foot that has gone to sleep. A lot of witty things are said, and above all it pleases R. that he can always refer to me as Frau Wagner. I am happy that an old and trusted friend of R.'s is glad to see his destiny placed in my hands.

*Monday, August 29*   I feared R. would have a bad night, since he had not been for a walk and the meal had been somewhat richer than we are used to; but to my joy he tells me in the morning that he slept well. "I believe it was your quiet and gentle sleep which calmed me, my dear good angel," he says. We take leave of the kind family and arrive back here. Loldi is considerably better, and the remaining children lively and healthy; apart from cards of congratulation there is nothing awaiting us. But at the Zurich railroad station R. brought me a French newspaper, *Paris-Journal*, the reading of which threw me into boundless amazement! The plan of campaign is deduced from the Crown Prince's jealousy of Prince Friedrich Karl, then the *French victories* are extolled, disharmony reported between the men from Württemberg, Prussia, and Baden, plunderings by Germans described and finally virulent attacks made on the German people! It is quite unbelievable, and German reports do not come anywhere near conveying an impression of the feelings in France. The ministers are always smiling, confident of victory. The French government has not permitted the wounded to be transported via Luxemburg; in consequence their own wounded have to wait, since the Germans take care of their own first. — Horrible weather. (Letter from Prof. Nietzsche in Maximiliansau.) In the evening Frl. v. M[eysenbug]. Before going to bed, we once more, before parting, look at Loldi in her bed in my room; a touching sight, we have to weep before the sleeping child! "Heaven forbid she turns into a saint," says R. "Those I will not tolerate in my house."

*Tuesday, August 30*   Letter from Elisabeth Krockow, who cordially rejoices in my marriage. Loldchen had a good night, but she is still feverish. The doctor calls her illness catarrh of the lungs. Richter tells me at midday that he saw a little wren seized by a crow, he also heard its piteous cry. Visit from Frl. M[eysenbug] from afternoon till evening; R. reads from his essay *What Is German?* and is surprised that I know it virtually by heart. We also make music before taking leave of our excellent friend. — Wishing me a good night, R. says, "You are my good life," and he says to Frl. M. with sweet impulsiveness, "Oh, I am so happy!" To me it is like a dream that I am really sufficient for him, indeed am permitted to make him happy! — We tell our friend an anecdote which Dr. Wille told us about Gottfried Kinkel and the Polish Count Plater; the latter had completely won over the former to the Polish cause; they came together in Dr. W.'s house and asked to be allowed to withdraw from the company for important discussions. At one point Frau W. goes in to offer them something, and she hears Kinkel say to Plater: "No, you must understand we cannot give you Danzig." Frl. v. M. laughs heartily, saying it is typical of all democrats—how often had she heard them bargaining about Trieste!

*Wednesday, August 31*   The doctor says a battle is expected today or tomorrow between MacMahon and the Crown Prince, God be with our troops! Very nice and touching letter from R.'s sister Ottilie, who shows how unutterably she has been suffering with us. R. says she has inherited their mother's truly pious nature. Loldi still very ill. I write to Claire and to Judith, God knows if the letters will get through! Go to meet R. on his walk. In the evening he reads us Byron's description of the capture of the fortress in Izmail; very remarkable and gripping; R. says, "He is the only true poet of this century who watched and described contemporary events; Goethe and Schiller turned their backs on them."

*Thursday, September 1*   Frau Wille sends some photographs of the wall paintings in Pompeii. Splendid things, in comparison with which all our art looks so contrived. R. has had a nice letter of congratulation from P. Cornelius. Loldi somewhat better, but R. indisposed. In town we learn that MacMahon has been beaten at Beaumont. Splendid feeling, damped only by some lines from Prof. Nietzsche (in Hagenau), who describes the terrible state and inadequacy of the medical care on the battlefields. Is it now over at last? . . . Prof. N. says the French are still talking about the conquest of the Rhine!

*Friday, September 2*   The great event of the Tribschen household is the arrival of a *goose*—we do not know from where; the children very pleased, the dogs very astonished. Lessons with the children; Loldi gets up for a few hours. The doctor comes and is addressed with terrible vehemence by R., because he is of the opinion that it is "not good" *to take Alsace and Lorraine away from the French!* R. enlightens him as to the disgracefulness of a neutral policy. Visit from Countess B., she reports that the French have been talking of their victory! (I write to E. Krockow, to M[athilde] M[aier], to Prof. N., etc.) Meanwhile we learn in town that the pursuit of the French is continuing and also that Bazaine, who tried to withdraw from Metz, has been thrown back on it. I receive a nice letter from Dr. Alfred Meissner, who tells me that in May 1865, when he visited me, he already suspected how things stood with me. We read nothing in the evening, since we are much too excited by the news.

*Saturday, September 3* Day of unsavory letters; our friend Kietz is in Zurich and does not know what to do with himself; he has been *expelled!* Herr Müller von der Werra sends a victory poem, which he wants R. to set to music, and he promises to take care of the distribution of the work through correspondence in the American newspapers! Schuré turns out to be a fanatic Frenchman, and that in the truest high-school manner. (From Hans Herrig and Dr. Pusinelli, however, very nice messages of congratulation; to judge from the former, it seems to have been maintained all over Germany that R. would not marry me.) — To compensate for these unpleasantnesses we receive from Colonel Am Rhyn in the evening the news that MacMahon has been wounded, the entire army under Wimpffen has capitulated, Napoleon III has surrendered to the King!!! What a christening present for Fidi! 9 battles within a month, all victorious, and now this conclusion!

*Sunday, September 4* The news is correct, we have seen the bulletin. God in Heaven, what an outcome! "I am bad for the Napoleons," R. says. "When I was six months old there was the Battle of Leipzig, and now Fidi is hacking up the whole of France." Letter from his sister Luise, her 18-year-old grandson has died. R. is expecting a *coup d'état* in Paris. Yesterday R. told me he would like to compose funeral music for the fallen, and wished he could be commissioned to do it. Not a victory hymn—that he could not do. I write to Marie Muchanoff about this, so that she might use her influence to get him the commission. At 3 o'clock arrival of the Wille family, then the Bassenheims, at 4 o'clock the christening takes place. *Helferich Siegfried Richard Wagner* behaves passably well. Merry gathering afterward. Semper's hanging lamp is inaugurated. Dr. Wille brings a silver cup but loses it on the journey, and arrives in a bad temper; suddenly an old woman appears and returns it. Then a terrible thunderclap as the christening begins.

*Monday, September 5* Congratulatory letters from Dr. Sulzer, Nuitter in Paris, etc. In the morning I drive to the railroad station to greet the Willes once more, then take a copy of Doré's Bible to the parson. With Countess B. I go to read the dispatches; a republic in Paris! The Emperor in Wilhelmshöhe, the Empress fled to Belgium. How unimportant it all seems! This eternal round of storming City Hall and Tuileries, with not a single word of sense being spoken. — Great vexation in the afternoon—through the negligence of a servant my pretty coat (velvet with fur) has been entirely ruined. My sorrow has nothing to do with the value of the article, but with its significance to me, a present from R. But I restrain my sorrow and vexation and bring myself at last to the point of regarding this accident as a sacrifice, which I willingly make in order to avert suffering of another kind. The *Illustrirte Zeitung* prints pictures of French soldiers (taken from life), and from them all the wretchedness and degeneracy of the people stare out at me—indeed all the misery of mankind. In these sensual, bestial, besotted faces one sees complete idiocy. A picture of Alsatian peasants in flight moves me to tears. What madness—they are fleeing from their German brothers! — The mail brought a letter from the lawyer Simson; in answer to my inquiry about my liabilities, he says that Herr von B[ülow] has decided to bear all the costs of the suit. This distresses me, but there is nothing I can do about it. — My union with R. is like a palingenesis, a reincarnation which brings me nearer to perfection, a deliverance from a previous erring existence; yet I feel, and tell him, that it is only in death that we shall be united completely, freed from the barriers of individuality. When I try to tell him how much I love him, I feel the complete impotence of existence, and know that only in our last living embrace will I be able to tell him! That is why I always start to weep when I try to come close to him and tell him how my soul worships him. Before going to bed he once more asks me not to spend so much time bringing up the children. He says, "No mother brings up her children alone." "Yet I believe my children will be grateful to me for having been so much to them." "You were also not brought up by your mother." "I might have turned out better if I had had a mother to care for me." He does not like to hear me say that and becomes angry. We part between tears and smiles.

*Tuesday, September 6* "Do you love me?" I call out to R. in the morning, still half in a dream. From his room he answers me: "I have no business, no *bisogna*, in the world but to love you alone." Many letters of good wishes. "Congratulations come welling," R. says. "The earth has reclaimed us." — The composition of the provisional government in Paris is quite ridiculous, and the first thing they do is to talk and talk and declare that the world is watching them in wonder. In all this it seems to occur to nobody that Germany has freed them from Napoleon! — R. says all this old round of processions to the Hôtel de Ville, the Tuileries, etc., reminds him of an old aria from *Norma*, ground out on a barrel organ. I walk with R. to town after having worked with the children in the garden in the morning. In the evening we read *Richard II*; Shakespeare is the only one who stands the test now.

*Wednesday, September 7* Violent fever, I have to stay in bed, the doctor comes and thinks it is smallpox, since I have a bad headache. Under R.'s heavenly care I spend the day in great pain, without seeing the children. R. finishes his *Beethoven*.

*Thursday, September 8* I feel better, all that remains is a bad cough. I see the children again, and in the evening R. continues with the reading of R[ichard] II. (Loulou and Boni at Countess B.'s, where they are to help work out a *tableau vivant*. This little bit of nonsense is to take place in Lucerne for the benefit of the wounded.) Letter from Marie Muchanoff; she says that at the patriotic demonstration which followed the tremendous news of the capitulation of the French army the King did not make an appearance, so that the Prussian ambassador was the center of the delirious ovations. How very foolish of the King!! — She also says my father has written very sadly, he had wanted to visit the wounded, but worldly considerations had restrained him, something he now deeply regrets. She says he is more isolated than he himself realizes. A person who always looks to and acts for the outside world will soon develop an inner emptiness, and I do not think a belief in infallibility can ever fill this emptiness. (R. reads me the conclusion of his *Beethoven*.)

*Friday, September 9* Very bad night with constant coughing. I overdid it yesterday after all. The reports, proclamations, etc., from Paris are utterly ridiculous and repugnant. How and when can the war end? R. tells me that in Paris they have reports from St. Louis (near Basel) that the defenders of Strassburg made a sortie in which *10,000* Prussians were captured, killed, and God knows what else. In Basel, however, no one has even heard of it, so it is just the same old lies again, one is getting really tired of it. In the evening R. reads *Die Aufgeregten* to Richter and me; he recalls that Heine once recommended this play by Goethe to Frau Laube, who was complaining of sleepless nights. It is unbelievably dull. I am vexed with Countess B.; she asked that my children take part in some *tableaux vivants* for wounded soldiers; I consented. Then I fell ill and discovered that, whereas Marie was to portray a noblewoman and young Elizabeth, my children had to appear as beggar maids. It should not really matter, and, praise God,

Boni and Loulou noticed nothing at all; but I understand what is meant by it, and I am sorry that maternal vanity should induce so magnanimous a woman as the Countess to act so inconsiderately. Even at the christening I noticed she was not at all pleased to see my children looking so pretty in their little curls. I resolve to tell her quite calmly what is in my mind. — I am very glad that Boni and Loulou noticed and understood nothing at all, but admired Marie's make-up and her important roles, and were quite content to take part as poor children. — *"General Holk"* is here again, attending to our fireplace in the upper *salon*.

*Saturday, September 10* Today I have completely lost my voice; whatever it is seems to be taking a little walk through my whole body. I nevertheless get up and sit down to lunch with R. and Richter. Soon back in bed, however, where I finish *Die Aufgeregten* and also read *"Der Gross-Cophta."* In the evening R. reads me the conclusion of R[*ichard*] *II*; every word a world in itself. The children, whom I sent to watch the *tableaux vivants*, did not return until eleven o'clock, which worries me. But then I take pleasure in the impartiality with which they admire the other children, how prettily they were dressed and made to look prettier still, and never give a thought to themselves. But when they are out of the room, I am foolish enough to weep; I tell R. that this instance shows me once again that I have far more sympathy for the Countess than she has for me; for she knows how anxious and concerned I am that my children should not be treated in a less friendly way than others. Well, may God help my dear good little ones! R. is heavenly, he comforts me, begs me to be calm and gives me a letter from Claire to distract my mind.

*Sunday, September 11* I get up early and write to Marie M[uchanoff], inviting her in R.'s name to come soon, in order to discuss *Bayreuth*. Then to Dr. Heigel, who sent us congratulations; since he is editor of the *Bazar*, I have requested him to start a new fashion. The news from Paris is always personal and drolly confused—phrases, nothing but phrases. The possibility has been mentioned of joining France to *Belgium*, that is to say, the Belgian dynasty should rule over both countries—a splendid thought, but a little far-fetched. Family lunch, for the first time in days all together again. In the evening *Henry IV*.

*Monday, September 12* Letters from C. Mendès, very elegiac, he thinks of dying beneath the walls of Paris; from Dr. Pusinelli, whose brother, after doing business with shipping firms in Le Havre for 30 years, has now been expelled with his ten children and has to seek a new occupation. (Claire's cook was also expecting to be expelled!) R. revises his *Beethoven* and writes in strong terms to Catulle, always reiterating: You got what you deserved. C. sent a *Proclamation to the*

Germans by V[ictor] Hugo—what utter nonsense the French now find good! Visit from Countess B.; owing to R.'s kind persuasions I am now sufficiently calm to receive her, and when we begin to talk of the *tableaux vivants* I say to her, "I did not send my children to you, firstly, because I could not be present, and secondly, because I feared my father would be surprised to hear that in the first little occasion in which they were called on to show themselves they were accorded no more favorable roles than those of beggar maids." We then slid away from the subject. — Very nice letter from Councilor Hagenbuch, congratulating us. — At something I say to R., he replies to me: "You must just be healthy and not have saintly ideas, for I want to enjoy my happiness down to the last drop." — In the evening conclusion of *Henry IV*. Before that read fairy tales with the children.

*Tuesday, September 13* Still indisposed, but able to give the children their lessons. Prof. Nietzsche writes to R., he is back in Erlangen and is ill. I wrote to Rothschild for my money—God knows whether I shall still receive anything. R. works on his *Beethoven*—too much, in fact, for he gets floating specks before his eyes. Letter from M. Meysenbug, who regrets the bombardment of Paris, which annoys R. We agree that what happens there must happen, and that it is great foolishness to jabber about these things.

*Wednesday, September 14* There is serious talk of treachery by the French at the capitulation of Laon, I consider them capable of anything bad. Work with the children, R. at his *Beethoven*. We are somewhat depressed by the continual bad weather. In the evening *Henry IV Part II*.

*Thursday, September 15* Letters from R.'s sisters, both (Klara and Cäcilie) are glad about R.'s marriage to me. Letter to me from Karl Tausig. We read Wolfgang Menzel's pamphlet on Alsace and Lorraine; it accords with R.'s views. The great question now is what the Germans will do—restore Napoleon, more and more of whose dirty financial transactions (the real cause of the war) are coming to light? Negotiate with the republic, which is still behaving in a hostile manner? R. is in favor of a long occupation and French disarmament, and is glad that the matter has assumed such dimensions. "The French," he said, "are driven by their fate, and the Germans borne along." Great joy in Fidi, who during our family lunch crawls everywhere; afterward I go with R. to find a winter hat for him—all of them too tight for his head! — As R. says good night to me, he declares, "I live on your love." I lay down, feeling that the only true thing in my life has been my union with him; everything else I have done, what I have suffered and experienced, all this I drag around like a bad dream, or like prison chains from which I have been released; an eternal warning and reminder in the bliss of

Paradise of how terrible life is and how wretched the mortal being. My contemplation ends with a prayer, a prayer of thanksgiving, a prayer for pardon, deep acknowledgment of my unworthiness.

*Friday, September 16* Letter from Prof. Nietzsche, who seems to be deeply upset; then from my mother, who is rather hurt by my frank opinion of France. R. has a letter from the publisher Fritzsch in Leipzig, he will print the Beethoven essay. Still cold, inhospitable weather, worked with the children. In the evening a letter of congratulation to R. from Frau von Schleinitz; to me one from poor Claire, who is quite disconsolate. — Paris is now cut off, we shall hear nothing for some while. — Yesterday we again began talking about the French character, and R. said one had only to look at their folk dance, the cancan, to know what sort of people they are. What a dance expresses —the wooing of the man, the flight, and then the renewed rousing of the woman, expressed with such charming naïveté in Spanish dances —all this one is expected to discern in this folk dance; he professes to see something of the cancan in the quadrille. — During the evening R. suddenly disappeared and did not return for a long time, then he came back, but sent Richter out, and so it went on mysteriously through the whole evening; I then found out that there had been five bats in R.'s room, everybody was alarmed, and R. did not wish to say anything about it to me, since he knows I am superstitious in this respect. It did upset me when I heard of it, but then, taking a grip on myself, I prayed that whatever disaster might threaten I might still carry out my duties as a Christian, a wife, and a mother.

*Saturday, September 17* Wrote to my mother and to Claire. Taught the children, then shopping for Fidi's wardrobe and for Loulou's birthday. Everybody is in fairly good health, thank God, and the sky is clearing. Nothing from outside, and inside reign love and harmony! God bless all who are suffering. —

*Sunday, September 18* In the morning R. much enjoys hearing the children romping about on the stairs. "Oh, I am too happy," he calls out, "much too happy!" — In the newspaper we read that Paris will be able to hold out for a long time still, also that Toul and Strassburg are still defending themselves stoutly, and it is said that Bazaine is still well stocked with provisions. When will it end, how many more sacrifices must our men make? — I write to Prof. Nietzsche. Family lunch, during which our good Richter, when *Wallenstein* comes up in the conversation, says, "Yes, it is a wonderful play, if only it were not for that boring affair between Thekla and Max." R. let him finish, then reproached him severely, indeed vehemently, for such crude statements. Recently he had said of Mozart that it was just as well he died, otherwise he would have fallen into mannerisms, or his ingratiating melodies would forever have made people incapable of grasping the art of Beethoven. R. reproached him earnestly for this, pointing out that Mozart had only just reached mastery when he died, and we could never know what treasures he might have given us. "One must not take the easy way and say that everyone dies at the proper time. What would I not give for Beethoven's tenth symphony! Even if I, too, believe that everyone as a general rule is given the chance to show what he is made of, a truly great genius always dies too soon; it is not as with Mendelssohn, Schubert, Schumann, minds of the second, third, or fourth rank." — I read parts of the manuscript of his *Beethoven* and am filled with admiration for its depth of thought and clarity. R. says to me: "I regret after all not having compared Beethoven with Schopenhauer. There would have been a fuss, and yet in Beethoven's world he does represent *reason*. I was recently reminded forcibly of Sch[openhauer]'s genius when I read what he had to say about the differences between human beings. He regards it as an ineptitude of Nature not to have created yet another species, since between gifted and ungifted human beings there is indeed a gap wider than between some human beings and animals. One only has to watch a theater audience, in which one person is utterly absorbed and concentrating, the other inattentive, fidgety, vapid. Between these two persons no understanding is possible, and therein lies the misery of the gifted person in a world in which he must regard as identical with himself a creature who no more resembles him than an ape does." — In the evening we read Ovid, the day before, Lucretius. R. says, "It is in effect literature for the refined people in their villas, there is nothing popular about it, but it captivates through its erudition and wit—in short, its refinement."

*Monday, September 19* Yesterday Richard spoke of making a trip to Berlin this winter, in order to give a lecture at the Academy to promote our performances in Bayreuth. He wants me to go with him, and misunderstands me when I say it would be better for me to remain here. He believes I am being restrained by worldly considerations, my previous relationship with Hans's family, whereas it is just my inner voice, which tells me, "You have nothing more to seek in the world; because you caused severe suffering, you have resolved to live now only within these four walls for the children and the One and Only." I do not wish to explain this to R., in order not to upset him, and God will help me to do what is right!

*Tuesday and Wednesday, September 20 and 21* Very fine weather, I let the children play and I read *Beethoven*, which R. has now finished. — We have an affliction in the household: poor Jakob has such a bad finger that there are doubts about how to care for it. A misunderstanding by R. also causes me concern; at lunch I say jokingly that I now have no money at all. R. took this as a reproach and became hard and bitter. I was able to explain what I had meant, but how swiftly is pain caused! — On Wednesday evening we read Schopenhauer; how this teaching affects me! On going to bed I asked myself whether I should not have acted much better in life if such things had been impressed on me in my youth; but very soon I had to tell myself: You had the teachings of Jesus, which were enough, if you had not been weak and sinful: a *mea culpa* from the depths of the soul and acceptance of all suffering as atonement for one's existence.

*Thursday, September 22* A letter to R. from a poor widow touches me, particularly since she appeals to him in the name of our marriage; I write to Düfflipp on her behalf. R. is looking for a publisher for his *Beethoven*. For the first time for several days German dispatches again: Paris is surrounded and the Corps Vinoy has been beaten by the Prussians at Lagny. Also the Italians are in Rome. The French are devastating their forests, pulling down their villas; like children they show their bravery in vandalism. — Our poor Jakob is in pain, I talk to the doctor, but he is not worried; Fidi has a cold, is hoarse and feverish. In the afternoon a visit from Mme Stockar-Escher, sister of Alfred Escher, who is very well known in Switzerland; she is one of R.'s oldest friends, he lived in her house in Zurich, and his dog Peps is buried in her garden. R. takes pleasure in introducing me to her, but after she is gone he says, "It seems to me so trivial to refer to you merely as 'my wife,' and I wonder how people must feel who previously used to see me, also with *my wife*." For me, on the other hand, it is a matter of the greatest pride to hear myself called his wife, and I can only counter my feelings of unworthiness by thinking in the morning with heartfelt gratitude of everything I have gained, and in the evening by immersing myself in rueful meditation on my unworthiness. Read Schopenhauer. (R. writes to Frau v. Schleinitz, Pusinelli, etc., etc.)

*Friday, September 23* Work with the children, because the weather is cold and dull. R. writes letters (J. J. Weber, etc.) and corrects his *Beethoven*. At lunch he says that the parts of the biography just received have taken him back to the Baltic Sea, and he suggests reading E. T. A. Hoffmann's story *"Das Majorat"* in the evening. The weather has cleared and we go for a splendid walk in the direction of Winkel, through many farms in charming and idyllic hill country. The lake stretches before us like a gulf, and the blue mirror of its surface ("Heaven at our feet") transfigures the whole landscape. We go past the "Fontaine de Soif" (as in earlier times we had christened a little stream)—for the first time since our marriage. A deep inner joy over our seclusion, but thinking at the same time gratefully of our little children. "Without them," R. says, "we should be too earnest, they provide distraction and draw us into the circle of their gay existence." In the evening R. reads *"Das Majorat,"* which has a curious effect on me. During the day R. had asked me whether horror stories would not frighten me. I smilingly denied it, but then began to think of ghosts and apparitions, deceased people, and finally of Daniel—this with a feeling of reproach; though his loss may have been due to my father's having sent him to Vienna on the advice of Princess Wittgenstein, yet I blame myself now for not having saved him by going with him to Cairo; also I fear that I did not consult the right doctor when he was lying ill in my house. All this occupies my mind, and now chance will have it that at the first appearance of a ghost in Hoffmann's tale the name *Daniel* should twice be called out. As R. spoke the name in that meaningful, penetrating tone so peculiar to him, I shivered—not in fear, but in unutterable pain. The story itself gripped me through the pregnancy of its description and the beauty of its atmosphere. I ask R. to permit me to sleep in his room, fearing otherwise to be unable to sleep on account of my melancholy thoughts. I am told I slept peacefully, yet the night was painful to me. — (Telegram of congratulations from Prince Georg of Prussia.)

*Saturday, September 24*   The publisher Fritzsch in Leipzig is very eager to have *Beethoven,* and R. will give it to him. R. believes the Germans will be in Paris before October 2. Heaven bring it to an end! . . . Lovely day, the children play, and I work in the vegetable garden. We decide on and carry through an outing to Stanz; nice drive in the carriage and charming journey back on the steamer, after a ritual family coffee in *Winkelried.* The children's great delight over the waves produced by our steamer and another sailing beside it; R. remarks on how the waves appear to be running along with us, whereas in reality they are constantly being produced by physical circumstances— the whole is a condition and a reflection of life. In Lucerne we learn in the tobacconist's of the capture of Toul, while the French newspapers are still publishing reports of exhausted Prussians, repulsed Germans, reinforcement of Toul, etc.! Renan has now replied to D. Strauss; his letter is very petty, he maintains that France does not share Germany's illusions, and he represents France as the oldest cultured nation, consequently does not appear to know what a long history Germany possesses, and he expresses a very shortsighted criticism of the Prussian monarchy. — In the evening we read *"Ritter Gluck"* with much enjoyment. Unfortunately R. is not very well.

*Sunday, September 25*   "I had an unusually fine dream about you," R. calls out to me. Later he tells it to me: "We had arrived in Hanover with the Ritters and were living together with them. Imagining that you had treated me harshly, I went out in a bad mood, had an encounter in the street with a man on a horse, but was everywhere greeted and treated with marks of the deepest respect. That, however, was your doing; I went back and saw the house you had furnished for me; it was simple, but in every way sensible, everything had been thought of, the wallpaper in my room red with little white stripes, curtains the same, the piano was in your room, and I was to work there. Then I noticed that the room was a great hall, and I thought: Here Cosima will receive her guests, and how well she will do that! When I recognized your love and your care in everything, I wanted to go to you, full of the tenderest gratitude, and throw myself at your feet. Then I woke up." Yesterday he told me he had dreamed of Minna, that she had been vindictive toward me. I told him that this test, if it had ever come about, would have left me very indifferent, since my heart would not have been touched. "Oh," says R., "it would have been bad enough, not to have been allowed to belong to each other, and that before the whole world. Secret relationships, even if they hold firm, always suggest that in essence it was all only a sort of game." — R. talks about our approaching journey; I should prefer to put it off, if not give it up entirely, but R. says it will do him good, and that decides the matter. He talks about his publisher Schott, who behaved well, paid him for the *Ms.* in advance. "That pleases me, if only because it proves how one stands in the world and shows that people do not after all want to get on the wrong side of me. That is also why Fritzsch's eagerness for the *Beethoven* pleased me."

Lovely day, the children play in the garden. Walk with R. after family lunch. Letter from Marie Muchanoff, she will come, but she announces her intention in a very off-putting way; I almost despair of my whole enterprise when I have to assume that a person basically so alien to us is to play a significant part in it. I keep reminding myself of the impressiveness of her character and the unconditional nature of her enthusiasm, and believe that it is only her French manner which is so distasteful to R. as she discusses these things which lie so close to his heart. — In the evening we are summoned by the children; on their own initiative they are presenting *tableaux vivants* in the gallery; they have arranged chairs in the dining room and now they summon the whole household, which duly assembles to form a lively demos. Everything is then, to our great surprise, performed under Loulou's direction, outstandingly well, by the children. I am deeply touched, with tears in my eyes. The play acting is forgotten, all I see is the gravity of life hanging over these four heads. Oh, children, my children, if only I could help you! Loulou distinguishes herself through much hard work and dexterity, Boni through her confident manner,

Eva with amiability and wit, Loldi, however, through a rare earnestness, which does not desert her even in the curtsy with which she and
her three sisters acknowledge our applause at the end. They had dressed
themselves up with great dexterity as peasant children and depicted
groups from their picture books. — Later in the evening talk about the
war brought us back once more to the misery of life. "And yet," says
R., "I enter this room and look at the Goethe portrait in its fine frame,
presented to me in love, and I feel happy and believe in happiness
here on earth." As I smile, he just continues: "I assure you that such
feelings make me a complete skeptic toward pessimism, since I tell
myself that such delight would not have been possible without great
suffering. Genuine love is as rare in this life as genius. The best way
is to regard life as a task, a piece of work; anything in it that delights
us comes from somewhere else."

*Monday, September 26* Very bad weather, cold and raw, and Fidi
ill. Obstacles everywhere, as R. says. I write to Marie M. and arrange
a meeting with her in Bayreuth. God knows what will come of it, we
go into it without much faith. News of an engagement in L'Isle de
Dame which is still going on! Utter anarchy, how and when will it
end? — R. is horrified with *"Die Wacht am Rhein"*; the *Illustrirte
Zeitung* prints it as a supplement. "I hope the French win," he cries. "It
is too pitiful"! If a witty Frenchman were to see that, he says, he would
regard our German fatherland with a mild, ironical smile for going
into battle with such a melody. R. is moved to tears by this prospect.
"We have sunk too low. Only our troops will rescue us, they are great,
and Bismarck." With a smile he adds, "He won't sing the '*Wacht am
Rhein*'!" I do not know what brings me to speak of Sappho, but R.
tells me that I will never be able to understand these poems, and from
there goes on to speak of the impossibility of our ever even envisaging
the Greek world—Christianity has made of us something completely
different, and between these worlds lies a chasm, an unbridgeable one.
— "We will try once more with the German fatherland, with Bayreuth;
if it doesn't succeed, then farewell the North and art and cold, we shall
move to Italy and forget everything." In the evening R. begins *"Der
Magnetiseur,"* which made a big impression on him when he was a
child. I soon ask him to stop, however, since the subject and the treatment of it displease me greatly. The previous evening *"Don Juan"*
had given me such enjoyment; Donna Anna and her death reminded
me of *Tristan* and Schnorr. And how keenly Hoffmann feels the triviality
of the so-called public vis-à-vis a great artistic figure! —

*Tuesday, September 27* Saint Cosmas Day; I tell R. I am curious
to see whether my father will send me a telegram as usual. — Fidi still
unwell, probably teething. Apart from that I am very embarrassed that

my picture has not yet arrived, though I was told three weeks ago that it had been sent off, and Lenbach, to whom I wrote on account of it, has not replied to me at all. Instead, I receive a parcel for the children full of little things which "their father" had bought for them in Venice. Their grandmother forwards these with a letter. Great joy among the children, I am touched that the parcel for Loulou is inscribed August 25, 1870, in Hans's handwriting. Visit Mme Stockar-Escher, return home in very fine weather. Very good article by the philosopher Vischer on the Germans and the French, tough home truths. R. says, "A pipe-smoking German like that has character." On the other hand, insane agitation on behalf of Herr Jakoby in all German newspapers. R. says, "As we well know, Jews have no interest in the formation of a German empire, but, on the contrary, are in favor of cosmopolitanism." Read Schopenhauer in the evening ("Death and Indestructibility").

*Wednesday, September 28* Letter to Loulou from my father; for me a touching letter from Karl Klindworth, who tells me that Hans was very happy with the news he gave him of Tribschen. The day spent in excessive worry about Fidi, who is very weak and run down; he has only four teeth so far, and the coming of the others seems to torment him so. — Strassburg has capitulated; on the other hand the talk between Favre and Bismarck has led to nothing, the French are afraid of one another, none dares recognize the situation as it really is, now they want to defend themselves to the death. According to their reports they have already repulsed the Prussians three times! But the English newspapers report the utmost disorder in Paris itself. God knows how it will all end. In the evening R. and Richter play Mozart's E-flat Major Symphony, then a conversation about Bayreuth. — (*Beethoven* sent off.)

*Thursday, September 29* Fidi still unwell, but had a better night. The muddles in France do not cease; nobody there can discuss the truth any longer, nor can he face it. Telegram to Herr Lenbach after I had confided to R. my distress regarding the picture. No news from outside. Walk with R., letter from M. Meysenbug. I write to Karl Klindworth. In the evening continuation of the "Death and Indestructibility" chapter. Before going to sleep R. calls out to me, "I am glad you are here." We had spent a long time talking about our certainty that our love could not die. "These are matters so secure and certain, yet they cannot be defined; one can only express them in sophisms, in word play, as in *Tristan*: Were I to die for my love, how could my love die, etc." — During our walk I had to laugh heartily: when we were talking about warmer climates and the senselessness of moving to *cold Germany*, R. said, "Cosima, what if the art of the future were to be a chimera!"

*Friday, September 30* Telegram from L[enbach], the picture was sent off yesterday. R. receives from his friend Herrig the reply that the publisher Stilke in Berlin does not want *Beethoven* even though, as Stilke says, after the Jewish pamphlet his things would now sell: the Jews would want to find out whether they contained something more against them. Letter from Fr[iedrich] Schmitt, the singing teacher, crude and unpleasant, but R. remains well disposed toward him, since Schmitt once behaved well toward him. R. replies to him kindly but firmly, saying that he has lost confidence in his methods. — R. is intrigued by and interested in the news, conveyed to us by Frl. v. Meysenbug, that Bakunin is organizing the workers in Lyon. There a Red government has been set up which takes no notice of Paris at all. R. feels we shall be hearing curious things from there, quite different from what people might expect, for "France is ripe for experiment." Lovely walk through the woods. Fidi somewhat better, though still plagued by a cough and still running a temperature. In the evening finished reading *"Der Magnetiseur"*; a gripping subject, but the treatment is weak.

*Saturday, October 1* In the mornings R. always enjoys Loulou's piano practicing in the downstairs *salon*, he says the childish sounds give him a real feeling of family life. Yesterday he read me something from his biography, and the shameless conduct of his wife toward him made me shudder. — When we returned yesterday from our walk, we found an Italian with a marmot in the courtyard; the children were playing with the animal. The beggar's countenance moved me deeply, the whole eclipse of a nation was reflected in it like a dream; the eyes, raised with difficulty, gave us a glimpse of lethargic melancholy. This fine race is likable, deeply instructive, touching, but I doubt whether it is still capable of active deeds. — Concern about Fidi, who always falls asleep in great weakness. Visit from Countess Bassenheim; she suggests that I send Loulou and Boni along with her daughter to a new school which is being opened. I find difficulty in agreeing; R. wishes it, to give me more rest, I must consider whether it would be of benefit to the children, either through giving them in communal learning a contact with other children or by perhaps providing them with better teaching than I can give them; I intend to see the schoolmistress. In the evening to *Knie's Circus* with the four children, R., Richter, and Hermine. Great excitement among the children; Loulou following everything with great concentration, Boni quizzical, Loldi full of wonder, Eva reflective, all very earnest; the Harlequin pantomime had the greatest impact. As always, the show made me feel melancholy; gazing at the four animated young faces I asked myself: How long will the peaceful, merry hours continue to strike for you? In the carriage R. embraces me, exclaiming: "That I am on such a pleasure outing with you and the children! It is a dream." Richter took Hermine in the char-à-banc, which turned out drolly, for our dear old Fritz was hopping on three legs and in the end had to be *pulled along* by Richter! — Somewhat concerned about my quarterly allowance, which Rothschild has not sent this time.

*Sunday, October 2* Letter from Herr L[enbach], the picture has now really been sent off, I conceal this from R., so as to give him a surprise. From France still nothing but lies, it disgusts one. R. drafts his *Proclamation.* As an exposition of the requirements of the Bayreuth performance it seems to be simple and persuasive, but he fears the obtuseness of the princes. Family lunch, then with the four children to the fair; Punch and Judy, waxworks, carrousels. In the evening R. reads the *Faust* puppet play. In the morning R. makes music with Richter (Beethoven quartets). In the evening the *Euryanthe* Overture, regarding which R. describes his youthful impressions; how the violin accompaniment on the G string sounded under Weber's own direction, and the unholy fascination it exercised on him as a child. "Childish impressions like that are irreplaceable if one has never had them." He also plays the *Coriolan* and *Egmont* Overtures, whose conciseness he finds particularly admirable, whereas in others—Schumann, for example—there is always a forte and then another forte, bits here and there which could have come from the great master, and yet the whole thing is smudged. R. also reads some passages from Weber's essays (parody of the German, French, and Italian opera). —

*Monday, October 3* Fidi getting better, infinite joy! Concern (slight!) regarding the elder children, because they are so given to telling lies. No money received from Herr Rothschild. To town with R. — Made music in the evening. (Yesterday three swans flew high in the sky above our heads, splendid sight.)

*Tuesday, October 4* I am learning to knit! I find it difficult, but I want to make some leggings for the children. Constantly with Fidi, whose recovery is progressing fast. Walk with R., in the evening [Aeschylus's] *Persae.* Sublime impact, and observation that all the present misery of France could never provide the basis for a tragedy, indeed hardly for a lament!

*Wednesday, October 5* Lenbach's fine picture is here! I had learned of its arrival yesterday evening and I awoke in the morning saying, "Now it is returning home, now you can depart." When Vreneli told me it was unpacked, she added, "But the black frame will give you a shock." It was not I who received the shock, but Richard, who thought he was seeing me dead or my father in monk's clothing—in short, the black frame made a violent impression on his imagination. But gradually the picture had its effect, and he has come to love it beyond words. Our mood was deeply serious all day long; we now have no delights except such sublime and solemn ones. — To Countess Bassenheim's, there meet the schoolmistress; I find it hard to give up teaching the children; only the thought that the children might perhaps prefer to work with other children could bring me to it. Introduced to the sister of Countess Moy from Munich, a great admirer of R.'s, who has seen *Tristan*. She is friendly, but all strangers upset me. — In the evening read [Goethe's] *Campaign in France* with much enjoyment. — R. writes to Lenbach.

*Thursday, October 6*  Always the picture! It is marvelously beautiful; R. yesterday dreamed of laburnum and says it signified the arrival of the picture. I write to Lenbach and to Marie M. — Family lunch; as we are finishing, the payment for the *Nibelungen* poem arrives from J. J. Weber in Leipzig (20 louis d'or). R. laughs a lot about it. Delightful evening walk with R., then, over *Job's juice*, as R. all of a sudden calls tea, resumption of *Campaign in France*. — Stimulated by the arrival of the picture, R. has again taken up the instrumentation of *Siegfried*. — Jules Favre's account of his meeting with Bismarck, unpleasantly sentimental. R. says it is a true reflection of his feelings, the French can no longer behave otherwise: indifferent to the sufferings of others and unable to bear their own in a worthy manner.

*Friday, October 7*  Most lovely weather, almost summer! The children play all day long, and Fidi taken out for the first time in the finery of the frock crocheted by me. R. goes for a walk alone. In the evening read the article about Spontini in the biography. R. calls the portrait "my elegant visitor."

*Saturday, October 8*  R. decides on an outing to Brunnen, the children are got ready; the sky clouds over, R. is about to tell the children that we are staying at home, but the dismay of the "regiment in blue" deters him, and we set off after all. Renewed lesson that we should not undertake anything outside; a foehn storm in Brunnen, we take a walk after lunch but are driven back by whirling dust. Richter stays in Brunnen with Herr Danike, Stephen Heller, Jaëll and wife; Jaëll, a Jew of the good-natured sort, comes up to me and converses with R. The fidgetiness of these people now has a horrible effect on me. Frl. Agathe Angermann sings us something, which causes R. to remark that naturalness is everything; this poor, unbeautiful person, already fifty or sixty years old, still has a charming voice, enunciates well, and, though her manner is very unpretentious and lacking in art, has no trace of lack of taste. Since the steamer does not stop in Brunnen (on account of the foehn) we drive to Gersau. There everything is quiet and peaceful, and we spend a happy hour on the terrace. Journey home in the dark, I give R. my hand, "the only hand"—he exclaims—

"I know what I am holding when I take this hand." His expression, nobly sad, moves me greatly. The children's games tear us from our contemplative mood; R. has to try on all the children's hats, and thus he romps around until we arrive in Lucerne. When we are about to descend the gangway we miss Rus, we call for him, and at last the captain tells us unconcernedly that he fell into the water. Awful moment, R. wants to go after him, we implore the captain not to let the ship sail, he reluctantly and surlily gives in, I have to hold on to the weeping children, I cry out to Richter on no account to let Wagner do anything; whistling, calling for Rus; if the ship moves, our dear dog will be done for. At last he swims ashore, at the place where the boats tie up, led there by his instinct. R. meets him sobbing. I turned to stone with anxiety for R. Thus ended this pleasure outing; always I hear the voice that cries out to me: Stay in the haven to which you have come! However, the children enjoyed themselves greatly. — We were unpleasantly affected by all the French we had to listen to; R. mentioned the *Campaign in France*, remarking, "So free a being, who sees everything, understands everything, shows such deep compassion, and yet remains so cheerful that he is always a help to others—how could he be anything but a German?" — (Herr Fritzsch sends the payment for *Beethoven*.)

*Sunday, October 9* [*C. W. originally wrote* "10," *afterward corrected it to* "9."] Seventeen years ago today I saw Richard for the first time! (Mistook the date—the anniversary is tomorrow.) Cheerful morning with R. and Fidi in spite of the violent storm outside; toward noon, thunder and lightning. Family lunch in almost total darkness, but cheerful and gay. In the afternoon, just as R. completes a page of instrumentation, I see, exactly between the two poplars on the terrace in front of the house, a wonderful rainbow. I call out to R.: a perfect triumphal arch! *Rheingold*, I say; Bayreuth, says R.; and at that very moment Prell, the bookseller, comes in to give us his notes on Bayreuth. A good omen, R. exclaims. Herr Prell tells us that it will be very easy for us to find a house in Bayreuth, and he commends the location of the town. He was also in Strassburg and entertains us with sundry details: how, for example, in a beer hall he came across some Bavarian soldiers who soon began singing songs about "Napoleon, the cobbler's apprentice," etc. — Yesterday R. was admiring a picture of General Moltke, and he said, "I should like to meet him and Bismarck, but without their knowing who I am; I should like to see and observe them as a secretary, a completely obscure underling." He says one can see something of Frederick the Great in the face of General Moltke, the deep solicitude, prudence, concentration. —

*Monday, October 10* To celebrate this cherished day the *A.A.*

*Zeitung* must needs choose to publish a disgraceful article by Herr Schletterer about R.'s writings. Since there is no reason for the timing of it (the writings being old), we suspect that certain gentlemen in Munich are frightened that R. might now be called back, and are seeking to prevent this by decrying him. "The sad thing about it," R. says, "is that, if I now come forward with my plan, people will feel it is permissible to treat it as the eccentricity of a charlatan." — It is also interesting to learn from this article that a second edition of the little pamphlet about Devrient has been published by Stilke in Berlin with R.'s full name attached—and this without R.'s knowledge and after he had paid Fleischmann in Munich 50 florins for bringing it out under a pseudonym! — Rothschild in Frankfurt says that the Paris office is making payments, and he does not know why my allowance has not been paid; nothing more, so I am left high and dry. R. suspects that the Jewish pamphlet may have had something to do with it. (Glorious moonlight yesterday evening, clouds lit up by it as they hastened silently across the sky, making the moon, R. said, look very much like a general reviewing his troops.) Very nice and touching letter from a friend in Berlin; I had almost forgotten her. R. reads Herr Schletterer's article and recognizes in it the definite purpose of influencing the King of Bavaria. "How wretched all these eternal reproaches over my well-being! I feel as if I have no right even to keep a dog." R. is not well; heavy, dull day, Fidi our sunshine. In the evening went through the old Germanic tribes with Loulou. — (Yesterday a letter from the conductor Herbeck, saying that *Lohengrin* has been revived with tremendous success in Vienna.)

*Tuesday, October 11* Concern for our troops in France, whose sufferings are being drawn out so long after all. Work with the children, drive, and little purchases for Loulou's birthday. R. not quite well, but continuing the instrumentation. In the evening a conversation about sense of duty, right and wrong. "What I recognize," says R., "is not the works but the belief—not to do what is right against my inclinations, but to do what is good from all my heart." I reply that I am aware of a conflict, and I have often found it difficult to do the right thing. "But you could not have done otherwise," he answers me. — We read the first canto of *Don Juan* together, and R. remarks that one is gripped not so much by the work as by the personality.

*Wednesday, October 12* Gay start to Loulou's birthday, birds, frock, etc. The usual festive music box, and this time Fidi as guest. Children's party, *tableaux vivants*. Richard unfortunately unwell. In the evening I make music with Richter, while R. looks through the proofs of the biography.

*Thursday, October 13* Letter from M. Muchanoff, to which I reply;

I scarcely think she will come. Walk with R., terrible foehn storm, which is probably responsible for R.'s feeling unwell. In the evening continued with *Don Juan*; we agree that times are wretched when such things can be written by a highly talented man. (Letter to Tausig with a photograph, and to Marie Much.)

*Friday, October 14* Orléans taken by Bavarian troops. "That we should live to see this, the humiliation of the French nation!" R. says. "And on top of that a wife and a son—is it not a dream?" He adds with a laugh, "Since I have known you, I have been unable to live without loving a woman." A ray of sunshine cheers us greatly, music, we think, and R. suddenly says: "I should like to know whether there is anything in any art more like this than the point in the *Eroica* where the theme is played in three different keys in succession. That is will, utterly freed and relieved of the weight of individuality. The material is always a limiting factor; one has only to think of human beings dancing, resting, drinking, sleeping, and so on—all that ceases to exist here." — He orchestrates, makes Fidi-music, as he says. Fidi with us at lunch. Afterward with the three girls to the fair; great delight in the Punch and Judy show, whose director distinguishes himself through his lively (Silesian) dialect and his good ideas, his puppets through their energetic movements. "The elegant visitor" standing beside the carrousel! I let the children ride on it, Rus runs after them. In the evening more *Don Juan*.

*Saturday, October 15* I let the children play in the garden, write to the headmistress of the school that I need her assistance only for English. At lunch R. says that Bavarian and Prussian troops are disputing with one another, the latter wanting to plant their black-and-white flag everywhere, the former insisting either that the black, red, and gold should be used for all, or the white and blue for Bavaria, the black and white for Prussia, etc.—and they are right. We deplore the Prussians' rigid and narrow-minded approach to this matter. Rainy day, R. goes through the second act of *Siegfried* with Richter; Fafner's last words to Siegfried move me beyond words, I told R. it was a feeling such as I had in seeing a dying animal, which is perhaps more touching than the sight of a dying person—or at any rate moving in a different way. R. replies, "With an animal the resignation is more instantaneous, because death comes to it unexpectedly, whereas a human being has been fighting against it all his life." We call Siegfried Kasperl and Fafner the animal which wants to gobble him up, R. says it is something along these lines. In the evening *Don Juan*; I realize that I do not understand much, indeed hardly any of the satire in it, but on the other hand thoroughly enjoy the sublime lyrical episodes, such as that about Haydee, which I read yesterday.

*Sunday, October 16* From Herr Rothschild in Frankfurt I receive the information that he can give me none. R. receives a telegram from Herr Schmitt, the singing teacher, which reads, "Lying was previously foreign to you, it is a disgrace to your name, etc." R. explains this delayed, yet so violent, reply to his letter as a sign of madness. Once again an old acquaintanceship sadly ended. In contrast, Herr Dingelstedt sends the contract for *Rienzi* with all sorts of compliments, and reports the triumphal progress made by *Lohengrin* in the new theater, calls *Tristan* a sunken treasure, and declares his intention of keeping the *Nibelungen* trilogy in mind! — Family lunch with R. in high spirits; he talks of Bohemia and Leipzig, which he much loves. After lunch we go for a walk; discussion of our artistic plan, R. thinks it might be a good idea, when the war ends, to send Bismarck his pamphlet *Art and Politics* along with a few lines. I agree with him, for so powerful a person must be made to see how important the theater is. Returning home, I find Loulou unwell and put her to bed; meanwhile the two little ones *romp around* with R., he cries to me that he is so happy: "Our love had marked us out for death, the children keep us alive." He is pleased and amazed that all the children always look so clean, he says he does not understand how it is done, and it always makes him feel so aristocratic. I am happy to see him well again; a bath, yesterday, helped him. In the evening *Don Juan*; the harem scenes disgust us, in spite of their talent. It is like in a comic opera, R. says, and it seems impossible that a European can depict this Oriental custom in all its naïveté. We are reminded of *The Arabian Nights*, which gives a very different insight into this world. Then, comparing Byron with Goethe and Schiller, R. says: "Everything in the lord's work is too violent, his work gives off a dry glow, for heat he certainly has. Our poets, just as clearly conscious of the hollowness and wickedness of the world, seek their salvation in other ways. And Goethe handles satire much more powerfully in his Mephisto. Byron is no good at drama, he can describe, but he cannot depict." — "You are my all, I your all-sorts," R. says to me.

*Monday, October 17* Loulou in bed. — In the music journal *Signale* there appears a report on *Die Msinger* in Berlin, in which a Herr G. Engel, one of the most insolent of R.'s slanderers, suddenly concedes that R.'s works alone can nowadays fill the theaters, he acknowledges their truly German character, also their noble artistic principles, and hopes that theater people in Germany will stop drawing their sustenance from Paris! — Wretchedly bad weather and nothing of significance; in the evening continued with *Don Juan*, very reluctantly on my part.

*Tuesday, October 18* Very nice letter to me from Franz Lenbach;

I am always gratified at having recognized him long before he was famous, and at having recommended him (though in vain) to the King of Bavaria. — R. has a letter from a Herr Fiege in Berlin, who tells him about the difficulties he encountered in placing some articles about *Die Msinger* in various newspapers. Small birthday gift to Loulou from her aunt. The newspaper publishes an article by Gregorius about the encampment at Metz; this gives us a vivid picture of the wonderful Prussian talent for organization. "What would Europe be without this Prussian strength?" R. exclaims. "Without this despised little corner, from which no one expected anything, but which has been getting itself prepared, so to speak, ever since the fall of the Hohenstaufens? Because its soil is sandy and unproductive, the people there have to rely on the strictest order, and it is this order which has led to the miracle of provisioning 600,000 men. Where would Germany be without Prussia? For that reason it is understandable that they do not wish to give up their Prussianness, for they can really say they do not know what Germany means." — Loulou sends the letter to her grandpapa, she is still unwell. — I am full of grief; our dear old Fritz has now been sacrificed, he had become completely incapacitated and he was ill, now he has been put to death. We do not speak of it in the house, but I feel as if I have committed a sin in recognizing and approving the need for a death. R. goes for a very long walk; the weather is glorious; I remain with Loulou and put the summer things away. In the evening *Don Juan*, which we are now discontinuing. We discuss the contrast with Aristophanes; compared with the Briton, how naïve and full of genius the Greek—not a poet, but a dramatist, and above all a musician. — Capture of Soissons by the Germans. R. dreamed of a friendly conversation with Moltke; we were both of the opinion that to such a person there is really nothing one could say, and people like us would be greatly embarrassed, were we to try to express our feelings to him. "Only the proclamations of a whole nation can do that," says R. I: "And a king." "Yes," R. says, "and that is why nations have instinctively chosen to place themselves under a select being, who must sacrifice a large part of his freedom in order to be able to speak when necessary for the whole community." —

*Wednesday, October 19* I remember my betrothal 15 years ago, under the auspices of the *Tannhäuser* Overture in Berlin. How I should like to make good the suffering I have caused Hans! Perhaps it will be given to the children to do it—I hope so. From France the news that Vesoul has been taken. Sitting beside Lulu, who is still in bed, I write to Franz Lenbach. After lunch to Countess Bassenheim's. In the evening, music; R. sings to me the wonderful scene in *Siegfried* between the Wanderer and Mime. — All day long I have been thinking of old

Fritz; I feel as if in him we have lost a guardian spirit.

*Thursday, October 20*   R. dreamed of his late wife. [*A sentence based on untranslatable word play omitted.*] We are not pleased that Paris has not yet been bombarded, for the longer the delay the more our poor troops must suffer. Garibaldi—the old fool—is organizing in the Vosges district! — Very bad weather; family lunch, then games with the children and Sicilian fairy tales. In the evening R. reads us Hoffmann's "Marino Falieri," the structure of which strikes us as very good, but the style— particularly in the love scenes—is very unattractive. — R. orchestrates the scene between Wotan and Siegfried and says its words are the finest he has ever written, then adds jokingly, "Wotan is tragic because his life is too long, Siegfried because his is too short." (Letter to me from Tausig, to R. from H. Herrig. Herr Stade sends his refutation of Hanslick's conception of beauty in music.)

*Friday, October 21*   The children better, are able to work with me. The Willes invite us for Wednesday; R. says he enjoys strutting about with me—Wille has only been persuaded that Richard is all right since I married him! We drive into town in spite of the bad weather, R. buys Richter a dressing gown. Richter is quite astounded by the introduction to the third act of *Siegfried*, which he is now copying; he discusses the instrumentation, particularly of the Norns' theme. R. laughs: "Yes, it sounds like a child shrieking. As well as something holy and sublime there is a demonically childish and shrieking quality in it, like a virgin who has never loved or borne children. One cannot imagine a witch's voice as anything but high and childish; it lacks the vibrating tones of the heart." — R. is not entirely well, the bad weather is a strain on him. — In the evening we read the folk play of *Fortunatus* with much enjoyment and remark that folk poetry never showed awareness of a moral purpose—that is an invention of our own time. — Richter has learned that *Die Walküre* is being given *subscription* performances in Munich! And there is nothing we can do about it! — When I was already in bed and we had said our good nights, R. came to me again, saying I could not possibly know how much he loves me; to him it was like a dream that I was there always, he had the feeling I had only been lent to him. This makes me send up a prayer; what blame can I lay on life, when— without merit of any kind, without a right, without anything that could explain it—I have found such happiness? And at the same time I see other, excellent people burdened with suffering. It is true I have my share of suffering, but it is on R.'s, on Hans's account, never my own.

*Saturday, October 22*   My father's birthday! From France the news that Bazaine, with whom negotiations are going on, will probably take things in hand and at last restore order in France. — Fidi unwell;

his teeth are coming in slowly and with difficulty, he has four so far, and he is also backward in walking and speaking. His only word is *Ati*. We drink to my father's health at lunch; R. suddenly laughs and says, "I did things differently from Wotan and Sachs, I married Brünnhilde and Eva right away; I let the good people say many excellent things, but I take care not to follow them." — Fine day, which I devote entirely to the children, play charades with them, etc. In the evening read *The Knights* by Aristophanes. (Letter from Marie Muchanoff—she is not coming.)

*Sunday, October 23* Mathilde Schuré writes to me; she is inconsolable about Alsace and Lorraine! — Read Herr Federlein's essay on *Das Rheingold*, which I find very good, and I suggest to R. that he have it printed as articles. — Family lunch; afterward walk with R. along the highway to Hergeschwyl. Once again we come upon an old acquaintance—a barking dog. R. says, "I could imagine walking the earth again as a ghost, just to satisfy my thwarted longing to thrash that dog." — Then he started to talk of the dramatic art of ancient Greece, of the cothurnus, which represents more or less the same as the doubling of the various wind instruments. "It is necessary when the room is too large, but it does not heighten the impression made by the single instrument playing the melody. The mask, the cothurnus, the megaphone—these brought forth a distinct art of their own, which could never have the variety of the Shakespearean drama. Instead, it is noble and monumental." — In the evening *The Peace* by Aristophanes. I suspect that R. has to skip many things in order to be able to read these plays to me; all the same I get immense enjoyment from observing this incomparable fusing together of people and poet, from the bubbling inventive talent and the reckless mixture of earnestness and humor. —

*Monday, October 24* Letter from Prof. Nietzsche, who, now recovered, has returned to Basel; he voices his fears that in the coming days militarism, and above all pietism, will make their pressure felt everywhere. R. very incensed by this thought. "I will tolerate anything," he exclaims, "police, soldiers, muzzling of the press, restrictions of Parliament, but on no account obscurantism. The only thing human beings can be proud of is the freedom of the spirit, it is the only thing which raises them above animals; to restrict or take away this freedom is worse even than castrating them." — I write to Frau Schuré, who (contrary to her usual custom) wrote to me in French. We discuss the woeful attitude of these Alsatians, who now want to use force to remain French, which they never were! — It is said that Mme Viardot has lost her whole fortune through the war and must take up singing again. We discuss this lady's remarkable talent coupled with what is —for us—her weird character; R. attributes it to her Jewishness:

"These people do not possess the soul of their gifts." — The returning foehn affects R. very badly. A bath relieves him. In the evening we read a pamphlet by Prof. Adolph Wagner from Freiburg, many good things about Alsace and Lorraine.

*Tuesday, October 25*   R. dreams again about his wife—that she was unwilling to recognize our marriage; again that permanent feature in R.'s dreams, that he is worried about her money, whether he has sent her any—a prolongation of his constant concern, in real life, to keep her well supplied. The day is spent in packing, our excursion to Zurich is fixed for tomorrow. — In the evening R. reads us the passages in his biography concerning Sulzer and Hagenbuch, whom Richter will also meet the day after tomorrow. (I write to Ottilie Brockhaus.)

*Wednesday, October 26*   Departure, grand leave-taking by the children. Yesterday *tableaux vivants* in Richter's room; [*a few words omitted as untranslatable*] all the children with him, and finally I and R., much noise; Eva presents "Mother and Child," forgets the mother, however, and just sets down Willy Stocker and then disappears into the wings (Richter's bed the curtain). Cheerful journey with R., balmy foehn atmosphere, the weather is mild. Met in Zurich by Arnold Wille, whose friendly conversation tires us a little. He talks about the Polish festival in Rapperswyl, Polish antiquities (library consisting of French novels, etc.), the Polish eagle cast in Berlin which was always falling down, etc. His mother, Frau Wille, delights us once again with her warm heart and her great and deep intelligence. At table a Professor Hellwig, who knows my father, and a Prof. *Bendof* (or Bender?). In the evening Richard reads parts of his biography (to Frau Wille and her husband alone); the excellent lady much affected, her clever husband interested. At table R. proposes a toast to Moltke, whose birthday it is today (the children are also drinking his health at Tribschen). Terrible foehn storm; R. and I can scarcely close our eyes.

*Thursday, October 27*   Breakfast with the family, with much feeling I take my leave of the excellent lady, who again had some wonderful things to say about R.'s biography. I then go alone to visit Frau Wesendonck. Despite my attempts to persuade him, R. would not accompany me—her poems ("A Call to the German People," etc.) had greatly displeased him; he also maintains that in the end she had behaved badly toward him. So now for the first time in eleven years I again entered the rooms in which I once played the role of a sort of intermediary and confidante. I found that the hospitable lady had now become a brunette, whereas in Munich four years ago she had been blonde; this disconcerted me; I was pleased by her friendly welcome, looked at her pictures, and on the way home reflected on the curious dreamlike quality of life. Eleven years ago, when I tried to make her feel more charitably disposed toward R., if anyone had then told me that I myself should be closely interwoven with his fate, I might indeed have believed it, but I should have been terribly alarmed. Her daughter Myrrha (!) is a good and devoted girl with fair hair. — From the Wesendonck villa to the Hotel Baur, where Councilor Sulzer, Professor Hagenbuch, and Colonel Müller (also Richter) came to see us. Dr. Sulzer in particular pleased and touched us; his suffering features, his refined, precise, but never harsh speech, his blindness, his whole reserved yet warmhearted nature, move me inexpressibly. He informs me that his family life (he has lost his wife and has 5 children) has been wiped out entirely by his participation in state affairs, and from this participation he can expect no satisfaction of any kind. I beg him to let his children visit mine. Our meeting is a gay one; for the first time the two state councilors met again at a friendly table, for in police affairs they are divided. When Hagenbuch mentions that he had driven past Tribschen, R. says he could really have turned the one extra little corner, and he tells a story about his mother; when he had once told her that Saint Boniface on his missionary travels had been in Guhr (?), a little village near Leipzig, she had answered, "Well, surely he could have covered the little extra distance to Leipzig." — Many memories crop up, old times come back to life among these friends, and everyone departs cheerful and stimulated. — We also visit Frau Heim, a former friend of R.'s, and find her with her hair powdered. This hair coloring makes both her and the brunette Frau Wesendonck seem literally like ghosts to me. But she was very delighted with our visit. Journey home with Richter, arriving there at about 10 o'clock to be pounced on by a beaming Loulou, the very embodiment of childlike devotion. The others are in bed. Letter from Math. Maier, also recalling vanished days. I am very worn out; R., too.

*Friday, October 28* Reunion with the children, followed immediately by lessons. R. tired, spends the morning reading the newspapers. After lunch R. overwhelms me with his heavenly love; he declares I am becoming more beautiful every day (oh, dear!) and he is dying of happiness. — Little is heavenly, he says, only Cosima is heavenly; looking at myself, I feel like the most inconspicuous of buildings which, in the rays of a sunset, can be made to look like the most splendid of sights. After he left me, he played a wonderful theme, which I begged him to write down. Then Loulou returned from her piano lesson and told us that Bazaine had surrendered! So another 150,000 Frenchmen to be cared for—it sounds like a fairy tale. And only this morning we were reading in the newspaper that Kératry had declared that Bazaine was about to surround the Prussians! — In the evening R. says to me, "It is nice that we have Bazaine, but it is very much nicer that I have you."

*Saturday, October 29*   Boni in bed with a chill; I hope it will not lead to anything. Loulou works in my room. R. orchestrates. At lunch I define my feelings about the present war with the words, "For France the war is not a misfortune, but a disgrace." R. agrees with this. Our student takes his leave, he has overcome all obstacles and is now to devote himself to natural science; he is going to Basel. In the evening we get on to the subject of *Tannhäuser*, and as a result R. plays and sings me the second act, which affects me unutterably. Biterolf (Moltke!), Wolfram, the Landgraf, they all move me to tears, but Elisabeth's "for him, too" (in this "too" lies Christianity, says R.) moves me to the depths of my soul. R. is almost alarmed by my reaction and disapproves of my emotion, he makes a joke of it and says: "You are Elisabeth, Elsa, Isolde, Brünnhilde, Eva in one, and I have married you. So I know nothing of love's tragedy, I care nothing for the world's soul, all I want is to keep you and to live a very long time." — I feel that such turmoil of the heart will be the death of me. — At midday R. defended the libretto of *Euryanthe* against Richter: he says it is not really as bad as it is made out to be.

*Sunday, October 30*   Fidi takes four steps! — Letter to Prof. Nietzsche, recommending our student to him. Reduced family lunch, with Boni ill, Loulou in disgrace for negligence (she has lost the Sicilian fairy tales). A drive with the two little ones. In the evening read Calderón's *La dama duende*, spoke about all sorts of things concerning it, such as its subtle argumentation, this subtle playing with concepts being the only way, without the help of music, to convey love, for example. Calderón's characters are not individuals, but masks, which the dramatist uses to express the most profound truths, but such art requires a theater in its prime, which Calderón could seize on in order to provide an insight into the world. — R. says he realizes that he will never write his projected plays (Luther's Wedding, Bernhard von Weimar, in whom he recognizes Dietrich von Bern), since the form alone (verse or prose) is a problem he cannot surmount; nothing without music. He quotes with appreciation something Dr. Herrig wrote to him—that music is the law of gravity according to which everything moves or stands, and the poet is one who attempts to stand outside this law. R. regrets that this promising young poet resorts to conveying a message as a substitute for the missing music. Calderón, he says, also conveys a message, but it is not a specific, politically historic one, it is the Christian, Catholic one, bearing the marks of a definite view of the world, and, as he had pointed out, Calderón had a flourishing theatrical period behind him to give it life. Also, such things succeed once and never again.

*Monday, October 31* "To kiss and kiss you as I may, and with your kisses fade away"—thus R. concluded yesterday. — Today a letter from my mother, who is living at Berg. Letters from the Schurés, still fanatically French! — Drove to Countess B.'s; her son tells in woeful detail about the sufferings of our troops at Metz. Gambetta's portrait in the *Illustrirte Z.* once more shows us the febrile, ineffectual character of a dying race. In the evening *Fuente ovejuna* by Lope de Vega; infinite delight in it. — R. rightly says that we onlookers can only be silent in the face of the grand and terrible events now taking place; no boasting of victories, no complaints about the suffering, simply a deep and silent recognition that God disposes.

*Tuesday, November 1* How horrible that Gambetta should so decry Bazaine and his armies after they had fought and suffered so terribly and yielded only to stern necessity! But our troops—how brilliantly they acquitted themselves in the most trying of circumstances! — R., indignant at the Alsatians, says: "They are incapable of acknowledging the truth, they have been ruined by French education; and everything depends on facing the truth, even if it is unpleasant. What about myself in relation to Schopenhauer's philosophy—when I was completely Greek, an optimist? But I made the difficult admission, and from this act of resignation emerged ten times stronger." — R. has given me a gold pen, with which I am now writing. In the afternoon a visit from young Count B. with his mother; he tells us of the panic, so far kept secret, which seized a Bavarian corps at Bitsch and sent them fleeing as far as Germersheim! He also tells us of the Jewish religious service outside Metz (prayer shawls and spiked helmets) and the bad organization of the nursing services. Also, like so many others, he is pessimistic about German unity. — In the evening Goethe's "*Triumph der Empfindsamkeit.*" The Prince reminds us of our royal master. The scene with Proserpina, the swallowing of the pomegranate seed, and the consequent immediate descent into Hell—this image, specifically quoted by Schopenhauer, leads me to a contemplation of the world, of life and death, then to the fate of the individual, and I go to bed in tears.

*Wednesday, November 2* All Souls' Day. Paris is to be bombarded— who has no ears to hear must feel it, to put it vulgarly. — I compose a prayer for the dead for the children. Yesterday R. said, with regard to the hymns our soldiers sing after their battles: "If someone were to ask me whether there is a God, I should reply: 'Can you not hear him? At this moment in which thousands of human beings are singing to him, God is alive, he is there.' To imagine him as someone watching and calling things good or bad is foolish; he exists in and for himself, but at certain moments in the life of nations or individuals, he is there, he awakes." — Letter from my mother, who, banished from the Jura, is seeking a refuge. Discussion with R. as to whether, for her sake, I should offer it to her here, in view of the fact that our seclusion, our German outlook, and our whole way of life would not be congenial to her. R. has received a letter from Herr van der Straeten with an article on the Weimar performances; the Catholic government in Brussels did not wish to see this published in the *Moniteur*, though the author had been sent to Brussels by the former, Liberal regime. Letter from the theater director in Mannheim, reporting that *Der Fl. Holländer* enjoyed a success there greater than any other opera, and with it many friendly remarks. "What can I do," says R., "if this compliment arrives 30 years too late?" The red curtain is placed around my picture. Eva is given the rod, for the first and probably the last time in her life, because of her ineradicable dirtiness.

*Thursday, November 3* The French declare that, even if Paris falls, they will not conclude a peace; it shows, as R. says, that they are no longer a nation, that no section has any feelings for another, and that once again a whole country has been undermined by the spirit of the Jesuits. Thoughts of having my children converted to Protestantism, since I want to bring them up as good Christians and find it impossible to accept the Jesuit teachings. Family lunch; Loulou's first English lesson. Visit from a *consul*, who turns out, after R. spent some time talking politics with him, to be a traveler in wine. Such a thing, says R., could only happen to him. Write to my mother and to Schuré. — In the evening Richter plays us passages from *Siegfried*.

*Friday, November 4* Rumors of an armistice, which bring us no joy; R. favors the bombardment. Very good articles by Ludwig Bamberger (material for a psychology of nations). Lessons with the children; I choose books for Christmas and am much moved by a description of the Indian religion. In the evening *El tejedor de Segovia*.

*Saturday, November 5* Gen. Moltke is said to be ill, the armistice is as good as certain, it all upsets us. R. works on his score without much heart: "All that has happened to me in the past two years is just too dismal—when I think of the people in Munich, putting *Die Walküre* in the program when they are otherwise in a fix! I suppose that is not too bad, but the King, the King—who can explain or understand such a character? Only a dramatist would be able to reproduce him, inexplicable as he is—that is why I say drama is the only really living art." With R. I take Loulou for her English lesson and hear her praises sung, and we recognize in her her father's brilliant intellectual gifts. In the evening music: Richter plays us the B-flat Major Symphony; music always makes me contemplative, brings me to a recognition of life and of myself; it is like a penance, it shows me all the guilt of existence, but in a conciliatory light. In bed I thought of Hans and all the suffering I have caused him; weeping, praying, I fall asleep. — At lunch R. expressed the wish to form a string quartet (Richter as violist, the other three to come from Zurich); I have my doubts on the financial side, but keep silent about them.

*Sunday, November 6*  Letter from Marie M., my father is not going to Weimar, out of sympathy for the French—so the gap between us is now beyond repair. She speaks of Napoleon's rehabilitation as probable! — I write to Frau Schuré. Read fairy tales to the children. R. brings home a letter from my mother, who encloses a letter addressed to the Crown Prince of Prussia, aimed at retaining Alsace for France!!! — R. says that the French government in balloons would be a subject for an Aristophanic comedy; a government like that, up in the air in both senses, would provide a writer of comedy with some splendid ideas. — In the evening *Othello*, every page an experience in itself.

*Monday, November 7*  Continual gray skies, which depress R., but he forces himself to work. (Yesterday evening arrival of the Brunswick sausage!) After lunch a drive with the children, Loldi in a brown silk coat with a collar—"the Marquis from *Le Postillon de Longjumeau*." In the evening the last three acts of *Othello*; unutterably moved; I tell R. that I shall never really get to know these plays, because I am always much too deeply affected by them to take in the precise details. R. reiterates his theory that "Shakespeare does not really belong to literature at all and cannot be compared with a poet and artist such as Calderón, for example. Through Shakespeare one can to some extent form a picture of a figure like Homer: what Shakespeare is to men of letters, Homer must more or less have been to the priests." I add in my thoughts: And what Richard is to our present-day men of letters and poets, who are quite unable to classify him. Lost my wedding ring on the way to Hergeschwyl!

*Tuesday, November 8*  Armistice or not, that is now the question. R. says the republic has no alternative but to declare: Not a stone, not an inch farther; well and good, reply the people, if you can do it; but the moment they start making terms with the enemy, the reaction would be quite different; that is why the men in power are behaving like fanatics. — Yesterday a man from Flanders sent us a raging, Germanic speech which we much enjoyed. R. says Germany has escaped by a hair's breadth from becoming, under French influence, a country like Belgium, all cultural activities French and only the humble people German in outlook. Just as in Spain the national theater disappeared immediately when the French influence made itself felt. — Fidi naughty to his papa! Around noon R. comes and calls to me that he wishes to read me something: it left him no peace, he had to sketch out a farce in the style of Aristophanes, *Die Kapitulation*; Richter can write the music for it, and then it can be played in the little theaters. His first thought was that I would be offended or worried because he had put aside his orchestration to do it, but I am content with anything that cheers and stimulates him. Anyway, he completed a page of the score in the evening. — We decide at lunch to drink to the venture, and R. says to Jakob, "The Baroness would like the Marcobrunner." I laugh at R. for using my old title. "Well, I still cannot really believe that you are mine, I still feel you have only been lent to me, you are the visitor from the fairy world who will soon vanish." — I intend to drive out to look for the lost ring, but sleep away the time in the afternoon; I send for the children, all five, and Willy Stocker as well; the four little ones leap about and crawl on the ground (the frog pond, says R.) and I read fairy tales to the two big ones; in the end I am left with Lusch alone, to whom I read Roman history. "We are truly in Paradise," R. tells me. The roses are still blooming in our garden; yesterday when I awoke I found three lovely roses with buds lying in my lap; R. had placed them there while I was sleeping. — In the evening the second part of *El tejedor de Segovia*.

*Wednesday, November 9* News of the death of a friend in Pest, Mosonyi. — R. begins to work out his farce, but his mind is not completely on it, he is unwell. Searched for my ring on the highway, but did not find it. Visited Countess B. In the evening began on Ranke's history of France. — The armistice has been rejected by the French.

*Thursday, November 10* Schiller's birthday. I find all these November days hard to live through, for my leaving Hans is constantly in my thoughts; one's own suffering grows less with time, it can indeed vanish entirely in devout renunciation, but the suffering inflicted on another weighs ever more heavily; I feel as if I might one day die beneath the burden. — *Der h. Krieg*, an illustrated periodical, gives us much pleasure with its fine portraits of people involved in the present war. "Moltke looks like an unearthed ancient stone," R. says; the French (Gramont, Benedetti, etc.) all repulsive. — Yesterday R. received a letter from Hans Herrig, who says the journalists have again been chasing after R. Then he says that at a performance of *Lohengrin* one old lady said to her neighbor, "Well, *Lohengrin*—W. wrote that a long time ago—he was not so *degenerate* then." Walk with the children, for the first time in ages saw the mountains again. In Paris they are putting on operas again, so as not to deprive the public of Rossini's and Meyerbeer's masterpieces!!

*Friday, November 11* It is reported in the newspaper that posters have been put up on the walls of Paris declaring that a republic has been proclaimed in Munich, R. Wagner's house stormed, and he himself beaten to death. With what rubbish people try to revive their spirits! R. is writing—though without much pleasure—*Die Kapitulation*. Bad weather, we do not go out. We discuss many things. For me the passionate side of love has disappeared, for R. it is still alive; when with constant dismay I am made aware of it, R. tells me that it is precisely this which gives him the great and calming assurance that our union is blessed by Nature; from that time onward a new life began for him, and he looked back on his previous life as into a ghostly pit. —

*Saturday, November 12* Yesterday in my bath I thought how I might encourage Lulu to devote her whole life to her father—may Heaven grant me the boon of achieving this! With every sacrifice one makes one throws from one's shoulders a part of the burden of life and walks more freely; self-will and self-love are the heavy ballast which restricts the soul's flight! — Very bad news: the Bavarians have been repulsed by the French at Orléans. Very depressed mood on this account, R. says, "One lurches from contempt for the world to the deepest sympathy with it." Letters from my mother and Prof. Nietzsche. I in a permanent state of inward contemplation; I think I am ripe for a convent. Went for a walk with the children. Made purchases for Christmas.

*Sunday, November 13* Write to Marie M. Nothing of significance; the German question seems to be held up by Bavaria. My mother writes me a long letter which shows that a mind drilled in French can never shake itself free of its fantasies! Richter goes to see *Fra Diavolo*, which starts R. talking about Auber and Rossini, allowing the former distinct precedence in regard to invention, wit, freedom from convention, but the latter in regard to feeling (example: the last act of *Otello*) and melodic flow. — In the afternoon, during their siesta time, Jakob comes in to announce that a woman brought back my wedding ring, which she had found on the parade ground—where I had not even been. What a remarkable stroke of fortune! Must I not gratefully recognize that the gods are kind and favorably disposed toward me? Amid ancient errors committed by me, which wrapped a veil around me, they have led me gently but firmly to the point at which I recognize where a woman's duty and happiness lie. Even in little individual happenings I must recognize the kindly hand! I tell R. that when I was searching for the ring on the road to Hergeschwyl I had mechanically repeated the little prayer of my searching childhood to Saint Antony of Padua. "Oh, you Age of Reason!" exclaims R. But to be happy is divine! R. embraces me in love and cries out to me, "You eternal 'Prize Song' of my life!" He repeats that he cannot even imagine what his life would be without me, he has no idea what would have become of him—"certainly an eccentric of the most reprehensible kind." —

We continue in the evening with Ranke; during this R. remarks that we have great historical researchers, but no writers of history to compare with the French and the English as far as the art of description is concerned.

*Monday, November 14* R. still somewhat indisposed, when I go to him in his workroom to ask how he is, he says only that during the night he had been thinking of how we discovered and united with each other: "It is a complete miracle, and I do not know how it was possible in this terrible world." With tears of joy I reply to him that it is for this reason that I am becoming ever more deeply and inwardly religious, I find it impossible not to express my gratitude, impossible, too, not to feel my unworthiness, impossible to forget the sufferings I have caused, impossible not to pour out my overflowing heart in prayer. In the afternoon an old acquaintance, Alfred Meissner, visits me. I have got over the fact that he once reproduced a conversation with me in Munich in a newspaper article, and I was pleased to see him again; only, when R. entered, the unfortunate man began to talk about the production of *Das Rheingold* in Munich, of the excellent *libretto*, of R.'s injustice in not going to see these things for himself, of the splendid settings! I was on tenterhooks. R. went away smiling, and I now begged the worthy gentleman on no account to speak about these things. — Read Ranke in the evening. — Prof. Nietzsche sends back *Beethoven*, remarking that probably few people will be able to follow R.

*Tuesday, November 15* At last sunshine again, and with it a conflict between Russia and Turkey! The day is a solemn one for me: two years ago today I took leave of Hans forever. R. says my religion dates from this Hegira, I pray with all my heart. In the night Fidi called; half asleep, I thought I was hearing Hans's complaining voice! — (Lusch photographed.)

*Wednesday, November 16* R. finishes his play, I think it is excellent. Richter is now to write the music for it. Alfred M. and his 17-year-old wife to lunch, both of them friendly and good-natured, but when he begins to talk about the Munich *Rheingold*, R. becomes serious and explains what it means to him. — Bavaria is making difficulties for the North German Confederation. R. regrets that Bismarck has so little imagination and has nothing to offer his allies but unconditional entry into the Prussian creation. In the evening a letter from my mother—she is not coming, we are too German for her. — Continued reading Ranke; in Calvin and Luther I can really feel the distinction between the Germans and the French, with the latter everything becomes so formalized and *boringly vehement*, as R. says. (According to Dr. Meissner Loldi will one day be a beauty of the first rank!!)

*Thursday, November 17*   Dr. Wille returns the biography. R. recalls that first morning two years ago: "How touching that was!" he says. "That is what so impresses people like Wille about my life: you are the dot on the *i*, my life's glory, what they envy me for." I thought yesterday of how I arrived, trembling, with the two children, hardly capable of uttering a word; I had shut the door of the world behind me forever, I had cut myself off from him forever. We learn through a musical periodical that our friend H. v. Bronsart, director of the theater in Hanover, had enlisted voluntarily as a soldier and has now been awarded the Iron Cross. That touches us deeply, it is the true Prussian spirit—God grant that it is not usurped by bigotry and military arrogance! Wrote letters, in the evening Ranke. R. received a letter from a French prisoner of war in Erfurt (Mercier), who wants to perfect himself in harmony. R. laughs as he breaks the commandant's seal, a rough, very cheap wafer, selected with Prussian thrift: "Oh, yes, music has affected everybody, it is a destroying, uplifting force—like Christianity when it first emerged." —

*Friday, November 18*   Arrival of the gold frame for the "elegant visitor"; it is handsome and gives R. much pleasure. In the evening a visit from the Meissner couple; unfortunately a conversation starts about poetry apropos of Heine. Alfred M. declares that some of H.'s poems are "as eternal as the stars," and speaks of hearing "*Ich grolle nicht*" with great delight at a concert in Zurich, whereupon R. says: "But just imagine what that means, hearing such bitter inner feelings recited with a bouquet in the hand in front of a concert audience, while people smile at it in enjoyment. Such acts of aesthetic demoralization make our audiences insensitive, they no longer pay attention to what is being said." The conversation broadens out to cover poetry in general, which R. says he would prefer not to see in print. The conversation produces a discordant note, and once again R. realizes that he can no longer manage with people around him.

*Saturday, November 19*   Work with the children as usual, take a walk with R., read with him in the evening. A letter from our friend Schuré, who encloses a furious French essay written by himself! R. is indignant about it and says I should ask him whether Poland, Ireland, and other nations had ever been as disloyal as Alsace is to Germany. — I am not very well, headaches cloud both my waking and my sleeping hours, bringing me feelings of the melancholy of life.

*Sunday, November 20*   A friend of Richter's writes that after the battle at Sedan the military band played the prayer from *Lohengrin* as the King of Prussia appeared! — Also that the King of Bavaria is having an affair with a Frl. Scheffsky (a singer). R. does not really believe it. A Danish scene-painter writes to R. and pays tribute to him as a composer, poet, and "*all-round* man of the theater." I write to my mother and to Schuré. — Fidi always at my side, like a polar bear in his fluffy coat. Melancholy thoughts about life; *to do one's work,* that is what matters. I read in the newspaper that Hans is conducting concerts in Florence. — žn the evening R. looks through the *Kladderadatsch* calendar, which leads to a discussion of Berlin humor. — (Letter from M. Meysenbug.)

*Monday, November 21* Garibaldi has captured 800 Prussians! Yet the mood in Paris is changing noticeably, the same people ([Edmond] About, etc.) who were once the most insolent are now advising greater compliance. Tresckow and the Duke of Schwerin have thrown back the Loire army, a battle is expected, and this, it is to be hoped, will be definitive. — For the first time in many months I again practice the piano, since R. desires to hear some sonatas with violin (Beethoven). Richter is composing *Die Kapitulation.* Concern about Grane, whom our ill-natured groom looks after badly and who has already taken fright a few times.

*Tuesday, November 22* Nothing except a glorious morning, which I spend with the children in the garden. R. orchestrates. I amuse the children greatly by telling them that a merchant ship called Hans Bülow has been captured by the French. — R. was despondent yesterday evening, he maintained that I was "not the same as before," but today he is cheerful again and tells me I should not be upset by the fact that he is so utterly dependent on me. In all my sad thoughts about life I am always uplifted by the knowledge that it was permitted to me to become necessary to him, that he really needs me in order that he may carry on effectively. In the afternoon piano practice, in the evening R. reads Hoffmann's story "*Die Brautschau.*"

*Wednesday, November 23* Again spent the morning in the garden; from the heights of the hermitage our promontory always presents a smiling, companionable aspect; to return home to this house, which contains everything that I love, is a divine feeling. Our quiet yet so busy life fills me with pleasure. — This morning at breakfast R. said to me, "You will always be a maiden, that is your true age—every person has an age when he is wholly what he is meant to be." I laugh and say that in that case I am an old maid. — R. is making sketches for the second act of *Götterdämmerung,* but he does not wish any notice to be taken of it. "Otherwise I lose the urge." I notice it from his agitated mood. But toward me he is always unutterably kind. — Richter, with his violin, pretends to the children that he is a water sprite; much jubilation. In the evening Hoffmann's story is read to the finish without particular enjoyment. — In the afternoon a Beethoven sonata (Opus 96) with Richter; R. says that when playing the piano I look too serious, my eyes turn brown, and I become so immersed in it that he feels afraid of me! I almost regret having played, concerned that it might not be what he really wants, though he himself requested it.

*Thursday, November 24*   Saint Catherine's Day, the feast of virgins; splendid weather, blooming roses and sunshine. R. exclaims in the morning that he has had a lively vision of Fidi as a youth. "Even if he does not excel in any one direction he is bound, with his big head and his sturdy character, to be quite a tremendous fellow. Then he will bring off all the things I was unable to do." — Thinking of my childhood yesterday (how Richter with his violin upstairs reminded me of Jozy, the gypsy my father adopted, who was always fiddling to us children), I voiced the opinion that happiness in childhood bears the same relation to happiness in life as Paradise to redemption. — R. composing. In the evening a letter from Prof. N., who announces his arrival on Saturday and is terribly pessimistic with regard to Germany. A letter in the newspaper from Carlyle pleases us greatly, he describes the gesticulating French precisely as they are. Read Goethe in the evening: "Shakespeare and No End" and the essay on [Calderón's] *La hija del aire.* The distinction he draws between Sh[akespeare] and Calderón pleases me greatly—the one the fresh grapes, the other the finished wine.

*Friday, November 25*   Night of mice, they frighten me from my bed. — R. always says he is being too well treated, is too happy with me and the children—oh, great Heavens! — Wrote to Malwida M[eysenbug]. Once again discussed with R. the question of the children's religion, I am above all for keeping their gaiety unclouded. — At lunch R. remembers how once, when he complained (of his physical condition), my father took up the *Nibelungen,* looked at him, and said, "He complains of abdominal troubles and writes things like this." R. goes on to say that without a doubt my father is the greatest man of originality and genius he has ever met, and after him Hans, because he has fire. "Thus does one think and work, contained within a very close circle of friends, and now this circle has been more or less split up. '*For when women come on the scene, they turn things upside down—things which had been going well up till then.*' That was Herwegh's comment on my *Nibelungen* poem!" — After lunch I play the piano with Richter. In the evening the music produces from R. the following remark: "Repetition! In that one sees the utter difference between music and poetry. A motive can be repeated because it is a personality and not just a speech. In poetry, on the other hand, repetition is ridiculous, unless it is a refrain and is intended to have a musical effect." — Read Ranke. I observed how curious it was that no Frenchman had ever chosen Coligny as a romantic hero. "That's because they are all

Jews," R. replies. "They know nothing except the Old Testament, for them it would be like writing Sanskrit."

*Saturday, November 26* R. reports in the morning that Paris is expected to capitulate next week. — When I pass on some news from the paper, he says: "You are so dear to me; however proud and refined you are, you are so familiar to me; you are my only intimate, everything else is alien. My life would no longer be possible without you. If you had said tut-tut and pulled back, I shouldn't have let go. I should have *toadied* to you like Turgenev with Mme Viardot—that would have been a fine sight!" — Talking of the third act of *Siegfried*, he says, "Siegfried's manner of wooing is really good, and the way he calls on his mother— well, that is religion: when the individual forgets himself and applies his happiness to the whole universe." — Moving on to Shakespeare, he says, "The fact that we know for sure that Sh. lived gives us proof of Homer's existence." In the afternoon arrival of Prof. Nietzsche. Music (Richter and I), in the evening R. reads aloud his *Nicht kapituliert*.

*Sunday, November 27* "Nothing is so dear to me as the room in which I bide, for near me dwells my fair neighbor side by side," sings R. to me in the morning; then he comes in and says, "There is a melody lying in bed, a really big one, you are my melody." Breakfast with Richter and the Prof.; I greatly concerned: the Loire army is described as very substantial (120,000) and is reported to be well led. Prof. Nietzsche says that he and his German colleagues in Basel are extremely worried! — We take a walk with the children. Then music; in the afternoon a visit from Count B. In the evening, first act of *Siegfried*. Richter has received some articles exposing Perfall, which make him glad.

*Monday, November 28* The largest battle in this war is now imminent. This permits no cheerful thoughts: may the Heavens be with our men! R. is not well, for which the cold, wet weather is to blame. I wade to Countess Bassenheim's house. In the evening read in Ranke about the Massacre of Saint Bartholomew. We come to realize that since Catherine de' Medici there have essentially only been factions in France, each fighting against the others. A letter from Hedwig Schröder in Berlin.

*Tuesday, November 29* Letter from my mother, who wants me to visit her, but I shudder at the thought of any separation from Tribschen. R., to whom I confide the news, says that he has no intention of undertaking anything without me. Toothache, piano practice, news of two victories, in Amiens and over Garibaldi. In the evening *Nicht kapituliert* sent off to the singer Betz with a letter of recommendation from R. (Frau Pohl has died.)

*Wednesday, November 30* R. tells his dream to his "dear miracle":

"I arrived with Minna in Constantinople and was so overwhelmed by the beauty of the place that I cried out that nobody could have any idea of such a thing without having seen it. Then I walked through strange alleyways, in which I imagined I recognized the places in which the Christians had concealed themselves in times of persecution. I passed all sorts of strange things—menageries, etc.—and suddenly noticed that I had lost Minna. I saw Rus approaching, and together we searched through a maze of streets, until I noticed that he had an injured leg. 'Dear God!' I exclaim, and tuck the huge, heavy beast under my arm. I arrive panting at an inn; there I inquire about a carriage and a boarding house. The landlady mentions one, *Sporchelt und Hausschild*, but as she is naming it she suddenly starts, having noticed a man listening as she gives me the address. 'Aha,' I think, 'they are all rogues here,' and I go away. The sight of the city again sends me into raptures, and during these raptures I must have fallen even deeper asleep, for, finding myself in a carriage driven by a Turkish coachman, I say, 'They put you in this carriage when you were asleep.' But Rus was missing. At last I find him beneath the seat of the carriage. But now I find my hat is missing, and I see it rolling down the hill behind me—somewhat like a dog following me; my coachman will not stop, and in my excitement I wake up." We laugh over the vividness with which in his dream he saw the Bosporus, the Golden Horn (which was, however, mountainous), etc.—all of which he has never set eyes on in real life! — Fidi the *Olympian*, that is what R. calls him, saying he will turn into something tremendous and cause us a lot of bother! — Nothing but dismal happenings to match the dismal weather. The news that Grane is ill, then Jews and travelers in wine; we are not well. (A nonpolitical letter from Schuré, on whom my statement that nothing throws a clearer light on Germany's pitiful fate than the defection of Alsace, compared with the loyalty which binds Poles, Hungarians, Irishmen to their race, seems to have made some impression.) In the evening, Ranke. (Victorious engagement against the bulk of the Loire army.)

*Thursday, December 1* Indisposition and worry. — The church is openly inciting war in France, which pleases R., since it makes the issue increasingly clear. — Family lunch. R. unwell, the weather overcast. I correct Schuré's translation of *Die Walküre*. In the evening conversation with R. — Late in the evening R. plays the Prelude to Act III of *Die Meistersinger*; it moves me to tears in the adjoining room. (Today cut off the first lock of Fidi's hair, since it was falling in his eyes. R. regrets it—"as if he had lost his first innocence.")

*Friday, December 2* Clear sky, R. at once better, he absolutely needs the blue of Heaven. Unfortunately it does not last long; when he comes home late in the evening, he is feeling pains in his back; he is vexed about it, he gets no pleasure from his work, the sight of the world fills him with melancholy, and also his eyes seem to be getting weaker. — This fills me with unutterable concern; once again I go to bed with Goethe's verse in my mind: "Who never ate with tears his bread, who never through night's heavy hours . . ." I will try to retain the favor of the heavenly powers by diligently performing my task through joy and sorrow. I am sometimes alarmed to see how we hang in the air, how completely without possessions and indeed without prospects we are, yet I also keep my eyes fixed on the worst misery, I tell myself that the worst was after all causing someone else suffering, everything else can be borne; and now let it be as God wills; He will continue to help, as good King Wilhelm says in his telegram!

*Saturday, December 3* R. still unwell and with no inclination to work; that is for me the hardest test, may Heaven help me to bear it! The children well, walk with them after work, then music with Richter. — (My cushion finished, started on leggings again!) In the evening continued reading David Strauss's lectures, begun yesterday. Much dissatisfaction with the book, the style of which is as slovenly as a student's and again very mannered. (Snow.)

*Sunday, December 4* Letter from M. Meysenbug, and fear that I am pregnant. R. has a cold and is despondent; a conversation which touched on the King yesterday has deeply upset him; the thought that "his work, his highest ideal, should be trampled underfoot to earn him his bread," depresses him, just as publications like Strauss's *Voltaire* annoy him, the contemporary world appears grotesque to him, and, as he confesses to me, he is now painfully aware of how much the world resembles a lunatic asylum. He forces himself to work. At lunch he exclaims: "What is the thing written down as compared with the inspiration? What is notation in comparison with imagination? The former is governed by the specific laws of convention, the latter is free, boundless. That is the tremendous thing about Beethoven, that in his last quartets he was able to remember and record improvisations, which could only be done through art of the highest, highest order. With me it is always the drama which flouts convention and opens up new possibilities." — I think I understand him, for the relationship of the written to the improvised is the same as speech to emotions. I could never express what is stirring my emotions at the present time, I feel as if my heart had been broken into pieces, and love, like a bird used to a cage, is fluttering around, knocking against everything, wounding itself—I want so much to express it now, but I just cannot! — Loldi doing a bear's dance, Eva leaping like a poodle to Richter's fiddling; Loldi amuses us with her affected speech, she talks as if she really spoke another language and had learned German quite separately. Prof. Nietzsche sends us Burckhardt's book on the Renaissance and a little treatise by Prof. Czermak on Schopenhauer's color theory; we read it during the evening, and R. is annoyed by the peculiar arrogance scientists show toward philosophers. He remarks, "Realists and idealists—they are and always will be worlds apart, but only the idealist can ignore the realist, never the other way around." And: "The scientist says, as it were: I, the individual, am nothing, but my science is infallible, and by being a part of it I am able to look down on the greatest philosophers." — The printed *Beethoven* has arrived. Sending copies off (wrote the poem to Hans).

*Monday, December 5* The night puts me in a mood for verse! Four or five little poems occur to me, but they are melancholy, like my whole outlook. Uncle Liszt sends me 15,000 francs in my father's name. At R.'s request I return them with the remark that I had asked for my affairs with Rothschild to be put in order, not for help in a time of embarrassment. The remittance vexes R. extremely. — Letter from our former cook, who is very touched. Christmas purchases. In the evening more Strauss.

*Tuesday, December 6* I tell R. of my pregnancy; he smiles and has no worries in his own behalf; I will willingly bear all the difficulties and face the problematic future without fear. R. says that in the past days he found himself thinking particularly of Egmont's words about the journey of life, during which one had only to clear away, to resist, to pay heed. (Yesterday a letter from Dr. Herrig about *Beethoven*, strange and somewhat incomprehensible.) In the evening the correspondence between Voltaire and Frederick. "A king should be just a king, not do other things as well, for the danger of Spandau, etc., playing a part in friendly relationships is too great," R. says. Much delight in both men in the letters, but particularly in the manner of the King. (Orléans has been taken.)

*Wednesday, December 7* I have to whisper in R.'s ear that I was wrong; this moves him to tears, for he had been pleased and had thought that Fate desired me to bring a child into the world without fear and in the full happiness of love. — To town to make Christmas purchases. Late lunch (5). In the evening more Strauss. Before that I come upon R. in conversation with Richter about Weber—how before the latter no one had any inkling of the sinister quality of certain instruments (oboe, clarinet); just as before Beethoven no one knew anything about *repetition*; what in Rossini is a sensual effect here becomes a form of melody; and everything combines to make it so, the instrumentation, the key, everything. — Telegrams from Leipzig about the great success of *Die Msinger* there.

*Thursday, December 8*   Letter from Dr. Heigel, who sends me his poem *"Die Majorin."* Report from the publisher that *Beethoven* is practically sold out. Another letter from Dr. Herrig about *Beethoven.* R. reads it slowly, he says he always seeks to immerse himself in such a personality. One can see, he adds, that Dr. H. has always gathered his impressions from books, never directly. Concern about the Jews seems unbounded, R. says. A letter from Herr W. Marr claiming that *Opera and Drama* has taken complete possession of him, is evidence of the same concern. Nice letter from the publisher Schott, saying that at the beginning of the war he had the impression that people were trying to liberate themselves from Verdi and Offenbach; the German nation, however, did not possess that amount of strength. Family lunch. Snow flurries, Grane ill, R. and I walk into town. In the evening more Strauss; the analysis of Voltaire's philosophical writings makes us remark how sad it is to see such a mind as V.'s involving itself in such torments of inextricable confusion by always seeking in outward things the explanation which can never come from outside. The Indians, says R., understood that; their Brahma myth is a symbolic interpretation of the world; by exaggerating the space relationships, for example, they produce the concept of spacelessness. How this wisdom continues increasingly to astonish me—beside it we look like barbarians!

*Friday, December 9*   There is talk of a religious movement in Germany; a free German church—that would be good. — The Loire army has now been defeated, but Trochu refuses to surrender, and Gambetta goes on lying about victories and triumphs. — Fidi says distinctly: Hermine. — Gambetta and Bismarck are now wooing the Holy Father; Bismarck requests an order from Rome that the Catholic population of the conquered provinces submit to the force of arms (as happened once in Poland). Europe is now busy admiring France again! And R. says: "Two opposing principles are clearly involved here; the Latin peoples, blinded by the French Revolution, have revived memories of the ancient world and expect from the republic bliss on earth; with the republic all evils are expected to disappear, including their own exertion and self-sacrifice. The individual German, on the other hand, suffers from no illusions; being wiser, he recognizes instinctively that no shibboleth can bring the world's salvation. In the Prussian officer's 'What my king commands, I obey,' which must certainly seem terribly stupid and narrow-minded to the French, there lies a deep meaning and a deep realization that there are certain matters one cannot discuss with semi-morons. I have lived through all these illusions myself and have now got to the point of understanding the meaning of a limited sense of duty." — In the evening, after playing a few bars, he exclaims: "Oh, all this world suffering, this childishly wailing nursery song of old men! I have given it expression in the thirds of the Norns, I feel as if I have heard it: now it is spring, now winter, now war, now peace, it is all the same." We again read Strauss's *Voltaire*. Remarking disapprovingly about Frederick the Great, R. says: "A king must be strong in endurance, he must reveal his heart by remaining untouched by many things. If in the Jewish affair he had banished Voltaire, that would have been in order, but he preferred to tolerate a humbled, rather than an independent friend. That is the way of kings, and it is brought about by their special position. I know beyond a doubt that, when at the end of *Die Msinger* the King summoned me to his box, he did it only in order to show those people who thought they had an influence over him that this was not so; the means he usually employed against me, he was in this instance employing against the others." *My Life* has now been bound; I beg R. not to make a present of it to the King, so that Fidi will not be deprived, on account of some possible indiscretion, of his only capital (publication after our death). — The demand from the steamship company—about 500 francs—brings us to a dismal theme; R. thinks I have a lot in the savings bank, and I have to explain to him that I have only 2,000 francs (the quartet and the hanging lamp used up the rest). This causes slight concern and arouses despondent thoughts of the children's future. I promise—as I had already decided in any case— to give no more presents, to spend nothing, and to put my allowance aside regularly. But shall I be receiving this? The state of affairs does not inspire confidence. But in God's name, I have certainly been given more happiness than I am worthy of, and I put my trust in God!

*Saturday, December 10* Fidi seeks out Plato for himself from his father's library! — Letter from Herr Wesendonck, to whom R. had sent his *Beethoven*. Work with the children and then Christmas shopping. R. comes to meet me in the darkness, he does not wish to let me return home on foot, has followed me and ordered a carriage (Grane is ill)! In the evening he falls into a gloomy rage about his work and the deplorable things that have happened to the first parts of it. This is for me the great test, the greatest of all, because here I cannot help him! I go sadly to bed. — (Letter from Grandmama in London, reporting the death of Hans's stepbrother Heinz von Bülow, who died at Châteauneuf; I weep a lot, for of course I knew the young man.)

*Sunday, December 11* Incalculable the duration of the war—who can love life when he experiences such horrors? Oh, God, individual suffering is unbearable enough, and now these mountains of sufferings! (Letters to Schuré and to Malwida, forwarding the cup with Loulou's picture for Hans.) Christmas matters. Herr Fritzsch cables for the additions R. had promised for *Beethoven*, but it is impossible for R. to work to order; he writes to the publisher that he has none to send. En route he was constantly asking himself what he was still supposed to say—though previously he had been full of the additions he wanted to make. In the evening finished *Voltaire*. "The deep source was missing, but it is the final flowering of the French spirit, as far as this can be taken; anything more—as attempted by J. J. Rousseau—just sounds false in them." R. astonished by the rough and crude diction of the conversation (Boulainvilliers). (Letter from Karl Klindworth.)

*Monday, December 12* Worked all day on a muff for Loldi. R. works, too; he says I should write to Countess Bismarck that a German emperor is predestined—he needs an emperor for the art of the future. I will do as he asks. — In the evening Loulou dictates to me her letters to her grandmama and to Heinz's mother. — In the morning R. says to me: "How I long to start studying the Indians! All of it is unqualified truth; their allegories express what cannot otherwise be expressed. With us everything is established in a sort of convention; for example, Goethe's *Tasso* is based on the tragedy of royal birth, which calls for unmixed blood, and that accounts for the Princess's noble renunciation; but along comes the great realist and says: 'What does it matter, you princes? You are human beings like ourselves.' With the Indians, on the other hand, even their caste doctrine is based on a profound knowledge of Nature." I mention R.'s poems as being of a kind which also frees us from convention. "That is the music," he says. I dispute this and maintain that even without music his poetry is unique. "*Das Rheingold,*" he says, "has this one advantage—that as in a peasant's trial it does clearly show us Wotan's guilt and fatal error and the urgent need for his renunciation."

*Tuesday, December 13* Richter sends Loldi to me with a very appreciative article about *Beethoven*; but R. does not want it read aloud; he says, "I am content to know that I have not been trampled into the dust and that I am not being talked about as if I were a charlatan; but to hear my praises sung is horrible to me." — He sends off, as requested, an autograph for associations for the wounded. He had been asked for *Meistersinger* songs, he writes a quotation from *Lohengrin*, "Ne'er shall the foe venture from his barren East," but alters this into "windy West"! — and then adds, "As a change from '*Die Wacht am Rhein.*'" In the evening R. is very worn out; he complains that thinking about his work robs him of so much time. — I told him today that we should have ourselves photographed, I kneeling before him, for this is my rightful position—it would be a family heirloom. He says that since having my portrait he wants no other possessions. (Letter to Lenbach.) In the evening Calderón's *Los dos amantes del cielo*; a little perturbed about the baldachins, the emeralds, etc. (Fidi very restless; I am anxious about him, since he fell off a chair yesterday.) Loulou writes to her grandmother.

*Wednesday, December 14* R. discusses with me the journey to Berlin next spring, I ask him whether I *have* to go, and he replies: "Definitely. Only with you am I something, together we form a whole; by myself I am no longer anything." So be it, then! We decide to avoid hotel life and to stay with a family if possible. — R. works; the children and I devote our day to needlework. Shortly after lunch R. plays some passages from the scene of Brünnhilde's awakening, which moves me unutterably—this genesis of love in a youth who does not even know what a woman is and who then enchants and rejuvenates this woman, who has already spun at the web of life and is his superior—this seems to me quite unique. And then the music! "Yes, I can still do it," R. says, laughing. "It is not so long since I did that, and afterward I even managed the horrible story" (the first act of *Götterdämmerung*). — Very nice and intelligent letter from Clemens Brockhaus about *Die Msinger* in Leipzig and *Beethoven*. Doris is engaged again, which her mother is reluctant to announce. — The cordial, familiar tone of R.'s nephew pleases me very much, I think of Fidi—that he might perhaps find a friendly relationship there. I am also touched by the decidedly friendly attitude toward me. "Oh, they know what is what," R. says. "Anybody who gets to know you can be in no doubt at all about you. It was ordained in the stars that you should dedicate yourself to me." Laughing, he adds, as he looks at my picture: "Oh, yes, the proud little lady was quite determined. I'll show you, she is thinking." Ate late in the evening, since R. was working. Finished Calderón's *Los dos amantes del cielo*; astounded by the coldness of the play and the flatness and shallowness of some of the scenes.

*Thursday, December 15* R. tells me in the morning that I am looking transfigured today—maybe the arrival of this mild, thawing weather, which always relaxes me, is to blame. I dreamed that at table Voltaire and R. got into a quarrel about Albrecht Dürer. Coming back once more to Calderón, R. says he is at his best in his comedies; the tragedies captivate through the themes they deal with. Christmas preparations. Family lunch. Letter from my mother with the familiar injustices toward Prussia.

I go into town with R.; there we find a letter from Schuré, who writes very understandingly about *Beethoven*, but in French, so R. does not even read it. — R. is writing another ending for his *Beethoven*. "One must not always butter the Germans up," he says. In the evening began Gibbon. — R. says he would like to be rich, move into an Italian villa with me, and there study in peace and at leisure. "I never read anything at all now, but to make up for it I live, I have you and the children." Loulou writes to Luise Bülow, I to Hedwig.

*Friday, December 16*   We are depressed about the news from France. Paris is reported to have laid in provisions during the recent fighting, and they claim to have 400,000 men mobilized. One cannot predict how long this slaughter will still go on, and I am beset by worry whether it will turn out as it should, in our favor. What still lies ahead? How will it end? I cannot apply myself to anything today, fear robs me of my breath. Letter from the Schurés, who are going to Lyon, she to tend the wounded, he probably to fight. Letter from Prof. Nietzsche: a Basel professor asked him whether Wagner's *Beethoven* was written *against* Beethoven! In the evening Richter plays us his music for *Die Kapitulation* and admits to us that he would find it embarrassing to put his name to it; he declares that the reason Betz does not reply to him is undoubtedly that he thinks Richter needs money and has therefore started to compose! — We laugh, and R. says how heavily one has to pay for such ideas; it had cost him a lot, too, to write the thing; but he had done it in order not to get into the habit of giving things up too easily. (Letter to my mother.)

*Saturday, December 17*   Beethoven Day! How to celebrate this unique occasion? R. admits that in order to give me pleasure he would have liked to conduct a symphony in Zurich today; we discuss how to make up for this. — The news from France fills us with mourning, it is being said quite definitely that even the fall of Paris will not mean the end of the war. — Betz returns *Die Kapitulation*: the theaters are frightened of the production costs. R. is basically glad, for the situation in Paris has changed, the mood is no longer the same, it is a decree of Fate. "To stretch out a hand to the outside world is a dead loss, to withdraw it and fold one's arms is wisdom and peace." — Fidi is Tribschen's Gambetta—howling! (says R.). He sees a creature like Gambetta as "in a fever of agitation, with a rose in his buttonhole." — Unpleasant experience with a dealer in art books from Berlin who has sent me disgraceful Christmas wrappers. — The bookbinder's assistant tells R. that he has read *Beethoven* and finds it very good, whereupon R.: "It is not very easy to read." "No, one has to give it some thought, but all the same I read it and find it very good." — R. works on *Siegfried*. (Letter to Dr. Heigel.) In the evening read Gibbon. (R. not well.)

*Sunday, December 18*   A discussion of Laube's behavior produces from R. the remark: "I find it so sad when people who have played a pleasant role in my life suddenly behave so badly—not only toward me, but altogether. Like young girls, a great many men have their *beauté de diable*, a time when they look promising, and later one is quite surprised to find there was nothing in them." I said it seemed to me that every person, man or woman, had a phase in life in which he was better than during the rest of it. R. replies: "Because in every individual all potentialities are contained, just as the whole universe is contained in cellular tissue. This is also why an artist can count on making an overall impression; I dare to maintain that even the most extreme of philistines can feel with Tristan and Isolde, for there has certainly been one hour in his life when he fought shy of falling in love." — Yesterday, in connection with the division of the Roman Empire into Latin and Greek provinces, R. says, "You can see at once how certain peoples, such as the Greeks, are unable to give up their language and their culture; the ancient Germans could not do it, either, while others, including the Gauls, became Latinized." — The way in which the war is being conducted is being bitterly condemned; it is said Moltke has ordered that Paris be merely surrounded, and that the pursuit of the Loire army was very halfhearted, the deployment of troops too scattered, leading to terrible losses. These things unfortunately dominate my thoughts entirely, and R. notes it with disapproval. I ought certainly to have concealed my agitation. At lunch R. asks Hermine whether she has been to church like a good girl—he himself went there only every 30 years in order to get married! — "What a fleeting, meaningless thing life is!" he exclaims after humming to himself the "Song of May 3." "When I think of these Poles—where have all those happy faces gone, the half-chivalrous, half-pedantic mood of that public holiday I told you about? The same people would have no idea what they looked like: it was all caused by the emergence of the idea of Poland." — I go to Countess B.'s. R., who had wanted to go for a walk with me (which I had not understood), hurries after me through meadows and marshes, and to my great astonishment I see him near the railroad striding along ahead of me on the other side with Rus. "You just don't realize how attached I am to you," he says. In the evening Gibbon.

*Monday, December 19*  Lusch touches my heart by telling me she has dreamed of her father, he had been in a corner between R. and Richter and had been unable to get away. — Letter to R. from an admirer of Schopenhauer in Pest, full of enthusiasm and veneration. R. works, I fully occupied with Christmas matters. The situation of our troops alarms me, a great mistake seems to have been made. R. says he would like to write a constitution for the German people— "to please you," he says jokingly. In the evening Gibbon. (2nd edition of *Beethoven*.) Countess B. comes and says a rumor is going around that Trochu has broken through. — Today, as I am plaiting my hair in various ways and I tell R. I enjoy doing it, he replies: "When I first read about the Spartans, who plaited their hair before going thus adorned into battle, I got my first impression of life as a lovely game, in which people sacrifice themselves gladly and seek to approach the gods adorned in a worthy manner. That is the one world, and the world of Saint Francis of Assisi is the other." Continued with Gibbon.

*Tuesday, December 20*   R. is not well. The foehn does not agree with him. His veins are swollen, and he had a bad night. His good muse, he calls me, but all his love cannot dispel my concern about his indisposition. — R[ichter] is in Zurich. I to town, where Count B. tells me there is a nice article about *Beethoven* in the *Nationalzeitung*. At the same time Herr Fritzsch sends R. more money for this work, which surprises R. exceedingly. In the evening Gibbon.

*Wednesday, December 21*   From General Headquarters Councilor Bucher sends his photograph. Still nothing encouraging concerning Paris, the French efforts have undoubtedly been underestimated by our people. R. has had another bad night. While we are drinking coffee in the downstairs *salon*, he looks up at the gallery and says he can recall the surprise he felt on his birthday in '69, when he listened there to the quartet and saw for the first time the painted windowpane. "You must prepare no more such surprises," he said, "for I can imagine how difficult it was for you all the time you were preparing it. In a love like ours it is surely almost unbearable having to conceal things from each other." I admit to him that when he questioned me about my correspondence with Herr Müller over the quartet and always accepted my answers without question, I did feel deeply ashamed. — I advise him to consult a doctor in Basel or Zurich about his indisposition. "Best of all I should have liked to go to Strassburg, since I hardly know it, so as to see something else at the same time. Were there any good pictures there?" I mention some which were destroyed with the library. "Yes, one has to make up one's mind whether all the treasures should be consigned to destruction without scruple, or whether one will put up with even the worst of conditions just in order to preserve them all." "And then they really will be destroyed," I said. "Yes, as the barbarians did with the Roman Empire. And what is art, after all? It is like the lovely blue flames which now and again flicker over a fire, while everything going on beneath them is destruction, annihilation. But that art should provide a light during a period rich in deeds—that indeed is the dream." — I reply to my friend in Versailles, write to Countess B. enclosing the Christmas gifts. In the evening read Gibbon.

*Thursday, December 22*   It is now being said that Paris has enough provisions to last until April, and there is hardly any likelihood of a bombardment, since the range of the guns is too short. This is certainly bad news. R. says, "Now the Germans can show what they are made of; they have always distinguished themselves through patience and perseverance." — Letter in *Latin* from Peter Cornelius, announcing the birth of his third child. Letter to me from Dr. Heigel, who has been asked to make a contribution to a book about the mothers of famous men and has chosen R.'s mother. I find journalism of this sort, which exploits everything, however private and intimate, quite horrifying; I shall tell Dr. H. that I am not willing to supply the required information. Richter brings along a violinist from Zurich, with whom our house quartets are to be arranged. — Yesterday R. spoke of our leaving Tribschen and then added, "Throughout my life there have been periods in which I was as good as dead and in which I sowed the seeds of a new life—thus Paris (after my jobs as music director), which led to my conducting engagement in Dresden, then Zurich following Dresden, and now Tribschen." I mention the remark that flight has always been a distinctive feature of his life; flight from Riga, flight from Dresden, flight from Zurich, flight from Munich (twice). It is to be hoped this is now at an end. — When I tell him of my delight in the Venus scene in *Tannhäuser* (added in Paris), he says: "How conscious I was in Dresden of the inadequacy of this scene, how modestly did I doubt my ability to become one of the great—someone capable of doing what he wanted! I was just glad that I could put my whole soul into whatever I did do. But the reappearance of Venus I added afterward, and from it I later developed the whole Paris scene." — Our conversation brings us to the large cities of France. "How dreary they are! Bordeaux, for example, is quite terrible, in spite of its magnificence; yet there I got to know a rector of the consistory; he gave a lecture on the Germanic character and maintained that the Saxon opposition to Charlemagne—that is to say, the Germanic versus the Latin—could be traced right up to Luther. I was absolutely Red in those days and I had a lively argument with this intelligent man, while Mme Laussot (who was not a bluestocking then!) listened in bliss." R.'s autograph is discussed in the *A.A. Zeitung*, it is expected to be auctioned for a very high sum.

*Friday, December 23* Nothing to report except Christmas preparations. I drive to town in a sleigh and return home half frozen. In the evening I decorate the tree. The children work in secret. Great excitement everywhere.

*Saturday, December 24* My day is devoted to laying out the presents, which I do with melancholy; the report concerning our people taken prisoner in Pau, and starving, dominates my feelings, and I also think of Hans. At 5 o'clock R. returns from town, bringing Prof. Nietzsche with him, at 7 o'clock we light the candles. It is the first Christmas on which I am giving R. no present and will receive none from him— so that is all right. A telegram from Dr. Sulzer says he is accepting R.'s invitation and will arrive at midday tomorrow from Bern. Everybody is happy and content, our good Stockers think we have done too much for them. — The children blissful!

*Sunday, December 25* About this day, my children, I can tell you nothing—nothing about my feelings, nothing about my mood, nothing, nothing. I shall just tell you, drily and plainly, what happened. When I woke up I heard a sound, it grew ever louder, I could no longer imagine myself in a dream, music was sounding, and what music! After it had died away, R. came in to me with the five children and put into my hands the score of his "Symphonic Birthday Greeting." I was in tears, but so, too, was the whole household; R. had set up his orchestra on the stairs and thus consecrated our Tribschen forever! *The Tribschen Idyll*—thus the work is called. — At midday Dr. Sulzer arrived, surely the most important of R.'s friends! After breakfast the orchestra again assembled, and now once again the *Idyll* was heard in the lower apartment, moving us all profoundly (Countess B. was also there, on my invitation); after it the *Lohengrin* wedding procession, Beethoven's Septet, and, to end with, once more the work of which I shall never hear enough! — Now at last I understood all R.'s working in secret, also dear Richter's trumpet (he blazed out the Siegfried theme splendidly and had learned the trumpet especially to do it), which had won him many admonishments from me. "Now let me die," I exclaimed to R. "It would be easier to die for me than to live for me," he replied.— In the evening R. reads his *Meistersinger* to Dr. Sulzer, who did not know it; and I take as much delight in it as if it were something completely new. This makes R. say, "I wanted to read Sulzer *Die Ms*, and it turned into a dialogue between us two."

*Monday, December 26* Aunt "Isa" sends the children some little things and exhorts them to think of their father! If the dear lady only knew how such thoughts are being kept alive in the children, she would leave the subject alone. At the same time Frl. v. M[eysenbug] reports that the cup and the poem have arrived and are being passed on to Hans. The whole day long I go about as if in a dream, my spirit listens for the vanished sounds and brings them back to birth for itself, my heart, oppressed by its emotions, seeks redemption in music; a twilight dream emerges—seeing nothing more, hearing everything in the depths of silence, love ruling supreme, boundaries melting away, an unawareness of existence—"the height of bliss." — In the evening R. reads aloud passages from the manuscript Prof. Nietzsche gave me as a birthday gift; it is entitled *The Birth of the Tragic Concept* and is of the greatest value; the depth and excellence of his survey, conveyed with a very concentrated brevity, is quite remarkable; we follow his thoughts with the greatest and liveliest interest. My greatest pleasure

is in seeing how R.'s ideas can be extended in this field. — Christmas
Eve brought us a letter from Alex. Serov, who made an official
journey from St. Petersburg to Vienna for the Beethoven festivities.
His highly original description of this shows that it was Judea which
celebrated the greatest of our heroes. All of it must have been absurd
and ridiculous and, for us, an affront. We would much welcome the
proclamation of the emperor as a fitting celebration for Beethoven,
but Herr v. Mühler's solution for Alsace does not give much cause
for joy! (Hermann Brockhaus invites us to his daughter's wedding.)

*Tuesday, December 27*   Played with the children in the morning.
(Fidi overexcited by the music and other Christmas pleasures—
could not sleep all night and kept on laughing and being skittish.
During the *Idyll* he pleased and captivated all the musicians with his
lively and spirited enjoyment of the music.) Letter from Frl. v.
Meysenbug; she maintains that Hans appears to be ignoring her entirely, which pained me, but it must all be borne. In the evening fetched
the children from Countess Bassenheim's in a sleigh. In the evening
we start on Hoffmann's *"Der goldene Topf,"* which we enjoy greatly.
R., embracing me as we part, says, "I want no change, I want only
that it remain like this forever." — We are concerned to have had no
news from the King at Christmas; R. fears that he is angry about not
having been sent *Siegfried.* (Things for the children from their grandmama.)

*Wednesday, December 28*   Letter from my mother; still the same
unwitting lies about the Germans' execrable conduct of the war!
Morning games with the children; R. with an effort writes his formal
letter of gratitude to the King. News of a Prussian victory in the North,
but our position is very serious. In the afternoon music from *Tristan,*
played by Richter for me and Prof. Nietzsche. In the evening we
finish H.'s *"Der goldene Topf,"* for which I place Hoffmann distinctly
above Edgar [Allan] Poe, although the latter has more art, because H.
is a poet. R. explains the profundity of his idea of looking upon the real
world as a specter, while the world of fantasy is his true home. "Of
course he does not succeed in making the latter plausible, because that
is impossible. Cervantes set it to one side and in *Don Quixote* showed
us only the negative aspect; for that reason his work is more perfect,
but in outlook Hoffmann is related to him." — (Yesterday visit from
our good student, Schobinger, who comes from Basel and assures me
he finds more pleasure in seeing me again than any of his relations.
Prof. N. helped him to get his scholarship.)

*Thursday, December 29*   Wrote to my mother, which unfortunately
brings me on to present events, a cause for the deepest mourning.
Loulou writes to her father, R. completes his very fine letter to the

King. Family lunch; after that, while R. takes his walk, the first act of *Tristan und Isolde*, played by Richter. In the evening R. reads us the words of it; but we wake up Fidi, and wander through the whole house, looking for a place to read the third act. It is cold downstairs, so we settle in the study, now given over to Prof. Nietzsche. But R. finds it too absurd, and he decides to read the third act in a lowered voice. The whole makes a tremendous impression on me. (Fidi very keyed up, dancing, laughing, etc.)

*Friday, December 30* Letter from Lieutenant von Gersdorff in Montmorency, thanking R. for the photograph he sent him. Arrival of an article about *Beethoven* by Herr H. Dorn, in which among other things R. is accused of toadying to the King of Bavaria! The article will be returned to its conductor author, now living on a pension. The music publisher [Peters] wants a coronation march and offers R. 1,500 francs for it; the only pity is that R. cannot write to order, and particularly not a coronation march. — The newspapers report the total dissolution of the Loire army. — God grant it is true! The bombardment of a fort has begun. R. writes his open letter to Herr Stade. Fidi very keyed up, cannot sleep, we abandon the orange room and spend the evening in R.'s workroom, after the tree has been stripped bare by the children.

*Saturday, December 31* Letter from Countess Krockow (reporting among other things that in *Saxony* there is great sympathy for the French). R. and I pay New Year calls to our clergyman Tschudi (whom R. greets not without emotion, since he was so friendly toward us). Then the Bassenheims, who are also in R.'s eyes hallowed and worthy of respect, since they were present at our wedding. The Countess tells us that Mont Avron has been taken. In the carriage R. gives me a long look and says, after joking that I have too much breeding, that my affinity is reflected so comfortingly in my face; he looks back over the past and says: "My position in regard to you I can only describe in Tristan's words in the second act—this attitude of hardly daring to believe which makes him a complete traitor toward Isolde; because poetry is always a step ahead, and only retrospectively can the reality prove how correctly the poet has seen things. How long did I suffer on Hans's account before I recognized that here, as in *Tristan*, a power reigned against which everyone was helpless." The reading of *Tristan* made me melancholy inasmuch as it reminded me of Richard's situation at that time in Zurich, and I cannot think of such false images, disappointments, and fleeting emanations of madness without tears; R. reproves me for these feelings and says I imagine things as far more significant than they had in fact been, though certainly in becoming aware of them I had matured. — In the afternoon the quartet players from Zurich, R. rehearsed them in the F Major Quartet, Opus 59 (a favorite work of mine, if one may speak thus of such divine things), then the last (also F Major). Toward eleven o'clock the musicians go away, we stay up, Prof. Nietzsche, our good Richter, and we two. Midnight arrives, we wish each other a Happy New Year. May God bring us all peace! —

# 1871

*Sunday, January 1*   Greeted R., the angel of my existence! And at the same time deep gratitude and a deep prayer of regret for all the good I have neglected to do and all the evil I have done. The children, all five, come with greetings, Loulou recites her English poem to me in a good accent and proves in this, too, her easy powers of comprehension, just as she yesterday delighted me with her lively attentiveness while listening to music. Boni also listened with devotion and cried when she had to leave. — Family lunch; at about 4 o'clock Prof. N. takes his departure. — R. has been *ruling lines* in his score, so this year will be *"nulla dies sine linea."* — Fidi starts the year with "Herr-mine," the word which to him expresses everything. — As some visitors arrived R. was just fixing his large pin (*Der Bauer als Millionär*) in a bright-green tie; when he told me he felt a little embarrassed, I answered him that he need not worry—to strangers he would look only like an archivist, a sort of *Lindhorst*. R. laughs and the name sticks: he calls me the Orange Lily and Prof. Nietzsche becomes the student Anselmus. — Yesterday morning, in great excitement, Richter brought us the news that Heinrich Porges has now really been appointed musical director in Munich. Since things were not going at all well in the theater, Baron Perfall played his favorite trick of proclaiming through the newspapers that it was all up with freedom in the Munich theater, since R. Wagner was having himself appointed manager. The object was to make *Porges*'s appointment look like R.'s work (because Porges is known *only* as a supporter of Wagner) and at the same time to secure the *permanent* appointment of Herr Wüllner, who is supposed to offset Porges, since it is known that the latter cannot conduct, or at least has never yet conducted. Things always remain exactly the same! But the King?

*Monday, January 2*   Richter has had a letter from his friend Servais, begging him in my father's name to go immediately to Pest, where plans to appoint him are progressing well; I advise Richter to approach my father directly for enlightenment. This notification saddens us further: "What a life this is, in which everything has to be sacrificed for bread!" R. says mournfully. — He goes into town, I stay at home and write letters (Meysenbug, Krockow, Serov). Fidi pays his first visit to Countess B., but her large figure dressed in mourning frightens him. In the evening finished reading [Hoffmann's] *"Klein Zaches,"* without much enjoyment apart from the originality of the main character; we are reminded of how often Bülow used to exclaim with a smile, "Little Zaches, known as Zinnober," when, for example, the raising of the musicians' salaries, effected by us, brought our good Baron Perfall a serenade, and when the lowering of the orchestra pit, demanded by R., was praised in all the newspapers as a good idea of Perfall's. — In Torgau, as Prof. Nietzsche tells us, the soldiers sing *"Götternot, nur Knechte knete ich mir,"* from *Die Walküre.*

*Tuesday, January 3* R. appeared in my room during the night, asking me whether I loved him, a bad dream had frightened him; in the morning I joke with him about it, and he says that any separation between us had always caused havoc in him, as in his dream, making him firmly convinced that we had come to grief. And on the many occasions when we had decided to separate, never to see each other again, our hearts had downright laughed at the impossibility of this resolve. This, he says, is what has given him the confidence to let people say what they like, for "what do they know of our sufferings and our love?" — He remarked yesterday that all our fine poets have got very quiet these days, giving us no more hurrahs at the very time we need a few words to give us new heart amid all the great sacrifices and sufferings. — Talking about freedom as it is understood today, R. says, "Freedom is the divine right of journalists to do and say whatever they please." — Long letter from Peter Cornelius, many complaints about his tribulations in the school and explanations of what he is and is not. "Everybody is prepared to admit that he has learned nothing, that he knows no Greek—but that he is not a genius, never." — One of our two little finches has died, causing great sorrow; to insure that the cock will not be left in solitary sadness without a hen, I drive into town with Loulou. In the carriage Lusch converses earnestly with me, asks me when I think peace will come, and about the German emperor. An article by Herr Gervinus brings R. to the subject of conditions in Germany, and its good fortune in still possessing princes, "only these princes should form the Reichstag and, after having found out from assemblies of various corporations what the interests of their own lands are, they should represent those interests there; in that way they would learn to do something again, and the absurdity of the monarchic system would disappear." — Letter to Prof. Nietzsche, who has been instrumental in getting *our* nephew Fritz Brockhaus called to Basel. — My birthday dove, too, has now died! The cold is severe and we are short of coal. — R. corrects his biography, and I tell him that with it we shall be bequeathing Fidi useful capital. R. replies, "If I can assume that my name will remain great in the history of art, then I also believe that the book will arouse interest." In the evening we once again discuss Prof. Nietzsche's thesis, and R. cannot praise it too highly.

*Wednesday, January 4*  Work with the children; R. is unfortunately not well, his nights are not good. Severe cold, we sit near the fire after lunch, and R. praises the stillness, saying: "It will seem strange when we come into contact with the outside world again. All we need ask of God is health, for we already have happiness." Speaking in general about the harshness of life, he says: "Everybody who is not an artist or a saint is a poor creature, indeed, a mere seven-day wonder. What life offers is always the same old thing over and over, a boring, monotonous affair, in which one can only discern differences of form." When I then quote Mephistopheles, "It drives one mad," he says: "Yes, that's what I call Goethe's Dionysian streak. *Faust* is one of the most wonderful things ever created by mankind; Faust and Mephisto— these are characters like Don Quixote and Sancho, except that they are brighter, which brings them much nearer in spirit to the Greeks, to whom the Germans alone are allied. Conceived in his flourishing youth, completed at the end of a long life—what a proof of vitality!" R. calls Fidi the blond Beethoven, he thinks he looks like him. (Letter to Prof. N. R. writes to Peter Cornelius, urging him to hold out at the school.) Compared to Goethe R. calls Schiller Apollonian. In the evening I read Gibbon to R.

*Thursday, January 5*  R. had a good night and went to work early. I with the children. The bombardment of Paris has now begun in earnest. Family lunch; afterward a visit from Countess B., who tells us to our great delight that the King has granted their fief. We accompany her home; on the return journey I make with R. through the deserted snow-covered fields, we find pleasure in what R. calls our "insane" life. Will the children ever be able to visualize it? — As we passed the Protestant church in the town, R. saluted it and said: "What a friendly wedding morn that was! One felt as if all one's cares were being smoothed away. All the people who took part in that ceremony are sacred to me." — In the evening Richter brings back a letter from a Herr Langer in Pest, on behalf of the management, offering him the conductor's post there. Richter will have to accept it, but for us it will be difficult to let him go—we look on him, after all, as our eldest son! — Talking again about E. T. A. Hoffmann, R. says he is always intrigued by the dilettantism in Germany, for to a certain extent all our greatest poets have been dilettantes, who produce sketches, in contrast to the Greeks, whose work always seems complete and assured. This leads us on to Prof. N.'s work, and R. says, "He is the only living person, apart from Constantin Frantz, who has provided me with something, a positive enrichment of my outlook."

*Friday, January 6*  At breakfast we are interrupted by Richter, who has received a telegram from my father, begging him to come at once. R. does not wish Richter to go before he has received a definite contract, and R[ichter] conforms to this wish. I am fearful of any interference in the fate of another. R. is in despondent spirits in view of Richter's impending departure. — (The birthday dove is still alive!) The children play at *staircase music*, Lulu conducts and they imitate the orchestra. An Englishman (Fitzgerald) introduces himself and believes the time is now ripe for making publicity for Wagner in England! He says the performances of the *Holländer* in London had made a deep impression. Another publisher also approaches Wagner with a commission for a musical work; R. laughs and says, "I see I was on the wrong track when I thought I could further my cause with literary work." Richter plays us passages from the 2nd act of *Siegfried*. R. is satisfied with Klindworth's arrangement.

*Saturday, January 7*  I had a sleepless, feverish night; R. came to me and told me that I had no idea what I meant to him, I had given him what he could not give me, I had made him the gift of his present life. The foehn has produced fine weather, the sun-drenched earth glistens beneath a clear sky. R. and I drive into town. At lunch R. notices that Richter is absent-minded and believes he wishes he were already in Pest. "I myself," says R., "am quite resigned, I am ready to give up everything at once. There is just one thing which must not be touched, but otherwise, if someone were to say to me, 'Here is a piece of property, here you may live with your wife and children, but you must never again listen to a note of your works,' I should accept the bargain at once. What do I get from performances except exertion and trouble, and just the satisfaction that nothing has gone wrong? But it leaves no impression. My things give me pleasure only up to the first working out in ink, when the nebulous penciled ideas suddenly emerge clearly and distinctly before my eyes. Even the instrumentation belongs too much to the outside world. One just gets too wearied by it. This English offer yesterday, for instance—of course I ought to be pleased, for an Englishman will certainly do things seriously and precisely, but it leaves me indifferent. Am I to feel pleased because things I wrote twenty years ago are now being noticed, when I have gone far beyond them—taking one step forward and two back? I have been much too battered around for that." (Letter to Klindworth.)

*Sunday, January 8*  Hans's birthday. The children celebrate it in high spirits; at lunch R. proposes his health: "Long live your good father, children, your mama's best and truest friend." — After the departure of the children, when R. wanted to speak about Hans, I asked him to be silent, for my heart was sore; that offended him, and so I had committed a great injustice. — Letter from my mother, who has persuaded herself that the French are worthy of admiration! — Showed the children slides on the magic lantern. In the evening we talk of our memories, particularly the unbelievable happenings in Munich. (I write a few lines to E. Ollivier.)

*Monday, January 9* With the children; R. orchestrates. In the afternoon sleigh ride with the two little ones. Bureau de Musique Peters (thus the signature) writes: "*I* am still hoping for the composition of the coronation march." The day before yesterday R. said to me, "If worst comes to worst, I shall write the march." The *Bureau* declares that the King and Queen of Prussia love R.'s music. —

At lunch R. said a true demonstration of how utterly Shakespeare's characters are living persons, and just as incomprehensible, is given in Hamlet's monologue. "When one sets out consciously to write a monologue about suicide, something emerges like Cato's monologue in Addison; but Shakespeare's is as incomprehensible as Nature itself." — I teach the continents to my "*favorite daughter,*" as R. calls Loldi. Letter to Loulou from her grandmother, who says that Hans was very touched by the cup. — I think of him a lot and hope so dearly that his children may one day give him pleasure, and I shy away from the thought of death. God help all us pitiful people!

*Tuesday, January 10* The news of the bombardment of Paris is good, and it seems the French themselves realize the hopelessness of their position. All the same a combined assault on the Vosges is being prepared. — Arrival of the Shakespeare which R. is giving me; a beautiful English edition. Visit from Countess B., who asks me to write down for her a criticism of the obituary of her father, with which she is not satisfied. Great weariness, which I fight against in order to do German history with the children. In the evening read Gibbon with R.: his childish views on the "barbarian" Germans made us laugh heartily, but also gave us cause for thought. Before that we had been truly shattered by Gellert's conversation with Frederick II, which we read again in Carlyle. How noble, enlightened, and modest does the poet appear, and how tragic the great German King who, blinkered by French culture, cannot recognize his own people!

*Wednesday, January 11* A young poet (Hartmann) sends us a printed account of his experiences with Herr v. Perfall! R. orchestrates. I write out the letter to Countess Bass. while the children are working. — At lunch we discuss the alliance with Austria and welcome this as a great German political deed on Bismarck's part. R., who had read a printed letter from G. Sand (my mother had sent it to me), feels a great urge to reply to it: "Of the philosophers, the Protestants of Germany of whom you speak, we know nothing, for they are *all infected by French culture*; I know only of a king whose minister had made him understand that the insolence of the French could no longer be tolerated, and of an army which is the people in arms." — I drive to Countess B.'s to deliver my little piece of work, with which she is satisfied. (Letter from L. Bucher in Versailles.) In the evening a technical discussion between R. and Richter, in which I am chiefly struck by what R. says about the horn: that it had recently (in the *Idyll*) sounded so indistinct to him, so blurred, which made him realize how carefully it had to be used, since it traced not the outline, but the color of a melody; that was also what made this instrument so romantic. — The Joachim-Mühler affair makes us smile. "It just goes to show the irony of the present world situation," R. says, "the Jesuit Mühler vanquished by the Jew Joachim." Of Beethoven: "He was the first to hear once more the melody of the people and to introduce it in music." — Ended the evening with Gibbon.

*Thursday, January 12* While yesterday laughing over Gibbon's childish description of the "barbarian" Germans, we find ourselves talking about J. Grimm's incomparable achievements, and R. read me a few pages from his *Mythology*, which does indeed open up to one an entire world. Family lunch, gay and companionable; afterward, visit from Countess B., in the evening Gibbon. R. works, but unfortunately he has caught another cold.

*Friday, January 13* Since my eyes are very weak, I consult the eye specialist; I have to take care of my eyesight. — A friendly New Year's greeting from Frau Wille, on the other hand an unpleasant exchange with Colonel Am Rhyn about the sleigh, he objects to our use of it; we give in immediately and hire one from the town. With R. fetched Loulou (from school). Richter has a letter from my father, sending greetings to "our great master." In the evening Gibbon; the field marshal *Successianus* gives us great delight, I observe that it would be a good nickname for Fidi. Richard is very much occupied with one passage in his instrumentation; he says he could not endow even the coronation march with more splendor than this scene of recognition between Siegfried and Brünnhilde.

*Saturday, January 14* Victory of Prince Friedrich Karl at Le Mans; the French on the other hand are still reporting brilliant triumphs. I said to R. that the relationship between the Germans and the French reminded me of the relationship between an intelligent man and a foolish woman (in an unhappy marriage). The latter always full of new fabrications, vexations, coquetries, etc., etc. Meanwhile our splendid Germans continue to make good progress, Heaven's blessings on them! — Our string quartet should have arrived today, but canceled their visit, to the very great sorrow of the children. — Yesterday Richard exclaimed to me: "The children in Augsburg—you sent them to me. Later you did not send them, but preferred to bring them yourself. What touching memories we have between us!" — Today he said how his heart laughed to hear the children going up and down the stairs fiddling. Boni recites us a fable by Gellert and afterward R. says he feels like writing a history of the German character. — Royalties from Berlin; *Lohengrin* maintains its position as Richard's most profitable opus (not opera). An unknown poet in Dresden asks R. to set his "Hymn to Peace" (with *tableaux*) to music! Nothing from Munich, nothing from the King. From Copenhagen 1,000 francs for *Die Msinger*. R. says, "Today I am Successianus—only in my relations with you am I *Perforianus*" (for he thought he had displeased me in something). Still reading Gibbon and still with great enjoyment.

*Sunday, January 15*  Games with the children all day, I reply to Frau Wille, who wrote to me yesterday and who had heard in Zurich about the morning music; I find it very difficult to touch on this theme, even to the best of mortals. Then a letter to my mother (still up in arms!). Richter brings me his arrangement of the "staircase music," it is excellently done; the three of us play it (Richter violin). At lunch R. tells us the story of a Prussian soldier, a tailor, who prepared a mitrailleuse and dummy and frightened the French with it. In the afternoon I perform theatricals with Lusch for the little ones, after Richter had utterly charmed us with an improvised accompaniment to Lully's *Armenian* Sonata; earnestly, discreetly, minutely he accompanied the child who, feeling important, sat and played with intense solemnity. R. said Richter had given us a consummate portrait of true chamber music. In the evening Gibbon.

*Monday, January 16*  My eyes are weak, I am not allowed to read, write, or sew. Richard orchestrates. In the newspapers it is still being reported that *Siegfried* is to be performed in Munich. God knows what will happen! — News that Bourbaki has scored a success; he is said to have 150,000 men; that disturbs us. I cannot believe that our Germans are really fated to be defeated by these hordes, yet everything which serves to raise the hopes of the French has a damaging effect. — At lunch R. talks again about [Wilhelmine] Schröder-Devrient and her performance as Romeo. "That really made me feel that everything hangs on the dramatic action; all the classicality (even quartets sound like so much squeaking!) crumbled in my eyes at the sight of this human warmth. In fact the libretto is not at all badly done, and it had its effect on me when I decided to reduce *Tristan* to three love scenes."

His intended work *The Destiny of Opera* is very much occupying R.'s thoughts, and many of his conversations now lead in this direction. The significance of the orchestra, its position as the ancient chorus, its huge advantage over the latter, which talks about the action in words, whereas the orchestra conveys to us the soul of this action—all this he explains to us in detail. Every utterance from him is doctrine to me. — Richard Pohl sends us a biography of his wife; a quotation from Bach's chorale *"Wenn ich einmal soll scheiden, so scheide nicht von mir"* moves me very much by reminding me of the impression I once received from the music. I mention this to R., and he says, "On such feelings I have built up my whole Parzival." Then we come to the subject of the Last Supper and the profound significance of the community *meal*; whereas now the priest performs it, and subtlety has turned bread into wafers, etc. — R.'s letter to Stade has appeared in Fritzsch's periodical. — First drive out with Fidi, in the new sleigh; Herr Am Rhyn has taken his away from us, we hire another, and R. and I and Fidi go to fetch Loulou. Besides this, Jakob announces the arrival of *Muni*; this is the bull which is to keep *Grane* company, since Herr Am R. has also taken away his horses, and the stable is very cold. R. takes great pleasure in the word *Muni*, we look for it in the dictionary of Middle High German, but cannot find it; learn then from Hermine that in Württemberg dialect a bull is called *Hagen*; *Hagen* and *Muni* give us much joy. — Of lyric tenors and heroic tenors, in the sense in which they are engaged and understood in present-day theaters, R. says: "The lyric tenor is one who has no voice, sings with his palate, and has a high falsetto. The heroic tenor is a certain fellow who has learned nothing." — About Munich R. says: "How clumsily people set about criticizing me! They need only to mention my appointments, such as that of Cornelius, Porges, and above all the singing teacher Schmitt, to reduce me to silence, for what can I say to make people understand that such men can only be of use under my direction? What I ought to be pardoned for is having believed in the possibility of such a thing!" In the evening Gibbon.

*Tuesday, January 17* Very nice letter from Malwida M[eysenbug] to R. "She knows we are happy," says R. "Oh, we are living here in Paradise! How we shall look back on it, long for it again, when once we have left it!" The subject of our conversation this morning: Homer, only possible before the invention of writing, and Fidi, who will lose his extremely lively facial expressions once he begins to talk! I have to kill time on account of my eyes. The day passes as usual in friendly harmony, I play with the children, Fidi *the librarian* rummages among his papa's books, and R. orchestrates. I tell him that he has certainly never in his life worked amid so many interruptions. In the evening Gibbon (Diocletian).

*Wednesday, January 18*  Letter from E. Ollivier, who is living in isolation near Turin. R. says, "He is a good and intelligent person, but shares his country's insolence, which robbed him of his senses and forced him into war." Our groom, Friedrich, is being taken from us, has to go as a soldier to the border, where fighting has been going on for the past two days (Werder and Bourbaki). — Icy roads, but I go with Richter to meet Richard; he brings me a letter from the musical director Weitzmann, who reports that an American wants to translate the Beethoven essay into English and at the same time assures us that the whole younger generation is full of enthusiasm for R. From Leipzig R. receives an anonymous card of congratulation with the assurance that Leipzig is proud of R., at the same time newspaper articles praising *Die Msinger.* R. says he undoubtedly owes this to his passage on Leipzig in the Jewish pamphlet. In the evening read Hoffmann's *"Die Königsbraut"* with much enjoyment. (My eyes are trying me sorely.)

*Thursday, January 19*  Snow again, winter is starting anew. R. orchestrates, I with the children. Then family lunch, Fidi sitting at table for the first time, great joy and gaiety. After lunch games with the children and reading. R. is pleased to see me sitting among the six of them (Willi Stocker is also there). Letter from Prof. Niet., he quotes some very fine words of his friend Rohde about *Beethoven.* In the evening Gibbon. Recalling his childish judgment on the Germans, R. says, "Yes, Jakob Grimm was a sort of mother figure." — As we part, late in the evening, R. exclaims to me, "You are the only person for whom I have respect." — Good heavens, and what would I be without his love?

*Friday, January 20*  Bourbaki has been repulsed after all. Bismarck's reply to Count Chaudordy's note gave us great pleasure yesterday; one takes heart and feels confidence in the German cause when one sees such firmness. R. is glad that he has put an end to diplomatic hypocrisy. I told R. I thought the main reason why the Alsatians were so afraid of becoming Germans again was the class distinctions which exist in Germany, whereas in France there really was freedom for the citizens. R. says this is indeed a drawback, but he hopes that the advent of an emperor will change things completely. — Seeing me today looking better, R. says: "You are my barometer. When you are well, I am happy. But when you are indisposed, I lose all my equilibrium." The children greet us: "What happiness it is to have the children! As the years pass by, one becomes dull and despondent, and what comes from outside one regards with increasing indifference —it is a sort of preparation for death. Then come the children, who are so full of lively impressions, in whom everything is alive, and they link us with the world again." He adds: "And all this you have done for me! Now at last the world must think there is something in me, since for me you abandoned everything and gave me everything!" — Boni is now developing in a way which gives us pleasure. To town with R. to fetch Lusch. Over his beer in the evening R. talks about Fidi's birth. After supper read Gibbon. (Wrote to Prof. Weitzmann and E. O[llivier].)

*Saturday, January 21* Chancy's army is reinforcing in Cherbourg— when will it all end? — Sunshine inside and out, though I did in fact dream that, flying with R., I was seized by a wild bird—but I laughed about it. At lunch R. describes the plan of the *Wanderjahre* to Richter in a wonderful way, though he then adds, "However, all this is only fully depicted in *Faust.*" — We attempt to take a walk, but the snow tires us too much. In the evening Gibbon, after spending the afternoon playing with the children, during which R. admires my gift of keeping them in order and making them obey; Fidi is already willingly obedient.

*Sunday, January 22* "We are living like gods, and there's nothing more to be said," R. exclaims to me in the morning, and then sings a melody from *La Straniera*, which reminds us once more of the effect of such things. "Vivid portrayal with it—an interesting singer—and goodbye to all classicality. That is where the drama must come in. I am no poet, and I don't care at all if people reproach me for my choice of words, in my works the action is everything. To a certain extent it is a matter of indifference to me whether people understand my verses, since they will certainly understand my dramatic action. Poets are nonentities compared to musicians, painters, and sculptors— it is only dramatists who can compete with them. The French people's great advantage is that they are playwrights, they derive the theater from their lives; it is a theater which resembles life. But it remains to be seen whether the Germans are capable of creating a theater which reflects the wildness of their nature." — Regarding the outcry in the press ("I should like to forbid that abstract word and insist on people's saying 'journalists'") against the bombardment of Paris, R. says: "Now at last I understand the Prussians and their stiff, buttoned-up character; it used to annoy me to see the King of Prussia in that uniform buttoned right up to the neck, even in his workroom. But now I can understand it; if it had been otherwise, we should be lost. Among the French there is too much slouching: our people are like inflexible machines." — Talking about musicians and indiscriminate composing, he said yesterday: "Everybody should improvise, every good musician can produce something interesting in his improvisation. But writing it down is quite a different process, then it has to be turned into a sonata, a suite, and so on, and it takes a lot to revitalize a familiar, defined form." "Beethoven was the first to write music which was listened to purely as music, all previous things were designed to enliven social gatherings or to accompany what was going on in the church or on the stage." Family lunch and later on the musicians; E-flat Major Quartet under R.'s direction, true bliss. In these tones one hears the lament of innocence over sin; if only one could transform the feelings they arouse into action, if only one could live according to them! The children happy, even the servants much moved; Hermine says she always finds herself looking at the portrait of Beethoven and wishing he could see how well Herr Wagner understands him. Only in intimate surroundings and through study are such things to be appreciated; symphonies, on the other hand, are written for the general public, and drama needs the people.

*Monday, January 23* The Bavarian Chambers have accepted the agreements—after all!! Our magnificent troops have put the French to flight at all three points, but that does not worry these good people, it is still "to the death." — I am very unwell, my eyes are becoming very weak and are painful, and even the great pleasure of yesterday was too much for me, I am having to pay for it today. R. is also not completely well, but he works all the same. He tells me he will embark soon on *The Destiny of Opera* and begin the second act of *Götterdämmerung* later, promises me (!!), however, to compose the two acts without interruption. Wrote to Councilor Düffl[ipp] (about costumes). Joy over our victories, which appear to be very great; vanished now is the fine European Court which was such a great humiliation for Germany; that is Bismarck's immortal achievement; Napoleon III, more cunning than any diplomat, was dependent on diplomacy, Bismarck realized that behind his wiliness there lay nothing. Gibbon in the evening. The name of Lady Milford causes an argument; I maintain she is called Johanna; R., Emilie. This leads us to read various scenes from the play. "I could read the whole thing again on the spot, from beginning to end, since the author does so arouse one's interest, just as every true word I hear about Beethoven—that he had been somewhere or other, seen this or that—grips me extraordinarily. — Yes, Schiller was a real playwright, he knew what he was doing. *Kabale und Liebe* will never die, for what roles it has—old Miller, Lady Milford, Luise, Ferdinand, Wurm, and so on."

*Tuesday, January 24* Bismarck (Lt. General!) refuses to give Jules Favre a safe-conduct to the conference; splendid! Everything reported about our people is great, and all the more does the world cry out against it. Taught the children the New Testament. After lunch sleigh ride with R.; at the post office we find a letter from a soldier in Blois; a sergeant named *Rudolph Nolte* writes to R. with touching enthusiasm and encloses letters from one of his friends (*Koch*, a student of philology), who is excited by the idea of a national drama. This reminds R. in the evening of his previously expressed wish that I send Countess Bismarck a copy of *Art and Politics*. I do not know why I find this so difficult to do, when I could so easily die for him. But thrusting myself forward in any way is something I find all but impossible. — In the evening Gibbon. (Letter from my mother.)

*Wednesday, January 25* We both had a bad night; mine was caused by the horrifying news which Jakob brought from town yesterday— that smallpox is reported to have broken out in Lucerne. May Heaven protect us! R. was unwell and worked on poems extolling the German troops; when he confided this to me, I encouraged him, but he replied: "Yes, but how? If I send it to the *N.A.Z.* without my name, it will receive hardly any attention at all. So should I sign it? With a name which any Jewboy can mock at as that of an opera composer one can't put oneself forward as a patriot." — Next morning his ideas had vanished. General Moltke has granted Jules Favre his safe-conduct. — The conductor Eckert sends a telegram from Berlin asking if he may send the "Ride of the Valkyries" to the Gewandhaus. R. replies: "Consider performance of 'Ride' an utter indiscretion, and use this opportunity finally to forbid any such thing." — When I go into his room in the morning, I notice that he is disconcerted, and turn to leave; he calls me back and tells me he has just hidden the paper on which he had after all written down his poem to the German people; he had been ashamed to let me see! At noon he reads it to me; I feel that it ought to be more extensive, and he intends to add another verse. Still snow and mist, no sun. We cannot go out. R. comes to the subject of the Queen of the Night's aria, and we laugh at the absurdity of regarding this as a jewel of characterization and classicality, when it is quite clearly a virtuoso aria for one particular singer. — Richter teaches the children the role of Kilian. In the evening R. sings several things from *Die Entführung*. We remark what a pity it is that such charming words get utterly lost in the ordinary opera house, since the audience has grown accustomed to art of much less refinement. Such things belong inside our school and must be dealt with like our quartets, then performed in front of an invited audience which has studied them. Bayreuth! — To follow *Mozart*, Gibbon. (Wrote to Bucher.)

*Thursday, January 26* R. reports that Trochu has resigned the high command, and nobody is prepared to take over the wartime govern-ment! So it will be dissolved. Garibaldi's success at Dijon has unfor-tunately been confirmed; as for the rest, it is still conquer or die! —

R. has added two verses to his poem, he reads it over family lunch, and, since I advise him not to have it published in a newspaper but, rather, to send it to Count Bismarck, he asks me to arrange this through Councilor Bucher. This brings the conversation to the people who have accomplished these deeds, and R. says: "There are individuals who stand above Fate and literally direct it themselves—these are the very rare geniuses like Frederick the Great. Then there are others who, though less talented, possess certain qualities which the Universal Spirit needs in order to achieve great things. Such a one is King Wilhelm, whose decency and trustworthiness are just what were required to bring about the downfall of the French. Where viability still exists, Nature literally clings to us, brings forth wonders, but, when there are organic defects, she gives up entirely; that is why there are now no men left in France. I expect much from the new empire; it is wonderful that a form arising from the nature of things, like the imperial status of Germany—whose previous downfall was due to its mildness and not to its power (the tactics of all foreign countries having been directed solely toward thwarting the Emperor)—it is wonderful that this should now rise up again, of its own accord, and should be recognized as legitimate, thus raising a barrier against the centralized state." — Visit from Count B. Jules Favre has brought peace proposals, but they have not been accepted. — In the evening Gibbon.

*Friday, January 27*  "My dear good wife," R. exclaims to me early in the morning, "Nature wanted me to bring a son into the world, and you alone could bear me this son; anything else would have been nonsense and absurdity. This gave me the strength to accomplish and bear unimaginable things in order to get us united. That must be our comfort, for Nature's purpose goes far beyond all else." R. has had a letter from the cathedral conductor in Eichstätt who wrote the pamphlet on the conducting of church music. He deplores the present state of things and says that, while Bülow was still in Munich, he could still hope, but now humdrum routine prevails everywhere. We think, in this connection, of our plan to make my father responsible for church music in Munich. "Yes, we could have turned Bavaria into a musical paradise, but it was not to be! We should have sacrificed ourselves, in our exaltation we were willing to separate; and so, when the first blow fell, the banning of my articles on art and politics, I was in fact inwardly glad. If our cause had triumphed, we should have had to become saints, and Fidi would never have come into the world." — "But since you came to join me I have had unlimited faith in myself, and want to live another 100 years with you." — I send off his fine poem to L. Bucher for Bismarck—what will the latter think of it?? —

Visit to Countess B., who calls Garibaldi the old hurdy-gurdy. It appears that the negotiations for peace are being taken seriously. At any rate Bismarck has put forward his conditions. — While R. is passing a picture shop in which portraits of the Prussian generals hang on display, he hears a boy cursing and saying, "All these fellows ought to be impaled and hanged." All these Swiss are riddled with sympathy for the French. In the evening we read Raimund's *Menschenfeind und Alpenkönig* (R. has just received his works); much, much enjoyment from this original play; with his writings the same thing happened to him as with his acting talents: best of all he would have liked to play great heroic roles, but Nature put them out of his reach; he would also have preferred to write that way in the main, like Shakespeare, but he was confined within the bounds of the Viennese popular theater. However, in that field he is an incomparable genius.

*Saturday, January 28* Work and children, all are well, and Fidi shining brightly. After lunch I lie down to rest, R. comes into the silent room and, uncertain whether I am asleep or not, says in Saxon dialect, "I am lighting a peace cigar, Paris has capitulated." Electrified, I leap to my feet and ask if it is true. It really is true—Jakob brought the news from town, completely phlegmatic in the usual Swiss way. It was not unexpected, yet it comes to me as such a surprise, so breathtakingly sudden. We shall not march into Paris, and that is splendid. In great excitement all evening, but read Gibbon attentively all the same.

*Sunday, January 29* No sleep, in a deeply religious mood thinking of the dead, of the living, of myself, my unworthiness, the inexpressible happiness of living for R. in this time of hope. — (Sent Minna five thalers, wrote to my mother and to Hedwig.) Gazing at me, R. tells me how touched he was in Starnberg to see all of my family reflected in my face—my father, Blandine, and Daniel—all the friendliness he had encountered from this direction was concentrated in me. — The five children at my bedside in their Sunday clothes. "Such dignity surrounding you," R. says, laughing, "and you are only a child yourself. All these beings depend on you—you are the axle on which it all turns." He says that yesterday he sent Frau Wille a telegram inviting her to lunch. Though I am pleased, I tell him how shy I am of the world, how nervous, and how I can only cling tight to him. "Well, what about me?" he asks. "Oh, the world is yours, you work for it and it loves you." "That is all silly rubbish, as you very well know." — Yesterday came news of Porges's failure as theater director. "It is a fine thing," says R., "the way all these sinister misunderstandings in Munich never cease. If only I could assure these people that I shall never again set foot in the dreary place!" At midday the musicians, and a bowl of

salad over my favorite dress! Studied the C-sharp Minor Quartet and
"*Es muss sein*"—great joy in Tribschen again. — No further news of
the capitulation.

*Monday, January 30*    Yesterday I was not feeling well, today I am
better. R. is pleased and says the quartet has cured me. "You are my
imperial crown," he says jokingly. We picture to ourselves the conversation between Bismarck and the puny Frenchman: "Where are you then,
little people?" Bismarck will say, searching like Polyphemus for the
tiny figures. — R. yesterday told the musicians that the difference
between the last quartets and the earlier ones lies in their tremendous
concision, and this is also where the difficulty of interpreting these
works lies; since everything in them is solid core and they no longer
contain any frills, each note must be played consciously, otherwise
the result is unclear; that is why these things have the reputation of
being incomprehensible, though, properly played, they are thoroughly
melodious and indeed easy to grasp. — Gambetta is reported to have
handed in his resignation; that would be a good thing. — After lunch
the musicians played us the *Idyll* in an arrangement by Richter; much
emotion! R. said how curious it seemed to him: all he had set out to do
was to work the theme which had come to him in Starnberg (when
we were living there together), and which he had promised me as a
quartet, into a morning serenade, and then he had unconsciously woven
our whole life into it—Fidi's birth, my recuperation, Fidi's bird, etc.
As Schopenhauer said, this is the way a musician works, he expresses
life in a language which reason does not understand. — "If I were a
young fellow," R. said, "how I should like now to complete my
Barbarossa, my Bernhard von Weimar! Frederick the Great still
occupies my thoughts, his state of mind is in fact a true picture of our
own up till now; the imagination French, but the essential being
thoroughly German; this division ought to give the work an extremely
interesting profile." — We still do not go out, fog and snow are too
dense. Nice letter from an old friend (*Alwine Frommann*), who is also a
friend of the Queen of Prussia; we are very pleased to receive a sign
of life from this lady of 70. — Always great delight in Fidi: "If nothing
comes of this one, then the devil take child making; one will have to
try it like Wagner with the Homunculus." —

*Tuesday, January 31*    The German Emperor's fine telegram; R. and
I are aglow with hope, may Heaven send us blessings! — A tenor
(Schleich) asks for an attestation that the role of Lohengrin cannot be
sung when one has catarrh; R. gives it to him. — R. has been composing
coronation marches during the night; he is thinking a little about it
because of the money. He replies to his friend [Alwine Frommann]
and describes his life with me in a way which I do not know what

I have done to deserve. How could I complain of life, when it has brought me so much more happiness than I could ever deserve? If all the world's sufferings had stormed me, I should have had no cause to complain, and now that I see R. in high spirits and the children well, I could spend all day in prayers, expiations, thanks! —

*Wednesday, February 1* Our friend Prof. Nietzsche is ill; the other friend, Schuré, sends us a raging pamphlet (by himself) attacking Germany. — We still fear French treachery regarding the capitulation. We drive into town and learn there that *85,000* French soldiers are coming to Switzerland, and Lucerne will have to take 5,000 of them. Immense excitement in the little town. — In the evening Gibbon as usual.

*Thursday, February 2* We believe that peace is assured; since the news of the capitulation I am sleeping well again. Family lunch, gay and talkative. Reply to friend Schuré, honest and to the point; also wrote to Judith and Claire. Sleigh ride, the Lucerne citizens in great fear of the *dear* French. In the evening Gibbon. (Arrival of the engraved conductor's baton used for the *Idyll.*)

*Friday, February 3* Nothing from outside, and inwardly at peace; R. reaches the end of the score of *Siegfried*, in a few more days it will be completed. Fetched Lusch from school. A letter from Marie Muchanoff, who also feels the Beethoven essay to be a revelation. R. laughs at me for spending all my time reading the "pamphlets" and being delighted with *everything* in them. I am worried about Evchen, who is apathetic and not herself toward us.

*Saturday, February 4* Letter to me from Councilor Düfflipp; my request regarding the costumes has been granted; but at the same time a letter to R., saying the King is asking about the score of *Siegfried*!! This puts a great weight on R.'s spirits. When I express my sorrow at being so helpless in the matter, R. says, "Your love is my token, *in questo signo vincet*" — I write to Marie M. that the bombardment of Paris is *not* barbaric, but a consoling token of the highest moral courage. — We are sorry that the colors of black, red, and gold have not been accepted for the flag, also that they had to sing the "*Wacht am Rhein*" at the peace celebrations in Berlin. — R. unwell, certainly as a result of that letter! —

*Sunday, February 5* Letter from E. O[llivier], very elegiac; we are both of the opinion that he cannot be exonerated; whatever he did, he should not have allowed himself to be dragged along by Gramont and advocate war against his original convictions. — Yesterday a cheerful and entertaining letter arrived from Cornelius; among other things he tells us that the old woman in the porter's lodge at the Court theater is still shouting in the corridors after the conductor, Wüllner, "You, where are you going?" — This critical view of the conditions there amused us vastly. — Plump Fidi is becoming a veritable Hercules! — Yesterday, when I read the children the story of Conradin, the last of the Hohenstaufens, we were all in tears, and R. pointed out Charles of Anjou to us as a typical example of French cruelty and lack of generosity: "Only the Germans behaved well." Loulou said she would have had the popes "tortured in the cruelest possible way" for their behavior toward Germany, and Loldi wanted to "beat them soundly" with Richter's help. R. completes his *Siegfried* today, I am beside him as he writes the last notes! This the day's happening which fills me with rapture. — Our conversation over beer brings us to the *Eroica* and the celebrated dissonance, which R. detests, because he cannot bear any form of eccentricity for its own sake; here it does not intensify the expression of the thought, but harms it, distracts from it.

*Monday, February 6* Nice letter from the painter *Pecht* about *Beethoven*. Luise Bülow writes a fine and composed letter to Loulou. Her son fell while crying out, "Dear Fatherland, you can rest in peace"— everything noble must always be mixed with a grain of absurdity, says R. I drive to town and there encounter Countess Bassenheim, awaiting the arrival of the French. She invites me to watch the spectacle, too, but I decline, for the sight would either sadden or disgust me. — In the evening Gibbon. — I forgot to note yesterday that, when R. went out after supper to get a breath of fresh air, he suddenly returned and asked Richter and me to follow him. We did so, and outside we heard the sound of a soft male voice; it came from the dark groom's lodge beside the stable: our new servant Jakob was singing alone out into the dark night. It moved us very much. R. went over and knocked, a rough voice replied, and the man who had been singing so peacefully said in his harsh prose, "Who's there?" But he was pleased by R.'s interest and was given cider. — (I send the letter off to Councilor Düffl[ipp].)

*Tuesday, February 7* R.'s Day, which I cannot celebrate this time— like everything else! — Nice letter from his sister Ottilie, who sends us caviar; arrival of the church music from Regensburg, which gives us both much pleasure. — Fidi is sent to see the doctor, since his tummy looks rather swollen; as we cuddle and kiss him, I ask R. whether Fidi will not one day have to pay for having had such a coddled childhood; R. thinks he will be happy and will reap the benefits. When we remark that he has a charming voice, Richter suggests he might one day become a tenor and sing his father's things. This alarms me terribly, and R. says: "I used to have the same ideas, that things in *our* theater should be as they were with the Greeks, when the noblest also took part; but we must give up the idea of the Greek world once and for all, it has gone forever, and the most we can do is to see to what extent our theatrical art can have an ennobling effect on the actors themselves. But I should also be horrified to see my Fidi beside Herr Betz putting on grease paint. I used to think, too, that I should have to play all my roles myself, otherwise they would never work!" In the evening we read the play which the young poet Josef Hartmann sent to R.; it contains quite outstanding scenes and is delicate and witty, its weaknesses are the young lovers and the 5 acts; I feel he would have done better to shorten the play into three.

*Wednesday, February 8* Frau Wesendonck sends me her *Friedrich der Grosse*; R. is utterly opposed to women's venturing into the market in this way, he sees it as a sign of lack of taste. From London he receives an invitation to write a cantata for the opening of the industrial exhibition. Naturally he does not accept, he says he has enough trouble already with the coronation march; he has a tremendous number of themes, but he lacks the concentration to select. Overcast weather; our sun is Fidi. R. writes a fine letter to the young author of *Die Propheten*. He is somewhat depressed by the weather and—Councilor Düfflipp!

*Thursday, February 9* I thank Frau W. for sending her book; I avoid praising the book itself, but speak earnestly and warmly about its subject. R., to whom I read my letter, is utterly against it and says to me, "What words are left for genuine things if we treat stupidities in this way?" When I reply that I find it impossible not to treat seriously people who have shown friendship toward him and for whom he has felt sympathy, he replies: "If you did it only out of consideration for me, it makes me feel downright degraded. To guard against any sentimental mistakes, I sent this lady her letters back and had mine burned, for I do not want anything to remain which might suggest it was ever a serious relationship. The fact that I once spoke in tones such as you use in this letter is something for which I have already had to pay dearly enough." — Family lunch, at which I notice that R. is despondent; in reply to my question he tells me that our friend Serov has died, suddenly and in a manner as gentle as his soul! In him we have lost a good, true friend of our cause, with the goodness of a child, and we can say that with him his country has also died, whose best representative he was for us. This news fills me with great melancholy. "How sad life is!" I say to R. My only help lies in the children; in order not to make them suffer for my melancholy I play with them as usual, and gradually I regain my normal appearance; what lies hidden beneath this outer guise is engaged in prayer. — We go into town, since the children want to see the Frenchmen. The behavior of the officers toward the ranks is hair-raising. — Splendid letter from Bismarck to Ollivier, who had written to King Wilhelm that, since he believed in God, he had also believed that he would save France: "Since you believe in God, the days of your life are not sufficient to beg forgiveness on your knees for the disaster you have brought on your fatherland."

*Friday, February 10*   R. exclaims to me, "You are my good half, I nothing without you, you nothing without me." — He has dreamed of my father and recalls his remark that Beethoven was not a Catholic: "Natural magic, which reveals itself to the world without divine help— that is something they fear." Another meditative letter from Dr. Herrig. R. says that the difference between North and South Germany can be seen in these two—the young man from Würzburg writes a play, the young man from Berlin ponders how the spoken drama is to be saved. "Write a good play," R. laughs, "and it is saved." — R. works on his march; I write to Klindworth, P. Cornelius (for the birthday poem), to England, and to Frau Wille. — The news of the French soldiers grows ever worse; it makes me indignant to think that such people fought our noble Germans. R. says that when one looks at these people, one has the feeling that the human race is a degraded form of the animal world, as if, so to speak, it were out of this rottenness that the true human being first emerged. Visit to Countess B., who also tells me the saddest details about these people. As always when I return home I am filled with the joy of reunion, and R., giving me his hand, tells me we are truly happy in spite of everything! The evening, however, lapsed into a mood of melancholy. Loldi began to cry out of naughtiness, I had to punish her, which always puts me in a fever, because I never do it in anger; a letter from Prof. Nietzsche, who is traveling to Italy without coming to say goodbye to me, arouses troubled thoughts in R.; and, finally, Richter gives us the impression of being tired of living. We, R. and I, are brought nearer to each other as much by melancholy as by cheerfulness, nothing but death can part us, and not even this: we vow not to part for even an hour of our life. — In the evening, when R. accompanied me to my room, he saw the hyacinths in it and said that these flowers always reminded him of *Manfred* and *Paradise and the Peri*, which he read in his uncle Adolph's translation in Leipzig, at a window at which flowers of this sort were standing. He does not like their scent, and nor do I; I only have them in the room because it touches me to see such plants suddenly spring into bloom after the long winter; also, it had been an attentive gesture on Jakob's part to place them in my room, and I did not wish to spurn it. — Kos our *Moblo!*

*Saturday, February 11*   Yesterday we were very touched by Eva; after I had punished Loldi, she went to her and said, "Oh, Loldchen, I almost had to cry but wasn't allowed to, here is my handkerchief; for this you will be given a nice birthday." — Besides our friend

Serov, 5 of our acquaintances have died: Prince Pückler, Baron Eötvös, Prof. Eckhardt, Prof. Schwind, Father Hermann (Cohen!). Snow again; the winter refuses to end. We do not go out, and I say jokingly to R. that this is not a good thing, for I shall torture him with my love. He laughs and says that if he were to go a single day without hearing me say I loved him, he would feel alarmed—he needed it. — In connection with our German history lessons I read the children the ballad of the Count of Habsburg, which makes a great impression on them. In the evening Gibbon.

*Sunday, February 12* The musicians cable that they are not coming, which disappoints the children greatly. — Yesterday afternoon sudden sounds of music startled us and enchanted the children; five German traveling musicians were standing out in the snow and had started to play without our having noticed their arrival. R. invited them into the hall, the whole household assembled on the stairs, and several things were played, to the great delight of the children. We gave the people beer and money and they departed in friendly spirits. I said to R. that no audience in the Bayreuth theater could be more spellbound by the first notes of the *Nibelungen* than the children were when the first notes of these poor musicians rang out in the snowy silence of solitary Tribschen. — Marie Bassenheim comes on a visit, which for the children makes up to some extent for the lost quartet. — The Frenchman Michelet has written a splendid book, *La France devant l'Europe* —he judges things just like the *Moblos* and *Turcos* in the barracks here. In Austria they really have set up a Czech Catholic cabinet: this move seems to have been the Emperor's own brainchild—where will it lead? Our old friend Princess Hohenlohe was very active at its birth! One hopes it will all be to Germany's advantage. — We discuss our Berlin plans. A letter from my former servant, saying that since the war the need of the people has exceeded all bounds, leads R. to say that large cities should cease to exist, since they produce mobs, and mobs are un-German; it is very much to be regretted, he says, that the first Reichstag is being convened in Berlin, he wishes that smaller towns, Erfurt, Halberstadt, etc., could be given new life, instead of the large cities' becoming ever larger and producing cancerous growths in the empire under the guise of prosperity. — R.'s astonishment that *Kladderadatsch* is edited by Jews, since the Jews have no wit of their own; though they are excellent subjects for witty observations, they themselves, he says, have no powers of observation. Heine an exception—the *daimon familiaris* of the evil conditions in the Germany of his time. — In the evening Richter brings the conversation around to Gounod, and that sets us off on a dreadful musical tour, *Faust, Le Prophète, Les Huguenots*, Bellini, Donizetti, Rossini, Verdi, one after another, I feel physically sick, I pick up and seek refuge in a volume of Goethe (*Paralipomena zu "Faust"*). But nothing helps, I suffer and suffer. It is too much for R. as well, and he begs Richter to stop after the latter sought to prove to him that Verdi was no worse than Donizetti. At last, God knows how, we come to Bach's organ fugues! Richter had to play two of them, and then we found ourselves back on a plane where we could contemplate and wonder to the full. I told R. that, as far as my own feelings were concerned, the difference between Bach and Beethoven lay in the fact that the former called on all my powers, to follow him was a test of intelligence and character, whereas I could give myself over to Beethoven without any effort of will. R. says: "Bach's music is certainly a conception of the world, his figurations, devoid of feeling, are like unfeeling Nature itself—birth and death, winds, storms, sunshine— all these things take place just like such a figuration; the idea of the individual, in Bach always extraordinarily beautiful and full of feeling, is the same which asserts itself in all this to-ing and fro-ing, as steadfast as the Protestant faith itself. Mozart gives us a picture of this juxtaposition of the two things in *Die Zauberflöte*, where the two guides sing to Tamino about eternal wandering and toiling; this is Bachian in feeling. And it belongs to the organ, which is as devoid of feeling as the universal soul, yet at the same time so powerful. In the themes dance motives alternate with hymns." — Thus R. continues for a long time to speak, and the Italian and Jewish ghosts are dispersed—but the feelings of nausea remained!

*Monday, February 13* R. called me to him around midday and said that he now had a clear first draft of the coronation march; he plays some of it to me and I like it very much. Sunshine and a merry mood at lunch. We go for a walk and at the post office find a letter from Frau Wesendonck, she accepts our invitation and invites us to lunch. — We let the children ride home, and there is tremendous jubilation as they drive past us. Three French officers were in our garden today, and they played with the children. They gave Boni 20 centimes (!), helped Eva ride on Rus, and gave Loldi a kiss! — When we see the wretched soldiers in the town, R. says, "Gambetta gathered armies together as the Jesuits did Christians in Asia—when one took a closer look there were none to be seen." We spend the evening in sweet nothings and do not get around to Gibbon. — In the morning I had read parts of *Götz von Berlichingen*; I was particularly struck by the melancholy mood in which Götz expresses himself to Sickingen, the whole difference between a character like his and Wallenstein's struck me; the ignoble man strives to deceive himself, "It must be night," etc., the noble man recognizes his perilous position and remains as resolute as he is resigned.

*Tuesday, February 14* Letters from Paris, our friend Nuitter wrote immediately (on January 31) after the capitulation. His touching letter has only just arrived, all this time he has been continuing the little payments for the life insurances! Claire also writes to me, with extraordinary self-control, talking only about small things, ignoring the whole disaster. When we speak of various friends who have no sympathy for present developments in Germany, R. says: "Who suffered more than I did under the drawbacks of life in Germany? Indeed, I even got to the stage of wishing to see the whole nation dissolved, but always in the hope of building something new, something more in line with the German spirit. It was a great joy to me to get a glimpse through Constantin Frantz of the German Empire; and who cannot feel at least some hope, now that the Germans have shown such strength?" — Later R. says: "One could explain the whole world by saying that those who belong together are separated and are seeking one another, and those who do not belong together are united, for which there are also chemical reasons; if everything that belonged together were to be united, we should have perfect harmony, but also an end of life—that would be the Nirvana of the Buddhists. There had to be a fundamental division in Nature, though of course we can no more comprehend this than the state of complete harmony which excludes life. That is the reason for the popular belief that Paradise would be a boring place." — Great ardor on R.'s part puts me into a despondent mood; best of all I should like to live my life here unnoticed, reaping only beaming glances; I have suffered too much to be susceptible to other pleasures!

*Wednesday, February 15* Hither and thither with Zurich; fears that we have been misunderstood. R. is unwell, he says to me, "Poor woman, you have already suffered much, and I don't deserve that." Yesterday he showed great displeasure with his march: "I can't do things when I can't imagine something behind it. And if I imagine something, it gets out of hand. A march is an absurdity; the most it can be is a popular song, but it is not meant to be sung, which is nonsensical. I must have some great vehicle, on which I can reel off my music; like this I can do nothing." Around four o'clock our musicians arrive; we start on the so-called *Grosse Fuge*, respectfully acknowledging that it can be interpreted correctly only by the greatest virtuosos and only after long study, and abandon it, taking up instead the Quartet Opus 130 (B-flat Major); we should have enjoyed it greatly ("The first part is our Beethoven—*pendule* Beethoven, one might say, to use a French expression," says R.), if Richard had not been unwell, so for me it was a fine lesson, but not a pleasure. When I tell R. that the scherzoso reminds me of Haydn, the finale of Mozart, he says:

"Yes, it is like with children, when we suddenly see unfulfilled voli-
tions planted by Nature in our ancestors putting in an appearance,
thus bringing to light the wonderful resemblances between succeeding
generations; it is like that here." I told him that for me the difference
between Beethoven's music and that of the others also seemed to me
to lie in the fact that his melodies arise out of the whole tonal fabric,
in the way that a flower arises out of the whole plant, whereas other
composers think up a theme with more or less ease, then append to it
their musical work, their fugues, canons, counterthemes, etc. When
yesterday we exclaimed, "Ah, that is Beethoven," I asked myself what
we meant by that. With other composers, Mendelssohn, for example,
when we say "That is he," we are defining some routine, an inborn or
assumed manner which crops up in unthinking moments; with Beethoven, however, we are recognizing the spirits which he alone can
conjure up. —

*Thursday, February 16*  Work with the children, then nothing really
except travel preparations; great excitement among the children,
because Eva's birthday is to be celebrated tomorrow in Zurich. I
write to Mathilde Maier. R. writes letters, works on his coronation
march, and late in the evening corrects his biography, while I
begin Calderón's *El monstruo de los jardines*, which I find very charming.

*Friday, February 17*  Brief birthday celebrations, in order to be
ready in good time. Letter from M. Meysenbug, read in the carriage.
Fine weather, arrival in good spirits (Belfort's capitulation). Tidied
ourselves up a little in the Hotel Baur, then drove to the Wesendoncks'.
After seven years I had brought him back there, and I was glad to have
succeeded. Frau W. was to all appearances pleased to see R. again—
and to see him looking so happy. Her black hair disturbed him a little,
but he grew accustomed to it and found her well disposed and friendly.
The children behaved splendidly, endured the long-drawn-out meal
with patience and good manners, and afterward they played with the
W. children. At 6 o'clock listened to quartets (E-flat Major, F Minor,
B-flat Major) in our hotel; the Wesendoncks and the Willes also there,
the musicians played very well, and a congenial atmosphere prevailed.
Only we were a little tired, R. and I.

*Saturday, February 18  Zurich.* Did not sleep a wink, consequently
great weariness, but in good spirits, the children very lively. When I
tell R. that old memories had returned in Frau W.'s boudoir, he says,
"The ugly grimaces of Fate." — At 11 o'clock drove to the Willes;
a merry day for the children; the Wesendonck house too fine for them,
children and toys too splendid, here everything much freer and more
amusing. But R. is very worn out. Frau Wesendonck arrives with her
daughter, and we invite them to visit us. Dr. Wille very clever and

original, as always. Frau Wille very kind, she always speaks to me with such deep sympathy and understanding. We all discuss the German situation, and R. sums up his attitude thus: "We have Bismarck to thank for keeping Germany from becoming a large Alsace." Took our departure at 6 o'clock, the children having again behaved very well. R. dead tired, I glad to be journeying home, we no longer belong among other people, we are only happy when alone in our own home. We welcome the sight of our "home" hill, our Tribschen, here we are away from the world! — An iron stove in the carriage was so overheated that it almost killed us. R. felt the consequence of it in the evening and looked very ill. I full of anxiety and concern, but sleep soon overcomes him and I feel very relieved.

*Sunday, February 19* Back again in Tribschen and a splendid morning, spring and Fidi there to greet us. "Dearest wife," R. exclaims to me, "the whole morning I have been thinking of you, how good and kind and lovely you are, there is nobody to compare to you." I had won this for myself with my report that I had had a good night! — Write letters for R. (to Hallwachs, Wittstein, etc., also to London, since they are repeatedly asking for the exhibition march!). R. tells me that what so wears him down in others is their talking to him— that is why he tends so often to express himself at great length, solely in order to spare himself certain questions which seem to him like an attack on his very existence. What had reconciled him in his re-encounter with Frau Wesendonck was, he says, the fact that she seemed to him to be a good person who was cordially pleased to see him now in a state of happiness. — Family lunch, then walk in the garden, Tribschen bursting into bloom! In the evening R. is still very tired, and we go to bed early.

*Monday, February 20* Prussia has rejected the Orléans claim in favor of a republic; there could be no greater triumph in the face of all the absurd things that have been said about Bismarck. R. works on his march and plays me his sketch, I believe it will be very fine. — Splendid weather, I let the children play out in the garden all day. With R. to town, where I find a letter from Baron Rothschild, sending me the 2,000 francs, though under the name Baroness von Bülow; this rightly annoys R., and he requests me to demand from my father a rectification. I am reluctant to demand this of my father, but after an inner struggle I decide to do so. R., who had been watching my face, says, "Your eyes are shining, as if you had decided to do me a favor," and indeed the thought that I was making a little sacrifice in his behalf had uplifted me. Bitter feelings about my father. R. has given me the score of *Siegfried*, bound, as a present. A new treasure for my room! . . . In the evening began Carlyle's *Frederick the Great*. R. says Carlyle is not a writer, but he has an original mind.

*Tuesday, February 21*   Foehn and a letter from the King, in his usual style; I remind R. that the clairvoyante *Katharina Dangl* in Munich had told him that the waxing moon was favorable in his relations with the King, and sure enough we now have a crescent moon. R. says that within such relationships it is impossible to be too mystical, and reasonableness would be the most mystical thing of all. The King asks R. to tell him his plans and complains about the political situation; we have to smile at the realization that, while everybody is applauding his German outlook, he is probably serving the German cause only very reluctantly, because he is obliged to. — I send the 2,000 francs to the savings bank—I now have 7,000 francs laid aside for the children. — Yesterday R. was looking for the origin of the word *Gam*, and when he found in the dictionary "of doubtful origin," he thought about it and came to the conclusion that it is the same as *Gaea* and both come from Sanskrit. — Long walk with R., and only then realized it is Shrove Tuesday. The *Illustrirte Zeitung* prints pictures from the war, and these lead us to talk of the fate of the horses. R. says the wickedness of human beings is shown at its clearest in this—one has only to think of such a life, starting proudly in a gentleman's stable and ending up old and tired pulling a cart, to shudder at the cruelty of the lords of creation! — In the evening Carlyle, whose style makes us suffer greatly.

*Wednesday, February 22*   Splendid weather; R. says, "Now I must see if I can make the inner sun shine, too," and works on his march. I with Fidi and the others in the garden. Richter has a letter from Munich, which says that Porges conducted *Lohengrin* so badly that he will not raise a baton again! — Nice letter from Herr Weitzmann in Berlin; R. has one from Brünn, where they are performing *Tannhäuser* and *Lohengrin*, and another from Leipzig, where they would like some-day to see R. conducting his own things. The autograph—the conductor Schmidt writes—has been sold for ten louis d'or. — R. to town, I to meet him; he says he cannot look at the French people, he turns his eyes away, he finds an alien element in them which he does not wish to study, whereas he would make a close study of any German, however bad or unsympathetic. — In the evening Carlyle; we skip the general chapters, which are too childish. During the day I read *El monstruo de los jardines*, which I find extraordinarily compelling.

*Thursday, February 23*   Spring! In the morning R. tells me that he has thought out his "petition" (to the King of Bavaria on the building of our theater). — He calls me his "angelic etching," of whom he can never see enough! I am sad, as always when his love overwhelms me. He asks me to write to Councilor Düfflipp in his name, which I do. He continues with his march; recently he asked me about a turn in it and approved my choice, a matter of the greatest pride for me, and yet I must always and ever say to myself, "Know not what he finds in me." In the afternoon I read the chapters of Carlyle which R. had skipped, and find to my great delight a reference to the opera house in Bayreuth. I tell R. when I walk to meet him in the evening. Returning home, saluting our house, R. says, "We are altogether too happy, and there's nothing more to be said." I tell him then that, when in the morning I was running up and down the hill opposite with the children and was downright intoxicated by the spring landscape with the cowherd yodeling in the distance, I thought with melancholy of the time when we should have to leave this place. The song "So fare thee well, thou silent house" came into my mind. "We must make an inscription when we leave," I say, whereupon R.: "So fare thee well, thou dear Am Rhyn, and servants of thy habitation; we go, ne'er to return agin: this our only consolation!" — In the evening Carlyle; we much enjoy the chapter on Friedrich Wilhelm I. — Evil doings in Russia, which we discuss at table, a conspiracy against the Emperor, because he is sympathetic to the Germans.

*Friday, February 24* Springtime gone; nasty foggy morning. Pleased with Bismarck, who has requested the *French* Alsatians to leave the country within 48 hours. Gave Loulou a piano lesson, since her teacher is much too lenient. I then go in the afternoon to fetch her from her English lesson, and since she told me to come at five o'clock, R. takes a gigantic walk in order to meet me. It transpires that Loulou is detained in school to read—behind my back—some musical fairy tales by Elise Polko, and the teacher takes pleasure in mocking the earnestness of my supervision of Loulou; it makes me very sad to see Loulou consenting to such things, and on R.'s advice I stop the lessons. R. says, "What is the point of all your worries, the pedantry in fact with which you keep all vulgar things away from the children, when all you get from other people is downright mockery?" I ask myself inwardly whether the children will not one day absolutely disown me, whether they will recognize my attitude, my way of doing things. . . . In God's name, I shall bear it all. Fidi causes us concern, his eye teeth are giving him trouble and he has a temperature. — A Countess Steinbach (70 years old) has become a Protestant; R. and I discuss when I shall do this. — As we returned yesterday from our walk, R. told me that he had met Stephen Heller, but had not greeted this "exile"; during his last visit to Paris the concert promoter Giacomelli remarked how well Stephen H. was behaving, whereupon R. visited him, but at once regretted it, since he realized how much too far he (R.) had gone and what a cold and shallow character he was— though perhaps not one of the worst. Since things had now gone badly for him, too, in Paris, Stephen Hell. had not repaid his visit. In this connection R. also tells me how, during his first visit to Paris, a man greeted him, and he was so pleased that someone should recognize and greet him there that he returned the greeting with tremendous cordiality, had then, however, to rack his brains over who the person could have been; after much exertion he at last realized it had been Mme Viardot's servant, which had "horribly vexed" him. — In the evening Carlyle; R. says he has a good mind to send him *Art and Politics.*

*Saturday, February 25*   Yesterday I woke up singing the trio from the Minuet of Haydn's D Major Symphony, which amused R. greatly, today Beckmesser's serenade. "You are my buskin, my crutch, my little *stilt,*" R. says to me in fine spirits. It seems to me as if I am always writing the same things here. Oh, could I but conjure up for you for all time the nature of our love, my children, so that in later times you might derive refreshment from it in this loveless world! — Discussion of our journey; we lack money; Hanover, Vienna, Dresden are making difficulties for us with their royalty payments. When R. yesterday observed Fidi's indisposition, he said, "It causes you such difficulty to bite, and when at last you are able to bite, you may have nothing to bite." "Are things so bad?" I ask. "God knows they are," he answers with a sigh. God alone knows—maybe we shall need much courage and patience, good children. — Fidi not well, sorrow. Also heavy thoughts in connection with the children's change of religion one day; I wish to assume the responsibility for this myself. Lusch tells me that she met the little Cambrinis and they did not greet her. "They are so proud." Whether this is due to hatred of the Germans or to a veto by the priest, who knows? Any disparagement of myself I find easy to bear, but I question myself when it falls on the children. May they just find strength in themselves and seek salvation always in themselves! After lunch R. plays us his march, to our delight. From town the children bring back several letters; one really startles us with its gigantic handwriting, R. guesses Bismarck, and truly it is Bismarck, thanking him for the poem. I believe R. would have been happier if he had not written, for he had not been expecting it, but the autograph gives me a childish joy. "Another treasure for Fidi." The children gaze with curiosity on the colossal sweep of the writing, and R. says his own *Leubald und Adelaïde* was written in a hand something like that. A letter from a publisher in Düsseldorf, who introduces himself as a *non-Jew* and wants to print the score of the "*Huldigungsmarsch.*" I say to R. that it really is a very good thing that the "bankers" are mentioned by name. Third letter from the exhibition committee in London; they have decided to perform the March from *Tannhäuser* and ask R.

to conduct it, for which they offer him 20 pounds! R., indignant, says: "For this, too, we have the Jews to thank—the fact that everything is so badly paid for. They have to make a noise in the world, and so they take on something like this conducting job for nothing, just because of their mania for pushing themselves forward and drawing attention to themselves. So people could always have Mendelssohn, Meyerbeer, not to speak of Hiller, who would give their names for nothing. Haydn, Jommelli, on the other hand, made them pay well." — While we are talking about the insolence of the Parisians, R. says, "The Germans never recognize the devil, even when he has them by the collar, Bismarck could say along with Mephisto." The French people in town are so brazen that R. has literally to push them aside to let me through. We hear one of them say aptly, "*Pas étonnant nos défaites,* [*one word unreadable*] *ils avaient des lunettes de marine, nos officiers des jumelles d'opéra.*" — In the evening Carlyle, whom we find very interesting, but with whose style we cannot become reconciled. R. says Gibbon would inquire with some justice, "Are we now writing for coachmen?" It is written without doubt for uneducated people, but his judgment is excellent, he sees his people and is capable of indignation.

*Sunday, February 26* Fidi had a really wretched night. R. has a wretched day; he intends to write to the King, and this involves him in a dismal round of reflections. All our experiences in Munich come back into our minds at lunch, and I end by saying that I thank God I now see the Rigi and Pilatus mountains every day instead of Pfistermeister or Düfflipp. — Fine day, R. goes out walking, I stay at home and play with the children. He brings back a letter from Sergeant Nolte, naïve and touching. In the evening Carlyle, whose truthfulness pleases us. — Fidi indisposed.

*Monday, February 27* The night not particularly good for any of us. R. says, "When one goes to bed it is as if one abandons oneself to subterranean forces, to mysterious demon voices which lie in wait." There are rumors that Metz is only to be razed, very unwelcome to R. "All these upsets—just to raze Metz!" R. works on his letter and tells me I would find it astonishing, it is truly a work of art. We talk again about the King, and R. says, half in fun and half in earnest, "People's good qualities are beyond comprehension, but their bad qualities are incomprehensible!" — Visit from Countess B., with news that the peace preliminaries have been signed. — Fidi very unwell. — Letter from Math. M[aier].

*Tuesday, February 28* Fidi did not sleep even for five minutes, so I, too, never closed my eyes. The doctor was called; it is thrush on the tongue which is so tormenting him. — R. finishes his letter and reads it to me; it is wonderful—may the King but understand it! Walk in the soft, warm air. In the evening Carlyle with R.

*Wednesday, March 1* Fine letter from our friend Nuitter, who takes a stand high above it all; the good Pasdeloup, however, is professing to hate the Germans, and he will not perform any of their works. *"Cela se calmera,"* Nuitter observes. In the Grand Opéra fragments from *Tannhäuser* have been performed, always with great success, in spite of newspaper protests. I feel that Pasdeloup would also be quite sensible if he did not have to appear before the public, something which turns every Frenchman into an actor; to win applause he must hate the Germans, etc. The members of the National Assembly certainly also express themselves in public in a way quite different from in private. — R. says how important and fruitful it has been to read Gibbon, since it has shown him that the idea of the Roman Empire still lives on as the wisest form of government, and it is only a matter of who puts it into practice. — Yesterday R. gave Richter a severe reprimand in connection with the *Jubelouvertüre*, which Richter had referred to in a dismissive manner. R. demonstrated to him how solemn and festive, in a popular way, the Overture is, a beloved king being received by his people: it is, as it were, an idealized round dance. In such a piece there could be no musical bones for musicians to gnaw on, it must be popular to the highest degree. To me R. intimated that a musician is guided by an idea, an image, that he designs his music in accordance with that, but it should never and must never be explained in pictorial terms. Richter was ashamed, and in fun we greeted him with the main melody of the Overture. Letter from my mother, incorrigible as ever, still abusing the Germans! In the evening Carlyle.

*Thursday, March 2* Fidi had a better night, Lulu on the other hand much troubled by a cough. I am still apprehensive about the entry of the troops into Paris. R. does in fact want the war to continue, but I do not. — Prince Pückler has succeeded in having his body cremated, and his ashes will be preserved in an urn; I wish this also for R. and myself, and that is one reason why I want to become a Protestant, so that I can be cremated and buried with him. After lunch R. reads Brünnhilde's last journey from the *Edda* (I think it was); I know it only through the *Ring des Nibelungen*, but the last verse makes an utterly overwhelming impression on me: "But I and Sigurd, we stay together!" — Today brought three letters from Russia, one from Karl Klindworth, another from an impudent Moscovite who claims it is R.'s duty to write something about Serov in the newspapers, and strangely enough one at the same time from Frl. v. Rhaden, lady in waiting to the Grand Duchess Helene, who thanks R. for the fine letter he wrote to the friend of Serov who informed him of his death. This brings R. to talk about his experiences in Russia. In town, news of the acceptance of the peace by the Assembly and the undisturbed entry of our troops into Paris. Two officers whom we meet, and who recognize R., say in voices of forced loudness, *"C'est une paix de dix ans!"* — Lusch is coughing very hard, which alarms me, Fidi is somewhat better. Carlyle thoroughly vexes us with his disagreeable way of describing things. — In the evening we walk by moonlight in our beautiful Tribschen grounds. R. sends off his letter to the King and then writes to Prince Hohenlohe in Vienna in an effort to obtain royalties on his earlier works (*Lohengrin, Tannhäuser*).

*Friday, March 3* Thiers has put forward the peace terms, with tears and the usual protestations of helplessness!! The same terms which he has spent so many weeks in negotiating! — Letter from Judith Mendès, suggesting that my letter has hurt her—I don't know why it should. They appear to have suffered very much. Friend Schuré informs us that he is definitely breaking with Germany and now regards Paris as his home, whereupon R. asks me not to write to him any more. Visit to Countess B. In the evening Carlyle, decided not to continue reading it. — In the evening R. and I —:"I and Sigurd, we stay together —that shall be the inscription on our grave." Fidi somewhat better, Lulu still unwell.

*Saturday, March 4* R. is not well, he is also complaining of financial embarrassments; he says, "We shall have to cancel Christmas and birthdays for ourselves, though of course the children's must still be celebrated." He is not well, yet in the morning he exclaimed to me, "The most awful time was when you were not my wife, I can no longer even imagine such a thing." — Letter from the poet Hartmann. Baron Perfall has offered to present his play if he will withdraw his pamphlet. Typical of Munich! The poet is not answering, which pleases us, and I write to him in R.'s name. I also write to Judith. The use of the word "God" as an exclamation is, as R. says, common to all peoples, "with the difference that they are not all thinking of that dreadful Jehovah." We recall the effect of this exclamation from Falstaff on his deathbed, even though only reported by that silly woman Mistress Quickly. In the evening the first scenes of *Julius Caesar*, to our renewed enchantment. R. is glad the time has come when one no longer needs to read the newspapers so avidly. — Conversation about Bayreuth—that we three, R., Richter, and myself, will do *everything*: no producer, no nothing, just a treasurer.

*Sunday, March 5* Will Fidi be a genius? I say *no*, geniuses are so rare. R. talks about it, about the genius's predestination—that a certain longing must be present and in the genius himself a dissatisfaction with things as he finds them. "Genius implies a huge imagination, with the strength to assimilate everything this imagination needs, hence a violent temperament, on top of that single-mindedness, no concern for life, hence in daily life unpractical." — Letter from my uncle: my father has done as I asked. — Family lunch; when the little ones speak of dying and Loldi declares she does not want to die, R. says, "There is a way of insuring against that; you must become French generals or emperors: they die, shoot, or poison one another, fling themselves into the heat of battle, but do not get killed!" — Loldi sings her lullaby: "Sleep, Süssliese, little child, the sun is there, the stars are there, sleep, little child, sleep." And Eva her song of *Siegerhauer*: "Siegerhauer is gone, Siegerhauer is no longer there." Who is Siegerhauer? "A gun." We go for a drive, Loulou stays at home. Beer in the nursery; R. regards Fidi with melancholy; will he lose us soon? Will we be able to protect him, will he also have to suffer like his father? Our delight in the children. — In the evening read about the death of Fr. Wilh. in Carlyle. R. observes that in his attitude toward French and German culture, Frederick the Great, one might say, is the spirit which always wants evil and always brings forth good. Splendid spring weather. R. begins his work on *The Destiny of Opera*; in the evening he dips a little into *Götterdämmerung* (1st act), and I was overwhelmed by the power of the music. — In the morning R. told me he had dreamed of a tooth which had been extracted from his mouth and which was terribly large; evil omen? Will we hear bad news of the King?

*Monday, March 6*   Lulu still unwell; R. working on his *Destiny of Opera*: "That one always has to go on chewing the same thing over and over!" Letter from Frau Serov, who informs me that my letter arrived in time to give her husband pleasure. From Winkel we go for a lovely walk, but return home tired. In the evening took up Gibbon again. Since I am coughing, R. rebukes me sharply for not wearing a neckerchief.

*Tuesday, March 7*   Early in the morning R. comes to me, hugs and kisses me, and says I can never know how much he loves me; if he gets angry, it is only out of concern for me. I laugh, for I had really forgotten what happened yesterday, so he felt everything was all right again. "The ending of *Tristan und Isolde*—that tells you everything, that explains us to you!" We vow never to part for a single day. Children's ailments, Loldi has caught a cold; Lulu is unwell. She cried because her father had not written to her, which pained me extremely. — Rumors that Bismarck has been shot—ridiculous as this is, I am dismayed, thinking of Lincoln's end. We go to town, it all turns out to be nothing. Letter from the publisher Peters; the military musician Prof. Wieprecht wants to orchestrate the march, but R. cannot bring himself to consent, and in the evening I find him ruling his orchestral score. This wretched money—I fear R. will never free himself of his embarrassments—in

God's name! Wrote all kinds of letters. In the evening R. reads me the beginning of his lecture on *The Destiny of Opera*. Then he goes back to work, and I look at Dürer's *Greater Passion* with renewed amazement and admiration.

*Wednesday, March 8* It saddens us that the soldiers could have had so little pleasure from their entry into Paris. "The best thing about it," says R., "is the effect it had on the Parisians." We laugh over their silent appearance on the boulevards; they cannot stay in their homes, and there were certainly some mourning clothes to be seen—"contrition hats, resignation jackets, revenge gloves," and so on! — Richter has been in Zurich since yesterday, we are again alone at table, so the talk is more intimate. Speaking of his life, R. says: "If we had not come together, I should have grown very old and apathetic. Your father noticed it when he visited me here (1866). That shook me." [*In the margin:* "My desperate mood at that time drove me to those extravagances which I so profoundly regret."] Lusch still unwell, her tears of yesterday go to my heart, but everything hard is good for one! We walk, R. and I, amid springtime storms into town, happy in our love, lots of birds in the trees. In the evening Richter returns; he tells us of a peace celebration held by the German students in Zurich; I feel offended that on such an occasion they did not think of R. "I am far away, am an opera composer, come perhaps a shade in front of Offenbach." — In the evening discussion about Bayreuth. Then R. reads me the splendid canto in the *Nibelungenlied* in which the mermaids encounter Hagen. R. says it is the mythical basis which gives this poem its peculiar character.

*Thursday, March 9* Loulou has had a very bad night, she stays in bed and I sit beside her. Family lunch consequently rather dismal. Nice letter from Frau Wille, though R. finds it too noncommittal. "I know why I love you, my treasure," he says. "All other relationships have proved so trivial." Regarding Frau Wesendonck, he says that her black hair has completely obliterated all memories. — Walk with R., in the evening Gibbon.

*Friday, March 10* "Do you believe in the '*reversibilité des mérites*'?" R. asks me. I had told him that Princess Wittgenstein, who always regards *Tannhäuser* through Catholic eyes, had put forward with matchless volubility "*la reversibilité des mérites*," that article of faith of the Catholic church, as the true explanation of it. R. goes on, "I believe in it, for it is your merits which have sanctified me." I am much out of sorts, owing to worry about Lulu. *The Arabian Nights*, which I read to Lulu, restores me a little. R. orchestrates his march. We go for a drive. Letter from A. Frommann, somewhat trivial. In the evening we hear that some Frenchmen forced their way into the Zurich celebrations and a fight ensued, which ended with the death of a French officer. "They have won equality, in fact to such an extent that freedom has become out of the question," R. says. — I stay beside Lulu's bed until late in the evening, she is still coughing violently.

*Saturday, March 11*    Letter from the poet Hartmann, who has made some alterations in his play, which improve it. R. works diligently on his *"Kaisermarsch."* Visit from Countess B., the incident in Zurich seems to have been very serious, the French and the Communists joined hands. In the evening Gibbon (Julian, who *believed* in Jupiter, surprised us.)

*Sunday, March 12*    Lulu had a better night, which is a deliverance for me! Otherwise the situation in Tribschen is not good, for R. is wearied by his rushed work on the *"Kaisermarsch"* and does not feel well. The affair in Zurich was more serious than we thought; I write to Frau Wesendonck to find out how they fared. Letter from my mother, who is coming here in about a week's time. In the evening Gibbon.

*Monday, March 13*    I wake up in the night with a very sore throat, think it is diphtheria, and have to laugh at myself in the morning, finding it almost gone. Herr Marr sends an essay on *Opera and Drama.* Otherwise only domestic annoyances. Fidi's nursemaid is leaving us, and we learn that the lower servants are in fact continually plotting against us. "We do not belong here," R. says .— My resolve to change to the Protestant faith is growing ever deeper; I shall do it in Bayreuth. But Bayreuth—when? The King keeps silent. R. tells me that last night he again had a dream which he had often had long before his meeting with the King of Bavaria; the King of Prussia, Fr[iedrich] Wilh[elm] IV, piled "judicious favors" on him, demonstrated unbounded love toward him, so that, when he first saw King Ludwig, he thought that his dream was coming true. We none of us go out of doors; I receive two letters from Berlin (Käthchen, Hedwig). R. orchestrates four pages, but is not well. We talk away the evening, discussing Bayreuth.

*Tuesday, March 14*    R. is working out a folk song for his march, to be sung by the soldiers. He is working hard, but it is a strain on him, for he is no longer cut out for having to complete things by a certain date. Lulu still unwell, Fidi and Loldi hoarse. Letters from Franz Lenbach, who wants to visit us in May. Delight in the starlings, who are making a fearful din in the trees.

*Wednesday, March 15*    Frau Wesendonck writes about the rowdy scenes in Zurich, which forced them to leave their villa for two nights and will perhaps persuade them to give up the city entirely. R. finishes his *"Kaisermarsch"* and sends it off to Berlin. I write to my mother and to Frl. v. Meysenbug. The children all unwell, on top of the dismal weather. Letter from Judith Mendès, she is nice and friendly and admits she was unjust. In the evening Gibbon.

*Thursday, March 16* R. tells me he woke up in tears during the night, he had dreamed of the time when we had separated and he visited me and I seemed to him like a departed spirit: "Those were the saddest of times." Jakob Sulzer says in his account of the Zurich affair that it was caused by hatred of the Germans. Letter from Constantin Frantz, who reproaches R. with belonging to the "National Liberals," and who is not prepared to "go along" with the German Empire. Thus the Germans—each has his own ideas. Family lunch, Lusch not present. The whole countryside covered with snow, the poor starlings will starve! We do not go out. R. drafts his poem; at first he thought of demanding 500 francs from the publisher for it, so as to have 2,000 francs for our journey (1,500 for the March). But he does not want it to be tacked on; his ambition is for it to be taken for a folk song, and for that reason it should sound quite artless. I come upon him at work, he is altering the words to fit the melody, and says: "Nothing worthwhile will come just from writing a good poem and then putting a melody to it. I can see how the irregularities of the Greek choruses arose; I also knew what I was doing when I constructed my *Nibelungen* meter—I knew it would accommodate itself to the music." — Regarding the folk song, I tell him there is nothing with which we can make money. At lunch he had also considered whether he could not send his march to the London exhibition, replacing *"Ein' feste Burg"* with "God Save the King." "That would mean 50 pounds, but it would spoil the March." — In the evening Gibbon; Julian's death reminds me of the ridiculous way in which his life was taught to us at school (he was said to have died saying, "Thou hast conquered, O Galilean!"). I am also surprised that no writer has made him the hero of a tragedy.

*Friday, March 17* Full of snow! R. working on *The Destiny of Opera*. The five children coughing, I in their room. Great sorrow over Lulu's having carelessly lost the letter R. once wrote to her; I chide her sharply for her untidiness and negligence, then regret it. In the evening I go upstairs to listen for whether she is sleeping or coughing. She is not coughing. Feelings of gratitude to God; acknowledgment that my good fortune is much, much greater than anything I have done to deserve it, utter identification of all pain with my need to atone. R. comes upon me thus and asks whether I have moods of which he knows nothing. — Some martial songs arrived yesterday, we thought they came from a soldier, and they were not very good; then we found out that they were by Heinr. Dorn, and the utter lack of taste disgusted us; when the folk style is imitated, only rubbish emerges. "They falsify everything nowadays," R. says. — In the evening discussed Bayreuth again. — At lunch R. says, "A poet must be a prophet and a singer." —

*Saturday, March 18*  R. tells me that last night he danced with me; that is to say, demonstrated something to the children. "Is that a bad omen?" he asks. — We discuss Bayreuth and Berlin, I ask him whether it would not be better if he refrained from giving a lecture and just tried to set up his subscription scheme; I shrink from any personal intervention. R. feels that, though it could do harm, it could also do a great deal of good, and defends his idea. I am apprehensive about it, I wish we could get things done without touching Berlin. . . . From the King we hear nothing, yet his approval is the most important of all. I am somewhat concerned that with my request for the military music I might have spoiled something, although I cannot imagine what effect it could possibly have. — R. corrects proofs and discovers through the Italian printer in Basel that the compositor is a *Hindu*! Drive into town to make purchases for Boni's birthday. R. writes to his friend Nuitter about the life insurance for the children. We are now short of money, and I really do not dare discuss this subject with R. — In the evening R. reads us some medieval German from Hahn's grammar (magic spells, then the *Lay of Hildebrand*). Great pleasure in the lovely sounds of the language and the lively constructions.

*Sunday, March 19*  I have made the difficult decision to change our doctor, since Dr. Seuther has now prescribed the 8th bottle of medicine and nothing has resulted except stomach upsets. Lulu still ill. — Fidi bothered by his teeth, but cheerful—"my life insurance company for both past and future," R. calls him. — Letter from my mother, she is arriving on Thursday. Quartets again at last; our three people arrive from Zurich and play with Richter the A Minor, which affects us deeply. Then Op. 95 and 74—somewhat "cold" music, as R. says, with wonderful passages. R. thinks that, at the time when his great reputation brought him many commissions, Beethoven fetched out earlier works, altered them slightly, and then published them. — Arrival of Lenbach's sketch (Eva!). R. does not recognize her, but I do. — While listening to music I realize ever more profoundly how much I love R.; life seems to me like a separation, I wish to die, in order to be "eternally undivided"! We take refuge, R. and I, in my room, I tell him of my feelings, he calls me his youth and his soul. — Fidi *"the rainbow."* — Marie Bassenheim was with the children, she makes a distressing impression on us all.

*Monday, March 20*  Celebrated Boni's birthday as well as possible. — R. and I both have headaches, the slightest change in our way of life upsets us. R. said yesterday: "This life is like being at a fair, strangers everywhere, one belongs nowhere. We draw nourishment from ourselves, what makes us happy is our love, our children. That is why the air outside is hostile to us, no one understands us. To them all we wish for is madness." — The King keeps silent, also Prince Hohenlohe, who could really put us in his debt. I go to Countess Bassenheim's with Boni, find there the pleasant wife of Archduke Heinrich. I informed the Countess of my worries concerning her daughter and tell her how I have succeeded, with much exertion, in never letting the children see anything of my sorrows, so that they may preserve their childish high spirits. Early to bed on account of my severe headache.

*Tuesday, March 21*   R. reads me the work he has begun; it is wonderfully fine, and it seems to me to matter not at all whether it makes an impression in Berlin—the main thing is that it should be said. — If Bayreuth is refused us, we shall think of Strassburg; and we have just read in the *Illustrirte Zeitung* that Herr *Cerf* (the name says everything) has received permission from the German Emperor to build a theater in Strassburg. Peters sent the 1,500 francs. Otherwise nothing but work and play with the children; R. declares that physically I am not up to it, but I think I can manage it, and it is what I wish. Going through *Robinson* [*Crusoe*] for the second time (now with Boni). — In the evening we read Raimund's *Bauer als Millionär*, one of the earliest impressions in R.'s youth. We enjoy it very much.

*Wednesday, March 22*   Start of spring. R. works and says, "Under your protection everything flourishes and succeeds." From the post office I bring the children a letter and a parcel from their grandmama. The old times rise up before me, I think sorrowfully of Hans; also of the old lady, whose life, I believe, I did make somewhat easier. As I enter the house, I ask myself: Why did it have to happen just like this? The sounds of *Tristan* answer me: Richter is playing the 3rd act, and I understand everything! (Drank the Emperor's health.)

*Thursday, March 23*   The day passes in preparations for my mother. I sort out papers and read old letters from my father, which show me once again that I had neither a father nor a mother. R. has been everything to me, he alone has loved me. — In Paris the insurgents rule the roost; they demand money from the bank and from Rothschild, and get it! Shoot generals, and people negotiate with them. Napoleonic intrigues are suspected. I teach the children R.'s *"Kaiserlied,"* which they sing very nicely. R. spends a long time considering how to add it to the score, for on no account does he want choral societies and glee clubs to sing it. Thought a lot about Strassburg.

*Friday, March 24*   Nothing from Munich. Instead, a letter of refusal from Prince Hohenlohe. "That is what has become of the aristocrats —they are all bureaucrats." — The situation in Paris is becoming more and more unbelievable. — At 1 o'clock to the railroad station to meet my mother. She does not arrive, which casts a slight shadow over the reception ceremony. But at 6 o'clock she arrives, and we spend the evening talking. She is well in spite of what she has been through and now faces.

*Saturday, March 25* Stormy day, talked over the past and future with my mother. She likes it here. I feel very strange toward her, but she is pleasant company because of her wide education. We talk a lot and about all sorts of things, the conditions in Paris are horrifying.

*Sunday, March 26* Letter from Prof. Nietzsche in Lugano. Family lunch; my mother finds the children very well mannered and well behaved, but they seem to her very pale, for which the cough which afflicted them all is to blame. In the afternoon quartets, but the players are not in such good form as usual. — Richter receives a letter from Munich. There people are talking of an arrangement between Tribschen, the King, and the Emperor to present the *Nibelungen* in Bayreuth. We compare this piece of news with the silence toward us and ask ourselves what it means; is there some mischief brewing? . . . I am fearful. (Rothschild sends the bill of exchange to "Frau Wagner.")

*Monday, March 27* Letter to Hedwig Neumann in Berlin regarding finding an apartment; also to Käthchen. Sent the 1,000 francs to the savings bank; I now have 8,141 francs laid aside for the children. Visit from Count Bassenheim, who inflicts a dismal afternoon on me, since I did not know how to get rid of him and R. does not like being alone with my mother; he says he can talk only to and with me, it depends on me whether he flies or creeps. My mother gets Richter to play many things from R.'s works and seems overwhelmed by this glimpse into a (for her) totally new world. — Everyone early to bed.

*Tuesday, March 28* A Silesian newspaper has published an article about *Beethoven*; the deliberate forgery puts into R.'s mind the idea of a "distraint," and he intends to prove the forgery, but I beg him to ignore it. — We also found out recently that the "Ride of the Valkyries" had been printed and sold in Leipzig; R. very indignant, writes to the conductor Eckert and to his publisher Schott, so that the latter may take the necessary steps with regard to this indiscretion. Wretched weather, we drive to Countess Bassenheim's, she is very friendly, but a little agitated. In the evening chatted with my mother.

*Wednesday, March 29* We learn that the life insurance cannot be sold; I write to the lawyer in Paris, who is also unable to send me anything in the present circumstances. Work with the children, whom my mother likes very much. In the afternoon a visit from Countess Bassenheim (calmer). Walk with my mother in a lovely sunset. In the evening R. reads the first act of *Tristan*, which impresses me with its sublime perfection and moves me indescribably.

*Thursday, March 30* Letters from Elisabeth Krockow, Claire, etc. Terrible weather and frightful news of Paris. I answer everything at once and work with the children. R. copies out his *Destiny of Opera*. Still nothing from the King. Great disturbances in church and state: the priest Egli in Lucerne, who will not recognize the dogma, and the nuncio, whom Bern is expelling. Only in Tribschen happiness. "Your love means the end of the world for me," R. says. "If you love me, I lose the outside world; if you do not love me, I lose both worlds." — In the evening Wagnerian music, the prayer from *Lohengrin* reduces my mother to tears.

*Friday, March 31* Lovely weather again, lovely walk to Winkel. In the evening music from *Tannhäuser*, otherwise just repetition of the difficulties with my mother. R.'s love is my only refuge, I know no other!

*Saturday, April 1* The children amusing themselves with April Fools' pranks; everything very quiet. R. copies *The Destiny of Opera*, I write some letters. Yesterday's lovely weather is followed today by the most dismal, on top of that the most atrocious of news from Paris. We kill time in conversation but the mood is despondent. (Noisy departure of our cook.)

*Sunday, April 2* My mother leaves us; R. thanks her for having come, I am very moved as I embrace her for the last time; all the sadness of life overcomes me! Dismal return home in dismal weather; R. offended by a joke on my part, I somewhat pained by his touchiness; everyone with colds and indisposed; nothing from outside which could count as bad. (Rothschild sends me 1,000 francs too many.)

*Monday, April 3* R. comes to my bed in the very early morning, kisses my hands and feet, says that if anything is guilty of casting a shadow between us it is the abundance of our feelings for each other that makes us so sensitive. Deep happiness, a feeling of redemption! — At breakfast Prof. Nietzsche is suddenly announced, he comes from Lugano and will spend some days here. He appears very run down. We go through the "*Kaisermarsch*," the German poem, and finally the lecture. Thus the day passes.

*Tuesday, April 4* A letter from Councilor Düffl[ipp]—the same old song! The King wants *Siegfried* and is offended by R.'s writing so truthfully about the performances in Munich. However, he wishes to send D. R. arranges for a meeting in Augsburg, but he is sad, for once again he has not been understood. Yesterday I received a letter from Frau Wesendonck, who is traveling to Germany with her family. Her letter is of no account, yet I am attracted by everything which comes from this quarter, since she was once so good to R. — Letter from Cornelius, my poem is not ready yet. Good article on *Beethoven* in an English periodical (*Academy*), the author (*Franz Hüffer*) a German acquaintance of Prof. Nietzsche's and a former opponent of R. Ottilie also writes, she is looking forward to seeing us. The thought of going away depresses me; I feel as if in leaving Tribschen I am not doing right.

*Wednesday, April 5* Prof. N. reads to me from a work (*The Origin and Aim of Greek Tragedy*) which he wants to dedicate to R.; great delight over that; in it one sees a gifted man imbued with R.'s ideas in his own way. We are spending these days in a lively discussion of our plans. Dr. Gruppe writes from Berlin that R. can give his lecture there on the 28th. Luise Brockhaus announces her removal and the marriage of her granddaughter to Arnold Frege, which makes me smile: hardly separated from this family, I am again connected with it through R.'s relations! The world is indeed small. (Walk to Winkel.)

*Thursday, April 6* Continuation of the reading; letter from Countess Krockow, who is anxious to see me and will come to Berlin. Councilor Düffl. also writes to me, he has sent off the costumes; only dear Cornelius is leaving me in the lurch. My father writes to Loulou and hopes to see us all soon! In the evening went through *Siegfried* (2nd act).

*Friday, April 7* Good Friday. The children do not go to church, their bad coughs are still persisting. Final reading of the essay. Letter from my friend Hedwig, the accommodation arrangements in Berlin have been made. And so everything is ready, and we leave next week. In the evening music from *Tristan*.

*Saturday, April 8* Prof. Nietzsche departs, after making the children happy with a green snake. Lovely, but rather enervating spring air. I write letters; R. drafts some lines to be distributed among the patrons of our undertaking. Great tiredness—why do I so fear this journey?

*Sunday, April 9* Easter eggs; the children search for and find them and are happy. Fidi also finds an egg; his "Papa" is already giving R. much delight. — In the outside world Döllinger and the Commune; when I went walking with R., he said, "I should like to tell all reformers to study human nature and to realize what a miracle it is that we have not all gobbled one another up, that things still go on as they do, and that they should consequently worship all such things as hereditary monarchy as divine manifestations, instead of emphasizing their absurd aspects; for by rights—men being what they are—we should have devoured one another long ago." — Over beer we discuss our prospects; my heart feels very heavy—God knows what now lies before us! All that remains for me is to be worthy of R. and never to show him any signs of faintheartedness. Today I had to weep on his shoulder; the King will demand *Siegfried*, and what then? In the evening at last took up Gibbon again.

*Monday, April 10* Loldi's birthday. Celebrations. — Twenty Jesuits shot dead in Paris. "Not the right way," says R. "These people should be destroyed only through the power of the state, that is to say, they should be driven out as corrupters of mankind." Letter from Claire. I write to my mother, who is waiting (in Geneva) for an early restoration of order in Paris. To Countess Bassenheim's; the rumor is going around that Döllinger is to be appointed minister of culture, which R. finds excellent, though we cannot understand how our young master came on this idea. — In the *Musikalische Zeitung* there is an article on Gluck which astonishes R. greatly; Gluck is quoted as talking about the performance of his works and declaring that the performance lacks soul when the composer is not present. R. announces to me that Richter is to leave us (because he wants to assist his mother in Vienna), and he asks me to lend him a thousand francs from my savings so that he can give Richter a small present. I do it willingly, though with a heavy heart; I feel as if we shall never be able to set anything aside, God help us! My mood regarding our journey is becoming more and more despondent, it seems like blasphemy for me to seek contact with the outside world again. Fidi indisposed.

*Tuesday, April 11* Very warm. Preparations for departure. Fidi very unwell; great concern; R. despondent. The face of a sick child hardly bearable. In the evening R. looks through Frau W[esendonck]'s *Friedrich* and describes it as "foolery." Letter from M. Meysenbug, full of disgust with the mess in France.

*Wednesday, April 12* R. decides to conduct a concert in Berlin for the Foundation for Disabled Soldiers, and I write to Karl Tausig asking him to announce this and to have the necessary arrangements made. (Long interruption, I restart my diary in Berlin on the 26th and must now see how I can reconstruct the days.) [*From this point the handwriting has been traced over. Some of the letters suggest R. W.'s hand.*]

*Thursday, April 13* My eye affliction troubles me so severely that I think seriously of going blind; how to bear this—not only to bear it but to welcome it as an act of atonement—occupies me throughout the night. When I wake, Fidi is brought into my room, his face is as white as a corpse, a terrible shock. Yesterday he had been wrapped in cold cloths (his feet), was left alone by his nurse, woke up, and cried; R. alone heard him, rushed to him, and found him standing up, prey to a chill. R. utterly beside himself, believes his appearance to be the result of this chill. The doctor reassures us. We had already given up our journey, but resume it.

*Friday, April 14* Day of packing and saying goodbye, family lunch and many tears!

*Saturday, April 15* At 5 o'clock kissed the (sleeping) children, then off, dread in my heart. (Thoughts of R.'s being murdered by a Berlin Jew.) A wait in Zurich, telegraphed and wrote to the children. In the evening neither Düfflipp nor Cornelius at the station, which surprises us. Misunderstandings—we come together in the Drei Mohren hotel, where attempts are made to whitewash the Moors. Düfflipp not difficult, tells us the cheerless news that the King has been thinking of performing the two acts of *Siegfried*, since the third is not ready. R. becomes very solemn and says he would burn his *Siegfried* before yielding it up like that, and then go out begging.

*Sunday, April 16*  Went to the museum with Cornelius while R. discussed matters with D. Lovely works, a very stylish Moretto, a very beautiful Holbein, and above all a head by da Vinci which had an indescribable effect on me. At 1 o'clock continued on to Nuremberg. Pleasant arrival there; en route a Bavarian officer who had been through the campaign and on whom we gazed with downright veneration.

*Monday, April 17*  A good night in Nuremberg; go out early in the rain, pleasure in everything we see there, but the overwhelming impression comes from Dürer's *Christus*, tears of emotion, this is the German character in all its goodness, its purely human and calm sublimity; it has nothing in common with Spanish ecstasy or asceticism; it is more moving than these, which can sometimes seem to us cruel, indeed even cold. Left at one o'clock, in Bayreuth at five. Charming impression of the town.

*[In the middle of the above entry the tracing is discontinued, apart from a few individual words in the subsequent lines.]*

*Tuesday, April 18*  Terrible night of worry and alarm. R. wakes up suddenly with fits of shivering; I send for the doctor, who is pensive, wants to wait and see how it goes, but cannot help laughing and saying: "The things that can happen to one! Who could have told me that I should this night be making the acquaintance of R. Wagner?" As he came in, he asked, "Are you *the* Richard Wagner, I mean the particular R. Wagner?" Whereupon R.: "If you mean the one who has written such pretty things—yes, I am he." — R. gets somewhat better, but has to stay in bed, I read [Goethe's] *Italian Journey* to him and receive a visit from Frau Raila, whose husband is a captain and was wounded at Sedan.

*Wednesday, April 19*  R. would by now be quite restored if a shocking noise in the hotel had not laid the whole night waste. Some gentlemen were giving a party and behaving like the roughest of coach drivers. We drive to the theater, a charming monument which tells us much about the productivity of German art in the 18th century. In the florid ornaments, shells, etc., of the eighteenth century one finds the same spirit of fantasy, though of course much distorted, which inspired German work in the 16th century. But the theater will not do for us at all; so we must build—and all the better. Now to find a house. With the curator of the palace we drive all over the town, nothing is quite suitable, so we must build for ourselves, too. Lovely drive to the Eremitage; the old curator there is delighted to see R. and says that it was only the priests who separated R. from the King, the people love him. In the evening R. is very tired. The Bayreuth population in an uproar over his presence.

*Thursday, April 20*   Left at 1 o'clock; at the railroad station an old ballad-singer, selling his poems (among others, about Richard)—this should really be the job of our Peter C[ornelius]. Another man, a cripple, terrible to look at, touches us deeply—how sprightly he makes one feel! How to atone for it? Infinite kindness, heartfelt sympathy. R. gives the man a little something, and, since the people rudely never shut the door, I beg the man to assume the duty of door shutter, which the poor creature performs with the utmost conscientiousness. At 10 o'clock in Leipzig, where Parson Clemens [Brockhaus] is at the station. Entry into the Hôtel de Prusse, laurel wreaths, poems, transparencies, and so on; rooms in the royal apartment. Spent the evening very pleasantly with Hermann Brockhaus and Ottilie.

*Friday, April 21*   In the morning the conductor Schmidt, the rehearsal at 12. Richard greeted with a flourish, everything well and good, but the orchestra! In despair R. takes the baton himself, but nothing sounds right—a terrible decline! R. so perturbed that he writes to Tausig, who had informed him that at the Emperor's command everything in Berlin would be at his disposal, telling him he does not wish to conduct the concert. Dinner with the Brockhauses and a Prof. Danz from Jena. R. makes much fun, particularly about the theater director Haase and his producer v. Strantz, whose inimitable dignity of comportment is to him like a ghostly breath from the past. He says this was what W[ilhelm] Meister was striving for; we laugh heartily at his funny demonstration. Hermann we find immensely engaging. — In the evening to Clemens in the parsonage; a very congenial gathering; in Hermann we recognize a charming and very original character, much depth beneath the refinement—"an engaging, eloquently intellectual, reserved character," as R. says.

*Saturday, April 22*   Morning with the family, at one o'clock on to Dresden, to escape the Leipzig *Meistersinger*, set down for today. At the railroad station Councilor Pusinelli, who has found us splendid lodgings in the Tower (Hotel Weber). Charming impression of Dresden, saw the house in which R. composed *Tannhäuser*. Then to his sister Luise; friendly but melancholy reception, for she has lost a grandson and son-in-law in the war. Spent the evening with the Pusinellis, homely family atmosphere—"*Seid umschlungen Millionen,*" for the children are innumerable.

*Sunday, April 23* Reunion with Countess Krockow, much to my delight. Went for a walk with her, the Brühl terrace, Wesendoncks, etc. At two o'clock to Luise's for lunch, she is pleased with her brother, finds he has become gentler, "fatherly," thanks me for my courage, my courage is my happiness. In the evening to the theater, the wooden barn does not displease R., it holds a lot of people; he observes everything with an eye toward Bayreuth. The actors beneath all criticism, their vulgarity, stupidity etc., etc., is now common throughout Germany. Sad impression.

*Monday, April 24* In the morning a knock at the door. Who is there? I. Who? Karl Pusinelli. A splendid boy, whom I earmark as a friend for Fidi. At 10 o'clock went to the picture gallery, above all to show R. [Titian's] *Christ and the Tribute Money*. At first he was downright disconcerted by the individuality of Christ's face, but then all the wonder of the work came through to him—he thought it "not without a hint of *aristocratic* superiority." My favorite Madonna by Titian also pleased him vastly, much to my joy. After her I show him almost the whole gallery, ending in meditation in front of [Raphael's] *Sistine Madonna*. As a painter he [Titian] is the greatest technician, his pictures kill the Veroneses, van Dycks and Rubenses, but not Raphael, the *Leda* of Michelangelo, or Holbein. At 4 to lunch with the Pusinellis. R. climbs the highest tree in the garden. After lunch we are both very tired; an infinite melancholy takes possession of me; while my friends are all attending the performance of *Die Meistersinger*, we wander in the evening through the streets of Dresden; when will death at last come to us? When we are with the children we are conscious of our duty to go on living, but when we are with other people, the longing for death comes over us with almost unconquerable force. I see the shop where R. sold Schiller's poems in order to buy cream puffs; and where he gave a disabled soldier money and was seen by his father from the house opposite. I also saw the gruesome "Stille Musik," and R. told me what effect the terrace, the Frauenkirche, etc., had on him in his youth. We near the theater, and I wish to hear how far they have got in *Die Meistersinger*; from far away we could hear it, but close to we hear nothing, then suddenly a run on the clarinet comes through to us—it sounds like *Tristan und Isolde*! We return home; it is cold outside and I cannot help weeping.

*Tuesday, April 25* Packed with the help of Countess Krockow; visited Frau von Marenholtz with R., a melancholy reunion. His sister Luise with us up to our departure, the members of the orchestra at the station: "If only we could play once more under your baton!" — Off to Berlin. I feel shut up inside, God knows I no longer belong among people. Arrived at 10 o'clock; met with flowers, to the hotel.

Marie Schleinitz very friendly and warm, everything Wagner asked for (3 rehearsals, so-and-so-many violins, etc.) has been granted. Wagner very pleased with the friendly lady.

*Wednesday, April 26* Many disturbances, visit to the office of the royal household, notifications of banquets and tributes, which alarm R., fears of the concert, in the evening with the conductor Eckert, all good people but, it seems, bad musicians.

*Thursday, April 27* Many visits, dinner with Frau von Schleinitz, Tausig so changed that we scarcely recognize him; amazement on my part at the tone in which Bismarck is talked about—"more luck than judgment, no character." Saw Lothar Bucher again, much joy. Johanna now the sentimental niece after having at the height of her career behaved very badly indeed. Hôtel du Parc, where we are staying, much besieged and noisy. After the ministerial banquet a walk through Berlin, we wish to visit our old friend [Alwine] Frommann in the palace; the guards are just closing the gates, but open them again for us, we wander through the courtyards, but no "academic artist" is to be found, we ask the Court apothecary, get lost several times, but at last find her. We ring. Long silence, then at last: "Who is there?" (in a complaining voice). Answer: "Wagner." Long silence, then, pitiably: "Oh, dear!" I: "Can we come in?" "Alas, no—I am in bed." "Will you have lunch with us tomorrow?" "Gladly." "At 2 o'clock?" "I shall be in the palace then." "At 3?" "People are coming to you then." — All this through the mailbox opening, as if it were coming from the cellar. R. and I are reminded of old Moor and feel like shuddering at this ghostly apparition. Earlier something unbelievable, even more sinister, had already happened to us: as we leave Frau v. Schleinitz, my foot is hurting me, R. summons a hansom, behind him a powerful voice cries, "Cabby!" He turns—*Dr. Julius Lang* is standing there! It makes us feel dreadful, for we believed him to be in Pest; has he turned up again to compromise R. here, as in Munich? What does it mean? — It results in a horrible night for me, I see nothing but Jesuit intrigues coiling themselves around R., everything seems to point in that direction, I feel like waking him, begging him to go away tomorrow, but I am held back by the consideration that a moment's sleep is more valuable than centuries of knowledge. Strange nightmares from which the morning at last frees me.

*Friday, April 28* Ever deeper into the miseries of the world! R. says, "One has only to want something, and one is at once vulnerable." But everyone so far friendly. At midday in the hotel a visit from Alwine Frommann, which gave us great pleasure. She is utterly *ancien régime* and in good humor, which we did not expect after the "old Moor" incident. We go for a walk with her. At 6 o'clock Dr. Gruppe calls to conduct R. to his lecture in the Academy. He comes home toward 9 o'clock; he laughs and says that the whole enterprise had been mad, he had expected large public sittings such as take place in Paris, but the Academy of Sciences was not even present, and at the green table he read his thing out to musicians, sculptors, and painters. He was introduced to each in turn, came to Joachim, who said, "It is a long time since I last saw you." "A long time indeed," R. replied. To Dorn R. said, "I should not have expected to see you here," whereupon the insolent man replied, "I am always interested in anything you do." And so on. In the evening we had guests, and R. related all this in front of Dohm, Heigel, Tausig, and young Hellwig, who is a bit green and pert.

*Saturday, April 29* We keep this morning free in order to visit the aquarium; great impression: it turns one into a philosopher, here one comes to realize that Man is also nothing but an animal with desires, here one understands that only renunciation can provide an ending to this terrible hell of existence; the grabbing plants are a horrible sight! We discover the human countenance everywhere, wherever one looks either stupid placidity or horrible covetousness. I feel the urge to tell R. here how much I love him, whereas he always, everywhere, and in front of everybody says that I alone knew how to help him, that he is literally submerged in me, that he wants nothing that excludes me. Breakfasted at home, in the evening with Frau von Schleinitz. R. reads *Parzival* to her and Princess Liechtenstein; indescribable emotion; if no single tone of it, no verse ever gets written, this draft is eternal and perhaps the sublimest vision R. has ever beheld. — Eckert calls to take R. to the banquet, during which Councilor Bucher visits me and tells me many interesting things about his stay in Versailles. The most curious thing about it is certainly, as we recently heard from Alwine, that the leading figures in the war were by no means of one mind. R. returns at about 2 in the morning. According to him the banquet was quite a handsome one, a nice toast was proposed to him (by Herr Tappert), whereupon he made a reply in which he described his idea in detail.

*Sunday, April 30* At 12 o'clock our old friend Weitzmann comes to conduct us to the Singakademie, where R. is to be received; it all takes place in the friendliest way; the orchestra, consisting of various poor musicians, plays the *Faust* Overture and the *Tannhäuser* March, not at all badly, so nicely, in fact, that R. feels disposed to say a few words and then to take up the baton and conduct the Overture again, amid great applause. Dohm's prologue (spoken by niece Johanna) was very pretty. R. was genuinely moved, and the whole thing was much better than expected. But afterward R. is very tired, we go home, he lies down; then a conversation with Prince Georg proves a tremendous strain on him, for the Prince, in spite of much good will, does not really know what it is all about, and is hardly capable of understanding. In the evening to Wallner's theater with our nice and modest friends the Neumanns.

*Monday, May 1* Dismal weather, but good news from the children, to whom I have been writing every other day. Visit from Karl Eckert, who brings all sorts of unpleasant news. First of all, I had been obliged to visit Frau Mallinger last Saturday in order to request her to sing, now I hear that she will not do so after all; then Walter telegraphs that he cannot come. The difficulty of making people understand that R. has really nothing at all to do with the concert, since he would prefer not to give it. R. is now writing to Councilor D[üfflipp], from whom we found a very discouraging letter awaiting us here; the King does not really like our project, he wishes to keep everything for himself in Munich. R. answers very earnestly, saying that this is his final plan; if it is not approved, he will give it up and live only for his family. He tells me how blissful he feels to be able to write about his family. He thinks of the children practically all the time with the most touching tenderness, he is happy to know these little creatures are waiting for us back there in Paradise. Everybody thinks he has grown so mild, and also that he is looking very well. Visit from Prince Georg. Then R. gets ready to visit Bismarck, *Bancroft* (who left a card here yesterday), and Countess Pourtalès. I am always in fear that he will not be able to see it through, yesterday he cried out when he saw a poor cab-horse which for sheer misery and exhaustion could no longer walk slowly, but lurched from side to side in a sad gallop; he then showed me the passage in his *Beethoven* depicting the different ways in which the saint and the artist bear the sorrows of life; in that connection, R. says, "I should never be able to live in a large city." At 9 o'clock with His Excellency, a mixed company, R. reads aloud his *Destiny of Opera* and excites interest in it. Reichensperger talks with him at length about it. All the same, we return home tired.

*Tuesday, May 2* Bad night for R., but at 10 o'clock to the rehearsal. R. greeted with a flourish; the orchestra seems to us better than previously, and the people exert themselves. R., however, when he is conducting, gives his heart's blood and a portion of his life, so I feel sad, even though enchanted. Arrival of the engravings; they do not satisfy me, but the engraver reports the tremendous success of the "*Kaisermarsch*" in Munich. R. goes to bed, I receive visitors. In the evening Tausig comes and plays Bach chorales for us. Lothar Bucher came and on Bismarck's behest asked R. to call on the Prince.

*Wednesday, May 3* (Day of Repentance) R. very indisposed, had another bad night! Betz rehearses "Wotan's Farewell," I go then to see Alwine Frommann, whose association is dear and valuable to me. At 4 o'clock dinner with Cäcilie Avenarius, then I go to the Repentance concert with Ernst Dohm. Bancroft sits beside me; bad acoustics, *Eroica* Symphony wretched. Everyone in black, since it is an occasion of mourning in honor of the fallen. Also the Violin Aria by Spohr and a banal Requiem for Male Voices by Cherubini; worldly stupidity and obtuseness! I return home and R. drives to see the Prince, who had invited him. [*For the rest of this entry all the words have been traced over, possibly by R. W.*] He returns highly satisfied, a great and simple character having been revealed to him. When R. gives expression to his respect, Bismarck says, "The only thing that can count as an accomplishment is that now and then I have obtained a signature." And then, "All I did was to find the hole in the crown through which the smoke could rise." R. is utterly enchanted with the genuine charm of his character, not a trace of reticence, an easy tone, the most cordial communicativeness, all of it arousing trust and sympathy. "But," says R., "we can only observe each other, each in his own sphere; to have anything to do with him, to win him over, to ask him to support my cause, would not occur to me. But this meeting remains very precious to me."

[*End of the third notebook of the Diaries.*]

*Thursday, May 4* Many visitors, among them Frau Mallinger, who says there has just been a rehearsal of *Mignon*; great vexation for Richard, who sees at once that he cannot put the orchestra to further exertion. All the same we drive at 2 o'clock to the opera house, and he asks the musicians whether they are prepared to work seriously with him; if they feel too tired, he would prefer to give up his undertaking. They unanimously declare in favor of the rehearsal. Great tiredness afterward. In the evening, arrival of the Krockows, with whom we spend the evening (the Eckerts also come).

*Friday, May 5* At 10 o'clock to the final rehearsal in the opera house; listened to it surrounded by friends; it goes very well. Before leaving, R. speaks once more to the stage technicians regarding a little dais for the singers, Herr v. Hülsen happens to be there, he rushes back into the wings, and I notice great embarrassment among the workers. I ask Käthchen whether anything has happened, and she tells me that "the large and imposing gentleman" (v. Hülsen) has just made a terrible onslaught on his people and told them they should not obey Wagner, the man has no right to give orders here, his job is just to wield the baton—and all this spoken in a towering rage, the poor harried, ignored manager! I say nothing to R., but send for Eckert and ask him to attend to it. I am overcome by overtiredness, am put to bed, giddiness, fainting fits, and God knows what else prevent my getting dressed; a quarter of an hour before the concert, when R. is about to cancel it on my account, I pull myself together, throw my dress over my head, and drive with R. to the concert. The auditorium in festive mood, the Court present, it all goes well, the orchestra makes a lovely sound (thanks to the acoustic barrier R. had erected), unanimous, unending applause. My main impression the C Minor Symphony. R. satisfied, and our dear good minister's wife beaming. (Beforehand another little Hülsen episode: he forbids the podium to be decorated and orders the box attendants to admit no one with flowers. Frau v. Schl[einitz] hears of this, confronts him with it, and receives the reply that it was a misunderstanding, so flowers were then thrown in plenty.) — R. reaches home in quite a good mood, feeling touched by the good will of the orchestra. Before the performance the first violinist came to him and begged his forbearance, saying, "You have no idea how these things (the symphonies) are rattled off here." —

*Saturday, May 6* We spend the day in bed and see only our good [Alwine] Frommann and [Elisabeth] Krockow. We get up in the evening to visit Johanna Jachmann. A large gathering; she sings "Elisabeth's Prayer," "*Blick ich umher,*" and the "*Abendstern.*" We are quite impressed with her husband, the district magistrate. We get to know Countess Danckelmann, a passionate devotee, and we seek support for Bayreuth.

*Sunday, May 7* Letter from the children; they are well. Longing for them; R. feels moved whenever he thinks of them, he also constantly asks me what people must think knowing that he has me, how relieved they must feel about him. My friend Frau Dirksen was quite amazed when he declared to her the day before yesterday that, if I were still ill, he had no intention of conducting the concert. On Thursday evening I asked him to promise me that we should die together, whereupon he replied that we had loved each other and had come together—Fate, the stars, would continue to look after us. — At 12 o'clock breakfast with Tausig at Marie Schleinitz's house. The minister tells us the Emperor claims never to have heard anything so perfect as this concert, it was *sublime.* General Beyer had heard R. conducting the *Faust* Overture in the morning concert and told the Emperor he had never heard anything like it. — After breakfast the selection of the committee members, whereupon I drive to the Wesendoncks' to invite him to take part, but obtain little satisfaction there. R. at the same time goes with Tausig to seek out "the touching Jew" Löser, orders cigars for him, and gives him his pamphlets in gratitude. On the journey he tells Tausig how and for what he is living, and speaks of Fidi, whereupon Tausig exclaims, "He must be a splendid boy." —

In the evening dinner with Eckerts, very pleasant, then some friends at home.

*Monday, May 8*    Early in the morning drove (with Elisabeth Krockow) to the cemetery, where I visit Daniel's grave. Somber mood; he was the victim of my father's and mother's thoughtlessness and the cruel indifference of Princess Wittgenstein; at the time I was too young and inexperienced to oppose them effectively and take firm measures. Much soreness of heart standing at this grave; where are you now, my brother, whither are you wandering, where is your pure spirit suffering or resting? In my soul you live on; have my children, Siegfried perhaps, absorbed your being? — Spoke about him with Elisabeth, who knew him well. Then departed from Berlin as if in a dream, all is vain to those who have looked upon death. At 5 o'clock arrived in Leipzig and were cordially welcomed by the Brockhaus family, with whom (Querstrasse 15) we spend a delightful evening. Ottilie and Hermann beings beyond compare.

*Tuesday, May 9*    Today Daniel would have been 32 years old. . . . Grandmama was also born on this day. — We wander, R. and I, through the city to make purchases for the children, who write me sweet letters. Councilor Düfflipp has now also written; the King will give 25,000 thalers toward our venture, but otherwise wants nothing to do with it, he is upset by the infallibility movement and is engaged in so much that his budget is completely committed. — In the evening a party consisting of young professors, to whom R. reads his *Nicht kapituliert*. Schuré's brother-in-law, Nessler, a musician, whom R. met by chance in the street, says that Schuré intends to have nothing more to do with politics. The Commune has taken care of that!

*Wednesday, May 10*    Hermann reports that the peace has now been ratified in Frankfurt. So Bucher was right when he wrote to me, just before leaving, that we would restore peace to the world. R. writes letters, then he shows me the house "Zum Roth und Weissen Löwen," and we visit the apartment in which he was born; I also see Jeannettchen Thomé's house. R. is very tired and goes to bed early, I stay up with the dear, kind family. (In the afternoon drove to the Rosental.)

*Thursday, May 11*    To the eye specialist *Ceccius* on account of my eyes, he says the affliction is of nervous origin; then purchases for the children. In the evening a party at the Brockhauses', with Prof. Ebers, the Egyptologist, and Prof. Czermak, with whom R. converses about his pamphlet on colors, which he sent to us at Tribschen; R. reproaches him for having written too thoughtlessly about Schopenhauer, to whom he does after all ascribe prophetic gifts. I learn this evening from Clemens Br[ockhaus] that Prof. Nietzsche has now dedicated his *Homer*, which he once dedicated to me, to his sister, and with the same poem. I had to laugh at first, but then, after discussing it with R., see it as a dubious streak, an addiction to treachery, as it were —as if he were seeking to avenge himself for some great impression.

*Friday, May 12* Visited Prof. Czermak's auditorium, which he, though now mortally ill, had built, also his house, there meeting his Jewish wife; little pleasure from any of this. The most pleasure from contact with the family—Hermann charming in both character and intelligence, Ottilie original and good, showing decided resemblances to R. in character. In the afternoon Prof. Ebers giving us a lecture with pictures of Egypt; he is a Jew and his talk is shallow and facile. Family evening with a discussion between R. and Hermann about beauty, which R. claims has vanished forever from the world, while Hermann, optimistically stressing the greatness of our times, confidently expects these to achieve beauty as well.

*Saturday, May 13* Affectionate parting from the dear people with whom we have felt so much at home. I pack once more for R., and he says it is like a dream, the way I scold him for his untidiness, it makes him feel so good, and everyone is amazed how well he looks. Booked tickets for Darmstadt, the joy of being alone together in the carriage; we talk about old times, R. says he does not wish to think of them, for we had been separated then, a wild and desolate dream! Delight in Thuringia, but melancholy feelings while passing Weimar, my father is there and I am not seeing him. At 8 o'clock in Frankfurt, went for a walk, thought of Schopenhauer, also of the day (August 1862) when I expressed to R. my willingness to sit in a wheelbarrow if he would push it, as he proposed in the Schwanplatz. Arrived at the Traube in Darmstadt at 10 o'clock, drank some punch, and went to bed.

*Sunday, May 14* Slept well, awoke in good spirits, at 10 o'clock the machinist Brandt, with whom R. discusses the arrangements for our future stage. During this I write to Richter, who from Vienna tells us of the rumor that royalty payments for *Lohengrin* and *Tannhäuser* have now been secured after all. God knows whether this is true, I had instructed Richter to tell my father of the behavior of Prince H[ohenlohe]. After lunch promenaded in the Court gardens, then continued the rail journey to Heidelberg. Lovely evening, saw the ruins in the splendor of a sunset, walked in the garden, had dinner on the terrace, then wandered home along the leafy garden paths in excellent spirits. R. has already been here, I ask him why he had never talked about it. He said it had been such a dismal time, he had walked here with Minna, it should not be difficult for me to imagine how distracted and indifferent his feelings. Reaching our street, we are on the point of going to look at the Neckar Bridge again when loud laughter coming from the square reminds me of the Kasperl theater I had noticed in passing during the day; I ask R. whether we should not visit it, and, since he assented, we had an evening of the most splendid entertainment. We stood there rooted to the spot till past 10 o'clock and drew veritable consolation from the various ideas and fancies; the folk wit of the Germans is still alive. Particularly delicious was the rapport between the audience (mainly little boys) and Kasperl, they talked to each other, and the smallest of the children joined in the action. Richard gave the woman with the collection box a florin, and that may well have spurred the man on, for he worked untiringly until at last Kasperl came on in a herald's cloak and said the show was at an end. Why? Because the lights were being "spat out." Going to bed, we agree that this evening with our walk and the Kasperl was the nicest moment of our whole journey.

*Monday, May 15* Made some small purchases, tried in vain to see Kasperl's master, but his "niece," who sits beside the stall, tells us he is at home. Does he come from here? we ask. "No, from far away." We walk once more to the castle; birds singing and flowers blooming. At 1 o'clock took leave of Heidelberg. Met Count Dunken on the train. At 8 o'clock in Basel, where we spend a nice evening in the hotel with Prof. Nietzsche and our nephew Friedrich Brockhaus.

*Tuesday, May 16* Going home! Great impatience to get there, dull weather, at 2 o'clock we at last arrived! Loulou and Boni weeping for joy, the little ones quieter, Fidi magnificent, plump and sturdy, all well. Family lunch and then distribution of presents; played the whole afternoon and evening. At bedtime R. says to me, "Remain kind to me, you dispenser of bounty." Feeling of utter bliss to be back in his world.

*Wednesday, May 17* A rainy day; letter from Judith M[endès]. They are in Orléans. Her husband was condemned to death by the Commune, concealed, and escaped! Once again working with the children; later tried on the costumes they are to wear on R.'s birthday. Visit from our good Count B., welcoming us home. In the evening we read Clemens's wartime sermons, they are not of much significance. Early to bed, for we have much sleep to make up.

*Thursday, May 18* R. reports that Bismarck will probably become Lord Protector of France, for the Commune intends to acknowledge him as Prince of the Peace. With the children to the fair; watched the apes at play; R. also with us. Delight in the little ones. Conversed in the evening.

*Friday, May 19* The poem at last arrives, the children learn it in the garden. R. writes to Frau von Schleinitz. Emil Heckel from Mannheim writes introducing himself, after having read the green pamphlet. In the afternoon to Countess B.'s, R. also. Walking through the fairground, we are annoyed to see that in the paintings on the stalls the war is depicted from the French viewpoint, MacMahon theatrically urging on his troops. In the evening searched in Frederick the Great's account of the battle of Torgau to see whether he really speaks so badly of Ziethen, and yes, he does, which offends us.

*Saturday, May 20* Still learning the poem. R. has written to the King, believing him to have made a great sacrifice in not demanding *Siegfried*. We rehearse our poem. I also write to my mother. In the afternoon a walk with R.; joy at our return, lovely light, warm everywhere, but no sun, a great, salutary quietness—this is our dream refuge. Never to part, in this union we can bear everything.

*Sunday, May 21* Gave the two children a piano lesson. The music teacher Federlein also offers his services and sends his essay (on *Die Walküre*). Richard is now out walking, I stay at home, write to Claire, and continue rehearsing with the children. In the evening read once again in Carlyle about the Battle of Torgau and came to the conclusion that we had allowed ourselves to be led astray by the popular assumption that Ziethen had saved the battle, and by the legendary embrace; Frederick rebukes him with justice, and he does so in a remarkably regal and dignified way, for Ziethen had spoiled things for him entirely. Thus the great man is right as always, and one must believe him, for he knows no envy. A week ago today we were in Darmstadt. At midday I told R. how curious it was that all performances (5th Symphony, *Tristan, Meistersinger*), no matter how good, leave me to a certain extent cold, but I feel ecstatic when R. talks to me about Beethoven, when he tells me of his first conceptions; I cannot put myself in the position of the audience but, rather, feel as if the work becomes disassociated from me as soon as it takes on an outer form. R. says he feels exactly the same way, and he knows that we shall regard our *Nibelungen* theater with cold pleasure, watching and observing. "For ourselves we do not need it, our pleasures lie in the idea." —

*Monday, May 22* Awake all night thinking of R.: how my life would be unthinkable without him, how little I can contribute to his happiness, how dearly I should like to spare him every atom of pain. The night before Hans had appeared to me with gray hair and beard, weeping; that moved me greatly, yet I feel I must devote myself to R. — God grant that I may do it to his complete benefit! Up at 4 o'clock to arrange the *salon*; set up the statuettes around R.'s bust, as if in a grove; later the children in their costumes, Loulou as Senta, Boni Elisabeth, Eva Isolde, each in front of her "man"; at about 8 o'clock we are ready (I at the foot of the bust as Sieglinde with Fidi in my arms). We do our piece well and R. is happy, indeed moved, he says that as Sieglinde I remind him of our return from Italy. All the children do honor to their names, and R. praises the costumes. Amicable breakfast with the children and the loveliest of weather for the loveliest of our days! (Letters from Richter, Düfflipp, Meysenbug.) In the afternoon visit from Countess Bassenheim, drove out to Winkel with her, R., and all the children. On our return we found Prof. Nietzsche in the house. We perform our birthday greeting once again. R. says it touches him all too deeply to see me in the guise of Sieglinde. Prof. N. tells us that he intends to found a periodical, under R.'s auspices, two years hence, till then he will be busy preparing it. —

*Tuesday, May 23* Slept sweetly, in the morning further birthday greetings from the King, from Lindner the engraver (very original!), and many from Berlin, Vienna, etc. The weather is splendid, I work with the children in the garden. How beautiful this country and this home of ours! How difficult it would be to take leave of it if the population were not so malicious! Two evenings ago R. came home quite agitated; as he was walking over the Am Rhyn hill our nasty milkman shouted two horrible *French* swearwords after him; the cowardice of it, then the French innuendo, the malice—all this made us deeply indignant; and the peasants, who are well disposed toward us, just stood there and said nothing. — In the afternoon a letter from Marie Schleinitz: my father is joining the committee and desires a few lines from me and a meeting in a neutral place! — In the evening discussion about two letters which Bismarck and Moltke have written to Oskar von Redwitz about his "German Song"! R. says the aesthetic outlook of these great men is terrible. But Moltke's letter is remarkable for his refusal to accept a comparison with the heroes of ancient times, on the grounds that the latter always held their own in misfortune, whereas the German warriors had simply enjoyed good luck.

*Wednesday, May 24* R. is arranging his writings, which he intends to publish in chronological order, since he does not wish to be regarded as a poet or an author. I teach the children. In the afternoon a visit from Professor Nietzsche, R. accompanies him to the railroad station. Grief over the death of a canary, which the children bury; Loldi speaks the funeral oration: "Now you will fly no more and must be put in the ugly earth, we shall not see you again," etc.

*Thursday, May 25* Letter from Tausig, sending the circular. R. calls out to me that Paris is on fire, the Louvre in flames, whereupon I let out a cry of anguish which, R. observes, hardly 20 people in France would echo. I write to Marie Schleinitz, explaining to her why I do not write to my father and why I wish to see him only *here*. With R. I discussed my previous life with great bitterness; he said as far as his own was concerned he had the same feelings as Röckel regarding his 13 years in prison: a great loss of time, but otherwise no memory of it. — In the morning we discussed music: "It is the element into which everything plunges, the fluid element, and that is why it is foolish to talk of 'classical' music. Can one imitate Bach, as with luck one can imitate the style of Goethe or Lessing? Bach's, Mozart's individuality plunged into music." R. very unwell, also the children again beset by coughs. — A lovely evening, which makes me feel happy.

*Friday, May 26* Letter from my mother; in the way the French have of never being able to stop admiring themselves, she finds "*beaucoup de vie dans nos folies et nos ruines*"! R. says that I should write to her that the trouble on both sides is that we have been judging by appearances —we had long regarded the French as something special, and they judge us by our jagged outlines and despise us (my mother writes that Claire belittles the Germans). — In the *A.A.Z.* an article by Karl Gutzkow, who is not above comparing *Die Meistersinger von Nürnberg* with Flaubert's *Madame Bovary* and a picture by Makart! — Did not allow the children to work much, for they are unwell again; the whooping cough is starting all over again, it is all so hopeless! Sitting on the terrace over coffee, R. again speaks about Beethoven. In his story he described him as *gaunt*, which he does not appear to have been; rather he was dumpy. Yet, R. says, he must have been able to make a fascinating impression, so utterly unique was he. "I shall surely leave the world with my great longing to have seen and known a man I truly venerate, who has given me something, unsatisfied. In my childhood years I used to dream I had been with Shakespeare, had conversed with him; that was my longing finding expression." — Everything in Paris is burning.

*Saturday, May 27* Wet weather, for me camphor and pepper for the winter things. R. writes his foreword, which he calls "a box on the ears for Gutzkow." I say G. is not worthy to come before the collected works. "And he won't come there—this is a leaflet for the publisher." At midday arrival of our nephew Fritz Brockhaus, who pleases us very much with his intelligence and his kind heart. Prof. Nietzsche does not come, the events in Paris have upset him too much.

*Sunday, May 28* Nice day again; I write to Baron Schack and send him some brochures. At midday arrival of Prof. Nietzsche (with sister), whom Richard had summoned (over the signature Lindhorst) by telegram. R. speaks sharply to him about the fire and its significance: "If you are not capable of painting pictures again, you are not worthy of possessing them." Prof. N. says that for the scholar such events mean the end of all existence. Spoke of Bakunin—whether he was among the arsonists . . . After lunch drove out to Winkel in two carriages. Very lovely evening by moonlight in the hermitage. — (A linnet we had set free has returned and wants to remain in its cage, it flies in and out and gives us much pleasure.)

*Monday, May 29*   A piano teacher in Vienna offers R. a portion of his income for the art of the future; it is profoundly touching. Walk without R., but with the rest of the company, to the farm. At lunch the conversation turns to Mommsen, and Fritz quotes him as dubbing Sulla a country squire, just as he dubs Cicero a writer of *feuilletons*. Fritz maintains that there are analogies between positions and persons, but R. denies it utterly. He says that is exactly where the difference lies: what we have is writers of *feuilletons*, what they had was Cicero. We then come via the Roman patriciate to talk about the German aristocracy and the German "rights of the estates," which R. tremendously praises, he says it represents the only type of freedom where one knows quite definitely what is being guaranteed, which is various defined freedoms; with the other, more general type of freedom one does not really know of what it consists. — After lunch discussion about Aeschylus and the misunderstood saying that "he was always drunk," about actors, and also, in passing, about Sophocles; and that tragedy had certainly evolved out of improvisation. All this contributed by Prof. Nietzsche, together with Sophocles's saying about Aeschylus, that "he does the right thing without knowing it," which R. compares with Schopenhauer's saying about musicians—that they speak the highest wisdom in a language which their reason does not understand. — Our friends leave; R. is very worn out, I on the other hand feel happy in the lovely sunshine. R. calls me "a salamander" and is glad when I tell him what feelings of gratitude a fine summer's day arouses in me. But his indisposition alarms me and destroys my happiness. He is also preoccupied. I ask him anxiously what is the matter, and learn that he has all sorts of worries on his mind; firstly, his obligations in Vienna, which have not been met, then the large wine bill, an old debt with Kahnt the publisher, and no income to cover it all. Then Herr Fritzsch, to whom he had promised a composition and to whom he would like to give the funeral music for Weber's reburial, if only he knew where to find it; then his collected works; and finally some songs of his which have suddenly been published without his consent! All this was now passing through his mind, when really he should be thinking only of his *Nibelungen*. — All the same I am glad he has told me all this; to feel with him unquestionably provides me with my only support.

*Tuesday, May 30*   The Louvre is saved. — R. wraps himself in blankets, in order to get rid of an obstinate catarrh. It does him good. He remarks cheerfully at breakfast how well I look. He says: "You are lovelier than you used to be: previously your face looked earnest and severe, now you have in your eyes the gleam of joy I have seen in so few faces. Your father has good will, kindness, cordiality, but he does not have joy, and that is the divinest attribute of a human face. On the stage I saw it only once, in [Wilhelmine] Schröder-Devrient." He works, I teach the children; write sympathetically to my mother, amid the twittering dialogue of two blackbirds. Letter from Paris, Nuitter again, writing at the first possible opportunity. He feels the French have given the world a great lesson in wisdom. "Always," says R., "seeing themselves as the Redeemer, suffering for the whole world! Always the godlike people who have to go through everything for the sake of others." Great delight in a speech by Bismarck in the Reichstag, R. says how inestimable it is that Bismarck can now say quite calmly that the Prussians are an object of hatred, the Germans on the other hand are loved. Letter from Marie Schleinitz, who understands why I want to see my father only here, but she asks me to write to him, since he had authorized her to tell me that he wished for such a letter. I talk to R. about this; we think of Hans—what would his feelings be over a reconciliation of this kind? I fear, very bitter. In the evening read Carlyle's *Frederick the Great* with much enjoyment (the time following Kolin). How right Moltke is when he says that in misfortune the great reveal what they are!

*Wednesday, May 31* Another man from Vienna who offers himself and his resources for the art of the future. The King also writes from Hochkopf, and in a friendly way. Walked to the woods with the children; R. meanwhile forwards his collected works (the Jewish pamphlet is not to be included), that is to say, he sends the list of contents to Fritzsch. At lunch R. sings a theme by Beethoven (the second in the first movement of the F Minor Sonata) and says, "No one before him or after him has ever given us anything like that; it is sublimity when it becomes pleasurable; when it has been caught and one floats in it." During coffee on the terrace R. is enchanted by the sight of a little sailing boat gliding over the lake. "What is a steamboat in comparison? One turns one's eyes away, our whole modern world is reflected in it; well, yes, it has its uses, but one cannot expect it to provide motives any more for the painter." I write to Marie Schleinitz that I am expecting my father to approach me, but I cannot write to him. In the evening Carlyle's *Frederick the Great*.

*Thursday, June 1* Worked in the garden with the children, it is splendid weather. R. goes through the essays of his youth for the collected writings. I copy out the first scene of *Tannhäuser*. Family lunch and afterward drove to Countess B.'s. In the evening had supper in the garden, designed our house. — Will we ever bring all this into being?? Schuré is now writing in German again!

*Friday, June 2*  The lovely days soon disappear, today it is cold and wet; on top of it news of eternal killings in Paris. "Against petroleum you can only use napoleum," says R. Letter from Käthchen, she wants to come here, to work for me again. Plaintive letter from M. Maier about our wish to build, we shall run ourselves into debt, etc. No walk, in the evening Carlyle.

*Saturday, June 3*  Still cold. The cask of wine has arrived from the King. Also letters, one from "Bureau Peters," he is willing to pay 1,000 thalers for an overture. Then a letter from Lindner the engraver, who reports blissfully that his plate of R.'s portrait was sold immediately in Berlin for 1,400 florins and has, as he reports with much gratitude, brought him many orders. Pity that the portrait is not better. R. is pleased, he says, "So one sees in the end what one is worth." — The news from Paris is horrifying, I can no longer bear to look.

*Sunday, June 4*  Copy of the pantomime from *Rienzi*. R. receives a very nice letter from Heidelberg, someone putting himself forward as a patron. Also one from Herr Fürstner in Berlin, he had to pay the Paris publisher 1,400 francs for the 3 songs, whereas R. could get only 500 francs from the Paris publisher. R. very indignant. Stayed indoors on account of the persistent bad weather. In the evening *Frederick the Great* by Carlyle. — Over supper we discussed our *indispensables* and classified them thus: Homer, Aeschylus and Sophocles, the *Symposium*, *Don Quixote*, the whole of Shakespeare, and Goethe's *Faust*.

*Monday, June 5*  Weather still not good; work with the children, letters (to the publisher Durand). Went out in the afternoon; read in the newspapers of the celebrations of R.'s birthday in Munich, where his bust was wreathed in flowers amid endless rejoicing. Then of Hans's intention of traveling to America. Dismal feelings; will his children see him before he goes, or indeed ever again? Heavy evening sunk in my thoughts, "the sword within my heart, speechless with bitter smart." — How do I come by all my happiness? Praying and supplicating I lay myself down to rest.

*Tuesday, June 6*  At 4 in the morning R. comes to me with good wishes on Fidi's birthday; at about 8 o'clock the congratulations; a rocking horse, the children clustered around! R., very happy, calls out to me: Cosima la Dieudonnée! — Large family lunch. Fidi's health drunk. In his high spirits R., proposing it, imitates his friend Heine in Dresden; since I am not very much taken with it, R. says, "You do not care for my friend—well, that was the world which brought forth *Tannhäuser* and *Lohengrin*." As I laugh, he continues, "And it is just the same with the *Nibelungen* and with *Tristan*—not a whit different." Letter from my mother, which I answer at once. In the afternoon R.

reads me his piece on the reform of the Dresden theater, in which I was particularly touched by his ardent desire to improve the existing state of things before beginning to think of revolution. I urge R. earnestly to include this piece in the collected writings. R. tells me how Herr v. d. Pfordten, when he was given the piece to read, wrote remarks in the margin, and among other things R. found written, opposite the passage dealing with the question of raising the conductor's salary: "This is the crux of the matter." Pitiful wretches! — In the evening the Battle of Zorndorf. ("Mine look like country bumpkins"!)

*Wednesday, June 7* Cold and frosty weather, in which I do not feel at all well. — Letter from Richter, reporting that many supporters will be found in Vienna for our venture. — R. says one is becoming blunted by the newspapers these days, one reads the most appalling things as if they were nothing. — Great alarm over Lulu, who in falling down almost gouged out an eye. With the children morning and afternoon; R. plays folk songs to them; after he has finished, Loldi points to him and cries out, "This is the friend who plays for us"—which makes all of us laugh a lot. The rocking horse the joy of the household. In the evening R. reads me his *Wibelungen* and says of it, "I am glad to see that I did not drivel on as much as I had feared." — Yesterday R. again thought actively about his story concerning Frederick the Great! The time after the Battle of Leuthen. Meeting in Breslau with Lessing (the latter is not named); discussion on poetry, F. extolling the French, the young man pointing on the other hand to the Greeks, to Frederick's great annoyance. The poet is then recruited, makes an error, and is set at liberty by Frederick, who, *though without expressing it*, feels immense respect for him, while the poet, who has seen and observed Frederick in action, breaks out in expressions of great enthusiasm for him.

*Thursday, June 8* Work with the children, then family lunch and later family games. The weather is cold, we stay indoors. R. is not well. My heart is at times really heavy; the recent news of Hans weighs it down. In the evening the Battle of Hochkirch; delight in the splendid Prussians; silent in their heroism.

*Friday, June 9* Letter from E. Ollivier, announcing the birth of his second son; he also asks me why last June I tried to advise him to give up his ministry. — R. works on his collected writings. After lunch we discuss the art of Berlioz, and R. says: "Just as in Hugo there is a blatant misunderstanding of Shakespeare, so in Berlioz there is a misunderstanding of Beethoven; here and there the main object is a garish highlighting of detail. French poetry is blown-up prose." — He then goes out, comes back, plays the first theme of the *Pastoral* Symphony, and says, "That is invention!" I ask him what had brought that up, and he says: "I went outside, heard the howling of the wind in the trees, and said to myself: We are just elements within elements. Then I heard this theme; how absurd are all spoken words, all declarations, compared with this direct revelation!" — In the evening a letter from Tausig; the committee is now in Weimar, and T. begs me to write to my father after all! He clearly wants a letter of some kind, never mind what. I cannot write to him, I must wait and see what happens. (To Cornelius, in an attempt to enlist his brother.) In the evening Carlyle, with ever-increasing enjoyment.

*Saturday, June 10*   R. in dismal mood; I ask him why; he has been asked to acknowledge his debt in Vienna and does not wish to, so as not to place a burden on Fidi in the event of our dying. He intends to write to Herbeck, to discuss once again the question of royalties. It stabs me to the heart to see him so worried and not to be able to help; I say, "How mean of Princess Hohenlohe not to have helped with such a reasonable demand!" Then R. relapses into bitterness and says he regrets every cordial and enthusiastic word spoken to such treacherous beings. "You alone are worth living for, but only you," he exclaims in a tone that brings only bitter tears to my eyes. When will this curse ever be lifted from him? — On top of this it is cold. Yesterday, in pelting rain, I went out to meet him; when he saw me in the distance he sang out loud, "*Ein' feste Burg ist unser Gott.*" Ever firmer is my resolve to make the children Protestants. — The Reformation saved the German spirit, and I wish my children to be true Germans (I am already planning my "show" for R.'s next birthday! This my recreation; R.'s recreation is planning our house in Bayreuth.) — *Very fine* letter to me from Ottilie, truly touching, revealing a large and cultivated heart. Herr Pecht also writes to me in a friendly manner and sends me his Shakespeare portrait gallery. R. receives from Fürstner (publisher in Berlin) 500 francs for "*Der Tannenbaum,*" which amuses him greatly. R. presents me with a very pretty new summer hat; he ordered it according to his own taste and it is decorated with a lovely big rose. — We talk about my father; what kind of reunion would that be, he in his religious robes, I on the verge of becoming a Protestant, so that I can at least rest with R. in a single grave? — R. tells me that when he was a child he made himself some cardboard clouds and fixed them to chairs, then tried to hover on them and was dreadfully annoyed that it did not work. "And that," he continues, "is still happening to me today: I cannot reconcile reality with idealism." In the evening the Battle of Züllichau. (He writes to the conductor Herbeck.)

*Sunday, June 11*   "Cosima, I shall still be able to compose," R. calls to me in the morning. He then goes to the piano and plays something which will, I believe, introduce the scene by moonlight between

Alberich and Hagen. Today is again fine; yesterday R. had the house heated again. — The proof corrections of the biography, which are piling up, are causing him vexation; but nevertheless a cheerful family lunch. Then a walk into town, during which we discuss Semper's polychromy, since I am at present reading his pamphlet on the subject. Herr von Schack has sent me some of his books, to my great delight; in connection with them R. says jokingly, "I demand so-and-so-many yards of satin, and he sends me security." (I had asked Herr v. S. to participate in our venture.) In the evening the Battle of Kunersdorf with an involvement as if it had been fought only yesterday. R. says: "The law of gravity rules the world, the appearance of a genius can do nothing to alter that, all he can do is try to place his pendulum in such a way that its working is also governed by the law of gravity. That is what Frederick the Great was obliged to do with his Prussian state, and that, if I may mention myself, is what I must do. My works will do nothing to change theatrical habits, accustomed routines; I must see that I get my own theater built."

*Monday, June 12* "We shall have our house one day," R. exclaims to me, "and in it we must have our Turkish coffee-table." Letter from Frau Neumann: the machinist Brandt has not yet been to see her husband, which we find disturbing. It is a lovely afternoon; after reading me his introduction to the first volume, R. suggests an outing to Stanz, and at about 3 o'clock we set off with the 4 girls. Beyond Winkel a cart with 3 horses and some drunken peasants runs into us, Grane takes fright, leaps aside on to the meadow, drags us madly across ditches and bogs, until the carriage breaks and he is at last brought to a halt, badly injured, by the coachman. The children in extreme fear, but R. and I calm enough to stop their screaming and make them sit still. No mishaps apart from Grane's injury, though that is severe. The cantonal magistrate makes a record of it, we continue the long journey on foot, R. heads for Tribschen while I take the children to the confectioner's. When I return home, R. says, "I see that I love you more than you love me; I stood a long time looking after you, and you did not turn toward me, you are not so much in need of connections as I am." (!) — He then tells me of the alarm in the household when the carriage was towed home by a cart, and Friedrich, still in a state of shock, found it impossible to say a word. But then Fidi's look of joy, when his father greeted him—"I do not know what to do for happiness," my One and Only tells me! — The fright strikes me dumb and I can only thank God in silence. R. says, "Throughout my life it has always been the same with the warnings of Fate—within an inch of an accident, but always coming through unscathed." — In the evening reading, only I am too tired and have to go to bed.

*Tuesday, June 13* In the morning R. comes to me: "So what is life? One sees, as Schopenhauer says, that it is all a kind of compromise —a whisker worse and it would not work at all. Yesterday we go for a drive, on the best highway, and put our lives in danger! It is gruesome, and it would be incomprehensible that people could consent to such an existence, if there did not exist in each one of us the illusion that things must go better for him. In the ancient world it was joy in overcoming misfortunes which inspired them; they acknowledged that life and the world were loathsome—'but I am stronger than they'; the strongest affirmation of the will." — Yesterday evening our poor horse was bandaged, it was done as the wind was carrying across to us some very wretched music from a beer garden in Lucerne. The poor animal is suffering, but the doctor says he will soon be better; the sad sight of the animal brought us once again to thoughts of a surgeon; to help, to help—may this be our son's mission in this awful world! In the evening we talked about Brahmanism and Buddhism; "not intelligence, but kindness," says the latter. Brahmanism the arrogance of the intelligence, yet despite its present petrifaction still far in advance of our pitiful hierarchy. — Herr von Schack writes a very friendly letter, but he cannot participate in the establishment of our theater, since he is devoting all his means to the pictorial arts. — Today saw the alpenglow for the first time.

*Wednesday, June 14* Grane is still very ill, he is feverish. Meanwhile the Swiss mills begin to grind. Jakob discovers in town that the magistrate in Horw, who wrote down our statement, has not yet made a charge of any sort to the law courts in Lucerne, because he is a Conservative, and the farmer who ran into us is also a Conservative. The police declare, on the other hand, that it has nothing to do with *them.* With Jakob's help the charge is made, and 8 people come to inspect the damage; Jakob asks us whether he should give them wine, since "a pound of good will is worth a hundredweight of ill will"! Everything is gone into in the usual Swiss manner, and our Friedrich, who is questioned, declares that he can say nothing, for his alarm was so great that he had not taken note of anything! And on top of that Jakob explaining things in his most pompous manner; we have resigned ourselves to the prospect of having to pay the court costs on top of all the damage. — R. is still not well; he reads through *The Artwork of the Future* and provides it with notes. In the afternoon a visit from Count B.; since he stays a long time, R. is annoyed and cannot understand that I do not know how to get rid of him. — Finished Herr von Schack's *Durch alle Wetter*, which I very much enjoyed. — In the evening went through *The Artwork of the Future* with R.

*Thursday, June 15* R. still not well; I tremble with fear that, once he has started composing, legal annoyances will interrupt him. — Döllinger's statement, signed by various people, pleases us very much, and R. says: "To people who think there is nothing positive about it one should reply that it is already something when someone says, 'I will not tolerate it.' To oppose and destroy a lie is to serve truth." — Family lunch in the garden, all in very good cheer. R. says: "Oh, if only I could make up my mind to abandon the art of the future, how good I should feel! But then I should have to make up my mind to let the King have the two last works as well, and then make money with them in other theaters, and that would be a bit too much cynicism." — R. is not well, and his mood toward evening is again depressed, which makes me sad, too. — We had to laugh recently when we read in the newspaper that all the theater managers had held a conference for the purpose of promoting art! Is perhaps the specter of Bayreuth looming in their minds?

*Friday, June 16* (Yesterday evening a nice letter from Malwida M.) Warm and sultry day, foehn approaching, R. very oppressed by it. Besides teaching the children, I draft a letter to Baron Schack about his writings. Disagreeable letter from Karl Tausig, the conference in Weimar seems to have been unfruitful. In the garden [Goethe's] line "All transient things are but an image" comes into my mind, and that leads us to talk of this drama [*Faust*, Part Two], "which does indeed belong on a stage, but a stage one cannot envisage." "The world of appearances, that is what is transient; inadequacy, shown here in action, that is what life shows us; the unseeable, that is what the drama sets out to reveal to us. And all this," R. continues, "in the tone of a mystical medieval saying, like something from Jakob Böhme; the coloring of Faust is retained throughout." — In the afternoon we read together the *Communication to My Friends*. The evening brought an inquiry from the publisher Fürstner whether "*Der Tannenbaum*" might not be dedicated to Betz. R. says no at my request; we then laugh over the high payment he has received for this one song. "I remember that in my early Paris days I was always being told about Demoiselle *Loïsa Puget*, who received 500 francs for each of her songs—now in my 59th year I have also achieved that."

*Saturday, June 17* Reading in the newspapers about the destruction in Paris, I am astonished to see that virtually everything of artistic value has been spared. "Yes," R. says, "the demon of mankind is at the same time its guardian angel; it thirsts for knowledge and, lashing out blindly (as it seems), protects the things which make this knowledge possible. Action is everything to it, in preserving as in destroying. Incidentally, the fact that the Communists really wanted to set fire to the whole of Paris is the one impressive feature; they have always disgusted me with their histrionic style of government, their hypocrisy, their pedantic administration with all its lace trimmings—it is the only way a Frenchman knows; but that their disgust with French culture should bring them to the point of wanting to set fire to it—that really is impressive. As for the Germans, they cannot imagine life without this culture; I realized that when I was planning my *Artwork of the Future.* I could see nothing developing in Germany, but I did see that the ground giving rise to all our evils was quaking, and so I began then to design a new world for myself." — In the morning R. exclaimed: "Do you know what note represents all modern music? It is C sharp, the C sharp of the first theme in the *Eroica.* Who else, either before or after Beethoven, could have uttered this sigh within the complete calm of a theme?" — Stormy foehn weather, making it very hot. Letter from my mother: she sees everything from the black side. I copy out my letter to Baron Schack and send it off. In the evening *Frederick the Great.*

*Sunday, June 18* R. has had a very bad night in consequence of the weather, which has now changed entirely; it is wet and cold again. Prof. Nietzsche sends back *Siegfrieds Tod,* he has copied it out himself! With it he also sends his essay. R. arranges his first four volumes and writes the foreword to the 3rd and 4th volumes, which he reads to me in the afternoon. In the evening we read his sketch for *Wieland der Schmied,* whose 3rd act in particular I find extremely gripping. We are suddenly called outside, the mountains are lit up, the Pope's jubilee, others think for the Gotthard railroad—the Catholic gentlemen have very cunningly conjured up the semblance of a festival virtually everywhere. When Eva sees the illuminations she cries, "That is Germany." In the garden Fidi is Laertes, on his rocking horse the Great Elector. (Begin copying for the King.)

*Monday, June 19* R. in very good spirits after having sent everything off to Fritzsch. I write to thank Prof. N. In the afternoon I ask R. whether he knows for certain that we shall not be divided in death. "Yes, because we have no longings, because we find complete satisfaction in each other. If we did not, we should have to be born again. Your dear father, for instance—he will be born again." A dream of roses. "I am so happy," R. tells me. "Now easily I could renounce the art of the future!" We go for a walk. During it I tell him how glad I am that through him Fidi will learn the right attitude toward everything—art, philosophy, Jews, religion, politics—so that he will be spared sterile misconceptions. Military music is wafted across to us from Lucerne, and R. says, "Military music is the most unbearable thing I know—the epitome of the world's vulgarity." Letter from Alwine Frommann describing the tumult in Berlin (ceremonial entry); everything one hears from there is exhilarating; Bismarck's speeches, the words of the Emperor, who now always speaks of "the people," which was never the case before.

*Tuesday, June 20*   In the morning R. embraces me and sings, "For my Redeemer liveth." Then he tells me he has been thinking how pitiful he would look if after the death of his wife he had married some good rich woman like Frau Eckert—everything was possible, since men are such bunglers. How noble must he now appear, having me! I have constantly to listen to such things, and I have no answer to them. R. is girding himself for composition; his first act both pleases and dismays him: "Shall I continue like this?" The scene between Waltraute and Brünnhilde he finds "utterly incomprehensible," so completely did he forget it. He says: "I should be uneasy if I did not know that everything I do passes through a very narrow door; I write nothing which is not entirely clear to me. The most difficult thing in this respect was the last act of *Tristan*, and I made no mistakes there." In the *Musikalische Zeitung* a Wagner devotee writes very severely about *Rienzi* (it has just been produced in Vienna). R. says, "*Rienzi* is very repugnant to me, but they should at least recognize the fire in it; I was a music director and I wrote a grand opera; the fact that it was this same music director who later gave them such hard nuts to crack—that's what should astonish them." — Raining furiously all day long, in the evening a splendid rainbow; I tell R., "That is the sign from Heaven that you are beginning your work again." — In the evening R. asks whether he should include in the printed score of *Siegfried* the poem which he wrote last year when sending it to the King for his birthday. He then reads the poem, and finds it rather cold and insincere: "What enabled me to finish the work was something quite different." This observation makes me feel melancholy in spite of myself, which worries R. very much; he says he cannot bear that anything he says gives me pain. — During the day I told him that I believed the German Empire would achieve wonders, for it was no accident that his *Nibelungen* coincided with Germany's victories. Whether we shall live to see it I do not know, but Fidi—! (Wrote to K. Tausig.)

*Wednesday, June 21*   Today, as I read the description of the entry of the troops into Berlin, I had to weep for joy and pride. R. is sorry that the memorial ceremony was not entrusted to him. — Then he said he was still thinking of writing down his thoughts on the Catholic church for Fidi; this had been the religion of the Roman Empire, it had held the disintegrating Empire together and had been adopted by all the subjugated provinces; Protestantism had come into being in the lands in which the Roman Empire had not held sway. — R. has given the name "the Gravelotte quartet" to the Emperor and his three friends B[ismarck], R[oon], M[oltke]. — R. is summoning up his strength for work. "God knows when I shall get down to it," he said. "You must be good. Do you know what I call 'good'? When you are not indisposed and not sad—then my spirits are raised, and I make music." — We are perturbed by the fact that the machinist Brandt does not reply—have they been working on him in Munich not to become involved with the building of our theater? — I work on my copy for the King and tell R. we really must complete this work. "Yes," says R., "up to your arrival here. Then Fidi can carry on." "Just when I should like to be composing something comfortable I come on all this emotional stuff! I have landed myself in a nice pickle." — At lunch we touched on the subject of Countess Pourtalès, R.'s former friend, who completely ignored his presence in Berlin. I tell R. I find it incomprehensible that such a woman should allow so mean-looking a man as Joachim to gain an influence over her. "Oh," says R., "such women know that it is only through deeds that they can mean anything to us, whereas people like Joachim fasten themselves to the individuals whose influence is important to them, and these they flatter. Besides, women are slaves to the *will*, which dominates them. 'Have you eyes?' asks Hamlet, but this is not a matter of eyes, it is something darker. It is the energy of the will, not intelligence, not beauty, which fascinates a woman. Perhaps Nature thinks this offers more protection for her and her brood. The man of intelligence is irresponsible, etc." — While I am playing ball with Lusch, a letter from Marie M. is brought to me; she beseeches me to write to my father; his dignity does not allow him to take the first step! Feelings of bitterness. I write at once—not emotionally, as my friend desires, but simply and soberly. R. says with a laugh, "I am all right, I can afford to be conciliatory, I have you!" Carlyle's *Frederick the Great* still.

*Thursday, June 22* The weather is taking a turn for the better. which makes us very glad. R. secludes himself, continually asking, "Shall I still be able to compose?" Family lunch; in the newspaper the entry of the troops into Berlin, which moves us indescribably, utter faith in Germany. Unfortunately the description is by a Jew (J. Rodenberg); R. says, "We are all part of it, but these people stand outside, look on, and exploit it." — In the afternoon a walk with the children; while we are out, strangers come to Tribschen, enjoy the view, admire Fidi, and ask whether this is not "the little Wagner." Hermine tells us about it, and R. much enjoys "the little Wagner." R. is completely taken up with his present views on the Catholic religion, he shows me the Germanic lands: "Where Catholicism predominates, that is where the Romans were, they built their cities there; but in the places they did not penetrate, where Hermann threw them back, that is where the German religion arose. And everything else has died out. I believe in a confederacy of the Germanic nations (Holland, Norway, etc.). The Latin nations, on the other hand, cannot unite—the Latvians are not a Latin race, nor are the Spaniards—what held them together was the church with its aim of world supremacy." —

*Friday, June 23* Midsummer Day! But bad news to mark it: Richter writes from Vienna that the funeral music has been brought out by Meser in Dresden; an act of unmitigated baseness; R. was just about to sell it to Fritzsch; without a single word the Dresden publisher has cheated him out of it. I feel very miserable at having to report this to R.; in order to restore his spirits to some extent I say to him that I feel some good may come of it, for he will at last be able to get his hands on Meser. This does in fact cheer him up, but I do not really believe it, and expect only the worst! — R. sends telegrams about it to both Tichatschek and Meser. But he settles down to work after all, and as we go to lunch he says: "I am now sketching out a big aria for Hagen, but only for the orchestra. It is incredible what a bungler I am—I can't transcribe at all. With me, composing is a curious affair; while thinking it up, I have it all in my mind, endless, but then comes the job of writing it down, and the mere physical actions get in the way. It becomes 'How did it go?' instead of 'How is it?'; not 'How is it to be?' but 'How was it?'—and then having to search about till one finds it again. Mendelssohn would raise his hands in horror if he ever saw me composing." We eat in the garden, for I want to enjoy Tribschen to the full as long as we still live here; this dream life—shall we ever be able to capture it again? While we are at lunch a bird is singing splendidly nearby. "How he talks," says R., "how very deliberately he breaks off! I am absolutely certain that they tell one another things and understand one another." When Jakob comes, we tell him to listen and tell us what sort of bird it is, but the bird, which had been singing the whole time, stops and sings no more: "The bad lad! Just try to pin Nature down!" — A nice day, we work in the afternoon, at 7 o'clock we walk into town, where Rus causes us much bother.

*Saturday, June 24* In the morning R. says to me, "Whoever possesses you becomes very poor, for he loses everything, wants nothing but you!" He is dating his pencil sketches from today, the true Midsummer Day. He has already half forgotten the Meser affair of yesterday. Only Brandt continues to cause both him and me concern. — Fearful thunderstorm and furious rain; in the morning I teach the children, in the afternoon copy for the King. We are expecting bad experiences with our Bayreuth venture, but at least it will show us where we stand. "Previously," says R., "after we had given each other up, we were dependent on great artistic successes; we had to submerge the sacrifice we had made in some great outward activity. That is why, when we did not achieve our aim, I was in fact inwardly glad—I felt it would bring us together. But things are different now. If this venture does not succeed, well, we still have each other, and we have the work of art, too. But it would certainly be bad if I had to yield up the last two parts of the work as well to the King in order to keep going; I could not do that." — In the evening a letter from Prof. Nietzsche.

*Sunday, June 25*  No word from Brandt. — Dismal weather; the silence from outside looks spiteful. R. works, however; he says: "If I could compose just anything, I could now make myself a lot of money. But I can't do that." Read Prof. Nietzsche's pamphlet with great interest, he is certainly the most outstanding of our friends. Then played with the children, and in the evening made plans for our house! —

*Monday, June 26*  Constant rain, no chance of going outdoors. Much work and play with the children; but R. works, and in the afternoon writes to Düfflipp; sent off 30 pages of the copy. Hearing nothing at all from outside makes us apprehensive. My father's and Marie Muchanoff's silence in particular displeases us very much. In the evening Carlyle with punch, since we were feeling so chilly. (Herr Meser makes excuses for himself!)

*Tuesday, June 27*  Still rain; but R. is working—that is my sunshine! When, visiting him while he is at work, I tell him that, he says: "And do you know what makes me feel so irresponsible toward everything? The fact that I have you; none of our evil experiences touches the nerve of things; so I, too, can be single-minded. If I had had you with me in Paris, I should not have let myself in for all those things. The only trouble is, we came together too late, I want to enjoy it for a long time yet." — Uncharitable feelings over my father's behavior. — R. has composed Hagen's aria. He says, "While doing it I was thinking of you asleep; I was uncertain whether to let him express himself in silence or not; then I remembered how you talk in your dreams, and I saw I could let Hagen voice his emotions, which is much better." — We are appalled by the triviality of the musical setting for the entry of the troops—a *"Kaiser Wilhelm* March" by I. von Bronsart!! "Music, if only bagpipes, haste! We have plenty of appetite, if not much taste." In the evening more Carlyle, with ever-increasing enjoyment. — R. has a pamphlet on the theory of music by a Dr. Carl Fuchs, which pleases him very much. —

*Wednesday, June 28*  Letter from Marie Schleinitz; she understands my conduct, but sees it all very shallowly, like a true woman of the world! — We are having to consult a lawyer in the matter of the carriage. The poet Hartmann rather gauchely sends us his revised *Propheten* again. — R. had a bad night, the weather is too oppressive; I was assailed by melancholy dreams, that Hans was in a bad way and complaining! — But R. works; at lunch he talks of the curious process of collecting one's thoughts, which looks like absent-mindedness; now he adjusts a cushion, now thinks of politics, but all the time he is collecting his thoughts, and suddenly it comes. But nothing from outside must intrude. "The difficulties I had in getting down the finale to the second act of *Die Meistersinger* were due to the fact that you had gone away. You will not believe me, will tell me I managed to work in my earlier days, but then I was drawing on my capital—now I am dependent." — In the afternoon a letter from Marie Muchanoff; she returns my letter, did not give it to my father, since he has changed his mind, thinks it is still too early!! We smile. R. digs out Holtei's *Lenore* for its songs from the Seven Years' War and sings them to the children. — In the evening Carlyle.

*Thursday, June 29* R. had a very bad night; the rain was coming down in a deluge. But Herr Brandt has sent a telegram, it seems everything is all right. Letter from Claire, my mother has become deranged again. "Your father and mother do not bring you much joy," R. observes. — Family lunch; in the garden again, the weather is fine; R. could not do much work, in the evening a walk. Very nice letter from Clemens Brockhaus.

*Friday, June 30* Letter from Judith, describing the horrible state of things in Paris. A dreadful, unprincipled nation. I write to Claire and to Judith, also go through Herr Hartmann's new play; it reveals much talent, but I find it unpleasant, and he himself seems rather tactless. Sultry heat, but a good letter from the machinist Brandt—all our worries were unfounded.

*Saturday, July 1* A fine day; R. at work, I with the children, then read Herr Hartmann's *Röschen*, which shows much talent but even more clumsiness. Visit from Count B., who tells us about a crime committed by a man in Lucerne against a child. R. says the punishment should be death, a person like that should be crushed like an insect. — R. unwell in the afternoon and in a rather bad mood, a lot of little irritations which upset him, since he had a very bad night, and there is thunder in the air, which keeps bursting out.

*Sunday, July 2* Wrote to Clemens Brockhaus and settled all sorts of business matters. Family lunch in the garden; R. in a good mood, has been working. After reading my letter to Clemens, he says: "You understand me only too well; this desolation when I think of my life, this absence of all traces! I find it horrible." R. considers Herr Fuchs's pamphlet to be very good. We spend all day in the garden. Fidi's mission in life? R. says he often thinks that, were he to die suddenly, his work would be uncompleted—who would finish it for him? It would not be too inconceivable that Fidi might have the same gifts as himself and might continue his life. I have my doubts, not believing in so swift a recurrence of genius, since there is no instance of it anywhere in history; I shall be happy if our son has a steadfast character and enlightened intelligence. "Yes," R. says, "for he would possess no individuality of his own if he were simply to follow in my footsteps. God knows what lies ahead for him." — I said that at the end of June we had celebrated the 7th year of our love. "Not that," R. said, "and also not its explosion, but the knowledge that we could no longer live apart from each other. And if Hans had been only a shade different, more trivial or more profound, we should not have been completely united, for what did we not attempt on his account?" We wander through the Tribschen grounds and settle down on the hill beside the hermitage, watching the curious cloud formations, in which a thunderstorm lurks. "We newer races are very restricted in our imaginings, not knowing the tropical regions—India, for example. How can I think of the God Thor behind Mount Pilatus? These myths all originated in the Himalayas." We come to the subject of the Egyptians, the veneration of the Nile and of the cow, and that leads us to Io and the curious dialogue between her and Prometheus. "The reason why the Greek legends have made such an impression on you is that they were seized on by such tremendous poets." We see a cow in the meadow, and R. points out to me how it moves just like a snake, the same stretching and elongating. A lovely moment in time, Richard! Life is beautiful after all! My exclamation brings Schiller's *Don Carlos* to my mind, the beauty of which, with its delicate and subtle language, its dignified tone, R. finds really unique. "Where did Schiller find his model for it? At most Shakespeare's *Henry VIII* could have served, but that play was not known then." — I do some copying, R. corrects the proofs of his biography. "My life," he exclaimed, "has so far not achieved the C major finale to the C Minor Symphony. Everything I can remember is trivial." After supper we sit on the steps in front of the house, gaze at the moon, gloriously reflected, and listen to a curious summer-night concert—frogs, cicadas, and toads—the last in the distance, like a chorus of the damned. The frog is the hero, and he makes himself very audible; the others are like a symphonic accompaniment. R. then plays some passages from *Euryanthe*, and the day ends with a few pages of Carlyle, always welcome. During our meal the bird struck up again as it did recently, whereupon R. says, "One can understand why poor lonely Siegfried listens to the birds in the forest, and it is his good fortune that the bird takes care of him; in this world we remain strangers eternally."

*Monday, July 3* Dull morning, then a shower of rain; yesterday was a gift, now the sad rule of gray skies takes over. — The newspapers downright disgust us with their reports of the review and the loan in Paris. After this war they hold a review of troops and congratulate themselves on having defeated the national guard! No shame, no pride! — R. is indisposed, but he works. I write to my lawyer [in Paris], who is not sending me any money. A long time reading Carlyle in the evening.

*Tuesday, July 4* Ugly pictures of the entry ceremonies in Berlin, sorrowful remarks about them; the women in chignons, little hats, tucked-up dresses, no sense of decency. R. says: "I should like to ask our artists, 'Have you so little influence on public life, or are you infected by it yourselves?' But," he adds, "we are wrong to judge these things aesthetically, we must be glad that such an occasion brings the whole town to its feet. This must make an impression on the young people, but what sort of young people are they?" R. gets down to his "toads, crows, and ravens concert," works long, and seems satisfied. He says a short sleep after breakfast helped him a lot and put him in the mood at once. I write several letters on his behalf. I am very annoyed at hearing nothing from my lawyer. — A two-hour walk with R. in the afternoon. Talked of all sorts of things, our memories, the snatched times of being together, then Schiller Shakespeare Goethe, the last "always between *Faust* and *Claudine von Villa Bella.*" In the evening Carlyle.

*Wednesday, July 5* Rain again! Letter from an American, J. Lang, whom I met 14 years ago in Berlin and who offers support (Bayreuth). C. Mendès sends us his book about the Commune. In Paris madness and baseness; R. is alarmed by the thought that Prussia might not have crushed the people sufficiently and might soon have to begin all over again! — At lunch R. tells me that he has had all sorts of trouble and difficulties with his work. Things look bad, it seems, with our lawsuit. "Why must one build golden bridges for the devil? I should have thanked God that we escaped as we did, and not thought of justice. There is a stupid sort of optimism about seeking justice. I have now resigned myself to having to pay all the legal expenses and heaven knows what else." Our landlord is also behaving badly, after R. has put so much into his house. R. says: "I feel as if one is always dealing with crooks; one is full of trust, but the other is merely waiting for one to lay oneself open through this trust." The town council now requires us to apply for a residence permit—just as we are thinking of leaving! — And on top of all that the wretched weather; we now reckon to have had 10 months of rain, cold, fog, frost. — With the children in the *salon.* In the evening R. tells me that the greatest male virtue— one of which the French know nothing—is obedience. "Fidi must be obedient, I will get a grip on myself and support you better than I do with the girls, when I always intervene, which is very wrong of me. A boy who has never learned obedience is lost. I grew up in the wildest of anarchy; it had to be, for then as later no known method ever fitted me, but how much should I have been spared if I had been accustomed to obeying! To my sister I was just a wild and forsaken being who never conformed." Letters from E. Ollivier, asking me for papers, on the assumption that my father had arranged a dowry for me as for Blandine; I reply that I was given nothing, and remind him of the jewelry which my mother's father had given me and Blandine, which I had signed over to Blandine and which he had illegally withheld from me; probably this will be met with silence! Letter from Claire; things look bad with my mother. Letter from C. Mendès. "One must treat these people like children."

*Thursday, July 6*  Wild night; I am troubled by wretched thoughts about Hans, how he is getting on; I wrote yesterday to M. Meysenbug to find out. How heavy one's heart always is! But R. slept well, "the devil of composition" is tormenting him, for he finds that he expended too much on the first oath (Hagen Gunther Siegfried), intends to transfer the orchestral interludes to the oath in the second act and compose something new—an experience quite new to him. — We talk about the biography, he says he is curious as to how Paris (1860–61) will come out in retrospect. "How insane it all was! That production of *Tannhäuser* and my domestic life! But my whole life has been thus, an insane dream up to the moment of understanding between us. Every association, every business arrangement, every conversation; I saw myself constantly as if I were walking in my sleep, and every minute I asked myself, 'Why don't you throw the whole thing away?'" — Family lunch, then a walk, and in the evening the War of Succession with much interest and enjoyment. — When we returned home from our walk, R. said, "I have something for you," and drew a heavily wrapped book from his pocket. It was the *Tribschen Pamphlets for Frau Cosima*, for, "You must always have something the others do not have." The splendid, kind man! — Dr. Heckel writes that a fifth certificate of patronage has been almost subscribed.

*Friday, July 7*  Fine weather again—at last! Yesterday the doctor we had summoned to examine Fidi set our minds at rest concerning his bone formation, and at the same time gave us his views on the weather: for the past year (since August) northerly and southerly winds have been battling together in our regions, and this battle has given rise to all the clouds. — When I tell R. of my mother's condition (she hits out and raves, then becomes quiet and gentle again), R. says: "How dreadfully human beings behave! No animal in a fury can behave like that; it is closer to Nature, which protects it; but what happens to a human being when his intelligence begins to waver, we can now see in your mother, whose intelligence made her so lovable and estimable. That is why we always look to the common people, in the hope that they have remained closer to Nature." — While I am working with the children in the garden, he calls out to me, "I have had a wonderful idea, but I can't tell it to you." I run up to his room, and there he informs me that the theme I had already heard and liked, which comes on Siegfried's sudden appearance from the bushes, is the same one which the vassals will sing when they laugh at Hagen; a sort of Gibichung song which expresses the curious and genial mood of Hagen. How blissful I feel when he tells me things like this! It is as if there has never been sorrow and can never be sorrow. — A walk, and great tiredness in the evening.

*Saturday, July 8* Another fine day. At breakfast R. tells me that in the early morning yesterday, when he watched our rooster and compared its outward appearance with its cry, he realized the connection between music and sculpture. For sound is also a very individual thing. — The fashion journal continues to arouse our indignation. "The world really is ripe for the art of the future," R. says, then informs me that he would like to learn more about the smaller theaters in Berlin which are presenting the Schiller plays. "One ought to know the base on which one is standing; and it was open-air concerts which gave me my popularity, whereas with my occasional compositions I was always ignored from above." I read C. Mendès's *Commune* and tell R. of certain invented words in it which shock me in French, such as *l'hideur*, though it has something of *laideur* in it, and one also has the word *horrible*. R. says, "Yes, you are right, there is a law for devils and ghosts, and also for the manufactured French language; it is the enforced language of Mephisto; German, on the other hand, is the language of Faust." — At lunch R. was very worn out and depressed, he says he is working so slowly, finds it difficult to get into the mood, all sorts of things distract him, he is getting another cold, etc. It makes me sad; Fidi, our small guest at table, provides a friendly diversion, and toward evening, after retiring upstairs, R. calls down to me: "It is coming, my atmosphere is forming. It is utter madness, the way I work— always such a grind!" The rebellious workers in Silesia are all Catholics, which is giving the Prussian government something to think about.

*Sunday, July 9* A fine, really hot day; R. works; I play with the children and write to Herr Hartmann, whose *Röschen* has given R. little enjoyment. The newspaper reports the Emperor as saying that he has no inclination at his age to concern himself with "religious follies" (the German church), which is certainly very regrettable. Family lunch in the garden in the gayest of spirits. In the afternoon I feel very unwell, probably on account of the thundery atmosphere. Still great delight in *Frederick the Great*. ("Today Alberich has disappeared," says R.)

*Monday, July 10*   My lawyer sends me 1,000 francs and uses the opportunity to pour abuse on the Commune. As we are looking at the very ugly pictures of the entry of the troops into Berlin, R. says, "Nobody thinks what effect this open contact between men and women can produce; all this sitting side by side in the theater stalls, this wearing in the street of clothes intended only for indoors, giving every man the right to gaze through his monocle on any woman, while the women also are quite willing to make an exhibition of themselves in the street; nobody seems to realize what a coarsening of the senses there has been." — *Peter Menzig* comes at noon; though he is our only witness, the magistrate has *not* summoned him! A court official in the town told Jakob that the matter had been delayed far too long. That's very nice, too! Now Jakob brings along Peter M. in triumph and tells me, "He'll swear to anything he is asked." "But, Jakob," say I, "he has only to tell the truth." "Hm," Jakob observes, "one must put an end to it somehow." Peter Menzig turns out to be a chatterer, and R. is now expecting us to be accused of bribing a witness! What use our lawyer is to us is not at all clear. — To town with R.; he comes home in an agitated mood, complains of making poor use of his time, then suddenly goes upstairs and starts to improvise. His work is making him very tense. — In the evening *Henry VIII*.

*Tuesday, July 11*   R. relates to me a comical dream: "I suddenly saw my old Aunt Friederike, but now much younger, and I wanted to bring her to you, thinking, 'What will Cosima say when I bring her the old aunt about whom I have dictated anecdotes to her?' I gave her my arm, she felt very heavy, so I asked if she was tired. 'Well, I should have preferred to ride.' So I went in search of a carriage. Suddenly I thought, 'But she is long since dead!' She hardly spoke. I look for a carriage, but see nothing but baskets of a sort, and I think, 'No, you don't want to put her in one of those, she should see how well you are living.' I ask, 'Isn't there another carriage?' And then someone rather like Pecht comes up and says, 'Kellar and Brandt have nice carriages, you should fetch one of theirs.' I: 'Oh, dear, we are almost at the house'; whereupon he: 'But Brandt is very busy, he has been in *Shepherd's* and made some bad bargains.' — Then the dream ended, but Shepherd's is a part of *Praeger*'s address—what a lot of nonsense it all is!" Jakob has taken the 1,000 francs to the savings bank, where I now have 5,641 francs; 3,500 in the steamship company, which so far has brought me in nothing; 2,000 francs with R., who is very angry if I do not assume that he will pay me back and in the meantime pay interest on them;

and 1,000 in the Paris insurance company. — R. works, but is much hindered by the weather, which has turned bad again. Fidi as table companion wrings from him the despondent remark that he will probably not see him grow up. — In the afternoon games in the *salon* with the children; R. makes corrections. In the evening read *Henry VIII* to the end, inexpressibly moved by it.

*Wednesday, July 12* (Worry.) — Our conversation at breakfast revolves around *Henry VIII*, an incredibly noble work. In the morning we are told that our witness (Peter Menzig!) is leaving next week; and so, if our case is not heard very soon, we are bound to lose it, says Jakob. Annoyance on R.'s part, he asks what we have a lawyer for. — He works; I tell him that in my eyes it is no accident that the completion of this work coincides with the founding of the German Empire, even if outwardly there is no connection between them. "And 21 years ago, during the first German Parliament, I planned the work." Then came to the subject of Eduard Devrient, his baseness; R. regrets that Devrient had turned the Grand Duke of Baden, whom he much respects, against him. "He probably described me as a daemonic character who spreads unrest wherever he goes—in other words, he alarmed the Grand Duke, who certainly liked me." — Loldi reports with tears in her eyes that Grane can walk again and has today been pulling the carriage. — While R. is working in my *salon*, he hears me moving around in the neighboring room. "What is rustling and bustling over there—could it be a rat?" I slip out and hide myself behind the portière of his bedroom; he searches for me, cannot find me, but when he wants to leave the door seems rather heavy and he discovers "the rascal." Much merriment over this little joke, which I played on him really only to prevent his feeling he was being spied on. R. walks to town, returns tired.

*Thursday, July 13* R. had a very bad night; he has been reading Mendès's *Commune* and says: "What play actors these Frenchmen are! As long as they were playing to the world, it worked, but now the world is no longer looking, they become Charenton inmates, imagining themselves to be this person or that." The abuse against the Germans does not cease. R. does not work, writes to the King, sends him the "*Huldigungsmarsch*," the orchestral score of which has just been published. Visit from Herr and Frau Schott in the afternoon, and since he was mayor of Mainz during the great period, they have a lot of interesting things to tell. They find my children well behaved and pretty, which gratifies me. — In the evening R. wonders whether or not to inform Bismarck of his plans; I observe that it would be better to wait until the finances are secured and then to send him a report which makes no demands on him.

*Friday, July 14* I inform R. of my wretched condition; he is good and angelic as always. — Letters from Dr. Kafka, who wants to look after our undertaking in Vienna, and from the King, very friendly as always. Letter from Claire—my mother is still ill. With Loulou to Frau Schott, who visits us again in the evening. — R. plays his first scene to me, wonderful! (Letter from Richter which does not please us.)

*Saturday, July 15* Same division of the hours, each at his own task; after work the children bathe in the lake. Very sultry and hot. Letter from Prof. Nietzsche. In this friendship, too, R. lavishes more love than he receives. I buy myself some blue spectacles, but do not know if I shall wear them.

*Sunday, July 16* Fidi was today given his new outfit, which he will now wear all the time; a shirt and vest with collar, with it a leather belt and pouch, he looks lovely in it. — At breakfast conversation about a letter from Luther to the musician Ludwig Senfl; R. says it will be of great use to him. — Yesterday evening R. said to me, "By marrying me, you seem to me to have entered a nunnery, all your qualities are now lost to the world." "I have indeed entered a nunnery," I reply, "but one I chose for myself, and which delivered me from the world and purified me." — Lunch with the children on the terrace, all in nice, gay spirits. A drive with the children; I, since our accident, filled with fear. In the evening R. reads *Das Liebesverbot*. His first volume is too thin, and he wonders whether to include his youthful works in it. However, he finds them too childish. — In his latest book Herr Julian Schmidt disposes of R. Wagner in four or five pages! (Anguish of heart.)

*Monday, July 17* R. exclaims to me, "I don't know if you are happy, but I am!" — Loulou called to give evidence in our accident case! She conducts herself there very well, relaxed and assured. — At lunch I am very painfully affected; we are talking about the art historian *Lübke*, who again without any reason has heaped abuse on R., and R. exclaims, "One can escape this misery only in death, that alone brings peace." Since my greatest pride is when R. wishes himself a long life, I am deeply disturbed, but R. chides me, saying, "It may not come for a thousand years, but I am saying it will come one day and put an end to the world's misery." "Lübke probably *Lübecker*, a Jew." — Yesterday I read a pamphlet by the theologian Overbeck, which Prof. Nietzsche sent me; it brings R. and me to a discussion of religion. "The Catholics are quite right when they say the Bible must not be read by profane people, for religion is for those who can neither read nor write. But they played such shameful havoc with their interpretations that Luther became the only one who could take his stand on the Bible.

He did indeed in that way also open the doors to science and to criticism, but Christ will continue to live all the same." *Siegfried* has arrived, R. corrects the proofs in the afternoon. — "Oh, if only we had a little place of our own and could live in it, and I could write my things and not have to think about what the world does with them!" R. exclaims as we are having our cozy lunch on the terrace. — Yesterday, on our drive, R. reminded me of the evening in Munich when he had sobbed so violently during a performance of *Preciosa*. He says: "The music reminded me of the indelible impression it made on me in my youth: all my ideas of southern fire and gracefulness are based on this impression. And how neatly the text was written, a short story could not be fashioned more finely. How clumsy in contrast what is being provided today!"

*Tuesday, July 18* Yesterday evening R. gave Eva a grave lecture about the importance of not tormenting animals, I hope it will have an effect. R. works; before lunch, when I go to greet him, he says: "How easy it would be if I could just write arias and duets! Now everything has to be a little musical portrait, but it must not interrupt the flow—I'd like to see anybody else do that!" After lunch he plays the 3rd act of *Siegfried* to me—wonderful beyond all words; he shows me the harp sounds he has added in Brünnhilde's greeting to Siegfried, like the harps of the skalds when they welcome a hero in Valhalla. These sounds are to be heard again at Siegfried's death. A profound, indescribable impression; a wooing of the utmost beauty; Siegfried's fear, the fear of guilt through love, Brünnhilde's fear a premonition of the approaching doom; her virginal and pure love for Siegfried truly German. — I try to imagine which people would be able to appreciate such things; my father, and also Tausig, come to mind. Friedrich returns from the post office and brings me a letter from Countess Krockow: she is in the Leipzig hospital with Tausig, who is dying of typhus! A great shock. Even if he recovers, he is in any case lost to our undertaking; what a lesson to us! To us his death seems to have a metaphysical basis; a poor character, worn out early, one with no real faith, who, however close events brought us, was always conscious of an alien element (the Jewish). He threw himself into Bayreuth with a real frenzy, but can this outward activity help him? . . . He is too gifted not to be weary of life. "I have no further wish to live in the world," R. says. "Now I have you, all I want is to care for the children and just look on; for no matter what one puts a hand to, ghosts arise. The Flying Dutchman was nothing compared to me." I tell him how happy we are in our solitude—I, for instance, should be quite unable to bear life in the world any longer. "Yes," says R., "it was a stroke of genius on my part when I cabled you from here, 'Casting anchor every seven years, I shall be united with you here.' No, to go along with the world, share its interests, etc.—I can no longer do that." — We walk in the sultry darkness into town to take my letter to Countess Krockow to the post office. Will it find Tausig still alive? R. says physically he is like a cat, perhaps he will recover. — Late in the evening read *Frederick the Great*, whose character captivates us with both joy and sorrow. (A year since the declaration of war!)

*Wednesday, July 19*  R. had five hours of good sleep. He works. Never-ending sultriness; we suffer under it; in the evening I am very sad, I do not know whether because of an incident between R. and myself (in which he was perhaps too impassioned, I too reserved), or because of yesterday's news, of which I am constantly thinking, particularly since this heat seems likely to be fatal for anyone with typhus. — In the afternoon R. corrects his biography, I read Semper's pamphlet on science, industry, and art, which I find absorbing. In the evening *Frederick the Great*.

*Thursday, July 20*  Terrible, stormy night; I do not sleep a wink. In the morning a letter from Elisabeth [Krockow] brings news that Tausig is dead; he died in the night between Sunday and Monday; when we received the news of his illness he was already dead. Complete stupefaction, then reminiscence—how many friends already gone, Uhlig, Schnorr, Serov, how many! In T. we have certainly lost a great pillar of our enterprise, but that leaves us indifferent. R. says: "I look upon it as upon a cloud; the vapors rise—will they be dispersed or will they form themselves into a life-bringing cloud? God knows. I just look on, my life seems to me godlike, for even its worries are now beautiful; they are about the children." — Contemplation of Tausig's sad life; so precocious, Schopenhauer already worked through at the age of 16; conscious of the curse of his Jewishness; no pleasure in his tremendous virtuosity, my father's even greater, and he too remarkable to see himself just as a pupil; the marriage with a Jewess, ended almost at once; completely finished at 29, yet still not a man. "What must the sleepless nights of such a person be like? What occupied his thoughts?" asks R., who shrugs his shoulders over the stupidity of Fate, snatching Tausig away at the moment when a great new activity would have brought him inner joy and satisfaction. — This was to be a sad day, in every respect; at midday Vreneli came in and declared that Kos could no longer be saved, he no longer had a moment's peace, neither day nor night, and Jakob would take him today to the apothecary. I said he should be shown to me before he was taken away, so that I could say goodbye to him, but they did not do so, and it pained me very much. The poor little creature shared with me the worst days of my life; Hans brought him to Zurich in '66 to give me "at least a little joy" in difficult, oppressive days. He was ill for the past 3 years; now he is gone and is buried here in Tribschen. — R. could not work this morning; he wrote to Dr. Gille explaining why he was not joining the society of authors, then to Herr Tappert in Berlin for Dr. Fuchs, whose pamphlet he thinks good. Dr. Fuchs had asked him to request the support of the King of Bavaria, and R. writes to say that the King protects only his person, not his ideas, and the fact that he will now have to produce his *Nibelungen* himself should show people clearly enough how things stand. Alarmed that R. should write like this to two entirely unknown people, I ask him to find another way; he is very angry, says he has no intention of writing banalities to a man whose book he admires, he cannot write more phrases, he is a truthful person. He tears up his letter; I am unutterably sad to have wounded him in what is surely one of the finest parts of his character; but it irks me to have the King spoken of to all and sundry. R. then regrets having been so violent and bursts into tears over the King, who knew everything, felt it all with him, and then abandoned him thus. He says he has taught himself to be honest in all directions, he stands in all simplicity, and now with this one lie he would have to go to the grave; he sobs violently. I stay with him, then leave him in order to supervise Kos's grave. When I return to him, he is reading *Faust* (Part One); he reads it out loud to me (5th act); this noblest of works calms, softens, grips, and cheers us; every word a jewel! R. says he would like to have *Faust* splendidly printed for himself on fine vellum paper, as a symbolic, holy book. The German monument, the German masterpiece. — In Munich the Jewish actor Possart recently welcomed King and Crown Prince in the theater, and after he had praised the alliance of the two men, they shook hands and thanked him!! — Talked a lot more about Tausig. I received a visit from Mr. Lang, an American, whom I met 14 years ago in Berlin and who, amicably remembering every detail, comes here to seek me out.

*Friday, July 21* R. dreams about Tausig. Last week he dreamed about teeth falling out of his mouth in great numbers; I also dreamed of a broken tooth, and asked him what dire event was here foretold. Then comes Tausig's death like a warning not to undertake anything in the outside world. I take it all very seriously. — Around noon R. tells me, "I have forced myself to work, but had little pleasure from it." — We come to talk about so-called cultural matters, and R. agrees with me when I tell him that I feel no trace of sympathy for the imposition of Christianity on others (Charlemagne and the Saxons) and that I would give the whole of discovered America in exchange for the poor natives' not having been burned or persecuted. He tells of Radbod, the Prince of Frisia, who, with one foot already in the font, leaped back when he heard that he would not meet his heathen father in Heaven (Siegmund!); that was why he had made his Ortrud, an inadequately converted heathen, a descendant of Radbod. The Roman conquest of countries much more humane, they did not impose their religion. — When I go to lie down after lunch, R. comes to my room, having just heard from Loldi that Kos is dead and buried. He weeps. When I come downstairs, he is still much affected. In the evening he looks back on his whole relationship with Kos and weeps bitterly— "such a good, friendly creature, so dependent on one!" — The American and his wife visit us; very nice people; Fidi and the four girls are presented to them, the former a great success. (Today Fidi's first bath in the lake, and now he has "lake-bath" to add to his very limited vocabulary.) We then talk much, R. and I, about the English language, which I enjoy speaking, but against which R. has an insuperable antipathy; he says a German can only regard it as a dialect, not a serious language. We remark on the fact that only the Germans have retained sufficient objectivity to pronounce Greek and Latin names without reshaping them; that the Germans alone have a pronunciation which conforms to spelling. A very significant factor. Shakespeare as triumph of the resurgence of the oppressed Anglo-Saxon spirit, he expresses (so to speak) the downfall of the Normans, those cunning, fierce, and powerful adventurers. This spirit culminated in Protestantism, since the Normans were also always associated with the Catholic church. — The name of Cromwell in *Henry VIII* makes a strange impression on R.: "One involuntarily thinks of an allusion, since Cromwell is shown as the only protector of Cranmer; then one tells oneself that just cannot be, and has the feeling of a poetic premonition." Thus our conversation goes from one subject to another, but we always come back to Kos. R. could not have said goodbye to him, for otherwise he would never have agreed to it, and yet his imposed death was inevitable. —

*Saturday, July 22* R. tells me: "I dreamed the two little girls (Eva and Loldi) went on a tiny, unsteady boat, and my shock gave me enough strength to wake up and break the dream. Then of Schröder-Devrient, I had a relationship with her." "Of what sort?" I ask. "As always, not of any sentimental kind. No, she could never have aroused love longings in me, there was no longer enough modesty in her, no mystery in which to probe." — Without mentioning Kos's name he says: "I believe that, since in a dog the mouth and its muscles have no expressive function, the whole power of expression lies in the eyes. How a dog's eyes regard one! The eyes of most people do not have this intensity, usually because they have become too used to dissembling." — Very fine weather; recently R. found very great pleasure in the crescent moon, he said he could understand why it had been adopted as a sacred symbol. — *Heimskringla,* newly acquired, also gives R. great pleasure; less, on the other hand, Herr Rodenberg's pageant (at the troop ceremonies in Dresden), in which he talks calmly of Rhine gold, of Siegfried's ring, as if these were quite commonly accepted things. R. says, "I feel as if I had swallowed an emetic." "Rodenberg and Redwitz are now the heroes of the day; after the wars of liberation it was Houwald and Müllner, but they were at least cleaner." A Count Amadei comes to visit R., a knowledgeable Wagnerian, but not one he finds very agreeable. By boat to town, to visit the Americans. Lovely homeward journey, despite my great fear, which R. says I should try to overcome. — In the evening Carlyle; the reunion between Wilhelmine and Frederick very moving; Frederick (through the execution of Katte) has suddenly become a man: "He has realized that life is no joke, he also wants to be a king, and he kisses the feet of his father, whose action arose from profound instinct." —

*Sunday, July 23* Letter from E. Krockow; in his final days Tausig had called us (Wagner and me) "two great natural forces"! Hermann Brockhaus sends the papers which Marie Muchanoff had entrusted to him for R.; she seems to have lost her head entirely. What will become of our affairs, God knows! — In the morning the two older girls to church, the two little ones with us, playing very nicely. As I am writing this, R. calls down to me from the upstairs *salon,* where he is working, "Cosima, where are you?" "Down here—I am writing my diary." "Are you writing nice things?" "Of course, but what makes you think of me now?" "Fool! What else do I ever think of? Where should I find the will to go on working except in this thought? I should like to know what would have become of me if I had not found you. Ruined, after committing one folly after another. Wasted away in misery." Then he goes back to his work. Unfortunately he is not well, he complained of heaviness and weariness. — In the afternoon visit from Countess Bassenheim; just returned from Munich, she tells us the most horrible things about the King, what ill-mannered jealousy he showed toward the Crown Prince (during the ceremonial entry of the troops), how the peasants scoff at him for having his hunting lodges gilded and furnishing them in Louis XIV style, etc., etc. R. very despondent about it—alas, this dependence on him! Our Americans (the Lang couple) both very nice and musical. But when he plays a difficult piece by my father, R. remarks that here something is being turned into a rule which was part of my father's personality: "The magic he conveyed in his playing, which suited the outer glamour of his life; now his pupils are learning his colossal technique and having to spend a colossal amount of time doing it." R. regards this, rightly, as a waste of time, since they lack the individuality from which it all sprang.

*Monday, July 24* R. in despondent spirits: the King, the King! Also, in order to deter people of note in Bayreuth, word is being spread that the King does not approve of our venture! — R. finishes the second scene of his act, but feels not at all well. We go out, he feels like a long walk but returns home very wretched; he complains that the diet is wrong, he cannot eat strawberries, etc. He goes to lie down, and I read Carlyle to him, which distracts him. — Our Americans have gone, after R. had decided that music is the new religion. "We could not get through to one another, so we made music together, and at once we understand one another." "Our life could be heavenly, but nothing must disturb it from outside."

*Tuesday, July 25* A dream of R.'s brings us to the subject of love. He told me that in his dream we had been separated, Hans had been delighted, R. had wanted to go away, and I had let him go; it had been the unhappy time in Munich. Then he adds, "Yes, love up to the point of complete union is just suffering, yearning." I: "And complete union achieved only in death—the whole of *Tristan* is saying that; this is what I constantly feel, I feel myself as an obstacle which I long to burst through. And yet I want as an individual to be united with you in death—how can one explain this?" R.: "Everything that is remains, what one already has persists, freed entirely from the conditions of its occurrence." I: "One has in the stars a good image for the appearance of things—as our eyes deceive us there, so, too, do our senses deceive us about the whole system of existence." R.: "The word 'eternal' is a very fine one, for it really means 'holy': a great feeling is eternal, for it is free from the laws of change to which everything is subject; it has nothing to do with yesterday, today, or tomorrow. Hell begins with arithmetic." "But God knows what else may still become associated with you?" R.: "Nothing, for I have believed in nothing deeply except you." — Yesterday I brought from Countess Bassenheim a spiked helmet and a saber for Fidi, he comes to us with them: "Achilles, Max Piccolomini." He looks very good in it and makes us feel happy. — From Berlin, Herr Davidsohn sends us an article about Tausig, very insipid and flat. "But we cannot say anything about it, no one would understand our point of view," says R. "He was altogether an unfortunate, interesting phenomenon." — R. does not work today, he is too worn out, he plays the two scenes for me, then lies down and reads. He says he would like to take a few days' break and write an obituary of Auber. — (Yesterday morning I wrote seven letters in connection with Bayreuth.) Loldi on the American, who is bald: "He has something naked on his head." — Melancholy in Nature and in myself, since Tausig's death I have no will for anything but business matters and the children's lessons; I just cannot manage to write personal letters. — In the evening I again read to R.; the emigration of the Salzburgers under Friedrich Wilhelm I moves us unutterably and strengthens me in my resolve to become a Protestant. R. regrets that Bismarck does not find the necessary drastic words in relation to the Catholics.

*Wednesday, July 26*   A portrait of poor Serov has been sent to us. R. receives a letter from Dr. Kafka in Vienna, undertaking to raise 100,000 florins in Vienna. During the night I was filled with fears, sad unto death, fearful for R., fearful for the children (their future), fearful for Hans himself, comfort only in complete resignation in all things and the firm resolve to do my duty at all times. — R. is still indisposed and in consequence despondent, but always divinely good to me. In the evening Carlyle, about which R. says that one must read it like a book called "Memoirs of a Grandfather" which one might have in manuscript. — I arrange R.'s papers—and come upon all sorts of things, among them letters to R. from his sister Rosalie, which surprise R. very much; he says he had not known how affectionate people had once been toward him. He then speaks of the dreariness—the ridiculous dreariness of his marriage.

*Thursday, July 27*   R. says to me around noon: "Do you know what I have done today? Thrown out everything I did yesterday. Hagen's call sounded *too composed*, I did not like it, it had to be altered." Family lunch; R. says that in the newspapers there are whispers about the King of Bavaria's ill-mannered attitude toward the Crown Prince—what will come of it? Walk with R. We are talking about all sorts of things when R. suddenly breaks off to say: "I feel like Kohlhaas, I have heavy thoughts that I shall never be happy and well again. The humiliation of being dependent on this King—it is scandalous and insupportable! If he would only take up a stand, if he had only supported my cause, one could justify both oneself and him. But like this—!" The beautiful countryside distracts us a little from these dismal thoughts. In the evening I continue arranging papers and read aloud passages from the letters to R. Much melancholy in this glance back over the past. — Passing the Fontaine de Soif, we talked of Melusina. "Christianity added something very touching to these natural spirits, and it brings to poetry a completely new quality; they are always good, but unredeemed, which makes them so sadly fascinating. Like this water sprite, to whom the parson's children come to tell her that she cannot be redeemed after all." — (The King has replied to Prince Albert, who asked him to come without fail to the banquet the town is giving in honor of the Crown Prince, "He can fetch his vivats by himself"!!)

*Friday, July 28*  Friend Nuitter sends R.'s articles from the *Gazette Musicale*, I look forward to translating them back into German. — At lunch, after Fidi has as usual eaten his strawberries with us, R. exclaims: "I curse this composing, this grind I am involved in, which will not allow me to enjoy my happiness! My own son has been here, and it all slips past me like a dream. This *Nibelungen* writing should have been finished long ago, it is pure madness, or I should have been made a wild creature like Beethoven. It isn't true, as you all seem to think, that this is my proper element; to live for my own education, to enjoy my happiness—that is my real urge. Earlier, it was different. I feel as if I were trying to build a house on the blossom of that catalpa; I should first have to fill in the thousands of gulfs which now separate me and my art from the people of today. Where am I to find my Hagen with his echoing, bragging voice? The fellows who have such voices turn out to be blockheads. It is utter madness. Idylls, quartets—that is what I should still like to do. And on top of it all this petty agitation about the production of the *Nibelungen!*" — Much indignation that Manteuffel, who literally led his troops to sacrifice, is also being given a grant, because King Wilhelm is especially fond of him. Concern over Loulou, because she has so little sense of order. Walk with the children, to whom we give ices; late homecoming, in the house find the Schotts, with whom we spend the evening.

*Saturday, July 29*  I begin translating R.'s articles, alternating between that and lessons with the children. R. works, but he is still not well, I think the climate here does not agree with him. The Wagner Society in Leipzig has also been in touch. In the afternoon, as I am working at my translation on the terrace, a stranger arrives, and I soon recognize in him R.'s old friend Praeger, whom we welcome heartily, but with whom we do not find very much to talk about. — R. was annoyed today to read that the Bishop of Munich had reprimanded someone with extracts in Latin from the papal bulls: "When I think that a German has to put up with that, I could explode with rage!" (Fidi visits Countess Bassenheim.)

*Sunday, July 30*  Things look bad in Bavaria, the Archbishop acts as if he were the King, and the King remains what he is! Prince Hohenlohe is said to have left Munich in anger. God knows what will come of it all. — At breakfast R. asks me whether I know the epic about Walther and Huldigunde, I say yes, and he continues: "I find in that the features I call truly German, the composure, bordering on humor, like the fight of Walther with the Gibichungs and then with Hagen, whose eye he hacks out and who hacks off his hand, after which they joke together about it. I believe one could find such things in the Prussian army." — Yesterday evening we talked again about

Berlioz, "who heard visual things wonderfully, and these awoke his powers of invention. Otherwise pitifully thin, restricted in form." — Yesterday when I came up to R. on his walk, he said to me, "The way Fidi just smiled at me, so nicely and sweetly and lingeringly, I feel quite shattered." Today he said: "How happy our children will still make us! You'll see." — R. is unwell, cannot work, and consequently very despondent. After lunch Herr von Gersdorff visits us, he is a friend of Prof. Nietzsche's who went right through the war and has all the noble and earnest characteristics of the North German. Naturally the conversation revolves around the war. (Letter from Frau Lucca, they want to do *Lohengrin* in Bologna.)

*Monday, July 31* Yesterday Countess Bassenheim took Loulou to a performance at the school, during which the pupils actually did a recitation about Ziethen and Frederick the Great—how the latter summoned Ziethen to his table on Good Friday, but Ziethen went to Communion instead, and Frederick could do nothing about it. A pretty jesuitical story! — R. very unwell, causing me concern. At table Herr v. Gersdorff, Prof. Nietzsche, Prof. Brockhaus, all equally pleasant. We spent our time in Tribschen, talking happily. —

*Tuesday, August 1* R. feels so unwell that he has taken refuge in cold packs. It indeed does him good, and at lunch he is lively and talkative. We have the same companionable guests, with whom I go out in a boat while R. settles some things in town. Lovely moonlight; late in the evening R. reads to us *"Die gerechten Kammacher"* by G. Keller; the talent it shows is greater perhaps than the unpleasantness of its subject, and we laugh a lot. — When the company breaks up and R. and I are left alone, we tend to embrace and rediscover each other with perhaps even more fervor than usual. R. says how beautiful he finds me, indeed he cannot imagine anything more beautiful, and I in my bliss say nothing. He is glad to have me running his house and entertaining people, and his contentment is my whole happiness.

*Wednesday, August 2* Very fine morning; with our guests and the children in the woods. — A letter to me from Clemens Brockhaus, and one to R. from Richter—for whom things are not going particularly well. — Lunch as on the previous days; in the afternoon R. plays passages from *Siegfried*. In the evening parts of Heinrich Kleist's posthumous works (political catechism).

*Thursday, August 3* Morning walk with the guests and the children, to the hermitage on the hill opposite. Lunch as yesterday; at five o'clock Herr von G. and Prof. Nietzsche leave us. The latter is certainly the most gifted of our young friends, but a not quite natural reserve makes his behavior in many respects most displeasing. It is as if he were trying to resist the overwhelming effect of Wagner's personality. Very pleasant evening with Fritz Br[ockhaus]; R. becomes heated about the custom of raising one's hat and its origin, and this leads us to Schopenhauer's rules for worldly wisdom, which R. reads to us. — Letter from Marie Schleinitz in Gmund[en], she is not so shattered by Tausig's death as I expected. Arrival of the piano scores of *Siegfried*.

*Friday, August 4* Gave the children their lessons. Lunch with Fritz and Herr Praeger. R. goes over my translation of his essays. To town by boat, visit the Lion, eat ices, home on foot. — Letter from friend Schuré, who is surprised that Karl Tausig did not send him a certificate of patronage; R. finds it repugnant to have him, a disloyal German, as a patron. Conversed during the evening. A man in Vienna writes asking R. to set his libretto of *Die Braut von Messina* to music, short and to the point. (Fritz tells the children the story of *Käthchen von Heilbronn*.)

*Saturday, August 5* Fritz, our excellent nephew, who has been very pleasant company, makes his departure. — A chance visit to the loft brings to light a letter from Frau Serov: it had been dropped by the maid who took the picture from its wrappings. Thus, fourteen days late, I see that she also sent me a copy of R.'s letter of condolence. I thank her at once, also write to E. Schuré and to Ottilie. — Yesterday R. caused me sorrow; Prof. Nietzsche had asked me for the *Idyll*, so that he could read it; after asking R., I lent it to him, requesting him on his departure to return it to me, but he forgot; after his departure R. asked about it; our absent-minded friend had left the little work lying on the piano, and R., assuming that I had been negligent, had taken it to his room in vexation; this pained me deeply, for my only mistake had been in assuming that Prof. N. had done as I asked and put the manuscript back in its place, which he knows. But the slight ill feeling is soon overcome. — We stay quietly at home and in the evening take up Carlyle again.

*Sunday, August 6* In the morning the machinist Brandt arrives from Darmstadt, and in the afternoon the Neumanns also arrive, and a little conference about Bayreuth takes place. At supper we drink to the Battle of Wörth. — R. made us literally shudder with his description of a duel (*The Corsican Brothers*) which he once saw in a little theater in London.

*Monday, August 7* Conference all day, in which our good Neumann conducts himself like "a bull in a china shop"; the excellent Brandt, however, efficient, intelligent, earnest, and inventive; he is utterly inspired by his task. The Neumanns depart after we also discussed our house, Brandt stays until evening.

*Tuesday, August 8* Wrote to Marie Schleinitz; R. to Karl Bechstein, requesting him to take Tausig's place on the committee. Told the children some German stories. Fidi, scared by the strange guests, no longer wants to come to us and causes me concern. As I lift him up to put him in his carriage, I feel a violent pain and become lame. I wonder what will ensue from it.

*Wednesday, August 9* Somewhat better, I can work with the children and translate, trouble with Fidi. R. also translates, but complains of having thus to fritter away his time. In the evening with Countess Bassenheim, with whom a Countess Ugarte, a former acquaintance of R.'s, is staying. I like her very much. But the unaccustomed act of leaving my home makes its mark on the evening.

*Thursday, August 10* Nightmares and wild dreams of helping to murder V. Hugo! — Fidi friendly again. Family lunch with Herr Praeger. Translated morning and afternoon, in the evening R. reads out loud *Walther und Huldigunde*. — Letter from R. Pohl and from Frau Serov—the latter, whom we hardly know, wants to pay us a visit, and speaks of all sorts of mysterious things: her child has been taken away from her, she has been virtually driven from Russia, etc. Shall I answer her? — Deep and sublime impression from an Indian legend (mother with her dead child, Buddha, the grains of mustard, the house in which nobody has died!).

*Friday, August 11* Emperor and King! The latter does not wish to see the former on his journey through Bavaria!! What will become of our young master? And consequently of us? R. dreamed that he had his *Nibelungen* scores offered to the Emperor through Bismarck, and, for the sake of the children, he asked for an advance of 4,000 thalers! — Thus does worry continue to creep like a ghost through his piteous fate. The Catholic movement is assuming greater proportions. — In the afternoon a visit from the two countesses; R. is indignant because Countess Ugarte asks him for a photograph; he says, "This is the extent of their interest in us!" — In the evening R. reads aloud his essay on the Overture. — Late in the evening R. tells me the confidences our poor guest imparted to him concerning his domestic troubles, which are indeed of a horrible kind!

*Saturday, August 12* R. talks in a high, thin voice, I ask with whom. Reply: "With Fidi, he must learn to respect me, must take me for an old woman!" — The King is visiting the Emperor after all!

I visit Countess Ugarte, whom I like very much. — R. still on his articles, which I have now finished. The balmy air does not agree with him, he says it is like a bad book. — We talk in the evening about Italian singers, to whom Rossini in effect owes his reputation, and when I wonder why there are no longer any of them about, he says: "Well, they are now all playing politics and waging war. Cavour, Garibaldi—the latter ought certainly to have sung the High Priest in

*Norma.*" Nice letter from Prof. Nietzsche. I write to Claire.

*Sunday, August 13*  R. said yesterday evening, "The reason why the great masters cannot be imitated is that each of them takes a path of his own and follows this to its utmost limits; if it could be pursued further, the master would have done so himself." — Lovely warm day; I copy for the King. Deep sorrow over a letter from M. Meysenbug; she relates that Hans hates the Germans so much that he would like to forget his German, and that last spring he was so agitated that his friends were seriously worried about him. — This the wound which will never heal; some days ago I dreamed that I had to convey the news of his death, written down in pencil on a piece of paper, to the children. The whole day, God help me, is overshadowed by this thought; I fight against it as much as I can. R. helps me, especially with his love and his playing (*Götterdämmerung*). I copy for the King; R. sends off his *Siegfried* to the Wesendoncks, Willes, and Mendèses.

*Monday, August 14*  Our poor guest takes leave of us and returns to his wretchedness! — I am still very weak and worn out, R. inspects my fingers and says, "These are not fingers at all, they are sensitive filaments, they could just as well be attached to wings, as on a butterfly." And: "Your father is a good man, and the cleverest thing he ever did is now mine!" — The day ended very badly; when I told Jakob to take my palm tree out and take good care of it, he replied with the assertion that the children had torn off the leaves; I denied this, R. confirmed it, whereupon I: "If the children are doing this, they must be punished for it." This put R. into such a rage that he forgot himself rather badly. — Sad evening. I go on the lake with the children. (Richter has been appointed conductor in Pest.)

*Tuesday, August 15*  Terrible storm and melancholy day. Thundery showers. Letter from Richter, he has definitely been engaged as conductor in Pest. This is good. What is not good is the despondent mood which possesses me; well, happiness, like glass, is fragile. . . . Copy for the King. — Nothing from outside, not even from the committee, which strikes us as ominous. —

*Wednesday, August 16*  The children look like boys; their hair has been cut off. Dull weather; R. prepares his essays. In the evening took up Carlyle again. — Something is brewing in the political field, Bismarck and Beust, with diplomatic retinue, are conferring in Gastein.

*Thursday, August 17*  Fritz Br[ockhaus] sends his book on the principle of legitimacy. Otto Wesendonck thanks us for *Siegfried*. Letters from Herr v. Gersdorff, Frl. Nietzsche, and Bechstein. Visit from Hänlein, the pianist, who reports that 10 certificates of patronage have already been taken up in Mannheim. — I send *Siegfried* to Prof. Nietzsche and make the copy for the King. R. has completed his articles; he now has as much material as is required for the first volume; he has tidied up his youthful pieces and much enjoyed this curious task; he says he enjoys being an author, it is so easy. "It's true the real genius has little to say. The fact that the Italians have not been very active as writers is really proof of their deep artistic instinct." In the evening he reads me the essays, and I remark, in connection with a simile, that the moon does not get its light from the earth, but from the sun, which he is unwilling to believe; we look it up in the encyclopedia and laugh when we discover that I am right!

*Friday, August 18* Our Sergeant Nolte, returned from the war, writes to R. that he has given up his university studies and wants to become a musician. R. emphatically advises him against it, tells him that musicians are born, not made; we intend to educate our Fidi as a surgeon, etc. — We plan an outing to Stanz, but have to give it up on account of a thunderstorm; games with the children in the *salon*, in the evening visit from Countess Ugarte, who tells me that in my outward appearance I look like George Sand's heroines!! — R. thinks about composing music without joy, indeed with a kind of repulsion, which pains me deeply.

*Saturday, August 19* Fourteen years ago I was married to Hans, the weather was dull like today. Solemn reflections; God give me strength and let me grow better until I go to my rest! Worked with the children, then drove with R. to Emmenbrück. Lovely sky at sunset, intimate mood of melancholy. Reverting to the sergeant, R. says, "When one takes up a book, one reads it; when one sees a picture, one examines it; but music one plays, one feels identified with it, and consequently imagines oneself to be a musician." —

*Sunday, August 20* Bechstein sends the portrait of Tausig; referring to the change which took place in our friend, R. says, "There are so many people who give the impression of being geniuses in their youth and who never in fact achieve intellectual puberty." He continues: "I remember that when I was at Dresden I told Röckel that I hoped to have written all my works before I was 40; I assumed that the sexual urge, with which all productivity is connected, would last until then. Röckel laughed at me and said I might assume that about Rossini, but with me it was quite different." Then he adds sadly: "But with age comes sorrow, the kaleidoscope of life is no longer so fascinating, one no longer expects miracles; this phase has to be overcome, to allow the serenity of old age to emerge." Visit from Frau von Abaza from St. Petersburg, a good and robust German character who tells R. many kind things about me. A gentleman from the Wagner committee in Vienna was also here. In the afternoon I visit Countess Ugarte. She wishes to take up a certificate of patronage for her daughter. — In the evening R. plays passages from *Oberon*, which we find very charming. "It breathes loyalty and faith, and that is the important thing—whether one is true to oneself or deceives oneself." — When I am already in bed, R. comes to me and says he cannot bear to see me so sorrowful. He talks to me for a long time, saying things which are beautiful, profound, and good, he weeps bitterly and I gently. I could have no idea, he says, how utterly he belongs to me, how much he loves me, that is the only thing that distresses him. I lie awake for a long time and pray to God.

*Monday, August 21* R. comes to me and says he needs no religion, for him I am the revelation of all that is good and beautiful, I am his fairy tale, the dream for which he lives; smilingly we admit that it is good when a shadow falls between us, for then we appreciate our happiness even more profoundly and fervently. Marie Schleinitz announces a visit. Letter from Dr. Standhartner (business affairs). Yesterday I had letters from Claire, Käthchen, Hedwig. — Visit from Marie Schleinitz along with Baron Loën; discussion about entrusting everything to small committees, nothing to my father or Marie Muchanoff; the Willes and Wesendoncks also entirely uninvolved. Baron Loën will take Tausig's place. — Arrival of a pineapple from Herr von Gersdorff. In the evening the Schleinitzes, Princess Hatzfeld, Baron Loën. — In the afternoon R. overwhelms me with love, which banishes all cares; but cares still exist; the King is said to be looking very bad. God knows what will become of us.

*Tuesday, August 22* Wrote many letters; R. to Councilor Düfflipp; he drives into Lucerne around noon to visit Herr von Schl[einitz]. In the afternoon a visit from Marie Schl., a few passages from *Siegfried* gone through. In the evening read Carlyle. R. and I are both tired. I was affected by a conversation with Marie Schl., particularly by what she told me about my father: he claims never in his life to have caused me any sorrow!!

*Wednesday, August 23* Terrible storm, the Hofkirche in Lucerne struck by lightning. Work with the children. R. writes letters in connection with Bayreuth; I go to town intending to pay visits. Our minister's wife gone to Brunnen, but she comes along later and spends the evening with us; the third act of *Siegfried* is gone through, and again much is said about my father. — As I returned home today in a boat, R. was waiting for me on the shore and greeted me with the "merry tune" from *Tristan*.

*Thursday, August 24* When other women come to see us, R. always says such nice and loving things to me that I could become really proud and arrogant, if it were not that such superabundant kindness induces feelings of profound humility in me. I write to dear Alwine

Frommann. From noon until 7 in the evening, Herr and Frau von Schleinitz; a very pleasant visit. R. and I then go for a walk in glorious moonlight to the opposite side of the lake. — The Schleinitzes tell us that the King of Bavaria was looking very run down; the Emperor had praised his discernment, but the people in the entourage thought he looked like a cretin!

*Friday, August 25* Our wedding day! R. comes to me early in the morning and congratulates—himself! — Letter from Councilor Düfflipp saying that he has been seriously considering asking for his dismissal, once again he can do nothing right for the King. Marie Schl. and Caroline Bass[enheim] send us flowers. R. says, "A fine coincidence, I must now compose 'Hagen's Wedding Call,' it is marvelously pretty!" — I write to Alwine Frommann, around noon I go to visit R. and find him unwell, he has had to break off his work! But when I come down to lunch he receives me with a melody he has written for this day, which the children are to sing to me on ceremonial occasions. In the afternoon drive with the children to Emmenbrück; coffee, honey, doughnuts, and the Titlis in all its glory. Beautiful evening. — After supper Carlyle.

*Saturday, August 26* R. had a very wretched night; he walked about until dawn, listened for a long time to a haymaker yodeling, then went to bed and dreamed that my father was treating him contemptuously, in an offhand manner, and R. said to himself, "Just you wait, you are not yet acquainted with my last score—you will treat me differently then, or have you already grown so stupid that you no longer will be able to understand it?" I had also dreamed of my father, wildly and hideously. — R. is still very unwell and cannot work. I write to Councilor Düfflipp and work with the children. In the evening, visit from Princess Hatzfeld and Frau von Schleinitz.

*Sunday, August 27* R. slept better last night and hopes to be able to work. He says to me with a laugh: "How different people are! I asked Friedrich about that haymaker who yodeled during the night, and he answered, 'He is a scoundrel.' Yet I found it touching that, having put up his tent in the meadow too far from the house, he yodeled out loud every time he woke up, in order to chase off his loneliness." — Yesterday evening R. again became very heated about the present spirit of the public, which profanes and degrades women. The woman who dresses up for the street is an absurdity, the conventional gallantry of men toward her a bad veneer concealing vulgarity of the worst sort. He is also in favor of marriages arranged by parents in the true interests of their families; nowadays, he says, everyone wants to live his own romantic novel and imagines that this rarest of things, love, over which whole epics have been written, is an everyday affair which happens to us all. — R. does some work. Family lunch. In the afternoon a visit by Princess Hatzfeld and Herr and Frau von Schleinitz; they say goodbye to us, since they are going to Engelberg. In the evening Carlyle. — The newspaper reports that Hans is to make concert tours during the winter, to Switzerland, Austria, etc. My gnawing grief never leaves me, and I do not wish to dispel it, but will carry it to my grave. — Rus is ill and very miserable.

*Monday, August 28* Fine day, with a touch of autumn already in the air. Work with the children. R. composes, and tells me that he does not intend to assemble a large chorus at "Hagen's Call," but individual vassals who appear from the farmsteads nearby. — Letter from Prof. Nietzsche, saying that Dr. Liebermeister in Basel strongly recommends iron and calcium for Fidi. R. goes for a long walk, I drive to meet him after taking Lusch through Bach's exercises for beginners. — Prof. Nohl sends another book about Beethoven and touches us by telling us that he had been in Lucerne, had looked at Tribschen from the outside, but had been reminded by the sign outside it, "Entry Prohibited," that everybody must be careful not to disturb. In the evening Carlyle.

*Tuesday, August 29* Richter writes from Pest; but he annoys R. because he has not been working for him and has not yet prepared the score of *Das Rheingold* for Schott. At 11 o'clock Baron Loën comes for a conference, he is taking Tausig's place, and R. is very pleased with him and his enthusiasm. We are glad to have found him and believe that things will now go more smoothly. Just as we are settling down to a siesta, Jakob announces Herr Bucher, and it really is our old friend, whom we welcome with joy to Tribschen. Then Louis Brassin, the doughty German musician from Brussels, also arrives. Talked about all sorts of things; Lothar Bucher horrifies us with the news that Duke Ratibor, Duke von Ujest, and Count Lehndorff had allowed Herr Strousberg to put down their names for 100,000 thalers in the Rumanian shares, and this had induced the smaller capital-holders to part with their money. The aristocratic gentlemen, since they gave nothing but their names, have escaped without damage, except to their honor, but the less well-to-do have lost everything.

*Wednesday, August 30* Still fine weather. R. works, I teach. At 2 o'clock dinner with Herr Brassin and our friend Bucher. Then a walk. R. tired and irritated because Herr Brassin entertains him with a constant stream of theatrical anecdotes and accounts of performances. Letter from Mme Ollivier.

*Thursday, August 31* Our friend intends to climb Mount Pilatus, and under adverse weather conditions. R. works, but he is tired. Herr Brassin's conversation was a great strain on him. Family lunch.

Letter to Loulou from Aunt Isa, she wishes to see her, which always gives me troubled thoughts. There is an article on Karl Tausig in the *Signale* by Hans; this—Hans exactly as I know him—makes no very favorable impression on us. — In the afternoon I visit Countess Bassenheim; heavy thunderstorm; when I return home I find R. in a very despondent mood; he says he has been drawing up the balance of his life and that, as I might imagine, I came out well in it; but he felt as if he were standing with me and Fidi on the top of Mont Blanc, abandoned in this solitary desert; and it was not just outwardly that everything had fallen away from him, no, it had crumbled within; I could see, he said, how hopeless he became when I left the house, if only for a single hour, how he cursed the world. — We read Carlyle. — At Countess B.'s I learn with dismay that they are staging a Wagner week [in Munich] and are performing *Rheingold* and *Walküre* again!!! Probably they want to make money.

*Friday, September 1* R. exclaims to me in the morning, "You know nothing at all; you don't know how I suffer when you are not there; with Bismarck I should have found a way of furthering my cause if you had been there, for: together with you everything, without you nothing—that's how it is." Fidi gives us great joy. R. says, "He will be all right; I am a kind of Siegmund, for whom there are always obstacles, he will have Goethe's world-conquering quality." — As he passes a hand over his forehead I ask him if anything is the matter. "My thoughts are itching." He works. We expect Lothar Bucher for lunch, but he does not come; at table R. says to me: "I have been thinking again about actors, poets, and so on, and have even made some notes on the subject in my sketchbook. An improviser such as an actor must belong entirely to the present moment, never think of what is to come, indeed not even know it, as it were. The peculiar thing about me as an artist, for instance, is that I look on each detail as an entirety and never say to myself, 'Since this or that will follow, you must do thus and such, modulate like this or like that.' I think, 'Something will turn up.' Otherwise I should be lost; and yet I know I am unconsciously obeying a plan. The so-called genius of form, on the other hand, reflects, 'This or that follows, so I must do such and such,' and he does it with ease." — Visit from Count Bassenheim, who gives us another shock with the news that the King has ordered a coronation carriage with 6 pictures from the Bible and 6 allegories about Louis XIV, for 20,000 florins. R. says we shall certainly soon receive news from that quarter of sudden insanity or death; deep concern, we will be without house or home. — R. goes to town and returns home with a Herr Hey, who wants to force his singing method on him at all costs; he is very agitated by this foolish interruption. After the good man has gone, R. tells me that he has had a dreadful scene with Eglin, the stationer; he had been unutterably rude and had even shouted after R. in the street, "May you suffer homesickness wherever you go!" — God knows who or what so stirs up these people against him; R. has been buying paper there for the past five years and is, if anything, too good to them; he was not satisfied with the sorts of paper, and then they behave thus. R. does not wish ever to go to Lucerne again.

*Saturday, September 2* In the morning R. says to me, "I was already composing in the early hours." "And what?" "The hawthorn tree no longer pricks." Written down? "Oh, no, things like that are done in the head." — At breakfast R. tells me again how pleased and touched he was yesterday when Fidi ran a long stretch toward him. He says he looked splendid. And so outside everything is worry and annoyance, inside all happiness and joy. — R. works, toward noon our friend returns from Mount Pilatus; happy lunch together. In the afternoon Hey, the singing teacher, who tells us that the Wagner Society in Munich is coming along well. Lovely moonlit night, R. gives L. B[ucher] *Art and Politics* to take to Bismarck. — In the night we are awakened by Rus's barking—a "crazy woman," as Jakob says, was prowling around Tribschen; R. thinks she was crazy enough to want to steal something.

*Sunday, September 3* Our friend has left. Letter from Vienna that Betz brought forth a real storm of applause in *Die Meistersinger*; this news is very welcome to R.—now at last *Die Msinger* is being given again in Vienna. Letter from M. Schleinitz, to which I reply straight-away, saying it will not be possible for us to visit them in Engelberg. — It turns out (through the vet) that Rus has been poisoned and that the woman from yesterday knew about it and, assuming his death, had planned a robbery attempt. I had heard footsteps and, during our evening walk, noticed that someone was hiding in the bushes, though R. laughed off my fears; Rus, however, who had at first growled, ran at once to the open *salon* door and lay down across it, the loyal watchdog. — Sultry afternoon, visit from Baron Uechtritz from Meiningen. In the evening Carlyle.

*Monday, September 4* A picture of the casino in Wiesbaden horrifies R.; women and men are both horrible: "And then one is supposed to think about the art of the future!" — Toward noon R. calls me and plays me his "inspiration"—Brünnhilde's reception by the vassals; her appearance will be characterized by the motive we heard when she becomes frightened of Siegfried, "when the *other thing* overcomes her," as R. says. — Great heat; I drive into town to make purchases for Loulou's birthday. R. brings me a letter from my mother, the first for several months; she complains of great weakness in the brain, but is thrilled by developments in France—the republic is assured, she says!! — In the evening Carlyle.

*Tuesday, September 5*  R. works "in ink"; after lunch I reply to my mother; letter from Marie Muchanoff with all sorts of objections from my father: not Bayreuth, but a national theater, etc.; R. laughs and says, "Ah, yes, I know, the Goethe Foundation." Then he becomes more vexed and says, "That is arrogance—not to accept another person's idea just as it is, being too unsettled himself even to be able to grasp it!" — Many disagreeable feelings, which are then swept away by an indescribable shock I experienced; I can distinctly hear the fluttering of a bird on the terrace, R. does not hear it, also does not hear the chirping of the cicadas; this impression starts a worry in me which no joy can dispel; all keenness of hearing is now accursed for me. Curiously enough, however, R. can hear quite distinctly the trickling of the fountain and the very distant sound of the breaking waves. A merciful God will help! — At lunch R. said, "The dying Englishman will turn up, you'll see—I have precedents in my life for hopes like that." I: "Apart from the King of Bavaria I know of none." "And yourself." "Oh, I do not belong there." "No, there you are right; it's just that I sometimes imagine how loathsome any sort of existence would be to me if you had not been born." — In the evening I have difficulty in concealing my overflowing mood from R.

*Wednesday, September 6*  I write to Marie M. — R., who reads my letter, says it suits its address just as little as his *Tristan* the Emperor of Brazil. R. works. Very close weather, we decide on a drive. In the morning R. told me he intended to write a short article on Weber, taking off from a very conceited statement the latter once made about Beethoven's lack of formal clarity, which he, Weber, took care not to imitate. R. wants to show that it was precisely in his misunderstanding of Beethoven that Weber's whole weakness lay, confining him within the boundaries of conventional form, stereotypes. — When I tell Wagner that I like the final ensemble number in Rossini's *Tell*, R. says: "Yes, it is incredibly lacking in ideas, but firstly it is dynamic in effect, and then the simplicity of this succession of chords, after all the operatic larks, does one good; it gives the effect of Nature." "I feel that in the opera the emptiness is concealed by the sunrise and the Swiss costumes, whereas in the symphony into which my father has transferred these effects the emptiness is very noticeable." — R. says, "Beethoven makes his effect mostly in similar ways, through continuity, but with him things are of course always quite different." — We start on our drive toward evening, and R. remarks, "These contours of low, wooded hills used to arouse feelings of longing and melancholy in me; I wanted to get beyond them, away, to the other side." I: "Yes, to the place where you are not—I know the feeling." "But now," R. says, "I wish to stay at home, I find going away utterly loathsome; I am glad of children around the house, the teeming life surrounding me—only I should like to be 15 years younger." — While getting ready to go out, he looked at the picture of his uncle [Adolph] and exclaimed: "How happy my uncle now is, how he will continue to live, in a way he certainly never expected! But without me—or, rather, without you— he would now be completely forgotten; nobody in my family would have given him a thought." On the journey he told me that at the age of 10 to 12 he had often visited an exalted lady, Frau Schneider; on account of lack of space, the books in her house were all kept in one little room, "and you should have seen me among those books in that little room!" — We talk of the love between Siegfried and Brünnhilde, which achieves no universal deed of redemption, produces no Fidi; *Götterdämmerung* is the most tragic work of all, but before that one sees the great happiness arising from the union of two complete beings. Siegfried does not know what he is guilty of; as a man, committed entirely to deeds, he knows nothing, he must fall in order that Brünnhilde may rise to the heights of perception. — We then discuss why German opera composers know nothing of the fire of love, with them love is just a sort of sentimental convention, its highest expression Ottavio in *Don Giovanni*. The French have more passion, but it is also very rare there. — Letters from Karl v. Gersdorff and M. v. Schl. In the evening cold punch, Carlyle, and lovely moonlight shining straight through our French windows.

*Thursday, September 7* The cold punch did not agree with R., he is unwell, but he works all the same. Family lunch with Fidi, who as a man is already demonstrating his superiority over his sisters. Drive after lunch; with the children. E. Ollivier has sent us his defense, he shows that it was France and not the government which wanted war. In the evening Carlyle and iced coffee. — When I went to R. as he was working he said to me, "I was just thinking about you and your religion; your feminine dignity was offended, and so you took refuge in religion!" — I am alarmed by the fact that R. leaves his window open during the night, I ask him to shut it, but do not dare tell him this is on account of his hearing. He does not shut it.

*Friday, September 8* Letter from Richter, who, it seems, is holding rehearsals, but is not doing his work for R., which vexes R. very much. He works in spite of the close atmosphere, continuing his composition even in the afternoon. I write to Thérèse Ollivier, giving her my candid opinion of the pamphlet, *Procès historique*, which E. O. sent me. I also write to little Daniel, I feel it would be a transgression against

Blandine were I not to attempt to come closer to this child and gain an influence over him. A drive with the children. Fidi's iron tonic is doing him no good so far, he has no appetite. In the evening Carlyle, who gives us much enjoyment. As R. says good night to me, he ends the day with a joke: "It must be very nice for a woman to have a husband who loves her so much." — I am frightened by a bat.

*Saturday, September 9* Bad and dull weather suddenly. R. receives a warning letter from a printer in Munich; our fine Dr. Lang, whom R. paid long ago, has not yet paid this man for printing *E. Devrient and His Style*; he demanded 60 florins from R., and now it comes out that the printers are asking only 40! He that toucheth pitch, etc. [besmirches himself]. The bat omen comes true: R. is very unwell and despondent, he says he takes no pleasure in his work, if only he could do things which would meet the needs of the world; what he does do is useless; nobody wants it. Marie M.'s letter has depressed him terribly; to submerge oneself on the one hand in the mightiest world of ideas, and on the other to be told nothing but platitudes! Another gift from the bat is an impertinent letter from the publisher Meser-Müller in Dresden, to whom R. had written. In the evening Carlyle.

*Sunday, September 10* Still the bat: Loulou suddenly falls ill. Violent fever and headache; I send for the doctor, he fears a throat inflammation. I spend the day with her. When I then go to R., I find him suffering from a pain in the foot; I tremble at the thought of gout; he has been suffering for two days now. — He is in dismal spirits, thinks of all the visitors we are expecting, fears a serious disturbance of his work, and wonders whether he will not have to break it off for a while. As we are talking, Prince Georg of Prussia is announced; his visit gives R. little pleasure, since the conversation turns out to be very flat and trivial. — Carlyle makes up for it in the evening.

*Monday, September 11* (Letter from Prof. Nietzsche.) Loulou had a better night, the danger is past; R. still suffers with his foot. — While I am still in bed and R. comes to wish me a good morning, he takes my hands and stretches them out, as if I were on the cross, at the same time saying, "I think that this horrible form of death did serve to spread Christianity—one would not have been able to accept a hanged man as a symbol; here one saw the mortal being in suffering—just dangling from a rope would have been impossible." A woman was here yesterday, well dressed and of a pleasant, modest appearance; she said her life's wish had been granted—she had seen the house in which R. Wagner lived. — In the afternoon we drive into town to make purchases for the children. As we ride home R. sinks into melancholy: "How pleasant it was for a person like Titian in the Venice of his day, what a part he could play in communal life—but our communal life, how pitiful! In Cologne Herr Hiller, in Dresden Herr Rietz, in Munich previously Herr Lachner—that is conformity, that is a harmony which people like ourselves can disturb only sporadically." In the morning we had seen in the *Illustrirte Zeitung* a picture of the Beethoven Festival under Hiller, which was truly alarming. Talking of Joachim and his wife, R. says, "One might think: Here are two capable artists, here only good music will be played; but what emerges?" Read a lot from the Greek legends to Loulou. Letter from Fritz Brockhaus.

*Tuesday, September 12* R. again had a very bad night; his foot is better, but his abdominal troubles are worse! Visit from Countess B. — Prince Georg wants to meet us this evening at her house. R. feels too unwell and ill-humored, and asks me to go alone, which I do reluctantly. — Lulu is somewhat better, but still in bed; Fidi is also unwell. Letter from Elisabeth Krockow in Gmunden. — The evening with Countess B. passes tolerably well; it must be very wounding for R. the way all his admirers, among whom Prince Georg can also be counted, carefully avoid talking about our venture! — R. does not like me to leave the house and he was a bit ill-humored when I came home, though in a joking manner.

*Wednesday, September 13* Loulou still in bed, but getting better; I stay with her and write letters and read Greek legends to her. In the afternoon did some shopping for her birthday. R. is unwell and despondent. Letter from L. Bucher. — *Fidi Albrecht Dürer* gives us much joy, only R. is sad at seeing so little of him, he is full of cares. "People tell me, when they see Tribschen, 'You are happy.' But can I remain here? And my new establishment—with what troubles is that connected! I could almost wish that a doctor would forbid me ever again to write a note of music, and I could live with you somewhere on my pension. But how to demand of the King that he give up these things? And the King, who does so incomparably much for me, he must go and stage *Rheingold* and *Walküre* without me! One is in a constant state of emotion and upset. Our earlier relationship, how that grieved us once; it has been smoothed out in the nicest way—but now apprehension about our very existence!" Thus he complains. . . .

*Thursday, September 14* At 4 in the morning R. comes to inquire how I am, for I was indisposed yesterday evening and still am. Then he could no longer sleep, and went downstairs to write Herr Brandt a letter, asking him for a first estimate of the cost of putting in the foundations of the theater; he would then lay the foundation stone in the middle of October, if Baron Loën makes a favorable report, and would make a speech. "Then," R. says, "the whole thing, as far as I am concerned, can hang fire for years. My speech, which will afterward be published as an appeal, ought to make some sort of impact." It fills me with sorrow to see R. so worried and agitated that he cannot possibly continue his creative work cheerfully and remain in good health. He said yesterday, "I am so churned up inside that even something like Tausig's death goes in one ear and out the other, and that is not good." — I do not wish to look even a day into the future, so dizzy does it all make me feel. — R. told me he thought he had seen me come to him in the night and say to him in a very clear voice, "Tichtel." But as even in his dream he remembered that I was hoarse, he believed it was a ghost, and cried out, waking himself up. Then he also dreamed that he had stolen something and had been put in prison; we laughed, and I remembered how he had once said, when we were talking about impossible things: "Murder, even in anger, would certainly be impossible for me, but stealing, from a rich banker when I was certain it would not be discovered, I believe I could do that. And yet, no, for I should constantly have to tell lies about where I got the money, and I couldn't." — Family lunch. I feel indisposed and cannot go out, R. goes into town. Before that he plays some of the second act, the reception of the Gibichungs—"a nice family," says R., "who are greeted by their vassals with love and respect—a decorous, not a turbulent reception." "But I can neither play it nor sing it; when I am done with this little opus I mean to content myself like Falstaff with only two shirts." — He is worried because Fritzsch, his publisher, sends him no word. I have another worry, namely, that Baron Loën will be restrained by his master, the Grand Duke of Weimar, from taking part in our venture; the Grand Duke has in fact flatly rejected Marie M.'s request to become a patron! But I do not tell R. this. — As we were driving home yesterday, R. sang to me Beethoven's song "Heart, oh heart, what means this feeling?" and said, "Everything there lies in the first rhythmic movement; what keeps a theme from sounding trivial lies in the composer's loyalty and faith, certainly not in the notes he chooses; a song can never be too simple." "There is youthfulness in this song," I said. "Yes," says R., "and it is more Goethe than Beethoven." — Lothar Bucher sends R., who had asked him for it, the derivation of the word *talent* (from a Greek word meaning "weight"). — R. is not well and is despondent, his income at the moment is small, and he told me that he did not know how to finance our journey if we have to make it next month. —

*Friday, September 15* I write to the banker Joachim in Berlin regarding the investment of my money for the children. R. works. and says to me, "I am now getting into the musical mood, that is why I am so agitated." The children in better health, but Eva is sleepy. In the afternoon a letter from Frau Wesendonck; she says she is going to Munich to see *Rheingold* or *Walküre*, but does not mention our Bayreuth venture in even a single word. R. is extremely annoyed about it, asks me not to reply, and complains of having spent his whole life consorting with pitiful creatures. "For," he says, "she knew all about it; our whole intercourse revolved around this production of the *Nibelungen*—and now just to ignore it all! The worst of it is that one cannot wipe out experiences; one can remove them from one's heart, but they remain in one's life." The bare mention of the production in Munich is like a dagger in his heart—"and now I am supposed to continue with my work, but how can I?" — His grief makes me miserable. He knows that all his friends will go running off to Munich again and none will give a thought to him! — *Frederick the Great* provides some slight distraction.

*Saturday, September 16* Hermine has had to go home, so the entire quintet is left in my hands; Loldi, the only one who misses Hermine, becomes ill; great woes. R. works, reverts to yesterday's wretched experience: "Yes, the Bible talks of princes and merchants, and it is right; but I am expecting a miracle, and it will come, you will see— I don't know how or where, but it will come." I tell him that I also believe this; to me the miracle is that he is working! He tells me to ignore Frau W. entirely; but I find it impossible to offend someone who once played a role in his life, and I tell her in a few words what these Munich performances mean to us. . . . At lunch—for what reason I do not know—R. told me that in his youth the worst thing he could imagine was to take leave of somebody forever, and he knew now that he could never have had Fritz and Kos put to death if he had had to say goodbye to them. I understand that; I once had to take leave of somebody, and from that hour, which also brought me my first gray hairs, I realized the true meaning of life; up till then everything I had read in the poets about the dreadfulness and blameworthiness of life I could feel only intuitively; but when I gave Hans my hand in farewell, I felt it all inside myself, and the veil of illusion was torn forever. From then on I understood life and death, and from then on I have wished for nothing more. — I put Loldi to bed and go for a drive with the other children; Fidi is also not quite well. The day is rather tiring, but I love such emergencies, and it does me good to know that the children enjoy being alone with me! —

*Sunday, September 17* Loldi had a terrible night, I stayed up with her throughout; in the morning, however, she is a bit better; but the doctor fears diphtheria. Marie Schleinitz writes that Bülow is to conduct the Wagneriana in Berlin, but I can scarcely believe it. Richter's National Theater in Pest has been burned down. — [*A few words about Fidi's speech omitted.*] I spend the day in anxiety at Loldi's bedside,

to M. Schleinitz with a verse saying: If you call genius the power that brings forth a true work of art, I call love and loyalty the favor with which the world repays its debt.

*Monday, October 2* R. exclaims to me: "What a happy couple we are! When it is so stormy outside, I am reminded that our storms are past. But the fact that you love me does not make it the best of worlds —if you didn't love me, it would simply cease to exist for me." Letter from Claire. — R. works so long that we do not eat until after two o'clock. R. overwhelmingly good and kind; he says to me, "You are the fulfillment of everything life never even promised me!" — I drive to town; purchases for Wilhelm. I bring back a nice letter from Herwegh, who, however, is still stuck fast in the Liberal mold. In the evening R. reads me passages from the *Edda*. — (Moltke at the head of the Protestant Association!)

*Tuesday, October 3* Very unsettled night; Fidi did not sleep a wink and never stopped talking. — Yesterday R. told me some very touching things about the women of the 17th and 18th centuries, among others Gessner's wife; they produced great men through their loyalty and enlightened outlook. The Gessner couple very moving, I ask whether this is the Gessner who wrote idylls, and this leads us on to Bodmer, the dedication of the *Nibelungenlied* to Frederick the Great, and his judgment on it. R. links to this the remark that great statesmen are not governed by historic thoughts, but do at the proper time what the exigencies of the moment demand; in political life the historical viewpoint fulfills roughly the same function as museums in art. "Oh, after all, if music is not meant to give new life to the whole world, it is not worth very much." — R. works and then plays me the splendidly daemonic *"Helle Wehr"* of poor Brünnhilde. Often, he says, he shudders to think that he might suddenly grow tired of writing this work —"but," he consoles me, "now that I have got so far, I shall finish it." Wrote to Rothschild, who has again not sent me my money! — Am indisposed, very tired. R. brings a letter from Luise von Bülow, Hans's stepmother, to Daniella; she wants to see the two eldest children; difficult as I find it, I decide at once to send the children to Weggis tomorrow. R. scolds me, says she can visit the children here, but I do not like isolating the children from their family, and in God's name—!

*Wednesday, October 4* Saying goodbye to the children, vigorous waving of handkerchiefs on both the steamer and the banks of Tribschen. The absence of the children makes me melancholy. — R. works; afterward family lunch, with Wilhelm, since it is his birthday. Then a drive, later put Fidi to bed. He puts out his own light, laughing, and then lies down quietly, which touches R. very much, he says he sees in it the symbol of a noble, free, fine death. In the evening our nephews return; I do not enjoy their company as much as usual, because I am too tired. Vreneli, returning from Weggis, brings me many regards from *Luise von Bülow* and says she was overjoyed to see the children.

*Thursday, October 5* The children back; sad at hearing that Boni had been exceptionally boisterous there and, in spite of the fact that everyone was in mourning, had allowed herself to be tempted into downright wild jubilation. Spent a lot of time with our nephews, who are becoming increasingly close to us. Through Boni I am plunged into deep melancholy, which I can talk about only to R., to whom I confide everything. [*In the margin:* "With R. prolonged contemplation of a comatose butterfly on a tree; a wonderful red admiral."] In the evening to the circus with the children and both nephews. R. remarks that the clown is the human being as an animal; he has no sense of honor at all, is sensitive only to physical pain. Contemplating the orchestra, which plays not at all badly, he says, "One mustn't forget it is from there that musicians come!" — Though the noise affects him very much, he is extraordinarily gay, delighted with the children's joy. . . .

*Friday, October 6* While R. is working, a long walk with children and nephews; *Eva* also walks a good German mile with us. R. receives letters from Baron Loën, Dr. Kafka, and Herr Heckel, all of them in effect agreeing to the laying of the foundation stone. In the evening *tableaux vivants*, which the children arrange and which please our nephews enormously.

*Saturday, October 7* Letter from Herr Rothschild; he ignores the fact that he made me no payments at all during the siege of Paris and sends me nothing for this October, reckoning that from January onward he has paid me for the whole year 1871. I am making inquiries and want simply to know whether, after my marriage to R., my father perhaps gave orders to pay me nothing; otherwise I do not understand R[othschild]'s mistake. I write to him. On top of this unpleasantness comes R.'s talk of the need to receive and entertain the people who come to the laying of the foundation stone in Bayreuth, though we do not really have the means for it, and R. still has several debts to pay. Deep concern over this; I realize with sorrow that in this matter I cannot share R.'s cheerful spirits, I would rather do without even the most important things than be in debt; also, I have no confidence about the earnings R. expects to make. I overcome all my worries and keep silent; but how hard life is, how dismal! Who would want more of it? In the afternoon went to meet our nephews, who had driven out to Flüelen in the morning and are now going back to Basel. — The children on the velocipede carrousel. — Hermine still not back, although I had urgently begged her to return. Wrote to Frau Tausig, still in connection with *Tristan,* but she knows nothing, either.

*Sunday, October 8* Very dismal experience with Blandine; I am told that recently she read aloud from a book, "There was once a nasty mama, she left the papa and married someone else; that was very nasty, I shall never do it." And that in front of two maidservants, who are telling others about it. All that is left for me to do is to look after this child as I have so far done and do without her love—God will aid me. At first I wanted to ignore the whole thing, but my mother's heart cannot bear to regard the situation as hopeless, and so I chose the end of family lunch to tell the children and R. what Boni had done. Great consternation; I hope it will not be forgotten. In the course of the day I am persuaded by various reports that Hermine has been a bad influence on the children, and, in spite of the difficulties in which I find myself at present, I write her not to return. We also have to dismiss the groom, since he downright torments poor Grane. However, R. goes on working steadily, despite these domestic turmoils. In the evening we read some pages of Carlyle. R. writes to Ottilie about a nursemaid, and I to Käthchen.

*Monday, October 9* Wet weather; the five constantly around me. R. works; around noon I hear him cry, "And if Cosima should fall begging at my feet, I shall not compose another note today." Everything now in the balance: foundation stone, domestic arrangements, relations with my father, Rothschild, *Tristan* manuscript, etc. — R. writes to his brother-in-law Avenarius, who has lost his son Max. In the evening Carlyle.

*Tuesday, October 10* 18 years ago today I saw R. for the first time. It was in Paris, he read *Götterdämmerung* to us—"which I am only now completing; without you it would never have dawned," he says! — I did not have a good night, since Fidi kept coming to me. Around noon R. calls me, in order to read to me Brünnhilde's "*An wen?*" ["To whom?"] which, addressed to Hagen, occurs in the "duet," and in which one sees that the wild woman of the rocks is the personification of melancholy. In the afternoon we receive two issues of the *Süddeutsche Presse*, full of invective against *Rheingold* and *Walküre*. R. beside himself over the scorn and abuse he has to put up with. — Visit from R. Pohl in connection with the Bayreuth exhibition affair. — R. telegraphs to Herr Bratfisch about *Tristan*, reply paid, but no reply comes. — Rothschild informs me that he cannot pay me!

*Wednesday, October 11* I write to Eduard Liszt about the Rothschild matter; to Marie Schleinitz—who had written to us—and to Councilor D[üfflipp], sending him the abusive articles, with a humble request to the King now at last to withdraw *Rheingold* and *Walküre*. — R. works and plays me what he has written. R. Pohl to lunch, and then a walk with him and the children. In the evening R. reads passages from the biography and plays from *Tristan* and *Siegfried*. Both R. and I in melancholy mood; the cessation of music in particular is for me like the death blow which returns me to life!

*Thursday, October 12*  Loulou's birthday, lovingly celebrated as usual. R. Pohl departs. The children play, R. works, I write to Herr von Gersdorff, entrusting the *Tristan* affair to him. Hermine's sister writes me a letter full of invective; R. takes this matter into his own hands and sends her 100 florins. Still no news from anywhere regarding nursemaids. While the children are at a puppet show with Vreneli, I converse with R. about my father and his influence on people with such things as "Norma," "Somnambula," etc. "He was the illustrator of a vanishing world," R. says, "as, for example, with his gypsy airs, which have no particular pretensions. The center for that sort of thing was Paris, now dead and gone." In the evening Carlyle, after I showed the children slides on the magic lantern.

*Friday, October 13*  R. works diligently, although he had a bad night. I nothing but children, but wrote a few lines to Claire. Mannheim sends money for *Rienzi*, which is used to pay Hermine. Letter from my father, who seems to have got pleasure from mine. In the evening sang songs with the children, and Fidi joined in roaring, which made us all laugh loudly. My mother sends a copy of the *Revue Positive*, in which the notable scholar Littré says the same silly things about Germany as any ordinary Frenchman.

*Saturday, October 14*  Clemens Br[ockhaus] writes very nicely to Loulou. R. works. As I greet him around noon, he exclaims, "You and I are in fact doing the same thing, devoting ourselves like mad people to one single aim, and that is absurd!" Käthchen writes that she cannot come for another five weeks, which upsets R. very much. He writes to Hedwig Neumann, asking her to get things settled. God knows, I am very tired, and regret being able to do so little for R. Fire in the rooms.

*Sunday, October 15*  Letter from my mother; also from R. Pohl, who is making difficulties. — The dying gnats and flies arouse R.'s pity, he cannot remember any poet's having written about this— usually they talk only of fading flowers. Walked a lot with the children. Fidi splendid, gives me much joy. An Englishman, Mr. Sweet, offers his services for the Bayreuth venture. R. works, but is very agitated, since he has so much to do (correcting).

*Monday, October 16*  Richard spends the morning on corrections, to my sorrow, since I should prefer to see him getting on with [*Götter*]-*dämmerung*. But this is still occupying him, he is even thinking of the third act, and yesterday ran back upstairs, though he had already broken off, because "the right thing had just come" to him. Letter from Marie Schleinitz, who is very much in favor of the laying of the foundation stone. But no news from Brandt, none from Käthchen, nothing which could be regarded as definite. I am constantly with the children, which tires me greatly. In the evening still a little Carlyle.

*Tuesday, October 17* A package for Loulou from her grandmother, something which always brings me bitter thoughts, which I try, however, to resist and dispel. The only possible thing to do in this case is one's duty, and nothing more; God will help! Very fine letter from Cl. Brockhaus, on whom Tribschen seems to have made a deep impression. R. works, I nursemaid, so that I can find time to write in this book only with difficulty. Yesterday wrote a hasty letter to my mother. The children come along suddenly with a little dog, which refuses to leave our yard; Loldi first discovered him, and he bears a remarkable resemblance to our poor Kos. The children are hugely pleased about it. In the evening R. is tired; he has written letters (to the Englishman), and I send my father a birthday greeting.

*Wednesday, October 18* No help, replies which are none, Brandt sends a telegram, saying he was waiting for R.'s reply! And Ottilie writes that she has found the right person for our children, but unfortunately she is already engaged! — R. is very worn out, does not work, but is thinking of it all the time; he has the theme for the Rhine-maidens in the third act, but he says he will have to make an alteration to the text, which he does not like doing. At lunch I talk about a clothing ceremony I once attended, that brought us on to the subject of religious orders, and R. said they arose from the feeling that the church is a servant of politics and that pious people should seek refuge from it in silent solitude. "Saints," R. continued, "did in fact exist before Christ, just as the verb came before the noun and the poet before poetry, that is to say, the gift of seeing, of contemplating, before the activity; the ecstasy of a soul, intent on renouncing life, came genetically earlier, and it fashioned for itself the symbol of the sacrificed innocent. All the same, it is foolish to try to analyze such things, which one cannot really grasp." — Jakob took the little dog to the market, thinking it would then find its way back to its master, but the dog followed him everywhere and returned home with him. We are increasingly struck with his resemblance to Kos and think he may have been his son, since there are no others of this breed in Lucerne. This thought moves and pleases us all very much, we are calling the little stray *Vito* and hope to keep him. — In Bavaria the minister Lutz has delivered a very strong statement from the Catholic party; this suggests that Bismarck is in earnest. — It is reported in many newspapers that the Bayreuth venture is assured. — Uncle Eduard does not reply. — In the evening read Carlyle.

*Thursday, October 19*   15 years ago the *Tannhäuser* Overture and my engagement to Hans. Today resolved to approach him directly regarding the conversion of the children. — R. better—gets down to his work; this morning he said to me, "On your account I should like to be very rich; we have everything else, our happiness, but you should have things a little easier!" — In the afternoon visit from Countess Bass-[enheim]. R. walks into town and brings back letters; the architect Neumann thinks one should not start a building in the winter, but should wait till March. His wife will try to get Käthchen to come here; Marie M. writes to me from Heidelberg that Tausig probably gave the *Tristan* score to Countess Dönhoff! Inquiry to El. Krockow in this connection; still no answer from Cousin Eduard! — In the evening Carlyle.

*Friday, October 20*   In a dream last night I saw myself dancing a quadrille, which does not please R. He works and I do mine, still without any news of outside help. At lunch R. told me he had seen a Jesuit in his ceremonial vestments: "What a face! You would need a painter to reproduce it, for neither a poet nor a musician could do it justice; its predominating expression one could only describe as cold, sheer hatred—it looked to me so strange, so un-German. I have never seen friendly blue eyes in a Jesuit." In the afternoon a letter from Herr von Gersd[orff], to whom I at once reply (regarding the manuscript). In the evening we get much enjoyment from the episode with Maupertuis in Carlyle, and we come to the conclusion that C. describes things well, even if he is a bad writer.

*Saturday, October 21*   Splendid, bright weather, scent of violets, golden tints; a long time with Fidi in the garden, watched beautiful butterflies, melancholy feelings; am also very tired, since I did not sleep a wink all night. Letter from Prof. Nietzsche, he wants his book to be published by Fritzsch. R. works long, but is very worn out. With the children I fetch Lulu from her piano lesson, she tells me of a dream she has had: she saw her father dying, he asked for my letters and hers to be placed in his grave, and died with the words "dear Cosima," after telling her, "Uncle Richard will now be your father." I was very touched. — In the evening Carlyle, after R. had warmly recommended Prof. Nietzsche's manuscript to Fritzsch. (Lulu is not well.) Regarding Voltaire, R. says: "One hardly looks at his writings any more, it is above all his personality which fascinates. Whereas with really great geniuses one seeks everything in their works." — Letter from old Herr Weitzmann in Berlin.

*Sunday, October 22*   My father's birthday, I send the children to church. R. is unfortunately very unwell and cannot work. I write to Marie Schleinitz and Clemens. Family lunch. Letter from Frau Neumann, saying that Käthchen will be here in a week's time. May God grant it! Great preparations in Bologna, but I fear a catastrophe. — Lulu unwell, put to bed early. In the evening R. reads me some pages from a book by Freytag about Frederick the Great, and he adds that the significant thing about him was that he revived German patriotism, which had completely vanished with the advent of the Habsburgs; Luther, Gustavus Adolphus, Frederick—those were the men who had helped the Germans, and now Bismarck. The plague of this nation has always been the Habsburgs, whom I one day hope to see thrown out; for this reason Bismarck's instinct to throw everything against Austria was the right one, and I hope the war with France was just an intermezzo on the way to the complete destruction of this shameful dynasty. Frederick also had the instinct: everything against Austria.

*Monday, October 23* Lusch under medical care, I read to her, receive a letter from Karl v. Gersdorff; Papa Tausig will do nothing more in the matter of the manuscript, and it seems no legal steps can be taken, which means that this affair has come to a bad end! But I do at least demand a public appeal. — At lunch R. tells me: "While I was composing, Frederick the Great's character became clear to me in the way Beethoven's character became clear to me—from within, as the will to live. What an artist sees, such a person lives—he is scarcely to be grasped or understood as an individual. What individual urge makes a man go through such tribulations as the Seven Years' War? And then this nation, suffering so terribly, yet always inspired and ready for sacrifices, participating in an idea, a great character—this is whence comes the pride of being a Prussian. Who could be proud of being a Württemberger, or a Bavarian, or a Saxon? But a Prussian, yes!" — Letter from a Turk, Prince Caradja, who asks for an autograph and receives along with it a certificate of patronage. Great tiredness in the evening; R. sad that I exert myself so much. (Wrote on R.'s behalf to the Luccas and to Mariani in Bologna, saying that he would have gone there for rehearsals, but never for the ovation to which they invite him after the second performance!)

*Tuesday, October 24* Letter from Clemens with enclosures from Herr Feustel and Herr Kolb in Bayreuth, which testify to the excellent sentiments of the people there. The disclosures of Benedetti, together with the reply of the *Reichsanzeiger*, bring me much enjoyment. R. works, says at lunch he has had an inspiration: Siegfried will blow on his horn at the wedding. Loulou is unwell, I read to her the first two acts of *Siegfried*. Before that I drive into town with all four and hear that Marie M[uchanoff] is to arrive tomorrow. Letter from Baron Loën; he now has about 25,000 thalers and has no doubts about success. — I write to Hedwig N[eumann] asking for assurances concerning Käthchen. Still reading Carlyle, during which R. remarks how immeasurable Frederick's influence was; without him no literature would have existed, he breathed courage and boldness everywhere; without him one would have tended to follow his own literary tastes— imitation of the French; one would not have dared to be original.

*Wednesday, October 25* Nice letter from Claire and from Alwine Frommann, the latter thanking us for sending the writings. These collected writings give R. great pleasure, he is so glad to have managed them, and so successfully, too. He is pleased that his writings should bring him some money: "*Siegfried*—what use is that? As soon as it appears, then the troubles will really begin, whereas the writings are quite complete in themselves—and there will be a second edition, you will see. I must just stay alive. But if I had died 10 years ago I should not have had much from life—not enough to have made it worth the trouble of living." Alwine sends some poems (unpublished) by Prof. Werder. R. says of them: "All these lyric poets make glosses on things which are not there; the true poet is seen in the characters he creates, a Faust, an Egmont, etc." — Today R. has completed the penciled sketch of his second act; may each and every god and benevolent spirit be blessed and thanked! Today the "altar stone" came to him, to the sound of which the bridal procession goes off, and to which they at the same time lead Brünnhilde. Brünnhilde's expression!! — Continually with the five children, in the garden and the nursery; but Lusch is causing me concern. "Oh, this mortal life!" . . . But the happiness of belonging to R. outshines everything. Yesterday he said to me jokingly, "If you were now to hear that nothing was to come of Bayreuth, and that we could continue to live quietly for ourselves, how happy you would be, for you have a slight latent tendency toward philistinism!" I laugh and do not know whether to affirm or deny it; the fact is, I fear everything. — Kaulbach's pictures are being exhibited; when I tell R. that I can see nothing in this man, no wit, talent, etc., he says: "There is also not a trace of truthfulness in such a character. Heine, for example, really had wit, and the difference between them is: Kaulbach makes something of his life, Heine made nothing." — In the evening Carlyle. R. is worn out, but still indescribably kind to me.

*Thursday, October 26* Letter from my uncle Eduard, who now, realizing that I am right, is writing to Rothschild; whether it will do any good we shall see. — R. reads me an alteration he has made in Brünnhilde's last words; I beg him to leave it as it was, and he agrees, saying that the new version comes too close to literary drama. — He works. Lulu still unwell. In the afternoon visit from Marie M., discussed many things with her. R. joins us, bringing the first volume of his writings and the news that the theater in Darmstadt has been burned down; a satanic stroke—it means our Brandt will now have no time to work for us. R. had known of it since morning, but said nothing to me, then forgot it because of Fidi and Loldi. "It is a calamity, such as always strikes me when I find somebody."

*Friday, October 27*   Letter to me from Hans about what he intends to do for the children! (Lulu's dream occurred on the day he wrote! . . .) — Telegram from Bratfisch, saying he has the manuscript of *Tristan* and is returning it to us. — Wonderful day! — R. says to me, "I have thought so much about your father; the fact that he is your father makes me forgive everything." In the afternoon surprise visit by Prof. Nietzsche from Basel. He tells us the title of his book, which will be called *The Emergence of Tragedy from Music.* Marie M. and Caroline B[assenheim] visit us. In the evening R. reads us his essay on Auber, begun today.

*Saturday, October 28*   Letter from Rothschild, who now at last has sent me my 1,000 francs. Visited Marie M. with Prof. N.; great admiration for this good friend, who spends the evening with us, along with Countess B. R. still working on *Auber.* I still much pressed, with child cares and hostess duties. — Marie M. relates that the Empress of Germany does not like the *"Kaisermarsch"*!!

*Sunday, October 29*   I write a long and detailed letter to Hans and ask him for permission to have the children converted to Protestantism. Family lunch and children's games until Marie M.'s visit. After she has gone, I read the children Tieck's *"Blonder Ekbert,"* which makes a great impression on me, too. Late in the evening, Carlyle.

*Monday, October 30*   Curious, anonymous letter from Graz: the eldest daughter of Paradise commissions a Mass for the Holy Grail, which will be demanded when the time comes. "Obey, keep silent or you will die"—signed Easter Flower. Addressed to the Mastersinger R. Wagner in Berlin, from the new Easter Realm. — I visit Marie M. and there meet Frau von Loë, who makes no great impression on me. In the evening our friend comes to us; we talk about the King of Bavaria; he is said no longer to be permitted to ride—he has a hernia; and many unpleasant things which alarm me very much. God knows! — R. relates that it was maintained in the *Musikalische Zeitung* that he (R.) was no true musician; the proof of that could be seen in his never having ventured into the field of the symphony. "Well," R. says, "I should like to know who has ever written a symphony, except for Beethoven! How idiotic to make a generic term out of one man's most individual characteristic, as if everybody had to write symphonies like that." He plays us the Norns' scene and Siegfried's entry from *Götterdämmerung,* stirring our emotions indescribably.

*Tuesday, October 31*　Took our friend to the station, where we parted from this unique woman with feelings of sadness. At home R. tells me that in Austria the Bohemian Cabinet has fallen. — In the evening he reads me his magnificent essay on Auber. — He took it amiss that in my letter to Hans I spoke only of 10,000 francs which I had set aside, taking that to mean I was assuming that the 3,000 francs I had lent him were now lost!!

*Wednesday, November 1*　Today, when I tell R. that Marie Muchanoff asked me to advise him to write to Roggenbach about Bayreuth, R.'s pride rose in protest; he said, "That is a matter for my friends; after having proclaimed my cause throughout the world, I cannot approach everyone individually with bowed shoulders." — He applies himself again to his second act. After lunch I go for a drive with the children. — Arrival of the score of *Tristan und Isolde*! Overwhelming joy! In the evening R. plays extracts from *Der Templer und die Jüdin* with enjoyment, laughs over its clumsiness and insipidity, but takes great delight in the fine dramatic passages. "That is the Germans all over," he says, "clumsy and stupid, but capable amid all their idiocy of catching fire and producing ideas. It is the same soil from which Beethoven sprang, here the quantity of genius decides the quality of it, for in quality it is not basically very different." [*In the margin:* "Easter Flower has written again, sending a photograph! — Modern, wild hair style! She tells R. to flee from Berlin." "Feelings of anguish, as always when music is played."]

*Thursday, November 2*　R. works, I with the children; write some letters. Telegram from Bologna that *Lohengrin* has had a tremendous impact there. Nice letter from the conductor Bratfisch. R. goes out and takes care of my little money transactions. He says at lunch, laughing, "If somebody would finish composing my *Götterdämmerung*, I should willingly make him a present of the *Lohengrin* success in Bologna!" Visit from Countess Bassenheim; in the evening arrival of Käthchen!

*Friday, November 3*　Very nice letter from Marie M. — I send 10,000 francs off to the banker J[oachim] and beg L. Bucher to see he takes great care of them. R. works till he is weary. I go for a drive with the children. R. writes letters to Dr. Standhartner, Herr Feustel in Bayreuth; business affairs, in short. Then an inscription in a copy of *Siegfried* for Bratfisch. [*Inscription based on word play omitted as untranslatable, but see notes.*] From town R. brings Hans's Beethoven edition, which Cotta was instructed to send him—probably by Hans himself!

*Saturday, November 4*　I send the children into town, where the St. Gotthard railroad is being celebrated with a torchlight procession, etc.; a German flag is waving, but the Catholics are not joining in the illuminations; a connection between Germany and Switzerland is being fêted—in short, a little victory for our cause. May God bless it! In Vienna the Czechs have also gone, thanks to Bismarck! —

*Sunday, November 5* Letter from Hans! He consents to my wishes, although—as he says—he hates everything German. Melancholy. From Bayreuth a very heartening reply from Herr Feustel—they are starting a Wagner Society there, too! — Countless letters from Bologna about the success of *Lohengrin*. — R. is working, "still bloodthirstily"; recently he said to Prof. Nietzsche, "From the fact that I am now composing nothing but bloodthirstiness one can deduce whether I was in love when I wrote *Tristan*." Now we have too much to do; R. wants to write an open letter to Italy, on top of that he has the essay on Auber to revise and all the frightful correspondence. I write to Grammann, to Härtel, to A. Frommann, and to Clemens. Very nice letter from Fritz Brockhaus about his uncle's first volume. In the evening Carlyle for the last time.

*Monday, November 6* Marie Schleinitz writes and reports that Herr Löser is taking up 60 certificates of patronage for the Wagneriana and responsibility for the engagement of the orchestra for Bayreuth. Letter from my mother. Taught the children, in spite of a very bad night, which I owe to Fidichen. Engaged an Italian teacher. R. works on *Götterd[ämmerung]* in the morning, and in the afternoon drafts his fine letter to the Italians. — We talk about art, reality, etc., come to *Kabale und Liebe*, which R. finds so remarkable because it gives a complete picture of its time—thus far can reality reach in our art—but he adds with a laugh, "The German will always keep his idealism as a hiding place." In the evening we read in Thucydides the splendid discussion between Athenian and Melian. "They were too intelligent, those fellows," says R., "they could not last." — "The religion of the saints, that is what I understand best, that one does not claim to be God, but says, 'This is the ideal to which I offer myself up.'" — Of the chorus in the 2nd act of *Lohengrin*: "I wanted in fact to show how a folk song evolves." — Herr Pecht sends Shakespeare drawings, which do not give us much pleasure. — R. is now laughing about his own present productivity.

*Tuesday, November 7* The chorus singers in Bologna send R. their respects. A friendly nation! Lucky he who earns his living there! Worked with the children. R. copies out his letter to Italy and writes other letters. Nice missive from Ottilie; but she still has found nobody for the children. Melancholy evening, spent in writing letters! — I find the month of November hard to bear.

*Wednesday, November 8* Mme Lucca writes that the fourth performance proceeded brilliantly and people are now taking to the second act as well. R. works, is astonished not to have received proofs of the second volume; a printers' strike, perhaps? I write to the painter Herr Pecht and give him my opinion of the unsuccessful Hamlet. Letter from Herr Heckel with proposals for the Wagner Societies. We are in melancholy spirits, R. and I; R. maintains that I am leading a wretched life! Because I devote myself to the children!! — We take up Gibbon again, then look through Constantin Frantz's new book in great dismay. "Clumsiness and envy, those are the characteristics of the Germans," says R. The chapter on Bismarck makes one really angry. — Today's sensational news is the resignation of Beust!

*Thursday, November 9* Wretched night, due once again to Fidi; but arose cheerful. I write to Hans. R. works. Family lunch. Walk in the garden in mild weather, melancholy thoughts of our having to leave here one day. Richard brings me a lovely rose, the last. In the Robbers' Park everything is gleaming gold, a splendid but sad color. First Italian lesson. R. corrects the proofs of *Lohengrin* and is glad to find in this poem no word needing alteration. In the evening we begin Plato's *Republic*.

*Friday, November 10* Schiller's and Luther's birthday. Splendid autumn day, sunshine and gold. R. works busily, he hopes to have the second act finished soon. Letter from Karl v. G[ersdorff] about setting up the Wagner Society in Berlin. At lunch R. tells me of a remarkable bookbinder in Leipzig whom his uncle recommended to him; he always read the books he bound, so one could not get them back from him. "He was a sort of Hans Sachs," R. said, "and he fascinated me very much in my youth." — R. maintains I am becoming more and more beautiful (I think myself already very old) and says when he sees me he is always terribly vexed not to be 15 years younger. — Wrote to Marie M. Much out of doors; in the evening looked through the catalogue of Uhland's library with R.; when we come to Luther, R. says, "The fellow was like me, had the writing itch, scribbled about everything." When I begged him at lunch to go out for a while and enjoy Nature, he replied with a laugh, "A composer is [*sentence uncompleted*]."

*Saturday, November 11* Still Italy—*Lohengrin* seems to pull everything along with it in Bologna. Could this lead to anything? R. works very busily; I give lessons to the children and write to the Luccas on R.'s behalf. In the afternoon a messenger arrives from Herr Bruckmann in Munich and brings a new photograph of R., based on a drawing by Herr Jaeger; not too badly done, but still terrible. One sees it has been put together again from all sorts of pictures. R. walks into town and brings back proofs of the second volume; for us the student (Dolder) comes—he turns out to be the son of a former acquaintance of R.'s in Zurich; he is very well-mannered and teaches well. In the evening R. plays his second act. — We talk about my father—has the correspondence come to an end?? — Since my banker is silent, I feel anxious and ask whether he has received the money order.

*Sunday, November 12* Letter from Malwida Meysenbug in Florence. I write to Fritz Br. Ottilie reports that she has engaged somebody for the children. R. works a little, but is not quite well. Visit from the little Bassenheim girl. — R. makes corrections in *Die Wibelungen*; he says he is in fact still thinking of doing something on Friedrich Barbarossa, in order to bring out this one single feature—his magnificent, barbaric, noble, and indeed divine inexperience. "And how remarkable it is," R. adds, "that this German Empire, the most inconceivable thing of all, is probably something which will outlast all monarchies." — "I am glad," he says, "that I have an eye for this connection between legend and history. In the popular view Caesar was connected with Ilium, and Saint Gregory of Tours speaks of a Frankish Pharamund who was a descendant of Priam. The compilation of the Nibelung Saga, which was hardly understood any more, began with Friedrich I. But with history one cannot take liberties; the historian cannot concern himself with such things—only the poet and the philosopher can do that." — In the *Signale* appears another of those familiar items of news about R.; it is claimed that he wrote to Napoleon asking that *Tannhäuser* be performed and at the same time abjured "his youthful buffooneries." R. is replying. — In the evening the *Republic*.

*Monday, November 13* R. had a very bad night; at breakfast he says to me: "Do you know what comes into my mind and alarms me on such bad nights? That I shall very soon have to make a journey without you and shall be separated from you for some days." — Winter is here, snow, wind, and cold. R. says, "I should like to read an intelligent book about Tellus and Sol and their influence." Then he quotes Semper, who once told him that Michelangelo's *Madonna* in Florence is tellurian. — The banker sends no word; a real worry! Worked with the children. R. on his act, but cannot work much. In the evening read Plato's *Republic*. —

*Tuesday, November 14* R. says, regarding Constantin Frantz's book, "When he says of Bismarck that this is how Germany looks from Pomerania, Bismarck could reply that he now also knows what Germany looks like from the Ritterstrasse." "Germans are like that—when things are going badly, they are envious and awkward; but when they are doing well, they become Jews, elegant and indifferent!" — R. is unfortunately not well and cannot do much work. I with the children; Lulu also unwell again. I go to do some Christmas shopping, also visit Countess B. — In the evening read Plato's *Republic* to R. with much enjoyment. — Before that R. read from Freytag's book about the times of the wars of liberation, always delighting in the German people and being shocked by the wickedness of the German princes.

*Wednesday, November 15*  My banker still silent; great concern. — Joy in Fidi, during his sleepless night R. considered Fidi's future career and is increasingly taken with surgery, "in which compassion will harden him against weakness." — R. unwell, cannot work. Thought a lot about our house in Bayreuth; a newspaper report that the Schiller celebrations in Berlin had been [*word indecipherable*] by bad jokes makes R. exclaim, "Never will I go to Berlin or any other city; nowhere is there even a morsel of soil for my seeds—I must create an alternative, which will then attract the rays." — Toward evening he calls to me, "Are you now on your way here?" Three years ago I left Munich. God forgive me the evil I have done and bless the good I wished to do! R. shows me how Freytag in his book writes *adelich* instead of *adelig*, thus seeing no difference between the suffixes *-lich* and *-ig*; R. says, "Wait till I have my *Bayreuther Blätter!*"

*Thursday, November 16*  R. greets me as "the only, the best, the loveliest," thanks me for coming to him, and says he cannot imagine what he or indeed the world itself would be like without me! — While working with the children I receive from the banker the dismal news that he has not received the money order. How to bear it? First resolve: not to tell R. while he is working; second: to keep the children as much as possible from noticing anything. All my little savings now probably lost—I have to weep bitterly, though I know that many others suffer similar misfortunes. — At lunch R. notices that Jakob is not serving, I have to inform him that I have sent him to the post office concerning the lost money order. It gives R. a great shock. Jakob returns home bringing the receipt. Has it been misappropriated by the Prussian mail, or even perhaps by the banker himself? The name Joachim was ominous! — On top of this misfortune, Grane took fright in town and knocked down a child, badly injuring it. Compensation troubles. To add to this, domestic worries, which I had felt coming, and—worst of all for me—Lulu unwell again, plagued by a severe headache! — Hans Herrig sends some articles about Schopenhauer, very green. — The success of *Lohengrin* is still growing in Bologna. But over and above it all our love!

*Friday, November 17*  Letter from my father: he is leaving Rome. Two very foolish letters, one from P. Cornelius, the other from a Herr Barth. Grün in Pest, who begs R. to venture into other branches of art, to write a Louis XVI symphony, etc. — R. had a bad night, but works all the same. He tells me that, when he could not sleep, Sol and Tellus came back into his mind, and with them genius and love. — After lunch we receive the news that the banker in Frankfurt has not paid out on the money order, so in consequence my money is safe. This is a happy outcome; but the matter with the horse is looking bad; the child is dying, and its people are turning the tragedy to their own advantage, regarding it as "a stroke of luck." — In the evening Plato; then us, always we ourselves, R. and I, who can never say often enough how much we mean to each other; R. says: "If only I had ever felt a millionth part of such feelings toward another person! But one only needs to discover the genuine thing once to know what the ungenuine, however gifted, meant to one: nothing at all." "You are Eve and Mary to me." — "A rough genius is watching over you," meaning Fidi, who is becoming very sturdy.

*Saturday, November 18* The city councilors of Baden [-Baden] intend to invite R. to build his theater in Baden; that, at any rate, is what R. Pohl writes us. R. works. I thank Frau Standhartner, who has very kindly asked me to stay with her if we go to Vienna. — To town to do some shopping. In the evening, the *Republic.* — Newspapers from Italy, further confirming the success. The mother of the injured child comes and shocks us with her cynical lack of affection for the boy; all she cares about is the compensation, and sympathy means nothing to her. Telegram from Mannheim: Herr Heckel says the newspapers are reporting that the theater in Darmstadt will be placed at R.'s disposal.

*Sunday, November 19* At midday Richard brings me his completed 2nd act and says, "Now I have written you one act every year." Great joy! — The snow lies thick around the house, but the sun shines and so we can go for a walk. Thought of Christmas. In the evening R. suddenly says to me, half joking: "I should still like to meet a magician, I understand magic making, I often have the feeling I could do it myself, like, for example, in certain conditions jumping over a huge distance. And my music making is in fact magic making, for I just cannot produce music coolly and mechanically. Even the soprano clef of a five-voice piece by Bach upsets me, I feel like transcribing it, but in a mood of ecstasy I can lead my voices through the most hair-raising contortions without a moment's hesitation; it all pours out so steadily, as if from a machine; but I can do nothing coolly." He says what he would now like to do is to write his essay on Weber's statement about Beethoven. "I recently read that Hanslick had spoken of Beethoven's naïveté. A donkey like that can of course have no idea of the wisdom of genius, which, though it comes and goes like lightning, is the highest there is. One could, rather, call Mozart naïve, because he worked in forms he did not create himself—only what he said within them was his own. The wisdom of genius is of course entirely spontaneous, not considered. But what do these people know of the enraptured state of a productive artist?" — In the evening Plato.

*Monday, November 20* Hans sends an Italian grammar for the children. R.'s letter appears in Italian. Letter from a member of the orchestra in Bologna. The success of *Lohengrin* constantly increasing. The Italian letter has been published, very weakened and watered down which prompts R. into some observations on the Italian people. Christmas excursions, and to Countess B.'s in that connection. A Count Spee has made off with 70,000 francs—we regarded him as the most honest of men. In the *A.A.Z.*, a news item saying R. had offered himself to Darmstadt; again quite typical. R. cuts out this item and the one in the Mannheim paper and sends them to Councilor Düfflipp, for presumably it is all aimed at the King. — In the morning R. plays me his second act, which is awesomely sublime! — In the evening, the *Republic*.

*Tuesday, November 21* R. is not well, and very resentful about the copy he has to make for the King. He says it gives him no pleasure. — Herr Heckel sends his organizational plan for all Wagner Societies and their function after the performance of the *Ring*. I have to pay the banker 75 francs for the lost money order! — *Lohengrin* is now being taken to Florence as a guest performance of the Bologna opera. Lovely afternoon walk with R.; the Fontaine de Soif is flowing. The children are well, thank God. In the evening discussed the furnishing of our house in Bayreuth with R.

*Wednesday, November 22* The *Signale* prints R.'s reply regarding "his youthful buffooneries." I write to M. Schleinitz. Lessons for the children. Walk with R. — No news of my money order, but I am supposed to pay the banker here 75 francs. R. cables for copyists for the King. He promises Herr Heckel to conduct the concert in Mannheim at the end of December, "in order to give you a birthday symphony," he tells me. (Found the last wasp today near the stove.)

*Thursday, November 23* R. finds that he is 100 pages short for the fifth volume and is looking for material; is thinking a lot about Weber. I work all day on Christmas and make myself unwell. In the evening Plato. Letter from the Baden city councilors.

*Friday, November 24* R. receives a very nice letter from his publisher Lucca, who declares himself to be "*felice e superbo*" on account of *Lohengrin*; letters from Richter and Boito. Arrival of Herr Spiegel to copy the sketch for the King; no very pleasant addition to our household. In the afternoon Countess B., to prepare the folio for Hans. In the evening the *Republic*.

*Saturday, November 25* R. is sketching a history of the *Nibelungenring* for the 5th volume. He now dreams constantly that he is on the point of departure, I am supposed to accompany him but do not really want to—"very melancholy," he says. He sends his writings to Herr Wesendonck and Frau Wille. I do nothing but Christmas things. In the evening Plato. — No news of my money order.

*Sunday, November 26* Prof. N. recommends a poor musician, but it is now too late; certainly we would prefer the poor wretch to the smooth Spiegel, but it cannot be helped. I write letters (my mother, Claire, von Gersdorff). Family lunch with Spiegel. Afterward magic lantern, in the evening finished the *Republic*.

*Monday, November 27* More news of Bologna, and ever more pleasant. I still taking care of Christmas; worry over Lulu and Boni (lies, untidiness), it upsets me deeply; R. thinks I should not take it seriously: "Youth and virtue do not mix." — Frau Wesendonck sends a tragedy, *Edith*, which I read at once; R. wants me to ignore both letter and play, he declares that it compromises him. To town with R.; returned alone. Letter from Brandt, asking pardon for the newspaper report and saying that the machinery cannot be ready before '74. R. replies. All newspapers print Herr Heckel's appeal to the Wagner Societies except the *A.A.Z.*, which also prints nothing regarding Baden-Baden or Bologna. In the evening Schopenhauer. Glanced during the day through his wretched collected poems. Richter writes that the *Tristan* Prelude caused tremendous jubilation in Pest. —

*Tuesday, November 28* Telegram from Bremen; with it news from Bologna; in Bremen *Die Meistersinger* has been performed and aroused great jubilation. — R. still dreams of a sorrowful departure. 8 years ago today he declared his love for me, it was on a Saturday; he left immediately afterward, and I had no thoughts, but was sad unto death; I still am today—I find life difficult; but I do not want to be ungrateful, and all I ask is that the children will turn out well. Will? — They must, for it is ordained in the stars, what does care have to do with it? — Upstairs R. plays the *Idyll*, I write to Frau W. about *Edith*, friendly but honest. A harpist from Munich offers his services for Bayreuth. Lulu writes to Marie Bassenheim, who has been saying spiteful things about her. — In the evening Schopenhauer. — Minister Lutz distinguishes himself in the Reichstag; Bishop Ketteler replies furiously that the South Germans are all revolutionaries.

*Wednesday, November 29* Letter from Marie Muchanoff, strongly advising acceptance of the Baden councilors' proposals. Long discussion with R. about all the difficulties connected with the establishment of our future home—is life worth all this trouble? — R. embraces me and says I should not imagine that his love for me was not the highest and deepest worry of all! — I reply to Marie M. and send Herr Pecht an autograph by R. — R. goes for a walk, I stay at home with the children. On his return R. says to me, "Prometheus's words 'I took knowledge away from Man' came to my mind and gave me a profound insight; knowledge, seeing ahead, is in fact a divine attribute, and Man with this divine attribute is a piteous object, he is like Brahma before the Maya spread before him the veil of ignorance, of deception; the divine privilege is the saddest thing of all." — We are now living our lives in theory, surrounded by a gray fog. In the evening R. pastes his *Auber* together, making a brochure of it; this reminds us of the Christmas here for which we made the pictures together.

*Thursday, November 30* Domestic trials and tribulations arising out of the Bassenheim affair; sorrowfully I ask myself during the night whether I have really done all I can for the children, whether I could not have spared them certain contacts, whether the influence has not been bad; I review my situation, feel I have done the only possible thing, yet still reproach myself. To R., who notices my preoccupation in the morning, I tell a part of my worries, and he comforts and encourages me, as always. May God give us His blessing, we have many difficulties to bear and to overcome, but if love does not falter, the strength will also remain. — Count Gergenté, a Bourbon, has committed suicide here, but it is being hushed up so that he can be buried in consecrated ground. — I am very touched when Loulou tells me that last night in a dream she saw me finely dressed and dancing—with Herr Spiegel! She woke up laughing. This must have coincided with the moment when, thinking of the children, their dispositions, their development and future, I was bitterly weeping. R. walks into town, I accompany him. R. in very good spirits at lunch. In the evening a remark by Herr Spiegel brings R. to the subject of the Germans; he becomes very lively, indeed emphatic, and to our great astonishment our copyist is much affected by his outburst and says he can now see how much W. loves Germany when he can grow so violently heated about the shortcomings and the wretched social conditions of the nation. With ice-cold fingers he presses the hands of R., who feels quite moved. — In the evening Schopenhauer; we feel uplifted by it—"a golden book," says R. With the words "We are after all happy," we part.

*Friday, December 1* Herr Hartmann sends us copies of his *Propheten*, prefaced with a letter from R., and *Neidhart*, with a letter from me, which truly appalls me, since my distaste for print and public attention grows ever greater. R. thinks my letter good and says jokingly I also have the advantage over him that it contains no misprints, whereas in his there are some which completely distort his meaning. He works on his pamphlet about the history of his *Ring des Nibelungen*. In the evening a letter from Frau Wesendonck, who has not understood me and gives me a lesson in world history; her tone annoys R. so much that he wants me to put off her visit next Tuesday. Letter from Countess B.; it seems that Lulu has been obstinately lying; I am very sad about it and consider what I should do to punish her. In the evening Schopenhauer, with great enjoyment. — We wanted to go out in the afternoon, but fear of the outside world kept us at home. R. preferred to stay with me and say nice, loving things to me. But in the evening he scolds me for taking Frau W. so seriously. "You really are silly," he says, "but the dreadful thing about it is that you are so clever in your silliness!"

*Saturday, December 2*   Talked to the children, much sorrow. Also letters of all kinds (Gerson, Rothschild, Frau Tausig, Countess B., Marie Schl.). R. works on his essay. Report from Italy, Verdi at a performance of *Lohengrin*, applauded by the public on that account, but he stayed at the back of his box so as not to distract from the solemnity of the performance. We continue reading Schopenhauer. Feelings of exaltation regarding life.

*Sunday, December 3*   Spoke very seriously with the children, wept and prayed with them, brought them to the point of asking me for punishment. (Incidentally, heard very unpleasant things about Herr Spiegel.) As I am talking to them, a letter comes from Hans; he asks me to make the children practice the greatest reserve toward their grandmother and aunt; the family is tormenting him (to take the children away from me), but he is turning a deaf ear. Then he tells me that my father agrees with my decision to convert with the children, to Protestantism. Important matters! That the family, annoyed by seeing me treated with respect, wishes to affront me under the pretext of furthering the children's interests, while in fact not considering them at all—that does not surprise me; but I am despondent about it, and am guilty of the great injustice of letting R. see that I am. How weak we poor mortals are! — A Wagner Society is being set up in Mainz, under the aegis of R.'s wine merchant! A report from Munich in the *Musikalische Zeitung* says that the orchestra always plays W.'s things well, but the classical things badly, and this is not right. What the good people forget, however, is that the works which go well were rehearsed by R. and Bülow, the classical works, on the other hand, by the present conductors! — My mood has affected R., he is sad. But gradually we manage to restore our spirits, and I put my trust in God!

*Monday, December 4*   Saint Nicholas's Day; snow and frost. R. exclaims to me, "You are a philosophical concept, *causa efficiens et finalis*, basis and cause of life." Great joy over the arrival of Anna Stadelmann for the children. Hope that better order will result. Wrote to Ottilie. Worked and played with the children. Letter from M. Muchanoff, Frl. Liszt, etc. In the evening Schopenhauer. Lucca writes that the Bologna company is now going to Florence to perform *Lohengrin* there. (R. writes to the King.)

*Tuesday, December 5* No letters, either received or written; R. works. At 2 o'clock visit from the Wesendonck family; he, good man, very ponderous and tiresome, but she friendly and kind; we promise to celebrate the New Year with them. In the evening we are tired and can only converse a little about the past and future.

*Wednesday, December 6* R. says, "Even if we had to put up with much further suffering in life, we could no longer be made unhappy." He works on his *Nibelungen* history and will soon have it finished. Moved the children's rooms, to separate them entirely from the servants upstairs and to get things running more smoothly. May God send his blessings! I write to my father. Purchases in town, Boni's photograph, etc. — In the evening a letter from Dr. Kafka, asking whether R. is really coming to Vienna on February 2, 4—we had heard nothing about it! In the evening Schopenhauer.

*Thursday, December 7* Domestic trouble, in which many ugly things come to light. A thousand pities that R. should hear of such things; all I can do is to suppress all signs of ill humor. Wrote to M. M. R. completes his report to the Wagner Society; he is somewhat hurt that I neglect to ask him about the ending, but I am so tired and also so sad (the children have again been lying!) that I may perhaps be excused. Shall I take Lulu to Mannheim after all, in spite of having told her she must stay behind as a punishment for her recent bad transgressions?? — This question weighs on my mind.

*Friday, December 8* Preparations for R.'s departure. On top of it, continuing domestic discord; many things have spread and taken root through kindness. The moral of Frederick the Great should be applied in this respect. R. reads me his report; I write to R. in Munich, though he is still here! Disturbed, sad day; on top of it a dismal letter from Math. Maier; they seem to have lost all they possess. — Supper with the children. Then upstairs; R. says that everything will turn out all right, Fate will not forget its role—it has been good to us! As he goes off to bed he says that when he is in such moods folk songs always come into his mind—now it is "Red today, dead tomorrow."

*Saturday, December 9* At five o'clock took R. to the station; the cold cruel; final sorrow. Home alone, to bed. It must all be borne in God's name! At 10 o'clock telegram from R. in Zurich, announcing a letter. Lunch with the children. Wrote to Hans, afterward fetched my letter; it had arrived, and later still a telegram from Lindau! — R. had a cold journey, very cold, but "his heart kept him warm." Frau W. sends some dolls. Loldi dictates a letter, I write to R. — Telegram from Lucca in Florence, saying *Lohengrin* is making fanatics of everybody there! — Shared everything with the children.

*Sunday, December 10* Dreary day, longing and depression! — From R. a telegram that he has arrived safely and that he had just written me a little letter. — Letter from Clemens; I can write to nobody and get Lusch to reply. Looked through a Christmas catalogue. Went out with the children. Read, played, ate with them, everything, but mourned alone. My heart is heavy, heavy, heavy. I write to R., but do not know where the letter will find him! — Newspaper from Florence, reporting that the national guard met the *Lohengrin* company from Bologna at the railroad station.

*Monday, December 11* Disappointment in the morning, since no letter from R. — At midday went to fetch some dear, cherished lines. Then Christmas shopping. Children's noises and children's work. Letter from Herr Pecht. In the evening wrote to R. (not sent). Longing!

*Tuesday, December 12* Letter from the town council in Reichenhall, they claim to have heard that agreement could not be reached with Bayreuth and they offer their little nest instead, send a photograph on which is indicated with a little German flag the site they want to give! — In the afternoon Christmas shopping; but first made sure of my letter! Heavenly letter!! R. is satisfied with Düffl. and is sitting for Lenbach. I wander about with pride, happiness, longing, and humility in my heart. Oh, our love! . . .

*Wednesday, December 13* Rather unwell, but still strong enough to work with the children. Toward noon a telegram from R. that everything has been approved and he is leaving in great satisfaction for Bayreuth this evening. I cable a word of thanks to him in Munich. Some hours later R.'s letter of Monday; he had not yet heard from me and tells me a lot about his sittings in Lenbach's studio.

*Thursday, December 14* Into town early. News from M. Meysenbug that *Lohengrin* had an unparalleled success in Florence; letter from an Italian impresario, who wants to tour the towns of Italy and Germany (with *Lohengrin*!). Telegram from R. in Bayreuth, then letter; somewhat sad. I gnawed by worry about him—the nearer the reunion, the harder, almost, the separation! — Called the doctor: Fidi has a touch of eczema, and his stomach is very swollen. Dispatched copies of the second volume of the writings, in the evening wrote to R. in Mannheim. Anxious day—God help me—why do I feel so worried?

*Friday, December 15* From R. a short letter from Munich, then a telegram from Bayreuth that all arrangements are in excellent shape. Also receive a pheasant and a bashlyk, sent by him. Worked with the children and then walked into town. Letter from poor Mathilde Maier, who now in her dire need is learning photography! Nothing to report beyond activities with the children. Great sorrow not to be taking

Lulu with me, God grant that by this means untruthfulness will be driven from her heart forever. My one consolation is that the cold is so intense that the punishment might turn out to have been prudent. May God be at my side in everything; things are never made easy for me.

*Saturday, December 16* Preparations for departure; left at 5, said goodbye to the children, found in the waiting room a few more lines from R. In Basel at 9 o'clock; evening with Fritz Br. and Prof. Nietzsche.

*Sunday, December 17* Coffee with the two Basel professors at 3 o'clock; after steadfastly reading Schlegel's lectures on history, arrived in Mannheim. Three gentlemen who were sitting in my compartment get out before me, so that R. does not see me; I wait on the platform, and at last he finds me! Lengthy joking about this occurrence, R. says I was standing there like a saga, so earnest and long! — Good reports on everything: "I have managed my affairs well"; many good things about Feustel and all the Bayreuth people, good, too, of the King. In the evening visit the Wagner Society; excellent people (Heckel, Koch, Zeroni).

*Monday, December 18* Did not sleep, but in good spirits; R. looks very well and splendidly handsome. First rehearsal; displeasure, people have not eaten, prefer not to rehearse the A Major Symphony; feeling that this will be the last concert R. conducts. Very fine apartment in the Hôtel de l'Europe; dinner with R. alone; afterward visit from Baroness Reden-Esebeck, a Hungarian, first met in Szegsgard, who is married to a baritone singer in Mannheim. Then Frl. Reis. In the evening rehearsal, *Zauberflöte* Overture and A Major Symphony—indescribable impression; unfortunately Mme Serov sits down beside me, which annoys R. very much. Tears that our communion in music can be disturbed by such ugly faces! Arrival of Prof. Nietzsche, who has literally run away from Basel. — Yesterday R. told me of a dream he had in Bayreuth: he had seen me, and I had teeth which gleamed like opal, and he had "kissed me to death." — R. to bed after each rehearsal, since so worn out.

*Tuesday, December 19* Morning rehearsal (*Lohengrin, Meistersinger, Tristan*); glorious, utter liberation of the soul. Letters from the children, they are well. Wander through the dreary city while R. is resting. Visit from a conductor from Pressburg who went into the army and is now asking R. to help him! — Arrival of the Ritters, who had already seen R. in Würzburg. In the evening final rehearsal, wonderful. R., however, very tired, cannot sleep, and has a cold. — In the evening Pohl, Ritters, and Nietzsche.

*Wednesday, December 20* R. dreams of suddenly seeing many moons in the sky; he watches them for a long time before discovering that it is the Pleiades, vastly magnified, he is seeing; turning away suddenly he catches sight of a shadow (me!) creeping off downstairs. Rehearsal, the *Idyll*, great sorrow on my part to see it performed in front of so many strangers, but it sounds lovely. Returned to the hotel. Dinner with Ritters, Pohl, Nietzsche; R. animated, talks about the *Idyll*, and in the process hurts me very much. In between, arrival of a tailor with a waistcoat and a request for the protection of the King of Bavaria for his son, in addition a bill for 23 florins for the waistcoat. R. in a great rage, but calms down. Arrival of Betty Schott, bringing good cheer. At 6 o'clock in the evening the concert; Grand Duke and Grand Duchess, also many Jews. R. already vexed at rehearsals by the universal success of the *Lohengrin* Prelude! — In the evening a banquet; very fine toast by Dr. Zeroni, which moves R. to reply in spite of great hoarseness. Usual talk, and in particular a serenade by a male vocal choir, very pitiful. Many *vivat*'s and hurrays, during which R. relates that when he arrived at Mannheim and was greeted by the gentlemen with cheers, his traveling companion got a sudden shock, thinking he had been traveling with a member of royalty; he stood up quickly and bowed low, but when he saw R. companionably shaking hands with the cheering group he looked very relieved! — (At the first rehearsal, on Monday, the conductor Lachner, who otherwise spends his life intriguing against R., had insisted on introducing R. to the orchestra; in doing so he made the most absurd of speeches; R. standing in dignified silence, he meandering on, at one time comparing him with the German Emperor, at another speaking of his artistic and literary activities, which for decades had *held the world enthralled*—Franz Moor trying to pray, said Dr. Zeroni.) After the concert R. tells me about his conversation with the Grand Duke and the Grand Duchess, which took place in public during the intermission; horribly superficial, the Grand Duke turning as red as a beet when R. mentioned the King of B. and said he owed the completion of his *Nibelungen* to him.

*Thursday, December 21* Neither of us slept; rose late, hairdresser who saw *Tristan und Isolde* in Munich and loves it above everything else. Departure at 12 o'clock, escorted by all our friends. — Very unsatisfactory letter from Baron Loën. Traveled with Levi, the conductor, and Pohl; of the former, R. says he respects him for the very reason that he calls himself Levi straight out, not Löwe or Lewin, etc. Evening in Basel with nephew and friend. R. relates much about Bayreuth; foundation-stone laying fixed for May 22; the Stuckberg site presented to R. by the town. The mayor proposed a toast to me and Fidi. R. says, "This will be our creation, you will be the Margravine of Bayreuth"!

*Friday, December 22*   Return to Tribschen! Day spent with the children, R. touched, happy, many blissful tears, high spirits, melancholy, joy, hope!

*Saturday, December 23*   To town in connection with Christmas; arrival of our nephew. In the evening punch and decorating the tree. (Fidi splendid; "approving.")

*Sunday, December 24*   Letter from Hans with photographs and remittance for the children. Melancholy. (During my absence her grandmother wrote to Lulu, asking about religious instruction and Hermine!!) Prepared the presents, in the evening jubilation around the Christmas tree, but R. is sad because the picture by Lenbach, meant for me, has not arrived; this deeply distresses him; he also feels that the Mannheim treat—his real birthday present for me—had been spoiled. Long and tender conversation till past midnight. Then to bed.

*Monday, December 25*   The children wish me many happy returns, but R. declares I must remain aged 33 until New Year's Eve. — I write to Hans to thank him, he is sad about leaving Italy. Two Hildesheim bowls from L. Bucher; also some things from Marie M.; quiet and peaceful day. Our nephew very pleasant company, we grow more and more fond of him. (Visit from Countess B. and her son, who considers it expedient to be a *new* Catholic.) Children's games, family lunch, all happy and merry. I contemplative, as always on my birthday. Fine letter from Prof. Nietzsche, who has sent me a musical composition. R. reads out loud to us his New Year's letter to Fritzsch. Nice evening of conversation with our nephew.

*Tuesday, December 26*   Wrote letters, played with the children; R. settles business affairs; much in our nephew's company. A peaceful existence, Tribschen happiness! Kissing me, R. says, "This is the holy Urdar Fount from which I draw wisdom."

*Wednesday, December 27*   R. writes to the King, I many various letters. For lunch Professor Hirzel, a former acquaintance of R.'s. Pleasant conversation throughout the day. In the morning a letter from Herr Lindau, inviting R. to contribute to a review; the foreign words "essays," which he uses, and "review," are quite enough for R. — Herr Bratfisch sends us souvenirs of poor Tausig.

*Thursday, December 28*   Good letter from my mother. Wrote a lot of letters. Loulou to her father. R. to the town councilors of Baden, Reichenhall, etc. Enjoyed the companionship of our dear nephew, discussed all sorts of things, and always of the same opinion. Nice article in the *Mannheimer Zeitung*. — In the evening R. reads to Fritz from his pamphlet *On Conducting*. R. makes us laugh a lot with his remark about how terribly vexed he is by the fact that I am so beautiful and so young, while he already has such gray hair. Then he says that the morning reception in Berlin was the only time he did not feel embarrassed by this because, in being greeted and cheered by so many people, he felt he was not begrudged his happiness. — Of Bayreuth he says, "You'll see, it will be like the discovery of America, which killed off the Hanse cities—our miserable artistic world will also be brought to a halt." It occurs to me that I quite forgot to note down the remarkable things R. said to us in Mannheim about the *Zauberflöte* Overture; this charming work made an indescribable impression, and R. said that its pattern came to him during a sleepless night; the teeming of night, a world of little gnawing creatures, rats and mice, tamed by the flute, dancing to the flute, and in between the appearance of the sun, of day (Sarastro) in all its tender glory.

*Friday, December 29* Letter from Claire; also from my father, short and despondent. Arrival of the *Lohengrin* cake and Holy Grail bread from Bologna! — R. says he is frittering his time away, and we really do spend a large part of the day talking to our dear nephew. In the evening a nice letter from Clemens.

*Saturday, December 30* Still writing letters while R. is in town with the children making purchases for me for the New Year, divine good man that he is! They all come home in great excitement, having drunk some hot chocolate, and bringing all sorts of good things with them! Harmonious afternoon in spite of household cares; our landlord, Herr Am Rhyn, who has been behaving very badly, nevertheless feels the urge to visit R. and to apologize, more or less. In the evening a long conversation about Balzac; R. reads the arrest of Vautrin from *Père Goriot* and admires Balzac's mastery.

*Sunday, December 31* New Year's Eve; the children and we ourselves very merry. R. discovers, to his dismay, that he left a letter from me to Frau Wesendonck (putting off our visit) lying around for a week, so I write to her again; I also write to Herr De Gubernatis, the Sanskrit professor in Florence, and R. signs it; he does not wish to copy it out, he says he is glad that people should see what I am to him. Nice letter from the Wagner Society in Mannheim; "the disciplined man, the man of Tribschen, the master of ceremonies, the speaker, and the strategist"! The King sends photographs of *Tristan*! In the afternoon we light the tree again and dance around it; R. plays for us. Stayed up until midnight, looked back on our year and found it good; affectionate good wishes. Between one and two we go off to bed.

# 1872

*Monday, January 1* Children's voices wake me, they are singing "All hail to the mother" and come garlanded to my bedside; very touched by the singing, the faces, and the goodness of R., who rehearsed them. I am made to go downstairs while things are set up, then I am summoned, the garlanded children sing once more, bring me their gifts on cushions, and I see R.'s picture by Lenbach and a portrait of my father (also by Lenbach). Joy beyond words over the masterpieces and the whole presentation ceremony! But immediately afterward I become aware that Lulu is unwell; I put her to bed, the doctor discovers that she has a high temperature; sorrow and concern, "the sad tune." Arrival of the report to the Wagner Societies. (Yesterday we read J. Grimm's speech on Schiller, which arrived for R., along with other very interesting things from Uhland's library.) — Letter from Alwine Frommann, very nice.

*Tuesday, January 2* Lulu had a tolerable night. Departure of our nephew in fine sunshine. Letter from Richter. The piano tuner comes, R. prepares himself to start on his third act; this makes me boundlessly happy, indeed lighthearted, in spite of my concern over Lusch; and, since the very splendid weather gives us a view of the gleaming mountains which we have long been without, we go for a walk, I almost overpowered by my high spirits. We return home and drink tea with Lulu, she herself having to consume much lime blossom tea, "for he who will not hear must feel, he who has a cold must sweat," R. tells her. — I stay with Lulu, but promise R. to go downstairs; since, worried about Lulu's delirious ramblings, I cannot do this, R. comes up to me and is offended; so offended that he reproaches me with not having understood his desire for my presence downstairs! In the evening he improvises wonderfully, and when I am in bed he comes to me and asks me to forgive his anger! I to have to forgive him for anything!! . . . He says it would be better if we did not love each other so, for then he would not torment me so much. Recently we had a long talk about love and being in love; he said the latter often occurred without the former, and that was very bad, but the former without the latter was a play of the imagination and possessed no power; one needed both together, but that was a miracle, so rare is it. (He writes to Dr. Standhartner and Kafka.)

*Wednesday, January 3*   R. asks me not to give any thought to yesterday —he had been drinking too much beer! Arrival of Prof. Nietzsche's book. Very nice letter to me from M. Meysenbug, R. reads it while I am with the doctor, and when I come downstairs I find him regarding Fidi with tears in his eyes. "You and the family are my sunshine," he says. "Now I understand Lenbach's portrait—a person who is as happy as I am dares to face life and he accepts the world's challenge; he neither makes melancholy eyes nor lets his head hang; the only trouble is that I do not want to die." [*A sentence based on untranslatable word play omitted.*] Lenbach's portrait pleases me more and more, although I know that R. can also look quite different, as, for example, when I saw him at the railroad station in Mannheim, beaming, transfigured, and with such a sweet expression on his face that his features looked small and delicate; here everything is sharp and energetic, unyielding; R. is humorously vexed that he is so ugly. Spent the morning with Lulu; at midday I find R. very excited and stimulated by Prof. Nietzsche's book, he is happy to have lived to read it; he says after me comes N. and then Lenbach, who painted his picture, and he observes how dreary his life would have been if he had died ten years ago; in what universal chaos ("a region to which I now gladly consign many things!") would his memory remain! He calls me his priestess of Apollo —he says I am the Apollonian element, he the Dionysian, but we made an alliance, a pact, and from it came Fidi! Silly letter from Prof. Werder to Alw. Frommann, correcting the account of the meeting in Berlin after *Der Fliegende Holländer*; as if anything mattered except the impression which R. received! — R. has today begun his third act; thrice-blessed day! — But my Lulu is still ill, and I stay beside her, hardly seeing the other children. — Letter from Marie Schl., I myself attend to all sorts of business affairs in the morning, among them Herr v. Rothsch[ild], who has again sent me no money! — On the subject of my father's *Christus*, which he is now having performed in Vienna and about which Marie Much. is concerned on account of the bad conductor (Rubinstein), R. says: "How curious your father is! He allows the most horrible performances to take place, smiling when I talk of model performances, yet he wants his things to be performed in front of an audience for which he thinks anything is good enough. It is all just a matter of appearances, that is how the world judges things, and people like us are regarded as peasants when they prefer to produce nothing, rather than something false." — In the evening we read Nietzsche's book, which is really splendid; R. thinks of the people who at the moment set the tone in Germany and wonders what the fate of this book will be; he hopes in Bayreuth to start a periodical, which Prof. Nietzsche would edit.

*Thursday, January 4*  Lusch much better, a quiet night. While with her in the morning I write to Mama and to Lenbach (thanks for the splendid pictures). R. works and sings me the ravishing song of the Rhinemaidens. The joy of creativity has now returned to this house— may God preserve it! Drove into town, home with R., fog, darkness, and snow, thought of the times when I lived here against all the rules, like a dream figure, and when this landscape seemed so appropriate. (Letter yesterday from Marie Schl., but otherwise no positive news of the material situation.) We read in the newspaper that Baron Perfall has been promoted to the title of "Excellency"; every time it begins to look as if the King were showing favor to R., he hastens to restore the balance in this manner; strange, unaccountable being! — In the evening read more of Nietzsche's book, which gives R. ever-increasing satisfaction, but we wonder where the public for it is to be found. — R. ends the day by saying, "My love for you is both Dionysian and Apollonian." Yesterday he told me of a ceremony he had attended in Heiligenstadt near Vienna, when a plaque was fixed to the house in which Beethoven had lived, stating that here B. had composed the *Pastoral.* "Well, says R., "you have only to see that place, its barren nature, to see what the relationship is between the work of genius and its creator's life."

*Friday, January 5*  Spoke much about the King; what shall we still experience through him? A lady from Transylvania sends R. thanks and blessings for the impressions she owes to him (Amalie von Könyvas-Tóth, in Torda). — R. works, and laughs at my being so happy about it: he says, "Yes, I know, I am just a composing machine." R. sends for me and sings me the second verse of the Rhinemaidens, he corrects something which he thinks sounds too "Altenburgian"—"for what is very bold must seem natural." — At lunch he becomes very high-spirited and says how lovely it is that we are married, "that all this is here, the children and you—now I enjoy talking about my earlier days, for *'nessun maggior piacer, che ricordarsi del tempo infelice nella gloria.'*" He goes into town and returns with the news that his sister Luise is dead! We had not even heard that she was ill.

*Saturday, January 6*  Yesterday we read [Nietzsche's] new book, with solemn feelings and with ever-increasing pleasure. — Two problems are still occupying us, the construction of the theater, what a theater should actually be like; looking at Semper's drawing and not being satisfied with the solution of the exterior, R. says it was perhaps fortunate that it was never built! I ask R. why it should not be constructed with a dome like a church, so that the stage section would not stand out so? . . . — Then he tells me he still wants to fulfill my wish and perform Beethoven's great Mass, but he has his own ideas about it; he would like to place the orchestra in the middle of the hall, with the chorus surrounding it as in a circus; everyone should join in the singing (the Latin text, however, scarcely audible), for this music is not just to be listened to, the true impression is gained only by those who are swept along inside it—he discovered that with the Ninth Symphony in Dresden. In fact, he says, all music is designed for its executants, a sonata for a solo player, a trio ditto; the princes kept musicians, but the musicians went one better and wrote for themselves. — Unfortunately R. had a very bad night and can do little work. Lulu somewhat better; I constantly with her, write letters to M. Meysenb. and to Marie Schl. Thaw and foehn. — Finished Prof. Nietzsche's book in the evening. "This is the book I have been longing for," says R. — He has received a fine poem anonymously from Heidelberg.

*Sunday, January 7* Letter from the King in the usual tones. R. works; I write to my father and to Alwine Frommann. Yesterday evening put away files. A letter comes addressed to "Herr R. W., theater director in Bayreuth"; R. says, "Laube at least got as far as theater director in Vienna!" Talking of Laube, R. says, "The idea of modernity ruined him; whatever is modern is always best." In the evening we begin the *Oresteia*, very powerful impact; talked a lot about Nietzsche's book. (We read some malicious things about my father's *Christus* in the newspaper; R. very indignant, intends to make it a condition, if he conducts a concert in Vienna, that no critics will be admitted.)

*Monday, January 8* Hans's birthday! — R. unfortunately did not have a good night. From Bayreuth the banker Feustel and the mayor suddenly announce a visit! They actually come, spend the day with us, and please me very much. They offer another site for the theater, better than the one previously chosen, and we settle on moving there in the summer. (Letters from Herr v. Loën and Councilor Düfflipp.) In the evening the completion of *Agamemnon*. When I tell R. that not only the tremendous naïveté but also the tremendous mastery of it move me so much, R. says, "Not just mastery, but craftsmanship—it is as if carved in stone."

*Tuesday, January 9* R. still not having good nights, Councilor D.'s letter gave him little pleasure. "But I must always increasingly respect and admire the way the King keeps to the original position and fulfills my wishes despite everything." The councilor wrote that with his 25,000 thalers for certificates of patronage the King had really had in mind sending people there (perhaps Herr v. Perfall?). — R. could not work yesterday, but today he sits down again at his loom. Unfortunately he does not feel well. We go for a drive together; a fine, sunny morning has transformed itself into a wild, snowy afternoon. In the evening read *Choephoroi*, which deeply moved us.

*Wednesday, January 10*   Again R. did not have a good night! At breakfast we again discuss musical performances—how to arrange them so that the audience can take an active part, not just listen. Yesterday R. disclosed to me his decision to combine a musical performance with the laying of the foundation stone, and I had to dance for joy, for I had had this very thought myself, but had been scared of expressing it, fearing to cause him yet further excitement and to appear (as it were) to be saying that the laying of the foundation stone was not enough for me. I ask for the Ninth Symphony. And R. intends to put an appeal in the newspapers, saying that he is going to perform the Symphony in Bayreuth, is prepared to pay travel and living expenses, and now invites musicians to come along; he needs 300 singers and 100 orchestral players, and his only condition is that they have to have taken part in a performance of the Symphony before. He says he will then see how far his power extends confronted with conductors, managers, choral institutions, etc. "Hardly has the cur got over his blows than he is back again nibbling!" The dear man is working! He shows me Brünnhilde's last words again and says he wants to use some of the new verse, but I beg him to alter Wunschheim and Wahnheim, which I find somewhat artificial. R. goes into town and takes care of my affairs; I now have 12,000 francs for the children with the banker and 182 francs laid aside in the savings bank, and, since R. insists that I reckon the other 3,000 francs with that, the total would be 15,000. Prof. Nietzsche writes that he is ill, whereupon R. writes him a touching and affectionate letter. In the evening read the *Eumenides*.

*Thursday, January 11*   R. still sleeping badly! But works nevertheless; yet he is vexed about his constant indisposition. Family lunch. R. is still pleased about the letter received yesterday from Karl Klindworth, who speaks very nicely about the "*Kaisermarsch*" (and from the point of view of a musician). Conversed in the evening, R. is quite indisposed and is looking worn out; he occupied himself a lot with our house.

*Friday, January 12*   Again R. did not sleep; letter from our tailor Chaillou-Ghezzi in Milan, who really wants to work for R.; delightful Italian ambitiousness. R. works; I am very unwell, but give the children their lessons. In the afternoon arrival of the photographs from Munich; they do not appeal to me very much, but R. is satisfied with them. R. is constantly working on the plans for our house; he suddenly says, "And if the King dies, everything will be lost." — Unutterable feelings of love for R. — R. says, "I say nothing, I just feel very happy, don't know whether I love you, only know that I take a heavenly joy in you, and my only vexation is having so much to do that I cannot enjoy my happiness fully." — In the evening talked a lot about Aeschylus. "The remarkable thing about this truly great being is that one hardly notices the way it is done! It does not appear to be art at all, because it is in fact something much higher: improvisation. With Schiller, one can imagine how things came into his mind and how he considered manipulating them; but not in Shakespeare or Aeschylus." "I should like to die in you," I say to R.—a poor expression for my feelings, my longing to be nothing apart from him.

*Saturday, January 13* Designed my dress for the foundation-stone laying; R. thinks of his speech and says he will conform to Luther's rule: "Enter boldly, open your mouth, shut it soon." He works, and in the afternoon goes into town, from where he brings back a childish letter from Herr De Gubernatis enclosing *König Nala* (a dramatic poem) and a request to compose the music to it! In the evening the *Bacchae* of Euripides, very distasteful impression, but on the other hand one scene from *Iphigenia in Aulis* (the parting of Achilles and Clytemnestra) brings back to me all the beauty of Greek literature. — R. completes the plans for our house.

*Sunday, January 14* R. works, I write letters; some more Lohengrin sweets have arrived from Italy, and also sweetmeats from the Mendèses. The statutes of the Wagner Society in Brussels also arrive, and a report that a similar society has been formed in Cologne. Marie Schleinitz writes to R., but nothing positive, it is to be hoped Cohn will soon tell us how things stand. Many bills, which vex R. He goes into town on business matters. In the evening took up Schopenhauer again. Explanation of the name Bayreuth—*beim Reuth* ["beside the clearing"]. Heaviness of heart, only love helps—to love through every moment! — The children are high-spirited and lively, they are all becoming quite pretty. Letter from Dr. Kafka; the Wagner Society in Vienna is very active.

*Monday, January 15* Letter from Richter, saying that Hans was in Pest, looked very well, was very pleasant, his playing perhaps even more outstanding than before. — After we had been reading Schopenhauer yesterday, R. says, "A Bach fugue is like a crystal forming, then solidifying on the pedal point." Then he said of Beethoven and Mozart, "As far as fugues are concerned, these gentlemen can hide their heads before Bach, they played with the form, wanted to show they could do it, too, but he showed us the soul of the fugue, he could not do otherwise than write in fugues." — Arrival of the manuscript of the 9th Symphony; infinite joy; this manuscript, well preserved by Schotts', is now more than 40 years old, and now it has come into my hands! R. says jokingly, "You have stored up my whole life around me— without you I should know nothing of my life." — R. works; he says he again has to write fateful episodes, which he cannot bear; things like

the *Lohengrin* Prelude, the "Bridal March," etc., he enjoys doing. —
The arrangements of the *Five Songs* for violin also arrives. R. says:
"With my so-called love affairs it was just as with my marriage; Minna
married me when I was in a very wretched position, attacked even as
a conductor, utterly without glory, and she was pretty and much sought
after, but all the same I was quite without influence over her. And thus it
was, too, with the other relationships, they all belonged in another
sphere, and the only unaccountable thing about them is the power I
exercised in passing, making Minna marry me, for example." He then
adds, "Incidentally, no one else would have suited or fitted me better;
you were the only one who complemented me; with all the others I
spoke in monologues." In the evening we read Schopenhauer, in
great exaltation. [*In the margin:* "I ink in the sketches of the 3rd act of
*Siegfried*."]

*Tuesday, January 16* Prof. N. sends the copies of the de luxe edition.
We consider how to prevent his books being killed by silence. R.
works and is very agitated when he comes down to lunch. I ink in and
give the children lessons. In the afternoon R. goes into town, then he
starts the preface to the fifth and sixth volumes of his collected writings.
I read *The Four Sons of Aymon* to the little ones, but have to break off
at the death of the horse Bayard; we talk about this aspect. R. explains
it as a noble killing off of the will, I say that it is only a step from there
to Peter Arbués, who did not bother with laments and tears, and in
my opinion Aymon's sons should have perished along with the horse—
what is the use of atonement and a holy life after such a deed? — R.
agrees with me and says, "The sacrifice of Bayard is in fact a piece of
infamy; a thing like that is alien to the Hindus and also to Christ, it is
specifically Catholic." In the evening read a lot of Schopenhauer and
philosophized till one o'clock in the morning.

*Wednesday, January 17* We discuss the performance of the 9th in
Bayreuth, how to organize it. When we talk of the Symphony itself,
R. says, "When the theme in fifths recurs in the middle of the first
movement, it always strikes me as a sort of Macbethian witches'
cauldron in which disasters are being brewed—it does literally seethe."
Richard works, I give lessons and ink in. In the afternoon we go for a
walk together in the loveliest of weather. R. finishes the preface to his
fifth and sixth volumes in the evening. Later we read Schopenhauer
again. (In the morning R. brings me the second volume of the *Renaissance*.)

*Thursday, January 18* Yesterday Herr Heckel sent us the photographs
of his Alpine flora. I write to Prof. Nietzsche while R. works. Then I
go for a walk with the children; later family lunch. Letter from
Clemens: the Nietzsche book has not been understood there; R. replies

to him at length, telling him what he thinks of the book and its author. Fidi sings *"Heil Mutter, unsre Mama"*—almost the whole song! R. says that it reminds him of his second year, when he saw *Wilhelm Tell* lying on the ground and said, "Ell, Ell." He was praised for knowing the name, whereas his feeling was of pleasure at getting his tongue around it. In the evening Schopenhauer.

*Friday, January 19*   R. works a lot, but is angry with his "composing," maintaining that it keeps him from enjoying his happiness. He so longs to be with the children, whose every word is gold. I go out with the children in splendid sunshine. Letter from Marie Schleinitz, but still nothing from Baron Cohn; God knows how things stand; nobody knows at all how business is progressing. R. very annoyed about it. R. is made honorary member of the Society of Friends of Music. An article about "Hans von Bülow" by Herr Schelle in Vienna has been sent to me. It leaves no pleasant impression. — A palm which R. gave me two years ago has died; I entrusted it to the servants, and now the tree looks at me so reproachfully that I feel a stab in my heart. — R. returns from his walk in a bad humor, but is cheered up by a tale from the *Pañcha tantra*, which he reads to us and which charms us all. In the evening Schopenhauer.

*Saturday, January 20*   R. tells me he dreamed of me and my steadfastness; then, however, perihelion and aphelion kept going through his mind. He works; I give the children lessons and then go for a walk with Fidi. Lusch to her piano lesson. In the afternoon, as I am working with the children, and R. on his proofs, Prof. Nietzsche pays us a surprise visit, which pleases us very much. Many things discussed: plans for the future, school reform, etc.; he plays us his composition very beautifully.

*Sunday, January 21*   Still fine weather; we go, 6 of us, for a morning walk; in the afternoon went through the second act of *Götterdämmerung*. In the evening discussed the Werder episode. Our friend means very much to us.

*Monday, January 22*   Feustel reports that he has rented a floor in the Fantaisie for us, also mentions a letter sent off on the previous day, which we have not received. R. works until nearly two, then the letter comes, and it states that Cohn has not yet sent anything, and that the credit for the whole building operation must be secured before work can begin. At the same time R. receives a letter from Baron Cohn, showing a subscription of 20,000 thalers! Baron Loën had spoken of 50,000 and reported that he himself had signatures for 28,000 thalers in his portfolio, yet for Baron Cohn he lists only 12,000! R. very alarmed at this news; we walk to town in silence and return home; R. has the idea of making a journey in order to come to an understanding with the Wagneriana. Were it possible to let this cup pass from us! Sent a telegram to Heckel, asking whether he could set out at once as R.'s plenipotentiary. Perhaps he can be spared the journey. The only comforting thing: a spider which runs persistently over Cohn's letter by lamplight. Heavy, silent evening!

*Tuesday, January 23*   R. feels he will have to make the journey— so goodbye now to the working mood—oh, how sad, how sad! I feel crushed. Herr Heckel replies by telegram that he cannot leave his business for any length of time, and he asks for details of the time and place. R. says, "It was just a shot in the dark, it would have been a miracle to have hit straightaway on the right person who could place himself at my disposal at once." He writes down his plan and a survey of the situation. So dive down deep, Rhinemaidens—alas, for how long?

In the afternoon a letter from Lenbach, saying he has nearly finished another portrait of R. — R. preparing for his journey; children in tears over his departure, I as if wiped out. On top of it all a Hamburg enthusiast asking for a letter. Childish friendship against calculated hostility. — Bülow is now in Berlin, which is also an embarrassing factor.

*Wednesday, January 24*   Departure today; Bernhard Löser is in Berlin; this the main transaction; then Cohn and Loën, to whom R. has written. R. leads me to the piano and plays me the last page of the first scene. "Yes," he says, "when the donkey feels his oats, he goes for a dance on the ice. I complained of having to compose, now things see to it that I can't continue. But this doesn't touch the vital nerve— that is safe; you are the driving force and embryo for everything, and I have you. Now I am going, but that is better than if you went." Contemplating the children at lunch, he says, "Only dreams help!" At one o'clock to the railroad station. "I remain in your protection," he says to me. "I am happy—just look at me: an old man like me, and what a beautiful wife I have been given!" Embracing and waving, and then gone! I have no urge to go home, do some shopping. Back at 5 o'clock; toiling and moiling with the children, in the evening upstairs, melancholy. (Letters from E. Krockow and Marie Muchanoff. Arranged files; to bed around midnight. Began a letter to R.)

*Thursday, January 25*   Telegram from R.; he is in good heart! I write, ink in, teach, go for a walk with the children, and think as little as possible. Prof. N. writes sympathetically from Basel, where he saw R. I write to Marie M. and spend the evening alone in the upstairs *salon.*

*Friday, January 26*   Splendid weather and a good telegram, saying there is hope of a good and easy settlement! I write to R. and feel better. Walk in the garden, spring sunshine and air. Glorious moonlight in the evening. The great, yet mild, indeed fair, melancholy of life. (Read *Beethoven*.)

*Saturday, January 27* No telegram, anxious mood; pale sunshine and the air cold. Letter from my father, with reports on Hans's great successes in Vienna and Pest. He sends the libretto of his *Christus*. Toward evening a telegram from R.; he is in need of rest, has decided what to do, and is returning via Weimar, Dessau, Bayreuth. — In the evening read *Tasso* with great enjoyment.

*Sunday, January 28* Everything vanished, mountains, sun, blue sky; fog, snow, and frost! I ink in the penciled sketches. Lusch writes to her grandmama and receives a letter from her with good news of Hans in Berlin. Drove to town with Fidi; bought cakes for the evening party, having invited my four daughters to tea! Much delight among the little ones, who dress themselves with the utmost elegance. But we soon have to put an end to our pleasure, since Loldi is unwell. Toward half past ten, after I have finished *Tasso* and am going off to bed, I hear a loud knocking, and Fitzo barks; I call Käthchen, who had already heard the noise (knocking) and was up; we look around, but see or find nothing; great fear. I have my mattress put on the floor in Käthchen's room and sleep (or, rather, lie awake) thus.

*Monday, January 29* Telegram from R. in Berlin, he is just (8 A.M.) leaving for Weimar. "Business settled"—so the warning was not on his account! — Loldi seriously unwell; I put her to bed and stay beside her. In the evening a letter from R., everything seems satisfactory, if not exactly brilliant; our conquest is Feustel, who took R. by surprise for the third time, came into his room, and is being helpful in everything. In the evening I write to R.—also to Frau Wesendonck and Pohl.

*Tuesday, January 30* Loldi somewhat better; with her the whole day. Then toward evening went to town to inquire about dancing lessons for the children. Melancholy mood; one does not belong here, but where in this life does one belong? Feelings of being a stranger all over the world! Telegram from R. in Weimar, he is well, traveling to Bayreuth tomorrow. I write to him in the evening. Vexation over this dry correspondence by telegram. — (A week ago I was touched to read of the death of Msgr. Bucquet, my first father confessor; the best priest there can ever have been and the friend of my childhood; he also knew Daniel and Blandine and was very dear to all three of us.) — In the night a curious knocking again.

*Wednesday, January 31* Loldi much better. Letter from my mother. With Loldi in the morning; in the afternoon to town. Letter from R. in Berlin, short, but good all the same. In the evening read Nietzsche's book. (R. sends some caviar from Leipzig.)

*Thursday, February 1* Chimneysweep upsets; Loldi still in bed, but somewhat better. Telegram from R. saying he has arrived safely in Bayreuth, but has much to do. Letter from Judith Mendès. Children all day, to town for clothes and shoes. Telegram from R.; he has acquired the site for our house, attended a ball at Herr von Lerchenfeld's, and is staying with Feustel.

*Friday, February 2* Terrible day! My children walk into town with Anna, take Fitzo with them, return home weeping, and tell me that Fitzo has been run over by the locomotive. I run to the spot and bury our poor little dog. It is a holiday, people come and go, the sun shines, and I feel as if I were to blame for his death. Today, when the bell rang and I did not hear his barking, I felt so desolate; I cannot help thinking that recently Kos was calling Fitzo; Fitzo heard the knocking and wanted to fly to me for protection. I feel as if I had lost Kos twice, and the terrible sight of that poor, mangled body will never leave me.

*Saturday, February 3* Went sadly to bed; rose despondent! A new snowfall, which covers poor Fitzo. The children do not seem to be thinking about him, I shall probably be the only one in whom the poor creature will live on. — In the afternoon a letter from R.; he is going to Munich; for what reason I do not exactly know. He really did see the Grand Duke in Weimar. He is happy about everything in Bayreuth, Feustel, Fantaisie, house, everything. — God give him His blessing. (Letters to Fritz and Judith.)

*Sunday, February 4* Telegram from R.; he is returning tomorrow, at the same time the sunshine returns. It is Saint Richard's Day, which I always used to celebrate; today the sky celebrated it with northern lights such as I have never seen before; the countryside looked indescribable, *Götterdämmerung* lights! — (Letter from Elisabeth Krockow, sending me a few lines from Countess Dönhoff, to whom Hans had said that he would be seeing "Wagner and his wife" in the course of this year. Prof. Nietzsche writes me that Hans thanked him for sending his book and said he would be visiting Basel in March.)

*Monday, February 5* Day of return! I expect R. at 12, and he really comes! Happiness, joy, delight, bliss; all, all of this for us in this hour of reunion. R. says that my letters always seemed to him like a voice from the Ganges, and now he is back again on the Ganges! Much to be related; the Wagneriana vanished into thin air, much Jewishness to put up with; but, on the other hand, Bayreuth, "my greatest practical stroke of genius." The Wagneriana had withdrawn their signatures because at the banquet in Berlin Tausig had not introduced the members by name, thus, so to speak, denying them. Jewish sensitivity and Jewish revenge. Cohn unbelievably brazen. R. a profound repugnance for

Berlin. — The evening passes in all sorts of talk, I recount to him the contents of letters which arrived during his absence. The infinite joy of seeing each other, having each other again!

*Tuesday, February 6* R. tells me in detail about his audience with the Grand Duke of Weimar, who greeted him with particular warmth as a poet and said to him that, if *Tannhäuser* were, so to speak, a local Thuringian work for the people of Weimar, *Die Meistersinger* had stirred up genuine German feelings. His reports on the Jewish community, on the other hand, ever more diverting and incredible. During the afternoon, as we blissfully sit beside each other, R. says to me: "I should like to know in what way I should have come to grief if I had not won you! For since we have been intimate, I have never had the faintest feeling that we could ever be separated, it was just the nature of our union which remained unclear to me, and out of sympathy I wanted it to remain so." — Yesterday he spoke a lot about Gustavus Adolphus, whom he is coming to respect more and more; his hero's popular way of speaking in particular gives him great joy, as for example to the Brandenburgers: "I shall seize you roundly by the ears." Some articles by Herr Riehl seem to us very pitiable: malice—everything is made to look as if it is being done only for the sake of Bayreuth —and stupidity. — A criticism of *Tasso* by Herr Hettner also fills me with disgust, as I have just recently received a profound and very definite impression from this consummate poetical work. — Prof. Nietzsche has sent me the book *Caroline*, without a doubt the most insipid thing it is possible to imagine. Conversed in the evening; on Riehl: "How deep-rooted it must be that such a goodhearted philistine, who has his merits, suddenly turns so malicious and nasty."

*Wednesday, February 7* A good night. I write, and R., too, he in connection with the 9th Symphony, and I to Lenbach about his latest sketch, then to my father, etc. — R. goes to town; the breaking up of our household is giving him trouble. In the evening glanced a little through *Caroline*: very pitiful stuff!

*Thursday, February 8* R. talks of the wretched present times, he says he will just have to put his trust in a new generation; he has now lived through three: his own, which grew up under the influence of Weber, up to the 1830 Revolution; the generation from then until '48, which, like Hans, received its youthful impressions from Meyerbeer, the people of the 1849 Goethe jubilee, who after our painful experiences found everything good and celebrated with jubilees. "Now I am living through the third, and this third saeculum I am living through I owe to you," he then says to me. He works, and at midday is able to play me his sketch for the Prelude. I write to Prof. Nietzsche and give the children lessons. In the afternoon I go for a walk with R., and on the quay we see a poor dog run over; a yelp, a cowering, then a wild leap into the air before falling back, then tossed aside. "That's how it was with Fitzo," R. exclaims. "It is as if it were being shown to us—he, too, was tossed aside in that way, like an old rag." Then I could no longer keep silent, and I told him how it had been with Fitzo. We are very despondent. "A human being should not feel pity," R. says. "Nature doesn't want it; he should be as cruel as the animals; pity has no place in the world." I suggest that pity should not be expressed, just acted on. R. is very oppressed, he cannot forget the dying animal's leap into the air. — We read Schopenhauer; then I tell Richard about the "barbarian advantages" on which Goethe says we must courageously insist. "Yes," says R., "*Faust*, the Ninth, Bach's Passions are barbarian works of that kind, that is to say, works of art which cannot be compared with a Greek Apollo or a Greek tragedy; which affect the individual, do not become part of the general picture; it was this feeling which brought me to the art of the future." — Fidi gives us much, much joy. "I am too happy," R. says. "I do not enjoy my happiness enough. I am still afraid of leaving the world without having enjoyed it." — I cannot bring myself to like the sketch of R. which Lenbach sent me to look at, and R. says, "I feel really sad that artists see in me only a sharp caricature or a thorough philistine!" — Frau Wille announces the engagement of her son to a Comtesse Bismarck.

*Friday, February 9* R. works; at lunch I ask him, and he promises, to dictate an account of his journey, which is given below. (A Herr Voltz, wine merchant in Mainz, claims to have found a way of enabling R. to receive earnings from his works and from performances of them.) Fine spring weather.

### Dictation

*On January 24 via Basel, where I spent several hours with Nietzsche and Fritz B., on the night train to Berlin; although I tried to keep up a brave face in front of them, a letter from N. which followed me showed that he had recognized the evil necessity behind my journey and truly regretted it. With me in the train from Erfurt to Weimar was Herr von Loën, whom I had invited to join me in this way for a talk; he was able to some extent to put my mind at rest regarding the state of things, since I realized that what I had to complain about was more his negligence as an administrator than the success of our enterprise in general. At the station in Berlin I was met by the good Gersdorff and the mysterious leading figure, to satisfy myself about whom had been the main point of my journey: Herr Bernhard Löser, founder of the Wagneriana, that society on which all our secret hopes had been set. He accompanied me to a bad hotel of his own choosing, and the little room set aside for me he had stuffed so full of plants and bushes in celebration of my arrival that their scent made me feel bad. [In the margin: "He dreamed that he was sick."] After a sleepless night I rose next morning feeling ill. Before receiving my mysterious benefactor, I was surprised by friend Feustel, who—in his now habitual, very pleasing way —came quite unexpectedly into my room, along with* Neumann, *whom I had invited. Since some differences had arisen between the Bayreuth building authorities and Neumann concerning the building estimates, Feustel had immediately journeyed here to put matters right, and his arrival showed that he had been sent to me by Fate. This soon became completely clear after I had spent some time conferring with Herr Löser. From him I wished to learn exactly what was this Wagneriana, which in the eyes of our friend Marie Schleinitz looked something like a choir of angels. Obviously, if this society really possessed the considerable funds of which Tausig had spoken, I should be well advised to put it in charge of the business side of our great Bayreuth enterprise. It cost me much effort to extract from Herr Löser's expatiations the true state of things, but in the end the Wagneriana dissolved into the usual Jewish fog. All that clearly emerged was that the founder of this society of names, rather than people, had succeeded through Tausig in making an impression on Frau v. Schl., but he was now to collapse into pathetic misery, being forced to admit that my previous good opinion of him had been quite without foundation. —*

*Saturday, February 10* Here R. broke off and observed that I knew it all exactly and would tell it better than he could, which I consequently intend to do. We read Schopenhauer on the subject of death. — This morning R. woke me up with the blissful "Dream Song." Then he pours abuse on his profession, which forces him to compose instead of living with us peacefully and happily: "I am always in convulsions, always preoccupied." — He works, I write letters (to Judith) and teach the children. The weather is splendid, I go into the garden with the children; R., however, again does not go out, which has a bad effect on him. In the evening Schopenhauer.

*Sunday, February 11* "What is God, is there a God? The answer is, 'A mighty fortress'—that is God; and the apotheosis of Isolde is immortality. What is faith? The 'Pilgrims' Chorus' from *Tannhäuser*." He works, but is not well; he finds the coal fire unpleasant, the fumes upset him. In the afternoon he corrects proofs, in the evening I read Schopenhauer to him. Of *Opera and Drama*, which he is correcting, he says: "I know what Nietzsche didn't like in it—it is the same thing which Kossak took up and which set Schopenhauer against me: what I said about words. At the time I didn't dare to say that it was music which produced drama, although inside myself I knew it."

*Monday, February 12* Nice letter from Marie M. R. works, I with the children. R. has now done the "Song of the Rhinemaidens" in ink; the children sing it in the garden; and R. says, "If I had an audience of Italians and French people for that, all hell would be let loose in this first scene—it's just as well that I can reckon on German stick-in-the-muds to preserve the unity of the impact." When I asked him whether he had read a scene from a Sardou play, which was quoted in *Die Gegenwart*, he said, "No, I thought it was something German, so I immediately looked in the other direction." Pleasure in Bismarck, who is starting his battle with the Catholic party: "He is doing enough already, he doesn't need to think of the art of the future." R. corrects proofs. A letter arrives from Mrs. Lang in Massachusetts with a signed certificate of patronage. Eliza Wille's novel *Johannes Olaf* also arrives, and I read parts of it to R. We like it.

*Shrove Tuesday, February 13*  I have a very bad night and fall asleep only in the early hours, R. wakes me with the "Song of the Rhine-maidens." Some days ago, R. told me that perhaps the finest thing in this act would be the orchestral Prelude following Siegfried's death; when his theme had finally died away, Gutrune would come out, thinking she had heard his horn. — Yesterday, as we read about Iceland: "Ghastly, desolate places," R. says. "I see them sometimes in dreams, a memory of my former voyage." — The fog has returned, all is gloomy and gray outside: "That's how the world looks to me," says R. But he works all the same. We go for a walk as far as Seeburg, both silent—so much lies in front of us, so much behind. Letter from *Chicago*: they want to "honor your German masters" and have performed the choruses from *Die Msinger*. Letter from Herr Heckel; in Berlin Herr Löser, that most useless and pathetic of Jews, wants to organize a lottery along the lines of the one for Cologne Cathedral; R. is protesting. In the evening read more of Frau Wille's novel; it is a bit slow. — Punch and doughnuts for the children.

*Wednesday, February 14*  Ash Wednesday; foggy as well. R. works; I write to Chicago. Letter to R. from Hamburg, asking his terms for conducting a concert there! — Letter from Alwine Fr., describing the entire Berlin fiasco. Some articles in the *A.A.Z.* about K[*aspar*] *Hauser* horrify us: how easily is the general public deceived! — In this instance the criminal succeeds completely. In the evening read Frau Wille's book with enjoyment.

*Thursday, February 15*  Letter from Prof. Nietzsche. R. at work, I with the children; family lunch; Fidi very exuberant and lusty. R. goes for a walk, but is not well; in the evening we read together. — I forgot to note that on his journey R. spent much time thinking of Gustavus Adolphus, whom he is coming increasingly to respect; when I tell him that he reminds me of Dietrich von Bern, he agrees. [*A repeated entry omitted.*] — In Prussia people are now talking of Bismarck's downfall! — (The post office has paid me 50 francs for the lost money order.)

*Friday, February 16*  R. unfortunately had a very bad night; to add to that, snow and fog. He also thinks of Fitzo's death (14 days ago today!). "All are dying," he says, "one is left alone." I am very despondent, overcome by indescribable fears for his life; how gloomy everything is when he is unwell! — In the evening I read him the novel; a quotation from Dante brings R. to the magnificent genius of this poet: "He has given us the entire Middle Ages."

*Saturday, February 17*  Nice foehn weather; Eva's birthday; R. to work after reading Döllinger's lecture on the Greek church. A walk in the afternoon; in the evening I am very unwell. Severe headache; R. reads me Frau Wille's book.

*Sunday, February 18*  Eva has brought us the spring; the weather is splendid; I feel somewhat better, R. works, after lunch we are able to go for a drive. Returning home, we are surprised by a visit from Prof. Nietzsche, to whom R. then gives an account of his journey. — (Letter from Clemens Brockhaus concerning my conversion.)

*Monday, February 19*  R., who had a good night, after breakfast plays the first scene to our friend, and that upsets him so much that the whole day through he can eat nothing and is very run down. All the same, there is much discussion of the reform of educational establishments, also of the German character. "So far," R. says, "we have been great in *defense*, dispelling alien elements which we could not assimilate; the Teutoburger Wald was a rejection of the Roman influence, the Reformation also a rejection, our great literature a rejection of the influence of the French; the only positive thing so far has been our music—Beethoven." "And *Faust*?" I ask. "It is really just a sort of sketch," R. says, "which Goethe himself looked upon in puzzlement, as a curiosity—he himself did not consider it a finished work of art." — The dean of Bayreuth sends his book *Pax Vobis* (on the reconciliation of Protestants and Catholics) with some very friendly words for me.

*Tuesday, February 20*  R. still very run down. (In the *Illustrirte Zeitung* a nice picture and an article on Bayreuth and the *Nibelungen* dramas.) — R. always comes back to the small towns, for, he says, "we have no real large towns, it is always—in Berlin, for example—as if they were masquerading as large cities." — "People can perhaps be divided into those who cry 'Evoe, Evoe' and those who cry 'Kohe, Kohe' (from *Das unterbrochene Opferfest*)." — R. works, but is still not well, which in turn robs me of all my strength. In the evening continued reading Frau Wille's very insipid book.

*Wednesday, February 21*  R. had a good night; let us hope things will now go better. But alas, too much lies ahead! — R. is editing the 8th volume of his writings and is glad to be giving in it a picture of his work in Munich and his trials there; it starts with the essay *State and*

*Religion* and peters out in the sands of Hiller! — R. works and completes Siegfried's reply to the Rhinemaidens, cutting two verses, which are too reflective: "Siegfried is all action—though he does recognize the fate which he has taken on himself." He plays me what he has just completed—sublime and tragic impression! — Fog and spring showers; we go for a drive, R. and I, he returns home alone on foot. In the evening we read *State and Religion*, but at 10 o'clock we are interrupted: Jakob announces that Vreneli's time has come; I stay with her until three o'clock, when she gives birth to a girl: suffering and fellow suffering!

*Thursday, February 22* Letter from Herr De Gubernatis, who sends all sorts of things, says he has had *my* letter published in the newspaper and that it was much applauded, which amuses R. and me very much: "Where the French language is concerned, I can rely on my wife." — R. works; I with the children. Read Saint Paul; otherwise rested, for I am very tired. Muddles in the outside world; none of the musicians has understood R.! In the evening we finish *State and Religion*. The third volume of the collected writings has arrived. — "When I was recently immersing myself in my writings, I thought: Cosima will no doubt be jealous that I am thinking so busily about other things besides her, and yet all I do is always together with her—it is because I have her that I feel free to do it." "If things had gone better for us earlier, we should have felt the misery of separation even more painfully, but we had experienced so much unhappiness that we were conscious only of the joy of seeing each other again." — He speaks about Gustavus Adolphus, how, when he left Sweden and exhorted his people, he concluded with the moving words, "As far as I am concerned, I know that I can hope for no more rest except the eternal one." — Riehl and Hiller are put in their places, "and yet I can never forget," says R., "that it was from Hiller that I first heard Beethoven's *33 Variations*."

*Friday, February 23* R. is well and works; at lunch we talk about the Rhinemaidens' scene; he shows me how the maidens come very close to Siegfried, then dive down again, consigning him amid laughter and rejoicing to his downfall with all the childlike cruelty of Nature, which only indicates motives and indifferently sacrifices the individual —thus, in fact, demonstrating a supreme wisdom which is only transcended by the wisdom of the saint. — We go for a drive, R. returns home on foot, I visit the parson, Herr Tschudi, who is very friendly; returning home late, I hear that Voltz, our former wine merchant, who wants to help R. receive royalties from his operas, has announced his coming. He arrives with a lawyer also, and business is discussed. —

R. receives a telegram from Hellmesberger, promising him eleven players for the 9th. I receive letters from M. Meysenbug, Math. M., etc. —

*Saturday, February 24*  The discussion affected R. badly; he had a wretched night, and now he has to devote this morning as well to giving these two people authority to act on his behalf! I am disconsolate and ask myself what will come of it. So a day of business, the two gentlemen have lunch with us and then go with R. to the law courts. — Letter from Friedrich Feustel: Baron Cohn is unwilling to collect the contributions, and Baron Loën does not write. Much vexation and despondency. "The only beautiful thing in my life was you, all the rest was rather ugly!" In the evening Schopenhauer, with great enjoyment. At least we are once more together and united; indescribable feelings of love for R. —

*Sunday, February 25*  R. had a good night and is able to work; he has now completed the first scene in ink. "I have given Siegfried a cry! The fellow cries out like a wild goose." I write letters (to Malwida and Fritz). Cohn's uselessness is disturbing R.; if only he can finish his work uninterrupted! — There is talk of an assassination attempt on Prince Bismarck. A Pole and a Jesuit. — At lunch our conversation turns on Calderón's comedies, and R. praises the way in which he makes his heroes all much the same—the loving man, the jealous man— in order to leave as much room as possible for the manipulation of chance. Otherwise one falls into the modern habit, in which one character constantly repeats a proverb, another sneezes, and so on. — Storm; R. goes out, however. In the evening he works on the foreword to the essays (Riehl, Hiller, etc.). We see a little black dog, very like Fitzo, wandering around the meadow during the storm; we try to catch it, but it disappears into the Robbers' Park. News comes from Karlsruhe that almost the entire orchestra wants to play, which means that the performance of the 9th Symphony would be assured; but what about everything else? — Vreneli, whom I went to see, made me very happy with a remark: she said that R. has become so much calmer and gentler, that his present manner cannot be compared with what it was in Munich. — In the evening we read Schopenhauer, and when I ask R. for some explanations, he gives them in so lively a manner that I tell him he reminds me of the professor of philosophy in Molière's play, who in the end lashes out with his fists. This amuses him greatly. — "The way the will sometimes takes matters into its own hands can be seen in me," R. says. "It had its ideas for me, and since I should otherwise have stopped cooperating, it brought us together in real life—independent of the fact that outside of time and space we belong to each other anyway—with the result that I started cooperating again. It's just like an employer raising the wages when he sees his employees leaving him."

*Monday, February 26* A night of bad dreams, I go for help to R., who, curiously enough, was just dreaming that something had happened to me. — He works, I finish the 3rd act of *Siegfried*. Over coffee after lunch R. says after a short pause: "Where was I just now? I was on the road to Possendorf—which I so often walked in a mood of gloom. Yet those were my productive, lonely walks, and it is strange how certain things are linked in my memory with the themes which came to me then. With '*Ich flehe um sein Heil*' in *Tannhäuser*, for instance, I always see a fence just in front of the big garden in Dresden, where this theme occurred to me." — I: "You also once told me that a theme in *Die Walküre* was connected with a certain walk in Zurich." "Yes—curiously enough, for these external things really have nothing to do with it; living impressions, as far as creation is concerned, are somewhat like the box on the ear which was given in earlier times to the youngest member of the community when the boundary stone was set, so that he should remember it." — In the evening dancing lesson, and later Schopenhauer.

*Tuesday, February 27* Rain and snow—"Let us betake ourselves to the day's crutches," says R. — Nothing of importance, except that R. works. In the evening Schopenhauer; doctrine of renunciation.

*Wednesday, February 28* R. sings something from *Die Zauberflöte* and says to me, "Sarastro—that, you see, is German: this mild aura of humanity beckoning to one through all the stupidities of opera." — Yesterday he read me his foreword to the articles, a sad look back on the times in Munich. He dreamed in three sections of a great party I had given without his knowledge. — Fidi sends Rus away from the fire, he has noticed that we cannot bear that; R. says to him, "You'll be a doctor, you're so clever." "No—emperor," replies Fidi. — R. works, but he is not well and complains of his sickly condition, which prevents his enjoying his happiness. Letter from Karl von Gersdorff, it seems that Baron Cohn is collecting the money after all. Walk, Countess B., dancing lesson. In the evening Schopenhauer. (We hear from the Nuremberg theater manager. Success of Batz and Voltz.)

*Thursday, February 29* Very good letter from an architect in Berlin, who wants to set up a student society for all Germany (for Bayreuth). A student in Heidelberg also writes to me on the subject of Bayreuth, and a man from Vienna, Herr *August Hahn*, reviews the performance of *Lohengrin* there excellently. "Little by little one gets through," R. says, "all I need is time." Wrote all sorts of letters in connection with Bayreuth. R. works and is satisfied; he feels better. Family lunch; walk after lunch; we talk about the theme in the march in *A Midsummer Night's Dream*, which begins as a return to the theme, and it certainly makes a very surprising effect in C major; but as a march theme it is in fact very absurd, and it is based on a joke, over which he always saw Mendelssohn smiling contentedly. — Reading the chapter yesterday in which Schopenhauer describes the nature of genius, I felt he had written it about R. R. writes to Herr Coerper; in the evening read Schopenhauer. Sad feelings of my unworthiness; how to become worthy of R.; to earn the happiness of his love? His goodness and his greatness I recognize ever more profoundly—how to repay him for so needing me?

*Friday, March 1*   R. calls out to me: "What is the difference between Wotan and Siegfried? Wotan married Minna and Siegfried Cosima." He then tells me he dreamed that I had beautiful golden locks. He works. We go for a walk after lunch. In the evening we receive letters, I a very nice one from R.'s sister Klara, which makes me very glad, for everything that has to do with him is very dear and valuable to me. (Letter from Judith.)

*Saturday, March 2*   R. had a good night, which he says he owes to a late glass of beer. Letter from our good Feustel. Much confusion with the Ninth Symphony; instead of 200 singers Herr Stern allocates 38; then people from Schwerin want seats for the performance of the *Nibelungen*, and the mayor of Schweinfurt offers to beat a drum; on top of that, people asking R. to find them lodgings—much foolishness. R. works. In the afternoon our nephew Fritz arrives, an always welcome guest. We spend a cozy evening conversing.

*Sunday, March 3*   Letter from Hans Richter, who is sending 1,000 florins to Bayreuth, the proceeds of a concert which he conducted. A Wagner Society is also being formed in Pest. Marie Schleinitz also writes and seems glad to be giving up the Israelite connections. R. does no composing, but works on his 8th volume. He starts the day fairly well and lively, but in the evening he is run down—visits unfortunately always tire him. Prof. Nietzsche sent us several letters, among them one from Prof. Ritschl to him, very ironical in tone. R. still does not know how things stand with the 9th Symphony, since all he is getting is confused letters. The mayor of Schweinfurt offers to play the drum! The evening conversation unfortunately brings us to K. von Holtei, whose intervention in R.'s life was certainly the most repulsive of all.

*Monday, March 4*   Letter from a Herr Dannreuther (very good), who reports the setting up of the Society in London. Splendid spring day, but R. is not well and is very unsettled, which sours for me the blue sky and the gleaming mountains, the singing birds and the fluttering

butterflies! Out of doors a lot with Fritz, who leaves us in the afternoon; R. has done some work after all. In the evening he is tired, we
read a little Schopenhauer. God give him strength and courage to
complete his work! Blessings on him! [*End of the fourth notebook of
the Diaries. The next begins:* "In the fifth year of my happiness, March
1872." *In the margin of the first entry:* "'Papa always pomade,' says
Fidi as he goes into his father's room and finds him shaving."]

*Tuesday, March 5*   Letter from my father, short and unexpansive.
On the other hand, M. M. writes that the fires of the south seem to
have harmed our friend Schuré, and we should help to deliver him.
R. is not completely well: outside it is spring. R. said yesterday that,
when he read Döllinger's recent lecture, it had struck him that in the
18th century many people had gone back to the Catholic church on
account of the drying up of the Protestant church; it then occurred
to him that, as the Lutheran hymn had rescued the soul of the Reformation from the dust of disputations, so, too, had Bach's music in the
18th century. — We drive to Winkel, R. and I; in the carriage he waxes
indignant against present-day writers, historians who will not acknowledge the full greatness of a man of destiny such as Gustavus Adolphus,
for instance; instead, they talk of the state of things, politics, etc.,
whereas, but for his heroic faith, there would not be a Protestant left
in Germany. — We also speak of the Crown Prince of Prussia, who has
suddenly become anti-Wagnerian through his wife and belongs to the
Joachim clique. Unfortunately R. is not completely well; we go for a
long walk, and in the evening we read Schopenhauer. Melancholy
thoughts of my father.

*Wednesday, March 6*   "Yes, this is my wife, whom I love forever and
ever"—R. calls out this hexameter to me on a lovely spring morning.
Arrival of a medallion from Neusel, not very satisfactory. R. works.
In the morning much joy in Fidi. In the afternoon we go out—I to
the dancing lesson, R. by himself. Returning home in the evening, I
find him in a very bad humor; he has no news from Dresden or Vienna,
and in Karlsruhe difficulties have arisen, so he has no idea whether the
thing can be done at all. Much vexation: how can he keep his head free
for his work in such circumstances? He writes several letters and sends
off several telegrams. In the evening help comes from Schopenhauer,
whose chapter on music particularly delights me.

*Thursday, March 7*   In the evening talked a lot about the Middle
Ages, which—utterly dominated as they were by Catholic ecstasy—
are almost as far away from us in spirit as the ancient world. R. works
and is somewhat better, thank God. Outside the foehn is raging, we
do not go out. Letters arrive, among others a very remarkable one from
Josef Rubinstein, beginning "I am a Jew" and demanding salvation

through participation in the production of the *Nibelungen*. R. sends him a very friendly reply. Also a telegram from Herr Hellmesberger in Vienna; he is successfully recruiting singers there. In the evening read Schopenhauer's chapter on genius. Profound awareness of our love; my request to R. that he feel convinced that I have utterly no will of my own, and that my only happiness lies in understanding him in everything and standing by him. Oh, if I could really help him! (In the afternoon he played passages from the first act of *Götterdämmerung*; in the morning he showed me Hagen's laughter: "*Was er nicht schmiedete, schmeckte doch Mime.*")

*Friday, March 8* Our lovely Weymouth pine, under which I have so often sat, has been destroyed by the storm! Recently, to my almost greater sorrow, the little palm R. gave me two years ago died. — Warm spring weather—the children out of doors, R. very persistently at work, for he is feeling better. Deepest, purest happiness between us! — Yesterday, when the foehn was coloring the lake, we thought of the fairy tale of Ilsebill, and R. said he had once thought of dramatizing it, till he realized that everything would have to be invented, and it is a great mistake to assume that tales which are complete in themselves can be turned into drama—they can only be spoiled. — I write to M. Meysenbug, R. corrects *Opera and Drama*. Rossini melodies keep coming into his mind, inspired by Schopenhauer's quaint worship. He wishes to have the piano scores of this curiously talented composer. Talking about *Die Zauberflöte*, he said: "This is folklorish. If it can be said of us Germans that we have no art, we can at least reply that we do have a folk tradition; art stands midway between academicism and folklore, for there have really been no genuine artists since the Greeks. Schiller was in a certain sense a dramatic artist." — R. tells me that he is extremely interested in Garrick's rediscovery of Shakespeare at a time when English taste was under French influence. The devices he evolved to replace the Shakespearean theater seem to him excellent. — We go for a walk; in the evening we read Schopenhauer's critique of Kant. — In general R. criticizes Schopenhauer for not having paid sufficient attention to the male and female elements, into which everything in this world is divided. — Before going to work he tells me that he cannot see the name Siegfried without thinking of Fidi. "What will the boy one day say and think about it?" — Before we begin the criticism of Kant, R. reads me the conversation between Gustavus Adolphus and the envoys from Brandenburg; splendid insight into the fine character of the Swedish King. (R. plays me the theme of the end of the world; "Siegfried is in command.")

*Saturday, March 9* R. tells me that he once tried to grasp the idea of the "thing in itself" by considering the mountain in Zurich (the

Uetli). He went for a walk with an acquaintance (Prof. Eschenburg) and said to him, "There is the Uetli—that is to say, in a certain light and at this or that distance it appears to us to be that, a mountain, but what is it in itself?" His companion replied, "Oh, you are an incorrigible metaphysician," which amused R. greatly. The *Rivista Europea* prints a nice article by Schuré about the Bayreuth venture, and in Italy a Wagner subscription fund is now being opened; the periodical itself has started it off with 150 francs. R. works. In the afternoon letters arrive, all very unsatisfactory. Lauterbach, the concertmaster in Dresden, is behaving badly. Betz agrees to sing in the 9th, but says Niemann is feeling offended by R. At such times one is struck by all the misery of life. We go for a walk, R. and I, then I to the dancing lesson. Bismarck's splendid speech in the Upper Chamber enlivens our evening. Then we read *Maria Stuart*, during which we are conscious of Schiller's weakness for too much talk; R. says, for instance, that in the scene with Maria the role of Mortimer is unplayable.

*Sunday, March 10* Hellmesberger writes at last; the results in Vienna are good; our concert fixed for May 12. Around 12 o'clock Frau *Heim* from Zurich, whom we were expecting. But since I was not yet dressed and I assumed that R. was finished with his work, I had her shown in to him, and this disturbed him in his work, which distresses me. Apart from that, the visit is agreeable, for Frau Heim is a good and intelligent person. Prof. Nietzsche sends Hase's *Polemik* and a letter to him from my father, who claims precedence for Golgotha and Tabor over Helicon and Parnassus. Played charades with the children, in the evening finished *Maria Stuart*. — Sad feelings over the departure of the baby, which the Stockers have given away. — (Wrote letters to M. Schl., Schuré, etc.)

*Monday, March 11* Wrote letters. R. works, thanks be to God! I write to Richter, Hellmesberger, Prof. Nietzsche (who tells me Hans will be giving his concert in Basel within the next three weeks). In the afternoon I go by boat to see the Stockers' baby, whom the crossing had made ill. R. sends the score of *Tannhäuser* to Dr. Standhartner, to have the first scene copied. In the evening Schopenhauer's critique of Kant. — While we were talking yesterday evening about the aphorisms of Schiller's heroes, R. said that, like Sancho Panza, they speak in proverbs.

*Tuesday, March 12* Somewhat indisposed; R. claims it is the dancing exercises I give the children which so wear me out, he says I am making him hate the idea of duty! He works, and toward noon plays me the splendid death symphony. "That is his heroic ode, thus will he and his ancestors be sung in later times." "Siegfried lives entirely in the present, he is the hero, the finest gift of the will." When we come down, we find the plans of our house, to our great joy. R. goes out alone and brings me a letter from Richard Pohl, who has seen Hans in Mannheim, where he was giving his 40th concert; he was friendly and in good spirits; he is giving a concert every day and sleeps in the train. This alarms me greatly. — In the evening we read *Romeo and Juliet*—Romeo as the spirit of death entering the house with a flaming torch, his love for Rosaline a kind of premonition of a terrible fate, Mercutio's being snatched away a symbol of the evanescence of life, all of it incomprehensible, inexplicably truthful, the magic of a dramatist!

*Wednesday, March 13* We begin the day talking about Romeo; R. then goes to work, I with the children. At lunch he says he is horribly envious of Shakespeare, whereupon we continue in very lively spirits to speak about the play, which, to use R.'s expression, evokes with its marvels moods which are not artistically satisfied. (As with the Greeks.) R. goes out, I go to meet him, he has found some bock beer in town, which has refreshed him. Pitiful letter from Herr Lauterbach: no musician from Dresden will take part! "That's how it is everywhere I lived and worked—that's how people behave." He writes to Councilor Düfflipp to tell him why he is not inviting the Munich Court orchestra. In the evening finished R[*omeo*] *and* J[*uliet*]; the short scenes, the at times overemphatic speech (like Juliet to Paris), the wailing in *words*, Romeo's spoken description of the apothecary's shop (though very correct in feeling) damp our emotions. (Lovely crescent moon.)

*Thursday, March 14* R. had a very wretched night—he will not be able to work! — As a consequence of the recent battles over the schools law, our friend L. Bucher has been made a privy councilor, on which I congratulate him. — R. is very unwell, does not go out, finally wraps himself in blankets. Telegram from Pest; they have again given a concert there.

*Friday, March 15* Letter from Hans in Zurich, saying he will not be able to see the children. He tells me of his journey to America, and I feel apprehensive, because he is traveling at the same time as Rubinstein, who has an insanely high contract, and whose sponsors must therefore do all they can to ruin his competitors. Should I write to him about this? — R. is feeling better and he works. After lunch he receives —from a member of the Dresden orchestra—the most extraordinary revelations concerning Herr Lauterbach, who has, it seems, just been thwarting our attempts! R. writes letters. In the evening I read him Döllinger's speech about the Church of England. "Always politics," R. says, "I see nothing of religion. Not a word about the wonderful dogma of redemption." Yesterday, when I read some of Hase's *Polemik* to him, he said, "I feel as if I were listening to an army of 10,000 idiots; and there is only one thing that needs to be done: to trust in the Son, the Redeemer, and to tell the faithful that the Father is the Son's secret; he must certainly have known of another world, since he went so willingly to his death." Frau Heim sends a water color by Semper, the Acropolis, and R. accuses me of pride, since I at once start thinking of a gift in return. — After Döllinger we read *Opera and Drama*. "When the rose adorns itself, it also adorns the garden, said my aunt as she adorned herself," R. joked.

*Saturday, March 16* Herr Riedel from Leipzig wants to supply more than 300 singers and says people are begging on their knees to take part. R. is well, thank God! As I am sitting with the children downstairs, he comes in and says, "I have succeeded in making an extension, my dear good wife, I have just been discussing it with you, for when something succeeds, I always discuss it with you; that is what I wanted to tell you." — I wrote 4 letters (Riedel, Betz, Bachmann, Heim). R. works; at 2 o'clock in fine weather to Weggis—Fidi's first excursion into the world! Back at 5 o'clock, I to the dancing lesson, R. indoors, where he edits his invitation. In the evening read *Opera and Drama*.

*Sunday, March 17* R. says he is very tired of composing, he has already done so much, and on the arrival of Siegfried's corpse he could in fact just write in the score, "See *Tristan*, Act III." — We read in the newspaper that Baron von Lerchenfeld has had an audience with the King, and this makes an unpleasant impression on us, since we know the King will certainly not give people confidence in our venture! — I write to Clemens. R. works, but is quite indisposed, which makes me disconsolate. — Yesterday he said jokingly to Fidi, "Your youth is supposed to be the support of my old age, but now my old age will have to be the support of your youth." — The weather is splendid, I go for a walk with R., there is a fine sunset. "All that leaves me indifferent now; maybe the mountains are beautiful, but I no longer notice them. It would be different if we had decided to stay here permanently." Yesterday he says to me, "Rapture at the sight of the moon and stars is now a bygone thing, we shall encounter it again in the children." R.'s indisposition casts a shadow over our whole life, he is spitting up a little blood and his digestion is so bad. He thinks work is a great strain on him. Alas, happy—who is ever happy? Spent the evening quietly with R. — Anonymous letter from Bayreuth, the Railas there seem to be behaving badly. Unpleasant impression. Herr Betz writes that Niemann would like to sing the solo part in the 9th.

*Monday, March 18* R. had a good night, but is still very run down. Letter from Dr. Kafka, who reports that 99,000 florins have been subscribed in Vienna, and 50,000 florins will definitely have been collected by the time of the concert. R. cannot work, which says everything as far as I am concerned, he also looks very run down. In town with the children; found letters, one from Hans, full of ill humor against Germany and all things German. — Package from Herr Franz Hüffer in London with an article, "Richard Wagner," in a review. Dancing lesson, storm, spent the evening quietly with R.

*Tuesday, March 19* A Count Deym sends an opera libretto, *Melusine*; R. is still run down. Yesterday, when I showed R. the photograph of Moltke, he exclaimed, "He is like Fidi," and it is true, there is something in his look. Very nice letter from Clemens, who is worried that his previous one may have hurt me; friend Bucher sends Lulu some lovely stamps and a very nice letter. Spring has vanished, storms, snow flurries, all sorts of things. If only R. were well, everything would be all right; but he is quite unable to work. In the evening read Menzel's *Roms Unrecht*.

*Wednesday, March 20* Boni's 10th birthday; celebrations, holiday, snow and sunshine outside. — I informed R. yesterday that Herr Hüffer was opposed to Ortrud's appearance and the transformation of the swan in the 3rd act. "These people have no idea of theater," he answers. "How would Lohengrin ever have got away otherwise without everyone's running after him? The point here was to create a diversion and to make Lohengrin's departure an unexpected surprise. But that's the way of people, to talk without thinking; he should just tell me how he visualizes it on the stage." — At lunch he tells me that once in Dresden he told his wife that he must get up very early in order to work since he had that day to conduct Mass in the church, and the whole day was arranged accordingly; after working (*Tannhäuser*) he went dreamily to the window, saw Wächter, the singer, who made conducting motions and pointed toward the church; R. looked at the clock; it was half past twelve and he had completely forgotten the Mass he was supposed to conduct—but it went all right without him. — R. is able to work, and he calls me to show me how he has effected Brünnhilde's entry after the raising of Siegfried's hand. — In the afternoon he plays me the 1st act of *Götterdäm.*; I listen amid snow flurries and flickering flames; profound impression. Then we go out; I accompany the children to their dancing lesson, R. fetches a letter of apology from Herr Lauterbach. In Karlsruhe they are preparing Gounod's *Faust* for Whitsuntide and consequently cannot supply R. with any great contingent—which R. finds very revealing. Up till now E. Devrient had at least prevented *Faust*'s being given in Karlsruhe. Read Menzel in the evening.

*Thursday, March 21* Much joy in our bright Fidi; yesterday, as he was drinking his chocolate, I asked him, "Fidi, what do you wish for your birthday?"; whereupon Eva: "Wish for an appetite!" — Our nephew Fritz arrives around noon, to everybody's satisfaction. R. has also been working: Brünnhilde's first words, "*Schweigt eures Jammers,*" etc. Letter from E. Krockow (answered at once), H. Neumann, and to the children from their grandmama. Herr Lauterbach has apologized. — Much conversation with our nephew. R. says to me in the evening, "I have stopped telling you that I love you, because we are one and the same, and so it is foolish to keep on saying it." Spoke a lot with Fritz about the *Vehmgericht.* — He brings us Prof. Nietzsche's lectures in Basel.

*Friday, March 22*  Letters to R. from Herr Feustel and Herr Neumann, also from Herr Raila in Bayreuth. R. is not very well, but he does some work. In the morning I converse with Fritz. In the afternoon a curious darkening over the lake, a flock of starlings comes over from the opposite bank and hurls itself at the tree as with a single wing beat. "There one sees the life of a species," R. says, "and yet each one is a complete entity in itself." — R. tells us about his attempts to ride, in the Bois de Boulogne, on a pitiful nag which did not wish to advance; in the end he had to turn back—and that in Paris, at the time of *Tannhäuser!* Farewells to Fr[itz].

*Saturday, March 23*  Letters from E. Schuré and the publisher Lucca, who is taking up two certificates of patronage. R. works. I with the children. In the afternoon a letter from the conductor Lassen, the Grand Duke of Weimar offers his orchestra for Bayreuth. With the children to their dancing lesson, home on foot in lovely moonlight. In the evening the first two of Prof. Nietzsche's Basel lectures. —

*Sunday, March 24*  Fidi touches us with his good behavior; today I took away his usual egg on account of his fatness; he sees it still on the plate and says nothing! — Letters from Lenbach, Schäfer, etc., they are giving amateur performances in Munich for the benefit of Bayreuth. — Herr Jacques Offenbach is being banished by the French as a German —a *quid pro quo* about which whole books could be written, says R. — Recently he spoke about the fire at the library in Alexandria: "There, according to all accounts, the universal spirit had established a place of eternal enlightenment, everything collected, put in order; culture seemed assured, and a Turkish empire destroys it all." — Family lunch, to end the day a discussion on death, which will not divide us! R. says he recently imagined himself dying in my arms, but the thought of my grief worried him. — He tells me about a curious and complicated dream, with musical tributes being paid, George Sand as audience, a coach which got away from him, and he says one should always note down one's dreams at once. — In the evening read Prof. N.'s third lecture. — Sad discussion with R. concerning the children.

*Monday, March 25* Gloomy mood; snow. — R.'s article about Riedel in the *Musikalische Zeitung.* — Letters. Prof. N. announces a visit. R. does not work. The 4th lecture affects us very much.

*Tuesday, March 26* Lovely day; cheerful surmounting of all worries; R. works again. Much time in the garden with the children. Long letter from Clemens, who sends me the Augsburg Confession and the Lutheran catechism. In gay spirits R. walks into town and returns home with a changed expression: he found a letter from Councilor Düfflipp at the post office! We were not wrong to have been alarmed by Baron Lerchenfeld's audience; the King now wishes it brought to our notice, firstly, that he has learned that the cost of our theater undertaking would far exceed 900,000 thalers, and the many festival performances would cause the Bayreuth people much expense; secondly, that the Bayreuth newspapers were talking of the luxury of our house, which was very unpleasant for the King; thirdly, that the King requires *Siegfried*, since he acquired it by purchase. I at once beg R. to return the house to the King, that is to say, to ask Düfflipp to cancel the purchase of the site; to say that the score of *Siegfried* is not yet completed; and finally to say that he knows where these statements, of which he had heard nothing, came from. — And so we are once more exposed to the old misery! Long conference with R.; he will ask the people in Bayreuth for a statement; should this be subdued in tone, we will abandon the whole project, for we cannot succeed if the King himself is against us. R. would probably also have to give up his allowance, and we to manage as best we could.

*Wednesday, March 27* R. awakes early; he is thinking of giving everything up, making a contract with Schott, assigning the *Nibelungen* to them for a lot of money, and traveling with me to Italy. "This proud Bayreuth edifice was based on my personal independence, and this root is defective." We intend to await the outcome of the two letters to Munich and Bayreuth! — With all this he is expected to compose! Yet he showed me a theme which he had worked out in his notebook early this morning. Naturally enough our conversations keep coming back to this latest trial. — The only musician in Dresden to volunteer for the performances in Bayreuth is the cellist Grützmacher, and there is also a cellist from Italy—while we ourselves are wondering whether we shall now remain in Germany! — Letter from M. Meysenbug. More Menzel in the evening.

*Thursday, March 28* R. calls to me that he is thinking of requesting an audience with Bismarck after the concert in Vienna. Strassburg? Only a few days ago he had been voicing his sorrow over Bismarck's lack of interest, and I had resolved to write to Lothar Bucher. — Toward noon arrival of Professor Nietzsche, who brings Lulu 100 francs in coins from her father. He saw a lot of Hans in Basel and found him contented and in good spirits. In the evening he reads us his 5th lecture. (I write to my father.)

*Friday, March 29* Good Friday; warm, soft air; 6 years ago we went on a walk to the Grütli, R. and I: "It was a solemn impression," R. says, remembering it. Lulu is unwell, I put her to bed and stay with her while R. goes out with Prof. N. Conversation in the evening. The manager of the Stuttgart theater writes nicely to R. and gives his consent for some musicians.

*Saturday, March 30* In the morning went out with Prof. Nietzsche in fine spring weather while R. worked. In the afternoon R. plays music, the scene between Waltraute and Brünnhilde. Yesterday evening we went through *Templer und Jüdin*, in order to wonder at the "drunken lack of culture"—as R. puts it—of so undeniably talented a musician. In the afternoon a great storm, and because of it read the fairy tale of the fisherman and his wife.

*Sunday, March 31* Lulu is out of bed again, and with the professor's help I hide eggs for the children. Then I go for a walk; but the foehn wind affects me very badly. In the afternoon I make music with Prof. Nietzsche. Lovely rainbow. R. brings back a friendly telegram from Feustel, announcing a letter. Richter has also written. But R. waxes very indignant about his publisher J. J. Weber, who, it seems, has the right to refuse *Der Ring des Nibelungen* for the collected writings. The terrible contract R. concluded with this publisher years ago makes him look back very ruefully on all his previous connections.

*Monday, April 1* A slight sore throat forces me to remain in bed. R. is also depressed. Prof. Nietzsche takes his leave. Yesterday we tried without success to make a table move; we had spoken about it at lunchtime. R. explains it as a matter of will power, I as fraud. — R. comes frequently to my bedside and relates, among other things, how, from his very earliest childhood, the thought of becoming great had possessed him (inspired probably by his mother's declaration that his father had wished to make something of him). He said he could remember once having written to a friend, inviting him to his home so that they might together read the exploits of the great Napoleon. When he had written *Rienzi* and *Der Fliegende Holländer* he asked himself doubtfully whether he would ever belong among the chosen few great men. This feeling had diminished with time, but he said he could imagine that in some people it persisted and induced them to try everything, even without the proper qualifications: on no account be a nobody! — Toward evening I get up, but am very weak. R. is also very run down. Herr Schäfer sends a program from Hans's concert in Munich with a vignette, a goddess of victory pointing to the building.

*Tuesday, April 2* My father's name day. I get up again, only to hear sad things about the children: Lulu has taken to lying again; this pains me so deeply that I feel quite numbed. R. works. At lunch he becomes heated about the Renaissance, which he maintains had an enormously damaging effect on German development; this period had understood and respected antiquity just as little as it did Christianity, and men of tremendous genius had worked in the service of a power which corrupted everything. As always, the naïve Germans had let themselves be so awed by foreign culture that their own aesthetic sense had been almost ruined. But strangely enough, though everything had been directed toward destroying the German identity, they had not succeeded entirely. — First thunderstorm; spring is here; but R. is very run down and none of the children really well. He writes to the Stuttgart theater manager. In the evening we read the 9th Epistle of Plato and joke about the analogy of Plato's relationship to Dionysius and Richard's to the King of Bavaria. He is also still occupied with Menzel; he says one can feel a real disgust with religion when one thinks of all the mischief it has caused.

*Wednesday, April 3* Everyone indisposed, the children hoarse and stuffed up; the climate here does not suit R., and then his thoughts—always "disgust, sorrow, worry, and with it the fear of not keeping up with my work." — I write to Riga regarding *Die Bärenfamilie*. — Italy, perhaps one day our place of refuge, but very alien to R. And we can also expect nothing in the future, since the next German Emperor, egged on by his mother and his wife, is proving unfriendly, though he was once enraptured by R.'s art! It is all melancholy! We hear from Munich that *Rheingold* and *Walküre* are being performed there as a matter of course. Also, the children are unwell: bringing them up causes me worry and sorrow; I pray that I may discover the right way here. In the evening confided my worries to R. (In the Italian *Rivista* the first public mention of Prof. Nietzsche's book.)

*Thursday, April 4* More annoyance! J. J. Weber writes, claiming to have the right to issue new editions of *Der Ring des Nibelungen*—again a duel of constant annoyance! — Rich. just goes on with his work but he cannot achieve much in this evil atmosphere. At lunch he says: "I have cut several things, for example, '*Glücklich in Leid und Lust*,' etc. I shall retain it in the reading text, but what is this maxim doing in the drama? One knows it anyway, having just gone through it all. It would seem almost childish if she were yet again to turn to the people to proclaim her wisdom." — After lunch to town with R.; we separate at the post office, R. sends Richter a telegram, I go to see Countess Bassenheim, who shows me in the *N.A.Z.* an appeal by the students in behalf of Bayreuth, which is very fine. — No letter from Bayreuth,

I am also apprehensive because no announcement of the 9th Symphony has yet been made by the management committee—it looks as if we are surrounded only by treachery. — Children's coughs; Fidi is in bed; his friendly ways are very touching.

*Friday, April 5* I dream of a great ovation for R. in Berlin. R. is fairly well, but his work gives him no pleasure. "And how could it?" he says. "I always have three things in front of my eyes: the King, who is only waiting for the works to be finished in order to desecrate them; Schott, who is demanding the copyright, in order to sell them to the theaters; Weber, who wants to publish the texts as he pleases; so I would rather destroy it all." When I beg him again to write to Bismarck, he is not averse to the idea, thinks of breaking off his work entirely. We go out together; in the post office we find very splendid letters from Herr Feustel and the mayor, which R. immediately sends to Councilor D. They say that in the Bayreuth newspapers not a word has been said about our house, which so bothered the King! The old story. —

In the evening we read some of Somadeva's fairy tales. Talked again a lot about the visual arts. — A panegyric of Frau Wille's novel by Herr Lübke in the *A.A.Z.* displeases us greatly; a feature of the book which we had suspected—namely, that she did not dare admit the deep influence exerted on her by *Tannhäuser*, but ascribed it to some ancient church music—becomes a certainty in our minds, and it angers R. extremely. "Nothing Frau Wesendonck does surprises me," he says. "She is weak in the head and has never known what things are all about; but from Frau Wille this is treachery, a cowardly and infuriating act of treachery designed to disarm the critics."

*Saturday, April 6* Letters from Dr. Kafka and from Hans Richter; R. is tired, he says he has taken too much on himself, and what he is experiencing is too upsetting. He works all the same. — I go to town, there meet R., who looks very run down. In the evening read more fairy tales; the laughing fish gives us much delight, also the cursing bear. — When we recently spoke of the Joly people, R. said they were both cantankerous fellows who affected a love of quietness and modesty because they hated great things.

*Sunday, April 7* Feustel sends 900 certificates of patronage for signature; R. had already signed 200 in Bayreuth. Reinhart Schäfer also announces 4 certificates in Munich. Clemens sends me the poem for R.'s birthday. R. writes Feustel a letter which both moves and perturbs me, so truthful is it with regard to our position and the King. The children write letters; I to my mother. Family lunch without Fidi, because he sleeps through it. R. has done a little work. Spring day, a short while in the garden. In the evening talked about Italian melody and music. "The Italians knew what it was all about, only they were too poor in invention and technique. But one can also discern the spirit of their painting in their music." He comes back to the impression [Wilhelmine] Schröder-Devrient made on him—"I owe many of my life's impressions solely to her." —

*Monday, April 8*   Letter from Feustel: Neumann has done no work on the plans all winter, so must be dismissed. R. sends a telegram to Brandt, the machinist, who is also keeping silent; R. thinks he has been lured away by Munich, a view confirmed by a telegram from his son: "Father away from home." Spring weather: "Now just one more shower," R. says, "and everything will open up like umbrellas." — Letter from Councilor D., saying "everything will remain as it was before"—the only pity being that we no longer want that! R. is very melancholy at the thought of his abandoned house. I do some shopping in town. (Letters to K. v. Gersdorff and to Clemens.) In the evening read the Indian fairy tales.

*Tuesday, April 9*   R. gets up in good spirits in spite of all and everything; he comes down early and has completed the pencil sketch of the third act! Yesterday he improvised on it for the children, and they danced furiously to it! —
Letter from Stern, the music director, giving the names of the people who will come to Bayreuth from Berlin to sing in the chorus; people of all (railroad) classes! It makes R. laugh a lot. — Councilor D. also writes, he is annoyed that R. made such a fuss about the matter! — At lunch we come to the legend of Count von Gleichen, and R. says, "It goes against our modern feelings, and yet for me it has always contained the true German quality of compassion." When I tell R. that I can fully understand the wife's behavior, he says, "That's why we are one heart and one soul—because you always share my feelings." — To town in the afternoon—R. does not like my buying things in the shops here. In the evening read Indian fairy tales, the lovely story of the Brahman who burned his poem page by page after reading it to the animals.

*Wednesday, April 10*   Loldi's birthday; present giving, Fidi in a bad mood, because no chocolate! R. has written out the last page of the sketches for Loldchen. At lunch yesterday he told me that he would send a little gift every year to the Protestant church here, because our wedding ceremony had been the most beneficent thing in his whole life, the one real favor from the outside world. — But his mood today is sad, the thought of where and how to settle down. He prepares for his performance of the 9th Symphony. Telegram from the agents: Brussels has been saved, and *Der Fliegende Holländer* has brought in 50 francs. In the evening R. in a very curious mood concerning his position. Fine letter from Dr. Rohde, pouring out his whole heart in a glorification of R. In the evening read the fairy tales.

*Thursday, April 11* [*In the margin:* "R. cried out loudly in the night; he had dreamed that my father was trying to kill him with an instrument of torture, and I withdrew with cold eyes to the adjoining room, having been instructed by my father to guard the door!"] Our morning conversation leads us to the myths of Nature; the interpretation of Elpenor as a premature spring held back. R. says, "That is what gives Homer's poetry its stamp of eternity—that every episode has a mythical quality; it is not, as in Ariosto, for instance, an arbitrarily invented adventure." — R. is annoyed at the bad penmanship of people today, who write just for themselves and never for others—"and then they talk about education." Of himself he says, "The only solution, when one has to write unpleasant letters, is to write them very slowly and beautifully, so that the technical aspect of the matter absorbs one and helps one over the content." — The loveliest of days; in the morning R. signs 311 certificates of patronage, helped by Lulu. After lunch, coffee in the garden, then went out with R. He is delighted with his Schiller and Lessing, which he has had newly bound; what made him choose mauve and green for Schiller was a childhood memory of a performance of *Die Braut von Messina,* in which Don Manuel—played by [Wilhelmine] Schröder-Devrient's handsome husband—appeared in mauve velvet and green silk, so that these colors have become in his mind the symbol for Schiller, for gentle manhood. All his impressions of Schiller have been boyhood impressions. — I take a bath; Fidi comes to say good night and is frightened; R., to whom I tell this, says that when as a child he saw the sky reflected in a bowl of water he was both horrified and fascinated, for him it was like an earthquake, a fluctuation of all known laws, he did not know where he was. — Conversed in the evening; the performance of my father's *Festklänge* and the friendly review of it in the newspaper makes us wonder how it has come about that hostility toward my father has ceased. R. thinks such things disappear with time, I believe it is because my father no longer stands in anybody's way, he no longer plays the piano, conducts, or has any interest in any position, etc. (Letters from Marie Schl.) [*Between this page and the next a piece of paper containing some dried flowers and the inscription:* "Last violets from Tribschen."]

*Friday, April 12* Letter from Feustel; Herr Neumann quite impossible; all else not exactly heartening. — A Wagner Society is being set up in Darmstadt. R. prepares for his performance of the 9th. In our personal affairs we declare an armistice. R. reflects with sorrow that he—though he has a family—has no home; will his old longing never be satisfied? — Letter from the agents, who are achieving much. Walk with R., most gorgeous weather. In the evening the fairy tales.

*Saturday, April 13* R. says to me in the morning that everything is so muddled in the world. The good, the bad, the noble, the contemptible, all this stands outside time and space; if one were to think of all these various things as chains laid side by side, then everything would be in order, but the muddling influence of time makes it all seem as crazy as a set of building blocks which a child has thrown into confusion. The chain is eternal, its various links, thrown into confusion, give one the eternity all at once. R. writes letters to all quarters concerning the performance. In the afternoon he comes to the dancing lesson and takes the little ones to the confectioner's.

*Sunday, April 14* R. still busy with the performance; I send a telegram to Herr v. Gersdorff about the planetarium. Loveliest of days. We walk in the afternoon to the friendly farmer's nearby; R. talks about music, *Der Freischütz* and then the *Pastoral.* "There you see the true German," says R. "What do the French express with their Arcadian rustics? What mawkish stuff! Beethoven writes a *Pastoral* and in it shows us the whole of Nature." In the evening read Menzel's book, which interests R. very much. (Letter from Claire—Mama is ill again.)

*Monday, April 15* R. tells me his dream: he went out in curious finery with a wig on his head and a doctor's gown; behind him some acquaintances were walking, rather like the Heims, and they said he was an eccentric, he always dressed like that; he turned around and cried out, "No, I want to marry my wife, and in Berlin this is expected of me." — In the afternoon the painter Zelger, who buys our superfluous frames from us. R. proposes remaining here throughout the summer and completing *Götterdämmerung.* We go for a walk into town in the beautiful weather; but on the way home we meet Countess B., and R. is vexed because I leave his arm and walk beside her; he says he does not belong to this world and does not wish to sacrifice his peace to it.

*Tuesday, April 16* A telegram came yesterday from Marie Schl., the Berliners are giving a concert for Bayreuth and wish, to R.'s annoyance, to include the "Magic Fire Music" and "Siegmund's Love Song." Letter from the landlord of the Fantaisie, R. cannot easily get out of his commitment there, and since the climate here does not agree with him and he is also required in Bayreuth for a conference, he decides that we shall spend the summer at the Fantaisie. Feelings of melancholy. Letter from Herr Feustel: the Bavarian Ministry of the Interior has forbidden the governmental architect to concern himself with the erection of our theater! Herr Neumann impossible, because of his unreliability and negligence. To town with R. — Grane a bad horse, he has kicked Joseph; the head equerry knew what he was doing when he sent the horse to us! — In the evening read Menzel. R. not well, the only thing that cheers him up is the dream he had last night, from which he was awakened by a cheer; from the bottom of his lungs he had called for three cheers for "the brother of the King, our future Emperor," since he felt not enough enthusiasm was being shown. — The separation from him weighs like a ton on my heart; he is going on Saturday and I follow with the children on May 1.

*Wednesday, April 17*   Mood of sadness in dull weather; R. prepares for his departure, I help where I can. We feel depressed—where are we going, what is in store for us, where our home? R. says, "Since I have you, the worst can no longer affect me, we are no longer separating, we are just preparing for our reunion." In the afternoon we take a short walk, all the trees are in bloom or soon will be: "Nature has been scattering face powder, green and white." R. hears the cuckoo. — Concern about Lulu, who, we believe, has again been untruthful. Fairy tales in the evening. We were much amused by Fidi with two sticks, carefully preparing revenge against Bernhard.

*Thursday, April 18*   R. is not well. He looks through his pencil sketches, those splendid things! When will he find peace to complete the work? . . . In the afternoon he goes to see Herr Am Rhyn and is glad to find him in a gentlemanly mood, so that our departure will take place without unpleasant disputes. Conversed in the evening, matters melancholy, pleasant, and sweet. (Family lunch without Fidi, who sleeps too much.) R. sang Elsa's beginning to the duet in the 3rd act of *Lohengrin.* "That is German," he says, "without passion, but deeply felt and warm—he has come from where she longs to go, but in the encounter their hearts must break."

*Friday, April 19*   Letter from the conductor Seifriz in Stuttgart. "He complains like a Hamlet of lack of progress," R. says, and this joke causes us to take up Shakespeare's play again; the impression and enjoyment we get is as if we had never even known it before. "Whatever else, no history," R. exclaims, "just communion with the few great spirits and the few great men in history who have forced it onto a different path through their personality, like Frederick the Great, the great German emperors, Luther." I remark that it is only German history which has produced such characters (apart from *Cromwell* in England). — When yesterday R. went into his workroom to fetch a book and light a fire, he spoke about this great discovery, which at once places human beings on the level of the gods, which banishes the night; and how rightly and beautifully the Greeks had distilled it all in the legend of Prometheus—the bringing of fire. — He goes into town. Telegram from the mayor of Bayreuth that the conference with Brandt has taken place and has led to substantial economies.

R. fixes his departure for next Monday. — In the evening read *Hamlet*. — From his room R. calls to me, "You are the only person who is close to me, the only one with whom I can be completely truthful."

*Saturday, April 20* The violinist Singer agrees to play in Bayreuth. At breakfast R. says he is sorry that Goethe or Schiller did not write a play about Frederick the Great, beginning with the execution of Katte and dealing with life at Rheinsberg up to the death of his father and the last, great conversation between them. "It could have become a companion piece to *Hamlet*, and it would have been interesting to see whether a period so close to us could be depicted in a work of art. Heinrich Kleist would have had the necessary skill." — R. is satisfied with his pencil sketches, only, he says, he needs much peace and time—at least two months—to complete them in ink. *Hamlet* in the evening. "My noble wife," R. called me today. Oh, how can I become worthy of this name, how can I serve him, show him how much I love him? Telegram from Herr Feustel, asking R. to go to Darmstadt, to Herr Brandt! —

*Sunday, April 21* Wrote several letters, R. sketches out his speech for the foundation ceremony, which moves me to tears; arrival of a very fine manifesto from the Academic Society. Family lunch. We are expecting Professor Nietzsche, but he does not come. Herr Am Rhyn comes to say goodbye and is visibly moved. In Fritzsch's paper there is a quotation from the Catholic *Volksbote* in which mud is flung at Hans's concert for the Wagner Society and at the whole enterprise. One sees from which direction the wind is blowing! Nice letter from El. Kr[ockow] and Fr. Lenbach. — R. is greatly vexed because the royalties from Berlin do not come—a deliberate act of malice on the part of Herr von Hülsen, who is now particularly annoyed, because the Emperor has allowed the Wagner Society the use of the opera house in Berlin. — In the evening Herr Josef Rubinstein suddenly arrives from Kharkov—a curious spectacle and experience; with him a Dr. Cohen, his companion, who, concealed in the boathouse without the young man's knowledge, wants to tell us that he needs to be treated with great consideration! — R. is infinitely kind to the young man and advises him to take things easy, offers him access to Bayreuth.

*Monday, April 22* Last morning together in Tribschen; melancholy activity! — The mail brings the letter from Berlin, and R. has to laugh, since this quarter has brought in so much (1,000 thalers); the performances must always have been full to bursting. Departure! R. left at one o'clock. I had a nervous night. God help poor us! Returned home with Vreneli, had a heartfelt conversation with her; then busied myself with the papers, sorted them, R.'s letters to Minna!! — In the evening a telegram from Basel, R. walking around there for 9 hours. (Prof. N. writes today from Geneva.)

*Tuesday, April 23* Wrote to R. and cabled Niemann's consent to sing in the 9th Symphony, just received. During the day sorted papers, in the evening telegram from Darmstadt. Wrote again to R., since Stuttgart manager has promised orchestral players.

*Wednesday, April 24* Still sorting papers, from morning to evening. In the evening telegram from R. in Bayreuth, he has arrived safely! Letters from Standhartners, Levi (who reports the downfall of the director Kaiser and hence participation of Karlsruhe orchestra in the performance). I report it all to R. —splendid sunset, alpenglow, trees in blossom, the cuckoo calls, the cowbells tinkle, a blackbird calls, melancholy farewell! Glorious moonlight across the water, shining stillness all around me—how different things will be now!

*Thursday, April 25* Up early, continued sorting; Countess B. comes to say goodbye. Toward 6 o'clock sudden arrival of Prof. Nietzsche from Montreux. — Finished with all the papers today; very melancholy summary of life. — R. cables from Bayreuth; affairs in good shape, but he is tired.

*Friday, April 26* No telegram today! — Walked to town, last boat ride. In the afternoon to Fontaine de Soif, packing in between. In the evening some music, Prof. N. plays for me.

*Saturday, April 27* Nice telegram from R., then letter, he is content with everything. — Purchases. Walk to Winkel. Prof. Nietzsche gone. Great weariness!

*Sunday, April 28* (These are the first words written at the Fantaisie.) — Telegram from R., he is worried that I have not yet signaled our departure; so I resolve to set off tomorrow. Much work in consequence, and letters besides. Said goodbye to Countess Bassenheim. Then went to see Vreneli's baby at the farm; last journey home by boat. Idyllic impression. In the evening prolonged ramble through the whole of Tribschen, full of gratitude to the gods for granting me such happiness here; it was always lovely, even the difficult times.

*Monday, April 29* Packed, cabled R., said goodbye to Vreneli, who is very grieved, telegram from R., departure at 1:20; my five children with Anna, Käthchen with baby, Jakob with Rus. First stop in Zurich; concern for Lulu, who has a cough. Terrible storm, crossing in the night steamer, Loldi fell into a puddle, darkness, endless hand luggage, streaming rain, customs examination, at last boarded the train at Lindau, said goodbye to Jakob, I to look after Rus, all goes well as far as Augsburg, then the luggage car is too full, the dog car impossible, so take him in the compartment with us, astonishment when I lead him out and give him a drink. At long, long last arrival in Bayreuth on *Tuesday the 30th* at 4:30, the children lively, Rus well, and R.

to greet us! In the evening went immediately for a walk around the Fantaisie, splendid park, even more remote from the world than Tribschen. R. happy that we are here, calls me his vital force. Conversed with R. until 10 o'clock, then to bed.

*Wednesday, May 1* R. unfortunately did not sleep well; Rus barked loudly. But he gets up early in order to show the children the splendid park immediately; peacocks fill the air with their wild call, which we so love; R. says, "I always feel as if I were hearing Sanskrit words." A turkey, "almost certainly the prototype of the sailing ship," gives us great delight, swans, guinea fowls, etc. The day before R. paid his visit to the Duke of Württemberg, whom he found very kind and gracious. We have complete freedom here. R. then holds a conference with the new architect of the theater, Brückwald (? He built the theater in Leipzig); our Herr Neumann had got a carpenter to draw up the plan of the theater! Brandt is beside himself with relief at not having to have anything more to do with that man! Lunch at 1 o'clock with the children. A telegram from Pusinelli in Dresden, they are giving a concert there with various pieces R. composed in Dresden. — In contrast, horrible behavior from J. J. Weber, who writes that he has pulled the chestnuts out of the fire for R.! R. says what he really meant to say is that he had gone through bad times with him, and has made a slip of the pen; but he will not permit Fritzsch to print *Der Ring des Nibelungen*. R. intends now to get rid of him on good terms or bad, and in that the agents Voltz and Batz must help him; they are conducting themselves splendidly—from Leipzig, for instance, they got 1,500 thalers; R. hopes to win a fortune through the new copyright law. Feustel (incomparable) writes from Munich that six musicians will come from there. Düffl. seems to be ashamed of himself. Fine weather; a magic dream world here, as in Tribschen! — In the afternoon, visit from a consistorial councilor, Kraussold, a onetime member of the Burschenschaft; a resilient, friendly man. Walk to the Schweizerei; meeting with an 82-year-old patron (v. Braun); splendid weather, very nice atmosphere. At home a letter from Councilor D.—they seem to want everything to be resolved in a friendly spirit. In the evening punch. R. is contented and happy, the children blissful! Piano has arrived.

*Thursday, May 2* R. had a good night and is in cheerful spirits; morning walk in the splendid park. Wrote some letters. Family lunch. Then with the children to Bayreuth, visit to Frau Feustel and Frau Muncker, inspection of our site, then of the house we are to rent. At the post office a letter from Berlin has arrived, also received a letter from Vreneli. Went into the opera house, splendid impression, the proscenium taken out by R., the building revealed in all its original glory; very moved by the knowledge that all these preparations and provisions are being made for the sake of Beethoven's splendid work— its creator could certainly never have dreamed of it! — R. told me that on my arrival the melody from the first movement had come into his mind and he had said to himself, "You have never done anything like that." He reminds me that, when we visited the opera house last year, I had said to him: "Impossible for the *Nibelungen*, but how fine for concerts!" — "You see, I do everything you say," he adds! — Home around 7 o'clock; there had been music at the Fantaisie; they had played the *Tannhäuser* March, and since she much regretted not having heard it, Lusch went down with our permission and asked for it again; they played it, but unfortunately like a march of "hollow priests," as R. puts it. We go out on the balcony with Fidi, and R. remembers having seen Weber in the same way with his child; Fidi very impressed and handsome (but he has a swelling on his head from falling off the sofa). Conversation with R. in the evening. The patrons have not yet all been identified; very bad behavior from Baron Loën, who does not reply—spite or negligence?? . . . My father? . . . R. says the Wesendoncks are also not to be found on any list, and he remarks, "It is really humiliating when one assumes that people will behave well and are on one's side, and then suddenly receives proof of the contrary." (Blots by Lulu.) [*This refers to ink blots over the whole page.*]

*Friday, May 3*   Business letters; R. still working on his orchestra, he needs second oboists. I write letters, we talked a lot about the 9th Symphony, which is so awkward in many technical details, yet throughout so intoxicating in the power of its thought. "It is the true 'tragelaph,'" R. says, laughing. He feels it would be very much to the advantage of the work if much of it were to be reorchestrated. "In regard to form Mozart seems a true Alexandrian master compared with Beethoven." Also talked a lot about Strassburg University; I tell him how disgracefully the German professors, who had screamed loudest about the Alsatian problem, had used their appointments there for purposes of blackmail. "The German spirit, where has it gone? We are a pitiful nation, our culture utterly undermined." — Walk after lunch; to Eckersdorf via the Salamander valley; very delightful scenery. Pleasant evening on the balcony; the children all day long in the park.

*Saturday, May 4*   R. did not have a good night, the weather is changing. Letter from Herr *Wilhelmj*, the violinist, announcing his arrival on the 9th. — We read details of the terrible conditions in Naples, Vesuvius in violent eruption. R. is vexed by the latest explanation of earthquakes as internal collapses caused by the erosion of underground springs—this seems to him much too gentle. — Then he speaks of the Jesuits and how everything always turns out to their advantage; their banishment of the Protestants from Bohemia produced a hatred of the Germans, which was of use to them—a terrible irony! — Roman, Latin culture, sentimentality, glossing over of brutality and inartistic Nature, subtlety, all play their part in it, feelings, but no feeling. — When we expressed our pleasure in the lovely park and the air here, R. said: "Yes, this is German. I believe going to live in Italy would have meant my early death; perhaps I should have stayed alive, but become childish." — This morning R. woke me with a passage from the *Idyll*. Eternal times now past! We drive into town, R. holds his conference, and I make purchases, my first in Bayreuth! The agents Voltz and Batz send 535 florins. The first beginnings. Home rather late and then to bed.

*Sunday, May 5* Packed; Käthchen is coming with us; the children's goodbyes are cool, which worries R., though I had indeed forbidden them to cry too much. Left at five o'clock; the mayor with his wife at the station; good journey as far as Schwandorf, but there a wait of 1½ hours. The unpleasant, silent gaping of the people. R. does not sleep, drafts his plans for the ceremony on the 22nd. Berlioz melodies; the difference between B. and Schumann, the latter getting impressions only from works, none at all from life, Berlioz very strong impressions from the world, if no very heartfelt or deep ones; he is a mirror—if only a small and broken one.

*Monday, May 6* In Linz R. is given good coffee; the country around Vienna pleases him, he can imagine Beethoven in it and recognize the atmosphere of many of the sonatas, Penzing! "All the past before our coming together was folly!" — Arrival at 10 o'clock, many Wagner Society-ites, reassurance concerning Kafka, nice accommodation with the Standhartners. Unfortunately, after lunch Herbeck expecting us to attend a performance of one of the Wagner works. *Rienzi* is finally approved, since so unfamiliar to R. In the evening, walk in the Volksgarten. Early to bed.

*Tuesday, May 7* R. slept well; went shopping with him, we are glad to be in Vienna *together*—which of us would ever have dreamed it? After lunch, visit from Countess Dönhoff, pretty and charming, a unique personality among the best Wagnerians. In the evening wandered again through the city with R. (at midday Saint Stephen's made R. angry, workers hammering in the cathedral while Mass was in progress). In the evening the excellent Dr. Kafka, also an enthusiast of a peerless kind. But when he spoke of the lack of influence of the press, R. felt impelled to ask whether the complete absence of indignation in face of malice was not ascribable to its activities! They cannot prevent people's going to the concert or the works' being played, but they can drag all the seriousness of the occasion through the mud, etc. —

*Wednesday, May 8*   First letter from the children, they are well. Drove to the rehearsal; nice reception, the players glowing with pleasure at playing under R. (music from *Tannhäuser* and *Tristan*). R. allows the students from the Conservatoire in, much cheering. After the rehearsal he lies down and I return Countess D.'s visit; heard nice things about Hans, am told he speaks of me with respect, says how happy he is that his children have the best of mothers, while he is the worst of fathers. — Then the Countess talks of Rubinstein, who left Vienna in a fury over its Wagnerianism. His wife had also flown into a rage over Wagner's music and had walked out of the performance of *Die Msinger*. — And finally of the aristocracy, which is completely passive toward Bayreuth. — In the afternoon Herbeck brings a heap of papers to justify himself in the *Meistersinger* affair; I prefer not to look at them, telling him that among friends no papers are necessary. — At 7 o'clock *Rienzi*, execrably played to a brilliant audience.

*Thursday, May 9*   To the photographer's, he had begged hard; then R. and I with Countess Dönhoff to Makart; saw the large picture of Caterina Cornaro; great talent, but again everything influenced by pictures, no living impressions! But an outstanding talent. — Countess D. says there is much in the newspaper about me and my life with R.—and also asserting that she had paraded with R. in the foyer— this miserable press! Thank God that it will stay away from Bayreuth— the *Nationalzeitung* has already written to R. offering to send Herr Gumprecht, but he is being firmly repulsed. — Birthday lunch, then drove out to Dornbach. In the evening a party at Dr. Nettke's; patrons, members of the Wagner Society, Lenbach, and Makart. Herbeck proposes a toast to Bayreuth, R. replies that he puts his trust in the German spirit. Unfortunately too much to eat and drink.

*Friday, May 10*   Headache. Letter from the children. In the Belvedere with Lenbach; splendid Titians. At 9 o'clock rehearsal, R. dissatisfied, the orchestra has got 10 percent worse in 10 years. — Letter from A. Frommann. — R. says the orchestral players clapped too much, out of idleness, to produce an easy-going atmosphere. R. is also indignant over the absurd situation in which ovations put him. A very curious thing: Frl. Gallmeyer, the soubrette, was at the rehearsal, in a corner, with tears in her eyes. Princess Liechtenstein, Countess Rossi (daughter of Henriette Sontag), Count and Countess D. at the rehearsal. — The trombones produce no tone, for there are no natural trumpets left in the orchestra. Dr. Standhartner reports that people wish to form a Wagner Society in Prague and are inquiring through a member whether

Wagner would agree to Czechs and Bohemians being represented in it in equal numbers. Wagnerian art is the only kind which unites hostile elements. — In the evening Dr. Kafka and some friends.

*Saturday, May 11* Final rehearsal; much time spent on the *Eroica*; R. has forbidden ovations, peace and quiet. Arrival of Count and Countess Krockow. R. not dissatisfied. Intimate lunch at home. R. talks of our relationship, tells how it all came about, what we went through, calls me his royal wife—great emotion. — Went for a drive; first to Count Lanckoronski's to see a splendid Rembrandt; then to the Prater. Lovely evening sunshine. In the evening Count Dönhoff with his charming wife, Lenbach, and some Wagnerians. Also Countess Rossi. —

*Sunday, May 12* Deputations from the Academic Choral Society and the Conservatoire, with laurel wreaths and silver plate. Nice speeches and fine replies by R., who says he is relying on youth. Drove to the concert at 12. I, in the director's box, can follow every movement of R.'s face. Fine, packed hall, an indescribable reception, mounds of laurel leaves; at the conclusion, since the calls do not cease, R. speaks a few words. During the "Magic Fire Music" a thunderstorm broke, which added a lot more still to the effect; R. said that the Greeks regarded this as a good sign and he would do the same, and he expressed his hope of receiving true sympathy and support in Vienna for his German venture. — (With Gluck's Overture dropped, the program is: *Eroica*, music from *Tannhäuser*, *Tristan und Isolde* Prelude, "Magic Fire Music.") R. says this is the last concert he will conduct, presenting fragments from his works is particularly repulsive to him. But he would always be glad to conduct a Beethoven symphony. — At lunch arrival of Richter, just as usual, splendid and excellent, he makes his singers pay fines when they alter something in the operas! — In the evening to Countess Dönhoff's; but R. is tired and we soon go home. (Prints of the photographs not bad.)

*Monday, May 13* Packing; R. busy with the musicians; I to the Albertina with Elisabeth Kr.; splendid things; Raphael drawings sent to Dürer. — Farewell from Countess D.; she talks about Rubinstein's rage over Wagner: "Gounod has more talent; he (Rubinstein) must leave, there is no place for him in Vienna, where he is respected only as a pianist; W. has turned all heads, particularly those of the beautiful women." — Affectionate parting from our excellent hosts and friends; at 5 o'clock departure with Richter. Sleepless night.

*Tuesday, May 14* Arrival at 8 o'clock; nice reception by the mayor, who arranges everything quietly and prudently. Busy in Bayreuth until nearly eleven o'clock; then on to the Fantaisie. Loldi sees us first; great joy at reunion, Fidi very moved; distribution of presents, for Fidi his first knee breeches. Arrival of a portion of our things; unpacking, great weariness. R. pleased with the children and the quietness here. Peacock calls greet us; fine weather; the people in Bayreuth say R. has brought it with him.

*Wednesday, May 15* R. had a good night. Letter from my father. The cellist Grützmacher, who had volunteered his services, withdraws without giving reasons—obviously suspended by Hiller and Co.; with the oboists things are also not looking good. Much trouble in getting things arranged; little help, since everyone so far away. But constant delight in the beauty of the surroundings. R. thinks with emotion of the many joys which still lie ahead as the children grow up, even when they marry and have children in their turn and euthanasia comes, a gentle fading out. "That could turn one into a downright optimist!" My father's letter conventional, like ours. He is attending the music festival in Kassel! R. goes into town with R[ichter?]; unpleasant muddles, the self-importance of Herr Riedel, who asks whether *"Ehrt eure deutschen Meister"* should not also be sung at the stone-laying ceremony, after the *"Wach' auf"* chorus. Frau Jachmann inquires about her trunks (!), etc. R. very vexed with all the drawbacks of existence. Richter is delegated to receive everyone.

*Thursday, May 16* Paper hangers at 5 in the morning, much work; our landlords muddled and unmethodical. But the children always lively and enjoying themselves. Family lunch, then with them to the Schweizerei. The location here pleases us more and more, the close proximity is worth so much to R., that and the cultural atmosphere. Our rooms have now been furnished, pictures hung, etc., and R. is content. It is almost quieter and more peaceful than Tribschen! — Fidi overexcited in the evening, sings in bed until late. — The violinist Herr de Ahna has withdrawn, allegedly because of jury duty, but I suspect pressure from Joachim. What else lies in store for us? It is unthinkable that these gentlemen should not try everything in order to thwart our efforts. When will R. at last be left in peace to get on with his work?

*Friday, May 17* R. again had a wretched night! He is trying to concentrate on his speeches, "to memorize them like Beckmesser!" — But then he decides to write the speech down and read it, since he does not wish to prepare himself like an actor, but is also unwilling to improvise, since the speech is to be preserved as a document. I call on Frau von Lerchenfeld; the district president himself is out of town during these days! Purchases for the birthday. Feustel still magnificent, the mayor as well. In the afternoon visited the festival site with R. and the children, fine impression; our home here!

*Saturday, May 18* No real recollection of the morning, in the afternoon arrival of Prof. Nietzsche, Herr v. Gersdorff, and the Ritters. Herr Heckel of Mannheim is also here, is spending the night at the Fantaisie with Richter. Cheerful, companionable atmosphere, we all belong together. Many of the musicians already here. (R. writes to my father and in splendid words invites him here.)

*Sunday, May 19* Whitsunday and many visits; arranging the laurels just arrived from Vienna; on top of that Cornelius, Porges, Schäfer, not very pleasant, later Ritter, Nietzsche, Gersdorff, then Countess Krockow; finally, and most charming, Frau v. Schleinitz and Countess Dönhoff. R. in town greeting the singers, much coming and going, but gay spirits. Rain, shortage of carriages.

*Monday, May 20* First rehearsal, fine and touching welcome to the musicians from R., all in solemn mood, the only ones out of place the critics Gumprecht and Engel, who, in spite of R.'s veto, have taken up certificates of patronage in order to be here. Much to be learned; the musicians as yet have no idea of the interpretation. Another rehearsal in the afternoon, this time with the singers. Frl. Lehmann very good. — Malwida Meysenbug also here, to our great delight. Several from Florence. In the evening I with Marie Schleinitz, Baron Loën from Weimar, Ernst Dohm, Prof. Rohde, Nietzsche, Gersdorff, etc. R. to bed immediately after the rehearsal; tired, but very exhilarated by his success. All the tribes of Germany are represented, and none has any other interest beyond his pleasure in art.

*Tuesday, May 21* Morning rehearsal, many Bayreuth people in my box, but friends, too, among them Dr. Standhartner, who has come all the way from Vienna. Johanna Jachmann gives no pleasure and does the occasion no honor, since she does not even know her part. Lusch and Boni at the rehearsal. It goes well, indeed splendidly, R. very affected, but the musicians and all of us even more so, greatest triumph of genius! — At a moment of foreboding Schiller wrote his words to joy, which nobody perhaps understood until Beethoven came along and understood them and made us in moments of foreboding understand them, too, but ununderstood they remained until, in a sublime and foreboding moment, Richard made them resound in words and music. — All of us, so various in ourselves, were assembled here in a single faith and hope! Niemann kisses R.'s hand; Betz has not yet quite achieved the accents R. wants for *"Freunde, nicht diese Töne"* (trembling indignation)—but he is trying. In the evening, driving home, we see columns of people making a pilgrimage to the Fantaisie; singers of both sexes in open farm wagons, since there is nothing else to be had. The choral society sings a serenade to R. We go down to join the people, which pleases them greatly, and, although he is hoarse, R. speaks a few words to them in his uniquely affecting way. In our apartments upstairs many friends, and we part in a general mood of joyous uplift.

*Wednesday, May 22* Birthday! I wish R. many happy returns very simply this time, for he is preparing the great treat himself. Daniella recites to him a little poem written by *Clemens*, the children present him with a Bible; Fidi very pretty in the blouse embroidered by Countess Bassenheim. Everything in good order, but rain and rain, not a single ray of sunshine in the offing! — R. relates that in a dream he saw Fidi with his face full of wounds. What can this mean? — We drive to the meeting place, Feustel's house, rain, rain, but despite it all in good spirits. Arrival of the King's telegram, which is to be enclosed in the capsule with other things. R. then goes to the festival site, where, in spite of the rain, countless people—including women—had gathered, and lays the foundation stone. The speeches, however, are made in the opera house. In Feustel's house I give Herr Julius Lang (who in a letter from Vienna had told me that he had sent Prince Bismarck a telegram about the concert in Vienna) a piece of my mind concerning his compromising activities with regard to our affairs during the past 10 years. I did it in fear and trembling, but I did it, so as from now on to be rid of such an individual. — In the opera house R. fetches me from my box to sit with the five children on the stage beside him. Very fine impression, even the gravest among the men have tears in their eyes. Dinner at the Fantaisie with Standhartner, who, like everybody else, praised the behavior of the children, particularly of Fidi, at the ceremony. At 5 o'clock the performance, beginning with the "*Kaisermarsch*." The 9th Symphony quite magnificent, everyone feeling himself freed from the burden of mortal existence; at the conclusion sublime words from R. on what this celebration means to him! — Then to the banquet. Before the concert a Frau von Meyendorff, just arrived from Weimar, handed over a letter from my father— the letter very nice, but the woman, unfortunately, very unpleasant. Her manner is cold and disapproving. — At the banquet R. proposes the first toast to the King, then to Bayreuth; we leave at about half past nine. Niemann and Betz had left earlier out of wounded vanity. I sit with Frau von Schl. and attempt to converse with Frau von Meyendorff; because of her obstinacy the conversation takes place in French. R. enters during it and is vexed with the ugly note here introduced; an angry mood on his part, sorrow on mine. In the end he returns to the banquet, I stay behind with Marie Schl., Marie Dönhoff, and Count Hohenthal. Home at 12 o'clock. (Count Krockow gives R. a leopard which he shot in Africa.)

*Thursday, May 23* R. dreams of a room which he is obliged to enter and on which is written "*Ici on parle français*," then of Betz and

Niemann, with whom he had quarreled. Up early and into town, R. to the patrons' meeting, which decides unanimously to build the theater; I with Frl. von Schorn from Weimar and Elisabeth Krockow (beforehand tried to appease Frau Niemann). To Frl. von Sch[orn], who invites me to go to Weimar, I say that I shall do this only along with Wagner—either a complete reunion, or none at all. Breakfast with Marie Schl.; visit to the festival site, then farewell to many friends; in the evening, however, still a great many of them with us, among them the splendid Mme Lucca from Milan, of whom, R. says, Nature originally intended to make a man, until it realized that in Italy the men were not much use, and quickly corrected itself. R. very tired in the evening, but cheerful. The weather fine today; we persuade ourselves that with yesterday's wretched weather we had paid our debt to Fate and, because of that, worse things had been spared us. But the nicest thing was that this misfortune had not been able to spoil our mood. — A curious scene took place yesterday at the banquet; Herr Gumprecht and Herr Engel got into an argument with Herr Coerper from Berlin, the latter probably feeling their presence there to be unseemly; a Bavarian army captain, Herr von Baligand, intervened and said merely that the journalists should be thrown out if they behaved badly, and this was done, whereupon the entire Jewish contingent from Berlin stood up as one man to defend the gentlemen of the press, and forced Coerper to apologize. This last act, when we heard of it, made R. and me extremely indignant. The unseemliness of journalists' being present is accepted without murmur, the impropriety of one incensed person on the other hand is punished; out of fear of the press—that is the truth of the matter. Besides this, so we hear, many cases of wounded vanity, but nothing can cloud the picture we keep in our hearts. (News of Clemens's engagement.)

*Friday, May 24* Touching letter from a working man, who asks us to be godfather and godmother to his child, born on the 22nd. We consent with pleasure. — Unpleasant feelings concerning the publication of the King's telegram despite R.'s veto; R. cables to Councilor D. to point this out. The children to the Eremitage with our excellent friend Malwida. Many visitors, among them an English journalist who was very disappointed with the music festival in Düsseldorf and very delighted and impressed with ours. After him Herr v. G., the Ritters, Malwida, who stayed all evening. — In the morning a conference took place with Brandt, who is quite an outstanding person, fully aware of the difficulties involved but always ready to help with imaginative ideas. Herr Porges was also here this morning; R. had to tell him a few home truths, which affected him painfully—an unhappy character.

*Saturday, May 25* Unfortunately R. had a very bad night, he would like to be able to sing, "*Ruhe ward dem Wurm gegeben!*" — Brückwald, the architect (nothing is heard of Herr Neumann), comes in the morning, many things are discussed, I advise letting the stage tower rise boldly above the whole building as its main feature and not concealing it, but keeping the auditorium as low as possible as a sort of low entry hall to the stage. — Yesterday R. sent to the *Tageblatt* a message of thanks to Bayreuth, but it has not yet appeared. R. rests a bit, we once more discuss the Jewish question, since the Israelite participation in the Berlin Wagner Society leaves us with a very bad taste. R. says he still hopes that this whole phenomenon is a sickness which will disappear; an amalgamation is impossible, and we cannot believe that the Germans will be subjugated by the Jews, our military exploits have shown us to be too strong for that. — Telegram from Niemann, he is appeased; R. writes to Herr Nettke, who was also offended at not having been personally noticed!! Herr v. Gersdorff to lunch; he relates that one of our friends (Herr Falko), while walking in the palace gardens, heard a man (with decorations) say, "Well, if Wagner causes too much scandal here, we shall take steps." About Herr v. Lerchenfeld of the Catholic party we also hear curious things. — As we are having supper with Herr v. G., four young people who want to "register" are announced; they are four of R.'s singers who had heard that R. wanted to know the names of his people, and after an outing in the surrounding countryside of Franconian Switzerland they have now come to take their leave. Good, vigorous people, one of them from Saxony. R. is very touched by them. Then our friend Gersdorff takes his leave with tears in his eyes. And so it has all gone past like a dream—who was not there? what did not happen?—all vanished now, a lovely dream!

*Sunday, May 26* R. slept somewhat better. Telegram from Betz, he is also appeased. Visit from an American newspaper correspondent who, already very well informed, is told by R. why the participation of America and England is important to him. Malwida with us at lunch, went for a walk with her in the Salamander valley, a sense of being in the heart of Germany. In the evening read an article by Prof. Rohde on Nietzsche's book; not suitable for the general public. Frl. von M. tells us she has heard that Bismarck is very concerned for our undertaking and is following it with interest as a matter of national importance, which pleases us very much. — Letter from Vreneli, foxes are stealing the chickens at Tribschen, so quiet is it there!

*Monday, May 27* R. slept only five hours and is very run down, but he works out his plan for keeping his singers free of firm engagements; he recommends Marie Lehmann to Milan; Wilhelmj is to set up a sort of school, and R. looks forward to the activities facing him.

In the afternoon went for a walk with R., paths of great beauty. Saw the Hummelbauer, whose children sing us folk songs. Back home, a nasty letter from Hans, reproaching me for having gone on the stage with the children. Bad impression. In the evening a visit to Malwida Meysenbug.

*Tuesday, May 28* Since yesterday working again with the children; wrote to Hans, also to Fritz and L. Bucher concerning Herr Lang. Visit from *Diener*, the tenor, who has a good voice but also all the bad habits of present-day singers, who can only produce bursts, no sustained notes; R. engages him for Milan and will try to save him from the "theater lark." Talked a lot about the 9th Symphony; what gave B. the idea of setting Schiller's poem to music? R. believes that he meant from the start to write a great symphony of joy in the spirit of the Freemasons and to precede it with struggle and mourning, but I have the feeling that he wrote the more somber movements first and then, finding, as it were, no finale, resorted to words. — But a work such as this remains a mystery; R. says how remarkable in B. is the hatred of trivialities, the avoidance of dominants, for example, and the enormous artistic instinct. Isolated passages are also splendidly orchestrated, such as the opening of the Adagio. We are, however, more and more convinced that such compositions as the first movement of this symphony do not belong in front of an audience, which never achieves the concentration necessary to grasp such mysteries. — With M. Meysenbug to the Sophienberg, a pleasant countryside, everything friendly and human. In the evening R. reads *Nicht kapituliert*, to our great delight.

*Wednesday, May 29* R. still finds no rest, he is not yet sleeping well and everything tires him. Around noon the architect Wölffel, discussion about our house; walk with M. Meysenbug, but without R., who is too run down. Very fine letters from Prof. N. to R. and to me. Certainly few people have so much feeling for our sufferings and joys as he.

*Thursday, May 30* R. had a very wretched night! He writes his letter to the King, asking him for patience as a reward for his perseverance. In the afternoon we walk to the town. Passing the churchyard, R. says: "I now think happily and calmly of my death. But I always have the feeling that you will soon leave me, that you have only been lent to me and will soon go back up there to a star." We are quite tired in the evening and go to bed early.

*Friday, May 31* R. had his first good night! Great gladness on this account. Up till now his mind was always filled during the night with the 9th. I work with the children and answer letters (M. Maier, etc.). Claire Charnacé writes about my mother, whose condition is still bad. R. drives into town to deal with various things; the mayor is happy about the success of the festival and is utterly devoted to R. — I walk to the Schweizerei with the children and our friends. Returning home, I am perturbed by a notice in the *A.A.Z.* Herr Weissheimer's opera (*Theodor Körner*) has been performed, the reviewer says one can tell from the sound of it that the composer belongs to the "music of the future" and has joined the Bayreuth camp with bag and baggage— and that no doubt had opened the doors of the Munich opera house to him. Indignant over this despicable distortion of the facts, I conceal this latest piece of malice from R., for Herr W., furious with R. for not wanting to recommend his *Körner* to the King of B., severed his connections with R. in the most offensive way, and it was this breach which won him the support of Herr von Perfall; now that this attempt has come to grief, they try to extricate themselves in this way!

In the evening we read Gottfried Keller's legends; initially I find them quite pleasing, but then the manner of relating ecstatic experiences in tones of *bonhomie* becomes very repugnant to me. "Goethe told legends in a different way," says R.

*Saturday, June 1* Letter from Marie Schl., which I answer at once, she wants to try to win over Princess Margherita, who is now in Berlin, for Bayreuth. (Yesterday R. expressed his gratitude to the minister.) As bad luck would have it, R. comes upon the page of the newspaper containing the notice about Herr W[eissheimer], and is greatly incensed by this malicious fabrication. He writes first of all to Herr W., demanding a correction, then sends the *A.A.Z.* a notice for insertion. I am quite indisposed and cannot walk much. R. visits Dr. Falko, the mental specialist who is our neighbor and who has been very friendly toward us; there he has to listen to a great deal about Herr Gutzkow, once the glory of the mental hospital! In the evening R. reads our friends passages from his biography, they are very affected by it.

*Sunday, June 2* Left home at ten o'clock, christening day, first R. and myself alone, then M. Meysenbug with my three girls. I have to leave Daniella at home, because yesterday she again caused me great sorrow with her obstinate lying, with her joy in bearing tales and her roughness toward her sisters. R. is in favor of sending her to a boarding school, but I am very much against it. Many sad thoughts, and in consequence a sleepless night. — Before the christening visited Frau Kolb, Frau Landgraf (the wife of the doctor), and finally the excellent Dean Dittmar, a magnificent old gentleman who receives us with the most lively friendliness; he talks with much fire about the performance, but admits that the "*Kaisermarsch*" made more impression on him than the 9th Symphony. He talks a lot about the pleasure all the strange people had given him, he had been particularly glad to make the

specialist), the Gutzkow room again, etc.; then surprise visit from *General* Heine, the former stage decorator, a braggart not seen for 29 years; besides that a letter in the *A.A.Z.* to R. from Herr W[eissheimer], the nastiness of which completely crushes me, and finally the arrival of the so-called Hugo letter, also bristling with nastiness. — R. has to atone for having recently allowed himself to take notice of the lying report in the *A.A.Z.*; firm resolve to read no more newspapers. — (Herr J. Rubinstein announces a visit.)

*Sunday, June 9* Not a good night, in consequence of the vilenesses; I reproach myself for not having urged R. more firmly to take no notice of this rubbish; I am too easily persuaded by R., and because I want to spare him unpleasantness, I do not perhaps help him with my judgment as much as I could. He drafts a final word for the *A.A.Z.*; I do not yet know whether that is a good thing, he feels it is. — Visit from the Feustels. — We then go through *Christus* and come to the conclusion that the style has not changed in the Catholic church; as in the 18th century the castrati served both opera and church, now it is grand opera which influences the church style of my father—strict old church modes are interwoven in the works of Halévy, Meyerbeer, etc., and it is these which exercised a decisive influence on my father in his youth. — At lunch our friends and unfortunately also the "general," who makes an increasingly bad impression on us and whom Wagner calls a "blown-up, buccaneering bag of nothingness." In the afternoon R. plays and sings passages from *Götterdämmerung*, but he is melancholy because it has become so alien to him, he sees the necessity of getting down to music again. Letter from Prof. N., who sends us Herr von Wilamowitz's pamphlet attacking him. Observations arising out of this newest example of nastiness; R. sees the present state of the world as a sad one; professors educating more specialist professors, no humanistic education spreading its influence—the jurist, for example, never thinks of studying philology and philosophy, just all specialist subjects.

*Monday, June 10* Our friends leave us, to our great regret. They are to see *Tristan* in Munich. Letters from De Gubernatis in Italy: the subscription he opened has not been successful, because all the newspapers screamed that financial aid must be restricted to Italy, that art is a national affair, and rubbish of that sort. R. reads Herr von Wilamowitz's pamphlet and is provoked by it into writing an open letter to Prof. Nietzsche, which he reads to me in the evening. Walk with the composer Svendsen and his wife. In the evening took up *Christus* again, with ever-mounting sorrow. A great talent has here been almost entirely destroyed.

*Tuesday, June 11* R. works on his letter, which he completes and which I find quite masterly; after some domestic crises I go into the garden with the children. Read some of our nephew's *Prudentius*. Took a long walk with R. in the splendid park; roses, acacias, jasmine, everything blooming and smelling sweet, behind it the pine wood— how easy it then becomes to forget what a wicked world we live in! I am writing these lines on our balcony while R. copies out his essay; blackbirds, orioles, thrushes twitter and sing, the children are well, I have hopes that R. will return to his work—thus I am happier perhaps than any other creature in the world and thank God in humility, penitence, and joy. — In the evening finished *Christus*.

*Wednesday, June 12* Up between three and four in the morning; birdsong and sunrise, a little deer runs past quite close to me, a cuckoo with three notes; happy mood. — But R. is not pleased with my morning walk, so that I come to regret it. — The sun soon went in, and now it is raining. Fidi is unwell, a back tooth is coming in. R. sends off his article. He goes for a walk and discovers a ravine, the Wolfsschlucht, after having sat a long time for Scharff, the medal maker.

*Thursday, June 13* Letter from Cornelius with an amazing description of the Weissheimer success; he returns the letter which R. had written to W. in the first instance and which he then demanded back by telegram; in place of it R.'s last statement in the newspaper. Sitting; the medallion will be good, I think. R. plays his second act and is satisfied with it, which pleases me all the more since he was recently depressed over the first act. Family lunch. Then to town with R. First to our architect, R. very satisfied with the execution of his plan for our house. Then to the Feustels', from there to the festival site; the working men make a fantastic impression on us. Back to the Feustels'; late in the evening home in our Fantaisie coach with its indescribable coachman, who always hastily puts on white gloves when he sees us coming, wears on his head a peasant's hat from Dürer's time, and has horses to match it. Today we were also in the editorial offices of the *Tagblatt* to lecture the editor on an unseemly report ("Pen War Between Weissheimer and Wagner") and to forbid him to mention R.'s name except in connection with the Bayreuth enterprise.

*Friday, June 14* R. dreams of a rosebush which was growing at the head of his bed and on which the roses were so large that he thought to himself, "You must show them to Cosima." Then they fell off like camellias; one remained, which he was just about to pluck when it fell, shed its petals, and revealed a core something like a pineapple, which Loldi ate; he was just wanting to show that, too, when he woke up. — Arrival of cigars from Havana ("the delicious weed," writes the supplier); it is a present from Herr Nettke. Last sitting for the medal maker, which unfortunately means another morning lost, but I hope it will turn out well. R. then again plays *Götterdämmerung* and is looking forward to working on it. When will he at last find the peace and quiet for it? In the afternoon with Fidi and Eva to the Schweizerei (the others are in the town). Then for a walk alone with R. Fine weather, lovely rest. In the evening the four girls work on R.'s head and make curl papers for his locks! — Early to bed, since R. is not well, sudden disturbance by a telegram: Herr Batz, the agent, is coming—another disturbance.

*Saturday, June 15* The whole morning lost! Herr Batz here from 9 until one o'clock—I could weep for grief! — When, oh, when the peace to work in? I should like to take a vow, if that would help procure it! . . . R. told me yesterday that Pastor Sydom was attacked by the whole consistorial council because he said Christ was a divinely appointed mortal. "The old Jewish God always ruins the whole thing," R. observes. "What one can clearly see is that religion is dying: it only keeps going by making fools of the people. The Liberals also do not know how to help except with their indifference; no one will abandon the old God, but for that very reason they are denying Christ; there is confusion everywhere, wherever one looks." — I dreamed of an E Major Symphony; R. had told me yesterday that the symphony of his which Mendelssohn lost and which he would like to find again, just to demonstrate how well he knew his job, was in E major. —

"If you take things as they come without discrimination, You will remain calm and still in love as in tribulation." This old verse, quoted in Gutzkow's novel *Fritz Ellrodt*, touches me very much and will become my motto. (The novel was sent me by friend Feustel, because it has to do with the history of Bayreuth.) — Long walk with R. through the woods and the cornfields, which are full of cornflowers; I tell R. my idea for the reverse side of the medallion, about which our medal maker was uncertain; I am thinking of myth and music creating drama, and when I tell R. that this should take the form of portraits to keep the allegory from seeming cold and stiff, he suggests Ludwig Schnorr and [Wilhelmine] Schröder-Devrient. — Happy mood during our walk, as always when we are together and undisturbed. Recently in the carriage he said to me, "If I take my eyes off you, it is only to consider how to give you real pleasure—" Our return is spoiled by the "general," whom R. espies at the window. R. decides to let him come up late in the evening. His coarseness appalls us, and his presence at the Fantaisie seems to us vaguely sinister. R. very put out. (Letters from Herr v. G[ersdorff], who is pleased with R.'s article, and from

Malwida, who tells us of the "general's" importunities and the continuation of the dispute with Weissheimer, of which we hear nothing, thank God.)

*Sunday, June 16* Wild night filled with nightmarish images! But the morning is fine, I in the garden with the children, write to Malwida M., while R. gets down again to his work. God give him blessings and peace! Later, walk with the Svendsens, who are thoroughly nice people. Late in the evening the "general," but—thank God—to take his leave. — In the afternoon I read *Hermann und Dorothea* and felt that the hexameter form does much to impair the impression of a splendid naïveté in Goethe's characters. R. agreed with me and said, "One sees by that to what extent everything with us was a seeking and groping; the people who don't understand call it classical, since it uses a Greek form which does not suit it at all and which gives everything an air of affectation." —

*Monday, June 17* R. has a buzzing and stabbing sensation in his ears, something he also had severely 8 years ago in Starnberg. It both worries and alarms me, and I am also worried by the very great expense of our life here—alas, the poor dear man has much to bear! — He is not at all well, can do little work, and does not go for a walk. In the evening the good Svendsens come and he has to leave, for he can talk to nobody. — We are very upset by the news that the dean is seriously ill. Are we now being threatened with a loss? His last office was administering Communion to our friend Feustel, who has gone over to Protestantism. R. says, half in fun, half in earnest, "Have certain gentlemen been giving him a dose for that?"

*Tuesday, June 18* R. had a tolerable night and is able really to work; he is in good spirits and goes to town on foot, I then go to meet him with the two little ones. He has been to inquire about the dean, who is somewhat better. Cheerful evening. Talked a lot about *Reineke Fuchs*, which I am just reading. News of Alfred Meissner's death.

*Wednesday, June 19* I very unwell, but one must pull oneself together. Wedding breakfast of Frl. Feustel in the Goldener Anker; 90 guests, music at table, toasts, and finally dancing, from 1 o'clock until 8. We are thoroughly tired, and I am particularly affected by the noise, R. vexed by the old women with flowers. He says, "The curious thing is, one feels in the first moment that one won't be able to stand it, the shock is enormous, but then one becomes deadened."

*Thursday, June 20* R. works in the morning, but is sad at being so often disturbed, as again yesterday by the wedding. Family lunch. Fidi naughty to his papa, from whom he receives his first punishment. In the afternoon a walk with R., after the arrival of some books (the life of Moscheles, etc.) had once more made us feel astonished at the

toothache—the growth of her teeth is causing me concern. I am never for a moment free from worries about the children, alas! Will I experience through them the proud joy of having brought up good and capable human beings? — R. has a cold and cannot work today; in Darwin (*The Origin of Species*) he reads the case of a dog which, while being dissected, licks the hand of its master, who is doing the operation; the fact that the latter does not then stop upsets R. greatly: "One needs always to visualize such things to recognize among what sort of people one is living, to whom one belongs, and to become humble." It moves me to utter silence—forget, forget! Oh, this life of ours! We reckon up our experiences since the festival: (1) Hans's letter; (2) the Weissheimer affair; (3) the "general"; (4) Wilamowitz; (5) Johann Herbeck; (6) Julius Lang! Regarding (5), R. surmises that they would like to have *Die Walküre* for the World's Fair, but are not saying so. In the afternoon drove to the dentist. Lulu in considerable pain, her teeth are bad. In the evening Gibbon. — R. says: "If I am still able to establish my school here, it will give me much joy to express my views on *Die Zauberflöte*, *Figaro*, *Freischütz*, Gluck, too, and their cultural significance. *Zauberflöte*, *Freischütz* belong to the popular theater, the *Didone Abbandonata*'s, on the other hand, to the Court theater. — But, alas, how is culture possible when religion has such defective roots, and even terminology is so little defined that one can talk of spirit and Nature as if they were antitheses?" — I entertain R. with an account of my visit to the dentist, where I really got to know *"les mystères de Bayreuth."*

*Sunday, June 30* R. had an exciting night, he dreamed of a performance of *Tannhäuser* in Vienna in which Lulu and Boni were to have appeared, but it fell through; suddenly, after Elisabeth's exit, he heard a cabaletta being sung which he had found inserted in the theater score and had cut; speechless with rage, he leaped onto the stage and there encountered his sister-in-law, Elise Wagner, who said to him, "But it all sounds very lovely," while he, searching desperately for words, at last said loudly and clearly, "You swine!" and woke up. — Talked at breakfast about the Spanish theater, the activity of the popular spirit, which in Italy never found expression, being too much tied down by academies, the seat of the church, and excavations of the ancient world. Popular trends such as produced Shakespeare in England. — Lulu in much pain. — Bismarck, publicly denounced by the Pope, affords us pleasure; R. is wishing for an alliance between Rome, France, and Austria; "then perhaps we shall achieve a German church and put an end to the Habsburgs, that arrow in our flesh." R. works. In the afternoon children's party. — Letters, from M. Muchanoff in Kassel: she invites me to visit her in Weimar and to visit my father, then my father would come to Bayreuth! — M. M[eysenbug] writes from Munich, where *Tristan* was performed; I am always beset by bitter feelings when I think about these performances, which delight our friends, taking place in our absence. (Prof. Nietzsche and Herr v. G. were also there.) "N. had his tragic mortal dished up there," says R., thinking of Tristan.

*Monday, July 1* Vexation over the bad hotel management. — But Lulu's toothache is subsiding. — Yesterday evening I read R.'s letter to M[arie] W[ittgenstein], which appears in the 5th volume, and I could not get over my astonishment—shared by R.—that at the time Princess Wittgenstein saw nothing in it but an attempt to wriggle out of recognizing my father. Stupid world! — R. is reading Darwin with enjoyment, only regretting that he did not know Schopenhauer, which would have made so many things easier for him. — Hopes set on Prof. N.; regret that things of such significance make no real impression, attract no attention. But was it ever different? Certainly Kant's *Critique of Pure Reason* seems to have attracted very great attention. — Talked about Princess Marie Hohenlohe; R. relates what she said to him in her youth and says it is an enigma to him how such characters can entirely wipe such things out of their lives, completely ignore them. — R. works and is satisfied with his work. In the evening read Gibbon. — In the afternoon the district president with his family in the hotel garden, nearby the Duke and his wife eavesdropping in a covered arbor!! — R., Fidi, and I to the Schweizerei, where the other children then joined us. On the way home Fidi is willful; in order to punish him I make him walk by himself (he only wanted to give me his hand), and that puts R. out of humor—which distresses me. In the evening R. says I must forgive him his moody manner; either he is not in a working mood, and then he is despondent, or he is in it, and then he could complete his work to the end without interruption, and everything—eating, drinking, sleeping, speaking—becomes an obstacle which causes him suffering and vexes him. — Alas, what distresses me is simply not having the power to smooth his path completely.

*Tuesday, July 2* While I am sleeping, R. brings his photograph to my bed—"it was supposed to beg forgiveness." — Unfortunately R. is very unwell, and much domestic vexation comes on top of it. We always seem to end up with a "bohemian household." — Telegram from Marie Muchanoff, she is arriving tomorrow. — R. cannot work. Melancholy; at lunch he says: "If it were not for the children, I would ask you whether you would not like to leave the world with me. But there they are, and with them hope—without them we should feel all too dismal in this world." — Which the greater, Wotan or Sieg-fried? Wotan the more tragic, since he recognizes the guilt of existence and is atoning for the error of creation. — Walk; fight between Rus and another dog, R. pulls huge Rus by the tail, which takes a lot out of him. — Darwin is giving him pleasure, and he agrees with him that, in comparison with the old world, there is moral progress in the fact that animals are now accepted as part of it. — In the evening Gibbon (death of Theodosius) with continued enjoyment. "The right reading for aristocratic English statesmen." R. agrees with me when I say it seems likely that Constantine embraced Christianity in order to rejuvenate the crumbling Roman world with new strength and to salvage the Roman idea of world dominion after the disappearance of Roman personalities. All of it politics, as right up to the present day, which is also why they (the priests) cannot give up the thought of world dominion. We cannot get over our astonishment that dramatists do not go for their material to Gibbon, who has done so much spade-work, brought the characters so individually to life—the episode of Gregory of Nazianzus, his triumph and subsequent defeat; Ambrosius and Theodosius—all of them tremendously interesting conflicts involving human beings. "Yes," says R., "the figures are there, but the 'figurers' are missing."

*Wednesday, July 3* Troubled night; Dr. L[ang]'s insults return to my mind, I have the feeling of being utterly without protection or defense, and, determined as I may be to live only within my own four walls, to think and breathe only for R. and the children, nevertheless it seems that anyone can throw mud at me to his heart's content—a wretched feeling. — Telegram from Marie M[uchanoff] that she is arriving tomorrow, in consequence of which family lunch and grand moving of furniture, since she wishes to live near us and there are no more rooms to be had in the hotel. The children move downstairs, six in one room! . . . R. is also in melancholy mood, but on returning from his walk he tells me that he felt curiously comforted by fireflies which he saw swarming in the darkness of the woods; he wept in the woods with emotion.

*Thursday, July 4* Into town early, but after R. had done some work; lunch with the Feustels, bad news of Ottilie's son-in-law (v. Berckefeld), who appears to have been reduced to seeking a job with the railroad! At 3 o'clock arrival of Herr v. Gersdorff, much about *Tristan*, tremendous impression on everybody, a Herr Hillebrand is reported to have said, "It is like the Eleusinian mysteries." At 9:15 our friend [Marie Muchanoff]; R. buys sausages, and I accompany our friend to the Fantaisie. The great joy of seeing her is soon clouded over by reports of *this* world. She relates among other things that Frau von Meyendorff complained of the poor reception she was accorded here! Yes, Herr v. G. had heard about that in Tegernsee, etc. — The four of us alone in the evening, talking about all kinds of things.

*Friday, July 5* While R. is working, I spend the morning with our friend; she herself always above reproach, pleasant and interesting, but all accounts of the outside world upset me, these eternal lies! Thus a Frau von Dewitz claims to have seen a letter from me to the bookseller Stilke, in which I spoke about R.'s letter to Tausig and Dr. Lang!! I feel like Erda, *"wüst und wirr"* ["muddled and confused"]— how gladly would I remain in ignorance of it! Walk in the afternoon; Herr v. Gersdorff informs me of a plan by which Prof. Nietzsche will issue an appeal for a collection in which all who cannot buy certificates of patronage, or do not wish by means of single contributions to join a Wagner Society, can take part. Our evening meal is enlarged by the presence of a Herr Krebs from Frankfurt am Main who, polite and well-educated, has come here with a curious request. He brings a sheet of paper which depicts, in a remarkably childish manner, Greek tragedy awakened by Wagner's genius; this is to be reproduced in gigantic size (like the *Symposium* of Feuerbach!), and he wants R.'s approval. R. advises him to read Nietzsche's book and gives it to him. He makes curious assertions—that one must now paint ideas, etc. After he has gone we are lost in astonishment over this curious apparition, and in the end have to laugh a lot over all these confusions.

*Saturday, July 6* A walk we took yesterday has given me a cold, in consequence of which I have entirely lost my voice. R. works. Coach muddles; I drive alone with our friend and Fidi and Lusch to the opera house, which she thinks splendid (Fidi says, "Papa concert"), and to the festival site (Fidi: "Fidi's house"). In the evening conversation on various topics with both friends. (The Emperor, on catching sight of the heavily compromised courtier: "Good morning, Duke of Strousberg, or, rather, Banker Ujest.") — R. plays us "Hagen's Call" and the Rhinemaidens from *Götterdämmerung*. (R. works.)

*Sunday, July 7* Departure of Herr von Gersdorff. The children in church, R. at work, I and Fidi with our friend; still voiceless. Afternoon visit to the Svendsens, who tell us all sorts of nice things about Kassel. In the evening the unhappy Herr Krebs again: his peculiarly obstinate insistence, despite anything one might say to him, suggests to our friend that he is emotionally disturbed. He departs in a bitter mood.

*Monday, July 8* I accompany our friend to the railroad station; she seems content with her stay here, the children behaved very well; yesterday, among other things, when the atmosphere became sultry (Herr Krebs!), I hoarsely instructed them to talk about something, and Lusch and Boni at once began to speak about the little Svendsen, how he fell into the water, etc. — Though we ourselves got great pleasure from her visit, it has nevertheless left behind a melancholy impression; the restless and joyless life of this outstanding woman, and particularly what she relates of the outside world, is so gloomy and sad (tragedy without dignity, as Schopenhauer says), that we always avert our eyes in disgust. Emotional parting from her. — R. was unable to work today, there has been too much distraction around him. It is very hot. In the evening we take the children to look for glowworms in the park. Meeting with the Duke, a fight between our dogs, but the Duke extremely friendly. In the afternoon I drafted a letter to Baroness von Meyendorff and was glad that preoccupation with form—that is to say, the attempt to express myself well—made me forget entirely the reason for my letter; even the most trivial exercise of art brings salvation. — R. is very pleased with a little notice in the newspaper that the town council is to permit the sale of sausages on the festival site. Regarding the building of the theater, R. says, "It is curious, I never really think about it; when I see the people working, it all seems quite natural to me; and if nothing were to come of it, I would still have the feeling that something different and greater would take its place." — Telegram from the Luccas (the day before yesterday), asking whether R. could go to Milan next February for *Lohengrin* and offering 9,000 francs. — R. replies yes, if *Lohengrin* is done according to his wishes. — Today R. set about reading *Die Ahnfrau*, in order to revive childhood memories; he was not shocked by the work's monstrosities, but he certainly was by the silliness of its language.

*Tuesday, July 9* Some unsigned lines from Herr Krebs, whose writing we know: "With Hamlet I have learned to recognize the nature of the world and I find it disgusting," the last words underlined three times! — Letter from a Herr Bergmann in New York, they would like to have the "Magic Fire Music" there, etc., and he inquires where certificates of patronage can be bought. — R. works, though with melancholy, since his impressions are all too discouraging, and I copy out my letter to Frau von M[eyendorff]; with this my pleasure is also at an end, for now I must expect replies, etc., and all the nonsense and deceit of the outside world. — R. goes into town, he inspects the site of our house, and it moves him very much to see the work well advanced. Letter from nephew Fritz; I should like very much to bring about a marriage between him and my Liszt cousin in Vienna.

*Wednesday, July 10* A gentleman from Coburg—*Dovris*, I believe —sends drawings for the King of Bavaria, recommending a "historic oven" he has made—unutterable nonsense! Yesterday Herr Tappert once more suggested an association with *Löser*, with the object, firstly, of supporting Bayreuth, then of producing the *Nibelungen* in Berlin!! — My only joy is the children, Fidi a constant source of hope. R. works. After lunch to town. To the Feustels'; the house we are to rent, etc. Splendid weather; home on foot from the Schweizerei, splendid birdsong, on which R. at once builds a symphonic movement. In the evening read a little Gibbon (on the religion of Christ and of Constantine, "supernatural or base reasons").

*Thursday, July 11*   Minister Schleinitz sends Lulu a nice assortment of seals; I thank him at once and write other letters, too. R. receives a not-very-successful medallion of Schubert. He works. After lunch R. visits the Svendsens, to ask whether he could undertake the copying for the King. Then we go for a walk. R. says: "How pleasant is literary work! Once a book is done, carefully corrected, and published, it is there, however much it may be criticized, and gives one pleasure. But a score—that might as well not exist until it has been performed. And with these works of mine I am addressing the most grotesque section of the public—a theater audience!" — The goings-on in the world, into which the visit of our friend gave us an insight, disgust us to the depths of our souls: "The only salvation is to take refuge in the *regions of august ancestors,*" says R. Just as we read no newspapers, we resolve quite seriously to see as few people as possible, except in connection with our task. What, for example, has come out of R.'s so well meaning invitation to my father? "The devil's own mess—let it be a lesson to us!" In the evening, Gibbon. —

*Friday, July 12*   Great heat, worked with the children in the garden, "a poet" wants to read poems to me! — R. works, "a few lines." After lunch to town, R. has to visit the law courts in connection with a theater manager in Chemnitz. We visit our site, on which work is proceeding vigorously. R. is pleased to see it. We return home at five o'clock and find the Kraussolds there. In the evening the Svendsens; R. had wanted him to do the copying, but he, himself a composer, shows no eagerness.

*Saturday, July 13*   Again and again R. comes back to the pleasures of literary work. "The fact that Lessing, Schiller, Goethe were melancholy would be incomprehensible if one did not know that they were possessed by an artistic urge which could not be developed in their own lifetimes. That is what makes them tragic; but otherwise literary work is a pure joy." Worked with the children; in the afternoon and evening the Feustels, also J. Rubinstein, arriving from Munich. The latter's piano playing pleases us greatly, in particular a fugue by Bach (from the *48 Preludes and Fugues*, D-flat Major) puts us into ecstasies: "It is as if music were really being heard for the first time," says R. When I tell R. that this scherzando has filled me, curiously, with tremendous melancholy, R. says: "I can understand that; it is like a restless forward striding, as if he were saying: 'Here you have everything with which you will later work, where you will lie down and rest; I know it all already, I must go on.' A sphinx—but that is German. How shallow and conventional does the sonata form—that product of Italy—seem in comparison! It was only by breathing such tremendous life into the accessories of this form that Beethoven brought music back close to Bach. One hears in it the lament of Nature (animals and plants)." For me it is, rather, the inorganic world, stones and mountains, which I hear calling. — (Letters from Marie M. and Malw. M.)

*Sunday, July 14* In the little church, sang hymns with much emotion, along with the Hummelbauer people; from such community comes devoutness, for what one feels in seeing these poor people, and what this divine service *in song* gave to me—that is prayer. As we sang "We have a God who helps us" I had to think of the times when the Protestants, with this cry on their lips, laid down their lives for their beliefs. I thought of Luther and his gigantic struggle; and the undecorated church, the standing, not kneeling congregation, the sung prayer, put me in a God-fearing mood. How gladly do I make contact with the world in this way, how well I understand their feelings and their faces! Unfortunately the "Herr Hofrat's" sermon was not at all in harmony with the mood, he drew distinctions between justified and unjustified concern for one's life, talked a lot about Satan—how dearly I should like to be a priest among the peasants, and how differently I should speak to them! — R. works. Family lunch. I am still not well; with the little ones in the park (Loldi indoors on account of inflamed eyes). Never has birdsong so affected me as here; I feel as if I were hearing it and understanding it differently from hitherto; like a strange call. I should like to feel no more evil and follow the call. I thought yesterday that every work of art should speak to us like birdsong, incomprehensible, unanswerable, yet at the same time understood and silently answered. For me art is all but spoiled, since for its sake one comes so much into contact with people—and not with good people. But nothing can spoil for me the song of the birds, the shadows of the trees, the blooming of flowers, and I feel a close relationship with the poor people who cultivate these things here, amid sweat and travail. The Duke is both philanthropic and unsociable, a condition to which life brings good people. — In the afternoon Herr R[ubinstein] comes and makes music with R.—everything inside him in a very raw state, which must be developed. (In the evening wrote to Marie M.)

*Monday, July 15* Recently Herr Heckel sent us a newspaper report which suggested that Hans was going to Mannheim; since we cannot at all understand this, we avoid talking about it; Heaven forbid that it should mean anything bad for Hans! In the garden with the children (Loldi indoors on account of her eyes). R. works. In the afternoon

Herr R[ubinstein] plays our piano while we walk to the Schweizerei with the children. Lovely atmosphere after some thundery rain; we watch a salamander making its laborious way into the meadow, birds warbling, the sound of church bells! Beside a stone Fidi suddenly asks, "Mama, what stands written here?," which makes us laugh a lot. R. says the sight of his head is real bliss to him, he can understand why the Greeks took such delight in male beauty, the strength and intelligence which emanate from it, whereas in feminine beauty there is only longing. In the evening went through the third act of *Siegfried* with Herr R. It is curious how *Siegfried* seems to be so completely unknown and misunderstood, even among devoted Wagnerians; I should have expected it to be seen as a thoroughly popular work. (Wrote to Fritz.)

*Tuesday, July 16*  Loldi still unwell, and wretched weather; spent the morning indoors. Richard works. In the afternoon he works out his plan for the orchestra for Wilhelmj. With the children in the Schweizerei; R. comes with Herr Rub. to join us. In the evening the Svendsens and— first act of *Siegfried*. Herr R. reveals great powers of understanding, and his handwriting in the copy is excellent.

*Wednesday, July 17*  Letter from friend Lenbach, he will now start on R.'s portrait. — The headmaster of a school in *Eisleben* sends R. an essay on medieval poetry, containing a (seemingly very good) chapter about *Tannhäuser*. R. works, I in the garden with the children (still with the exception of Loldi, whose eye is still inflamed). In the afternoon letters from Prof. Nietzsche and Frau von Meyendorff, the latter, though trivial, suggesting the desire to maintain good relations. A walk with J. Rubinstein; R. questions him about his study of Schopenhauer, which soon leads the conversation to very deep levels. I listen devoutly to R.'s teachings; who is not filled with a thirst for salvation? — In the evening Herr R. plays *Tristan*. All these musicians seem to find it difficult to get the tempo right.

*Thursday, July 18*  R. receives the contract for our house for signature; he recently dreamed of his burial beneath the chestnut trees on our terrace, which were already very large, so that he felt he would live for a long time, since we have only just planted the chestnut trees. He is now reading a life of Garrick (in French) and observes that it was a good mixture, French Protestant and Anglo-Saxon. He also comes to the conclusion that a really great actor is as rare a phenomenon as a great poet. — At lunch he says that, in order to visualize the Romans of the 5th century, one should imagine the present-day Frenchmen's having been beaten by the Americans and, after the invasion, amalgamating with them; what would emerge from that would certainly be something very remarkable. — Family lunch. R. then goes for a walk, I stay at home with Loldi. Herr R. comes, plays Chopin. In the *Tagblatt*

Cosima, Blandine, and Daniel Liszt in Weimar, 1855
Drawing by Friedrich Preller

Caricature of Wagner's relationship with Cosima and Hans von Bülow

Cosima von Bülow, Baron Augusz, Franz Liszt, and Hans von Bülow in Budapest, 1865

Tribschen, with Mount Pilatus in the background
Copy of a lost watercolor

Cosima Wagner

Judith Gautier-Mendès, 1875

Siegfried Wagner as Young Siegfried,
in the original costume of 1876

Cosima Wagner, 1877

Richard Wagner, 1877

Beethoven!" — Much joy in Fidi; but Loldi still troubled with her eye. — Letter from the agents that Herr Fürstner in Berlin has bought up Meser's business; R. very pleased, would like to sever all connections with Schott. Letter to me from A. Frommann: she has left Berlin and is asking the Empress to release her. — Nothing from my father; it looks as if Frau v. M[eyendorff] has achieved her aim.

*Monday, July 29*  Storm in the night, with it much peasant song. At breakfast we recall a funny incident yesterday: Herr Rubinstein wished to sing us a song of his own and began on "I will plunge my soul into the lily's cup!" His childish delivery, the text, and finally a break in his voice make all four of us break out into such uncontrollable laughter that it is just not possible to continue. — Letter from R.'s excellent publisher Fritzsch, who reports that the collected works are selling very well, which pleases R. all the more in view of the fact that the other publishers always claimed that there was no demand for any of these things. R. is still correcting the biography; in the afternoon he takes Herr Diener in hand, gets him to sing Wolfram's song slowly and softly, and is very happy with the way he manages it; less so with Herr Rubinstein, whose playing is still very undisciplined. They take up *Die Walküre*; tremendous impression on me, as if I did not know it at all. In the morning R. prepared the text of the *Ring* for Herr Fritzsch and wrote in the final verses. — In the evening he is a little vexed over always having only immature people to deal with, and having to begin with them right from the start.

*Tuesday, July 30*  Much, much worry over Loldi's eyes, which are very inflamed; yesterday and today I went with her to the hospital. R. writes to a scene designer in Vienna, Herr Hoffmann, who, it seems, would like to take on the work for Bayreuth. — For Fritzsch's periodical R. today writes a response to the errors in Herr Lang's biography. — He prepares his essay *Actors and Singers*. — At lunch he talks about the "*Kaisermarsch*" and says that on the first page (after the first four bars) he would like to reorchestrate the passage in which the chords are repeated; to start with, some powerful instruments, and then gradually introduce the full orchestra; as it is it sounds monotonous. — He completes the corrections to his third volume and laughs over the fact that he begins it with the reunion with Minna in Zurich and ends it with their reunion in Paris. "All this squandering of my life's and my soul's energies!" he exclaims. "The nonsense of all these relationships; I really believe that I must live only for my mission in life, for in Paris, for instance, nothing of a positive value emerged, I gained nothing from it; I just became harsher and harsher. Today I was correcting proofs of the time of the third act of *Tristan* and thought: If only the Grand Duke of Baden had offered me asylum then! But I was destined for other things, it all had to come about other than by a direct route." He concludes, "You are my element, my atmosphere, I exist only in you and the children." — But, as everything has to be paid for, a wicked fate decreed that while in this expansive mood R. should fetch Dr. Lang's article in order to read parts of it to me, and I must needs ask him to tell me nothing of what it contains; R. is hurt, does not understand that the mere mention of that name pains me—and so the payment is made. On the Sappho sofa with the children; then, with R., drank milk in the Schweizerei. In the evening two scenes from *Die Walküre*. (Letter from Malwida Meysenbug.) Big thunderstorm.

*Wednesday, July 31* R. is somewhat disgruntled at having to concern himself with immature ("stupid") people. "The only pleasure I get from my things is when I have written the sketch and sing it to you— after that it is all gone." Loldi still indisposed; R. and I take up the biography again, on a wet morning. — At lunch we talk about the impossibility of making oneself understandable through speech; speech is a convention; only love, which overcomes egoism, or an exaltation gained through art, enables one person to understand another. "Your father and Princess W. understood me just as little as utterly stupid persons." — Yesterday evening Herr Diener told us that Rubinstein wanted to build a theater of his own to perform five Biblical works. "Not very original," says R., laughing, "but why do these good people always begin everything from the outside? I wrote my work first, then began to think about the means of performing it." We learn that during Joachim's absence the Academic Wagner Society received permission to advertise its meetings on the staircase of the Academy; when Joachim returned, this was forbidden! — In the afternoon a visit from Herr Krausse, a historical painter from Leipzig, who reports that Wagnerianism has assumed enormous proportions in Leipzig. — In the evening the last scene of the second act of *Die Walküre*.

*Thursday, August 1* R. and I work on the biography, Loldi always at our side. Family lunch. In the afternoon visit from Frau Landgraf, then went for a walk with R. In the evening Herr Diener sings something from *Tannhäuser* and then attempts the "Forging Songs."

*Friday, August 2* Quaintly enough, I dreamed of Sainte-Beuve and Schuré, and when I tell R. this, he says he was also thinking only this morning about Schuré, and deciding that his high opinion of the French must have come from his having such a pleasant experience with Sainte-Beuve (who got him into the *Revue des Deux Mondes*). We work on the biography and reach the point of Minna's arrival in Paris, where R. now wishes to break off. — In the afternoon into town with "Stirb-Stirb" (Lulu tells us that our peasant coachman is called

works on his essay, I in the garden with the children. In the afternoon a visit from the von Hagen family—the son, a student of philosophy, had requested the journey to Bayreuth as a birthday present. Music is played, the third act of *Götterdämmerung* up to Gutrune's entrance; utterly splendid, and as a whole new even to me. — In the evening went for a walk by moonlight; a sad difference of opinion between R. and me, "the stupidest thing that can happen." Having read in the newspaper about a man who had celebrated two silver wedding anniversaries, R. talks of the possibility of our own silver wedding anniversary and says: "There would never be another celebration like it! Oh, I wish I were much younger—not just to relive past events, but to enjoy the present longer!"

*Wednesday, August 14* Visit from our good dean, who always brings us joy; he agrees to hold the christening in Frau Svendsen's house. In the afternoon continuation of the third act; overwhelming impression; I come to realize that all the characters invented by a true poet are enigmas, like the figures in the pictures of the great masters; it is as if the poet above all *sees* his characters, and language is only an inadequate tool with which to reproduce them exactly as he sees them; he sees them walking, standing, acting, suffering, but he does not really know their motives, and thus he stands above the law of cause and effect. The reason why the French write better plays than the Germans (the mediocre ones!) is because, though a French writer also may not see his characters from the inside, he does at least have before his eyes living actors, for whom he shapes his things. Our modern German writers, on the other hand, who get everything from books, see their characters from neither the inside nor the outside; nor are there any enigmas in their works, it is all shallowness, clear but at the same time insipid. — In the evening our watchman annoys us by telling us that our house will be very damp. R. says, "How people love telling one unpleasant things!" I understand why—in this way they save themselves from feeling envy. — R. is now enjoying reading A. W. Schlegel's critical essays. — Great joy in Fidi's kindness of heart. (Arrival of the medallion for the King.) — While we are talking about Josef Rubinstein's piano playing, R. says how curious it is that Jews seem neither to recognize nor to play any themes; he recalls that Levy in Dresden (not the Viennese one) played through the whole of the *Holländer* without recognizing the Dutchman's theme.

*Thursday, August 15* Early to town with the three eldest, at 10 o'clock the christening with Frau Svendsen and her boy, R. and I (godparents) very affected. — Weeping, R. remarks that every time the words "This is my body," etc., are spoken, one's heart is literally torn in two. The dean very moved and moving. Then visited our new quarters and the house, returning around 2 o'clock; our washerwoman draws a pistol in honor of the new Christian and presents flowers! — R. very tired; we wander through the lovely park, visiting various places. In the evening read Gibbon. — Bad news from Brückwald, the architect, who is too casual; in contrast, a good letter from Hoffmann, the scene painter in Vienna, who seems to understand his task. — Herr Hartmann, the poet, turns up again with a *Päpstin Johanna* and at the same time as *captatio benevolentiae* with a suggestion of crowning R. like Petrarch—miserable!

*Friday, August 16* Since I tell R. all my thoughts about literary and dramatic art, he says, "It is always the same things which occupy us, and our understanding of them is so identical that we are always considering and enriching each other's ideas." I write several letters, and among other things send Herr Hartmann his *Päpstin Johanna* back. R. works on his essay. In the afternoon to the Schweizerei with 7 children. Letters from A. Frommann and a very interesting one from a cellist, Herr De Swert in Berlin, whom Wilhemj has engaged for the Bayreuth orchestra and who explains his absence at the Ninth Symphony by telling us that Herr de Ahna—a former Wagner supporter who was entrusted with finding players in Berlin—had been so intimidated and influenced by Joachim that he had (1) not engaged the good players in the orchestra and (2) canceled everything at the last moment—which had at the time struck us as very reprehensible. — Final evening with the Svendsens; cordial parting from these dear, excellent, and very well educated people, who are now going to Christiania.

*Saturday, August 17* We read the novel *Um Szepter und Kronen* yesterday and were astonished by the truthfulness of its descriptions; two people whom we know, Klindworth and Beckmann, could have been photographed; also the motivation for the events of '66 seems very plausible. R. not very well, amuses himself with the book. — In the afternoon Herr Niemann and Herr Levi, the conductor; the former goes through part of Siegmund with R.; the latter tells us about a letter from Herr Weissheimer, offering him 1,000 thalers and wine for life if he would bring out *Körner* in Karlsruhe! — Bad news of Bavaria; the King did not see the German Crown Prince when he passed through, and they say that Herr Windthorst, the leading Catholic, may become minister for Bavaria. Very bad.

*Sunday, August 18* The children in church, I with Fidi in the garden, write letters to M. Meysenbug and A. Frommann. R. is worn out, but works a little on his essay. Family lunch. Afterward the musicians—five in number—R. plays them the third act of *Götterdämmerung*, which absolutely stuns them. Herr Niemann says that no one will ever be able to perform it like R. himself. At supper Herr Levi

and even praise their work. — We talk about vital relationships, and R. ends by saying, "You are the only person who has given me anything, to whom I have listened willingly and attentively; you and Uncle Adolph; otherwise nobody has brought me a thing."

*Monday, August 26*   A fair! Yesterday in the woods I heard a great deal of music and singing which pleased me a lot, and today the noise is even greater, peasant dances right up to the house. R. has to go to town early today; it makes me sad to let him go, but Brückwald and Brandt are there, and there are many things to be discussed. All day long with the children; worked in the morning, in the afternoon with them to the Salamander valley. More letters from Marie M., she worries me with the report that Hans would dearly like to remain in Munich. His concert for Bayreuth (sonatas) is said to have been brilliant. R. returns home at about 7 in the evening; completely hoarse! He also brings some money. I am sad that so much is spent, alas, and I worry over our moving to a new house, worry because our expenditure is always increasing and our income not, worry because R. is becoming so involved in his enterprise before the certificates are signed. — My only help is the grateful belief that God, who has protected us so far, will continue to protect us! R. is very pleased with his machinist. But he is very tired!

*Tuesday, August 27*   R. is so worn out that he begs me to drive into town, to look at the plans, and make his excuses at the architects' office; this I do, and at the same time visit our house. R. works. Herr Brückwald at lunch, which is a bit difficult for us, but over which we finally joke. In the evening talked about the journey of the Crown Prince through Bavaria, very humiliating for the King, but how to change that? — Discussion over the wretched state of teachers and clergymen. A shame that it is so, need for a sweeping reform—but who is even thinking of it? — Letter from my mother, she seems to be quite well.

*Wednesday, August 28*   Once more Marie M. asks me to visit my father! Unsatisfactory discussion with R.; great misgivings, this journey seems to us foolhardy—God knows what we shall decide; whichever way, we shall feel apprehensive. — R. works, I with the children; write to Marie M. about Herr von P[erfall] and my doubts about the journey. In the afternoon I read my mother's history of the Netherlands, R. the writings of A. Schlegel, which he finds very interesting. In the evening young Rubinstein is with us, and I beg R. to read us his work as a whole, which to my great delight he does. — I took the children to the Schweizerei, there we met R. with Rus, drinking milk. — Fidi very willful; R. remarks that he would like to find him a male playmate, to remove him from the constant companionship of women.

*Thursday, August 29* Letter from Herr Schäfer: the concert in Munich has brought in 1,400 florins! Renewed discussion with R. about the Weimar visit; he becomes angry, and I ask him not to talk of it again. At noon he tells me he felt the urge to come to me, take me in his arms, and tell me that I should go to Weimar and that he would come to fetch me. This seems to me a good solution, but since at family lunch R. remarks ironically, regarding this journey, "Yes, one must play at diplomacy," etc., I again beg him to think no more of the matter, we shall simply let it rest. [*Here the page is smudged, with the remark:* "Fidi's doing!"] He resolves then to write to my father himself, which he does at once, declaring our readiness to visit him, but demanding a word from him, then touching on the episode of the visit of his friend [Frau v. Meyendorff]. The letter is wonderful and clears up the situation at once. — With the children to the Schweizerei, R. meets us there; home through the woods, Fidi: "But, Mama, this is a funny path." — In the evening our good Josef R[ubinstein], whom we find a little tiresome. We read Schlegel's conversations about language; when I single out what he says about Homer's simplicity, R. remarks, "Times are sad when one has to write about such things—if our theater were blooming, I should certainly not be writing about actors and singers." He remarks how Goethe and Schiller were distracted from their true work as poets by their criticial investigations—*Elpenor, Die Braut von Messina* were the outcome of this period, significant in cultural history, but artistically unproductive, and it lasted until Schiller decided to become exclusively a dramatist and Goethe returned to his *Faust*, which he did not rate particularly high aesthetically. "Music is the only naïve art—up to Mendelssohn. Beethoven did not ponder over the nature of the symphony."

*Friday, August 30* R. had a very bad night: "What I call being healthy is being able to follow one's inclinations, and my inclination is toward productivity; now, alas, I have to spend my mornings running around instead of sitting still and working." When I tell him how happy his letter to my father has made me and how much I love him, he says, "But I you much more, and you are more beautiful and more complete than I am"!! When we speak of that woman [Mathilde Wesendonck] who, in spite of her long contact with him, absorbed his ideas so little that she could now write literary dramas, R. says, "Associations of that sort were a constant stirring of the pot on my part; what was in the pot can only be judged once the stirring has ceased and the grounds have settled." — Fine letter from the King, he applies King Marke's words to the *Nibelungen* ("this wonderful work, which my desire, etc."), and R. finds this extraordinarily witty. R. works; went into town in the afternoon, did some shopping in case my father summons us; also bought things for Fidi. In the morning Fidi makes us laugh heartily. We had forbidden him to put his feet on the table, now he placed them there and hit them, said, "Feet, go away!," and threatened them with a stick, holding it above his head and watching us slyly. Letter from Malwida, at the same time one from Herwegh. On behalf of the Herzen children, the former had asked Herwegh for the letters their mother had written to him; she received from him a rude refusal, and, since Malwida had told him she was applying to him with R.'s consent, H[erwegh] also writes here. "He is dripping with importance now," R. says. The pitiful creatures! In the evening R. does some revision.

*Saturday, August 31* Letters from Chicago (R. is invited to inaugurate the new opera house during the celebrations of the revival of the city); from Herr Löser—more proposals! And all sorts of rubbish. R. works on his essay and reads me what he has added in the afternoon. I write the replies to the letters, which he signs. In the evening to the Schweizerei with the children, R. comes to meet us, bringing with him J. Rubinstein, whom he had called for out of pity, though he finds his restless Jewish character very unsympathetic; during the recent reading he could not stay still for a moment, and R. says, "Though the rustling of a beloved woman's dress might entrance one as a sign of the stirring of her intense concentration, this masculine deportment is not exactly encouraging." — R. reads passages from Schlegel's essay on Bürger, and thinks him in the right concerning Schiller. I find my mother's history of the Netherlands very interesting, and it seems to me very good. — I had been half expecting a telegram from my father, but nothing came. [*In the margin:* "Fidi's new hat 'Mambrino's helmet.' "]

*Sunday, September 1* When I tell R. my dream and say it dealt with a time before he loved me, he replies, "You foolish woman, as if we could love each other now as we do, if we had not always loved each other!" — We come by chance to talk about the curiously lax attitude of Catholics among the ordinary people; R. calls it a lack of honor, and he agrees with me when I say that indulgences are to blame for people's not being able to take anything seriously. — R. works; I with the children in the garden. In the afternoon I read my mother's history of the Netherlands and find it excellent; I express to R. my surprise that W. of Orange has been so little used in tragedies, and he replies: "What do you expect? Eckert once composed him—he was his poet-murderer." I am now reading Schiller on Bürger and have to take Schiller's part; there is a note of ignoble sentimentality in Schlegel.

A letter from my father has not yet arrived; the children in church; R. at work, I with Fidi in the garden. In the afternoon with the children in the park; they play. R. joins us at the playground, brings a nice letter from my father, and we resolve to make the journey. Hasty packing during the evening.

*Monday, September 2* We leave at 11 o'clock amid the fluttering of Sedan flags; fine sight of the harvest festival in Liebenstein; goose boy and shepherd! Bonfires and illuminations—arrived in Weimar at 9 o'clock! My father well and pleased, pleasant time together in the Russischer Hof.

*Tuesday, September 3* Visited my father during the morning in the pretty Hofgärtnerei, lunched with him and R. at one o'clock, then unfortunately many people (before lunch visited Frau v. Meyendorff with him). We part just before 5 o'clock, to meet at his house again in the evening, with the Loëns (whom we visited in the morning) and Frau v. M. That is a lot for such recluses as ourselves—the best of it was that my father played me *"Am stillen Herd"* and the *"Liebestod."* I am terribly upset by my father's weariness of soul. In the evening, when he scarcely spoke and I related all sorts of things, and R., in order to do his bit toward sustaining a cheerful atmosphere, jokingly disputed with Baron Loën about his (R.'s) supposed popularity, I saw the tragedy of my father's life as in a vision—during the night I shed many tears! (Early in the morning my father had sent me roses from the Court gardens.) Telegram from the children that all is well with them.

*Wednesday, September 4* I send a note to my father asking whether he has had some rest—my melancholy regarding him remains with me to such an extent that, when Frau von Meyend. returns my visit and asks me how I find him, I cannot help bursting into tears, which gives her a shock. Other visits are returned, then to the Erholung with my father and Dr. Gille in the burning heat. Very pleasant, merry and earnest atmosphere! Afterward with my father to Frau Merian-Genast. Later our dear old Alwine Frommann, and in the evening at Baroness Meyend.'s house, where my father plays us the andante from Beethoven's G Major, the preludes of Chopin, and his own *Mephisto-Walzer* at my request. He talks a lot about old times, when together we bought fruit in the market in Berlin—and the old feelings of familiarity are recaptured. [*In the margin:* "R. introduces as a standard aside, whenever a French word is used, 'As the Latinists say.' "] R. is in very good spirits, asks Dr. Gille whether he is any relation to the Spanish Gil with the green hose, which, since the unhappy man casts a fleeting glance at his nether garments, makes us all laugh very much, laughter which I in my naïveté only increase by explaining to my father, "The Spanish play is a very decorous play, since it is a woman who was wearing the trousers."

*Thursday, September 5* [*In the margin:* "R. complaining humorously of his lack of popularity in Weimar; nobody recognizes him. He goes into the Anker, swears that he saw *bedbugs* there, and says that is where one must go in order to get to know one's fellow countrymen."] I write to Mar. M.—then we visit our dear old Alwine Frommann, in whose little apartment, with its portrait of La Roche Jacquelein (!), we feel very much at home. Home at about eleven, my father comes to fetch us. I notice at once that his mood has changed—he has had to pay for having shown his great affection for me yesterday! We went to his house to make music, *Götterdämmerung*—but the music making would not work. He came to Baroness Loën's, where we were all invited for lunch (with the Bojanowskis and Baroness Meyendorff), and was silent and fatigued; Frau v. M. also silent, but content. After lunch we returned to Fräulein Frommann's and stayed there some time before going on to my father's. The same mood—R. very charming, helping out with witticisms: "I wish I had your eyebrows," he says to my father, which makes us laugh a lot. My father plays us the adagio from [Opus] 106—but everything with reserve, he hardly looked at me at table, spoke only to Frau v. M.—and of his idea, put forward explicitly yesterday, of accompanying us as far as Eisenach, nothing more has been said.

*Friday, September 6* Up at half past three, off about five, my father has breakfast with us and takes us to the railroad station; quiet farewell. I depart in sorrow—it is not the separation which pains me, but the fear of entirely losing touch. In the train R. has an outburst of jealousy toward my father, but he is soon pacified. Glowing heat and dust, and R. gives vent to his annoyance with the railroad, which destroys all good manners. At 4 o'clock arrived in Bayreuth, joyous reunion with the children; Fidi in a mauve velvet suit. Very tired in the evening, off to bed at seven-thirty.

*Saturday, September 7* R. very unwell, but he writes the epitaph for Tausig's grave, which I find wonderfully moving. In the garden I work out the notes to a laudatory discourse which my father entrusted to me. In the afternoon I write to him and send him my work. R. sends him his works with a dedication "in the style of Hans Sachs." To the Schweizerei with the children, there met the lawyer Käfferlein from the management committee, who has no doubts about the success of the enterprise. — Loldi, seeing his three dogs, says, "One of them belongs to him, the other two have been invited." — R. indisposed, becomes angry when I speak of giving up my bedroom in the new house to my father. — The whims of the particularist administration in Bavaria have led to nothing.

*Sunday, September 8* R. still unwell and in bitter mood; he recalls how nobody was prepared to help him, etc. —

*Monday, September 16*  While putting the new house in order I take up my diary again. Every day since Monday the 9th I have been driving into town at 8 o'clock, returning to the Fantaisie in the evening at 6, even 7 o'clock; many furnishing difficulties, but in good spirits. R. always comes to fetch me. On Sunday the 15th stayed at the Fantaisie all day; R. reads me his splendid work, completed on the previous day. On the first day of the moving the military band at the Fantaisie made a truly magical impression on me; as I arrived home they were playing the "Prize Song" from *Die Msinger*—my tiredness was gone. The moonlight on the huge trees also helps me—but it disturbs R. to see me refreshing myself in this way. — Nice letter from my father (Wednesday), announcing a visit. Later one from Frau v. Meyendorff (I had asked my father to write to her), as friendly, I think, as it is in her to be. During this time R. received a diploma making him a freeman in Bologna, which pleased him greatly and really puts the German cities to shame. R. again has trouble with his architect, Herr Brückwald, the matter of the scene decorations is also not progressing, and how things stand with the funds I do not know—only that Baron Loën is paying nothing either in or out, after giving us the figure of 70 certificates of patronage. R. has, alas, taken too much on himself! Nice letter from Marie M.—also from my mother, who is now well. — R. gave me great pleasure yesterday evening by reading to me Görres's foreword to *Lohengrin*; the connection between the myth of the Holy Grail and other myths of antiquity, profoundly stimulating and gripping. — R. also reads me a charming poem by A. Schlegel ("Saint Luke"), which had reminded him of my "passion for the visual arts." Today (Monday) wrote to M. Muchanoff; R. calls for me at four o'clock, tells me in the carriage that he "howled like a chained watchdog," he was reading the dedication to *Faust*. Following on our conversation, we take up the first part of it again in the evening, and R. reads it to me—in a way I shall never again experience. He was seeking to make clear to himself the tone in which it should be spoken, simple and natural throughout—all would be lost, he says, if the actor were to give the impression of being conscious of its metaphysical content. "Land and sea, this is the complete map," R. says. "In it Goethe's optimism seeks refuge; he is thinking: these are after all facts, which continue to exist, whatever happens." I go to bed deeply affected and comforted in the highest sense by his reading and his remarks.

*Tuesday, September 17*  R. corrects his manuscript and sends it off; I pack a few things, send them into town, and go for a walk with the 5 children. Lunch with the children, in the afternoon a splendid walk with R. through woods, fields, and villages, lovely autumn air; right at the start a meeting with Herr v. Lerchenfeld ("he looks like a

Spanish lackey"), who almost became a minister, but nevertheless puts on a friendly air! — Lovely moonlight. "That is the cheerful moon," says R. "The waning moon is the sorrowful one, which utterly dismays one when one suddenly catches sight of it during the night, penetrating to one over city towers, through narrow windowpanes." This brings him back to *Faust*. "It is truly a poem of great culture," R. says. "However folklorish its characters, modeled literally on Kasperl, however abstract its objects, it reflects the whole development of mankind." The preface to *Lohengrin* he finds very gripping. "How curious," he says, "that I should come up on this again and be reading it just now, when I am so occupied with thoughts of the Roman and German civilizations." The suggestion, mentioned in the newspapers, of a kingdom of Alemannia, with the Grand Duke of Baden as king, pleases him greatly. "That would be the finest German country of all," R. says.

*Wednesday, September 18* (still at the Fantaisie). Unfortunately R. had a very bad night. A word he let fall yesterday cast a complete mantle of grief over my spirits: he said he believed there was something wrong with his heart! After our walk we had supper at Donnweyer's (the Goldener Pfau in Eckersdorf); did something he ate there perhaps disagree with him? . . . He corrects his manuscript, I go into the park with the children, and we take a walk of almost 4 hours with Fidi, the children very merry, Fidi incredibly lively, with not a sign of tiredness, I taking leave in my heart of the trees I have come so much to love. We return to find R. looking unwell, and after lunch he becomes ill-humored. We drive into town in deep silence, and as we are passing the cemetery, R. points a finger toward it— The house still very behindhand; the Stockers have packed things immensely unskillfully—half of them, the most necessary, still missing. On top of that, R. has a very unpleasant encounter with a Herr Kastner, who had been recommended to him as a copyist by Herr Lassen in Weimar, the conductor with whom we once had a bad experience (though we have forgotten the details). This Herr Kastner makes a very unpleasant impression on R., though he affects very great enthusiasm (would rather be a copyist here than a conductor anywhere else, etc.). — Quiet journey home, quiet evening. Always moonlight, in joy as in sorrow—

*Thursday, September 19* R. had a better night, but he has a headache and is feeling despondent. — "You alone keep me going. If I had not found you, what urge would I have had to do anything? Disgust would have defeated me. People knew instinctively that I would do no more, and I felt the same. And it is pitiful, too, what I have achieved; nobody really listens to me. If only I were to be asked, even once, by someone high up for my views on the reform of the theater—but being completely ignored like this! — All our best minds are turning to the world of machines, the sons of good families are becoming engineers and emigrating to America whenever they can, and those who stay behind and devote themselves to science are unintelligent." However, he takes pleasure in Fidi and says he would like to know if he was like that as a child. "Yes, one has to do everything for oneself, we had to make Fidi for ourselves." Wet weather, I write off for *Delikatessen*; R. makes his corrections, he knows that all great men have felt as he does. "Goethe kept himself going with his scientific loves." (My father wrote to him yesterday, to thank him for the dedication in the style of Hans Sachs.) He goes into town, I with the children to the Schweizerei, where the rain surprises us. Georg, coming from town, overtakes us, he has with him the photographs sent by Brück-wald and a letter from Marie Schleinitz, reporting that the Sultan is taking 10 certificates of patronage, a piece of news which gives R. little pleasure, since it wounds the pride of our *German* enterprise. R. returns home rather late, but we are still able to read a little of Görres's preface, which—particularly since it is completely new to me—I find extremely gripping. — A wet day ends nicely with moonlight.

*Friday, September 20*  Last walk around the Fantaisie with the children, Fidi with us the whole time; it is beginning to look melan-choly here, all our little possessions are being packed—"I turn my back gladly on the past, toward something with a future." Our spirits are also damped by news of a great fire in town which this morning struck our decorator, too—he is said to have had severe losses, and his son is reported to have been killed. (R. learns from A. Röckel's son, who is seeking employment as a chorist, that Röckel has completely gone to seed! This leads to a review of all past relationships—alas, how wretchedly most of them have ended!)

*Tuesday, September 24*  (in the new house in town). Moved out and in on Saturday; lunch in the Sonne, much misery; no cook, not even a housemaid! *Sunday*: difficulties with breakfast, the refined temporary cook makes us no coffee, uses up all the water; coffee is at last made around 10, and our watchman pours it away, which at any rate turns our ill humor into loud laughter. In the afternoon arrival of our nephew Fritz Brockhaus—not exactly convenient, since everything still in a state of disorder and R. unfortunately not at all well. *Monday*: the day goes by better; shopping, accompanied Fritz to the railroad station with the five children; lunched haphazardly at home, R. still unwell; in the evening played through some Beethoven sonatas. (Visit from Herr Feustel, who tells us many things about the discord between Prussia and Bavaria; the King upset the Crown Prince by failing to

please to send them money so that they can travel to Munich to see *Tristan*—direct and to the point!

*Friday, November 1* Lovely autumn weather; sent Boni to school, so that our journey will not interrupt her studies. The people in Vienna do not reply, and now the contracts should be settled—I hope to God that we are not facing wretched disappointments! — In the morning continued sorting the children's things. Boni returned from school highly pleased, it is to be hoped she will become more lively intellectually there. R. has a final discussion with Brückwald. — At three o'clock to the railroad station, Marie Muchanoff had sent a telegram announcing her arrival; she comes from Munich, very tired and agitated; she says *Tristan* had much affected her; it had gone very well under Bülow's direction. She tells us all sorts of curious things about Hans, which do not surprise me. On one occasion, she says, he would be extremely cordial, on the next downright rude, so that one never knew quite how to approach him. All kinds of things about the German Empress, of whom she has seen much and whom she loves dearly. She spends the evening with us and dismays us with her restlessness.

*Saturday, November 2* To our friend early, accompanied her at 11 o'clock to the railroad station, where R. joins us. When shall we see our poor friend again? We are concerned about her. — I visit the dean in order to give him a small offering for his people, and stay talking with him for quite a while about the German church. R. visits the law courts in connection with the Düsseldorf theater director and returns home very annoyed by the incomprehensible silence in Vienna. At supper we discuss the news which Marie M. brought us concerning the King, which is very alarming; among the people there is already talk of insanity, and on top of that the King's hatred of Prussia, his only protection! . . . I beg R. to put all worries on this score out of his mind, since predictions of a catastrophe can neither improve nor alter the situation. — Later R. comes to the subject of our holy event: "How beautiful it was in that little vestry, how powerful the voice of our dean sounded—like the voice of a lion emerging from a cave! What substitute could there be for the feelings aroused in one when the indescribably moving words 'This is my body' are spoken?" The monotonous sound of the Liturgy also touched his heart. "I could almost say—if I did not shrink from the word in this connection—that it all made an artistic impression, even the little acts of pouring wine, etc." — Afterward we talked about the children—worries!

*Sunday, November 3* To church; Councilor Kraussold preaches on the connection between the Reformation and the present-day church movement, all of it excellent, but I noticed a peasant woman leaving the church in the middle of the sermon, and that told me everything! The hymns move me very much—how I enjoy singing with the congregation—and I recall the trials undergone amid these sounds by the Protestant community. — Many letters received (Father, Krockow, Marie Schleinitz, Math. Wesendonck, Claire, Judith Mendès—the last very despondent), invitation from Clemens to his wedding. I write to Frau v. Meyendorff, Marie Dönhoff, Marie Schleinitz, and pass on to the last R.'s suggestion of staging a new production of *Lohengrin* in Berlin, which he would conduct for the benefit of Bayreuth. In the evening our copyists—R. plays and sings to them from *Die Walküre*. They have not much that is edifying to say about the singers in the Munich *Tristan*. (The children write to their father.)

*Monday, November 4* In the morning R. says that he has again been thinking about the birth of drama from music: "As the baby is nourished in the womb by the mother's blood, so does drama emerge from music; it is a mystery; once it emerges into the world, the outward circumstances of life begin to exert their influence." Yesterday evening we once again came to the topic which is always preoccupying us— that of the Reformation, and also Gustavus Adolphus. I told R. that in my eyes he was a German. "Of course," says R., "he is just as much a German as Alexander the Great was a Greek." Today R. said: "I spend more and more time reflecting on what being a German means, and for me it is becoming a matter of pure metaphysics; Slavs and Celts are mixed in with us, and we have absorbed them; it is only the Roman Empire, the eunuch system, with which we have nothing to do. Grimm, it seems, did not take the Celtic character nearly seriously enough. I have been thinking about that; the bloody lance comes from a bardic mystery, Parzival is also Celtic, after all. Thus I am quite happy to liken the Germans to the Greeks in the way they handle legends. The Greek mysteries knew nothing of a World Creator, they worshiped the supremacy of Nature, because they feared it, and when Plato talks of a god, it is a misunderstanding of the Egyptian mystery— and yet God as a symbol of the mystery, of the inexplicable, that one can accept." — At lunch, as an instance of a spontaneous understanding, I told him that yesterday, as he was singing Siegmund's "*Waffenlos höhnt mich der Feind*," I found myself thinking: My God, where will he find a sword for his fight with Hunding? Will he perhaps pass by a smithy?! — This makes R. laugh, and he tells me that just on the previous day, while reading Hunding's threat to Siegmund in the copyists' room, he thought to himself: My God, have you not made a vital blunder there? Where is Siegmund to get his sword?! This makes us laugh a lot. — In the afternoon we go for a walk; first we walk, then inspect our house, and R. takes me up on the scaffolding; while

Prof. Nietzsche tells me that in Munich a Dr. Puschmann, lecturer at the university there, has just published a paper in which he proves psychiatrically that R. is mad. That such things are possible and are tolerated!)

*Monday, November 25* Karlsruhe in sunshine. R. jokes, "I too, have almost got to the point of acknowledging the French as superior beings, for truly the way our dear Germans behave gives one no pleasure; in the French there is still the last glimmering of that Greek culture which enlivened the Roman world." Marie Much. tells us things which make me see how difficult Bismarck's position still is; the native aristocracy hates him and the Upper Chamber affair is also alienating the Protestant aristocracy. He is and remains our greatest German. We have a table d'hôte lunch, and I sleep away almost the entire afternoon, since I am very tired. In the evening *Tannhäuser*; the tempi either dragged or hurried by good Herr Kalliwoda, the conductor; the production dating from Herr Devrient, ridiculous and impossible (the guests in the 2nd act perform a veritable *chasse* [?] *anglaise*, then in the 3rd act Elisabeth disappears into the forest, since Herr Devrient did not consider it plausible that she could climb the hill and return as a corpse in such a short time; she is discovered in the forest, and so all Wolfram's gazing after her and the idea of the evening star also disappear; this among other things). One good singer (Venus). R. tells me that he can no longer bear these theaters in which everything is so close—it all seems so crude. The curtain, also made with Herr Devrient's approval, matches the pyramid which actually stands in Karlsruhe; everything gray, colorless, and pretentious. — At home in the evening R. reproaches me for not making things easier for myself—he says that it pains him, for instance, to see me packing and unpacking by myself, etc.; and that he would rather I remain at home than do that. I never know what to reply to such statements.

*Tuesday, November 26* "Some people are never aware of their good fortune in having you, and that is why they torment you," R. exclaims to me today, and so everything is all right again. He has applied to the Grand Duke and has been granted an audience at 12 o'clock. He was received in the most cordial manner ("in the old style") in the Grand Duke's study, and there he put forward his request, which is that the Grand Duke support the Bayreuth undertaking, now that it is so far advanced. When he told the Grand Duke that he was the first German prince whom he had approached, the Duke thanked him and said he could well understand how difficult R. must find it to apply for help, and he was very grateful to him. R. made the company (the Grand Duchess was also there) laugh a lot when he said he was now traveling around like the Marquis in *Le Postillon de Longjumeau*. The

Grand Duke spoke of the complete transformation of taste that had taken place since the appearance of Wagner's works, and how the influence of these was still spreading. Finally they talked about a performance for the benefit of Bayreuth, and R. left with a very favorable impression of the Duke's cordiality and integrity, as also of his friendly modesty. We miss the one o'clock train and leave at half past two, traveling to Mainz via Mannheim, where the Heckels and Dr. Zeroni come to greet us. In Mainz we are met by Mathilde Maier. In place of the advertised *Fidelio*, the opera house is doing *Stradella*. We stay in our hotel and in the evening merely accompany our friend home, through the narrow and confusing little lanes.

*Wednesday, November 27*  Not a very good night, the trains pass close to our hotel, the walls of the fortress rise forbiddingly outside our window; we decide to move to Wiesbaden, from where I write to the children. Mathilde comes over and spends the afternoon with us. R. strayed into the casino and was almost on the point of playing, but could not bring himself to do so. He brings me a good Gustavus Adolphus almanac.

*Thursday, November 28*  We did not have a good night, rose late to see a man who had advertised his old wardrobes, etc., to us; a lot of nonsense—9,000 florins for a *soi-disant* Poussin. — R. visits his business associates and finds all the books in good order. At midday the military band of the 85th Regiment comes and plays for us; after the first two pieces (*Tannhäuser* and *Oberon*) R. gets up, sends the conductor off for a meal, and himself conducts the Prayer and Finale from *Lohengrin*. Then he drinks with all the people out of a large tankard. In the afternoon we take a little rest, then to the theater in Mainz after paying a visit to Mama Maier; *Fidelio* much better than we expected; afterward a banquet at the Mainz Wagner Society, with more military music and a choral group. We return to the hotel at about one o'clock, not overtired. Herr Schott comes into our box in the theater, is very friendly, and presides over the banquet. — Although R. finds the theater better than a few years ago, he confirms that there has been a decline in military music, and he was very indignant when he heard that in Prussia the conductor has the rank of sergeant and the players are increasingly badly paid. They also take all their tempi from the theater, dragging and hurrying. R. says, "There one sees where conservatoires can be useful—everything is influenced by the theater." — Of theater people who always address the audience directly, he recalls the anecdote about the Jew who asked: "Why does he tell me that? Why doesn't he tell my neighbor?"

*Friday, November 29*  Devoted entirely to rest—that is to say, Richard writes letters to the Grand Duke, to Düfflipp, Feustel, etc., but we remain undisturbed. At lunch our conversation leads us to dreams and apparitions; R. informs me of Daumer's views, I tell him that I do not like all these interpretations—I believe in apparitions, but their inexplicability tells me more than all explanations. Curiously enough, R. dreams virtually always about states of mind, rather than apparitions. He believes that, after his last bad dream, his first wife has now taken leave of him and he will no longer see her in his dreams. Mathilde arrives at about 6 o'clock and stays the night with us. R. goes for a walk, meets his two business associates, and in the evening brings them to the hotel; this is somewhat tiring. (Wrote to the children.)

*Saturday, November 30*  Departure from Wiesbaden, I leave regretting not having found time to visit the cathedral in Mainz. Poor Mathilde, cut off from us through her deafness, touches us very much. Lovely journey along the Rhine, lovely colors, a deep impression; R. sings my father's melody to the "Lorelei" and praises the vividness of his themes; we talk of him: "It is all interesting, even when it is insignificant," and he adds, laughing, "a canto whose bass line is difficult to write." We pass Nonnenwerth, where my father and sister once stayed; yesterday memories of Daniel took such a firm hold on me that I had to talk of him and his character to R., who knew him. "Euphorion," he says. Spoke a lot about Fidi, R. imitates his walk and takes pleasure in strange children in the corridor, since they remind him of ours. In Cologne around 6 o'clock. We are met by Herr Lesimple and Herr Ahn, the heads of the Wagner Society, and the tenor Diener. Letters of all kinds—notes from Marie Schl. concerning *Lohengrin*; announcement of the death of our good Lucca. Nice letter from an Italian in Bologna, who reports that at the third performance of *Tannhäuser* even the *italianissimi*, who had so hissed the first performance because they were upset by his letter to the mayor, had capitulated and applauded, even though the performance had not been very good. Good news of the children; and from New York the news that they have already collected 5,000 dollars. The W. Society here has a difficult territory—not only because Herr Hiller is powerful (says Herr Ahn), but also because he is an intriguer and, by undermining us, forestalls us in places where we might have been able to gain a little ground. We go to bed really tired. The Hotel Disch, in which we are staying, is the first we have liked—it is very comfortable and not at all modern.

*Sunday, December 1*  R. writes letters and I fetch him to come and look at pictures I have already discovered in the museum—the *Pipers and Drummers* of Dürer, splendid! "He was a complete Shakespeare," says R. — After that a visit to the cathedral—cold impression; it is the power of the Church which speaks in it, not devoutness of soul; how much do I prefer Strassburg Cathedral! The guides repulsively sugary—

we think of the Medusa we saw just before in the museum. "There," says R., "one has all the ideality of the world, a creature which was never seen and never existed, but which fills us with such dread." — A table d'hôte lunch, not very pleasant on account of the importunities of the people. Drove out to see the flora and the zoological gardens. In the evening *Die Zauberflöte*—appalling. Not a singer of talent, a stupid conductor, and the stamp of vulgarity on everything—here it is the opulent broker who sets the tone. When R. talks to people about this, they say the audience is such and such. "Don't talk to me about audiences," R. replies. "That is a world one does not criticize, but accepts just as it is; the fault lies entirely with the artists—they can seize an audience out purely for entertainment and raise it up. An audience does at least show a lively interest in everything; if a few people turn head over heels, it does at any rate laugh, which means it is better than these pygmies of conductors and producers, who don't know that, when the Queen of the Night appears, it must be night on the stage—one must put out the lights. Just as in church—when things are done properly, as they seldom are—a soul finds refuge from the petty pressures of its own miseries, is raised above them, and acknowledges the wretchedness of the world, so in the theater the audience is raised up by means of its desire to enjoy itself!" Various things are said about Herr Hiller, among others that he came running to Herr Lesimple after the first performance of *Tannhäuser* in Bologna and said, "Now T. has been hissed, too!" — R. says, "The curious thing about these people is that they want to play an important role before they have done anything, whereas first they should show what they can do, and then their influence would follow." — Letter to the children.

*Monday, December 2* In the Cologne museum; examined as much as I could; then the Church of Saint Gereon. R. is meanwhile writing letters, among others to Eckert, who is said to be offended that the *Tristan* score was refused him. R. then goes into a beerhouse, the landlord approaches and asks whether he does not recognize him—he was the landlord of the restaurant on the Rolandseck where 10 years ago a bank note for 100 florins, which R. had lost, was restored to him; he had written an account of it on this bank note, with which R. had then paid the bill, and an Englishman had offered him 200 florins for it. (The joke makes us laugh a lot, for we had recalled this little episode during our journey here; I had also been present.) — In the afternoon inspected the rare antiques of our landlord (Herr Disch); after that an audition, the singers whom we had not heard in the opera sing various things for R. (Diener, too). Not much to be gained here. R. talks about the miserable state of the theater; no tradition left, no example, the conductors straight from music schools, though an old and experienced

the masters, who take us around and offer us a second breakfast. Following that, a visit to the stock exchange, whose dignified air strikes R. as very different from the exchanges in which Jewish traders predominate. — Fine impression of the Town Hall chamber with its staircase. A table d'hôte lunch, at which R. is cheered. We had added this day in order to get a Wagner Society started, but I very much fear we have not succeeded. Herr Reinthaler, who has monopolized us here and at the same time—so it seems to me—isolated us, is "an opponent," as people express it, and his one worry is that on such an occasion he might be circumvented; he belongs to the clique of musical bigots. In the evening we are taken to the Rathauskeller restaurant, and a little circle gathers there, once again with the Reinthalers at its head. It leaves me with a very unpleasant impression, and I am foolhardy enough to say so to R., who immediately agrees; the only consolation is that there were some young people there who will presumably take up the idea—carefully evaded by the head people—of a W[agner] Society. — (Thought a lot about the children, *Freude schöner Götterfunken!*)

*Tuesday, December 10* R. had a very bad night, the oysters, the inexpert and slow service, but particularly my observations cause him nightmares; all the acts of disloyalty committed against him go through his mind. We leave around 11 o'clock; amicably escorted by the young people. At 7 o'clock in Magdeburg; after supper we go for a little walk. R. shows me the house and the hotel gable from which he once called down to *Rüpel*, his clever poodle, who had been missing for several days; the dog, who was walking down the street, looked around, suddenly saw him, and ran upstairs to him, there to remain. We are in the Stadt London, where the concert with Schröder-Devrient took place. The landlord has respected the incognito which R. enjoined on him by telegram. The reason for this was that the theater director Asché (*c'est tout dire!*) had cabled all sorts of ridiculous and impertinent things, and so R. resolved to stay here only until tomorrow morning and not to visit the theater at all. — On the Breiter Weg, the main street, we are moved by three poor women, gazing admiringly into an elegant clothes shop! — From the outside the theater is still as R. knew it; he tells me how, when he was conducting there, he felt himself in Heaven—in his sky-blue dress coat with its huge cuffs. He shows me the street in which Minna lived, with whom he "spent the whole day"; also the Stadt Braunschweig, where he had to pacify (settle with) his creditors!

*Wednesday, December 11* At last R. had a good night again, thanks to our quiet evening. We walk in the morning through the town, visit the beautiful cathedral, recalling the terrible events which drove the poor people to gather inside it. The tomb of Otto the Great sets us talking about the great emperors; R. summarizes the merit of the present one by saying he has enabled a great man to stay at his side and bring to fruition a great deed which could only be achieved through legitimate power. — At three o'clock arrival in Dessau; met by the conductor Thiele, who was R.'s predecessor in Magdeburg. At 6 o'clock to the theater, a very handsome and elegant auditorium. The manager, Herr von Normann, receives us very charmingly; the performance begins with the Prelude to *Die Msinger*, at the end of which the curtain rises to disclose a *tableau vivant*, "The Crowning of Hans Sachs"—it touches us deeply. Since part of his company is absent through illness, the ingenious manager seized on this expedient, and with it, achieved the finest of effects. However, it was the performance of *Orfeo* which revealed to us all the worth of this remarkable man; splendid the first act with the chorus, the second no less so, and, if there were a few mistakes in the Elysian fields, they did not prove at all disturbing. The first really artistic impression from our whole journey! We return home deeply affected by this unexpected discovery, amazed that more is not known about the intelligent management of this theater.

*Thursday, December 12* R. had a very bad night and feels so unwell that he asks the Duke for a postponement of his audience. He goes there at 12 o'clock. He had been invited to a meal, but refused the invitation, saying he was not seeking marks of honor, but wanted simply to lay his proposition in front of the Duke. He returns very charmed by the Duchess as well as the Duke, both earnest, sympathetic, encouraging. — We leave at 2 o'clock, after Herr von Normann showed me around the palace. In the evening in Leipzig, the whole family, Clemens with his young wife, Hermann, the rector of the university, Ottilie, and Anna. Very pleasant, but R. is tired.

*Friday, December 13* Lunch with the Brockhauses; good news of the children. In the evening a banquet at the Hôtel de Prusse. Richard speaks of the three generations he has experienced here in Leipzig: the first, the time of *Oberon*, pleasant and exciting; the second, at the time of his first return from exile, completely alien to him; the third now friendly toward him, making him feel at home in his birthplace. Several people reply, more or less well. We return home around midnight.

*Saturday, December 14* We visit Clemens in the *Johannisturm*! Afterward did some shopping; had lunch again with the Brockhauses, also present being the brother, Heinrich Brockhaus, who had insisted on a "reconciliation" with R. The deaf and blind man made a horrible impression on me, reminding me of the evil servant in Raimund's play —here, too, someone has unjustly taken possession of another's

# 1873

*Wednesday–Saturday, January 1–4* New Year activities; various things by mail, among them a folder of manuscripts from Prof. Nietzsche containing forewords to unwritten books. Otherwise nothing to give us pleasure; the people in Vienna more and more incomprehensible, nobody knows how much there is in the bank. We work out a plan for a concert in Berlin and a reading in Frau von Schleinitz's house before the assembled might of intellect and breeding. It is such a gloomy phase which we are now entering, as if everything were against us; one is literally set upon by ugly things, a newspaper is sent to us which reports that someone had asked for an album leaf, whereupon R. sent him two certificates of patronage, which he dutifully signed! No wonder that R. is utterly dispirited and ill. He has written to London asking if it would be possible to earn a large sum there—God knows! — In the evening we read Prof. N.'s forewords; we also read Aristophanes, bits from *The Birds*, which enchant us. On the 2nd, a conjurer, Herr Smith, came and enchanted us with his amazing dexterity. R. says, "A person like that is a wild character—in fact, a flawed rogue; something has held him back from becoming one, a certain fear, and now the urge finds expression in this way." — Prof. Nietzsche's manuscript also does not restore our spirits, there are now and again signs of a clumsy abruptness, however deep the underlying feelings. We wish he would confine himself principally to classical themes. (Wrote all kinds of letters to all corners of the earth.) Today (the 4th) Richter arrives, bringing good news of my father. (During these days R. continues work on his articles.) R. amused me very much with his description of a dispute with the dean, who is reading Hartmann's *Philosophy of the Unconscious* with much enjoyment; R. argued heatedly against a philosophy that gives pleasure, the dean against Schopenhauer, whom he has not read. The 7th volume of R.'s writings has been published. — Yesterday we went through *Le Nozze di Figaro* (last scene) and afterward read the same scene in Beaumarchais, and once again felt the transfiguring influence of the music. "In the play they are like beetles, struggling laboriously on the ground, in the opera they are butterflies playing in the air."

*Sunday, January 5*   Very fine weather—still no winter; I go for a walk with the children after having talked again with R. about the strangeness of these times in which everything is against us; our good Weitzmann wrote so fearfully about the projected Berlin concert that it became quite ridiculous; Dr. Pusinelli writes that Dresden is not worth bothering about, etc. Nevertheless, a cheerful lunch with Richter and the children (despite sorrowful talk of Bismarck's leaving the Prussian government; the greatest deeds can do nothing for the greatest of men: Bismarck has created Germany, R. a German theater, and both have to keep starting again from the beginning). — R. visits our house with Richter and is very pleased with it. I write to A. Frommann, from whom I received an excellent letter (she says of the Grand Duchess, "She saves, and she is in a bad mood"—this as an occupation!). — The copyists come in the evening (without Herr Kastner, who has fulfilled all our worst misgivings), and Richter, who tells us all sorts of unpleasant things about Hans: his unbounded rudeness, etc.; that makes me very sad. Thank goodness, R. goes through parts of Act III of *Götterdämmerung*, then *Tristan*, and finally the *Idyll*, which charms us all. "Yes," says R., "that was our poetic period, the dawn of our life, now we are in the full glare of the midday sun, my dear wife, and climbing the mountain." The memory moves me to tears, but much more the work itself. Alas, what gifts have here been deposited in an earthly frame, how well I understand what he must suffer when life eternally keeps him from pouring out these gifts! He must be in a continual state of convulsion, like a poor bird kept from flying!

*Monday, January 6*   In the night thought much again about the nature of art, in consequence of Prof. N.'s forewords; R. dreamed that King Ludwig II had been shot dead, he tried to find me in order to tell me, could not find me, was bitten by an angry dog, comforted himself with the thought that it was Louis-Philippe who had been shot, since he had often enough been the target, then woke up, still not entirely well. (I note that the Lerchenfelds have not returned our New Year's greetings—probably on instructions from higher up.) Loldi today went to school for the first time! — (Yesterday evening R. read us the rules of the mastersingers' art as laid down in Wagenseil's book—remarkable how R. extracted all the essence for his own work, leaving out the peculiarities and using only what was most characteristic.) He said, "The names must all be genuine, invented ones are valueless." — Around noon drove with R. and Richter to the building site; indescribable impression! It is like a path to the underworld, or the foundations of an Egyptian temple! And then the charming, peaceful surroundings. — Lunch with Richter, in the evening with the Feustels, very

of which is that the performance is put off for a year. — I write to Marie M., in order to explain to her that W.'s true friends must stop urging him to conduct concerts. — In the afternoon and evening Brandt and Brückwald—a rather difficult occasion, and R. is kind enough to admire the courage with which I, *à tort et à travers*, guide the conversation and keep it going.

*Sunday, March 9* R. had a better night; he then gets up early and is amused to find me reading his "Letter to Berlioz" in bed. Our conversation leads us to reflect what a pity it is that no businessman ever came along with sufficient vision to pay R. an advance on the certain appreciation in value of *Rienzi, Holländer, Tannhäuser,* and *Lohengrin,* and then to recover his advance, leaving R. in possession of his works, which so far have only cost him money. R. feels that businessmen are too demoralized; Goethe had Cotta, Schiller Göschen, the second half of the 18th century had made great advances, but with the Restoration in the post-Napoleonic era things had gone from bad to worse; E. Devrient's Goethe celebrations were a scar over the wounds, the Schiller celebrations arranged throughout the world by Jews— appalling! — We talk about French expressions in the German language, and R. says they are essential for purposes of irony, just as in philosophy such words as "immanent" are essential—only a deep religious faith would be of any use in this connection, such as existed among the Indians, who could play with the most awesome things, since they were firm articles of belief. — About the Holy Roman Empire—how everything lay in its name. — President Grant's speech, placing his trust in a language and a state, thus virtually letting art be buried! . . . R. wanted to work on his essay, but was disturbed by a visit from Feustel with a *patron* from Augsburg, which vexed him a great deal. — Family lunch. (I write to Clemens and to Marie Schleinitz.) Silly, nonsensical letters. The Quatuor Society in Milan wants R. for a concert, the Court brewery in Berlin wants a composition from him for the opening of their concert hall, the Society of Fine Art in London sends poems, but with regard to things it would be important for us to know, silence reigns everywhere: Löser, Dannreuther, the people in Vienna. Mme Lucca has now resigned herself to the fact that we are not going to Milan and has withdrawn *Lohengrin.* — R. has a bad foot, we go for a walk together in the palace gardens, a feeling of spring (in the morning we heard finches). R. preoccupied with his undertaking, constantly thinking of it. Schott writes that he wishes to exhibit the score of *Das Rheingold* in Vienna, R. writes on it an inscription: "Started in reliance on the emergence of a German spirit and completed to the glory of his noble benefactor, King Ludwig of Bavaria." — In the evening we work on the biography. I remark jokingly to R. what capital we are bequeathing to Fidi: he will receive the house (the decorations of which are keeping us much occupied at the moment), then until 30 years after our death our royalties, and at the end of these 30 years he can publish the biography. "And then," says R., "he can compose *Parcival.*" I shake my head, and R. continues: "Yes, who can lay such things down? He must cut himself off from us entirely—if not to the same degree, nevertheless in the same way that I cut myself off from my family. Impressions will influence him, naturally—if I had not received my impressions from Weber and the symphonies of Beethoven, God knows what would have become of me. But he must develop in his own way, which we cannot foresee, and then he may amount to something." —

*Monday, March 10* R. drank some yarrow tea late in the evening on our doctor's advice and it helped him gain a good night's sleep. He plays passages from the 3rd act of *Lohengrin* as he puts on his clothes; how very preoccupied he always is when he is dressing, how high-spirited—indeed how productive! — He says he has a good mind to tell his joke in public (that it was his misfortune that Napoleon had not won, for then Napoleon would have become Germany's ruler, would have familiarized himself with German things at once and have built R.'s theater for him). The Duke of Dessau has taken up two certificates of patronage. R. finishes his essay on the 9th Symphony. — In the afternoon we go for a walk together, to the Feustels', then visit our house, concern about its dampness; thoughts of Fidi—if there is no fortune for him, he can shut off the bottom story and live very comfortably above it. I hope he will cherish this property which keeps his father so busy in his behalf! — In the evening the biography; oh, all these meaningless trials! No amount of love and care, I feel, can ever make up for them! I tell R. this in my own way, whereupon he replies jokingly: "You are not content when people are everything to each other—they have to keep on saying it!"

*Tuesday, March 11* R. had another bad night and is run down, but all the same our conversation at breakfast is cheerful, even lofty; he again touches on the 7th (A Major) Symphony and says: "It is quite wonderful how, due to their separation in time, the same original thought has appeared under two different guises. For me this work is a complete portrait of a Dionysian festival. One won't, of course, think of that when one hears it, but if an imaginative composer had wanted to portray it, he could not have done it except in this way. At the start the herald and the tibia players, then the gathering people (the scale), after that the charming theme, whose swinging movement gives the idea of a procession, and so on. The Andante is the tragedy, the sacrifice of the god, memories of Zagreus, 'you, too, have suffered,' then the rustic celebrations, the vinegrowers and other country people with their thyrsi, and to end with, the bacchanale. But the music is, of course, very much more idealistic than any of that, and it would be silly to draw up a program; the picture emerges only in meditation and memory, and even in retrospect it remains utterly idealistic—it is not like a festival in which one is actually taking part." — When I talk about the perfection of these symphonies as a whole, R. says, "Yes, the other great masters were still in the grip of convention; the jesuitical style, which set its seal on architecture, also gave rise to the sonata form, and Mozart was too easygoing to break fully with convention." R. gives me the conclusion of his wonderful essay to read; talking to me about it, he says, "I have the right to suggest certain alterations in places where even the best of performances cannot adequately bring out the melodic content, for in all else I insist throughout on correctness of execution and tell people that, if they understand and play only the nuances as indicated by Beethoven, they will find themselves on the right path." Since he had left me, I sent him back the manuscript with a message that *it was splendid*; he tells me that the child said it beautifully. — But we are not allowed to spend too long on this delightful exchange of thoughts: Herr Am Rhyn is demanding more and more, supported by all the other rogues—and from Vienna the Academic Society reports that it will not be able to guarantee the sum (10,000) which R. asked for! . . . — Yesterday we spoke of the stimulus the Schlegel brothers had given to Indian studies, and I asked R. whether the French and the English had not been before them in that. "Without a doubt," he says. "They had possessions there, and in any case we can never pride ourselves on being ahead in anything; the honor of taking the initiative we must leave to the Latin peoples, but then one must look at what the Germans make of it all. They had no possessions which made it advisable for them to study, but it was they who discovered the basic relationship with their language and their spirit—and that no other nation succeeded in doing." When he was speaking about Beethoven and some of the nuances which would have to be altered in performance, since Beethoven had been unable to hear them, I asked how it was with Weber. "Oh," says R., "he was extremely careful, he had, I should say, a romantic acuteness." — R. goes for a walk, returns home in the evening very tired; during the afternoon I had begun the *Vikramorvasi*, and in the evening I read parts of it to him; but he begins to feel weary, although the wonderful work impresses him, and goes to bed early. From Cologne Herr Lesimple writes to say they would be unable to bear the costs of the concert, but net receipts of 5,000 thalers could be expected.

*Wednesday, March 12* R. had a very wretched night—for which the infamies in Lucerne are to blame; another conference with Hoffmann, the clerk, as to whether we can expect to be taken to court here. Family lunch, after which Fidi put to bed, very unwell; the doctor is called and ascribes it to slight indigestion. Around midnight I visit the nursery once more and find them all sleeping peacefully. We begin with great enjoyment the Indian drama *Mālavikāgnimitra.*

*Thursday, March 13* R. had a good night, thanks be to God! But Fidi is ill, a warm forehead and fast pulse. R. sorts through his books and shows me among other things *Maximilian's Prayer Book* by Dürer; I remark that I had once brought it to him in Munich to show him and left it there, he declares that he never even looked at it: "At that time I was angry with everything that was supposed to take my mind off the one and only thing, and I didn't want to have anything to do with it." — Now he looks at it, and with very great delight: "Dürer and then Bach and Beethoven—those are our German characters." R. suddenly asks himself how Bach would have listened to such a good symphony. I suggest: With the feeling that he could have done it himself. R. says he understands very well what I mean, "for convention in Bach's time was somewhat different from that in Mozart's. For Bach it was religion, ritual; raising himself up to this form out of four-part music was to create a whole new world." Gladness over Lulu's and Boni's health, sorrow over Fidi's. Great melancholy over a poor, handsome, and good-hearted bookbinder's assistant who will probably die on account of having made a journey home on foot, because of poverty, thereby bringing on pneumonia. R. is reminded of Pohl, his poor, faithful dog in Munich, who died on account of an overlong journey! R. at the Thursday gathering, in Councilor Kraussold's house opposite; I alone, writing, Lulu practicing the piano, all asleep, Fidi, too—melancholy thoughts, but great peace, all desires stilled, not really a single wish remaining; gratitude, a feeling of utter gratitude! . . .

Yesterday I asked R. whether he thought the *Vikramorvasi* would be good adapted as an opera text and set to music. "No," he says, "it would have to be done for a Court of a kind we no longer possess." In the *Mālavikāgnimitra* we are fascinated by the descriptions of Court etiquette. "Everything which we nowadays claim to be original is reflected here, but how stiff and crude Louis XIV seems in comparison!" When I express my surprise at the freedom of the women, R. says, "Wherever there is a Court such a relationship will be found, and this is as it should be—only in the French does one find it repugnant."

*Friday, March 14* R. arrived home yesterday toward midnight and laughed to find me deep in the work of Palla[dio] [*name not clear in original*], which was giving me great pleasure. He was not dissatisfied with the discussions, but the tobacco fumes and the beer had given

Seligsberg, and then play through Hagen's part as copied by Herr Zumpe. Great consternation over its difficulties! — In the morning R. sang a pretty theme by Auber; when I observed how French it was and remarked that the Germans should not try to imitate such things, for they could not succeed, R. says, "Yes, not even a German Jew— Meyerbeer is clumsy in comparison." Auber's being a musician is proof that music is the art of today—in another period he would perhaps have been a wood carver.

*Thursday, March 20*   We have a poor live capon, kept in captivity, and every night it mournfully heralds the arrival of day; it wakes me, and its sad tones speak to me of the misery of life. Whoever in youth could understand such tones—how could he forbear turning his back on life and seeking salvation in resignation and atonement? — Herr Strauss's *The Old and New Faith* has reached its fifth edition—in a single year, I believe. "What does he mean by *new faith?*" says R. "Where does he get that word, for he certainly does not mean by it respect for the incomprehensibility of great men." — Letter from my father. Loldi in bed on account of a small abscess. R. busy on the part of Hagen. We go out together, tell the mayor about our concern for the [bookbinder's] assistant; terrible state of the district of Nordhalben—wretched condition of the people everywhere; strikes! A man says to me: "I have enough for myself and I spend it in the Sonne. The community takes care of my family." The laws are made by journalists and lawyers, it all looks humanitarian, but it is barbarous. The people sink lower and lower, the churches empty in favor of the taverns. The land, sucked dry by its previous rulers, is left by their successors in the condition to which their predecessors brought it! — The motto at breakfast this morning was [Mephisto's] "My pathos would cause thee laughter, hadst thou not forgotten how to laugh." R. finds the treatment of God absolutely unique, and he says, "*Faust* ought to be regarded as the new Bible, everybody should know all its verses by heart." The Thursday gathering in our house this evening; I stay upstairs and write to Malwida Meysenbug regarding her move here. R. is not dissatisfied with the conversation with his friends; they discussed Strauss's book. (At the antiquarian's I bought an old glass painting which I find pretty. Sent off the two pictures of my father and R. to Lenbach for the World's Fair.)

*Friday, March 21*   The Lucerne Am Rhyn affair not too upsetting, after all. I spent the morning downstairs with the children, since Loldi has to stay in bed. R. prepares his 9th volume. During lunch a telegram comes from Mme Lucca, saying that *Lohengrin* has triumphed against great opposition in Milan and the second performance will take place tomorrow. — Went out with R., we separate, he goes to Herr Feustel's, and learns that many certificates of patronage have been ordered from Mainz, where a large movement is beginning to emerge! . . . — In the evening chance puts some essays by Carlyle about Goethe and Schiller into our hands, and we are edified to read his fine words of praise for Goethe, uttered on the very eve of his death. Carlyle's words on how little one really knows about great men and in what a shadowy guise they appear to posterity make me think of these diaries, in which I want to convey the essence of R. to my children with all possible clarity, and in consequence try to set down every word he speaks, even about myself, forgetting all modesty, so that the picture is kept intact for them—yet I feel the attempt is failing: how can I convey the sound of his voice, the intonations, his movements, and the expression in his eyes? But perhaps it is better than nothing, and so I shall continue with my bungling efforts. I am much moved by the praise for Goethe, which also fits R. like a glove—the genuineness, the truth, the courage, the kindness, the prophetic powers. R. likes Carlyle, he says that despite his many banalities and completely unphilosophic mind one recognizes in him a man of original ideas with a feeling for the genuine and the great. (He thinks for a moment of sending Carlyle his *Beethoven*.) In his analysis of the soul Strauss shows complete ignorance of the basic conceptions of philosophy. Strauss probably an Israelite.

*Saturday, March 22*   First day of spring, Goethe's dying day; he came into the world at noon on a hot August day and left it on the threshold of spring; fire and mildness! I reflect how R.'s nature consists, like his works, of a mixture of great strength and delicacy; his mouth, ears, skin are as fine and delicate as a woman's, his bone structure sturdy, even gnarled. — We greet each other very cheerfully at breakfast; Herr Zumpe, the copyist, had told me of a text in which cardinals silently light candles to one another, and we are still amused by it today. — "Oh, how I should like to write poetry, to start on a poem and to close my eyes and ears to the world!" I ask him whether he does not feel inclined to work on his score, but he is fearful of being interrupted. Fidi pleases me; yesterday he recognized the parade ground and said, "It's always muddy there, because of all the soldiers trampling." At lunch R. thinks of his song *"Dors, mon enfant,"* he laughs and says, "You can see I didn't know then what it was to have a child, it was something like that, too, with Tristan and his Isolde. No, once the thing is already there, the work of art turns out more realistic, like the '*Schlafe, Kindchen, schlafe*' in the *Idyll*." In the afternoon a walk with R., to Herr Gross, Feustel's gaffe in asking the Duke of Coburg for letters of recommendation to England. In the evening dictation, but it now unfortunately puts a strain on R. Talked about Fidi; R. says, "I should like quite deliberately to put him out of the reach of my influence, so that he is free of me, as Siegfried was of Wotan—he might even stand up to me as an opponent!" (The Emperor's birthday celebrated with toasts and cheers.)

*Sunday, March 23* Today we are celebrating Boni's birthday. Hans has sent her a book; Frau Ritter wrote that he had stayed a while in Würzburg, tired from his many journeys; he is going to Karlsruhe to give three concerts for Bayreuth under the sponsorship of the Grand Duke, then to London. Fritzsch announces in his periodical the start of a new literary supplement, which R. finds very remarkable, the first indication that his ideas might be realized! — Also the fact that among other things Herr Tappert castigates journalists for the way they mishandle the German language pleases R.—he sees it as at least a small shadow cast by him. — R. glances at Shakespeare's *Macbeth* and is greatly affected by the very first line he reads: Macbeth's aside when the first confirmation (that he is Thane of Cawdor) comes, and they end, "And nothing is but what is not." "Those are the naked words of feeling which arise in such a breast; the poet grasps the feeling and then finds the words for it, which are consequently right and natural, even when a person does not himself find any." Schiller's translation shows that he did not grasp the feeling. — I asked R. whether the news of Goethe's death had not shattered him in his youth; he says that his uncle had been very upset by it, but he himself had not really known very much about Goethe—or, to put it more accurately, [thought] he had fallen among the scribblers! Schiller, he says, did a tremendous amount to spoil Goethe for him with *Die Räuber, Fiesco, Kabale und Liebe* —he had found *Elective Affinities* boring, and regarded the popular scenes in *Egmont* as mere imitations of Shakespeare. That is how one is in one's youth. All sorts of letters—from London one which makes us decide not to go there, despite the theatrical organization which wants to arrange everything according to R.'s ideas! — Splendid spring weather, I go for a walk with R.; up to the theater, slow work, strange thoughts! "Not a plank in it," says R., "which national feeling has brought me, only personal sympathy, and a kind of blackmail arising from this." — In the evening, dictation—this time happily, in cheerful spirits.

*Monday, March 24* Still lovely weather, but Evchen put to bed; a sore throat. R. arranges his ninth volume. In the supplement to the *Conversations-Lexikon* there is an entry under his name to the effect that, after R.'s friends had sought in vain to secure for him the post of musical director in Berlin (Joachim's Hochschule had stood in the way!) and his stay in Berlin had consequently proved unsuccessful, he threw himself into Bayreuth with redoubled energy. Should such lies be allowed to go unchallenged for all time?? — "Proudest lady, joy to you, your Richard writes his works for you!" was today the motto (sung to Marschner's "Proud England") for our breakfast hour which, now that R. is having good nights, is always friendly and cheerful. Made the decision not to go to London. A walk with the children in splendid weather. In the evening dictation. — At a very late hour R. sang the first theme of one of Beethoven's last quartets: "What is the most exalted of words compared with that?" When the melody sounds, he says, it is as if the blotting paper is at last removed and the true picture emerges before one's eyes.

*Tuesday, March 25*  Evchen still unwell, but happily there is no danger. . . . Richard talks to me about the article on Bayreuth which he is writing for the 9th volume and in which he speaks of Tausig. Thoughts of his death and of Schnorr's, in the same month, almost (I believe) on the same day, and both at a time in which they were most vital to R.'s cause, when relationships should have been growing closer: "One asks oneself what Fate was trying to tell one—it was all quite in the natural order of things, and yet it seemed like a demonic hint!" — Fine all day, we go to the building site. In the evening dictation—still dreary Paris. R.'s dreams are very curious: he, who has no tendency toward—indeed, no understanding of—personal vanity, had nothing but vain visions!

*Wednesday, March 26*  R. says that his article will be quite different from that originally envisaged: "The limits I set myself in creating something always melt away, and I get into a sort of frenzy of inspiration, from which everything I achieve then emerges." Jokes about my incorrigible datives and accusatives—"though you know the language like a beggar knows his pockets." — Yesterday he drafted his reply to the article in the *Conversations-Lexikon*; though I well know how despicable the attitude of these highly learned gentlemen is toward R., I am still utterly shocked by the malice and perfidiousness of this article. — When I ask R. how far Baron Erlanger's sympathy for him went, he says, "Up to the point where I had no further chance; in such cases one is like the bird who became arthritic and was pecked to death by his loving mate." — At lunch he reads me his essay on Bayreuth, which moves me to tears. — Feustel has reported that the performance in Munich brought in 550 florins and one certificate of patronage!! — In the evening, with R. and the two eldest children to an amateur performance in the beautiful opera house. The performance not at all bad, the most dreadful thing about it being the entr'acte music. Also the clothes, and particularly the hair styles of the women annoy R.; he says he cannot understand how a man can embrace such a woman, how he can help feeling disgusted. — The printed letter has arrived, accompanied by an impertinent note from the editorial staff of the *N.A.Z.*

*Wednesday, April 16* Schott inquires about the score of *Götter-dämmerung*, R. replies, saying why he cannot send it. Discussions back and forth about a concert in Mainz!! — In the afternoon drove to the Riedelsberg with the children. Before that a statement from Berlin (royalties), from which we see that during the most profitable season, when he also had the singers for it, Herr v. Hülsen gave hardly any performances of R.'s works, in order to make us atone for the *Lohengrin* project! — Great tiredness in the evening. — Our main joy at the moment is the library; today R. read the story of Hamlet in Saxo Grammaticus; we really had to laugh over the Latin rhetoric in which Hamlet indulges during his speeches. Some remarkable features, but still more remarkable what Shakespeare preserved and what he cast aside.

*Thursday, April 17* Sultry heat; all sorts of things to be seen to before our departure; my arrangements for R.'s birthday give me a lot to think about, and I fear nothing will come of them. R. visits the house and gives his orders. In the evening resumed work on the biography, much to my joy. — Our conversation over coffee was about Cromwell, and I remarked to R. how stupidly and injudiciously we are taught in our childhood—for example, to hate this great man. R. describes as the most remarkable thing about him his high opinion of the advantage of birth, against which he could see no weapon except religious fanaticism. — When R. goes off for his afternoon rest he laughs at the way we once again got immersed in lively discussion. "We are a pair of enthusiasts," he jokes.

*Friday, April 18* Fidi helps his papa arrange books, hands him Creuzer's *Symbolik*! The musicians' convention in Leipzig is holding up work on the new pamphlet, and R. is very vexed about it. Sultry air and finally a great thunderstorm, very unusual for Bayreuth at this time of year; everything is in bud, and were it not for the preparations for our journey, one could be merry! In the evening the biography—"a useless waste of energy," R. exclaims as he completes the Paris period. —

*Saturday, April 19* Preparations for the journey. Worry about the children, which R. understands and shares, a deep, everlasting worry! . . . In the morning conversation about the Germans and the French, there is talk of civil war breaking out among our neighbors. "If only we could reach the point of no longer looking to them for our ideas!" R. says. "How low they have sunk one can see by the fact that they imagine they can get things done by maxims based on reason. As if anything ever comes of reason! If men were reasonable, they would not live or congregate together in bad regions, leaving the finest lands uninhabited. The emigrations, the evil behavior which this seems to cause among the people concerned, show that morality is closely interwoven with established customs, from the cradle to the grave. A great statesman is one who recognizes the prevailing influence of unreason and guides it as best he can without the use of maxims. But only religion and art can educate a nation—what use is science, which analyzes everything and explains nothing?" — He quotes to me some of Jean Paul's titles, and when I say I find these very mannered and affected, he says, "Yes, and yet he had some original ideas, such as death after death, but was unable to express them in any other form than the one which looks affected to us." — The Pope is dangerously ill. — Letters from Cologne, no very good news from there, and we consider whether under the circumstances we should not give up our journey there. We ask to be informed by telegram in Würzburg. In the evening dictation, despite the mood of vexation (conclusion of the 3rd volume).

*Sunday, April 20*　Took leave of the children, who are well, thank goodness! Also of the mayor, and R. tells him not to expect too much. R. tells me how embarrassing he finds this play acting for the sake of keeping up people's spirits, etc. He feels happy only in an atmosphere of complete truth. Pleasure in the scenery, the widening of the river Main. In Würzburg at 5 o'clock, once again at the Kronprinz; I have some trouble in talking to the Ritters about the birthday, since R. does not leave me alone. A pleasant sort of trouble! . . . Lovely walk in the splendid palace gardens, in the evening at the Ritters'; he relates a remarkable story: he sent a petition to the King urging the reform of the music school in Würzburg, his plan is adopted, but the position given through Lachner's agency to one of the chief musical bigots, Herr Kirchner! Thus it is everywhere. Telegram from Cologne, revealing nothing.

*Monday, April 21*　Birds twittering in the early hours, then military music and artillery, less enjoyable. Very cordial parting from the Ritters; I hope they will come to Bayreuth; I feel the need to preserve R.'s relationship with all the people to whom he was once close, so that he can find compensation for the sad instability of his previous outward life in the continuity of his inner relationships. Lovely journey from the valley of the Main, "the cradle of German civilization," to the valley of the Rhine, "that fanatic expression of Nature." "But the best of all," says R., "is that we are journeying through it together; they are insignificant excursions, but what help would it be to us to travel through the length and breadth of Berlin, for example?" I tell him I wish to get to know every little corner of our Franconia and to awake in our children a love and interest for what is close to them and belongs to them, instead of allowing their gaze to stray to distant

strength of the 100,000 already in hand. In the evening looked through catalogues.

*Wednesday, May 14* R. still not well, today cannot even work; I write on his behalf to Marquise Pepoli-Hohenzollern, who is looking for unpublished compositions for an Italian charity concert. I am having many difficulties with my secrecy, have to call the Thursday gathering for today, so that I can secretly go to the rehearsal. R. suspects nothing so far—how dearly I wish to give him a little pleasure! Sascha Ritter arrived today—he also here in secret. — In the evening, while the meeting was going on, went to the rehearsal—it will be all right! . . . The discussion at the meeting chiefly concerned the financial crisis, which seems to be very substantial; Vienna is said to be bankrupt, nobody can make do; this the result of copying Paris.

*Thursday, May 15* R. tells me in the morning that he dreamed we were together in Berlin and a friend visited him; after I had left the room he asked this friend, "Well, what do you think of my wife?" "Oh," he replied, "I had thought she would be very domestic in outlook, but now I see that everything in her comes from a completely different direction!" On that R. woke up with tears in his eyes. He then dreamed he had received 600 francs in gold; when he got up he discovered that Fritzsch had actually sent him nearly this sum. After breakfast he settles down to his morning reading and soon comes to me, laughing loudly, and reads me Holtzmann's quotation about *Villemarqué*—again magnificently French! — Great delight in the blackbirds in the trees in front of our windows! — R. goes out and returns in high spirits—the palace gardener has been ordered to construct our gate! Happy enjoyment of this victory! The house! Valuable now because we have a son, otherwise pointless. — "Often I really have the feeling that I am being borne along and sustained by the fairies." (Meanwhile I hold a theater conference.) — Unfortunately our high spirits are much damped by a letter from Herr Fürstner in Berlin. He intends to publish *Tannhäuser* in French and German, and what is the point of this affront, except to bypass R. by buying the new scenes from Flaxland? So from one Jew to another! Yet he feels no shame in telling R. of it! In the evening we read some excellent articles, *The Semitic and the German Races in the New German Empire*, which a Herr *Beta* has sent to R., requesting permission to dedicate them to him.

*Friday, May 16* The wretchedness of Herr Fürstner gives R. no rest, he writes to him early in the morning. We have to laugh, because I, too, was already sitting pen in hand early in the morning. (I wrote to Brandt about *tableaux vivants*.) — The children come up; R. says, looking at Fidi, "He will turn out better than I, but that will be counterbalanced by the fact that he will not have such a wife as mine—though

I hope not the 30 years of my first marriage, either!" . . . He remembered yesterday evening that it was 10 years since he had settled in Vienna—all these attempts, leading to nothing. — In the morning, in splendid weather, to a very disagreeable rehearsal of the *tableaux vivants*. When I return home, R. is in a very bad humor: a Herr Fiege has written concerning a reviewer named Wuerst in Berlin. On the occasion of Diener's singing Lohengrin this reviewer said: From this one could see how much the performance would be worth, since Diener was Wagner's chosen singer. Herr Wuerst goes on to warn his readers against Wagner's falsification of Beethoven; he says that in one passage Wagner talks of the horns ceasing to play, when in fact they continue to play. Now, R. had meant by that—and Herr W. well knows it—that the horns cease playing the main role, and the trumpets have to dominate. What wretchedness! And because of it a whole, splendid morning's work is lost! . . . In the afternoon I go with R. to the new house. I leave him in order to visit the Ritters and am scolded by him, at half past seven in the evening, for coming home so late and deserting him to go for a walk by myself. We finish reading the very interesting articles, but immersing oneself in such a subject is really unsavory.

*Saturday, May 17* R. is still finding great pleasure in the Holtzmann book; "the Breton fraud, once uncovered, restores the bards to us," and after Holtzmann has explained the *Bar* in Barditus, R. explains the *ditus*, which means *diut*, the people—thus the verse people. He also writes to the man in Berlin, advising him to dedicate his work to Prince Bismarck through the agency of Bucher. He notices from my involuntary start that this advice does not please me, and thinks it is because he has mentioned my name in connection with it without asking me first, whereas it was in fact only the feeling—which I always have regarding virtually all people—of wishing to make no demands of even the most trivial kind that came over me. This misunderstanding causes me much sorrow! . . . In the afternoon I go to meet R. on the assumption that he had gone to the Riedelsberg (Feustel), meanwhile he has gone to the palace gardens, where he waits for me! Astonishment and reproaches. — We read the metaphysical discussion in *Ardinghello* and find this much-disparaged book very full of good sense. Renewed discussion of the morning *contretemps*, to which R. links angry remarks concerning the impending journey to Weimar—grief! I ask myself what I must do to convince him that everything he considers right is agreeable to me, even if now and again my first reaction is one of surprise.

*Sunday, May 18* R. is concerned about what happened yesterday, says he feels stunned, he is not worthy of me, I am too good, and other such melancholy things. Choir rehearsal, I tell the ladies and gentlemen

he calls me Melusina. — Nothing from Fritzsch, nothing from my father or those around him, nothing from Marie Schl., either—very strange. Instead, all sorts of uninteresting things. Great heat again, and with it the Schotts, whom we shall now have to entertain in the evening! Feeling of unreality. R. unfortunately not well; the house causes much vexation and the theater building much worry, and on top of it the Office of the Royal Household is being tiresome about the gate— self-importance and malice . . . .

*Wednesday, June 11* Kept to the early working hour. R. feels very unwell, the thundery heat is back again. With the children to the theater and then to the Bürgerreuth, charming view, the countryside pleases us more and more—may it provide a friendly home for the children! I feel as if I am no longer really living, but just dreaming, so lacking in desires am I on my own behalf, and when I hear R. wishing for a carriage and horses I am glad that he is so young and full of strength—but I endeavor to insure that my great tiredness does not tempt me to let things drift. — R. works on his score, but he is not well.

*Thursday, June 12* R. still working, though he is not well. The doctor insists on his drinking Ems mineral water, and this seems only to make him more excitable. There are in any case too many worries: the estimate for the house grows ever larger, the children need more and more things, but our income does not increase. Luckily our thoughts are not always of this kind, and they fly heavenward. With the children a lot; in the evening went through *Rheingold*, great delight.

*Friday, June 13* Melusina still! At the same time, worry that my children may be led astray by our style of living into imagining themselves to be rich and taking insufficient care of their belongings. — The King of Bavaria has again appalled everyone with a cabinet order commanding the military to line the route for the Corpus Christi procession, thus countermanding General von der Tann's order forbidding it! Hopeless! — Letter from Frau von Mey[endorff], saying that Hans is now in Weimar with my father. — Nice afternoon in the garden; Fidi, gardening, reminds R. of a book, *Christ the Essene*, which he once read in Thun and which, in spite of its rationalistic tone, he found very moving—the meeting of Christ the gardener with Magdalene. — R. wants a life-size picture of Fidi as he now is. — In the morning R. talked to me about his poem dedicating *Tannhäuser* to the Grand Duke of Weimar. It runs something like this: in medieval times priests and monks despised life, and knights rescued it through their poetry, the outward symbol of this was the Wartburg; now the Wartburg, once again under a magnanimous prince, will rescue art from mercantilism. — The dedication—submitted through my father—has been refused. In the evening went through *Rheingold*. — The letter on actors has at last appeared in Herr Gettke's almanac.

*Saturday, June 14* Reconciliation at last with my child, and the hope that she has learned her lesson. — Wrote some letters (Klara), spent much time with the children. A cloudburst, Bayreuth flooded. Letter from Marie Schl.: the Khedive has taken 11 certificates of patronage. In the evening conclusion of *Rheingold*. Departure of Sascha R[itter] and young Kummer. [*Ten lines describing an untranslatable conversational misunderstanding omitted.*]

*Sunday, June 15* R. has the idea of asking Herr Wesendonck to advance the second 100,000 thalers. Thoughts of including Herr Riederer and Herr Erlanger as well—constant brooding. Herr Voltz arrives but brings no particular news. A short walk (with the children). In the evening pleasure in being once more by ourselves, we continue *Ardinghello* with great interest, and R. keeps recalling the effect this book had on him and the influence it had on his conception of *The Artwork of the Future*. (In the morning R. worked on his score.)

*Monday, June 16* Violent downpours, Fidi has caught cold, is coughing; besides that, bad news of our poor little Putz—with every new creature arises a new wellspring of torment. We send the veterinary surgeon to Weidenberg and hope for an improvement. — I did not sleep well, worries about the children beset me. R. is somewhat better, works on his score. He is pleased with Fritzsch's literary periodical, which contains a very good description of the Young Germany movement and the relationship between the literature it produced and true poetry. R. talks about foreign words and the whole idea of literature and says, "What we cannot express in our own language has no value for us." He shows me J. Grimm's *Ancient Germanic Law*, which he has now received and which he is glad to possess. When I expatiate on the excellence of a person like J. G., who has so much feeling for the German identity, R. says he feels downright offended by the way Grimm is nowadays taken to task, just because of a few weaknesses he showed (as, for example, regarding the Celts). — Terrible news of the death by drowning of a child who went to school here, the only child of a man in Hof. Oh, God, all these ways of bringing about misery! Herr Kietz is here again, to make a bust of R. In the evening we take up *Ardinghello* again, and I have to ask R. to stop reading, so angered and vexed am I by certain descriptions which I cannot consider to be Greek but, rather, French.

*Tuesday, June 17* At last fine weather again. At breakfast we come to the subject of *Ardinghello* and R. tells me splendid things about the Greeks and the sculptors; he ends his talk by calling Saint Cecilia the liberator. I go for a walk with the children; as I return home, R. calls (drafting letters, giving up the celebration, etc.). In the morning a visit to Makart's *Abundantia*, which is being exhibited here and which truly delights me; pleasure that a German is now so original in his conception and so bold in his execution, no imitation of any known model to be detected. Sad that no house can be found to buy this picture and that it has to tour around like a menagerie, for the very fact that it was designed for a particular room and a particular country (Hungary, which accounts for its Serbian, Turkish, modern Greek coloring) contributes much to its excellence; but now it has to wander around homeless, badly lighted, and Makart goes on working for art dealers, earning a lot of money certainly, but degenerating in the process! The picture interests me so much that I return home and persuade R. to leave his corrections of the 9th volume to come and view it. He shares my feelings. — R. wants to have a bust of me, he says: "If only I could be of such help to you with it as you have been with mine!" — In the afternoon to the new house, then R. goes to the Riedelsberg, where the Thursday gathering is now being held. He returns home talking of a *plan*—the good people want to undertake a journey together as they do each year, and they invite R. to join in. He says, "It's all right for those who are glad to get away from their wives, but for me—!" He wishes that I and the children might also go, but that would hardly be possible. — I remain in the garden a long time, listening to the birds; two blackbirds are conversing, the sun goes down in a fiery glow, profound solace! The grave lies there in silence, "soon, soon thou shalt rest, too." — Read *Saint Paul* on my own. When we were speaking of what the Schlegel brothers did for the German cause, R. said, "Goethe and Schiller did not concern themselves much with the German idea, their attitude toward it was like Frederick the Great's attitude toward them."

*Friday, July 4* Fine weather again at last, R. works, I with the children in the garden; after lunch conversation about Siegfried and Brünnhilde, the former not a tragic figure, since he does not become conscious of his position, there is a veil over him since winning Brünnhilde for Gunther, he is quite unaware, though the audience knows. Wotan and Brünnhilde are tragic figures. — In the afternoon I read *Saint Paul* and am much affected by the greatness of this being. To be sad in God's, not the world's sense of this word—how moving this doctrine is! A serene disregard for all worldly things, silent and deep sorrow over one's guilt! Saint Paul's submission to the command of the Jerusalem church to cut his hair and take the oath (Nazarite) sets the example of how one should respect the commandments and enter the church, in a spirit of Christian love. I am much moved, and tell R. about my feelings. We walk to the new house, and the thought that it is the book of a man accused of heresy which has put me in such a religious mood makes me laugh. The bust is beginning to look quite good. Then a little walk, and in the evening reading (R. pleased with "the Saxon soldiers," as he calls the blue of the sky and the green of the trees). The chapter about Rüdeger moves us into admitting that this second part of the *Nibelungenlied* is superior even to the *Iliad* with its tender depiction of a devotion to duty which, as one reads it, utterly breaks one's heart. — "You should have married a god," R. says to me, at which I observe, "Well, I did!" — As he goes into his workroom he says: "Now everything has a meaning—my books, my desk—because you are here with me. When I think of my earlier moves, the despair with which I arranged everything—!" "Your first wife would no longer be young enough for you now," I say to him today. "My dear child, if things had remained as they were, I should be very old by now."

*Saturday, July 5* Richard is not at all well and had a bad night; but he works a little. In the afternoon to the sitting, from there via the theater to the Bürgerreuth. A feeling of fear, which I cannot describe, overcomes me when I see the giant scaffolding and the wide auditorium! As long as it was all just an idea inside us, I was not alarmed by its remoteness from reality, but now, taking shape in front of our eyes, it frightens me with its boldness, and it all looks to me like a grave (the Pyramids!). I keep my feelings to myself, and we eat our supper gaily in the Bürgerreuth before returning home to bed.

*Sunday, July 6* To church with the children, then again went to see Makart's picture; family lunch, then to the house—the fountain and the sitting! In the evening Uhland. Unfortunately R. is not quite well.

*Monday, July 7* Nursemaid ill, I have to step in for her. R. works, before it reads Holtzmann's *Germanic Antiquities*, which he finds very absorbing. — Letter from Barcelona, a Wagner Society has been founded there for the promotion of his works, they ask for a concert program and write very touchingly. To the sitting. In the evening Uhland.

*Tuesday, July 8* Charming letter from Marie Dönhoff with 3 new certificates of patronage. R. works, but is dissatisfied, having to write one page again. To the new house, the bust is finished, and is really quite good. In the evening Uhland. (France has become prey to insane bigotry, Switzerland on the other hand very stouthearted.)

*Wednesday, July 9* R. tells me a curious dream he had last night: he had stood with a prince, whom he called "Your Highness," in a similar relationship as with the King of B.; this prince reproached him in a friendly manner for having ridden in a special train on his (R.'s) birthday, asking him not to do so again; R. assured him that this had not been the case, and pressing his hand, calmed him. But as he went

tions, whereupon R. works out the following program: Part I: Rebuff at Oldenburg; II: Scherzo, Travels in the East; III: Meeting at Lake Constance; IV: Joy of the Saxon People! . . .

*Sunday, August 31* Sent the children to church, then with them to the new house. R. works and says at lunch that he enjoys what he is at present doing, a quartet accompanying a conversation, but when reason ceases and has to be replaced by musical ecstasy—that he finds horrible; now he can fit three groups of staves on one page, and that pleases him. After lunch we finish *Coriolanus* in the garden, with indescribable emotion. I tell R. that whoever has not heard him read it does not really know the play, any more than one knows a Beethoven symphony without having heard it conducted by him. We come more and more to the conclusion that it is impossible to imagine these works just by reading them. In the evening music with our copyists; *Meistersinger* and *Faust* Overtures; then R. sings from *Die Walküre*, at the end of it we are all of the opinion that *Die Walküre* is the most emotional, most tragic of all his works, *Tristan und Isolde* is much more conciliatory, and in *Götterdämmerung* Hagen at least is a folk figure, which Hunding is not. "*Fons amoris*," R. calls out to me in the evening as he bids me good night, after lamenting that constant assaults from the outside world prevent his enjoying his happiness.

*Monday, September 1* R. has a headache and cannot work, he comes to sit with me and remembers how he first heard the news, "You have a son!" "One can't believe in one's good fortune. Oh, if only I could renounce all ideals and just enjoy what I have, relinquish control of my works, earn money with them, and not bother my head any more about German culture, how happy I should be! Now it's only scoundrels who seek my favor, people like Herr Löser and the gentlemen from Vienna, whereas it should be Monsieur Bismarck." Sorrow and worry are consuming us, and perhaps only for chimeras—will things one day be better for our son? — In the afternoon walked with R. to the theater, he striding out vigorously. Met Herr Koch, our patron from Nuremberg, and elaborated with him the idea of a subscription. In the evening began the *Myth of Odin*. Conversed a lot about the French, who are really very diverting at the moment.

*Tuesday, September 2* Sedan Day and consecration of the colors by the veterans' organization; unfortunately we have no flag, but we are very moved as the people march by our window and give us a friendly greeting, looking very well and vigorous. "We are not a peace-loving nation," R. finally exclaims. "We are a warrior nation and have a warrior's culture." He reads to me the passage with which Holtzmann ends a chapter of his book, and it is very remarkable. "All we have is our army, our general conscription, our discipline, all our virtues are revealed in war; whether anything will emerge in times of peace still remains to be seen!" — Resolve to take Malwida into our home when we move into the new house. — In the evening the chapter on the Vanir in Uhland's *Myth of Odin.* — A Herr v. Miller wants to form a Wagner Society in Troppau. Since the weather was bad in the afternoon, I played passages from *Die Meistersinger* with R., he worked in the morning.

*Wednesday, September 3*  A dream which I relate to R., and in which he figured, gave him cause to remark, "That must have been your father." This joke dominates the whole day—to Malwida he says, "How glad I shall be, at the time of his next visit, to have you as a companion," for when I am together with my father, he claims, everything else is forgotten! The diverting way in which he says this makes us laugh heartily. But with regard to the house he unfortunately finds much to vex him; scarcely any house can ever have been built with so little supervision. — R. has done some work, and now he is reading a book about Italic antiquity, always in relation to the question that interests him (German and Roman). In the evening we continue reading Uhland; R. says he no longer has the veneration for these Norse songs which he used to have, he cannot discern in them the original Germanic myths, but, rather, the poetic embroideries of the skalds, in which the original features appear in a mixed form. — When I tell him he should choose our evening reading entirely according to his own wishes, he replies that in this matter he feels like Siegfried with Brünnhilde—he can hear me, and takes delight in that, not concerned with the sense. — At table he says he was thinking: "My God, if Cosima were to have seen the company among which I lived in Königsberg, for example! Those play actors who attended my first wedding, Frau Hübsch, the director's wife, like a gypsy in her poppy-red satin dress! Oh, where did I crawl out from!" — After supper he plays passages from *Preciosa* and tells me what an impression the march with the triangle made on him when he heard it for the first time from the proscenium box as an 8-year-old boy. "And the magic sound of the clarinet—I still often think of that. What Beethoven did unconsciously in his instrumentation Weber chose consciously; an engaging German character." R. describes Mozart's choice of the *Don Giovanni* libretto as a remarkable piece of boldness, the urge to free himself from the academic conventions of Metastasio. —

*Thursday, September 4*  Dispatching the circulars. In the course of it, R. breaks the gold pen with which he wrote *Tristan, Die Meistersinger,* and in fact everything since '68. It grieves me all the more since it happened while he was just pointing with the pen to the place on which I was to put a stack of the circulars. R. is not well, the business of dispatching is a strain on him. After lunch in the garden, where very unexpectedly Schuré comes rushing toward us! A hearty welcome in spite of everything! At supper, when he asks for Bordeaux wine "out of patriotism," and I reprove him for trying to provoke us, R. explains to him earnestly and at length what it means to be and to wish to be German, that is to say, to feel a longing which cannot be fulfilled in Latin countries; here in Germany, he says, the question can at least still be asked; our armies have shown that strength is still there, and now we are anxiously waiting to see whether this strength can extend to other fields. "My dear friend," he concludes, "I am not to be counted among the ranks of the present-day patriots, for what a person can suffer under present conditions I am already suffering—I am, as it were, nailed on the cross of the German ideal." — After supper R. very charmingly takes out Berlioz's memoirs, which Schuré gave me, and asks me to read from them the anecdotes about Cherubini, which then transport us right back to France.

*Friday, September 5* R. works; at lunch we have friend Schuré and Malwida, and after lunch we visit the theater; the question of the flags is already being raised, because the poles which are to be set up on the roof have to be painted. Just German flags, or those of all the patrons, Turkey, Russia, etc.? R. wants to consider it. An unpleasant disappointment from Hamburg—instead of the 20 certificates we regarded as certain, Herr Zacharias has paid for ten, though we had assumed that these were in addition to the 20 certain ones! In the evening our friends with us again. — R. talks a lot about the Romans, their difference from the Germans, etc., etc.

*Saturday, September 6* I go to the garden to listen to a reading by our friend Schuré on the history of music and poetry. In the garden I meet our friend Kietz, who has come here really and truly at R.'s behest to make a bust of me, which gives me little pleasure. Schuré's work, apart from a few bits of Alsatiana, is very interesting—he really has understood R. — On returning home, R. reads me a nice letter from Hoffmann, our painter—he seems to be a very decent man. But where the aid? The King keeps silent—R. jokes that he is singing the words from the requiem, *ad patronem.* My father sends notepaper and many French books, among them Littré's dictionary and a work by Princess W[ittgenstein]. The dedication to my father is enough in itself to show what a gulf lies between us—I find it incomprehensible that a woman should publicly address the man she loves in such terms! — For this half of the day we were in good spirits, but at the house R. met with such real vexations that he exclaimed, "We shall be moving into our grave before we move into our house!" Besides that comes the news that the German Crown Prince will be coming to Bayreuth within a week; his adjutant has announced a visit to the historical society—he wants to see the documents. A real blow for us, however the visit turns out—whether he shows any interest in the theater or not, in either case it is awkward. The evening arrives, the dean, Feustel (who reports that Bismarck is again in disgrace), Kietz, Schuré, and Malwida. R. very agitated (before the arrival of the guests I had conversed with Schuré in French, as was our habit in the past, and that also annoyed him), and he hardly departs from the topic of France and Germany all evening; this makes me feel embarrassed, particularly for Schuré, who strikes me as defenseless here. When the guests leave early, I unfortunately remark to R. that the evening was uncomfortable, and he gets very angry!

*Sunday, September 7* Wretched night, R. peevish, cannot work, has no pen, with all the terribly neglected proofs of *Die Walküre* to be read. — I go to Malwida's to listen to the continuation of the reading by Schuré. Silent lunch—how different all of a sudden from yesterday! Silence and melancholy. Yesterday R. told me that, when he thought of the old, warlike Germans, always restless and always fighting, at home only in their cold Nordic forests, he wondered how music emerged among them; then he would suddenly see the moon rising over the forest, the silent night shadows forming, and a melody like that of the Andante in the *Kreutzer* Sonata would begin to sound in his ears. We spend the day with no other reading than, for me, the manuscript of our friend Schuré, to whom R. has given Holtzmann's book on the Celts and the Germans for information.

*Monday, September 8* Marie Dönhoff sends four signed certificates of patronage. Discussion of the Crown Prince's visit brings me dismal thoughts that the Prussians must consider the situation in Bavaria quite untenable, and therefore they no longer need to show consideration. First sitting with friend Kietz. In the evening he and Schuré with us; we make music, first from *Die Msinger*, then from *Götterdämmerung*, the Norns' scene and the Rhinemaidens. R. kept from his work—what I call his real work!—by the corrections to *Die Walküre*. A grief to me— sometimes I ask myself in alarm whether he will ever be able to finish this score.

*Tuesday, September 9* Our watchman gives me his notice; R. laughs and says in this matter he admires me in the way that Fr[iedrich] W[ilhelm] IV, after his abdication, admired the regent, his brother, for having so quickly got rid of Manteuffel, whom he had wanted for years to see removed. — R. writes to Düffl[ipp]. Friend Feustel is to visit him, God knows whether it will help—I fear not! . . . R. tells me he dreamed about me last night, I had smelled strongly of violets, he had asked me not to go away, but suddenly I had vanished, had called him, he had answered no, it was beautiful here. Strangely enough, yesterday I had clumsily sprinkled my handkerchief so strongly with essence of violets that I was unwilling to take it out of my pocket; but R. had not smelled it, since his snuff always prevents him anyway! — Sittings in the morning and afternoon, in the evening a reading of *Hamlet*. Regarding the words of advice Laertes gives his sister, R. reminds me what it is that makes such books (for example, *Mémoires d'une idéaliste*) so disagreeable to him—it is because he finds men infinitely coarse, shallow, conceited, unworthy of troubling a woman's heart; the way Laertes takes Ophelia's chastity very seriously, but his own very lightly —men are permitted. Indescribable impression on us all (Malwida, Schuré, Kietz) of R.'s delivery—Hamlet seen by each of us as if for the first time. R. says that after Hamlet has spoken to the Ghost he lacks restraint, the blinkers which everyone needs in order to be able to act.

*Wednesday, September 10*   I am supposed to have sittings with our dear Kietz, but the autumn weather is so cold and I feel so unwell that I stay at home, attending to letters and other things. R. is also having difficulties all around, his circular has produced nothing but spiteful remarks in the press and meaningless consternation among his friends, who are alarmed by his proposal to turn the theater into a joint-stock enterprise. He talks about the freedom of the press, then about the jury system, comparisons with the lay assessor's court. Do we owe anything at all to the Revolution of '89? An emphatic no, we have been diverted by it from our own true development onto foreign sidetracks— parliamentarianism, freedom of the press—whereas in fact all interests should be represented by corporations, and once these interests have become satisfied, decisions should be announced, without the arguments of people who know and understand nothing about it. Politics, he says, have become a free-for-all, like philosophy in Byzantium, where a barber could talk to a church father about proofs of the Trinity. — In the afternoon music—from *Götterdämmerung* "Hagen's Watch," "Hagen's Call," The "End of the World"—and after supper R. reads us his *Parcival*. Ever-increasing astonishment at this divine power of his—I am reminded of what Schopenhauer says about the reaction of Nature, which produces many twins after big wars. In the same way, I imagine, the emergence of a Shakespeare was a powerful reaction against the oppression of the Anglo-Saxon spirit, which then broke through in this tremendous way; the emergence of Wagner is an equally powerful act of salvation for the German spirit. Doubtless in all this Nature is only looking after itself, and is then indifferent to the awful gap which is created, as if stating, as it were, that though the race may be destroyed (mixing with the Jews, insuperable Latin influences), the spirit is saved, the image remains. The difference between these volcanic outbreaks of genius and its blossoming from the normal development of things in Greece. — But when I see R., who is never tired when he is active in his element, worn out and pulled in all directions because of the gap between him and his fellow beings, then I feel an unutterable grief and, like Falstaff, I could wish it were bedtime and all well. — Warning for Fidi! We decide to bring him up to be glad that he has inherited a little property, and then to protect his independence with the utmost frugality, to traffic with the world only on the basis of compassion, and to desire and demand nothing from it, for this way lies hell. He should make do with the top story of the house, keep only one servant, and, with the help of his books, be diligent and free; and remember what his father had to suffer because he was dependent on other people, who did not understand him. — R. writes to Councilor Düffl., asking him to receive Feustel.

*Thursday, September 11*　Foolish letter from Gedon, the sculptor; silly communication from Herr Herrig, who has written a *Barbarossa* and an article on the theater, in this latter he makes proposals for a playhouse! — Arrival of the box containing the original scores of *Lohengrin* and *Fl. Holländer*; the unpleasant feeling that my father has sent it without love; we had asked him for a copy of the parts not yet published; now he sends us the whole thing, and I know what comments others will make about this. Angry letter from Herr Batz, who says someone was about to form a W. Society in Frankfurt, but had been frightened off by the circular. Oh, how happy we would be if R. could decide just to work, and not to worry about what becomes of his works! — In the afternoon a sitting—in the house, which is also an object more of vexation than joy. — It is said the Crown Prince is not coming. Our last evening with friend Schuré, whom we now with a quiet conscience yield to France. When we were talking together about London, R. said, "In Paris everyone going out on business looks as if he is going for a walk, and in London everyone going for a walk as if he is on business."

*Friday, September 12*　R. writes to the Grand Duke of Oldenburg and the King of W[ürttemberg] in behalf of his undertaking. My heart is so heavy—how many days is it now that he has been unable to work on his score? I feel a real fear that, if things go on like this, he will never get his score finished. We are thinking again about concerts. — And the King of B. has just bought himself a castle for 200,000 florins! Letter from Herr Zacharias with many words of advice, but less sense, and even less activity. The newspapers are reporting that the performance of the work is now in doubt. Much worry. In the evening we read Lichtenberg's letters about Garrick. R. is happy with the progress of my bust. Herr Krausse, the painter, comes to carry out the *sgraffito* panel on our house. I constantly feel that R. is again becoming much too much involved in commissions, but I do not dare to speak, for fear of exacerbating his great worries with my worries.

*Saturday, September 13* R. could not sleep, he was thinking of his patrons! He writes to Otto Wesendonck, invites him to come and see the theater, I write to Herr Zacharias, encouraging him to set an example, rather than give advice. The Crown Prince is coming after all, his arrival is suddenly announced. Much ado about putting up flags. [*A few words based on word play omitted.*] R.'s good mood comes to us like a blessing of God; although he has not got down to his work for weeks and is having nothing but unpleasant experiences, he is today full of good and amusing ideas for the sculptors! . . . He says the good progress of my bust is giving him pleasure. Sitting twice daily robs me of much time, but if it brings him the least little bit of satisfaction, that is reward enough! — My mother writes for the first time since February. My father also writes, only to say the original scores of *Lohengrin* and *Holländer* are a gift, but alas, alas, I cannot accept this, for it is being done without feeling! — At 7:30 arrival of the Crown Prince; the question of whether our theater should be illuminated is answered by the mayor in the affirmative, and like an apparition, like Wotan's castle, it rises twice into view, bathed in a red light. The people give the Crown Prince a nice, spontaneous welcome; thoughts of the King —how everything takes its course. Very moved by the sight of the theater, we embrace each other, and R. says, "It is colored red with our blood!" . . .

*Sunday, September 14* Friend Feustel, arriving from Munich in the early morning, has hopes that the King will take over the guarantee! Splendid weather; the sun of the Hohenzollerns shone today as yesterday: "I must be sure to order it for my festival," says R. The Prince visits church, opera house, palaces, but not our theater, which stands there by itself, solitary and remote, the cross to which we are nailed, the temple in which we pray. — Sitting in the morning; at lunch Malwida; when she speaks approvingly of the participation of women in the legislature, R. reads her the chapter on women's emancipation from Constantin Frantz's *Naturlehre des Staats,* and we are full of admiration for its classical clarity of style and the preciseness of its thinking. "Another truly German original," says R. — The Crown Prince departs and takes the good weather with him. In the afternoon in the garden. In the evening read Lichtenberg's letters about the German theater with great enjoyment; very impressed by his description of Garrick's French costumes in *Hamlet.* R. agrees with Garrick; everything is just a masquerade nowadays, he says, even if one decides to present the tragedies of Racine in Louis XIV costumes, as was very rightly done in Racine's own time. "That is why I went back to the myth," R. says, "to Siegfried, who goes around more or less in shirt sleeves and wears a hat such as one can still see being worn here and there by peasants." One can learn from Lichtenberg how one should deal with a genius—not criticize, but learn, ask oneself: Why does he do that? — The Crown Prince has taken the good weather away with him, rain is now falling from the heavens in streams.

*Monday, September 15* At last R. gets down again to his score, though he still has no pen which he likes. I write to my father (sending back the scores), my mother, the Englishman who sent a fine translation of *Die Walküre*, etc., and complete this book. Written always in haste and without leisure, it does, I believe, contain a picture of our life, which I want to be able to give my son Siegfried, along with all the opinions of his father. We hope things will go better for him. "I am quite content to be the Siegmund," R. said today, and he is glad he is old enough not to become an impediment to his son. "If I can do the festivals, and if they lead to the consequences I expect, he will be able to lead a truly Periclean existence." I want him to recognize his father truly, to know everything about him, and that is why I continue with these pages: through these he may learn what his father will not perhaps be able to say himself. My blessings on him and his sisters!

[*End of the sixth notebook of the Diaries.*]

> Dear God, make me devout,
> that I may go to Heaven,
> but if I do not become devout,
> take me away from this earth,
> take me into thy celestial kingdom,
> make me be like thine angels.

This volume shall begin with Fidi's prayer, the same one which R. spoke in his childhood, and I hope that Fidi's children will all speak it, too. — In the afternoon a sitting with our good Kietz, who R. says has made him downright happy with the lovely bust he has made of me. Wretched state of the trades here, not a molder to be found. R. is thinking of suggesting a vocational school with workshops, under a commission which would look after the orders. The worker here is constantly drunk. — In the evening we take up Uhland again; after the reading R. plays the third act of *Tristan*, the bliss of melancholy, the desolation of the sea, profound calm, Nature's sorrow, Nature's consolation—all, all here in this most wonderful of poems! When I speak of it to R., he says, "In my other works the motives serve the action; in this, one might say that the action arises out of the motives." When I tell him I should like to die to these strains, he says, "But better to the strains with which Siegfried dies."

*Tuesday, September 16*  Friend Feustel tells us that the Crown Prince made the King's jealousy his excuse for not viewing more things here. Frankness is the order of the day; we agree that at least something has been won by not having to look upon the Crown Princess as if she were God; we must make up our minds to look on the Hohenzollerns as the guardians of the German Reich, and all the rest, impetus and art, the Reich must discover for itself. — Very bad weather, the sun smiled only for the Prince! R. in difficulties with the corrections to *Die Walküre*, nobody is helping him; with the house, which is making absolutely no progress, nothing but difficulties; the need for a vocational school with workshops is becoming increasingly clear to us, there is no molder to be found here, while in Swabia even the tiniest village has them. In the evening we read Grimm's essay on cremation and are dismayed by the dreadful piling up of quotations, which make a complete mockery of the argumentation; these confirmations could very well be printed as an appendix.

*Wednesday, September 17*  R. spends the morning teaching the copyists how to correct! For me, sittings. Nice letter from Dr. Hemsen, who has the task of bringing the Bayreuth undertaking to the attention of the King of Württemberg. Dr. Coerper also writes, wanting concerts! A gentleman in Stettin wants concerts, too, in order to be able to send a Herr Kossmely to the performances here!! — In the evening read Uhland, the section about runes. When I read that, in addition to Thurs, Noth was also a magic symbol, R. exclaims, "Then I made a very good choice with the name for my sword—I did not know that."

*Thursday, September 18*  We are thinking about a performance of *Lohengrin* in Berlin (not in the Court theater); R. writes replying to Herr Coerper with this in mind. — At lunch he talks about Beethoven's 4th Symphony and says, "One could not understand the striking difference between it and the *Eroica* if one did not see that it contains the seeds of that unworried mood (containment of emotion) which first emerged in the *Eroica* and the quartets and rose to a godlike humor—a runner-up to the 8th! Mendelssohn's absurd explanation of B.'s alarm following the *Eroica* and a return, so to speak, to the norm. That's the way scribblers think when, having done something that cost them a great effort, they write something easy again." Recently R. played the *Coriolan* Overture to me and Malwida, a wonderful picture, the struggle within a soul, everything takes place within the hero's breast, nothing external, not even the voice of his mother, which we hear only as an echo in the son's heart. — Great vexations for R., as much with the house, on which the people say they no longer wish to work, as with Gedon. In the evening the Thursday gathering, Herr Kraussold relates in the dryest possible way some insipid anecdotes concerning the Crown

Prince. Our excellent Heckel notifies us of 3 certificates of patronage. Herr Wesendonck announces his impending visit. In Hamburg the crisis in Bayreuth is greeted with pleasure! God knows! . . . Yesterday R. gave me a great shock when he declared he felt no urge to work; all the many annoyances had utterly deprived him of it, he said.

*Friday, September 19*  R. writes letters to Gedon and Heckel, this time regarding the equipment. I work with the children, in the afternoon a sitting. A brighter sky, R. in consequence feeling better. In the evening R. reads to me and Malwida the report on the execution of Marchner, the murderer, and the executioner's remarkable appeal to the soul of the wretched man. R. speaks once more about his idea of capital punishment and how this should be carried out—once the condemned man has given his consent, it should be entirely the work of religion, which, like music, starts with the first scream, proceeds to lamentation (and the artistic display of lamentation), and ends with salvation; the executioner Steller gives the impression of being a most remarkable person and he does what the monk and the judge should be doing. Participation of the community in the extermination of one of its members in a ceremony of mourning. R. recalls the court in the chapter on Dietrich in the *Amelungen Saga*, and we read the episode of Rutlieb and the Red Man with deep emotion.

*Saturday, September 20*  R. is able to orchestrate again; he receives a very nice letter from a patron in reply to the circular (Herr Max Pauer of Schloss Gutenhaag in Styria). I again have a sitting. In the evening read Uhland and then *Egil's Saga*. A difference with R. with regard to the children; in view of their great carelessness I have had tin mugs made for them to drink from; R. will not tolerate the punishment; I give way, but am inwardly sad about it. Letter to R. from Prof. Nietzsche, after a long silence; but his eye trouble is not yet cured. — Visit of the King of Italy to Berlin, on which certain hopes are set; it is said to have been brought about by Bismarck (who is unfortunately unwell). The Catholic party press is conducting a veritable campaign against the new Reich.

*Sunday, September 21*  Dull, close day; R. had a bad night; he cannot work. I go for a walk with the children, chance leads me to the cemetery, we go inside; thoughts of death within me, yearned-for rest for R. and myself. R. leaves the lunch table to go for a long walk. In the evening continued reading Uhland with Malwida and R., the recognition of Christianity by the gods makes a very fine impression, moving picture of Wotan (Nornagest), who himself lights the candle of his life and dies beside the font. "One knows nothing like this among the Greeks," R. observes. "These German myths are so serene, so touching." How ridiculous Saint Olaf looks, throwing a missal after the venerable, omniscient man and god! "It could not have been easy," R. observes, "to drive these gods out of the hearts of the people." — Before our reading we spoke of the visit of the King of Italy to Germany and the hopes attached to it. "How noble kings are made to look by the importance attached to their decisions! They are like marionettes in the hand of God; we others are still lying in the box and need enormous efforts of genius to crane our necks over the side!"

*Monday, September 22* R. cannot understand that I attach importance to upholding a punishment once imposed on the children; he is also not well, and has much writing to do besides. An illustrated calendar with a picture of Herr Paul Lindau gives us food for thought! The Prussian men of state (Falk, Möller, Stosch) arouse confidence with their proficiency and earnestness, but everything that has to do with literature looks horrifying. "With the others one has nothing to do, they impress one with their sense of duty, but here we have an ape pure and simple, and people like Laube, etc., are competing for his favor!" R. replies to Prof. Nietzsche, on whose pamphlet there is a nice article in the *A.A.Z.* In the evening we play music from *Die Meistersinger*, and R. says he always has the feeling that he wrote this work in parentheses. Before we went off to bed he said to me, "I have much to thank you for, I was just thinking about *Die Meistersinger*, and felt how much I owed to you."

*Tuesday, September 23* Earnest reflections on the children's education —whether I can possibly carry it out in the present circumstances; much worry on this account. R. also does not get down to his score, and there is no reading in the evening, letters and a sitting. In the morning a long walk to St. Georgen.

*Wednesday, September 24* Long discussion with R.; resolve on my part to use no more strictness toward the children, and even to stifle all thoughts of what I hold to be good in this matter. My father sends his Wartburg songs! I have my last sitting for the bust. In the evening read Uhland. Before that a discussion with a clergyman named Baum about the children's lessons in school; much shocked by the barrenness and shallowness of such an intellect. Impossible to make him understand how the children here should be taught—that bad teaching in French and English is foolish, the German language should be learned thoroughly, and the foundation should be German history and geography, on which the family should be encouraged to build further. The good man complains of the obtuseness of the pupils and wishes to overcome it with the help of the French language! . . . Before this interview visited the theater in lovely weather; splendid decoration supplied by the supporting beams, which are simply to be painted over—thus a downright primitive art form results: no deliberate ornamentation—

the bricks provide the red background, the beams provide the lines which, painted yellow, gleam in the sunshine like gold. The whole thing stands there like a fairy tale in the midst of clumsy reality. God knows what will come of it. R. said the building supervisor was so pleased by the success of his work: "Everyone will laugh when we weep." — And yet how one's energies droop! It is only one's little bit of intelligence which still flutters and takes pleasure, now as before, in the great and the beautiful.

*Thursday, September 25* Once again sittings, and for R. a little work on the score. The weather continues fine, the children go for a drive with Malwida and R., and I catch up with them later. In the evening R. has his Thursday gathering and reads aloud to the good people— somewhat to their dismay—two chapters from Nietzsche's pamphlet. Meanwhile with Malwida I read Uhland's fifth volume to the end.

*Friday-Saturday, September 26–27* Arrival of my sister-in-law Ottilie with her son Fritz; the two days are devoted to them and pass very pleasantly—from their astonishment at the beauty of the theater I recognize the effect which the malicious drawing in *Die Gartenlaube* had. — R. receives a letter from Councilor D., saying the King will *not* give the guarantee; he has taken on too much himself! . . . At midday a military band from Meiningen comes along and pays a little tribute to R., they play very nicely, and I am much affected by this sign of popular sympathy for R. Unfortunately, the finale to the first act of *Lohengrin* spoils the mood, the players dragging and then rushing in the wrong places. R. shows them how it should go, conducts it himself from the ground-floor window, and they understand him at once; he drinks with them from a tankard and is delighted with these nice, lively people. In the evening we read in the newspaper about the expenditure of the French billions and are alarmed by its application exclusively to military purposes; but R. sees the reason and says: "We must remain armed right up to the teeth, for everyone is hostile to us, we are surrounded by enemies. Bismarck has the right instinct. The nation is rich enough to take care of the rest, it does not need the government's support." R. has the feeling that the King of Italy's visit to Germany actually means an alliance between France, Italy, and Austria against Germany; Berlin is visited, as well as other places, in order not to make things too obvious, but genuine cordiality was seen only in Vienna. The Catholic party is probably out to ensnare a King of Italy, crowned by the Pope and under the Pope's control, working together with France against Prussia.

*Sunday, September 28* In the garden with children and relations; an all-but-angry interchange with Ottilie concerning Prof. Nietzsche; she is so bound up in university ways that she talks about the book *The*

*Birth of Tragedy* without stopping to consider that N. has jeopardized his whole career for the sake of her brother, and that it is therefore insensitive of her to pass on to us the contemptuous and libelous opinions of the top academics; I see from the sentiments of W.'s sister toward her brother's most loyal supporter how even the warmest heart can cool when it is constantly confronted with power! Lunch and then a drive together to the Eremitage. Nothing of significance, except that R., referring to himself, says he is like Robin Hood, so out of step with the world. [*A few untranslatable words omitted.*]

*Monday, September 29* Will work on the theater have to be stopped? That is the question which alarms and occupies us. R. writes to Councilor Düffl. and to Herr Zacharias, instructing the latter to form a consortium of patrons. I write to Emil Heckel. As we have just completed these letters, Loldi comes to tell us that a worker has fallen to his death from the top scaffolding of the theater. A sad shock—I had felt it to be a blessing that no such accident had yet accompanied the building work; now it has happened, and the sign is received in silence. The sky is overcast, as if rain is on its way, but the air is mild; it accords with the atmosphere in my heart, which is also mild and melancholy! In the evening sister-in-law, nephew, and the good dean.

*Tuesday, September 30* Departure of our relations, which leaves me in a mood of great melancholy; I see clearly that the way in which R. and his undertaking are spoken of in my sister-in-law's circles has had an influence on her, and her heart is not big enough to follow him. — R. writes letters, clearing things up so that from tomorrow on he can get to work on the score. My bust is packed away; departure of the excellent Kietz. From Munich Herr Baligand reports that the W. Society there is again sending 1,500 florins.

*Wednesday, October 1* R. goes back to his score—a great joy, for then things are easier to bear. Otherwise nothing of note, the Grand Duke of Oldenburg thanks us for sending the plans and brochures, but says nothing further. Schott pays for *Götterdämmerung* (10,000 francs) and is thus behaving agreeably. But this is probably our last large piece of income, and our growing expenses fill me with worry. R. has an unquenchable confidence in himself, and I an all-absorbing mistrust in Fate. In the evening started on Uhland's 6th volume, also read the article on Loki in Grimm's *Mythology.* (Alliance between Germany and Italy after all.)

*Thursday, October 2* R. had a curious dream: Semper with a plaster mask, annoyed at being recognized, the Wesendoncks, I suddenly vanished, anxious searching, till suddenly my voice, as clear as silver but frightened, is heard calling, "Richard." He cannot reply, which surprises me, but at last, struggling to wake up, he calls out, "Here I am." — I also had a wretched night, the desertion of R.'s relations hurt me more than I thought; it had been an article of faith, and it has now vanished. R. works, but he does not feel well; he badly needs a walk, but can walk only very little on account of his painful foot. He talks about being unable to envisage himself outliving the performances! What may not yet intervene? . . . In the evening read Uhland, "The Song of the Mill," a great and sublime impression. After it R. reads us the story of the four deaf men from Rückert's Indian sagas.

*Friday, October 3* "The strict governess," as Fidi calls her, is here; another new being. Letter from Herr Voltz: we shall probably receive nothing from the Haase lawsuit. R. works and says jokingly that he would like to score everything for horns. Very nice letter from a Frau Emilie Basler in Munich, who says she has saved up 100 thalers without her relations' knowledge and wishes secretly to buy a third share in a certificate of patronage. In the evening we read in Uhland the legend of the nocturnal conjurations of Angandy's daughter—quite splendid. To conclude the evening R. reads us another Indian story (the four foolish Brahmans).

*Saturday, October 4* R. dreamed that he was in his theater, surveying from the princes' gallery the whole lovely, completed auditorium. "How will we feel when we come to the performances?" he asks. "After all that has gone before, one is so tired that one has no feelings at all— one is in a complete dream state, as I was when I sat in the King's box at the first performance of *Die Meistersinger*." While we are talking about the old Nordic sagas, R. says he knows what Odin whispered in Baldur's ear, that insoluble riddle; resignation, the breaking of the will—the ethical theme of *Der Ring des Nibelungen*. R. works, and during his work comes to the following conclusion: "There are two ways of looking at the orchestra: as a homophonous body in which one instrument stands in for another; or my way, where every instrument is regarded as an individual standing by itself; that is why I am so annoyed when an instrument does not possess a particular note." Fidi in front of the two busts of R. (Kietz and Zumbusch): the two of them are dead, and then they meet. R. told me he did not wish to have a second son, for if he did not turn out to be like Fidi, how terrible that would be— "and one can hardly expect a repetition." — R. visits the theater and returns home in silence—the workmen are making no progress with the shell of the building! The worker who fell from the scaffolding did not die, but he is much mutilated. In the evening the *Saga of Hrolf Kraki* in Uhland. Great delight in it; superiority, the virtue of the Germans. R. observes that Bruno Bauer was right to point out in his study of the Jesuits that the Jesuits were unable to get the better of this superiority, which was not much concerned with death, Heaven, and Hell:

"They have always carried their Valhalla deep in their hearts." — "Much patience and a little crying," according to Charles V the only remedy for gout; R. puts it forward as a remedy for life—one should cry a little at times! This quotation brings me to Titian's portrait (Charles V in Madrid); difference between the painter and the dramatist; we know Falstaff and Hamlet thoroughly, but cannot visualize them; the painter sees, propounds, and solves a riddle. — In the evening R. declares that he hardly hears me when I am reading: he watches me and is enchanted. "How happy we are!" he exclaims. . . .

*Sunday, October 5* I find the following piece of paper [*not discovered*] on my table, laid there by R., who found it in the American newspaper, which he otherwise never looks at. [*See note headed* "R.'s appearance at Löwenberg" *under this date.*] It makes us laugh heartily. After lunch R. talks about his first parents-in-law and the proletariat; his contacts with these strange poor people (the father used periodically to disappear with some woman) during the conception of *Lohengrin* and *Tannhäuser!* . . . My mother writes; she encloses newspaper clippings which report on the theater in Bayreuth; she also tells me that E. Ollivier bears a grudge against me for my German feelings! Sitting over his score, R. says: "Two *corni!* That used to be the first thing to do—to write down the Italian words when one was writing a score." Recently he spoke of his inability to show brilliance (musical embellishments, etc.): "For me it was never a choice between brilliance and earnestness—I just could not provide the former. Or runs—I find such attempts to please repellent, even when these occur in Beethoven—when the virtuoso is supposed to step forward and show what he can do." — Talked about Shakespeare's early death (R. says he finds Guizot's 86 years encouraging, but none of the politicians have a heart), his withdrawal to Stratford, doubtless disgusted with the theater, except for one or two good actors; he would have had the same attitude toward his company as Bach had toward his choir pupils, and what would he have found, apart perhaps from a Lord Seymour? Doubtless the worm gnawed at his heart—oh, if only one knew! "His works did not create a culture, otherwise they could not have disappeared." — R. praises in Nietzsche's work his remark about the *"seekers"*—we do not have any classical figures, i.e., no flourishing period, after which a line could be drawn. "They all console themselves with the word '*Epigonentum*' and are fortified in their slovenliness." — Read Walachian fairy tales with the children, and in the evening *Frithiof's Saga* and the *Saga of Rolf and His Warriors* in Uhland. Ever-growing delight in this Germanic literature, so much closer to us than the Greek. Our amusement over the American newspaper persists all day; R. says, "I am just surprised that any of these clumsy mortals notices anything." From this same article I also read aloud something concerning R.'s appearance in Löwenberg, but he cannot bear hearing his own person described. — At supper R. said how touched he had been to meet two little girls (aged 6 and 4), the elder of whom was carrying a sack of potatoes on her back and yet, in spite of the heavy load, was continually joking with the smaller child; he spoke to them, and the girl replied politely and clearly. He then gave them some money, which she accepted gratefully, saying, "My mother will be very pleased when I bring her this, for my father is ill and cannot work." — As we are joking together about the fairy stories which are being spread around concerning R., he says, "I have become a veritable Robin Hood."

*Monday, October 6*  Herr Zacharias maintains his silence—a repetition of our Löser experience, though with better manners. I pay some calls while R. works on his score. In the afternoon he goes out, and returns home in a despondent mood; his foot hurts him, and the doctor seems unable to help; with regard to our undertaking, silence reigns everywhere again; the house is not progressing and is still causing us expense. On top of all that he finds at home a letter from a music dealer in Königsberg, who claims to have heard that R. intends to give a series of concerts and who, experienced in this field, now offers his services. At a moment when the pain in his foot hardly allows R. any movement, a real mockery. In the evening read Uhland; what he has to say about Hamlet's gift—to smell out foul deeds, the result of bitter experience—makes me think of ourselves. . . . We are almost in the same situation. — R. tells about an encounter with a boy, who asked him for alms; R. refused, then behind his back heard how the boy let out a great sigh; turning around, he asked him what was the matter. Reply: "How can I find a bit of bread to eat?" Seeing his clean clothing and well-soled feet R. cried, "Where are you from?," whereupon the boy gave him a sharp look and to R.'s utter amazement ran off like a madman in spite of all R.'s friendly shouts.

*Tuesday, October 7*  In spite of R.'s telegram, Herr Zacharias continues to keep silent; instead there comes from the Liszt Committee in Pest an invitation to me and R. to attend the ceremony marking my father's 50 years of professional activity. R. very vexed about it, I still undecided whether I shall *have* to go. Best of all is that R. is remaining true to his vow of working every day on his score. I make inquiries about the titles of the head of the Committee, Archbishop Haynald, before making my decision. Went to the new house, where work is practically at a standstill, to R.'s great vexation. In the evening Uhland —fine *Saga of Syrnit*, who will not open her eyes—very touching moments. All day long seeing clergymen in the street, they have come to attend the synod here, and the bells are continually ringing! — The trial of Bazaine has begun.

*Wednesday, October 8* In spite of a violent headache, R. spoke a lot with me early this morning about the German language, which has in his opinion not yet displayed all its riches, "for Lessing, finding it in the state it then was, constructed words based on foreign conceptions, which then dominated everything. It is fortunately true that these constructions were in the spirit of the German language, but the language has not yet undergone a development coming from its own roots." — Yesterday we discussed the children's financial situation after our death. According to the arrangements Voltz and Batz have made, Fidi can count on 6,000 florins annually, of which only 4,000 can be spent by him or on his behalf, so that, during the 30 years in which this pension will be paid to him, 2,000 florins can be put aside for him each year, and he will then have a capital of about 65,000 florins, counting the interest. His sisters will receive their provisions from the shares I have saved. We hope to have 20,000 francs for each of them. What Hans has saved will provide the dowries for the two elder girls, and my capital the dowries for the two younger ones. On top of that there is the house—though of course all of it only with God's blessing! — R. is very unwell, he forces himself to work, which worries me, what with his headache, his sore foot, his abdominal troubles, and on top of all those his depression arising from our situation. The single purest joy is our Siegfried, a ray of cheerfulness. Some days ago Lindner, the engraver, was here; he told us that R.'s picture had won him a prize at the exhibition in Vienna, and this had led to further orders. He would like to make another one. In the evening read Uhland, the two sagas of *Harald Hyldetand* and *Starkardr* move us tremendously—the hero who is always marked out for victory, yet receives mortal wounds in every fight, reminds me of R. — Speaking of the ancient Germanic tribes, R. divides them into Franks and Saxons: these were certainly the main tribes, the first being rougher and more adventurous, the second regarding war more as a matter of defense and loyalty. — The morning brings me 100 thalers from our good Frl. Basler, then the gift of the first book of sketches for *Götterdämmerung*. For R. it brings a visit from the dean, who first of all reports that the Crown Prince spoke at length and significantly about R. with the mayor, calling him the first "to have represented the German ideal in art." Then he announces the arrival of a Herr von Thon (with wife), who is a member of the Wagner Society in Regensburg and who is suggesting a banker who wishes to put money into our undertaking! . . . This couple does in fact arrive during the afternoon. Baron von Thon is a delegate to the synod and a district magistrate as well as a member of the Wagner Society in Regensburg; both make an excellent impression on us. — Can we really count on help? — A pitiful letter full of sentimentality from Frau Wille, making a veritable exhibition of her lack of participation (they prefer to remain in their flower meadows, etc.). An equally pitiful one from Herr Zacharias—gout, lack of authority, all sorts of things serve him as an excuse for not calling the conference together. — Only a few of the patrons have replied to the invitation. — A fountain is splashing in our greenhouse—to celebrate the birthday of Cervantes, I say jokingly; and for that reason we read two of his interludes, "The Alert Sentry" and "The Magic Theater," and amid all the humor, which reminds us of Shakespeare, think of the great writer and his sad, sad life.

*Friday, October 10* R.'s nights continue to be wretched, his nerves are terribly strained. We return Baron Thon's visit and take him and his wife to the building site. Will we get help from this quarter?? — We talk about the German word *dichten* ["to create poetry"], and R. remarks that not even the Greeks had such a fine word; the Greek word for it means "to make." Herr Beta writes to R., sending the dedication of his pamphlet; he wants to print a letter from R. as a preface! "Schemes are the mark of a poor man," R. remarks. — R. vows to think only of his score, he cannot produce the money. Our evening is mainly spent in discussing the trial of Bazaine, in which we detect the same French characteristics which so appalled us during the war. A poor German musician in Australia asks for help and sends some verses, a composition, and a photograph, with details of his life!! Herr Beta sends the dedication of his book (to Prince Bismarck, whose acceptance surprises us).

*Saturday, October 11* Spent a long time in town, looking for birthday presents for Lusch; R. buys her a beautiful medallion. We are just discussing with R. how to arrange our reception today when Baroness Thon comes and says her husband is ill. Another curious experience, another hope, it seems, that has come to nothing. In the evening more Bazaine.

*Sunday, October 12* Lulu's birthday; we celebrate as best we can with gifts and treats, and in my heart with melancholy blessings! In the afternoon we go to the railroad station to meet Marie Schleinitz, who in her charming way is paying us a visit. She has just seen and heard Hans in Munich and tells us wonderful things about his playing, but he is still capricious in his moods; he boasts, however, of having put aside a fortune for his children! — Our sympathetic friend wants to know all about our situation here, but what we have to tell her does not make very pleasant hearing. Letter from my father in Rome, with the program of the festivities; R. says it is like *Ragnä Röer*—everything known in advance! My father apparently expects me to go.

*Monday, October 13* Fine morning, I drive with our friend to the Eremitage, which looks very delightful, and after that lunch at home with the mayor and friend Feustel, who is not downhearted in spite of the bad state of things; he urges R. to go with him to Munich and to present himself to the King—he says the last word has not yet been spoken in this affair. God knows! . . . Drove with our friend to the theater, and from there home, where we spend the evening. R. plays *Tristan* (3rd act), making my heart almost break with emotion.

*Tuesday, October 14* Drove with our friend to Neumarkt and there said goodbye to her; in the meantime R. completed his page of orchestration. After lunch, he wondered whether the Greeks ever read their great dramatists; probably they did at the time of Aristotle; the quotations presumably all from memory, but they probably read Aeschylus and Sophocles as well as Homer. — The Baron from Regensburg keeps silent! Our family in Leipzig is also silent—in both cases ominous and puzzling. In the evening read Uhland. Before that, pleasure in Bismarck's decision to take over the railroads—a great step against the profiteering. The recognition of Bishop Reinkens is also a very gratifying deed.

*Wednesday, October 15* Insignificant letters; I write many myself; everything again in its usual order. R. works, but he is still unwell, having bad nights (dreams of two importunate Jewesses). He has a conference with Feustel and the mayor, which reveals that by no means all is lost. Friend Feustel wants at all costs to take R. with him to Munich, he declares that the King only wants to be asked, fundamentally he is annoyed at not being the patron and only requires a little pushing—God knows! R. is very reluctant. In the evening Uhland and Bazaine.

*Thursday, October 16* R.'s bad foot worries me greatly. We discuss my possible journey to Pest, a great disruption in our lives. But R. is working regularly. Visit to the new house, the conservatory has been stocked and the fine, green plants give me much pleasure, though as with all property the sight makes me melancholy. A word from Baron Thon, mentioning by name the banker Haymann in Regensburg, who is willing to make a loan against security. I do not much trust Israelite aid. — In the evening read the story of Wieland the Smith in the *Vilkina Saga*. [*A few untranslatable words omitted.*] We hear worrisome things about the King! . . .

*Friday, October 17* I write to my father, leaving to him the decision whether I go to Pest or not. R. works and says if he continues with the score as he is now doing, it will never be finished. Yesterday he spoke to me about the English horn, which he is using to express Gutrune's utter innocence. A student in Leipzig says that he has just heard

*Tannhäuser* for the first time and wishes to express thanks for the overwhelming impression. "I must build on the younger generations for the sake of Fidi's royalties," R. says. — I do not remember what it was that caused R. to remark that there are no rectangles in Nature, and that quadrature is the form specifically needed by the human intellect to express certain things. When I was walking today with the children under our veranda, which has no greenery covering it, I noticed how beautiful, how idealized the landscape looked through the red pillars, and I was forced to conclude that art lies in the framing, in limitation. Walk through the meadows with R. and the children, saw the theater in all its glory, then to the house, where much vexation, as usual. In the evening Baron Thon with his wife and the poor dean, who is worn out completely by the synod and its deliberate hardness of hearing. The banker Haymann is discussed, Baron Thon fears a design on royalties. R. again becomes angry, since the dean rather stupidly dismisses his situation and his torments as if they were something quite normal.

*Saturday, October 18* Correspondence between the Pope and the Emperor, the latter's reply splendid—the first free acknowledgment of Protestantism since Luther—dispatched on Sedan Day. Discussion with R. concerning the religious situation—how to avoid throwing out the baby with the bath water? "The unfortunate thing," says R., "is that the naïve and beautiful faith of the people has met with a civilized world, and that has corrupted it." Our Protestant clergy, under whom the good dean is now suffering so much, are behaving so badly that one must almost believe in the future of a *tabula rasa*. I am reading a book by Princess W[ittgenstein] which might truly be called the *pirouettes* and *entrechats* of scholastic theology (*De la matière*).

The restlessness of such intellects looks strange in comparison with the wisdom and equanimity of the Nordic heroes. Reflections on the magnificent Roman world, which was great and humane until it came into contact with the Germans; fear then made it treacherous, attempts were made to effect what the legions could no longer achieve by moral means. A children's party in honor of Lusch, in the evening Uhland. R. is working so regularly and so concentratedly that in day-to-day matters he is absent-minded.

*Sunday, October 19* In church, not enough edification; then on the battlements, where the sun is shining splendidly and I can sit with Malwida while the children play. R. works. In the afternoon R. shows us pictures of old Roman coins; the picture of Hadrian particularly strikes him. Talked about the splendors of the Roman world and the blessings of a good prince (king); a good king can do more good than a bad one can do evil, hence the advantage of a monarchy. Regarded the heads—what serenity, what nobility, what solicitude is expressed in them! Went for a walk with R. and Fidi—the other children are tired. No reading in the evening, conversed on various subjects, glanced through Gryphius. At the end of the evening R. played me the Andante from [Haydn's] Symphony in D (*London* Symphony); infinite delight in his masterly art; Haydn, spurred on after Mozart's death by Mozart's genius, became the true predecessor of Beethoven; varied instrumentation, and yet so artistic; everything speaks, everything is inspiration: "All the bold deeds of these modern people mean nothing to me—they are not inventions, just accumulations."

*Monday, October 20*  Domestic upsets, the new manservant has to be dismissed. R. does not understand that servants here do not become attached to him. He works. I for a walk with the children. Attempt to design a hat for myself from the dreadful fashions, which really seem to have been created just for disreputable women. No reading in the evening, but a Haydn symphony (in D) played as a piano duet with R., great delight in it.

*Tuesday, October 21*  Hailstorms and cold, house inspection, still full of annoyances. In the afternoon arrival of Senator Petersen and daughter, pleasant memories of Hamburg, the Senator an outstanding person, very individual—in character he reminds me a little of Sulzer, however different in appearance. He observed some encouraging signs in South Germany, the German Emperor's preacher (Frommel) listened to in Gastein by the whole Catholic population and much respected. A peasant in Lower Austria said, "If only we had a minister of culture like Falk!," etc.

*Wednesday, October 22*  My father's birthday. Yesterday, after our guests left, R. utterly overwhelmed me with endearments, and in the end we had to laugh. Did Tristan and Isolde also laugh so much? "Of course, otherwise they wouldn't have been so sad during the day." — Heavy rain, but despite it we took our guests to see the theater, the Senator seriously impressed. During our meal together heard many interesting things about Hamburg past and present. The evening also spent with our guests, and very pleasantly, too.

*Thursday, October 23*  R. not well, as always after too prolonged contact with other people. Much domestic activity for me. Took leave of our friends at the railroad station. With R. feeling unwell, conversation in the evening—Bazaine, the French—pitiful.

*Friday, October 24*  R. cannot work today, either! Letter from Herr Haymann—he much regrets! . . . Herr Erlanger keeps silent. R. promises Herr Feustel to go to Munich with him around November 15 — Berlin surprises us with a royalty payment of 234 thalers for two performances in the off season, and Batz reports that a settlement is being worked out with the management with regard to Wiesbaden,

Kassel, and Hanover. — Read Uhland again. Recently R. spoke of E. Sue's book about Joan of Arc, how well the author seeks the reasons for her emergence in the impressions that she received during her adolescent years; her emotional turbulence in this period is thus directed entirely toward a hatred of the English and a longing to drive them out of France; her development into a woman was passed over, as it were— she remained a maiden.

*Saturday, October 25*   R. had a very bad night and today hardly works at all. Visit from the dean, who is indignant about our newest Jewish experience (Haymann). R. goes to the theater and comes home via the house, which he calls his *Gräfe-Coeur*, since every time he goes there the foreman Gräfe stops him and gives him some unpleasant news. — R. is very upset when he hears about the possibility of my journey to Pest, and concludes some bitter remarks with the joking observation, "Good, if you go to Pest, I shall visit the World's Fair in Vienna!" — In Paris a monarchy seems assured, and we come to the conclusion that this would be the best thing for both France and the world; anybody except a legitimate ruler in that country would always be obliged to foment war; a hereditary monarch would not, however, and perhaps things would then develop as in Belgium—freedom, welfare, unproductivity, and Jesuitry. In the evening Uhland.

*Sunday, October 26*   My father relieves me of the necessity of traveling to Pest; R. both glad and sorry about it, says that I have to give up so much on his account! So a heavy sacrifice on my part is over and done with. R. still not well and cannot work—in the morning we go for a walk together; in the afternoon first long rest in the conservatory! In the evening Uhland, and, when Malwida has gone and I feel provoked by a curious book by Princess Wittgenstein (*De la matière*) to ask R. some questions, our conversation leads us to the mystic Meister Eckhart; R. begins to read a sermon by him, which fascinates us to the highest degree. Everything turned inward, the soul silent, so that in it God may speak the hidden word! — Then read a lovely Danish poem ("Aage the Knight and Else") in Uhland—*Lenore* seems barbaric in comparison. Helgi and Sigrune. — At lunch the statement of the gladiators—"*Morituri te salutant*"—cropped up. — The word *morituri* cannot be expressed in other languages in a single word; the German language has lost these potentialities because it took its cultivation from the languages of the Latin countries, that is to say, from the languages based on Latin in an emasculated form. R. very unwell. Our only joy Fidi's high spirits and cheerfulness—it is almost impossible to remain serious with him, even when one is trying to scold him.

*Monday, October 27*   R. again slept badly. Constant vexation with the house; on top of that no prospect of a solution regarding the theater. —

Prof. Dahn sends some poems in which the whole love story between himself and his wife is portrayed—the present lack of sensitivity is incomprehensible, I cannot understand a woman who reveals such secrets. Morning and afternoon in the conservatory—wrote to my father. Life is again difficult, R. is unwell, and we see no patch of blue in the sky. — In the evening started Meurer's life of Luther—great pleasure in the true German character, in which we recognize Goethe, Beethoven, and all that we venerate among the Germans; and here it is not a game, it concerns the very nerve center of life. "The absence of all ideality brings the soul blissful peace," says R., "and the way to this peace is through Jesus Christ." — To be stubborn in one's piety (Luther)—splendid creatures, steadfast in their faith.

*Tuesday, October 28*  Talked with R. about Buddhism and Christianity. Perception of the world much greater in Buddhism, which, however, has no monument like the Gospels, in which divinity is conveyed to our consciousness in a truly historic form. The advantage of Buddhism is that it derives from Brahmanism, whose dogmas can be put to use where science reveals gaps, so far-reaching are its symbols. The Christian teaching is, however, derived from the Jewish religion, and that is its dilemma. Christ's suffering moves us more than Buddha's fellow suffering, we suffer with him and become Buddhas, through contemplation. Christ wishes to suffer, suffers, and redeems us; Buddha looks on, commiserates, and teaches us how to achieve redemption. We laugh heartily at Mathesius's saying, that priests do everything for their congregation, read masses, pray, etc.—would they also go to hell for them? Also at the honest sins of Staupitz, who moves us with his address to Luther on the subject of providence. God is not angry with you, you are angry with him—all the profound words of these profoundly religious natures. The great folk quality of these personalities is balm to us. R. says, "All great people in Greece and in India were close to the folk culture, it was the Latin peoples who invented the word *elegant*." R. had a better night. Professor Nietzsche sends us his "Appeal to the Germans" but who will be prepared to sign it? . . . R. works. Our house affair is at last being taken in hand by Herr Feustel. Unexpected and startling visit from Herr Heinrich Brockhaus! — In the evening R. plays passages from *Le Nozze di Figaro*: "We Germans can be proud of showing the Italians their true nature—how it looks in German eyes." The French text is important in this work, "for when an Italian abandons his folk qualities he becomes superficial; the Frenchman, who has no folk qualities, has something to offer in this sphere of comedy." — The importance of the masks in Italian comedy, in which speech is just an illustration of the masks—the miming is all-important. That does not work in tragedy, for suffering must be individual—the Italians were unable to produce tragedy. Continued with the biography of Luther, a profound impression. R. observes that scholasticism bears the same relation to Aristotle as French tragedy to Greek—a misinterpretation.

*Wednesday, October 29*  R.'s nights somewhat better, he is working regularly. Today I have the task of driving with Herr Brockhaus to the theater. When R. today heard the sounds of a cadenza in a Mozart sonata coming from the nursery, he said, "If I had never had the experience of Weber's things, I believe I should never have become a musician." Today, as we thought amusedly of the Italian priest's *passa passa* to Luther during the Mass, R. related how one day, as a boy in the Thomasschule, he wanted to play the organ, and the headmaster took him to accompany the hymn; but when, between the verses, he improvised in the way he believed it should be done, he became so immersed that the headmaster stopped him: "The congregation wants to go home." — Did not read the Luther biography in the evening but, after taking Heinrich Brockhaus to the theater, had supper with the poor man, during which R. was pleased with my gift for speaking to the deaf. Friend Feustel helped.

*Thursday, October 30*  Letter from Prof. Lenbach: he saw my father in Vienna, and he had remarked that it would be too great a sacrifice for me to travel alone to Pest. R. is vexed by this. Distraction provided by the arrival of our good friend Heckel, who tells us all sorts of curious things, for instance, of a traveling salesman who told him he would not give a cent for Bayreuth, even if he were a millionaire. "Why not?" He liked the *first* works—*Tannhäuser, Lohengrin, Die Meistersinger*—but to build a theater especially for *Rienzi*—no!! On the other hand, a Herr Schön, whose wife became dangerously ill and cried out on her sickbed; "Now I shall never be able to go to Bayreuth." They made a vow, should she recover, to buy two certificates of patronage—and this is what happened! And an opponent (*Cahn*) was so overcome when he heard the "Love Song" at a concert that he wrote some very fine, detailed articles on *Der Ring des Nibelungen* for *Die Grenzboten*. Plans, projects. — In the afternoon a meeting in the street with Prof. Nietzsche. He, completely outlawed, tells us unbelievable things: that the International is reckoning him as one of their own, encouraged in that direction by a writer in *Die Grenzboten*, whose article, entitled "Herr Nietzsche and German Culture," exceeds all bounds and actually denounces our friend!

*Friday, October 31*  Went through Prof. Nietzsche's very fine "Appeal" with him. Is it wise to issue this—but what use is wisdom to us? Only faith and truth can help. They are maintaining here (the dean and others) that R.'s circular has had a discouraging effect; but I am so pleased it was issued—it tells the truth! — Reformation Day and bad weather. "The Hohenstaufens never had any luck," says R. All too few people have come to the meeting, and God knows whether anything advantageous will come of it, but what else can we do? . . . In the evening a little banquet at the Sonne with the delegates and management committee. The meeting resolved not to proceed with the "Appeal"; the Societies feel they have no right to use such bold language, and who apart from them would sign it? All the proposals of the excellent Heckel are adopted. Herr Wesendonck creates real indignation by sending proposals and demands (cost estimates, etc.) which amount to a vote of no confidence in the management committee, whereas this committee has achieved wonders with the little money it has. The evening ends merrily.

*Saturday, November 1* Today the sun is shining, and yesterday the poor patrons had to view the theater in the worst weather! We shall have to get used to these edicts of Fate. Today there is another meeting of delegates and they adopt a proposal by Dr. Stern for a simple appeal for subscriptions. Lunch with Prof. N., friend Heckel, and Malwida, very nice and cheerful. In the afternoon we go to the theater, which looks splendid. In the evening the same company, plus Dr. Stern; R. in very gay mood. Then, in all seriousness, he talks about the German language, its arrested development, the great intellects searching around for foreign models—"Is it still possible now to return to the source, to think again about the wealth of inflections, etc.?" — Friend Nietzsche tells us all sorts of dismal things about the position of the excellent Fritzsch, his health, and the state of his business. Our friend also relates how he is being tormented in connection with the International, a Frau Nilsson, a friend of Mazzini's, announced herself to him as a servant of the cult of Dionysus, she wants to advance Fritzsch money and if possible also to take over his business. Our friend greatly agitated by these curious happenings! He showed the importunate woman the door, she threatened him, etc. — Our Prof. Rohde in Kiel has been advised that he will never become a full professor. Curious situation.

*Sunday, November 2* All Souls' Day! I go to confession and Holy Communion—the dean administers it. Feelings of communion with everyone, including the dead and departed; with those whom I have offended, with those who have offended me, with the lowly and the exalted—it is all just suffering, every act of malice a hideous suffering; the only true communion with people is before the altar, sorrow and concern dissolve in repentance and meditation; not only is no doubt possible in the truthfulness of this faith, but also no thought—oh, could this mood but persist! But a fair blessing that it is possible at all! None is excluded, neither the dead nor those who stand outside; sin, thus deeply acknowledged, does not torment, but dissolves in a repentant prayer; an unspoken love reigns, and my soul reaches out to the solemn, furrowed countenances of the peasants: this is yourself and everything is yourself, all who are born of flesh and marked for salvation; eternal rest, no desire waking, no sorrow searing, no pain wounding, no sin tormenting, at all levels there is peace, you feel no stirring, and now you, too, are at rest! — I do not believe that in this place any wish is being spoken, that a mother is pleading with God to save her sick child, for all is accepted and nothing considered, all such things are semblance and delusion, and as such fall apart. — Departure of friend Nietzsche, who is causing us profound concern. — I am very tired all day and cannot go out in spite of the splendid weather. Boni also indisposed, she keeps me company; agreeable impression of the settled nature of this child, whose strength and harmony lie in her reserve. Read *Luther*.

*Monday, November 3* R. has had a letter from Baron Erlanger, saying he is prepared to promote the undertaking to the best of his ability. R. writes to the King, once again appealing to him for a guarantee and announcing his visit on the 15th. — At the house, which is now making progress; I in the conservatory until moonlight falls on the leaves. In the evening conversed with R., since Malwida did not come.

*Tuesday, November 4* Very fine day, which I, however, spend in discussions with the paper hanger. But R. writes a page of his score. In the afternoon in the garden, in the evening *Luther*. It seems now to be all over with the monarchy in France, after Count Chambord very properly pointed out to the French that they themselves no longer knew how to behave toward a legitimate prince! Gloomy thoughts on my part concerning the house. R. always inclining toward new acquisitions, I constantly worried. — Boni still unwell.

*Wednesday, November 5* Real spring weather, walk with the children in the garden. Many domestic cares. In the afternoon to a Kasperl theater with the children, very gripping and interesting. As we leave, a splendid moon shining brightly, lovely impression of town life, pleasure at being in this little town. The Franconian dialect of the puppet play gave me much enjoyment, it imparts so much life. — At lunch R. told us about a melancholy dream; he saw Schnorr again, singing in an opera by Gluck, yet all the time he knew that Schnorr had died, and, in his astonishment and wonder at the impossibility of it all, he woke up. "How fine you are!" he had told him. "You are like Apollo!" — In the evening *Luther*, to our great edification and enjoyment—this is German.

*Thursday, November 6* Spent the morning with the painter Maurer from Nuremberg; we hope to have done some good. In the afternoon in the Kasperl theater again, with R. and Malwida; red cushions on our seats and Kasperl thanking R.! Bonichen still unwell, unfortunately. In the evening, *Luther*. The borrowed habit in which he journeyed to Augsburg brought R. around to extolling poverty for religious zealots; he cannot approve of Bishop Reinkens' accepting the appanage of a bishop, for the people believe in and trust poverty. — Fidi's face "lively as summer lightning," says R.

*Friday, November 7* Fidi unwell, Boni ill with catarrhal jaundice, with it fine weather and all kinds of gloomy thoughts! Made some purchases for the house; R. works; wrote letters (Herr Wesendonck has apologized); in the evening *Luther*; his address to the German nobility—splendid! R. says, "I understand this prayer." — R. seems to regret not having persuaded me to go to Pest.

*Saturday, November 8* Sad dispute with R. in consequence of my not making the journey. He has written a verse for the festival committee. — The hat I invented, since I cannot wear the present-day extravaganzas, pleases R. — Dr. Martin Perels, editor of *Die Deutsche Schaubühne*, offers to give lectures on mental illness for Bayreuth!!! — The children unwell. R. dreamed that I was conducting [Beethoven's] A Major Symphony at a concert which Rachel was attending, though he knew her to be dead; after it he was supposed to conduct the 9th, but I was doing so well that he asked himself whether he could possibly perform the same office! — In the evening *Luther*.

*Sunday, November 9* To church with Lusch, wretched preaching; a dismal spirit holds sway over present-day theology. So chilled, both without and within, that I feel no urge to go out again. In the evening *Luther*—the march to Worms—quite wonderful, incomprehensible that any servants of Rome still remained: "Just because there are always good people and bad people," says R. — Luther's saying that he hardly knew now whether he would again undertake the march to Worms in so joyous a spirit brings from R. the remark, "Yes, joy—it can disappear."

*Monday, November 10* We send off the verse to Pest. I walk with the children to the theater, which grows ever more splendid! R. occupies himself with German grammar—origin of the word *Demut* [humility], *Dienen* [serving], etc. He reads a lot of Grimm, in whom (under the word "think") he finds a quotation from Lessing which makes our hearts laugh: "A woman who concerns herself with thinking is like a man who paints his face." In the evening Malwida brings along a very pleasant Russian, Prince Mestshersky, very cultured and lively.

*Tuesday, November 11* Winter is here. R. works, I am more or less submerged in domesticity. Walk with the children; Fidi remains at home; R. suspects molars. When, at coffee during the afternoon, he is sitting beside us, happily playing on his own, R. says, "I myself was something like that, I think, playing at puppet theaters; in later years I was a complete romantic, I ran around the countryside and had a mania from the earliest times for imitating musical instruments, the fiddles as they appeared to me, whispering, whistling, and so on." Fidi sang a few notes of his own: "That's how composition begins," says R. — In the evening Luther at Worms; his prayer moves us to tears. During the night I am seized by feelings of bitterness that I did not go to Pest for my father's jubilee. I have to shed tears over this separation between us.

*Wednesday, November 12* Very fine weather, though cold. Walk with the children. Lunch with Malwida. R. works. The King sends word that he cannot receive R., but says nothing about the guarantee! . . . In the evening *Luther*; splendid letter to the Elector as he leaves the Wartburg. — The power of faith! R. also finds splendid what Luther writes to Karlstadt (?) about the preservation of traditional customs: "Do not cast out for other things that with which you have grown up and gained strength, now that you, already strengthened, no longer need it." R. observes that Prof. Overbeck could have linked his pamphlet to that.

*Thursday, November 13* Reflections, worries. My work today consists of a letter to Archbishop Haynald, summarizing my feelings about the festival and my absence from it. [*Attached to this entry is a newspaper clipping about the Liszt Jubilee in Pest on November 10.*] A walk around noon. The house a torment for R. — In the evening, due to a misunderstanding, the dean and the consistorial councilor, who thought the Thursday gathering was in our house. R. had the copyists with him and went through the *Egmont* Overture and [Mozart's] E-flat Symphony with them. Feelings of melancholy that so few people know his interpretations, and accordingly no tradition is built up. The character of the E[*gmont*] Overture is agitated accents throughout, though one must take care not to hurry it; everything must sing, but see that you do not fall asleep! In music one must always look for the melody, and if there is none, the music is bad. In cadenzas, formal phrases, one can never be too fast, etc. R. discusses with the consistorial councilor the original form of the hymn, how much lovelier they used to be, what steadfastness of faith the people who sang them expressed, what scope for a free and completely folk culture lay within them! But now they had been invested with the 1, 2, 3, 4 of a military march and had become completely trivialized. — The dean tells us that for two days running, until half past one in the morning, the King sat in the opera house and had ballets and French pieces performed just for himself.

*Friday, November 14* [*Attached to this entry is a newspaper clipping concerning a concert in Paris in which Pasdeloup played the* Tannhäuser Overture. *According to the writer, this produced a scandal, and a member of the audience commented,* "The hisses were for the Prussian, the applause for the composer."] Various enclosures, a French pamphlet about R., addressed "R. Wagner, Prussian—his admirer nonetheless"; also a German pamphlet, *Socialism and Art,* which describes R. as the final manifestation of aristocratic art. — R. writes to Düffl. to inquire whether the guarantee will be given. Hoffmann announces his arrival, and now one must decide whether one can go ahead with a commission. "The worst of it is," says R., "that I cannot, like Luther, sing, 'A mighty fortress is our God,' for God cares little about art, it's a matter of indifference to him." — In the afternoon with R. to the house. Conversed in the evening and read Part Two of *Faust.* Wonderful impressions: creation of the Homunculus, the brevity of it, yet the wealth of wit; one does not need anything in it *explained,* so gripping is it. Also the Baccalaureus with Mephisto, splendid, all so human. Gryphons and sphinxes, Chiron we also read with real enchantment—who will ever know enough of this work? . . .

*Saturday, November 15* R. works very diligently, but it tires him. Our good little Dönhoff sends us a certificate of patronage, but otherwise our affairs are very tepid. With R. to the house; wallpaper questions. In the evening again read *Luther*—the preachings following his return from Wittenberg—wonderful; everything from within, nothing revolutionary as with the French, but preserving, letting things remain, no iconoclasm, no violent abolishings, always just preaching the Word! He could protect the elector prince more than the prince could him! Indescribably uplifting and moving—the true folk hero.

*Sunday, November 16* We go on talking for a long time about the impact of the preachings; how different the reformers and revolutionaries in Italy and France, how different Savonarola! But that is the nature of the Germans. — When I asked R. how he had slept, he replies: "With worries! I go to bed with worries, and I get up with worries. I find it embarrassing to speak even to my own people here." — Malwida not at lunch, but here in the evening; it is too cold (first snow). We continue reading *Luther* for ourselves. — R. is trying to clarify the origin of the name Parcival. He was looking for it in Greece, since the Celts (Germans) came first of all into contact with the Greeks. — Lusch asks me questions about Hell, Heaven, the soul; I answer as best I can, directing her to the Gospels; R. says I can describe the soul as the Immutable by contrasting it with the mutability of appearances. Regarding the way babies come into the world (does God mold them? but the girls in school were saying the mothers are always ill at the time), she asks Malwida, and I tell her to say to Lusch: From their mothers, as with animals. — R. speaks of the influence of Rome through its officials, who introduced Roman law, the sapping of the warrior spirit of the Germans. Frederick the Great scarcely trusting his people, recommending noblemen as officers in his will. — In the evening R. plays the music for Klärchen's death in *Egmont*. "These things impress themselves on one's mind like revelations. I know that I first encountered the *Egmont* music as a boy through my sister Luise in Leipzig. What an indelible impression! It is these sounds of Klärchen's death which have accompanied me ever since." — Of the French pamphlet, R. says he finds it impossible to read such things, and I had to admit that the French, though correct in their feelings, are in their judgments too confused and uneducated, they couple Meyerbeer with Beethoven, Wagner with V. Hugo. The Italians even worse—for them Dante and Rossini are one and the same.

*Monday, November 17*  R. works hard, he is now orchestrating the scene between Waltraute and Brünnhilde. After lunch the children's playing causes us to exclaim, laughing, "Oh, how these sounds rupture my ear!" and this brings us to *Die Jungfrau von Orleans*. "Schiller has presented the problem splendidly," says R., "but it is just that, presented; one does not believe in her love for Lionel." R. agrees when I say that Schiller might perhaps have done better to let Joan tell about her meeting with the Briton (he looked into my eyes, I let the sword fall, etc.), as R. did in *Tristan und Isolde*. R. says yes, some soldiers might remark that after this meeting she is no longer her usual self, since her wild courage has been broken; she hears this and realizes that she has broken her vow and lost the strength of her chastity. — "There was no basis for it," R. says, "which shows what a living thing myth is, and how one cannot abandon it without becoming lifeless. Lionel has no place in the story of the Maid. But Ophelia is in the [Hamlet] saga, he has to be tested by a maiden, and so Shakespeare imagines this maiden. In the same way the relationship of Siegfried to Brünnhilde could not have been invented. The saga or history must provide the guidelines, and the poet then visualizes the characters." — Of Fidi R. says: "There stands a glory. He will bring it about. He forms the third in our pact. I have no other." R. visits Feustel and returns with a heavy heart. Feustel is of the opinion that the conference with Brandt and Hoffmann should be put off. R. is against that, though he does not really know from where help is to come, for Wesendonck says nothing! In the evening our dear Luther, who was also spared no bitter cup! . . .

*Tuesday, November 18*  R. makes plans for a journey to Munich to speak with Councilor Düfflipp, since he does not reply. R. is finding work very difficult because of his constant preoccupations. Interruption by Maurer, the painter from Nuremberg—I am very hesitant to order things, fearing that here, too, we might go beyond our resources. I know of no deprivation which I could not bear more lightly than this worry! . . . Luckily my intellectual interests always intervene and make me forget my worries at once. Thus—since I am reading the history of the Crusades with Daniella—I talked with R. about the 90-year Latin empire in Constantinople and asked him to consider buying Villehardouin for his library; he takes up the idea and talks about the great significance of this story, observing that it was here that the marriage between Faust and Helen took place. We then speak about Louis IX of France, his greatness and his limitations. "Yes," says R., "that was France's lovable, productive period. It is full of characteristics which present them in a lovable light, but they lacked wisdom, restraint; all their virtues were tinged with levity." Yesterday a picture of the new fashions arrived, and we were appalled by their depravity— as if the complete woman were only to be seen from behind, when one turns around to look at her! Much disgust with the nation which invents such things, and shame for the nation which imitates them. — In the evening Luther's marriage, very fine; R. returns again and again to his idea of a comedy on the subject. "One must have seen Dürer's women (in Bamberg) to understand these marriages. Certainly there is nothing in them of the searing love which devours the man, as in *Tristan,* or in *Antony and Cleopatra,* where we have the additional knowledge that the woman is bad. It is this love which Brünnhilde exalts, and it was very remarkable that in the middle of my work on the *Nibelungen* I felt the need to deal exhaustively with this one aspect, which could not be dealt with fully in my huge poem, and so I worked out *Tristan.* All of it subconscious, just always driven on. Among the Rhinemaidens love is just a phenomenon of Nature, to which it returns in the end, after, however, having been turned through Brünnhilde into a world-destroying, world-redeeming force." — We also talked again about *Die Jungfrau von Orleans*: her dread of her actions, far transcending her female propensities, should be felt and expressed by her before the encounter with Lionel, and here too much is asked of even the greatest tragedienne. Lionel must also be too noble in appearance—too much is left to chance. — This more or less our conversation, after which R. plays me some of the *Egmont* music and then reads me the scenes of Klärchen's misery and death. Who will ever hear it as he read it? "Already I walk in Elysian fields"—so simple and so heartrending! — Brackenburg's monologue helps us over our tears, we smile and are able to talk about the play again. Malwida did not come, which worries me and makes me fear that she will soon have to leave us—on account of her health.

*Wednesday, November 19* R. works, I spend much time with the children. Melancholy dream of Hans. Recall with R. earlier difficult times—it is now five years since I came to him. He declares that the next morning I said to him, "Now start on *Siegfried.*" — He goes to see Herr Feustel and confirms his departure tomorrow—just in order to demonstrate that he fears no disturbance, but without a shred of hope! — In the evening read *Luther* and finished Meurer's first volume. In Audin's Jesuitical *Life of Luther* we read the chapter on Katharina von Bora and are appalled by its meanness and triviality. Audin draws his view of this very simple and uncomplicated relationship from scurrilous songs and cartoons—as if one were later to base an account of R.'s life on contemporary newspaper reports!

*Thursday, November 20* R. off at 11 in the morning with Herr Feustel and wife—God's blessing on him! The house seems empty and dreary. At 1 o'clock wrote to R. Spent the evening with Malwida, started on Köppen's history of Buddhism. Deeply impressed, definition of Brahma! . . . In the evening wrote to R.

*Friday, November 21* Various domestic cares, two telegrams as well, here attached [*not discovered*]. Malwida to lunch, talked a lot with her about the children. Will my desire for one of them to devote herself unselfishly to her father be realized? I doubt it. They will not believe my teachings, will make their own mistakes, and not seek the bliss of bearing the cross rapturously on their shoulders—will not *choose* that. How sad it makes me to know that my experience can spare them nothing! Spent the evening with the children, later read Köppen at Malwida's home.

*Saturday, November 22* R. is on his way home—bad weather; I work in the house, clearing up, so as not to have too much to do during the move; I do so with the teachings of Vedanta constantly in my mind; strange how moved I am by this teaching of a Brahma who leaves and returns to himself; I can even understand the division into castes, there is a deep knowledge of the world in it. The only legend which stands above Buddha is that of Christ, since in the latter the action touches the heart—the crib, the supper, the cross; Buddha does not move one, he teaches; Christ teaches by moving us. — R. home at 3 o'clock, I meet him with Fidi. He is glad to be back—says when he saw Munich again and thought, "I once lived here," he felt like Giordano Bruno among the priests! — He was given hope of a favorable decision from the King by Councilor Düfflipp, who received him very affectionately. But of the King himself alarming news: every day he has some inspiration, and has hardly been persuaded out of it when he returns to it again. He no longer goes out of doors, takes his midday meal at 7 o'clock, has 60 candles lit in one small room, in which he remains, eating again at 11 o'clock and going to bed at 2 A.M., then, since he cannot sleep, taking pills! He would see nobody except his equerry, who conveyed a reprimand to the adjutant, Count Hohenstein— whereupon the latter resigned his post! . . . Worry upon worry. I cannot sleep a wink. In the evening I read R. a curious account of the festival in Pest—countesses, gypsies, journalists, the Archbishop, and among them my father, always his incomparable self, performance of *Christus*, purely personal enthusiasm. — Afterward had a long talk with R. about the Indians, the relationship of the Sankhya philosophy to the Vedanta (the latter a religion, the first just a philosophy). — While I cannot sleep, R. wakes up suddenly, tells me he has dreamed about me: that I had rebuked Fidi for wanting to give away his meat again, whereupon R. himself had reproached me! "One glance from you," R. tells me, "teaches one all about the illusory quality of things."

*Sunday, November 23* Melancholy morning, I try to persuade R. not to hasten the furnishing of our house by taking out loans. — He does not receive this well, finding me timid. This makes me weep, for I have absolutely no more wishes of my own, and am only haunted by catastrophes which I see looming on all sides. I try hard to get a grip on myself and hope to give no further impression of melancholy. Malwida's indisposition is also worrying us. The children (Daniella and Blandine) present a puppet play, Boni surprising us with her wit and calm, Daniella excitedly directing it all. R. plays the overture and entr'acte music. [*Attached to this entry a handwritten theater program*: "Sunday, November 23, for the 1st time: *The Abducted Maiden, or: Sunshine Follows Rain*, play in 6 acts. Beginning 4 o'clock precisely, ending around 6 o'clock."] In the evening R. reads to us the little sketch of *Die Sieger*. How splendid! I hope to God, who protects me, that he will complete this work—God will hear me, and I want, mean to force him to it through this prayer! . . . Read the original legend in Burnouf. R. says he will write *Parcival* when he is 70 and *Die Sieger* when he is 80, I say when he is 65 and 70. He says yes, if I do not hold him back through my timidity, but allow him to get the house finished quickly. We laugh; but I always restraining my tears. — Talk about the pedantic elaborations of the Indians, their divisions, circles, etc: it looks pedantic, but if one examines it more closely, one sees it is always profoundly meaningful—as, for example, that the Chandalas stem from the marriage of a Sudra with a Brahman woman, bad seed in a noble soil produces dreadful things. The Greeks also possessed this pedantry, it seems to me; it is like the arithmetic of music; in Christianity, in the mystics, it is not present to the same degree. It is as if this aid is required, like the apparatus of a diver, to plumb the depths. — R. has the feeling that the Kshatriyas, who were overcome by the Brahmans, were the ancient Germans—the warrior caste.

*Monday, November 24* R. dreams of a path which grows ever narrower: "Never mind," he says on waking, "I know this already, have already dreamed it several times." He is not quite well and does not wish to go out of doors. I start on my Christmas expeditions, peaceful lunch with the children. In the evening read *Luther* with Malwida; the quarrel about the sacrament—how important and significant Luther's decision! And how irreligious of Zwingli to touch on this very point, which can hardly be spoken about! The Bible—that was the thing on which Luther took his stand. Nowadays, when rationalism has so gained the upper hand, he can hardly be comprehended, and yet his decision was such an important one.

*Tuesday, November 25* Once more talked with R. about the Indians. The idea in Scandinavian mythology of a new world to follow the downfall of the gods is maybe a stray offshoot of the Indian religion. The governing of all actions by rites—this is true religion, and what distinguishes human from animal existence. The natural tendency of Germans toward corporate bodies, which restrict individual freedom. Came back once again to the acknowledgment that the human spirit needs barriers, a formula. — Arrival of my bust, which delights R.; he places it above his writing desk and sings, "Nothing is so dear to me as the room in which I bide, for now I have my fair neighbor standing by my side." In the evening we go to the amateur concert—*Egmont* Overture and R.'s overture (the one from his birthday); it makes him laugh to remember that on its first performance it was included in the same program with just this *Egmont* Overture—which pleased his mother even better. In the evening we read the play *Die Familie Posa* by Herr von Meyern!! . . .

*Wednesday, November 26* R. was very dismayed yesterday by the conductor Zumpe; he had been through both the *Egmont* Overture and the Mozart Symphony with him, and the good man had taken in nothing, or he overdid it all. "I will talk to them again about tempi," R. says and wonders whether he was perhaps like that himself in his youth, so dense and inattentive. — He works, I go to see Malwida, and since she feels wretched in her apartment, I beg her urgently to move in with us, which (since she finally accepts) means for me some rearrangements in the house. Visit from the dean, who talks very impressively about the wretchedness of the Protestant church today: the clergymen cannot bring themselves to consent to be pastors and no longer officials; he seeks in vain to prove to them that they can never be deprived of their influence over children, the poor, and the sick— all they do is abuse Prussia and Bismarck and look to their "dear God, who is still in charge and can put his foot down!" A reform in the church is the only thing which could help us, he says, and this cannot

remain invisible, just protecting, watching, serving! The house and the building on the outskirts lie like a nightmare on my soul. I fear the house will lead us into expenditure beyond our means—and the theater? . . . We hear nothing about the subscriptions.

*Tuesday-Saturday, December 9–13* Spent my days in Christmas preparations, constantly sewing dolls' clothes. Received no news from outside, R. working on his score. Read the Euphorion episode, thinking throughout of its stage presentation possibilities. Faust's soliloquy to the cloud splendid, beauty of form, so long sought after and longed for, sinking down utterly into nothingness, leaving only the beauty of the soul behind. — Helen could succeed Gretchen, but not outlast her —by remembering her, Faust attains his salvation! — Bazaine sentenced to death—the final and most wretched comedy of the war. How pitiful does this nation seem! One play actor after another, and not even for the victim can one feel any sympathy! — I have again to dismiss a thief among the servants and do it this time without inner agitation. But the servant problem is a worrisome one—what will come of it? The church has no more influence, through its own fault. Yesterday (Friday) R. earnestly reproached Malwida for not having her ward baptized. This was not right, he said, not everyone could fashion his religion for himself, and particularly in childhood one must have a feeling of cohesion. Nor should one be left to choose; rather, it should be possible to say, "You have been christened, you belong through baptism to Christ, now unite yourself once more with him through Holy Communion." Christening and Communion are indispensable, he said. No amount of knowledge can ever approach the effect of the latter. People who evade religion have a terrible shallowness, and are unable to feel anything at all in a religious spirit. — Fidi very handsome now with his "tousled" hair; R. worried about him, because he seems so sensitive, he feels he should soon have other boys to play with. — The two elder girls, having been taken on the ice several times, are now beginning to conduct themselves more expertly on it. Camellias in the conservatory. The little ones play very nicely at acting, Loldi thinks up and sings a dirge for a deceased sister, very solemn—then immediately starts playing the clown. — One morning recently we talked again about Titian's *Tribute Money*, the picture which lives deepest in my heart: I can still see the facial expression, the movement of the hand, its dying away, mildly pained, contemptuous—it has the same effect on me as music, and how ineffable the painting technique! — (Baron Weichs has died. Archbishop Rüdiger is refusing him burial. — Dr. Landgraf tells me that someone in the Baden Chamber has said that some of the strands connected with the recognition of the Old Catholic Bishop Reinkens were spun in Bayreuth.) Letter from E.

Heckel, the subscription seems to be making very tepid progress! The good man has now written to the theater managements—which is very repugnant to R. R. is very tired of his score, he hopes to have finished the first act by the New Year. He has piled too much on himself— house, theater, score, etc. — Recently, as we were eating hare for lunch, Lusch asked him whether he had ever hunted. He said yes, once in his youth, on Count Pachta's estate in Bohemia. He had shot at random, without taking aim, and was told he had hit a running hare in the leg. At the end of the hunt a dog had discovered the poor animal and dragged it out; its cry of fear pierced right through him. "That is your hare," he was told, and there and then he swore never again to take part in such a sport. The way people had come down from the useful and dangerous hunting of bears and lions to chasing hares, deer, and stags was a shameful degradation of this sport, he said. — In the evening read more *Luther*—his sermon at the funeral of the Elector Prince powerfully moving; his very remarkable character, naïveté, simplicity, graciousness, subtle sharpness, great wisdom, refusal to destroy anything that was not positively evil: "Goethe grew out of him," says R. "He applied his wisdom to the search for beauty." "There are no great men without religious feeling." "Christ is our intermediary, he leads us out of this life." Recalled Fidi's baptism with emotion, R. says he will never forget the occasion, how beautiful, how comforting it had been; how earnest the faces of the people who were present—only in a common faith can people come together like that. Religion is a *bond*, one cannot have religion by oneself.

*Sunday, December 14*  R. spoke much about the bad relations between servants and master, and said they would only get worse, yet one despised the way the Greeks and Romans had solved the problem. When he is alone, R. laughs, having remembered a musical play by Angely he saw as a child, *Seven Girls in Uniform*, in which seven girls dressed as men rescued their lovers. His sister Rosalie had played one of the girls, and Weber was asked (by the Saxon Court) to conduct; he still remembers seeing Weber conduct the music, which included a piece from *Preciosa*. — R. curses the "fire-and-water affairs" he is now having to orchestrate once again. I am still busy on the dolls' things and do not get out of doors. Our good mayor visits us; he is not in despair, even though our affairs are so much at a standstill. I once again read out loud something from *Luther*.

*Monday, December 15*  R. is not well, he goes for a walk in the morning to chase away a headache, but he does not succeed. I receive a letter from E. Ollivier, who intended bringing up his son as a soldier, in order one day, etc.—his own happiness was twice destroyed, he says, through not being a soldier! And so my sister's only son will be estranged from me and brought up as a Prussian-hater! — The house is making good progress, thanks to the Nuremberg painter. Very icy roads today, bad Christmas weather. In the evening, having used the quotation "He jests at scars, that never felt a wound," R. reads the first act of *Romeo*, as always indescribably moving. R. says that to one's complete discomfiture, one finds everything here, everything already done. I ask R. whether he believes that people who have never loved—that is to say, felt love's compulsion—could understand this play; he says no, to appreciate it inwardly one must have felt oneself that separation would mean death. The curious conversation with the apothecary somewhat surprises R., he says it offends one, coming after the news of Juliet's death; I observe that it contains a sort of ecstasy of suicide—for the despairing youth all emotion is at an end. — Today I myself am indisposed, and the thought of my own death draws nigh— how should I wish to die? Begging with all my heart the pardon of those I have offended; uttering the sublimest words of love to him whom I love; with all my strength forgiving those who have done or wished me evil; imparting to my children with my blessing a lesson which in this moment would surely take root in their hearts! But now my prime duty is to hold sacred the life which has brought me so much, such infinite, indescribable happiness. I feel as if R.'s love for me and mine for him are always growing; from this comes the cheerfulness, indeed the gay, happy mood which enables him to bear all his adversities.

*Tuesday, December 16*   Letter from Herr Hoffmann, he is demanding 1,500 thalers for the work so far done, and later 300 thalers a month. Herr Feustel will see whether Baron Erlanger will at least pay the 1,500 thalers, having subscribed 3,000. R. works, I still have a lot of errands to run, Christmas delights and vexations. In the evening we read a canto (the first) by Ariosto, but I cannot get much enjoyment from it, despite my admiration for the light and amusing action. — Very nice letter from Alwine Frommann. R. works diligently on his score.

*Wednesday, December 17*   A huge pile of old opera music arrives from friend Schuré, and we spend the evening with Auber's *Lestocq* (nice and witty) and scenes from *Semiramis* by Catel; this latter work really astounds us with its nobility and refinement. What has become of this French nation, which once produced so much and is now so horribly sterile? R. writes thanking Schuré, saying he wished all the Germans had opted for France, then they would all be delightful people. A lot of nonsensical letters to R.: a student in Alsace asks him to read an opera libretto and write music to it; Grandmongin writes from Paris: "*moi Grandmongin à Richard Wagner*—from man to man without distinction of nationality," etc. But there is also a very fine anonymous letter from an architect in Vienna who has some doubts concerning the acoustics in the Bayreuth theater and offers advice, but he writes so warmly and enthusiastically that I feel utterly moved. (A man in Brussels asks "the giant philosopher" to compose a *Macbeth* and a *King Lear!*)

*Thursday, December 18* Our love grows ever deeper, ever greater, we ask ourselves how we could ever have lived without each other. Blissful thoughts of Tribschen, the mornings, the evenings there, the Robbers' Park, the feeling of being away from the world, protected. Now indeed we are unprotected and very much exposed. Fidi's birth, my arrival with the children, the moonlight on the lake. — No one else will perhaps ever enjoy the peninsula with such deep inner feelings. — R. works. In the evening a letter arrives from the district president, telling R. that he has been asked to hand over the decoration to him. With some lack of tact, it seems to me, he invites R. to visit him tomorrow morning. R. finds this very repugnant, he says he does not know how he should come to be given instructions by anyone. I beg him not to let any vexations arise from this useless affair, but to suffer it in silence. Our evening is somewhat soured by this interlude.

*Friday, December 19* Visit from our friend Gersdorff, returning home from Italy via Basel; I enjoy the presence of this excellent man, who is utterly lacking in vanity, always open, truthful, and serious. R., too, thinks a lot of him. He spends the whole day with us. In the evening R. reads out passages from *Henry IV*, since these eternal things always affect one like springtime, the flowers, the sunny blue sky, as if one had never enjoyed them before. R. remarks on the rare dignity and loftiness of Shakespeare's kings, then the way in which he suddenly describes a subsidiary scene, such as that between Hotspur and his wife, in loving detail, as if it were the main theme. As far as Prince Hal is concerned, the aim was to portray him as a noble figure, but since Sh. is always truthful, he turns out unsympathetic. At the conclusion of the evening R. plays passages from *Wilhelm Tell* (first act); we enjoy its expansive atmosphere, in comparison with which the refined and witty Auber seems very threadbare, but the remaining acts are terribly boring. — At breakfast a volume of poems by Frau Wesendonck brings R. and me to the subject of women's emancipation. It is hard to form a fair judgment in this matter; since the position of women is such that they are very often obliged to support their families and to work like men, one cannot blame them for also demanding the rights of men. But one thing I cannot understand: that a woman should voluntarily seek a public position, for her own enjoyment. Her experiences in life must, I feel, tend to make her more retiring and bring her back to her main function, which is to raise upright men and good women.

*Saturday, December 20*  This day, too, devoted to our friend. R. works, he wishes to complete the instrumentation of the first act by Christmas. In spite of much indisposition, vexation, worry, and exhausting work, he remains, thank goodness, in gay spirits and is utterly good and kind. "With your picture (the bust)," he says, "I worship idols while I am orchestrating—if you only knew all the things I say to you!" — Yesterday he went to fetch his decoration, today he is congratulated on it; the president—very courteous, but a very dry official—did not make a graceful ceremony out of it. — In the evening he reads us Calderón's *El médico de su honra*; though I place our German dramatists, not to mention Shakespeare, very much higher, and feel emotionally much closer to them, I must nevertheless admire this fanciful artist, whom I might almost call a virtuoso of life's misery. Don Enrico's passionate nature, Donna Mencia, fearful as a beast being led to the slaughter, Guttiere with his subtle earnestness, Don Pedro and his humorous brand of popular justice—besides these the artistic and lively action, the King's forebodings of death leading to Enrico's removal, and the songs to him which his brother is obliged to listen to in the street—all this is highly effective, one has the feeling of being in tropical climes, but it is alien, alien, one is captivated, powerfully fascinated, but one is not moved—oh, Desdemona, Juliet, Gretchen, Klärchen, Thekla—what very different characters! In the Germans, Nature is in conflict with itself and with life; in the Spaniard, it is Man with his conventions—the barriers he has himself created. But the artist in Calderón is always worthy of admiration.

*Sunday, December 21*  Visits of congratulation! Some letters besides; friend Lenbach writes expressing great satisfaction with Hoffmann's sketches. An unknown man in Brussels reports the great success of *Tannhäuser* there. None of this exists for R. at all, he does not even read the letter. Departure of our good friend Gersdorff, who is now beginning a new career as a farmer, to some extent at our urging. R. outlines to him the fine activity now facing him and how he might turn out to be of use to his friends by offering them a refuge and saying to them, "Abandon your cares and do as you please, without thoughts of earning a living." In the evening we read an article by Herr Hillebrand attacking Gervinus; the aim very laudable, but the execution dry and blunt. "One can see," says R., "that a man like this has never reflected on the problems of existence and eternity, does not have that eye for the nature of all things which makes one so tranquil and serene; he is a stranger to those feelings which enable one so lightly to bear the transient, vexatious nature of things, indeed not to notice them at all." — As we are talking about the way in which J. Grimm regarded language, using quotations even from the *Vossische Zeitung*, I ask R.

whether one might not say that he saw language the way a dramatist sees a character, as a living entity, and had also presented it in the same way, without making critical remarks about what would or would not become it well.

*Monday, December 22*   A wet day, but I still have to do some shopping. R. works busily, without thoughts of the difficulties that surround him! Yesterday I put the little ones to bed and prayed with them —oh, how feelingly, how ardently—a formulation of, a leading up to the unconditional acceptance of life's difficulties! — At lunch today R. spoke about history—how it can be summed up in the exertions and sufferings of great individuals: "What else is the history of the Reformation but the sufferings of Luther? What became of the Reformation after him?" — Spent the evening gilding fir cones and threading them. — To bed at about one o'clock, kept from sleeping by the indisposition of Daniella, who has caught a cold.

*Tuesday, December 23*   Slept until nearly midday, yet despite that very tired. R. works; we go out in the afternoon, to *Ärgersheim* ["Vexation Hall"], as we call the house, since we are always finding something there that has been missed or forgotten. Home in the rain at about five o'clock, when Lusch—who has to keep to her room—gives presents to a poor child. In the evening I decorate the big fir tree, R., loving and kind as ever, comes to join me and reads to me and Malwida the Walachian fairy tale of Bagalla, which we greatly enjoy. What above all makes me happy is R.'s good mood; all day long he keeps us in fits of laughter with his incredible sallies, and I thank Nature for her kindness in bestowing on him this divine gift of humor.

*Wednesday, December 24*   Much to do from early morning until five in the afternoon; the only interruption at lunchtime, when our conversation brought us on to *Elective Affinities*. Malwida expressed her dislike of Eduard, whom she finds spineless, whereupon R. gives her a very lively answer: "What makes people significant? That something takes possession of them which wipes out everything else—for a great man this is some idea, for a less gifted one it is love. Eduard tries everything: he goes to war to seek his death, survives, and sees in that a sign that he can win Ottilie after all; he tries, the child dies, and now he wants only one thing—that the two of them, dying in silence, at least see each other; one might call these two people ascetics of love. And Goethe has shown us in detail the world they inhabit, Luciane, the Count, and the Baroness, etc., in order to show us the difference between them and these lovers. And how calmly he expresses it, how anecdotal the love scenes! A superficial person can perhaps scarcely realize how tragic the book is." During his discussion of the book I have to shed tears, our own fate flits past our eyes, and, embracing,

above the king—through it the weak dominate the stronger. The imperishable nature of nourishment, wonderful chapter, the *son* as *propitiator*. I cannot note down here everything which grips me, particularly as interpreted to me by R. We talk about the divine wisdom of these people who, in order to express something which cannot really be expressed in words (like, for example, that reason stands above the heart—yet without a turbulent heart genuine reason is not attained, though a turbulent heart by itself is evil) invented all these gradations —Atma, Purusha, the endless subdivisions. Through this wisdom they really have succeeded in building a religion on abstract conceptions which an ordinary person can never hope to understand. We cannot read much of it at a time. — And after a short pause, led there by the winter of our discontent, we pick up R[*ichard*] *III* and cannot get away from it—not even in our conversation! Among other things that interjection—"Margaret." "Richard!" "Ha!"—is one of those lightning flashes which sharply emphasize the truthfulness of a scene, while making the poet himself even more invisibly elusive. What was he like, this incredible man before whose might all must vanish? — What other poet of any place or time would ever have permitted his hero constantly to supply the program of his actions without making us lose our belief in him? But here one believes it all: thus it was, thus were they. We once again feel completely overwhelmed.

*Thursday, January 15* "You set a crown on me with your tenderness," R. says to me early in the morning. "You are the crown not only of my life, but of the whole world as well." — Alas, and I can do nothing for him! He writes Heckel a letter for the Grand Duke of Baden and says, "One does this, but one has no faith, no belief in it all—one does it just so as to have left nothing untried." At lunch he tells me he dreamed about Emperor Wilhelm, that the Emperor was very friendly toward him, and when R., touched, thanked him in extravagant terms, he reproved him with the remark, "None of this twaddle," to which R. replied in some consternation; but the Emperor throughout amiable and kind. — Walked to the house; as I am leaving to return home, an old woman stops me and asks whether she may walk across the building site. It was late, Fidi had wet feet, I tried to make her understand that she would gain nothing by walking through, but she was deaf; she went on her way, leaving me with remorse enveloping me like a shadow. Why had I not done as she asked, even if she was mistaken? She did not understand me and must have had bitter feelings about possessions and lack of possessions. Even wearier than she, I dragged myself home, cursing my prudence and my complacency, but above all my suspiciousness—I was afraid she had dishonorable intentions. But what could she have done if I had led her through? Fidi could have managed the few additional steps—I can find no excuse, and feel I should like to atone for it. — In the evening Upanishads and R[*ichard*] *III* — Before this R. suffered more vexation: the water for the second fountain, dug with great difficulty, turns out to be bad.

*Friday, January 16*   R. is not well, though the weather has improved. He has too many worries churning around inside him. Both of us in the house in the morning, positioning the Hildebrand water colors. In the afternoon as well, while the children are skating. Fidi, given two pieces of gingerbread there, hands the larger piece to Eva, then gets into a rage about it: "I always have to do that, so that people will say something!" — R. copies out his letter (to friend Heckel). In the evening continued R[*ichard*] *III* and finished the Upanishads. Found Schopenhauer's dream theory in it.

*Saturday, January 17*   R. had a bad night with wild dreams, among others that Frau Wesendonck showed him a newborn child, remarking that in her case this does not cease; then, with the utmost naïveté, she gave the child the breast; it had a curious decoration on its head and looked precocious, making R. think it had white hair. "How naïve people are here!" R. said. Then a great, powerful hawk attacked the mother and child, R. drove it off, but it kept swooping down on them again. — Then he woke up. — After that he met me in the street in Paris, dressed in black and looking very pale and sad, and he wanted to take me home. "But, my God, Minna is still alive—she'll again say she has nothing in the oven. A stop must be put to this nonsense." In silence we had then started on our way, losing ourselves in the streets, which became more and more confusing. — Yesterday I took delight in a budding cyclamen; I had given the little pot to Malwida, she went away, now the little plant is putting forth its blossoms. It is not as little children I should like to be, but as plants, soundlessly inhaling elements poisonous to mankind, soundlessly exhaling balm, silently giving joy, silently fading, striving toward the light, stretching out protecting arms. — When I tell R. about the blossoming cyclamen, he says: "Yes, you are still grateful—you have this gift, or you are still so young that you can take pleasure in something amid all this vexation. I cannot." — The children skating very prettily. On his return home R. finds a letter from our good Heckel, who did not write to Herr Wesendonck as had been decided here: instead of returning to this gentleman's proposal, he made him another one, which Herr W. has of course turned down. That's how it is—everyone thinks he knows best— R. laughs a lot when I tell him that in this matter one requires not the faith of an infidel, but the patience of a Christian. In the evening played Beethoven quartets with R.; the composure of the heart spoken of in the Upanishads is thus miraculously attained, and on this composure a ringing delight floats as on clear, still water. Here is *Brahman*, devoutness achieved, this is nonexistence and one is close to the All-Seeing. — When I spoke of the purity and chastity of this music, R. says, "Yes, it is German, and that was his foundation; it also occurs in Mozart, though his true foundation was the ingratiating art of Italian opera." — [*A passage based on untranslatable word play omitted.*]

*Sunday, January 18* R. had a bad night: "If only one had the strength not to keep thinking about it!" It is thoroughly depressing that a debt of 25,000 florins still remains. How ironic all the news which keeps coming in: Wagner concerts in London, success of *Die Meistersinger* in Cologne, requests for autographs, etc.! R. thinks of presenting the theater to the town, so as to be able to raise a mortgage on it. Visit from the mayor; the shock of the elections—Germany in no way suitable for a general franchise. The good people, satisfied with the government, abstain, and only the bad are active (Jews, Catholics, Socialists). R. is not well, consequently in a very angry mood. In this spirit he works out a poem on *pâté de foie gras*, which he wants to give Herr Feustel for his birthday. I beg him not to send the poem.

*Monday, January 19* Yesterday evening I read by myself the 12 anonymous letters of an aesthetic heretic; thoroughly healthy views, yet one does not really understand why the author felt the need to express them—and anyway it is all taken from *Beethoven* and *Art and Politics*, though lacking the philosophical basis. — In the conservatory. [*A few untranslatable words omitted.*] Chose carpets and curtains. Letter from Richter: he has not been able to arrange anything in Vienna. In the evening we begin a book about India by a missionary from Basel. Richard finishes *R[ichard] III*—great pleasure in his address to his troops. In him Shakespeare shows us the last convulsions of Norman power—but for the dream apparitions he would appear undefeated, unpunished—he does not care about his life, and is convinced of his right to the crown over such weaklings as Edward and Clarence.

*Tuesday, January 20* "Whoever acknowledges no nation as his own might just as well not have been born." "I am one of them," I say laughing. "A woman takes the nationality of her husband; men have always taken foreign wives, who are designed, like birds, to carry the seed hither and thither. A woman follows her love—if she loves a German man, she is German." R. is orchestrating the 2nd act—this the best news of the day! Utterly springlike today, starlings twittering in the palace gardens. In the evening continued reading the book on India. Before that, a visit from the dean, who strangely enough is expecting Bishop Ketteler to found the German national church. — The Protestant clergy are said to have voted almost wholly for the

Catholic party, and from the womb of this fragile, desiccated church nothing more can be expected.

*Wednesday, January 21* Herr Feustel's birthday; I send the children to his house with the *pâté de foie gras*, in connection with which R. and I vow never to touch this ingenious product of human cruelty. R. works. I write to Dr. Standhartner regarding the concert in Vienna. Eye troubles chain me to the house and idleness. In the evening I ask R. to read the text of *Der Fliegende Holländer* to the children (Daniella and Blandine), which he kindly does. My anxious desire to plant or cultivate the noble seed in my children grows daily. — R. plays passages from Beethoven's Quartet Opus [*left blank*], my favorite, and when I think about the effect such music has on me, I come to the conclusion that it is exactly like the feeling a mother has when the child first stirs in her womb—the movement of Eternity in her heart, the source of all things, usually silent, unmoving, resounds and stirs. I have the feeling that, just as the root shatters the earthen vessel, my existence, too, must yield to this striving.

*Thursday, January 22* R. works and in the afternoon goes to Herr Feustel to congratulate him, returns home in gloomy spirits, and would prefer not to talk at all. He finds great indifference prevailing there and a purely business attitude. 30,000 florins are still said to be owing on the building. — Shocking news of the suicide of Prof. Ott. In the evening continued reading the missionary's book; R. deplores the fact that only people who are not qualified to do so deal with these matters, treating them like curiosities.

*Friday, January 23* In America a second edition of *Beethoven* is being published, and it is described there as one of the most significant books of our time—a very remarkable sign! The people in New York also send 2,000 thalers, the people in Vienna 600, Lenbach 300, and Antonie Petersen five pounds—in all about 3,000 thalers. — All the same, next to nothing when one thinks what is needed. In the evening still occupied with India, a real spiritual release.

*Saturday, January 24* The long-awaited royalties from Berlin arrive at last—it seems Herr von Hülsen always sends them with chagrin, and R. must always cable for them. For this quarter they amount to 1,400 thalers, and show that R.'s works produce the biggest receipts. Eye trouble keeps me from writing or reading, and R. takes over the evening reading. After it we converse until nearly midnight. "I have what I want," he says, "you, and with that I am content, all the rest I let slide." Today he hit upon the idea of suggesting to Schott six overtures, which he intends to write starting next year, against an advance of 10,000 florins. Once before he promised me to write these overtures— "Lohengrin's Ocean Voyage," "Tristan the Hero," and "Dirge for

Romeo and Juliet." The others he does not yet know.

*Sunday, January 25* The children attend the funeral of poor Prof. Ott and are very solemnly impressed by it. Prof. Hoffmann writes that people are jamming his studio to see the sketches. He also asks about the commission for them. How and what is one to reply? I have to admire R. for remaining so cheerful amid all the depressing worry and uncertainty. He keeps telling me that it is I who keep him on his feet— which always makes me want to say an Ave Maria! — We go for a walk together, the avenue leading to the Eremitage, delight in the pretty scenery, much peace and merriment in the fields. In the evening, India. —

*Monday, January 26* English translation of *Das Rheingold* and *Siegfried,* soon the whole *Ring* will appear (Alfred Forman). Letter from Malwida in San Remo, she was ill, but is now enjoying the south —I thank God for every bright cloud I see here, and R. observes it is just a matter of degree, the poetic spirit will be awakened just as much here as down there. The gemstone flashes but faintly, nevertheless it flashes! — Repeated news from Cologne: *Die Meistersinger* seems to be a great success there—the only sad thing is that this success means nothing to us! — The Indians in the evening, penetrated further, saw that Buddhism was the fulfillment of Brahmanism, the first directed toward pure knowledge, the latter toward ethics. To end with, R. reads me some of Aristophanes's *Lysistrata*—great fun.

*Tuesday, January 27* Went to the house early; when I return home, R. shows me a letter from the King which he did not wish to read—I should tell him what it contains. I see at once that it is very friendly. The King promises never to give up his mission in life, and says the delay was forced on him only by the state of his purse. He treats Prof. Dahn's poem as sycophancy and knows that R. has better things to do than to embellish such verses. But still we are left in uncertainty—will he grant the guarantee or will he not? . . . Heckel has forwarded the letter to the Grand Duke of Baden. In the evening made more progress with the new Brahmanism. Before our reading we talked about the people who had all drifted away from him, such as the Brockhauses, Karl Ritter, the Willes, Laube—a vast number R. can trace throughout his life. I tell him he can also say, of his *Ring des Nibelungen,* "Those who listened to the first songs no longer hear the last!" He replies: "I don't care much about that. For me these people have passed away before they have actually died, and I have what I want: you!" — Today he played the end of the second act, the richest, most varied piece of work he has perhaps ever written, and the most acute in its dramatic accents.

*Wednesday, January 28* The question which was this morning tormenting R. is whether he should write to Prof. Hoffmann in Vienna that the whole undertaking has been indefinitely postponed, or whether, relying on the King's letter of yesterday, he should count on the guarantee. While I am paying some calls he makes up his mind, but I do not dare ask him in what direction; I am just glad to distract him a little, if it lies in my power. Over coffee we come once more to the subject of "the icebergs which have melted in the sea of inferiority," among them K. Ritter. R. maintains that it was the *Judaism* article which destroyed him, as it did poor Tausig, for he had Jewish blood in his veins. R. takes a long walk, goes out to the theater, and there meets a peasant woman, with whom he has a cheerful conversation. He talks to her about the long, poor path she has before her on the way back to her village. "My dear sir, if you've had to walk it every day for 30 years, you stop thinking about whether it's good or bad." — In the evening, after we had read some more of the Basel book, R. wanted to read me Aristophanes, but it was impossible—there is too much licentiousness, in which women can take no part. While R. was out walking, I sat for a long time in the moonlight in the conservatory, quite unable to take my leave of the gentle rays and the great stillness.

*Thursday, January 29*   Spent the whole morning walking in the palace gardens, keeping an eye on the children on the ice. R. works on his second act. After lunch he goes to see Herr Feustel, who cannot understand the King's remarks about the Dahn poem, since in Councilor Düfflipp's office he had seen telegrams from Eisenhart, the secretary, reporting that the King was feeling extremely ungracious toward R.! — The bank in Coburg is prepared to advance 50,000 florins on the spot, once the guarantee is given! Well, at least the men have now been paid 10,000 florins. — In the newspaper we read as a piece of literary and theatrical news that Laube and Dingelstedt have now been reconciled after an estrangement of many years, and that as a result, *Faust,* Parts One and Two, are to be performed (with stage design by Makart, etc.) over six days. I have to laugh over these miserable people. Of *Faust* R. says: "Such works tower like sphinxes over our incompetent culture. The German drama is past rescue, the opportunity was missed, now music has taken over and swept everything away." — Today it was also my lot to be put to a fearful test. When the two elder children came upstairs to say good night, I joked with Blandinchen about coming times. As the children leave, I notice that Daniella is saying something and call Blandinchen back to ask about it. "How boring," is what she had said about my joke! . . . R. horrified, I preserving silence, bidding my soul to be calm, and in this calmness stammering a prayer of submission. All I can do here is accept. With distress I now realize that blame lies not in my divorce from Hans, but in my marriage to him. Profound effort to control my soul, to raise it to the level of thanking

God for my punishment, resolve not to let the cheerfulness fade which is so vital to R.; holding back my tears, praying!

*Friday, January 30* I find it difficult to speak to R. about anything except what happened yesterday! . . . But I do not let my sorrow show. Daniella, returning from school, wants to beg my pardon for having so offended me, but I reply that she does not have to beg my pardon, since she had not offended me; I told her that when she misbehaved, lied, or was impertinent, I should continue as before to punish her; but when, after a day spent in harmony, she makes such a remark about an affectionate little joke addressed to her sister, I could make no punishment, no reproach—for me it had been a revelation, and on this level I could only commune with God, who bestows both blessings and curses. I allow her to work beside me, treat her as usual, and bear no bitter feelings against my lot, no grudge against my child, and believe I have thus achieved understanding. R. wants her to be sent away, but I fight against this, for I believe that despite everything she is happier here than anywhere else and that the good aspects of her character will be brought out better. If in my heart I am sorrowful and if I humbly bear this pain, perhaps I shall not be denied the blessing of seeing my child become a good person; and the fact that my way of doing things remains a mystery to her is of course of no importance to her. — Letter from my father; he says that the wreath presented to him by the Wagner Society at his appearance in Vienna had aroused mixed feelings in him, he tells himself that there is nothing better he can do than place his fingers at the disposal of the Wagner Societies. Yesterday Marie Schleinitz wrote in a very chastened spirit, saying that the mood in Berlin was so depressed that she expected nothing from the petition to the Emperor. She also tells us that Hans and Dohm had been in Meiningen at the same time, as guests of Frau von Heldburg, and that Hans had been in splendid spirits and had professed himself extremely satisfied with his success and his earnings in London. May his children bring him joy! — Walk with R., Fidi, and Eva, snow flurries—I feel unwell, as if my heart is being suffocated, but I manage to keep control over myself, and praise God for silence! In the evening with R. to Frau Gross's for a housewarming. — Earlier a letter from Herr Schott, who seems, apart from a few ifs and buts, to be interested in R.'s suggestion.

*Saturday, January 31* R. writes to Herr Schott and is pleased with the success of his scheme. Outing with the children in the afternoon. — In the house the first of the Hildebrand water colors has now been put up. In the evening—my eyes are still weak—R. starts to read *Timaeus,* but he soon gives up, since, as he remarks, it is not profound metaphysics but artistry that one expects from the Greeks, and in Plato it is the artist and not the philosopher who enchants us. Behind all the fantasies of the Indians there lies a deep philosophy, in them it seems that proper knowledge can only be won through these fantasies.

*Sunday, February 1* Farewell, January, with all your sorrow and pain! It is good the way one divides up time, for then one says to oneself: This month was bad, the next will be better; but there is also a kind of experience that alters nothing. — Today to the photographer's! R. can scarcely be painted—how can one photograph him? Conversing about it, we decide that photography's claim to replace painting is like that of science to replace philosophy. — I gaze upon the Brussels portrait of R. and say to him, "What fills me with melancholy is that in it your eyes never seek mine." "They are not seeking anything," he replies. "For me the world is completely dead." — A walk in the afternoon, the weather is cold, and R. loses patience. We return home. In the evening Fr. Schlegel's book on Greeks and Romans, read with interest the chapter on Diotima.

*Monday, February 2* R. writes to the King, discusses in his letter the vocation of the German princes (Councilor D. wrote to me that the winds blowing from Hohenschwangau seem more favorable now to our enterprise than previously). In the afternoon our new servants arrive—a man, his wife, and 3 children, from Berlin. In the evening picked up our old Gibbon again after a long break, with great enjoyment (Honorius, death of Stilicho, etc.).

*Tuesday, February 3* To the new house in the morning, to see how the newly arrived family (complete with canary and Bible) is getting along. R. finishes his letter to the King. In the evening the copyists' group enriched by a Macedonian, Herr Lalas, sent by Richter (who has now become director of the opera in Pest). R. goes through Haydn's D Major Symphony with them, then he plays the Andante (G minor) from another symphony, explaining its beauties, above all its concision—everything expresses something, no arabesques, the two themes circle around each other like sun and moon. Of Weber's *Jubelouvertüre*, R. says that it made him for the first time conscious of the brilliance of the key of E major. — At the end of the evening a strange conversation with the Macedonian, who claims to descend from the ancient Greeks and prefers the German neo-Greek pronunciation to the Greek (Idipus instead of Oidipos)! . . .

*Wednesday, February 4* Herr Schott seems interested in R.'s proposal. Yesterday R. sent off his letter to the King—I have not read it. — Went to the photographer's, the children in their costumes, for the King. Returned home late, which vexes R.; he is in a state of torment just now, wondering whether the date can be adhered to if the King now gives the guarantee, and he is worried about the turmoil which will result. A gloomy evening in consequence. — My sick eyes condemn me to idleness, and I am becoming more and more turned in on myself—at times I feel that I shall never be able to speak again.

*Thursday, February 5* Went to the house in the morning; when I return I find R. beside himself with rage. Herr J. J. Weber is laying claim to the rights in the text of *Der Ring des Nibelungen* which R. has assigned to Herr Schott. I manage with difficulty to calm R. down over this bit of sharp practice. It is the fact that nobody is indignant over Herr Weber's behavior which so upsets him; I tell him: "We have the theoretical knowledge of Man's wickedness, the others the practical knowledge; that is why they are never indignant, but just protect themselves with provisos. They do not want to acknowledge the theory, because the doctrine of the sin of existence and the wickedness of the human race contains too much ugly truth for them." — In the afternoon a letter from friend Heckel, saying the Grand Duke of Baden regrets not being able to do what R. asks, since he is convinced the step would prove unsuccessful! And Herr Wesendonck is prepared, "with reservations," to subscribe 700 thalers to the guarantee fund. We, R. and I, cannot help laughing. "One has done one's best," R. says. "I didn't expect much, but one acts as if one expects something and leaves nothing untried." In the evening Gibbon, always with enjoyment. Unfortunately my eye is not yet sufficiently restored to allow me to do the reading. R. still very indignant over Herr Batz and Herr Weber.

*Friday, February 6* My eye prevents my reading or writing. R. takes over the reading in the evening. As we are admiring individual acts of heroism among the last of the Romans, R. says, "They go down like men, the French like apes." — They are preparing to do *Rienzi* in Venice.

*Saturday, February 7* Springlike weather, went for a walk with the children in the morning and with R. in the afternoon (Rollwenzel). Great inner weariness, longings for death. The sight of the theater now actually offends me. "Perhaps something still unforeseen will come along," R. says, "since the known factors on which we built have so completely deserted us." Read Gibbon. In the night I am beset by a congestion of the heart which drives me to R. It gives up after a little while, but I am left feeling very limp.

*Sunday, February 8* Snow flurries! The weather throws us this way and that. More and more I get the feeling that R. and I have been banished from the world. "Can you say where our home is?" R. has invited the copyists, along with Herr Runckwitz; nice, good people. The building supervisor tells us about the harshness of the foremen, who have been declaring in all the taverns that they intend to sue the management committee unless they are paid. The sum involved is now only 5,000 florins, and R. and I decide to pay them from my small savings if the King deserts us again. — They are preparing *Rienzi* in Venice and send a telegram asking whether Orsini is a *"Baryton absolu,"* to which R. replies that he has no knowledge of either a relative or an absolute baritone and that in Germany singers count it an honor to appear in his works. R. tells me about a dream in which he attended a performance of *Der Fl. Holländer* with me, and in the 3rd act, after the Dutchman's declaration of jealousy, the scene suddenly changed back to the spinning room, in which there were three policemen; in despair R. had cried out, "Heavens, what are they doing with my things?" — In the evening Gibbon (Chrysostom) and a play sent by the secretary of the University of Strassburg, Dr. Schricker; based, so the author assures us, on impressions received from *Lohengrin, Meistersinger,* etc.— the play, *Bertha the Spinner,* is the most pitiful hotchpotch one can possibly imagine! — R. reads me a sentence from his *State and Religion* about the duties of a politician, and says: "Bismarck could quote that against me, though in any case, if he does do something for my undertaking, he will not be acting like a politician. In the whole of history only one man—Pericles—has ever found a nation which supported his ideals." — Another sad piece of behavior from Daniella (some derogatory words about the copyists) has wounded me deeply. I have an image of the heart as a block of granite which has been broken up, and now its original pattern is being pieced together like a mosaic— one still recognizes it—but it is in pieces. However, the skeleton stays firm, and in me there arose a complaint against this physical strength which persists unimpaired though the heart is already in pieces. Fervently I longed for death—for one of the main tasks of my life I shall be unable to achieve. — Reflected on the Chandala maiden!

*Monday, February 9* Letters from Herr Schott, R. and he conclude the contract, which, in R.'s words, "is equally honorable for both sides." In the afternoon comes a letter from friend Feustel, saying the King has asked for a formulation of the guarantee and at the same time for an expert opinion from the management committee. Considerations as to whether the performances will be possible (in the year '75) after all. R. writes to Brandt and Hoffmann in this connection.

*Tuesday-Monday, February 10–16* Did not write in my diary all week, my eyes being bad. R. has many troubles: part of the piano arrangement of *Götterdämmerung* arrives and is unplayable and un-understandable, the middle voices too prominent, so that the main theme is obscured. He cannot find time for his score, which worries him a lot. "What I should like to do is to keep on producing, to get down to *Parcival,* but I am held up by things which other people ought to be doing. No school, no stage, no one to help me, there I stand and still have to spend long years working on my past creations to put them in proper order." Herr Schott sends the 10,000 florins, and R. reflects on the overtures: "Lohengrin's Journey," "Tristan," "Epilogue to Romeo and Juliet," "Brünnhilde," "Wieland the Smith." Unfortunately R. still has troubles with the house which I cannot take over for him, and his mood has a very depressing effect on me — I am like someone coming down with an illness: hindered, but not really ill. My eye ailment is also an obstacle. R. very kind, always reading to me in the evening—Gibbon. The present time seems to us likewise a time of decay, in which great individuals perform great deeds which, however, have no real meaning. R. deplores the fact that through the introduction of Latin the peasants were suddenly cut off from all culture— that had not been the case previously. — Brandt writes that it will probably not be possible to put on the performances before '76, which is probably a good thing. If only R. does not overexert and exhaust himself! This fear will not leave my heart. — Recently Siegfried caused me sorrow for the first time—he went to his father, looked at the library, and said, "This will one day belong to me, when I am big, you will be dead then." — The mayor recently touched R. greatly by the way he said, "An undertaking like this must be brought to completion; a deed so selfless as this of R.'s must receive recognition; for R. has no need of fame and does not need his name and his works spread around, etc." — The barber says that a play was produced in Passau entitled *Wagner's Dream*, in which all the characters R. had created came to greet him. — Bechstein is sending us a new grand piano, the old one is sent away, and the Erard again installed in our house—for me a host of memories come flying back.

*Tuesday, February 17*  Eva's birthday. — Today, too, she is greeted with the master melody to which she was born. I remind R. how at her birth he whispered in my ear, "I have never loved before." He replies, "Whoever loves you has never loved before." Recently, when after a day of vexations for R. we fell into each other's arms, he said to me in the evening, "I understand now how one can die for love; I believe the full power of love is felt only when one is my age: today, when I was holding you, I was close to losing consciousness." — I cannot tell him how much I love him, and I suffer in consequence; in this case one must just act, for one cannot describe one's state of being to another. Children are invited, running through the new house. R. unfortunately still much weighed down by corrections—if only Richter were here! — Read Gibbon in the evening. Before that R. reads me from Freytag's book a passage about the itinerant people, with whom he associates Luther. "The writer of the *Nibelungenlied* must certainly have been that sort of itinerant, a genius," says R., "for the theme he sang about was utterly despised at that time, and it was especially hated by the clergy, on account of its old heathen flavor. What would we know about Shakespeare, for example, but for the art of printing?"

*Wednesday, February 18* Today R. told me his dream: how he had been in a theater box and it had suddenly seemed like a precipice; to his horror Minna had suddenly come in and, reproving him in a friendly way, helped him in his peril; as they tried to walk down the steps, a series of cows' heads appeared, ever more and more, until he woke up. — Much domestic trouble, a wretched governess; on top of that, R. not well—he cannot work, spent the morning reading Daumer's new book attacking the Old Catholics, Strauss supporters, etc., defense of miracles. We thought we might find something profound in it, but find ineptitude; in his polemics against the others he is quite right, but in positive matters he is very superficial, even childish. On all these subjects Schopenhauer alone is profound and acute. — The new copyist, the Macedonian, visits me and tells me what disgraceful opinions about R. prevail in the Munich Conservatoire; he also tells me about Brahms, how this gentleman at first spoke against the propagation of W.'s music, but when he saw that the young musician was a Wagnerian, he simply observed that this music was too difficult for young people! — I am foolish enough to talk to R. about this, and it brings him back to the subject of the decoration, he wonders how he can make his opinion about this known. — Friend Feustel writes from Munich that there are no difficulties in the way of the guarantee—just that another formulation is being demanded. Worries that maybe there will be an insistence on keeping to the year '75, or after the performances some hold over the works. — In this case, R. says, he must do everything to insure that not a cent is paid out of the King's purse! —

*Thursday, February 19* R. had a bad night, constantly thinking about the decoration affair, then the dangers of the guarantee. He reads Daumer, but in the evening Gibbon, to me. — The Women's Wagner Society sends 550 florins as the first proceeds of their lottery. Apart from that, nothing of significance. R. tells me that for Winkler's newspaper he signed his short story about Beethoven "Richard Wagner, music setter in Paris." — R. tells Loldi the story of William Tell, and in connection with this we admire the way Schiller handles the main scene, making Bertha and Rudenz burst in (on Gessler); Tell literally disappears, as if defeated, and suddenly one hears that the apple has been struck. —

*Friday, February 20* R. dreamed of the Brockhauses, that they behaved in a pitiably embarrassed way when we visited them in Leipzig!

. . . Went on the ice with the children, R. in the afternoon to Feustel's, for the conference. The King does not wish to give a guarantee, but will advance money up to a limit of 100,000 thalers; until this money is refunded, the stage decorations, etc., etc., will belong to him. . . . R. returned from the conference in an ill humor; the committee was downhearted, because of the impossibility of keeping to the original year, and Feustel once more talked of concerts. — Feustel remarked that Düfflipp had been in a very bad mood. In short, nothing good, and especially no joy. In the evening Gibbon. (On our site they have at last struck water.)

*Saturday, February 21*  Bad eyes, which refuse to function any longer. The doctor does not know what to do. We think of the water at Lourdes, of which R. has read much in Daumer's book! . . . Busy with the house; R. again to Feustel, who is going to Vienna. Hoffmann, the painter, is ill. Fine speech by Count Moltke about the extraordinary exertions the French are making in connection with their army. — The piano teacher Heintze sends 100 thalers for our undertaking. In the evening Gibbon.

*Sunday, February 22*  I write to the King and send him photographs of ourselves and the children. R. gets down at last to his score. In the morning he reads a book by a headmaster in Danzig about Gallicisms in the German language, which pleases him. In the evening we read Nietzsche's recently arrived book on the uses of history; it starts off in a very abstract way and consequently seems somewhat arbitrary.

*Monday, February 23*  Armed with a green eyeshade, as in my childhood—but R. is working busily. We continue with our friend's book and delight in it—great courage, great fervor, very acute judgment. R.'s example has opened his eyes to the triviality of the whole modern world.

*Tuesday, February 24*  For me still no activity possible, my eyes are very painful. No news from the outside world, the house making slow progress. In the evening finished the book with great interest.

*Wednesday, February 25*  Our friend's treatise forms the topic of our conversation, the fiery wit with which it is written is quite astonishing. R. works. In the afternoon we go to the house, and in the evening the dean visits us, delighting us with his warmth and his originality. He speaks of the awful turn the religious question has taken through the fact that Rome seems conciliatory; if peace is proclaimed, they will be the victors.

*Thursday, February 26*  The Emperor's note shows our good dean to have been wrong; the mood in Prussia seems very determined. — R. works. From Hamburg he has received 60 thalers as the result of a concert given for the benefit of Bayreuth by the military band in

Hamburg. Still very touching proofs of interest. Delight in the pictures based on the *Nibelungenring*, which have been affixed in the hall of our house. R. is delighted for Fidi's sake; I tell him I wish he, R., had had such things done for him. Fidi's constant high spirits please him. "That is life's flowering, it is how the Will shows pleasure; this is what drives it to produce childhood." In the evening we read the introduction to the book on Gallicisms; Frederick the Great speaking of *M. Quantz* amuses us very much, although his deep insight exalts us at the same time. "How terrible, how sad," says R., "that such a being shows characteristics which are downright grotesque, and which turn him merely into a subject for anecdotes!" "Latin was to Charlemagne what French was to Frederick." Praising our Emperor, R. says: "It is only as a man of culture that he shows up badly, that is to say, only when he comes into contact with our culture. Otherwise he is truly a hero."

*Friday, February 27* R. still at work, but he also does a lot in connection with the house, which gives him pleasure. Fidi's constant cheerfulness gives him much joy: "There is no silly vanity, no arrogance, no wickedness in the wake of cheerfulness. Those qualities belong to melancholy, to lack of freedom." "He will reap the harvest," he says, looking at the house. "I am glad: he will have no longings for wealth and fine living and will be able to despise all outward things." — Today, when I pose a riddle to the children—"When I bring it about, I bring it about, but if not, it happens just the same"—Fidi guessed *"an accident,"* which did rather amaze us. In the evening Gibbon. In great pain with my eyes.

*Saturday, February 28* R. still busily at work. In Vienna friend Feustel is working out a contract with Professor Hoffmann, who expects to have his work completed by 1875; but there can be no question of that. In the morning I walk to the house with the children, in the afternoon R. In the evening he reads to me some of the Gallicisms, which make one wonder what will become of the German language. Also read Gibbon. Over coffee we once more talked about the *Nibelungenlied*, and R. said, "A poet literally grows with his task, as Shakespeare did in *Antony and Cleopatra*; in the beginning he is just compiling, but then he sees more and more of the tragedy in it." Incidentally, the dean recently pleased us greatly—when he was talking about rare impressions which he had had and which made an immediate impact on him, whether in music, painting, or literature— by quoting the scene in which the wounded Antony has himself carried up to Cleopatra. "This shows," R. says to me, "what repressed fires and emotions lie concealed in our friend." —

*Sunday, March 1* R. tells me two dreams he had last night; in one of them he was taking leave of Minna, whom he suddenly asked in alarm, "My God, have I given you any money?" She, in a friendly manner: "So you think of that now!" Then a cordial parting, he, however, saying to himself, "You will be able to tell her better in writing that we cannot go on living together." The second dream was set in Paris, in the foyer of the Grand Opera, where R. was to produce and conduct one of his works, and he was received scornfully by the members of the orchestra. One of them: "I suppose you think you write pretty things and will please the audience." "I suppose you want to perform your work here!" R. seeks to pacify them by saying he has never tortured an orchestra, but they will not listen. When it is time to begin the rehearsals, he loses his hat and looks for it, and amid mocking laughter the members of the orchestra bring him all kinds of children's hats—then he woke up. — I go to church; the hymn "*O Haupt voll Blut und Wunden,*" followed unfortunately by the sermon. R. works. At lunch the Macedonian, to whom R. addresses some remarks on tempo. "Of course," R. says, "one must have some idea of it; one must know, having heard it done well and then badly, that they are not the same thing." In this regard the metronome is of no use. [*An untranslatable witticism omitted.*] — When the stranger has departed and R. and I embrace, he says to me, "You are unfadingly beautiful!" — In the morning he told me that Minna had once threatened to publish her memoirs, which makes me laugh a lot. — When he is talking about tempo, he again tells how [Wilhelmine] Schröder-Devrient had come to a rehearsal of *Guillaume Tell* and asked him please not to take the *Tyrolienne* so fast. "She could not bear slapdash work," says R. In the evening we intend to put the etchings in order, but we do not succeed, and return to Gibbon.

*Monday, March 2*   Again R. did not have a good night, but he works all the same. Splendid spring weather; I take Daniella to the elementary school to be registered and deep within myself pray to God that she may perform the pious act of improving herself. Lunch alone with R., afterward he goes to look for Herr Feustel, who has now returned from Munich; he returns home in a despondent mood, and tells me that friend Feustel has not been to see Düffl. because of the unpleasant treatment he had received on their last meeting; Prof. Hoffmann's demands were unclear and carping, and Brandt has not made any at all; on top of all this, the King is in debt. God knows what lies ahead of us! — In the evening R. reads to me from the *Pictures of German Life.*

*Tuesday, March 3*   At breakfast, when we were talking about his wife, R. said to me, "I should know nothing of the reality of my whole former life if I did not have the few operas I wrote then." — At lunch R. said, "If I had to say something to the Socialists, I should set up these three axioms: (1) there are good people and bad people; (2) the rich man is no happier than the poor man; (3) if you do not have the peasants with you, are not in agreement with them, your whole movement is not worth a cent." — Walk with the children morning and afternoon. In the evening a telegram from Brandt, also full of vague stipulations; R. very unpleasantly affected by it, says he feels as if everyone is taking him too lightly. Yesterday he wrote to Councilor Düfflipp, asking for a quick decision. — Malwida writes; as R. is reading the letter with a somewhat ironic air, I say to him, "You were not always so sharp toward your female friends." "I did not know any better—and they carry no scars." Read Freytag and appalled by his style. "What are our schools for?" — We end the evening with the hymn "*O Haupt voll Blut und Wunden.*" "It is true, at that time there were no great men, but there were solemn hours," R. says.

*Wednesday, March 4* "Help me to have a good day," R. says early in the morning. Then he addresses the picture of his mother, before which I am lying: "What have you got to say," he cries, "now that I have won this woman for myself?" — He then talks about a play in the manner of *Die Kapitulation* which he would like to write, in which all the literary figures would appear by name (Lucius Freytag, Fabius Rodenberg, etc.) with their manners of speech; and with them a peasant. "I only wish some theatrical genius would arrive who would describe all this plainly, sparing nobody, though not treating them as real persons. But the audience would not understand him anyway, for we have no public life, and these men are really just phantoms, they don't exist for the people. In Germany you must shout from the rooftops, as I do; solemnity is the only thing which has an effect on the Germans, and music is the only arcanum." — R. works; still no news from Munich. Since the weather is fine, I spend the whole afternoon in the new house with the children. In the evening the copyists and Herr Runckwitz; go through the *Meistersinger* Prelude, then the C Minor Symphony and *Joseph*, the last the object of much admiration on R.'s part, he tells how Simeon's aria had gripped him as a young man. "He (Méhul) has taught us the art of letting something die away, the [*word illegible*], he uses it twice: after the father's curse and after Simeon's aria. Joseph's entrance—that is true art. People were better than they are now—they enjoyed such things, and the period which could produce three such works as *La Vestale, Les Deux Journées,* and *Joseph* was no trivial one. Today's rulers are Flotow and Offenbach." — Speaking of conductors and orchestras, he says: "For an intelligent orchestra player who feels and knows everything it must be terrible to have the time beaten for him by a stupid conductor, as all of them are nowadays. And what care is taken nowadays to insure that people without fire are engaged everywhere! When a young foreigner such as our Macedonian friend comes to Germany in search of culture, all he encounters is spiteful mediocrity."

*Thursday, March 5* R. tells me that during the night he saw me in the room with Fidi, who had some curious spots, and I said to him, "The boy will not go to bed, it is past his time, he is so excited." — Herr Gross comes in the morning to tell us that the King has signed the agreement. I write to Malwida. In the afternoon at the house. R. very worn out, he writes to Richter to find out if in 3 months' time he can be at his disposal (from May). In the evening the Thursday gathering; the question of hotels during performance season debated with Karl Kolb. Delight in Fidi; but when, with some alarm, I notice him pulling many faces, R. says to me, "He won't become a play actor, he will have the same distaste for it as I have; the idea of going in front of an audience with a painted face and getting myself applauded would appall me—it has never occurred to me to do that." — "What prince except for the King of Bavaria has a sense of honor?" R. recently exclaimed during a conference.

*Friday, March 6* R. works; I to the house with the children. Concern over the great amount of money being spent. In the afternoon there again, in the evening discussed the difficulties of the children with R.; resolve to send the eldest ones to an aristocratic institute. Spent the whole night in thoughts and worries of this kind. — It is indeed wonderful that a glance at the brightly shining moon should be able to bring me solace; no word from another human being could, I believe, be of help to me, but a flower, a moonbeam, comforts a sore heart.

*Saturday, March 7* Governess affairs. — R. writes to Niemann and Betz; then also to other singers (Hill, etc.); the state of the male ensemble is good, but with the women the situation is bad. In the evening R. is upset by an official letter from the management committee, asking him to keep to the year 1875 and to give concerts to this end! R. answers in great detail and also raises the question of accommodations for the patrons coming here. In the evening read Gibbon. (Sad letter from Frau v. Meyendorff, my father seems to have deserted her; R. feels no sympathy for her, he says that only genuine relationships arouse his concern.)

*Sunday, March 8* The children in church, I write to Marie Schl., and R. writes more letters. In the afternoon to the house, in the evening R. shows me what he read this morning in Tieck's critical studies, in consequence of which we also go through the second act of *Der Prinz von Homburg*; slight disappointment—the idea incomparable, but some flaws in the execution, it also lacks the expansiveness which breathes in Schiller's works. In the afternoon, while R. was resting, I read parts of *Wallenstein* and was again overwhelmed by its beauty; happy the nation which possesses such a poet! R. talks about Tieck's unfairness toward Schiller, which was certainly due to envy. — They held Goethe to be above competition and simply admired him. R. remembers having seen in his youth the production of *Der Prinz von Homburg* of which Tieck writes, as well as Tieck's own efforts for the stage: "He had the right dramatic instinct, though it was somewhat sketchy, but he came to grief over the modern German theater, such as it is." Tieck's interpretation of *Der Prinz von Homburg* pleases us greatly. — Telegram from Vienna reporting on the success of the concert for the benefit of Bayreuth.

*Monday, March 9* Today, after an interruption of several days, R. wanted to get down to his score again, but then Herr Feustel arrives with Herr Riederer, the latter showing not the slightest trace of any willingness to help in providing new hotels. Quite by chance a hotel owner, Herr Albert from Mannheim, arrives in the afternoon and puts forward some plans; R. takes him to see Feustel, but brings home little that is encouraging or edifying: friend Feustel declares that no corporation could be formed here to promote such things—the town is too poor. On the other hand, one cannot expect strangers to bring their capital here if the town is unwilling to invest in it. — Gloomy evening; R. did in fact manage by sheer will power to complete a page of his score, but he is thoroughly depressed by the great difficulties of his task, and on top of that Richter, the only one who could help him, is now a theater director! "It's as if I wanted to become the minister of trade!" R. says. — Schopenhauer's annotations to the *Parerga* give R. great pleasure "at a time when philosophy comes out of apothecaries and clinics." He also says, "I can't help feeling sorry for our European culture, which is based on a monotheistic belief."

*Tuesday, March 10* R. receives a letter from Brussels, from a German who encloses some sonnets to the Nordic gods, and this brings us to the subject of the old myths and legends. Regarding the latter R. says: "If we had a true poet, there would be material enough for popular dramas (*Rolf Kraki, Nornagest,* etc.); however, they should not be conceived in three acts and with all the usual stiff apparatus, but, rather, should be put before us like a picture. I myself would find such a task attractive, if only I had the time." At 3 o'clock a women's coffee party at Frau Dr. Käfferlein's house! . . . R. meanwhile at a conference with the management committee, the subjects to be discussed being the contracts with Hoffmann and Brandt, the preservation of '75 as the opening date, and, finally, accommodations for the guests. In the end Herr Albert is brought in, and he makes such a good impression that the mood improves and agreement is reached. Did not do much reading in the evening.

*Wednesday, March 11* R. talks in the morning about a capital city for the German Reich—how he would like to see it built where the river Main flows into the Rhine. "One can't blame the Alsatians for preferring Paris to Berlin. Cultural ideas have been forgotten, and all that remains of the Reich is the Prussian uniform." — Much delight in Fidi; R. says, "He is the finest testimony to our love." When I tell him that, because of the shade our boy had placed aslant on his head, I had managed to see one of his eyes singly and had been very surprised by its beauty and brilliance, R. says, "Yes, a single eye would certainly make more effect than two, and the fact that Nature gave us two shows that in this connection it was more interested in the question of seeing than in that of being seen." Letter from Marie Schl., the excellent woman is arranging *tableaux* in Berlin for the benefit of Bayreuth. In the evening read some of Tieck's critical studies and much enjoyed his account of a popular play. — R. told me that his uncle once spoke about the essays on Goethe and Shakespeare which Tieck was planning to write and had told him that all the things Tieck wanted to say sounded wonderful; but Tieck was "lazy," never completed anything.

*Thursday, March 12* R. had a bad night and complains bitterly to the doctor when he comes to visit him; all the same, he works. Richter writes, happy about the news he has received: he will manage to get himself freed. Frau v. Meyendorff has chosen me to be her confidante, but how can I give advice between her and my father? I cannot even tell her that I knew about my father's intentions long ago. — Continuing unpleasantnesses regarding the fountain. In the evening R. goes to the Thursday gathering at Councilor Dittmar's house; I pass the time conversing with the two big girls and seeking in a joking way to implant the good seed in them. May God give His blessing!

*Friday, March 13* R. relates all sorts of things concerning the Thursday gathering, which shows that he enjoyed being in the company of these men. — Despite snow and bad weather, at the house morning and afternoon. R. also finds much to vex him there and returns home in gloomy spirits, but works on his score in the morning and afternoon. Two very nice letters from the singers Betz and Niemann, who agree unconditionally to work for R. and are demanding no fee. In the evening we read some of Tieck's theater criticism (*Letters on Shakespeare,* etc.) with great interest, and we are delighted with what he has to say about Hanswurst and the comparison he makes with the dramatists of today, his description of *Julius Caesar* in London, and also of *Lear* in Dresden. In connection with the last of these, R. tells me about the actor Hellwig—how fine he was and how upset R. had been as a child to hear he had gone mad; he had a dog called Leuko

—all these things had infinitely fascinated him in his childhood.

*Saturday, March 14* In good spirits we discussed at breakfast what we had read yesterday. Then, as we are both about to begin our daily tasks, we receive from the bookseller Giessel the news that 19 letters written by Richard and his wife between the years 1860 and 1867 are being advertised for sale in the *Reichsanzeiger*—with the comment that they are highly interesting! What can this mean? — I suspect Malwina Schnorr, who, probably egged on by Munich, has chosen precisely this time to publicize these things—she was an intimate friend of ours. This, God knows, will certainly put an end to our being granted credit! R. turns to the lawyers for help, but there seems little hope of taking any effective steps, and there is nothing for it but to put up with this new piece of malice. — Paid some calls. Back home looked through R.'s letters to his first wife to see whether any had perhaps been stolen. Got a sad impression from this glance into R.'s troubled past. On top of this an alarming letter in the evening from Herr Feustel, who sees huge financial difficulties piling up on our undertaking; and I have to perform an act of judgment on my nursemaid and dismiss her at once from the house, which upsets me terribly; punishing wickedness weighs more heavily on my heart than experiencing it. — In the evening R. reads me a long letter from him to his first wife; dismal to see how he strove in vain to bring this low-minded woman into a nobler frame of mind; in the margin of his letter, which from this point of view is truly sublime, she has written in her distress: Schopenhauer lies. Shabby and crude!! — In the evening a melancholy prayer—who would not grow weary on this hard path?

*Sunday, March 15* Together a lot with the children morning and afternoon; did not go out on account of great tiredness; pleasure in the warmheartedness of them all. In the morning R. sings me Sieglinde's theme to Brünnhilde and says, "That is you—" In the evening the copyist musicians, who, however, give R. little pleasure.

*Monday, March 16* Early this morning a visit from friend Feustel, who has at last received friend Brandt's calculations and again plunges us in gloom. R. works, though in despondent spirits, and I have things to do in the house, both morning and afternoon; I miss the dismissed governess very much, also from a practical point of view, and on top of that the ever-increasing expenses. — I feel it as a true liberation when R. reads me some scenes from *The Tempest* in the evening. — Recently we were truly appalled to come upon a piece of work by E. v. Hartmann—a defamation of *Romeo and Juliet*! (Mimi Schl. writes about an approaching auction of works of art in aid of Bayreuth.)

*Tuesday, March 17* Very bad weather; many errands in connection with Boni's birthday. R. works, but is unwell. News of the success of

*Rienzi* in the Teatro La Fenice, an ironic impression; in Brussels, *Tannhäuser* with a ballet in the second act finds favor! — R. says that his creative work no longer gives him pleasure, he has forgotten the moments of inspiration and can only remember the difficulties and sufferings he has gone through on account of his works. In the evening read Tieck, the critique of *Wallenstein*; we do not agree with everything he says, but we are pleased by the great warmth and acute observation in this essay. Tieck was also earnestly aware of the level to which the theater has sunk.

*Wednesday, March 18* Spring storms and many domestic cares, great melancholy, yet pleasure in the children. In the evening R. reads me from Freytag's book about Myconius's visit to Tetzel and the business of the indulgences—very interesting. Marie Schl. is organizing, not *tableaux*, but an auction of pictures in aid of Bayreuth.

*Thursday, March 19* R. corrects his biography, I write some letters and do some housework. In the evening to the rehearsal of the amateur orchestra with R., who actually gives the poor conductor, Zumpe, a few suggestions to help him along.

*Friday, March 20* Snow flurries, at the same time flowers from Malwida in Italy! At the house with R. In the morning a letter to Prof. Nietzsche about his treatise; R. accuses me of forgetting my German, he is very jealous of the fact that I have been receiving and writing so many letters in French. Feeling of sadness. In the evening Tieck's essay on ways of reciting verses.

*Saturday, March 21* Sent our revered dean some cigars, wrote letters, at the house with the children, R. works. — In the evening read *Twelfth Night*; much, much enjoyment from it, long discussion about it. R. says Malvolio is like E. Devrient, who equates dignity with pedantry and has curious ideas besides (that he is an actor and Mendelssohn's poet). Of Olivia he says, "In her one sees those melancholy, glowing Southern eyes, those faces which are all eyes." But a veritable school has now arisen against Shakespeare, and who is defending him? Bodenstedt, Dingelstedt, and consorts. — We find what Tieck has to say about men playing the women's roles very illuminating and full of the right feeling.

*Sunday, March 22* To church with the two elder girls, before that talked with R. about Paul de Lagarde's essay, in which he comes out strongly against Saint Paul. R. says, "I was also against him when I knew nothing about him—that was because of my anti-Mendelssohnism." I do not believe there would be any Christians without Saint Paul, though I think I understand what P. de Lagarde means when he wishes one to be evangelical rather than Christian. — After church gave presents to Boni, whose birthday is being celebrated today. After that the visit from Dr. Käfferlein, who says the bookseller is offering the letters for 100 thalers, which we do not have at present! But there is no other protection against such indiscretions. We consider the question from all angles and finally decide to buy the letters. — Children's party, with them and R. in the garden of the new house. In the evening the musicians, they play as a piano duet the E-flat Major Quartet which R. and I played so often in Tribschen; with its finale (Allegro commodo) which R. calls the alpenglow. Indescribable beauties! . . .

*Monday, March 23* All kinds of letters to write—to the Italians about *Rienzi*, the legal matters, things for the house—all kinds. R. is good enough to sign them. He also decides to buy up the letters. Reflections on a legal system which never hinders a wicked deed, but punishes it only after it has perhaps caused damage. How many similar offers can now be made to us? — In Parliament they are quarreling about the defense bill; it is not enough that a man like Moltke speaks in favor of it; all the other gentlemen insist on having their say. "By permitting a general franchise Bismarck has given the German Reich the weakness of Napoleon," R. says, "he has given it the character of a usurpation, something illegitimate." — After lunch he quotes to me that fine saying of Luther's in his *Table Talk*—that everything comes about through ignorance, and if he had known what the Pope and his retinue were like, he would not have hoped to influence them, and consequently would never have bestirred himself. Conversed in the evening, though there is indeed little enough that is pleasurable to chat about. Early to bed.

*Tuesday, March 24* Perfect spring weather, but R. unfortunately still not well, he cannot work. He receives a letter from Fritzsch, which shows once more that a letter from R. (to a Herr Luckardt) has been misused—against Fritzsch himself; R. replies. Another headline, "Latest Wagner Swindle," reports that he has summoned Frau Mallinger to Bayreuth to study the part of Elisabeth. Firm resolve to write no more letters to anyone—Israel will not be appeased. The dean said today, that whenever R. is spoken of, it is only the Jews here who react bitterly. I read some quotations from a novel by Disraeli—how he claims for Israel all the great men in art, science, even religion (the first Jesuits, he says, were Jews). A very curious phenomenon. — The Berlin schools are said to be teaching *Der Ring des Nibelungen* side by side with the *Edda*. Again spent the evening conversing.

*Wednesday, March 25* R. still not well, but he rises early and works. I morning and afternoon in the new house with the little ones, much work there. When R. comes, there is much vexation because the construction work reveals many serious flaws! R.'s foot is very painful: he

melancholy one from our friend Nietzsche, who is tormenting himself. R. exclaims, "He should either marry or write an opera, though doubtless the latter would be such that it would never get produced, and so would not bring him into contact with life." — I go to the house and then pay some calls; R. takes his first bath in the house and feels so good in it and so well after it that he comes home a different man. A cheerful lunch in consequence, happy enjoyment of what we are to and have in each other! In the afternoon to the house, arrival of the "Kauders," the children's laughter, much merriment. In the evening I read R. poor Frau v. M[eyendorff]'s letter, which brings the conversation to my father. Then we read some of the Indian proverbs, feeling ever more deeply this curious link between the highest world-renouncing wisdom and the acutest perception of life.

*Sunday, April 5*  To church with the children; afterward hid the eggs in the house. R. takes another bath, after doing some work. "I shan't be really healthy until I am rid of this 'Kauder,'" he says. "By that I mean *Der Ring des Nibelungen.*" — Chatting from afternoon till evening with the children, who are making themselves masks. — R. says, "I shan't write another score until Fidi is able to orchestrate it for me." — In the evening Ollivier's book, which has been sent to me, about Lamartine and his nonelection to the Academy. Early to bed. — Today R. was pleased with my bust and said, "It is pleasure of a different kind from your presence; when I gaze on you, feelings are always involved, but here, looking at this bust, it is the idea which dominates." He is also pleased with Kietz's bust of himself. "I want to be happy," he says, "another twenty years." — Early this morning we heard the hymn being played from the church tower, and R. played me the "Pilgrims' Chorus." "Here I should like to see something changed; in the words '*Alle Welt*' the '*Alle*' is too long. At that time I was not very good at handling the various metrical forms, and the false intonation has always embarrassed me." — Yesterday some anonymous person sent R. an Easter poem with the remark "If you set this to some good music, I shall reveal who I am." R. thinks he must be a prince—"Reuss Schleiz Greiz." —

*Monday, April 6*  Consistorial visitors. R. works. Troubles with the ducal hens, which are suddenly proving difficult. Continued reading *Wallenstein* to Lulu; R. rouses Wallenstein at Lützen with a loud "Cock-a-doodle-doo," suggested to him by the troubles with the hens. In the afternoon the children all unwell and put to bed. We read Schopenhauer ("On Forms of Cognition," I think the chapter is called)—and are amazed as always by the profundity of the thought, the lucidity of expression. — Letter from my uncle in Vienna: my father is staying with him and today is giving a concert at Princess Auersperg's residence.

*Tuesday, April 7*   Everybody ill, even I plagued by a headache and hoarseness. R. divinely good, takes over all commissions for the house and remains in a good, cheerful mood.

*Wednesday, April 8*   A new governess! May God give His blessing! R. teaches her the latest prayer for Fidi: "Dear God, tomorrow it would be nice if you could give me the largest slice!" — R. goes to the house, I with him, he takes a bath but does not feel very well after it. After lunch he sings a melody from a Beethoven quartet and says: "Beethoven is the best of them all, because he has beauty. There are really only two forms of art, sculpture and music, the latter infinitely greater than the former, because it owes nothing to the realities of life. Literature one can't really acknowledge as an art form; Goethe, who thought himself born to be a sculptor, felt that, and that is why he did not balk at making those terrible alterations in *Romeo and Juliet.*" — News of Kaulbach's death—a false deity already discredited. — In the evening R. reads to me from Schopenhauer's comment on his own philosophy and the opening pages of Finlay's history of Greece. The latter very interesting—every contact with the genius of Greece grips and uplifts one. R. is particularly pleased with the appreciation of Alexander.

*Thursday, April 9*   I had a bad night and in consequence have to stay in bed, hoarse and running a temperature; the children all have colds, too. — In the morning R. reads the latest work by our friend Nietzsche and summarizes his opinion thus: "It is the work of a very significant person, and if he ever becomes famous, this work will one day also earn respect. But it is very immature. It lacks plasticity, because he never quotes examples from history, yet there are many repetitions and no real plan. This work has been brought out too quickly. I don't know anybody to whom I could give it to read, because nobody could follow it. The basic idea has already been stated by Schopenhauer, and N. would have done much better to throw light on it from a pedagogical point of view." — I am attaching telegrams from the King and the Prince to this page, since I find them very gratifying. [*Attached are newspaper clippings reporting that King Ludwig II of Bavaria sent a telegram to Bismarck congratulating him on his fifty-ninth birthday and wishing him a speedy recovery, and that Bismarck sent a cordial reply.*]

*Friday, April 10*   Loldi's birthday celebrations have to be postponed, we are all in the grip of spring. R. writes a page of his score; he tries something out on the piano and then returns to his desk: "A stitch in time saves nine," he says, laughing. — Herr Peters-Friedländer writes of the continued success of the *"Kaisermarsch"* and offers 5,000 marks for an overture! And yesterday Herr Eckert wrote to say that this quarter had brought in 1,750 thalers in Berlin, houses continually sold out and prices raised.

*Friday-Tuesday, April 10–14* Spent more or less in bed. Nothing significant has happened, two fine spring days, but otherwise gray and stormy weather. R. also not well, and slow progress in the house. My father writes me that he will not be visiting us this summer, he is going to Rome for 6 to 8 months. R. is working regularly, if slowly.

*Wednesday, April 15* Dull gray weather, I spend morning and afternoon with the children, writing letters. R. works, goes to the house twice during the day, has a bath, and also keeps an eye on everything. In the evening some more fine scores arrive from Paris, and R. plays me parts of *La Vestale*—Julien's plea to the High Priestess, the crowning of Lycinus, and above all her monologue enchant us, and R. says, "A person who has written things like that is sacred to one."

*Thursday, April 16* Still under house arrest, and the house looking like a desert, since curtains and furniture have already been removed. R. does not work, but writes to the King's secretary, "amiably" complaining that though a great favor has been granted him, he has received no word about it. In the evening R. goes to the Thursday gathering, where Prof. Fries, who has just seen *Die Meistersinger* in Nuremberg, remarks that it was the greatest artistic experience of his life. — R. tells me that when a boy asked him for alms he at first refused, but then called the boy back, moved by his pitiful expression; he gave him a florin and said he should see if his mother would buy him something with it; then he should come again and would receive another florin. R. is scolded for that by his colleagues at the gathering, but he cannot understand why there should be so much poverty in so small a town. — The well in the house at last made to function with a pump, a lot of chickens in the yard; besides this a barometer purchased and an excellent gardener acquired: Konrad Rausch, who himself looks just like an old root. — *Lohengrin* has been performed in New York.

*Friday, April 17* R. plagued by a headache in consequence of the Thursday gathering, he cannot work and goes to the house; I cannot give him support, since, being beset by a severe cough, I have to stay at home. In the evening R. says to me: "I believe it would not take much now to make me feel an insuperable disgust for the whole Bayreuth undertaking and regret having written my works, just as Goethe regretted ever having had anything to do with the theater. Today I saw a theater journal, and the mere thought of people sending such things to me, of my having any contact with such people, filled me with repugnance." — In the evening he reads me Freytag's account of the 30 Years' War in *Pictures of German Life* — terrible.

*Saturday, April 18* I am again confined to my bed and am now a completely useless member of the family! — I ask R. to bring me *Wood-stock*, and he is glad that I wish to read it, saying, "I was thinking only recently that history is only enjoyable in the hands of an artist such as W[alter] Scott; otherwise it is the dreariest, most forbidding thing possible." — R. has been much distracted from his work today and has decided to write the last page tomorrow. And so it is: the last thing written in the old house is *"bei des Speeres Spitze,"* and in connection with this R. remarks that there will never again be those religious states of mind in which every object is held sacred, every deed dedicated to the gods. From the 19th to the 28th all the exertions of moving, during which I receive a terrible blow with the news of Marie Much-anoff's mortal illness and awful pain . . .

Many treasures from the rich contents of mind and heart are now lost to this book for ever, since, numbed by the shock and in any case over-worked, I only take up my pen again in the new house (the final happi-ness) on 29th. But isolated details I can still note down. R. packs his books away, and we keep out only Shakespeare, the Indian proverbs, and Schopenhauer. The last of these was the only one to which I could listen on the day I received the news that my friend was dying. Then we read *Julius Caesar*, which always impresses me as the most tragic of all tragedies: from the very beginning all is lost, and the people seem like ghosts; curious how Sh. here so closely reflects the impressions of people and things that one received from Plutarch in one's youth. — Within the last few days R. had a strange dream about Mendelssohn, who did not wish to write something for Schröder-Devrient, since she had not sung at his funeral! Then again and again the old dream about Minna, who was still alive, and R. kept asking himself, "My God, what is going to happen with Cosima? Well, she can't live forever"—and with these words he wakes up. — The last letters I receive in the old house are from my mother and E. O[llivier]; the former cannot send me my 40,000 francs, and the latter will not return my jewelry (left with my sister Blandine)! — At last—

*Tuesday, April 28*  —move into the new house! It is not yet finished, far from it, but we shall conquer. Nice lunch at the Feustels'; at 4 o'clock consecration of the dining room with a conference among Herr Hoffmann, Brandt, Brückwald, the management committee, and the Brückner brothers, scene painters from Coburg. At Prof. Hoffmann's suggestion, the task of preparing the scenery according to his sketches is entrusted to these two. R. tells me about the fine mood which pre-vailed throughout, and how everyone was filled with a spirit of com-plete dedication to the cause. The house could have been accorded no finer consecration. Cozy supper; the three little ones, Eva as leader, thank us for having given them such nice rooms. Fidi has a room of his

him if we were to die now, otherwise he will be spoiled! — In the evening the second act of *Siegfried*!

*Tuesday, June 16* The weather has turned mild again. Worked much with Lusch. — A lot of bills are coming in; I remark to R. how curious it is that I, who have never known real financial need, should be in a constant state of worry, whereas he, who has suffered so much from it, never feels any alarm. — Dr. Haase has won his lawsuit. — Some articles about Andreas Hofer affect me greatly, and I observe that he was a tragic figure. R. says he once worked out a libretto for Röckel on the subject, and as usual he immediately saw it in three acts, of which the first would be the gathering of the people in the mountains. But Röckel did nothing about it! . . . Our conversation led us to *La Juive*, and R. says that, after his taste had been completely ruined, it was this score which gave him back his feeling for pure music. We talk about Mozart's instrumentation, and R. mentions the introduction of a clarinet in Gluck's *Armide* which makes one wonder where he got it from, so lovely and moving is it. — Richter goes to see *Don Giovanni* and thinks he has discovered a Valkyrie in the Elvira.

*Wednesday, June 17* Marvelous clear weather, yesterday R. pointed out to me the crescent moon with the evening star, that lovely celestial emblem. The marble slabs bearing the motto are affixed to our house, people in the street watching curiously. We receive reports about *Tristan und Isolde* in Weimar, a very nice one from G. Davidsohn, saying it was all very fine, though he does not even mention King Marke, that symbol of moral order and consequently herald of death. At the quotation "night of love" R. says, "That is Wahnfried." We resolve to explain the motto to nobody. R. works. We think often of his family in Leipzig, finding their attitude toward us incomprehensible. In the evening the musicians, the third act of *Siegfried* is gone through. News of visits of not the most welcome sort. — *Maneia Manteia Wahn*: R. explains to Richter that he is in fact mad to undertake something like the festival theater when everyone keeps saying: My God, every opera house in the world is open to him, and still he is not satisfied! To these people, rational people, he is a madman, and yet from madness of this sort all greatness springs—like, for example, the ideal of a united Germany as well; analogy with animal instinct—also "mad." — Finally he makes a joke, saying people ought to see that he can make concessions—was he not now writing an opera which could be produced even in Bayreuth?!

*Thursday, June 18* First visitor in the morning: friend Lenbach; great joy at seeing him again. At one o'clock the little Countess [Dönhoff], friendly meeting. Lenbach delights us with his pleasure in Bayreuth, which he finds interesting. Drive to the Eremitage. Richter returns home on foot with the children, but sprains his ankle on the way. Serious interruption of the work, but luckily no danger.

*Friday, June 19*  Fine morning, drive with our friends to the Fantaisie, at lunch the mayor and the dean. In the evening R. reads *Parzival* to our two friends. Whether they appreciate it I do not know, but it again moves me unutterably.

*Saturday, June 20*  In dull weather accompanied the charming little Countess to the railroad station. Is anyone happy? Spent the rest of the day with Lenbach. My father writes that Hans has 150,000 francs set aside for the children. Visit of Herr v. Gersdorff to my father. Friend Feustel with us in the evening; he says that twenty families from Nuremberg have come to live here.

*Sunday, June 21*  Spoke a lot with Lenbach about a lot of things, discovered in him a noble, selfless, unusually talented person; R. is also coming to like him, about which I am glad. Departure at four o'clock, which does not come easily to any of the three of us. — Much with Richter, who is not allowed to move around.

*Monday, June 22*  Many things to catch up on, as always after visitors have been here. R. works. News of *Tristan* in Weimar, friend [Alwine] Frommann reports that the older people were in particular completely bewitched by it. Nice articles by Frau Merian in the *Weimarische Zeitung*. Great heat, we read nothing more in the evening, but keep Richter company for a while.

*Tuesday, June 23*  Telegram from the Grand Duke of Weimar to R., expressing his emotion regarding the performances of *Tristan*. R. does not wish to thank him, so I do it for him. R. works, though very often asking himself whether he is not orchestrating too opulently!! Again worked a lot with Daniella.

*Wednesday, June 24*  Correspondence of all kinds, R. has some difficult business arrangements, I think; I live in fear that our standard of living is far beyond our means! And I can find no way to reduce it, for R. wishes to have it this way.

*Thursday, June 25*  A Rhinemaiden presents herself (Frau Pauli from Hanover), good voice, but no conception of enunciation. Richter attempts to accompany her, but cannot yet hold himself properly upright. Celebrations in Nuremberg for Hans Sachs, but nobody has the idea of inviting R. to them! . . . Speeches, music, all sorts of things, but not a note of *Die Meistersinger*.

*Friday, June 26*  Today it is a Mime who introduces himself; R. is shocked by the unclear speech of these people, who all possess no consonants, particularly no *S*'s. — Visit from Franz Kolb, coming from the Rhine—curious repetition of the behavior of the Brockhaus family, to whom he is related! —

*Thursday, July 9* Prolonged struggle against melancholy, aroused in me by two dreams; in the first I saw Hans, with a pale face but a kind expression on it, I presented Daniella to him and wanted to tell him about the way in which I had tried to bring her up; he did not speak, but looked at me lovingly and kindly. Then I was in a hotel room with Marie Muchanoff and she was in tears as she took leave of me. I was sobbing; she: "Why am I crying? In a month I am going to die." — R. receives a letter and a photograph from Frau Materna, highly recommended by Herr Scaria; attractive, if you like, but so ungainly! A Hamlet-like mood overcomes him, he almost loses all inclination to concern himself with these people! But shortly after writing the last lines, I am shown that one should never give way to vexation through making the acquaintance of three singers. In Frau Grün from Coburg we have made a real discovery: the voice is lovely and her whole character reveals a good musician and a fine woman. Besides her, a good bass and a good baritone (Fasolt and Donner). The fragments from *Tannhäuser* sung by Frau Grün move me profoundly—I do not know why *Tannhäuser*, of all R.'s works, affects me most deeply. — The many things we heard before this encouraging experience had not been very pleasant; Richter told us that a representative of the *Neue Freie Presse* in Vienna was now here and had asked him for news, whereupon Richter, to the man's utter consternation, had told him his opinion of this newspaper, which from the very beginning had published nothing but scandalous reports about our undertaking. Then Richter tells me of an article in the *Börsencourier* which deals maliciously with the singers and the sacrifices they are making in our behalf, and which adds that I (Frau Cosima Wagner) will now no longer have any cause to doubt the keenness and self-sacrifice of these people. The last words are printed in quotation marks, so as to give the impression that I had said some such thing, thereby offending the singers and possibly stopping them from coming here. Very pitiful stuff—and the way they always drag me in, in God's name! . . .

*Friday, July 10* R. receives a letter from Councilor Düfflipp: the King sends friendly greetings to him and me. He orchestrates a page of *Götterdämmerung*. In the evening the musicians again; we learn that the article, which has been reproduced in all newspapers, has alarmed some singers, who however much they would like to appear here, do not have the means to do so without payment. In such ways can this unholy press cause damage and difficulties! — It is also a curious thing that the inscription on our house has been spread throughout the world in a false form, since the first person to read it read it wrong: instead of *Wähnen* ["illusion"] with its pregnant meaning—having something to do with *Ahnen* ["surmise"]—they speak of *Wahn* ["madness"]! —

*Saturday, July 11*    A prolonged and good spell of work with Lusch—literature, English, French. In the afternoon arrival of Herr Betz, who came together with Herr Brandt. Since "an engineer" had been announced, I took (as a result of my weak eyes) Herr Betz to be this man, and when R. entered and embraced his singer, my misunderstanding gave rise to much merriment. Pleasant evening, R. recites a scene from *Die Walküre* (Wotan and Fricka).

*Sunday, July 12*    R. studies with Herr Betz, very enjoyable. After that lunch to celebrate the completion of the *salon*, with the Feustels and the Grosses; R. drinks to his guests and says that a heathen god (Wotan) has given us his blessing. Feustel then rises and speaks very handsomely about the enrichment of his life through meeting R., and how uplifted he feels in being able to devote himself to our cause. Music in the evening: Herr Betz sings the riddle scene between Wotan and Mime.

*Monday, July 13*    Further study between R. and his singer. Family lunch with Herr Betz as guest. In the evening, news of the assassination attempt on Bismarck. Great consternation. One can almost see it as a sign of good fortune—how a star shines over the German Empire. I remark to R. that the King's greetings and his signs of friendship toward us always coincide with his gestures of friendliness toward Germany as a whole—as, for example, his granting of the credit with his telegram to Bismarck, and now his message of greetings with his resolve to drive out to meet the Emperor and to welcome him. — The evening passes in agitated discussions of the assassination attempt, after R. has visited Herr Betz, who is hoarse, in his hotel.

*Tuesday, July 14*    A tenor, Herr Unger, is introduced to us today—perhaps for Loge. With R. paid a call on a very pleasant family here named Braun. Family lunch, with no guests. In the evening R. goes through the 3rd act of *Siegfried*. He is very worn out by it.

*Wednesday, July 15*    Much worry about my wardrobe—R. thinks I do not have enough to wear! At lunch Herr Betz, who admits to me that he is happy to have come here and thus got to know R. really well personally—he has also seen how happy he is! Rehearsal with Herr Unger, Loge not yet decided. In the evening Herr Betz and the "Kanzlei"; Josef Rubinstein distinguishes himself by playing from the manuscript of the 3rd act of *Götterdämmerung*. — Fine speech by Bismarck, saying to his intended murderer that it is not good for a man to shoot at a fellow countryman. — Friend Richter causes R. concern. — There is a report in the *A.A.Z.* about the ill-starred inscription on the house—and yet it is they who have read it incorrectly!

*Thursday, July 16*  Wrote some business letters, in the afternoon to a coffee party in Frau v. Braun's house, for me a somewhat strange experience. In the evening the singer Alexis. — When all have gone, R. looks at the picture of me in his folder, which was done at the time when we were separated: "It is all like a dream, and yet when I think back to the times this picture reflects, I feel moved to tears."

*Friday, July 17*  I feel quite indisposed and can hold myself erect only with an effort. Glorious weather, an incomparably fine summer, the heat not oppressive. R. works on his third act, but has many vexations, among other things the loss of the arrangement of the 2nd act of *Götterdämmerung*, which would now be very necessary to him. In the evening visit from the Feustel family. No music.

*Saturday, July 18*  R. again dreamed his traditional old dream about his wife, whom he did not know how to fit into his new life, until the problem was solved by his waking up thinking, "But she is dead." — R. works morning and afternoon; I do a lot of work with Lusch and hope to inculcate in her, without trouble, a good and noble education. In the evening a somewhat abortive attempt to bring an Alberich into being.

*Sunday, July 19*  R. reads me the printed letter of an unnamed leading figure in the Catholic party to a French bishop, which sounds really ominous for Germany. In this connection R. quotes Cromwell's words to his soldiers at Worcester: "Put your trust in God and keep your powder dry." We stay at home, R. works morning and afternoon, and I amuse myself with the children. They sing pretty songs, and then go on singing to us through the window. In the evening R. and I enjoy being alone together.

*Monday, July 20*  Frau v. Schl. sends us a photograph of the Menzel water color sold in support of Bayreuth: very peculiar! — R. works; no further news about singers; domestic unpleasantnesses; in the evening rehearsed Gunther with Herr Alexis. (Wrote to my father.)

*Tuesday, July 21*  Worked with Lusch, R. on his score, is pleased with the *salon*, unfortunately not an unalloyed pleasure, since domestic difficulties are increasing. In the evening Frau Grün again comes over from Coburg; she sings "Brünnhilde's Awakening," which causes a certain amount of embarrassment, since she cannot sing Brünnhilde.

*Wednesday, July 22*  Paid some (card) calls. Strange mood in spite of all my activity—it finds expression in my taking up my old favorite Eugénie de Guérin again. One could scarcely imagine a calling as different from mine as hers, and yet no one lies as close to my heart as this Breton girl, and in this book I love the French very much. — In the afternoon we drive out to the theater; in the evening Frl. Oppenheimer from Frankfurt, who will probably sing Erda; with Frau Grün she sings the duet from *Lohengrin* (Ortrud and Elsa). R. has a lot of things to point out, but he is satisfied with their eagerness to learn.

*Thursday, July 23*  The whole day and evening devoted to Herr Hill; R. reminds me that I had remarked, after the first few bars he sang in Schwerin, "This is the most remarkable of them all." An unusually powerful personality with great fire—in short, all the qualities which R. needs. — He complained about Prussia and the Prussian Court, saying that, when he had once sung some songs by Schumann there, the German Empress had come up to him and asked, "Do you not sing any of Gounod's songs?" He sings to us from *Lohengrin* and *Holländer*— tells us that the Court in Schwerin is very well disposed toward both R. and me, also talks about the sullenness of Frau Schnorr, whom he met in Brunswick. On the other hand, Frl. Oppenheimer tells us touching things about R.'s former friend Friederike Meyer, who is now living all by herself in Jugenheim, devoting herself entirely to bringing up her two children.

*Friday, July 24*  While I was attending to various things outside, R. had to deal with some domestic difficulties, and that brings us after lunch to talk about all sorts of things concerning the world and the artist, his absent-mindedness with regard to the realities of life. In this connection he tells me how once, on an outing with Dr. Wille and Herwegh to [*place name left blank*], he became so tired that he asked the two men to leave him at a certain point and to go on without him; Dr. Wille, believing in his insensitivity that it was simply idleness, had then given him a shove in the back and told him to get moving; R.'s rage had vented itself in a vulgar expletive, and during this scene the whole of Loge's address to the Rhinemaidens (words and music), which he had not originally had in mind, came to him. "The way it just flies into one's mind—impossible to say how it happens! When I sit down at the piano, it is just to refresh my memory, nothing new comes to me there, I am just trying to find the things which occurred to me now and then during the most exasperating situations. This used to upset Minna, my first wife—the way I would keep calm during the terrible scenes she was making, because something had occurred to me for *Tristan* or *Walküre*." He feels that, because in anger a person's powers are stretched, his true nature is also goaded into activity in spite of all the incongruities; only for working out one's ideas are tranquillity and a certain bodily well-being necessary, artistic work demands these things, but inspiration laughs at all difficulties as well as all comfort. He reminds me that he had not been satisfied with the quintet in *Die Meistersinger* and I, coming in while he was composing, had begged him to retain it. His dissatisfaction had been due to his feeling that the original inspiration had been a different one, and then

scene from *Götterdämmerung*. — Surprised at midday by the painter Krausse, who brings with him the whole completed cartoon for the *sgraffito* on the front of our house. A matter of great alarm for me— only the day before I had discussed with R. how fortunate it was that Herr Krausse, from whom we had heard nothing for a whole year, seemed to have forgotten us! —

*Tuesday, September 8* Early in the morning to our friend, who then goes to fetch her husband in Neumarkt. Spent the whole afternoon very pleasantly together; the minister, just come from the confirmation of the Crown Prince's son, tells us of the Prince's admirable profession of faith. But he confirms that the Prince's left arm is crippled. Visit to the theater. — Concern over Lusch's health, the beginnings of puberty. — R. again dreamed that he was on intimate terms with Bismarck and that, when he addressed him as "Your Excellency," Bismarck replied, "Say, rather, 'Your Majesty.' "

*Wednesday, September 9* Isolde surprised us yesterday with a complete historical lecture, which Fidi brought to an end (it was about the quarrel between Louis the Pious and his sons) with the remark, "They squabbled as in a chicken coop."

Farewell visit from our friendly sponsors, who were extremely kind to the children. Erection of the scaffolding [for the *sgraffito*]. Discussed all sorts of things with "Cousin" Krausse. I with many letters to write, R. doing some work on the score. Great tiredness.

*Thursday, September 10* Herr Hoffmann the painter is turned away; expected here on August 25 at the latest, he made his appearance only today. Question as to whether this will lead to a lawsuit. — Today I begin work again with the children, R. works on his score. Letters of various kinds have to be dealt with. In the evening we read Tieck's fine preface to his *Vorschule*.

*Friday, September 11* Very bad night, during which I drafted amid tears an invocation to music for Marie Muchanoff. Bath with Lusch, work with the children, and after that wrote seven or eight letters. In the evening read *The Witch* by Greene, without pleasure—a genius has no predecessors. (Before that attended a coffee party at Baroness von Reitzenstein's.)

*Saturday, September 12* R. works (after a bad night—"The whole of Nature is fizzing like bicarbonate of soda," he calls out jokingly during the night storm). I work with the children morning and afternoon. In the evening we begin [Calderón's] *La niña de Gomez Arias*. I am very tired.

*Sunday, September 13* Letter from Herr Hoffmann, who wants very much to talk to R.; we decide to invite him and his wife in the evening. R. is at first very agitated, but then calms down, it is agreed to have the maquettes sent back here from Coburg. — The advertised Poets' Congress with all its clauses alarms one in its brazen stupidity. [*A newspaper clipping on the conference attached; see notes.*] Cold, occupied with winter clothing.

Did not write in my diary from Monday, September 14, to Wednesday the 23rd. Work with the children, writing letters for R., afternoon parties, discussions with Herr Hoffmann—all this preventing it.

*Tuesday, September 22*   Worked with the children, began W. Scott's *Quentin Durward* with Lusch. R. worked on his score despite a bad night, he is plagued by eczema on three fingers. At noon Herr Hoffmann and wife, R. has at last persuaded him to make a new sketch! Afternoon party, which I attend solely in order to keep contacts open for the children; R., on the other hand, always against it, says he cannot understand life when I am not there, that house and children seem meaningless to him. — Fine letter from the King, thanking R.; I remind R. of what an old fortuneteller in Munich once told him—that the King would always be sympathetic to him when the moon is waxing. — We have been having the most beautiful moonlit nights. In the evening our artist of the *sgraffito*; the work on it makes me very nervous. — Read a nice paper by a local district councilor, according to which the Fichtel Mountains were the cradle of ancient Teutonism, which pleases us. R., coming back to *La niña de Gomez Arias,* says it is too bad that these Moors, regarded as something to be stamped out like pests, once more provide the only decent characters: religion really existed only among the heathen, he says. — R. tries in vain to make our Macedonian understand that the Greeks no longer exist, and that the Russians will one day unite all these Slavs. — Regarding his score, R. tells me that during Siegfried's narration in the forest, the "Forest Murmurs" from *Siegfried* would only be hinted at in the orchestra, for here it is Siegfried's fate which must make an impact, and a natural phenomenon must not be allowed to obscure it; there was a difference, he said, between then, when he wanted the rustling of the forest itself to make an impression, and now; and anyway he could never just repeat anything, in such cases he could not even find the right notes for the transcription.

*Wednesday, September 23*   R. again had a very bad night; the barber gave him coal-tar packs, and these irritate him; he does not work, and we visit the kindergarten, considering whether perhaps to send Friedel [Fidi] there; but we cannot bring ourselves to like it, and come to the conclusion that, excellent institution though it may be, it is only suitable for lower-class children in large cities. Long letter from Herr Ullmann, setting out for the King's benefit all kinds of matters regarding the virtuosos in London, and giving advice on how to achieve an understanding with the press; finally, concerning Frau Nilsson, whom he himself proposed, he says that she would probably not be able to take part in the Bayreuth performances because of the vengeful feelings of the French, etc. Letter from Frau Betty Schott, saying she herself is too unwell to come, but her manager would represent her, which makes R. very glad. The financial situation does not seem at the moment to be very favorable—I notice that my small savings have been used up and have proved insufficient, and also our living costs are very high. — Sent the children to the Fantaisie while I deal with correspondence, later with R. to meet them. In the evening began Xenophon's *Anabasis*. Lovely moonlight, wandered with R. in the garden before parting for the night.

*Thursday, September 24* Still bad nights for R., so bad, in fact, that he cannot work much. I work with the children. At lunch the painter Krausse, who is working diligently on the *sgraffito*. In the afternoon a walk with R. and the children, R. is very worn out, and he is upset by our present financial situation; the theater in Pest has still not paid the 1,000 florins (long overdue) for *Rienzi*, and there are so many bills to pay. Early to bed.

*Friday, September 25* For both a very bad night; R. also dreamed that I wanted to leave him together with Fidi, and he could only resolve silently never to let me for a moment out of his sight! — He cannot work and is despondent, but always finds pleasure in Fidi, he says he finds it a perpetual joy to watch him. I work with the children. In the afternoon walked up to the theater with R. and the children. Fine evening, but R. unfortunately not well, no reading except for some bits from a book of sketches about St. Petersburg society, very trivial.

*Saturday, September 26* Again a very wretched night for R., who has now been unable to work for some days. I in the morning with the children as usual. In the afternoon sent them to the Eremitage, in the evening visit from Professor Schulz, an architect from Würzburg, who gives us some advice regarding our *sgraffito*. — Magical moonlight, I leave my little gray room; I should like to enjoy it all night, but R. does not wish it; however, during the night he does pull back the curtains.

*Sunday, September 27* R. again dreamed that I left him—he declares that the expression on my face when I said "The moon is my friend" had made him jealous and caused the dream, in which I stole away from him in fine clothes, only to be with him again, dressed in a gray woolen jacket! — He writes to the King, who has asked for a detailed report on everything. — "They've made a new dragon," our servant informs us regarding the *sgraffito*. A letter from painter Hoffmann (woeful friend, breaking wanly through the painted panes, R. exclaims, laughing!), which causes me to write to the Brückner brothers. R. reads me parts of a 15th-century folk song which enchants us ("To My Loved One"): "The chaste glance which troubles the heart!" — Today is my name day—my father does not write, which somewhat troubles me. In the evening we read with much emotion the story of Krespel in [E. T. A. Hoffmann's] *Serapionsbrüder*. A remark by the professor surprises us with its great perspicacity; curious the sense of what the ridiculous can at times imply.

*Monday, September 28* R. has been writing to the King for several days, his letter grows and grows, at the King's wish he is writing a complete report on our undertaking, also on our life here. — I work with the children. In the afternoon R. tells me that he knows why it would nowadays be impossible for a great poet to emerge—because everyone shares the same shallow and optimistic philosophy, one which makes it impossible to perceive the world profoundly and truthfully. We come to the conclusion that the great power of the Jesuits lies not in their external means, but in their correct recognition of the world's wickedness; their attempts to turn this recognition to their own advantage is what makes them so execrable. In the evening we begin on Xenophon's *Anabasis*.

*Tuesday, September 29* R. still on his letter; at lunch Prof. Schulze, Herr Mazière, manager of Schott's, here to revise the agreement (not yet achieved), and our *sgraffito* artist. In the afternoon I have much correspondence to deal with, enthusiastic students, etc. In the evening music, Strauss waltzes, kindly sent to us from Pest by the publisher Rózsavölgyi and played to us by Herr Rubinstein, to our great enjoyment. Letter from my father: Princess Wittgenstein is very seriously ill in Rome. Friend Feustel has seen Councilor Düfflipp in Munich and found him in an extremely bad mood. If another demand were made regarding the theater, he would strenuously resist it! Feustel told us in the morning that money is very short. R. is thinking of giving a concert in Pest. Great unpleasantnesses with the painters Brückner and Hoffmann, God knows how they will be settled.

*Wednesday, September 30* R. goes on writing, and I work with the children. A walk in the afternoon; the whole countryside completely parched. It is reported in the newspaper that the King is only waiting for the performances in Bayreuth before setting up a regency and going on a journey to India. Strangely enough, this news coincides with the King's request to R. to tell him exactly to the day when the performances will take place. — In the evening *Anabasis*, with great enchantment—it is as if one were looking into a purer air. R. praises its naïveté, its utter lack of a striving for effect. How stilted and colorless are our present historians in comparison! —

cancan! . . . Schott's is behaving well, agreeing to R.'s demands.

*Wednesday, October 14*  Walked to the theater in the morning with friend Gersdorff. Said goodbye to him. He found the sight of the theater in the morning light truly magical. The unceasing activity amid all the splendors of Nature has its effect on me, and how movingly! — After lunch R. and I recall our times in Tribschen: "Those were sacred times," says R. — In the evening visit from Herr Rubinstein's father. The painter Hoffmann at last got rid of, and indeed on good terms! Friend Feustel with us in the evening, speaks against the arrest of Count Arnim. Young Rubinstein plays us a fantasy and fugue by Bach, and R. tries to give friend Feustel an idea of what Bach means.

*Thursday, October 15*  R. did not have a good night and has to write letters in the morning, which always upsets him. Yesterday a telegram arrived from friend Richter, announcing his engagement; we congratulate him all the more joyfully since he is said to have chosen a good and pretty girl from a good family, with means of her own. R. sends my father the score of *Die Walküre*. The painters Brückner arrive and say how happy they are to be rid of Herr Hoffmann. They make no demands of any kind and are now going joyfully to work. — In the evening finished *Anabasis*. R. complains to me that he still has 50 pages of his score to write!

*Friday, October 16*  Making provisions for my departure tomorrow, R. is complaining about it and making more difficult what is already difficult enough for me! But I cannot give it up, and I now close this book with its account of the fulfillment of a maternal duty. From September 16, 1873, to October 16, 1874—what misery and suffering does it contain! How little pleasure from the outside world, but in compensation an ever-deepening tranquillity within the confines of our home! Blessings on Richard, blessings on the children, forgiveness for myself—this is what I here beseech. I lost a cherished spirit, it took me a long time to overcome my grief, but I rediscovered my old attitude toward death and life: they are forms which cannot harm us— Marie is not lost to me! —

Desultorily, indeed always hastily written, this volume will still, I believe, give my Siegfried a picture of our life; what he himself has meant to this life, how the dear countenance of his father always shone as he gazed on him—this I could not always state; but he will find it here unspoken, the love which surrounds him. Farewell, year—I gladly grow older, for with every gray hair a selfish thought is extinguished!

*[End of the seventh notebook of the Diaries. The eighth begins with the entry: "October 1874. Dedicated to my Siegfried." Before the first daily entry there is a page containing notes on payments to be made and holiday dates*

*(obviously in connection with the boarding school in Dresden), as well as a list of laundry and household items.]*

**Friday, October 23**   Yesterday I returned home from Dresden; I have kept no diary of my stay there, since R. was unable to accompany me. I went to see a dentist, and also to visit the Luisenstift. It made a good impression on me, and I think I shall do well to send the girls there for a few years. On Thursday the 22nd, I left Leipzig at 6 o'clock with the two girls, having spent the evening there in the company of Frau v. Meyendorff; at 12 R. met me at Neumarkt with the three children. He had written to me every day, yet how much we still had to say to each other on our reunion! He was unwilling to receive anyone during my absence: "They should know what it means when you are at home." At home he showed me the book about the war which he has been studying; it throws a curious light on the Crown Prince, who, it seems, was unwilling to have a battle waged without him and who kept General Hartmann waiting. The Battle of Weissenburg also seems to R. to have been a scene of quite unnecessary slaughter. — In the evening we drink to my father's birthday, and then go early to bed. — Today R. is well and cheerful; he says, "When you are away, the hook is missing on which I hang, and then I fall down in a heap." The many interruptions make it difficult for R. to work; I write to Hans, informing him of my plan to send the children to the boarding school. After lunch we try to find a place for the little Dürer table. While R. goes off for a rest, I begin reading Prof. Nietzsche's paper *Schopenhauer as Educator*, which R. has already read and which absorbs us to the highest degree. In the evening I read some of it out loud to R.

**Saturday, October 24**   R. works, and I write some letters, after having tidied things up. I caught cold on the journey and cannot do much beyond continuing to read the professor's pamphlet, which I find really very stimulating. In the afternoon R. goes out with Fidi; in Angermann's a stranger addresses the child: "Can you drink beer, too?" Fidi is silent, then shyly says yes, whereupon R.: "The boy does not know you, my dear sir." . . . R. takes much delight in Fidi, says, "To have a boy like this beside me who calls me Papa and asks all sorts of questions —how wonderful it is!" — I arrange the *Dürer* as a flower table. R. finds a letter from Councilor Düfflipp, demanding that the patrons' money be paid into the treasury; R. replies to him, pointing out that in this case the royal credit would be of no help. — In the evening the musicians, a Haydn symphony is gone through, then the *Tannhäuser* Overture.

**Sunday, October 25**   R. works; I feel rather unwell and take advantage of the children's day off work to rest and to finish Prof. Nietzsche's fine paper. Cheerful lunch, then sent the children to the woods, R. goes to meet them, is pleased when he sees them in their *Freischütz* hats, and returns home in very high spirits. But unfortunately, when he is about to go to work, the mayor visits him, and this keeps him from his work; when I rejoin him at supper he is in a very ill humor. During the evening he complains about his work and the fact that he cannot even talk about the things which are obsessing him.

*Monday, October 26* I had a bad night and spend part of the morning resting; when I awake, I find R. at the coffee table, occupied with the Battle of Spichern; he reads some of it to me, then goes to his work. Our *sgraffito* is now all but finished. In the evening R. works on his score and strikes Gunther dead, as he puts it.

*Tuesday, October 27* Yesterday I had to write to Herr Vitzthum in Hanover: he had notified us of the visit of his wife (a singer) and she did not arrive—due, we suspect, to the maliciousness of the theater manager's wife, the composer [Ingeborg] von Bronsart. — Betz writes from Berlin and seems to have settled the matter concerning *Der Fl. Holländer.* — Still reading about the Battle of Spichern. News of the death of Herr Wolfram, R.'s brother-in-law; R. writes a fine letter to his sister. — "Much despised and much acclaimed," R. called out to me in the early morning; yesterday evening he had reproached me for the little economies by means of which I am trying to keep our domestic budget from rising unduly. . . . — Our *sgraffito* is costing us more than 400 thalers; I would rather have left our house unadorned, but I say nothing about this to R., who is pleased with the ornament. Early to bed—R. is tired.

*Wednesday, October 28* Departure of the painter, who thanks us for the "material and moral benefits" which he received here. R. again immersed himself in the Battle of Spichern and was restless in consequence. — Yesterday evening Fidi entertained us with his account of the 12 boys ("I've had enough of girls") with whom he would one day live, and how he would examine his sisters' nails before allowing them to touch his books, etc. — Herr Runckwitz came in the afternoon—trouble with the orchestra pit in the theater, there has been some miscalculation. — News of the death of Peter Cornelius: another being swept away whose fate was in many ways linked with our own! —

*Thursday, October 29* R. again has a restless night; he dreamed at first that his first wife mocked him, that he then struck her and she poisoned herself, and that some drops of the poison fell on him; then that he was jealous of Lenbach on my account, and Mimi Schl. tried to console him! — I write to Peter Cornelius's poor widow. — R. works, says he is preparing his plan as if for a battle, advancing now with these forces, now with those. If the gods grant him tranquillity, he will need another month to finish it. "Completed the wondrous work!" —

Tears fill my eyes at the thought. — In the evening the children play us an improvised comedy, in which Boni—usually somewhat noncommittal—distinguishes herself with her ideas and her liveliness. We then read the Battle of Spichern, after I received yet another sad impression of Daniella's roughness and ungracious manner toward her sisters. Hans has received my letter.

*Friday, October 30* R. sings something from the conclusion of *Götterdämmerung* and says he noticed yesterday in the way things come together in this conclusion that he can do anything when he wants to; when I reply with a laugh that I can well believe it, he says, "No, as a rule I am very much lacking in routine—I have to want something." — I am working now with the two younger girls, while the elder ones are in the sewing school and the high school for girls. In the afternoon, following their walk, I work with Lusch. Letter from Hans, agreeing very kindly with my boarding-school idea and wishing for only one thing—the preservation of my maternal authority and the avoidance of any discordant impressions for the children. I am now asking myself whether I am doing right to send the children away from their home. Deep concern—oh, if only a God would enlighten us! . . . In the evening R. studies [Beethoven's] *Les Adieux* Sonata with Herr Rubenstein. In his playing the usual fault of making an emotional work of this kind almost unrecognizable through an unfeeling, unaccented rendition can be discerned again. R. explains to him that the difficulty of interpreting the works of B.'s middle period lies in the fact that they appear to preserve the old forms, whereas the themes and figurations go far beyond them—they are full of passion and deep emotion.

*Saturday, October 31* Arose with my mind full of worrying thoughts, to be resolved in silent self-communion. Worked with the children while R. discussed business affairs morning and afternoon with his agents, Herr Voltz and Herr Batz, and with friend Feustel, who again distinguished himself through his acute perception and firm judgment. In the evening Councilor Dittmar with Frl. v. Zerzog. There are rumors that the King is turning to the Catholic party. — Herr Rubenstein plays us some pieces by Chopin, during which R. professes his antipathy toward the modern, richly decorated school of piano music.

*Sunday, November 1* The children in church, R. on his score, I dealing with correspondence. In the afternoon from 4 o'clock on a great business debate with the two agents Voltz and Batz; friend Feustel asks me to remain in the room. It concerns the question whether to appoint them mandataries rather than assignees (which would one day severely restrict Fidi). The matter remains undecided, since they oppose it with all their might; they are coming again in the middle of next

of peace until the children leave—and afterward?? . . . — R. works; he receives a letter from Herr Friedländer, the publisher of the "*Kaisermarsch*," offering him 9,000 marks for an overture—simply in order to wrest from Schott's the prestige of being Wagner's publisher. — R. sends C. Frantz a number of pamphlets (Nietzsche, etc.) to show him that he does not belong to the National Liberals! The more we discuss the works of this man who is certainly by no means insignificant, the more indignant we become over them—they impede the good cause in a thoroughly unpatriotic way. The poor mathematics teacher, *Vogler* here (he is giving Lusch lessons in arithmetic); he is pleased with the new coinage, saying it is handsome and noble and a German can be proud of it, even if he knows very well that it will increase his expenses and not his income. — To give vent to such feelings is a sin when one does not have the power to create something better than that which one censures. The powerless person who is discontented must keep silent. At the same time he knows South Germany and particularly Bavaria just as little as the attackers and present-day defenders of Christianity know Christianity. — The church councilor brings me *The Self-Destruction of Christianity*—a very pitiful affair. In the evening I read Tyndall's address to the British Association for the Advancement of Science to R. He is very tired.

*Friday, November 13* R. at his work, I at mine; at eleven he calls me down to show me how the sun is falling on my Lenbach portrait and transfiguring it! R. quotes from "The Knight of Toggenburg," how the knight waits for the loved one to show herself. He does not go out today. In the evening I discover him utterly depressed—as long as the children are present he does not speak, but when they have left he bursts out: "What is the point of all this hard work with which I have burdened myself and which will only be abused? Who cares about it? Even the best of them, Liszt and Bülow, seek only to get on top of it as quickly as possible. What encouragement have I for working it all out so laboriously except the thought that it might be enjoyed? It is madness—where am I supposed to get the strength?" I try to cheer him up as far as my poor abilities allow. Reading (the conclusion of [Tyndall's] address) gradually distracts him. The address interests me very much; R. is always roused to indignation by new evidence of how little known Schopenhauer is, but apart from that, he also finds it an interesting example of English culture.

*Saturday, November 14* We laughed heartily yesterday over a little paper entitled *Goethe in Dornburg*, which Prof. Overbeck sent me in connection with a conversation I had with him. — Worked with Lusch and Loldi; R. on his score. Yesterday Brünnhilde leaped into the flames, today he had some alterations to make and spent so long reflecting on them that he did not finish his page. In the afternoon we go out together; the sun is shining brightly, but the wind is cold and our walk unenjoyable. Worked morning and afternoon with Lusch. In the evening we read *The Self-Destruction of Christianity* and are amazed that such a meager, indeed stupid thing can cause a stir.

*Sunday, November 15* Fine cold morning in the garden with the children—R. works, groaning, on his monster. In the evening some guests, music is played, Mozart's D Major Symphony, which R. uses to show the difference between M.'s genius and Haydn's—how much more greatly Mozart was influenced by ideality. Herr Rubinstein plays us Beethoven's A Major Sonata. The first movement, flowing, ambling along, but at the same time full of sensitivity, is impossible to analyze.

*Monday, November 16* At breakfast we discuss the music of yesterday; I tell R. that with regard to myself the curious thing has always been that from the moment music begins to sound, all images, concepts, the whole world of appearances and of the intellect, disappear. He says he has always sought the mystical significance of things; for example, in the introduction of [Beethoven's] A Major Symphony he always thinks of the passage in *Faust*: "Passing gold buckets to each other, how heavenly powers ascend, descend!" — and perhaps indeed this is what it might signify! — When I go down to him at about eleven, he says, "I am just writing 'Hagen in great alarm perceives the Rhine-maidens.'" Much snow, cozy atmosphere indoors. In the evening read the report of the general staff.

*Tuesday, November 17* R. dreamed of an audience with the King of Hanover, during which one of the King's dogs constantly got in the way of his feet and snapped at him when he tried to remove it, though the King kept assuring him, "He won't hurt you." Today he writes the 399th page and hopes to be finished before the week ends. I am very sad about being unable to give him a present to mark the occasion—but I cannot permit myself to. The children drive me around in the sleigh. Worked in the morning with Loldi, in the afternoon with Lusch. In the evening R. gets into a rage over my father, who really seems to have believed what the newspapers say—that we wished him to play the piano at this concert. At least this is what Frau v. M[eyendorff] tells me. — Visit from Herr and Frau v. Künsberg.

*Wednesday, November 18* R. works and compares himself with Moltke bringing up his battalions, but having always to keep something in reserve; he says, "I am convinced I could conduct Mars la Tour, too." At lunch he tells me very movingly of a general who in one of these battles hands the flag to his captain of cavalry before dying, but still utters the cry, "Long live the King!" — He finds pleasure, indeed comfort, in the organization of the army, tells me about how the ordinary ranks salute the officers in Angermann's, standing stiff and straight, and how an officer then sits down together with the men. Also about a conversation between two officers: "Good day, fellow countryman." "Where have you been? Surely on duty." Decorum and freedom are both observed. — I find R. reading *Oedipus* in the evening, after his work, comparing the translation with the text. "It is like a Persian carpet," he says, "a torrent of beauty—now vanished forever: we are barbarians." We then come to the *Oresteia*, the scene of Cassandra with the chorus, and R. declares it to be the most perfect thing mortal art has ever produced. In the evening went through Beethoven's Second Symphony and the first movement of the *Hammerklavier* Sonata. Of the latter R. says he knows of no symphonic movement, with the exception perhaps of the first movement of the *Eroica*, that is more effectively carried out; it seems like a play of the most tremendous imagination, containing everything—longing, pain, joy, everything. (In Paris a battle at a Pasdeloup concert over the *Tristan* Prelude, victory for the Wagnerians.)

*Thursday, November 19* We talk a lot more about music in the morning—R. goes to his work, I occupy myself with the children but am slightly interrupted by domestic concerns. In the evening Herr Rubinstein brings the pages of the score he has copied, and R. agrees with me that this strange man's behavior toward R. is utterly extraordinary, since he has never in the least been encouraged to settle here. — In the evening we read about Mars la Tour amid shudders, for it appears that a great deal of blood flowed unnecessarily. General Alvensleben, march on Toul, very interesting; also the very strange misunderstanding between Bazaine and the German general staff. He wanted simply to concentrate on Metz and allow the Germans to bleed to death, whereas they thought he wished to break through—

*Friday, November 20* I awake this morning from a melancholy dream, utterly shaken and suffering. — I dreamed that, for the sake of the two little girls, I had agreed with R. to remarry Hans; correspondence with the latter, wedding in a white dress edged with bright flowers carried out to the strains of Riedel's choral society, at last the double doors opened, and R., pale, silent, strangely transported, had to leave, convulsively I held him fast, screaming loudly, until I awoke! — R. says he has often had such dreams—of how I left him, turned back toward him, he with my spectacles in his hand saying, "She is short-sighted, she can no longer see you." — Domestic cares—but R. works. In the evening read Moltke's book.

*Saturday, November 21* Thrice sacred, memorable day! Toward the hour of noon R. calls to me upstairs, asking me to bring him the newspapers; since he had yesterday complained how worn out he felt and had also assured me that he would not finish before Sunday, I thought that tiredness had prevented his working any longer, but I was too shy to ask him; to distract him, I put down my father's letter, which had just arrived, thinking—since my father was friendly toward our projected journey to Pest—thus to distract him. The noon hour strikes, I come to him reading the letter, he asks me for explanations, I tell him what I intend to reply to it, and purposely refrain from looking at the page of the score, in order not to offend him. Offended, he shows me that it is finished and then says bitterly to me that, when a letter arrives from my father, all thought for him is entirely swept away. I repress my pain at lunchtime, but when R. afterward repeats his complaint, I cannot help breaking into tears, and I am still weeping now as I write this. Thus have I been robbed of this my greatest joy, and certainly not because of the slightest bad intention on my part! *"Dass wissend würde ein Weib"* ["That a woman should learn to know"]. The fact that I dedicated my life in suffering to this work has not earned me the right to celebrate its completion in joy. Thus I celebrate it in suffering, bless the fair and wonderful work with my tears, and thank the malicious God who ordained that I must first atone in suffering for its completion. To whom impart, to whom complain of this suffering? With R. I can only be silent; so I confide it to these pages, to my Siegfried—that it may teach him to feel no rancor, no hatred toward the miserable creature that a human being is, but only boundless pity. And thus I am glad of my suffering and fold my hands in grateful prayer. — What imposed it on me was nothing evil, let my consolation be to accept it with my whole soul, without bitterness for my lot, without reproach for anyone. — May other suffering be atoned for by this, the most un-utterable of all! The children see me weeping and weep with me, but are soon consoled. R. goes to his rest with a final bitter word, I search the piano for *Tristan* sounds; every theme is, however, too harsh for my mood, I can only sink down inside myself, pray, worship! How could I spend this day more piously? How could I express my gratitude other than through the destruction of all urges toward a personal existence? Greetings, eventful day, greetings, day of fulfillment! If a genius completes his flight at so lofty a level, what is left for a poor woman to do? To suffer in love and rapture.

*Thursday, December 3* Since that day I have been unable to write in my diary, I was too upset. In the evening, after I had written down those lines, R. came to me, embraced me, and said we loved each other too intensely, this was the cause of our suffering. We had to go to a party at Herr Gross's, and my face was completely tear-stained. On Sunday the 22nd, we celebrated the completion of the work, but then R. had many business letters to attend to. On Monday the 23rd, I make

F Minor Quartet, after R. had explained to them his nuances and his tempi.

*Monday, February 15* Today I had the feeling that one must atone for all delight! R. catches cold, vexed by the present state of things. Feustel tells us how the government has meanly deprived him of the lease of the Kissingen waters. The only happy event the arrival of Frl. Nietzsche; pretty, friendly, cheerful, she is to stay here during our absence.

*Tuesday, February 16* Devoted the whole day to Frl. Nietzsche, introducing her to the household as well as to our circle of friends. Fine weather. In the evening Herr Brandt from Darmstadt, says he has completed all his preparatory work. R. very worn out; Hill, on whom we so firmly counted, suddenly writes to say he cannot come, the people in Karlsruhe are behaving badly and refusing even the people in Darmstadt permission to participate; the Mannheim theater committee is making it impossible for Herr Knapp to come!

*Wednesday, February 17* Eva's birthday. The good and modest child quite overcome by suddenly being the center of all attention. R. plays her melody to her! — Discussion with friend Feustel; very embarrassing financial situation; R. wishes to break with Schott and make an agreement with Peters, who is offering him three times as much for an overture. Proof that Messrs. Voltz and Batz have been stealing (Frankfurt theater). R. is afraid of breaking off with them, since there is nobody else to look after his affairs. Feustel very concerned about our situation. A new loan. R. deeply upset. In the evening a conversation about the accommodation of guests for the performances. The town is doing nothing. I cannot understand how R. can bear all these worries. On top of that, confusing news about the concert in Vienna. The whole thing was undertaken on the assumption that Richter would participate, and now he cannot get leave—which he, incidentally, already knew when he asked for his wedding vacation!! I feel comforted only when I see R. go off to bed, and sleep wipes all these towering worries from his mind. "But one also dreams!" — Eva very worn out.

*Thursday, February 18* Paid further calls with Elisabeth N. Resolved to have a word with Karl Kolb about the question of guesthouses; R. busy with—and, I fear, perturbed by—all sorts of things. Feustel visits him again for a talk. A further ground for worry is that I have suddenly been advised very strongly against the Luisenstift; its pietism is said to be quite frightening!! I do not have the courage to catalogue all the difficult questions now hovering about our heads—and then the exertion on top of all these worries! It is said that the day on which the concert was first advertised brought in 4,000 florins. Frl. Brandt sends the part of Waltraute back, does not reply to my letter. Nowhere a Sieglinde. Or a Siegfried. — On top of that, domestic annoyances. Karl Kolb in the evening, we explain the position to him; at first he gives us the same overconfident answers as the mayor—the people here have their parlors, the guests are coming on R.'s account and are not interested in comfort, etc. To this R. reacts very violently, I calmly but insistently, and in the end Kolb declares himself convinced and promises to help.

*Friday, February 19*   R. not well—I literally creep past him, refrain from asking questions, try only to help him to forget. When once he laughs heartily, I feel as if I have triumphed over the forces of life. Many preparations for our departure tomorrow. On top of that the cook gives notice, all the servants are ill. The children, thank God, well and very happy with Elisabeth. I write up the days from the 13th till today and close now until Vienna.

When, one morning during this week, I went to R., he told me that my picture had comforted him, the rays of the sun had fallen on the picture and I had looked at him as if transfigured! —

*Saturday, February 20*   Packing and saying goodbye, arrangements made. Waved to the children from the train. R. and I *"the first time alone"* for a long time, which means momentarily relieved of our cares. We feel our spirits rise; can trust, too, that the children are being well looked after. A lot of fun, a lot of sausages, a lot of Marcobrunner—moonlight, a cold but good night. In Vienna at 10 o'clock on Sunday; Standhartner, the *Academic* W. Society, 80 young people, and all sorts of others. Taken to Standhartner's house, cordial welcome. At 2 o'clock Marie Dönhoff; in the evening Lenbach for a moment, spent the evening with the Dönhoffs.

*Monday, February 22*   R. slept very well, I not at all, thinking anxiously about the house. Calls with R.; to Makart's astonishing studio, a sublime lumber-room. To Angeli, in the evening to *Fidelio*, not too atrocious a performance. R. not with me. (Saw Uncle Liszt again.)

*Tuesday, February 23*   Wrote to the children (for the 2nd time), did some shopping. Drove in the afternoon to Princess Hohenlohe's, our first meeting in 15 years, curious impression. Then with charming Marie D., saw Prince Liechtenstein again. R. holds a rehearsal with Frau Materna and Glatz; the latter makes no very good impression, but Materna glorious. In the evening at Marie D.'s with Lenbach.

*Wednesday, February 24*   First rehearsal—much trouble caused by Richter's incredible neglectfulness (he has not sent the tubas, and the tuba players, promised us quite definitely, will not come!). Nevertheless, since the orchestra is good at sight-reading, the effect is overwhelming. It puts everything so far experienced into the shade; what passes through my ears is like the most powerful forces of Nature, and even more—it does not pass through, either, but stamps itself on my mind forever. — R. not too tired after the rehearsal; he lies down afterward and comes to table quite fresh. Very nice letter from the four children. In the evening a small party at Marie Dönhoff's, made the acquaintance of Countess Andrássy, charming and beautiful, and also Countess Festetics, ladies in waiting to the Empress.

*Thursday, February 25* Second rehearsal; though the tubas are now there, Richter has forgotten to have the harp parts copied. Decision not to go to Pest, or at any rate not to give a concert there. The orchestra rebellious; since these people always have bad conductors, who can only get through by giving in, discipline has now completely vanished; they also have so much to do—concerts, in the theater every evening (playing to empty houses on account of the general bankruptcy)—that their irritability can be excused. But much that is splendid is already emerging, and the orchestra is better than it was three years ago. After the first rehearsal a sitting at Lenbach's. Saw Marie Muchanoff's portrait! . . . Spent the evening quietly at home, also all day, unpleasant domestic news; instructions to be given.

*Friday, February 26* With R. to Haas's shop, looked at Oriental objects and bought a few things. R. visits his friend Princess Metternich, who despite her affected hatred of Germany receives him very joyfully and makes a decidedly pleasant impression on him. I visit Countess Andrássy with Marie Dönhoff, to find my extremely pleasant impression of her on our first meeting confirmed. In the evening with R. to the ballet *Robert und Bertrand*—woeful impression! This magnificent, expensive theater—and the use that is made of it! . . . It seems to me indisputable that Vienna can never become a metropolis. They imitate Paris, have display pillars of news, etc., which nobody stops to read!

*Saturday, February 27* Received and answered letters; many domestic cares. Rehearsal from two until six o'clock, in my box the Countesses Andrássy, Dönhoff, Widenburg, Amadei. It goes well, though there are still signs of rebellion in the orchestra. Materna splendid, Glatz neither very laudable nor very audible! Utterly overwhelming impression! Spent the evening at home.

*Sunday, February 28* Arrival of Heckel and Pohl. In the evening a nice dinner at the Dönhoffs', after that a visit to Frau v. Meyendorff, just arrived.

*Monday, March 1* Dress rehearsal from 9:30 to 12. It goes splendidly. The concert at 7 in the evening. Unprecedented reception, unending applause for R., whole heaps of laurels with fine inscriptions: "To the savior of German art," "to the master of humor," "to the creator of

*Die Meistersinger*," "to the connoisseur and renovator of the ancient saga," "to the reformer," "to the sublime master," "to the dramatic poet," "to the greatest of masters," etc. R. has to address some words to the audience, he thanks the splendid Viennese public, which today, as on previous occasions, has followed him and taken to itself these fragments which are so difficult for the imagination to grasp. Called back again, he brought Materna with him and said he was leaving Vienna a pledge in the person of this outstanding artist. The worthy Glatz, on the other hand, was a complete failure.

*Tuesday, March 2*  We are all very tired; Countess Dönhoff is even ill. Wrote letters. The Academic Society presents an address. Heckel to lunch; visit from Prince Rudolph Liechtenstein, who says that people who otherwise never go to the theater or to concerts were present at this concert, "the lame and the blind." Departure of Frau v. M., who is going to Pest.

*Wednesday, March 3*  R. calls on Rubinstein and is pleased to hear that he is longing to return to Bayreuth. Received calls, in the evening a *soirée* in Makart's studio in R.'s honor—Count and Countess Andrássy, Count and Countess Széchenyi, Countess Festetics, lady in waiting to the Empress, who told me in the morning that for her R.'s art is like the creation of the world . . . Countess Wickenburg, Count Hoyos, Countess Wilczek, Prince Liechtenstein, the Standhartner family, the Liszt family, Herr and Frau von Angeli, Dr. Mosenthal, Prince Metternich, the Hellmesberger Quartet, Semper (whom R., seeing him for the first time in 8 years, does not at first recognize), Countess Dönhoff, Frau Wolter, and many others—perhaps 60 people in all. A pleasant occasion, everyone looking his best, face and clothes, and the general mood very cheeful.

*Thursday, March 4*  Went to the Belvedere with Rich., then to poor Semper, whose plans we looked at; in response to my slight surprise over the dome with the four little domes, he says it was done as a concession to his colleague! Very sad impression. — Despite his commissions and the Emperor's protection he remains poor, so poor that he does not venture to take a carriage, and he looks so worn out that I do not believe he will live long. Yet, in spite of it, all these colossal plans for a crumbling state! The Court is divided into two factions, the Hungarians and the Germans, the former, staunch Catholics, full of hatred against the German Empire, the latter in favor of an alliance with Germany, and liberal. A curious conflict, the Emperor a tragic figure between them, irresolute, uncertain. Poor Semper, ignored throughout Germany, is now erecting buildings for this state and going to pieces in the process! In the evening went through the third act of *Götterdämmerung* in Standhartner's house, with piano accompaniment.

dinner; mutual observations about the misery in Germany; everywhere fraud and bad work, the rich people have all their furniture sent from Paris; our friend traveled to London to have some clothes made. — Regarding Bismarck, he says that he wished to bring all the attacks on the Catholic clergy to a head at one time, but experienced so much trouble with *all the powers* that he will now (as he himself expressed it) have to cut off the dog's tail in sections. R. says that four years ago he was recommending the Jesuits, now he is recommending the Jews! Bucher also feels that they are gobbling us up—one Israelite is now even a minister (Friedland)! — In the evening Scholz, Dohm, and Niemann; I meet them again when I return from the opera house where *Die Maccabäer* was performed; a curious impression of this opera—it definitely seems that one can nowadays only make an effect if one writes in the Wagnerian style.

*Wednesday, April 21* Day of Repentance, everything closed, but in spite of that I succeed, with Prof. Doepler, in getting the museum opened; great delight in the old objects and those newly acquired, especially a head by van Eyck and a portrait by Velasquez. Returning home, I find R. in great difficulties, lots of visitors, on top of that the necessity of drawing up the programs for Vienna, where a third concert is being planned. Photographers ceaselessly pestering! Calls with R. (British ambassador, Usedoms, etc.). At 5 o'clock with our niece Johanna; very nice dinner with the lady in waiting to the Crown Princess, Countess Brühl, Dohm, etc. After that spent the evening with a few friends in the Office of the Royal Household.

*Thursday, April 22* Rehearsal at 10 o'clock; the orchestra is becoming ever better and more fiery, as always after a certain amount of contact with R. . . . But he very tired. — He lies down for a while and I pay some calls, take care of the distribution of tickets for the dress rehearsal. In the evening we entertain some friends, among them Frau Wesendonck. — Before that R. and I went for a little walk in the Tiergarten, looked at the curious victory column!! — Recently R. said that the best thing Germany had recently produced was the Prussian army constitution, but he had little sympathy for what this army was now protecting. Herr Tappert tells us the most curious things about the pressure exerted by the School of Music against all who have not been through it; when in a newspaper he (Tappert) recently called Wilhelmj the leading violinist, the editor was attacked by the people in the ministry and from all sides, saying that the leading violinist is Joachim! Poor music teachers who do not swear by this god gradually lose all their pupils. In the school itself no note by my father may be played; but if one asks about the accomplishments of the head of this institution, one is told that he plays the violin well! However, he has the

Ministry of Culture and the Crown Prince and Princess behind him, and so any sign of independence is at once stifled.

*Friday, April 23* Dress rehearsal, R. not well, however; we drive there with Frau Wesendonck. Many friends; and great emotion (Prof. Helmholtz constantly in tears as he listened to these divine things). I utterly shattered, the whole finale in fact a paraphrase of the words not set to music, "Not the glitter of gold, etc.—in joy and sorrow let love alone prevail." — The entire world of the gods, the forces of Nature, the heroes—all serve, as it were, to glorify the noblest of women! [*In the margin:* "The victory column!"] . . . At the conclusion of the rehearsal R. says to me: "Here comes the awakener! You are always in my thoughts, for it is you who awakened everything in me again—love, creative power, everything." — He is longing to be back with the children. Lunched at home, I pay some calls, in the evening a *soirée* at the Office of the Royal Household in honor of Frau Materna. (R. decides on Schroetter for Siegfried.)

*Saturday, April 24* R. slept well, in good spirits; I pay some calls with my friendliest friend (to Helmholtz, Luise Oriola, Princess Biron). At half past seven the concert; I in Mimi's box with Baroness Loë, Frau v. Bülow (wife of the Undersecretary of State), Prince Liechtenstein, etc. Great enthusiasm by Berlin thermometers, though the performance was not good and R. greatly exhausted and in consequence out of humor. In the evening, visit from the Jachmanns and Frau Wesendonck with the Bissings. The former tells me that R. has an expression he never before had—contented. Count Redern visits me in the box, declares that R. has not changed since the year '47. Bucher affected by music for the first time, in the concert hall he literally cries out, which, coming from this taciturn man, sounds very strange.

*Sunday, April 25* A long sleep, after which we immediately got dressed for the second concert, at 12 o'clock. Atmosphere very nice and cordial, a better performance, audience friendly, Materna and Niemann in tears, R. very cheerful afterward. Dinner at Poppenberger's, with the Niemanns, Materna, the Eckerts. In the evening at Helmholtzes'; made the acquaintance of Mommsen, who looks, as R. says, "as if he had put on a professor's mask for a fancy-dress ball." Worked out a plan with Herr v. Radowitz to force the state to intervene in Bayreuth affairs!

*Monday, April 26* Preparations for departure; visit to Menzel, whose brother-in-law welcomes us with strains from *Götterdämmerung*; looked at folios. To the hotel at one o'clock, lunch with Lothar Bucher, laughed a lot over Mommsen, his dishonest behavior and that of other scholars in the Lauenburg affair. Spoke about the Prince [Bismarck], whose policies were actually thwarted by the Empress's intrigues (outside Paris, for example, it was impossible to attack, since the shells did not arrive; it eventually turned out that the trains had all been commandeered by the Empress and Princess Victoria to take provisions to the Parisians!). Matters of the most important kind have to be postponed because the Empress plagues the Emperor about them so much that the doctors fear a stroke. Bismarck downright incensed, ill. — Many visitors to be received afterward, at 5 o'clock dinner in the Office of the Royal Household. There I talk to the editor of *Kladderadatsch* and demand the support of his periodical for Bayreuth. — Departure at 7 o'clock; the two concerts have brought in about 6,000 thalers—a lot in view of the unfavorable circumstances. Journeyed through the night, glad and happy to be back on Bavarian soil.

*Tuesday, April 27*   In Bayreuth at 8 o'clock, the children at the station, well and full of glee. We both very sleepy. In the evening Feustel, who tells us about a curious meeting with Councilor Düfflipp, who was extremely rude to him! . . . On the other hand, in Vienna a complete triumph for R.'s views, the opera schedule being adapted to them completely. Much delight in the children.

*Wednesday, April 28*   A day of correspondence and accounts, on top of that the house in disorder. — We hear that Hans has been swindled out of fifteen hundred pounds in England; grievous news. The lawyer Skutsch; another mortgage! . . . In the evening great tiredness. R. had wild dreams, an uprising of the rabble in Paris against him, he attempts to appease them through eloquence, someone eventually comes forward from the crowd, kisses his hand, and tells him he has convinced him, whereupon all calm down. Probably this wild dream was brought on by the news, given to us by Bucher, that Bismarck was constantly receiving threats and warnings. Among other things Bucher quoted to us a letter which is utterly crazy and enough to turn other people crazy, too. Bismarck recently declared that he was glad of the urchins who always accompanied him in the street, for then he could be sure that nothing would come on him from behind—he could take care of what lay in front! . . .

*Thursday, April 29*   A good night for R., he looks very well, thank goodness; much disturbance in the house. In the afternoon a walk in the palace gardens, visit from the mayor, discussed the accommodation question, great hardness of hearing. In the evening an amiable conversation with R., about children and what makes them what they are.

*Friday, April 30*   R. definitely wants me with him in Vienna, I should like to stay at home to keep an eye on the house. He composes the concert ending to "Hagen's Watch," which puts him in good spirits. In the afternoon a drive to the theater; terrible impression again— nothing done about the ground clearance, all the rubble still lying around, no plantings possible this year! . . . Dismal mood; in the evening some calming down and restoration of spirits.

*Saturday, May 1*  Long sleep; nasty letter from Feustel; R. resolves to return a part of the site to the town, since it is so mean about doing anything. I am always comparing R. to the poor hare in the fairy tale, wearing himself out while the two hedgehogs look calmly on! . . . In the afternoon drove to the theater in fine weather, Rus following behind, barking and leaping; there inspected the orchestra pit once again; firm decision made. In the evening unpleasant discoveries for R.: Herr v. Reichenberg, engaged for Fafner, can think of nothing better to do than describe R.'s indoor garments in the newspaper, he also says the silliest things about the house. R. gives him his notice.

*Sunday, May 2*  A sad day—we are told of Rus's death from a ruptured lung, caused, it seems, by our drive yesterday. With him we certainly lose one of our best friends. I noticed again yesterday how anxious and concerned for R. he was as R. climbed down into the orchestra pit. If one of us were to have died, the dog would doubtless have known it in advance, but we are taken by surprise—this on top of everything else. I write to the children. In the evening some acquaintances—we are despondent.

*Monday, May 3*  R. talks of a possible performance of *Tannhäuser* in Vienna, with Materna. [*A few words based on untranslatable word play omitted.*] At 12 o'clock burial of Rus; when I told Fidi of his death, he said: "Oh, good heavens, what will his wife say when she comes?!" Fidi knew that we had ordered a mate for Rus. At 5 o'clock left for Vienna, tolerable night journey; arrival at the Standhartners' at 9.

*Tuesday, May 4*  Not good news of the concert at all, the proceeds will be small. At lunch we are visited by Baron Hofmann and the opera director Jauner; the former really has changed the operatic arrangements in accordance with R.'s views; Richter, now a conductor there on R.'s recommendation, also presents himself, but does not make a pleasant impression. — In the evening *Around the World in 80 Days,* the present great success, utterly devoid of wit, a lack of any sort of imagination.

*Wednesday, May 5*  Rehearsal, "Hagen's Watch" very beautifully sung by Scaria. Voice of the very darkest coloring— R., tired, goes to bed, I pay some calls. After lunch Herr Jauner, Prince Rudolph Liechtenstein, in the evening friend Lenbach. During the afternoon I visited Princess Hohenlohe in the Palais Augarten with R.

*Thursday, May 6*  Concert at 12 o'clock—fine impression, "Hagen's Watch" repeated. But R. is tired. I then visit the picture and flower exhibition with Prince Liechtenstein and Standhartner. — In the evening Semper, very interesting—he literally comes to life in conthe station. My father apparently well. Spent the evening with him.

*Thursday, June 17* Wrote to R. and the children—at 12, rehearsal for the memorial service for Marie, the service at 3 o'clock, very moving. Lunch with Frau v. Meyendorff, my father very worn out. In the evening I alone with Alwine Frommann.

*Friday, June 18* A letter from R. in French! . . . My father unfortunately very unwell, a shock for me! With torn feelings to the performance of *Tristan und Isolde*—much absurdity and shoddiness, but I beg the Vogls to come to Bayreuth.

*Saturday, June 19* R. sent me a very curious letter from Herr Brahms, as artificial and unedifying as his compositions. — At 9 o'clock took leave of my father, heartbreaking, he is very, very wretched! . . . Sad journey to Eisenach, a wait of 5 hours, I visit the Wartburg. At 11 in the evening met by R. in Neumarkt—much to tell him, among other things, about my two-hour conversation with the Grand Duke of Weimar.

*Sunday, June 20* Good awakening, R. tells me that he does not really live at all when I am not there, nothing has any meaning, he did not even have the gas lit. — I write the better part of 10 letters during the day; R. has many inquiries from Americans and is reckoning on these to fill his hall in the end—nothing for the Germans to be proud of! — In the evening some friends, went through Berlioz's *Le Bal*. The guesthouse problem constantly in our minds . . . When our guests have left, R. says that, no matter what people come, it always seems to him absurd to receive them.

*Monday, June 21* Wretched night with bad dreams; at breakfast discussed with R. all the behavior of the Reich authorities toward his undertaking; R. intends after the rehearsals to approach them again, but then, if nothing comes of it, the Americans. Inquiry to Frl. Tietjens, who is said to have sung Ortrud magnificently, whether she would take on Sieglinde. In the afternoon arrival of the dressing case which the King of the Netherlands presented to my father and he now to me, along with the manuscripts (*Lohengrin, Tannhäuser*), melancholy feelings. — R. continues to study with the singer Unger, some hope after much exertion! . . . We drive to the theater; Brandt returns home with us; complaints about the lack of interest among the local people.

*Tuesday, June 22* Conference on apartments. R. afterward in a very bad humor and unwell. When I think that he could be working on *Parzival* and has to sacrifice his time and strength to such things, I could despair. What power keeps us on our feet?? — In the afternoon Herr Unger, who pleases R. a lot through his application, but it is a strain on him. Good letter from Lusch, though she has been ill.

*Wednesday, June 23* R. had a very bad night; too many worries—

and on top of that bad news of my father! . . . Since the worry is almost more than I can bear, I send a telegram and am told that things are improving. In the afternoon R. tries out the desks! — The custodian is demanding 600 florins a month for a rented apartment, great worry about this problem, shared by nobody else here. In the evening Prof. Doepler with sketches of the costumes; much in them very fine.

*Thursday, June 24* Up at half past four to deal with letters it was impossible to write yesterday. Dull weather, then worked with the children. — For lunch Prof. Doepler, then some Bayreuth ladies, in the evening Prof. Doepler and friend Feustel. Again the accommodation problem, it seems definite that a hotel cannot be built, and now it is a matter of making the necessary arrangements. The question of the cost of the costumes is also discussed. "My undertaking looks to me like a will-o'-the-wisp over a marsh," R. says to me. (Yesterday he dreamed about his mother; rouged and painted, she was furnishing a magnificent house for him, he himself so alarmed at not having given her money for it that he could only think of how to escape, and he ran away, even leaving his dog locked in to die of starvation!)

*Friday, June 25* Better night for R. He tells me about a letter from Herr Jauner in Vienna, promising him the royalties and 2,000 florins for each work produced personally by him; R. considers this and comes to the conclusion, in view of the present state of the theaters and their attitude toward the singers (who have in their contracts permission to make cuts, etc.), that it is not possible for him to accept. In the evening Prof. Doepler.

*Saturday, June 26* Domestic day, payments, during which the many requirements of our life here always fall heavy on my heart. R., having had no reply concerning Frl. Tietjens (Sieglinde), sends a telegram and receives the reply that she will probably accept, so it is still unsettled. Herr Scaria inquires whether he might come later—various difficulties of this kind. But the singer Unger is giving R. pleasure. In the evening we read Prof. Werder's *Hamlet* lectures, an almost comic impression! (In the afternoon with Frau Kolb.)

*Sunday, June 27* Children's games and for me correspondence, both morning and afternoon; R. also has much correspondence. Prof. Hey from Munich to take part in Herr Unger's studies. The latter sings the "Forging Songs" before our quite numerous Sunday gathering in a way that gives grounds for hope. —

*Monday, June 28* Lessons for the children, during them two boys for Fidi to play with (Erich Braun and Ludwig Reitzenstein). In the afternoon to Turkish coffee with friend Lalas; what he has to tell us about Albanians and Turks is highly interesting; the Albanians possess no state, but in their customs there is more culture than among our-

willingness to conduct concerts all over the place following the performances, but this is insufficient security for borrowing money. It is pointed out that R. might die! R. asked me whether I believed our undertaking would ever come to anything. — R. remarks that it is now once more four years since he last wrote a note of music; how this pains me! . . . Herr O. Beta has sent us his pamphlet on the Jews, privately printed; it is badly written, without style, but contains remarkable insights into the present nature of things; the comparison between Antonio's melancholy toward Shylock and the present behavior of the Germans toward the Jews is very apposite. — In the evening Herr Gross brings a letter from Herr Scaria: he is demanding 2,700 thalers for the month of August and 250 marks for each evening rehearsal— R. dispenses with the services of this gentleman. Now he has to look around for a new Hagen! . . . In the evening a little music-making with Herr Rubinstein. R. in cheerful mood in spite of everything and everybody.

*Thursday, December 23* Fine day, R. in good spirits in spite of an ugly dream (he concealed himself, was apprehended, taken prisoner), I likewise, in spite of profound, probably never-ending sorrow! Silent decoration of the tree as the sun goes down; nuts and apples gleam in the golden light, tranquil melancholy—how willingly would I bear everything, if only I could spare others being put to the test! I do not complain that this is my lot, everything we suffer is just—I complain on behalf of others, another! . . . Continued decorating in the evening, while R. selects at random from his library a volume of the *Correspondance générale de Voltaire* (Volume VIII) and reads some letters from it, to our very great amusement. We think of Goethe and Frederick the Great—how pleasant this refined, lively, cultured spirit must have seemed to them!

*Friday, December 24* Preparations from morning till evening, in the evening R. gives me a lovely dress, but loveliest of all are his words to me: "The only god I possess is my love for you." After the distribution of presents in the evening, R. reads *Don Quixote* aloud, and we laugh as heartily as if there were no such things as sorrow and concern.

*Saturday, December 25* I thank Heaven and earth for my existence, since I was given a mission and permitted to perform it, remorsefully I beg forgiveness for the suffering caused by me, and I will courageously bear what my courage refuses to put into words! Breakfast with the children; birthday cake with candles, singing! R. unfortunately not well. — Yesterday he answered a letter from the editor of the *Weser-Zeitung*, who asked him whether he ought not reply to all the lies about him in the press—R. says that unless he were to do it for the honor of the *press* itself, he could let it rest, for the press, though it might hinder him, could not destroy him, as it would so much like to do. — In the evening read [Dozy's] history of the Arabs.

*Sunday, December 26* We had a wretched, separated night, the night lights were not working properly, on top of that R. had a bad dream, that I went mad and wanted to leave him! I spend the morning and afternoon writing letters; in the evening finished reading the story of Almansor.

*Monday, December 27* R. dreamed that the Queen of Prussia declared herself to him to be his mother! . . . "Justice is a precious word, lust is not to be deterred," he suddenly exclaims at lunch, laughing. — Yesterday he listened to the conversation of some people in the beer-house: villages becoming destitute, no one willing to work, the Jews are buying up woodlands and cattle, they raise the prices, everything goes to ruin! — R. feels very disgusted with the composition for America, says it is not worthy of him! — Bitter feelings against Bismarck. — Dependent entirely on Feustel and a few young people! "If it turns out well," R. says, "you and I will have nothing but sobs and tears, for we have suffered too much; if it turns out badly, we will be upheld by vexation and pride." — Oh, God, if only I could help! In the evening read Grimm's legends and Semper's pamphlet on architectural styles.

*Tuesday, December 28* Although I have a firm arrangement with R. not to discuss unpleasant things, but to fight against them or bear them, and only to talk about the beautiful things, I manage to inform him of Mimi's letter; thereupon he drafts a letter to Prince Bismarck, a copy of which I sent to Bucher. Everything gloomy and harsh can be borne in love! — But in the evening I am plagued by a violent headache. — We read Goethe's "The Secrets" and some fine poems translated from the Chinese.

*Wednesday, December 29* Still writing letters until further notice! Friendly letters and business ones, among these last belongs an inquiry to Baron Seydlitz regarding the advance! . . . Always delight in Fidi. The children skating! In the evening went through some sonatas by Scarlatti, without great pleasure. — Went for a long walk in the palace gardens with R.; almost impossible to speak, our minds too full, we cannot ignore the embarrassing subjects, and what point in discussing those?

*Thursday, December 30* I dreamed that Kinowsky got into a train in order to murder R. R. on the other hand had pleasant dreams, and Fidi had a nice dream about his father's birthday, which coincided very nicely with my own thoughts, which are already frequently occupied now with R.'s birthday. — R. writes to Frau Wesendonck, also in connection with the advance! . . . I pay calls. In the evening I receive a

Christianity suddenly entered, how moving the death of Saint Ferdin-
and! How familiar to us! It is the *humility* behind it which so moves us.
Fell asleep thinking tenderly of Hans.

*Sunday, January 9* R. dreamed of an ink blot which he made on a
page of the score, to his great annoyance, then it turned out that the
score was not one of his. Morning prayers with the children—then to
the ice with them. R. has good news of Herr Unger, God grant that no
disappointments will arise here! Mimi Schl. writes advising a petition
from the management committee to the Reichstag, Bucher believes the
mood to be favorable. In such a difficult situation, anyway, it is impossible to do more damage, since nothing helps! . . . R. in despondent
mood, I try to persuade him to start again on the biography tomorrow,
and he promises. God forbid any obstacles!

*Monday, January 10* Lessons for the children very early in the morning, then *dictation*! In the afternoon to the ice with the children and
worked with them in the evening before supper. R. was with the mayor,
who is very much against a petition to the Reichstag. R. writes to
Councilor Düfflipp to inquire whether H. M. would take this ill! — In
the evening some scenes from *Hamlet*.

*Tuesday, January 11* The same routine as yesterday, pleasurably
melancholy images from the past rise up, the spirit of my sister hovers
between us! — Everything vanished! . . . In the afternoon a letter from
our nephew Jachmann about the Fürstner affair. R. is thinking about
going to Berlin. In the evening Marke alarms us with a howl of
lament—Brange was not there. Profound effect of this animal sound. —

*Wednesday, January 12* No dictation today! R. is thinking of business
matters; he is deeply annoyed at being referred to the Reichstag, when
he had appealed to the Emperor's grace. After lunch we come to the
subject of *Tannhäuser*—how the fate of this work is linked with an unbroken series of experiences of the most wretched kind. [*In the margin:*
"I am very shocked to learn that Pusinelli was never paid (about 5,000
thalers), and here I solemnly say to my son Siegfried that it is his duty,
should he ever be in possession of a fairly large amount of capital, to
pay off this debt to Dr. Pusinelli's heirs."] Despondent mood in the
evening.

*Thursday, January 13* Worked with Boni 9–11, dictation 11–12:30,
then with the children on the ice; from 5–7 worked with Boni and the
little ones, in the evening with R. read about Mohammed in Gibbon.

*Friday, January 14* Letters, a very good one from Standhartner with
an account of the royalties, then a nice one (as always) from the King,
a sad one from Councilor Düfflipp, complaining of the difficulties of
the royal treasury; R. sends a telegram saying he has decided not to
approach the Reichstag, and to give concerts in Brussels. A conference

yesterday with Feustel and the mayor did in fact reveal that the emergency is not such a dire one, and that a rebuff from the Reichstag would discredit our whole undertaking—Bismarck probably only too anxious for this rebuff, in order to justify his own behavior. In the evening finished Dozy's history of the Arabs: Motamit! — R. says they are less congenial to him than the Christian heroes of Castile.

*Saturday, January 15* It turns out that R. has once again been swindled in connection with a contract; in the contract with Vienna they have omitted the subscription proceeds, so that if the theater has a rise in its fortunes (and indeed most probably because of R.) and the number of regular subscribers increases, R. will suffer a significant drop in royalties, just because he relied on having his stipulations (based on the Berlin arrangement) taken into account in writing as well as in conversation! . . . Work with the children and dictation. R. writes to Herr Jauner, complaining of this.

*Sunday, January 16* Nephew Jachmann reports that R.'s presence is not utterly necessary; we celebrate R[ubinstein]'s return from Berlin. In the evening he plays us several things, among others a composition by Mihalovich, *Hero & Leander,* which, while giving evidence of a decided talent, arouses great misgivings in us.

*Monday, January 17* R. wrote down a theme which came to him during the evening, and discovers that the countertheme can be found in a simple reversal of it; he says there are melody spectra for the ear just as there are light spectra for the eyes. Dictation; visits with R. — ͏ ͏ ͏ ͏ ͏ s us a note from Feustel; the latter has received a which makes it seem advisable after all to approach the Prince personally with a request. R. very much against it. Bismarck's secretary writes somewhat confusedly, but also seems of the opinion that the difficulties would be less if one were to approach the Reichstag! R. replies that he cannot approach the Reichstag for an *advance,* also that he is appealing to the Emperor's grace and the understanding of the Reich Chancelor, not, however, to the views of the gentlemen in the Reichstag.

*Tuesday, January 18* The King sends us a life-size photograph of himself; Dr. Strecker (successor of the "Sons" in the firm of *B. Schott's Sons*) visits us, bringing the score of *Siegfried.* He pleases us with his very good manners. More dictation, and work with Boni. — In the evening we begin the pamphlet *On the Present State of the German Reich,* which Prof. de Lagarde has sent me; it contains excellent things (Austria's task, criticism of present-day schools), but much confused theology.

*Wednesday, January 19* Dictation and work. Also, arrival of royalties and calculation of expenditure. Baron Hofmann writes of bad attendance in the theater; the disastrous financial situation is causing very great alarm everywhere. "The fact that only a man like Bismarck can help us," says R., "shows that we are lost." — Herr Jauner cables that he will arrange matters according to R.'s wishes, reports at the same time that as a condition of his engagement Herr Scaria is demanding 2,500 thalers from July 15 onward, to be paid now *in advance*. This makes R. so indignant that he feels like dispensing with Scaria right away, but he cables Betz first, inviting his and Niemann's opinion. — Continued Prof. Lagarde's pamphlet in the evening.

*Thursday, January 20*  Further dictation and lessons; R. receives Herr Betz's opinion that Scaria will have to be dispensed with. R. writes to Herr Jauner accordingly. How will Frau Materna now react? . . . Change of daily routine (lunch at 3 o'clock), squabbles between governess and parlormaid, on top of that trouble with my eyes! . . .

*Friday, January 21*  Lessons and dictation; R. to Feustel with good wishes on his birthday— In the evening continued Prof. Lagarde's pamphlet. Many excellent things in it. More and more we are considering, R. and I, the question of education; thoughts of establishing a model school, with Nietzsche, Rohde, Overbeck, Lagarde. Could the King be induced to sponsor it? . . .

*Saturday, January 22*  Still the same activities; R. continues to occupy himself with the Arabs through the work of Baron Schack. In the evening Shakespeare's R[ichard] II, my favorite among the historical plays—reading one act gives rise to endless amazement, admiration, re-reading, discussion—it is as if one had never grasped it all before, a complete revelation! . . .

*Sunday, January 23*  Dictation; walk; in the evening visitors, a Haydn symphony, and Rubinstein's latest piece from *Der Ring des Nibelungen*.

*Monday, January 24*  The same life, lessons, dictation, but besides these many business matters for me to settle; in the evening conclusion of R. II, which moves me so much that I lose my night's sleep on account of it.

*Tuesday, January 25*  Tired day—yesterday I wrote to friend Bucher, to tell him the reasons why we have not approached the Reichstag, and to ask him not to allow any *official* notification to reach us before our visit to Berlin (March). — In the evening *Henry IV*.

*Wednesday, January 26*  R. not entirely well; displeased with a letter from Betz; Fricke is recommended for Hagen. In the evening a ball at the district president's house! . . . Following which an intimate hour for R. and me on the homeward journey!

*Thursday, January 27*  R. spends the day writing to the King, I with lessons and business matters, in the evening *Don Quixote*.

*Friday, January 28*  Dictation, my eyes are causing me trouble; fine

Indian saying: He who produces fine works throughout his life has overcome sensuality. Letter from the editor of the *Weser-Zeitung*, Herr Hofmann; he says if anyone were to attack the press openly in R.'s behalf, he would have the whole pack after him. Herr Bauernfeld has published a play in which, so it is said, R. is ridiculed, and the editor of a large newspaper in Leipzig recommends the book as *useful, desirable,* etc.

*Saturday, January 29* Dictation and lessons; visit to our poor good friend Schenk; R. in bad humor. Lothar Bucher writes, telling us on no account to undertake anything just now, the Prince is the only person on whom one can rely, and he is ill. — In the evening *Don Quixote*.

*Sunday, January 30* Correspondence day, the children have a holiday! Wrote to R. L[iechtenstein], also dictation. In the evening Bayreuth company, enriched by Frau v. Staff.

*Monday, January 31* Work with the children and dictation. R. has a conference in the afternoon, from which he returns very depressed. To contemplate going on with the performances looks like foolhardiness! Only 488 patrons so far! And the expenditure is mounting, the press closed to us even for announcements! — In Paris, it appears, *Le Figaro* has published a libelous article about R., a Herr Ullmann begs R. to reply to it, if only for the sake of *Lohengrin*, which is to be performed in Paris. . . . R. answers that he reads no newspapers, and the task of replying belongs to those who honor the press with their attention. — In America Hans also seems to be exposed to this vile blot on our public life.

*Tuesday, February 1* Small dinner party in our house, Staffs, Künsberg, etc.; afterward R. attempts to skate, but he can no longer do it. In the evening *Don Quixote,* our only source of pleasure at the moment. Yet now and again R. thinks of *Parzival*; the name Gurnemanz keeps coming into his mind.

*Wednesday, February 2* Candlemas—little illumination around us, in me a longing for peace. "Perhaps," says R., "there will emerge after the performances a rosy blush of shame, which will turn into the rosy dawn of a new age." — In the evening a reception given by the local patrons—a trial for R.

*Thursday, February 3* R. makes preparations for Herr Unger's debut in Vienna, he wants him to sing the scene from the 3rd act of *Siegfried* with Frau Materna. All we hear from Vienna is that royalty payments will not be paid on the subscription proceeds. Frau v. Staff and Frau v. Künsberg with us at lunch. In the evening *Don Quixote*.

*Friday, February 4* Dictation; deep, deep melancholy; Siegfried the only source of amusement. R. wanders up to the theater, it is like a desert up there! The preparations for accommodations are having to be pursued very casually, since nobody has the slightest idea who will come! — My pessimism is such that I can scarcely believe any more in the money value of curiosity! — R. would like to explain the position to a patron. A nice book from an English lady, Helen Zimmern, a biography of Schopenhauer, done with great understanding. — In the evening *Don Quixote*.

*Saturday, February 5* R. says if our journey to Berlin were not impending he would start work on *Parzival*. But unfortunately we shall have to make this excursion. R. has a conference with his management committee, and it does not upset him; he tells them they are engaged in a complete game of chance, but the good people are not losing their confidence. — In the evening *Don Quixote*.

*Sunday, February 6* Snowfall: "Winter learns in its old age to turn white," R. says. — He has a headache; I write letters, to Prof. Lagarde, Mimi (she wants to arrange a performance of *Tristan* in support of our theater), etc. R. goes for a walk with the dogs, his only pleasure now in the outside world. It is being said in Meiningen that Hans has bought a house there and intends to marry a beautiful Russian woman; how gladly I would believe this, but I have no hopes in this regard. I am having to struggle against an increasing melancholy!

*Monday, February 7* R. wakes up whistling loudly; he was dreaming of a festival here, but of *Holländer* and *Tannhäuser,* and he was conducting them from a piano in a neighboring room with the help of a mirror; around him were gathered Schröder-Devrient and others who preferred being with him to watching the performance itself, and he could not open the piano for wreaths and flowers; suddenly he hears strange sounds and runs into the theater, where he sees *Ocean Waves* being performed, a ballet (so his singers tell him) by Servais which had been inserted in *Holländer*: "And you put up with that!" he exclaims, runs into the theater again, and lets out a mighty whistle! . . . Telegram from Madrid that *Rienzi* has been performed there with great success. — Herr Hoffmann is traveling around with *Walküre* and *Götterdämmerung* and is not to be restrained! . . . A bailiff arrives, and we rack our brains wondering what he wants, all sorts of possible and impossible things occur to R.; then to our great amusement it turns out that a woman in Vienna is laying claim to Scaria's earnings here; we are told he owes her 25,800 thalers and is under an obligation to her. At least we are glad to have an explanation for Scaria's unbelievable behavior! — *Don Quixote* in the evening.

*Tuesday, February 8* Children's lessons and dictation: "We are getting on with the *Life* like a house on fire," R. says when he sees how much I have already written down. In the evening an amateur concert, Mendelssohn's *Reformation* Symphony, the second movement makes

R. think of Tetzel: "When the money in the cashbox rings, the soul at once to heaven wings."

*Wednesday, February 9*  No dictation today, R. works on his composition for the Americans (opening of the World's Fair, Centennial of Independence); he has asked for 5,000 dollars for it—we wonder whether the promoters will agree to this. When I go to lunch, he is playing a gentle, rocking theme—he says nothing occurs to him to represent American pomp. Sleigh ride, little real success; in the evening Beethoven trios, the D Major and B-flat Major, great impression particularly from the latter, regret that Beethoven does not conclude the Adagio but, as with the crack of a whip, as R. says, launches straight into the finale. — A Herr Ritter from Heidelberg brings along a new kind of viola, which R. finds excellent and intends to introduce into his orchestra. But after such evening amusements R. is always tired.

*Thursday, February 10*  R. at his composition, I busy with the children, Boni is working well, is willing and friendly; in the evening *Don Quixote*. The editor of the *Weser-Zeitung* announces his intention of becoming R.'s champion, Standhartner writes that *Lohengrin* will be possible in Vienna only on March 2.

*Friday, February 11*  R. works morning and afternoon on his piece; as he says, it is the first time he has ever written for money! *Don Quixote* is our restorer in the evening.

*Saturday, February 12*  I teach, R. composes, unfortunately without enjoyment. In the evening—reading. Dispatch of the management committee's quarterly report to the patrons.

*Sunday, February 13*  Day of general correspondence for me while the children play; I thank the English lady who has written to us and sent an excellent biography of Schopenhauer. Wrote to R. L[iechtenstein] and Marie Dönhoff.

*Monday, February 14*  R. still working, complains of being unable to visualize anything to himself in this composition; it had been different with the "*Kaisermarsch*," he says, even with "Rule Britannia," where he had thought of a great ship, but here he can think of nothing but the 5,000 dollars he has demanded and perhaps will not get. A conference in the evening; friend Feustel brings along and reads to us an article from the *Frankfurter Zeitung* entitled "R. Wagner and the Critics," which is really excellent. The situation is tolerable on the whole, though Feustel informs us that Bismarck has declared to Jachmann that, since we had not followed his advice to go to the Reichstag, where he would have exerted all his power in behalf of our cause, he wished to hear nothing more about the matter! . . .

*Tuesday, February 15*  A thaw, not favorable for R.; all the same, he works both morning and afternoon. In the evening the editor of the *Weser-Zeitung* writes and declares that he is the author of the article in the *Fr. Zeitung.* — Yesterday a man from Italy sent an inquiry: the Italian newspapers are reporting that the performances will not take place, and he says this has confused him and several acquaintances who want to attend them! . . . R. enlightens him. A poor teacher applies for a certificate of patronage, to be paid for from his savings; after having seen the piano scores, he says, he must attend the performances at all costs. — In the evening *Don Quixote*; we note how Cervantes became more and more of an artist and discovered, as it were, more and more in his material.

*Wednesday, February 16* I take a lot of trouble with my lessons— with profit, I wonder? . . . Herr von Hülsen writes very nicely, saying *Tristan* cannot be given until March 15, on account of the difficulty of the work. R. agrees with this. After lunch he shows me his latest album leaf, "an attempt to be American," and says it is the chorus the women will sing to Parzival: *"Komm, schöner Knabe!"* . . . He is thinking a lot about *Parzival* and is grieved that so many things intervene. Among other things, a letter from Herr Simson, who wants all possible dates, etc., etc. — The children celebrate Eva's birthday in advance, I write to Marie Hohenlohe for her birthday (18th). In the evening *Don Quixote,* the fine episode with the lions.

*Thursday, February 17* R. under much pressure on his composition; but we celebrate Evchen very merrily. In the afternoon R. goes through several things by Handel and is astonished at their banality; no depth, no Christianity, a proper Jehovah worship. The only excellent thing he remembers is the "Ode to Saint Cecilia." — R. persists in saying he himself is no musician! — A letter from Countess Danckelmann makes us despondent: she wants to know whether she should bring her cook with her, and inquires about the apartments here! Are we not facing a complete catastrophe in this respect, even if everything else succeeds? . . .

*Friday, February 18* Springtime, the starlings are here; but R. is unwell, he thinks because he has too many things on his mind—*Tristan* in Berlin, court cases, accommodation matters, *Lohengrin* in Vienna, on top of that the American composition is supposed to be finished by March 15! And will he be paid the 5,000 dollars anyway? He is so worn out that he cannot read to me in the evening.

*Saturday, February 19* R. works, I give lessons. Recently Herr Niemann cabled for the parts of the so-called love song for a Court concert in Meiningen—the first direct sign of life from him since he returned the part of Siegmund; when I ask R. whether he intends to send them, he replies, "You don't look a gift Siegmund in the mouth!"

— In the evening a little of *Don Quixote,* but splendid (puppet-theater episode)—how many people appreciate this? Know it?

*Sunday, February 20* Free day, that is to say, letter day for me; R. has completed his draft, plays it for me, it is splendid, much good cheer about this. — In the evening some local acquaintances.

*Monday, February 21* I am busy with plans for R.'s birthday, besides my lessons. R. is very vexed by a telegram from Jauner, saying that one half of the proceeds plus the daily expenses are to go to the theater, so that only about 2,000 florins will be left for the chorus from the performance of *Lohengrin.* In the evening conference about apartments, also cloakroom arrangements, etc. — Everything here in blissful calm!! . . . Only Herr Brandt deeply worried, and ourselves.

*Tuesday, February 22* R. writes to Herr Jauner, asking whether the performance could not be put off to another time, since conditions are now so bad. — In Germany the losses are said to amount to 1½ billion, and that by the small property owners; the rich bankers only pretend, economize as a precautionary measure, but they have profited from the general misery. Whole branches of industry are lying idle! . . . Brandt complained yesterday that one can get nothing in Germany; he needed pink glass for a sunrise, and had to order it from France. "Bismarck," says R., "has handled the country's welfare like a student." — In the evening *Don Quixote,* the splendid episode of the bark. —

*Wednesday, February 23* Correspondence with the music festival committee in Aachen, which boasts of having performed compositions by R. in '57 and suffered much trouble on that account; for this reason they wish for Herr Vogl at the beginning of June!! . . . R. annoyed with Vienna; journey there unlikely. He begins the orchestration of the march, but has to write the first two pages again! — Herr Feustel reports that the cash supply (for the undertaking) is exhausted. Vexation; on top of that R. has rheumatism in his right hand. — Spring is approaching. In the evening *Don Quixote.*

*Thursday, February 24* R. had a good night, probably because of his decision not to go to Vienna. But now Herr Jauner cables to say that only the daily expenses are to be withheld from the chorus, and that he will discuss everything personally with R. R. sends a telegram in the evening, asking whether it would not be better, since they do not dare charge high prices under present conditions and he is anyway feeling unwell, to postpone this performance of *Lohengrin* under his direction to the fall. — Apart from that R. orchestrates; I work with the children and in the evening receive a letter from Hans, who has decided to remain in America. — Will I ever, if only to my Siegfried, disclose the pit of sorrow which has been dug inside me? . . . I believe that I shall dumbly take refuge in the land of silence! . . . Thus amid tears I heard

regrets this, however, and cordially begs pardon of the B.'s. But then he decides not to visit the restaurant any more, deeply grieved by his excessive reaction.

*Thursday, July 13* No rehearsal; we drive up to the theater, however, since R. wants to discuss the last scene (the appearance of Wotan) with Brandt and to see the Doepler figurines. I am much grieved by them, revealing as they do an archaeologist's fantasy, to the detriment of the tragic and mythical elements. I should like everything to be much simpler, more primitive. As it is, it is all mere pretence. Some friends in the evening. Discussion of the new biography of R. by Glasenapp, in which several things are inexact, but astonishing research. — The piano rehearsals ended with the wholesale dismissal of Herr Rubinstein, who here once more displayed all the dismal characteristics of his race.

*Friday, July 14* Vexations of various sorts; the ducal palace takes advantage of the problem of finding accommodation for Frau von Schl. to show rudeness to us! . . . In the afternoon rehearsal of *Rheingold*. — Herr Niemann "graciously" present, as I say to him in fun. We remain in the restaurant after all, since R. wishes to "invent" something with Brandt so that the glare from the orchestra will not spoil the effects in *Rheingold*.

*Saturday, July 15* Herr Siehr at rehearsal; R. satisfied with him, engages him for Hagen! In the evening final rehearsal of *Das Rheingold*; many vexations for R. in the course of it, the rainbow bridge wrong (so far), the steam fails to work, because Herr Brandt, warned by the management committee about the need for economy, could not produce the proper vapors! The Brückner brothers have painted in haste, so there are ineradicable mistakes in the decorations! . . .

*Sunday, July 16* Letter from the King, signifying his intention to come, forbids any sort of ovation, wants to see nobody. Mimi's arrival, great joy over this, we spend the day together. It is doubtful whether the German Emperor will come.

*Monday, July 17* First act of *Walküre*, Frl. Scheffsky terrible! Herr Niemann *does* it well. Got Mimi installed, also spent the day with her. R. very tired, little demand for seats.

*Tuesday, July 18* Second act of *Walküre*, Frl. Scheffsky even more horrible; she previously at lunch, an excess of ungainliness and gracelessness! Conference over whether to get rid of her at all costs. Fears that another singer would no longer have time to learn it. (Also Scaria-like troubles.)

*Wednesday, July 19* Most of my time spent with Mimi. In the evening 3rd act of *Walküre*, splendid impression. Herr Brandt's "Magic Fire" magnificent, Herr Doepler's representations of the Valkyries not good yet.

*Thursday, July 20* First act of *Siegfried*, Herr Unger quite good, in spite of the players' not giving him enough support. Unfortunately Herr Schlosser has forgotten a lot of Mime through having had to sing all sorts of different things in Munich.

*Friday, July 21* A good day for the box office today—5,200 marks come in—enough to keep us for 2 days. Trouble about the candelabra in the auditorium. The final scene of *Götterdämmerung* is given shape— with human forms, not transparencies. Nice telegram from the King, thanking us for the Nietzsche pamphlet. 2nd act of *Siegfried*, Herr Unger in very good voice! The previous evening Herr Niemann had declared that he (Unger) would not have a note left in his throat for the 2nd act! . . . R. very tired. He sleeps now only until 3 or 4 in the morning!

*Saturday, July 22* A vague rumor brings the news that Hans may possibly come here! . . . Rehearsal of 3rd act of *Siegfried* to the jubilation of all. R. tired. At 11:20 in the evening I go to fetch Lusch. She has grown, and looks nice, strikingly like her father! R. wakes up as I come home, goes to the window, greets the constellation of the Great Bear, which is shining most beautifully. "Good star, protect my wife and my children, do with me what you will!" He tells me he has been thinking of his death. He embraces me tenderly, saying that nobody knows all the things he owes to me. He is pleased with Lusch.

*Sunday, July 23* Pleasure in Lusch, who has become quite grown-up. Paid some calls with her. Several guests in the evening. In the meantime great vexation. Without telling R. anything about it, the management committee has advertised a public rehearsal with seats at 3 marks. R. beside himself.

*Monday, July 24* All seats are said to have been sold within half an hour, which delights friend Feustel! R. has the good idea of inviting Feustel, Gross, etc., to lunch. Prof. Nietzsche has also arrived, and the Dannreuthers and several others. First act of *Götterdämmerung*; Princess Barjatinsky, Mimi, and I in the princes' gallery, the children with us. In the evening supper with the children.

*Tuesday, July 25* Dinner with Princess B., Mimi, Count Wallis, who enthusiastically plays the organ in our house, Wilhelmj. Afterward the 2nd act in public; Herr Siehr very good as Hagen. After the audience has left, second rehearsal. Afterward Herr Brandt offended, declares his intention of leaving, because he is described in a program by Herr Giessel merely as a machinist!! I try to calm him down and to prove to him that R. knew nothing about the whole thing. With difficulty I half succeed!

*Wednesday, July 26* R. opens a letter written yesterday by Herr Feustel, who announces his resignation from the management committee—because R. had admitted the fire brigade to the rehearsal free of charge! R. writes back jokingly, and Heckel mediates! In the evening 3rd act, we remain in the restaurant with Mimi and Princess B. — Increasing awareness of the imperfections in the representation!! The performance will lag as far behind the work as the work is removed from our own times!

*Thursday, July 27* News today that Herr von Baligand has quarreled with the management committee and departed!! Who will now prepare the palace for the princely guests? Absurdities like this a daily occurrence now! At dinner the Niemanns, Wilhelmj, the Richters. In the afternoon costume rehearsal, little pleasure in it, much conventionalism, lack of beauty, little inventiveness, and too much ornateness. R. again splendid in his patience and kindness! — On top of all this servant troubles at home! . . .

*Friday, July 28* R. had a bad night, but he remains in a cheerful, friendly mood. Light lunch with the Wilhelmjes, the wife very pleasant. In the evening costume rehearsal; on my request to Professor Doepler to make Siegfried's clothes a little less close-fitting and to dress Gutrune's ladies less brightly, the poor man becomes so angry and rude that I realize for the first time what a hack one is having to deal with! The costumes are reminiscent throughout of Red Indian chiefs and still bear, along with their ethnographic absurdity, all the marks of provincial tastelessness. I am much dismayed by them and also rather shocked by the professor's manner. R. is having great trouble with Wotan's hat; it is a veritable musketeer's hat!

*Saturday, July 29* R. goes to the theater; rehearsal with Prof. Doepler, who behaves like a "schoolboy." French dinner, Schurés, Monod, etc. In the evening first *Rheingold* rehearsal in costume, R. very sad afterward, because Herr Brandt himself is in error. The singers very good, particularly Herr Vogl as Loge. After the rehearsal R. and I at home by ourselves, R. deeply worried— The King inquires whether R. is satisfied with the scenery!

*Sunday, July 30* In the morning R. goes straight to the theater, I to pay all sorts of calls. Dinner with Herr and Frau v. Schl. Afterward, garden party at the Feustels'; some Bayreuth people and all our artists.

*Monday, July 31* Fetched Princess Barjatinsky from the railroad station, then Niemann's little daughter. Get a fleeting idea of what floods of ugly talk and opinion are always flowing about here. What most shocks me is the falseness and mendacity behind it, and I feel very much like wishing, with our good Falstaff, that it were bedtime and all past. — In the evening *Walküre*, rehearsal of the entr'actes.

*Tuesday, August 1* Visitors of all kinds, and finally fetched my father from the railroad station. He is very well, and R. decidedly refreshed by his arrival. In the evening opening of the second restaurant, R. makes a speech thanking his artists. Regret that many are missing.

*Wednesday, August 2*   Many arrivals, family lunch with my father; Olga Meyendorff also here. Lulu considered very well mannered. In the evening *Siegfried*, Unger quite good. Herr Niemann is very prejudiced against him. Much that is unsatisfactory. The costumes, particularly Alberich's, almost ludicrous—Alberich with coat and epaulettes; overwhelming impact of the work, transcending everything.

*Thursday, August 3*   Deep inner despondency! Hans in Godesberg is said to be so very, very unwell! . . . The tidings oppress my soul like an overwhelming shadow, joy is unthinkable, only patience and work! — R. holds a scenery rehearsal of *Götterdämmerung*, reception in the evening, before that a small dinner party with the Danckelmanns, Schleinitzes, Frau v. Meyendorff.

*Friday, August 4*   Slept little, submerged in thought, thoughts, sighs, and entreaties; a return of the inexorable powers! I take up writing again on September 8—will my memory serve me sufficiently? . . .

*Saturday, August 5*   R. goes at midnight to fetch the King, I accompany him as far as the railroad station near the Eremitage, then R. drives away with the King and returns home late, but in raptures about his kindliness.

*Sunday, August 6*   Several arrivals, among others Prince Liechtenstein; cheerful lunch, in the evening dress rehearsal without an audience, the King sends for me as well and tells me I should never have doubted that he would remain loyal to us. The rehearsal goes very well. Great illuminations and cheers for the King.

*Monday, August 7*   Rehearsal of *Die Walküre* in front of an audience, since it improves the acoustics. Much abuse with the tickets. Public rehearsals also on 8th and 9th, R. with the King throughout; R. professes to have detected a certain ill feeling as he takes his departure— the King has forbidden any sort of ovation, yet he seems astonished when none takes place. — On the 12th arrival of the Emperor, the Grand Duke of Schwerin with wife and daughter, the Grand Duchess of Baden, Anhalt-Dessau, Schwarzburg-Sondershausen, etc., etc.; R. goes to meet the Emperor, who, in very friendly mood, talks about a national festival. At last, on

*Sunday, August 13*, first performance of *Rheingold*, under a completely unlucky star: Betz loses the ring, runs into the wings twice during the curse, a stagehand raises the backdrop too soon during the first scene change and one sees people standing around in shirt sleeves and the back wall of the theater, all the singers embarrassed, etc., etc. — Each of us returns home separately, R. at first very upset, but gradu-

Walk through the Piazza San Marco with R. and the children. Ate at 6 o'clock, afterward a serenade by the Società! Workers in the dockyard who delight us and regale us with songs, lighthearted, devout, and serious; I ask them for the *"Canzone del Tasso,"* which moves me greatly. Indescribable pleasure in this music, the soul of the people!

*Wednesday, September 20* To San Marco—for a poorhouse I like its luxury! I more at home in San Zeno. Divine air. No desire to think, dream! . . . Meeting with Tesarini, the *corbo bianco,* the earliest Wagnerian in Italy, a true Venetian. Spent the evening on the Piazza San Marco.

*Thursday, September 21* Rainy day. Wandered through the streets of Venice, went into an antique dealer's, R. not well, the air does not much agree with him. In the evening to the theater—*Nerone,* a new play showing more talent than Herr Wilbrandt's play of the same name; it is also acted quite well, though the style is very mannered. — Visited the Palazzo Giustiniani (see tomorrow).

*Friday, September 22* Made the acquaintance of Countess Luise Voss, went inside the Doge's Palace with her, a veritable feast of opulence and beauty; in the afternoon a trip to the Lido, in the evening a play, *Parini,* not very enjoyable.

*Saturday, September 23* Fine letter from the King, he has truly grasped the idea of Bayreuth—this our greatest triumph! Less pleasing letter from friend Feustel, who reports debts amounting to about 120,000 marks. Discussion with R., plans, projects, much effort in store, a whole baggage train of activities. — Went by myself to the Academy of Fine Arts, since R. feared it would tire him. Indescribable impression, as if I had never seen colors before; the *Ascension,* as if I were hearing a Beethoven symphony for the first time. I am enraptured by the *Madonna* of Giovan. Bellini in the same gallery, and the galleries themselves so unexpectedly beautiful and lavish. Like in a fairy tale or, better still, in the cave of Montesinos: nothing from the outside, but inside, this dazzling of the spirit! In the afternoon a ride along the narrow canals. In the evening R. is unfortunately still unwell, but he was on the S. Marco.

*Sunday, September 24* On foot to Santa Maria dei Frari, fine impression [*In the margin:* "Titian's *La Pali dei Pisani*!!!"]; reflected on the Renaissance and the 18th century; the latter, to judge by the tombs, with more feeling for the monumental, but less tasteful; on the whole I find little pleasure in Renaissance sculpture, with a few exceptions. [*Added at end of entry:* "*The Great Elector* by Schlüter finer than the very fine *Condottiere* here."] Drive to the Giardino Papadopoli. Spent the evening with Countess Voss, R. unwell! —

*Monday, September 25* In the morning to San G[iovanni] e Paolo, inspected it thoroughly, then to the splendid hospital adjoining it;

strangely and unutterably moved by the sight of the sick people in these beautiful rooms! — Then to the Gesuiti for [Titian's] *Saint Lawrence,* after that the *Saint Barbara* of P. Vecchio and the picture by Giorgione, then the Bellini picture in a small church. — The sacristan in the Gesuiti the lower stage of the Döllinger type of person. These trips on foot with the children provide the liveliest pleasure, though in the streets hardly anything but poverty is to be seen. In the afternoon Santa Maria Salute, and in the evening Piazza San Marco, where a Prof. Hertel from Berlin joins us.

*Tuesday, September 26*   To the Accadèmia di belle Arti, R. giving me pleasure by accompanying me there, as difficult to part from these divine things as from Venice itself, which we leave at 1 o'clock. How very sad a city in which those who dwell in it seem like worms, utterly alien to the noble, diversified body! But I did not contemplate this living element, seeing only the eternity; from few human beings have I found it harder to part than from this city, which went straight to my heart as I know no other will ever do. — Arrival in Bologna at 5 o'clock. Walk to the Piazza Vittorio E[manuele]; gloomy impression. I write up the days in Venice here, melancholy that they were so fleeting.

*Wednesday, September 27*   Drive through the city with R., then outside the city to S. Michele and the Church of Saint Luke. Spent the evening indoors. Made the acquaintance of the syndic (Count Tacconi), who greets R. as an honorary citizen and makes a pleasant impression on us. Visited the Archiginnasio; the city is built horizontally, as if by people who had a lot of room to spare; it is very solid.

*Thursday, September 28*   Went out shortly after 9 in the morning and did not return until 3:30, visited the museum, the university, churches, and palaces. Much pleasure in the Francia pictures; in the museum formed a fairer view of Domenichino and Carracci, though without veneration. A *Madonna* by Cima very lovely. When painting becomes too violent, fantasy is aroused, speech, the restriction governing all art—the bounds are transgressed and one demands to hear the screams of these tormented people. Thus, in music, drama must be kept for the stage; the greatest genius, such as Titian, extends the boundaries as far as possible, but his figures may still remain silent. The Ninth Symphony the proof of the human need for speech. — One can gaze upon the preceding painters with great pleasure, but not those who follow after; the furthest boundary was reached by the greatest masters, and those of the greatest talent (Domenichino, Carracci) are forced, as it were, to go beyond it. — Left at 2 in the morning, reached Naples at 10 in the evening, Hôtel Vittoria; during this long and very tiring journey in immense heat the children remained good-natured, Siegfried in particular is indefatigably cheerful and good.

*Saturday, September 30*  A long rest, after that a little walk; in the afternoon siesta and reading (Sismondi). In the evening a trip on the sea and on the Chiaia.

*Sunday, October 1*  R. and I journey via Castellamare to Sorrento to look for an apartment; fine day, many remarkable views. Returned to Naples in the evening.

*Monday, October 2*  To the museum in the morning; in the afternoon the drive over the Posillipo very fine! R. very much enjoys the hectic life here, and it really is the liveliest city imaginable; popular in the most extravagant sense of the word. In the museum today I saw only the antique statues and wall paintings; a serious and noble impression, like the calm of immortality over the struggles of existence. Outside the liveliest reality again; I think a lot about Venice the silent, the needy, where I should feel more at home.

*Tuesday, October 3*  Went to the museum again and stayed there till noon. After lunch, drive to Capo di Monte and back along the Via Vittor. Emanuele. In the evening in San Carlino, Punchinello as a street vendor, very vigorous acting, but not much of a play.

*Wednesday, October 4*  In the museum again, this time with Boni, to make her acquainted with certain things. R. catches up with me, I show him the Hercules Farnese, after that, drive to the Mercato Vecchio; in the evening a walk on the Chiaia. After our return a street fiddler pleases me greatly with the style of his playing.

*Thursday, October 5*  Departure for Sorrento; as the ship leaves, beggars swim around in the water, among them a boy who stands out on account of his brown skin, his beauty and liveliness and agility— "like something direct from Nature's workshop," says R.—he gathers the coins thrown into the sea in his mouth. On the ship singers and guitarists and fiddlers, cheerful and mournful popular songs, at the same time wickerwork and oysters being bartered, all languages being spoken; while a dark-blue sea sings its eternal lullaby, and the blue line of hills encloses it all—a curious dream! Is it its strangeness or its familiarity which makes us feel so melancholy—a gentle yearning, I might call it, but for what? Not for living! — A gentleman from Magdeburg speaks to R., he was at our performances and speaks very nicely about them. Sorrento, the Hôtel Vittoria, we have taken the little cottage beside the hotel, wonderful peace. — During the siesta hours R. and I read, to ourselves, Sismondi's *Les Républiques d'Italie*.

*Friday, October 6*  Picked up lessons with the children again; they have forgotten quite a bit! In the afternoon a very lovely donkey ride to the Deserto, R. and I admit to each other that all our delight lies in the delight of the children; up above, a good Franciscan, splendid terrace, but in the little church two pupils playing dance music of the most wretched kind. Merry ride home, my donkey called Fantasia! The driver promises it *macaron tutto formaggio* to liven it up. [*In the margin:* "Walk to the ravines."] — At home the news that M. Tribert has deposited my 40,000 francs with the lawyer.

*Saturday, October 7* Still lovely weather, work with the children, sea baths, reading Sismondi, and—alas!—many, many worried thoughts. The ride to the Deserto, entered for yesterday by mistake.

*Sunday, October 8* Wrote to Claire, in the afternoon drove to Massalubrense, a none-too-successful outing.

*Monday, October 9* At 8 o'clock set sail for Capri, breakfast in the Hôtel du Louvre, whose ridiculous name amuses us greatly; ride to the Villa Tiberio; stop at the Leap; our donkey girls dance the tarantella for us; the eldest of them with great passion, but one of them is not permitted to dance, says her husband is jealous. Our ride home through narrow lanes resembles an Arab wedding procession, everything splendid! The poverty of the people in comparison with the richness of Nature astonishes one; but this poverty would not exist—or at least the mania for profit—if there were not strangers here to beg from. I felt shame, too, in making them dance the tarantella. Journey home amid shooting stars and phosphorescent waves! Unforgettable impression; the white houses in all that green, the splendid flowers, later the calm sea, a perfect summer night. Unfortunately, however, the shadow of gloomy thoughts at home. R. is wondering whether he should repeat the performances! Not a single one of the princes, having distributed decorations to all the participants, has asked R. what can be done for him, how he might be helped or supported! . . .

*Tuesday, October 10* 23 years ago I saw R. for the first time, being led by my father, coming to see us children; practically all those then with me are now gone! . . . Give lessons to the children while R. is writing his address to the patrons. Spent the afternoon on the splendid terrace, from which one looks out over an olive grove and the sea. In the evening wrote to my father and to M. Tribert to thank them (my 40,000 francs are to be paid to me).

*Wednesday, October 11* Lessons, bathing, reading, a resumption of our Tribschen life, unfortunately with many reflections for and against; for R., how to get the performances started again? A pamphlet by Hans Wolzogen starts out by giving us much enjoyment, but further reading arouses great displeasure in me; R. Wagner and—Jordan!!

*Thursday, October 12* R. not well; perhaps the soft air does not agree with him? He is not sleeping well. — Lulu's birthday today, we drink to her. — Spent the afternoon sitting on the little terrace, on one side the olive grove, on the other the sea. We read Sismondi together with great enjoyment. Nice letter from Herr Hill, advising R. not to make any changes in the cast.

*Friday, October 13* R. begins a sort of spa cure (*eau de Vichy*), and the pretty morning walks seem to do him good. He writes to Herr von Schl., telling him something of his situation and saying that the only thing at the festival which was really successful was what the Schleinitzes themselves brought about! Walk in the afternoon—in the evening the tarantella danced by Sorrento people in the hall of the hotel; also some of their plays. One of the women extremely graceful in an unstudied, natural sort of way. At the end "*Die Wacht am Rhein*"! Our waiter confessed to us that he had been in Berlin and had brought it back and taught it to the people here!

*Saturday, October 14* Fidi slightly unwell. Lessons for the children. R. writes to Herr v. Radowitz, asking him for his opinion about what should be done. I give the children lessons; in the afternoon a walk; this spot here is becoming increasingly dear to me; the paths between two walls with overhanging trees, the ravines and rocks, the olive trees, it has all become so familiar to me, and I also hear nothing upsetting here. Only R.'s worries can hardly be banished, even for a few moments, and so the horizon is clouded.

*Sunday, October 15* A free day for the children, for me a day of writing letters and reading (Sismondi and Nietzsche's paper again). Sirocco.

*Monday, October 16* Moving; we leave the pretty cottage, which is slightly damp, and move to the 3rd floor of the big hotel. I am always rather reluctant to change rooms, it makes me feel melancholy.

*Tuesday, October 17* Lessons for the children, resumption of music lessons. Sirocco, the sea rough. R. still somewhat worn out, but in cheerful spirits. Talked a lot about Goethe; *Faust* much more valuable than the *Divina commedia*, but less variability in it. — Read the story of Emperor Heinrich IV of Germany with indignation.

*Wednesday, October 18* The boat which carries the mail from Sorrento to Capri capsized yesterday, seven people were saved, but one was drowned. Such things are reported and heard with indifference here, and how indifferent, too, the whole outside world, romping in the sun again today! . . . Wrote on R.'s behalf to the secretary of the Royal Academy in Stockholm, with thanks for his nomination. R. starts a long letter to the King, once again describing the whole situation to him and suggesting that he take over the whole thing. Watched the sunset with R. from the terrace; thoughts of Odysseus swimming. I already feel quite at home in this country. In the evening read with R.

the touching story of Pope Celestine V. — Frequent thoughts of giving up the festival entirely and disappearing—but would that be good for the children?

*Thursday, October 19*   At 5 o'clock tolling of the canonical hour, an ugly jangle indeed, our German bells speak with a different voice! — R. not well, has to go to bed, where he remains for part of the day. I give the children their lessons, read the life of Dante, two cantos of the *Purgatorio* and parts of the *Républiques italiennes*.

*Friday, October 20*   R. still unwell, which throws me into a truly melancholy mood. My own salvation, work with the children; bathing in the sea very strange, for the waves very powerful. In the afternoon R. gets up, he is somewhat better, but still very weak; the weather clears up, I take out a boat and float for a while on the sea, constantly changing, in eternal motion, neither wave nor cloud pays heed to my woe, and the motionless mountain throws it back; movement and rigidity, deaf and unreceptive; will a mortal being hear the sound? Perhaps a mother's heart! — We talk to R. about the beauty of this spot. "Yes," he observes, "if one did not always bring one's thoughts with one."

*Saturday, October 21*   Stormy night, hail, thunder, and I don't know what else. R. dreamed of my execution: I had come to an agreement with my father that, in order to atone for my marriage to R., I must be executed, only Lulu should accompany me; he had not believed it at first, but when he saw me being carried off on a bier (because I could not walk), he had cried out, and his cry woke him up. Before that he had dreamed that *Siegfried* was being performed and something went wrong on the stage. "Brandt, the lights are going out!" — With these words he woke up! — Lessons for the children, R. finishes his letter to the King, to whom he makes the proposal either to recommend our festival to the Reich through a representative or to take the whole thing over himself. — Read Sismondi. Spent much time reflecting in the evening, firm resolve to fight against melancholy, which is threatening to drive me mad.

*Sunday, October 22*   "'Tis a consummation devoutly to be wish'd"— these words come into my mind as I think of my father's birthday and wonder how he must look back on his life! — Today is a letter day for me (11!), R. writes to Frau Lucca, apologizing for not being able to give her the cuts she requested for *Rienzi* in Bologna. In the afternoon a lovely walk to Capo di Sorrento—a terrible thunderstorm during the night has cleared the sky and refreshed the earth. The walk does R. good, we let ourselves go in one of those endless conversations which have always taken place between us; this time about the Normans, fascinating in their influence in the South, unsympathetic in the North against the Saxons.

singers, that Herr v. Perfall is demanding a direct request from R. before giving leave to Schlosser, likewise Herr v. Hülsen and the Grand Duke of Schwerin, even the conductor Wüllner before releasing two students from the Conservatoire, etc., etc. On top of that, alarming letters from Herr Ullmann, giving his opinion that we shall *not* achieve financial success. He also talks about having received a dismal letter from Hans! . . . Visit from friend Feustel.

*Wednesday, March 28* God be praised! R. is continuing to work on *Parsifal*, even though it means we sometimes have to deal with repugnant business matters till late in the night. Herr Hodge asks for a postponement of the guaranteed payment, we grant it to him through the lawyer. — Arrival of Richter, very vulgarly bringing the 20,000 marks, with the request that R. should sign a declaration of consent to the performance of the other three works. R. is standing by what my father has written to Standhartner. R[ichter] praises *Die Walküre* in Vienna—from my father's account, I gather that it lacks all dedication and nobility.

*Thursday, March 29* Maundy (mourning) Thursday—many tears in my heart, may the Saviour receive them graciously! Richter departs, our good Heckel arrives, he is going on from here to a Wagner Society meeting in Leipzig. R. tells him he would like the Societies to remain in existence, even though he cannot yet say for certain whither their activities should be directed.

Today R. concludes the first act of *Parsifal*!

*Friday, March 30* Good Friday, prayer, church, the Passion according to Saint John with the younger children. Stillness and meditation. In the evening my father plays his *Funérailles* and *Saint Francis Preaching to the Birds*, to the great delight of R. and myself. — Contemplative day, *one* wish to the Redeemer! . . .

*Saturday, March 31* For R., all-too-many London problems, which I actively share to the extent that I have to write the letters; Herr Unger sluggish, alarmed by having to learn Tristan! Problems with orchestra parts, nobody yet sure where to obtain them all. And Messrs. Hodge and Essex are getting nervous about the costs. But music at home nevertheless—*Hungaria* and *Tasso*; in the minuet of the latter my father says, "What is proper."

*Easter Sunday, April 1* No church for me on account of preparations for the evening, for which I have invited about 100 Bayreuth people. It comes off very well, since my father is kind enough to play (*Saint François de Paule marchant sur les flots*) and R. is in good spirits.

*Monday, April 2* My father's name day; R. gives him his *Life* with a dedication which deeply pleases and touches my father; in the afternoon R. reads his wonderful first act to us, and in the evening my father plays his sonata. A lovely, cherished day, on which I can thank Heaven for the comforting feeling that nothing—no deeply tragic parting of the ways, no malice on the part of others, no differences in character—could ever separate us three. — Oh, if only it were possible to add a fourth to our numbers here! But that an inexorable Fate forbids, and for me every joy and every exaltation ends with an anxious cry to my inner being! . . .

*Tuesday, April 3* Departure of my father; I accompany him as far as Neumarkt, where I watch him leave on the train to Meiningen; he covers his face as I wave to him for the last time—shall I ever see him again? Home at 1 o'clock, family lunch, in the afternoon London letters for me and R., who writes to Dannreuther and Wilhelmj; in the evening a letter from Mr. Hodge, complaints regarding the high cost of the singers; also, upsettingly enough, a telegram from Richter! He had refused to come to London to conduct the rehearsals; finally persuaded by R. while he was here, he was supposed to apply for leave, and my father wrote in that connection to Prince and Princess Hohenlohe; now they would dearly like to repeat the game they played last year with *Die Walküre*! . . . R. wanted to send Richter an indignant telegram, I beg him not to.

*Wednesday, April 4* Saint Richard's Day; R. at his writing, I with the children and the books, from which I see that we spent 14,999 marks in the last quarter, which worries me very much. — Letter from the King in his usual kind and enthusiastic style! — In the evening Aristophanes's *Plutus*, which seems to us utterly splendid! How sublimely the downfall of this most talented people is reflected in the humor of their deeply discerning dramatist!

*Thursday, April 5* Work with the children. R. busy with Klingsor. R. has now seen Tappert's *Dictionary*, but it makes him deplore the malice of humanity. — He dreams of a performance of the *Ring* before a number of people now dead, Tausig, Gaspérini, his sister Luise, but all horribly unrecognizable. — In the afternoon we are surprised by a visit from Herr Essex, who requests another postponement of the guaranteed payment. We consent, since personally Herr Essex makes a good impression and Wilhelmj pleads in his behalf.

*Friday, April 6* Today's stranger is our good Lalas, coming here from Salzburg to say goodbye—he is returning to Monastir. Memories of the *Nibelungen* days! After he has departed we start on the preface to Karl Ritter's *Der milde Welf*, dealing with verse meter in the German tragedy. It looks very much as if all he says in it comes from his conversations with R. and from R.'s writings, but he does not once mention him. R. very vexed by the reading.

*Saturday, April 7* A gloomy, very gloomy day! — Herr Gross visits me, to report that Düfflipp has told his father-in-law in Munich that, according to the contract made in 1865, R. has no right to sell the *Nibelungen* work to Vienna or anywhere else; a copy of this contract has also been sent to the firm of Feustel and Gross. R. much agitated and vexed about this, he writes to Councilor Düfflipp, requesting that the contract be annulled, since in view of the failure of his Bayreuth plans he has no alternative but to release the work. He adds that he no longer has any objection to its performance in Munich. — At one o'clock arrival of Frau Dr. Herz from Altenburg; at my request she examines the children. I am thunderstruck when it turns out that Isolde is very round-shouldered and should be sent to the institute in Altenburg. Silent tears! . . . My father forwards a letter from Herr Ullmann, who has seen Hans in Paris and describes the utterly demoralized mood in which he found him! Prayers and more prayers.

*Sunday, April 8* Gymnastic exercises; discussion concerning Loldchen's going away, departure of Frau Dr. Herz, who now, so much a stranger to me, is to have my dearest one with her. In the evening picked up Karl Ritter's *Der milde Welf*, R. wishes to hear no more, and I end it by myself. Began Plutarch with Daniella.

*Monday, April 9* Spring has arrived! I sort out Loldchen's things after giving my lessons. Wrote some business letters. In the evening R. reads me Hoffmann's "*Die Räuber*," which is very good up to the two final letters, which ruin everything.

*Tuesday, April 10* Loldchen's birthday! Celebrated amid tryings-on and packing, her bed and other things to be dispatched by rail! But she has her children's party, which she much enjoys. In the evening, call on Frau von Parseval with Lusch. — A mild, fine day, R. very kind and affectionate toward me, memories of earlier times. In the morning he works steadily on *Parsifal*.

*Wednesday, April 11* Work and troubles. Telegrams from Richter, saying he will be given leave only if the three works are granted! . . . R. writes to him, saying that nothing can be got from him this way. — Herr Staudt asks for payment. Besides that, begging requests from all sides, and particularly requests to us to become godparents, some of them very touching.

*Thursday, April 12* Domestic worries for me; but R. is able to work, and that is the main thing. In the evening a visit from our friend Gross, who is not at all happy about the position with the guaranteed payment. Various rumors and finally definite news of Bismarck's leave of absence. — Our trade and industry in a deplorable state.

*Friday, April 13* Today R. completes the 2nd act of *Parsifal* and is cheerful and happy, despite the fact that there is again no lack of "rats and mice," as R. calls them. For example, Herr Mazière writes to say that Messrs. Brandt, Brückner, Hoffmann, and Doepler are demanding royalties for all performances of the *Nibelungen* everywhere (though they have already been overgenerously paid for their work), and that they have appointed Herr Batz their representative! R. says he cannot imagine how he will ever be able to compose *Parsifal* with all these bogeys constantly in his mind. He is thinking of securing Richter's release and transferring the whole thing to him and Heckel, under my control, just as if he were already dead, in order to insure leisure for his work. In the evening he inks in his penciled manuscript, while I write to Countess Voss.

*Saturday, April 14* Lessons for the children, who afterward rub out the traces of pencil in the manuscript. In the afternoon R. reads me the 2nd act, and when he sees how profoundly affected I am by it, he says, "This is our secret, from me to you, do not ask me to read it to anyone else." — In the evening we take up [Goethe's] *Jery und Bäteli*, which R. tells me made a very lively impression on him when he saw it on the stage during his childhood. We enjoy it very much, except for the operatic conclusion, I observe that one ought to turn all the verses back into prose.

*Sunday, April 15* Packing for Isolde! R. is worried about London, since Messrs. Hodge and Essex do not seem very safe after all. From Vienna a not-at-all-nice letter from Richter, in which he says that Prince Hohenlohe must by now have written expressing the Emperor's wish; Jauner is waiting for R.'s consent before approving Richter's leave of absence, since R. is the one who is making demands. R. sends a telegram saying that his consent depends on negotiations with Munich and various other things; but if Richter's leave is not approved, *a complete break*. A letter from Herr Schlesinger and a telegram from London, also not encouraging. The £1,500 have still not yet been paid; it also seems that no supervision of the sale of tickets is possible, since they are sold in 20 different places. All this plus grief at Isolde's going away is not calculated to produce good cheer, but we control our feelings sufficiently to take up and read a play by Lope de Vega, *La Carbonera*, with great enjoyment. Drama, no poetry, yet much romance and humor.

*Monday, April 16* Departure! I take Isolde to Altenburg. With this genuine sorrow I now close this volume. The gloomiest forebodings have settled in my heart, but I wrap them up with slumber like night birds during the day; like the dreadful goddesses in the temple of the god of light, they hide themselves away and sleep, but they are still there. Farewell, my companion of nearly three years! Begun on my return home after a separation, concluded with my journey toward a parting! I beseech you all, ye eternal, invisible guardian spirits, bless my child, bless the paths of him who suffers through the sin of my existence, let me suffer with equanimity, that I may never forget my mission—bless this mission, take pity on all others, not on me! [*End of eighth notebook of the Diaries.*]

Left at 1 o'clock with my little girl, a most painful moment as she says goodbye to her sisters and brother, she remains silent throughout the journey. Arrival at 7, supper, then wrote to R. Curious feelings.

*Tuesday, April 17*   First gymnastic exercises for Loldchen, then introduced her to the head of the school, then paid calls with her. Rough weather. The little girl accepts her lot uncomplainingly; a very nice parson's daughter and another child help her to do this. I spend the evening with the Gerstenbergs. Conversation about Bismarck's position, he has been abandoned by all his friends, offended by the Court, supported in the Chamber by only the slenderest of majorities. The lack of efficient men in Berlin is said to be very noticeable. The minister Hofmann just a bureaucrat.

*Wednesday, April 18*   Breakfasted with Loldchen. I then lunch with the Gerstenbergs; in the afternoon with my child once more. At Frau v. Braun's in the evening. Telegram from Richard.

*Thursday, April 19*   [*In the margin: "Parsifal* is finished!"] Final parting; a night of great sorrow. My little girl examined. She does not emerge from it well. Weeping, but no complaining. Left at half past one. Apathy! Memories of another parting. In Neumarkt at 8 in the evening, R. there to meet me; with Plutarch. He tells me the contents of telegrams between Prince Hohenlohe and himself. A cheerful evening, in spite of pain and worry, due to reunion!

*Friday, April 20*   Work again with the children, one fewer, it does not make things easier, quite the contrary. R. very irritated after lunch by the whole situation, he has cabled Councilor Düfflipp that he must have a reply. Now he is expecting deceit and treachery, as everywhere else. He says he ought to be glad that theaters are inquiring after his *Nibelungen* work, that things are not as they were with *Tristan*; but it would be madness even to think any more about *his* ideas. In London the business side is still unclear, but the rehearsals are said to be progressing better than expected. In the evening R. reads me the 3rd act of *Parsifal* and then gives me the poem, which I regard as my greatest solace in life's misery.

*Saturday, April 21*   Gave the children lessons. R. writes to friend Standhartner, setting out the terms for the use of the *Nibelungen*: ten percent instead of seven; 20,000 marks as an advance (not as a gift); in return, exclusive rights for the Austrian monarchy. A letter from Councilor Düfflipp informs us that the King would like consideration to be given to the repayment of the money borrowed (for our theater). In the evening we finish Lope de Vega's *La Carbonera* with great interest and enjoyment.

*Sunday, April 22* R. says he wakes up feeling heavy, and with such heavy thoughts. — We discuss the release of the works to the various theaters and come to the conclusion that it would be a good thing, for the sake of the Society of Patrons which is now being established, to insist on a clause in the contracts with the various theaters to the effect that, should the Society succeed in its efforts to achieve a repetition of the festival, the theaters holding rights in the work should support this festival, enabling a sort of model performance to be given here in Bayreuth. R. also writes in this vein to Councilor Düfflipp, offering the decorations, costumes, and machinery in repayment of the advance; or he might sell all these things to the theater director in Leipzig and then pay the money to the King. R. cables to Dr. Förster, asking him at last to engage Unger and thereby to secure the performing rights for Leipzig, with priority in all North Germany. R. says he now sees his way a little more clearly; he is also demanding support for his festival in Bayreuth on a cooperative basis, should the Societies of Patrons have raised funds for it. Amen. I have only one thought in mind: the possibility of gaining time for R. to work, and the hope of seeing *Parsifal* completed. We start on Lope's *La quinta de Florencia*, but without enjoyment—it lacks warmth.

*Monday, April 23* Lessons for the children and various things, news from England not very encouraging; a request to remove *Tristan* from the program, the tiny double basses are said not to sound well, on top of that still great uncertainty on the business side, Messrs. Hodge and Essex are certainly in no position to deposit the guaranteed sum. Some of the singers to whom contracts have been sent are behaving very injudiciously, and we are leaving in a state of worry. First letter from Loldi! Somewhat nicer weather, though still not springlike.

*Wednesday, April 25* Lessons for the children and letters. R. receives the consent for Herr Unger's engagement in exchange for rights in the N., which is one great burden the less. From friend Standhartner a telegram saying that neither the Prince nor the management is raising any significant objections to R.'s proposals (10 percent, 20,000 marks advance). In the evening we take up an *auto* by Calderón (*Llamados y escogidos*) and are downright appalled by its Jesuitical ornaments, its hair-splitting, superficial depiction of religious matters. Oh, Parsifal!

*Thursday, April 26* Work with the children and some visits. R. settles his business affairs, Dr. Förster is engaging Herr Unger, paying 10 percent and an advance of 2,000 thalers, is receiving in exchange the rights in the work in North Germany. — Fine speech by Moltke on the necessity for the 13th captain.

*Friday, April 27* Letters from Loldi! R. still has business affairs to settle, none of them encouraging. I give lessons and write the necessary letters. — War has broken out between Russia and Turkey. At the same time, our industry in such a pitiful state that one cannot help feeling concern.

*Saturday, April 28* Final lessons and domestic arrangements. Many unpleasantnesses for R. Herr Batz, his agent, turns up as representative, against R., of the rights of Messrs. Brandt, Brückner, Hoffmann, Doepler! R. also has to write to Councilor D. regarding Leipzig and Vienna. On top of this the W. Societies are upset by this turn of events, and news of the legal action against Fürstner! R. very vexed. Also Herr Unger helpless and complaining, though it was R. who got his engagement in Leipzig!

*Sunday, April 29* Packing and disposing! Apprehensive departure; after saying goodbye to the children, left on Monday the 30th at 6 A.M. with the mail train; at 1 o'clock in Würzburg, where we ask the good Ritters to ride with us as far as Aschaffenburg. Welcomed in Mainz by M. Maier, in Cologne our good Lesimple managed to get us a sleeping compartment, in which we then get some quite tolerable rest.

*Tuesday, May 1* In Brussels in the early morning, in Ostend at 10 o'clock after receiving a nice, pleasant impression of the scenery. In Dover at 1 o'clock, after a very disagreeable crossing for R.: he is utterly seasick, so that I feel almost ashamed at feeling nothing of this wretched condition but, rather, taking a kind of pleasure in this unusual journey. Dover makes a powerful impression on us, and the first drive through London not only a powerful, but also a pleasing impression. Almost the entire orchestra is gathered on the platform at Charing Cross, with Wilhelmj, Dannreuther, Seidl, Fischer, etc. We are living very pleasantly and comfortably with the Dannreuthers; the night passes very quietly. Visit to the Albert Hall, which we like very much, in spite of its enormous dimensions. Our singers have already arrived. Then I drive with R. in a hansom cab; the fog gives everything a ghostly appearance and it is precisely here, in this center of the utmost activity, that I feel most closely aware of the ideality of things and the dreamlike quality of life. The huge buildings cannot be ignored, are there, and then vanish. The low houses and large gardens give a feeling of freedom and comfort. If I had to choose a large city, it would be London. Received some calls in the afternoon and in the evening, too.

*Thursday, May 3* I have to give R. bad news regarding the state of our business here; H. and Essex seem to be very good people, but they are very inexperienced, and the whole of Israel is once more working against us. R. accepts what I have to say calmly. [*The following passage, enclosed in square brackets, has a slanting line drawn through it; this, as the entry for the following day makes clear, is because it is entered in the wrong place.* "He is very cheered by the sound of the orchestra and by the very good orchestra—he says as long as that gives him pleasure he can put up with everything else. In the afternoon I enjoy several hours in Kensington."] In the evening we were to go to see R[*ichard*] *III*, but R. feels indisposed and goes to bed at 9 o'clock. I write to friend Gross, telling him how our affairs look here.

*Friday, May 4* Rehearsal (*there was none yesterday, I wrote letters, among others to the children in the morning*), to R.'s great satisfaction, as already reported. In the afternoon rehearsal at home with the singers. In Kensington. Dinner in the evening at Herr Schlesinger's with the poet Browning, the painter R. Lehmann, Wilhelmj, Richter, etc.

*Saturday, May 5* Fine day in spite of great cold; I visit the National Gallery, make the acquaintance of Reynolds with great pleasure, gain a fairer impression of Hogarth, and receive light and warmth again from the Italians. In the afternoon rehearsal at home with the singers, in the evening we have some guests, all of whom were in Bayreuth at the performances. R. annoyed at the visitors.

*Sunday, May 6* Wrote letters, visited the Zoological Gardens, made the acquaintance of George Eliot, the famous woman writer, who makes a noble and pleasant impression. In the evening dinner at Herr Sainton's with Lüders, R.'s two old friends.

*Monday, May 7* Full rehearsal; R. tired, not by the event itself, but by the signs of negligence, for example, in the parts, etc. He is really very tired! And what confronts us here is not, alas, calculated to restore his spirits! The concert at 8 in the evening; I sit with the two Leweses in the *grand tier* and am horrified by the sound, a double echo, no impression possible! On top of that, our singers very feeble. Sad feelings, despite the brilliant reception for R.

*Tuesday, May 8* Rehearsal, after which a nice lunch with Wilhelmj and the D[annreuthers] in Kensington Museum. Cheerful spirits in spite of everything. In the evening *Rip van Winkle, superb* performance by an American, Mr. Jefferson.

*Wednesday, May 9* Rehearsal, in the evening the concert, an even greater success; afterward I go to a reception given by Lady Lindsay in the Grosvenor Gallery, 400 people, very magnificent.

*Thursday, May 10* It turns out that things are even worse than we had supposed; Messrs. H. and E. are on the verge of bankruptcy! The last concert brought in £600—in such circumstances there is no question of even covering the costs! Great despondency. In the evening went with R. to R[*ichard*] *III*; the company not good, but some things in it gripping and well done, such as the scene in the tent and the scene with the aldermen.

*Friday, May 11* Rehearsal, very moving. After this obliged to discuss our position with R. America?? Then never again a return to Germany! . . . Visit to the British Museum. On the homeward journey saw R. in a cab in Regent Street, after him, caught up with him finally in the sea of vehicles, laughter!

*Saturday, May 12* Crystal Palace, flower show, and then our 3rd concert in the afternoon; Materna magnificent in *Walküre*; the "Ride of the Valkyries" repeated. R. is received by the Prince of Wales, who says he was present at the Philharmonic concert 20 years ago, R. repeats something the Queen said to him then—that all the Italians here were Germans and in consequence R.'s works could very well be performed here. — But R. very depressed, we spend the evening quietly at home; I write some letters. Herr Batz impertinently approaches us again on behalf of Herr Brandt.

*Sunday, May 13* I go to the High Church to hear a famous preacher (Rowssell), did not understand much, and the preceding service soul-destroying, much worse than ours—I can see why the Roman Catholics are making so much propaganda here, as I have been told. While I am there, R. writes to Herr Feustel, asking him to start a subscription to help clear up the deficit. Thoughts of America—never again back to Germany. In the afternoon I have some calls to pay, in the evening a German dinner at Herr v. Ernst's; Dr. Schliemann, the archaeologist, a guest, not very impressive; on the other hand, Dr. Siemens very impressive, to all appearances. R. very cheerful and friendly.

*Monday, May 14* Rehearsal till 1 o'clock, after which I to Mr. and Mrs. Lewes' for lunch and then with them to the studio of the Pre-Raphaelite painter Burne-Jones. Pretty, delicate pictures, he himself very pleasant. At 8 in the evening the concert, a substantial number of the royal family and a fairly full house. Herr Unger already shows signs of hoarseness in the *Lohengrin* duet, and he declares he will be unable to sing the "Forging Songs"; it is decided to repeat "Wotan's Farewell," but Herr Hill has already gone home—persisting confusion, finally Mr. Hodge tells the audience that the "Ride of the Valkyries" will be played instead of the forging scene, but the concert ends, after all, with the farewell scene between Siegfried and Brünnhilde, though indeed only Frau Materna can be heard. This is the last straw—that now the program cannot even be adhered to!

*Tuesday, May 15* Rehearsal; great concern, the Court complains about the alterations in the program, but there is absolutely no chance of keeping to it, since Herr Unger will certainly not recover in time; the public, already intimidated by the press and by Herr Joachim and consorts, will doubtless become even more timid, despite the brilliant reception given every time to both R. himself and all the pieces played.

Requests are being made from all sides not to alter the program, but how can it be adhered to? — At home R. finds a plaintive letter from Mme Lucca, Herr Schott is refusing her something, though R. does not tell me what—nothing but torment from all sides. — I attend a session of Parliament with Miss Cartwright. At 10 in the evening Herr Hill sends word that he is hoarse. R. has to go over to see Richter, in order to discuss the program once again!

*Wednesday, May 16* Rehearsal from 10 until 1 o'clock, in the evening concert, great impact of *Götterdämmerung* with Materna, the "Ride of the Valkyries," *Meistersinger* Prelude as well. Visits between rehearsal and concert. [*Added later:* "Between rehearsal and concert drove through the City with R."]

*Thursday, May 17* To the British Museum to see the drawings, then rendezvous with R. at the railroad station to visit Windsor. There he is received by the Queen and Prince Leopold, who talks to him about Rus, whom he once saw in Lucerne. Windsor makes a powerful impression, though its interior furnishings are much out of keeping with its exterior; and even the lovely van Dycks, the splendid Holbein, and the miraculous Rembrandt do not match it. How different the palaces in Italy! In the evening Lewes for dinner, then some others, to whom R. reads *Parsifal*.

*Friday, May 18* Rehearsal. Afterward R. has a long conference with Messrs. Schl., Hodge and E., the secretary of the Albert Hall, etc., about giving 3 more concerts. He thinks he has convinced them, and is very upset when he learns from Herr Schl. that only 2 instead of 3 concerts will be possible, and that only in 10 days' time. We again go for a drive together.

*Saturday, May 19* Today I am indisposed and have to force myself to attend the concert. It turns out brilliantly; proceeds of £1,600 and a very animated audience—very un-English, we are told. R. crowned with a laurel wreath, speech from the orchestra and unending cheers. — Ate in a restaurant with our good friends the Dannreuthers. To bed early in the evening.

*Sunday, May 20* Went twice to Westminster Abbey to hear the dean. Fine impression. — R. unfortunately not well. I have to go by myself to dine with the painter Millais.

*Monday, May 21* I have to speak to the singers, asking them (Hill, Frau Grün) to reduce their exorbitant demands somewhat, since R. will now have to pay them himself! R. is not well. I go out alone to breakfast and dine, visit the studio of the painter Watts, in which there hangs a quite amazing picture of Joachim; I can read the whole biography of this thoroughly bad person in this picture; that is not what the painter intended, but it is the very thing which reveals his talent—that he has depicted the truth without realizing it! Indeed, by trying to express something splendid.

*Tuesday, May 22* R.'s birthday! Very nice letters from all the children and all sorts of greetings besides. In the evening a banquet, at which R. distributes the medallions which I gave him: probably the last work of Semper, the great master! Materna, Richter, Wilhelmj receive them. — R. speaks very movingly, expressing gratitude for his reception, and, quoting Semper, he compares moments with years—such moments, he says, make him forget the years. The celebrations otherwise a little loud, very German; Fidi's health is drunk!

*Wednesday, May 23* R. is very tired and today goes only to the Athenaeum, where Dr. Siemens has arranged a small dinner for him; I visit Westminster Abbey, Canon Hartford shows me all the features of this remarkable house of God; I found it very moving that "Elisabeth's Prayer" was played on the organ at the conclusion of the service; the crowds dispersed in silence, and above their heads this pure soul spread her wings; they return to their lives, silent and unheeding, while she yields herself singing to Death! — In the evening a letter from Loldi which affects us very much, I reply to her at once, promising to visit her. (R. thanks the King for his telegram of congratulations.)

*Thursday, May 24* R. receives unpleasant letters from Leipzig and has to break off negotiations there, which is perhaps a good thing. Meanwhile, however, there is Herr Unger to look after, who has already proved very expensive and not very rewarding! Session with the photographer, not to be avoided! In the evening we hold a reception.

*Friday, May 25* Good letter from Councilor Düfflipp, according to which they seem willing in Munich to buy the machinery. R. replies by return. I visit the British Museum again and take pleasure in the splendid drawings. Afterward rendezvous with R. at Charing Cross and fish dinner in Greenwich. Return home by steamer, very successful, mild, gray weather, tremendous impression, R. says, "This is Alberich's dream come true—Nibelheim, world dominion, activity, work, everywhere the oppressive feeling of steam and fog." — In the evening *Tannhäuser* in Italian! Oh! . . . All of it terrible, only the orchestra wonderful, but unfortunately directed by a conductor who is not at all good. Our friend Wilhelmj ill.

*Saturday, May 26* Visit to the Tower of London with R., enjoyed the sentries, the Beefeaters; lunch with R. in the aquarium. Paid some calls. In the evening to *Don Giovanni*.

*Sunday, May 27* Sitting for the painter Herkomer, then lunch at the Schlesingers' and visit to the Leweses', where it was decided that I should sit for the painter Burne-Jones. At home in the evening.

*Monday, May 28* Rehearsal for the concert; it ends at 12 o'clock and the concert begins at 3; it goes quite well; Wilhelmj absent owing to illness.

*Tuesday, May 29* Rehearsal from 10 to 1, Herr Unger sings the "Forging Songs" and "Brünnhilde's Awakening" very well; after the rehearsal a sitting for Burne-Jones, then a nice walk in fine weather through Holland Park and Kensington Gardens. In the evening the concert; Herr Unger produces not a single note, does not ask to be excused, but stands there utterly unperturbed, with poor Materna exerting herself in the awakening scene, Richter cursing, R. sending him looks to turn him to stone, not making the slightest effort; R. tells him afterward that he was not hoarse, but had lain down tired after eating too much and had clogged his palate. This tops everything. The audience very good-natured.

*Wednesday, May 30* Another sitting for Burne-Jones. After that, accounts; it turns out that, after R. has paid everything off, £700 will remain for Bayreuth; it is some relief to me, for I was expecting the worst; but R. is very depressed.

*Thursday, May 31* Farewell visits, sitting for Burne-Jones, in Kensington in the evening, party of engineers.

*Friday, June 1* Stormy weather! All the same, we plan to leave tomorrow. In the evening dinner with Herr Ionides, brother of Charicleas Dannreuther. Made the acquaintance of the writer Mr. Morris. — D.'s child ill.

*Saturday, June 2* Departure impossible on account of the storm; attended the Caxton celebrations in Westminster Abbey; very curious impression; Mendelssohn's *"Lobgesang"* ["Hymn of Praise"] as much out of place there as all the monuments. — In the evening dinner with Herr Schlesinger, whose handsome womenfolk (wife and sister-in-law) are full of London society.

*Sunday, June 3* Journey to Hampton Court with R. and the Dannreuthers, return via Richmond, lovely impression; in the evening with D.'s very pleasant sister.

*Monday, June 4* Left London! Very mixed feelings. Calm sea, R. in good spirits, I melancholy as always with any change in my circumstances! Cramped cabin and bunk: "The latitude here must be very narrow," R. says with a laugh.

*Tuesday, June 5* Arrival at 6 o'clock in Ems, where R. is supposed to take the cure. The children (except for Loldi) at the station; Fidi's gaze fixed in tender sympathy on his father. The *Bayreuther Tagblatt* is said to have published some really disgraceful articles about the London concerts; the boy seems to have heard about them, and that is why he now looks at his father thus!

*Wednesday, June 6*  Siegfried's birthday! My darling child! Distribution of gifts all around. A construction set for Fidi, acquired in London by R. personally. Bad weather, consequently no outing. Letters from Feustel! Rebellion among the people who had been put off with promises till after the London concerts. I beg R. to make use of my 40,000 francs—along with the London proceeds that makes about 50,000 marks. I firmly believe that my children will not hold this against me, and I know that God will bless them for it. — The negotiations have been broken off with Leipzig and taken up with Hanover; Herr Unger, I hope, after his behavior in London, done with. — God bless you, my child!

*Thursday, June 7*  R. begins his cure. The place is pretty and the weather good. Walk in the woods; R. writes to Herr Feustel. Besides our great worry there is trouble with the house, on which substantial repairs have become necessary owing to the negligent work of the Bayreuth people.

*Friday, June 8*  I start copying out *Parsifal* and resume lessons with the children. Drive to the tomb of Herr von Stein; walk in the Schweizer Valley, three hours on foot. I read my mother's *Souvenirs*. R. reads Rémusat's *Abélard* on my recommendation and finds it very enjoyable.

*Saturday, June 9*  Still business matters, *Parsifal*, and lessons, in the afternoon to the pavilion. *Tannhäuser* Overture from the distance. —

*Sunday, June 10*  Boat trip down the Rhine, dinner in Bingen; memories of 14 years ago! . . . I am very tired.

*Monday, June 11*  I take delight in *Parsifal*. — Great heat. R. gives us delicious descriptions of the ladies in the pump room, fat, with discontented, indeed malicious expressions, but with roses on their hats. He thinks of the Spartans, who killed off all their superfluous people.

*Tuesday, June 12*  The same life, which unfortunately remains oppressive on account of the worries in the background.

*Wednesday, June 13*  With the eldest girls to the French theater, which is playing here for the Emperor; *Tigre du Bengale* very enjoyable, but the preceding play revealing all the wretchedness of present-day Parisian literature.

*Thursday, June 14*  Feustel sends the papers for signature; letter from the King, beside himself over the news that R. intends to emigrate to America. R. had written to Feustel saying he would perhaps have to go to America, in which case he would not return home again! "Without illusions, but full of hope," Guizot says of Cromwell in his *History of the English Revolution,* which R. is now reading. — Of certain people R. says, "In them what is called character is simply bad play-acting." . . . Still on the subject of the Society here, he says, "Everything is done to music—that is what I find so strange." — Much birdsong, recently nightingales singing during a heavy night thunderstorm. R., when I tell him this, says, "They take the thunder for applause."

*Friday, June 15* R. dissatisfied with his cure, believes the doctors have made a mistake. I continue copying out *Parsifal*. R. still oppressed by his situation. I am deeply worried about it, but how can one expect worry to end except with one's life?

*Saturday, June 16* Arrival of the Emperor. Very little enthusiasm, but considerable heat. — R. decides to take the Marienbad instead of the Ems waters. — In the evening went with R. and the children to see the illuminations.

*Sunday, June 17* To church with the children, a simple service. Walk to the pump room. R. works out his plan to go to Munich, possibly in order to get the theater management there to take over the Bayreuth performances.

*Monday, June 18* For me copying *Parsifal* and lessons for the children, for R. Guizot's *History* and some business matters with Feustel. My father sends us a letter from Herr v. Bronsart to him, from which it transpires that Herr von Hülsen is utterly hostile to the idea of having the *Nibelungen* performed in Hanover. "Are you quite blind to the fiasco in Bayreuth and the fiasco in London, where the people streamed out of the hall during the *Ring* pieces?" Hülsen writes to Bronsart. So this is what comes from the lying newspaper reports! However, R. does not mind at all now that there will be no performances in Hanover.

*Tuesday, June 19* The last volume of Glasenapp's biography has appeared, and it touches me deeply. All R. has to say is, "What he has got from other people is not always quite correct, but what he writes himself is sensible and profound." Math. Maier visits us. We also make the acquaintance of one of Malwida's sisters, and R. of the deputy *Windthorst*, head of the Catholic party, who is supposed to be very witty. Unfortunately we see him between two priests, eagerly reading a newspaper they have brought him—not a pretty sight.

*Wednesday, June 20* Hülsen's words to Bronsart have much upset R.; this helplessness in the face of lies and hostility! I no longer feel aggrieved, I just feel as if I were melting away, as if there were nothing of me remaining but a curious mirage.

*Thursday, June 21* Daniella and the children spend the whole morning in the pump room with R., then they return to do some work with me. — Visit from one of our nicest patrons, Count Pourtalès, conversation about the Germans; the National Liberal party, which is making difficulties for Bismarck! . . . It is indeed difficult to make any progress with the Germans!—In the evening Herr Heckel arrives— R. thinks in order to make a report to him, to put forward proposals; but no: nothing is happening, and the party, feeling powerless to help, relapses into inactivity. R. very depressed.

*Friday-Saturday, June 22–23* R. leaves Herr Heckel to me, since he wants to draft his reply to the King. I go for a walk with our friend, and the good man tells me, among many other disagreeable things, that the *Neue Freie Presse* is now advertising that it has bought up some letters from R. to a milliner and intends to publish and annotate them. When R. now talks about emigrating to America, I no longer have the courage to speak against it. Unfortunately I have finished copying *Parsifal*, which for me kept the whole real world at bay. Visit from Herr Voltz; R. declares that he is unwilling to receive any further letters from Herr Batz.

*Sunday, June 24* To church with the children. Before that, letters from London; little hope for the subscription. From this day until *July 1* visit from Herr Niemann, who also reports that Herr von Hülsen is hostile to the *Ring*. The curious man wants to read *Parsifal*, R. gives it to him, and it makes a great impression on him. Made the acquaintance of the former minister Windthorst, a very unhandsome but, we feel, a decidedly gifted man. R. gives him *Art and Politics* to read. Belief that war may break out, owing to present French confusions. Visits to the pump room increasingly difficult for us on account of the bad music. The theatrical performances also fill us with melancholy, and a most pitiful regatta! . . . R. is very annoyed at all this, but the cure seems to be doing him good. — Councilor Düfflipp writes that he is expecting us in Munich and hopes with all his heart that a satisfactory solution can be found. In the meantime Herr Rosa, a theater director, with proposals for America, operatic performances, etc. Herr Ullmann also making proposals . . . Otherwise nothing much is doing. But the "inventive mind" is hatching out plans for a school. He says he is so incorrigibly rash that he can imagine going to America and then returning home after all to "commit some foolish act," by which he means putting on a performance.

*Monday, July 2* Promenade in spite of the rain, then a rest; R. is now reading a book by Maxime Ducamp about *Paris*, the chapter on the *malfaiteurs* amuses him. In the evening the Reichstag deputy Windthorst; he comes with the volume of the collected writings which R. had lent him under his arm, and talks with acuteness and sense both about this and about other political matters. He seems to belong to the Catholic party only as a politician and has a free outlook on affairs generally, but probably the party is too powerful for him not to be led in directions he does not wish to go. R. was eager to talk to him, became heated about the war between the Russians and the Turks, since our guests were not on the side of Russia, for whom R. advocates the possession of Constantinople; but the conversation calms down and remains very interesting.

*Tuesday, July 3* Nice weather, promenade in the morning. To Lindenbach in the afternoon, Frau Wesendonck and her daughter there. R. finds conversation somewhat difficult, a sort of intimacy devoid of any context.

*Wednesday, July 4* Letter from Herr Gross: Count Magnis Ullersdorff has sent 5,000 marks toward the deficit. Besides that, news from Herr Simson that R. has won his case against Herr Fürstner in the court of appeal as well. Both very pleasing. Final walk to Lindenbach after receiving farewell visits of all kinds. In the evening Count Pourtalès and Frau Wesendonck with her daughter; R. says to the Count, among other things: "What are we Germans? We don't know; all we know is that we are stripped bare by the Jews and clothed by the French."

*Thursday, July 5* Farewells of all kinds. I send Fidi to the Kurhaus to give a bunch of cornflowers to the Emperor. Fidi sees and also speaks to the very friendly old gentleman. Probably for the first and last time. Departure at 10 o'clock, great merriness and high spirits from R. and the children, only Fidi with a slight sore throat—it gets worse, and when we arrive in Heidelberg, we decide to stay, since the Schlosshotel is very pleasant. In the evening Herr Heckel, Dr. Zeroni, Herr Lang, a serenade by the choral society; 6,000 people present. (R. conducts *"Gaudeamus igitur"* from the balcony.)

*Friday, July 6* Fidel still indisposed, his tonsils inflamed, we take a stroll on the splendid terrace. But we are tired. In the evening, visit from our Mannheim friends with an Old Catholic priest. Like her mother, the Grand Duchess of Baden is supporting the Catholic party; the Reich Chancelor said to the deputies for Baden in the Reichstag, "Your Grand Duke has always been very good to me, but now I hear he has fallen among the women." Letter from my father.

*Saturday, July 7* Fidel has to remain in bed all day, I almost do likewise, so tired do I feel. R. continues reading Maxime Ducamp's book. The chapter on the *malfaiteurs* interests him very much. Walk in the palace gardens, delight in the splendid trees; a blackbird which accompanies the *Gazza Ladra* Overture with its song gives us great enjoyment.

*Sunday, July 8* Drive in the morning to the Königstein, splendid woods. At lunch our friends from Mannheim and R. Pohl—also Prof. Nohl! In the evening R. reads out loud his *Parsifal*, whose impact on me grows more profound each time. After the reading a conversation develops with the Old Catholic priest about religion; R. speaks in favor of reviving the monasteries, from which all activities should originate —visiting the poor, the imprisoned, all those who are suffering in any way. He says, "If, before I met my good wife, I had known of any such monastery, I should have entered it and not lightly left it again."

*Monday, July 9*  Each day we like it better here, and though Fidi is still not entirely well, we are enjoying our stay very much. Today we visit the town with the 3 girls; it seems to us very orderly and clean.

*Tuesday, July 10*  Fidi lively again, I on the other hand confined to my room; consultation with Dr. Zeroni, milk diet. R. and the children go for a walk to the Wolfsbrunnen. We are still reading Maxime Ducamp's *Paris*, each with a different volume, and R. comes to the conclusion that one class of people there—roughly the middle class, made up of employees—stands out, but its sole function is to protect the upper classes, which are bad, from the lower classes, which are equally useless.

*Wednesday, July 11*  Morning drive to Schwetzingen, no particular pleasure in frivolity and decadence, but cheerful spirits throughout; on the homeward journey we see a falcon circling high above our heads; we welcome it as a good omen. — In the afternoon a concert, the conductor Rosenkranz asks to be put right on certain tempi, but it does not much help.

*Thursday, July 12*  R. had a bad night, following an unhealthy diet; he says, "Perhaps it was just so that I should see the falling star," and he tells me that a magnificently shining object sank before his eyes— he at once thought of the King. When the falcon was circling, he said to me, "That falcon is thinking, 'Wagner must be given good fortune, for beside him is the only being for whom it is worth putting up with life.' " — Around noon we go with the children to see the students' wine cask. In the evening a wonderful drive to the Wolfsbrunnen; magnificent sunset. Evening on the terrace, a perfect idyll. Eight happy days! And on the homeward journey another lucky omen, a green spider on R.'s hat—"spider at night"—In no other district have we felt so much at home; hardly anywhere else have we been so much left to ourselves.

*Friday, July 13*  On the terrace R. shows me two doves sitting quietly on the edge and says, "Those are our souls, which have stayed here since our conversation yesterday evening." I visit the castle with the children; then R. improvises a drive to Mannheim, where we are joined by our friends in the Pfälzer Hof. It seems that friend Heckel may really be appointed to the theater committee, which is significant insofar as the gentlemen of the school of malice have played the vilest tricks on him here in Mannheim and have almost completely destroyed his business—the conductor Frank, the theater committee, etc. He also tells us that, when he proposed the engagement of Hans as conductor here, the committee approached Herr von Perfall, who declared that Hans was impossible to work with! And with this wretched man we shall now have to negotiate in Munich! As I was writing this page, R. came in to report another lucky omen; at the moment when he put his hand in his pocket and jingled his money, he had caught sight of the moon in the first quarter! — Evening on the terrace, one after another the lights come on in the city like huge glowworms, we feel ever better and more at home here, where no stupid tricks come between us. Even the worst possibilities of our life together, such as the journey to America, we can talk about gaily; R. says, "In order to keep down costs, I will ask your father to engage me for matinée performances and give concerts with me there—he will play, and I sing." This proposed, we discuss all the details of the situation amid growing laughter, from the nursing of his voice and raw eggs to the embarrassed welcome, *à la* Beckmesser. [*Postscript added after the July 14 entry*]: Our joking was interrupted for a moment by a child's song; a girl, returning home in the evening, is singing in a voice which is loud, but very pure and clear [Weber's] "I am lonely, not alone." She strolls about, accompanied by someone with a bright lantern; a very pretty impression. — I have the feeling that only the sounds of Weber could emerge from this beautiful, dense greenery: this is where his graceful spirit sits weaving.

*Saturday, July 14* R. did not have a good night. I went to bed with strange forebodings, chance always brings three lights into my room, and the happiness we are feeling here I find almost alarming. — R. had what he calls his "dreams of cowardice"—lack of money, contemptuous treatment by other people, my wish to have nothing more to do with him. — Visit from our friends Pohl, Nohl, Heckel. Went for a walk to the Wolfsbrunnen. Conversed in the evening. R. talks about London and says he had the feeling of much individual good will, to which he was unable to respond.

*Sunday, July 15* R. early in the morning to the fountain, Fontaine de Soif, then breakfast. As he is resting a while and reflecting, he exclaims to me, "All of it is possible only because I have you; even peace and solitude appeal to me only when I can tell myself that you are with me." . . . A wet day; in the evening, arrival of General Grant and his family, and we have a short meeting with him. He can speak neither German nor French!

*Monday, July 16* Drive to Heilbronn, the town hall and the Church of Saint Kilian make an impression, particularly the altarpiece carved in wood; R. is utterly captivated by the four figures, Pope and cardinal below, and two bishops; I am also much fascinated by the Death of Mary and by what I take to be the Ascent to Heaven. A strange impression in the house of Justinus Kerner: a pretty woman, clearly dressed for a social occasion, a rather mysterious house, an excited, mesmerizing Court councilor, an interesting picture of the visionary of Prevorst, and a fine portrait by Lenbach.

*Tuesday, July 17*  Packing, a sad occupation—another departure! Cheerful evening with the Zeronis, a Mrs. Monro, and a Dr. Scheibner, geologist and Wagnerian. The conversation ranges from the Ice Age to the present state of affairs; the customs laws in Germany seem to be designed to lay waste our industry and to benefit trade, like the new coinage, which is in step with no other and benefits nobody except clever bankers! Herr Scheibner tells of a recent speech in Brussels by Lord Derby, in which he said that the German people, with their abilities, would soon overtake all others, if only their governments were not so bad. But nobody listens. It is also mentioned that young Englishmen formerly were sent to the forestry school in Tharandt, but they were so disregarded there that now they are being sent to Nancy. The Russians have been defeated in Asia. Much enjoyment from this conversation with intelligent English people!

*Wednesday, July 18*  At 10 o'clock left the cozy spot where we have spent such lovely, quiet days. R. tells me he is always enraged that we did not discover each other 15 years earlier: "How much silly nonsense would I have been spared!" Nice journey; in Freiburg a large crowd of Wagnerians, including Heckel and his wife, at the railroad station, flowers, beer, and toasts. In Oos friend Pohl told us that the Russians were now beyond the Balkan Mountains. R. laughs: "How silly of me to be glad! Both the Sultan and the Khedive bought certificates of patronage, but the Russians did nothing at all for me; people will think me very ungrateful." — Yesterday we talked about the tragedy of life, about Hans! The nearer I come to the places I know in Switzerland, the more I feel as if someone were talking about my past life, with gentle melancholy; it has ceased to exist for me, yet the melancholy remains. Nice letter from the King about *Parsifal*. Also, before our departure, one from Loldi. Arrived here (Lucerne) in the evening, to our great surprise Richter on the platform, then Countess Bassenheim, the Stocker family, in short, our whole past. — Unfortunately also a letter from Dr. Herz which dismays me: diphtheria has broken out in Altenburg. All the signs of ill omen come back to my mind—last night we were 13 at table, the three lights, the dead horse, the bloody star; we intend to travel on Friday—; why is my mind so full of disaster? —

*Thursday, July 19*  It is raining; in the morning conversation with Countess Bassenheim; in the afternoon a drive to Tribschen in spite of the rain; it is neglected and overgrown, some French Jews are living there: "Too much for one time," says R. — Visit from the Stockers. The sky remains gloomy, as if we were being told not to grieve that the Tribschen days are past.

*Friday, July 20* Early departure. Walk in Zurich, very pleasant boat ride on Lake Constance. R. points out the Säntis to me, which he climbed with Uhlig. In Munich around 8 o'clock in the evening. Friend Lenbach at the station.

*Saturday, July 21 Munich* At 8 o'clock Councilor Düfflipp, I go out, so that R. can speak to him more unrestrainedly, and show the children the city. When I come home, R. declares to my surprise that we will leave tomorrow, since we have nothing more to do here. The King has given no instructions of any sort with regard to our affair, and since he himself is in financial difficulties, he is just afraid of being obliged to pay further advances, indeed also of not getting his advances back. Councilor Düfflipp suggests that R. talk to Herr von Perfall; R. consents, and at 11 goes to Düfflipp's office; Herr v. P. voices lengthy protestations of respect, R. replies that he is willing to accept him as a new acquaintance. It is proposed that the Munich theater management present the festival next year in Bayreuth, and then in Munich. This proposal is now to be worked out between Herr v. P. and Düffl. R. says to me, "I must be glad that, when the master sends me away, the servants give me something to eat!" Drive with R., the children, and friend Lenbach through the English Garden and the older parts of Munich. Sad news of Semper, who is nearing his end; it is terrible to see the emergence of this mad craving for life, after everything that makes life horrible has been tried and all illusions concerning it have been lost!

*Sunday, July 22* Departure in the early morning, arrival in Nuremberg at 11 o'clock; with R. and the children visited the town hall, the Church of Saint Sebald and the wonderful Church of Saint Lorenz, the fortress, etc. *Meistersinger* atmosphere; near Hans Sachs's house found the street of the 2nd act again. Unfortunately the Hans Sachs Platz much disfigured by the synagogue, insolent and sumptuous. — On the Rosenau common a small crowd gathers to see R. In the evening the enthusiastic music master; R., however, flaring up when he is told of the love the Nuremberg people bear him, recalls that *Die Meistersinger* was played here last of all, that, when he offered it to the theater in aid of the Hans Sachs monument, without demanding anything for himself, he did not even receive a reply. Then he is vexed with himself over his useless rage.

*Monday, July 23* Went to see [Dürer's] *Hieronymus Holzschuher* in the G[ermanic] Museum, the splendid picture pleases R., too. "I should have known this man," he says, "he would have understood me." —

Departure for Weimar. Arrival at 7 o'clock, found my father very well, thank God. He tells us of his conversation with the Crown Prince and Princess in Potsdam, both of them completely "Wagnerian"! —

*Tuesday, July 24* Frau v. Schleinitz and friend Dohm come here to greet us, very friendly meeting. In the evening met the Grand Duke in my father's house; R. in scintillating mood. *Arrival of Loldi!* . . .

*Wednesday, July 25* Joyful reunion with our child, who, just like [Schiller's] unknown maiden, seems to us transfigured by joy and sorrow. — R. had sent to Altenburg for her so that we could visit my father with the whole family. — Frau v. Schl. tells us all sorts of curious things about Berlin; Bismarck, who literally hates both her and her husband, gets the newspapers to declare that Bayreuth is only a subterfuge for her Catholic party intrigues, etc. Absurd, angry rubbish. — In the evening departure of our friends, they are returning to Berlin, where things are looking topsy-turvy.

*Thursday, July 26* Lunch in the Erbprinz, with us my father and Frau v. Meyendorff with her son. The Grand Duke pays us a call and sits down at our table to say many friendly things to R. about *Die Msinger.* — In the evening at Frau v. M.'s, my father plays wonderfully but looks tired.

*Friday, July 27* Went to Eisenach with R. and the children, very nice evening in the restaurant above, after visiting the Wartburg. The evening star; through *Tannhäuser* this spot seems to be my soul's home.

*Saturday, July 28* R. and the children to Bayreuth, I with Loldchen to Weimar; telegram from R. at midday; spent the evening with my father.

*Sunday, July 29* Visit to the castle, in which there are some fine pictures and drawings; in the afternoon a drive with Loldi to the Belvedere, fine old trees; in the evening read *Parsifal* with my father. Schnappauf arrives, bringing a sweet letter from R. —

*Monday, July 30* Packing and departure, taking leave of my father. Unexpected wait in Leipzig, in Altenburg at midnight.

*Tuesday, July 31* A talk with Frau Herz, great blow for my Loldchen, she must stay another 6 weeks! . . . Sorrowful day with her, we go for a walk, in the evening to the castle and listen together to the "Pilgrims' Chorus" and the "Evening Star." (Telegram from R.)

*Wednesday, August 1* Departure at 5 o'clock, no farewells, so as not to upset her too much. Arrival in Bayreuth at 1 o'clock. R. at the station with Fidi, a dear, kind, and tender welcome. Once again in Wahnfried. Friend Standhartner.

*Thursday, August 2* I receive the lovely letter which R. wrote to me in Altenburg and in which he told me everything, including the news that the "tempo school" will now probably be set up, the mayor has no doubts that the town will provide funds for it. Dinner with the theater director Baron Loën, his wife, and his son. R. afterward not quite well, as always when his routine is even only slightly disturbed. But he has arranged his studio for *Parsifal*, and today I heard a few of the first notes!

*Friday, August 3* R. unwell; friend Standhartner departs. Many household duties for me, the fight with the dragon, as R. calls it—that is to say, against the excessive spending.

*Saturday, August 4* Still the house! — R. was much pleased yesterday that the general (Osman Pasha) who has just unexpectedly beaten the Russians at Plevna is the same man who some time ago sent him a pamphlet attacking the Jews. When I tease him about his preference for the Russians, he says, "One mustn't allow oneself to be beaten—it is silly."

*Sunday, August 5* Still fighting with the dragon, difficult to get into the heads of the servants that we are methodical people with no wish to squander. Lulu quite helpless in this connection, the poor child in a state of great confusion, still lacking in seriousness and application. Well, with God's help—! . . . Yesterday evening read Lucian with much enjoyment. This evening a short discussion with the mayor.

*Monday, August 6* Resumed lessons with the children, my time until evening divided without interruption between them and the house; in the evening read Lucian with R. with much enjoyment. "Lucius or the Ass" recently made a great impression on him. — News that the Russians have again been heavily defeated! — A merchant in Viersen, Herr Schmidt, has written an appeal to the patrons, very fine and moving. R. is much occupied with plans for the school.

*Tuesday, August 7* R. really working, I occupied with the children and the house; sent off medallions to our festival colleagues. In the evening Lucian, "The Carousal or the Lapiths," the old philosophers remind us of our professors!

*Wednesday, August 8* Same life, busy, cheerful, tender. The Turks' successes give us much to talk about! Lucian in the evening.

*Thursday, August 9* Somewhat indisposed, I stay in the upstairs room; however, the children have their lessons and R. comes to have coffee and tea with me; he takes pleasure in the nursery and the garden, the lines of trees. Lucian's "The Dream or the Cock" also gives us great pleasure.

*Friday, August 10* R. dreamed that I wanted to go away, was sitting in the carriage, and the horse reared up against me—I discuss with R. the curious connection between his dreams and my thoughts. When I am troubled by sad thoughts which I keep to myself, he sees me during the night in danger! — He works or reflects, I also in my own way, in the evening we continue with Lucian. Night of shooting stars; R. says he does not care for them since the falling star in Heidelberg deceived him so: "But why did I apply it to the King? Perhaps it meant the manufacturer in Viersen?"

*Saturday, August 11*  Expecting the arrival of my father, he cables that he will not come till tomorrow, melancholy return home. Then many affectionate outpourings and finally the revelation of "*Nehmt hin mein Blut*" ["Take ye my blood"]—R. tells me he wrote it down shortly before my return, with his hat and coat on, just as he was about to go out to meet me. He has had to alter the words to fit it, he says; this scene of Holy Communion will be the main scene, the core of the whole work; with the "Prize Song" in *Die Meistersinger*, too, the melody came first, and he had adapted the words to it. He had already told me yesterday that one must beware of having to extend a melody for the sake of the words—now today the chief passage ("*Nehmet hin mein Blut um unsrer Liebe willen, nehmet hin meinen Leib und gedenket mein' ewiglich*") is there complete, in all its mildness, suffering, simplicity and exaltation. "Amfortas's sufferings are contained in it," R. says to me. — Its impression on me is overwhelming, and I am incapable of putting my mind to anything. A long time after this R. reads me the first scenes of *Hamlet*, which one thinks one knows by heart and yet never knows. R. agrees with me when I remark that H.'s outburst about the reveling occurs when he is in a state of great agitation, when one talks only in order to speak, not to say anything in particular; the cold night, gruesome expectation excite in H. this urge to work himself into a passion; and from a dramatic point of view, too, nothing could be more felicitous than this diversion of attention from the expected apparition, allowing it to make its impact suddenly; as always in Shakespeare, the height of artistry coincides with the waywardness of real life.

*Sunday, August 12*  Went to fetch my father, he arrives at the same time as friend Dannreuther. R. says it is a happy day and presents the children with the 4 thalers he still has left from our traveling expenses. Cheerful, indeed exuberant mood!

*Monday, August 13*  R. already somewhat tired, as always when his day's routine is not strictly adhered to. Several telegrams arrive, commemorating this day last year. In the evening some Americans, R. very, very irritable, jealous of my father on my account.

*Tuesday, August 14*  Oh, this mortal life! When one is happy, a breath can turn it—putting an end to joy, peace, and work, and no one in the least to blame! . . . In the evening my father plays us his "*Divertissement à la Hongroise*" enchantingly, but R. remains disturbed.

*Wednesday, August 15*  Departure! At the station the Riedel Society, going to Nuremberg for the jubilee celebrations of the Germanic

Museum; my father very indignant that R. was not invited to them; also that it did not occur to Eisenach to make R. an honorary citizen! . . . In the evening a sculptor from Leipzig who has been commissioned to make a large bust of R. for the theater; a private citizen is donating it. R. is reluctant to sit for it.

*Thursday, August 16* R. begs me most movingly to forgive his bad mood, he is so unwell, physically, that it takes nothing at all to bring on black thoughts. I could see that from his dreams, he says. — Friend Dannreuther brought with him £500 from our English friends, decision to return the money with thanks. The conductor Herr Levi sends us an article from the *Blätter für literarische Unterhaltung* entitled "The Festival and Its Reviewers," probably written by Prof. Bernays (it is signed Uhde); it is very well disposed toward the festival and well written, but it is upsetting to see all the press's trivialities paraded once again. R. says the great mistake was being obliged to demand payment for admittance and having in consequence to allow such people in as well.

*Friday, August 17* Lessons and household for me; for R., I fear, no resumption of work yet; in the evening Herr Zumpe comes along with a ballad opera; R. very concerned, asks him where he learned the things he is now showing him—certainly not from him! — His resolve to found a school strengthened!

*Saturday, August 18* Lessons and house and correspondence. In the afternoon a drive up to the theater, strange impression; going inside, a tremendous impression, as magnificent as the work itself. On the other hand, the costumes, the photographs, arouse in R. an utter repugnance against concerning himself with the *Ring* again. Spent the evening in the Bürgerreuth, nice atmosphere, pretty scenery, and friendly moonlight.

*Sunday, August 19* "He sighed, and his sighing was a prayer"— My wedding day, 20 years ago now. Went to church—sermon on the healing of the deaf-mute—oh, could my sighing but turn into a prayer and bring blessings on others! When I come home from church, R. tells me he does not know whether he should surprise me, and he shows me the poem he has written for the *Idyll*—Schott wants something; the poem moves me to tears, but the thought of publication dismays me. There is nothing I can say, since R. is clearly under compulsion to publish it. At lunch he says that he should have kept all his works for himself and his friends, since none of them had brought him joy after publication. In the evening R. reads us Shakespeare's *The Tempest*.

*Monday, August 20* Work with the children; R. still not returning home to *Parsifal*! — In the afternoon he drives with us to the Eremitage. In the evening we finish *The Tempest*; its concision and attention to de-take over control, yes, even for a lengthy period, but should not put it in his pocket.

*Saturday, September 22* Another operation, R. bears it patiently, says that yesterday, while it was going on, he was composing! Departure of Mr. Jenkins, who utterly declines to accept any money from R. In the afternoon R. has a conference about the school with the mayor and Herr Feustel, after which he writes to friend Klindworth, to see whether he can secure him for it. — An open letter to my father from Herr Hiller, sent to us by Herr Lesimple, reveals once more to our astonished eyes how far impudence can go in its lack of shame or self-reproach. Nice letter to me from Herr von Wolzogen.

*Sunday, September 23* Departure of Fritz, who cannot get over his surprise at R.'s cheerfulness and good spirits. — After lunch went with R. for a walk in the palace gardens, he tells me that these gardens have a connection with his work, as localities always do—there is a modulation, for instance, in the girls' school on the corner. — On our return home he writes all sorts of letters, among others to Herr Pollini, who has written to him about presenting his works in London, saying there is no sacrifice he would not willingly undertake in order to do it. R. of course refuses, but reminds the impresario of his *"German"* obligations; in the same connection he writes to Herr Voltz, exhorting him to protect all his rights in this matter. — An embarrassing altercation with the governess, who has given vent to her bad temper. In the evening R. plays a splendid theme and says he would be able to play me the whole prelude if he had yet written it in ink.

*Monday, September 24* Resumption of usual routine. R. works, telling me that when he writes music he feels as if he were always beginning again from the start. In the afternoon he writes his appeal for the school. In the evening we are visited by a Herr von der Leeve, who was a patron and who requests an occupation in the school for Dr. Fuchs, whom he would be prepared to support. (Another Turkish victory over the Russians!!)

*Tuesday, September 25* R. feels he would find it easier to reach an understanding with a Prussian lieutenant than with the most educated Frenchman—the language is too great a gulf. — He works and in the afternoon goes to view the site for the school. — In the evening I show him my newly arranged manuscript folders, and afterward he reads me, with much amusement, Voltaire's article on Aristotle in the *Dictionnaire philosophique.* The boldness of its flights of imagination leads us to Beethoven, and R. says that, were he to try to visualize Beethoven "in all his starry glory," he would surely think of the second movement of [Opus] 111 (Adagio with variations); he knows nothing more ecstatic, he says, yet at the same time it is never sentimental. The Larghetto of [Opus] 106 he finds too long and somewhat academic; it grieves me to observe that what one of the greatest does is not always acceptable to another of the greatest, even in his most mature works.

*Wednesday, September 26*  A curious, wonderful day! — At the start worked with the children; in the afternoon did accounts, figured out the third quarter of the year! In the afternoon, toward evening, I see R. busily writing. And in the evening he says (with fatigued eyes), "It has to be finished in time for Saint Cosmas!" He plays me the Prelude, from the orchestral sketch! My emotion lasts long—then he speaks to me about this feature, in the mystery of the Grail, of blood turning into wine, which permits us to turn our gaze refreshed back to earth, whereas the conversion of wine into blood draws us away from the earth. Wonderful mingling in the Prelude of mysticism and chivalry. The D major modulation is for him like the spreading of the tender revelation across the whole world. But in order to impart the spiritual quality of Christ's words, their detachment from all material things, he intends to use a mixture of voices: "A baritone voice, for example, would make it all sound material; it must be neither man nor woman, but neuter in the highest sense of the word." We continue for a long time to talk about Christ, the Gospel account of the day before his death the sublimest thing ever produced by Man, incomparable, divine! He plays me once more the passage in which, as he says, "the transfigured gaze breaks." — With the words *"Es gibt ein Glück, das ohne Reu,"* I fall asleep following these consecrated hours. — R. had relapsed into joking, but was brought back to our theme every time by my tears.

*Thursday, September 27*  "Greetings from Saint Cosmas!" I ink in the page in the nursery. An old and enjoyable occupation, of which I have been deprived for many years. R. lamented the fact that we did not find each other and unite 20 years ago, I observe that it is at any rate a good thing that we did so 13 years ago. — My patron saint brings me a splendid day, we go for a walk, R., Lusch, and I, and enjoy the sun and the sky. Letter writing for us both before supper. In the evening Euripides's *Phoenissae*, whose influence on Goethe and Schiller was immeasurable, R. observes. Then R. plays me the Prelude once again. "I also have some accents for Mademoiselle Condrie, I already have her laughter, for instance." A long time lost in our memories, gladdened by our earlier times together, saddened by the intermingling of fellow suffering. I beg my good patron saint to lay his healing hand on all wounds, for my greatest feelings of happiness always remind me of the sufferings of another. — R. recalls how much we have already achieved together

the obituaries of Ludwig Geyer and Adolph Wagner, which Herr Glasenapp has tracked down with such touching diligence. — 22 years ago I heard the *Tannhäuser* Overture for the first time—my very first encounter with R.'s works for orchestra. My fate sealed by it, betrothal to Hans, and all the sorrow and joy which was our lot!

*Saturday, October 20* Installation of my picture—"Kundry in Klingsor's magic workshop," as R. says. He works on the copy for the printers. I am very worried that his foot ailment prevents his going out of doors, which is such a necessity to him. In the evening the *Interludes* of Cervantes—"*Los habladores*" and "*El rufián viudo.*"

*Sunday, October 21* R. completes his copy. He receives a letter from a theater director in Melbourne, according to which *Lohengrin* last month made its ceremonious entry there, too. — Splendid autumn weather, R. unfortunately unable to enjoy it. In the evening friend Gross, discussion about the periodical; there have been no applications yet for the school.

*Monday, October 22* My father's birthday. — Letter from friend Pohl, reporting that the concert in Baden was a great artistic, but not a financial success. R. gets down to his work again. In the afternoon we walk in the garden, slowly on account of his foot; a young singer stops him, she wants to join the school, and she sings "Elisabeth's Prayer." R. writes several letters, gives Baron Loën permission for *Das Rheingold* without any conditions. In the evening two of Demosthenes's Corinthian speeches and parts of Pfaffe Lamprecht's poem *Alexander*. — (R. dreamed of a large tooth, which he extracted himself.)

*Tuesday, October 23* R. again had a wretched night; abdominal troubles—he reads Darwin (*The Descent of Man*), feels cold. I cannot say how sad it makes me to see him, at the start of his great work, so hindered by bodily ailments. However, he works in the morning. In the afternoon he writes a long letter to Dr. Eiser in Frankfurt, who wrote a detailed report about our friend Nietzsche's state of health. R. says, "He (N.) is more likely to listen to the friendly advice of a medical man than to the medical advice of a friend." In the evening friend Wolzogen reads us the preface to his translation of [Euripides's] *Bacchae*.

*Wednesday, October 24* R. had a bad night, I come up on him reading Darwin! . . . Work in the house; in the afternoon I go for a drive with R., but the weather is dull, and he does not feel well. I recall one of my last drives with Daniel in Berlin at the end of October. Back home, I am soon summoned by R., who does not feel well and wants me near him. "I only hope it is not heart trouble," he says. We walk up and down in the *salon*, the foliage on the trees is faded, the sun sinks palely to rest, my heart is heavy, but I leave R. with spirits restored, he settles down to work by lamplight. "In ink!" I give a lesson. In the evening R. reads to us from Pfaffe Lamprecht's *Alexander*; very little poetry in it, and little art—how much superior the heroic sagas, because in them the poets knew what they were doing! — Concern about Fidi, the longed-for company with other boys has turned out thoroughly vulgar!

*Thursday, October 25* At last a good night for R., and work. I ink in another page which he gave me; he works, tells me afterward that he is seizing every opportunity to conjure up a little musical paradise, as, for example, when Amfortas is carried to the lake. In the afternoon R. goes walking in the garden, while I arrange the rooms for Frau von Wolzogen, who is arriving this evening. Letter from Herr Pollini in Hamburg, he wants *Die Walküre*. R. replies that he will give *Die Walküre* only to directors and managers who intend to perform the whole of the *Ring des Nibelungen*. Arrival of Frau v. W.—the first move to Bayreuth on our account.

*Friday, October 26* R. at least had a tolerable night. — Yesterday afternoon, as he was working in ink, he said to me, "I have had a few good ideas." — In the evening he plays piano duets with Herr Seidl, without much enjoyment.

*Saturday, October 27* R. did not sleep very well, but he works; at lunch he tells us that the ugly distortion of his advocacy of the viola caused him to write to the editor of the *Augsburger Abendzeitung*, telling him not to publish it. In the evening he writes to Councilor Düfflipp, asking when *Siegfried* would be produced in Munich, since he would not be able to withhold it from the other theaters. Then to Herr Fritzsch about the publication of the *Bayreuther Blätter*. — Around midday he played me what he had so far worked out "in ink," unimagined currents of sublimity flow through my soul and soothe away all sorrow and suffering! — In the evening he goes through the 1st act of *Der Holländer* with Herr Seidl; from *Holländer* to *Parsifal*—how long the path and yet how similar the character! — Following the music, R. talks about the influence of the "cosmos," the outside world, on characters who, though basically good, do not perhaps possess the strength to resist it, and who then become quite exceptionally bad, indeed perverse. "Nothing from the outside world is of benefit to such characters!" — As we are saying good night, R. says to me, "We will understand each other till we die!"

*Sunday, October 28* R. had a good night. I go to church with the children. When I recently woke up in concern, wondering whether R. was sleeping, and saw him enjoying some real rest, I expressed my gratitude in prayer and felt how close the godhead had come to my joy. Oh, take every thorn from my heart, take everything which means

"I," the only thing I have to fear! Soften all harshness, break down all desire—this I cry unto thee from the depths! . . . Gladly do I utter this prayer in church. . . . R. tells me before lunch that he had a bad headache, but composed it away! . . . The trees now bear only yellow leaves on their crowns; "The journey home is nigh," the journey into eternity, a golden gleam still resting on the treetops; I reflect on our journey home. Frau Lucca reports on the performance of *Der Fl. Holländer* in Bologna and of *Lohengrin* in Rome, complains of R.'s infrequent letters; he replies humorously that he has not written, because otherwise all he would have been able to do would be to ask her for a half of her great fortune! — The *Musikalische Zeitung* reports some very foolish resolution passed by the W. Society in Berlin; they want to give their support, not *solely* to R.'s ideas, but to art in general! — Read Indian proverbs.

*Monday, October 29*   R. had a tolerable night and works, but when he comes down to lunch he complains bitterly of abdominal pains. — On account of my eyes, I unfortunately have to interrupt my inking in of the penciled sketches, but I begin instead on the translation of *Parsifal* into French, and R. and I have to laugh a lot over the difficulties arising for me from this unyielding and prosaic language. Walk with R. to the neighborhood of Konradsreuth; he talks about the "magnificent, unsurpassed" fugal passage in the finale of Mozart's C Major Symphony, and deplores the way in which it is immediately followed by a banal "boom-boom," which robs the whole thing of style. The walk is pleasant, but afterward R.'s foot is unfortunately very painful. — Herr Gross brings me some news; Baron Perfall writes that the King desires the performance of the *Ring* as soon as possible, and in order to meet this request, Herr Seitz and others from the Munich Court theater will be coming to Bayreuth to make an inventory and take away the things which will be needed in Munich. Friend Feustel writes saying we should stop and consider before handing over any articles in the theater, since that would at once lead to legal action by the creditors, whose claims have been kept at bay only with the greatest difficulty. Herr v. P[erfall] also says that he intends to give a concert in support of the reserve fund! — Herr Porges writes that Prof. Bernays has become active in the W. Society in Munich and has signed his name to the appeal there. — In the evening the 2nd act of *Holländer*, then the scene with Launcelot Gobbo. R. says one always ought to read these things separately, otherwise one does not really get to know them, for every pause, every comma, every period is important. Much merriment, and then much tenderness between us. R. reads Dr. Eiser's work and is pleased with it; it reminds him touchingly of the interest his singers showed; he says he wants to bring them all together again for a banquet next year, for what they had achieved was extraordinary, considering the background from which they come and the conditions they are normally used to—he also thinks of Betz, acknowledging the excellence of much in his interpretation. Various inquiries regarding the school.

*Tuesday, October 30*   R. works, I with the children and doing a little on the translation. Despite November weather R. goes for a little walk and feels somewhat better. He writes to Dr. Eiser about his work, very nicely, in the evening the 3rd act of *Holländer*. Herr Pollini writes to R., accepting R.'s conditions, but he wants to begin with *Die Walküre*; he will give an advance of 16,000 marks, which will be earned by the year '80; up till then 4 percent royalties, and after that 8 percent.

*Wednesday, October 31*   R. works, I do a little bit of inking in, translate, and give the children their lessons. R. settles with Herr Pollini. And so the splendid work has now been given away! R. says again and again that he would like one day to give the world his final word! — However, he still retains his divine sense of humor; as we were talking about arithmetic, and among other things about planimetry, he says, "I know about that, I practiced it throughout 30 years of marriage, but I never really mastered it." In the evening a story by Lope de Vega, uninteresting. Foehn, memories of Tribschen. But R. also recalls that at one time I did not like Kietz's busts, that grieves him, because he loves mine greatly; I also feel sad at having said it, we weep, lament, and embrace. "Oh, dear! I must give up love," says R. "I am like Schmitt, the singing teacher—at my age it is too intense."

*Thursday, November 1*   All Saints' Day. "I do not just love you, I am immersed in you!" R. tells me. — He is able to work. In the afternoon I go with the children to lay a wreath on the grave of our old friend [Dean] Dittmar, recalling as I do all our deceased, Daniel, Blandine, sister Rosalie, R.'s mother, every one of them. R. comes to meet me. In the evening R. reads Sophocles's *Electra* to me; while listening, one ought not to think of Aeschylus's *Choephoroi* and the playing around with grief, arising from the false news of Orestes's death, has an unpleasant effect: "It is unworthy of a great artist," says R., who also calls the tutor's narration "a fine piece of Italian opera"—but the impression is terrifying, and its truthfulness, overcoming all artificiality, quite overpowering. Human beings confront one another with the wild, naïve cruelty of animals and inspire dread and awe.

*Friday, November 2*   Yesterday R. came to meet me as I returned from the cemetery and said he had been considering that in 10 years' time he would be 75, and he was terribly vexed that our happiness was not of longer duration: "You made such a silly mess of things with your first marriage," he told himself—however long it may now last, we cannot make up for that lost time. "I shall love you till I die," he says today in reply to my question. — All Souls' Day! I bid you welcome and linger with you! Compared with this life below, mostly in shadow, how gently you dwell within me! — R. works, in the afternoon some inspiration which he had thought good in the morning sounds garish to him—he closes the lid of the piano to damp it down, finds his way again, and, in order to give me, as I work above with the children, a signal that he is satisfied, plays the charming theme from the coda of the first movement of Mozart's C Major Symphony. In the evening we read Huxley's address on education and find it excellent, apart from his opinion of German universities, which suggests a certain degree of ignorance.

*Saturday, November 3* Indisposition and work. R. also at *his* work! Read Huxley in the evening with great enjoyment. Of the Germans R. says humorously that Moltke made them worth shooting at, but out of uniform they are not worth a shot. Wrote to Herr Strecker telling him our condition for releasing the *Idyll*, i.e., that it should wipe out the debt.

*Sunday, November 4* Translation; great difficulties—the simplest of things cannot be expressed in French. Took the children to the children's theater, *Snow White*. R. comes to fetch us; in the evening some scenes from *Love's Labour's Lost*.

*Monday, November 5* Yesterday R. received a letter from Councilor D. with the news of his resignation: his successor is said to be a devotee of W.'s works. The King has ordered a performance of *Siegfried*, but does not want the Bayreuth decorations, which he says did not please him. Düffl. suggests that friend Feustel visit Baron Perfall in Munich to arrange matters as circumstances permit. — R. writes a very friendly reply, Düfflipp is someone with whom he has had a lot to do over the past 11 years. — Regarding the Russo-Turkish War, R. says that a turn of events is probably imminent. Plevna is reported to be surrounded, and the Turks now appear to be finished in Asia. R.'s foot slightly better.

*Tuesday, November 6* My weak eyes keep me from continuing the translation, as they did the inking in of the pages. R. is also not completely well, he wanted to come to meet me and embarked on a longish walk, and now he again felt pains in his foot! — In the evening went through the first act of *Tannhäuser* with Herr Seidl; R. says he has in mind shortening the new first scene considerably, it weighs the rest down too much, there is a lack of balance, this scene goes beyond the style of *Tannhäuser* as a whole. — I argue in its defense, saying that it casts over the audience the magic spell which causes Tannhäuser's downfall, and thus it makes the 2nd act more understandable; it is also fitting that the magic underworld is different from the simple world

above. "That is what I told myself," R. observes, "but it is not right."
— The problem occupies him greatly.

*Wednesday, November 7*   Worry about R. keeps me awake. Why am I
worried? R. observed to me yesterday how right Calderón was to say
that the worst thing on this earth below was a happy love, for then one
could only be the loser, living in dread rather than hope! . . . Nice
drive in splendid weather to the Waldhütte. In the evening a paper by
our old friend Constantin Frantz about present-day political parties;
very admirable and absorbing.

*Thursday, November 8*   R. dubs me the "district judicial medical
officer," the title of our physician, because I have discovered the right
breakfast diet for him; he works morning and afternoon, in the evening
we continue Constantin Frantz with much interest.

*Friday, November 9*   R. had a curious dream that he was still a conductor in some obscure theater and, owing to the illness of the other
conductor, was faced with the task of having to conduct [Marschner's]
*Der Vampyr* in the morning and *Tannhäuser* in the afternoon; he turned
to Hans, to ask him to take over one of the works, but Hans just
looked at him in astonishment; the dream ended, after a few more
grotesque images, with his being unable to write to me for 6 weeks,
being prevented by all kinds of trivialities and his own desire to write
me a particularly good letter; his fear that all this would make me uneasy woke him up. What again strikes me about this is that the grotesque happenings were, as usual, the same ones that had come into my
mind during the night when I was unable to sleep; I was sleepless
because I was worrying about the sort of night he was having; since he
was sleeping, I thanked God, but was unable for a long time to overcome my worries and was troubled by all sorts of things as I lay awake.
— R. works. Letter from Herr Pollini, who has now acquired the *Ring*
but is unwilling to accept R.'s recommendation that he employ Herr
Brandt and Herr Hoffmann. In the evening quartets played by the
Munich Court musicians; [Opus] 135 by Beethoven; indescribable impression of the adagio, arousing real yearning—these sounds are like a
legacy from the greatest of mortals, a heart's treasure—inexpressible
emotions of release within me! — Before that a Haydn quartet, infused
with masterly intellectual vigor, and then one by Mozart, unfortunately very banal. Only in the adagio is there one page which soothes my
ears like the comforting words of an angel. Mozart's sweet melody in
all its grace, but unfortunately an isolated instance, the work as a whole
insignificant. — During it R. noted a theme which came into his mind,
but afterward it no longer pleased him, or he could do nothing with
it.

*Saturday, November 10*   Herr Peters is inquiring about the *Idyll*, the

Sonata in A-flat Major, and the Overture in C Major. Herr Strecker has not yet replied. — R. talks about his attitude toward the world and how utterly isolated he feels in it, having been so forsaken in connection with his undertaking and now so ignored with regard to his school. He has me and the children, he says, but otherwise nothing. — Terrible news of the sudden death of our nephew Clemens. [*From this point to the middle of November 12, the entries are written in a strange, childish hand; they were evidently dictated to one of Cosima's daughters, presumably Blandine, on the evidence of the reference to "Boni" on November 14.*] R. incapable of work because of it. In the afternoon he and his lawyer formulated for Herr Simson in Berlin his terms for the Court theaters. In the evening the quartet; Opus 135 again, with tempo indications by R., and B-flat Major; at the end, the wonderful Adagio from Haydn's Quartet Opus [*left blank*], R.'s great favorite. The lovely evening gives R. much delight: "What I like best is being with professional musicians, they know how to do things." All kinds of strange rumors about Councilor Düfflipp's resignation; it is said the Linderhof castle is to be rented out.

*Sunday, November 11* R. works a little again; I prevented by a headache from doing anything. Telegram from Fritz Brockhaus saying his mother wishes R. to be present at Clemens's funeral. I take it upon myself to ask the doctor to cable that he has advised R. against the journey. In the evening friend Heckel, who asks for *Die Walküre*, to be presented at Mannheim in the normal repertory; we are surprised by his request; but he at once abandons it.

*Monday, November 12* I admit to R. the responsibility I took upon myself; he thanks me for it. Negotiations with Peters and Strecker regarding *Parsifal* and the *Idyll*. R. works; I prevented by eye trouble from writing this myself. [*From here on continued in Cosima's own handwriting.*] After several days somewhat better. R. in good and cheerful mood, talks of our tomb, how he designed it and how mice and rats have got in: "He who digs a pit sees others fall into it." Much laughter about this. — He takes me for a little walk. In the evening friends Heckel and Fischer; at lunch we were 13 at table, an unpleasant feeling. R. writes to the firm of Gebrüder Hug for his sonata.

*Tuesday, November 13* Still troubled with my eyes. But R. works and says he does not wish to be disturbed. In the afternoon he called me into the *salon* in order to play me what he had just played: the beginning of Gurnemanz's narration, "*In heiliger Nacht neigten sich die Boten*"—it is wonderful! — Shortly after this, Herr v. W[olzogen] tells me that the public prosecutor in Berlin regards it as an insult to compare Bismarck with R., since R. W. has the public reputation of being a megalomaniac! . . . Continued with C. Frantz's paper in the evening. In political theory the constructive part is always the more difficult, for what does not happen can for that very reason not happen, and this produces a deceptive view of the prevailing factors in public affairs.

*Wednesday, November 14*  R. works, I do a little translation with Boni's help, but have to take great care of myself, my eyes are terribly weak. — Continued in the evening with C. Frantz; R. says it costs an effort to concern oneself so closely with the world of appearances, when one's thoughts are in fact more concentrated on the thing-in-itself, but we find our reading very absorbing. —

A letter from Herr Pollini, R. dissatisfied with it, since Pollini wishes to engage Seidl, whom R. recommended to him, only as director of the chorus. — Leipzig is also inquiring again about *Der Ring des Nibelungen*, they say they have heard that Berlin is to do it first, and perhaps R. might now propose different terms, since they no longer have the first rights! . . .

*Thursday, November 15*  R. in cheerful spirits, though dissatisfied, as he says, with a *canon*. We read C. Frantz in the evening; when I ask him what is meant by the *Potenzen* ["powers"], he says most probably the *Popanzen* ["bogeymen"]. Much laughter about this, as also about a sally concerning his barber Schnappauf, who has given a charity concert. [*A sentence containing untranslatable word play omitted.*] — For me, further correspondence with publishers, despite trouble with my eyes.

*Friday, November 16*  R. dreamed about Uncle Liszt, that he came here, embraced us very tenderly, but then said reproachfully to me, "Why, my niece, do you paint your face?" Whereupon I, with great dignity: "I hide neither my youth nor my age, I often look young and often old." — R. works. But at midday a letter from Herr Batz, making renewed demands on behalf of the *Ring* "assistants"! . . . R. very annoyed, I reproach myself for not having intercepted the letter. — Walk with R., the damp, misty weather does not agree with him. But he works, completing yesterday's canon. In the evening *La verdad sospechosa* by Alarcón, with great enjoyment.

*Saturday, November 17*  R. up almost the whole night! His annoyance of yesterday has upset his entire digestion. — He tells me most comically about an absurd dream: he was in a carriage with me, more and more people kept coming, but at last we were alone, then ever-increasing numbers of horned animals advanced on us; one of them very strange, with huge antlers but a body like a bush, I just alarmed, but R. watching—suddenly a large house with a party going on; R., much fêted, is to dance a *galop* down a flight of stairs with Hans's mother, he declares that he is better at waltzes—suddenly great thirst; he cries out, "Georg, Georg, a glass of beer!" No one understands his cry—then a crocodile-like creature comes up to him and cries in a quavery, metallic voice, "You have stolen my *Kox*," whereupon he wakes up. — The news that Clemens died of trichinosis horrifies us! — In the evening R. plays his *"Fantasie"* from the year 1831; very touching! Inner absorption in the example of the great masters, dreamy simplicity—how different the juvenile works of today! —

*Sunday, November 18* The "dwindling Batz" permits a better night. Feustel has returned from Munich, tells us Baron Perfall is offering 1% of the proceeds for the *Ring*; friend Feustel has refused this illusory aid and says legal measures will accordingly be taken at the end of the year. — R. works. — Letter from the firm of Gebrüder Hug, R.'s public threat has had its effect, for they send the copy of the A Major Sonata. In the evening *Hamlet*. R.'s reading is unutterably affecting, he himself nobly sublime, deeply moving both personally and artistically. In the afternoon we went for a walk together in the fields.

*Monday, November 19* The *Idyll* is sent off today; the secret treasure is to become public property—may the pleasure others take in it match the sacrifice I am making! — R. works, we then go for a walk, quite a long one, unfortunately it brings back the pain in his foot. — In the evening he writes to the mayor of Bologna, who had kindly written to inform him that, though there was much opposition at the first performance of *Der Fl. Holländer*, the 2nd was a complete triumph. — In the evening the last three acts of *Hamlet*, during which I felt more clearly than ever before the harmony of the whole work, the rightness of its proportions.

*Tuesday, November 20* R. did not have a very good night, but he works. In the evening he plays me Gurnemanz's narration about the coming of the angels to Titurel. Then we go through the first act of *Parsifal* (in French).

*Wednesday, November 21* R. works; I likewise, with the children. In the evening R. plays "Klingsor's Hermitage" and *"Die Wege, die kein Sünder findet,"* wonderfully beautiful. . . . Concluded *my* first act!

*Thursday, November 22* R. had a very bad night. . . . He works nevertheless, and in the evening plays me "Klingsor's Magic Garden" in Gurnemanz's narration. Evening spent in conversation—assassination attempts everywhere, against the Sultan in Turkey, a planned one in Russia against the Tsar, the same in Prussia by a Pole against the Emperor and Bismarck, others in Spain and in France!

*Friday, November 23* R. again had a very bad night; I should dearly like to ascribe it to the foehn weather, but my concern makes me call the doctor. He does not seem at all alarmed. — R. finishes Gurnemanz's narration; however, at my request he does no more work. In the evening the 1st act of *Henry VI Part I*. Dannreuther writes to say that Hans has once again made an unaccountable attack on English musicians; but my worry about R.'s health makes me impervious to everything else. Thus is one saved by one worry from another! In the evening, first act of *H. VI.*

*Saturday, November 24*    R. had a good night—mine was disturbed by worry! I was awakened from sleep by a dream—I heard R.'s voice asking me, "Have you ever heard that I have got dropsy?" — Much praying and beseeching on my part for the scarcely appreciated pleasure of his good night. — In the evening recently, R. told me about his method of working, and observed that only in old age could one love and work at the same time! In the evening the second and third acts of *Henry VI*; wonderful the scene between Mortimer and his nephew—it is usually omitted in present-day stage performances of the play. R. was married 41 years ago, we play with our wedding rings (I am wearing his, which he wore for 30 years!).

*Sunday, November 25*    To church with the children, heartened by the news that R. slept well. He works and tells me at lunch that he had had an inspiration which would please me: as the esquires repeat the saying about the *"reine Tor"* ["pure fool"], both the arrow and Parsifal make their appearance on the word *"Tor,"* so the saying is not spoken to the end. — He reads in a book by Herr Proelss a description of theater life in Dresden, based on documents (among them a very dismal one by Johanna Wagner); R. writes to the author, explaining one of the documents to him (letter to Herr von Lüttichau). In the evening we finish *Henry VI Part I.* R. does not care much for the scene between Talbot and his son, finds it too monotonous and sentimental.

*Monday, November 26*    R. slept well! He told me recently that I cured him of worry; I thank thee, God, for that! Great joy in the gift of the manuscript of the Sonata in A Major, which Gebrüder Hug have suddenly sent of their own free will. R. plays it, I like it, but R. suddenly has doubts about publishing his youthful works and this A Major Sonata. — We read a scene from *Henry VI Part II.* Arrival of R.'s portrait from the exhibition. A really good, fine day, for R. worked as well; continued with his work for more than an hour past his usual time, we lunched happily at 2:15.

*Tuesday, November 27*    R. slept well again, much excitement about the "conductor's clock" which R. gave me a long time ago and which was stolen from the house during my journey to Italy, unceasing investigations, now a glimmer of hope that it will be found; the police here like those in *Much Ado About Nothing.* — In my merry mood I yesterday wrote much nonsense to Marie D[önhoff], who had written to me again after a long silence. — R. says at lunch that he once again dreamed that during an emergency he had to sing in *Tannhäuser*—we talk about dreams, etc., and, when Frau v. Wolzogen remarks that one cannot control one's dreams, I say I have the feeling that deep inside myself there is a power which rules over everything and can avert disaster, whether dreamed or real, but this power either is lying fallow or, more likely, does not choose to exert itself. R. says that Goethe expressed this feeling so beautifully, and in the Pythian way befitting a poet, in his lines: "The God above my powers enthroned." — [Frau Lucca's] Italian menu card brings us on to the subject of the Italians, and R. tells us what he once replied when Sgambati spoke of the *dolce far niente* of Italian music: "With German musicians, on the other hand, it is a case of laboriously saying nothing — *penible dir' niente.*" — Letter from Herr Tappert—he thinks he has discovered R.'s symphony! . . . And he has a lot of other interesting things to say. Much, much joy over this! — In the evening two acts of *Henry VI*; Gloster's departure and return after the vilifications of the lords strikes R. as one of the most remarkable features in Shakespeare.

*Wednesday, November 28* Alas, a very bad night again! And today is an anniversary for us, which I planned to celebrate! — The music box gives R. pleasure. — He says: "Oh, it is better now than it was then! We shall be the decoy birds, the Timoleons, who make others see what happiness is possible on this earth, but a happiness such as ours will not occur again." — R. shows the box to the children, plays with it at lunch, and delights in the sparkling gems. Then he says to me, "This is how we and our children will one day twinkle in the sky, like these flower gems on this box." — Mild, unpleasant weather, which does not agree with R. He thanks Herr Hug for sending the manuscript. In the evening the 2nd and 3rd acts of *Henry VI Part II,* most moving of tragedies! When one thinks what the hacks do with such works in order to make them "human," like Herr Dingelstedt, or "stage-worthy," like others, one might well ask oneself for what purpose such eternal works have been created! —

*Thursday, November 29* R. again had to get out of bed once, but the night was better than the last, during which he read his *State and Religion* and noticed an example of negligent style: in*creasing* de*crease*— how they elude one despite all care! — Letter from the "Gralsritter-schaft" ["Knighthood of the Holy Grail"] — R. and I go for a walk in spite of the unpleasant, dark day. On our return home he writes the public dedication for the *Idyll.* The happiness we are permitted to enjoy seems to me like a blissful time already past, rather as it will one day appear to our children. My feelings of unworthiness mount daily— dear God, I thank you for your grace, make me worthy of it! 4th and 5th acts of *Henry VI.* — R. still delighted with the music box, which he has named Klingsor.

*Friday, November 30* R. had a good night and he works (kills off the swan!). Unfortunately the weather is still damp and gloomy, so that our walk provides no refreshment beyond the pleasures of our conversation. We thought of Tribschen, our walks there, the hedgehog which we once encountered. We are then pleased with the house when we return home. In the evening the first two acts of *Henry VI Part III.*

*Saturday, December 1* Indisposed, my eyes increasingly weak; but R. had a good night and is able to work. Yesterday morning he sang me the theme from the finale of [Beethoven's] A Minor Quartet and said there is no longer anything in music as beautiful as the modulation and the conclusion of this theme. — In the afternoon he goes for a walk alone, since I am unable to accompany him; he returns home and says that, as it did yesterday, the sky bore a *"faux air von soleil couchant"* ["false air of a setting sun"], as if it were saying, "I could, but I don't want to." In the evening the 3rd and 4th acts of *Henry VI Part III*; R. finds Edward's wooing of Lady Grey a masterpiece of dramatic virtuosity, in spite of its naïveté—we cannot stop talking all evening, indeed even when we are in bed, about the power of this poet: he can express what otherwise remains unsaid. R. says he himself has no bent for historical plays, but, if he had ever written his *Barbarossa*, he would have cast it in the light, rhyming verse of the literature of that time, in order to introduce a popular element into it. But we are now too remote from these subjects, he says; Shakespeare was still bound by tradition to his.

*Sunday, December 2* R. tells me he dreamed of having announced a concert in which he was to sing ballades by Loewe and play Beethoven's A-flat Major Sonata, but when the time came to begin, he felt uneasy and sent for Anton Rubinstein, who was among those present, and asked him to play in his place; he himself went to a restaurant to refresh himself, and there (it was in Zurich) Baumgartner told him of Rubinstein's tremendous success. R. then wanted to sing, but Baumgartner told him the people were already leaving, quite satisfied with the recital, but somewhat offended at R., who was annoyed about not having given his recital. — R. works, and after lunch he says, "I am writing *Parsifal* only for my wife—if I had to depend on the German spirit, I should have nothing more to say." After the 4th act of *Henry VI* he says to me, "I still intend to write my music of mourning for the fallen, but there won't be any apotheosis at the end, you can be sure of that." — When he returns from his walk today he says, "For the sake of the house I shall end my mourning music with the buzzings of *A Midsummer Night's Dream*—those are the chuckling Jews." — Worry about Fidi: we have tried to find boys for him to play with, but it has brought us nothing but coarseness, vulgarity, mean idleness, quite horrifying. In the evening the children play *Cinderella* for us, and Fidi plays one of the ugly sisters very amusingly. After this very funny comedy we conclude the tragedy, our admiration and emotion increasing all the time. Each newly introduced character alive and completely individual, the conversation between Warwick and Gloster incredible in its humor. Yesterday R. remarked particularly what a tragic effect is produced when the impostor's wife cries out in the 1st act of *Part II,* "We did it for pure need." A horrifying excuse, which goes unheeded even by the noble Gloster; the people, rendered quite stupid by this contempt and unable in consequence to listen to the good and high-minded Henry, finds its brutal expression in the figure of Jack Cade. The nobles show no trace of feeling, only a magnanimous interpretation of Fate in relation to themselves. We continue for a long time to talk about the poet, who sees, feels, and describes absolutely everything, without ever giving a sign of his own feelings. We think of friend Nietzsche, who rebelled against Sh[akespeare]: "He always demands a certain kind of form," says R., "and this is a malformation of sublimity and revelation." And so we take leave of the work which has provided us with a complete picture of the dreadfulness of life. If only I could describe how fine, great, sublime in expression, sound, and gesture R. appeared as he was reading it! How much I enjoy the privilege of perceiving and watching him like this all by myself, yet I would still like to let the whole world share it! I now feel as if we were once more living our Tribschen life—once more we have turned our backs on everything, R. is working, the children flourishing, and I forget everything in contemplating his kindness and his love!

*Monday, December 3* At last some sunshine! R. slept well and works; we lunch alone together upstairs, since I am not able to move about much and he does not like eating without me. In the afternoon he goes with Fidi to see friend Feustel and discuss his general and personal (deficit) position; they agree to ask the King for 10% of the proceeds for the *Ring* to pay off the deficit. In the evening R. sends for Fidi's teacher, in order to discuss with him the boy's education, but his horizon does not extend beyond the limits of the teachers' training college. Afterward, as we are discussing the boy's education between ourselves, R. says: "God, to send a boy out into such an evil world! And it is growing steadily worse; what should we bring him up to be? Maybe an African explorer!" . . . At which we laugh heartily.

*Tuesday, December 4* R. had a tolerable night and he works. But school and periodical ("*Schule und Schournal,*" as in fun he alliteratively says) are causing him difficulties; he would most prefer not to start anything new outside, and the enrollments are so few that it seems almost absurd not to turn down the half-dozen people concerned. However, the presence here of H. v. W[olzogen], who is otherwise of much value to us, obliges R. to find some activity for him. — And so the periodical! — The idea of addressing any more words to the public is distasteful to R., and my only desire is that he have tranquillity in order to create. A curious situation. In the evening R. and I laugh heartily about it, in spite of the worry it causes us.

*Wednesday, December 5* R. works. Visit from our friend Pohl, to whom we announce the abandonment of the school. Main activity of our friends is now to be the organization of the Patrons' Society and, through this and on behalf of this, the publication of the periodical; the ultimate aim of the Society the performance of *Parsifal*. I settle all this with Herr v. W. and report on it to R., who is very satisfied and says he will give me a power of attorney, so I can do just as I wish! Merriment. So now, I hope, enough has been done to insure that everything that might hinder him in his creative work has been removed from his path. — R. tells me he has concocted a fine *mélange* for the esquires as they remove the dead swan: Amfortas's theme, Herzeleide's theme, and the swan motive from *Lohengrin*.

*Thursday, December 6* Work, I am able to do some translation; R. had a tolerable night, too. In the afternoon I visit Herr Feustel, and have then, unfortunately, to inform R. that he is very surprised by the latest decisions. R. very upset by this, and in consequence unwell! In the evening we take up Dozy's history of the Arabs, which R. wants to read again.

*Friday, December 7* R. had a very wretched night, and I wonder to myself how I can keep things from him, so that he can live solely for what really matters to him. — The mild, dull weather also does not agree with him. Yesterday I felt I had to tell him about my visit to Herr Feustel, but now I think I should have kept silent, let come what may, rather than torment him. But the few people who have enrolled must indeed be told not to come, and friend Feustel did not wish to do this without first consulting R. — This pains me unutterably; the only point of my existence is to protect him, to shield and take care of him! He does manage to work a little in the morning. But in the evening the proofs of *Parsifal* cause him great annoyance; the print is too large and the appearance of the whole is not pleasing. On top of that, Herr Seidl made such a bad copy that R.'s work has been doubled. — To Herr Feustel in the evening to meet the mayor. As we are driving there, R. recalls various times when he went out like this in the evenings, and he says, "There are no forms and faces hovering near me, nothing lives in my memory, I look back into the mists of the past, everything before our time together is dead inside me." — Herr Feustel and the mayor comply with R.'s wishes, though it is decided only that the school will not open *for the time being*. — We return home in cheerful spirits, and

R. thanks me! Oh, God! — When he said to me today, "I am hard to put up with—one has to unload one's vexation and worry on the person one loves best," I did not know what to say: the only thing I find hard is to see him suffering!

*Saturday, December 8* R. did not sleep much, but at least he had no attacks of cramps and did not get up. He spends the morning correcting the *Parsifal* proofs and will demand from Dr. Strecker a different type-face from the "elegant roman" in which, as we note with laughter, he has announced the poem. In the evening we continue with Dozy's history of the Arabs.

*Sunday, December 9* R. got up once during the night, but he says he did not sleep too badly; worry kept me awake. — Christmas errands. R. works. In the afternoon a short walk. Grief on my return home—R. tells me that the *Idyll* has already been performed in Mainz, and he reads me the stupid words which accompanied the performance (that in it Fidi's joys are depicted!). — I knew when I made the sacrifice just what a sacrifice it really was, yet curiously enough this review affects me as if I had never foreseen it! — I could not be more estranged from the world than I am, never less involved in its joys, less sympathetic toward its doings, yet at this very time I am obliged to yield to it my most cherished possession! I have the feeling, since I was obliged to yield it up, that I have proved unworthy of it—and I hasten to my room, there to weep and lament and once again accept within myself that my hard lot is just, that what I cherish must be yielded up as too sublime for me. Why should I alone be made happy, I alone be blissful? . . . I see all the tears I have shed, hear the sound of all my lamentations, and my complaining relapses into silence, my tears dry up. To you alone I confide them, my Fidi—when you read these lines after I am dead, hear these sobs after I have vanished from sight, think of your mother—how she loved you and sadly sent you outside into a world from which she was already severed in her lifetime! In the evening with the Wolzogens and the entire "flock" to see *Die Teufelsmühle*, an old memory of R.'s—but the performance worse than bad.

*Monday, December 10* Anniversary of Daniel's death. — Herr Eckert, the conductor, wrote yesterday to say that Herr v. Hülsen wants *Die Walküre* and would also like to make some cuts in the 2nd act. R. decides not to hurry with his reply. The corrected proofs of *Parsifal* arrive, and the whole thing looks much better than it did, so that R. decides to put up after all with the "elegant roman type." We continue with Dozy in the evening. Fine winter weather, R. walks around the house in the evening—"like Gloster," he says—and returns saying that he has never composed an "opera" under such friendly auspices, with all the others there had been trials and tribulations. "This should bring us in a lot of money!" he adds with a laugh. The memory of Daniel's death arouses violent anger in him against the people whom he sees, not without justice, as having been responsible for his death; he deplores the fact that one still remains on good terms with these people; feelings are weak, he says.

*Tuesday, December 11*   R. works; during the night we laughed heartily because yesterday, in his agitation, he went downstairs instead of going to bed; becoming worried after a while, I left my bed and crept downstairs after him; he was sitting in the *salon,* asleep, the lamp alight, Schlegel's *Greeks and Romans* at his side. Much relieved, I waited until he woke up, which soon happened, and the situation caused us much laughter. The distichs quoted in the book had sent him to sleep. The rest of the night passed peacefully. He does a little work. I start to translate the 3rd act. In the evening the history of the Arabs and Hoffmann's story about Daucus Carota.

*Wednesday, December 12*   R. works, he spent quite a tolerable night, though he had to get up once. A conversation about the events in Munich, his departure at the King's request, causes him to remark, "It was better it should have happened like that." I: "Yes, it left me with an unconquerable faith." R.: "Faith in what is good and genuine; that stands firm, nothing can affect it, it is there, whatever else happens." — Walk with R. in the palace gardens, during which he guides me along the most wonderful paths, so that we walk for three quarters of an hour in this small space without ever using the same path twice. — A letter from Herr Eiser in the evening arouses unpleasant feelings—the concert in Frankfurt ended with a deficit of 3,000 marks; yet people will persist in dallying with these useless activities, which gives them a kind of importance. — We finish [Hoffmann's] tale, which we find very entertaining.

*Thursday, December 13*   R. dissatisfied with his morning's work, intends to discard it. Ill humor in consequence. Dr. Eiser's reply to Herr von W.'s invitation to merge the local Societies into the general Patrons' Society is also not calculated to raise our spirits. — In the evening Herr v. W. reads us an excellent article he has written about Heinrich Kleist, in which he indicates quite outstandingly the peculiar nature of the poet's genius and the special qualities of both *Die Hermannsschlacht* and *Der Prinz von Homburg.* — After that R. plays us some passages from *Die Meistersinger*—splendid work!

*Friday, December 14*   R. says he has now "put right" yesterday's errors—one must be careful, he observes, not to let oneself be led astray by the melodies—that happened to him yesterday, and it had put him right out of the mood. The weather still dull; but here in our home the sunshine of love and creative work. R. plays and sings to me

Parsifal's replies to Gurnemanz! In the evening he gives Herr v. W. a theme to study and work out—"the contrast between rhetoric and German style." He says it can be traced right through the development of the arts, particularly that of music, this rhetoric which is still a principal ingredient of French teaching and the educational methods of the Jesuits. The principle derived from a false understanding of the Greeks, and it dominates our whole culture, its antithesis being the German style. We talk a lot about this, finding many examples. Then R. plays passages from *Die Meistersinger*, to our great bliss. — The *Idyll* is now being reeled off everywhere; to bear this trial cheerfully takes all my efforts! We are now beginning a new Tribschen life, and only R.'s indisposition can cloud it. All that seemed hard in my life has been transformed into blessings, and Fate has graciously guided me by force wherever I resisted; and so, unworthy in every way, thoroughly undeserving, here I stand, loved and protected by God, in grateful astonishment, full of an unshakeable faith, moved to the depths of my soul by this mission which has been vouchsafed me, the privilege of serving the highest—I, unworthy as I am! . . . Thus I know only devotion and work and deep humility in my sacred happiness!

*Saturday, December 15* R. had a good night, and he works; I with the children. Short walk with R. in the palace gardens, since the damp air does not agree with him. I remain outside in the garden and, after a few turns in the gloom, am suddenly bathed in light: the moon is shining brightly down on me, and a star sends me a mild and friendly greeting—it is as if they have understood my thoughts and are blessing me, the one with courage, the other with comfort! With a full heart I go indoors, to find R. dissatisfied with an advertisement announcing "a sketch for a sonata"—he would like to see the work described as "a fantasy for an album," thus explaining its "elegant triviality"; altogether he is displeased that it should have been published without his being sent a proof. In the evening the history of the Arabs again, and some passages from *Die Msinger*.

*Sunday, December 16* Church and snow! R. works, he has at last brought Kundry into the bushes, he tells me at lunch. In the evening we take delight in the house and the hall (lit from above); as we separate, he to his work and I to some reading with the children, I remark how hard it is to have to part. He replies: "But being together, though not side by side, is just as nice. When we are side by side, we also talk about other things, but when we are separated, we can be wholly together in spirit—while working, I would be unable to speak to you, and yet I am wholly with you." — Herr v. W. reads me his very fine essays on the *Ring des Nibelungen* and on Christianity. In the evening the history of the Arabs and some music from the *Pastoral* and the Ninth Symphonies,

R. plays. Before supper he shows me what he has already worked on in ink, the shining men of *Parsifal*! . . . At table his whole countenance radiates genius and goodness! He told me recently that his vehemence had been given him to compensate for his softness. He shrank away, to the point of cowardice, from saying harsh things to anybody. And it is true, people might consider him to be completely ungenuine, for he does not like telling people what he thinks of them, and for that reason his only defense lies in seclusion. Beethoven's birthday!

*Monday, December 17*   "If you say you are happy, then I say that you have made me exuberant." — But unfortunately he is again not quite well today. He works nevertheless. In the afternoon he goes to the tailor's to see about a Christmas suit for Fidi. — He has a mind not to reply to the conductor Eckert at all. — Many thoughts come my way, things said to me under the influence of all kinds of situations, feelings, and occasions. I should like to write them all down for the children. — Over coffee R. spoke to Herr v. W. about what he said in his essays concerning the disconsolate metaphysics of Schopenhauer: "What greater consolation can there be than to tell people that this existence is a trivial one? We can then feel inside ourselves hope for another existence, which we cannot in any way visualize and about which nothing can be said, but the feeling alone enables us to enjoy it." He also says that W[olzogen] interprets Faust from too Christian a viewpoint, there is no love in Faust, love comes from above, at the end, and it is to Goethe's eternal credit that he concluded his work thus. In Faust himself there is nothing but restless striving. — In the evening the history of the Arabs. — Much amusement over Fidi, who sings a sort of Turkish music in his sleep.

*Tuesday, December 18*   R. dreamed that I was embittered, estranged from him, I dreamed of a fight between swans and dogs, in which R., going to the help of Rus, was dragged into the water, but emerged again from it at once. — R. works and plays me Kundry's "withdrawal to the bushes" and the subsequent words of Gurnemanz. It is utterly splendid, and when I manifest my delight in it to him, he says, "Yes, one must be good to me, then everything is all right." "Am I worthy of being good to you?" "Yes, beyond all bounds you are, and in you I know what that means, for you are someone who makes an impression." Laughter. In the afternoon he goes out, and afterward tells me that in the palace gardens he saw a man beating the snow regularly with his stick; he kept out of his way, having no desire to be hit on the head and murdered by a lunatic. We laugh over this fear. [*Written across the margin of this whole page:* "News of the capitulation of Plevna on very honorable terms for Osman Pasha."] He corrects the "album sonata." In the evening the history of the Arabs, then two preludes from [Bach's]

*48 Preludes and Fugues,* played very movingly by R.; of the one in [*key left blank in text*] he says: "That gave me my direction. It is incredible how many things in music passed me by without leaving any impression, but that determined me. It is infinite! No one else has ever done anything like it!" — Weber's birthday!

*Wednesday, December 19*   R. says he needs nobody, he has everything he needs for his happiness, everything, he wants only to enjoy it in peace. — He works. Arrival of a large Gloucester cheese from Herr Schlesinger, which gives R. great pleasure. In the evening we hear from London of the dispatch of another cheese—Stilton—which makes us laugh. — R. was once again followed by an individual who inspired no great feeling of trust in him. He said: "I wouldn't have offered him a pinch of snuff from my box." Sorrow over Fidi, who, quite contrary to his usual habit, does not share something we gave him with his sisters.

*Thursday, December 20*   R. does not feel very well, he tries to work but is not satisfied with what he does. He does not go out, but he has a good appetite in the evening; he laughs over it and says: "If you knew what is bothering me! It is a rhythmical battle. This morning I suddenly understood none of my things." In the evening read the history of the Arabs. Early to bed. — I struggle with feelings of alarm, which always assail me when R. is not quite well. — We joke a lot about MacMahon, who declares amid tears that people wish to take away his honor, which he would sacrifice for the well-being of his country! —

*Friday, December 21*   Viennese artists are planning a Germanic procession, and they ask R. in extravagant phrases to compose the music for it! How very curious, the disparity between devotion of this kind and what really inspires R.'s spirit! . . . Took care of Fidi's Christmas with R. R. has survived his rhythmical battle and tells me when he comes from his work, "Today I have set a philosophical precept to music: 'Hence space becomes time.' " — He says he is now about to start on something in which "bits of dramatic nonsense" will be of no help to him! — In the evening the history of the Arabs, in which I am put off both by Herr Dozy's view of the Goths and also by Count Baudissin's negligent translation. "None of these people know our language," says R. "They haven't studied Grimm, and are still basing themselves on Lessing. Good God, whether '*für*' or '*vor*'—how vivid Grimm makes it all!"

*Saturday, December 22*   Arrival of the copies of the *Parsifal* text; R. works, is satisfied with a "middle voice" he wrote today. We go out together, once more to the tailor's, then to the palace gardens. In the evening the history of the Arabs and an interlude from Rapp's collection.

*Sunday, December 23* Decorating the tree; R. works and is feeling tolerably well. Unfortunately the first reactions to *Parsifal* to reach us have to be a very silly and sprawling letter and a review in the *Börsen-courier*! . . . But despite these R. works in the afternoon. — In the evening he reads the children a very pretty and moving story from the *Fl[iegende] Blätter*, called "The Yellowhammer." Then, in the middle of a general conversation, he picks up a volume of Goethe and points significantly to the words "But nothing could compare with their contentment . . ." which have echoed so profoundly throughout our life together. . . . A moment of deep emotion, enjoyed in silence! — Continued with the history of the Arabs, while reading the stories about the martyrs R. exclaims to me, "That would have been a time for you—you wouldn't have stayed two days alive!"

*Monday, December 24* R. dreamed of a friendly association with Lachner, who, in a performance of *Fidelio*, cut out the Allegro in the Overture. "This might have a deeper significance," R. thought to himself, "since the Overture does not really fit the work." But when he discovered that L. had inserted a chorus of his own (reapers or something of that sort) into the beginning, he lost patience. Then he found himself in a hall full of ancient busts, but they were talking, and it seemed that one of them was [Wilhelmine] Schröder-Devrient, whereupon R. said to himself, "I would not like to dream that I kissed her, for it is not good to kiss dead people in dreams." — R. does some work; I occupied all day long by the *Christkind*. At last, at about 6 o'clock, I come into the *salon* and am greeted with a song, "Welcome, dear Christ!" When he came home and saw the house and "all its joys," it had occurred to R. that Christ was not only a "bringer of salvation," but a "bringer of joy" as well! Under Lulu's supervision the children learned the words at once and sang them very nicely. R. had built up a splendid pile for me, including the "manuscript," inscribed "from the one who loves you" (he wrote "*ript*"—Loldi's word for "*liebt*"—to rhyme with "*Manuskript*"!); he says, "One must be able to joke about the sublimest of things"—that is a sign of happiness! And a thousand other things, all sought out with kindness and loving care. [*Attached to this page a water-color drawing with the inscription:* "Japanese négligé given to me by Richard, Christmas 1877."] All this had led to a long correspondence between him and Judith, during which it had unfortunately become clear to him that even the best of French people cannot overcome certain limitations! For instance, Judith cannot believe that it is impossible to translate *Parsifal* into French! But of course they do not know *the other thing*! — Splendid evening, the children bubbling over, memories of Italy, Eva sings "The Olive Boy of Sorrento." Everything merry, joyful, sublime, tears of

Lessing and the Simrock set of folk tales: Gotthold Ephraim Lessing (1729–1781), the great German writer, dramatist, and critic, best known in English for his work on aesthetics, *Laocoön*, and his plays *Minna von Barnhelm* and *Nathan der Weise* (*Nathan the Wise*). Karl Simrock (1802–76) brought out his *Deutsche Volksbücher* (*German Folk Books*) in several volumes between 1839 and 1843. • His second visit to London: Wagner was engaged by the Philharmonic Society to conduct eight concerts in London between March and June 1855, and during one of them was presented to Queen Victoria.

JANUARY 14
• The *Lohengrin* "Battle Song": presumably the king's address and chorus at the beginning of Act III, Scene 3. • Kos: a pinscher dog, a present to Cosima from Hans von Bülow in 1866. • Hebbel: Wagner got to know the dramatist Friedrich Hebbel (1813–63) during his stay in Vienna. • Nestroy: Johann Nepomuk Nestroy (1801–62), the great actor-dramatist of the Viennese popular theater (the *Volkstheater*). • His niece Ottilie in Dresden: daughter of Wagner's sister Luise Brockhaus. • Letter from Milan (his publisher): Francesco Lucca (1802–72), whose wife Giovanna was also active in the business, which was taken over by Ricordi in 1888.

JANUARY 15
• The failure of our great undertaking: this probably refers to Hans von Bülow's abortive attempt in the late 1850s to write an opera on the subject of Merlin, for which Cosima prepared a libretto with the help of Ernst Dohm, the editor of *Kladderadatsch*. • *"Ein' feste Burg ist unser Gott"*: the hymn by Martin Luther (*Hymns Ancient and Modern*, no. 378, "Rejoice today with one accord"). • *"Alles Vergängliche ist nur ein Gleichnis"*: from Goethe's *Faust*, Part Two.

JANUARY 16
• Mitterwurzer: Anton Mitterwurzer (1818–76), baritone singer at the Dresden opera, much respected by Wagner; he sang Wolfram in the first performance of *Tannhäuser*, 1845, and Kurwenal in the first performance of *Tristan und Isolde*, 1865. • The King: Ludwig II of Bavaria (1845–86), ascended the throne in 1864, at the age of eighteen, on the death of his father, Maximilian II; a devotee of Wagner's music since his boyhood, he read in 1863 the preface to the published text of *Der Ring des Nibelungen*, in which Wagner appealed for the patronage of a prince to enable him to complete and produce the work, and vowed to undertake this task when he became king. When that happened a year later, he immediately sent for Wagner. Though most of their plans for Munich came to nothing and Wagner retired to Switzerland, the king continued to support him financially and to correspond with him, though they did not meet personally in the period between the first performance of *Die Meistersinger* in Munich in 1868 and the opening of the festival theater in Bayreuth in 1876. The handsome young king was shy by nature and did not enjoy his monarchical duties; many of his psychological difficulties were no doubt related to his homosexuality. Their correspondence, edited by Otto Strobel, was published in 5 vols. between 1936 and 1939. • The painter Lenbach: Franz von Lenbach (1836–1904), the most successful German portrait painter of his time, came to live in Munich in 1868 and became a friend of Cosima, whose portrait he painted. • Claire: Claire Christine, a daughter of Cosima's mother by her husband, Count Charles d'Agoult, before the liaison with Liszt, was born in 1830 and married Count Guy de Charnacé in 1847; they lived in Versailles; Claire wrote literary works under the pseudonym de Sault. • Karl Ritter (1830–91): son of Julie Ritter, who supported Wagner financially while he was writing the *Ring* in the early years of exile in Zurich; he enjoyed a close friendship with Wagner during those years, when Wagner tried to help the young man in his musical career; Ritter visited

Schopenhauer (1788–1860) in 1855 and talked to him about Wagner; Wagner himself never met the philosopher he so much revered. • Letters to his wife: i.e., to Minna, née Planer, whom Wagner married in 1836 in Königsberg; born September 5, 1809, she was an actress before her marriage; she died on January 25, 1866, in Dresden. • Schiller's poems: *"Worte des Wahns"* and *"Das Glück."*

JANUARY 17

• Daniel: Daniel Liszt (1839–59), Cosima's only brother and youngest child of Liszt and Countess d'Agoult, died in the home of Hans von Bülow in Berlin.

JANUARY 18

• Götz or Egmont: the main characters of Goethe's plays *Götz von Berlichingen* and *Egmont*; Georg is Götz's henchman and Klärchen is Egmont's mistress.

JANUARY 19

• Bismarck, Countess Bismarck: Count Otto von Bismarck (1815–98), the German statesman, married Johanna von Puttkamer (1824–94) in 1847; prime minister of Prussia from 1862, he became chancellor when the states of northern Germany were formed into the North German Confederacy in 1867; Wagner, who had previously been critical of Bismarck, turned into a supporter in 1866, after Prussia's defeat of Austria at the battle of Königgrätz. • *German Art and German Politics*: Wagner wrote his *Deutsche Kunst und Deutsche Politik* for the *Süddeutsche Presse*, where it appeared from October to December 1867; King Ludwig's veto on it before it reached its end led directly to Wagner's leaving Munich and quarreling with Fröbel; he published the essay in pamphlet form in 1868 (publisher, J. J. Weber, Leipzig). • Loewe's ballades: Karl Loewe (1796–1869) composed some 150 ballades, which are dramatic narrative poems set for solo voice and piano accompaniment. • *Henry VI*: by Shakespeare; A. W. Schlegel (1767–1845) translated 17 of Shakespeare's plays into German between 1798 and 1810, and his work on them was continued by J. L. Tieck (1773–1853); their translations are still in regular use.

JANUARY 20

• Preller's illustrations to the *Odyssey*: Friedrich Preller the elder (1804–78). • Esser, the musical director in Vienna: Heinrich Esser (1818–72), conductor at the Court opera in Vienna 1857–69. • Dingelstedt: Franz von Dingelstedt (1814–81) was director successively of the Court theaters in Munich (from 1851), Weimar (from 1857), and Vienna (from 1867); though not basically unsympathetic to Wagner's work, he crossed swords with the composer several times on financial terms; Cosima might have had an extra reason to think ill of him, since it was apparent differences with him over the production of Cornelius's opera *Der Barbier von Bagdad* in 1858 that led Liszt to give up his position as musical director in Weimar. • Goethe's *Faust*: presumably Wagner was thinking here of Part One of the play, which the author did not divide into acts in the usual way; though the more philosophical Part Two of the play is divided into five acts, it was not intended primarily for stage presentation. • Schiller's poem "The Fight with the Dragon" (*"Der Kampf mit dem Drachen"*).

JANUARY 21

• The Lessing biography: *G. E. Lessing, sein Leben und seine Schriften* (*G. E. Lessing: His Life and Works*) by Adolf Stahr, published in 2 vols. in 1859; for Stahr, see note for June 10, 1870. • Kasperl: roughly the equivalent of Punch in the puppet theater.

JANUARY 22

• Our nephew Clemens: Clemens Brockhaus (1837–77), theologian, a son of Wagner's sister Ottilie. • Pasdeloup: Jules Etienne Pasdeloup (1819–87), French conductor and founder of the very successful Concerts Populaires (Popular Concerts) in Paris; though he was a fanatical admirer of Wagner's works and played a number of excerpts from them at his concerts despite the audience's hostility, the composer always treated him with some reserve; director of the Théâtre Lyrique in Paris from 1868, he gave *Rienzi* (1842) its first performance in France there in 1869.

JANUARY 23

•Weber (the publisher): Johann Jacob Weber (1803–89) founded his publishing house, J. J. Weber, in Leipzig in 1834. • Mme Laussot: Jessie Laussot (born c.1829) was English by birth (née Taylor) and was married to a French businessman in Bordeaux, Eugène Laussot, at the time of her love affair with Wagner in 1850; after her divorce from Laussot, she married the German historian Karl Hillebrand, with whom she lived in Florence.

JANUARY 24

•Dr. Lang: Dr. Julius Lang, editor of the periodical *Blätter für die bildenden Künste* (*Fine Arts*). • R.'s passion for silk materials: Wagner liked to dress himself in fine, soft fabrics when he was working. • The King of Saxony: this was not the king (Friedrich August II) who issued a warrant for Wagner's arrest after the Dresden uprising of 1849, but his brother, Johann, who succeeded to the throne in 1854; the pardon, reluctantly granted to Wagner in 1862, did not mean, however, that he was personally forgiven; hence King Johann's apparent delight in *Die Meistersinger* in Dresden was a noteworthy event. • *Jesus von Nazareth*: synopsis for a drama made by Wagner in 1849, depicting Jesus Christ as a propagator of social revolutionary ideas. • Princess Wittgenstein: Carolyne, Princess Sayn-Wittgenstein (1819–87), daughter of a Polish landowner (née Ivanovna); married Prince Wittgenstein, a Russian landowner and Court official, at the age of seventeen and bore him a daughter, but the marriage was unhappy. Liszt met her while on a tour to Russia in 1847, and they settled in Weimar, but were unable to marry because of opposition from both the Tsar of Russia and the Pope; she went to Rome in 1860, but from there she continued to exercise a possessive influence on Liszt. Her relations with Wagner were cordial at first, but became increasingly hostile; Cosima had particular reason to dislike her, for her possessiveness toward Liszt and jealousy of Countess d'Agoult did much to sour the childhood of Blandine, Cosima, and Daniel in Paris. • Ludwig Schnorr von Carolsfeld (1836–65): Wagner's ideal *Heldentenor*, he sang at the Dresden opera from 1860 until his death, and was chosen by Wagner to sing Tristan in the first performance of *Tristan und Isolde* in Munich in 1865. His death on July 21 of that year was long thought to have been due to the strain of singing this role, but it seems more likely that he caught cold during it, and this led to a fatal illness; Wagner considered his premature death one of the greatest catastrophes of his own life. Cosima's quotation is taken from Wagner's *Erinnerungen an Schnorr von Carolsfeld* (*Reminiscences of S. v. C.*), a moving tribute to the singer written shortly after his death; in it Wagner described his feelings regarding Schnorr's performance in Munich as Tristan: "I came to feel it a crime to think of this deed as something which should be performed repeatedly in an operatic repertory, and at the fourth performance, after Tristan's curse on love, I felt constrained to declare quite definitely to all around me that this would be the final performance of *Tristan*; I would allow no more."

JANUARY 25

•Al[exander] Müller (1808–63): music teacher and chorus master in Zurich; Wagner lived in his house from July to September 1849. • Vreneli: Wagner's housekeeper, Verena Stocker (née Weidmann), the wife of Jakob Stocker, in Wagner's service from 1859; she died in 1906.

JANUARY 26

• The visit "of his wife to Versailles": i.e., to visit her stepsister, Claire, who lived

there. • To stay in Genoa: during their tour of Italy in September of the previous
year. • Pastor Brockhaus: Clemens Brockhaus, Wagner's nephew; see note for
January 22, 1869.
JANUARY 27
• "Robbers' Park": Der Räuberpark, part of the grounds surrounding Tribschen, a
name invented by the children. • Devrient's book about Mendelssohn: Eduard
Devrient (1801–77), German stage and theater director, with whom Wagner fell
out when the projected first performance of *Tristan und Isolde* in Karlsruhe in 1859
failed to materialize; his book, *Meine Erinnerungen an Felix Mendelssohn-Bartholdy und
seine Briefe an mich* (*My Reminiscences of F. M.-B. and His Letters to Me*), was published
in Leipzig in 1869.
JANUARY 29
• The scene in which Sachs tries the shoe on Eva: *Die Meistersinger,* Act III, Scene
1. • *Augsburger Allgemeine Zeitung:* founded in Stuttgart in 1798, the newspaper
moved to Augsburg in Bavaria in 1810, there becoming one of the leading newspapers in Europe; its official title after 1810 was simply *Allgemeine Zeitung,* but
since it is almost invariably referred to (by Cosima as well as others) as *A.A.Z.,*
the "*Augsburger*" is here retained. • Rietz, the conductor: Julius Rietz (1812–77),
composer and, from 1860, conductor in Dresden.
JANUARY 30
• His father Geyer: Ludwig Geyer (1778–1821) was an actor, dramatist, and portrait painter; he married Wagner's mother on August 28, 1814, fifteen months after
Wagner's birth, and was thus the only "father" he knew; in his autobiography
Wagner relates with gratitude that Geyer told his wife on his deathbed that he
hoped to "make something" of young Richard, then only eight years old. • His
mother: Wagner was very attached to his mother (1778–1848), who, widowed
twice by the time she was forty-three, brought up her large family with great
practical and domestic efficiency; her youngest son inherited from her both her
small stature and her energy; though poorly educated, she possessed, as he once
said, "extreme intellectual sensibility." The probability that she was not in fact the
true daughter of Johann Paetz, the baker of Weissenfels, but that of Prince Constantin of Weimar, is discussed at length in vol. 2 of Ernest Newman's biography
of the composer. For family relationships see also the introduction. • A councilor
Jeorgie: correctly, Kriegsrat Georgi, a friend of Ludwig Geyer.
JANUARY 31
• Goethe's correspondence with Knebel: Karl Ludwig von Knebel (1744–1834),
translator and master of the household to Prince Constantin of Weimar.
FEBRUARY 1
• The old Cologne School: the reference here is to Schopenhauer's discussion of the
painters Jan van Eyck and Hans Memling in section 234 of his *Paralipomena.*
FEBRUARY 2
• If Frau W[esendonck] had conducted herself well then: Mathilde Wesendonck
(1828–1902) and her husband, Otto (1815–96), both Germans from the Rhineland,
settled in Zurich, where Wagner got to know them in 1852; Otto, a prosperous
businessman, built a villa for his family on the outskirts of Zurich and adapted a
little summerhouse on the grounds (Das Asyl) for Wagner's use. Wagner's love
affair with Mathilde, reflected both in the first act of *Die Walküre* (Siegmund and
Sieglinde) and in *Tristan und Isolde,* aroused the jealousy of Wagner's first wife,
Minna; Wagner gave up Das Asyl and took to traveling; it is this situation to which
Cosima is here referring.

FEBRUARY 4
• The first letters R. wrote me (from Starnberg): in 1864; the accompanying poem, entitled "*An Dich!*" ("To Thee!"), is dated October 1, 1864.

FEBRUARY 5
• "Forging Songs": sung by Siegfried in Act I of *Siegfried.* "Now Begin" ("*Fanget an!*"): Walther's trial song in Act I of *Die Meistersinger.* Schnorr von Carolsfeld sang the songs mentioned by Cosima at a private concert for King Ludwig given on July. 12, 1865, in the Munich Residenztheater, with Wagner himself conducting.

FEBRUARY 6
• Hiller: Ferdinand Hiller (1811–85), composer and conductor, active in Leipzig, Dresden, Düsseldorf, and, from 1850, in Cologne. Wagner's relations with him when they were colleagues in Dresden do not appear to have been unfriendly, though Wagner had no great opinion of his talents as a composer; Wagner's essay *Judaism in Music* was certainly the main cause of Hiller's subsequent active enmity, for Hiller was a Jew converted to Christianity.

FEBRUARY 7
• Levi, the conductor: Hermann Levi (1839–1900) was Court conductor in Karlsruhe from 1864 to 1872, when he moved to Munich; in spite of his Jewish birth, he remained throughout his life a great admirer and loyal supporter of Wagner, and he conducted the first production of *Parsifal* in the Bayreuth festival theater in 1882.

FEBRUARY 8
• Mme Viardot: the singer Pauline Viardot-Garcia (1821–1910), a younger sister of Malibran; she began her brilliant operatic career in 1839 in Paris, where Wagner met her; she left the stage in 1863. • Dr. Nohl: Ludwig Nohl (1831–85), a writer on music and an authority on Beethoven.

FEBRUARY 9
• *Proteus* by Dr. Marbach: a satirical play written in 1864 by Oswald Marbach (1810–90), husband of Wagner's sister Rosalie, who died in 1837; a writer and lecturer in philosophy. • Halm, Geibel: Friedrich Halm (pseudonym for Eligius Franz Joseph Baron von Münch-Bellinghausen) and Emanuel Geibel were contemporary German writers, dramatist and poet respectively. • Daumer's *Book of Ghosts*: Georg Friedrich Daumer (1800–75) published his *Das Geisterreich in Glauben, Vorstellung, Sage und Wirklichkeit* (*The Realm of Ghosts in Belief, Imagination, Legend, and Reality*) in Leipzig in 2 vols. in 1867.

FEBRUARY 10
• Winckelmann's biography: Johann Joachim Winckelmann (1717–68), son of a cobbler, became the leading authority on classical art in his time; his work was immensely influential in Germany. In 1763 he was appointed president of the Collection of Antiquities in the Vatican, and was also concerned with the early excavations in Pompeii and Herculaneum; Wagner appears to have possessed his *Collected Works* (published in 12 vols. between 1825 and 1829), and the biography to which Cosima refers is probably that by Joseph Eiselein printed in the first volume. • Born in a land that at the time hardly possessed a language: it is not clear whether Cosima is referring to Winckelmann's actual birthplace (Stendal, in the Altmark part of Brandenburg) or to Germany as a whole, which Wagner considered to have no true literary language before Lessing (born 1729). • "Once more you hover near me, forms and faces": Philip Wayne's translation of the first line of the dedication in Goethe's *Faust*—"*Ihr naht euch wieder, schwankende Gestalten.*" • His article on Devrient: "Eduard Devrient," published in vol. 8 of Wagner's collected writings. • Calderón's *El secreto a voces* (*The Secret in Words*). • Albrecht Dürer's letter on

receiving the news that Luther had been arrested: the great German artist (1471–1528) from Nuremberg heard of Martin Luther's arrest on May 17, 1521, and wrote about it in his *Tagebuch der Reise in die Niederlande* (*Diary of a Journey to the Netherlands*).

FEBRUARY 11

• That comedy with Luther as hero: Wagner wrote a sketch for a play about Martin Luther in August 1868; it is referred to several times in the Diaries, but he never carried it out. • "More to listen than to shine": a quotation from Calderón's *El secreto a voces* in the translation by Schlegel (under the title *Das laute Geheimnis*).

FEBRUARY 12

• Calderón's comedy *Los enredos de la suerte*: might be translated as *The Complications of Chance*.

FEBRUARY 13

• A 74-year-old musician (Claudius): Otto Claudius (1795–1877), a pupil of Wagner's teacher in Leipzig, Theodor Weinlig. • The King's secretary Düfflipp: Lorenz von Düfflipp, secretary to King Ludwig II from 1866 to 1877. • An advance, to be deducted regularly from his allowance: King Ludwig paid Wagner an annual allowance of 8,000 florins. • Semper's claim: the architect Gottfried Semper (1803–79), a friend from Wagner's Dresden days, prepared the plans for the special theater that King Ludwig wanted to build in Munich for Wagner's works; when the plan fell through in 1868, Semper put in a claim to the royal treasury for the work he had done; he was finally paid, but his action upset both the king and Wagner and led to an estrangement between Semper and Wagner. • Rubinstein compositions: the Russian composer Anton Rubinstein (1829–94).

FEBRUARY 14

• Fräulein von Meysenbug: Malwida von Meysenbug (1816–1903), an important friend frequently mentioned in the Diaries, was a German writer who championed the democratic movement and workers' and women's education; expelled from Berlin in 1852, she moved to London, then after 1861 to France and Italy; Wagner first met her in London in 1855 during his concert tour; she wrote novels and books of reminiscences; probably it was one of the latter, *Mémoires d'une idéaliste*, published anonymously in Switzerland in 1869, which she sent to Wagner: it was the first version of her three-volume *Memoiren einer Idealistin* (*Memoirs of a Female Idealist*), published in 1876. • When he had Weber's ashes moved to Dresden: Wagner was responsible for having the remains of the composer Carl Maria von Weber, who died in London in 1826, moved to Dresden in 1844, and he composed funeral music for the occasion.

FEBRUARY 15

• Hans's mother: Franziska von Bülow (née Stoll) (1800–88) had separated from her husband in 1849; a domineering woman, of whom Hans von Bülow himself stood in awe, she disliked Cosima and, above all, Richard Wagner.

FEBRUARY 16

• *Die Horen*: a periodical edited by Schiller in the years 1795–97. • Vasari: Giorgio Vasari (1511–74), whose biographies of Italian painters are an important source. • The hours two years ago: just before the birth of her daughter Eva in Tribschen on February 17, 1867.

FEBRUARY 17

• "Prize Song": sung by Walther in Act III of *Die Meistersinger*.

FEBRUARY 20

• If only I had a mother: it is doubtful whether Countess d'Agoult was entirely to blame, since after their separation Liszt sternly forbade her to have anything to do with her three children by him, putting them in the care of his own mother; but, with her literary activities (she wrote under the name of Daniel Stern), she was probably not a maternal type of woman anyway. • Judith Mendès: Judith Mendès-Gautier (1846–1917) was the daughter of one French writer, Théophile Gautier, and the wife of another, Catulle Mendès (1841–1909), whom she married in 1868; she was still a child when Wagner first met her in Paris in 1861 at a rehearsal of *Tannhäuser*. • Quotation from Goethe: the sentence, not quite correctly quoted, is spoken by Verazio in Act I of Goethe's *Lila*; it should be "*Jeder, der in sich fühlt, dass er etwas Gutes wirken kann, muss ein Plaggeist sein.*"

FEBRUARY 21
• *N.A. Zeitung: Norddeutsche Allgemeine Zeitung,* founded 1861.

FEBRUARY 22
• Bettina: Bettina von Arnim (1785–1859) wrote a work of fiction, *Goethes Brief-wechsel mit einem Kinde,* in 1825 (her own English translation, *Goethe's Correspondence with a Child,* was published in 1837); in her book, dissatisfied with Ottilie's atonement by starvation in Goethe's *Die Wahlverwandtschaften* (*Elective Affinities*), she wrote, "Is it not also a penance to bear happiness, to enjoy happiness?" • "Oh, that a man might know . . .": Brutus in Act V, Scene 1, of Shakespeare's *Julius Caesar.*

FEBRUARY 23
• H. Franck: Dr. Hermann Franck (died 1855), a friend of Wagner's in Dresden; his piece on *Tannhäuser* appeared in the *Augsburger Allgemeine Zeitung* on October 19, 1845. • Wagner: meant here is Faust's amanuensis.

FEBRUARY 25
• As in Terburg: meaning as in a picture by Gerard ter Borch, the Dutch painter.

FEBRUARY 26
• Frau Marenholtz: Bertha von Marenholtz-Bülow (1816–93), a teacher specializing in kindergarten schools.

FEBRUARY 27
• Eckert: Karl Eckert (1820–79), conductor at the Court theater in Berlin, was a friend and supporter whom Wagner first met during one of his visits to Vienna, where Eckert was then engaged; he moved to Stuttgart in 1860, and Wagner was with him and his wife there when King Ludwig's invitation (to Wagner) to go to Munich arrived in May 1864. • Herr von Hülsen: Botho von Hülsen (1815–86) had been director (*Intendant*) of the Berlin Court theater since 1851, responsible since 1867 also for the theaters in Hanover, Kassel, and Wiesbaden; though both Wagner and Cosima looked upon him as an enemy, there is evidence that he had considerable respect for Wagner's works, however little they appealed to his own tastes. • Hans Richter (1843–1916): first came into contact with Wagner and Cosima when he was invited, on the recommendation of the conductor Esser in Vienna, to Tribschen to do some copying work on *Die Meistersinger*; at that time he was a horn player in a Viennese theater orchestra; in 1868 he was appointed a conductor in Munich at Wagner's request; his subsequent development is fully catalogued in Cosima's Diaries and need not be outlined here. After Wagner's death he became one of Europe's leading conductors, his work centered mainly on Bayreuth, Vienna, and England, where he conducted the Hallé Orchestra in Manchester for many years. • R. has given me Gibbon (in English): Edward Gibbon's *History of the Decline and Fall of the Roman Empire* was published in London in 6 vols. between 1776 and 1788.

MARCH I

• "Winter tempests": "*Winterstürme*," a reference to Siegmund's "Spring Song" in Act I of *Die Walküre*.

MARCH 2

• The song with which Wotan wakes the Wala: at the beginning of the Wotan-Erda scene in Act III of *Siegfried* (Wala is another name for Erda). • Marbach's adaptation: Oswald Marbach (Wagner's brother-in-law) published his adaptation of Shakespeare's play, under the title *Antonius und Cleopatra*, in Leipzig in 1861.

MARCH 3

• The *Faust* Overture: composed by Wagner in 1840, revised 1855. • "Bid that welcome which comes to punish us . . .": spoken by the dying Mark Antony in Act IV, Scene 14, of Shakespeare's play. • "Let that be left . . .": Mark Antony in Act III, Scene 9, of the same play.

MARCH 4

• With the love of Eduard: a principal character in Goethe's novel *Die Wahlverwandschaften (Elective Affinities)*. • The verse at the conclusion of *Tasso*: the concluding lines of Goethe's drama *Tasso*, "Thus at the end does the sailor cling tight to the rock on which he foundered." • Beethoven's grandnephew: Ludwig van Beethoven, a son of Beethoven's adopted nephew, Karl; in 1867, when he was in need, Wagner approached King Ludwig on his behalf; see also July 28, 1872.

MARCH 5

• Through Schuré: Edouard Schuré (1841–1929), a French writer and musical historian who championed Wagner's cause in France. • The Grand Duchess of Weimar: possibly Cosima means here the former Grand Duchess, Maria Paulovna, who had been Liszt's friend and supporter and was now dead, rather than the present one, Sophie Luise, who succeeded with her husband, Karl Alexander, to the grand duchy in 1853. • Herr von zu Rhein's collection: a celebrated collection of coins owned by Prince Alexander von Hessen und bei Rhein (1823–88).

MARCH 6

• Little Wilhelm: the son of the servants Jakob and Verena Stocker, also referred to as Willi.

MARCH 8

• Schott: the music publishers in Mainz, headed by Franz Schott (1811–74); Wagner's main publishers from 1859 on.

MARCH 9

• *Gallery of Famous Germans*: published by Breitkopf und Härtel, Leipzig, Wagner's principal publishers before he moved to Schott.

MARCH 10

• Baron Sina: a Viennese banker.

MARCH 11

• Berlioz has died: the French composer Hector Berlioz (born 1803) died on March 8, 1869. • All the deaths in this year: meaning the past twelve-month period, since of the persons mentioned, three—Berryer (a French lawyer), Genelli, and Rossini—died in 1868. • "My Richard Wagner letter": a letter addressed to Judith Gautier about the forthcoming production of *Rienzi* in Paris was published in the French periodical *La Liberté* on March 10, 1869; though signed by Richard Wagner, it was apparently written by Cosima. • The approaching Vatican Council: the First Vatican Council was held in Rome by Pope Pius IX from December 8, 1869, to October 20, 1870; the main issue was the promulgation of the doctrine of papal infallibility.

MAY 2

• *Wilhelm Tell:* drama by Schiller. • *Der arme Heinrich (Poor Henry)*: an epic poem by Hartmann von Aue (c.1165–c.1215), one of the *Minnesänger*.

MAY 5

• Marie Bassenheim: daughter of Count and Countess Bassenheim, born in 1861. • Herr Drumont: Edouard Drumont (1844–1917), a French journalist, contributor to *La Liberté*; gained prominence later as a leading anti-Semite with his book *La France juive (Jewish France)*, 1885.

MAY 6

• *"La Nature paraît . . ."*: correctly, *"Il paraîtrait qu'elle [la nature] nous a fait plutôt pour devenir des postillons que des philosophes"* ("It would seem that it has fashioned us to become postilions, rather than philosophers"); from the correspondence with d'Argens.

MAY 7

• Heralds of peace: these figure in the cast of *Rienzi*.

MAY 8–11

• The people from Paris: the string quartet. • *Réveil:* a republican periodical in Paris, 1868–71. • Honorary membership in the Berlin Academy: on May 7, 1869.

MAY 12

• Apel's story *"Der Freischütz"*: together with Friedrich Laun, Apel edited the *Gespensterbuch (Book of Ghosts)*, 1815; it contains the story *"Der Freischütz"* ("The Marksman"), on which Weber based his opera.

MAY 13

• Léon Leroy: Belgian musician and writer and friend of Wagner's in Paris 1860–61. • Gaspérini: Auguste de Gaspérini, a physician, who died in 1868, also became a close friend of Wagner's at this time. • *La France Musicale:* a musical weekly founded in Paris in 1838 and edited by the brothers Marie and Léon Escudier; it ceased publication in 1870.

MAY 14

• *"Après cela . . ."* ("With this I will have rendered a service to my country by acquainting it with those privileged beings who are the glory of mankind").

MAY 15

• Frau Wille: Eliza Wille (1809–93), née Sloman, a close friend of Wagner's after he visited her and her husband, François Wille (1811–96), on their estate at Mariafeld, near Zurich, in 1852; staunch republicans, they left their native Hamburg in 1851 to settle in Switzerland; Wagner's friendship belonged more to her than to her husband, a somewhat duel-scarred journalist who had been a fellow student of Bismarck's at Göttingen and Jena; she wrote novels. • *"On m'a inquiétée . . ."* ("I have been made uneasy on your account; may God watch over you").

MAY 16

• Old Prince Wallerstein: Ludwig, Prince zu Öttingen-Wallerstein (1791–1870) was the father of Countess Bassenheim, in whose home he now lived; he had held high office in Bavaria under the kings Maximilian I, Ludwig I, and Maximilian II, and was prime minister 1847–48 (when Lola Montez was granted citizenship); he was then a member of the opposition in the Chamber of Deputies until 1862, when he retired to Lucerne. • *Euryanthe*: opera by Weber.

MAY 17

• Professor Nietzsche: the philosopher Friedrich Nietzsche (1844–1900); Wagner's first meeting with him had been on November 8, 1868, in the home of his brother-in-law Hermann Brockhaus in Leipzig; in 1869 Nietzsche, at the early age of twenty-five, was appointed professor of classical philology at the University of

Basel, and, finding himself living close to the composer he so much admired, he paid an early visit to Tribschen—the first of many.
MAY 19
• Several themes that date from the "Starnberg days": Cosima is referring here to that summer visit in 1864 to Wagner's villa on Lake Starnberg during which their first child, Isolde, was conceived; though it is known that the melody in Act III of *Siegfried* set to the words *"Ewig war ich, ewig bin ich"* ("Eternal I was, eternal I am") —sometimes called the "Peace Motive," but better known as the opening theme of the *Siegfried Idyll*—originated in Starnberg, it has not been possible to establish with certainty that the second theme of the *Idyll*, used by Wagner in *Siegfried* for the words *"O, Siegfried, Herrlicher! Hort der Welt!"* ("Oh, Siegfried the magnificent, treasure of the world"), also originated then; Cosima's reference here to "several themes" strongly suggests that it did—and perhaps some other themes not yet identified.
MAY 22
• Richard Wagner's fifty-sixth birthday. • Hungary: the birthday telegram from there was signed by eight Budapest musicians, among them Friedrich Altschul, Mihály Mosonyi, and Gyula Rózsavölgyi (the music publisher), according to the *Neue Freie Presse* of June 1, 1869.
MAY 27
• Uncle Adolph: though Cosima always spells his name this way, he is more usually referred to as Adolf Wagner (1774–1835); the younger brother of Richard Wagner's father, he was a writer and translator who lived in Leipzig; see also the introduction.
MAY 29
• The "great" Riehl: Wilhelm Heinrich Riehl (1823–97), a German art historian and writer on music. • Rheinberger's new opera: *Die Sieben Raben* (*The Seven Ravens*) by Joseph Rheinberger (1839–1901), teacher since 1867 at the music school in Munich.
JUNE 1
• *Tristan* . . . with the two Vogls: since the death of Schnorr von Carolsfeld there had been no further performances anywhere of *Tristan und Isolde*, Wagner feeling that no singer could ever replace Schnorr; of Heinrich Vogl (1845–1903) he had a very low opinion and described him as "a thoroughly incompetent singer" in a letter to King Ludwig dated March 30, 1868; he later revised his opinion sufficiently to cast Vogl as Loge in his production of the *Ring* at Bayreuth; against his wife, Therese Vogl (1845–1921), he was less prejudiced, and he offered her the part of Sieglinde in *Die Walküre* in his Bayreuth production; she sang this role in the first production of *Die Walküre* in Munich in 1870.
JUNE 3
• Wolfram's poem about the birth of Parzival: Wolfram von Eschenbach (c.1170–c.1220); his courtly romance *Parzival* was based on the Holy Grail stories of Chrétien de Troyes.
JUNE 8
• Letter from Villot: Frédéric Villot, curator of the Louvre and one of Wagner's Parisian friends (see also October 25, 1876).
JUNE 9
• *"Leuchtende Liebe, lachender Tod"* (in Andrew Porter's singing translation, "Light of our loving, laughter in death"): the final words of *Siegfried*, sung to the so-called *Jubelmotiv* ("Joy Motive").
JUNE 11
• Chaillou: Cosima's tailor, Chaillou-Ghezzi, Milan.
JUNE 12
• The C Minor Symphony: Beethoven's Fifth.

JUNE 13
• "The great Zenobia": after Calderón's play, *La gran Cenobia*.
JUNE 14
• "*Témoignage* . . ." ("A testimony of my inexpressible admiration").
JUNE 16
• Eckermann-Goethe: Johann Peter Eckermann (1792–1854) published his *Gespräche mit Goethe* (*Conversations with Goethe*) between 1837 and 1848; a new edition appeared in Leipzig in 1868. • His "*Attente*": Wagner wrote the song "*L'Attente*," to words by Victor Hugo, in 1840. • Doré edition of *Don Quixote*: an edition of Cervantes's novel illustrated by Gustave Doré (1832–83). • Cornelius: Peter Cornelius (1783–1867), a German artist who produced, among other things, illustrations for *Faust*.
JUNE 18
• Alberich: the dwarf in the *Nibelungen* who fashioned the ring to gain ascendancy over the gods. • His essay *What Is German?* (*Was ist Deutsch?*): written for King Ludwig in September 1865, published in 1878 in vol. 10 of Wagner's collected writings. • *Antigone*: the drama by Sophocles.
JUNE 20
• This performance of *Tristan* in Munich: with the Vogls, conducted by Hans von Bülow and produced by Eduard Sigl.
JUNE 22
• The "*Cinque Canti*": after the Italian title of the five songs to words by Mathilde Wesendonck (the *Wesendonck Lieder*). • Tellus and Sol: in Roman mythology Earth and Sun. Councilor Pfistermeister: Franz Seraph von Pfistermeister (1820–1912) was the man Ludwig sent, on his accession in 1864, to find Wagner and bring him to Munich; he was Cabinet secretary to the king until December 1866, when he resigned—because, it is said, he resented Wagner's interference in affairs of state. • Sauer, the adjutant: Karl Theodor von Sauer, Ludwig's aide.
JUNE 23
• The feather on my bed: this is not clear, but it must have been a single feather to remind Wagner of Lear's line in Shakespeare's play, "This feather stirs; she lives!" • Gozzi: Count Carlo Gozzi (1720–1806), Italian dramatist whose fantastic plays based on fairy tales were once very popular; Wagner used one of them, *La donna serpente*, as the basis for *Die Feen*, his first completed opera (1833).
JUNE 25
• Röckel: August Röckel (1814–76), an Austrian conductor, composer, and writer, was musical director in Dresden from 1843 to 1848, during which time Wagner and he became close friends; Röckel played a leading part in the revolution of 1849 and was sentenced to life imprisonment; while he was in prison, Wagner wrote him a number of important letters that shed much light on the genesis of the *Ring*; released from prison in 1862, he wrote a book about the revolution and his experiences in Waldheim prison, published in 1865; Röckel came to live in Munich, and the friendship was resumed, but it died when Wagner began to suspect him of having spread gossip in Munich regarding his, Wagner's, relations with Cosima. • The trumpet calls in the second act: Cosima's mistake—she means the third act of *Lohengrin*. • Count Platen: Julius, Count von Platen (1816–89) became manager of the Dresden opera in 1867. • The *Nibelungen* belongs to the King of Bavaria: under the terms of a contract signed on October 18, 1864, by Wagner and Julius von Hofmann, the Cabinet treasurer.
JUNE 27
• Countess Nako: Bertha Nako, née Gyertyánanffy de Bobda (1824–82); during his

stay in Vienna between 1862 and 1864 Wagner visited the Hungarian Countess and her husband, Count Coloman Nako, on their estate at Schwarzau, near Vienna, in the hope of winning some financial support from them; he was unsuccessful. • Barbarossa: Frederick I (c.1122–90), Holy Roman Emperor, also known as Rotbart or Redbeard; Wagner had in fact begun a drama about Barbarossa in 1846, but he gave it up to concentrate on Siegfried, with whom Barbarossa was closely identified in his mind. • *Die Sieger*: Wagner wrote a prose sketch for this music drama on a Buddhist theme in May 1856; he never gave up his intention of writing it.

JUNE 28

• *"Lieben, leiden, lernen"* ("to love, to suffer, to learn").

JUNE 30

• Ollivier, my brother-in-law: Emile Ollivier (1825–1913), a French politician, the husband of Cosima's deceased sister, Blandine; a lawyer, he entered politics in 1857, and in 1870 was to form Napoleon III's first parliamentary government.

JULY 1

• Kaulbach: Wilhelm von Kaulbach (1805–74), a German painter and head of the art academy in Munich. • *Oedipus*: tragedy by Sophocles.

JULY 2

• Villiers de l'Isle-Adam: Jean-Marie Villiers de l'Isle-Adam (1838–89), French poet, satirist, and writer of fantastic tales, etc. • Lübke's wretched essay on *Die Msinger*: Wilhelm Lübke (1826–93), an art historian, published in 1869, together with the Austrian critic Eduard Hanslick, a pamphlet, *Über Richard Wagner* (*On Richard Wagner*).

JULY 3

• A volume of Droysen: Johann Gustav Droysen (1808–84), author of a two-vol. history of Alexander the Great's successors (*Geschichte des Hellenismus*). • Schopenhauer at the chapter on music: chap. 39 of vol. 2 of *Die Welt als Wille und Vorstellung* (*The World as Will and Idea*).

JULY 4

• Met G[eorge] Sand: this famous French writer (1804–76) was a friend of Cosima's mother. • *"Diesen Kuss der ganzen Welt," "Seid umschlungen, Millionen"*: lines from Schiller's "Ode to Joy," which Beethoven set to music in his Ninth Symphony; the lines should be in reverse order; they have been translated by E. A. Bowring as "Welcome, all ye myriad creatures! Brethren, take the kiss of love!" • The theater manager a coward: Karl, Baron von Perfall (1824–1907), director of the Munich opera since 1867; Wagner considered him an archenemy, though he himself had favored Perfall's appointment at the time. • *"Hepp, hepp"*: anti-Semitic invective of unknown origin, widely used in Germany during the nineteenth century.

JULY 7

• Hornstein: Robert von Hornstein (1833–90), a composer; Wagner made his acquaintance during the Zurich years; they fell out when Hornstein inherited his father's estate in 1861 and refused Wagner's request for financial support.

JULY 8

• Perfall: see note for July 4, 1869. • Anna in Munich: Anna Mrazéck, who, with her husband Franz Mrazéck, had been Wagner's servants in Vienna; they resumed work for him in Munich in 1864, and after Wagner had left for Switzerland, Franz was given employment at the music school in Munich.

JULY 9

• Serov: Alexander Serov (1820–71), Russian composer and writer, a devoted supporter of Wagner's music. • His Russian national opera: *Rogneda*, first produced in Moscow in 1865.

*feste Burg"* in his opera *Les Huguenots*. • Nohl's *Gluck und Wagner*: Nohl's book was published in Munich in 1870.

FEBRUARY 21
• Tischbein: Johann Friedrich August Tischbein (1750–1812), cousin of Goethe's artist friend Wilhelm Tischbein; Johann Tischbein painted his portrait of Schiller in 1805.

FEBRUARY 22
• Daniel Defoe in the pillory: the author of *Robinson Crusoe* (c.1660–1731) was put in the pillory in London for his pamphlet *The Shortest Way with the Dissenters* (1702).

FEBRUARY 23
• Her son, just returned: Count Friedrich Bassenheim (born 1844).

FEBRUARY 24
• The Fritschi procession: the annual carnival procession in Lucerne, named after its initiator in the fifteenth century, a Herr Fritschi. • Archduke Heinrich (1828–91): son of Archduke Rainer and grandson of Emperor Leopold II of Austria, had married the actress Leopoldine Hoffmann on February 4, 1868. • *Hermes Odysseus*: a poem by Karl Wilhelm Osterwald (1820–87). • The rabbi: in a letter to Nietzsche dated March 1, 1870, Cosima mentions this dancing rabbi and comments, "I thought it must have been a fancy dress, but now I discover that this 'synagogue infallible' in fact gives dancing lessons."

FEBRUARY 25
• The Munich "Schäfer": probably Richter's friend, Reinhard Schaefer; see note for September 4, 1869.

MARCH 1
• The bookseller Lesimple: August Lesimple, later active in the Wagner Society in Cologne. • The music festival in Bonn: in connection with the centennial of Beethoven's birth in 1770 in that city. • The condition which he imposes on the woman: Lohengrin, a knight of the Holy Grail, marries Elsa on condition that she does not demand to know who he is.

MARCH 3
• Beethoven's A Major Symphony: the Seventh.

MARCH 4
• Constantly heard R. speaking of Méhul: Wagner thought highly of the opera *Joseph* (1807) by the French composer Etienne Nicolas Méhul (1763–1817) and, indeed, conducted it in 1838 in Riga. • Alexander: Alexander the Great. • Cromwell: Oliver Cromwell. • Charles: King Charles I of England.

MARCH 5
• *Petitcriu*: meaning "little creature," the name of the dog in Gottfried von Strassburg's epic, *Tristan und Isolde*. • Baireuth: old spelling; Wagner first set eyes on the little town of Bayreuth in July 1835, when he passed through it on his way from Karlsbad to Nuremberg. • Gretchen: in Goethe's *Faust*, Part One.

MARCH 6
• With a little verse at the bottom: the verse, entitled *"Braunschweiger Wurst für Lohengrin"* ("Brunswick Sausage for Lohengrin") appears incomplete both in Wagner's *Braunes Buch* and in the collected writings; the version Cosima attaches to her diary reads: *"Zu Worms ein Krug Einbecker Bier | der labte Luther's Durst: | Held Lohengrin nach dem Turnier | zu Braunschweig stärkt' ihn Wurst. || Daraus nehm' Jeder sich die Lehr': | nicht Pfaffenmarkt noch Fürstenwehr | hilft ihm von seinem Durst, | doch stellt auf Gott sein Sache er, | und wenn die Welt voll Teufel wär', | dem Deutschen ist alles dann Wurst."* In prose translation this means: "In Worms a jug of Einbeck ale quenched

Luther's thirst; after the joust in Brunswick Lohengrin restored his strength with sausage. So let each learn this lesson: neither priest nor prince will save him from his thirst; but if he puts his trust in God, though the world is full of demons, then no German needs to fear." (The joke lies in the last line, which means literally, "All is sausage to the German"—an idiom for "It's all the same . . .") • Kindermann: the singer August Kindermann (1817–91), who sang Wotan in the first performances of *Das Rheingold* and *Die Walküre*, in Munich. • In Rio de Janeiro: in 1857, while he was working on the second act of *Siegfried* in Zurich, Wagner was approached by the Brazilian consul in Leipzig with an invitation from his Emperor, Dom Pedro II, to stage performances of his works in Rio de Janeiro in Italian; this aroused in him thoughts of writing *Tristan und Isolde* for production there; however, after sending the emperor the piano scores of *Der Fliegende Holländer, Tannhäuser,* and *Lohengrin,* he heard nothing further.

MARCH 7
• The folder with the portrait of Geyer: containing correspondence between Geyer and Wagner's mother; the letters had been returned to him by his stepsister Cäcilie. • The new director, Kaiser: Wilhelm Kaiser (1813–92), Court conductor at Karlsruhe from 1869. • *Catarina Cornaro*: Franz Lachner's most successful opera, first performed in Munich in 1841.

MARCH 8
• *"Höllendämmerung"*: "The Twilight of Hell."

MARCH 9
• Frau von Schleinitz: Marie, Baroness von Schleinitz, née von Buch (1842–1912), wife of Alexander, Baron von Schleinitz (1807–85), the Prussian Minister of the Royal Household; she had been a close and confidential friend of Cosima's in Berlin and was later to become one of the leading lights in the founding of the Bayreuth festival.

MARCH 11
• Simrock's *Heldenbuch* (*Book of Heroes*).

MARCH 13
• The quartet *"Es muss sein"*: "It must be"—Beethoven's String Quartet in F Major, Opus 135.

MARCH 14
• The *Trois Mélodies*: the three songs written in Paris (see note for January 20, 1870).
• Baronne de Caters: née Lablache, a singer.

MARCH 15
• Siegfried's arrival: at the Court of the Gibichungs, the opening of Act I of *Götterdämmerung*; the introduction contains the Norns' scene, the parting of Brünnhilde and Siegfried, and the orchestral interlude known as "Siegfried's Journey to the Rhine."

MARCH 24
• The conductor Hagen: most probably Johann Baptist Hagen (1818–70), conductor at Wiesbaden since 1856.

MARCH 28
• Doris Brockhaus's fiancé: the man named Richard Wagner; see November 30, 1869.

MARCH 29
• Perrin: Emile Perrin (1814–85), director of the Comédie Française in Paris.

MARCH 31
• Marburg: town in the German *Land* of Hessen, where Saint Elizabeth of Hungary,

after the death of her husband, the Landgrave of Thuringia, lived as a Franciscan tertiary. • The story of Saint Alexis: a saint in the fifth century who left his bride and went traveling in poverty; the story was told to Goethe by his hostess in a house in which he stayed on the St. Gotthard, and he recorded it in his *Briefe aus der Schweiz* (*Letters from Switzerland*). • Fétis's 86th birthday: François-Joseph Fétis (1784–1871), a Belgian musicologist, founded in 1827 the French periodical *Revue Musicale*. • Mathilde Mallinger (1847–1920): soprano singer in Munich (1866–69)—where she sang Eva in the first performance of *Die Meistersinger*, in 1868—and in Berlin (1869–82); though Wagner thought highly of her performance as Eva, she seems to have resisted all his attempts to make use of her again. • The aged Moscheles: Ignaz Moscheles (1794–1870), pianist and composer, teacher at Leipzig from 1846.

APRIL 1
• Concerning the serenade: in connection with Wagner's birthday celebrations on May 22.

APRIL 2
• Louis Köhler (1820–86): a pianist, conductor, and writer on music. • *Bereuter*: Wagner's pun on Bayreuth is obvious enough, but the subsequent reference to the stable lads is subtler; *Bereiter* means "horse trainers." • The death of Clitus: Clitus, friend and foster brother of Alexander, had saved the king's life in battle; Alexander killed him in a state of drunkenness.

APRIL 3
• The King of Italy: Victor Emmanuel II, King since 1861.

APRIL 4
• Letter from Herr von Gersdorff: Karl von Gersdorff (1844–1904), a close friend of Nietzsche, who encouraged him to write his letter to Wagner; Gersdorff subsequently became a friend of both Wagner and Cosima.

APRIL 5
• "We want to be a single nation of brothers" ("*Wir wollen sein ein einzig Volk von Brüdern*"): from Schiller's *Wilhelm Tell*. • Members of the Burschenschaft: student organization of nationalist outlook founded in 1815; banned between 1819 and 1848, so Wagner must have been a very young child at the time.

APRIL 6
• Horawitz: Adalbert Horawitz (1840–88), Austrian historian and cofounder of the Academic Wagner Society in Vienna. • Diotima: a fictional prophetess in Plato's *Symposium*.

APRIL 8
• The former Lieutenant Müller: Hermann Müller, Wilhelmine Schröder-Devrient's lover, was obliged to resign his army commission in 1849, because of her connection with the rebellion, and he went to Switzerland. • *Art and Revolution*: Wagner wrote his long essay *Die Kunst und die Revolution* in 1849 after his flight from Dresden; it contains the first intimations of his ideas on the music drama and its function in a reformed society. • Prytaneum: in ancient Greece, the meeting place of the authorities in power.

APRIL 13
• R. writes a poem for the King (*dernier effort!*): Wagner's poem is printed in his *Braunes Buch* under the title "*An den König (dernier effort!)*" ("To the King (last attempt!)"), but when he sent it to King Ludwig he gave it the title "*Beim Herannahen des dritten Mai*" ("On the Approach of May 3"); it was in fact May 4 and not May 3, 1864, when Ludwig came to his rescue, a deed of which Wagner wished to remind him in the hope of averting the production of *Die Walküre* in Munich. • Too

much Makarie: Makarie is a character in Goethe's novel *Wilhelm Meister*, a saintly elderly lady, much interested in the heavenly constellations, withdrawn from the world, and full of sage advice.

APRIL 16

• "Green eggs for Richard Geyer": up to the age of fourteen Wagner was known by his stepfather's name; the inscription *"Grüne Eier für Richard Geyer"* rhymes in German; the uncle here referred to was Carl Friedrich Wilhelm Geyer, a goldsmith in Eisleben, with whom the eight-year-old Richard was staying. • The Lehmann brothers: two German-born artists, Heinrich, or Henri (1814–82), who lived in Paris, and Rudolf (1819–1905), who lived in London and became a British subject.

APRIL 17

• A new musical periodical: the *Neue Berliner Musikzeitung*. • The conductor Schmidt: Gustav Schmidt (1816–82), Leipzig.

APRIL 18

• Julius *Cohen* Rodenberg: Julius Rodenberg (1831–1914) was born Levy; he was a writer and journalist in Berlin and in 1874 founded the *Deutsche Rundschau*. • The poet Hans Herrig (1845–92): wrote historical plays, librettos, and essays. • Reissiger: Karl Gottlieb Reissiger (1798–1859), a fellow conductor in Dresden whom R. rather despised for his easygoing ways.

APRIL 21

• *Non possumus* ("We cannot"): the expression customarily used by the Pope in refusing secular demands.

APRIL 26

• Since chignons and *bibi* hats: the German text has here *"seit Avignon und Bibi-Hut,"* but since the *bibi* is a type of hat that came into fashion in the 1830's, the association with the chignon (for which Wagner seemed to have a particular aversion) appears a more likely one. *Phaedrus*: dialogue by Plato.

APRIL 27

• I no longer enjoy hearing the cuckoo: it is a German superstition that the number of calls a cuckoo gives when first heard denotes the number of years one still has to live.

APRIL 28

• No diary?: Wagner continued to make occasional entries in his *Braunes Buch*, but they are mainly jottings in connection with his artistic work. • Our friend von Bronsart: Hans Bronsart von Schellendorff (1830–1913), a former pupil of Liszt's, became director of the opera in Hanover in 1867. • *Ivanhoe*: the novel by Walter Scott.

APRIL 29

• The conductor Marpurg: Friedrich Marpurg (1825–84), conductor at Darmstadt since 1868.

MAY 1

• England-Greece Marathon: on April 11, 1870, a group of English people visiting the battlefield of Marathon had been taken as hostages by a band of robbers, and when the Greek government refused to pay a ransom or grant an amnesty, three of the tourists were shot dead; this led to strained diplomatic relations. • The three J's: Jews, Jesuits, journalists.

MAY 4

• Moritz's mythology: Karl Philipp Moritz (1756–93) published his *Götterlehre oder Mythologische Dichtungen der Alten* (*Religious Mythology, or The Mythological Writings of the Ancient Greeks*) in 1791.

published 1844, made a case for a new form of national music drama based on the German saga, and on the *Nibelungen* legend in particular. • Herr Jakoby: correctly, Johann Jacoby (1805–77), a German democratic politician, opposed to Bismarck and the annexation of Alsace-Lorraine. • "Death and Indestructibility": from the supplements to the 4th bk. of *The World as Will and Idea* (in the translation by R. B. Haldane and J. Kemp, "On Death and Its Relation to the Indestructibility of Our True Nature").

SEPTEMBER 28

•Favre: Jules Favre (1809–80) became French foreign minister in September 1870.

SEPTEMBER 30

• The publisher Stilke: the second edition of Wagner's *Herr Eduard Devrient and His Style* was published in 1869 by the Berlin firm of Stilke & van Muyden (see October 10, 1870). • Fr[iedrich] Schmitt (1812–84): former singer turned singing teacher; Wagner, whose friendship with him dated back to the time when they were both beginners at Magdeburg, invited him to Munich in 1867 to teach at the music school; there his rather rough manners caused difficulties, and the cordial and intimate friendship of earlier years faded. • Bakunin: Michael Bakunin (1814–76), Russian anarchist, took part in the Dresden uprising of 1849, during which time Wagner was strongly under his influence; sentenced to death and then deported back to Russia, he escaped from Siberia and eventually settled in Switzerland, becoming a leading figure in the International.

OCTOBER 1

•Char-à-banc: a long carriage with rows of seats facing forward.

OCTOBER 2

•His *Proclamation*: concerning Bayreuth, published April 1871. • The *Coriolan* and *Egmont* Overtures: by Beethoven.

OCTOBER 5

•*Campaign in France* (*Kampagne in Frankreich 1792*): Goethe accompanied the duke of Weimar on an invasion of France in the year 1792.

OCTOBER 7

• An asterisk beside the date of this entry in the manuscript is interpreted by the German editors as indicating the beginning of a menstrual period, since it is repeated at roughly monthly intervals for some time; however, the German editors decided to omit the asterisk throughout. • The article about Spontini: in his autobiography, Wagner describes in great detail how at his instigation the Dresden opera invited the composer Gasparo Spontini (1774–1851) to supervise a new production of his opera *La Vestale* in 1844.

OCTOBER 8

•Herr Danike: not known. • Stephen Heller (1813–88): Hungarian composer and pianist, living in Paris from 1860. • Jaëll: Alfred Jaëll (1832–82), Austrian pianist.

OCTOBER 9

•Prell: a letter from Cosima to Nietzsche dated June 24, 1870, reveals that this Lucerne bookseller came from Wunsiedel (near Bayreuth); though he had been asked for information about Bayreuth, he would certainly not have known why Wagner wanted it, because the idea of producing the *Ring* at Bayreuth was still a secret at this time, known only to Wagner's closest friends.

OCTOBER 10

•Schletterer: Hans Michel Schletterer (1824–93), a writer on music, an editor with the *A.A.Z.*, and conductor at Augsburg cathedral. • With R.'s full name attached: Wagner's essay *Herr Devrient and His Style* had first been published by Cäsar Fritsch in Munich under the pseudonym Wilhelm Drach.

OCTOBER II
• *Don Juan*: by Byron.
OCTOBER 15
• Fafner: the giant who has turned himself into a dragon to guard the Nibelung hoard; he is slain by Siegfried in the second act of *Siegfried*.
OCTOBER 16
• In the new theater: the new Vienna Court (later State) opera had been opened in 1869.
OCTOBER 17
• G. Engel: Gustav Engel (1823–95), German music critic of the *Vossische Zeitung* in Berlin from 1861.
OCTOBER 18
• Fiege: a contributor to the *Norddeutsche Allgemeine Zeitung* in Berlin. • Gregorius: not known. • The fall of the Hohenstaufens: members of this German family were holy Roman emperors during the years 1138–1254, the most renowned being Friedrich Barbarossa; the male line became extinct in 1268 with the execution of Conradin (see note for February 5, 1871).
OCTOBER 20
• Omitted passage after "R. dreamed of his late wife": "She is not my blessed wife, but you are, as the expression was used in the Middle Ages" (the play is on the word "*selig*," which means both "late" and "blessed"). • Garibaldi . . . organizing in the Vosges district: Giuseppe Garibaldi (1807–82), the great Italian freedom fighter, organized an unsuccessful feud with German troops in Burgundy in 1870 in an attempt to aid the French. • "Marino Falieri": the actual title of this story about the doge of Venice is "*Doge und Dogaressa*," and it appears in E. T. A. Hoffmann's *Die Serapionsbrüder*. • Stade: Friedrich Stade (1844–1928), a musicologist in Leipzig, published his "*Vom Musikalisch-Schönen. Mit Bezug auf Dr. Ed. Hanslick's gleichnamige Schrift*" ("On Musical Beauty—with Reference to Dr. E. Hanslick's Essay of the Same Title") in 1870; Wagner's "*Offener Brief an Dr. Stade*" ("Open Letter to Dr. S."), dated December 30, 1870, appeared in the *Musikalisches Wochenblatt* of January 1871; see also December 30, 1870, and January 16, 1871.
OCTOBER 21
• The folk play of *Fortunatus*: second part of a fifteenth-century prose novel, dramatized by Hans Sachs, 1553, and in English by Thomas Dekker (*Old Fortunatus*, 1600).
OCTOBER 23
• Federlein: Gottlieb Federlein (1835–1922), a music critic (later in New York).
OCTOBER 24
• Her Jewishness: Pauline Viardot was the daughter of the Spanish singer Manuel del Popolo Garcia; she was not Jewish. • Prof. Adolph Wagner (1835–1917): German economist, professor at Freiburg from 1868, at Berlin from 1870.
OCTOBER 26
• Arnold Wille: son of Eliza and François Wille. • The Polish eagle: a black marble column erected to commemorate the hundredth anniversary of Poland's liberation movement. • Prof. *Bendof* (or Bender?): Otto Benndorf (1838–1907), professor of archaeology at Zurich, 1869–71, participated in the excavation of Samothrace.
OCTOBER 27
• I once played the role of . . . confidante: Cosima's second visit to the Wesendonck home in Zurich in August 1858, when the jealousy between Mathilde and Minna was at its height. • Frau Heim: Emilie Heim, a singer, wife of Ignaz Heim, director of music in Zurich.

MARCH 3
• Thiers: Adolphe Thiers (1797–1877), French statesman, President of the Third Republic 1871–73.

MARCH 7
• Prof. Wieprecht: Wilhelm Friedrich Wieprecht (1802–72), director general of the Prussian military bands and part inventor of the bass tuba. • Dürer's *Greater Passion*: a series of twelve woodcuts.

MARCH 13
• Fr[iedrich] Wilh[elm] IV (1795–1861): Wagner made several efforts during his Dresden years to further his career by winning the favor of Friedrich Wilhelm, King of Prussia from 1840; though the king appeared to like his work and ordered *Rienzi* performed in Berlin after seeing it in Dresden, nothing tangible ever resulted. • Käthchen: presumably Käthchen Eckert, wife of the conductor Karl Eckert. • Hedwig: presumably Hedwig Neumann, wife of Wilhelm Neumann, inspector of the royal buildings; Neumann was later invited to produce plans for the festival theater in Bayreuth.

MARCH 16
• R. drafts his poem: Wagner wrote down his *"Kaiserlied"* ("Emperor's Song") on this day in his *Braunes Buch;* though he set it to music in such a way that it could be tacked on to the *"Kaisermarsch,"* he did not regard this as essential or even desirable; the march in its orchestral form had already been completed and dispatched the previous day.

MARCH 18
• The Italian printer in Basel: Bonfantini. • Hahn's grammar: Karl August Hahn (1807–57) published grammars for Old, Middle, and New High German, all in Wagner's library.

MARCH 19
• "Eternally undivided": quotation from *Tristan und Isolde,* Act II, Scene 2 (*"So starben wir, um ungetrennt, ewig einig ohne End"*).

MARCH 20
• Prince Hohenlohe: Konstantin.

MARCH 21
• Herr *Cerf* (the name says everything): it is not clear why, except perhaps that it was a Jewish name; the former theater in Strassburg had been destroyed in the bombardment of the city in 1870.

MARCH 22
• Drank the Emperor's health: it was his birthday.

MARCH 23
*"Kaiserlied"*: the choral adjunct to the *"Kaisermarsch"*; see note for March 16, 1871.

APRIL 3
• The lecture: *The Destiny of Opera.*

APRIL 4
• Franz Hüffer (1843–89): born in Germany, he settled in London in 1870, where he Anglicized his name into Francis Hueffer; he wrote for several periodicals before becoming music critic for *The Times* in 1878; he may formerly have been, as Cosima states, an opponent of Wagner, but he turned into one of his main champions in England, publishing *Wagner and the Music of the Future* in 1874 and a biography of Wagner in 1881; he was the father of the novelist Ford Madox Ford.

APRIL 5
• *The Origin and Aim of Greek Tragedy*: this was the first draft of Nietzsche's *Geburt der Tragödie* (*The Birth of Tragedy*). • Arnold Frege (1846–1918): an agriculturalist,

son of an aunt and uncle of Hans von Bülow, Professor Woldemar Frege and his wife Livia, née Gerhardt.

APRIL 8

• A green snake: on April 13 Cosima wrote in a letter to Nietzsche, "The snake has given Eva very great joy, after the inevitable preliminary alarm."

APRIL 9

• The Commune: the revolutionary Commune ruled in Paris from March 18 to May 29, when it was savagely suppressed by French troops.

APRIL 10

• Our young master: King Ludwig. • His mother in Vienna: Josephine Csazinsky (died 1892), a former singer in Vienna, had become a singing teacher.

APRIL 15

• The Drei Mohren hotel: in Augsburg; the name means "The Three Moors"; hence the joke about whitewashing.

APRIL 18

• Frau Raila: she and her husband were residents of Bayreuth, and will be mentioned a few times again in passing.

APRIL 19

• We drive to the theater: the Markgräfliches Opernhaus, the Court theater of Friedrich, the Margrave of Bayreuth, and his wife, Wilhelmine (a sister of Frederick the Great), was completed in 1748 and is still in use today, one of the finest examples of baroque theater architecture still in existence; the architect was the Italian Giuseppe Galli-Bibiena, who was assisted by his son Carlo. • The Eremitage: a rococo summer residence in fine parklands just outside Bayreuth; both this and the former margraves' palace in the town were now the property of the King of Bavaria.

APRIL 20

• The job of our Peter C[ornelius]: a reference to Cornelius's delay in supplying the poem Cosima had requested from him for Wagner's approaching birthday.

APRIL 21

• Prof. Danz: Heinrich Aemilius August Danz, a lawyer and writer on Roman law. • Haase: Friedrich Haase (1825–1911), director of the Leipzig opera 1870–76. • V. Strantz: Ferdinand von Strantz, producer at the Leipzig opera 1870–76, afterward at the Court opera in Berlin.

APRIL 23

• The Brühl terrace: a celebrated promenade built in 1738 on the south bank of the river Elbe.

APRIL 24

• The picture gallery: the Zwinger, renowned as one of the finest collections in Europe. • "Stille Musik": a narrow corner in Dresden.

APRIL 26

• The office of the royal household: Count von Schleinitz was minister of the royal household in Berlin.

APRIL 27

• Johanna: Johanna Jachmann-Wagner (1826–94), adopted daughter of Wagner's eldest brother, Albert, her mother, Elise Gollmann (1800–64) having become Albert's wife in 1828; Johanna married a district councilor, Alfred Jachmann, in 1859; she was the first Elisabeth in *Tannhäuser* at Dresden in 1845, when she was only eighteen; this led to a brilliant singing career in Dresden and Berlin, which sometimes got in the way of Wagner's plans to make use of her, hence Cosima's sour remark; losing her singing voice in 1862, she turned to acting, but later she recovered her voice sufficiently for Wagner to invite her to sing at the foundation-laying ceremony of the Bayreuth festival theater, and also at the first festival, in 1876. • Old Moor: a character in Schiller's play *Die Räuber*, who in Act IV is heard speaking from a dungeon in a ruined castle.

APRIL 28
• He read his thing out: *The Destiny of Opera.* • Hellwig: Cosima actually wrote "Herwig," but he has been identified by the German editors as the son of the actor Friedrich Hellwig; see note for March 13, 1874.

APRIL 29
• Herr Tappert: Wilhelm Tappert (1830–1907), musicologist and lecturer at the Neue Akademie der Tonkunst (New Academy of Music) in Berlin (not Joachim's, but a rival establishment).

APRIL 30
• Wallner's theater: Franz Wallner (1810–76), theater director in Berlin.

MAY 1
• Walter: Gustav Walter (1834–1910), a tenor in Vienna from 1856. • Bancroft: George B. Bancroft (1800–91), American statesman and historian, American ambassador in Berlin 1868–74. • Countess Pourtalès: widow of Albert, Count von Pourtalès (1812–61), Prussian ambassador in Paris from 1859 until his death; Wagner became friends with them in Paris while preparing the production of the revised *Tannhäuser*. • Reichensperger: August Reichensperger (1808–95), member of the Prussian Lower Chamber and the Reichstag.

MAY 3
• The Violin Aria by Spohr: Spohr's Violin Concerto No. 8.

MAY 4
• *Mignon*: opera by Ambroise Thomas.

MAY 6
• *"Blick ich umher"* and the *"Abendstern"*: these were in fact written for baritone, being Wolfram's songs in *Tannhäuser* (Acts II and III, respectively). • Countess Danckelmann: Countess Hertha Danckelmann, née Moltke.

MAY 7
• Frau Dirksen: wife of a councilor in the Department of Foreign Affairs, Karl von Dirksen. • General Beyer: commander of an army corps during the Franco-Prussian war. • Löser: Bernhard Löser, a financier, founder of the Wagneriana, a society that aimed at establishing a Wagner festival in Berlin.

MAY 9
• Nessler: Viktor Ernst Nessler (1841–90), active at this time as a choir conductor, but later to achieve success as an opera composer (*Der Trompeter von Säckingen*, etc.).

MAY 10
• "Zum Roth und Weissen Löwen": this is the correct name of the house in which Wagner was born, though Cosima in fact writes "Weissen und rothen Löwen"; the address is Brühl 88; a newspaper clipping found in a later volume of the Diaries records that on Wagner's sixtieth birthday (May 22, 1873) a plaque was affixed to the house, describing it as his birthplace. • Jeannettchen Thomé's house: a large house in the market square in which Adolf Wagner and his sister Friederike lived; Jeannettchen Thomé was part owner of the house.

MAY 11
• Prof. Ebers: Georg Moritz Ebers (1837–98), professor at Leipzig since 1870, was a novelist as well as an Egyptologist, most of his novels being set in Egypt. • Prof. Czermak: see note for December 4, 1870.

MAY 13
• Thought of Schopenhauer: Schopenhauer lived in Frankfurt. • The day (August

1862): Cosima incorrectly wrote 1863; the event, as described by Wagner in *Mein Leben*, is quoted in the introduction (page 12).

MAY 14

• The machinist Brandt: Karl Brandt (1828–81), technical director of the theater in Darmstadt; he enjoyed a high reputation throughout Germany, and Wagner had great respect for his talents; he took an active part both in the building of the festival theater in Bayreuth and in the production of the *Ring* there in 1876. • Prince H[ohenlohe]: Konstantin.

MAY 15

• Count Dunken: possibly Wilhelm, Count von Dunten (1800–78).

MAY 19

• The poem at last arrives: from Peter Cornelius. • Emil Heckel (1831–1908): a music dealer in Mannheim, he suggested the establishment of Wagner Societies in various towns to raise funds for the Bayreuth festival, and founded the first of them in Mannheim. • The green pamphlet: a pamphlet by Wagner, bound in green, entitled *Über die Aufführung des Bühnenfestspieles "Der Ring des Nibelungen"* (*On the Production of the Stage Festival Play* Der Ring des Nibelungen), published in April 1871; Wagner later included the text of this in his *Schlussbericht über die Umstände und Schicksale, welche die Ausführung des Bühnenfestspiels "Der Ring des Nibelungen" bis zur Gründung von Wagner-Vereinen begleiteten* (*A Final Report on the Fates and Circumstances That Attended the Execution of the Stage Festival Play* Der Ring des Nibelungen *up to the Founding of the Wagner Societies*); this is published in vol. 9 of the collected writings.

MAY 21

• The Battle of Torgau: in which Frederick the Great defeated the Austrians in 1760. • Ziethen: Hans Joachim von Zieten (or Ziethen) (1699–1786), Prussian general.

MAY 23

• Oskar von Redwitz (1823–91): German writer and poet, wrote the anonymous article that appeared in the *Augsburger Allgemeine Zeitung* of February 19, 1865, entitled *"Richard Wagner und die öffentliche Meinung"* ("R. W. and Public Opinion"), which was intended to alienate King Ludwig from Wagner by pointing to his extravagance.

MAY 26

• *"Beaucoup de vie dans nos folies et nos ruines"* ("Much life among our follies and our ruins"). • Karl Gutzkow (1811–78): German playwright and novelist, dramaturg in Dresden 1847–49, from 1869 in Berlin. • Makart: Hans Makart (1840–84), Austrian painter, mainly large historical subjects; Wagner and Cosima were later to meet him in Vienna. • In his story: *"Eine Pilgerfahrt zu Beethoven"* ("A Pilgrimage to Beethoven"), written by Wagner in Paris in 1840.

MAY 27

• "A box on the ears for Gutzkow": Wagner's foreword to his collected writings, printed at the beginning of vol. 1, contains only a passing reference to Gutzkow, whose views on music he describes as "very coarse."

MAY 28

• Baron Schack: Adolf Friedrich, Count von Schack (1815–94), German writer and translator and founder of a picture gallery in Munich. • Lindhorst: see note for January 1, 1871. • The fire and its significance: though the fire started by the Communards in Paris destroyed the Tuileries, it in fact touched only the corner of the Louvre that contained the library.

for the unification of Italy, 1860/61. • *Norma*: opera by Bellini.

AUGUST 17

•Book on the principle of legitimacy: in this book, entitled *Das Legitimitätsprinzip* (1868), Friedrich Brockhaus deals with the principle that usurpers and conquerors should not be recognized as long as the legitimate rulers are alive or have not abdicated. • Hänlein: A. Hänlein, a member of the committee of the Mannheim Wagner Society, one of the "five just men" (see note for December 31, 1871).

AUGUST 20

•*Oberon*: Weber's last opera.

AUGUST 21

•Princess Hatzfeld: Marie, Princess Hatzfeld, née von Nimptsch (1820–97), mother of Marie von Schleinitz; Prince Hatzfeld was her second husband.

AUGUST 23

• The "merry tune" from *Tristan*: the melody played by the shepherd in Act III when he sees Isolde's ship.

AUGUST 28

•Another book about Beethoven: *Die Beethoven-Feier und die Kunst der Gegenwart* (*The B. Centennial and the Art of Today*) by Ludwig Nohl, 1871.

AUGUST 29

•Louis Brassin (1840–84): pianist and teacher, from 1869 at the Conservatoire in Brussels. • The Rumanian shares: in the Rumanian railroads; see note for June 3, 1870.

AUGUST 31

•An article on Tausig: "Karl Tausig," by Hans von Bülow, in *Signale für die musikalische Welt* of August 22, 1871.

SEPTEMBER 1

•A Herr Hey: Julius Hey (1831–1909), a singing teacher who appears in the Diaries later, since he coached Georg Unger for the role of Siegfried in the Bayreuth *Ring* of 1876; in his book of reminiscences, *Richard Wagner als Vortragsmeister* (*R. W. as Producer*), published posthumously in 1911, Hey states that he had been a pupil of Wagner's friend Friedrich Schmitt and that he first met Wagner in 1864, when he called on him in Starnberg, the meeting having been arranged personally by King Ludwig.

SEPTEMBER 3

•Baron Uechtritz: Friedrich von Uechtritz (1800–75), a writer.

SEPTEMBER 5

•R. works "in ink": it was Wagner's practice to write his first composition sketch in pencil and to ink it over when he was satisfied that it met his intentions. • The Goethe Foundation: on the centennial (1849) of Goethe's birth, Liszt wrote an exposé (*De la Fondation Goethe à Weimar*) proposing an olympiad of all the arts under the patronage of the Grand Duke of Weimar; lack of funds prevented its realization, but Liszt never abandoned his plan; Wagner replied to Liszt's plan with an open letter to him dated May 8, 1851, and entitled *"Über die Goethestiftung"* (*"Concerning the Goethe Foundation"*); it is published in vol. 5 of the collected writings. • "The dying Englishman . . .": a jocular reference to Peabody; see note for February 10, 1870.

SEPTEMBER 6

• Just as little as his *Tristan* the Emperor of Brazil: see note for March 6, 1870. • "The symphony into which my father has transferred these effects": Liszt's symphonic poem *Ce qu'on entend sur la montagne* (1848–49).

SEPTEMBER 7

• E. Ollivier has sent us his defense: *Le Procès historique* (1871).

SEPTEMBER 8

• Little Daniel: the son of her sister, Blandine.

SEPTEMBER 11

• Joachim and his wife: Amalie Joachim, née Weiss (1839–99), a contralto singer, gave up her operatic career at Vienna and Hanover in 1866, three years after marrying the eminent violinist, but continued as a *Lieder* singer, gaining international fame, and visiting both England and the United States.

SEPTEMBER 14

• Beethoven's song: "*Herz, mein Herz, was soll das geben?*" Words by Goethe.

SEPTEMBER 15

• Our whole intercourse revolved around this production of the *Nibelungen*: referring to his friendship with Otto and Mathilde Wesendonck while he was composing *Die Walküre* and the first two acts of *Siegfried* in Zurich.

SEPTEMBER 20

• A Herr Hugo von Sänger: correctly, Senger (1835–92), musical director in Geneva from 1869 and a supporter of Wagner.

SEPTEMBER 22

• Jeremias Gotthelf (1797–1854): eminent Swiss novelist who wrote, mainly in Swiss dialect, about peasant life. • His work on Prudentius: Clemens Brockhaus's *Aurelius Prudentius Clemens*, dealing with the fourth-century poet of the early Christian church, was published in Leipzig in 1872.

SEPTEMBER 23

• "*Albumblatt für Fürstin M.*": i.e., for Princess Pauline Metternich, written in 1861.
  • The sonata which Frau Wesendonck had: the Sonata in A-flat Major, written for Mathilde Wesendonck in 1853. • That piece for Countess Pourtalès: "*Albumblatt für Gräfin Pourtalès*" in A-flat major, 1861.

SEPTEMBER 24

• The meeting of Old Catholics: the first congress of Old Catholics met in Munich, September 22–24, and devised a program for church reform, pastoral duties, and communal activities.

SEPTEMBER 27

• The old Frau von Schleinitz: Jenny, Baroness von Schleinitz (born 1809), was the widow of a brother of Marie von Schleinitz's husband and the mother of the two nieces mentioned on September 24.

SEPTEMBER 29

• "Let the ghost do what it likes" ("*Lass das Gespenst doch machen, was es will!*"): in Goethe's *Faust*, Part Two, Act I, after the appearance of Helen of Troy.

SEPTEMBER 30

• Herr Batka: Johann Nepomuk Batka (1845–1917), a music critic.

OCTOBER 3

• Gessner's wife: Judith Heidegger married the Swiss engraver and writer of prose idylls Salomon Gessner (1730–88) in 1761. • Bodmer: Johann Jacob Bodmer (1698–1783), Swiss man of letters, discoverer and editor of several medieval German poems, including *Das Nibelungenlied*. • "*Helle Wehr*" ("Shining Steel"): the opening words of Brünnhilde's oath swearing vengeance on Siegfried in Act II of *Götterdämmerung*.

OCTOBER 10

• Herr Bratfisch: Karl Bratfisch (1829–1901), military band leader and organist in Glogau, later in Stralsund.

OCTOBER 12
• Such things as "Norma," "Somnambula," etc.: Liszt's fantasies for piano on themes from the operas by Bellini. • His gypsy airs: Wagner probably means Liszt's "Hungarian Rhapsodies."

OCTOBER 13
• Littré: Maximilien Paul Emile Littré (1808–81), French philosopher and philologist, author of the French dictionary *Dictionnaire de la langue française.*

OCTOBER 18
• The minister Lutz: Johann, Baron von Lutz (1826–90), a Bavarian minister of state involved in the negotiation of treaties setting up the German Reich.

OCTOBER 19
• Countess Dönhoff: Countess Marie Dönhoff, née Princess di Camporeale (1848–1929), married to Count Karl Dönhoff, first secretary in the German Embassy in Vienna; she later married Bernard Prince von Bülow, who was chancellor of the German Reich 1900–09; Wagner met Count Dönhoff in Paris during the 1860–61 period.

OCTOBER 22
• A book by Freytag: Gustav Freytag (1816–95), German writer; the work mentioned is *"Aus dem Staat Friedrichs des Grossen"* ("From the Nation of Frederick the Great"), a chapter in his 5-vol. *Bilder aus der deutschen Vergangenheit*, 1859–67 (English translation in two volumes published 1862–63 under the general title *Pictures of German Life*).

OCTOBER 23
• Mariani: Angelo Mariani (1821–73), who conducted the first performance of *Lohengrin* in Bologna on November 1, 1871.

OCTOBER 24
• Feustel: Friedrich Feustel (1824–91), a banker in Bayreuth who was to become one of the leading figures in establishing the festival there, as well as a close personal friend. • Kolb: Johann Ludwig Georg Kolb (1822–84), head of the Laineck-Friedrichsthal flax mills and member of the Landtag; or Karl Heinrich Sofian Kolb (1824–95), director of the cotton mills, both Bayreuth. • The disclosures of Benedetti: in his recently published pamphlet, *Ma mission en Prusse (My Mission in Prussia)*, Benedetti set out to disprove Bismarck's allegation that France had been trying for years to enlist Prussia's help in annexing Belgium and Luxembourg; see July 15, 1870, and note.

OCTOBER 25
• Prof. Werder: Karl Friedrich Werder (1806–93), a dramatist; his poems were not published until after his death. • The "altar stone": the passage at the end of Act II of *Götterdämmerung* when, according to Wagner's stage directions, Siegfried and Gutrune are borne to the temple to make sacrifices before their marriage. • Brünnhilde's expression: Wagner's stage direction reads, "Brünnhilde looks fixedly at Gutrune, who waves to her with a friendly smile."

OCTOBER 27
• *The Emergence of Tragedy from Music (Die Entstehung der Tragödie aus der Musik)*: Nietzsche finally gave it the title *Die Geburt der Tragödie aus dem Geiste der Musik (The Birth of Tragedy out of the Spirit of Music)*; it was published by Fritzsch in Leipzig at the beginning of 1872. • His essay on Auber: *Erinnerungen an Auber (Reminiscences of Auber)*, published in vol. 9 of the collected writings.

OCTOBER 30
• The new Easter Realm: a literal translation of *Oster-Reich* (the German name for Austria is Österreich). • Frau von Loë: Franziska, Baroness von Loë (born 1833),

was a daughter of Prince Hatzfeld, who subsequently married Marie von Schleinitz's mother; she was the wife of Baron Walther von Loë (see note for August 17, 1870).

NOVEMBER 1

• Roggenbach: Franz, Baron von Roggenbach (1825–1907), a member of the Reichstag and opponent of Bismarck. • *Der Templer und die Jüdin* (*The Knight Templar and the Jewess*): opera by Heinrich Marschner (1795–1861), cofounder with Weber of German romantic opera; it is based on Scott's *Ivanhoe*.

NOVEMBER 3

• An inscription in a copy of *Siegfried* for Bratfisch: since Bratfisch means "fried fish," Wagner's punning spirit inevitably had him swimming in butter; the inscription runs, "*Weil er in der Treue-Butter geschwommen, soll Bratfisch auch den Siegfried bekommen.*" • Hans's Beethoven edition: an annotated edition by Hans von Bülow of Beethoven's piano works from Opus 53 to Opus 111, published by Cotta in Stuttgart.

NOVEMBER 4

• The St. Gotthard railroad: on October 28 the German Reich joined the agreement between Switzerland and Italy to build the St. Gotthard tunnel.

NOVEMBER 6

• His fine letter to the Italians: "*Brief an einen italienischen Freund über die Aufführung des 'Lohengrin' in Bologna*" ("Letter to an Italian Friend [Arrigo Boito] About a Performance of *Lohengrin* in Bologna"), in vol. 9 of the collected writings.

NOVEMBER 8

• Constantin Frantz's new book: *Das neue Deutschland* (*The New Germany*), 1871.

NOVEMBER 10

• Uhland's library: the poet Ludwig Uhland (1787–1862), who had been a professor of German language and literature in Tübingen up to 1833, was keenly interested in literary research, and Wagner's library contains his 2-vol. *Alte hoch- und niederdeutsche Volkslieder* (*Old High and Low German Folk Songs*), 1844.

NOVEMBER 11

• Herr Bruckmann: Friedrich Bruckmann (1814–98), owner of an art and book publishing firm in Munich. • A drawing by Herr Jaeger: Carl Jaeger (1833–87) produced in 1870/71 twelve half-length portraits of various composers for a "gallery of German composers."

NOVEMBER 14

• What Germany looks like from the Ritterstrasse: the street on which Frantz lived. • From Freytag's book: *Bilder aus der deutschen Vergangenheit* (*Pictures of German Life*). • The wars of liberation: 1813–15.

NOVEMBER 15

• *Bayreuther Blätter*: the title of the periodical Wagner was intending to found in Bayreuth.

NOVEMBER 19

• His completed 2nd act: of *Götterdämmerung* (orchestral sketch).

NOVEMBER 24

• Herr Spiegel: a music teacher from Zurich; he prepared a copy for King Ludwig of Act II of *Götterdämmerung* (orchestral sketch).

NOVEMBER 25

• A history of the *Nibelungenring*: "*Epilogischer Bericht über die Umstände und Schicksale, welche die Ausführung des Bühnenfestspieles 'Der Ring des Nibelungen' bis zur Veröffentlichung der Dichtung desselben begleiteten*" ("Report on the Fates and Circumstances that Attended the Execution of the Stage Festival Play *Der Ring des Nibelungen* up

AUGUST 9
• Emil Devrient: actor (born 1803) and brother of Eduard and Karl Devrient, died on August 6, 1872.

AUGUST 12
• "You're a full 30 years old!" ("*Schier 30 Jahre bist du alt!*"): a quotation from Karl von Holtei's "*Mantellied*" ("Cloak Song") in his play *Lenore* (1827). • A Herr von Hagen: Edmund von Hagen (born 1850), philosopher and writer on Wagner.

AUGUST 14
• Levy in Dresden (not the Viennese one): i.e., not the conductor Hermann Levi, but a horn player in the orchestra during Wagner's years in Dresden.

AUGUST 15
• *Päpstin Johanna*: Pope Joan. • Crowning R. like Petrarch: the Italian poet Petrarch was awarded the laurel crown of the poet by the senate of Rome, and the coronation took place on the Capitol in Rome in 1341.

AUGUST 16
• Herr De Swert: Jules de Swert (1843–91), cellist and professor at the Hochschule in Berlin 1869–73.

AUGUST 17
• *Um Szepter und Kronen*: a novel by Gregor Samarov, pseudonym for Oskar Meding (1829–1903); English translation under the title *For Sceptre and Crown*. • Herr Windthorst: Ludwig Windthorst (1812–91), a Hanoverian statesman and a leading member of the Center party from 1870.

AUGUST 18
• Louis Schneider (1805–78): German actor and writer in Berlin. • The awakening of Barbarossa: according to legend, the Holy Roman Emperor Friedrich Barbarossa sleeps in a limestone cave in the Kyffhäuser hills in central Germany and will one day arise to restore the greatness of Germany.

AUGUST 19
• Frl. Lehmann: Lilli Lehmann (1848–1929), the celebrated Wagnerian soprano, was then only on the threshold of her career, having been engaged in Berlin in 1870 after appearances in Danzig and Leipzig; her mother, Marie Loew (1807–83), had been the leading soprano at Kassel under Spohr, and she trained both her daughters, Lilli and Marie Lehmann. • Mme Lucca: Pauline Lucca (1841–1908), celebrated Austrian soprano, at the Berlin opera since 1861.

AUGUST 21
• His brother-in-law Wolfram: Heinrich Wolfram, husband of Wagner's sister Klara.

AUGUST 22
• How he betrayed him in Paris: by causing Wagner great difficulties when singing the title role in the revised *Tannhäuser* in Paris in 1861.

AUGUST 23
• With his mother: Maria, née Princess of Prussia (1825–89). • *Natura lo fa . . .* ("Nature fashions him and then smashes the mold").

AUGUST 25
• The victory tower: the Siegesturm on the Hohe Warte, the hill behind the festival theater; it was erected to commemorate the war of 1870–71. • *Medea, Sappho*: plays by Grillparzer. • *Phèdre*: by Racine.

AUGUST 30
• King Marke's words: in Act II of *Tristan und Isolde;* King Ludwig in fact adapted the words in his letter of August 27, for Marke says, "This wonderful woman . . . whom my desire renounced in timid veneration" ("*Dies wunderhehre Weib . . . Der*

*mein Wunsch Ehrfurcht-scheu entsagte"*). • In behalf of the Herzen children: Natalie
and Olga, daughters of the Russian philosopher Alexander Herzen (1812–70) and
his wife Natalie, née Zacharinya (1817–52); the latter eloped with Georg Herwegh,
but returned to Herzen after a short while; after her death, Malwida von Meysenbug
became foster mother to the two girls.

AUGUST 31
• The revival of the city: after the great fire of October 1871. • Bürger: Gottfried
August Bürger (1747–94), author of the ballad *Lenore* (1773) • In the right concerning Schiller: in a review (1791) of Bürger's poems, Schiller had dealt harshly
with the poet; August Wilhelm Schlegel, in his essay on Bürger (1800), declared
that Schiller's review was morally unjustifiable. • "Mambrino's helmet": *Don
Quixote*, bk. I, chap. 21.

SEPTEMBER 1
• W. of Orange: William the Silent, Prince of Orange (1533–84), founder of the
Dutch republic.

SEPTEMBER 2
• Sedan flags: the day of the Battle of Sedan was celebrated in Germany as a public
holiday until the First World War.

SEPTEMBER 3
• Hofgärtnerei: the residence of the grandducal master of the gardens in Weimar;
Liszt had been given an apartment in it (now a Liszt museum). • "*Am stillen Herd*":
Walther von Stolzing's song in Act I of *Die Meistersinger*. • "*Liebestod*": sung by
Isolde in Act III of *Tristan und Isolde*.

SEPTEMBER 4
• The Erholung: a restaurant in Weimar. • Frau Merian-Genast: Emilie Merian-
Genast (1833–1905), a German *Lieder* and oratorio singer. • Beethoven's G Major:
the Fourth Piano Concerto. • The Spanish Gil with the green hose: in *Don Gil de
las calzas verdes*, a comedy by Tirso de Molina (1584?–1648).

SEPTEMBER 5
• La Roche Jacquelein: Louis Duverger Marquis de Larochejacquelein (1777–1815),
French Royalist general and supporter of Napoleon. • The Bojanowskis: relatives
of Hans von Bülow, whose sister Isa was married to Viktor von Bojanowski. •
[Opus] 106: Beethoven's *Hammerklavier* Sonata.

SEPTEMBER 7
• Epitaph for Tausig's grave: written down in the *Braunes Buch*, Wagner's words
were later inscribed on Tausig's gravestone. • Käfferlein: a Bayreuth lawyer. • The
whims of the particularist administration: i.e., opposition to a centralized German
state.

SEPTEMBER 16
• The new house: Dammallee 7, Bayreuth—a rented villa occupied by the family
pending the completion of Wahnfried. • Görres's foreword to *Lohengrin*: Johann
Joseph Görres (1776–1848), editor of *Die teutschen Volksbücher* (*German Folk Books*,
1807).

SEPTEMBER 18
• A Herr Kastner: Emmerich Kastner (1847–1916), a member of Wagner's group of
copyists, the so-called Nibelungen Kanzlei, up to January 1873.

SEPTEMBER 19
• The Sultan: Abdul-Aziz (1830–76), Sultan of Turkey from 1861.

SEPTEMBER 24
• Herr v. Gasser: Rudolf, Baron von Gasser (1829–1904), councilor of state and
Bavarian envoy.

September 26
• The ancestral lumber: *Urväterhausrat*—a quotation from Goethe's *Faust* (in Bayard Taylor's translation).
September 27
• Frau v. Helldorf: probably the wife of Otto Heinrich von Helldorf, a member of the Reichstag. • *Hanswursts Hochzeit* (*The Clown's Wedding*): a sketch for a farce by Goethe, 1775.
September 28
• The excitable Israelite: J. Rubinstein. • The taciturn Magyar: Anton Seidl (1850–1898), from Pest, later to become one of the greatest Wagnerian conductors, particularly at the Metropolitan Opera in New York.
September 29
• *"Signor Formica"*: a story in E. T. A. Hoffmann's *Serapionsbrüder,* and a possible influence on *Die Meistersinger von Nürnberg* (it concerns an elderly man who serenades a young girl).
September 30
• The Genelli: *Dionysus Being Educated by the Muses*; Cosima acquired it from Friedrich Brockhaus, knowing Wagner's admiration for it. • "In your 'Pilgrimage to Beethoven' ": in Wagner's story (*"Eine Pilgerfahrt zu Beethoven"*) a young man travels to Vienna on foot in an attempt to meet Beethoven.
October 1
• His letter to the people of Bologna (*Schreiben an den Bürgermeister von Bologna*): in it he thanks the mayor for granting him the freedom of the city; in vol. 9 of the collected writings. • Frl. Spitzeder: Adele Spitzeder, a former actress; owner of one of the so-called Dachauer banks, set up in Munich in 1871/72; she was sentenced in 1873 to three years in prison for fraud.
October 2
• Empress Charlotte (1840–1927): daughter of King Leopold I of the Belgians and wife of Maximilian, the Emperor of Mexico; she came to Europe in 1866 to beg help from Napoleon III and Pope Pius IX but was unsuccessful; after the execution of Emperor Maximilian in 1867, she went insane.
October 13
• The plays of Gozzi: a German translation of Gozzi's plays, in 5 vols., was published in Bern 1777–79.
October 14
• *Hasenauer*: Karl, Baron von Hasenauer (1833–94). • Maurice of Nassau (1567–1625): succeeded his father, William the Silent, as stadtholder in the Netherlands and expelled the Spaniards; his former friend Jan van Olden Barneveldt (1547–1619) became leader of the Republican party and opposed Maurice's war policy; at a national synod in 1618, Barneveldt was found guilty of treason and beheaded.
October 15
• Cardinal Hohenlohe: Gustav Adolf, Prince of Hohenlohe-Schillingsfürst (1823–1896), a cardinal since 1866, was the brother of the Princes Chlodwig and Constantin Hohenlohe, and a friend of Princess Wittgenstein.
October 18
• R. proposes a toast: this rhymes in German (*"Ein edler Geist, ein guter Christ, es lebe Franz Liszt"*).
October 19
• *"Je ne donnerai . . ."* ("I shall not give a cent for Bayreuth"). • The 300,000 thalers: the sum Wagner hoped to raise for Bayreuth by the sale of certificates of patronage.

OCTOBER 21

• Emile Ollivier sends a book by himself: *Une Visite à la chapelle de Medicis: Dialogue sur Michel-Ange et Raphaël (1872).*

OCTOBER 24

• Bernhardt: Joseph Bernhardt (1805–85); his portrait in oils of Wagner was painted in Munich in April 1868. • *Barbares et bardits:* the book concerned is *Le Mystère des bardes (The Mystery of the Bards)* by Adolphe Pictet (1799–1875), a French Swiss linguistic expert who sought to define the culture of prehistoric peoples through an investigation of their vocabulary.

OCTOBER 25

• A very fine reply to the Wilamowitz pamphlet: by Erwin Rohde, entitled *"After-philologie—Sendschreiben eines Philologen an Richard Wagner"* ("Pseudo-Philology—a Philologist's Open Letter to Richard Wagner").

OCTOBER 26

• Babett: not identified. • "Copyistery" (*"Kopisterei"*): a word invented by Wagner or Cosima to define his group of copyists, later dubbed the Nibelungen Kanzlei; the four men were Anton Seidl, Franz Fischer, Hermann Zumpe, and Emmerich Kastner. • An essay on the term "music drama": *"Über die Benennung 'Musikdrama,'"* published in vol. 9 of the collected writings; it first appeared in the *Musikalisches Wochenblatt* of November 1872.

OCTOBER 27

• Daru's history of Venice: *Histoire de la république de Venise* by Pierre Antoine Bruno Daru (1767–1829); the Council of Ten was a secret committee of the Venetian senate, wielding almost absolute power from the fourteenth to the eighteenth centuries.

OCTOBER 28

• Daniella: Cosima's eldest daughter, hitherto referred to as Lulu or Lusch; the name is correctly spelled Daniela, but Cosima always writes it with two *l*'s. • *Hermann und Dorothea:* a lengthy idyllic poem by Goethe. • Herr Lenbach cables: the telegram is placed between the pages of the Diaries. • Menzel's picture of Frederick and Voltaire: in a set of sketches dealing with the times of Frederick the Great by Adolph von Menzel (1815–1905).

NOVEMBER 4

• *"Waffenlos höhnt mich der Feind":* more a paraphrase than a direct quotation of Siegmund's words in Act I of *Die Walküre,* as he wonders where he is to find the sword promised him by his father, Wälse, in his hour of need; the point of the joke here is that the sword was all the time stuck in the tree in Hunding's hut, only waiting to be pulled out—something that Siegmund did not yet know, though both Wagner and Cosima did. • Beethoven's B-flat Sonata: the *Hammerklavier,* Opus 106.

NOVEMBER 5

• *Reineke Fuchs:* the German name for the fable of Reynard the Fox.

NOVEMBER 6

• *Frithiof's Saga:* one of the Icelandic sagas, dealing with the exploits of a Norwegian hero.

NOVEMBER 7

• A wonderful poem by Emperor Heinrich VI: the 2-vol. *Sammlung von Minnesingern (Collection of Minnesingers)*, published in Zurich 1758–59, opens with a poem by Heinrich VI (1165–97), the son of Friedrich Barbarossa; Heinrich was a minnesinger (a composer of courtly love songs), belonging to that group of medieval German poets somewhat similar in style and outlook to the troubadours. • Wolfram: Wolfram von Eschenbach (c.1170–c.1220), German poet; he plays a

of 1851, it was re-erected in the suburb of Sydenham for purposes of popular entertainment, and from 1855 on, symphony concerts were given there every Saturday.

JANUARY 11
•" The Battle" ("*Die Schlacht*"). • "The Diver" ("*Der Taucher*"). • His poem to the King: vol. 8 of the collected writings ends with three poems, of which the second, "*Bei der Vollendung des* Siegfried" ("On the Completion of *Siegfried*"), is obviously the one meant here; in it Wagner asks how he could have completed this work without the inspiration of his youthful friend. • *O Kosel* . . . : since Kosel is a nickname for Cosima, and *Getosel* is a diminutive form of the word for "din," perhaps the nearest one can get in translation is to describe Cosima as "a fair little nuisance"!

JANUARY 12
•Klopstock: Friedrich Gottlieb Klopstock (1724–1803), the German poet. • The complete "*Fanget an*": a reference to Walther von Stolzing's "Trial Song" in Act I of *Die Meistersinger,* the symbol of genuine artistic expression free of convention or foreign influences. • Samiel lurking in the bushes: in Act I of *Der Freischütz.* • From the drinking song to the end of the act: Act I of *Der Freischütz.*

JANUARY 13
•Queisser: Friedrich Benjamin Queisser (1817–93), a member of the Dresden Court band 1842–85 and teacher at the music school there, a friend of Wagner's since the first production of *Tannhäuser* in 1845.

JANUARY 17
•Lepsius: Karl Richard Lepsius (1810–84), Egyptologist, professor in Berlin. • Helmholtz: Hermann von Helmholtz (1821–94), physician and physiologist, professor in Berlin. • Delbrück: Martin Friedrich Rudolf Delbrück (1817–1903), Prussian statesman, head of the Reichskanzler's office. • The Crown Prince of Württemberg: Wilhelm (1848–1921), nephew of King Karl I, whom he succeeded in 1891. • Countess Oriola: Luise (born 1824), lady in waiting to Empress Augusta. • Princess Biron: Helene, Princess of Curland, née Princess Mestschersky (born 1820), wife of Calixt, Prince of Curland (1817–82). • Countess Voss: not identified for certain, but presumably not the Countess Luise Voss whose acquaintance Cosima made in Venice on September 22, 1876 (unless Cosima had forgotten meeting her before). • Frau von Rochow: presumably the wife of the Prussian envoy in Stuttgart, von Rochow.

JANUARY 19
•Marie (Jacoby): daughter of Wagner's brother Albert, married since 1851 to a Hamburg businessman, Carl Jacoby.

JANUARY 20
•C Minor Symphony: Beethoven's Fifth. • Dr. Baumeister: Hermann Baumeister (1806–77), from 1853 President of the City Parliament (*Bürgerschaft*). • Senator Petersen: Karl Petersen (1809–92), Chief of Police in Hamburg from 1860, Mayor in 1876.

JANUARY 23
•Prince Carolath: Heinrich zu Schönaich-Carolath (1852–1920), a member of the Prussian Upper Chamber.

JANUARY 24
•Herr *Zacharias*: a merchant and banker, friend of Feustel's.

JANUARY 25
•Minna's wickedness: in May 1837 Wagner's wife Minna ran away from Riga with a merchant named Dietrich; Wagner pursued her to Dresden but was unable to persuade her to return (though she eventually did so); he traveled back alone and

in August 1837 had to remain in Lübeck several days, because of bad weather. • *Barbiere*: Rossini's *Il Barbiere di Siviglia*. • Herr von Wolzogen: Alfred, Baron von Wolzogen (1823–83), from 1868 director of the Court theater in Schwerin; father of Hans von Wolzogen.

JANUARY 26
• The Grand Duke: Friedrich Franz II of Mecklenburg-Schwerin (1823–83), grand duke from 1842. • Herr Schmitt: Aloys Schmitt (1827–1902). • The singer Hill: Karl Hill (1831–93), an official in the postal service before being engaged as a bass singer at Schwerin in 1868.

JANUARY 27
• Von Bülow: Bernhard von Bülow. • Schmale: Wilhelm Schmale (born 1792), producer at Schwerin from 1836; Wagner was conductor at Bad Lauchstädt and Magdeburg when he met him, in 1834.

JANUARY 29
• The Duchess of Mecklenburg: Grand Princess Katharina Michailovna, wife of Duke Georg of Mecklenburg-Strelitz. • Countess Brühl: Hedwig (born 1835).

JANUARY 31
• Dr. Brandis: probably Johannes Brandis (1842–1927), archaeologist and secretary to Empress Augusta.

FEBRUARY 1
• The two *Maries*: Muchanoff and von Schleinitz. • A paper on Hesiod: *"Der Florentinische Tractat über Homer und Hesiod, ihr Geschlecht und ihren Wettkampf,"* published in the *Rheinisches Museum*, Frankfurt, 1873.

FEBRUARY 2
• General Tresckow: Hermann von Tresckow (1818–1900), a Prussian general. • Count Solms: Eberhard, Count of Solms-Sonnenwalde (1825–1912), a Prussian diplomat. • A foreign princess: the Crown Princess Victoria was a daughter of Queen Victoria of Great Britain and Ireland. • The lawsuit concerning Pastor Grote: not identified. • Guelph money: Guelph was the family name of the Hanoverian monarchs; the last king, Georg V (deposed in 1866), was still making attempts at restoration.

FEBRUARY 3
• Count Usedom: Count Guido Usedom (1805–84), a Prussian diplomat, director of the royal museums in Berlin since 1872.

FEBRUARY 6
• Herr Jäger: Ferdinand Jäger (1838–1902): though Wagner did not engage him for the *Ring* in 1876, he subsequently took Jäger under his wing, even to the extent of giving him the title role in *Parsifal* in 1882, but his respect for the tenor was always fluctuating.

FEBRUARY 7
• *The Old and New Faith* (*Der alte und der neue Glaube*): by David Friedrich Strauss, published in 1872.

FEBRUARY 9
• Kahnt's journal: *Neue Zeitschrift für Musik*. • Dr. Moritz Heyne: (1837–1906), lecturer in Halle and Basel.

FEBRUARY 10
• Laplace: Pierre Simon, Marquis de Laplace (1749–1827), French mathematician and astronomer, propounded important theories on the origin of the solar system.

FEBRUARY 11
• Düntzer: Heinrich Düntzer (1813–1901) published his study of Goethe's *Faust* in 2 vols. in 1850/51.

FEBRUARY 14
• Robert Franz (1815–92): composer of songs and director of music at the University of Halle. • Prof. Bachofen's *Tanaquil*: Johann Jakob Bachofen (1815–87), professor of Roman law, published *Die Sage von Tanaquil* in 1870. • Ille's *Tannhäuser*: Eduard Ille (1823–1900), a historical painter in Munich, produced a series of water colors, among them *Tannhäuser*.

FEBRUARY 16
• The *Völsunga Saga*: one of the later Icelandic sagas (thirteenth century) dealing with the Nibelungen material.

FEBRUARY 18
• Herman Grimm (1828–1901): a German art historian who wrote lives of Michelangelo, Raphael, etc.

FEBRUARY 21
• Poem to R. by Herwegh: this poem, enclosed with the Diaries, pokes fun at Wagner for currying favor with the emperor by conducting a concert before him in Berlin on February 4, predicting that it will not bring him much financial help.

FEBRUARY 25
• A distich to Herwegh: Wagner's reply to Herwegh's poem, written in his *Braunes Buch* on February 24, accuses him of being "a democratic doggerel poet" (*"der demokrat'sche Bänkelsänger"*).

FEBRUARY 27
• The first part of the third volume: of Wagner's autobiography, *Mein Leben,* dealing with his exile in Zurich, 1850. • The passage concerning *Elective Affinities*: a description in *Mein Leben* of a walking tour with Herwegh in the Swiss Alps in 1853, during which Wagner reread Goethe's novel (*Die Wahlverwandtschaften*) and argued with Herwegh about it. • The trip with my father and Herwegh: in July 1853, to the Vierwaldstätter Lake.

MARCH 1
• His essay on the 9th Symphony: *Zum Vortrag der neunten Symphonie Beethovens,* published in vol. 9 of the collected writings. • Herr Zumpe: Hermann Zumpe (1850–1903) joined Wagner's "Nibelungen Kanzlei" in 1872, straight from his studies in Leipzig; he eventually became a prominent conductor, holding appointments in Stuttgart, Hamburg, and Munich.

MARCH 2
• Philipp Wackernagel (1800–77): published his edition of Luther's sacred songs (*Luthers geistliche Lieder*) in 1848.

MARCH 3
• Goethe's Iphigenie: *Iphigenie auf Tauris,* classical drama, 1787. • Menzel's new book: *Geschichte der neuesten Jesuitenumtriebe in Deutschland,* by Wolfgang Menzel. • The bad years following '48: the reactionary mood following the revolution of that year.

MARCH 4
• We resume work on the biography: at the paragraph beginning "With the New Year of 1860," against which in the manuscript Cosima wrote, "Resumed March 4, 1873, Dammallee, Bayreuth."

MARCH 5
• Schlegel's book on the language of the Indians: *Die Sprache und Weisheit der Inder,* by Friedrich Schlegel, 1808.

MARCH 7
• [Mathilde] Mallinger's portrayal of Eva: in the first production of *Die Meistersinger* in Munich, 1868.

MARCH 8
• *À tort et à travers*: at random.

MARCH 9
• "Letter to Berlioz" ("*Ein Brief an Hector Berlioz*"): written in Paris in February 1860 and reprinted in the collected writings, vol. 7. • Cotta: the publisher Johann Friedrich Cotta (1764–1832) paid his authors (including both Goethe and Schiller) very well. • Göschen: the publisher Georg Joachim Göschen (1752–1828) lived in the same house in Leipzig as Schiller and supported him. • President Grant: Ulysses Simpson Grant (1822–85), President of the United States of America 1869–77.

MARCH 11
• The tibia players: flautists in Ancient Rome. • Zagreus: Dionysos. • The child: presumably Cosima sent one of the children with the manuscript and the message. • The *Vikramorvasi*: a play by the Indian poet Kālidāsa (4th/5th century), translated into German under the title *Urwasi: Preis der Tapferkeit* (*The Price of Courage*) in 1837.

MARCH 12
• *Mālavikāgnimitra*: another play by Kālidāsa, translated into German in 1856.

MARCH 13
• *Maximilian's Prayer Book*: while in the service of the Holy Roman Emperor Maximilian I, Dürer drew illustrations in the margins of a specially printed book consisting of psalms, gospel texts, hymns, and prayers; the purpose of the book (printed in 1513) is not known.

MARCH 14
• When the morality of the thing was being discussed: by Wotan and Fricka in Act II. • *Robert le diable*: opera by Meyerbeer. • Another Mathilde: Mathilde Maier.

MARCH 16
• *Illuminati* (*enlightened ones*): a name assumed by several religious sects and secret societies.

MARCH 18
• Our tomb in the garden: Wagner and Cosima had decided to erect at once a vault in the garden of Wahnfried; both were eventually interred there. • R. dictates five pages to me: of *Mein Leben*. • The two women: his wife Minna and Mathilde Wesendonck.

MARCH 20
• "My pathos . . .": Goethe's *Faust*, Part One, Prologue in Heaven (Mephistopheles addressing God).

MARCH 21
• Essays by Carlyle: there are several essays on Goethe and Schiller in the 5 vols. of Carlyle's *Critical and Miscellaneous Essays*; the essay in praise of Goethe first appeared in *Fraser's Magazine*, no. 26 (1832), beneath an illustration of Stieler's portrait of Goethe, and contains the remarks: "Reader, within that head the whole world lies mirrored, in such clear ethereal harmony as it has done in none since Shakespeare left us. . . . The clearest, most universal man of his time."

MARCH 22
• "*Dors, mon enfant*": a song written by Wagner in Paris in 1840. • "*Schlafe, Kindchen, schlafe*": a little nursery song written by Wagner on New Year's Eve 1868, after he had been joined at Tribschen by Cosima along with Isolde and Eva; he later incorporated it (slightly modified) in the *Siegfried Idyll* (bars 92–148); it is "more realistic" because it warns the child to whom it is addressed that, if she does not go to sleep, a sheep will come and bite her, whereas "*Dors, mon enfant*" rhapsodizes

over "a child full of charms." • The Duke of Coburg: Ernst II (1818–93) was the elder brother of Queen Victoria's deceased consort, Prince Albert.

MARCH 23

• Goethe's death: Goethe died in 1832, when Wagner was nineteen.

MARCH 24

• Marschner's "Proud England": in the opera *Der Templer und die Jüdin* (based on Scott's *Ivanhoe*).

MARCH 25

• The article on Bayreuth: this article, *"Das Bühnenfestspielhaus in Bayreuth,"* is printed in vol. 9 of the collected writings; it contains an account of the foundation-laying ceremony.

MARCH 26

• Datives and accusatives: Cosima's German is not always quite correct grammatically. • His reply to the article in the *Conversations-Lexikon*: it appeared in the *Musikalisches Wochenblatt* (1873, p. 197). • Baron Erlanger: Baron Emil Erlanger, a banker in Paris; the reference has to do with the performance of the revised *Tannhäuser* in Paris, 1861. • The printed letter: presumably Wagner's letter of March 18, addressed to the Berlin Wagner Society, about the proposed production of *Lohengrin*; see March 17, 1873.

MARCH 27

• Schiller's unknown maiden: the poem *"Das Mädchen aus der Fremde."* • A good claim on the district: Bayreuth was Prussian from 1791 to 1810. • Eduard Brockhaus: Heinrich Eduard Brockhaus (1829–1914), son of Heinrich Brockhaus and a partner in the publishing firm from 1854.

MARCH 28

• The "Resurrection Hymn": the angels' chorus in the first scene (Night) of Goethe's *Faust*, Part One; it is based on a medieval German Easter hymn. • The *"Sehnsuchts-Walzer"* ("Waltz of Longing"): appears under this title in Beethoven's *15 Waltzes*, but is in fact one of Schubert's Opus 9 collection, in which it is called *"Trauerwalzer"* ("Waltz of Mourning").

MARCH 29

• He has lithographed *Lohengrin*: the firm of Breitkopf und Härtel first published the full score of *Lohengrin* in August 1852. • Niemann's cynicism: in connection with the catastrophic performances of the revised *Tannhäuser* in Paris in 1861; out of consideration for Niemann's relatives, some passages concerning him were omitted from the first public edition of *Mein Leben*; they were restored in the German edition of 1963.

MARCH 31

• The Rollwenzel tavern: an inn on the road from Bayreuth to the Eremitage, formerly much patronized by the writer Jean Paul (Bayreuth's most eminent citizen apart from Wagner).

APRIL 1

• *Europäische Minen und Gegenminen* (*Mines and Countermines*): Gregor Samarov's sequel to his *Um Szepter und Kronen*.

APRIL 4

• A Herr Tesarini: Luigi Tesarini, an Italian supporter of Wagner; see note for September 20, 1876. • Ricordi: G. Ricordi, the Italian music-publishing firm.

APRIL 5

• "The sources of the Iamblichus": an allusion to Rohde's treatise, *Die Quellen des Iamblichus in seiner Biographie des Pythagoras* (*Iamblichus's Sources in his Biography of*

*Pythagoras*); Wagner is referring jokingly to the twin sources of the river Main, both in the vicinity of Bayreuth. • Having second thoughts about the duel: a speculative translation, the German original being rendered additionally obscure by an illegible word; but the idea of the king of Bavaria setting himself up, like Lohengrin, as a champion of virtue, only to back away from the duel (with Telramund), seems to accord both with Wagner's view of King Ludwig's conduct toward himself, and with the behavior of Scott's hero in *The Fair Maid of Perth*. • A castle . . . above Tegernsee: incorrect; no such castle was built. • "Longing" (*"Die Sehnsucht"*). • He has once experienced my leaving for Pest: in August 1865, Hans von Bülow took Cosima to Pest for several weeks to separate her from Wagner; though she wrote to him from there, he could not reply, but he wrote his answers to her letters in a diary, so that she could read them later; this was the origin of the so-called *Braunes Buch*.

APRIL 6
• Gedon: Lorenz Gedon (1843–83), architect and sculptor; his works include the Schack Palais in Munich.

APRIL 7
• Paper about the philosophers before Plato: *"Die vorplatonischen Philosophen,"* a lecture given by Nietzsche in Basel in May 1873.

APRIL 8
• Prof. Paul Lagarde: Paul de Lagarde (1827–91), professor at Göttingen from 1869; his book, published 1873, was *Über das Verhältnis des deutschen Staates zu Theologie, Kirche und Religion*. • Karl Hillebrand (1829–84): German historian living in Florence; he later married Jessie Laussot; the book to which Cosima is referring is his *Frankreich und die Franzosen in der 2. Hälfte des 19. Jahrhunderts (France and the French in the Second Half of the Nineteenth Century)*, 1873.

APRIL 9
• "The sons of Thales": Thales (6th century B.C.) was the first of the Seven Sages of Greece; the others named were his pupils or successors.

APRIL 10
• *"Barbaros"* is translated as "un-German": Wagner wrote the following in his *Braunes Buch*, probably on the same day: "We must understand a thing in *our own* language, if we really want to understand it. (Barbaros—un-German. Luther.) That is the meaning of a 'German' culture. That in the Greek character which we can never understand, in any language, is what wholly separates us from them, e.g., their love—in—pederasty." • Megalissus's *The Un-German Catholics (Der undeutsche Katholik)*: Megalissus is a pseudonym for Georg Litzel (1694–1761). • *El médico de su honra (Physician of His Own Honor)*.

APRIL 11
• Our friend's music-making pastimes: it is not entirely clear whether this remark applies only to Nietzsche's composition *"Une monodie à deux,"* written in 1873 for the wedding of Olga Herzen to Gabriel Monod, or to his composing attempts in general—quite possibly both!

APRIL 13
• Tieck's preface to his *Vorschule Shakespeare's*: correctly, *Shakespeares Vorschule*, a collection of pre-Shakespearean plays in 2 vols., Leipzig, 1823–29.

APRIL 16
• Saxo Grammaticus: a twelfth-century Danish historian whose works include legends as well as facts; the story of Amleth was one of Shakespeare's sources for his *Hamlet*.

APRIL 19

• Conclusion of the 3rd volume: this volume of *Mein Leben* ends with a parting from Minna in Frankfurt in 1861 and the words "Here a short time ago Schopenhauer died."

APRIL 20

• Herr Kirchner: Theodor Kirchner (1823–1903), a composer much influenced by Schumann; director of the music school in Würzburg 1873–75.

APRIL 21

• Walter Scott's novel: *Count Robert of Paris* (1831).

APRIL 24

• Concert: in the Gürzenich Hall; according to the program, inserted in the Diaries, the works played were Beethoven's *Eroica* Symphony, the *Tannhäuser* Overture, the "Prize Song" from *Die Meistersinger*, the Overture to that work, the Prelude to *Lohengrin*, the "Spring Song" from *Die Walküre*, and the "*Kaisermarsch*"; Diener was the soloist in both songs.

APRIL 25

• The master of the Lipporger Passion: Meister der Lipporger Passion, a fifteenth-century Westphalian painter.

APRIL 27

• *Eisleben*: the young Wagner spent a year in this little town in Saxony (the birthplace of Martin Luther) immediately after the death of his stepfather, staying with Ludwig Geyer's younger brother, a goldsmith, and his old mother; writing about his childhood at the beginning of *Mein Leben*, Wagner remarks, "I always felt the desire to visit it again, to confirm the vividness of my memories, but curiously enough I have never done so." • The painter Rigault: correctly, Rigaud, Hyacinthe (1659–1743), the French portraitist. • Fair: the annual Easter Fair (furs, leather, cloth).

APRIL 28

• A theological work by Prof. *Overbeck*: in this month Overbeck completed his manuscript "*Über die Christlichkeit unserer heutigen Theologie*" ("On the Christianity of Our Present-day Theology"); Fritzsch published it later in the year.

APRIL 29

• Inserted beside this entry is a sheet containing some childish verses, making fun of Zumpe's love of beer.

APRIL 30

• R. drafts a fine letter: the article "*Das Bühnenfestspielhaus in Bayreuth*" ("The Festival Theater in Bayreuth") is prefaced in vol. 9 of the collected writings with a letter to Baroness Marie von Schleinitz, "to whose indefatigable zeal and support my great undertaking almost exclusively owes its progress."

MAY 1

• *Frauen Treue* (*A Woman's Loyalty*): by the thirteenth-century German writer Konrad von Würzburg.

MAY 3

• The muse of Parnassus: a reference to the "Prize Song," which contrasts the incorporeal muse of Parnassus (poet's dreams) with the corporeal Eve in Paradise and ends in rapture at finding the two combined in Pogner's daughter Eva ("Parnassus and Paradise"); Wagner had considerable difficulty composing his "Prize Song," and it came together in its final form when Cosima joined him (though not yet permanently) in Tribschen in 1866.

MAY 5

• "In the dead . . .": from Aeschylus's *Eumenides* (translation by Herbert Weir

Smyth). • Count Castell: Gustav zu Castell-Castell, Master of the Household to Ludwig II. • The Germans had paid the 5 billions: the sum of 5 billion francs was what France had to pay Germany as reparations after the Franco-Prussian War; the meaning of this sentence perhaps becomes a little clearer if one assumes that Cosima wrote "the Germans" when she meant "the French."

MAY 6

•Prof. Ott: Johann Christoph Ott (1811–74), an art teacher in Bayreuth.

MAY 7

•My good nephew: Alexander Ritter, in Würzburg, who was helping with the birthday preparations.

MAY 8

•Désirée Artôt's troupe: the French singer (1835–1907) made several tours, above all to Russia. • A prize from the Academy: Marie d'Agoult was awarded a prize by the Académie Française for her history of the Netherlands. • "Well thought out, Pater Lamormain . . .": a quotation (not quite correct) from Schiller's *Wallenstein* (*Die Piccolomini*).

MAY 11

•Paul Heyse (1830–1914): German writer and poet.

MAY 12

• A book by Holtzmann: Adolf Holtzmann (1810–70), professor of Sanskrit as well as of German language and literature; his book, *Kelten und Germanen*, was published in 1855.

MAY 14

• Marquise Pepoli-Hohenzollern: Princess Friederike von Hohenzollern-Sigmaringen (born 1820), married Marquis Pepoli, the Italian ambassador, in 1844. • Sascha Ritter: Alexander Ritter.

MAY 15

• *Villemarqué*: Hersart Vicomte de la Villamarqué (1815–95), editor of ancient Breton tales, poems, etc. • *Tannhäuser* in French and German: in acquiring *Tannhäuser* from the publisher Meser, Fürstner took over the original Dresden version; the new scenes in the revised Paris version had been set by Wagner to French words, and the rights in them belonged to the publisher Flaxland in Paris; for the production of the revised version in Munich in 1867, Wagner translated the French of the new scenes into German; in all other theaters the work was still being played in the Dresden version. • Herr *Beta*: Ottomar Beta (born 1845), a writer and journalist in Berlin; the article he wished to dedicate to Wagner ("*Die semitische und die germanische Race im neuen deutschen Reich*") appeared in the *Krämersche Freie Zeitung*, Berlin, in 1874; see also December 21, 1875.

MAY 16

•Wuerst: correctly Richard Wüerst (1824–81), music critic and composer in Berlin.

MAY 17

•The man in Berlin: Beta. *Ardinghello*: a novel (published 1787) by Johann Jakob Wilhelm Heinse (1749–1803); in *Mein Leben* Wagner states that he was much influenced by its fiery spirit in 1834, when he was adapting Shakespeare's *Measure for Measure* into a libretto for his second opera, *Das Liebesverbot*.

MAY 20

•Franziska: Franziska Ritter. • Young Brandt: Fritz Brandt, the son of Karl. • Fallmerayer: Jakob Philipp Fallmerayer (1790–1861), German historian; his book, *Geschichte der Halbinsel Morea im Mittelalter*, deals with the history of Morea (the peninsula forming the southern part of Greece) during the Middle Ages.

MAY 21
• "The three Moors": the Ximenez brothers, a trio from Cuba. • Concertmaster Abel: Ludwig Abel (1834–95), violinist, concertmaster in Munich. • Buonamici: Giuseppe Buonamici (1846–1914), Italian pianist and composer, pupil of Hans von Bülow, from 1868 a teacher at the music school in Munich. • Karl Ritter: son of Alexander and Franziska Ritter.

MAY 22
• The painter Hübner: Julius Hübner (1806–82) lived from 1839 in Dresden, where Wagner met him. • Burnouf: Eugène Burnouf (1801–52), French Orientalist. • R.'s former library: in *Mein Leben* Wagner describes how in the 1840's he set up a library in his Dresden apartment (Ostra-Allee); this included much old German and medieval literature, including the "valuable" and "rare" old *Romans des douze pairs*; on his flight from Dresden in 1849, the library was claimed by Heinrich Brockhaus as a recompense for 500 thalers that Wagner owed him, and "I was never able to recover from him this characteristic collection." • The program: the works performed were a Concert Overture composed by Wagner in 1831; Ludwig Geyer's two-act play, *Der bethlehemitische Kindermord*; Wagner's song *"Träume"* (from the *Wesendonck-Lieder*) in his own arrangement for violin and orchestra; and finally a stage presentation put together by Peter Cornelius, using music Wagner had composed in 1835 in Magdeburg for a New Year's cantata, in which a series of *tableaux vivants* based on the pictures of Genelli was enacted; Cornelius's text was spoken by Franziska Ritter, and Alexander Ritter was the conductor of an orchestra made up of amateur players from Bayreuth and Würzburg; Geyer's play was performed by a professional company then giving a season in Bayreuth, and the stage manager was Fritz Brandt. • *Janna*: not identified.

MAY 23
• Kummer: Alexander Kummer (born 1850), violinist, a nephew of the cellist Friedrich August Kummer, Wagner's friend in Dresden; Kummer had played *"Träume"* in its violin arrangement at the concert, and now he added another of the *Wesendonck-Lieder ("Der Engel")*.

MAY 25
• The sculptor Kietz: Gustav Adolf Kietz (1824–1908), a sculptor in Dresden and brother of Wagner's friend in the early Paris days, Ernst Benedikt Kietz.

JUNE 1
• The last fugue: Beethoven's Fugue in B-flat Major, Opus 133.

JUNE 2
• Councilor Bluntschli: Johann Kaspar Bluntschli (1808–81), statesman and jurist, a leading authority on international law; in 1873 he founded the Institute of International Law.

JUNE 5
• The essay on the origin of language: Jacob Grimm's *Über den Ursprung der Sprache*, 1851.

JUNE 6
• The melody of the shepherd boy: *Tannhäuser*, Act I, Scene 3, *"Der Mai ist da, der liebe Mai."* • *Götz von Berlichingen*: Goethe's play was published in 1773, when he was twenty-four.

JUNE 8
• Schloss Colmdorf: an eighteenth-century palace in the Königsallee, Bayreuth.

JUNE 13
• General von der Tann: Ludwig Samson, Baron von und zu der Tann-Rathsamhausen (1815–81), a Bavarian general who commanded the First Army Corps

during the Franco-Prussian War. • *Christ the Essene*: not identified. • The Wartburg: twelfth-century castle near Eisenach in Thuringia associated with the "Battle of the Bards," which Wagner dramatized in *Tannhäuser*, and with Martin Luther, who translated the New Testament there.

JUNE 14

• The Khedive: Ismael Pasha (1830–95), Khedive of Egypt 1863–79. • Omission: Cosima describes a misunderstanding with Wagner, in which she thought he was talking about their garden gate when in fact he was talking about "the fool" King Ludwig (*Tor* means both "gate" and "fool" in German).

JUNE 15

• Herr Riederer: Carl Riederer, the hotelkeeper at the Fantaisie. • Herr Erlanger: Baron Viktor von Erlanger, a banker in Vienna.

JUNE 16

• The Young Germany movement: a literary movement in the 1830's and 1840's that held that art should be politically committed, in the direction of liberalism and national consciousness; Heine was for a while associated with it, as were Ludwig Börne, Karl Gutzkow, Heinrich Laube, and Georg Herwegh. • *Ancient Germanic Law*: J. Grimm's *Deutsche Rechtsaltertümer* (1828) deals with the influence of law and poetry on ancient traditions.

JUNE 18

• The plans are badly printed: Wagner's article "*Das Bühnenfestspielhaus zu Bayreuth*" includes six architectural plans of the festival theater (also in the collected writings, vol. 9). • "*Nie sollst du mich befragen . . .*" ("Never shalt thou question me, nor bear the burden of knowledge"): the student apparently objected to "*noch*" ("nor"), and wanted "*nie*" ("never") repeated. • The *Xenienkampf*: a 2-vol. book entitled *Schiller und Goethe im Xenienkampf* (*S. and G. in the Xenia Contest*) by Eduard Boas (1815–53) was published in 1851; it dealt with the series of "xenia," distichs in the manner of Martial, which Goethe and Schiller wrote in reply to their critics; these "*Xenien*" were first published in Schiller's *Musenalmanach für 1797*.

JUNE 19

• The Jew Lasker: Eduard Lasker (1829–84), a member of the Reichstag since 1867 and leader of the left wing of the National Liberal party.

JUNE 20–23

• Renan's *Saint Paul*: Renan published his *Saint Paul* in 1869 as the 3rd vol. of his *Histoire des origines du christianisme*. • Dürer's laboring angels: in *Das Leben der Maria*, twenty woodcuts (1510).

JUNE 24

• Hesekiel's biography of Bismarck: *Das Buch vom Grafen Bismarck* (1868), by Georg Ludwig Hesekiel (1819–74).

JUNE 25

• Uhland's history of poetry in legend: Uhland's *Schriften zur Geschichte der Dichtung und Sage* appeared in 8 vols. 1865–73. • *Ferwer*: no Persian poet of this name can be identified.

JUNE 26

• *Iphigenia, Alceste*: by the latter Cosima presumably meant *Armide*, the Gluck opera that Wagner conducted at Dresden in March 1843; the other opera by Gluck, *Iphigenia in Aulis*, he conducted at Dresden, in a new version of his own, in February 1847. • "Two students on vacation": the first of these two articles, entitled "*Theaterreform*" (1849), was signed "J. P.—F. R., actors without an engagement," and the second, entitled "*Nochmals Theaterreform*" ("Theater Reform Again"), published in the same year, bore just the initials "J. P.—F. R."; both are included in vol. 12 of the collected writings (published after Wagner's death); the four initials are derived from the full name of the writer Jean Paul (Johann Paul Friedrich Richter).

JUNE 28

• *Une Nuit dans la Forêt*: complete title *Deux Mots, ou Une Nuit dans la Forêt (Two Words, or A Night in the Forest)*, an opera in one act by Nicolas Dalayrac (1753–1809), first produced in Paris in 1806. • The Landgraf: in *Tannhäuser*.

JUNE 30

• Dahn: Felix Dahn (1834–1912), German poet and novelist, mainly on historical subjects. • The Wartburg war: the "Battle of the Bards." • Heinrich von Ofterdingen as Tannhäuser: it was Wagner who gave the role of the minnesinger Heinrich von Ofterdingen in the "Battle of the Bards" to Tannhäuser, a minnesinger historically of later date; Elisabeth was also an invention of Wagner's, though she is given both the name and character of Saint Elisabeth of Hungary.

JULY 2

• Bleichröder: Gerson Bleichröder, a Berlin banker closely associated with Bismarck. • Wolfram: Wolfram von Eschenbach. • "None is of freedom . . .": Goethe's *Faust*, Part Two, in the translation of Philip Wayne.

JULY 3

• "Soon, soon thou shalt rest, too": quotation from Goethe's poem *"Über allen Gipfeln ist Ruh."*

JULY 4

• A man accused of heresy: Renan's *Life of Jesus* (1863) was the subject of bitter controversy in orthodox Catholic circles.

JULY 9

• Demanding the plans: of the projected Wagner festival theater in Munich, which was never built. • Otfried: Otfried von Weissenburg, author of a versified life of Christ (c.870).

JULY 10

• "Who trusts in joys . . ." (*"Wer auf Freuden vertraut, der zimbert auf den Regenbogen"*): an epigram by Freidank, an early-thirteenth-century itinerant poet from Swabia. • Set the fountains going: fountains of the most ingenious and intricate kind are a prominent feature of this rococo summer palace.

JULY 11

• The noble, fiery Mariani: Angelo Mariani died on June 13.

JULY 13

• Hildebrand's Echters: there was a series of frescoes, depicting scenes from *Der Ring des Nibelungen* by Michael Echter (1812–79), in the royal palace at Munich; Ludwig II had these copied in water colors for Wahnfried; the copies were made by the painter Franz Heigel (1813–88) and not by Eduard Hildebrand (1818–69); some water colors by Hildebrand were, however, inset in the wall of the gallery at Wahnfried.

JULY 14

• Reichsofen: the French name for the Battle of Wörth, at which, on August 6, 1870, the French cuirassiers distinguished themselves.

JULY 15

• R.'s barber: Bernhard Schnappauf was more than just the local barber—he was also the family factotum, running messages, helping out at social functions, attending to minor ailments; in 1877, he accompanied the family on their tour of Italy.

JULY 20

• "Believe me, who the ancient leaven . . .": Mephistopheles in Goethe's *Faust*,

Part One; Cosima quotes it incorrectly—the lines (in Bayard Taylor's translation) are, "Believe me, who for many a thousand year / The same tough meat have chewed and tested, / That from the cradle to the bier / No man the ancient leaven has digested!" • Daumer's book on Kaspar Hauser: Daumer had connections with the foundling Kaspar Hauser, who lived in his house, and he published three books on the subject; Cosima is probably referring to the third, published 1873 and entitled *Kaspar Hauser, sein Wesen, seine Unschuld (K. H.: His Character, His Innocence)*. • His teacher Humann: in *Mein Leben* Wagner describes him as "a private tutor . . . from whom I received real, if very sketchy, piano lessons."

JULY 22

•A poem on "the moderns": included in vol. 12 of Wagner's collected writings. • Herr Keil: Ernst Keil (1816–78), founder of the periodical *Die Gartenlaube*, published in Leipzig from 1853. • To play a trick on the Grand Duke of Baden: it was rumored that Kaspar Hauser was the grand duke's child. • Dr. Julius Meyer: Meyer, the son of one of Kaspar Hauser's teachers, presented the view, in a work published in Ansbach in 1872, that Hauser was not a prince of Baden, but a fraud.

JULY 24

•Herr von Meyern: Gustav, Baron von Meyern-Hohenberg (1820–78), a jurist, director of the Court theater in Gotha 1860–68.

JULY 28

•A Turkish colonel: Osman Nuri Pasha (see August 4, 1877, and note). • A book by Prof. Overbeck: *Über die Christlichkeit unserer heutigen Theologie* (1873).

JULY 30

•The *Riddles* by Weitzmann: *Musikalische Rätsel*, canons for piano duet (1870).

AUGUST 1

•*Bergsymphonie*: German title of Liszt's symphonic poem *Ce qu'on entend sur la montagne*.

AUGUST 4

•Inserted beside this entry was a copy of the *Bayreuther Tagblatt* of August 4, which contains, among other things, a report entitled "The Charge Against Bazaine," the poem "On the Roof-Raising Ceremony," and a report on that event.

AUGUST 7

•Franconian Switzerland: the northern part of the Franconian Jura is known locally as *"Die Fränkische Schweiz."*

AUGUST 8

•Prof Nietzsche's pamphlet: the first of the *Unzeitgemässe Betrachtungen (Thoughts Out of Season)*, entitled *David Strauss der Bekenner und der Schriftsteller (D. S. the Confessor and Writer)*, published by Fritzsch in Leipzig in 1873. • A certain Herr Bennett: if this was William Sterndale Bennett (1816–75), one might wonder why it should be called "a German endeavor"—unless because this English composer studied in Leipzig, where he was hailed by Schumann as an ascending star; since 1866 he had been principal of the Royal Academy of Music in London.

AUGUST 9

•A Dr. Brée: not identified.

AUGUST 15

•The first edition: Goethe's play *Götz von Berlichingen* was first published anonymously in 1773.

AUGUST 16

•Charlotte von Kalb (1761–1843): a friend of Schiller and Jean Paul, died blind and in poverty, leaving behind letters, reminiscences, and a novel, *Cornelia*.

MARCH 24
• A Herr Luckardt: Fritz Luckardt, who made a photographic portrait of Wagner in Vienna in 1872. • Disraeli: Benjamin Disraeli, later Earl of Beaconsfield (1804–1881), British statesman and novelist.

MARCH 29
• C-sharp Minor Quartet: by Beethoven (Opus 131). • "A certain Reichard": Wagner was teasing Lalas; the character "R." in "A Pilgrimage to Beethoven" is fictional, though there are plain autobiographical features.

APRIL 1
• "It was the very first thing that came to me in Paris": Wagner jotted down the melody for the *"Wach' auf"* chorus in Act III of *Die Meistersinger* in January 1862; it came to him, as he relates in *Mein Leben*, "as I was strolling through the galleries of the Palais Royal on my way to the Taverne Anglaise." • "The prelude to the third act will be the main thing": in fact the main theme of this prelude, as noted down by Wagner in Biebrich in May 1862, differs considerably from its final form, which did not emerge until 1866, when Wagner was living at Tribschen; however, the intention to use the theme of the *"Wach' auf"* chorus in the prelude to the third act was clearly present from the start.

APRIL 2
• *Die Piccolomini*: the first part (following the prologue) of Schiller's *Wallenstein* drama. • "That's what Lessing bequeathed us": a reference to Lessing's play *Nathan der Weise*, which deals with religious tolerance.

APRIL 3
• Parzival flowers: in his *Annalen* for 1866 Wagner, during a journey with Cosima through Switzerland, jotted down, "Grütli flowers. (Good Friday.)"

APRIL 4
• Arrival of the "Kauders": this seems to be the name for the hens from the Duke of Württemberg, which clearly (to judge by the succeeding entries) made a considerable impact on Wagner's domestic life!

APRIL 5
• "Reuss Schleiz Greiz": presumably an invention, satirizing the lengthy and peculiar names of some German princes.

APRIL 8
• Schopenhauer's comment on his own philosophy: *"Einige Bemerkungen über meine eigene Philosophie,"* sect. 14 of *"Fragmente zur Geschichte der Philosophie"* in vol. 1 of *Parerga und Paralipomena*. • Finlay's history of Greece: the English historian George Finlay (1799–1875) published his *History of Greece from the Roman Conquest to the Present Time* in sections between 1843 and 1861; the volume *Greece under the Romans* (1844) includes a characterization of Alexander the Great in its first chapter.

APRIL 9
• The latest work by our friend Nietzsche: the second of the *Unzeitgemässe Betrachtungen* (mentioned on February 22, 1874).

APRIL 10
• Herr Peters-Friedländer: Julius Friedländer, proprietor since 1860 of the music-publishing firm C. F. Peters.

APRIL 16
• *Lohengrin* has been performed in New York: it was not the first performance there (*that* took place—in German—in 1871), but a production in Italian.

APRIL 18
• *Woodstock*: a novel by Walter Scott, 1826. • *"Bei des Speeres Spitze"* ("on the point

of this spear"): sung by both Siegfried and Brünnhilde in the oath-taking scene of *Götterdämmerung* (Act II, Scene 4).

APRIL 28

• The Brückner brothers: Max (1836–1919) and Gotthold Brückner (1844–92) prepared the scenery both for the *Ring* in 1876 and for *Parsifal* in 1882, and continued working at Bayreuth for Cosima after Wagner's death. • "The Final Happiness" (*"Zum letzten Glück"*).

MAY 4

• A place called Wahnfried in Hesse: correctly, Wanfried; it is near Eschwege. • This juxtaposition of the two words: the German word *"Wahn"* has many shades of meaning impossible to match in a single English word: "madness," "illusion," and "delusion" are all contained in it; *"Friede"* means "peace."

MAY 7

• R. finds the verse for our house: *"Hier, wo mein Wähnen Frieden fand, 'Wahnfried' sei dieses Haus von mir benannt"* (translated by Ernest Newman, "Here where my illusion found peace, be this house named by me 'Peace from Illusion' ").

MAY 8

• A Herr v. Gerstenberg: Dr. K. von Gerstenberg. • The travel adventures of Vorstel and Will: nicknames for Cosima and Wagner respectively, after the title of Schopenhauer's *Die Welt als Wille und Vorstellung* (*The World as Will and Idea*); the travel adventures are Wagner's notes in his *Annalen* of journeys made with Cosima before they finally came together, among them the weeks in Switzerland in March 1866 spent house-hunting and culminating in the discovery of Tribschen.

MAY 11

• Herr Schott has died in Milan: the publisher Franz Schott died on May 8.

MAY 12

• "And marble statues . . ." a quotation from Goethe's "Mignon" ballad.

MAY 13

• The parson in Possendorf: Wagner gives his name (Wetzel) in a footnote in *Mein Leben*, but the curate Heine is not mentioned.

MAY 14

• A saying concerning Greece: in his *Greece Under the Romans* Finlay quotes this saying (preserved by Polybius) as, "If we had not been quickly ruined, we should not have been saved."

MAY 17

• *Pericles*: though this play is included in most English editions of Shakespeare, there is still doubt whether the text as published is entirely his work; Tieck did in fact translate the play into German but included it in a volume entitled *Alt-Englisches Theater oder Supplemente zu Shakespeare* (*Old English Theater or Supplements to S.*), 1811.

MAY 19

• The old German federation: the federation in 1815 of thirty-nine petty kingdoms, known as the Germanic Confederation.

MAY 28

• A Glinka opera in Milan: *A Life for the Tsar*, first produced in Milan on May 20.

MAY 29

• The arrangements for confession: certain sections of the Lutheran church in Germany retain a form of general confession, differing from the Roman Catholic in being limited to assent to a prayer spoken by the parson.

MAY 31

• Max's picture of Gretchen: Gabriel Cornelius Max (1840–1915) produced among other things illustrations to Goethe's *Faust*, one of which, *"Margarethe vor der Mater Dolorosa,"* was re-executed in oils in 1869.

JUNE 9
• The "Nibelungen Kanzlei": the copyists. • The great scene between Wotan and Fricka: in Act II of *Die Walküre*.

JUNE 14
• The telegram from *N. Homolatsch*: see June 27, 1870.

JUNE 16
• Andreas Hofer: the Tirolean freedom fighter (1767–1810). • *La Juive*: opera by Halévy. • Discovered a Valkyrie: the singer was in fact Friederike Sadler-Grün (1836–1917), the Fricka and Third Norn of the first festival in 1876.

JUNE 17
• *Maneia Manteia Wahn*: aspects of "madness"—*"maneia"* (correctly, *"Mania,"* Greek for "madness"), *"manteia"* (Greek for "power of divination"), *"Wahn"* (German for "illusion").

JUNE 22
• Frau Merian: Emilie Merian-Genast; see note for September 4, 1872.

JUNE 25
• Frau Pauli: a singer from Hamburg who sang Orfeo in the performance at Dessau of Gluck's *Orfeo ed Euridice*.

JUNE 27
• Frau Löper: not identified.

JULY 1
• Herr Ullmann: an impresario. • [Kristina] Nilsson (1843–1921): Swedish soprano who made frequent appearances in foreign cities, including London and New York. • Frau v. Schleinitz's lottery: inserted in the Diaries is a copy of an invitation to a sales exhibition at Wilhelmstrasse 73 (Berlin) on December 9–11.

JULY 3
• Nicolai: Otto Nicolai (1810–49), composer of the opera *Die Lustigen Weiber von Windsor* (1849) and founder of the Philharmonic concerts in Vienna (1842). • *Fra Diavolo*: opera by Auber, 1830. • "Oh, stay a while . . .": Faust in Goethe's *Faust*, Part One (referring to a moment in time). • General Concha: Manuel Gutiérrez de la Concha was killed on June 27, 1874, during an attempt to wrest Estella from the rebel Carlists, supporters of the Spanish pretender, Don Carlos.

JULY 4
• "The *Decameron*": presumably the people settled on the stairs reminded Wagner of the group of young people who assembled in a country house and told the one hundred tales that make up Boccaccio's *Decameron*. • Isouard's *Joconde*: an opera by the French composer Niccolò Isouard (1775–1818), first produced in Paris in 1814; Wagner had a particular liking for it.

JULY 5
• The new form of interment: cremation, still at that time a subject of much controversy in Europe. • Herr Monod: Gabriel Monod (1844–1912), French historian, from 1869 teacher at the Ecole des Hautes Etudes in Paris and copublisher from 1873 of the *Revue Critique d'Histoire et de Littérature*; in 1873 he married Olga Herzen, Malwida von Meysenbug's ward. • The story of *"Der Freischütz"*: in *Das Gespensterbuch* (*The Book of Ghosts*) by Johann August Apel and Friedrich Laun, 1815. • V. Lutz: Johann Baron von Lutz (1826–90) was a Cabinet secretary during Wagner's time in Munich, and Wagner considered him an adversary; it was he who in November 1865 brought Wagner King Ludwig's letter telling him he

would have to leave Munich; a minister of state from 1867 to 1871, Lutz became Bavarian prime minister in 1880.

JULY 6

• The harpist: Peter Dubez; as a result of Wagner's discussions with him, a new harp part was issued as a supplement to the score of *Das Rheingold*, which was already printed; the harp parts in the remaining parts of the *Ring* were altered before publication in accordance with Dubez's advice.

JULY 7

• "The Hostage" ("*Die Bürgschaft*," also translated as "The Pledge"). • "The Diver" ("*Der Taucher*"). • "The gigantic shadows of evening": Cosima quotes incorrectly, for Schiller wrote (in "*Die Bürgschaft*"), "*Der Bäume gigantische Schatten*" ("The gigantic shadows of the trees").

JULY 8

• The conductor Doppler: Albert Franz Doppler (1821–83), conductor and flautist.

JULY 9

• Frau Materna: Amalie Materna (1844–1918), Austrian soprano, made her debut in 1864 as a soubrette; her first appearance at the Vienna opera was in 1869; she sang Brünnhilde at the first festival in 1876. • Frau Grün: Friederike Sadler-Grün; see note for June 16, 1874.

JULY 10

• The article, which has been reproduced in all newspapers: inserted in the Diaries is a clipping from the *Wiener Presse*, similar in content to that from the *Börsencourier* mentioned on July 9. The Viennese article reads: "As proof of their unselfishness and devotion to his person and to his works, Richard Wagner has demanded of all artists summoned to Bayreuth that they work completely without pay, both at rehearsals, spread over two years, and at the performances in 1876. Niemann and Betz have already agreed, as has Scaria, though on certain conditions. In the meantime the above-named artists continue to draw their salaries from the Berlin and Vienna Court theaters. But the salary problem is more difficult for those artists who belong to private or commercial theaters. The promoters concerned are utterly opposed to paying salaries to Richard Wagner's singers, and Frau Cosima Wagner feels herself obliged to dispatch letters full of indignation over 'these egotistic play actors completely devoid of idealistic impulses.' The long-sought Siegfried has been found in the person of a 19-year-old student, who has already immersed himself in his studies in Bayreuth. Hans Richter, Wagner's right-hand man, is ill as the result of a fall, but this does not prevent his keeping the young army of musicians and choristers busy. The scores and parts already fill several packing cases. The horses for the Valkyries and for Brünnhilde, the last of whom has to leap with her horse into a burning funeral pyre, are expected to arrive any day from the royal stables in Munich for the necessary training in Bayreuth." Another clipping, from the *Oberfränkische Zeitung* in Bayreuth, reads: "In yesterday's edition we printed a report from the *Wiener Presse* without any comment; it provides evidence enough of the way in which so-called reporters here are attempting to discredit the enterprise. The following remarks are aimed at contradicting these suspicious rumors. The completion of the interior works of the theater, whose external structure is already finished, is utterly assured, due primarily to the munificence of His Majesty King Ludwig of Bavaria. A contract has been signed with the Brückner brothers, Court painters in Coburg, for preparing all the decorations, designed by the court painter Hoffmann in Vienna and approved by R. Wagner. . . . Whoever has any acquaintance with Frau Cosima Wagner, however slight, will know that she could never have written letters containing such words as the *W. Presse* ascribes to her. Hans

production he became Wagner's right-hand man in the field of grouping and movement, and left in his book, *Bayreuth vor dreissig Jahren* (*Bayreuth Thirty Years Ago*, 1908), a vivid account of those rehearsals.

JULY 30
• The shrug of the shoulders: at the first performance in Paris of the revised *Tannhäuser*, which was received on March 13, 1861, with a hostile demonstration.

JULY 31–AUGUST 23
• "*Vollendet der Bau*": correctly, "*Vollendet das ewige Werk*," Wotan's greeting to Valhalla in Scene 2 of *Das Rheingold*. • The Schirmers: Gustav Schirmer (1829–93), American music publisher, and his wife, Mary, née Fairchild. • His "Saint Francis Legend": there are in fact two, written in 1865 and dedicated to Cosima, "*St. François d'Assise*" and "*St. François de Paule marchant sur les flots.*"

AUGUST 26
• Baumgarten-Crusius: headmaster of the Kreuzschule in Dresden, which Wagner attended from 1821 to 1827; Wagner professes in *Mein Leben* to have had a high regard for him, though he left the school suddenly to avoid what he considered to be an unjust punishment by the headmaster. • Telegram from Richter: sent express from Vienna, dated the same day: "Deeply revered master. Forgiveness for the penitent. Please write to me all you wished to say, so that I can acknowledge my wrong completely and repent. Regretting my absence, assure you never to have wavered in my loyalty. Your life-long devoted Hans Richter."

AUGUST 28
• His circular: announcing that the festival would be held in 1876.

AUGUST 29
• "*Quasimodo*": the hunchback in Victor Hugo's novel *Notre Dame de Paris*.

SEPTEMBER 2
• San-Marte on Parcival: San-Marte was the pseudonym of Albert Schulz (1802–93), who wrote, in addition to a life of Wolfram von Eschenbach, *Parzival-Studien*, 3 vols., 1861–62.

SEPTEMBER 3
• The poem "*An Dich*" ("To Thee"): a poem of seven stanzas addressed to Cosima, written in Starnberg on October 1, 1864.

SEPTEMBER 4
• The new *Tannhäuser* scene: the enlarged Venusberg scene in Act I, written for the Paris production of 1861 (see note for May 15, 1873); Fürstner had acquired the publishing, but not the performing rights of *Tannhäuser*.

SEPTEMBER 5
• Netty Mrazek: Anna Mrazeck.

SEPTEMBER 6
• "*Dans le siècle . . .*": correctly, "*En ce siècle . . .*" ("In this foul and horrible century"), a quotation from the satirical "*Bible*" of the thirteenth-century French poet Guiot de Provins, who traveled as far as Palestine; a German translation by Wolfhart and San-Marte appeared in 1861.

SEPTEMBER 9
• "Oh, now we were Night's vassals": "*O! nun waren wir Nacht-geweihte*," from Act II of *Tristan und Isolde*.

SEPTEMBER 11
• "The worst society . . .": paraphrase of Mephistopheles's words in the scene in Faust's study (Goethe's *Faust*, Part One), "The worst society thou find'st will show thee / Thou art a man among the rest" (Bayard Taylor's translation).

SEPTEMBER 14

• The Hirschsprung: correctly, Hirschensprung, a wooded hill to the west of Karlsbad. • Where 30 years ago R. and Apel had enjoyed themselves: in fact it was forty-one years since Wagner had been there (in June 1834) with his friend Theodor Apel (1811–67), a writer. • See biography: Wagner describes his journey with Apel in *Mein Leben*.

SEPTEMBER 15

• The Schlackenburg: a castle near Teplitz; Wagner wrote the prose sketch of his opera *Das Liebesverbot* there.

SEPTEMBER 17

• The Baumgarten: a park in Prague on the banks of the river Moldau.

SEPTEMBER 19

• Niemann wants to sing all three roles: Loge, Siegmund, Siegfried.

SEPTEMBER 21

• The Bocchesi: inhabitants of the southernmost tip of Dalmatia, part of Austria from 1814; they rebelled when conscription was introduced in 1869, but were pacified by a payment of 40 florins to each man.

SEPTEMBER 26

• There will be damages to pay: as a result of breaking Unger's engagement in Düsseldorf to enable him to study in Munich with Hey.

SEPTEMBER 27

• Kinowsky's misery: nothing has yet been discovered about him and his connection with Käthchen König, a distant relative of Wagner's.

SEPTEMBER 28

• Frau Wilt: Maria Wilt (1834–91), a soprano engaged at the Vienna opera from 1867 to 1877; she also made appearances at Covent Garden in London, and in Italy; she did not sing Elisabeth in Vienna. • Captain Schenk: Wilhelm Schenk, Baron von Stauffenberg, Ludwig's adjutant during the festival of 1876.

OCTOBER 2

• Trevrizent: in *Parzival*, a hermit who tells Parzival how to reach the Grail. • Scherbarth: Karl Scherbarth (1837–86), director of the Düsseldorf opera. • The "one-eyed Swedish Jew": Leonard Labatt (1838–97), singer.

OCTOBER 3

• "Here comes Galathea! . . .": a reference to the "Classical Walpurgisnacht" in Goethe's *Faust*, Part Two. • The complaint of the Herzegovinians: the Christian inhabitants of Herzegovina, part of the Ottoman Empire since 1479, started an insurrection in July 1875, an act that led finally to the Russo-Turkish War of 1877–78.

OCTOBER 4

• Goethe's *Annals*: *Annalen*, a continuation of his autobiography, *Dichtung und Wahrheit*, in the form of a year-by-year account up to 1822, published in 1830.

OCTOBER 5

• Fritz's silence: Fritz Brockhaus, Clemens's brother. • *Orbis Pictus*: not the book of that name by Comenius mentioned on July 27, 1869, but an illustrated encyclopedia issued in parts.

OCTOBER 6

• All things transitory: an adaptation of Goethe's famous words at the conclusion of *Faust*, Part Two: "*Alles Vergängliche ist nur ein Gleichnis.*"

OCTOBER 7

• The green-and-golden tree of autumn: an echo of Mephistopheles's words in

Goethe's *Faust*, Part One, "Gray are all theories, and green alone Life's golden tree" (Bayard Taylor translation).

**OCTOBER 8**

•Goethe's speech on Wieland: the eulogy "*Zu brüderlichem Andenken Wieland's,*" spoken on the death of the German writer Christoph Martin Wieland (1733–1813); in it Goethe spoke of Wieland's habit of writing, correcting, and copying all his works very neatly with a fine quill.

**OCTOBER 10**

•Saw R. for the first time: this was 22 years earlier, on October 10, 1853, when Liszt introduced his three children to Wagner during a visit to Paris. • General Herz: not identified.

**OCTOBER 11**

•The Brocken: the highest peak in the Harz Mountains.

**OCTOBER 14**

•R.'s toast to his nephew Kurt Kessinger: "*Kurt und gut, von unters zu Oberst, mein lieber Neffe ganz besonders, bleib mir gut!*" • Prof. Haeckel: Ernst Haeckel (1834–1919), the German naturalist, wrote many accounts of his travels; Brussa (Brusa) was in Asia Minor, present-day Turkey.

**OCTOBER 16**

•Herr v. Gerstenberg: von Gerstenberg Edler von Zech was from 1867 a minister of state and administrator of the domains of Duke Ernst von Sachsen-Altenburg. • Herr Schweitzer: Jean Baptist von Schweitzer (1833–75), a Social Democrat deputy in the Reichstag and playwright.

**OCTOBER 17**

•Triller's "*Der Prinzenraub*": correctly, "*Der Sächsische Prinzenraub*" ("The Abduction of the Saxon Princes") by Daniel Wilhelm Triller (1695–1782). • *Deutsche Rundschau*: a monthly literary periodical founded in Berlin in 1874 by Julius Rodenberg. • Princess Marie of Sachsen-Weimar: Maria, Princess of Sachsen-Weimar-Eisenach (born 1849) married Prince (Heinrich) Reuss (1825–1906) in February 1876.

**OCTOBER 18**

•His circular to the singers: an invitation to his singers to take part in the festival of 1876, dated November 1, 1875. • *The Mabinogion*: a collection of eleven Welsh prose tales from the eleventh to the thirteenth centuries.

**OCTOBER 19**

•Omitted sentence: "*Der Vice-König von Ägypten, will man einen Orden, er gibt'n.*"

**OCTOBER 21**

•The Catholics' petition: presented by Jörg, who was opposed to Bismarck and a united German Reich.

**OCTOBER 22**

•*Héroïde funèbre*: a symphonic poem by Liszt (also known as *Heldenklänge*), 1857.

**OCTOBER 25**

•Professor Gosche: Richard Gosche (1824–89), literary historian, wrote among other things *Richard Wagners Frauengestalten* (R. W.'s Female Characters).

**OCTOBER 26**

•*Pandora*: a festival play by Goethe (1807–08).

**OCTOBER 27**

•Inserted in the Diaries are two clippings from the *Fränkische Zeitung* of this date; one deals with Jörg's petition to Ludwig II (see October 21); the other is an appeal to "the tradesmen and small shopkeepers in Bayreuth" to take part in an exhibition during the festival year; the report states that attempts had been made at a meeting on the previous evening to prevent it, apparently "because Herr Richard Wagner does not wish an exhibition to be held at the same time as the stage festival"; however, the report continues, people should not be hindered from taking advantage "in these bad times" of the influx of strangers due to this event, "when we have been reminded so often of the significant honor and profitability of this occasion for the local citizens."

OCTOBER 29
• The third scene from *Die Walküre*: Siegmund and Sieglinde's love duet in Act I.
NOVEMBER 2
• Ellen, now the wife of the Duke of Meiningen: see note for January 30, 1874. •
Verdi's *Requiem*: its first performance had taken place in 1874 in Milan; this performance in Vienna was conducted by Hans Richter.
NOVEMBER 3
• *Carmen*: this was the first new production of Bizet's opera after its première in Paris in March 1875, and the first time that it was given with Guiraud's recitatives, the Paris performances having been with spoken dialogue; in Vienna it was sung in German.
NOVEMBER 5
• Rehearsals: of the Paris version of *Tannhäuser*.
NOVEMBER 8
• Bignio: Louis Bignio (1839–1907), a baritone at the Vienna opera from 1863.
Frau Niemann: Hedwig Niemann-Raabe (1844–1905), an actress and singer.
NOVEMBER 9
• Schönbrunn: the Austrian Emperor's summer palace.
NOVEMBER 10
• Mosenthal: Salomon Hermann Mosenthal, who wrote the libretto of Goldmark's opera, *Die Königin von Saba*.
NOVEMBER 11
• Dozy's *The Moors in Spain: Histoire des Musulmans d'Espagne*, by the Dutch historian Reinhart Dozy (1820–83), was published in 4 vols. in 1861; the 2-vol. German edition appeared in 1873.
NOVEMBER 12
• *L'Africaine*: opera by Meyerbeer (1865).
NOVEMBER 13
• Harry Arnim's pamphlet *Pro Nihilo*: see note for October 8, 1874.
NOVEMBER 14
• Mendelssohn's *Lobgesang*: symphony-cantata, Opus 52 (1840).
NOVEMBER 16
• Wettin: a noble German family dating back to the tenth century; at their height in the twelfth and thirteenth centuries with Konrad I and his successors. • Widukind: leader of the Saxons against Charlemagne in the eighth century.
NOVEMBER 18
• Brahms . . . piano quartet: in C Minor, Opus 60, completed that year.
NOVEMBER 20
• Prince Hohenlohe: Konstantin, Marie Wittgenstein's husband.
NOVEMBER 22
• The performance of *Tannhäuser*: inserted in the Diaries is a newspaper clipping containing a review, which reads: "Richard Wagner's *Tannhäuser* has surely never before been performed in Vienna in so festive a manner as on this evening. The presence of the composer exercised an encouraging influence not only on the

interpretation of the singers and musicians concerned, but on the audience as well. The production was inspired in the highest degree and unusually correct; the energetic hand of the master was visible in every detail, every feature of it; besides that, it was of particular interest in that it was based, with some modifications, on the revised version for Paris, hitherto unknown here. We shall be talking of that in more detail on a later occasion. For the present we can report that Wagner, the participants, and, outstandingly and deservedly, the conductor Hans Richter celebrated a veritable triumph. We can only pay our own unreserved tributes to all the participants, the chorus and orchestra included. But it was in particular Frau [Bertha] Ehnn as Elisabeth who gave us the pleasantest surprise, for her interpretation and performance of the role put all her previous attempts at it completely in the shade. Every possible moment was seized for an enthusiastic demonstration of applause, of which the other participants—Frau Materna, Fräulein Siegstädt, and the Herren Labatt, Scaria, Bignio, etc.—also received their full share. If the participants were able to bask in such a remarkable show of favor, for Richard Wagner himself the evening amounted to a brilliant ovation. After each act there were thunderous calls for him. In the early intermissions he came each time to the front of his box, in which Frau Cosima Wagner and Countess Dönhoff were also seated, and acknowledged with a bow the applause of the cheering, handkerchief-waving audience. But at the conclusion of the opera he appeared with the soloists on the stage, where a wreath was thrown to him, and, since the applause showed no sign of ceasing, he addressed the audience approximately as follows: It was about 15 years ago that he heard his *Lohengrin* here for the first time, and he would never forget the cordial reception he had received then. Today the same thing seemed to be happening again. The applause given to his artists would encourage him to continue with the production of his works, as far as the means allowed, and he hoped that they would in this way become clearer to the public than they had so far been. In this sense he would like to express his thanks once again for the fine encouragement he had received."

NOVEMBER 24
• The singers hurt by his speech: it was suggested that Wagner's words "as far as the means allowed" were a reflection on their abilities. • "The Prophetess of the Morning": from the *Pañcha tantra*.

NOVEMBER 26
• Wilbrandt's *Arria und Messalina*: a play (first produced 1874) by Adolf von Wilbrandt (1837–1911), who became director of the Burgtheater in Vienna in 1881.

NOVEMBER 27
• My father's *Hunnenschlacht*: a symphonic poem by Liszt (1857).

DECEMBER 6–17
• A wonderful performance of *Lohengrin*: conducted by Richter, the cast included Amalie Materna as Ortrud and Emil Scaria as the king; with the Lohengrin (Georg Müller) and the Elsa (Ludmilla Kupfer) Wagner was not at all satisfied, but he was so pleased with the chorus that he offered to return to Vienna in March 1876, to conduct another performance for their benefit. • Prof. Holtzendorf: Franz von Holtzendorf (1829–89), professor of law in Berlin and Munich. • Brange, Marke, Putz: dogs. • Ross, Rausch, Viktor; people (servants at Wahnfried).

DECEMBER 20
• Frl. Siegstädt: sang the shepherd boy in the *Tannhäuser* production in Vienna; she did not appear at Bayreuth. • Herr Lewy: Richard Lewy (1827–83), musical supervisor (*Oberinspektor*) at the Vienna opera 1870–80.

DECEMBER 21–22

• A composition for the opening of the exhibition: the Centennial Exposition at Philadelphia to mark the first centennial of the American Declaration of Independence.

DECEMBER 26

• Almansor: Al-Mansur (939–1002), the Moslem Regent of Cordoba, who extended Arab rule in Spain and was a patron of the arts; Dozy, whose book Wagner and Cosima were then reading, deals with him at length.

DECEMBER 27

• "Justice is a precious word . . ." ("*Gerechtigkeit ein schönes Wort, Geschlechtlichkeit wirkt immer fort*").

DECEMBER 28

• Goethe's "The Secrets" ("*Die Geheimnisse*"): a fragment of an epic poem, written 1784–85.

DECEMBER 29

• Baron Seydlitz: Baron Reinhard von Seydlitz, artist and writer, became president of the Munich Wagner Society in 1876.

DECEMBER 31

• Fortunes are told with lead: this is done by pouring molten lead into cold water and then interpreting the solidified shapes.

# 1876

JANUARY 3

• Old Wieck: Friedrich Wieck (1785–1873), the piano teacher and father of Clara Schumann; his account of his visit to Beethoven, first published in the *Dresdner Nachrichten*, gives the date as May 1826, but it may have been two years earlier; they discussed living musicians, and Beethoven improvised for an hour on the piano. • Czerny: Carl Czerny (1791–1857), piano teacher whose studies are still much used; he was a friend of Beethoven, and his letters contain several descriptions of their encounters. • "Only in times of storm and stress . . ." ("*Nur wenn alles bricht und kracht, geht Richard Wagner einst befrackt*").

JANUARY 4

• The Schnorr experience: the difficulties with Schnorr's widow, Malwine (see note for July 28, 1872).

JANUARY 6

• Lope [de Vega]'s *El peregrino* (*The Pilgrim in His Native Land*): a novel, 1604.

JANUARY 8

• The curtain in the Gibichung's hall: Act I, Scene 1, of *Götterdämmerung*.

JANUARY 14

• Motamit: presumably al-Mutamid (1040–95), ruler of Seville and a poet.

JANUARY 15

• The subscription proceeds: under the so-called *Abonnement* system, common in European countries, whereby one pays an annual subscription for seats in the theater at stipulated performances.

JANUARY 16

• *Hero & Leander*: an orchestral ballade by Mihalovich.

JANUARY 18

• Dr. Strecker: Ludwig Strecker (1853–1943) took over the management of the firm of Schott in 1875—not, in fact, as successor to the "Sons," since Franz Schott was a grandson of the original founder, Bernhard Schott; Strecker, who eventually became proprietor of the firm, kept a diary of his visits to Bayreuth, and these have been published in his son's book, *Richard Wagner als Verlagsgefährte* (R. W. as *Publishing Colleague*) by Ludwig Strecker (1951). • *On the Present State of the German Reich (Über die gegenwärtige Lage des deutschen Reiches*): by Paul de Lagarde, appeared in 1876.

JANUARY 22
• Baron Schack: Adolf Friedrich, Count von Schack, published his *Poesie und Kunst der Araber in Spanien und Sizilien (Arab Poetry and Art in Spain and Sicily)* in 2 vols. in 1865.

JANUARY 26
• Fricke: August Ludwig Fricke (1829–94), bass-baritone at the Berlin opera from 1856; he did not sing at Bayreuth.

JANUARY 28
• Herr Bauernfeld: Eduard von Bauernfeld (1802–90), Austrian poet and playwright, wrote in 1876 the comedy *Die reiche Erbin (The Rich Heiress)*.

JANUARY 29
• The Prince: Bismarck.

FEBRUARY 4
• Helen Zimmern (1846–1934): author of *Arthur Schopenhauer: His Life and His Philosophy*, published in London in 1876.

FEBRUARY 6
• Hans has bought a house there: Hans von Bülow did eventually become musical director at Meiningen, but not until 1880; there he married (in 1882) an actress, Marie Schanzer (1857–1941).

FEBRUARY 8
• *Reformation* Symphony . . . Tetzel: Mendelssohn's symphony (Opus 107) uses Luther's hymn *"Ein' feste Burg"* in its final movement; the second movement is, however, a scherzo, and there seems no clear reason why it should have reminded Wagner of Tetzel, the fifteenth-century Catholic monk who sold indulgences; the rhyme (*"Wenn das Geld im Kasten klingt, die Seele in den Himmel springt"*) was a popular saying satirizing Tetzel.

FEBRUARY 9
• His composition for the Americans: see December 21–22, 1875, and note; the composition became the *"Grosser Festmarsch,"* known in English as the "Centennial March." • Beethoven trios: the piano trios Opus 70, No. 1, and Opus 97 respectively. • A Herr Ritter: Hermann Ritter (1849–1926), inventor of the "viola alta," which was used eventually by other composers besides Wagner; Ritter, a student of philosophy at Heidelberg at the time of his visit to Wagner, played in 1876 in the Bayreuth festival orchestra, and from 1879 taught the viola at the music school in Würzburg.

FEBRUARY 10
• The editor of the *Weser-Zeitung*: Hofmann; see January 28 and February 14 and 15.

FEBRUARY 16
• *"Komm, schöner Knabe!"*: correctly, *"Komm', komm', holder Knabe"* ("Come, fair youth"), sung by the Flower Maidens in Act II of *Parsifal.* • Simson: the lawyer in Berlin who acted for Hans von Bülow in the 1870 divorce (see note for January 22, 1870) and was now representing Wagner in his lawsuit against Fürstner concerning the rights in *Tannhäuser.* • Episode with the lions: *Don Quixote*, pt. two, chap. 17.

FEBRUARY 19
•Love song: Siegmund's *"Winterstürme"* from Act I of *Die Walküre.* • Puppet-theater episode: *Don Quixote*, pt. two, chap. 26.
FEBRUARY 21
•Only about 2,000 florins will be left for the chorus: the performance of *Lohengrin* was to be given for the benefit of the chorus of the Vienna opera.
FEBRUARY 25
•His contacts with Rio de Janeiro: in connection with *Tristan und Isolde*; see note for March 6, 1870.
MARCH 2
•R.'s magical conducting: this was the only occasion on which Wagner ever conducted *Lohengrin*.
MARCH 5
•Frau Voggenhuber: Vilma von Voggenhuber (1845–88) made her debut as a soprano in Pest in 1862, performed in Berlin from 1868; she was to sing Isolde, and Niemann Tristan, in the production of *Tristan und Isolde* that Wagner had come to Berlin to supervise.
MARCH 6
•The main singer: Niemann.
MARCH 7
• A Herr Kögel: Josef Kögel (1836–99), bass singer at the Hamburg opera 1874–84.
• My mother's death: Countess Marie d'Agoult died in Paris on March 5; the newspaper report reads: "Countess d'Agoult, known as a writer under the name of Daniel Stern, died on Sunday in Paris at the age of seventy-one. The deceased, much talked about in former times because of her relationship with Liszt, was the mother of the late wife of Emile Ollivier and the present wife of Richard Wagner."
MARCH 9
•*Theologia Germanica*: or *Theologia Deutsch* (*German Theology*), mystical text written c.1400 by a priest (*"Der Frankfurter"*); Luther edited it in 1516.
MARCH 13
• Queen Luise: the graves of Queen Luise and her husband, King Friedrich Wilhelm III, are in the gardens of the palace of Charlottenburg, marked by marble figures.
MARCH 14
•M. Tribert: a French writer.
MARCH 16–20
•Count Harrach: Ferdinand, Count von Harrach (1832–1915), a painter, professor at the Berlin Academy of Arts from 1868.
MARCH 22
•Messrs. Bote & Bock: a music-publishing firm in Berlin.
MARCH 25
•The music director Thomas: Theodore Thomas (1835–1905), born in Germany, emigrated with his family at the age of ten to the United States, where he became one of the leading orchestral conductors of his time.
APRIL 3–6
• Taine's *Les Origines de la France contemporaine* (*The Origins of Contemporary France*): by the French historian Hippolyte Taine (1828–93), published in 6 vols., 1875–94.
APRIL 7
• 13,000-odd marks: though the German text has *"13 und so und so viel Mark,"* which could perhaps be translated as "13 marks more or less," Ernest Newman in his biography of Wagner sets the sum earned for Bayreuth by the special first performance of *Tristan und Isolde* in Berlin at "nearly 14,000 marks," giving as his source

Julius Kapp's *Geschichte der Staatsoper Berlin* (*History of the Berlin State Opera*, 1937); the sum of "13,000-odd marks" would confirm Kapp's figure, and it seems a much more likely one, for Cosima would surely have had more to say if the yield had been only 13 marks!

APRIL 9
•A novel in which the heroine's name is Cosima: *Benediktus*, by Karl von Heigel (1835–1905), appeared in 1875.

APRIL 15
•To get the law carried through: presumably the copyright law, issued on June 11, 1870.

APRIL 16
•Prof. Bernays: Michael Bernays (1834–97), literary historian, professor in Munich since 1873. • Dr. Schönaich: Gustav Schönaich (1840–1906), a journalist, stepson of Dr. Standhartner; apparently Wagner did not much care for him.

APRIL 21
•[Minna] Lammert (born 1852): singer at the Berlin opera 1873–96, sang Flosshilde in the 1876 festival. • Eilers: Albert Eilers (1830–96), bass singer at Coburg from 1865; he sang Fasolt in the 1876 festival.

APRIL 23
•Frl. v. Pretfeld: not identified. • Frl. Scheffsky: see note for November 20, 1870. • Waive the audition: presumably of Unger (mentioned in entry of April 1, 1876).

APRIL 26
•The new currency: the Reich currency law of July 9, 1873, set the value of the mark at one-third of a thaler; the southern states of Germany had now adopted the Reich currency.

APRIL 29
•Herr Krolop: the singer Franz Krolop (1839–97), from 1873 at the Berlin opera, was Vilma Voggenhuber's husband.

MAY 1
•Herr von Gilsa: Baron von und zu Gilsa, director of the opera in Kassel from 1849. • Frl. Haupt: Marie Haupt; she sang Freia and Gerhild in the 1876 festival, subsequently married the singer Georg Unger.

MAY 2
•[Goethe's] *Trilogy of Passion*: three poems, "*An Werther*," "*Elegie*," and "*Aussöhnung*" ("Atonement").

MAY 3
•"*Sangst du mir nicht dein Wissen* . . ." ("Didst thou not sing to me that thy knowledge . . ."): sung by Siegfried in Act III of *Siegfried* to the motive known variously as "Love of Siegfried" and "World Inheritance." • The correspondence between Goethe and . . . Wolf: Friedrich August Wolf (1795–1824) was a philologist at Halle and Berlin; his correspondence with Goethe (*Goethes Briefe an Friedrich August Wolf*) was edited by Bernays and published in 1868; the introduction deals with Goethe's attitude toward Ancient Greece.

MAY 4
•The E-flat Concerto: Beethoven's *Emperor* Concerto.

MAY 6
•Berlioz took up *le divin Shakespeare*: a reference to Berlioz's "dramatic symphony," *Roméo et Juliette* (1838).

MAY 10
•Menzel's pictures: during the rehearsals in 1875 Adolph von Menzel had made two drawings of Wagner in the festival theater. • The conductor Frank: Ernst

Frank (1847–89), conductor in Mannheim from 1872. • Herr Herrlich: a singer recommended by Lilli Lehmann but not accepted by Wagner.

MAY 12

• Telegram from America: dated New York, May 12, the telegram (inserted in the Diaries) reads, "Herald writes March will outlive next centennial, tremendous applause, Steinway." • *Lalla Rookh*: Félicien David's opera, based on the poem by Thomas Moore, was produced first in Paris in 1862, and in Munich the following year.

MAY 18

• The children's dancing lesson: under the tuition of Richard Fricke. • Young Brandt: Fritz, son of Karl. • Swimming machine dubious: a specially constructed machine in which the three Rhinemaidens were to be moved during the opening scene of *Das Rheingold*; there were fears that the three singers would not dare entrust themselves to it.

MAY 22

• *"Hört ihr Leute"* ("Hear, good people"): the night watchman's song in Act II of *Die Meistersinger von Nürnberg*.

MAY 24–29

• Herr Brassin: Gerhard Brassin (born 1844), brother of Louis Brassin.

MAY 30

• Sultan Abdul-Aziz: of Turkey. • The conference: between Bismarck, Count Julius Andrássy (the Austrian Foreign Minister), and Prince Alexander Mikhailovich Gorchakov (the Russian Foreign Minister) prior to the meeting of the three emperors in Reichstadt in 1876.

JUNE 2

• Rehearsal between Alberich and Mime: Karl Hill and Karl (Max) Schlosser.

JUNE 3

• The Rhinemaiden singers mount the machines in person: Lilli and Marie Lehmann and Minna Lammert. Richard Fricke provides a description of the occasion in his reminiscences (*Bayreuth vor dreissig Jahren*); Marie Lehmann was persuaded to make the first attempt: "Amid many 'Ohs' and 'Ahs,' cries and squeaks, we strap her in firmly and the ride starts—very slowly. She begins to lose her anxious expression, laughs, and says it is going quite nicely. Now Lilli decides to make the attempt, too, and—what do you think?—within a few seconds she is the more intrepid of the two. Now Fräulein Lammert joins them, and all three are swimming amid delighted laughter. Wagner appears; the whole scene is played right through. And on top of it the three ladies sing their parts enchantingly."

JUNE 12

• Eilers: as Hunding, a role in which he was subsequently replaced by Niering (from Coburg).

JUNE 13

• *Memento mori* (Remember you must die).

JUNE 19

• August Röckel's death: he died on June 18 in Budapest.

JUNE 20

• Frozen despair . . . enraptured exultation: when Brünnhilde tells Sieglinde of the child in her womb.

JUNE 22

• Countess Usedom and daughter: Countess Olympia Usedom, née Malcolm (died 1888), wife of Count Guido Usedom, and Countess Hildegard Usedom (born 1852), their daughter.

JUNE 27
• Looking bad in Turkey: the Turkish Parliament had refused to grant the rebellious Bulgarians and other regions the right of self-government, one of the causes of the Russo-Turkish War of 1877.

JUNE 29
• The mechanics in London: Richard Keene (see note for July 7, 1875); in fact, parts of the dragon in *Siegfried* did not arrive in time for the performances—apparently the missing pieces had been dispatched by mistake to Beirut in Lebanon!

JUNE 30
• Arrival of the English governess: presumably Mrs. Cooper (or Miss, since Cosima writes "Misses" before her name in later entries).

JULY 1–11
• A splendid piece by Nietzsche: *Richard Wagner in Bayreuth*, the fourth of the *Unzeitgemässe Betrachtungen*, published by Schmeitzner in Schloss-Chemnitz in 1876; Nietzsche, in a letter to Gersdorff dated July 21: "Wagner has written, 'My friend, your book is tremendous! Where did you get to know so much about me?' "

JULY 13
• The new biography of R. by Glasenapp: Carl Friedrich Glasenapp (1847–1915) originally planned his biography in 2 vols., the first of which (covering events up to 1843) appeared in 1876; vol. 2 was published in 1877; Glasenapp later extended the biography to 6 vols., the last of which (up to Wagner's death) appeared in 1911.

JULY 15
• Herr Siehr: Gustav Siehr (1837–96), a bass singer at Wiesbaden, sang Hagen at Bayreuth in 1876 and Gurnemanz in *Parsifal* in 1882.

JULY 21
• Nice telegram from the King: dated July 21, thanking Wagner for Nietzsche's *Richard Wagner in Bayreuth*, which he found "extraordinarily gripping."

JULY 23
• A public rehearsal: of Act II of *Götterdämmerung*, in order to test the acoustics of the theater with a full auditorium.

JULY 24
• Princess Barjatinsky: presumably the wife of the Russian Prince Victor Barjatinsky, who held a certificate of patronage. • The princes' gallery: a row of boxes at the back of the auditorium in the festival theater.

JULY 25
• Count Wallis: Rudolf, Count von Wallis from Bohemia. • Herr Brandt offended: according to Fricke's reminiscences, Brandt had already shown signs of dissatisfaction before this, objecting to being described as "head machinist" ("*erster Maschinenmeister*") instead of "stage manager" ("*Bühnenleiter*").

AUGUST 4
• I take up writing again on September 8: Cosima's failure to keep a daily account of events during the first Bayreuth festival has resulted in a disappointingly sketchy description; for fuller descriptions readers must go to biographers such as Glasenapp and Newman and to participants who wrote reminiscences, among them Richard Fricke and Lilli Lehmann (*Mein Weg*, 1913). The cast of the three performances of the *Ring* given during the festival (all conducted by Hans Richter) was: Woglinde, Lilli Lehmann; Wellgunde, Marie Lehmann; Flosshilde, Minna Lammert; Alberich, Karl Hill; Wotan, Franz Betz; Fricka, Friederike Sadler-Grün; Donner, Eugen Gura; Froh, Georg Unger (second and third performances, Robert Engelhardt); Freia, Marie Haupt; Fasolt, Albert Eilers; Fafner, Franz von Reichenberg; Loge, Heinrich Vogl; Mime, Karl (Max) Schlosser; Erda, Luise Jaide (second

performance, Hedwig Reicher-Kindermann); Siegmund, Albert Niemann; Sieglinde, Josephine Scheffsky; Hunding, Joseph Niering; Brünnhilde, Amalie Materna; Valkyries, Antonie Amann, Luise Jaide (her role taken over at the second performance by Marianne Brandt), Johanna Jachmann-Wagner, Marie Haupt, Minna Lammert, Lilli Lehmann, Marie Lehmann, Hedwig Reicher-Kindermann; Siegfried, Georg Unger; Woodbird, Lilli Lehmann; First Norn, Johanna Jachmann-Wagner; Second Norn, Josephine Scheffsky; Third Norn, Friederike Sadler-Grün; Gunther, Eugen Gura; Gutrune, Mathilde Weckerlin; Hagen, Gustav Siehr; Waltraute, Luise Jaide (second performance, Marianne Brandt); the musical assistants (coaching, conducting groups or individual singers behind the scenes, etc.) were Franz Fischer, Demetrius Lalas, Felix Mottl, Joseph Rubinstein, Anton Seidl, and Hermann Zimmer.

AUGUST 5

•R. drives away with the King: Ludwig stayed at the Eremitage; he was accompanied only by his head equerry, Count Max von Holnstein (1835–95), and an aide-de-camp.

AUGUST 7

• Much abuse with the tickets: they were being bartered for prices of up to 20 marks each. • Schwarzburg-Sondershausen: Günther Friedrich Karl II (1801–80), Prince of Schwarzburg-Sondershausen.

AUGUST 13

• The Emperor of Brazil: Dom Pedro II (1825–91); for his previous contacts with Wagner see March 6, 1870, and September 6, 1871, and notes; he arrived in Bayreuth without any ceremony and put up at a hotel, where he filled in an ordinary registration form, giving as his occupation "Emperor."

AUGUST 18

• The final chorus from *Faust*: in Part Two of Goethe's drama, "*Alles Vergängliche ist nur ein Gleichnis . . . Das ewig Weibliche zieht uns hinan.*" • A wonderful toast to my father: during his speech Wagner suddenly pointed at Liszt and exclaimed, "Here is the man without whom you would perhaps have heard not a single note from me today"; he then embraced him.

AUGUST 20

• The King writes quite wonderfully: in his letter from Hohenschwangau, dated August 12, Ludwig wrote, "Through hearing this ravishing, magnificent, profound poetry, so blissfully transfigured and consecrated by the divinely inspired music in which it is clothed, I have been transported to such a pitch of emotion, raised to such a state of happiness as never in my life before. . . ."

AUGUST 24

• Saint-Saëns: Camille Saint-Saëns (1835–1921), French composer; Wagner had met him while in Paris in 1860 preparing *Tannhäuser*, and described him in *Mein Leben* as "an extremely talented young French musician." • Mme Minghetti: Donna Laura Minghetti (1829–1915), wife of the Italian statesman Marco Minghetti (1818–86); her first marriage had been to Domenico Beccadelli di Bologna, Prince of Camporeale, and Marie Dönhoff was the daughter of that marriage; in *Mein Leben* Wagner describes a private occasion in Vienna in 1861 when he had "the curious experience of hearing Isolde's final scene sung by a Neapolitan Princess Camporeale [the subsequent Mme Minghetti], with a good pronunciation of the German words and a surprising sureness of intonation," accompanied on the piano by the "very efficient" Saint-Saëns.

AUGUST 26

• Bovet: also a member of the festival orchestra.

SEPTEMBER 1
• The Opus 106: Beethoven's *Hammerklavier* Sonata.

SEPTEMBER 19
• The Società: a choral society. • *"Canzone del Tasso"*: presumably settings of poems by the Italian poet, Torquato Tasso (1544–95).

SEPTEMBER 20
• Tesarini: Luigi, a piano teacher in Venice (Wagner spells his name "Tessarin" in *Mein Leben*, where he describes their meeting when he himself was living in Venice in 1858); Tesarini described himself as a *"corbo bianco"* ("white raven"), since he was an Italian with a taste for German music.

SEPTEMBER 21
• *Nerone: Nero*, a drama by Pietro Cossa (1830–81). • Palazzo Giustiniani (see tomorrow): presumably Cosima intended (but forgot) to say more about this house, in which Wagner lived in 1858 while composing the second act of *Tristan und Isolde*.

SEPTEMBER 22
Countess Luise Voss: née Countess Henckel von Donnersmarck (born 1820); she became a close friend of Cosima's, the introduction having been made by Marie von Schleinitz. • *Parini*: author not identified.

SEPTEMBER 23
• The cave of Montesinos: in *Don Quixote*, pt. two, chap. 22.

SEPTEMBER 24
• *The Great Elector* by Schlüter: this statue of Friedrich Wilhelm by Anderas Schlüter (c.1660–1740) now stands outside the Charlottenburg palace in Berlin. • *Condottiere*: equestrian statue of Bartolommeo Colleoni by Andrea Verrocchio (1436–88).

SEPTEMBER 25
• A Prof. Hertel: probably Albert Hertel (born 1843), a painter and professor at the Berlin Academy of Art.

SEPTEMBER 30
• Sismondi: Jean Charles Léonard Simonde de Sismondi (1773–1842), French Swiss historian, whose works include *Histoire des républiques italiennes du moyen age* (*History of the Italian Republics During the Middle Ages*), published in 16 vols., 1807–24. • The Chiaia: Riviera di Chiaia, a thoroughfare to the west of the ancient city of Naples.

OCTOBER 4
• The Hercules Farnese: a statue from the Thermae Caracallae in Rome, part of the Farnese collection in the national museum in Naples.

OCTOBER 9
• The Leap: the Salto di Tiberio, a rock rising nearly a thousand feet from the sea, from which the Emperor Tiberius had his victims thrown.

OCTOBER 10
• His address to the patrons: *"An die geehrten Patrone der Bühnenfestspiele von 1876"*; it brought no positive results.

OCTOBER 11
• A pamphlet by Hans Wolzogen: *Der Nibelungenmythos in Sage und Literatur* (*The Nibelung Myth in Legend and Literature*), by Hans von Wolzogen (1848–1938); the son of Baron Alfred von Wolzogen (see note for January 25, 1873), he came to Bayreuth at Wagner's invitation and became editor of the festival magazine, the *Bayreuther Blätter*; an influential figure in Bayreuth right up to his death. • R. Wagner and—Jordan!!: a reference to Wilhelm Jordan's epic poem *Die Nibelunge* (see note for July 24, 1872).

OCTOBER 17

• The story of Emperor Heinrich IV (1050–1106): excommunicated by Pope Gregory VII for refusing to give up his right to invest German bishops; he was forgiven only after making a pilgrimage in the snow to the pope at Canossa; Heinrich later deposed the pope and appointed one of his own, but he was eventually forced to abdicate.

OCTOBER 18

• Pope Celestine V: Peter von Murrone, elected pope in 1294, abdicated after five months and died in captivity; he was canonized in 1313.

OCTOBER 22

• " 'Tis a consummation . . .": meaning death (*Hamlet*, Act III).

OCTOBER 24

• His cousin Fredi: son of his uncle Geyer in Eisleben. • The oboist Wieprecht: Paul Wieprecht, Berlin. • Fleischhauer: Friedhold Fleischhauer, violinist, concertmaster in Meiningen.

OCTOBER 25

• His preface for Villot: this essay, written in 1860 as a preface to a French prose translation of the texts of *Der Fliegende Holländer*, *Tannhäuser*, *Lohengrin*, and *Tristan und Isolde*, was reprinted in vol. 7 of the collected writings under the title *"Zukunftsmusik"* ("The Music of the Future"); the subtitle is "Open Letter to a French Friend [Frédéric Villot]." • A reply to Herr Monod's letter: in this letter addressed to Professor Gabriel Monod in Paris and dated October 25, 1876, Wagner describes his attitude toward France. • Castruccione: Castruccio Castracani (1281–1328), Italian general who fought a protracted war in the Ghibbeline cause against the Florentines. • A Herr Dunkl: Johann Nepomuk Dunkl (1832–1910), a pupil of Liszt, published *Aus den Erinnerungen eines Musikers* (*The Reminiscences of a Musician*) in 1876.

OCTOBER 26

• His *Romeo and Juliet* theme: written down in Wagner's *Braunes Buch* on May 7, 1868, at the time he was writing his essay on Schnorr von Carolsfeld, with whose death it was apparently connected in his mind; though Wagner spoke more than once of using it in a symphony in memory of the fallen, he did not in the end carry it beyond that first sketch in the *Braunes Buch*.

OCTOBER 27

• Arnold of Brescia (died 1155): an Italian monk who campaigned against the temporal power of the pope; Emperor Friedrich I (Barbarossa) broke his promise and gave him up to Pope Adrian IV; he was taken to Rome and hanged. • Dr. Rée: Paul Rée, (1849–1901), a philosopher, friend of Nietzsche's from 1873, accompanying him on several of his journeys; this was Nietzsche's first meeting with Wagner since he fled from Bayreuth just before the opening of the festival.

OCTOBER 30

• Some of Herr v. Hagen's writings: Edmund von Hagen (see August 12 and 13, 1872); according to Glasenapp, an essay by him about the first scene of *Das Rheingold* had appeared in June 1876 and had given Wagner great pleasure; Hagen was one of the guests at the reception in Wahnfried on August 3, 1876. • Judith [Mendès-Gautier]: now divorced from Catulle Mendès, she had renewed acquaintance with Wagner in Bayreuth during the festival and was corresponding with him regularly.

NOVEMBER 2

• With our friends Malwida and Prof. Nietzsche: this was Wagner's last meeting with Nietzsche.

# Index
# R.W.'s Musical Compositions